Numerical Methods Using Kotlin

For Data Science, Analysis, and Engineering

Haksun Li, PhD

Apress®

Numerical Methods Using Kotlin: For Data Science, Analysis, and Engineering

Haksun Li, PhD
Hong Kong, China

ISBN-13 (pbk): 978-1-4842-8825-2
ISBN-13 (electronic): 978-1-4842-8826-9
https://doi.org/10.1007/978-1-4842-8826-9

Managing Director, Apress Media LLC: Welmoed Spahr
Acquisitions Editor: Steve Anglin
Development Editor: Laura Berendson
Coordinating Editor: Gryffin Winkler
Copyeditor: Kezia Endsley

Cover designed by eStudioCalamar

Designed by rawpixel.com / Freepik

Distributed to the book trade worldwide by Apress Media, LLC, 1 New York Plaza, New York, NY 10004, U.S.A. Phone 1-800-SPRINGER, fax (201) 348-4505, e-mail `orders-ny@springer-sbm.com`, or visit `www.springeronline.com`. Apress Media, LLC is a California LLC and the sole member (owner) is Springer Science + Business Media Finance Inc (SSBM Finance Inc). SSBM Finance Inc is a **Delaware** corporation.

For information on translations, please e-mail `booktranslations@springernature.com`; for reprint, paperback, or audio rights, please e-mail `bookpermissions@springernature.com`.

Apress titles may be purchased in bulk for academic, corporate, or promotional use. eBook versions and licenses are also available for most titles. For more information, reference our Print and eBook Bulk Sales web page at `www.apress.com/bulk-sales`.

Any source code or other supplementary material referenced by the author in this book is available to readers on GitHub (github.com/apress). For more detailed information, please visit `www.apress.com/source-code`.

Printed on acid-free paper

Dedicated to my beloved children, Tintin, Yiyi and Abigail, who will one day find the one sentence in this book about how to solve any problems.

Table of Contents

About the Author

Haksun Li , PhD, is the founder and CEO of NM DEV PTE. LTD, NM Education LTD, NM Optim LTD, and NM FinTech LTD. The NM group of companies has the single mission of "Making the World Better Using Mathematics." Under his leadership, the company group serves security houses, hedge funds, high-net-worth individuals, multinational corporations, factories, and plants all over the world. See `https://nm.sg`.

NM DEV PTE. LTD is dedicated to the research and development of innovative computing technologies for business operations as well as quantitative wealth management. Haksun and the team have developed a suite of programming libraries for mathematics. They created the S2 platform, a next-generation data science toolbox that offers high performance and easy deployment. See `https://nm.dev`.

NM Education LTD is an online tutoring service to teach pre-university kids mathematics using an innovative learn-by-coding approach. Traditional math teaching often asks students to repeatedly do exercises mechanically. Traditional programming classes mainly teach language constructs and syntax and ask students to code toy problems. Haksun and his team have designed a new teaching methodology to teach math using programming. Kids are asked to code the math concepts to solve real engineering problems. Consequently, not only do students gain hands-on experience applying new skills, but they also gain deeper understanding of how math actually works. See `https://nm.education`.

NM Optim LTD helps factories and plants streamline operations, improve productivity, and increase revenue by applying operations, research, and optimization theories. It is the bridge between industries and academia. Haksun leads a team that is revolutionizing the workflow of factories by making more efficient use of resources and offering better scheduling, better management, better pricing, and so on, all based on mathematical models, hence upgrading companies to Industry 4.0. See `https://nmoptim.com`.

NM FinTech LTD develops financial analytic systems for quantitative portfolio managers worldwide. For the U.S. equity market, Haksun created a risk-management system, together with a factor library and tools for portfolio construction. For the China bond market, Haksun created SuperCurve, which is to date the only accurate yield curve publicly available for pricing Chinese bonds, together with a suite of fixed-income analytics. See `https://nmfin.tech`.

Haksun is the associate dean and a professor of the Big Data Finance and Investment Institute of Fudan University in Shanghai, China. He was an adjunct professor with multiple universities. He has taught at the National University of Singapore (mathematics), the Nanyang Technological University (business), the Fudan University (economics), and the Hong Kong University of Science and Technology (mathematics). Prior to that, Haksun was a quantitative analyst and a quantitative trader at UBS and BNP Paribas New York, Tokyo, London, and Singapore.

Haksun holds a bachelor's degree in mathematics and a master's degree in financial mathematics from the University of Chicago, as well as a master's and a doctoral degree in computer science and engineering (with specialization in artificial intelligence) from the University of Michigan – Ann Arbor.

About the Technical Reviewer

Mark Wickham is a software developer based in Dallas. Prior to returning to Texas in 2020, Mark lived in Beijing for nearly 20 years, where he worked for Motorola, Inc., as a software engineering manager, and in various program management and product management roles for the Asia-Pacific region. Mark got his start in Java and Android when Motorola produced the first Java-based mobile phone and he wanted to write his own apps.

Mark was a regular speaker at some of the well-known Android developer conferences and has written two books for Apress, *Practical Java Machine Learning* and *Practical Android*.

Before embarking on his professional career, Mark obtained a degree in physics from Creighton University in Omaha, with a major in computer science and a minor in mathematics. Mark later obtained an MBA from the University of Washington and also studied at the Hong Kong University of Science and Technology.

An Iowa native, in his free time, Mark enjoys gravel bike riding, sports photography, and his latest new passion, disc golf. For more information about Mark, connect with him at `linkedin.com/in/mark-j-wickham`.

Acknowledgments

I never knew that writing a book would be such a tremendous effort, especially for this book with such wide coverage. It started out as a one-year project and then was extended to become an almost two-year project. For eight months in 2021, I basically did nothing other than write this book, pretty much every day. What would be a better thing to do during the indefinite COVID-19 lockdown?

This book covers a lot of topics in basic college applied mathematics, supplemented with a lot of sample code and more than 300 images for illustration. It was a tremendous effort to put the materials together. I want to thank my team for their incredible support throughout the writing of this manuscript. They are amazing and this book would not have happened without them: Kehao Feng, Jingqi Guo, Shihao Liu, Yang Lu, Hengyu Luo, and Dr. Xueying Ni.

Although we have never met in person, I thank Steve Anglin for inviting me to write this book, something that I have wanted to do for a long time but never found sufficient motivation to do. I thank you Mark Wickham for carefully reviewing my book and making a lot of good comments and suggestions. Last but not least, I must thank Mark Powers for pushing me to submit the manuscript. He provided a huge push for me to sit down at my computer and start typing and meet the always-missed-and-always-late deadlines. I thank you all for your patience!

Preface

When I was a boy, I liked to organize my math notes. I did not really like math (or any studies) at all until I met my first math teacher, who enlightened me. It was Professor Bīn Hé (何斌) who showed me how interesting math could be and taught me math at the Sun Yat-sen University in the summers when I was in junior high school. To him, I am forever grateful. Mathematical training shaped the way I think and opened the door to learning other science subjects like physics. Those summers changed my life from being a mediocre student to a top one.

I found mathematics interesting because there are structures in numbers. For example, prime numbers build all numbers; there are no "holes" in the real number line. There are so many ways to prove the same thing, e.g., the Pythagorean theorem. There are again structures and relationships among geometric shapes, as well as between shapes and numbers. It is fascinating *why*. I thought I was pretty good at mathematics until my first year taking an honor's class in real analysis at the university. Some of my classmates were way beyond my league. I did not see myself becoming a mathematician, so I switched to computer science in graduate school, thinking that it might be easier.

Studying computer science is never about learning to program. It turned out that I was a pretty good coder, or so I thought, after coding C++ almost a decade at universities. I had the good aptitude of spending hours and even days doing nothing other than debugging a segmentation fault, fixing a memory leak, or comparing numbers down to the last decimal place. (I still remember when it took me three days to figure out a very obscure bug at UBS.) It turned out that I was ignorantly over-confident when my first mentor introduced design patterns to me. Dr. Anil Kumar asked me to design a singleton during a job interview and guided me through designing the double-checked locking pattern. Luckily, he still hired me onto his team for my first job. I am thankful for his training, guidance, and mentorship, which jump-started my career of becoming a professional quantitative trader.

My training in mathematics and computer science, with a specialization in artificial intelligence, has been powering my career as a quantitative trader and applying mathematics to solve business problems. It is a rare combination of skills. Most mathematicians cannot code (Excel/MATLIB/R is not really professional coding), and most programmers do not read mathematics. We often needed to translate R code into Java code and back and forth between the mathematicians who created the trading models and the programmers who implemented them in an order-execution system. So, one day I decided to make myself useful by creating a programming library of mathematics, using both of my skills. This is kind of a continuation of my childhood hobby of organizing my math notes, because now I am organizing math algorithms in a more useful form. The objective is that quantitative programmers can code mathematics in the same language that they use to build applications. There will be no more "lost in translation" issues.

I was lucky to hire Dr. Ken Yiu in 2007, starting out as an intern and then going full-time, who is a cofounder of the startup. Ken is the best software engineer I have ever met. He is smart, quick-witted, careful, and above all responsible. I cannot thank him enough for traveling with me through this adventure of learning and building the math library, trading strategies, and systems. He has taught me a lot about computer science and programming.

In 2008, Dr. Kevin Sun joined the team as an intern. I was fortunate to have Kevin later join the startup as another cofounder. He is now the brains behind our team and is the key person creating many mathematical models in trading and gambling. He has excellent mathematical-thinking and problem-solving skills. I am still impressed by how he could back then (and still can) solve in a nice and elegant way just about every problem we threw at him. He always saves the team before deadlines with his incredible math and R skills. He has taught me a lot about mathematics and statistics.

Also, I am forever grateful to my brother, Kevin, for all his moral support, teamwork, contributions, encouragement, advice, connections, precious time, and financial assistance through all the ups and downs, laughs and tears, and hopes on this journey with me. Nothing would have been possible without his tremendous effort and resources. I thank God for having him in life.

This is the story of how NM Dev, the math library, started. Today, the library has been adopted by big-name commercial organizations as well as academic institutions. NM Dev is the cornerstone of all the work that we do. We build trading strategies, financial analytics (AlgoQuant), fixed-income analytics (SuperCurve), data-driven decision-making systems (NM Optim), and high-performance solvers and optimizers (NM Solver) based on this Java numerical programming library.

Source Code

All source code used in this book can be downloaded from `github.com/apress/numerical-methods-kotlin`.

CHAPTER 1

■ ■ ■

Introduction to Numerical Methods in Kotlin/S2

When I coded the first line of a matrix multiplication algorithm, the classical $O(n^3)$ version, in the attic of my London apartment during an evening back in 2009, it was nothing more than a hobby. I was coding a trading strategy in Java but could not find a good Java math library to use (namely, one that was professionally maintained, well documented with examples, solidly object-oriented, and had an extensive open data structure). A large part of the strategy code was developed in R/MATLAB and the trade/order execution system was in Java. However, making Java talk to R/MATLAB and vice versa was a nightmare, let alone the many other IT nuisances (e.g., multi-thread safety, multi-instances, debugging, R/MATLAB was very slow, and the mysterious who-knows-why-not-working issues).

I thought that the world would benefit from having a Java math library much like the then-ubiquitous "numerical recipes in C". One easy way to create one was to (auto) translate the C code into Java. Yet, this gave me a bunch of functions (procedures) that did only what the functions did. There was no data structure or module or (sub-)algorithm that I could reuse to build my new data structures or algorithms. A vector should not just be a bunch of numbers or an array. A vector is a mathematical concept that is well-defined with properties and operations. Any algorithm that works with vectors should understand them, and not have to re-code the properties and operations.

While there were a few Java numerical libraries at the time, most notably Apache Commons Math, none of them was designed to be high performance. Modern computing has come a long way since the FORTRAN/C era. We now have concurrent programming, more efficient algorithms (for matrix multiplication, etc.), new hardware like GPUs, and so on. Simple translation of FORTRAN/C code or textbook implementation of algorithms would not leverage these advances. Performance would be very slow. We needed a multi-threading, highly optimized data structure as well as efficient algorithms. For example, instead of using the simple $O(n^3)$ algorithm for matrix multiplication, we implemented a parallelized version of the Strassen algorithm. Due to a lot of team effort twisting, experimenting, and testing things during these ten years, the end result is that we now have arguably the fastest linear algebra implementation in Java.

Another problem that I had with the existing Java math libraries was that they were very limited in scope. A quantitative trading strategy can be as simple as a moving average crossover, but it can also be very complicated, involving solving stochastic differential equations. It certainly involves a lot of statistical analysis. Last but not least, it also takes a suite of solvers to optimize things like strategy parameters. Pretty much all statistical procedures involve some optimization, for example, regression and maximum likelihood. There is no free or cheap optimizer that is good and is in Java. Professional ones such as Gurobi and Mosek are expensive.

Something might have hit my head and made me do the unthinkable. I resigned from my trader job with the investment bank and embarked on a great adventure. I set out to create a Java math library that was well designed with data structure and software engineering, easy-to-read for humans (not machines),

© Haksun Li, PhD 2023
H. Li, PhD, *Numerical Methods Using Kotlin*, https://doi.org/10.1007/978-1-4842-8826-9_1

leveraged modern computing technologies, enjoyed high performance, and was extensive, including linear algebra, Calculus, statistics, time series analysis, optimization, stochastic differential equations, and so on. I didn't realize how difficult this would be when I quit my job. I didn't know how many Herculean tasks there were to overcome. I just thought that it would be fun to create something to (hopefully) share with the world. When I was a teen, I used to write my own math books by organizing my mathematics notes. I supposed then that organizing algorithms in code would be much more useful, a sort of continuation of my childhood hobby.

It turned out that building a math library, especially a good one, was very challenging. It was much more than translating math formulas into code. First, we needed to understand every detail in the algorithms. For many of them, we read the original publications. Some old publications were written in an ancient and arcane language that was very difficult to understand. Many papers had details missing. Many papers had errors and typos. For each algorithm that we implemented, we had to re-derive every step in the mathematics to make sure that we understood all the details and that the algorithm was correct. This was nothing like learning from textbooks, which are usually well written and illustrated with plenty of examples.

There are many concepts that we are used to using without even thinking about the details. For example, we use eigenvalues and eigenvectors of a matrix all the time, but few of us care how decomposing a matrix actually works. To code a linear algebra package, we needed to understand the many different decompositions and factorizations of a matrix, their pros and cons, precision, numerical stability, debugging and testing, API design, and user friendliness — all little details. This process was non-trivial.

Second, we had to verify that our code was correct. If the paper came with examples, we reproduced them to make sure that our results matched theirs. They were usually very few simple illustrative examples. We needed to try for a wide range of test cases, corner cases, stress tests, and performance tests. Our benchmark was R. We would always match our results with Rs. When there were differences, we had to explain every one of them. We were very serious about the accuracy of our code and were constantly fixing bugs in each release. In some cases, our code was even more accurate than the Rs. For example, we didn't know that R has for Johansen tests only a few critical points — e.g., 10%, 5%, 1% — and did a linear interpolation between them for the other values (from the R's source code). On the other hand, we computed the asymptotic distribution for Johansen tests using the exact distribution functions. That was many hours of debugging and reading the R source code.

Third, we designed the software so that it was user friendly and in line with good software engineering principles. Most popular math libraries, such as Netlib, were written decades ago in FORTRAN/C. They were neither user friendly nor used good programming (because there was not much computer science at that time). One most annoying thing to me was that a function often took dozens of parameters with impossible-to-decipher-and-remember names (because the concept of "object" and data structure did not exist back then; names were limited to eight characters). I often could not remember what the variables meant, missed putting in some arguments, and messed up their orders. They were not user friendly by modern standards.

The code was often very difficult to read. Good code should read like English and should be easy to maintain by other professional programmers without the author sitting next to them. When we coded our math library, we made every effort to have the lines mirror the paper so that another person can follow our logic by comparison. This was so that others could fix our bugs, extend our work, translate it to another language (e.g., C#), and port it to other hardware (e.g., GPU). They needed to understand our code to do so. My opinion was that it was next-to-impossible to do this with the decades' old FORTRAN/C code. I bet that once those authors were gone, no one could do anything with that code other than run it, having faith that it had no bugs. I coded up ALGORITHM AS 288 in Java from reading the original paper. I tried to understand the AS 288 FORTRAN code (see Figure 1-1) for comparison, but have still failed to do so to this date. The FORTRAN code just seems to move variables around for no obvious reason and somehow gets it right magically.

```
      SUBROUTINE MSAE(K, N, KPN, IMAX, JMAX, X, XBAR, Y, YBAR, ALPHA, B,
     +  LSAE, IDEP, IFAULT, A, C, IS, NB)
C
C     ALGORITHM AS 108  APPL. STATIST. (1977), VOL. 26, NO.1
C
C     Computes the minimum sum of absolute errors (MSAE) estimates of
C     unknown parameters ALPHA, B(1), B(2), ... , B(K) in the linear
C     regression equation:
C
C     Y(I) = ALPHA + B(1)X(1) + B(2)X(2) + ... + B(K)X(K)
C
C     The regression line passes through the point
C     ( XBAR(1), XBAR(2), ... , XBAR(K), YBAR ) ,
C     where these are the mean values of these variables,
C     though the values of XBAR() and YBAR are input by the user, and
C     could be any point through which the line is to be forced.
C     Users should read the criticism of this algorithm on page 378 of
C     volume 27 of Applied Statistics (1978).
C     One way to use this algorithm would be to fix the XBAR's, say
C     equal to the means, but to vary the value of YBAR until the minimum
C     value of LSAE is found.
C
C     An alternative source of Fortran algorithms for this task is:
C        Gonin, R. and Money, A.H. (1989) Nonlinear Lp-norm estimation,
C        Dekker: New York.
C
C     N.B. The user should check the output values of both IFAULT & IDEP.
C
      REAL A(IMAX, JMAX), B(K), C(KPN), X(N, K), XBAR(K), Y(N)
      INTEGER IS(IMAX), NB(JMAX)
      LOGICAL DONE
      REAL SMALL, TOL, ZERO, ONE, TWO
      REAL LSAE
      DATA SMALL/-1.E+10/, TOL/1.E-08/, ZERO/0.0/, ONE/1.0/, TWO/2.0/
C
C     Check for parameter consistency
C
      IFAULT = 0
      KP1 = K + 1
      KN = K + N
      NP1 = N + 1
      IF (K .GT. N) IFAULT = 1
      IF (IMAX .NE. NP1) IFAULT = 2
      IF (JMAX .NE. KP1) IFAULT = 3
      IF (KPN .NE. KN) IFAULT = 4
      IF (IFAULT .GT. 0) RETURN
C
C     Set up the initial tableau.
C
      LCOL = JMAX - 1
      DO 1 J = 1, JMAX
    1 A(1, J) = ZERO
      DO 10 I = 1, K
        B(I) = ZERO
        C(I) = ZERO
        NB(I) = I
   10 CONTINUE
      DO 20 I = KP1, KPN
   20 C(I) = TWO
      DO 30 J = 1, K
        DO 30 I = 1, N
          A(I+1, J) = X(I, J) - XBAR(J)
   30 CONTINUE
      DO 40 I = 1, N
        IS(I+1) = I + K
        A(I+1, JMAX) = Y(I) - YBAR
   40 CONTINUE
C
C     Determine the variable to leave the basis.
C
   50 H = -TOL
      ICAND = 0
      DONE = .TRUE.
      DO 80 I = 2, IMAX
        AA = A(I, JMAX)
        IF (AA .GE. H) GO TO 80
        DONE = .FALSE.
        H = AA
        ICAND = I
   80 CONTINUE
      IF (DONE) GO TO 200
C
C     Determine the variable to enter the basis.
C
      JCAND = 0
      RATIO = SMALL
      DO 110 J = 1, LCOL
        IONE = 1
        AA = A(ICAND, J)
        IF (ABS(AA) .LT. TOL) GO TO 110
        RCOST = A(1, J)
        IF (AA .LT. -TOL) GO TO 90
        IONE = -1
        IF (ABS(NB(J)) .GT. K) RCOST = RCOST - TWO
   90   R = RCOST / AA
        IF (R .LE. RATIO) GO TO 110
        JCAND = J * IONE
        RATIO = R
        RSAVE = RCOST
  110 CONTINUE
C
C     Determine if an ordinary simplex pivot is unnecessary.
C
      IT = IS(ICAND)
      II = ABS(IT)
      CJ = C(II)
      IF (RATIO .GT. -CJ) GO TO 140
      IS(ICAND) = -IS(ICAND)
      DO 130 J = 1, JMAX
        A(1, J) = A(1, J) + CJ * A(ICAND, J)
        A(ICAND, J) = -A(ICAND, J)
  130 CONTINUE
      GO TO 50
C
C     Perform ordinary simplex pivot.
C
  140 WUN = ONE
      IF (JCAND .GT. 0) GO TO 160
      JCAND = -JCAND
      NB(JCAND) = -NB(JCAND)
      WUN = -ONE
      A(1, JCAND) = RSAVE
  160 PIVOT = A(ICAND, JCAND) * WUN
      DO 170 J = 1, JMAX
  170 A(ICAND, J) = A(ICAND, J) / PIVOT
      DO 190 I = 1, IMAX
        IF (I .EQ. ICAND) GO TO 190
        AIJ = A(I, JCAND) * WUN
        IF (AIJ .EQ. ZERO) GO TO 190
        DO 180 J = 1, JMAX
          A(I, J) = A(I, J) - A(ICAND, J) * AIJ
  180   CONTINUE
        A(I, JCAND) = -AIJ / PIVOT
  190 CONTINUE
      A(ICAND, JCAND) = ONE / PIVOT
      IS(ICAND) = NB(JCAND)
      NB(JCAND) = IT
      GO TO 50
C
C     Compute ALPHA and the vector B containing the slopes.
C
  200 ALPHA = YBAR
      DO 220 I = 2, IMAX
        WUN = ONE
        II = IS(I)
        IF (ABS(II) .GT. K) GO TO 220
        IF (II .GT. 0) GO TO 210
        II = -II
        WUN = -ONE
  210   B(II) = WUN * A(I, JMAX)
        ALPHA = ALPHA - XBAR(II) * B(II)
  220 CONTINUE
      LSAE = -A(1, JMAX)
C
C     Inspect the final solution for dependencies amongst the predictor
C     variables.
C
      IDEP = 1
      DO 300 J = 1, LCOL
        IF (ABS(NB(J)) .GT. K) GO TO 300
        IDEP = 0
        RETURN
  300 CONTINUE
C
      RETURN
      END
```

***Figure 1-1.** It is very hard to remember the meanings and order of A, B, C, K, N, X, Y (AS108)*

Our first attempt in building such a library was SuanShu, named after one of the earliest known Chinese mathematical treatises, 算数书, which was written around 200 B.C. Since 2009, it was a decade of effort. It started as a basic linear algebra package and grew to be an extensive library covering Calculus, optimization algorithms, statistical analysis, differential equations, and so on. It started being my personal hobby and then dozens of experts, professors, PhDs, students, and practitioners around the world contributed to the library. It was adopted by some big-name commercial organizations as well as academic institutions. In 2018, we decided to discontinue the sale and support for SuanShu. We made the codebase open-source as of June 2012.

Leveraging our decade of experience with numerical programming, NM Dev is a fresh new numerical library that succeeds SuanShu. We have collected a large amount of feedback from users and bug reports in the last ten years. We want to have a new software foundation and architecture to account for all these good suggestions.

1.1. Library Design

The objective of SuanShu and hence NM Dev is to enable very easy programming of engineering applications. Programmers can program mathematics in such a way that the source code is solidly object-oriented and individually testable. NM Dev source code adheres to the strictest coding standards so that it is readable, maintainable, and can be easily modified and extended.

NM Dev revolutionizes how numerical computing is traditionally done, for example, Netlib and gsl. The repositories of these popular and "standard" libraries are collections of ad hoc source code in old languages, such as FORTRAN and C. One problem with such code is that it is not readable (for most modern programmers), hence it's unmaintainable. For example, it is quite a challenge to understand AS 288, let alone improve on it. Other problems include, but are not limited to, the lack of data structure, duplicated code, being entirely procedural, very bad variable naming, abuse of `GOTO`, the lack of test cases, insufficient documentation, the lack of IDE support, inconvenient linking to modern languages such as Java, unfriendly to parallel computing, and so on.

To address these problems, NM Dev designs a framework of reusable math components (not procedures) so that programmers can put components together like Legos to build more complex algorithms. NM Dev is written anew so that it conforms to the modern programming paradigms, such as variable naming, code structuring, reusability, readability, maintainability, as well as software engineering procedures. To ensure very high quality of the code and very few bugs, NM Dev has thousands of unit test cases that run daily.

1.1.1. Class Parsimony

We decided to make the class library as parsimonious as possible to avoid method pollution. This is inspired by the jMatrices' whitepaper.[1] The challenge is to organize the methods by minimal and correct packages. We illustrate this with the NM Dev matrix package.

The `Matrix` class has only 26 methods, nine of which are constructors and the related methods, three are overrides for the `AbstractMatrix` interfaces, and eight are overrides for the `MatrixSpace` interfaces. Only six of them are class-specific, to make calling these methods convenient for the user. The other dozens of matrix operations — such as the different factorizations, properties like rank, and transformations like inverse — are grouped into multiple classes and packages. In most cases, each of these operations is a class on its own. For instance, the inverse operation is a class inheriting from `Matrix`. The constructor takes as input the matrix to invert. For example, to find the inverse for the following:

$$A = \begin{bmatrix} 1 & 2 & 3 \\ 6 & 5 & 4 \\ 8 & 7 & 9 \end{bmatrix}$$

The NM Dev code in Kotlin is as follows:

```
val A = DenseMatrix(arrayOf(
        doubleArrayOf(1.0, 2.0, 3.0),
        doubleArrayOf(6.0, 5.0, 4.0),
        doubleArrayOf(8.0, 7.0, 9.0)))
val Ainv = Inverse(A)
Ainv
```

[1] http://jmatrices.sourceforge.net/

The output is as follows:

```
3x3
     [,1] [,2] [,3]
[1,] -0.809524, -0.142857, 0.333333,
[2,] 1.047619, 0.714286, -0.666667,
[3,] -0.095238, -0.428571, 0.333333,
```

It is important to note that the `Ainv` object is of the `Matrix` class; it's created as a new instance of the `Inverse` class. In summary, we choose to have hundreds of classes, rather than to have one class with hundreds of methods. Each class is kept deliberately short. This class parsimony principle is a key design decision that guides the whole library development.

1.1.2. Java vs C++ Performance

FORTRAN/C/C++ have traditionally been the languages for mathematics because of their bare metal performance. Modern Java performance is comparable to that of C++. There was the wrong perception about Java slowness. The bad impression was by-and-large because Java 1 in 1995 was indeed slower than C++. Java has improved a lot since then, for example, hotspot. It is now version 17 LTS (or 18). Java is now a competitive technology compared to C/C++. In fact, in order to realistically optimize for C/C++, you need to find the "right" programmer to code it. This programmer needs to be aware of all the performance issues of C/C++, including profiling and code optimization such as loop unfolding, and may even need to write code snippets in assembly. An average programmer coding in C/C++ is probably not any faster than coding in Java. (I am in general against code-optimization techniques because they make the code unreadable to humans, hence unmaintainable, such as a lot of the FORTRAN/C/C++ code found in Netlib and Statlib.)

More importantly, most modern software runs on multiple cores. Code-optimization techniques are dwarfed by parallel-computing technologies. It is significantly easier and more efficient (and more enjoyable) to write concurrent programming code in Java than in C++. Therefore, to code high-performance software, I personally prefer to code multi-core, multi-CPU, and cloud in Java rather than doing code optimization in C/C++.

In general, among the general-purpose programming languages, I like to use Java instead of C/C++, FORTRAN, Assembly, and so on, whenever possible because Java is a very easy programming language to learn and work with, without a sacrifice in performance. It has been the most popular language for building systems and applications.

(As For FORTRAN, I am not sure why it survives in 2022. How are you supposed to read thousands of lines of code all in upper- and lowercase with a bunch of Cs and `GOTO`s everywhere?)

1.2. Java Scripting

To do data science and analysis, the main problem with using Java is that you cannot work on the data in interactive mode. That is, I would like to type a command to work on the data, such as to extract the first six rows from a table, take a look at the result, think about what to do next, and then type another command. The ability to work in interactive mode makes MATLAB/R the most popular tool in data analysis. See Figure 1-2.

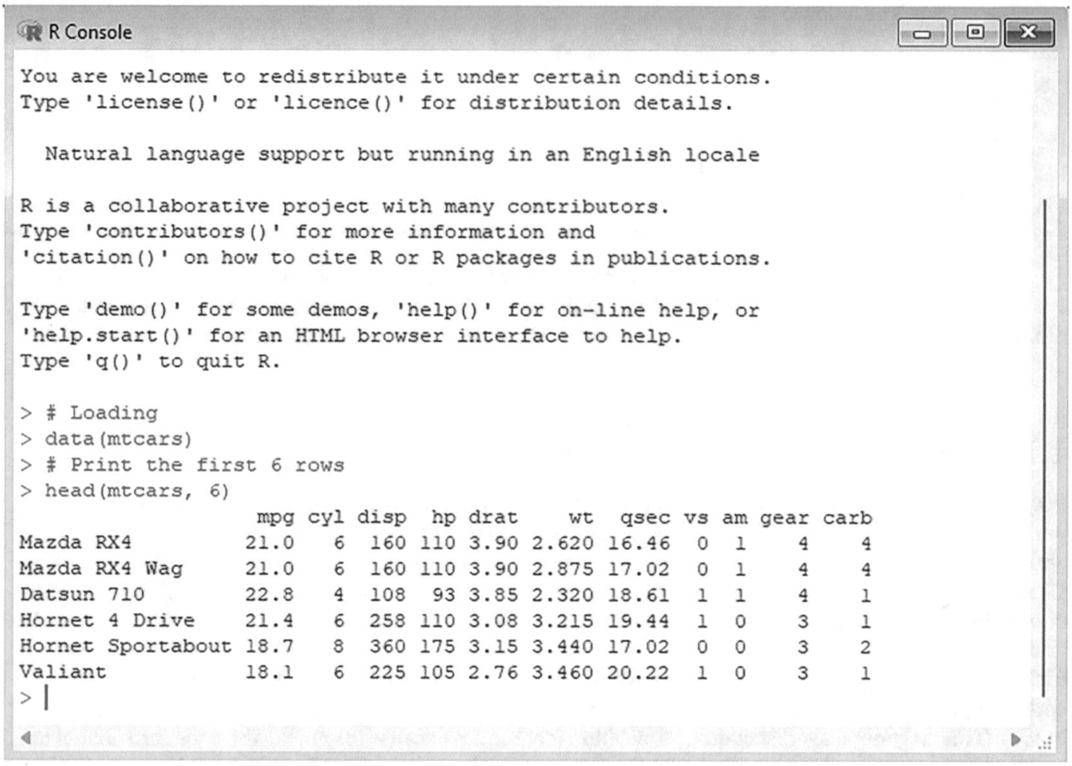

Figure 1-2. *Print out the first six rows in a data set in R*

By contrast, when using Java, you always have to write, compile, and then run the whole program. There are many problems with this approach. First, it is very annoying to always have to repeatedly compile, deploy, and execute the code. Second, Java is verbose. It has too much boilerplate code. There are sections of unnecessary code that have to be included in many places with little or no alteration. You need to write a lot of code even for simple things like printing out a number. Third, it is very time consuming to run the whole program from the beginning each time. Fourth, you often do not know what program you want to write without examining, understanding, and experimenting with the data. Java does not allow programmers to try different things with the data, such as look the first six rows versus the first hundred rows. Fifth, you cannot pause a Java program in the middle of a run to examine the intermediate results. In a nutshell, Java is not the right tool for prototyping and developing data science code. You need a Java-based scripting language that lets you interact with data.

There are a few Java-based scripting languages that fully interoperate with existing Java code and libraries, most notably Clojure, Scala, Groovy, and Kotlin. (I do not count JRuby and Jython because they are simply Java implementation of Ruby and Python, respectively. Their goals are to make Ruby and Python code run on JVM.) I do not like Clojure, a dynamic and functional dialect of the LISP programming language on the Java platform, because there are too many parentheses to read and they hurt my eyes and brain.[2] I can read English-like

[2] My first class in computer science at the University of Chicago used the text book *Structure and Interpretation of Computer Programs* by Harold Abelson, Gerald Jay Sussman, and Julie Sussman. It was very annoying to have to parse all those parentheses in my head. It was also useless for my career, as I have never once used LISP in my life after finishing that class. I would think that teaching Java or C++ would be more useful and practical. I used C++ for my PhD and Java for my work.

sentences much faster than LISPs. Scala is a strong, statically typed general-purpose programming language that supports both object-oriented programming and functional programming. Designed to be concise, many of Scala's design decisions are aimed to address the criticisms of Java. My problem with Scala is its learning curve. I cannot figure out what the lines mean at the first glance, especially with all the symbols like :, ::, :::. I want a language that I can pick up and use right away without spending time learning it.

Groovy is easy to learn and read. I did not spend any time learning it. I simply copied, pasted, and modified the code and was able to get things working. Groovy is a Java-syntax-compatible object-oriented programming language for the Java platform. It is both a static and dynamic language with features similar to Python. It can be used as a programming language and as a scripting language, is compiled to Java Virtual Machine (JVM) bytecode, and interoperates seamlessly with other Java code and libraries. Groovy uses a curly-bracket syntax similar to Java's. SuanShu used to support Groovy. For example, the following two-line Groovy script evaluates a definite integral. See Figure 1-3. More examples can be found in Figure 1-4.

```
I = new Riemann();//create an integrator
v = I.integrate(
      ['evaluate' : {x -> return x * x}] as nivariateRealFunction,//integrate the
                                                                   function y = x^2
      0, 1);//limit: [0, 1]
```

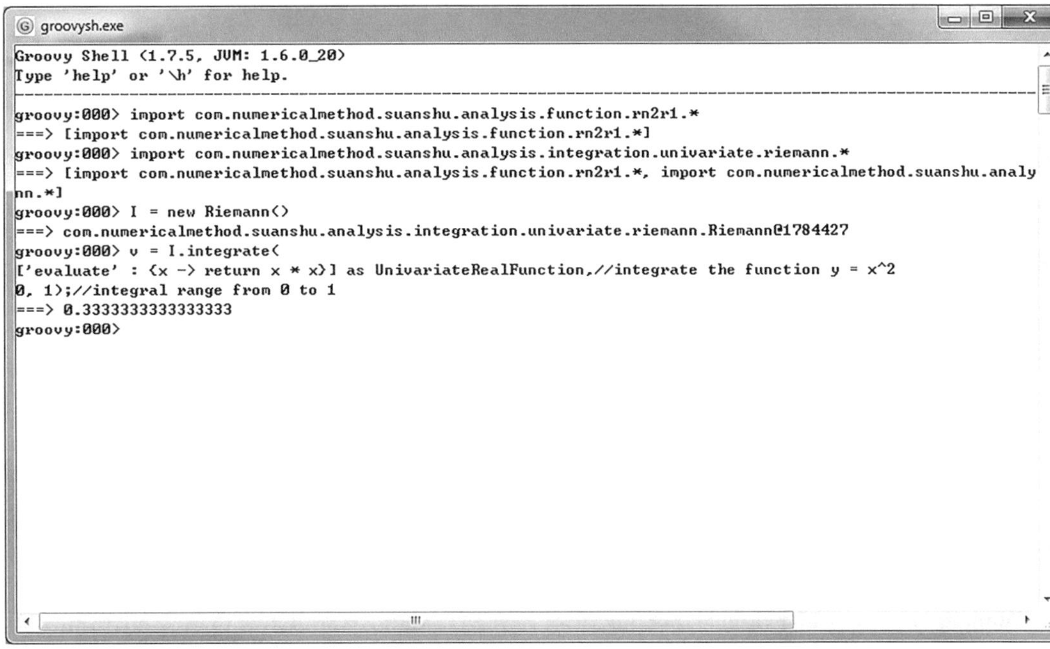

Figure 1-3. *Evaluate a definite integral using Groovy and SuanShu*

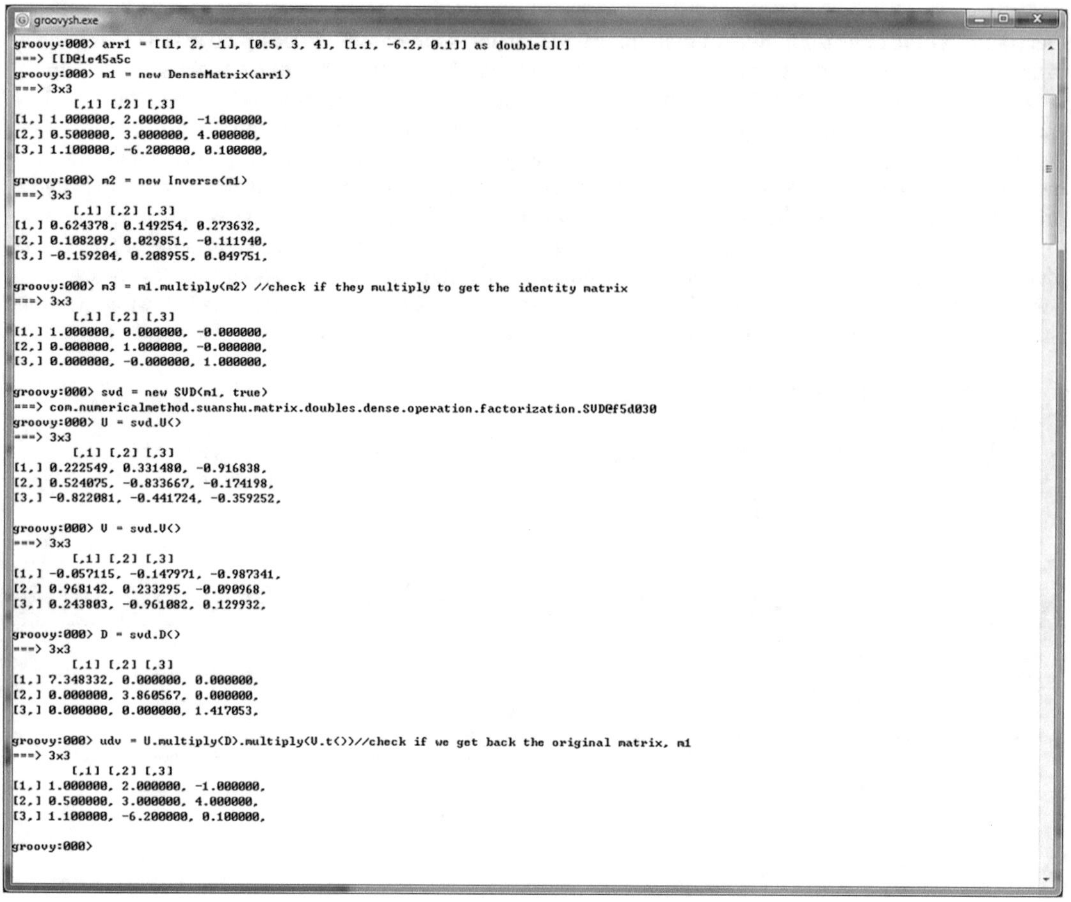
groovysh.exe
groovy:000> arr1 = [[1, 2, -1], [0.5, 3, 4], [1.1, -6.2, 0.1]] as double[][]
===> [[D@1e45a5c
groovy:000> m1 = new DenseMatrix(arr1)
===> 3x3
[,1] [,2] [,3]
[1,] 1.000000, 2.000000, -1.000000,
[2,] 0.500000, 3.000000, 4.000000,
[3,] 1.100000, -6.200000, 0.100000,
groovy:000> m2 = new Inverse(m1)
===> 3x3
[,1] [,2] [,3]
[1,] 0.624378, 0.149254, 0.273632,
[2,] 0.108209, 0.029851, -0.111940,
[3,] -0.159204, 0.208955, 0.049751,
groovy:000> m3 = m1.multiply(m2) //check if they multiply to get the identity matrix
===> 3x3
[,1] [,2] [,3]
[1,] 1.000000, 0.000000, -0.000000,
[2,] 0.000000, 1.000000, -0.000000,
[3,] 0.000000, -0.000000, 1.000000,
groovy:000> svd = new SVD(m1, true)
===> com.numericalmethod.suanshu.matrix.doubles.dense.operation.factorization.SVD@f5d030
groovy:000> U = svd.U()
===> 3x3
[,1] [,2] [,3]
[1,] 0.222549, 0.331480, -0.916838,
[2,] 0.524075, -0.833667, -0.174198,
[3,] -0.822081, -0.441724, -0.359252,
groovy:000> V = svd.V()
===> 3x3
[,1] [,2] [,3]
[1,] -0.057115, -0.147971, -0.987341,
[2,] 0.968142, 0.233295, -0.090968,
[3,] 0.243803, -0.961082, 0.129932,
groovy:000> D = svd.D()
===> 3x3
[,1] [,2] [,3]
[1,] 7.348332, 0.000000, 0.000000,
[2,] 0.000000, 3.860567, 0.000000,
[3,] 0.000000, 0.000000, 1.417053,
groovy:000> udv = U.multiply(D).multiply(V.t())//check if we get back the original matrix, m1
===> 3x3
[,1] [,2] [,3]
[1,] 1.000000, 2.000000, -1.000000,
[2,] 0.500000, 3.000000, 4.000000,
[3,] 1.100000, -6.200000, 0.100000,
groovy:000>

Figure 1-4. *Matrix operations using Groovy and SuanShu*

Unfortunately, the company Pivotal Software ceased sponsoring Groovy in April 2015. I was looking for an alternative that was motivated by commercial interest with better resources and support.

1.2.1. Kotlin Programming Language

Kotlin was invented by the company JetBrains. It is a cross-platform, statically typed, general-purpose programming language with type inference. Kotlin is designed to interoperate fully with Java and existing Java libraries. Kotlin mainly targets JVM, but it also compiles to JavaScript (e.g., for frontend web applications using React) and native code (e.g., for native iOS apps sharing business logic with Android apps).

On May 7, 2019, Google announced that Kotlin was its preferred language for Android app developers. It was the third language fully supported for Android, in addition to Java and C++. In 2020, Kotlin was the most widely used on Android, with Google estimating that 70% of the top 1000 apps on the Play Store were written in Kotlin. Google itself has 60 apps written in Kotlin, including Maps and Drive. Many Android apps, such as Google's Home, are in the process of being migrated to Kotlin.

In addition to its prominent use on Android, Kotlin is gaining traction in server-side development. The Spring Framework officially added Kotlin support with version 5 on January 4, 2017. To further support Kotlin, Spring has translated all its documentation to Kotlin and added built-in support for many Kotlin-specific features, such as coroutines. In addition to Spring, JetBrains has produced a Kotlin-first framework called Ktor for building web applications.

With all the commercial interests and community momentum, Kotlin is likely to remain a mainstream language and be well supported. Kotlin will likely (and hopefully) stay for a very long time. Therefore, I chose Kotlin as the scripting language to do math computing and data analysis.

One major advantage of Kotlin over Java is that Kotlin code is concise. It has little boilerplate code, is shorter and more readable. Also, Kotlin is very easy to learn. I have never read any tutorials on the Internet or books about Kotlin. I simply copy, paste, and modify existing snippets. This approach seems to work for me and proves how easy Kotlin is to use and read. In fact, all sample code in this book was coded in this fashion.

For example, to add two numbers, you do the following:

```
1 + 1
```

The output is as follows:

```
2
```

To multiply two numbers, you do this:

```
2 * 2
```

The output is as follows:

```
4
```

To define a constant, you do the following:

```
val A = 1.0
```

To print out a variable, you simply type its name. For example:

```
A
```

The output is as follows:

```
1.0
```

To define a variable, you do the following:

```
var x : Double = 1.0
```

This statement says that `x` is a variable whose value can change. It is of type `Double`.

To change x, you can add 1 to it.

```
X = x + 1
x
```

The output is as follows:

```
2.0
```

A for loop is, for example:

```
for (i in 1..3) {
    println(i)
}
```

The output is as follows:

```
1
2
3
```

The following snippet defines an array and prints it out.

```
Val arr1 = arrayOf(1.0, 2.0, 3.0, 4.0, 5.0)
for (I in arr1) {
    println(i)
}
```

The output is as follows:

```
1.0
2.0
3.0
4.0
5.0
```

The following snippet defines a function:

```
fun add1(x : Double) : Double {
    return x + 1.0
}
```

To call the function, you do the following:

```
add1(2.0)
```

The output is as follows:

```
3.0
```

There are many good books and tutorials on the Internet to learn how to code Kotlin. The official Kotlin Foundation website has a lot of information about Kotlin, its development, news, and community.

`https://kotlinlang.org`

They also have an online course to get beginners started on coding Kotlin.

`https://kotlinlang.org/docs/getting-started.html`

1.3. S2

S2 is an online integrated development environment of data and analytics for data science and numerical computing. It is developed by the company NM DEV PTE LTD. The official S2 website is:

`http://nm.dev/s2`

S2 contains all numerical algorithms in the NM Dev library and some mathematics, science, machine learning, graphing, plotting, financial, and other commercial libraries. S2 lets users create their math algorithms by calling all these built-in libraries in a simple manner using Kotlin.

1.3.1. R Replacement

S2 is designed to be a modern-day replacement for R. You can do a lot of things in S2 that you can do in R and S2 does them faster. Moreover, R code runs inside only the R environment. It is very difficult to deploy the code anywhere else such as in embedded devices like microwaves, automobiles, or space rockets. S2 code runs in any JVM environment. There are now 15 billion devices that run JVM!

S2 is an online IDE for numerical computing and coding numerical algorithms. It is like an online calculator. Let's start with 1+1, as shown in Figure 1-5.

Figure 1-5. *S2 1+1*

With 1+1 working, you can do pretty much anything in numerical programming, which is just a more complicated series of many 1+1 computations. For example, integration is shown in Figure 1-6.

```
[10]: %use s2

val exp_2x: UnivariateRealFunction = object : AbstractUnivariateRealFunction() {
    override fun evaluate(x: Double): Double {
        return Math.exp(2 * x) // exp(2x)
    }
}
val I: Double = Riemann().integrate(exp_2x, 0.0, 1.0)
println("integrate exp(2x) from 0 to 1 = $I")

integrate exp(2x) from 0 to 1 = 3.1945280494653288
```

Figure 1-6. *S2 doing integration*

S2 supports a few dozen type of graphs, charts, and plots. See Figures 1-7 through 1-12 for examples.

```
// construct a box plot
val plot = ggplot(data) {x="cond"; y="rating"} + // supply data; set legends
    ggsize(300, 200) + // plot size
    geom_boxplot() {fill="cond"} // draw a colored box plot
// display the plot
plot

{cond=[A, B], rating=[-3.3812632581654454E-4, 1.3530503384104802]}
```

[3]:

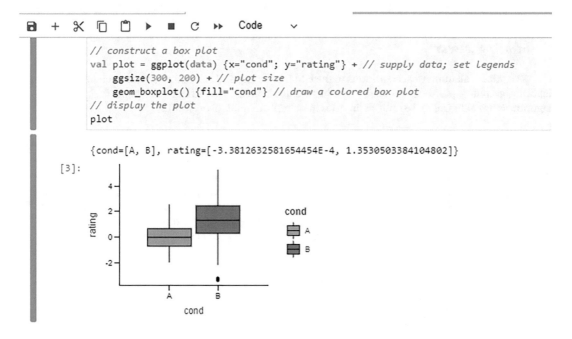

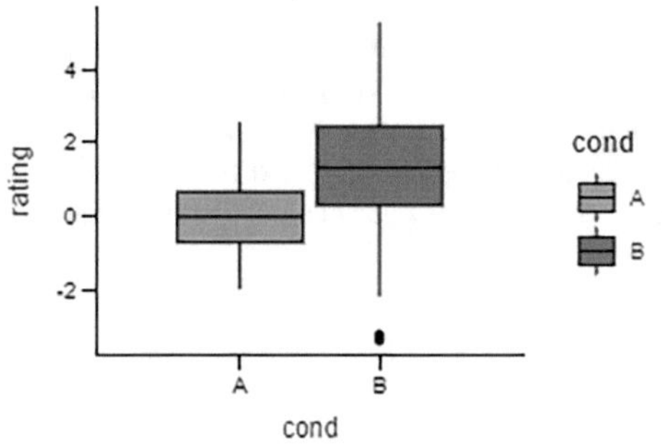

Figure 1-7. *S2 box plot*

```
// construct a density plot
val plot = ggplot(data) {x="rating"; color="cond"} + // supply data; set legends
    ggsize(500, 250) + // plot size
    geom_density(alpha=.3) {fill="cond"} // density plot with semi-transparent fill
plot
```

[1]:

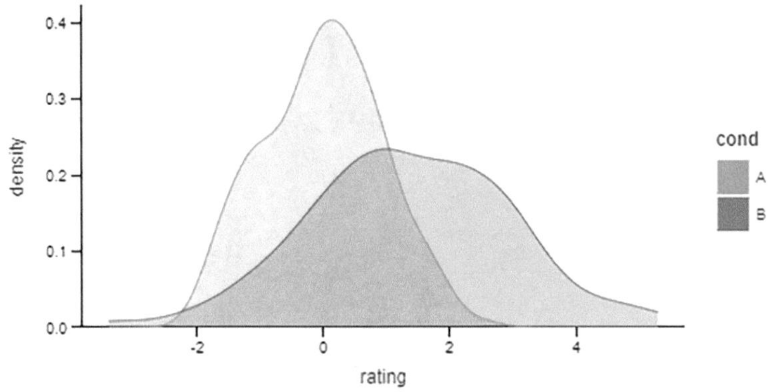

Figure 1-8. *S2 density plot*

```
// construct a scatter plot
val plot = ggplot(data) { x = "xvar"; y = "yvar" } + // supply data; set legends
    ggsize(300, 250) + // plot size
    geom_point(shape = 1) // draw a basic scatter plot
plot
```

[1]:

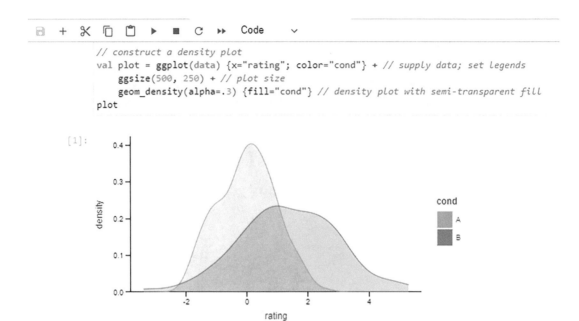

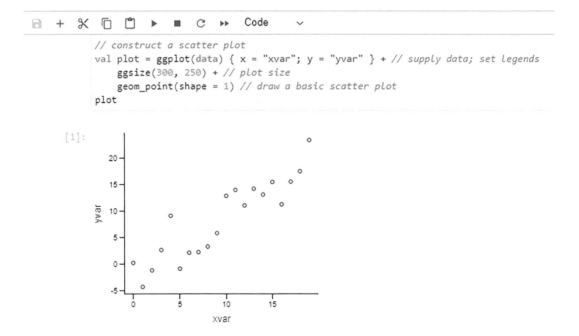

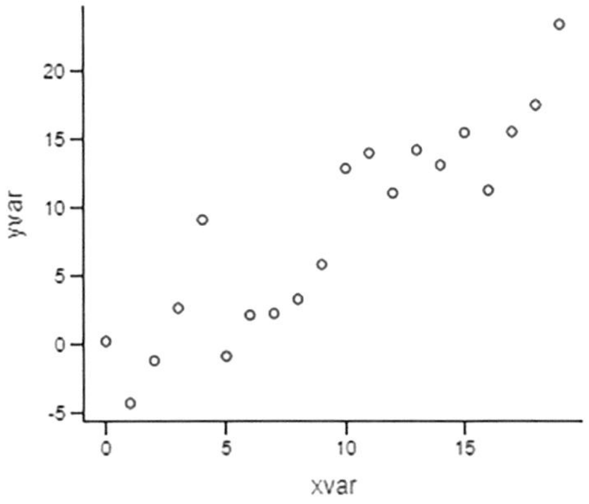

Figure 1-9. *S2 scatter plot*

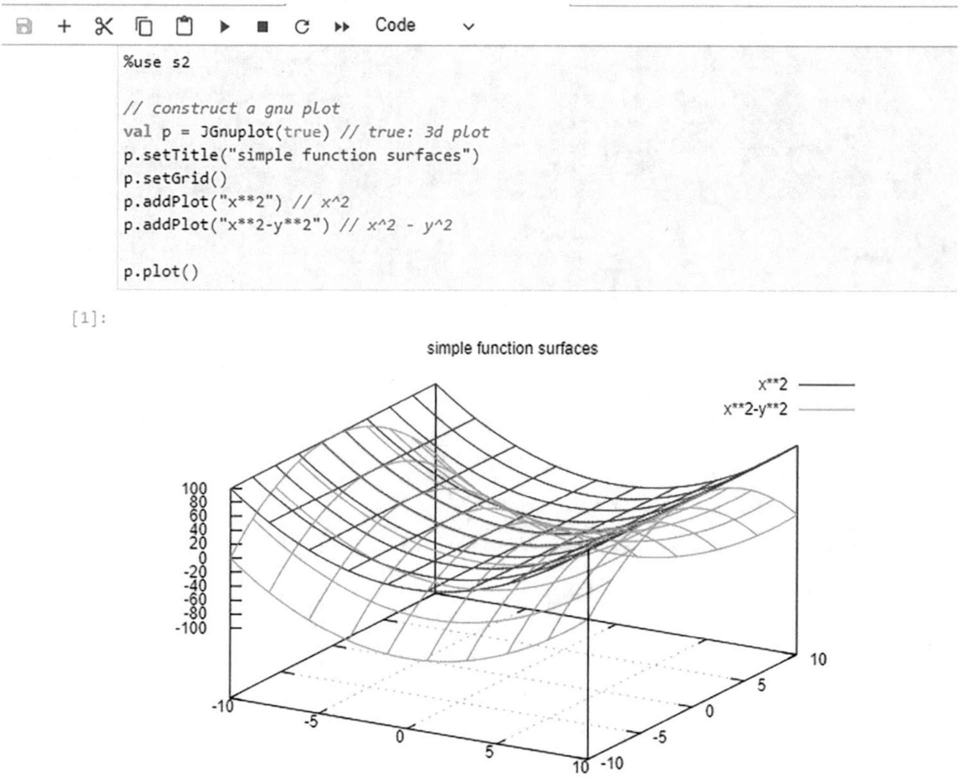
Code
%use s2
// construct a gnu plot
val p = JGnuplot(true) // true: 3d plot
p.setTitle("simple function surfaces")
p.setGrid()
p.addPlot("x**2") // x^2
p.addPlot("x**2-y**2") // x^2 - y^2
p.plot()
[1]:
simple function surfaces
x**2
x**2-y**2
100
80
60
40
20
0
-20
-40
-60
-80
-100
-10
-5
0
5
10
-10
-5
0
5
10

Figure 1-10. *S2 surface plot*

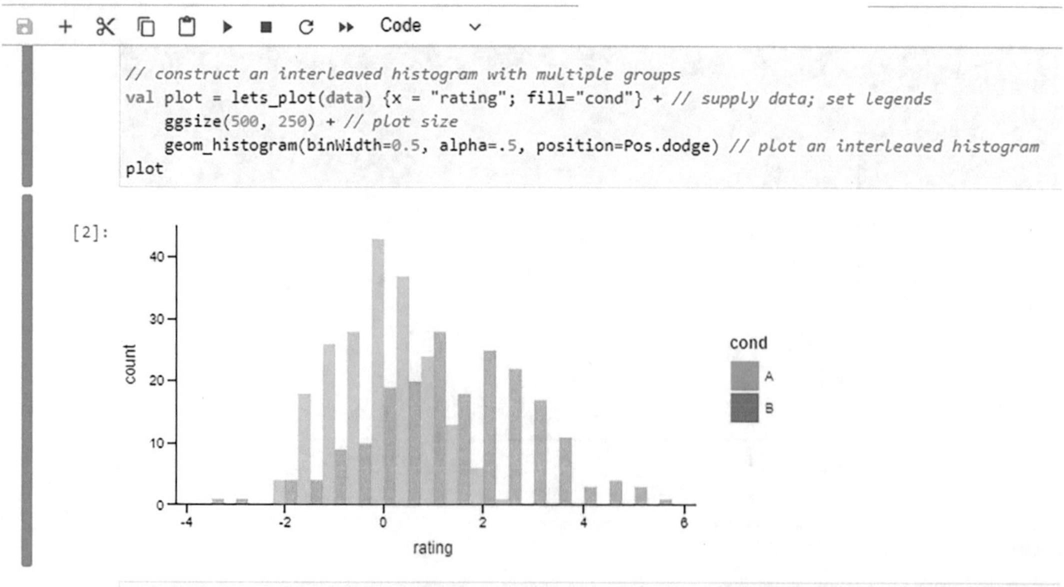
Code
// construct an interleaved histogram with multiple groups
val plot = lets_plot(data) {x = "rating"; fill="cond"} + // supply data; set legends
    ggsize(500, 250) + // plot size
    geom_histogram(binWidth=0.5, alpha=.5, position=Pos.dodge) // plot an interleaved histogram
plot
[2]:
40
30
20
10
0
count
-4
-2
0
2
4
6
rating
cond
A
B

Figure 1-11. *S2 histogram*

```
// download the data from the Internet
val dp1 = DataSetPlot(FileDataSet(BufferedReader(InputStreamReader(
    URL("https://s2-nmdev.s3.eu-west-3.amazonaws.com/resources/immigration.dat")
        .openStream()))))
dp1.setUsingColumns("6:xtic(1)")
p.addPlot(dp1)

// use the same data set
val dp2 = DataSetPlot()
dp2.setUsingColumns("12")
p.addPlot(dp2)

val dp3 = DataSetPlot()
dp3.setUsingColumns("13")
p.addPlot(dp3)

val dp4 = DataSetPlot()
dp4.setUsingColumns("14")
p.addPlot(dp4)

p.plot()
```

[3]:

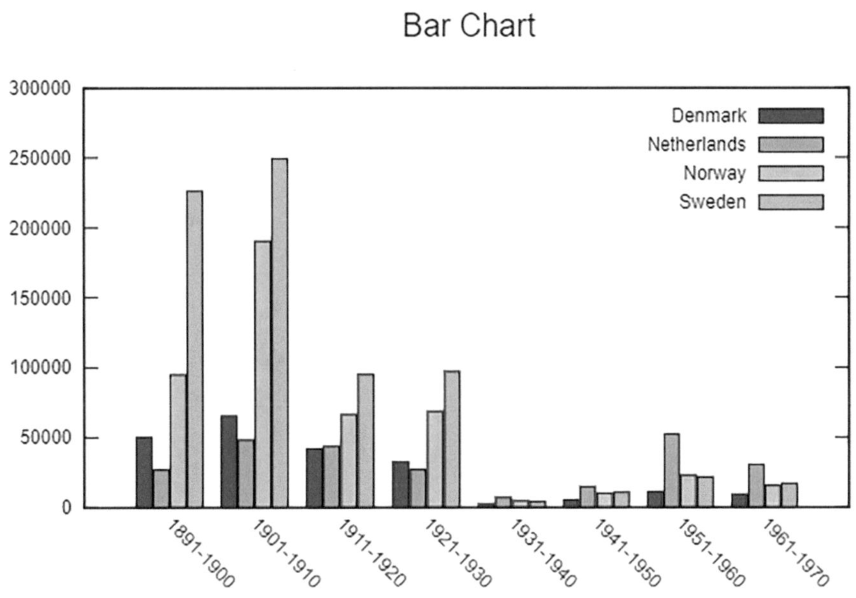

Figure 1-12. *S2 bar chart*

S2 has a very comprehensive statistics package. It supports almost all types of linear regressions and their statistics, OLS, GLM, and logistics. See Figures 1-13 through 1-16 for examples.

```
// construct a linear model problem
val problem = LMProblem(
    DenseVector(df["y"].asDoubles()), // Y, the dependent variables
    DenseMatrix(DenseVector(df["x"].asDoubles())), // X, the independent variables
    true) // true if to additionally add an intercept term to the model
// run OLS regression
val ols = OLSRegression(problem)

// the regression coefficients
val beta_hat = ols.beta().betaHat()
// the error terms
val residuals = ols.residuals()
println("beta_0 = ${beta_hat[1]}, beta_1 = ${beta_hat[2]}")
println("R^2 = ${residuals.R2()}")
println("expected value of y at x = 50 is ${ols.Ey(DenseVector(50.0))}")
```

```
beta_0 = 1.0143353551195182, beta_1 = -0.4618107736611625
R^2 = 0.9891203611402716
expected value of y at x = 50 is 50.254956982314745
```

[2]:

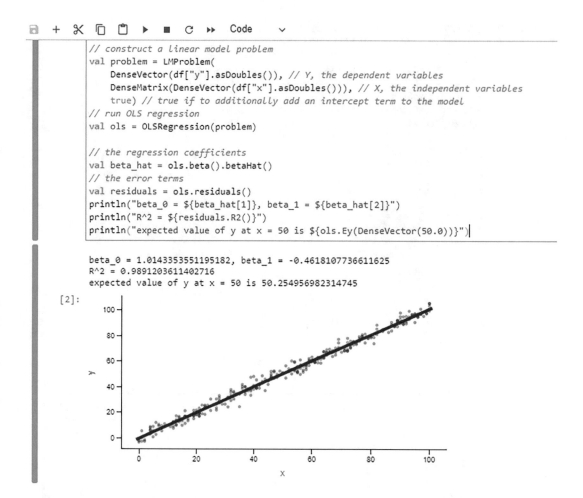

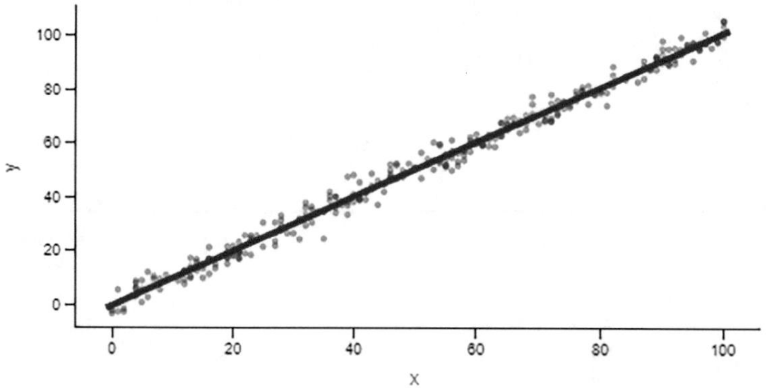

Figure 1-13. *S2 OLS regression*

```
%use s2

// construct a GARCH(1, 1)
val model = GARCHModel(0.2, doubleArrayOf(0.3), doubleArrayOf(0.6))
// construct a GARCH RNG using a GARCH  model
val sim = GARCHSim(model)
sim.seed(1234567890L)
// generate the time series
val xt = RNGUtils.nextN(sim, 10000)
// print the first 10 items
for (i in 1..10) println(xt.get(i))
```

```
-0.0926032543005452
0.7837011446480964
-0.9359209612784913
0.03514612681843151
0.18996782228284192
0.3995042160014833
-1.9745439876565025
-2.3272872886509064
0.2653638132622115
-1.0311449251140137
```

Figure 1-14. *S2 time series analysis*

```
%use s2
import java.util.*

// the number of data points to generate
val N = 10
// construct a random number generator for uniform distribution
val rng: RandomNumberGenerator = UniformRNG()
// generate the random numbers
val values = DoubleArray(N)
for (i in 0 until N) {
    values[i] = rng.nextDouble()
}
println("uniformly generated random numbers:\n%s".format(Arrays.toString(values)))
```

```
uniformly generated random numbers:
[0.14304131409153342, 0.8694100854918361, 0.5969358449801803, 0.05194615200161934, 0.9407
0.18347151833586395]
```

Figure 1-15. *S2 random number generation*

```
[1]: /**
      * Print the properties of an F-distribution with the given parameters,
      * where the quantile and the density are printed for the given values.
      *
      * @author Haksun Li
      */

     %use s2

     // the first degree of freedom
     val df1 = 12.0
     // the second degree of freedom
     val df2 = 11.5
     // construct an F distribution
     val F: ProbabilityDistribution = FDistribution(df1, df2)
     println("mean: %f, var: %f, skew: %f, kurtosis: %f".
             format(F.mean(), F.variance(), F.skew(), F.kurtosis()))

     // the quantile
     val x = 0.1
     // the cumulative distribution function
     println("F($x) = %f".format(F.cdf(x)))
     // the quantile function
     println("the quantile at %f = %f".format(x, F.quantile(x)))
     // the density function
     println("the density at %f = %f".format(x, F.density(x)))
```

```
mean: 1.210526, var: 0.700123, skew: 2.937297, kurtosis: 20.765328
F(0.1) = 0.000183
the quantile at 0.100000 = 0.463739
the density at 0.100000 = 0.009245
```

Figure 1-16. *S2 statistical distributions*

Solvers are the foundation of the future of mathematics. They are the core of AI and Big Data analysis. You need solvers for any problems that do not have a closed form solution. That is pretty much any modern problem nowadays. S2 supports a full suite of all known standard optimization algorithms. See Figures 1-17 through 1-19 for examples.

```
// construct an LP problem in canonical form
fun problem(): LPCanonicalProblem1 {
    // min c'x
    val c = DenseVector(arrayOf(-1.0, -1.0, -1.0))

    // subject to Ax <= b
    val A: Matrix = DenseMatrix(arrayOf(
        doubleArrayOf(1.0, -1.0, 1.0),
        doubleArrayOf(-1.0, 1.0, 1.0),
        doubleArrayOf(1.0, 1.0, -1.0),
        doubleArrayOf(-1.0, -1.0, -1.0)))
    val b = DenseVector(arrayOf(-2.0, -3.0, -1.0, -4.0))

    val problem = LPCanonicalProblem1(c, A, b)
    return problem
}

// construct an LP solver for canonical problems
val solver = LPCanonicalSolver()

// solve the LP problem
val soln: LPSimplexSolution = solver.solve(problem())
val minimizer = soln.minimizer()
val minimum = soln.minimum()
println("minimizer:\n$minimizer\nminimum: $minimum")
```

```
minimizer:
size = 1
[3.500000, 0.500000, 0.000000]

minimum: -4.0
```

Figure 1-17. *S2 linear programming*

```
// An initial guesses for a solution. Note that the initial guess must satisfy the constraints!
val x0: Vector = DenseVector(2.0, 2.0, 3.0, 3.0)

// construct an QP solver
val solver = QPPrimalActiveSetMinimizer(
    1e-8, // precision
    100) // max number of iterations

// solve the QP problem
val p = problem()
val soln: Solution = solver.solve(p)
val qpSoln: QPSolution = soln.search(x0)
val minimizer = qpSoln.minimizer()
val fx = p.f().evaluate(minimizer);
println("minimizer: $minimizer, fx = $fx")
```

```
minimizer: [2.000000, 0.000000, 4.500000, 3.500000] , fx = 27.5
```

Figure 1-18. *S2 quadratic programming*

```
// Uses interior point method to solve the given problem from a given starting point.
val x0: Vector = DenseVector(1.0, 0.0, 0.0, 0.1, 0.0, 0.0, 0.1, 0.0, 0.0)
val s0: Vector = DenseVector(3.7, 1.0, -3.5, 1.0, 0.25, 0.5, 1.0, -0.35355, -0.1767)
val y0: Vector = DenseVector(-3.7, -1.5, -0.5, -2.5, -4.0)
// an initial guess
val soln0 = PrimalDualSolution(x0, s0, y0)

// construct an SOCP solver
val solver = PrimalDualInteriorPointMinimizer(
    1e-8,
    20) // max number of iterations

// solve the SOCP problem
val p = problem()
val soln: IterativeSolution<PrimalDualSolution> = solver.solve(p)
soln.search(soln0)

// the solution
val y = soln.minimizer().y
val fx = p.f().evaluate(y);
println("minimizer: $y, fx = $fx")
```

```
minimizer: [-1.707790, -2.044676, -0.852738, -2.544822, -2.485651] , fx = -1.7077904490804823
```

Figure 1-19. *S2 second order conic programming*

S2 supports a few machine learning libraries, such as WEKA. It is simple to create and train a Neural Network (NN) in S2. The example in Figure 1-20 is a simple script that trains an NN to learn the Black-Scholes formula from a data set of stock prices and option prices.

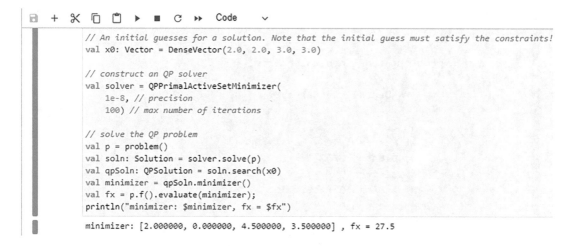

```kotlin
/*
 * build and configure an ANN
 */
// number of epochs (full passes of the data)
val nEpochs = 1500
// batch size: i.e., each epoch has nSamples/batchSize parameter updates
val batchSize = 200
// network learning rate
val learningRate = 0.0001
val conf = NeuralNetConfiguration.Builder()
    .seed(0)
    .weightInit(WeightInit.XAVIER)
    .updater(Adam(learningRate))
    .list()
    .layer(0, DenseLayer.Builder().nIn(5).nOut(10).weightInit(WeightInit.XAVIER)
            .activation(Activation.RELU).build()) // first hidden layer
    .layer(1, OutputLayer.Builder().nIn(10).nOut(1).weightInit(WeightInit.XAVIER)
            .activation(Activation.IDENTITY) // output layer
               .lossFunction(LossFunctions.LossFunction.MSE)
               .build())
    .build()
val net = MultiLayerNetwork(conf)
net.init()
val iterator = ListDataSetIterator<DataSet>(trainSet.asList(), batchSize)

/*
 * train an ANN
 */
val scores = ArrayList<Double>(nEpochs)
var lastScore = 0.0
var sameForNEpochs = 0
for (i in 0 until nEpochs) {
    iterator.reset()
    net.fit(iterator)
    val score = net.score()
    scores.add(score)
    println("epoch: $i, score: $score")
    if (abs(lastScore - score) < 1e-6) {
        if (++sameForNEpochs > 4) {
            println("Score hasn't changed for 5 epochs. Early stop.")
            break
        }
    }
    sameForNEpochs = 0
    lastScore = score
}
```

Figure 1-20. *S2 neural network to learn the Black-Scholes formula*

The neural network converges in a few hundred epochs. The output is shown in Figure 1-21.

```
epoch: 1486, score: 6.617237813770771E-6
epoch: 1487, score: 6.598205072805286E-6
epoch: 1488, score: 6.5801100572571154E-6
epoch: 1489, score: 6.561859045177698E-6
epoch: 1490, score: 6.543863564729691E-6
epoch: 1491, score: 6.526190554723144E-6
epoch: 1492, score: 6.508601363748312E-6
epoch: 1493, score: 6.490883533842862E-6
epoch: 1494, score: 6.472441018559039E-6
epoch: 1495, score: 6.453620735555887E-6
epoch: 1496, score: 6.434681708924473E-6
epoch: 1497, score: 6.41579506918788E-6
epoch: 1498, score: 6.396765820682049E-6
epoch: 1499, score: 6.377637037076056E-6
Given stock price:                 23.75
      strike price:                15.0
      risk-free rate:              0.01
      volatility:                  0.35
      time to maturity:            0.5
=============================================
option price by the Black-Scholes model: 8.879159263714119
option price by the ANN model:           8.776679039001465
```

[1]:

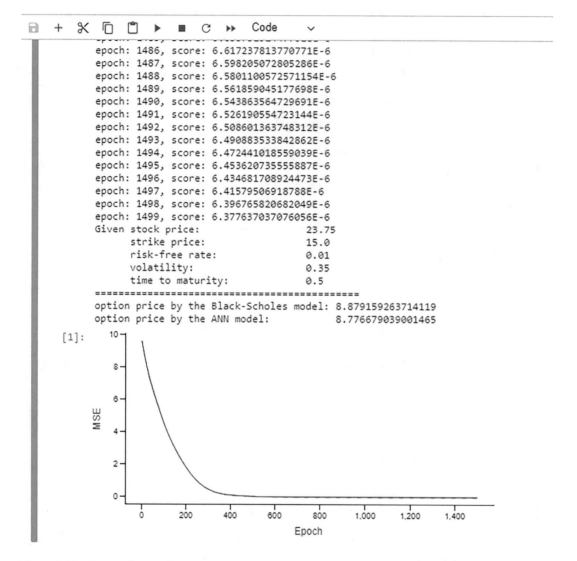

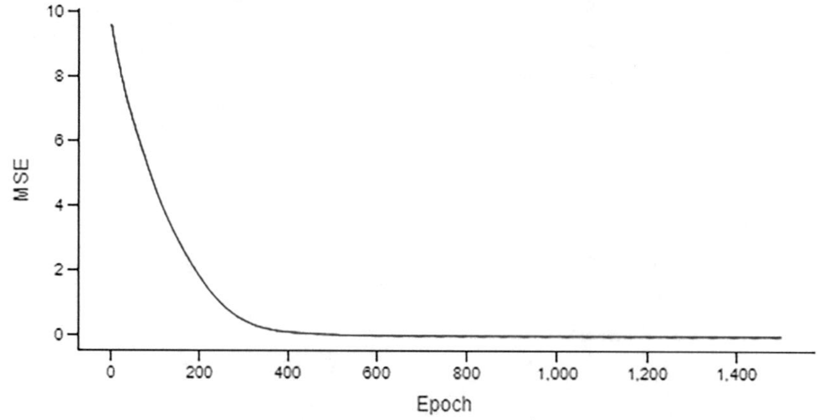

Figure 1-21. *S2 neural network convergence*

1.3.2. Python Replacement

S2 using Kotlin can challenge what Python can do in data science. The problems with Python are that it's scripting or interpreted language is slow, and it is very difficult to deploy code to other devices due to numerous versioning of dependencies and an assorted array of libraries in FORTRAN, C, C++, and so on. S2 is fast and runs on the billions of devices with a JVM by copy-and-pasting jars. Python does two good things: It treats scripting as a glue to combine many components to do data analysis, and it supports array/tensor programming. S2 does those as well, but better.

Python is slow, very slow.[3] Secondly, Python scripts run only in the Python environment. You cannot port it to your phone, watch, router, automobile, rockets. Worst of all, Python deployment can be a nightmare. It runs fine on your machine, but it can take a lot of effort to make it run on another person's machine due to the numerous versioning, compatibility between libraries, and machine dependent executables. In contrast, S2 scripting, compiled to Java bytecode, is orders of magnitude faster than Python. It runs on any (embedded) device that runs JVM, hence there is no deployment problem.

S2 scripting acts as the glue that combines many components, but with much better performance. The following case shows a scheduling system built for a large steel manufacturing plant. The steps are as follows:

1. Read the job data.
2. Read the machine data.
3. Schedule the jobs to the machines.
4. Plot the job-shop schedules to maximize utilization.

All these steps are done in an S2 script in 12 lines! See Figure 1-5. This same code can be deployed on S2, on a stand-alone application, or on a cloud using REST.

[3] See `https://belitsoft.com/java-development-services/java-vs-python-tried-and-true-vs-modern-and-new`

```
%use nanjingironsteel, krangl

// download the job data
val jobs = Job.parseJson(BufferedReader(InputStreamReader(
    URL("https://s2-nmdev.s3.eu-west-3.amazonaws.com/resources/jobs.json")
        .openStream())))
// print the jobs
for (job in jobs) {
    println(job)
}

// download the machine data
val machines = Machine.parseJson(BufferedReader(InputStreamReader(
    URL("https://s2-nmdev.s3.eu-west-3.amazonaws.com/resources/machines.json")
        .openStream())))
// print the machines
for (machine in machines) {
    println(machine)
}

// do the scheduling
Files.createDirectories(Paths.get("./img"))
val scheduleResultJson = NJSteelJsp.schedule(jobs, machines) // run the scheduling algorithm
val scheduleResult = DataFrame.fromJsonString(scheduleResultJson) // get the results
scheduleResult.print(maxRows=100)

// display the Gantt chart of schedules
val filePath = "./img/gantt.svg"
val svg = String(Files.readAllBytes(Paths.get(filePath)))
MimeTypedResult(mapOf("image/svg+xml" to svg))
```

```
订单:
        订单编号: 2020-NM-1
        轧制序号: 2020-OPTIM-1-1
        工艺流程: BP2

订单:
        订单编号: 2020-NM-1
        轧制序号: 2020-OPTIM-1-2
        工艺流程: BP2
```

Figure 1-22. *S2 script to solve a job-shop scheduling problem*

The output is a job schedule and a Gantt chat, as shown in Figure 1-23.

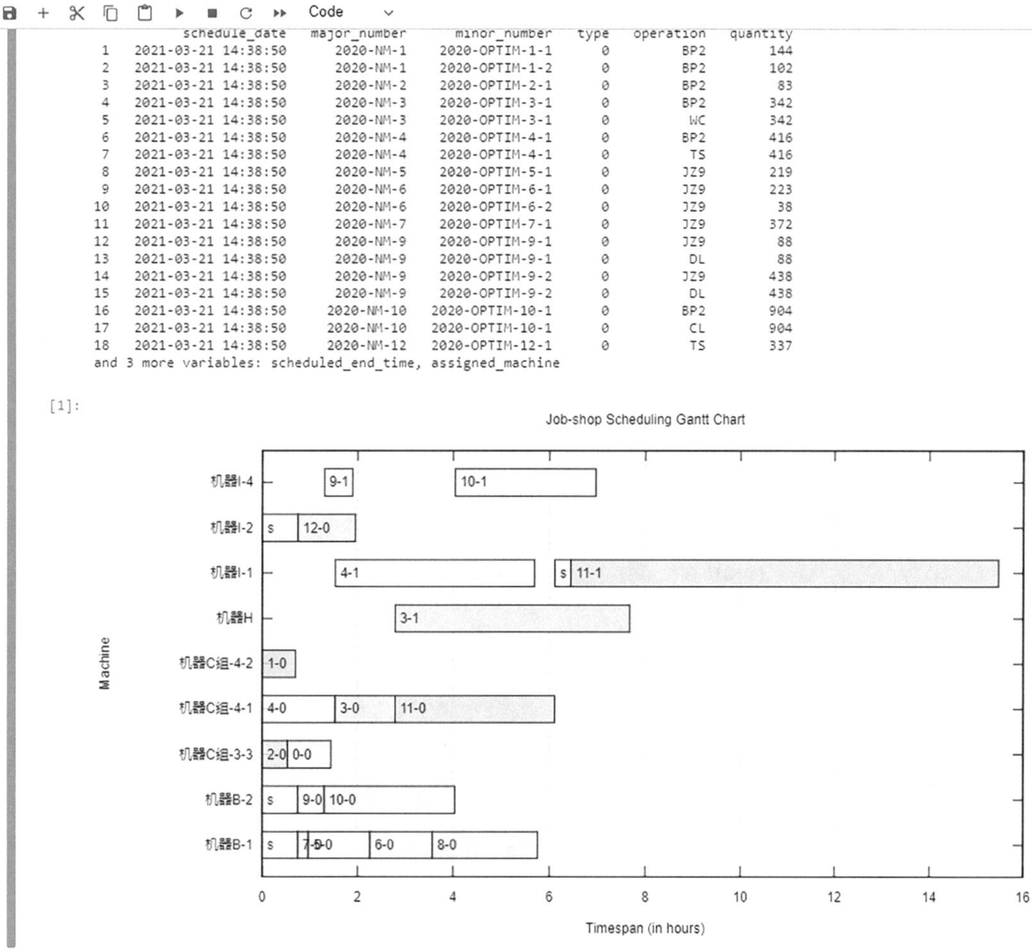

	schedule_date	major_number	minor_number	type	operation	quantity
1	2021-03-21 14:38:50	2020-NM-1	2020-OPTIM-1-1	0	BP2	144
2	2021-03-21 14:38:50	2020-NM-1	2020-OPTIM-1-2	0	BP2	102
3	2021-03-21 14:38:50	2020-NM-2	2020-OPTIM-2-1	0	BP2	83
4	2021-03-21 14:38:50	2020-NM-3	2020-OPTIM-3-1	0	BP2	342
5	2021-03-21 14:38:50	2020-NM-3	2020-OPTIM-3-1	0	WC	342
6	2021-03-21 14:38:50	2020-NM-4	2020-OPTIM-4-1	0	BP2	416
7	2021-03-21 14:38:50	2020-NM-4	2020-OPTIM-4-1	0	TS	416
8	2021-03-21 14:38:50	2020-NM-5	2020-OPTIM-5-1	0	JZ9	219
9	2021-03-21 14:38:50	2020-NM-6	2020-OPTIM-6-1	0	JZ9	223
10	2021-03-21 14:38:50	2020-NM-6	2020-OPTIM-6-2	0	JZ9	38
11	2021-03-21 14:38:50	2020-NM-7	2020-OPTIM-7-1	0	JZ9	372
12	2021-03-21 14:38:50	2020-NM-9	2020-OPTIM-9-1	0	JZ9	88
13	2021-03-21 14:38:50	2020-NM-9	2020-OPTIM-9-1	0	DL	88
14	2021-03-21 14:38:50	2020-NM-9	2020-OPTIM-9-2	0	JZ9	438
15	2021-03-21 14:38:50	2020-NM-9	2020-OPTIM-9-2	0	DL	438
16	2021-03-21 14:38:50	2020-NM-10	2020-OPTIM-10-1	0	BP2	904
17	2021-03-21 14:38:50	2020-NM-10	2020-OPTIM-10-1	0	CL	904
18	2021-03-21 14:38:50	2020-NM-12	2020-OPTIM-12-1	0	TS	337

and 3 more variables: scheduled_end_time, assigned_machine

Figure 1-23. *S2 output for a job-shop scheduling problem*

The power of Python comes from these three libraries: scipy, numpy, and pandas. Together, they allow users to put data in a high-dimensional array (aka tensor) so that they can dice, slice, cut, and sample the tensor in however way they want. More importantly, they magically "convert" any Python script into parallel execution code for high performance. They split a pandas DataFrame into several chunks, spawn a thread to operate on each chunk, and puts them back together.

S2 supports exactly this kind of array/tensor programming for parallelization, and all kinds of dissecting, slicing, cutting, dicing, sampling, massaging data frame using ND4J. We have a paralleled version of the Black-Scholes formula application example. The formula is applied concurrently to all the rows in the stock share price/option price table/array, in the same fashion that Python does with pandas (see Figure 1-24). The code can be found at:

```
https://s21.nm.dev/hub/user-redirect/lab/tree/s2-public/Examples/Neutral%20Network/
Black_Scholes_learning_asynchronous.ipynb
```

```
/**
 * Generate a random set of data of option prices for a range of parameters.
 * This is the training set fed to the ANN.
 */
suspend fun generateData(N: Int,
                         sRange: DoubleArray,
                         xRange: DoubleArray,
                         rRange: DoubleArray,
                         sigmaRange: DoubleArray,
                         tauRange: DoubleArray): DataSet {
    val xs = Nd4j.zeros(N, 5)
    val ys = Nd4j.zeros(N, 1)
    val rowPromises = ArrayList<Deferred<DoubleArray>>(N)
    for (i in 0 until N) {
        val row = GlobalScope.async {
            generateDataAsync(sRange, xRange, rRange, sigmaRange, tauRange) }
        rowPromises.add(row)
    }
    rowPromises.forEachIndexed{index, deferred ->
        val row = deferred.await()
        val input = Nd4j.create(row.slice(0..4))
        val output = Nd4j.create(row.slice(5..5))
        xs.putRow(index.toLong(), input)
        ys.putRow(index.toLong(), output)
    }
    return DataSet(xs, ys)
}
```

Figure 1-24. *S2 script to apply the Black-Scholes formula to a big table of stock share prices to compute the option prices*

1.3.3. S2 Online IDE

To use the S2 online IDE for numerical computing, you need a browser and access to an instance of the S2 server. A few free instances are available. For example, open your browser to this web page:

```
https://s21.nm.dev/
```

S2 will start loading and create a workspace for your session (see Figure 1-25).

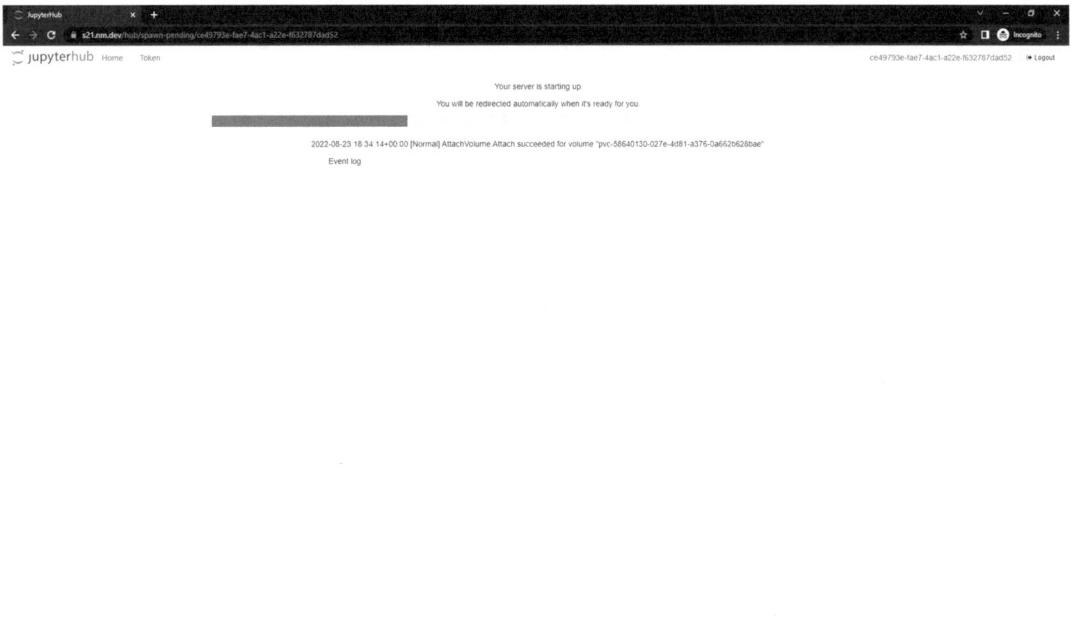

Figure 1-25. *S2 loading*

After S2 is loaded, you will see the welcome screen shown in Figure 1-26, with some public files on the left panel and a launcher on the right panel.

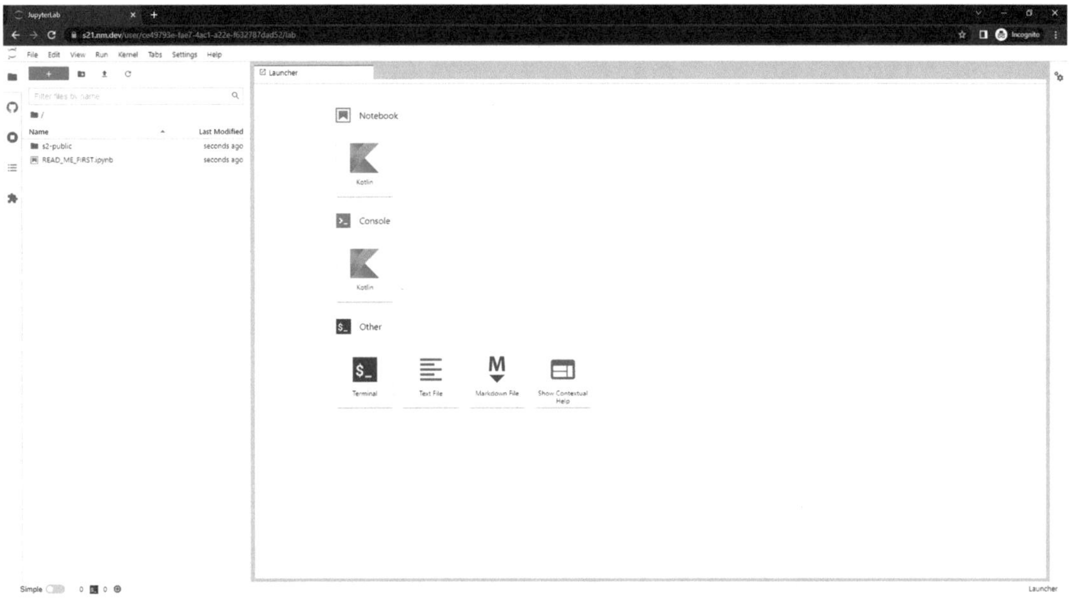

Figure 1-26. *S2 welcome screen*

If you are an absolute beginner, the first file that you should read is `READ_ME_FIRST.ipynb`. It contains a brief tutorial on using S2 and Kotlin. Double-click the filename to open it. See Figure 1-27.

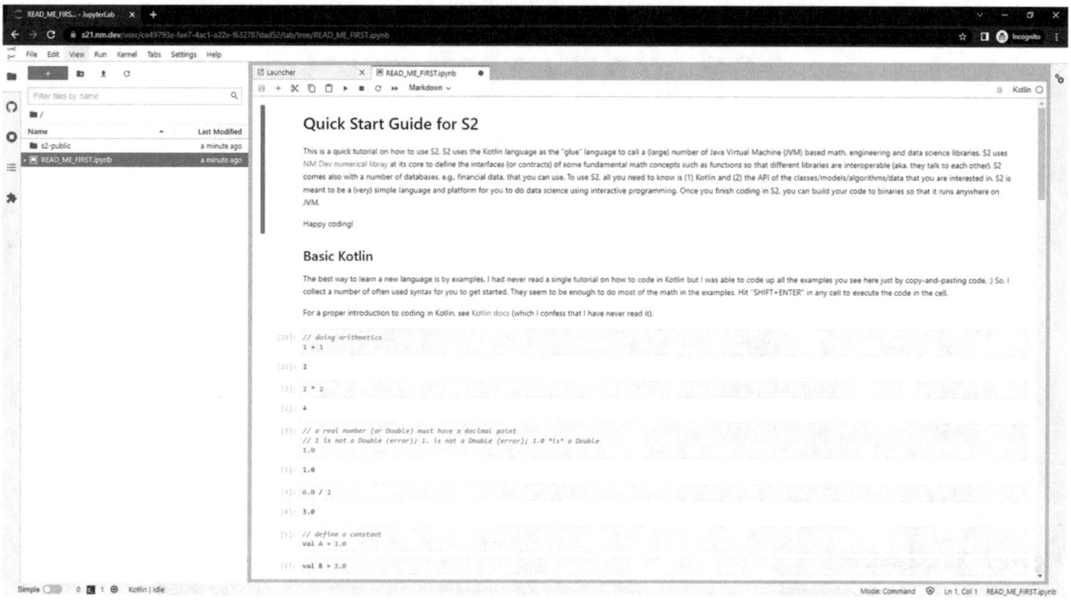

***Figure 1-27.** S2 Quick Start Guide*

To run a Kotlin statement, click the cell and press Shift+Enter.

To open a new blank session, go to the Launcher and create a new notebook, as shown in Figure 1-28.

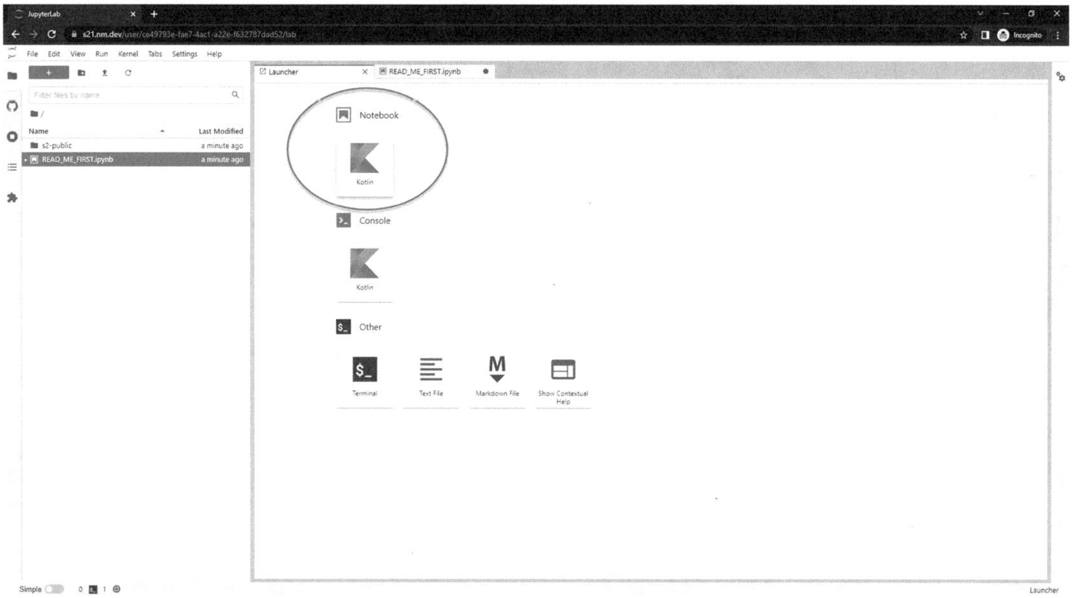

Figure 1-28. *S2 launcher*

You will create new blank notebook, as shown in Figure 1-29.

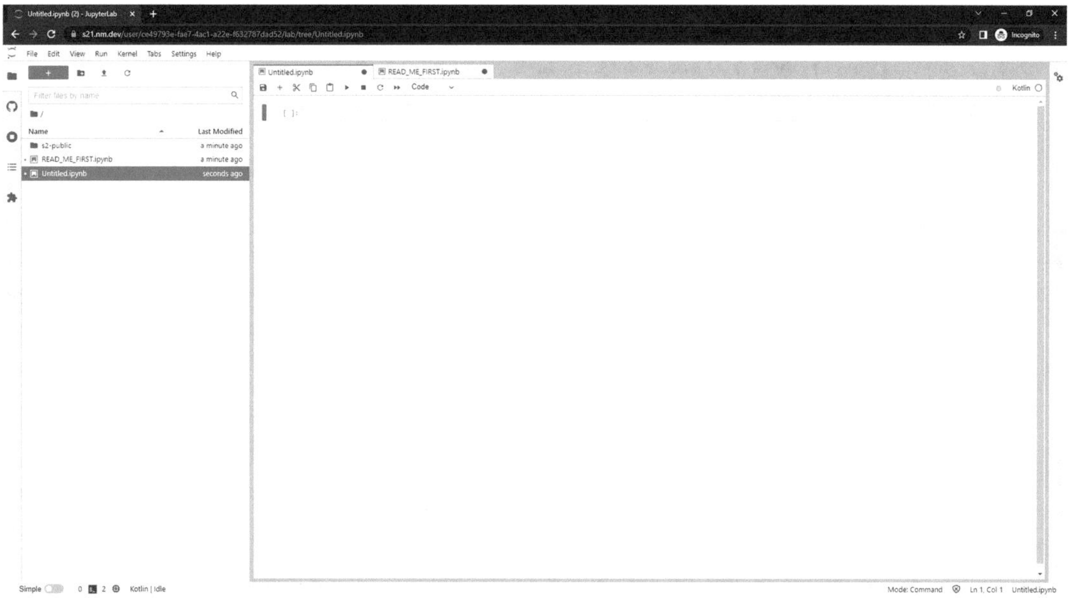

Figure 1-29. *S2 a new blank notebook*

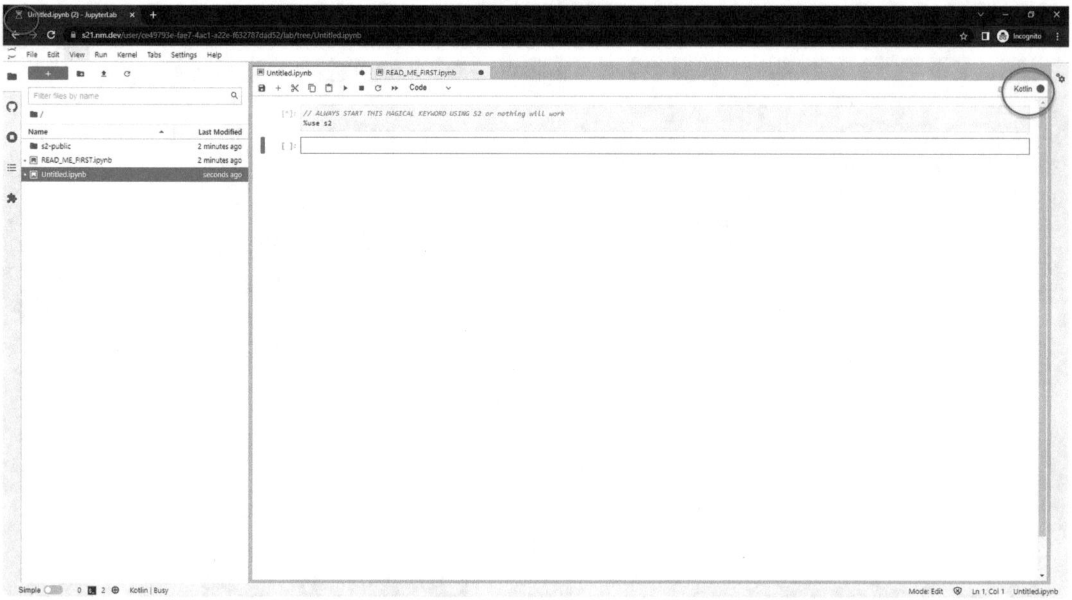

Figure 1-30. *%use S2*

Before you can use an S2 library, the first command you need to type is:

```
%use s2
```

Type your first S2 code, and then press Shift+Enter.

```
1+1
```

It will give you this output (see Figure 1-31):

```
2
```

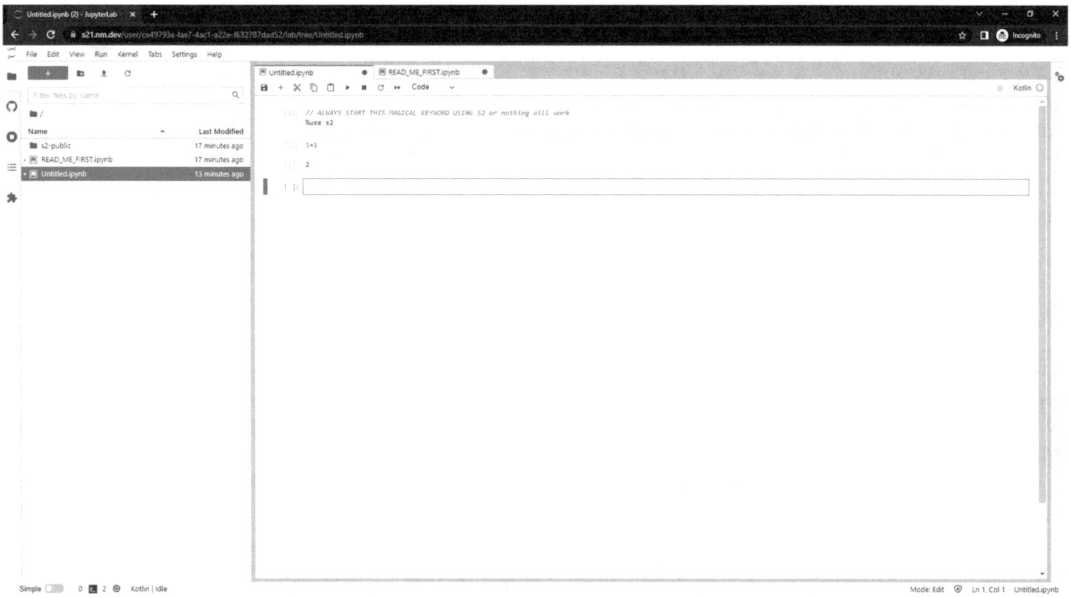

Figure 1-31. *S2 1+1*

Congratulations on your first S2 numerical program! More S2 and Kotlin examples can be found on GitHub (see Figure 1-32) at `https://github.com/nmltd/s2-public`.

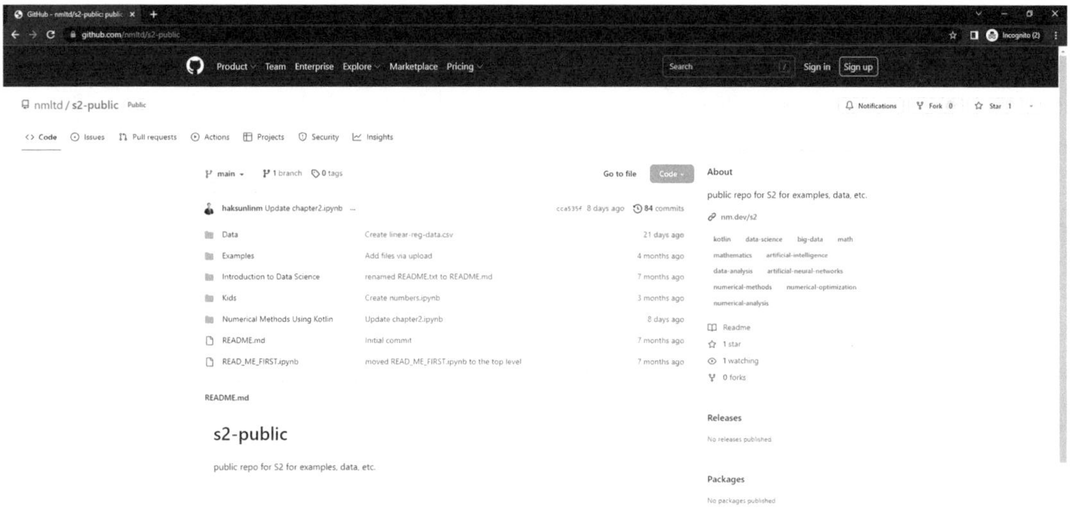

Figure 1-32. *S2 examples in GitHub*

S2 has a large collection of math algorithms, including linear algebra, solving equations, curve fitting, numerical differentiation and integration, ordinary and partial differential equations, linear programming, quadratic programming, second-order conic programming, semi-definite programming, sequential quadratic programming, integer programming, genetic algorithm, basic statistics and probability, random number generation, time series analysis, linear regression and time series analysis. More information can be found in the NM Dev Javadoc.

`https://nm.dev/html/javadoc/nmdev/`

1.4. About This Book

This book covers a wide range of the basic college applied mathematics. This is not a typical mathematics textbook. Most people find learning mathematics difficult and boring. The main reason, I think, is that most people are not good with symbols, abstract reasoning, technical definition, and rigorous proof. For example, the technical definition of limit is as follows.

A function f with domain D in $\mathbb{R}$ converges to a limit L as x approaches a number $c \in \text{closure}(D)$ if given any $\varepsilon > 0$ there exists a $\delta > 0$ such that if $x \in D$ and $|x - c| < \delta$ then $|f(x) - L| < \varepsilon$.

This definition of limit is made very precise and technical because it is the foundation of modern mathematics. Mathematicians can work with it, but most people cannot. Most people are put off simply by those ε and δ. Mathematicians are trained to visualize sentences in symbols and construct images mentally. It would be so much easier for most people if we simply say that the limit of a function is the value that it is approaching if you try different values of x, getting closer to c, with the aid of the graph in Figure 1-33 in mind.

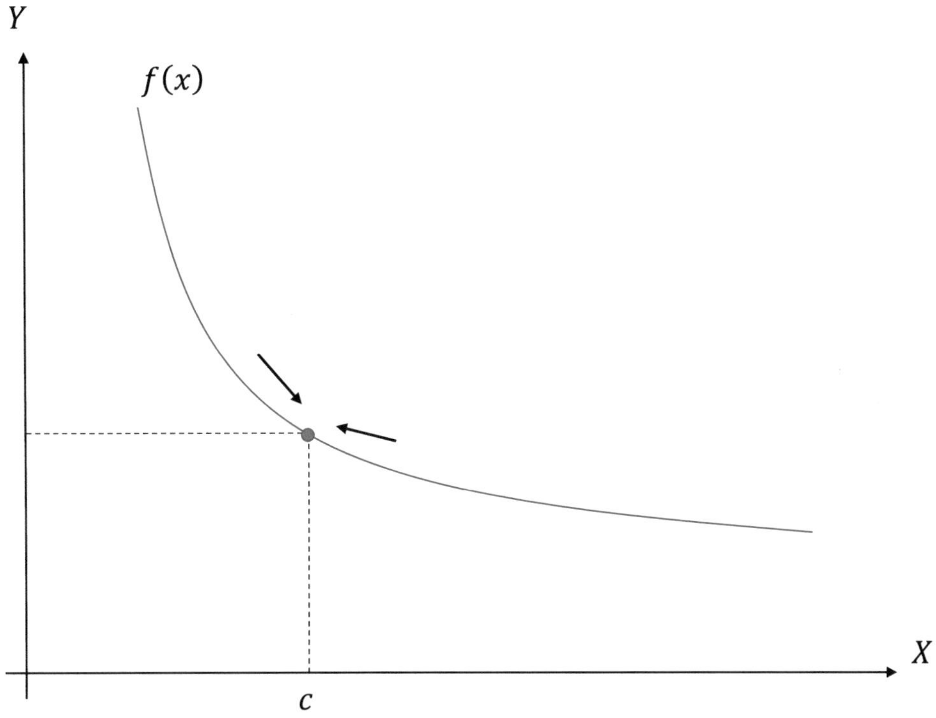

Figure 1-33. $\lim_{x \to c} f(x)$

Likewise, to prove that $\lim_{x \to c} f(x) = f(c)$ if and only if *f* is continuous is not difficult but rather technical, because we would need another definition of continuity and work with the ε-δ definition of limit. It would be so much easier to say, look at Figure 1-33 it is so obvious. Of course, mathematicians do not work like that. What is so obvious to most people cannot be "just obvious" to mathematicians; what is obvious to mathematicians is usually not obvious to non-mathematicians.

For most practitioners of mathematics, the technicality and rigorousness is neither important or necessary. This book is written for engineers who apply mathematics rather than mathematicians who create mathematics. Instead of technical definitions, I give ideas of math concepts supplemented with pictures and diagrams. Instead of rigorous proof, I try to use intuition, which makes it easy to see why things make sense. More importantly, each concept in this book comes with sample code. It is easier to learn a new math concept when you can actually play with it. For example, instead of proving that linear regression is best-fitting a line across a data set in terms of $\boldsymbol{\alpha}$, $\boldsymbol{\beta}$, $\boldsymbol{\varepsilon}$, $\boldsymbol{y}$ and $\boldsymbol{X}$, you can use the code to draw the line in your own data set. Instead of just listing the formula for a normal distribution, it's more fun if you can generate some random numbers from the distribution and see for yourself. Playing and twisting things around (aka experiments) is the best and most fun way to learn and practice mathematics. It makes concrete the ideas that would otherwise be too abstract to grasp. As the Confucian scholar Xunzi pointed out, "What I hear, I forget. What I see, I remember. What I do, I understand."[4]

4 **《儒效篇》 荀子曰:「不**闻不若闻之, 闻之不若见之, 见之不若知之, 知之不若行之; 学至于行之而止矣。」

1.4.1. Sample Code

The sample code in this book is in this format:

```
val v = DenseVector(arrayOf(1.0, 2.0, 3.0))
v
```

It is usually followed by the corresponding output like this:

```
[1.000000, 2.000000, 3.000000]
```

You can copy and paste most of the sample code in the S2 IDE and it should work. Some of the code references a (large) data set that I do not copy in the book. To make things easier, we uploaded the source code and the data sets (in the folder `resources`) to GitHub. The addresses are as follows:

```
https://github.com/nmltd/s2-public/tree/main/Numerical%20Methods%20Using%20Kotlin
```

and

```
https://github.com/apress/numerical-methods-kotlin
```

The source code should compile, build, and run out-of-box. See Figure 1-34.

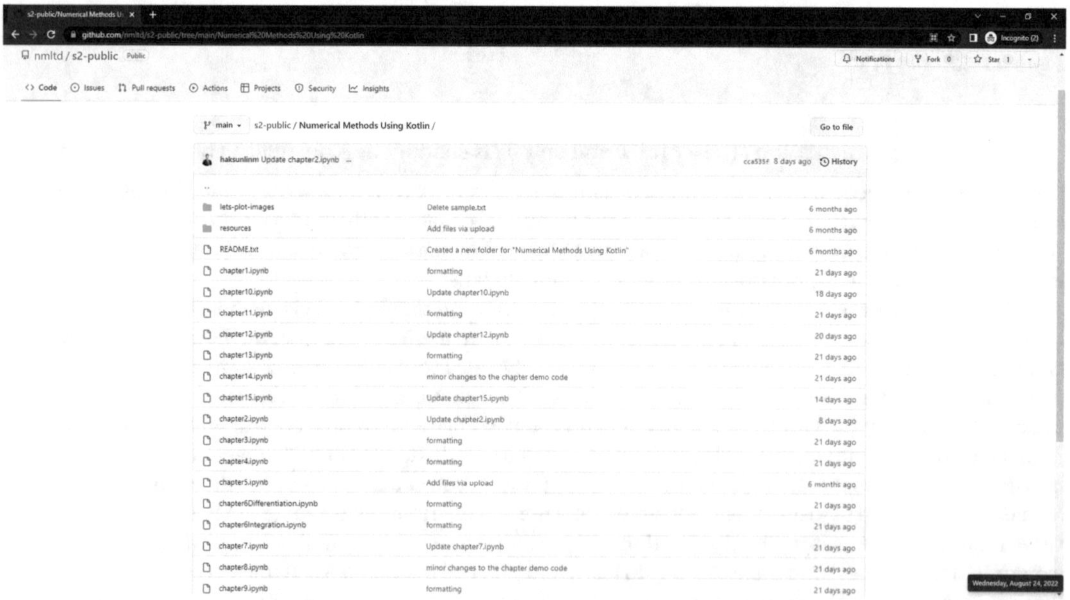

Figure 1-34. *Sample code in GitHub*

Happy coding!

CHAPTER 2

Linear Algebra

Linear algebra algorithms are the most important algorithms in numerical computing. They are the foundation of all numerical algorithms. Many numerical algorithms, however complicated they are, involve some linear algebra computation. For example, a nonlinear problem is often difficult (or impossible) to solve directly. A popular technique is to approximate the nonlinear problem using multiple smaller linear subproblems (as in calculus). A linear problem then usually involves some vectors and matrices because it has multiple variables. Vector and matrix arithmetic are ubiquitous in numerical computing. The theoretical algorithms may be the same for different libraries, but the implementations can be very different, leading to very different performance and accuracy. Therefore, the implementations of linear algebra algorithms, such as matrix decompositions, are critical to the accuracy and performance of many numerical algorithms or to numerical computing in general.

There are (at least) two challenges to producing a high-quality and professional linear algebra computing library: accuracy and high performance (fast computation). A computer can represent only a finite amount of numbers (a 64-bit computer can represent roughly about 1.8e19 numbers); put in another way, there are infinitely many numbers that a computer cannot represent. The (floating-point) value of a computation is usually just an approximation of the true theoretical result. This gets even worse when the computation involves a very big and a very small number. The result is often skewed toward the big number, ignoring the precision of the small number. In an iterative computation, such as those for optimization, tiny errors in each round accumulate. A theoretically tractable problem can sometimes become practically infeasible.

Correctly implementing a theoretical algorithm is therefore not enough. A professional numerical library also needs to handle the practical numerical issues, for instance, when handling a matrix whose elements range many orders of magnitude. Basic matrix operations that involve a series of consecutive row and/or column operations, mixing very tiny and very big elements, will lead to considerable rounding errors. One way to handle this problem is to permute the matrix beforehand, insofar as possible, so that the entries are rearranged in a monotonic order. You can apply permutation matrices to push smaller elements to the top-left corner. Then you do the operations starting from the bottom-right corner. Sometimes, choosing a better algorithm will also help. For example, the QL algorithm usually has smaller roundoff than the QR algorithm when computing eigenvalues.

In NM Dev, we deal with this issue of numerical stability seriously. We test our library over a large collection of benchmark problem instances and gather the ill-conditioned and degenerate cases. Then, we apply various numerical techniques to deal with these cases one by one. We carefully compare our results to other open-source and commercial software to make sure our results are good. This process makes our library more robust and capable of handling a wide variety of problem structures.

Speeding up the vector and matrix computations will consequentially speed up any numerical computation in general. There are many ways (and hence considerations) to do so using modern computing technologies: parallel computing (multithreaded, multicores, multi-machines, CUDA), faster algorithms,

H. Li, PhD, *Numerical Methods Using Kotlin*, https://doi.org/10.1007/978-1-4842-8826-9_2

more efficient data structures, in-place operations versus making copies of objects, inline operations versus virtual function calls, and so on. Some of these techniques speed up code execution (e.g., in-line operations), but they may make the code indecipherable to another human (or sometimes even the original authors) and hence are not maintainable. NM Dev tries to strike a balance between readability (for humans) and speed. We compared the performance of NM Dev to all other major Java math libraries that are publicly available. The comparisons were done on a Dual Intel Xeon X5650 2.66GHz (12 cores in total) machine with 24GB RAM running Windows 7 Ultimate 64-bit. The JVM used was Oracle Java HotSpot 64-bit Server 1.8.0_25. By our benchmarking, NM Dev is (probably) the fastest (Java) math library available to date. Here are a few benchmark comparisons. The source code of the full test suite and results can be downloaded from here:

```
https://nm.dev/html/benchmark/benchmark_chart.html?category=linearalgebra
```

NM Dev or SuanShu matrix multiplication is 182 times faster than Apache Commons Math and 14 times faster than R. See Figure 2-1.

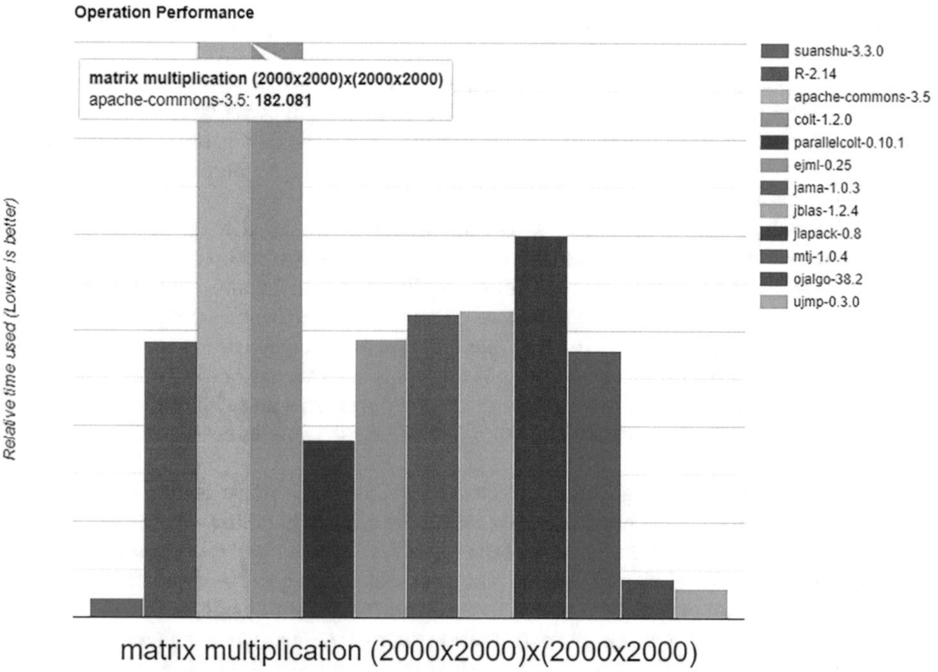

Figure 2-1. *NM Dev is 182 times faster than Apache in matrix multiplication*

This is because the NM Dev matrix implementation uses a parallel version of the adaptive Strassen's algorithm for fast matrix multiplication, which has a complexity of $O(n^{2.8074})$. Apache Commons Math and most other Java libraries that we are aware of implement the standard $O(n^3)$ algorithm. The performance advantage of NM Dev is significant for bigger matrices, especially when handling big data.

NM Dev matrix determinant computation is 31 times faster than Apache Commons Math. See Figure 2-2.

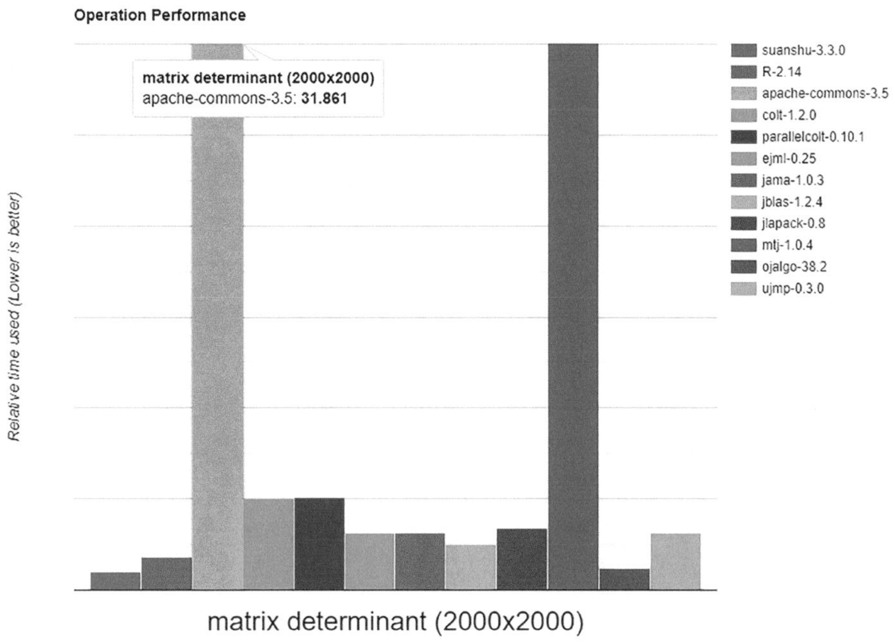

Figure 2-2. *NM Dev is 31 times faster than Apache in computing matrix determinant*

NM Dev LU decomposition is 32 times faster than Apache Commons Math. See Figure 2-3.

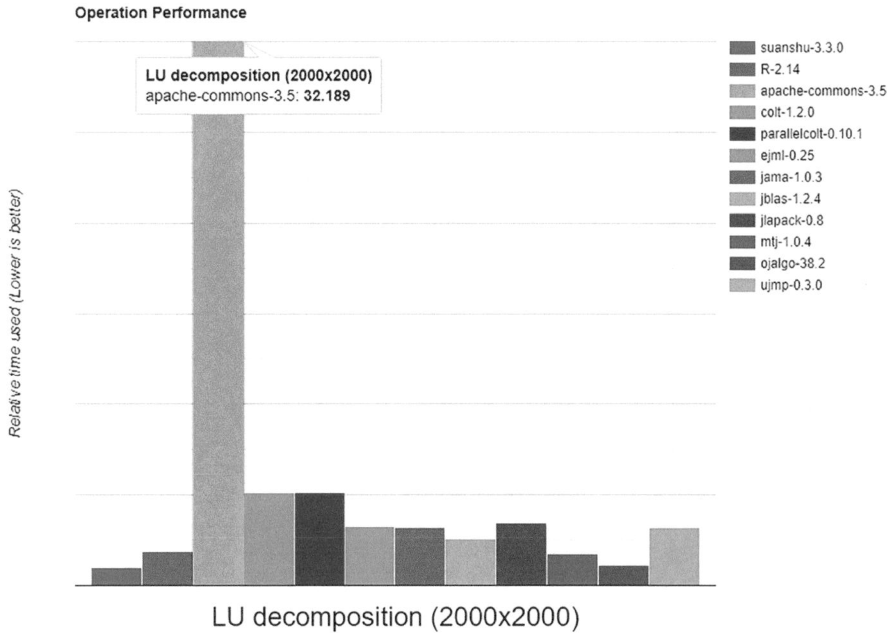

Figure 2-3. *NM Dev is 32 times faster than Apache in LU decomposition*

NM Dev QR decomposition is two times faster than R. See Figure 2-4.

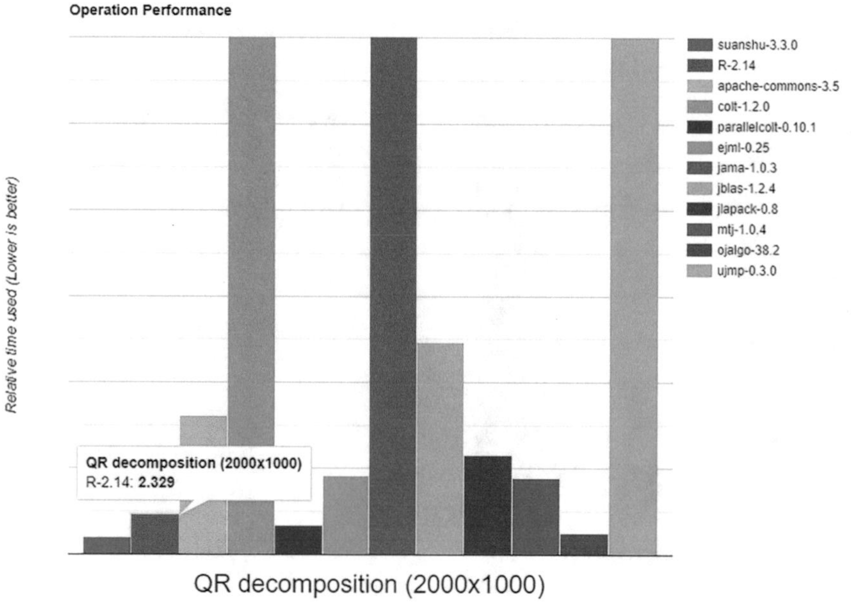

Figure 2-4. *NM Dev is two times faster than R in QR decomposition*

NM Dev SVD decomposition is two times faster than R. See Figure 2-5.

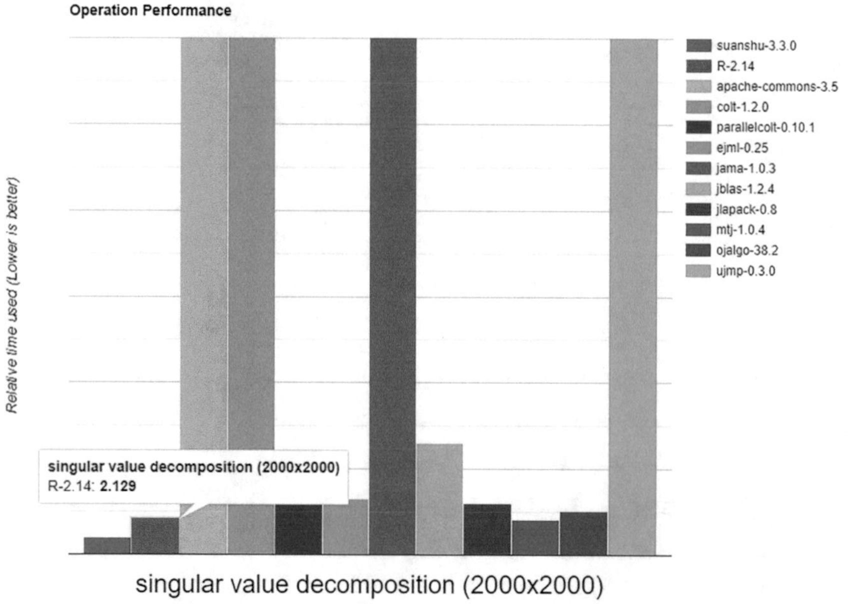

Figure 2-5. *NM Dev is two times faster than R in SVD*

NM Dev is six times faster than R in solving this system of linear equations. See Figure 2-6.

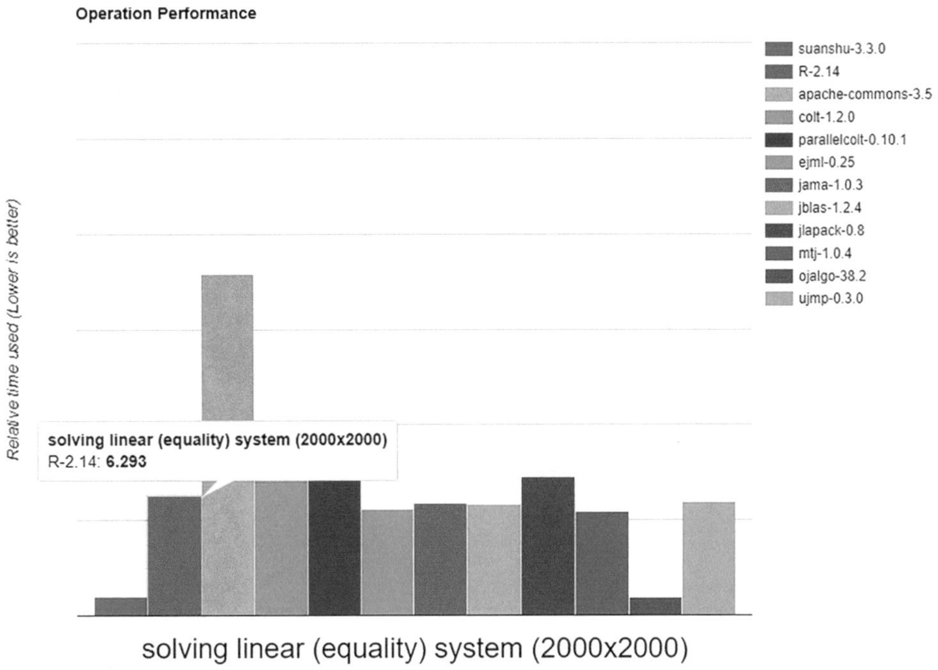

Figure 2-6. *NM Dev is six times faster than R in solving a system of linear equations*

The source code in this chapter can be run on the S2 platform here:

https://s21.nm.dev/hub/user-redirect/lab/tree/s2-public/Numerical%20Methods%20Using%20Kotlin/chapter2.ipynb

The source code can be found on GitHub:

https://github.com/nmltd/s2-public/blob/main/Numerical%20Methods%20Using%20Kotlin/chapter2.ipynb

2.1. Vector

In mathematics, a Euclidean vector is a geometric object that has a magnitude (or length) and direction. An n-dimensional vector can be represented as an array consisting of n scalar elements where each element is the length of the vector's projection on the corresponding dimension. For example, in a two-dimensional Euclidean space (denoted by $\mathbb{R}^2$), a vector a pointing from point $A = (0, 0)$ to point $B = (1, 2)$ can be denoted by the following:

$$a = \overrightarrow{AB} = (1,2)$$

In NM Dev, a vector is represented by the `Vector` interface. There are multiple ways to construct such an object. The most common one is to initialize a `DenseVector` with a double array, specifying each element. See Figure 2-7.

```
val v1: Vector = DenseVector(arrayOf(1.0, 2.0)) // define a vector
println(String.format("v1 = %s", v1)) // print out v1
```

The output is as follows:

```
v1 = [1.000000, 2.000000]
```

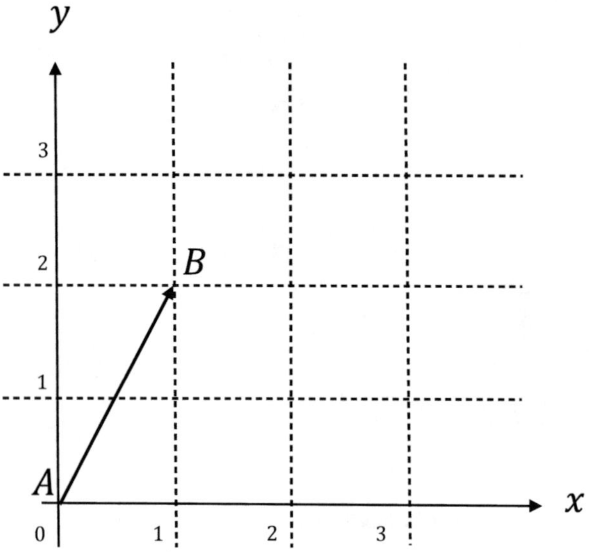

Figure 2-7. *A vector* $\overrightarrow{\boldsymbol{AB}} = (\mathbf{1},\mathbf{2})$

2.1.1. Element-Wise Operations

These functions access and modify a `Vector`:

```
/**
  * Gets the length of this vector.
  *
  * @return the vector length
  */
public int size();
/**
  * Gets the value at position <i>i</i>.
  *
  * @param i the position of a vector entry
  * @return <i>v[i]</i>
  */
public double get(int i);
/**
```

```
  * Changes the value of an entry in this vector.
  * This is the only method that may change the entries of a vector.
  *
  * @param i     the index of the entry to change. The indices are counting
  *              from 1, NOT 0.
  * @param value the value to change to
  */
public void set(int i, double value);
```

Computer scientists count from 0, while mathematicians count from 1. NM Dev counts an (vector and matrix) index from 1 instead of 0, following the mathematician convention.

Continuing with the previous example, the following code snippet changes the vector to (1, –2):

```
val size: Int = v1.size() // 2
println(String.format("v1 size = %d", size))
```

The output is as follows:

```
v1 size = 2
```

```
val v1_1: Double = v1.get(1) // 1.0
println(String.format("v1_1 = %f", v1_1))
```

The output is as follows:

```
v1_1 = 1.000000
```

```
v1.set(2, -2.0) // v1 becomes (1.0, -2.0)
println(String.format("v1 = %s", v1)) // print out v1
```

The output is as follows:

```
v1 = [1.000000, -2.000000]
```

In NM Dev, the arithmetic operations—addition, subtraction, multiplication, division, scaling, and exponentiation—on a vector are element-wise operations.

```
/**
  * \(this + that\)
  *
  * @param that a vector
  * @return \(this + that\)
  */
@Override
public Vector add(Vector that);
/**
  * \(this - that\)
  *
```

```
    * @param that a vector
    * @return \(this - that\)
    */
@Override
public Vector minus(Vector that);
/**
    * Multiplies {@code this} by {@code that}, entry-by-entry.
    *
    * @param that a vector
    * @return \(this \cdot that\)
    */
public Vector multiply(Vector that);
/**
    * Divides {@code this} by {@code that}, entry-by-entry.
    *
    * @param that a vector
    * @return \(this / that\)
    */
public Vector divide(Vector that);
/**
    * Adds a constant to all entries in this vector.
    *
    * @param c a constant
    * @return \(v + c\)
    */
public Vector add(double c);
/**
    * Subtracts a constant from all entries in this vector.
    *
    * @param c a constant
    * @return \(v - c\)
    */
public Vector minus(double c);
/**
    * Takes the exponentiation of all entries in this vector, entry-by-entry.
    *
    * @param c a constant
    * @return \(v ^ c\)
    */
public Vector pow(double c);
/**
    * Scales this vector by a constant, entry-by-entry. Here is a way to get a
    * unit version of the vector:
    * <blockquote><code>
    * vector.scaled(1. / vector.norm())
    * </code></blockquote>
    *
    * @param c a constant
    * @return \(c \times this\)
    */
public Vector scaled(double c);
```

The following code snippets demonstrate the vector arithmetic operations:

```
val v2: Vector = DenseVector(arrayOf(-2.0, 1.0)) // define another vector

// addition
val a1: Vector = v1.add(0.1) // add 0.1 to all entries
println(String.format("a1 = %s", a1)) // print out a1
val a2: Vector = v1.add(v2) // a2 = v1 + v2, entry by entry
println(String.format("a2 = %s", a2)) // print out a2
```

The output is as follows:

```
a1 = [1.100000, -1.900000]
a2 = [-1.000000, -1.000000]
```

```
// subtraction
val m1: Vector = v1.minus(0.1) // subtract 0.1 from all entries
println(String.format("m1 = %s", m1)) // print out m1
val m2: Vector = v1.minus(v2) // v1 - v2, entry by entry
println(String.format("m2 = %s", m2)) // print out m2
```

The output is as follows:

```
m1 = [0.900000, -2.100000]
m2 = [3.000000, -3.000000]
```

```
val s1: Vector = v1.scaled(0.5) // multiply all entries by 0.5
println(String.format("s1 = %s", s1)) // print out s1
```

The output is as follows:

```
s1 = [0.500000, -1.000000]
```

```
val t1: Vector = v1.multiply(v2) // multiply v1 by v2, entry by entry
println(String.format("t1 = %s", t1)) // print out t1
```

The output is as follows:

```
t1 = [-2.000000, -2.000000]
```

```
// division
val d1: Vector = v1.divide(v2) // divide v1 by v2, entry by entry
println(String.format("d1 = %s", d1)) // print out d1
```

The output is as follows:

```
d1 = [-0.500000, -2.000000]
```

```
// power
val p1: Vector = v1.pow(2.0) // take to the square, entry-wise
println(String.format("p1 = %s", p1)) // print out p1
```

The output is as follows:

```
p1 = [1.000000, 4.000000]
```

2.1.2. Norm

The ℓ_p-norm of a vector $\boldsymbol{x} = (x_1, x_1, \ldots, x_n)$ is defined as follows:

$$\| x \|_p = \left(\sum_{i=i}^{n} |\boldsymbol{x}_i|^p \right)^p$$

A *norm* is a function that maps a vector to a non-negative real number that behaves in certain ways like the distance from the origin. It commutes with scaling, obeys a form of the triangle inequality, and is zero only at the origin. In NM Dev, a vector norm is computed using the `norm(double p)` member method. In particular, when no argument is given, `norm()` computes the ℓ_2-norm. The ℓ_2-norm, or Euclidean norm, often denoted as $\|\boldsymbol{x}\|_2$ or simply $\|\boldsymbol{x}\|$, is the Euclidean distance of a vector from the origin. It is also the square root of the inner product of a vector with itself. The following snippet computes the ℓ_1-norm and ℓ_2-norm of a right triangle with side lengths 3 and 4. See Figure 2-8.

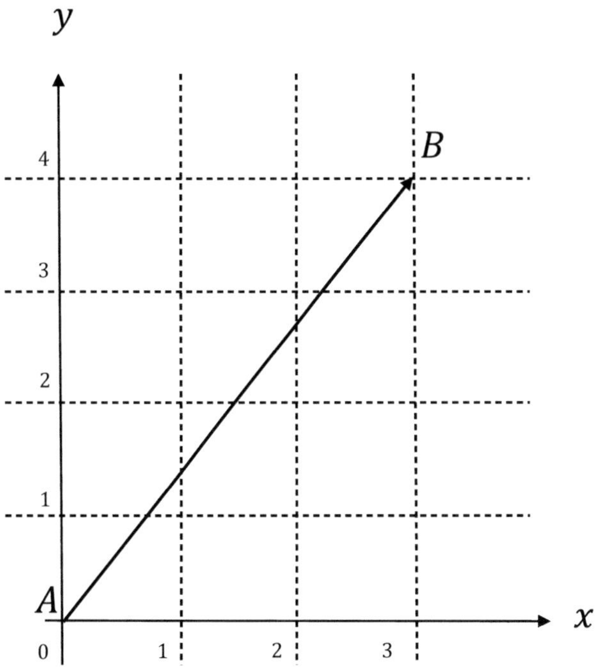

Figure 2-8. *A 3-4-5 triangle*

```
// norm
val v3: Vector = DenseVector(arrayOf(3.0, 4.0))
val norm1: Double = v3.norm(1.0) // l1 norm = (3.0 + 4.0) = 7.0
println(String.format("L1 norm = %f", norm1))
val norm2: Double = v3.norm() // l2 norm = sqrt(3^2 + 4^2) = 5, Pythagorean theorem
println(String.format("L2 norm = %f", norm2))
```

The output is as follows:

```
L1 norm = 7.000000
L2 norm = 5.000000
```

2.1.3. Inner Product and Angle

In a real n-space $\mathbb{R}^n$, the inner product of $\boldsymbol{x} = (x_1, x_2, \ldots, x_n)$ and $\boldsymbol{y} = (y_1, y_2, \ldots, y_n)$ is defined as follows:

$$\langle \boldsymbol{x}, \boldsymbol{y} \rangle = \boldsymbol{x} \cdot \boldsymbol{y} = \sum_{i=1}^{n} x_i y_i$$

The angle θ between $\boldsymbol{x}$ and $\boldsymbol{y}$ is as follows:

$$\theta = \cos^{-1}\frac{\langle \boldsymbol{x},\boldsymbol{y}\rangle}{\|\boldsymbol{x}\|\|\boldsymbol{y}\|}$$

See Figure 2-9.

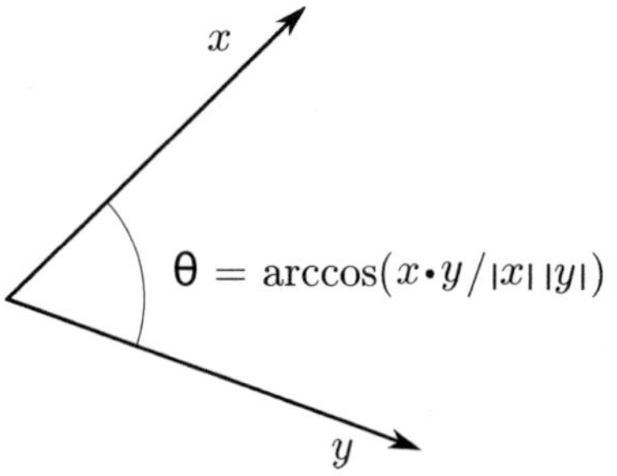

Figure 2-9. *Dot product and angle*

In particular, if the vectors x and y are orthogonal or perpendicular (their angle is 90°), then $\boldsymbol{x} \cdot \boldsymbol{y} = 0$. At the other extreme, if they are pointing in the same direction (their angle is 0°), then $\boldsymbol{x} \cdot \boldsymbol{y} = \|\boldsymbol{x}\|\|\boldsymbol{y}\|$. This implies that the dot product of a vector $\boldsymbol{x}$ with itself is $\boldsymbol{x} \cdot \boldsymbol{y} = \|\boldsymbol{x}\|^2$. In NM Dev, the signatures for the inner product and the angle are as follows:

```
/**
  * Inner product in the Euclidean space is the dot product.
  *
  * @param that a vector
  * @return \(this \cdot that\)
  * @see <a href="http://en.wikipedia.org/wiki/Dot_product"> Wikipedia: Dot
  * product</a>
  */
@Override
public double innerProduct(Vector that);
/**
  * Measures the angle, \(\theta\), between {@code this} and {@code that}.
  * That is,
  * \[
  * this \cdot that = \|this\| \times \|that\| \times \cos \theta
  * \]
  *
  * @param that a vector
  * @return the angle, \(\theta\), between {@code this} and {@code that}
  */
@Override
public double angle(Vector that);
```

Here's an example:

```
// inner product and angle
val v4: Vector = DenseVector(arrayOf(1.0, 2.0))
val v5: Vector = DenseVector(arrayOf(3.0, 4.0))
val dot: Double = v4.innerProduct(v5) // (1.*3. + 2.*4.) = 11.
println(String.format("<%s,%s> = %f", v4, v5, dot))
val angle: Double = v4.angle(v5)
println(String.format("angle between %s and %s = %f", v4, v5, angle))
```

The output is as follows:

```
<[1.000000, 2.000000] ,[3.000000, 4.000000] > = 11.000000
angle between [1.000000, 2.000000]  and [3.000000, 4.000000]  = 0.179853
```

2.2. Matrix

A matrix is a set of elements or entries arranged in a rectangular array or table in rows and columns. An $m \times n$ matrix is a rectangular array of m rows and n columns. The elements of a matrix can be numbers, symbols, or mathematical expressions. The following is a three-row, three-column matrix consisting of nine elements:

$$\begin{bmatrix} 1 & 2 & 3 \\ 4 & 5 & 6 \\ 7 & 8 & 9 \end{bmatrix}$$

The individual entries in an $m \times n$ matrix $\boldsymbol{A}$ are often denoted by a_{ij}, where i (the row index) and j (the column index) usually vary from 1 to m and n, respectively. To conveniently express an element of the results of matrix operations, the indices of the element are often attached to the parenthesized or bracketed matrix expression (for example, $(\boldsymbol{AB})_{ij}$ refers to an element of a matrix product). A matrix is tall if $m > n$, fat if $m < n$, and square if $m = n$. See Figure 2-10.

$$\begin{array}{c} \\ 1 \\ 2 \\ 3 \\ \vdots \\ m \end{array} \begin{array}{c} \begin{array}{cccc} 1 & 2 & \cdots & n \end{array} \\ \begin{bmatrix} a_{11} & a_{12} & \cdots & a_{1n} \\ a_{21} & a_{22} & \cdots & a_{2n} \\ a_{31} & a_{32} & \cdots & a_{3n} \\ \vdots & \vdots & \vdots & \vdots \\ a_{m1} & a_{m2} & \cdots & a_{mn} \end{bmatrix} \end{array}$$

Figure 2-10. *a_{ij} refers to the entry in the i-th row and j-th column*

In NM Dev, a matrix is represented by the `Matrix` interface. There are multiple ways to construct a `Matrix` object. The most common way is to use the `DenseMatrix` implementation and specify all entries (nonzeros and zeros) in a double array. The following code snippet constructs the 3×3 matrix shown previously:

```
// matrix construction
val m1: Matrix = DenseMatrix(
    arrayOf(
        doubleArrayOf(1.0, 2.0, 3.0),
        doubleArrayOf(4.0, 5.0, 6.0),
        doubleArrayOf(7.0, 8.0, 9.0)
    )
)
val m2: Matrix = DenseMatrix(m1) // copy the matrix m1
println(String.format("\nm1 = %s", m1)) // print out the matrix m1
println(String.format("\nm2 = %s", m2)) // print out the matrix m2
```

The output is as follows:

```
m1 = 3x3
        [,1] [,2] [,3]
[1,] 1.000000, 2.000000, 3.000000,
[2,] 4.000000, 5.000000, 6.000000,
[3,] 7.000000, 8.000000, 9.000000,
m2 = 3x3
        [,1] [,2] [,3]
[1,] 1.000000, 2.000000, 3.000000,
[2,] 4.000000, 5.000000, 6.000000,
[3,] 7.000000, 8.000000, 9.000000,
```

There are many ways to construct a `DenseMatrix`. The signatures are as follows:

```
/**
 * Constructs a 0 matrix of dimension <i>nRows * nCols</i>.
 *
 * @param nRows the number of rows
 * @param nCols the number of columns
 */
public DenseMatrix(int nRows, int nCols)
/**
 * Constructs a matrix from a 2D {@code double[][]} array.
 *
 * @param data a 2D array input
 * @throws IllegalArgumentException when {@code data} is a jagged array
 */
public DenseMatrix(double[][] data)
/**
 * Constructs a matrix from a 1D {@code double[]}. The array is a
 * concatenation of the matrix rows. A sample usage is to convert a vector
 * to a matrix. For example, to construct a column vector, we do
```

```
 * <pre>{@code
 * DenseMatrix V = new DenseMatrix(v.toArray(), v.length, 1);
 * }</pre> To construct a row vector, we do
 * <pre>{@code
 * DenseMatrix V = new DenseMatrix(v.toArray(), 1, v.length);
 * }</pre>
 *
 * @param data  the 1D array input
 * @param nRows the number or rows
 * @param nCols the number of columns
 * @throws IllegalArgumentException when the length of {@code data} does not
 *                                  equal to <i>nRows * nCols</i>
 */
public DenseMatrix(double[] data, int nRows, int nCols)
/**
 * Constructs a column matrix from a vector.
 *
 * @param v a vector
 */
public DenseMatrix(Vector v)
/**
 * Converts any matrix to the standard matrix representation. This method is
 * the same as {@link #toDense} if {@code A} is {@link Densifiable}.
 *
 * @param A a matrix
 */
public DenseMatrix(Matrix A)
/**
 * Copy constructor performing a deep copy.
 *
 * @param A a {@code DenseMatrix}
 */
public DenseMatrix(DenseMatrix A)
```

For example, this snippet creates a column matrix from a vector:

```
// create a vector
val v: Vector = DenseVector(arrayOf(1.0, 2.0, 3.0))
// create a column matrix from a vector
val m3: Matrix = DenseMatrix(v)
println(String.format("\nm3 = %s", m3)) // print out the matrix m3
```

The output is as follows:

```
m3 = 3x1
      [,1]
[1,] 1.000000,
[2,] 2.000000,
[3,] 3.000000,
```

2.2.1. Matrix Operations

When designing the NM Dev library, we made the class library as parsimonious as possible to avoid method pollution. This is inspired by the jMatrices' whitepaper. The challenge is to organize the methods by minimal and correct packages. The `Matrix` class has only 26 methods, nine of which are constructors and related, three of which are overrides for the `AbstractMatrix` interfaces, and eight of which are overrides for the `MatrixSpace` interfaces. Only six of them are class specific, which makes calling these methods convenient for the users. The other dozens of matrix operations, such as the many factorizations, properties like rank, and transformations like inverse, are grouped into multiple classes and packages. In most cases, each of these operations is a class of its own. For instance, the inverse operation itself is a class inheriting from `Matrix`. The constructor takes as input a `Matrix` to invert. For example, to find the inverse for this:

$$\mathbf{A} = \begin{bmatrix} 1 & 2 & 3 \\ 6 & 5 & 4 \\ 8 & 7 & 9 \end{bmatrix}$$

You would code the following:

```
// compute the inverse of an invertible matrix
val A: Matrix = DenseMatrix(
    arrayOf(
        doubleArrayOf(1.0, 2.0, 3.0),
        doubleArrayOf(6.0, 5.0, 4.0),
        doubleArrayOf(8.0, 7.0, 9.0)
    )
)

val Ainv: Matrix = Inverse(A)
val I: Matrix = A.multiply(Ainv)
println(String.format("%s * \n%s = \n%s", A, Ainv, I))
```

The output is as follows:

```
3x3
        [,1] [,2] [,3]
[1,] 1.000000, 2.000000, 3.000000,
[2,] 6.000000, 5.000000, 4.000000,
[3,] 8.000000, 7.000000, 9.000000,  *
3x3
        [,1] [,2] [,3]
[1,] -0.809524, -0.142857, 0.333333,
[2,] 1.047619, 0.714286, -0.666667,
[3,] -0.095238, -0.428571, 0.333333,  =
3x3
        [,1] [,2] [,3]
[1,] 1.000000, 0.000000, 0.000000,
[2,] -0.000000, 1.000000, 0.000000,
[3,] -0.000000, -0.000000, 1.000000,
```

NM Dev computes the inverse of A to be the following:

$$A^{-1} = \begin{bmatrix} -0.809524 & -0.142857 & 0.333333 \\ 1.047619 & 0.714286 & -0.666667 \\ -0.095238 & -0.428571 & 0.333333 \end{bmatrix}$$

It is important to note that the inverse of A Ainv is also a Matrix, created by the keyword new, not by a method call. In summary, we chose to have many classes, rather than to have a class with many methods. Each class is kept deliberately short. This class parsimony principle is a key design decision guiding the whole library development.

2.2.2. Element-Wise Operations

These functions access and modify a Matrix:

```
/**
 * Set the matrix entry at <i>[i,j]</i> to a value.
 * This is the only method that may change a matrix.
 *
 * @param i     the row index
 * @param j     the column index
 * @param value the value to set <i>A[i,j]</i> to
 * @throws MatrixAccessException if <i>i</i> or <i>j</i> is out of range
 */
public void set(int i, int j, double value) throws MatrixAccessException;
/**
 * Get the matrix entry at <i>[i,j]</i>.
 *
 * @param i the row index
 * @param j the column index
 * @return <i>A[i,j]</i>
 * @throws MatrixAccessException if <i>i</i> or <i>j</i> is out of range
 */
public double get(int i, int j) throws MatrixAccessException;
```

NM Dev counts an (vector and matrix) index from 1 instead of 0. The upper top-left entry is the (1, 1)-th entry. The following code snippet changes the diagonal entries to 0:

```
// getters and setters
val m1_11: Double = m1.get(1, 1)
val m1_22: Double = m1.get(2, 2)
val m1_33: Double = m1.get(3, 3)
println(String.format("\nThe diagonal entries are: %f, %f, %f", m1_11, m1_22, m1_33))

// changing the diagonal to 0
println("\nChanging the diagonal to 0")
m1.set(1, 1, 0.0)
m1.set(2, 2, 0.0)
m1.set(3, 3, 0.0)
println(String.format("m1 = %s", m1)) // print out the matrix m1
```

The output is as follows:

```
the diagonal entries are: 1.000000, 5.000000, 9.000000
changing the diagonal to 0
m1 = 3x3
      [,1] [,2] [,3]
[1,] 0.000000, 2.000000, 3.000000,
[2,] 4.000000, 0.000000, 6.000000,
[3,] 7.000000, 8.000000, 0.000000,
```

In NM Dev, the arithmetic operations—addition, subtraction, and scaling—on a matrix are element-wise operations. The signatures are as follows:

```
/**
 * <i>this + that</i>
 *
 * @param that a matrix
 * @return the sum of {@code this} and {@code that}
 */
@Override
public Matrix add(Matrix that);
/**
 * <i>this - that</i>
 *
 * @param that a matrix
 * @return the difference between {@code this} and {@code that}
 */
@Override
public Matrix minus(Matrix that);
/**
 * Scale this matrix, <i>A</i>, by a constant.
 *
 * @param c a double
 * @return <i>cA</i>
 */
public Matrix scaled(double c);
```

Here's an example:

```
val m1: Matrix = DenseMatrix(
    arrayOf(
        doubleArrayOf(1.0, 2.0, 3.0),
        doubleArrayOf(4.0, 5.0, 6.0),
        doubleArrayOf(7.0, 8.0, 9.0)
    )
)
```

```
// m2 = -m1
val m2: Matrix = m1.scaled(-1.0)

// m3 = m1 + m2 = m1 - m1 = 0
val m3: Matrix = m1.add(m2)

// not a recommended usage
val isEqual1: Boolean = m3.equals(m3.ZERO())
println(isEqual1)

// recommended usage
val isEqual2: Boolean = MatrixPropertyUtils.areEqual(m3, m3.ZERO(), 1e-16)
println(isEqual2)
```

The output is as follows:

```
true
true
```

The `ZERO()` method generates a zero matrix of the same dimension as the calling instance. The `equals()` function compares two matrices and checks whether they are equal in value. However, this function is not recommended because two theoretically same matrices can have different representations in a computer. The values of the entries may differ by a small amount. The `equals()` function will mistakenly treat them as different. The proper way to check whether two matrices are equal in value is to check, entry by entry, whether they are the same value within a threshold. The utility function `MatrixPropertyUtils.areEqual` serves this purpose. The advantage of this utility function over the `equals()` method is that you can input a tolerance threshold for floating-point comparison. The signature is as follows:

```
/**
 * Checks the equality of two matrices up to a precision.
 * Two matrices are equal if
 * <ol>
 * <li>the dimensions are the same;</li>
 * <li>all entries are equal</li>
 * </ol>
 *
 * @param A1      a matrix
 * @param A2      a matrix
 * @param epsilon a precision parameter: when a number |x| &le; &epsilon;, it is considered 0
 * @return {@code true} if all entries are equal, entry by entry
 */
public static boolean areEqual(Matrix A1, Matrix A2, double epsilon)
```

2.2.3. Transpose

The transpose $\boldsymbol{A}^T = \boldsymbol{A}'$ of a matrix $\boldsymbol{A}$ is defined as follows:

$$\left(\boldsymbol{A}^T\right)_{ij} = \left(\boldsymbol{A}\right)_{ij}$$

That is, it swaps the rows and columns. The columns become rows; the rows become columns. For example, for the following:

$$\boldsymbol{A} = \begin{bmatrix} 1 & 2 & 3 \\ 4 & 5 & 6 \\ 7 & 8 & 9 \end{bmatrix}$$

The transpose is as follows:

$$\boldsymbol{A}^T = \begin{bmatrix} 1 & 4 & 7 \\ 2 & 5 & 8 \\ 3 & 6 & 9 \end{bmatrix}$$

The following code implements this example:

```
val m1: Matrix = DenseMatrix(
    arrayOf(
        doubleArrayOf(1.0, 2.0, 3.0),
        doubleArrayOf(4.0, 5.0, 6.0),
        doubleArrayOf(7.0, 8.0, 9.0)
    )
)

println(String.format("m1 = %s", m1)) // print out the matrix m1
val m1t: Matrix = m1.t() // doing a transpose
println(String.format("m1t = %s", m1t)) // print out the transpose matrix
```

The output is as follows:

```
m1 = 3x3
        [,1] [,2] [,3]
[1,] 1.000000, 2.000000, 3.000000,
[2,] 4.000000, 5.000000, 6.000000,
[3,] 7.000000, 8.000000, 9.000000,
m1t = 3x3
        [,1] [,2] [,3]
[1,] 1.000000, 4.000000, 7.000000,
[2,] 2.000000, 5.000000, 8.000000,
[3,] 3.000000, 6.000000, 9.000000,
```

2.2.4. Matrix Multiplication

Matrix multiplication is a binary operation to obtain the third matrix from two matrices. The third matrix is the product of the first two, which is called the *matrix product*. If $\boldsymbol{A}$ is an $m \times n$ matrix and $\boldsymbol{B}$ is a $n \times p$ matrix, then their matrix product $\boldsymbol{C} = \boldsymbol{AB}$ is an $m \times p$ matrix. The m elements in each row in matrix $\boldsymbol{A}$ are multiplied by the m elements in the corresponding column in matrix $\boldsymbol{B}$, and the sum of these products is an element of matrix $\boldsymbol{C} = \boldsymbol{AB}$. See Figure 2-11. Mathematically, it is as follows:

$$c_{ij} = a_{i1}b_{1j} + a_{i2}b_{2j} + \cdots + a_{in}b_{nj} = \sum_{k=1}^{n} a_{ik}b_{kj}$$

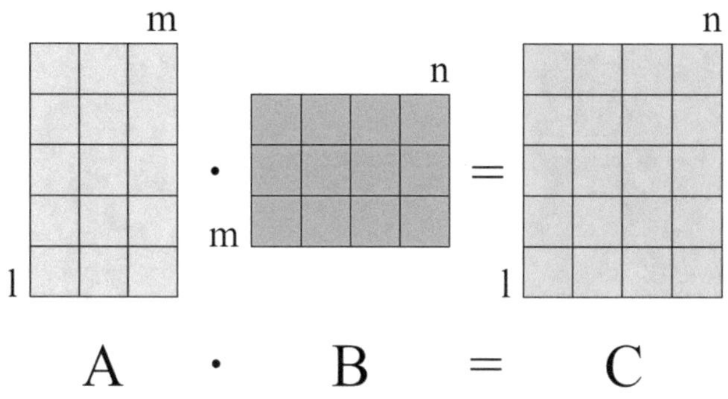

***Figure 2-11.** Matrix multiplication*

For instance, for a matrix such as this one:

$$\boldsymbol{A} = \begin{bmatrix} 1 & 2 & 3 \\ 4 & 5 & 6 \\ 7 & 8 & 9 \end{bmatrix}$$

You get this:

$$\boldsymbol{A}^T\boldsymbol{A} = \begin{bmatrix} 1 & 4 & 7 \\ 2 & 5 & 8 \\ 3 & 6 & 9 \end{bmatrix}\begin{bmatrix} 1 & 2 & 3 \\ 4 & 5 & 6 \\ 7 & 8 & 9 \end{bmatrix} = \begin{bmatrix} 66 & 78 & 90 \\ 78 & 93 & 108 \\ 90 & 108 & 126 \end{bmatrix}$$

Note that matrix multiplication is not commutative, meaning that ***AB*** is not necessarily the same as ***BA***. The following code implements this example:

```
val m1: Matrix = DenseMatrix(
    arrayOf(
        doubleArrayOf(1.0, 2.0, 3.0),
        doubleArrayOf(4.0, 5.0, 6.0),
        doubleArrayOf(7.0, 8.0, 9.0)
    )
)

val m1t: Matrix = m1.t()
val m1tm1: Matrix = m1t.multiply(m1)
println(String.format("%s * \n%s = \n%s", m1t, m1, m1tm1))
```

The output is as follows:

```
3x3
      [,1] [,2] [,3]
[1,] 1.000000, 4.000000, 7.000000,
[2,] 2.000000, 5.000000, 8.000000,
[3,] 3.000000, 6.000000, 9.000000,  *
3x3
     [,1] [,2] [,3]
```

```
[1,] 1.000000, 2.000000, 3.000000,
[2,] 4.000000, 5.000000, 6.000000,
[3,] 7.000000, 8.000000, 9.000000,  =
3x3
        [,1] [,2] [,3]
[1,] 66.000000, 78.000000, 90.000000,
[2,] 78.000000, 93.000000, 108.000000,
[3,] 90.000000, 108.000000, 126.000000,
```

Matrix multiplication occupies a central role in scientific computing with an extremely wide range of applications. Many numerical procedures in linear algebra (e.g., solving linear systems, matrix inversion, factorization, and determinants) can essentially be reduced to matrix multiplication. Hence, there is great interest in investigating fast matrix multiplication algorithms to accelerate matrix multiplication (and other numerical procedures consequently). NM Dev is already the fastest in matrix multiplication and hence linear algebra per our benchmark. See Figure 2-12.

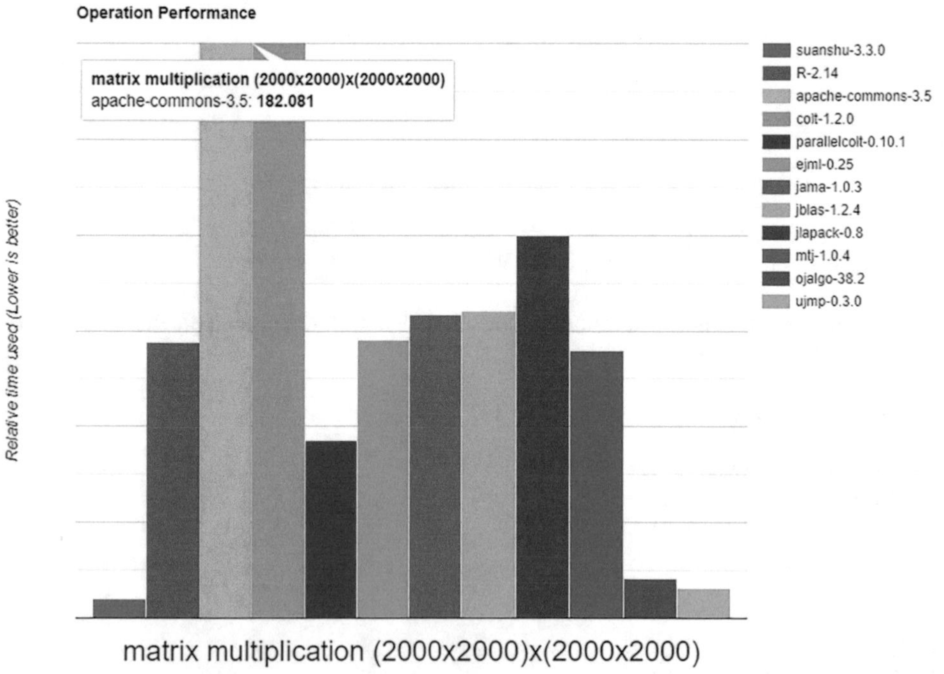

Figure 2-12. *NM Dev fast matrix multiplication*

NM Dev implements an advanced algorithm for fast matrix multiplication. We briefly describe this implementation of a matrix multiplication algorithm, which dramatically accelerates dense matrix-matrix multiplication compared to the classical IJK algorithm.

We first describe the benchmark method against which this fast algorithm is compared, the IJK algorithm. The classical IJK algorithm does the matrix multiplication using three loops and hence a time complexity of $O(n^3)$. Supposing **A** is $m \times n$, $\boldsymbol{B}$ $n \times p$, and $\boldsymbol{C}$ $m \times p$, the IJK algorithm is as follows:

```
for (i = 1; i < = m; i ++){
    for (j = 1; j <= p; j ++){
        for (k = 1; k <= n; k ++){
            C[i,k] += A[i,j] * B[j,k];
        }
    }
}
```

In NM Dev, this is implemented in parallel; the outermost loop is passed to a `ParallelExecutor`. As there are often more rows than threads available, the complexity of this parallelized IJK is still roughly the same as the classical version $O(mnp)$ or cubic time $O(n^3)$ for $m = n = p$. This is the implementation found in most other Java libraries, and we wanted to do much better than this.

The core of our fast multiplication algorithm, the Strassen algorithm, reduces the time complexity to $O\left(n^{\log_2 7}\right)$. The Strassen algorithm (Strassen, 1969) is based on the following block matrix multiplication:

$$\begin{pmatrix} \boldsymbol{A}_{11} & \boldsymbol{A}_{12} \\ \boldsymbol{A}_{21} & \boldsymbol{A}_{22} \end{pmatrix} \begin{pmatrix} \boldsymbol{B}_{11} & \boldsymbol{B}_{12} \\ \boldsymbol{B}_{21} & \boldsymbol{B}_{22} \end{pmatrix} = \begin{pmatrix} \boldsymbol{A}_{11}\boldsymbol{B}_{11} + \boldsymbol{A}_{12}\boldsymbol{B}_{21} & \boldsymbol{A}_{11}\boldsymbol{B}_{12} + \boldsymbol{A}_{12}\boldsymbol{B}_{22} \\ \boldsymbol{A}_{21}\boldsymbol{B}_{11} + \boldsymbol{A}_{22}\boldsymbol{B}_{21} & \boldsymbol{A}_{21}\boldsymbol{B}_{12} + \boldsymbol{A}_{22}\boldsymbol{B}_{22} \end{pmatrix}$$

The naive method of computing this involves eight submatrix multiplications and four additions. The Winograd's variant of Strassen's algorithm that we use forgoes one submatrix multiplication in exchange for 11 extra additions/subtractions, which is faster when the submatrices are large enough (Winograd, 1971).

The algorithm runs as follows (see Figure 2-13):

1. Split $\boldsymbol{A}$ into four equally sized quadrants **A11**, **A12**, **A21**, **A22**. Do the same for $\boldsymbol{B}$. (Assume for now that all dimensions are even.)

2. Obtain the following factor matrices:

$M_1 = A_{11}$	$N_1 = B_{11}$
$M_2 = A_{12}$	$N_2 = B_{21}$
$M_3 = A_{21} + A_{22}$	$N_3 = B_{12} - B_{11}$
$M_4 = M_3 - A_{11}$	$N_4 = B_{22} - N_3$
$M_5 = A_{11} - A_{21}$	$N_5 = B_{22} - B_{12}$
$M_6 = A_{12} - M_4$	$N_6 = B_{22}$
$M_7 = A_{22}$	$N_7 = B_{21} - N_4$

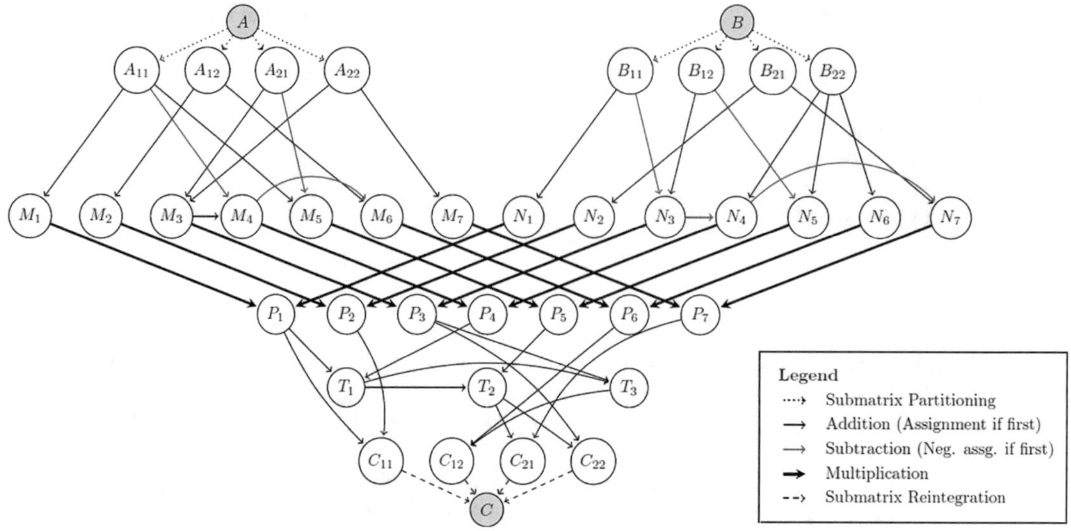

Figure 2-13. *Visualization of Strassen's algorithm (Winograd variant)*

3. Obtain $\boldsymbol{P}_i = \boldsymbol{M}_i \times \boldsymbol{N}_i$ for $i \in \{1, 2, \cdots, 7\}$. Depending on the dimensions, we either use Parallel IJK or make a recursive call to Strassen's algorithm.

4. The final product $\boldsymbol{C} = \boldsymbol{A} \times \boldsymbol{B}$ can then be obtained as follows. The $\boldsymbol{T}_i$ are temporary matrices.

$C_{11} = P_1 + P_2$	$C_{22} = T_2 + P_3$
$T_1 = P_1 + P_4$	$T_3 = T_1 + P_3$
$T_2 = T_1 + P_5$	$C_{12} = T_3 + P_6$
$C_{21} = T_2 + P_7$	

So far, we ignore the cases when $\boldsymbol{A}$ and/or $\boldsymbol{B}$ has an odd number of rows/columns. There are several methods of dealing with this. For example, you could pad the matrices statically so that the dimensions are always even until the recursion passes to IJK (static padding); or you could pad only when one of the dimensions is odd (dynamic padding). Alternatively, you could disregard the extra rows/columns until after the algorithm completes and then take care of them afterward. (In other words, if $\boldsymbol{A}$ has an extra row or $\boldsymbol{B}$ has an extra column, use the appropriate matrix-vector operation to calculate the remaining row/column of $\boldsymbol{C}$. If $\boldsymbol{A}$ has an extra column and $\boldsymbol{B}$ has an extra row, their product can be added on to $\boldsymbol{C}$ afterward.) NM Dev uses this method, called *dynamic peeling*, for this implementation.

Taken on its own, this basic version of Strassen's algorithm works well, provided both matrices are roughly square. In practice, you may encounter cases where either is highly rectangular (e.g., too tall or long). You can solve this by slicing the matrices into blocks that are nearly square and then using Strassen's algorithm on the submatrices. The blocking scheme is devised so that long or tall strips are avoided. See Figure 2-14.

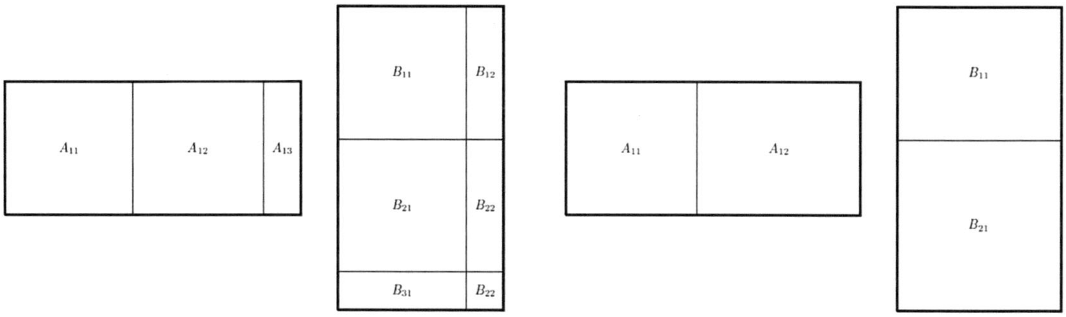

***Figure 2-14.** Blocking and tiling. Left: a strict blocking scheme (strips!). Right: an efficient blocking scheme (our implementation)*

The charts in Figures 2-15 through 2-18 show the performance of our hybrid Block-Strassen algorithm versus Parallel IJK on an Intel® Core i5-3337U CPU @ 1.80 GHz with 6GB RAM, running Java 1.8.0 update 40.

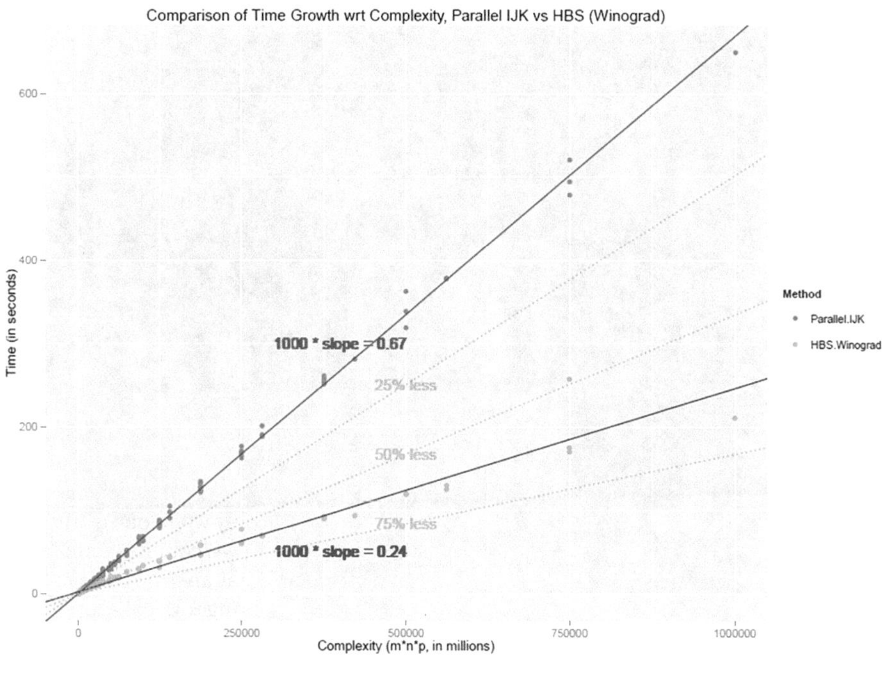

***Figure 2-15.** Multiplication time (by method) versus complexity $m \times n \times p$*

The tests were patterned after D'Alberto & Nicolau (2007). We ran $\boldsymbol{C} = \boldsymbol{A} \times \boldsymbol{B}$ for random matrices $\boldsymbol{A}$ $(m \times n)$ and $\boldsymbol{B}$ $(n \times p)$. For every triple (m, n, p) in S^3, where $S = \{100,500,1000,2500,5000,7500,10000\}$. This multiplication was done three times using Parallel IJK and then three times using Hybrid Block-Strassen (HBS). The average times using each method are compared and tabulated. See Figure 2-15.

Figure 2-15 shows the multiplication time plotted against the product $m \times n \times p$ of the dimensions. The multiplication time for IJK is $O(mnp)$, and our empirical results show that multiplication times for both Parallel IJK and HBS are strongly linearly related to complexity. HBS, however, has a significantly smaller gradient.

The gradients of the best-fit lines suggest that as complexity approaches infinity (ignoring memory constraints), HBS will take 63.5 percent less time than IJK. Several data points, however (e.g., $m, n, p \geq 5000$), show an even greater speedup. See Figures 2-16 and 2-17.

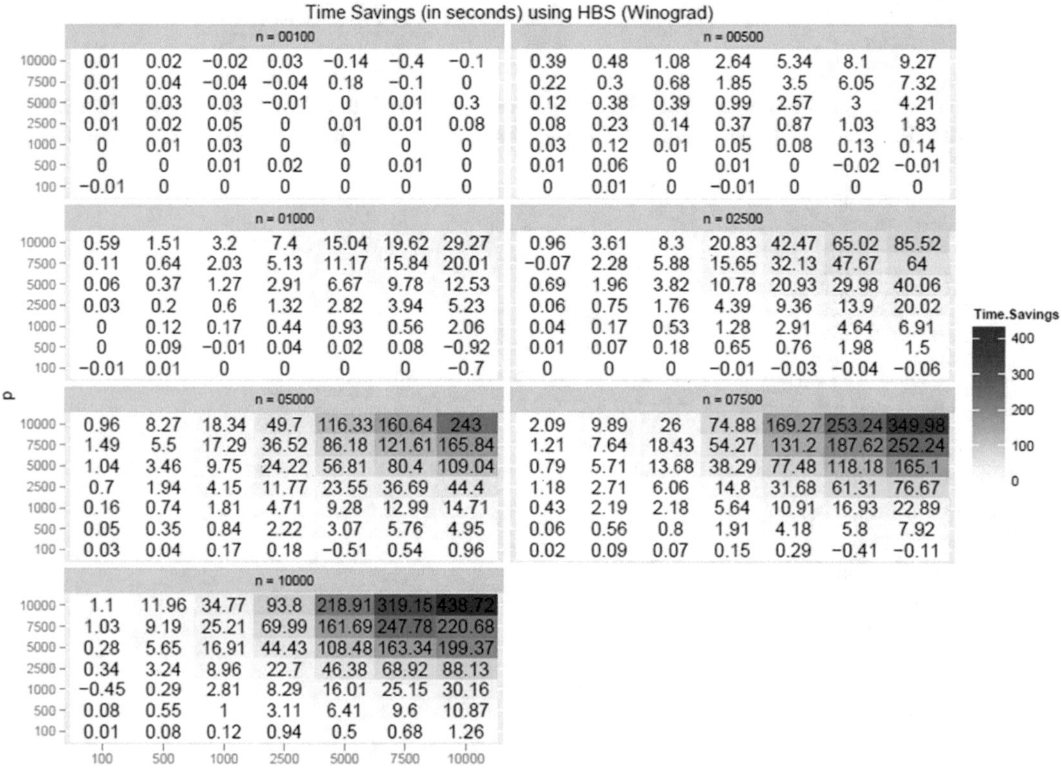

Figure 2-16. *Time savings (in seconds) using HBS versus Parallel IJK*

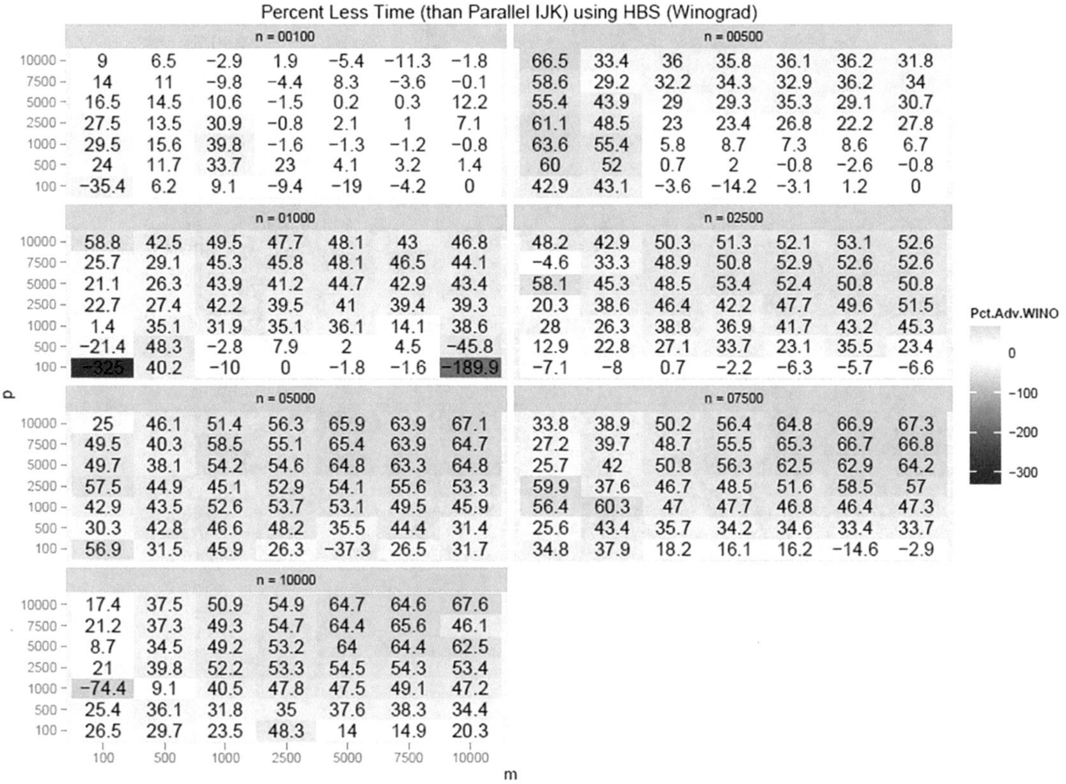

***Figure 2-17.** Time savings (as a percent of P.IJK time) using HBS versus Parallel IJK*

Figure 2-16 shows the time savings of HBS over Parallel IJK in seconds, and Figure 2-17 shows it as a percentage of the Parallel IJK time (Figure 2-17). Each table is for a specific value of *n* (number of columns of ***A***) and runs over the values of *m* (number of rows of ***A***) and *p* (number of columns of ***B***). See Figure 2-18.

Maximum Entry-wise Relative Error (versus P. IJK) (in units of 1e-15)

n = 00100

p \ m	100	500	1000	2500	5000	7500	10000
10000	0	0	0	0	0	0	0
7500	0	0	0	0	0	0	0
5000	0	0	0	0	0	0	0
2500	0	0	0	0	0	0	0
1000	0	0	0	0	0	0	0
500	0	0	0	0	0	0	0
100	0	0	0	0	0	0	0

n = 00500

p \ m	100	500	1000	2500	5000	7500	10000
10000	0	0	0	0	0	0	0
7500	0	0	0	0	0	0	0
5000	0	0	0	0	0	0	0
2500	0	0	0	0	0	0	0
1000	0	0	0	0	0	0	0
500	0	0	0	0	0	0	0
100	0	0	0	0	0	0	0

n = 01000

p \ m	100	500	1000	2500	5000	7500	10000
10000	4.5	4.2	4.6	5	4.7	5.2	5.2
7500	4.5	4.2	4.5	5	4.7	5.2	5.2
5000	4.5	4	4.5	4.7	4.7	4.8	5
2500	4.5	3.9	4.5	4.6	4.7	4.7	4.7
1000	4.1	3.9	4.4	4.5	4.4	4.6	4.7
500	3.7	3.7	3.9	3.9	4	4.2	4.2
100	3.1	3.7	4.1	4.5	4.5	4.5	4.5

n = 02500

p \ m	100	500	1000	2500	5000	7500	10000
10000	7.7	7.3	7.7	8.3	8.3	8.3	8.3
7500	6.8	7.3	7.6	8.3	8.3	8.3	8.3
5000	6.6	7.1	7.6	8.3	8.3	8.3	8.3
2500	6.3	7	7.6	7.7	8.3	8.3	8.3
1000	6.3	6.9	7	7	7.2	7.6	7.6
500	6.2	6.9	6.9	7	7.1	7.3	7.3
100	5.4	6.2	6.3	6.3	6.6	6.8	7.7

n = 05000

p \ m	100	500	1000	2500	5000	7500	10000
10000	9.6	10.3	11.1	11.7	11.3	11.6	11.6
7500	9.6	10.3	11.1	11.7	11.3	11.3	11.6
5000	9.6	10.3	11.1	11.7	11.3	11.3	11.6
2500	9.6	10.3	10.3	10.6	11.1	11.1	11.1
1000	8.3	9.9	9.4	10.3	11.3	11.3	11.3
500	8.3	8.6	9.9	10.3	10.3	10.3	10.3
100	7.6	8.3	8.3	9.6	9.6	9.6	9.6

n = 07500

p \ m	100	500	1000	2500	5000	7500	10000
10000	11	12.6	12.5	12.6	12.6	12.9	12.9
7500	11	12.6	12.5	12.6	12.6	12.9	12.9
5000	10.5	12.6	12.5	12.6	12.6	13.1	12.6
2500	10.5	12.6	12.3	12.6	12.6	12.6	12.6
1000	10.5	11.2	10.9	12.5	12.5	12.5	12.5
500	10.5	10.2	11.2	12.6	12.6	12.6	12.6
100	10.5	10.5	10.5	10.5	10.5	11	11

n = 10000

p \ m	100	500	1000	2500	5000	7500	10000
10000	15	15.3	15.3	15.7	16	16.8	16.2
7500	15	15.3	15.3	15.7	15.5	15.8	16.6
5000	15	15.3	15.3	15.7	15.5	15.5	15.7
2500	15	15.3	15.3	15.7	15.7	15.7	15.7
1000	15	15.3	15.3	15.3	15.3	15.3	15.3
500	12.2	15.3	15.3	15.3	15.3	15.3	15.3
100	12	12.2	15	15	15	15	15

MaxRelativeError
- 1.675005e-14
- 1.256254e-14
- 8.375024e-15
- 4.187512e-15
- 0.000000e+00

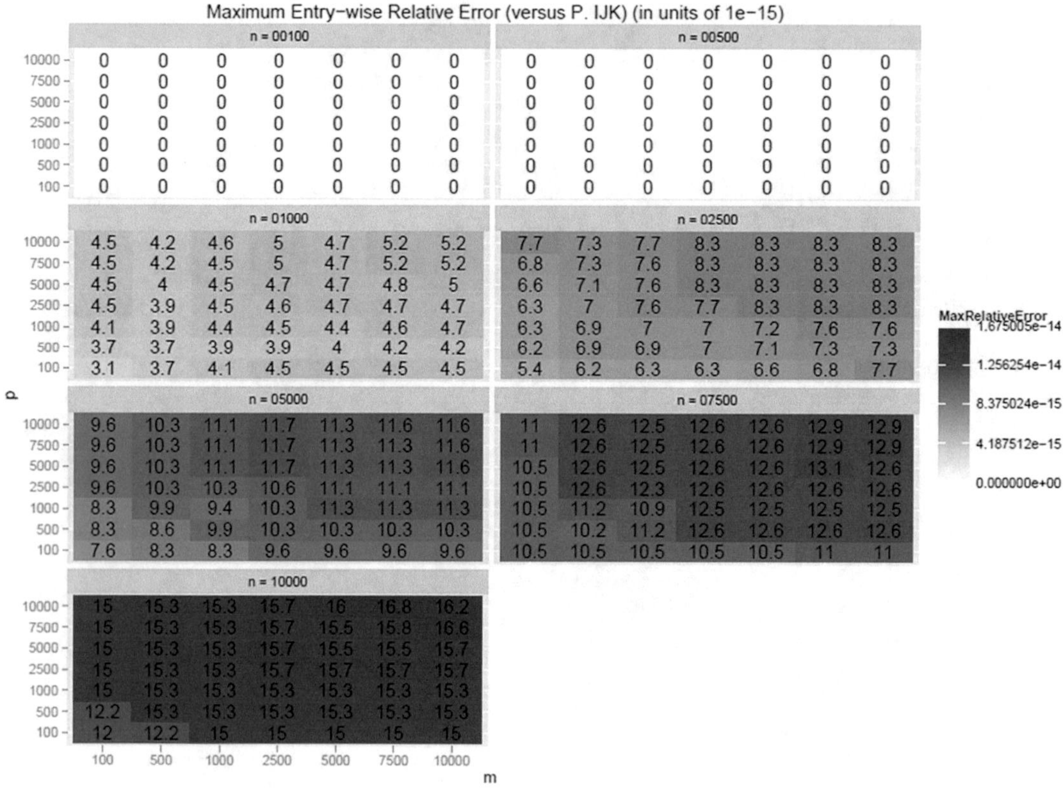

Figure 2-18. *Maximum entry-wise relative error of HBS versus PIJK (in units of 1e-15)*

Finally, an accuracy test was also run to address concerns regarding the numerical stability of Strassen's algorithm. Figure 2-18 shows the maximum entry-wise relative error, $\max_{i,j} \left| \dfrac{C_{i,j}^{IJK} - C_{i,j}^{HBS}}{C_{i,j}^{IJK}} \right|$, of the resulting product matrix. You can see that none of the errors exceeds 2×10^{-14}. Note that we did not run Strassen's algorithm completely to the scalar level; when the matrices Mi and Ni are too small, IJK is used. This reduces the error. This suggests that HBS is very accurate and is therefore a strong candidate for use in general-purpose contexts when speed is a priority. HBS is the default NM Dev implementation of matrix multiplication.

2.2.5. Rank

The column rank of a matrix A is the maximal number of linearly independent columns in A. Similarly, the row rank is the maximal number of linearly independent rows in A. The column and row ranks of a matrix are always equal, so they can simply be called the rank of a matrix rank (A). A square matrix is called a *full-rank matrix* if the rank is the same as the number of columns (or rows).

Here's an example:

$$A = \begin{bmatrix} 1 & 0 & 1 \\ -2 & -3 & 1 \\ 3 & 3 & 0 \end{bmatrix}$$

A has a rank of 2 because the first two columns are linearly independent. The third column, however, is a linear combination of the first two columns. Specifically, the third column is equal to the first column subtracting the second column. This is not a full-rank matrix.

Here's another example:

$$\boldsymbol{A} = \begin{bmatrix} 1 & 1 & 0 & 2 \\ -1 & -1 & 0 & -2 \end{bmatrix}$$

A has a rank of 1 because every column is a scalar multiplied to the first column.

In NM Dev, the utility function `MatrixMeasure.rank` computes the rank of a matrix. The following code computes the ranks of the two previous matrices:

```
val PRECISION: Double = 1e-15
val M1: Matrix = DenseMatrix(
    arrayOf(
        doubleArrayOf(1.0, 0.0, 1.0),
        doubleArrayOf(-2.0, -3.0, 1.0),
        doubleArrayOf(3.0, 3.0, 0.0)
    )
)

// calculate the rank of M1, treating numbers smaller than PRECISION as 0
val rank1: Int = MatrixMeasure.rank(M1, PRECISION)
println("Rank 1: ${rank1}")
val M2: Matrix = DenseMatrix(
    arrayOf(
        doubleArrayOf(1.0, 1.0, 0.0, 2.0),
        doubleArrayOf(-1.0, -1.0, 0.0, -2.0)
    )
)

// calculate the rank of M2, treating numbers smaller than PRECISION as 0
val rank2: Int = MatrixMeasure.rank(M2, PRECISION)
println("Rank 2: ${rank2}")
```

The output is as follows:

```
2
1
```

2.2.6. Determinant

Determinant is a function that maps an $n \times n$ square matrix ***A*** to a scalar. It is often denoted as $|\boldsymbol{A}|$. Denote the elements of the matrix ***A*** as a_{ij} and N_{ij} as the determinant of the submatrix of ***A*** that is created by removing the i-th row and j-th column from matrix ***A***. Then a recursive definition of the determinant of matrix ***A*** is as follows:

$$|\boldsymbol{A}| = \sum_{j=1}^{n} (-1)^{i+j} m_{ij} N_{ij}$$

For instance, when $n = 2$, you get this:

$$\begin{vmatrix} a & b \\ c & d \end{vmatrix} = ad - bc$$

Similarly, when $n = 3$, you get this:

$$\begin{vmatrix} a & b & c \\ d & e & f \\ g & h & i \end{vmatrix} = a\begin{vmatrix} e & f \\ h & i \end{vmatrix} - b\begin{vmatrix} d & f \\ g & i \end{vmatrix} + c\begin{vmatrix} d & e \\ g & h \end{vmatrix}$$

$$= aei + bfg + cdh - ceg - bdi - afh$$

Here's an example:

$$\begin{vmatrix} 2 & 1 & 2 \\ 3 & 2 & 2 \\ 1 & 2 & 3 \end{vmatrix} = 5$$

In NM Dev, the utility function `MatrixMeasure.det` computes the determinant of a matrix. The following code computes the determinant of the previous matrix:

```
val M1: Matrix = DenseMatrix(
    arrayOf(
        doubleArrayOf(2.0, 1.0, 2.0),
        doubleArrayOf(3.0, 2.0, 2.0),
        doubleArrayOf(1.0, 2.0, 3.0)
    )
)

// calculate the determinant of matrix M1
val det: Double = MatrixMeasure.det(M1)
println("Determinant: ${det}")
```

The output is as follows:

```
Determinant: 5.0
```

2.2.7. Inverse and Pseudo-Inverse

For a square matrix $\boldsymbol{A}$ of order n, if there exists a square matrix $\boldsymbol{B}$ of order n such that:

$$\boldsymbol{AB} = \boldsymbol{BA} = \boldsymbol{I}_n$$

where I_n is the identity matrix with order n, then matrix A is said to be *invertible*, and matrix B is called the inverse of matrix A. We often denote the inverse matrix of A as A^{-1}. That is, $AA^{-1} = A^{-1}A = I_n$. Only square matrices may have inverse matrices. A matrix is invertible if and only if it has full rank. Not all square matrices are invertible. Noninvertible matrices are called *singular* or *degenerate*. A matrix is singular if and only if its determinant is 0.

For example, consider this matrix:

$$A = \begin{bmatrix} -1 & \frac{3}{2} \\ 1 & -1 \end{bmatrix}$$

A is invertible. You can check that by computing the determinant $|A| = -0.5$. Specifically, you get this:

$$\begin{bmatrix} -1 & \frac{3}{2} \\ 1 & -1 \end{bmatrix} \begin{bmatrix} 2 & 3 \\ 2 & 2 \end{bmatrix} = \begin{bmatrix} 1 & 0 \\ 0 & 1 \end{bmatrix}$$

In NM Dev, the `Inverse` class constructs a new matrix, which is the inverse of an invertible matrix. The following code computes the inverse of the previous matrix:

```
// compute the inverse of an invertible matrix
val A1: Matrix = DenseMatrix(
    arrayOf(
        doubleArrayOf(-1.0, 3.0 / 2),
        doubleArrayOf(1.0, -1.0)
    )
)

val det1: Double = MatrixMeasure.det(A1)
println("det of A1 = " + det1)
val Ainv1: Matrix = Inverse(A1)
val I1: Matrix = A1.multiply(Ainv1)
println(String.format("%s * \n%s = \n%s", A1, Ainv1, I1))
```

The output is as follows:

```
det of A1 = -0.5
2x2
        [,1] [,2]
[1,] -1.000000, 1.500000,
[2,] 1.000000, -1.000000,  *
2x2
        [,1] [,2]
[1,] 2.000000, 3.000000,
[2,] 2.000000, 2.000000,  =
2x2
        [,1] [,2]
[1,] 1.000000, 0.000000,
[2,] 0.000000, 1.000000,
```

Consider another matrix, shown here:

$$A = \begin{bmatrix} 2 & 4 \\ 5 & 10 \end{bmatrix}$$

It is easy to check that this matrix is singular as $|A| = 0$. So, its inverse does not exist. Moore and Penrose define a generalized concept of inverse, called the Moore-Penrose inverse or simply the pseudo-inverse, denoted as A^+. The pseudo-inverse has the following four properties that define it:

1. $AA^+A = A$
2. $A^+AA^+ = A^+$
3. $(AA^+)^H = AA^+$
4. $(A^+A)^H = A^+A$

The A^H operator denotes the Hermitian transpose (also called *conjugate transpose*) of a matrix. You first take the transpose of the matrix and then replace the matrix elements with their complex conjugates, replacing $a + bi$ with $a - bi$. Specifically, the Hermitian transpose of an $m \times n$ matrix A is defined as follows:

$$\left(A^H\right)_{ij} = \overline{A_{ij}}$$

The overbar denotes a scalar complex conjugate. If all elements in A are real, then the Hermitian transpose is the same as the transpose. The third and fourth properties would simply mean that AA^+ and A^+A are symmetric. The pseudo-inverse of a matrix is uniquely defined. It always exists, even for nonsquare matrices. If a matrix is invertible, then the pseudo-inverse is the same as the inverse.

In NM Dev, the PseudoInverse class constructs a new matrix, which is the pseudo-inverse of a matrix (singular as well as invertible). The following code computes the pseudo-inverse of the previous matrix:

```
// compute the pseudo-inverse of a non-invertible matrix
val A2: Matrix = DenseMatrix(
    arrayOf(
        doubleArrayOf(2.0, 4.0),
        doubleArrayOf(5.0, 10.0)
    )
)

val det2: Double = MatrixMeasure.det(A2)
println("det of A2 = " + det2)
val A2p: PseudoInverse = PseudoInverse(A2)
println("The pseudo inverse is")
println(A2p)
// the first property of pseudo-inverse
println("Should be the same as the matrix")
val A2_copy: Matrix = A2.multiply(A2p).multiply(A2)
println(A2_copy)
// the second property of pseudo-inverse
println("Should be the same as the pseudo inverse")
val A2p_copy: Matrix = A2p.multiply(A2).multiply(A2p)
println(A2p_copy)
```

The output is as follows:

```
det of A2 = 0.0
the pseudo inverse is
2x2
      [,1] [,2]
[1,] 0.013793, 0.034483,
[2,] 0.027586, 0.068966,
should be the same as the matrix
2x2
      [,1] [,2]
[1,] 2.000000, 4.000000,
[2,] 5.000000, 10.000000,
should be the same as the pseudo inverse
2x2
      [,1] [,2]
[1,] 0.013793, 0.034483,
[2,] 0.027586, 0.068966,
```

Consider another example of a nonsquare matrix, shown here:

$$\boldsymbol{A} = \begin{bmatrix} 1 & 0 \\ 0 & 1 \\ 0 & 1 \end{bmatrix}$$

The pseudo-inverse is as follows:

$$\boldsymbol{A}^{+} = \begin{bmatrix} 1 & 0 & 0 \\ 0 & 0.5 & 0.5 \end{bmatrix}$$

The following code computes the pseudo-inverse of the previous matrix:

```
// compute the pseudo-inverse of a non-square matrix
val A3: Matrix = DenseMatrix(
    arrayOf(
        doubleArrayOf(1.0, 0.0),
        doubleArrayOf(0.0, 1.0),
        doubleArrayOf(0.0, 1.0)
    )
)

val A3p: PseudoInverse = PseudoInverse(A3)
println("The pseudo inverse is")
println(A3p)
// the first property of pseudo-inverse
println("Should be the same as the matrix")
val A3_copy: Matrix = A3.multiply(A3p).multiply(A3)
println(A3_copy)
```

```
// the second property of pseudo-inverse
println("Should be the same as the pseudo inverse")
val A3p_copy: Matrix = A3p.multiply(A3).multiply(A3p)
println(A3p_copy)
```

The output is as follows:

```
the pseudo inverse is
2x3
        [,1] [,2] [,3]
[1,] 1.000000, 0.000000, 0.000000,
[2,] 0.000000, 0.500000, 0.500000,
should be the same as the matrix
3x2
        [,1] [,2]
[1,] 1.000000, 0.000000,
[2,] 0.000000, 1.000000,
[3,] 0.000000, 1.000000,
should be the same as the pseudo inverse
2x3
        [,1] [,2] [,3]
[1,] 1.000000, 0.000000, 0.000000,
[2,] 0.000000, 0.500000, 0.500000,
```

2.2.8. Kronecker Product

The Kronecker product (or outer product or matrix direct product), denoted by $\otimes$, is an operation on two matrices of arbitrary size resulting in a block matrix. Specifically, if $\boldsymbol{A}$ is an $m \times n$ matrix and $\boldsymbol{B}$ a $p \times q$ matrix, then the Kronecker product $\boldsymbol{A} \otimes \boldsymbol{B}$ is the $pm \times qn$ block matrix, shown here:

$$\boldsymbol{A} \otimes \boldsymbol{B} = \begin{bmatrix} a_{11}\boldsymbol{B} & \cdots & a_{1n}\boldsymbol{B} \\ \vdots & \ddots & \vdots \\ a_{m1}\boldsymbol{B} & \cdots & a_{mn}\boldsymbol{B} \end{bmatrix}$$

Or more explicitly, as shown here:

$$A \otimes B = \begin{bmatrix} a_{11}b_{11} & a_{11}b_{12} & \cdots a_{11}b_{1q} \cdots\cdots a_{1n}b_{11} & a_{1n}b_{12} \cdots a_{1n}b_{1q} \\ a_{11}b_{21} & a_{11}b_{22} & \cdots a_{11}b_{2q} \cdots\cdots a_{1n}b_{21} & a_{1n}b_{22} \cdots a_{1n}b_{2q} \\ \vdots & \vdots & \ddots \quad \vdots \qquad\qquad \vdots & \vdots \quad \ddots \quad \vdots \\ a_{11}b_{p1} & a_{11}b_{p2} & \cdots a_{11}b_{pq} \cdots\cdots a_{1n}b_{p1} & a_{1n}b_{p2} \cdots a_{1n}b_{pq} \\ \vdots & \vdots & \ddots \quad \vdots \qquad\qquad \vdots & \vdots \quad \ddots \quad \vdots \\ \vdots & \vdots & \ddots \quad \vdots \qquad\qquad \vdots & \vdots \quad \ddots \quad \vdots \\ a_{m1}b_{11} & a_{m1}b_{12} & \cdots a_{m1}b_{1q} \cdots\cdots a_{mn}b_{11} & a_{mn}b_{12} \cdots a_{mn}b_{1q} \\ a_{m1}b_{21} & a_{m1}b_{22} & \cdots a_{m1}b_{2q} \cdots\cdots a_{mn}b_{21} & a_{mn}b_{22} \cdots a_{mn}b_{2q} \\ \vdots & \vdots & \ddots \quad \vdots \qquad\qquad \vdots & \vdots \quad \ddots \quad \vdots \\ a_{m1}b_{p1} & a_{m1}b_{p2} & \cdots a_{m1}b_{pq} \cdots\cdots a_{mn}b_{p1} & a_{mn}b_{p2} \cdots a_{mn}b_{pq} \end{bmatrix}$$

Here's an example:

$$\begin{bmatrix} 1 & 2 \\ 3 & 4 \end{bmatrix} \otimes \begin{bmatrix} 0 & 5 \\ 6 & 7 \end{bmatrix} = \begin{bmatrix} 1\begin{bmatrix} 0 & 5 \\ 6 & 7 \end{bmatrix} & 2\begin{bmatrix} 0 & 5 \\ 6 & 7 \end{bmatrix} \\ 3\begin{bmatrix} 0 & 5 \\ 6 & 7 \end{bmatrix} & 4\begin{bmatrix} 0 & 5 \\ 6 & 7 \end{bmatrix} \end{bmatrix} = \begin{bmatrix} 1\times 0 & 1\times 5 & 2\times 0 & 2\times 5 \\ 1\times 6 & 1\times 7 & 2\times 6 & 2\times 7 \\ 3\times 0 & 3\times 5 & 4\times 0 & 4\times 5 \\ 3\times 6 & 3\times 7 & 4\times 6 & 4\times 7 \end{bmatrix} = \begin{bmatrix} 0 & 5 & 0 & 10 \\ 6 & 7 & 12 & 14 \\ 0 & 15 & 0 & 20 \\ 18 & 21 & 24 & 28 \end{bmatrix}$$

Here's another example:

$$\begin{bmatrix} 1 & -4 & 7 \\ -2 & 3 & 3 \end{bmatrix} \otimes \begin{bmatrix} 8 & 9 & 6 & 5 \\ 1 & -3 & -4 & 7 \\ 2 & 8 & -8 & 3 \\ 1 & 2 & -5 & -1 \end{bmatrix}$$

$$= \begin{bmatrix} 8 & -9 & -6 & 5 & -32 & 36 & 24 & -20 & 56 & -63 & -42 & 35 \\ 1 & -3 & -4 & 7 & -4 & 12 & 16 & -28 & 7 & -21 & -28 & 49 \\ 2 & 8 & -8 & -3 & -8 & -32 & 32 & 12 & 14 & 56 & -56 & -21 \\ 1 & 2 & -5 & -1 & -4 & -8 & 20 & 4 & 7 & 14 & -35 & -7 \\ -16 & 18 & 12 & -10 & 24 & -27 & -18 & 15 & 24 & -27 & -18 & 15 \\ -2 & 6 & 8 & -14 & 3 & -9 & -12 & 21 & 3 & -9 & -12 & 21 \\ -4 & -16 & 16 & 6 & 6 & 24 & -24 & -9 & 6 & 24 & -24 & -9 \\ -2 & -4 & 10 & 2 & 3 & 6 & -15 & -3 & 3 & 6 & -15 & -3 \end{bmatrix}$$

In NM Dev, the KroneckerProduct class constructs a new matrix, which is the Kronecker product of two matrices. The following code computes the Kronecker products of the previous examples:

```
val A1 = DenseMatrix(
    arrayOf(
        doubleArrayOf(1.0, 2.0),
        doubleArrayOf(3.0, 4.0)
    )
)

val B1 = DenseMatrix(
    arrayOf(
        doubleArrayOf(0.0, 5.0),
        doubleArrayOf(6.0, 7.0)
    )
)

val C1 = KroneckerProduct(A1, B1)
println(String.format("%s ⊗ \n%s = \n%s", A1, B1, C1))
```

The output is as follows:

```
2x2
     [,1] [,2]
[1,] 1.000000, 2.000000,
[2,] 3.000000, 4.000000,  ⊗
2x2
      [,1] [,2]
[1,] 0.000000, 5.000000,
[2,] 6.000000, 7.000000,  =
4x4
      [,1] [,2] [,3] [,4]
[1,] 0.000000, 5.000000, 0.000000, 10.000000,
[2,] 6.000000, 7.000000, 12.000000, 14.000000,
[3,] 0.000000, 15.000000, 0.000000, 20.000000,
[4,] 18.000000, 21.000000, 24.000000, 28.000000,
```

The following is another example of Kronecker product:

```
val A2 = DenseMatrix(
    arrayOf(
        doubleArrayOf(1.0, -4.0, 7.0),
        doubleArrayOf(-2.0, 3.0, 3.0)
    )
)

val B2 = DenseMatrix(
    arrayOf(
        doubleArrayOf(8.0, -9.0, -6.0, 5.0),
        doubleArrayOf(1.0, -3.0, -4.0, 7.0),
```

```
        doubleArrayOf(2.0, 8.0, -8.0, -3.0),
        doubleArrayOf(1.0, 2.0, -5.0, -1.0)
    )
)

val C2 = KroneckerProduct(A2, B2)
println(String.format("%s ⊗ \n%s = \n%s", A2, B2, C2))
```

The output is as follows:

```
2x3
      [,1] [,2] [,3]
[1,] 1.000000, -4.000000, 7.000000,
[2,] -2.000000, 3.000000, 3.000000,  ⊗
4x4
      [,1] [,2] [,3] [,4]
[1,] 8.000000, -9.000000, -6.000000, 5.000000,
[2,] 1.000000, -3.000000, -4.000000, 7.000000,
[3,] 2.000000, 8.000000, -8.000000, -3.000000,
[4,] 1.000000, 2.000000, -5.000000, -1.000000,  =
8x12
     [,1] [,2] [,3] [,4] [,5] [,6] [,7] [,8] [,9] [,10] [,11] [,12]
[1,] 8.000000, -9.000000, -6.000000, 5.000000, -32.000000, 36.000000, 24.000000, -20.000000,
56.000000, -63.000000, -42.000000, 35.000000,
[2,] 1.000000, -3.000000, -4.000000, 7.000000, -4.000000, 12.000000, 16.000000, -28.000000,
7.000000, -21.000000, -28.000000, 49.000000,
[3,] 2.000000, 8.000000, -8.000000, -3.000000, -8.000000, -32.000000, 32.000000, 12.000000,
14.000000, 56.000000, -56.000000, -21.000000,
[4,] 1.000000, 2.000000, -5.000000, -1.000000, -4.000000, -8.000000, 20.000000, 4.000000,
7.000000, 14.000000, -35.000000, -7.000000,
[5,] -16.000000, 18.000000, 12.000000, -10.000000, 24.000000, -27.000000, -18.000000,
15.000000, 24.000000, -27.000000, -18.000000, 15.000000,
[6,] -2.000000, 6.000000, 8.000000, -14.000000, 3.000000, -9.000000, -12.000000, 21.000000,
3.000000, -9.000000, -12.000000, 21.000000,
[7,] -4.000000, -16.000000, 16.000000, 6.000000, 6.000000, 24.000000, -24.000000, -9.000000,
6.000000, 24.000000, -24.000000, -9.000000,
[8,] -2.000000, -4.000000, 10.000000, 2.000000, 3.000000, 6.000000, -15.000000, -3.000000,
3.000000, 6.000000, -15.000000, -3.000000,
```

2.3. Matrix Decomposition

A matrix decomposition or matrix factorization is a factorization of a matrix into a product of (simpler) matrices. There are many different matrix decompositions for different applications such as solving systems of linear equations and finding eigenvalues. They have different numerical properties such as precision and stability.

2.3.1. LU Decomposition

Lower-upper (LU) decomposition (or LU factorization) factors a matrix as the product of a lower triangular matrix and an upper triangular matrix. Computers usually solve square systems of linear equations (when the number of variables is the same as the number of equations) using LU decomposition. It is also a key step when inverting a matrix or computing the determinant of a matrix. Specifically, for a square matrix **A**, LU decomposition finds a lower triangular matrix **L** (all elements above the diagonal are zero) and an upper triangular matrix **U** (all elements below the diagonal are zero) such that:

$$\boldsymbol{A} = \boldsymbol{LU}$$

For instance, for a 3 × 3 matrix **A**, its LU decomposition looks like this:

$$\begin{bmatrix} a_{11} & a_{12} & a_{13} \\ a_{21} & a_{22} & a_{23} \\ a_{31} & a_{32} & a_{33} \end{bmatrix} = \begin{bmatrix} l_{11} & 0 & 0 \\ l_{21} & l_{22} & 0 \\ l_{31} & l_{32} & l_{33} \end{bmatrix} \begin{bmatrix} u_{11} & u_{12} & u_{13} \\ 0 & u_{22} & u_{23} \\ 0 & 0 & u_{33} \end{bmatrix}$$

This version may sometimes not be possible. For example, if $a_{11} = 0$, then either $l_{11} = 0$ or $u_{11} = 0$. This problem can be removed by simply reordering the rows of **A** so that the first element of the permuted matrix is nonzero. The same problem in subsequent factorization steps can be removed the same way. Therefore, the product sometimes includes a permutation matrix **P**. Specifically:

$$\boldsymbol{PA} = \boldsymbol{LU}$$

P is a row permutation matrix, which, when left-multiplied to **A**, reorders the rows of **A**. It turns out that all square matrices can be factorized in this form, and the factorization is numerically stable in practice. This makes LUP decomposition a useful technique in practice.

For example, say you have the following:

$$\begin{bmatrix} 0 & 0 & 1 \\ 1 & 0 & 0 \\ 0 & 0 & 0 \end{bmatrix} \begin{bmatrix} 1 & 2 & 3 \\ 4 & 5 & 6 \\ 7 & 8 & 9 \end{bmatrix} = \begin{bmatrix} 1 & 0 & 0 \\ 0.142857 & 1 & 0 \\ 0.571429 & 0.5 & 1 \end{bmatrix} \begin{bmatrix} 7 & 8 & 9 \\ 0 & 0.857143 & 1.714286 \\ 0 & 0 & 0 \end{bmatrix}$$

In NM Dev, the LU class performs the LU decomposition for a square matrix. It computes the matrices **L**, **U**, and **P**. The following code implements the previous example:

```
val A: Matrix = DenseMatrix(
    arrayOf(
        doubleArrayOf(1.0, 2.0, 3.0),
        doubleArrayOf(4.0, 5.0, 6.0),
        doubleArrayOf(7.0, 8.0, 9.0)
    )
)

// perform LU decomposition
val lu: LU = LU(A)

val P: PermutationMatrix = lu.P()
println(String.format("P = %s", P))
```

The output is as follows:

```
P = 3x3
         [,1] [,2] [,3]
[1,] 0.000000, 0.000000, 1.000000,
[2,] 1.000000, 0.000000, 0.000000,
[3,] 0.000000, 1.000000, 0.000000,
```

```
val L: LowerTriangularMatrix = lu.L()
println(String.format("L = %s", L))
```

The output is as follows:

```
L = 3x3
         [,1] [,2] [,3]
[1,] 1.000000, 0.000000, 0.000000,
[2,] 0.142857, 1.000000, 0.000000,
[3,] 0.571429, 0.500000, 1.000000,
```

```
val U: UpperTriangularMatrix = lu.U()
println(String.format("U = %s", U))
```

The output is as follows:

```
U = 3x3
        [,1] [,2] [,3]
[1,] 7.000000, 8.000000, 9.000000,
[2,] 0.000000, 0.857143, 1.714286,
[3,] 0.000000, 0.000000, 0.000000,
```

```
val PA: Matrix = P.multiply(A)
val LU: Matrix = L.multiply(U)
// verify that PA = LU
println(String.format("%s = \n%s is %b",
        PA,
        LU,
        MatrixPropertyUtils.areEqual(PA, LU, 1e-14)))
```

The output is as follows:

```
3x3
         [,1] [,2] [,3]
[1,] 7.000000, 8.000000, 9.000000,
[2,] 1.000000, 2.000000, 3.000000,
[3,] 4.000000, 5.000000, 6.000000,  =
3x3
```

```
        [,1] [,2] [,3]
[1,] 7.000000, 8.000000, 9.000000,
[2,] 1.000000, 2.000000, 3.000000,
[3,] 4.000000, 5.000000, 6.000000,  is true
```

2.3.2. Cholesky Decomposition

If ***A*** is a symmetric (or Hermitian if ***A*** is complex) positive-definite matrix, you can make it so that ***U*** is the conjugate transpose of ***L***. That is, you can write ***A*** as follows:

$$\boldsymbol{A} = \boldsymbol{L}\boldsymbol{L}^H$$

This decomposition is called the Cholesky decomposition. Cholesky decomposition or Cholesky factorization is the decomposition of a Hermitian, positive-definite matrix, ***A***, into the product of a lower triangular matrix, ***L***, and its conjugate transpose $\boldsymbol{L}^H$ (or simply transpose $\boldsymbol{L}^T$ if the matrices are real). $\boldsymbol{L}^H$ is an upper triangular matrix. The Cholesky decomposition always exists and is unique for a positive-definite matrix. Furthermore, computing the Cholesky decomposition is more efficient and numerically more stable than computing LU decomposition. When it is applicable, the Cholesky decomposition is roughly twice as efficient as the LU decomposition for solving systems of linear equations.

A variant of the classic Cholesky decomposition is LDL decomposition. That is:

$$\boldsymbol{A} = \boldsymbol{L}\boldsymbol{D}\boldsymbol{L}^H$$

L is a lower unit triangular matrix (having 1s on the diagonal), and ***D*** is a diagonal matrix (nonzeros only on the diagonal and zeros everywhere else). That is, the diagonal elements of ***L*** are required to be 1 (unitriangular) at the cost of introducing an additional diagonal matrix ***D*** in the decomposition. The main advantage is that the LDL decomposition can be computed and used with essentially the same algorithms but avoids extracting square roots. The LDL decomposition is related to the classical Cholesky decomposition as follows:

$$\boldsymbol{A} = \boldsymbol{L}\boldsymbol{D}\boldsymbol{L}^H = \boldsymbol{L}\boldsymbol{D}^{\frac{1}{2}}\left(\boldsymbol{D}^{\frac{1}{2}}\right)^H \boldsymbol{L}^H = \boldsymbol{L}\boldsymbol{D}^{\frac{1}{2}}\left(\boldsymbol{L}\boldsymbol{D}^{\frac{1}{2}}\right)^H$$

For example, say you have the following:

$$\begin{bmatrix} 4 & 12 & -16 \\ 12 & 37 & -43 \\ -16 & -43 & 98 \end{bmatrix} = \begin{bmatrix} 2 & 0 & 0 \\ 6 & 1 & 0 \\ -8 & 5 & 3 \end{bmatrix} \begin{bmatrix} 2 & 6 & -8 \\ 0 & 1 & 5 \\ 0 & 0 & 3 \end{bmatrix}$$

There are many ways to do Cholesky decomposition. In NM Dev, the `Cholesky` interface represents the many algorithms in the library. The `Chol` class wraps up a number of implementations to use depending on the input matrix. The default choice is the `Cholesky-Banachiewicz` class. The Cholesky-Banachiewicz algorithm starts from the upper-left corner of matrix *L* and proceeds to calculate the matrix row by row. NM Dev `Chol` implementation is highly optimized for performance because Cholesky decomposition is such a fundamental operation and appears in many linear algebra computations. For a big matrix, `Chol` runs the Cholesky-Banachiewicz algorithm in parallel. For a sparse matrix (a sparse matrix is a matrix with mostly zeros), it runs a sparse version. `Cholesky` computes the matrix ***L***. The following code implements the previous example:

```
val A: Matrix = DenseMatrix(
    arrayOf(
        doubleArrayOf(4.0, 12.0, -16.0),
        doubleArrayOf(12.0, 37.0, -43.0),
        doubleArrayOf(-16.0, -43.0, 98.0)
    )
)

val chol: Cholesky = Chol(A)
val L: LowerTriangularMatrix = chol.L()
val Lt: UpperTriangularMatrix = chol.L().t()
println(String.format("\nL = %s", L))
```

The output is as follows:

```
L = 3x3
         [,1] [,2] [,3]
[1,] 2.000000, 0.000000, 0.000000,
[2,] 6.000000, 1.000000, 0.000000,
[3,] -8.000000, 5.000000, 3.000000,
```

```
println(String.format("Lt = %s", Lt))
```

The output is as follows:

```
Lt = 3x3
         [,1] [,2] [,3]
[1,] 2.000000, 6.000000, -8.000000,
[2,] 0.000000, 1.000000, 5.000000,
[3,] 0.000000, 0.000000, 3.000000,
```

```
val LLt: Matrix = L.multiply(Lt)
// verify that A = LLt
println(String.format("%s = \n%s is %b",
        A,
        LLt,
        MatrixPropertyUtils.areEqual(A, LLt, 1e-14)))
```

The output is as follows:

```
3x3
         [,1] [,2] [,3]
[1,] 4.000000, 12.000000, -16.000000,
[2,] 12.000000, 37.000000, -43.000000,
[3,] -16.000000, -43.000000, 98.000000,  =
```

```
3x3
         [,1] [,2] [,3]
[1,] 4.000000, 12.000000, -16.000000,
[2,] 12.000000, 37.000000, -43.000000,
[3,] -16.000000, -43.000000, 98.000000,  is true
```

2.3.3. Hessenberg Decomposition and Tridiagonalization

In the two-dimensional space R^2, you typically use the x-axis and y-axis as the coordinates or basis. However, there is nothing special about these two axes, except that they are perpendicular (or orthogonal) to each other. You can equally choose another set of two orthogonal axes to label the coordinates, if it is more convenient. See Figure 2-19.

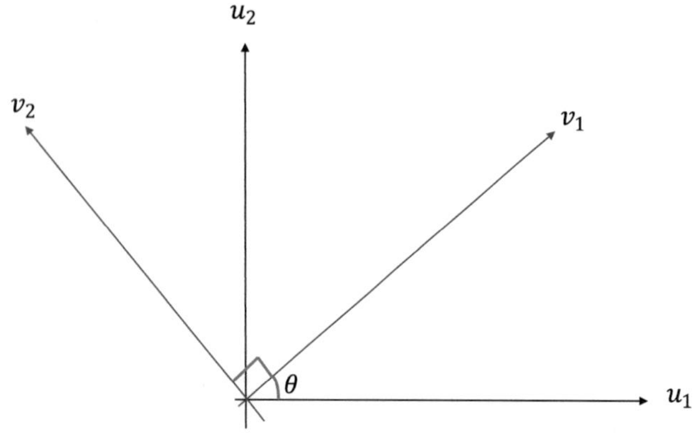

Figure 2-19. *Change of coordinate or change of basis*

For the example in Figure 2-19, suppose $\left\{ \boldsymbol{u}_1 = \begin{pmatrix} 1 \\ 0 \end{pmatrix}, \boldsymbol{u}_2 = \begin{pmatrix} 0 \\ 1 \end{pmatrix} \right\}$ are your typical x-y axes. $\{\boldsymbol{v}_1, \boldsymbol{v}_2\}$ is the new coordinate system or basis, which is a rotation of $\{\boldsymbol{u}_1, \boldsymbol{u}_2\}$ by θ. You can write $\{\boldsymbol{v}_1, \boldsymbol{v}_2\}$ in terms of $\{\boldsymbol{u}_1, \boldsymbol{u}_2\}$ as follows:

$$\begin{cases} \boldsymbol{v}_1 = \boldsymbol{u}_1 \cos\theta + \boldsymbol{u}_2 \sin\theta \\ \boldsymbol{v}_2 = \boldsymbol{u}_1 (-\sin\theta) + \boldsymbol{u}_2 \cos\theta \end{cases}$$

Or, equivalently in matrix form:

$$\begin{bmatrix} \boldsymbol{v}_1 \\ \boldsymbol{v}_2 \end{bmatrix} = \begin{bmatrix} \cos\theta & \sin\theta \\ -\sin\theta & \cos\theta \end{bmatrix} \begin{bmatrix} \boldsymbol{u}_1 \\ \boldsymbol{u}_2 \end{bmatrix}$$

By left-multiplying the change-of-basis matrix $\boldsymbol{P} = \begin{bmatrix} \cos\theta & \sin\theta \\ -\sin\theta & \cos\theta \end{bmatrix}$, you can write the new coordinates in terms of the original ones. The same change-of-basis concept applies to a higher dimension.

Two $n \times n$ square matrices $\boldsymbol{A}$ and $\boldsymbol{B}$ are similar if there exists an invertible matrix $\boldsymbol{P}$ such that:

$$\boldsymbol{B} = \boldsymbol{P}^{-1}\boldsymbol{A}\boldsymbol{P}$$

A and ***B*** represent the same linear transformation but in two coordinate systems with a different basis. The matrix ***P*** is the change-of-basis matrix. The coordinate of ***x*** in the new coordinate system after changing the basis is as follows:

$$\boldsymbol{x}' = \boldsymbol{P}\boldsymbol{x}$$

In the new coordinate system, the transformation can be written as follows:

$$\boldsymbol{y}' = \boldsymbol{A}\boldsymbol{x}'$$

In the coordinate system with the original basis, the transformation would be as follows:

$$\boldsymbol{y} = \boldsymbol{B}\boldsymbol{x} = \boldsymbol{P}^{-1}\boldsymbol{A}\boldsymbol{P}\boldsymbol{x}$$

Geometrically, the similarity transform operates in three steps: change to a new basis (***Px***), perform the simple transformation (***APx***), and change back to the old basis ($P^{-1}\boldsymbol{APx}$). A change of basis—for example, aligning the rotation axis with the positive z-axis—can result in a simpler form of the same transformation or matrix, such as more zeros in ***A***. Similar matrices have the same eigenvalues and multiplicities and the same determinant.

An (upper) Hessenberg matrix is a matrix that has zero entries below the first subdiagonal. The first subdiagonal is the entries right below the diagonal. In other words, a Hessenberg matrix has nonzero entries only on the first subdiagonal, the diagonal, and the upper part of the matrix. That is, $a_{ij} = 0$ when $i > j + 1$. For example, the following matrix is a Hessenberg matrix:

$$\begin{bmatrix} 1 & 4 & 2 & 3 \\ 3 & 4 & 1 & 7 \\ 0 & 2 & 3 & 4 \\ 0 & 0 & 1 & 3 \end{bmatrix}$$

Hessenberg decomposition finds, for a square matrix ***A***, a matrix ***Q*** such that:

$$\boldsymbol{Q}'\boldsymbol{A}\boldsymbol{Q} = \boldsymbol{H}$$

H is a Hessenberg matrix. **Q** is an orthogonal matrix, meaning that any two rows (or columns) are orthogonal or their dot product is 0. Equivalently, $\boldsymbol{Q}^{-1} = \boldsymbol{Q}'$. So, ***A*** and ***H*** are similar.

In NM Dev, the `HessenbergDecomposition` class performs the Hessenberg decomposition for a square matrix. It computes the ***Q*** and ***H*** matrices. The following code implements this example:

$$\begin{bmatrix} 1 & 0 & 0 & 0 \\ 0 & -0.348743 & 0.089751 & -0.932911 \\ 0 & -0.464991 & -0.880822 & 0.089084 \\ 0 & -0.813733 & 0.464862 & 0.348914 \end{bmatrix} \times \begin{bmatrix} 1 & 5 & 7 & 9 \\ 3 & 0 & 6 & 3 \\ 4 & 3 & 1 & 0 \\ 7 & 13 & 2 & 10 \end{bmatrix}$$

$$\times \begin{bmatrix} 1 & 0 & 0 & 0 \\ 0 & -0.348743 & -0.464991 & -0.813733 \\ 0 & 0.089751 & -0.880822 & 0.464862 \\ 0 & -0.932911 & 0.089084 & 0.348914 \end{bmatrix}$$

$$= \begin{bmatrix} 1 & -12.322250 & -1.533240 & -0.900742 \\ -8.602325 & 13.594595 & -1.657558 & 7.593136 \\ 0 & -5.460964 & 2.073954 & -1.404349 \\ 0 & 0 & 4.989271 & -4.668549 \end{bmatrix}$$

```
println("Hessenberg decomposition")

val A: Matrix = DenseMatrix(
    arrayOf(
        doubleArrayOf(1.0, 5.0, 7.0, 9.0),
        doubleArrayOf(3.0, 0.0, 6.0, 3.0),
        doubleArrayOf(4.0, 3.0, 1.0, 0.0),
        doubleArrayOf(7.0, 13.0, 2.0, 10.0)
    )
)

val hessenberg: HessenbergDecomposition = HessenbergDecomposition(A)

val H: Matrix = hessenberg.H()
println(String.format(
        "H = \n%s is Hessenberg, %b",
        H,
        Hessenberg.isHessenberg(H, 0.0)))
```

The output is as follows:

```
H =
4x4
         [,1] [,2] [,3] [,4]
[1,] 1.000000, -12.322250, -1.533240, -0.900742,
[2,] -8.602325, 13.594595, -1.657558, 7.593136,
[3,] 0.000000, -5.460964, 2.073954, -1.404349,
[4,] 0.000000, 0.000000, 4.989271, -4.668549,  is Hessenberg, true

val Q: Matrix = hessenberg.Q()
println(String.format(
        "Q = \n%s is orthogonal, %b",
        Q,
        MatrixPropertyUtils.isOrthogonal(Q, 1e-14)))
```

The output is as follows:

```
Q =
4x4
         [,1] [,2] [,3] [,4]
[1,] 1.000000, 0.000000, 0.000000, 0.000000,
[2,] 0.000000, -0.348743, 0.089751, -0.932911,
[3,] 0.000000, -0.464991, -0.880822, 0.089084,
[4,] 0.000000, -0.813733, 0.464862, 0.348914,  is orthogonal, true

// verify that Qt * A * Q = H
val QtAQ: Matrix = Q.t().multiply(A).multiply(Q)
println(String.format("%s = \n%s is %b",
        H,
        QtAQ,
        MatrixPropertyUtils.isOrthogonal(Q, 1e-14)))
```

The output is as follows:

```
4x4
         [,1] [,2] [,3] [,4]
[1,] 1.000000, -12.322250, -1.533240, -0.900742,
[2,] -8.602325, 13.594595, -1.657558, 7.593136,
[3,] 0.000000, -5.460964, 2.073954, -1.404349,
[4,] 0.000000, 0.000000, 4.989271, -4.668549,  =
4x4
        [,1] [,2] [,3] [,4]
[1,] 1.000000, -12.322250, -1.533240, -0.900742,
[2,] -8.602325, 13.594595, -1.657558, 7.593136,
[3,] 0.000000, -5.460964, 2.073954, -1.404349,
[4,] -0.000000, 0.000000, 4.989271, -4.668549,  is true
```

If $\boldsymbol{A}$ is Hermitian, this transformation reduces it to tridiagonal form. That is:

$$\boldsymbol{Q}'\boldsymbol{A}\boldsymbol{Q} = \boldsymbol{T}$$

$\boldsymbol{A}$ and $\boldsymbol{T}$ are similar. $\boldsymbol{T}$ is a tridiagonal matrix. A tridiagonal matrix has nonzero elements on the main diagonal, the first subdiagonal below this, and the first super-diagonal above the main diagonal only. That is, $a_{ij} = 0$ when $i > j + 1$ and $i < j - 1$. It looks like this:

$$T = \begin{bmatrix} a_1 & b_1 & & & \\ c_1 & a_2 & b_2 & & \\ & c_2 & \ddots & \ddots & \\ & & \ddots & \ddots & b_{n-1} \\ & & & c_{n-1} & a_n \end{bmatrix}$$

In NM Dev, the `TriDiagonalization` class performs the tri-diagonalization for a symmetric square matrix. It computes the $\boldsymbol{Q}$ and $\boldsymbol{T}$ matrices. The following code implements this example:

$$\begin{bmatrix} 1 & 0 & 0 & 0 \\ 0 & -0.40161 & 0.601902 & -0.690235 \\ 0 & -0.562254 & -0.756975 & -0.332956 \\ 0 & -0.722897 & 0.254368 & 0.64243 \end{bmatrix} \times \begin{bmatrix} 1 & 5 & 7 & 9 \\ 5 & 0 & 3 & 13 \\ 7 & 3 & 1 & 2 \\ 9 & 13 & 2 & 10 \end{bmatrix}$$

$$\times \begin{bmatrix} 1 & 0 & 0 & 0 \\ 0 & -0.40161 & -0.562254 & -0.722897 \\ 0 & 0.601902 & -0.756975 & 0.254368 \\ 0 & -0.690235 & -0.332956 & 0.64243 \end{bmatrix}$$

$$= \begin{bmatrix} 1 & -12.4499 & 0 & 0 \\ -12.4499 & 16.070968 & -7.692568 & 0 \\ 0 & -7.692568 & 1.696818 & 4.45481 \\ 0 & 0 & 4.45481 & -6.767786 \end{bmatrix}$$

```
println("Tri-diagonalization")

// define a symmetric matrix
val S: Matrix = SymmetricMatrix(
    arrayOf(
        doubleArrayOf(1.0),
        doubleArrayOf(5.0, 0.0),
        doubleArrayOf(7.0, 3.0, 1.0),
        doubleArrayOf(9.0, 13.0, 2.0, 10.0)
    )
)

val triDiagonalization: TriDiagonalization = TriDiagonalization(S)

val T: Matrix = triDiagonalization.T()
println(String.format(
        "T = \n%s is tri-diagonal, %b",
        T,
        MatrixPropertyUtils.isTridiagonal(T, 1e-14)))
```

The output is as follows:

```
T = 4x4
      [,1] [,2] [,3] [,4]
[1,] 1.000000, -12.449900, 0.000000, 0.000000,
[2,] -12.449900, 16.070968, -7.692568, 0.000000,
[3,] 0.000000, -7.692568, 1.696818, 4.454810,
[4,] 0.000000, 0.000000, 4.454810, -6.767786,  is tri-diagonal, true
```

```
val Q: Matrix = triDiagonalization.Q()
println(String.format(
        "Q = \n%s is tri-diagonal, %b",
        Q,
        MatrixPropertyUtils.isOrthogonal(Q, 1e-14)))
```

The output is as follows:

```
Q = 4x4
      [,1] [,2] [,3] [,4]
[1,] 1.000000, 0.000000, 0.000000, 0.000000,
[2,] 0.000000, -0.401610, 0.601902, -0.690235,
[3,] 0.000000, -0.562254, -0.756975, -0.332956,
[4,] 0.000000, -0.722897, 0.254368, 0.642430,  is tri-diagonal, true
```

```
// verify that Qt * A * Q = T
val QtSQ: Matrix = Q.t().multiply(S).multiply(Q)
println(String.format("%s = \n%s is %b",
        T,
        QtSQ,
```

```
        MatrixPropertyUtils.areEqual(QtSQ, T, 1e-13)))
```

The output is as follows:

```
4x4
        [,1] [,2] [,3] [,4]
[1,] 1.000000, -12.449900, 0.000000, 0.000000,
[2,] -12.449900, 16.070968, -7.692568, 0.000000,
[3,] 0.000000, -7.692568, 1.696818, 4.454810,
[4,] 0.000000, 0.000000, 4.454810, -6.767786,  =
4x4
        [,1] [,2] [,3] [,4]
[1,] 1.000000, -12.449900, -0.000000, 0.000000,
[2,] -12.449900, 16.070968, -7.692568, 0.000000,
[3,] -0.000000, -7.692568, 1.696818, 4.454810,
[4,] 0.000000, 0.000000, 4.454810, -6.767786,  is true
```

The SymmetricMatrix class constructs a symmetric matrix from the data in the lower triangular part of the matrix. The signature is as follows:

```
/**
 * Construct a symmetric matrix from a 2D {@code double[][]} array.
 * The array specifies only the lower triangular part (main diagonal inclusive) of the whole
 * matrix.
 * For example,
 * <blockquote><code><pre>
 *        new double[][]{
 *                {1},
 *                {2, 3},
 *                {4, 5, 6},
 *                {7, 8, 9, 10},
 *                {11, 12, 13, 14, 15}});
 * </pre></code></blockquote>
 * gives
 * \[
 * \begin{bmatrix}
 * 1 & 2 & 4 & 7 & 11\\
 * 2 & 3 & 5 & 8 & 12\\
 * 4 & 5 & 6 & 9 & 13\\
 * 7 & 8 & 9 & 10 & 14\\
 * 11 & 12 & 13 & 14 & 15
 * \end{bmatrix}
 * \] * This constructor uses lower instead of upper triangular representation for
   visual reason.
 *
 * @param data the lower triangular specification
 */
public SymmetricMatrix(double[][] data)
```

If the constraints of a linear algebra problem do not allow a general matrix to be conveniently reduced to a triangular one, reduction to Hessenberg form is often the next best thing. In fact, reduction of any matrix to a Hessenberg form can be achieved in a finite number of steps. Subsequent reduction of a Hessenberg matrix to a triangular matrix can be achieved through iterative procedures, such as shifted QR decomposition. In eigenvalue algorithms, the Hessenberg matrix can be further reduced to a triangular matrix through shifted QR decomposition combined with deflation steps. Reducing a general matrix to a Hessenberg matrix and then reducing it further to a triangular matrix, instead of directly reducing a general matrix to a triangular matrix, often economizes the arithmetic involved in the QR algorithm for eigenvalue problems.

2.3.4. QR Decomposition

QR decomposition or QR factorization is a decomposition of a matrix $\boldsymbol{A}$ into this product:

$$\boldsymbol{A} = \boldsymbol{QR}$$

such that $\boldsymbol{Q}$ is an orthogonal matrix (its columns are unit vectors and $\boldsymbol{Q}^{-1} = \boldsymbol{Q}'$) and $\boldsymbol{R}$ is an upper triangular matrix. If **A** is invertible, then the factorization is unique if you require $\boldsymbol{R}$ to have a positive diagonal (the diagonal elements in $\boldsymbol{R}$ are positive). If $\boldsymbol{A}$ has n linearly independent columns, then the first n columns of $\boldsymbol{Q}$ form an orthonormal basis for the column space of $\boldsymbol{A}$. More generally, the first k columns of $\boldsymbol{Q}$ form an orthonormal basis for the span of the first k columns of $\boldsymbol{A}$ for any $1 \le k \le n$. The fact that any column k of $\boldsymbol{A}$ depends only on the first k columns of $\boldsymbol{Q}$ is responsible for the triangular form of $\boldsymbol{R}$.

There are several methods for doing QR decomposition, such as by means of the Gram-Schmidt process (the `GramSchmidt` class), Householder transformations (the `Householder` class), or Givens rotations (the `GivensMatrix` class). In NM Dev, the `QRDecomposition` interface represents the implementations of the different QR algorithms. The signature is as follows:

```
public interface QRDecomposition {
    /**
     * Get <i>P</i>, the pivoting matrix in the QR decomposition.
     *
     * @return <i>P</i>
     */
    public PermutationMatrix P();
    /**
     * Get the orthogonal <i>Q</i> matrix in the QR decomposition, <i>A =
     * QR</i>. The dimension of <i>Q</i> is <i>m x n</i>, the same as <i>A</i>,
     * the matrix to be orthogonalized.
     *
     * @return <i>Q</i>
     */
    public Matrix Q();
    /**
     * Get the upper triangular matrix <i>R</i> in the QR decomposition, <i>A =
     * QR</i>. The dimension of <i>R</i> is <i>n x n</i>, a square matrix.
     *
     * @return <i>R</i>
     */
```

```
    public UpperTriangularMatrix R();
    /**
     * Get the numerical rank of <i>A</i> as computed by the QR decomposition.
     * Numerical determination of rank requires a criterion to decide when a
     * value should be treated as zero, hence a precision parameter. This is a
     * practical choice which depends on both the matrix and the application.
     * For instance, for a matrix with a big first eigenvector, we should
     * accordingly decrease the precision to compute the rank.
     *
     * @return the rank of <i>A</i>
     */
    public int rank();
    /**
     * Get the square <i>Q</i> matrix. This is an arbitrary orthogonal
     * completion of the <i>Q</i> matrix in the QR decomposition. The dimension
     * is <i>m x m</i> (square). We have <i>A = sqQ * tallR</i>.
     *
     * @return the square <i>Q</i> matrix
     */
    public Matrix squareQ();
    /**
     * Get the tall <i>R</i> matrix. This is completed by binding zero rows
     * beneath the square upper triangular matrix <i>R</i> in the QR
     * decomposition. The dimension is <i>m x n</i>. It may not be square. We
     * have <i>A = sqQ * tallR</i>.
     *
     * @return the tall <i>R</i> matrix
     */
    public Matrix tallR();
}
```

The decompositions discussed so far apply only to square matrices. QR decomposition works on square matrices as well as tall matrices with a twist. Specifically, for an $m \times n$ matrix $\boldsymbol{A}$ with $m \geq n$, you can do the following:

$$\boldsymbol{A} = \boldsymbol{QR} = \boldsymbol{Q}\begin{bmatrix} \boldsymbol{R}_1 \\ \boldsymbol{0} \end{bmatrix} = \begin{bmatrix} \boldsymbol{Q}_1 & \boldsymbol{Q}_2 \end{bmatrix}\begin{bmatrix} \boldsymbol{R}_1 \\ \boldsymbol{0} \end{bmatrix} = \boldsymbol{Q}_1\boldsymbol{R}_1$$

$\boldsymbol{Q}$ is an $m \times m$ matrix. $\boldsymbol{R}$ is an $m \times n$ upper triangular matrix. The bottom $(m - n)$ rows of $\boldsymbol{R}$ are zeros. $\boldsymbol{Q}_1$ is an $m \times n$ matrix, and $\boldsymbol{Q}_2$ is an $m \times (m - n)$. $\boldsymbol{Q}_1$ and $\boldsymbol{Q}_2$ both have orthogonal columns. $\boldsymbol{R}_1$ is an $n \times n$ matrix. The `Q()` function computes the $m \times n$ $\boldsymbol{Q}_1$ matrix. The `R()` function computes the $n \times n$ $\boldsymbol{R}_1$ matrix. The `squareQ()` function computes the $m \times m$ $\boldsymbol{Q}$ matrix. The `tallR()` function computes the tall $m \times n$ $\boldsymbol{R}$ matrix.

The NM Dev class `QR` is a wrapper class that performs QR decomposition. By default, it uses the Householder QR algorithm. The Householder reflection has a better numerical stability than the Gram-Schmidt process. The following code implements this example:

$$\begin{bmatrix} 3 & 2 \\ 1 & 2 \end{bmatrix} = \begin{bmatrix} 0.948683 & -0.316228 \\ 0.316228 & 0.948683 \end{bmatrix}\begin{bmatrix} 3.162278 & 2.529822 \\ 0 & 1.264911 \end{bmatrix}$$

```
val A: Matrix = DenseMatrix(
    arrayOf(
        doubleArrayOf(3.0, 2.0),
        doubleArrayOf(1.0, 2.0)
    )
)

// use the Householder QR algorithm
val qr1: QRDecomposition = HouseholderQR(A, 0.0)
println("\nRank = " + qr1.rank())

val Q1: Matrix = qr1.Q()
println(String.format(
        "\nQ = \n%s is orthogonal, %b",
        Q1,
        MatrixPropertyUtils.isOrthogonal(Q1, 1e-15)))

val R1: UpperTriangularMatrix = qr1.R()
println("\nR = \n" + R1)
```

The output is as follows:

```
rank = 2
Q =
2x2
        [,1] [,2]
[1,] -0.948683, -0.316228,
[2,] -0.316228, 0.948683,  is orthogonal, true
R =
2x2
         [,1] [,2]
[1,] -3.162278, -2.529822,
[2,] 0.000000, 1.264911,
```

```
// verify that Q1R1 = A
val Q1R1: Matrix = Q1.multiply(R1)
println(String.format("\n%s = \n%s is %b",
        A,
        Q1R1,
        MatrixPropertyUtils.areEqual(Q1R1, A, 1e-13)))
```

The output is as follows:

```
2x2
         [,1] [,2]
[1,] 3.000000, 2.000000,
[2,] 1.000000, 2.000000,  =
```

```
2x2
         [,1] [,2]
[1,] 3.000000, 2.000000,
[2,] 1.000000, 2.000000,  is true
```

```
// use the Gram-Schmidt QR algorithm
val qr2: QRDecomposition = GramSchmidt(A)
println("\nRank = " + qr2.rank())
```

The output is as follows:

```
rank = 2
```

```
val Q2: Matrix = qr2.Q()
println(String.format(
        "\nQ = \n%s is orthogonal, %b",
        Q2,
        MatrixPropertyUtils.isOrthogonal(Q2, 1e-15)))

val R2: UpperTriangularMatrix = qr2.R()
println("\nR = \n" + R2)
```

The output is as follows:

```
Q =
2x2
         [,1] [,2]
[1,] 0.948683, -0.316228,
[2,] 0.316228, 0.948683,  is orthogonal, true
R =
2x2
         [,1] [,2]
[1,] 3.162278, 2.529822,
[2,] 0.000000, 1.264911,
```

```
// verify that Q2R2 = A
val Q2R2: Matrix = Q2.multiply(R2)
println(String.format("%s = \n%s is %b",
        A,
        Q2R2,
        MatrixPropertyUtils.areEqual(Q2R2, A, 1e-13)))
```

The output is as follows:

```
2x2
         [,1] [,2]
[1,] 3.000000, 2.000000,
[2,] 1.000000, 2.000000,  =
2x2
         [,1] [,2]
[1,] 3.000000, 2.000000,
[2,] 1.000000, 2.000000,  is true
```

Here's a tall matrix example:

$$\begin{bmatrix} 1 & 2 & 3 \\ 6 & 7 & 8 \\ 11 & 12 & 13 \\ 16 & 17 & 18 \\ 21 & 22 & 23 \end{bmatrix}$$

$$= \begin{bmatrix} -0.034199 & -0.773841 & -0.359539 \\ -0.205196 & -0.507833 & -0.031675 \\ -0.376192 & -0.241825 & 0.868055 \\ -0.547188 & 0.024183 & -0.202929 \\ -0.718185 & 0.290191 & -0.273913 \end{bmatrix} \begin{bmatrix} -29.240383 & -31.121343 & -33.002304 \\ 0 & -1.209127 & -2.418254 \\ 0 & 0 & 0 \end{bmatrix}$$

$$= \begin{bmatrix} -0.034199 & -0.773841 & -0.359539 & -0.365120 & -0.370701 \\ -0.205196 & -0.507833 & -0.031675 & 0.361174 & 0.754023 \\ -0.376192 & -0.241825 & 0.868055 & -0.145512 & -0.159079 \\ -0.547188 & 0.024183 & -0.202929 & 0.667982 & -0.461107 \\ -0.718185 & 0.290191 & -0.273913 & -0.518524 & 0.236864 \end{bmatrix}$$

$$\times \begin{bmatrix} -29.240383 & -31.121343 & -33.002304 \\ 0 & -1.209127 & -2.418254 \\ 0 & 0 & 0 \\ 0 & 0 & 0 \\ 0 & 0 & 0 \end{bmatrix}$$

The NM Dev code to solve this problem is as follows:

```
val A: Matrix = DenseMatrix(
    arrayOf(
        doubleArrayOf(1.0, 2.0, 3.0),
        doubleArrayOf(6.0, 7.0, 8.0),
        doubleArrayOf(11.0, 12.0, 13.0),
        doubleArrayOf(16.0, 17.0, 18.0),
```

```
        doubleArrayOf(21.0, 22.0, 23.0)
    )
)

val qr: QRDecomposition = QR(A, 1e-14)
println("\nRank = " + qr.rank())

val Q1: Matrix = qr.Q()
println("\nQ1 = \n" + Q1)
val R1: UpperTriangularMatrix = qr.R()
println("\nR1 = \n" + R1)
```

The output is as follows:

```
rank = 2
Q1 =
5x3
         [,1] [,2] [,3]
[1,] -0.034199, -0.773841, -0.359539,
[2,] -0.205196, -0.507833, -0.031675,
[3,] -0.376192, -0.241825, 0.868055,
[4,] -0.547188, 0.024183, -0.202929,
[5,] -0.718185, 0.290191, -0.273913,
R1 =
3x3
         [,1] [,2] [,3]
[1,] -29.240383, -31.121343, -33.002304,
[2,] 0.000000, -1.209127, -2.418254,
[3,] 0.000000, 0.000000, 0.000000,
```

```
// verify that Q1R1 = A
val Q1R1: Matrix = Q1.multiply(R1)
println(String.format("%s = \n%s is %b",
        A,
        Q1R1,
        MatrixPropertyUtils.areEqual(Q1R1, A, 1e-13)))

val Q: Matrix = qr.squareQ()
println("\nQ = \n" + Q)
val R: Matrix = qr.tallR()
println("\nR = \n" + R)
```

The output is as follows:

```
5x3
         [,1] [,2] [,3]
[1,] 1.000000, 2.000000, 3.000000,
[2,] 6.000000, 7.000000, 8.000000,
[3,] 11.000000, 12.000000, 13.000000,
[4,] 16.000000, 17.000000, 18.000000,
```

```
[5,] 21.000000, 22.000000, 23.000000,  =
5x3
        [,1] [,2] [,3]
[1,] 1.000000, 2.000000, 3.000000,
[2,] 6.000000, 7.000000, 8.000000,
[3,] 11.000000, 12.000000, 13.000000,
[4,] 16.000000, 17.000000, 18.000000,
[5,] 21.000000, 22.000000, 23.000000,  is true
Q =
5x5
        [,1] [,2] [,3] [,4] [,5]
[1,] -0.034199, -0.773841, -0.359539, -0.365120, -0.370701,
[2,] -0.205196, -0.507833, -0.031675, 0.361174, 0.754023,
[3,] -0.376192, -0.241825, 0.868055, -0.145512, -0.159079,
[4,] -0.547188, 0.024183, -0.202929, 0.667982, -0.461107,
[5,] -0.718185, 0.290191, -0.273913, -0.518524, 0.236864,
R =
5x3
        [,1] [,2] [,3]
[1,] -29.240383, -31.121343, -33.002304,
[2,] 0.000000, -1.209127, -2.418254,
[3,] 0.000000, 0.000000, 0.000000,
[4,] 0.000000, 0.000000, 0.000000,
[5,] 0.000000, 0.000000, 0.000000,

// verify that QR = A
val QR: Matrix = Q.multiply(R)
println(String.format("%s = \n%s is %b",
        A,
        QR,
        MatrixPropertyUtils.areEqual(QR, A, 1e-13)))
```

The output is as follows:

```
5x3
        [,1] [,2] [,3]
[1,] 1.000000, 2.000000, 3.000000,
[2,] 6.000000, 7.000000, 8.000000,
[3,] 11.000000, 12.000000, 13.000000,
[4,] 16.000000, 17.000000, 18.000000,
[5,] 21.000000, 22.000000, 23.000000,  =
5x3
        [,1] [,2] [,3]
[1,] 1.000000, 2.000000, 3.000000,
[2,] 6.000000, 7.000000, 8.000000,
[3,] 11.000000, 12.000000, 13.000000,
[4,] 16.000000, 17.000000, 18.000000,
[5,] 21.000000, 22.000000, 23.000000,  is true
```

2.3.5. Eigen Decomposition

Given a linear transformation or its matrix, $\boldsymbol{A}$, an eigenvector $\boldsymbol{v}$ of $\boldsymbol{A}$ is such a vector that:

$$\boldsymbol{A}\boldsymbol{v} = \lambda \boldsymbol{v}$$

λ is called an eigenvalue of $\boldsymbol{A}$, corresponding to the eigenvector $\boldsymbol{v}$.

Geometrically, it means that when applying the linear transformation $\boldsymbol{A}$ to the vector $\boldsymbol{v}$, the transformation only stretches ($\lambda > 1$) or shrinks ($\lambda < 1$) the vector, but does not change its direction ($\lambda > 0$) other than flipping it to the opposite direction ($\lambda < 0$). $\boldsymbol{A}\boldsymbol{v}$ is parallel to $\boldsymbol{v}$. See Figure 2-20.

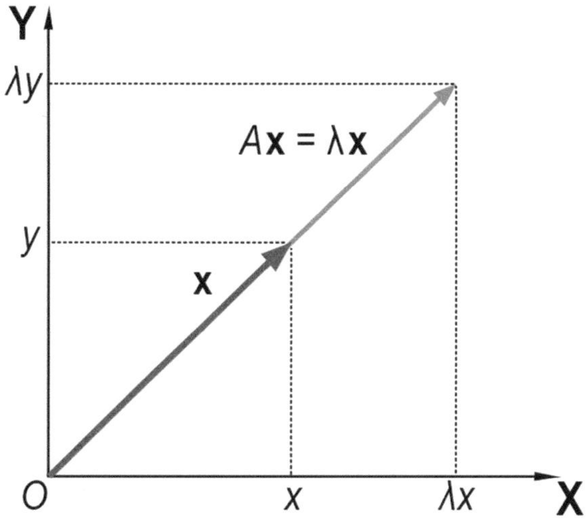

Figure 2-20. *Eigenvector and eigenvalue*

To see why this is important, consider a motivating example. Consider this diagonal matrix in R^2:

$$\boldsymbol{A} = \begin{bmatrix} a_{11} & 0 \\ 0 & a_{22} \end{bmatrix}$$

If you multiply $\boldsymbol{A}$ by the x-axis $\boldsymbol{u}_1 = \begin{bmatrix} 1 \\ 0 \end{bmatrix}$, you get this:

$$\boldsymbol{A}\boldsymbol{u}_1 = \begin{bmatrix} a_{11} & 0 \\ 0 & a_{22} \end{bmatrix} \begin{bmatrix} 1 \\ 0 \end{bmatrix} = \begin{bmatrix} a_{11} \\ 0 \end{bmatrix} = a_{11} \begin{bmatrix} 1 \\ 0 \end{bmatrix}$$

$\boldsymbol{A}\boldsymbol{u}_1$ and $\boldsymbol{u}_1$ are parallel, so the x-axis is an eigenvector. The corresponding eigenvalue is a_{11}.

Likewise, if you multiply $\boldsymbol{A}$ by the y-axis $\boldsymbol{u}_2 = \begin{bmatrix} 0 \\ 1 \end{bmatrix}$, you get this:

$$\boldsymbol{A}\boldsymbol{u}_2 = \begin{bmatrix} a_{11} & 0 \\ 0 & a_{22} \end{bmatrix} \begin{bmatrix} 0 \\ 1 \end{bmatrix} = \begin{bmatrix} 0 \\ a_{22} \end{bmatrix} = a_{22} \begin{bmatrix} 0 \\ 1 \end{bmatrix}$$

$\boldsymbol{Au}_2$ and $\boldsymbol{u}_2$ are parallel so the y-axis is an eigenvector. The corresponding eigenvalue is a_{22}. In fact, they are the only two vectors that work among all (infinitely many) other possible vectors. That is, for a diagonal matrix, the eigenvectors are simply its basis. The converse is also true. For any diagonalizable matrix, if you write the matrix in a new basis consisting of its eigenvectors, then the matrix in the new coordinate system is a diagonal matrix.

Mathematically, an $n \times n$ square matrix $\boldsymbol{A}$ is diagonalizable if there exists an $n \times n$ square matrix $\boldsymbol{Q}$ such that:

$$\boldsymbol{A} = \boldsymbol{QDQ}^{-1}$$

Or, equivalently:

$$\boldsymbol{D} = \boldsymbol{Q}^{-1}\boldsymbol{AQ}$$

$\boldsymbol{Q}$ is orthogonal and hence a basis. Its columns are the eigenvectors of $\boldsymbol{A}$, and they are all linearly independent. $\boldsymbol{D}$ is a diagonal matrix whose diagonal elements are the corresponding eigenvalues. This is called the *eigen decomposition* of matrix $\boldsymbol{A}$. This decomposition can be derived from the fundamental property of eigenvectors:

$$\boldsymbol{Av} = \lambda \boldsymbol{v}$$

$$\boldsymbol{AQ} = \boldsymbol{QD}$$

$$\boldsymbol{A} = \boldsymbol{QDQ}^{-1}$$

Finding eigenvalues and eigenvectors is important as they have a wide range of applications, for example, in stability analysis, vibration analysis, atomic orbitals, and facial recognition.

One important application in machine learning or data analysis in general is dimension reduction or principal component analysis (PCA). PCA is the process of computing the principal components and using them to perform a change of basis on the data, sometimes using only the first few principal components and ignoring the rest. Intuitively, PCA can be thought of as fitting a p-dimensional ellipsoid or data by rotating the axes so that the majority of the variances of the data land on only a few axes. If a (rotated) axis of the ellipsoid is small, then the variance along that axis is also small. You can remove that dimension, effectively projecting the data from a high-dimensional space to a lower-dimensional space.

To find the new axes of the ellipsoid, you compute the covariance matrix of the data and calculate the eigenvalues and corresponding eigenvectors of this covariance matrix. Then you must normalize each of the orthogonal eigenvectors to turn them into unit vectors. Once this is done, each of the mutually orthogonal unit eigenvectors can be interpreted as an axis of the ellipsoid fitted to the data. This choice of basis will transform the covariance matrix into a diagonalized form with the diagonal elements representing the variance of each axis. The proportion of the variance that each eigenvector represents can be calculated by dividing the eigenvalue corresponding to that eigenvector by the sum of all eigenvalues. See Figure 2-21.

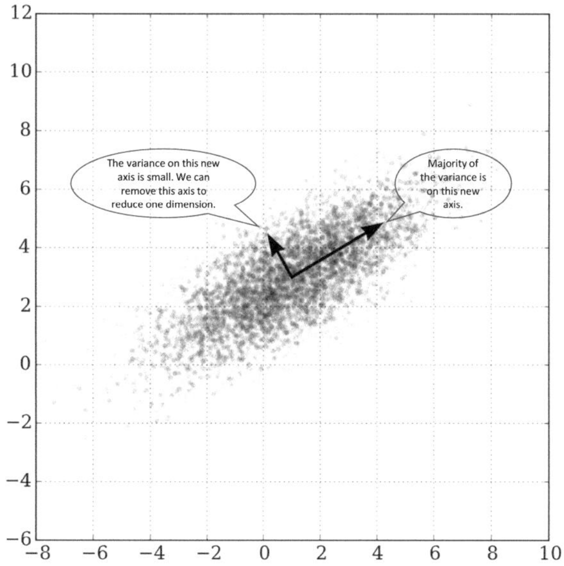

Figure 2-21. *PCA and dimension reduction*

There are several methods for doing eigen decomposition, such as by means of characteristic polynomial (for small matrices), DQDS algorithm (for tri-diagonal matrices), MR3 algorithm (for symmetric matrices), and QR algorithm (for general matrices). The implementations of all these algorithms and transformations are very involved. The NM Dev class called `EigenDecomposition` wraps all these algorithms and applies the appropriate one depending on the input matrix. The signature is as follows:

```
/**
 * Runs the eigen decomposition on a <em>square</em> matrix.
 *
 * @param A       a square, <em>diagonalizable</em> matrix
 * @param epsilon a precision parameter: when a number |x| &le; &epsilon;,
 *                it is considered 0
 */
public EigenDecomposition(Matrix A, double epsilon)
/**
 * Runs the eigen decomposition on a <em>square</em> matrix.
 *
 * @param A a square, <em>diagonalizable</em> matrix
 */
public EigenDecomposition(Matrix A)
/**
 * Get the diagonal matrix <i>D</i> as in <i>Q * D * Q' = A</i>.
 *
 * Note that for the moment we support only real eigenvalues.
 *
 * @return <i>D</i>
 */
```

```
public DiagonalMatrix D()
/**
 * Get <i>Q</i> as in <i>Q * D * Q' = A</i>.
 *
 * Note that for the moment we support only real eigenvalues.
 *
 * @return <i>Q</i>
 */
public Matrix Q()
/**
 * Get <i>Q'</i> as in <i>Q * D * Q' = A</i>.
 *
 * Note that for the moment we support only real eigenvalues.
 *
 * @return {@code Q.t()}
 */
public Matrix Qt()
```

The following code implements this example:

$$\begin{bmatrix} 5 & 2 \\ 2 & 5 \end{bmatrix} = \begin{bmatrix} 0.707107 & -0.707107 \\ 0.707107 & 0.707107 \end{bmatrix} \begin{bmatrix} 7 & 0 \\ 0 & 3 \end{bmatrix} \begin{bmatrix} 0.707107 & 0.707107 \\ -0.707107 & 0.707107 \end{bmatrix}$$

```
val A: Matrix = DenseMatrix(
    arrayOf(
        doubleArrayOf(5.0, 2.0),
        doubleArrayOf(2.0, 5.0)
    )
)

// doing eigen decomposition
val eigen: EigenDecomposition = EigenDecomposition(A)

val D: Matrix = eigen.D()
println("\nD = \n" + D)
val Q: Matrix = eigen.Q()
println("\nQ = \n" + Q)
val Qt: Matrix = eigen.Qt()
println("\nQt = \n" + Qt)
```

The output is as follows:

```
D =
2x2
        [,1] [,2]
[1,] 7.000000, 0.000000,
[2,] 0.000000, 3.000000,
Q =
```

```
2x2
         [,1] [,2]
[1,] 0.707107, -0.707107,
[2,] 0.707107, 0.707107,
Qt =
2x2
         [,1] [,2]
[1,] 0.707107, 0.707107,
[2,] -0.707107, 0.707107,

// verify that QDQt = A
val QDQt: Matrix = Q.multiply(D).multiply(Qt)
println(String.format("%s = \n%s is %b",
        A,
        QDQt,
        MatrixPropertyUtils.areEqual(A, QDQt, 1e-14)))
```

The output is as follows:

```
2x2
         [,1] [,2]
[1,] 5.000000, 2.000000,
[2,] 2.000000, 5.000000,  =
2x2
         [,1] [,2]
[1,] 5.000000, 2.000000,
[2,] 2.000000, 5.000000,  is true
```

While the EigenDecomposition class gives the decomposition, it is not convenient to extract the eigenvectors and the corresponding eigenvalues. To manipulate eigenvectors and eigenvalues, you use the Eigen and EigenProperty classes.

The signature for Eigen is as follows:

```
/**
 * Compute the eigenvalues and eigenvectors for a <em>square</em> matrix.
 * For each eigenvalue, there are infinitely many associated eigenvectors,
 * which forms a vector space. This implementation computes a set of
 * linearly independent basis, any linear combination of them qualifies as
 * an eigenvector.
 *
 * <em>
 * TODO: For the moment, we compute both real and complex eigenvalues,
 * but we do not compute the eigenvectors for complex eigenvalues.
 * </em>
 *
 * @param A        a <em>square</em> matrix
 * @param method   the eigen decomposition algorithm, c.f., {@link Method}
 * @param epsilon  a precision parameter: when a number |x| &le; &epsilon;,
 *                 it is considered 0
 * @throws IllegalArgumentException if <i>A</i> is not square
```

```
 */
public Eigen(Matrix A, Method method, final double epsilon)
/**
 * Use {@link Method#QR} method by default.
 *
 * @param A       a <em>square</em> matrix
 * @param epsilon a precision parameter: when a number |x| &le; &epsilon;,
 *                it is considered 0
 * @see #Eigen(dev.nm.algebra.linear.matrix.doubles.Matrix, double)
 */
public Eigen(Matrix A, double epsilon)
/**
 * Compute the eigenvalues and eigenvectors for a <em>square</em> matrix.
 *
 * @param A      a <em>square</em> matrix
 * @param method the eigen decomposition algorithm, c.f., {@link Method}
 */
public Eigen(Matrix A, Method method)
/**
 * Compute the eigenvalues and eigenvectors for a <em>square</em> matrix.
 *
 * @param A a <em>square</em> matrix
 * @see <a href="http://en.wikipedia.org/wiki/QR_algorithm">Wikipedia: QR
 * algorithm</a>
 */
public Eigen(Matrix A)
/**
 * Get all the eigenvalues, real and complex.
 *
 * @return the eigenvalues
 */
List<? extends Number> getEigenvalues();
/**
 * Get all real eigenvalues.
 * The eigenvalues are sorted in descending order.
 *
 * @return all real eigenvalues
 */
public double[] getRealEigenvalues()
/**
 * Get the {@link EigenProperty} by eigenvalue. Note that the number passed
 * in must be exactly the same as the eigenvalue in binary representation.
 * Passing in an approximate number (up to precision) will likely result in
 * an unmatched error, i.e., {@code null} returned.
 *
 * @param eigenvalue an eigenvalue
 * @return the {@code EigenProperty} of the eigenvalue
 */
public EigenProperty getProperty(Number eigenvalue)
```

The signature for EigenProperty is as follows:

```
/**
 * {@code EigenProperty} is a read-only structure that contains the information
 * about a particular eigenvalue, such as its multiplicity and eigenvectors.
 *
 * @author Haksun Li
 */
public class EigenProperty {
    /**
     * Get the eigenvalue.
     *
     * @return the eigenvalue
     */
    public Number eigenvalue()
    /**
     * Get the multiplicity of the eigenvalue (a root) of the characteristic
     * polynomial.
     *
     * @return the algebraic multiplicity
     */
    public int algebraicMultiplicity()
    /**
     * Get the dimension of the vector space spanned by the eigenvectors.
     *
     * @return the geometric multiplicity
     */
    public int geometricMultiplicity()
    /**
     * Get the eigenvectors.
     *
     * @return the eigenvectors
     */
    public List<Vector> eigenbasis()
    /**
     * Get an eigenvector.
     * Note that eigenvector is not unique.
     * This implementation always returns the first vector in the basis.
     * To get a complete set of the basis of the eigenvector space, use
     * {@link #eigenbasis()}.
     *
     * @return an eigenvector
     */
    public Vector eigenVector()
```

Note that there may be repeated eigenvalues for a matrix. The number of duplicates of an eigenvalue is called the *algebraic multiplicity of the eigenvalue*. The geometric multiplicity of an eigenvalue is the number of linearly independent eigenvectors associated with it. That is, it is the dimension of the null space spanned by the basis consisting of the eigenvectors associated with that eigenvalue. The geometric multiplicity is always less than or equal to the algebraic multiplicity of the eigenvalue.

The following NM Dev code computes, for a matrix, the eigenvalues, their associated eigenvectors, and the linear spaces spanned by each set of eigenvectors. A vector belongs to a linear space if it can be written as a linear combination of the basis vectors.

The following matrix:

$$\boldsymbol{A} = \begin{bmatrix} 1 & -3 & 3 \\ 3 & -5 & 3 \\ 6 & -6 & 4 \end{bmatrix}$$

has two eigenvalues: 4 and -2.

For the eigenvalue 4, there is one eigenvector $\begin{bmatrix} 0.5 \\ 0.5 \\ 1 \end{bmatrix}$. The null space spanned by it is a one-dimensional linear space (a line).

For the eigenvalue -2, there are two eigenvectors, $\begin{bmatrix} 1 \\ 1 \\ 0 \end{bmatrix}$ and $\begin{bmatrix} -1 \\ 0 \\ 1 \end{bmatrix}$. The null space spanned by them is a two-dimensional linear space (a plane).

```
val A: Matrix = DenseMatrix(
    arrayOf(
        doubleArrayOf(1.0, -3.0, 3.0),
        doubleArrayOf(3.0, -5.0, 3.0),
        doubleArrayOf(6.0, -6.0, 4.0),
    )
)

// perform an eigen decomposition
val eigen: Eigen = Eigen(A)
eigen.getEigenvalues().forEach {
    println("eigen value = " + it)
}

// the first eigenvalue
val eigenvalue0: Number = eigen.getEigenvalue(0) // count from 0
println("eigenvalue0 = " + eigenvalue0)

// get the properties associated with this eigenvalue
val prop0: EigenProperty = eigen.getProperty(eigenvalue0)
println("algebraic multiplicity = " + prop0.algebraicMultiplicity())
println("geometric multiplicity = " + prop0.geometricMultiplicity())

val basis0: List<Vector> = prop0.eigenbasis()
basis0.forEach {
    println("basis vector = " + it)
}
val vs0: RealVectorSpace = RealVectorSpace(basis0, 1e-15)
// check if this vector belongs to the vector space, i.e., a linear combination of the basis

val in0: Boolean = vs0.isSpanned(
        DenseVector(arrayOf(-0.4, -0.4, -0.8)))
println("is in the vector space = " + in0)
```

The output is as follows:

```
eigen value = 4.0
eigen value = -2.0
eigenvalue0 = 4.0
algebraic multiplicity = 1
geometric multiplicity = 1
basis vector = [0.500000, 0.500000, 1.000000]
is in the vector space = true
```

```
// the second eigenvalue
val eigenvalue1: Number = eigen.getEigenvalue(1) // count from 1
println("eigen value 1 = " + eigenvalue1)

val prop1: EigenProperty = eigen.getProperty(eigenvalue1)
println("algebraic multiplicity = " + prop1.algebraicMultiplicity())
println("geometric multiplicity = " + prop1.geometricMultiplicity())

val basis1: List<Vector> = prop1.eigenbasis()
basis1.forEach {
    println("basis vector = " + it)
}
val vs1: RealVectorSpace = RealVectorSpace(basis1, 1e-15)
val in1: Boolean = vs1.isSpanned(DenseVector(arrayOf(-0.4, 0.4, 0.8)))
println("is in the vector space = " + in1)

val in2: Boolean = vs1.isSpanned(DenseVector(arrayOf(-0.5, 0.5, 1.0)))
println("is in the vector space = " + in2)
```

The output is as follows:

```
eigenvalue1 = -2.0
algebraic multiplicity = 2
geometric multiplicity = 2
basis vector = [1.000000, 1.000000, 0.000000]
basis vector = [-1.000000, 0.000000, 1.000000]
is in the vector space = true
is in the vector space = true
```

2.3.6. Singular Value Decomposition

All the decompositions discussed so far apply to square matrices. Singular value decomposition (SVD) can be thought of as an extension to eigen decomposition, but SVD applies to any matrices, square, tall, and fat. That is, SVD applies to any linear transformations. Specifically, the SVD of an $m \times n$ matrix $\boldsymbol{A}$ is a product of three matrices:

$$\boldsymbol{A} = \boldsymbol{U}\boldsymbol{D}\boldsymbol{V}^T$$

U is an $m \times m$ orthogonal matrix. ***D*** is an $m \times n$ diagonal matrix. ***V*** is an $n \times n$ orthogonal matrix. The diagonal entries $\sigma_i = \boldsymbol{D}_{ii}$ are called the *singular values* of ***A***. The number of nonzero singular values is equal to the rank of ***A***. The columns of ***U*** and the columns of ***V*** are called the left-singular vectors and right-singular vectors of ***A***, respectively. You'll typically choose a decomposition so that the singular values $\boldsymbol{D}_{ii}$ are in descending order. In this case, ***D*** (but not always ***U*** and ***V***) is uniquely determined by ***A***. Mathematical applications of the SVD include computing the pseudo-inverse, matrix approximation, and determining the rank, range, and null space of a matrix. The SVD is also widely useful in all areas of science, engineering, and statistics, such as signal processing, least squares fitting of data, and process control.

Geometrically, SVD says that any linear transformation can be broken down into three steps, namely, rotate first ($\boldsymbol{V}^T$), stretch/scale (***D***) (not necessarily by the same amount in all directions; you could stretch the x-axis twice as much as the y-axis), and rotate again (***U***).

For instance, to transform a square into a parallelogram, you could rotate clockwise by θ (the value of this is not too important as long as you pick a sensible number, as the rotation matrices are not unique), scale the axes by different factors, and then rotate it counterclockwise again by θ. In terms of dimension reduction, you first "select the right axes" by rotation. Then you project away minor dimensions by ignoring (or replacing by 0) the smallest singular values. See Figure 2-22.

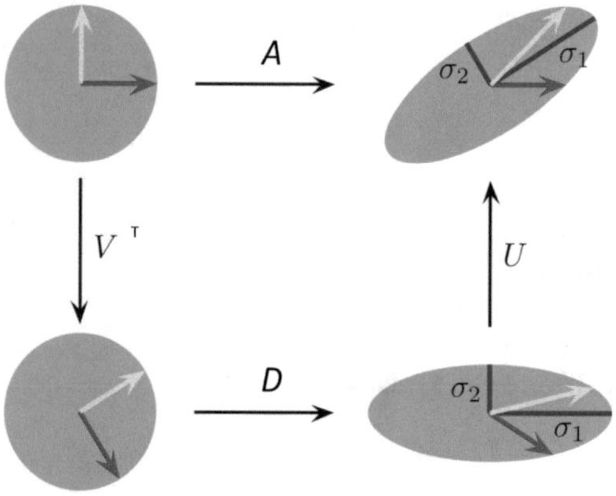

Figure 2-22. *SVD geometric interpretation*

There are several methods for doing SVD, such as by means of the Golub-Kahan algorithm for tall matrices, the QR algorithm for symmetric matrices, and Multiple Relatively Robust Representations (MRRR) for bi-diagonal matrices. The implementations of all these algorithms and transformations are very involved. The NM Dev interface called `SVDDecomposition` represents the different implementations. The signature is as follows:

```
public interface SVDDecomposition {
    /**
     * Get the normalized, hence positive, singular values. They may differ from
     * the values in <i>D</i> if this computation turns off normalization.
     *
     * @return the singular values
     */
    public double[] getSingularValues();
    /**
     * Get the <i>D</i> matrix as in SVD decomposition.
     *
     * @return <i>D</i>
     */
```

```
    public DiagonalMatrix D();
    /**
     * Get the <i>U</i> matrix as in SVD decomposition.
     *
     * @return <i>U</i>
     */
    public Matrix U();
    /**
     * Get the transpose of <i>U</i>, i.e., {@code U().t()}.
     *
     * @return {@code U().t()}
     */
    public Matrix Ut();
    /**
     * Get the <i>V</i> matrix as in SVD decomposition.
     *
     * @return <i>V</i>
     */
    public Matrix V();
}
```

The SVD class wraps all these algorithms and applies the appropriate one depending on the input matrix. It has the same signature as SVDDecomposition because SVD inherits from it. The following NM Dev code computes this example:

$$\begin{bmatrix} 1 & 0 & 0 & 0 & 2 \\ 0 & 0 & 3 & 0 & 0 \\ 0 & 0 & 0 & 0 & 0 \\ 0 & 2 & 0 & 0 & 0 \end{bmatrix} = \begin{bmatrix} 0 & -1 & 0 & 0 \\ -1 & 0 & 0 & 0 \\ 0 & 0 & 0 & -1 \\ 0 & 0 & -1 & 0 \end{bmatrix} \begin{bmatrix} 3 & 0 & 0 & 0 & 0 \\ 0 & \sqrt{5} & 0 & 0 & 0 \\ 0 & 0 & 2 & 0 & 0 \\ 0 & 0 & 0 & 0 & 0 \end{bmatrix} \begin{bmatrix} 0 & 0 & 1 & 0 & 0 \\ \sqrt{0.2} & 0 & 0 & 0 & \sqrt{0.8} \\ 0 & 1 & 0 & 0 & 0 \\ 0 & 0 & 0 & 1 & 0 \end{bmatrix}$$

```
val A: Matrix = DenseMatrix(
    arrayOf(
        doubleArrayOf(1.0, 0.0, 0.0, 0.0, 2.0),
        doubleArrayOf(0.0, 0.0, 3.0, 0.0, 0.0),
        doubleArrayOf(0.0, 0.0, 0.0, 0.0, 0.0),
        doubleArrayOf(0.0, 2.0, 0.0, 0.0, 0.0)
    )
)

// perform SVD
val svd: SVD = SVD(A, true, 1e-15)

val U: Matrix = svd.U()
println("\nU = \n" + U)
val D: DiagonalMatrix = svd.D()
println("\nD = \n" + D)
val V: Matrix = svd.V()
println("\nVt = \n" + V.t())
val Ut: Matrix = svd.Ut()
println("\nUt = \n" + Ut)
```

The output is as follows:

```
U =
4x4
         [,1] [,2] [,3] [,4]
[1,] 0.000000, 1.000000, 0.000000, 0.000000,
[2,] 1.000000, 0.000000, 0.000000, 0.000000,
[3,] 0.000000, 0.000000, 0.000000, 1.000000,
[4,] 0.000000, 0.000000, 1.000000, 0.000000,
D =
4x4
         [,1] [,2] [,3] [,4]
[1,] 3.000000, 0.000000, 0.000000, 0.000000,
[2,] 0.000000, 2.236068, 0.000000, 0.000000,
[3,] 0.000000, 0.000000, 2.000000, 0.000000,
[4,] 0.000000, 0.000000, 0.000000, 0.000000,
Vt =
4x5
         [,1] [,2] [,3] [,4] [,5]
[1,] 0.000000, 0.000000, 1.000000, 0.000000, 0.000000,
[2,] 0.447214, 0.000000, 0.000000, 0.000000, 0.894427,
[3,] 0.000000, 1.000000, 0.000000, 0.000000, 0.000000,
[4,] 0.000000, 0.000000, 0.000000, 1.000000, 0.000000,
Ut =
4x4
         [,1] [,2] [,3] [,4]
[1,] 0.000000, 1.000000, 0.000000, 0.000000,
[2,] 1.000000, 0.000000, 0.000000, 0.000000,
[3,] 0.000000, 0.000000, 0.000000, 1.000000,
[4,] 0.000000, 0.000000, 1.000000, 0.000000,
```

```
// verify that UDVt = A
val UDVt: Matrix = U.multiply(D).multiply(V.t())
println(String.format("%s = \n%s is %b",
        A,
        UDVt,
        MatrixPropertyUtils.areEqual(UDVt, A, 1e-14)))
```

The output is as follows:

```
4x5
         [,1] [,2] [,3] [,4] [,5]
[1,] 1.000000, 0.000000, 0.000000, 0.000000, 2.000000,
[2,] 0.000000, 0.000000, 3.000000, 0.000000, 0.000000,
[3,] 0.000000, 0.000000, 0.000000, 0.000000, 0.000000,
[4,] 0.000000, 2.000000, 0.000000, 0.000000, 0.000000,  =
```

```
4x5
        [,1] [,2] [,3] [,4] [,5]
[1,] 1.000000, 0.000000, 0.000000, 0.000000, 2.000000,
[2,] 0.000000, 0.000000, 3.000000, 0.000000, 0.000000,
[3,] 0.000000, 0.000000, 0.000000, 0.000000, 0.000000,
[4,] 0.000000, 2.000000, 0.000000, 0.000000, 0.000000,  is true
```

```
// verify that UtAV = D
val UtAV: Matrix = Ut.multiply(A).multiply(V)
println(String.format("%s = \n%s is %b",
        A,
        UtAV,
        MatrixPropertyUtils.areEqual(UtAV, D, 1e-14)))
```

The output is as follows:

```
4x5
        [,1] [,2] [,3] [,4] [,5]
[1,] 1.000000, 0.000000, 0.000000, 0.000000, 2.000000,
[2,] 0.000000, 0.000000, 3.000000, 0.000000, 0.000000,
[3,] 0.000000, 0.000000, 0.000000, 0.000000, 0.000000,
[4,] 0.000000, 2.000000, 0.000000, 0.000000, 0.000000,  =
4x4
        [,1] [,2] [,3] [,4]
[1,] 3.000000, 0.000000, 0.000000, 0.000000,
[2,] 0.000000, 2.236068, 0.000000, 0.000000,
[3,] 0.000000, 0.000000, 2.000000, 0.000000,
[4,] 0.000000, 0.000000, 0.000000, 0.000000,  is true
```

2.4. System of Linear Equations

A system of linear equations (or a linear system) is a collection of one or more linear equations involving the same set of variables. Here's an example:

$$\begin{cases} x + 3y - 2z = 5 \\ 3x + 5y + 6z = 7 \\ 2x + 4y + 3z = 8 \end{cases}$$

This is a system of three equations in three variables, *x*, *y*, and *z*. A solution to a linear system is an assignment of values to the variables such that all the equations are simultaneously satisfied. A solution to the previous system is given by the following:

$$\begin{cases} x = -15 \\ y = 8 \\ z = 2 \end{cases}$$

since it makes all three equations valid. The word *system* indicates that the equations are to be considered collectively, rather than individually.

The theory of linear systems is the basis and a fundamental part of linear algebra, a subject that is used in most parts of modern mathematics. A system of nonlinear equations can often be approximated by a linear system, a helpful technique when making a mathematical model or computer simulation of a relatively complex system. Computational algorithms that find solutions are an important part of numerical linear algebra, and they play a prominent role in engineering, physics, chemistry, computer science, and economics.

A general system of m linear equations with n unknowns can be written as follows:

$$\begin{cases} a_{11}x_1 + a_{12}x_2 + \cdots a_{1n}x_n = b_1 \\ a_{21}x_1 + a_{22}x_2 + \cdots + a_{21}x_n = b_2 \\ \vdots \\ a_{m1}x_1 + a_{m2}x_2 + \cdots + a_{mn}x_n = b_m \end{cases}$$

$x_1, x_2, \ldots, x_n$ are the n unknowns; $a_{11}, a_{12}, \ldots, a_{mn}$ are the $m \times n$ coefficients of the system; $b_1, b_2, \ldots, b_m$ are the m constant terms.

It is helpful to write each unknown as a weight for a column vector in a linear combination. This allows you to consider the problem in terms of vector space or linear space. For example, the collection of all possible linear combinations of the vectors on the left side is called their *span*, and the equations have a solution just when the right vector is within that span or exists in the spanned vector space. If every vector in that span has exactly one expression as a linear combination of the given left vectors, then any solution is unique.

Equivalently, you can write the vector equation in matrix form:

$$\boldsymbol{Ax} = \boldsymbol{b}$$

where

$$\boldsymbol{A} = \begin{bmatrix} a_{11} & a_{12} & \cdots & a_{1n} \\ a_{21} & a_{22} & \cdots & a_{2n} \\ \vdots & \vdots & \ddots & \vdots \\ a_{m1} & a_{m2} & \cdots & a_{mn} \end{bmatrix}, \ \boldsymbol{x} = \begin{bmatrix} x_1 \\ x_2 \\ \vdots \\ x_n \end{bmatrix}, \ \boldsymbol{b} = \begin{bmatrix} b_1 \\ b_2 \\ \vdots \\ b_m \end{bmatrix}$$

The number of vectors in a basis for the span is now expressed as the rank of the matrix, which is smaller than m and n.

A solution of a linear system is an assignment of values to the variables $x_1, x_2, \ldots, x_n$ such that each of the equations is satisfied. The set of all possible solutions is called the *solution set*. A linear system may behave in any one of three possible ways.

- The system has infinitely many solutions.
- The system has a single unique solution.
- The system has no solution.

Geometrically, for a system involving two variables (x and y), each linear equation determines a line on the xy-plane. Because a solution to a linear system must satisfy all the equations, the solution set is the intersection of these lines and is hence a line, a single point, or the empty set. See Figure 2-23.

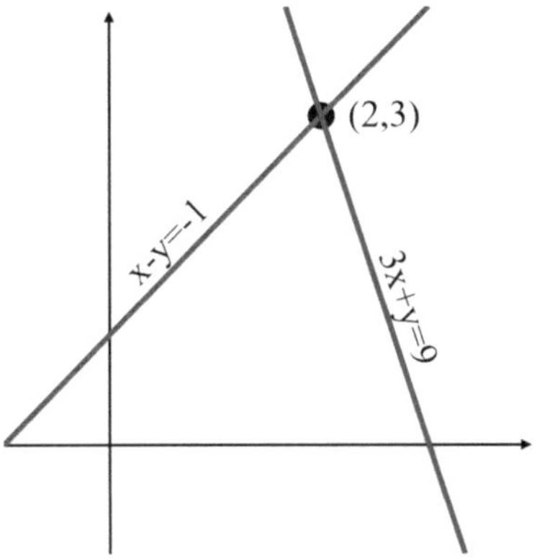

Figure 2-23. *Solution to a system of two linear equations*

For three variables, each linear equation determines a plane in three-dimensional space, and the solution set is the intersection of these planes. Thus, the solution set may be a plane, a line, a single point, or the empty set. For example, as three parallel planes do not have a common point, the solution set of their equations is empty. If three planes intersect at a point, the solution set is a single point. If three planes pass through two points, their equations have at least two common solutions; in fact, the solution set is infinite and consists of all the points on the line passing through these points. For n variables, each linear equation determines a hyperplane in n-dimensional space. The solution set is the intersection of these hyperplanes, which is a flat (or a Euclidean) subspace of any dimension lower than n.

In general, the behavior of a linear system is determined by the relationship between the number of equations m and the number of unknowns n. Specifically:

1. If $m = n$, the system has a single unique solution.

2. If $m > n$, the system has no solution. Such a system is also known as an *overdetermined* system.

3. If $m < n$, the system has infinitely many solutions, but it may have no solution. Such a system is known as an *underdetermined* system. The dimension of the solution set is equal to $n - m$.

Figure 2-24 illustrates this trichotomy in the case of two variables. The first system has infinitely many solutions, namely, all of the points on the blue line. The second system has a single unique solution, namely, the intersection of the two lines. The third system has no solutions, since the three lines share no common point. See Figure 2-24.

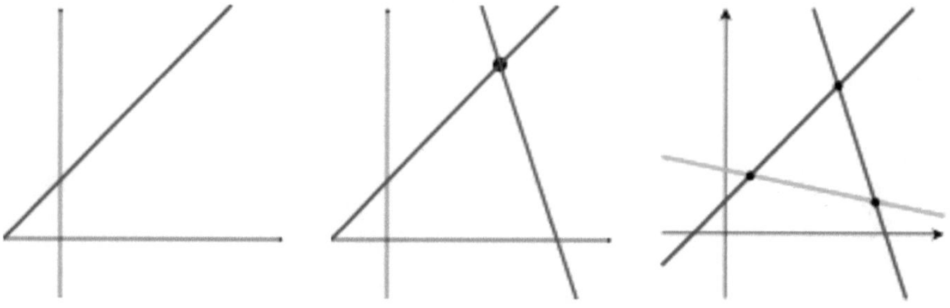

Figure 2-24. *Possible solutions to a system of two linear equations*

It is important to note that the images in Figure 2-24 show only the most common case (the general case). A system of linear equations behaves differently from the general case if the equations are linearly dependent (parallel lines/planes) or if it is inconsistent (no solution). For example, it is possible for a system of two equations and two unknowns to have no solution (if the two lines are parallel) or for a system of three equations and two unknowns to be solvable (if the three lines intersect at a single point). See Figure 2-25.

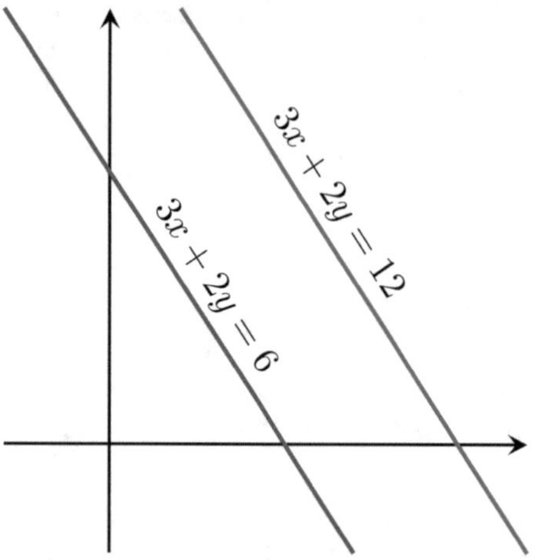

Figure 2-25. *System of two parallel lines are inconsistent and hence no solution*

NM Dev has a suite of tools to solve various types of systems of linear equations. It can solve square systems, underdetermined systems, and overdetermined systems. There are multiple algorithms (and multiple implementations for one algorithm) to solve for each type of systems.

2.4.1. Row Echelon Form and Reduced Row Echelon Form

Let's consider a motivating example of solving the previous system of equations:

$$\begin{cases} x+3y-2z=5 \\ 3x+5y+6z=7 \\ 2x+4y+3z=8 \end{cases}$$

You can write x in terms of the other two variables and plug it into the second and third equations. That is:

$$x = 5 - 3y + 2z$$

Then:

$$\begin{cases} -4y + 12z = -8 \\ -2y + 7z = -2 \end{cases}$$

You repeat the procedure and solve for y. Then plug it into the second equation. That is:

$$y = 2 + 3z$$

Then:

$$z = 2$$

Knowing z, you can back-substitute into the y equation to obtain y. Knowing y, you can then back-substitute into the x equation to obtain x. Finally, you obtain a solution:

$$\begin{cases} x = -15 \\ y = 8 \\ z = 2 \end{cases}$$

You can generalize this procedure and make an algorithm to solve systems of equations in general. First, you need a few concepts.

A matrix is in row echelon form if the following are both true:

- All rows consisting of only zeros are at the bottom.
- The leading coefficient (also called the *pivot*) of a nonzero row is always strictly to the right of the leading coefficient of the row above it.

These two conditions imply that all entries in a column below a leading coefficient are zeros. The following is an example of a 3 × 5 matrix in row echelon form (but it is not in reduced row echelon form):

$$\begin{bmatrix} 1 & a_0 & a_1 & a_2 & a_3 \\ 0 & 0 & 2 & a_4 & a_5 \\ 0 & 0 & 0 & 1 & a_6 \end{bmatrix}$$

A matrix is in reduced row echelon form (also called *row canonical form*) if it satisfies the following conditions:

- It is in row echelon form.
- The leading entry in each nonzero row is a 1 (called a leading 1).
- Each column containing a leading 1 has zeros in all its other entries.

This is an example of a matrix in reduced row echelon form:

$$\begin{bmatrix} 1 & 0 & a_1 & b_1 \\ 0 & 1 & a_2 & b_2 \\ 0 & 0 & 1 & b_3 \end{bmatrix}$$

Once you can make the system of equations in reduced row echelon form, it is easy to compute or read out the solution. The previous matrix is simply saying that the equations are as follows:

$$\begin{cases} x_1 + a_1 x_3 = b_1 \\ x_2 + a_2 x_3 = b_2 \\ x_3 = b_3 \end{cases}$$

You can read the solution for x_3 from the third equation. Once you know x_3, you can simply back-substitute it in the other two equations to get x_1 and x_2.

2.4.2. Back Substitution

Backward substitution solves a matrix equation in the form ***Ux*** = ***b*** by an iterative process for an upper triangular matrix ***U***. The process is so-called because, for an upper triangular matrix, you first compute x_n, then substitute that backward into the next equation to solve for x_{n-1}, and finally repeat this until x_1. Note that some diagonal entries in ***U*** can be 0s, provided that the system of equations is consistent. Here's an example:

$$\begin{bmatrix} 1 & 2 & 3 \\ 0 & 0 & 5 \\ 0 & 0 & 0 \end{bmatrix} \times \begin{bmatrix} 10 \\ 0 \\ 0 \end{bmatrix} = \begin{bmatrix} 10 \\ 0 \\ 0 \end{bmatrix}$$

The NM Dev class called `BackwardSubstitution` implements a backward-substitution algorithm. The following code solves this example:

```
val U: UpperTriangularMatrix = UpperTriangularMatrix(
    arrayOf(
        doubleArrayOf(1.0, 2.0, 3.0),
        doubleArrayOf(0.0, 5.0),
        doubleArrayOf(0.0)
    )
)

val b: Vector = DenseVector(arrayOf(10.0, 0.0, 0.0))

val solver: BackwardSubstitution = BackwardSubstitution()
val x: Vector = solver.solve(U, b)
println("x = " + x)

// verify that Ux = b
val Ux: Vector = U.multiply(x)
println(String.format("%s = \n%s is %b",
        Ux,
        b,
        MatrixPropertyUtils.areEqual(Ux, b, 1e-14))) // MatrixPropertyUtils.areEqual works
                                                      for vectors too
```

The output is as follows:

```
x = [10.000000, 0.000000, 0.000000]
[10.000000, 0.000000, 0.000000]  =
[10.000000, 0.000000, 0.000000]  is true
```

2.4.3. Forward Substitution

Likewise, you can use forward substitution, which solves a matrix equation in the form $\boldsymbol{Lx} = \boldsymbol{b}$ using an iterative process for a lower triangular matrix $\boldsymbol{L}$. The process is so-called because for a lower triangular matrix, you first compute x_1, then substitute that forward into the next equation to solve for x_2, and finally repeat until x_n. Note that some diagonal entries in $\boldsymbol{L}$ can be 0s, provided that the system of equations is consistent. Here's an example:

$$\begin{bmatrix} 0 & 0 & 0 \\ 2 & 0 & 0 \\ 4 & 5 & 6 \end{bmatrix} \times \begin{bmatrix} 0 \\ 0 \\ 30 \end{bmatrix} = \begin{bmatrix} 0 \\ 0 \\ 30 \end{bmatrix}$$

The NM Dev class called `ForwardSubstitution` implements a forward-substitution algorithm. The following code solves this example:

```
val L: LowerTriangularMatrix = LowerTriangularMatrix(
    arrayOf(
        doubleArrayOf(1.0),
        doubleArrayOf(2.0, 3.0),
        doubleArrayOf(4.0, 5.0, 6.0)
    )
)

val b: Vector = DenseVector(arrayOf(10.0, 20.0, 30.0))

val solver: ForwardSubstitution = ForwardSubstitution()
val x: Vector = solver.solve(L, b)
println("x = " + x)

// verify that Ux = b
val Lx: Vector = L.multiply(x)
println(String.format("%s = \n%s is %b",
        Lx,
        b,
        MatrixPropertyUtils.areEqual(Lx, b, 1e-14))) // MatrixPropertyUtils.areEqual works
                                                        for vectors too
```

The output is as follows:

```
x = [10.000000, 0.000000, -1.666667]
[10.000000, 20.000000, 30.000000]  =
[10.000000, 20.000000, 30.000000]  is true
```

In general, the NM Dev class LUSolver can handle upper and lower triangular matrices. The following code reproduces the previous two problems:

```
// an LSProblem
val L: LowerTriangularMatrix = LowerTriangularMatrix(
    arrayOf(
        doubleArrayOf(1.0),
        doubleArrayOf(2.0, 3.0),
        doubleArrayOf(4.0, 5.0, 6.0)
    )
)

val b1: Vector = DenseVector(arrayOf(10.0, 20.0, 30.0))

val solver1: LUSolver = LUSolver()
val x1: Vector = solver1.solve(
        // construct a Linear System Problem: Lx = b1
        LSProblem(L, b1)
)

println("x1 = " + x1)

// verify that Ux = b
val Lx: Vector = L.multiply(x1)
println(String.format("%s = \n%s is %b",
        Lx,
        b1,
        MatrixPropertyUtils.areEqual(Lx, b1, 1e-14))) // MatrixPropertyUtils.areEqual works
                                                        for vectors too
```

The output is as follows:

```
x1 = [10.000000, 0.000000, -1.666667]
[10.000000, 20.000000, 30.000000]  =
[10.000000, 20.000000, 30.000000]  is true
```

```
// another LSProblem
val U: UpperTriangularMatrix = UpperTriangularMatrix(
    arrayOf(
        doubleArrayOf(1.0, 2.0, 3.0),
        doubleArrayOf(0.0, 5.0),
        doubleArrayOf(0.0),
    )
)

val b2: Vector = DenseVector(arrayOf(10.0, 0.0, 0.0))

val solver2: LUSolver = LUSolver()
```

```
val x2: Vector = solver2.solve(
        // construct a Linear System Problem: Ux = b2
        LSProblem(U, b2)
)
println("x2 = " + x2)

// verify that Ux = b
val Ux: Vector = U.multiply(x2)
println(String.format("%s = \n%s is %b",
        Ux,
        b2,
        MatrixPropertyUtils.areEqual(Ux, b2, 1e-14))) // MatrixPropertyUtils.areEqual works
                                                        for vectors too
```

The output is as follows:

```
x2 = [10.000000, 0.000000, -0.000000]
[10.000000, 0.000000, 0.000000]  =
[10.000000, 0.000000, 0.000000]  is true
```

2.4.4. Elementary Operations

You can transform any matrix into (reduced) row echelon form by using a series of elementary operations. There are three types of elementary operations:

- **Row switching**: Switch the i-th row with the j-th row.
- **Row multiplication or scaling**: Multiply the i-th row by a nonzero constant.
- **Row addition**: Replace the i-th row with the sum of the i-th row and a multiple of the j-th row.

Row Switching Transformation

You can create an elementary matrix corresponding to the transformation by performing the operation on the identity matrix. An elementary matrix is a matrix that differs from the identity matrix by one single elementary row operation.

For example, the corresponding elementary matrix swaps the second and third rows of the 3 × 3 identity matrix. That is:

$$\boldsymbol{P} = \begin{bmatrix} 1 & 0 & 0 \\ 0 & 0 & 1 \\ 0 & 1 & 0 \end{bmatrix}$$

If you left (right) multiply any 3 × 3 matrix by $\boldsymbol{P}$, its second and third rows (columns) will be swapped. Here's an example:

$$\begin{bmatrix} 1 & 0 & 0 \\ 0 & 0 & 1 \\ 0 & 1 & 0 \end{bmatrix} \times \begin{bmatrix} a_{11} & a_{12} & a_{13} \\ a_{21} & a_{22} & a_{23} \\ a_{31} & a_{32} & a_{33} \end{bmatrix} = \begin{bmatrix} a_{11} & a_{12} & a_{13} \\ a_{31} & a_{32} & a_{33} \\ a_{21} & a_{22} & a_{23} \end{bmatrix}$$

Row Multiplying Transformation

Similarly, to scale the i-th row by a nonzero constant m, the corresponding elementary matrix is a diagonal matrix, with diagonal entries 1 everywhere except in the i-th position, where it is m. For example, the corresponding elementary matrix scales the second row of the 3 × 3 identity matrix by 2. That is:

$$\boldsymbol{D} = \begin{bmatrix} 1 & 0 & 0 \\ 0 & 2 & 0 \\ 0 & 0 & 1 \end{bmatrix}$$

Here's an example:

$$\begin{bmatrix} 1 & 0 & 0 \\ 0 & 2 & 0 \\ 0 & 0 & 1 \end{bmatrix} \times \begin{bmatrix} a_{11} & a_{12} & a_{13} \\ a_{21} & a_{22} & a_{23} \\ a_{31} & a_{32} & a_{33} \end{bmatrix} = \begin{bmatrix} a_{11} & a_{12} & a_{13} \\ 2a_{21} & 2a_{22} & 2a_{23} \\ a_{31} & a_{32} & a_{33} \end{bmatrix}$$

Row Addition Transformation

To add row j multiplied by a scalar m to row i, the corresponding elementary matrix is the identity matrix but with $a_{ij} = m$. For example, to add the second row of a 3 × 3 matrix by 2 to the first row, the corresponding elementary matrix is as follows:

$$\boldsymbol{L} = \begin{bmatrix} 1 & 2 & 0 \\ 0 & 1 & 0 \\ 0 & 0 & 1 \end{bmatrix}$$

Here's an example:

$$\begin{bmatrix} 1 & 2 & 0 \\ 0 & 1 & 0 \\ 0 & 0 & 1 \end{bmatrix} \times \begin{bmatrix} a_{11} & a_{12} & a_{13} \\ a_{21} & a_{22} & a_{23} \\ a_{31} & a_{32} & a_{33} \end{bmatrix} = \begin{bmatrix} a_{11} + 2a_{21} & a_{12} + 2a_{22} & a_{13} + 2a_{23} \\ a_{21} & a_{22} & a_{23} \\ a_{31} & a_{32} & a_{33} \end{bmatrix}$$

2.4.5. Gauss Elimination and Gauss-Jordan Elimination

Gauss-Jordan elimination is an algorithm for solving systems of linear equations. It can also be used to compute the rank of a matrix, the determinant of a square matrix, and the inverse of an invertible matrix. To perform row reduction on a matrix, you use a sequence of elementary row operations to modify the matrix until the lower-left corner of the matrix is filled with zeros, as much as possible.

Using these operations, a matrix can always be transformed into an upper triangular matrix, and in fact one that is in row echelon form. Once all of the leading coefficients (the leftmost nonzero entry in each row) are 1 and every column containing a leading coefficient has zeros elsewhere, the matrix is said to be in reduced row echelon form. This final form is unique; in other words, it is independent of the sequence of row operations used.

The term *Gaussian elimination* refers to the first step of process until it reaches an upper triangular or (unreduced) row echelon form. In this form, you can tell for a system of linear equations whether there are no solutions, a unique solution, or infinitely many solutions. Gauss-Jordan elimination, the second step, continues to use row operations until the solution is found. In other words, it puts the matrix into reduced row echelon form.

Equivalently, you can see that row reduction produces a matrix decomposition of the original matrix. The elementary row operations may be viewed as the multiplication on the left of the original matrix by elementary matrices. Alternatively, a sequence of elementary operations that reduces a single row may be viewed as multiplication by a Frobenius matrix. Then the first part of the algorithm computes an LU decomposition, while the second part writes the original matrix as the product of a uniquely determined invertible matrix and a uniquely determined reduced row echelon matrix.

The NM Dev class called `GaussianElimination` performs elementary row operations to reduce a matrix to the row echelon form. This is equivalent to multiplying the original matrix with invertible matrices from the left. For a square matrix, this algorithm essentially computes an LU decomposition. You have this:

$$\boldsymbol{TA} = \boldsymbol{U}$$

where $\boldsymbol{T}$ is the transformation matrix that is the product of a sequence of elementary matrices/operations. $\boldsymbol{U}$ is in the row echelon form.

Alternatively, you have this:

$$\boldsymbol{PA} = \boldsymbol{LU}$$

where $\boldsymbol{P}$ is the permutation matrix, $\boldsymbol{L}$ is the lower triangular, and $\boldsymbol{U}$ is in the row echelon form.

The signature is as follows:

```
/**
 * Run the Gaussian elimination algorithm.
 *
 * @param A           a matrix
 * @param usePivoting {@code true} if to use partial pivoting, e.g., for
 *                    numerical stability. In general, no pivoting means no row
                      interchanges.
 *                    It can be done only if Gaussian elimination never runs into
                      zeros on the
 *                    diagonal. Since division by zero is a fatal error we usually avoid no
 *                    pivoting.
 * @param epsilon     a precision parameter: when a number |x| &le;
 *                    &epsilon;, it is considered 0
 */
public GaussianElimination(Matrix A, boolean usePivoting, double epsilon)
/**
 * Run the Gaussian elimination algorithm with partial pivoting.
 *
 * @param A a matrix
 */
public GaussianElimination(Matrix A)
/**
 * Get the transformation matrix, <i>T</i>, such that <i>T * A = U</i>.
 *
 * @return <i>T</i>
 */
```

```
public Matrix T()
/**
 * Get the upper triangular matrix, <i>U</i>, such that
 * <i>T * A = U</i> and <i>P * A = L * U</i>.
 *
 * @return <i>U</i>
 */
public Matrix U()
/**
 * Get the lower triangular matrix <i>L</i>, such that <i>P * A = L * U</i>.
 *
 * @return <i>L</i>
 */
public Matrix L()
/**
 * Get the permutation matrix, <i>P</i>, such that <i>P * A = L * U</i>.
 *
 * @return <i>P</i>
 */
public PermutationMatrix P()
```

For instance, this NM Dev code computes this example:

$$\begin{bmatrix} 0 & 0 & 1 \\ 0 & 1 & -0.5 \\ 1 & -0.6 & -0.2 \end{bmatrix} \times \begin{bmatrix} 2 & 1 & 1 \\ 2 & 2 & -1 \\ 4 & -1 & 6 \end{bmatrix} = \begin{bmatrix} 4 & -1 & 6 \\ 0 & 2.5 & -4 \\ 0 & 0 & 0.4 \end{bmatrix}$$

$$\begin{bmatrix} 0 & 0 & 1 \\ 0 & 1 & 0 \\ 1 & 0 & 0 \end{bmatrix} \times \begin{bmatrix} 2 & 1 & 1 \\ 2 & 2 & -1 \\ 4 & -1 & 6 \end{bmatrix} = \begin{bmatrix} 1 & 0 & 0 \\ 0.5 & 1 & 0 \\ 0.5 & 0.6 & 1 \end{bmatrix} \begin{bmatrix} 4 & -1 & 6 \\ 0 & 2.5 & -4 \\ 0 & 0 & 0.4 \end{bmatrix}$$

```
val A: Matrix = DenseMatrix(
    arrayOf(
        doubleArrayOf(2.0, 1.0, 1.0),
        doubleArrayOf(2.0, 2.0, -1.0),
        doubleArrayOf(4.0, -1.0, 6.0),
    )
)

val ops: GaussianElimination = GaussianElimination(A, true, 0.0)

val T: Matrix = ops.T()
println("T = \n" + T)
val P: PermutationMatrix = ops.P()
println("P = \n" + P)
```

```
val U: Matrix = ops.U()
println(
        String.format("U = %s is upper triangular, %b",
                U,
                MatrixPropertyUtils.isUpperTriangular(U, 0.0)))

val L: Matrix = ops.L()
println(
        String.format("L = %s is lower triangular, %b",
                L,
                MatrixPropertyUtils.isLowerTriangular(L, 0.0)))

// verify that TA = U
val TA: Matrix = T.multiply(A)
println(String.format("%s = \n%s is %b",
        TA,
        U,
        MatrixPropertyUtils.areEqual(TA, U, 1e-15)))

// verify that PA = LU
val PA: Matrix = P.multiply(A)
val LU: Matrix = L.multiply(U)
println(String.format("%s = \n%s is %b",
        PA,
        LU,
        MatrixPropertyUtils.areEqual(PA, LU, 0.0)))
```

The output is as follows:

```
T =
3x3
        [,1] [,2] [,3]
[1,] 0.000000, 0.000000, 1.000000,
[2,] 0.000000, 1.000000, -0.500000,
[3,] 1.000000, -0.600000, -0.200000,
P =
3x3
        [,1] [,2] [,3]
[1,] 0.000000, 0.000000, 1.000000,
[2,] 0.000000, 1.000000, 0.000000,
[3,] 1.000000, 0.000000, 0.000000,
U = 3x3
        [,1] [,2] [,3]
[1,] 4.000000, -1.000000, 6.000000,
[2,] 0.000000, 2.500000, -4.000000,
[3,] 0.000000, 0.000000, 0.400000,  is upper triangular, true
L = 3x3
        [,1] [,2] [,3]
[1,] 1.000000, 0.000000, 0.000000,
[2,] 0.500000, 1.000000, 0.000000,
[3,] 0.500000, 0.600000, 1.000000,  is lower triangular, true
```

```
3x3
        [,1] [,2] [,3]
[1,] 4.000000, -1.000000, 6.000000,
[2,] 0.000000, 2.500000, -4.000000,
[3,] 0.000000, 0.000000, 0.400000,  =
3x3
        [,1] [,2] [,3]
[1,] 4.000000, -1.000000, 6.000000,
[2,] 0.000000, 2.500000, -4.000000,
[3,] 0.000000, 0.000000, 0.400000,  is true
3x3
        [,1] [,2] [,3]
[1,] 4.000000, -1.000000, 6.000000,
[2,] 2.000000, 2.000000, -1.000000,
[3,] 2.000000, 1.000000, 1.000000,  =
3x3
        [,1] [,2] [,3]
[1,] 4.000000, -1.000000, 6.000000,
[2,] 2.000000, 2.000000, -1.000000,
[3,] 2.000000, 1.000000, 1.000000,  is true
```

The NM Dev class called `GaussianElimination` performs elementary row operations to reduce a matrix to the reduced row echelon form. That is:

$$\boldsymbol{TA} = \boldsymbol{U}$$

where $\boldsymbol{T}$ is the transformation matrix that is the product of a sequence of elementary matrices/operations. $\boldsymbol{U}$ is in the row echelon form. This implementation makes sure that the leading 1s are numerically 1 for comparison purposes. Supposing there is a leading $u_{ij} = 1$, then `U.get(i, j) == 1` always returns `true`.

For instance, this NM Dev code computes this example:

$$\begin{bmatrix} -2.75 & 1.75 & 0.75 \\ 4 & -2 & -1 \\ 2.5 & -1.5 & -0.5 \end{bmatrix} \times \begin{bmatrix} 2 & 1 & 1 \\ 2 & 2 & -1 \\ 4 & -1 & 6 \end{bmatrix} = \begin{bmatrix} 1 & 0 & 0 \\ 0 & 1 & 0 \\ 0 & 0 & 1 \end{bmatrix}$$

```
val A: Matrix = DenseMatrix(
    arrayOf(
        doubleArrayOf(2.0, 1.0, 1.0),
        doubleArrayOf(2.0, 2.0, -1.0),
        doubleArrayOf(4.0, -1.0, 6.0),
    )
)
val ops: GaussJordanElimination = GaussJordanElimination(A, true, 0.0)

val U: Matrix = ops.U()
println(
        String.format("U = %s is in reduced row echelon form, %b",
                U,
                MatrixPropertyUtils.isReducedRowEchelonForm(U, 0.0)))
```

```
val T: Matrix = ops.T()
println("T = \n" + T)

// verify that TA = U
val TA: Matrix = T.multiply(A)
println(String.format("%s = \n%s is %b",
        TA,
        U,
        MatrixPropertyUtils.areEqual(TA, U, 1e-15)))
```

The output is as follows:

```
U = 3x3
         [,1] [,2] [,3]
[1,] 1.000000, 0.000000, 0.000000,
[2,] 0.000000, 1.000000, 0.000000,
[3,] 0.000000, 0.000000, 1.000000,  is in reduced row echelon form, true
T =
3x3
         [,1] [,2] [,3]
[1,] -2.750000, 1.750000, 0.750000,
[2,] 4.000000, -2.000000, -1.000000,
[3,] 2.500000, -1.500000, -0.500000,
3x3
         [,1] [,2] [,3]
[1,] 1.000000, 0.000000, 0.000000,
[2,] 0.000000, 1.000000, 0.000000,
[3,] 0.000000, -0.000000, 1.000000,  =
3x3
         [,1] [,2] [,3]
[1,] 1.000000, 0.000000, 0.000000,
[2,] 0.000000, 1.000000, 0.000000,
[3,] 0.000000, 0.000000, 1.000000,  is true
```

2.4.6. Homogeneous and Nonhomogeneous Systems

In general, a consistent system of linear equations has that the number of equations (m) is smaller than or equal to the number of variables (n), that is, $m \le n$. Otherwise, it is an overdetermined system that usually admits no solution. To understand the system of linear equations, as shown here:

$$\boldsymbol{Ax} = \boldsymbol{b}$$

you can view $\boldsymbol{A}$ as a linear transformation or a function that maps from one linear space $\boldsymbol{V}$ to another linear space $\boldsymbol{W}$. The kernel, or called *null-space*, of a linear map, ker($\boldsymbol{A}$), is the linear subspace of the domain such that the function maps all its elements to 0.

$$\ker(\boldsymbol{A}) = \{\boldsymbol{v} \in \boldsymbol{V} \mid \boldsymbol{Av} = 0\}$$

The rank-nullity theorem states that the dimension of the kernel and the dimension of the image equals the dimension of the domain. See Figure 2-26.

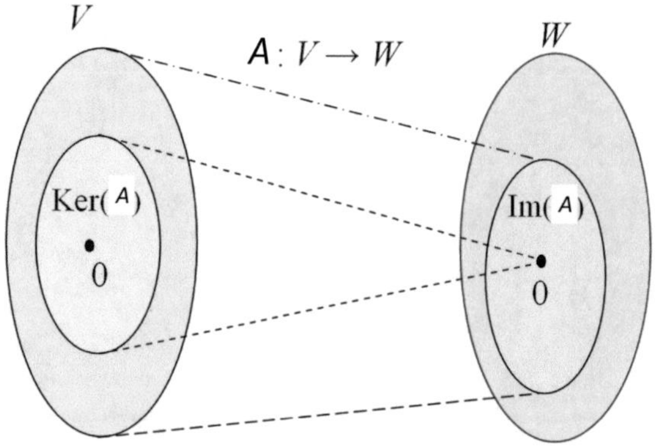

Figure 2-26. *Kernel and image of a linear map*

For any homogenous system of linear equations, as shown here:

$$\boldsymbol{Ax} = \boldsymbol{0}$$

There is at least one solution, known as the zero (or trivial) solution, which is obtained by assigning the value of zero to each of the variables. That is, $\boldsymbol{A0} = \boldsymbol{0}$. If the system has a nonsingular matrix ($\det(\boldsymbol{A}) \neq 0$), then it is also the only solution. If the system has a singular matrix ($\boldsymbol{A}$ is not full rank), then the dimension or rank of the kernel of $\boldsymbol{A}$ is not 0, $\ker(\boldsymbol{A}) > 0$. There is a solution set with an infinite number of solutions. Every vector in the kernel is a nontrivial solution. This solution set has the following additional properties:

- If $\boldsymbol{u}$ and $\boldsymbol{v}$ are two vectors representing solutions to a homogeneous system, then the vector sum $\boldsymbol{u} + \boldsymbol{v}$ is also a solution to the system.
- If $\boldsymbol{u}$ is a vector representing a solution to a homogeneous system and c is any scalar, then $c\boldsymbol{u}$ is also a solution to the system.

For a nonhomogenous system of linear equations, you have this:

$$\boldsymbol{Ax} = \boldsymbol{b}$$

Suppose $\boldsymbol{p}$ is a particular solution to the linear system, that is, $\boldsymbol{Ap} = \boldsymbol{b}$; then the entire solution set can be described as follows:

$$\{\boldsymbol{p}+\boldsymbol{v} \mid \boldsymbol{v} \in \ker(\boldsymbol{A})\}$$

Geometrically, this says that the solution set for the nonhomogenous system $\boldsymbol{Ax} = \boldsymbol{b}$ is a translation of the solution set for $\boldsymbol{Ax} = \boldsymbol{0}$. Specifically, the flat or Euclidean subspace for the first system can be obtained by translating the linear subspace for the homogeneous system by the vector $\boldsymbol{p}$. This reasoning applies only if the system has at least one solution. This occurs if and only if the vector $\boldsymbol{b}$ lies in the image of the linear transformation $\boldsymbol{A}$.

The NM Dev class `LinearSystemSolver` solves a system of linear equations in the form $\boldsymbol{Ax} = \boldsymbol{b}$. Assume that, after row reduction, $\boldsymbol{A}$ has no more rows than columns. That is, the system must not be overdetermined.

Note that the following system is not overdetermined. One of the rows is linearly dependent:

$$\begin{bmatrix} 1 & -1 & 0 \\ 0 & -2 & 0 \\ 0 & 0 & -1 \\ 0 & 0 & -2 \end{bmatrix} \mathbf{x} = \begin{bmatrix} -0.8 \\ -1.6 \\ 0.8 \\ 1.6 \end{bmatrix}$$

The system of linear equations is solved in two steps:

1. First, solve $\boldsymbol{Ax} = \mathbf{0}$, the homogeneous system, for nontrivial solutions.
2. Then, solve $\boldsymbol{Ax} = \boldsymbol{b}$ for a particular solution.

If **A** has full rank, this implementation solves the system by LU decomposition. Otherwise, a particular solution is found by $\boldsymbol{p} = \boldsymbol{Tb}$, where $\boldsymbol{T}$ is the transformation matrix of $\boldsymbol{A}$ to reduced row echelon form. The final solution is as follows:

$$\boldsymbol{p} + \ker(\boldsymbol{A})$$

Hence, the solution can be seen as the translation of the null-space of $\boldsymbol{A}$ by the vector $\boldsymbol{p}$.

For example, for the following linear system:

$$\begin{bmatrix} 0 & 1 & 2 & -1 \\ 1 & 0 & 1 & 1 \\ -1 & 1 & 0 & -1 \\ 0 & 2 & 3 & -1 \end{bmatrix} \boldsymbol{x} = \begin{bmatrix} 1 \\ 4 \\ 2 \\ 7 \end{bmatrix}$$

The basis for the kernel is such that:

$$\begin{bmatrix} 0 & 1 & 2 & -1 \\ 1 & 0 & 1 & 1 \\ -1 & 1 & 0 & -1 \\ 0 & 2 & 3 & -1 \end{bmatrix} \begin{bmatrix} -2 \\ -1 \\ 1 \\ 1 \end{bmatrix} = \begin{bmatrix} 0 \\ 0 \\ 0 \\ 0 \end{bmatrix}$$

A particular solution is such that:

$$\begin{bmatrix} 0 & 1 & 2 & -1 \\ 1 & 0 & 1 & 1 \\ -1 & 1 & 0 & -1 \\ 0 & 2 & 3 & -1 \end{bmatrix} \begin{bmatrix} 9 \\ 11 \\ -5 \\ 0 \end{bmatrix} = \begin{bmatrix} 1 \\ 4 \\ 2 \\ 7 \end{bmatrix}$$

The following NM Dev code solves this example:

```
val A: Matrix = DenseMatrix(
    arrayOf(
        doubleArrayOf(0.0, 1.0, 2.0, -1.0),
        doubleArrayOf(1.0, 0.0, 1.0, 1.0),
        doubleArrayOf(-1.0, 1.0, 0.0, -1.0),
        doubleArrayOf(0.0, 2.0, 3.0, -1.0)
    )
)
```

```
val b: Vector = DenseVector(arrayOf(1.0, 4.0, 2.0, 7.0))

// construct a linear system solver
val solver: LinearSystemSolver = LinearSystemSolver(1e-15) // precision
// solve the homogenous linear system
val soln: LinearSystemSolver.Solution = solver.solve(A)
// get a particular solution
val p: Vector = soln.getParticularSolution(b)
println("p = \n" + p)

// verify that Ap = b
val Ap: Vector = A.multiply(p)
println(String.format("%s = \n%s is %b",
        Ap,
        b,
        MatrixPropertyUtils.areEqual(Ap, b, 1e-15)))

// get the basis for the null-space
val kernel: List<Vector> = soln.getHomogeneousSoln()
// println("kernel size = " + kernel.size())

// verify that A * kernel = 0
val k: Vector = kernel.get(0)
println("kernel basis = " + k)
val Ak: Vector = A.multiply(k)
println("Ak = 0, " + Ak)
```

The output is as follows:

```
p =
[9.000000, 11.000000, -5.000000, 0.000000]
[1.000000, 4.000000, 2.000000, 7.000000]  =
[1.000000, 4.000000, 2.000000, 7.000000]  is true
kernel size = 1
kernel basis = [-2.000000, -1.000000, 1.000000, 1.000000]
Ak = 0, [0.000000, 0.000000, 0.000000, 0.000000]
```

The signature for `LinearSystemSolver` is as follows:

```
/**
 * Construct a solver for a linear system of equations.
 *
 * @param epsilon a precision parameter: when a number |x| &le; &epsilon;,
 *                it is considered 0
 */
public LinearSystemSolver(double epsilon)
/**
 * Get a solution for the linear system, <i>Ax = b</i>.
 *
 * @param A0 a matrix representing a linear system of equations (the
```

```
 *              homogeneous part)
 * @return a solution for the linear system
 */
public Solution solve(final Matrix A0)
```

Note that the solve function returns an object of the `LinearSystemSolver:: Solution` class. This object contains the homogenous and nonhomogenous solutions to the linear system defined by the input matrix. The signature is as follows:

```
/**
 * This is the solution to a linear system of equations.
 */
public static interface Solution {
    /**
     * Get a particular solution for the linear system.
     *
     * @param b a vector
     * @return a particular solution
     */
    Vector getParticularSolution(Vector b);
    /**
     * Get the basis of the homogeneous solution for the linear system,
     * <i>Ax = b</i>.
     * That is, the solutions for <i>Ax = 0</i>.
     *
     * @return the homogeneous solution
     */
    List<Vector> getHomogeneousSoln();
}
```

2.4.7. Overdetermined Linear System

A system of equations is overdetermined if there are more equations than unknows; that is, $m > n$, m is the number of equations, and n is the number of unknowns. The $m \times n$ matrix $\boldsymbol{A}$ is a tall matrix:

$$\boldsymbol{Ax} = \boldsymbol{b}$$

An overdetermined system is usually inconsistent (no solution). The only exception is in some cases that some equation occurs multiple times in the system, or equivalently some equations are linear combinations of the others. In general, each unknown gives one degree of freedom. Each equation introduced into the system restricts one degree of freedom. Therefore, the critical case occurs when the number of equations and the number of free variables are equal. For every variable giving a degree of freedom, there exists a corresponding constraint. This square system of equations can have one unique solution if consistent. The overdetermined case occurs when the system has been over-constrained, that is, when the equations outnumber the unknowns.

For example, Figure 2-27 shows three linearly independent equations such that the system is inconsistent and hence no solution.

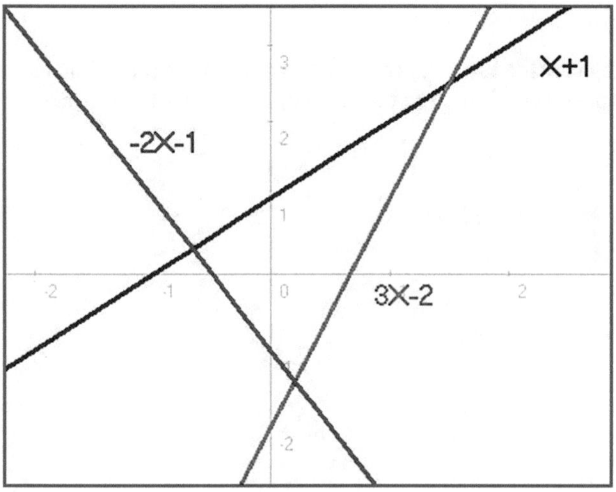

Figure 2-27. *An overdetermined system*

In Figure 2-28, one equation is linearly dependent on (in fact, the same as) another equation. The system has two variables and two (linearly independent) constraints, so the system is consistent and has one solution.

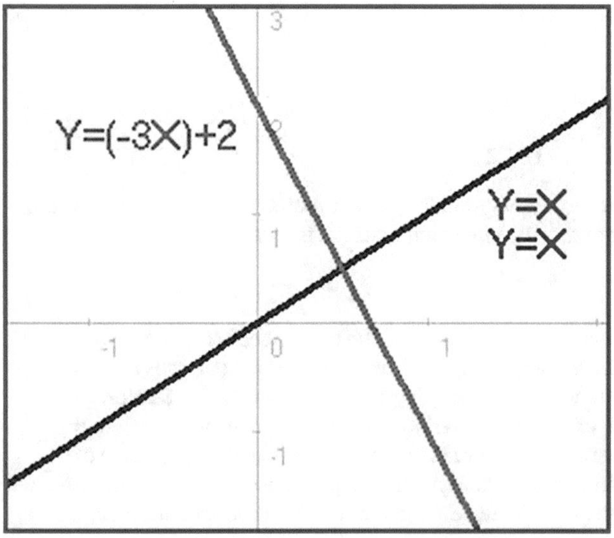

Figure 2-28. *One equation is linearly dependent on another; one solution*

For an overdetermined system where no solution exists, you should instead try to find the "best approximation." There are many ways to define "best approximation." The method of ordinary least squares (OLS) finds a solution $\boldsymbol{x}$ that minimizes the least square. That is:

$$\min_{x} \| \boldsymbol{Ax} - \boldsymbol{b} \|_2$$

Geometrically, OLS draws a (high-dimensional) line (or hyperplane) across the data points $\{(\boldsymbol{x}, \boldsymbol{b})\}$ so that the sum of squared distances is the smallest. See Figure 2-29.

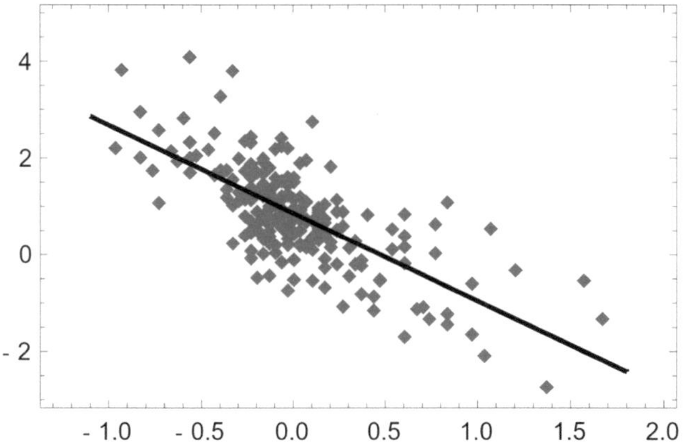

Figure 2-29. *The OLS solution to an overdetermined system*

The solution is given by this formula:

$$\boldsymbol{x} = \left(\boldsymbol{A}^T \boldsymbol{A}\right)^{-1} \boldsymbol{A}^T \boldsymbol{b}$$

With this formula, an approximate solution is found when no exact solution exists, and it gives an exact solution when one does exist, provided that $(\boldsymbol{A}^T\boldsymbol{A})^{-1}$ exists (or equivalently $\boldsymbol{A}$ has full column rank). In practice, however, we do not use this formula because of numerical stability problem when computing $(\boldsymbol{A}^T\boldsymbol{A})^{-1}$. Instead, we use orthogonal decomposition methods.

NM Dev has two implementations of the orthogonal decomposition methods, one based on QR factorization and the other on SVD factorization.

Using QR factorization, you can write $\boldsymbol{A}$ as follows:

$$\boldsymbol{A} = \boldsymbol{QR} = \boldsymbol{Q}\begin{bmatrix} \boldsymbol{R}_1 \\ \boldsymbol{0} \end{bmatrix} = \begin{bmatrix} \boldsymbol{Q}_1 & \boldsymbol{Q}_2 \end{bmatrix}\begin{bmatrix} \boldsymbol{R}_1 \\ \boldsymbol{0} \end{bmatrix} = \boldsymbol{Q}_1\boldsymbol{R}_1$$

The overdetermined linear system $\boldsymbol{Ax} = \boldsymbol{b}$ can be rewritten as $\boldsymbol{Q}_1\boldsymbol{R}_1\boldsymbol{x} = \boldsymbol{b}$. Because $\boldsymbol{Q}_1$ is orthogonal, you get this:

$$\boldsymbol{R}_1\boldsymbol{x} = \boldsymbol{Q}_1^{-1}\boldsymbol{b}\boldsymbol{x} = \boldsymbol{Q}_1^{\mathrm{T}}\boldsymbol{b}$$

As $\boldsymbol{R}_1$ is an upper triangular matrix, you can use backward substitution to solve the system.

The following NM Dev code solves this overdetermined system using the QR method:

$$\begin{bmatrix} 1 & 1 \\ 1 & 2 \\ 1 & 3 \\ 1 & 4 \end{bmatrix} \boldsymbol{x} = \begin{bmatrix} 6 \\ 5 \\ 7 \\ 10 \end{bmatrix}$$

```
// define an overdetermined system of linear equations
val A: Matrix = DenseMatrix(
    arrayOf(
        doubleArrayOf(1.0, 1.0),
        doubleArrayOf(1.0, 2.0),
        doubleArrayOf(1.0, 3.0),
        doubleArrayOf(1.0, 4.0)
    )
)

val b: Vector= DenseVector(arrayOf(6.0, 5.0, 7.0, 10.0))
val problem: LSProblem = LSProblem(A, b)

// solve the system using QR method
val solver1: OLSSolverByQR = OLSSolverByQR(0.0) // precision
// compute the OLS solution
val x1: Vector = solver1.solve(problem)
println("the OLS solution = " + x1)
```

The output is as follows:

```
the OLS solution = [3.500000, 1.400000]
```

Using SVD factorization, you can write $\boldsymbol{A}$ as follows:

$$\boldsymbol{A} = \boldsymbol{U}\boldsymbol{D}\boldsymbol{V}^T$$

The pseudo-inverse is $\boldsymbol{A}^+ = \boldsymbol{V}\boldsymbol{D}^+\boldsymbol{U}^T$, where $\boldsymbol{D}^+$ is by taking the reciprocal of each nonzero element on the diagonal and leaving the zeros in place. In numerical computation, only elements larger than some small tolerance are taken to be nonzero, and the others are replaced by zeros. The overdetermined linear system $\boldsymbol{Ax} = \boldsymbol{b}$ can be solved as follows:

$$\boldsymbol{x} = \boldsymbol{A}^+\boldsymbol{b}$$

The following NM Dev code solves the same example as earlier:

```
// solve the system using SVD method
val solver2: OLSSolverBySVD = OLSSolverBySVD(0.0) // precision
// compute the OLS solution
val x2: Vector = solver2.solve(problem)
// verify that Ax2 = b
// val Ax2: Vector = A.multiply(x2)
println("The OLS solution = " + x2)
```

The output is as follows:

```
the OLS solution = [3.500000, 1.400000]
```

The output is exactly the same as when using the QR method.

The NM Dev class called `LSProblem` constructs a linear system problem that can be solved by a number of solvers. This class uses the builder design pattern to construct an `LSProblem` that is customized to prescribe the behavior of a solver, such as number of iterations, precision, initial guess, and the left and right preconditioners. A preconditioner is the application of a transformation that transforms a problem into a form that is more suitable for numerical solving methods. This process is called *preconditioning*. Preconditioning is typically used to reduce the condition number of a numerical problem. The preconditioned problem is then usually solved by an iterative method. The signature of `LSProblem` is as follows:

```
/**
 * Constructs a system of linear equations <i>Ax = b</i>.
 *
 * @param A the the homogeneous part, the coefficient matrix, of the linear system
 * @param b the non-homogeneous part, the right-hand side vector, of the linear system
 */
public LSProblem(Matrix A, Vector b)
/**
 * Gets the homogeneous part, the coefficient matrix, of the linear system.
 *
 * @return the coefficient matrix
 */
public ImmutableMatrix A()
/**
 * Gets the non-homogeneous part, the right-hand side vector, of the linear system.
 *
 * @return the vector
 */
public ImmutableVector b()
/**
 * Gets the number of variables in the linear system.
 *
 * @return the number of variables
 */
public int size()
/**
 * Overrides the maximum count of iterations.
 *
 * @param maxIteration the maximum count of iterations
 * @return the new problem with the overridden maximum count of iterations
 */
public LSProblem withMaxIteration(int maxIteration)
/**
 * Gets the specified maximum number of iterations.
 *
 * @return the maximum number of iterations
 */
```

```
public int getMaxIteration()
/**
 * Overrides the tolerance instance.
 *
 * @param tolerance the criteria which determines when the solution converges and the
   iteration stops
 * @return the new problem with the overridden tolerance
 */
public LSProblem withTolerance(Tolerance tolerance)
/**
 * Gets the specified {@link Tolerance} instance.
 *
 * @return the {@link Tolerance} instance
 */
public Tolerance getTolerance()
/**
 * Overrides the initial guess of the solution.
 *
 * @param initialGuess the initial guess of the solution
 * @return the new problem with the overridden initial guess
 */
public LSProblem withInitialGuess(Vector initialGuess)
/**
 * Gets the initial guess of the solution for the problem.
 *
 * @return the initial guess
 */
public Vector getInitialGuess()
/**
 * Overrides the left preconditioner. If right-preconditioning is used,
 * leave this as its default value - {@link IdentityPreconditioner}.
 *
 * @param preconditioner the preconditioner
 * @return the new problem with the overridden left preconditioner
 */
public LSProblem withLeftPreconditioner(Preconditioner preconditioner)
/**
 * Gets the left preconditioner.
 *
 * @return the left preconditioner
 */
public Preconditioner getLeftPreconditioner()
/**
 * Overrides the right preconditioner. If left-preconditioning is used,
 * leave this as its default value - {@link IdentityPreconditioner}.
 *
 * @param preconditioner the preconditioner
 * @return the new problem with the overridden right preconditioner
 */
public LSProblem withRightPreconditioner(Preconditioner preconditioner)
```

```
/**
 * Gets the right preconditioner.
 *
 * @return the right preconditioner
 */
public Preconditioner getRightPreconditioner()
```

2.5. Sparse Matrix

In numerical computing, a sparse matrix (vector) is a matrix (vector) in which most of the elements are zero. There is no strict definition how many elements need to be zero for a matrix to be considered sparse, but a common criterion is that the number of nonzero elements is roughly the number of rows or columns. By contrast, if most of the elements are nonzero, then the matrix is considered dense. The number of zero-valued elements divided by the total number of elements is sometimes referred to as the *sparsity* of the matrix. For instance, the following sparse matrix contains only 9 nonzero elements, with 26 zero elements. Its sparsity is 74 percent, and its density is 26 percent.

$$\begin{bmatrix} 11 & 22 & & & & & \\ & 33 & 44 & & & & \\ & & 55 & 66 & 77 & & \\ & & & & & 88 & \\ & & & & & & 99 \end{bmatrix}$$

Conceptually, sparsity corresponds to systems with few pairwise interactions. For example, consider a line of balls connected by springs from one to the next: this is a sparse system as only adjacent balls are coupled. By contrast, if the same line of balls had springs connecting each ball to all other balls, the system would correspond to a dense matrix. The concept of sparsity is useful in combinatorics and application areas such as network theory and numerical analysis, which typically have a low density of significant data or connections. Large sparse matrices often appear in scientific or engineering applications when solving partial differential equations and optimization.

When storing and manipulating sparse matrices on a computer, it is beneficial and often necessary to use specialized algorithms and data structures that take advantage of the sparse structure of the matrix. Operations using standard dense-matrix structures and algorithms are slow and inefficient when applied to large sparse matrices because processing and memory are wasted on the zeros. Sparse data is by nature more easily compressed and thus requires significantly less storage. Some very large sparse matrices are practically infeasible to manipulate using standard dense-matrix algorithms.

In general, for an $m \times n$ matrix, the amount of memory required to store the matrix in the dense format is proportional to $m \times n$ (disregarding the fact that the dimensions of the matrix also need to be stored). In the case of a sparse matrix, substantial memory requirement reduction can be realized by storing only the nonzero entries. Depending on the number and distribution of the nonzero entries, different data structures can be used and yield huge savings in memory when compared to the basic approach. The trade-off is that accessing the individual elements becomes more complex, and additional structures are needed to recover the original matrix unambiguously.

NM Dev library supports two groups of formats.

- Those that support efficient modification, such as a dictionary of keys and a list of lists. These are typically used to construct the matrices.
- Those that support efficient access and matrix operations, such as compressed sparse row. These are typically used to support matrix operations.

2.5.1. Dictionary of Keys

A dictionary of keys (DOK) consists of a dictionary that maps (row, column) pairs to the value of the elements. That is, the nonzero values are hashed such that adding, removing, and retrieving values can be done in constant time. Elements that are missing from the dictionary are taken to be zero. The format is good for incrementally constructing a sparse matrix in random order, but it is poor for iterating over nonzero values in lexicographical order. You would typically construct a matrix in this format and then convert it to another more efficient format for processing.

The following NM Dev code constructs sparse matrices for this matrix using DOK in two ways. You can use either arrays or lists to specify the nonzero entries.

$$\boldsymbol{A} = \begin{bmatrix} 1 & 2 & 0 & 0 \\ 0 & 3 & 9 & 0 \\ 0 & 1 & 4 & 0 \end{bmatrix}$$

```
// the target matrix in dense representation
val A: Matrix = DenseMatrix(arrayOf(
            doubleArrayOf(1.0, 2.0, 0.0, 0.0),
            doubleArrayOf(0.0, 3.0, 9.0, 0.0),
            doubleArrayOf(0.0, 1.0, 4.0, 0.0)
))

// DOK
val B1: SparseMatrix = DOKSparseMatrix(3, 4, // 3x4 dimension
            listOf<SparseMatrix.Entry>( // specify only the non-zero entries
                SparseMatrix.Entry(MatrixCoordinate(3, 3), 4.0),
                SparseMatrix.Entry(MatrixCoordinate(2, 2), 3.0),
                SparseMatrix.Entry(MatrixCoordinate(1, 1), 1.0),
                SparseMatrix.Entry(MatrixCoordinate(3, 2), 1.0),
                SparseMatrix.Entry(MatrixCoordinate(2, 3), 9.0),
                SparseMatrix.Entry(MatrixCoordinate(1, 2), 2.0))
)

//verify that B1 = A
println(String.format(
        "B1 = A, %b",
        MatrixPropertyUtils.areEqual(B1, A, 1e-15)))

val B2: SparseMatrix = DOKSparseMatrix(3, 4, // 3x4 dimension
        listOf<SparseMatrix.Entry>( // specify only the non-zero entries
                SparseMatrix.Entry(MatrixCoordinate(3, 3), 4.0),
                SparseMatrix.Entry(MatrixCoordinate(2, 2), 3.0),
                SparseMatrix.Entry(MatrixCoordinate(1, 1), 1.0),
                SparseMatrix.Entry(MatrixCoordinate(3, 2), 1.0),
                SparseMatrix.Entry(MatrixCoordinate(2, 3), 9.0),
                SparseMatrix.Entry(MatrixCoordinate(1, 2), 2.0))
)
```

```
//verify that B2 = A
println(String.format(
        "B2 = A, %b",
        MatrixPropertyUtils.areEqual(B2, A, 1e-15)))
```

The output is as follows:

```
B1 = A, true
B2 = A, true
```

2.5.2. List of Lists

An list of lists (LIL) stores one list per row, with each entry containing the column index and the value. Typically, these entries are sorted by column index for faster lookup. This is another format that is good for incremental matrix construction.

The following NM Dev code constructs sparse matrices for ***A*** shown previously using LIL in two ways. You can use either arrays or lists to specify the nonzero entries.

```
// LIL
val C1: SparseMatrix = LILSparseMatrix(3, 4, // 3x4 dimension
        listOf<SparseMatrix.Entry>( // specify only the non-zero entries
                SparseMatrix.Entry(MatrixCoordinate(3, 3), 4.0),
                SparseMatrix.Entry(MatrixCoordinate(2, 2), 3.0),
                SparseMatrix.Entry(MatrixCoordinate(1, 1), 1.0),
                SparseMatrix.Entry(MatrixCoordinate(3, 2), 1.0),
                SparseMatrix.Entry(MatrixCoordinate(2, 3), 9.0),
                SparseMatrix.Entry(MatrixCoordinate(1, 2), 2.0))
)

//verify that C1 = A
println(String.format(
        "C1 = A, %b",
        MatrixPropertyUtils.areEqual(C1, A, 1e-15)))
val C2: SparseMatrix = LILSparseMatrix(3, 4, // 3x4 dimension
        listOf<SparseMatrix.Entry>( // specify only the non-zero entries
                SparseMatrix.Entry(MatrixCoordinate(3, 3), 4.0),
                SparseMatrix.Entry(MatrixCoordinate(2, 2), 3.0),
                SparseMatrix.Entry(MatrixCoordinate(1, 1), 1.0),
                SparseMatrix.Entry(MatrixCoordinate(3, 2), 1.0),
                SparseMatrix.Entry(MatrixCoordinate(2, 3), 9.0),
                SparseMatrix.Entry(MatrixCoordinate(1, 2), 2.0)))
//verify that C2 = A
println(String.format(
        "C2 = A, %b",
        MatrixPropertyUtils.areEqual(C2, A, 1e-15)))
```

The output is as follows:

```
C1 = A, true
C2 = A, true
```

2.5.3. Compressed Sparse Row

The compressed sparse row (CSR) or compressed row storage (CRS) or Yale format represents a matrix by three (one-dimensional) arrays, which respectively contain nonzero values, the extents of rows, and column indices. This format allows fast row access and matrix-vector multiplications $\boldsymbol{Av}$. The CSR format stores a sparse $m \times n$ matrix $\boldsymbol{A}$ in row form using three (one-dimensional) arrays (V, COL_INDEX, ROW_INDEX). Let NNZ denote the number of nonzero entries in $\boldsymbol{A}$. The arrays V and COL_INDEX are of length NNZ and contain the nonzero values and the column indices of those values, respectively.

The following NM Dev code constructs sparse matrices for $\boldsymbol{A}$ previously using CSR in two ways. You can use either arrays or lists to specify the nonzero entries.

```
// CSR
val D1: SparseMatrix = CSRSparseMatrix(3, 4, // 3x4 dimension
        listOf<SparseMatrix.Entry>( // specify only the non-zero entries
                SparseMatrix.Entry(MatrixCoordinate(3, 3), 4.0),
                SparseMatrix.Entry(MatrixCoordinate(2, 2), 3.0),
                SparseMatrix.Entry(MatrixCoordinate(1, 1), 1.0),
                SparseMatrix.Entry(MatrixCoordinate(3, 2), 1.0),
                SparseMatrix.Entry(MatrixCoordinate(2, 3), 9.0),
                SparseMatrix.Entry(MatrixCoordinate(1, 2), 2.0))
)

//verify that D1 = A
println(String.format(
        "D1 = A, %b",
        MatrixPropertyUtils.areEqual(D1, A, 1e-15)))

val D2: SparseMatrix = CSRSparseMatrix(3, 4, // 3x4 dimension
        listOf<SparseMatrix.Entry>( // specify only the non-zero entries
                SparseMatrix.Entry(MatrixCoordinate(3, 3), 4.0),
                SparseMatrix.Entry(MatrixCoordinate(2, 2), 3.0),
                SparseMatrix.Entry(MatrixCoordinate(1, 1), 1.0),
                SparseMatrix.Entry(MatrixCoordinate(3, 2), 1.0),
                SparseMatrix.Entry(MatrixCoordinate(2, 3), 9.0),
                SparseMatrix.Entry(MatrixCoordinate(1, 2), 2.0)))
//verify that D2 = A
println(String.format(
        "D2 = A, %b",
        MatrixPropertyUtils.areEqual(D2, A, 1e-15)))
```

The output is as follows:

```
D1 = A, true
D2 = A, true
```

2.5.4. Sparse Matrix/Vector Operations

In NM Dev, you can create a sparse vector using the `SparseVector` class. Here's an example:

```
// sparse vector construction
val v1: SparseVector = SparseVector(
        99, // vector size
        listOf<SparseVector.Entry>(
            SparseVector.Entry(1, 11.0),
            SparseVector.Entry(3, 22.0),
            SparseVector.Entry(53, 33.0),
            SparseVector.Entry(79, 44.0),
            SparseVector.Entry(99, 55.0)
        )
)

println("v = " + v1)
```

The output is as follows:

```
v1 = size: 99
[1] 11.0000
[3] 22.0000
[53] 33.0000
[79] 44.0000
[99] 55.0000
```

All these sparse matrix and vector data structures are fully interoperable with all other matrix and vector data structures. The sparse data structures fully support all matrix and vector operations, such as addition and multiplication. Here's an example:

```
// addition
val M1: Matrix = B1.add(A)
println("M1 = " + M1)
```

The output is as follows:

```
M1 = 3x4
        [,1] [,2] [,3] [,4]
[1,] 2.000000, 4.000000, 0.000000, 0.000000,
[2,] 0.000000, 6.000000, 18.000000, 0.000000,
[3,] 0.000000, 2.000000, 8.000000, 0.000000,
```

```
val M2: DOKSparseMatrix = B1.add(B2) as DOKSparseMatrix
println("M2 = " + M2)
```

The output is as follows:

```
M2 = 3x4 nnz = 6
(1, 1): 2.0
(1, 2): 4.0
(2, 2): 6.0
(2, 3): 18.0
(3, 2): 2.0
(3, 3): 8.0
```

```
val M3: LILSparseMatrix = C1.minus(C2) as LILSparseMatrix
println("M3 = " + M3)
```

The output is as follows:

```
M3 = 3x4 nnz = 0
```

```
val M4: CSRSparseMatrix = D1.multiply(D2.t()) as CSRSparseMatrix
println("M4 = " + M4)
```

The output is as follows:

```
M4 = 3x3 nnz = 9
(1, 1): 5.0
(1, 2): 6.0
(1, 3): 2.0
(2, 1): 6.0
(2, 2): 90.0
(2, 3): 39.0
(3, 1): 2.0
(3, 2): 39.0
(3, 3): 17.0
```

```
val v2: SparseVector = SparseVector(
        4, // vector size
        listOf<SparseVector.Entry>(
            SparseVector.Entry(1, 11.0)
        )
)

println("v2 = " + v2)
```

The output is as follows:

```
v2 = size: 4
[1] 11.0000
```

```
val v3: Vector = B1.multiply(v2)
println("ve = " + v3)
```

The output is as follows:

```
ve = size: 3
[1] 11.0000
```

NM Dev also supports a wide variety of other matrices for special structures, as follows:

- `DiagonalMatrix`
- `BidiagonalMatrix`
- `TridiagonalMatrix`
- `LowerTriangularMatrix`
- `UpperTriangularMatrix`
- `SymmetricMatrix`
- `PermutationMatrix`

These data structures have operations special to them, but they are also fully interoperable with all other matrix and vector data structures. They also fully support all matrix and vector operations, such as addition and multiplication.

2.5.5. Solving Sparse Matrix Equations

Solving systems of linear equations is fundamental to numerical computing. You can take advantage of the sparsity of the problems to handle much bigger problems that you otherwise would not be able to handle. For example, the solvers discussed in the previous chapters—such as LU, QR, and SVD factorizations—work with dense matrices. They fill the entire matrices (imagine they are millions by millions) with zeros and need to fill many of them over and over again. These many dense matrices may not fit into the computer memory. Operations of these full matrices are inefficient and wasted on the zeros. Algorithms to solve systems of linear equations, which are typically iterative methods, take advantage of sparse matrices and do not change the sparsity patterns, as they only involve matrix-vector products and do no filling.

An iterative method to solve an $n \times n$ (or nonsquare) linear system $\boldsymbol{Ax} = \boldsymbol{b}$ involves a sequence of matrix-vector multiplications. Starting with an initial guess of the solution, each iteration returns a new estimate of the solution. It is hoped that the estimates converge to a satisfactory solution (within a tolerance) after k iterations. For a dense matrix $\boldsymbol{A}$, each iteration takes $O(n^2)$ operations. An iterative method takes $O(kn^2)$ operations to converge. For a sparse system, matrix-vector multiplication takes only $O(\#\text{nonZeros})$, where #nonZeros is the number of nonzeros in the sparse matrix. Therefore, an iterative method can be much faster than a traditional direct method of solving a linear system such as taking an inverse. An iterative method using sparse matrices is much faster than one using dense matrices.

NM Dev supports a large range of sparse matrix linear system solvers. They are as follows:

- Biconjugate gradient solver (BiCG)
- Biconjugate gradient stabilized solver (BiCGSTAB)
- Conjugate gradient solver (CG)
- Conjugate gradient normal error solver (CGNE)
- Conjugate gradient normal residual solver (CGNR)
- Conjugate gradient squared solver (CGS)
- Gauss-Seidel solver
- Generalized conjugate residual solver (GRES)
- Generalized minimal residual solver (GMRES)
- Jacobi solver
- Minimal residual solver (MINRES)
- Quasi minimal residual solver (QMR)
- Steepest descent solver
- Successive overrelaxation solver (SOR)
- Symmetric successive overrelaxation solver (SSOR)

Here are some guidelines for choosing an iterative solver of a sparse system. For Hermitian problems, if the system is positive definite, use CG or MINRES; otherwise, use MINRES. To avoid doing inner products in CG or MINRES, you may choose stationary methods such as Jacobi, Gauss-Seidel, SOR, or SSOR. These methods save computation cost in each iteration, but the number of iterations may increase unless there is a good preconditioner.

For non-Hermitian problems, the choice is not so easy. If matrix-vector multiplication is very expensive, GMRES is probably the best choice because it performs the fewest multiplications. The second-best alternatives are QMR or BiCG. QMR is numerically more stable than BiCG. When the transpose of a matrix is not available, there are transpose-free methods such as CGS or BiCGSTAB. For nonsquare systems, there are CG methods for solving overdetermined systems, such as CGNR, and underdetermined systems, such as CGNE.

The use of preconditioner can significantly improve the rate of convergence of an iterative method. A preconditioner transforms a linear system into one that is equivalent in the sense that it has the same solution. The transformed system has more favorable spectral properties that affect convergence rate. In particular, a preconditioner $\boldsymbol{M}$ approximates the coefficient matrix $\boldsymbol{A}$, and the transformed system is easier to solve. Here's an example:

$$\boldsymbol{M}^{-1}\boldsymbol{A}\boldsymbol{x} = \boldsymbol{M}^{-1}\boldsymbol{b}$$

This has the same solution as the original system. The spectral properties of its coefficient matrix $\boldsymbol{M}^{-1}\boldsymbol{A}$ may be more favorable. Another way of preconditioning a system is as follows:

$$\boldsymbol{M}_1^{-1}\boldsymbol{A}\boldsymbol{M}_2^{-1}\left(\boldsymbol{M}_2\boldsymbol{x}\right) = \boldsymbol{M}_1^{-1}\boldsymbol{b}$$

The matrices $\boldsymbol{M}_1$ and $\boldsymbol{M}_2$ are called the left and right preconditioners, respectively. There are three kinds of preconditioning: left, right, or split. Left-preconditioning leaves $\boldsymbol{M}_2$ as `IdentityPreconditioner`. (This identity preconditioner is used when no preconditioning is applied.) Similarly, right-preconditioning leaves M_1 as IdentityPreconditioner.

In NM Dev, all the sparse matrix linear system solvers inherit from the IterativeLinearSystemSolver interface. The signature is as follows:

```
public interface IterativeLinearSystemSolver {
    /**
     * This is the solution to a system of linear equations using an iterative
     * solver.
     */
    public static interface Solution extends IterativeMethod<Vector> {
        @Override
        public IterationMonitor<Vector> step() throws ConvergenceFailure;//override the
                                                                          return and
                                                                          exception types
        @Override
        public Vector search(Vector... initials) throws ConvergenceFailure;//override the
                                                                            exception type
    }
    /**
     * Solves iteratively
     * <blockquote>
     * <i>Ax = b</i>
     * </blockquote>
     * until the solution converges, i.e., the norm of residual
     * (<i>b - Ax</i>) is less than or equal to the threshold.
     *
     * @param problem a system of linear equations
     * @param monitor an iteration monitor
     * @return an (approximate) solution to the linear problem
     * @throws ConvergenceFailure if the algorithm fails to converge
     */
    public Solution solve(LSProblem problem, IterationMonitor<Vector> monitor) throws
    ConvergenceFailure;
}
```

The following NM Dev code solves a sparse linear system using a number of nonstationary sparse linear system solvers. The general procedure is to first define a linear system problem using LSProblem. Then you construct a solver for the problem. There are many choices here. Solving the problem gives IterativeLinearSystemSolver.Solution. Using the solution object, you can start the iterative search from an initial guess (which is 0 in these examples). The search algorithm returns a vector x as the solution. You check the validity of the result by comparing the difference between Ax and x using the ℓ_2-norm. Here's an example:

```
/* Symmetric matrix:
    * 8x8
    * [,1] [,2] [,3] [,4] [,5] [,6] [,7] [,8]
    * [1,] 7.000000, 0.000000, 1.000000, 0.000000, 0.000000, 2.000000, 7.000000, 0.000000,
    * [2,] 0.000000, -4.000000, 8.000000, 0.000000, 2.000000, 0.000000, 0.000000, 0.000000,
    * [3,] 1.000000, 8.000000, 1.000000, 0.000000, 0.000000, 0.000000, 0.000000, 5.000000,
    * [4,] 0.000000, 0.000000, 0.000000, 7.000000, 0.000000, 0.000000, 9.000000, 0.000000,
    * [5,] 0.000000, 2.000000, 0.000000, 0.000000, 5.000000, 1.000000, 5.000000, 0.000000,
```

```
    * [6,] 2.000000, 0.000000, 0.000000, 0.000000, 1.000000, -1.000000, 0.000000, 5.000000,
    * [7,] 7.000000, 0.000000, 0.000000, 9.000000, 5.000000, 0.000000, 11.000000, 0.000000,
    * [8,] 0.000000, 0.000000, 5.000000, 0.000000, 0.000000, 5.000000, 0.000000, 5.000000,
    */
val A: Matrix = CSRSparseMatrix(8, 8, // matrix dimension
        listOf<SparseMatrix.Entry>(
            SparseMatrix.Entry(MatrixCoordinate(1, 1), 7.0),
            SparseMatrix.Entry(MatrixCoordinate(1, 3), 1.0),
            SparseMatrix.Entry(MatrixCoordinate(1, 6), 2.0),
            SparseMatrix.Entry(MatrixCoordinate(1, 7), 7.0),
            SparseMatrix.Entry(MatrixCoordinate(2, 2), -4.0),
            SparseMatrix.Entry(MatrixCoordinate(2, 3), 8.0),
            SparseMatrix.Entry(MatrixCoordinate(2, 5), 2.0),
            SparseMatrix.Entry(MatrixCoordinate(3, 1), 1.0),
            SparseMatrix.Entry(MatrixCoordinate(3, 2), 8.0),
            SparseMatrix.Entry(MatrixCoordinate(3, 3), 1.0),
            SparseMatrix.Entry(MatrixCoordinate(3, 8), 5.0),
            SparseMatrix.Entry(MatrixCoordinate(4, 4), 7.0),
            SparseMatrix.Entry(MatrixCoordinate(4, 7), 9.0),
            SparseMatrix.Entry(MatrixCoordinate(5, 2), 2.0),
            SparseMatrix.Entry(MatrixCoordinate(5, 5), 5.0),
            SparseMatrix.Entry(MatrixCoordinate(5, 6), 1.0),
            SparseMatrix.Entry(MatrixCoordinate(5, 7), 5.0),
            SparseMatrix.Entry(MatrixCoordinate(6, 1), 2.0),
            SparseMatrix.Entry(MatrixCoordinate(6, 5), 1.0),
            SparseMatrix.Entry(MatrixCoordinate(6, 6), -1.0),
            SparseMatrix.Entry(MatrixCoordinate(6, 8), 5.0),
            SparseMatrix.Entry(MatrixCoordinate(7, 1), 7.0),
            SparseMatrix.Entry(MatrixCoordinate(7, 4), 9.0),
            SparseMatrix.Entry(MatrixCoordinate(7, 5), 5.0),
            SparseMatrix.Entry(MatrixCoordinate(7, 7), 11.0),
            SparseMatrix.Entry(MatrixCoordinate(8, 3), 5.0),
            SparseMatrix.Entry(MatrixCoordinate(8, 6), 5.0),
            SparseMatrix.Entry(MatrixCoordinate(8, 8), 5.0)
        )
)

val b: Vector = DenseVector( // note that we can still use dense data structure
                    arrayOf(1.0,1.0,1.0,1.0,1.0,1.0,1.0,1.0)
                )
// construct a linear system problem to be solved
val problem: LSProblem = LSProblem(A, b)

// construct a sparse matrix linear system solver
val BiCG: BiconjugateGradientSolver
        = BiconjugateGradientSolver(
                10, // maximum number of iterations
                AbsoluteTolerance(1e-8) // precision
        )
```

```
val soln1: IterativeLinearSystemSolver.Solution = BiCG.solve(problem)
val x1: Vector = soln1.search(SparseVector(A.nCols())) // use 0 as the initial guess
println("x = " + x1)
val Ax1_b: Vector = A.multiply(x1).minus(b) // verify that Ax = b
println("||Ax - b|| = " + Ax1_b.norm()) // should be (close to) 0
```

The output is as follows:

```
x = [-0.041860, -0.003413, 0.117250, -0.112640, 0.024172, -0.107633, 0.198720, 0.190383]
||Ax - b|| = 3.4321107842718707E-13
```

```
// construct a sparse matrix linear system solver
val BiCGSTAB: BiconjugateGradientStabilizedSolver
        = BiconjugateGradientStabilizedSolver(
                10, // maximum number of iterations
                AbsoluteTolerance(1e-7) // less precision
        )
val soln2: IterativeLinearSystemSolver.Solution = BiCGSTAB.solve(problem)
val x2: Vector = soln2.search(SparseVector(A.nCols())) // use 0 as the initial guess
println("x = " + x2)
val Ax2_b: Vector = A.multiply(x2).minus(b) // verify that Ax = b
println("||Ax - b|| = " + Ax2_b.norm()) // should be (close to) 0
```

The output is as follows:

```
x = [-0.041860, -0.003413, 0.117250, -0.112640, 0.024172, -0.107633, 0.198720, 0.190383]
||Ax - b|| = 6.001732649867594E-8
```

```
val CGNE: ConjugateGradientNormalErrorSolver
        = ConjugateGradientNormalErrorSolver(
                10, // maximum number of iterations
                AbsoluteTolerance(1e-8) // precision
        )
val soln3: IterativeLinearSystemSolver.Solution = CGNE.solve(problem)
val x3: Vector = soln3.search(SparseVector(A.nCols())) // use 0 as the initial guess
println("x = " + x3)
val Ax3_b: Vector = A.multiply(x3).minus(b) // verify that Ax = b
println("||Ax - b|| = " + Ax3_b.norm()) // should be (close to) 0
```

The output is as follows:

```
x = [-0.041860, -0.003413, 0.117250, -0.112640, 0.024172, -0.107633, 0.198720, 0.190383]
||Ax - b|| = 1.6870268466872934E-9
```

```
val CGNR: ConjugateGradientNormalResidualSolver
        = ConjugateGradientNormalResidualSolver(
                10, // maximum number of iterations
                AbsoluteTolerance(1e-8) // precision
        )
```

```
val soln4: IterativeLinearSystemSolver.Solution = CGNR.solve(problem)
val x4: Vector = soln4.search(SparseVector(A.nCols())) // use 0 as the initial guess
println("x = " + x4)
val Ax4_b: Vector = A.multiply(x4).minus(b) // verify that Ax = b
println("||Ax - b|| = " + Ax4_b.norm()) // should be (close to) 0
```

The output is as follows:

```
x = [-0.041860, -0.003413, 0.117250, -0.112640, 0.024172, -0.107633, 0.198720, 0.190383]
||Ax - b|| = 6.817480703009663E-10
```

```
val CG: ConjugateGradientSolver
        = ConjugateGradientSolver(
                10, // maximum number of iterations
                AbsoluteTolerance(1e-8) // precision
        )
val soln5: IterativeLinearSystemSolver.Solution = CG.solve(problem)
val x5: Vector = soln5.search(SparseVector(A.nCols())) // use 0 as the initial guess
println("x = " + x5)
val Ax5_b: Vector = A.multiply(x5).minus(b) // verify that Ax = b
println("||Ax - b|| = " + Ax5_b.norm()) // should be (close to) 0
```

The output is as follows:

```
x = [-0.041860, -0.003413, 0.117250, -0.112640, 0.024172, -0.107633, 0.198720, 0.190383]
||Ax - b|| = 3.4321107842718707E-13
```

```
val CGS: ConjugateGradientNormalResidualSolver
        = ConjugateGradientNormalResidualSolver(
                10, // maximum number of iterations
                AbsoluteTolerance(1e-8) // precision
        )
val soln6: IterativeLinearSystemSolver.Solution = CGS.solve(problem)
val x6: Vector = soln6.search(SparseVector(A.nCols())) // use 0 as the initial guess
println("x = " + x6)
val Ax6_b: Vector = A.multiply(x6).minus(b) // verify that Ax = b
println("||Ax - b|| = " + Ax6_b.norm()) // should be (close to) 0
```

The output is as follows:

```
x = [-0.041860, -0.003413, 0.117250, -0.112640, 0.024172, -0.107633, 0.198720, 0.190383]
||Ax - b|| = 6.817480703009663E-10
```

```
val GRES: GeneralizedConjugateResidualSolver
        = GeneralizedConjugateResidualSolver(
                10, // maximum number of iterations
                AbsoluteTolerance(1e-8) // precision
        )
```

```
val soln7: IterativeLinearSystemSolver.Solution = GRES.solve(problem)
val x7: Vector = soln7.search(SparseVector(A.nCols())) // use 0 as the initial guess
println("x = " + x7)
val Ax7_b: Vector = A.multiply(x7).minus(b) // verify that Ax = b
println("||Ax - b|| = " + Ax7_b.norm()) // should be (close to) 0
```

The output is as follows:

```
x = [-0.041860, -0.003413, 0.117250, -0.112640, 0.024172, -0.107633, 0.198720, 0.190383]
||Ax - b|| = 1.0175362097255202E-15
```

```
val GMRES: GeneralizedMinimalResidualSolver
        = GeneralizedMinimalResidualSolver(
                10, // maximum number of iterations
                AbsoluteTolerance(1e-8) // precision
        )
val soln8: IterativeLinearSystemSolver.Solution = GMRES.solve(problem)
val x8: Vector = soln8.search(SparseVector(A.nCols())) // use 0 as the initial guess
println("x = " + x8)
val Ax8_b: Vector = A.multiply(x8).minus(b) // verify that Ax = b
println("||Ax - b|| = " + Ax8_b.norm()) // should be (close to) 0
```

The output is as follows:

```
x = [-0.041860, -0.003413, 0.117250, -0.112640, 0.024172, -0.107633, 0.198720, 0.190383]
||Ax - b|| = 1.0053497077208614E-15
```

```
val MINRES: MinimalResidualSolver = MinimalResidualSolver(
        10, // maximum number of iterations
        AbsoluteTolerance(1e-8) // precision
)
val monitor: CountMonitor<Vector> = CountMonitor<Vector>()
val soln9: IterativeLinearSystemSolver.Solution = MINRES.solve(problem, monitor)
val x9: Vector = soln9.search(SparseVector(A.nCols())) // use 0 as the initial guess
println("x = " + x9)
val Ax9_b: Vector = A.multiply(x9).minus(b) // verify that Ax = b
println("||Ax - b|| = " + Ax9_b.norm()) // should be (close to) 0
```

The output is as follows:

```
x = [-0.041860, -0.003413, 0.117250, -0.112640, 0.024172, -0.107633, 0.198720, 0.190383]
||Ax - b|| = 2.392209894095706E-13
```

```
val QMR: QuasiMinimalResidualSolver
        = QuasiMinimalResidualSolver(
                10, // maximum number of iterations
                AbsoluteTolerance(1e-8) // precision
        )
```

```
val soln10: IterativeLinearSystemSolver.Solution = QMR.solve(problem)
val x10: Vector = soln10.search(SparseVector(A.nCols())) // use 0 as the initial guess
println("x = " + x10)
val Ax10_b: Vector = A.multiply(x10).minus(b) // verify that Ax = b
println("||Ax - b|| = " + Ax10_b.norm()) // should be (close to) 0
```

The output is as follows:

```
x = [-0.041860, -0.003413, 0.117250, -0.112640, 0.024172, -0.107633, 0.198720, 0.190383]
||Ax - b|| = 5.933770145831627E-13
```

The following NM Dev code solves a sparse linear system using a number of stationary sparse linear system solvers:

```
println("solving sparse linear system using stationary iterative solvers")

var A: Matrix = SymmetricMatrix(arrayOf(
            doubleArrayOf(4.0),
            doubleArrayOf(1.0, 3.0)))

val b = DenseVector(arrayOf(1.0, 2.0))

// construct a linear system problem to be solved
val problem: LSProblem = LSProblem(A, b)

// construct a sparse matrix linear system solver
val gauss_seidel: GaussSeidelSolver = GaussSeidelSolver(10, AbsoluteTolerance(1e-4))
val soln1: IterativeLinearSystemSolver.Solution = gauss_seidel.solve(problem)
val x1 = soln1.search(SparseVector(A.nCols())) // use 0 as the initial guess
println("x = " + x1)
val Ax1_b = A.multiply(x1).minus(b) // verify that Ax = b
println("||Ax - b|| = " + Ax1_b.norm()) // should be (close to) 0
```

The output is as follows:

```
x = [0.090917, 0.636361]
||Ax - b|| = 2.8131430040989613E-5
```

```
// construct a sparse matrix linear system solver
val jacobi: JacobiSolver = JacobiSolver(10, AbsoluteTolerance(1e-4))
val soln2: IterativeLinearSystemSolver.Solution = jacobi.solve(problem)
val x2 = soln2.search(SparseVector(A.nCols()))
println("x = " + x2)
val Ax2_b = A.multiply(x1).minus(b) // verify that Ax = b
println("||Ax - b|| = " + Ax2_b.norm()) // should be (close to) 0
```

The output is as follows:

```
x = [0.090917, 0.636365]
||Ax - b|| = 2.8131430040989613E-5
```

```
val SOR: SuccessiveOverrelaxationSolver = SuccessiveOverrelaxationSolver(
                1.5,
                20, // need more iterations
                AbsoluteTolerance(1e-4))
val soln3: IterativeLinearSystemSolver.Solution = SOR.solve(problem)
val x3 = soln3.search(SparseVector(A.nCols())) // use 0 as the initial guess
println("x = " + x3)
val Ax3_b = A.multiply(x3).minus(b) // verify that Ax = b
println("||Ax - b|| = " + Ax3_b.norm()) // should be (close to) 0
```

The output is as follows:

```
x = [0.090909, 0.636344]
||Ax - b|| = 6.462981890138403E-5
```

```
val SSOR: SymmetricSuccessiveOverrelaxationSolver
        = SymmetricSuccessiveOverrelaxationSolver(
                1.5,
                20, // need more iterations
                AbsoluteTolerance(1e-4))
val soln4: IterativeLinearSystemSolver.Solution = SSOR.solve(problem)
val x4 = soln4.search(SparseVector(A.nCols())) // use 0 as the initial guess
println("x = " + x4)
val Ax4_b = A.multiply(x4).minus(b) // verify that Ax = b
println("||Ax - b|| = " + Ax4_b.norm()) // should be (close to) 0
```

The output is as follows:

```
x = [0.090904, 0.636348]
||Ax - b|| = 6.213495416129946E-5
```

CHAPTER 3

Finding Roots of Equations

A root-finding algorithm is a numerical algorithm that finds a value x such that $f(x) = 0$ for a given function f. This procedure is also called *finding zeros*. As a result, you can get no solution, one solution, or multiple solutions. NM Dev provides a few methods to find such roots. They is the Jenkins-Traub algorithm, the bisection method, Brent's method, the Newton-Raphson method, and Halley's method. With the exception of polynomials, you have the Jenkins-Traub algorithm, which calculates all the roots of a polynomial. In general, the zeros of a function cannot be computed exactly or there is no closed form. Most algorithms do not guarantee finding a root, even though one does exist. A root-finding algorithm is an iterative algorithm that approximates the root sequentially, finding a new root using the previous one (the first one needs an initial guess from the user), until the function comes close to zero within a certain prespecified tolerance. The efficiency of an algorithm depends on the function itself (continuity, smoothness aka differentiability, and the number of roots), initial guesses, the number of iterations, and a bit of luck. In practice, it may be a good idea to try a few algorithms on the same problem, compare their results, and adopt the best solution.

The source code in this chapter can be run on the S2 platform here:

```
https://s21.nm.dev/hub/user-redirect/lab/tree/s2-public/Numerical%20Methods%20Using%20
Kotlin/chapter3.ipynb
```

The source code can be found on GitHub:

```
https://github.com/apress/numerical-methods-kotlin
```

3.1. An Equation of One Variable

The first step to finding roots is to construct the equation to be solved. An equation can be represented by a polynomial or (generic) function. See Figure 3-1.

H. Li, PhD, *Numerical Methods Using Kotlin*, https://doi.org/10.1007/978-1-4842-8826-9_3

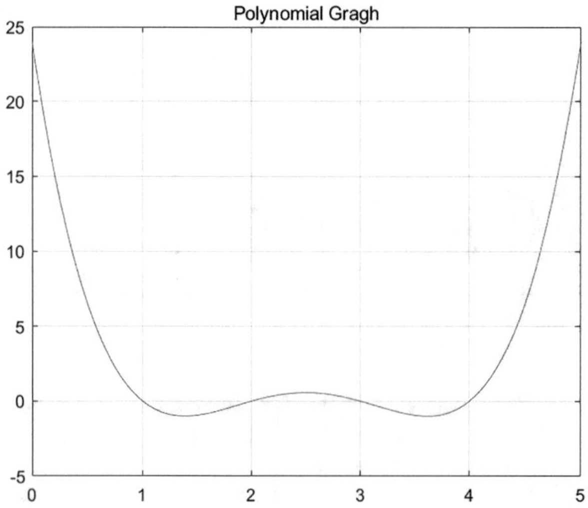

Figure 3-1. $x^4 - 10x^3 + 35x^2 - 50x + 24 = 0$

In NM Dev, a polynomial is represented by the `Polynomial` class. For example, to represent the polynomial $p(x) = x^4 - 10x^3 + 35x^2 - 50x + 24$, you construct a `Polynomial` instance, supplying the constructor with the coefficients starting from the highest-order term.

```
val p: Polynomial = Polynomial(1.0, -10.0, 35.0, -50.0, 24.0)
println("p(1) = " + p.evaluate(1.0))
```

The output is as follows:

```
p(1) = 0.0
```

In NM Dev, a function is represented by the `UnivariateRealFunction` interface. Typically, you use the `AbstractUnivariateRealFunction` class to simplify implementation. For example, to represent the $f(x) = x \sin x - 3$ function, you construct an instance of `AbstractUnivariateRealFunction`.

```
val f: UnivariateRealFunction = object : AbstractUnivariateRealFunction() {
    override fun evaluate(x: Double): Double {
        return Math.sin(x) * x - 3
    }
}
println("f(1) = " + f.evaluate(1.0))
```

The output is as follows:

```
f(1) = -2.1585290151921033
```

See Figure 3-2.

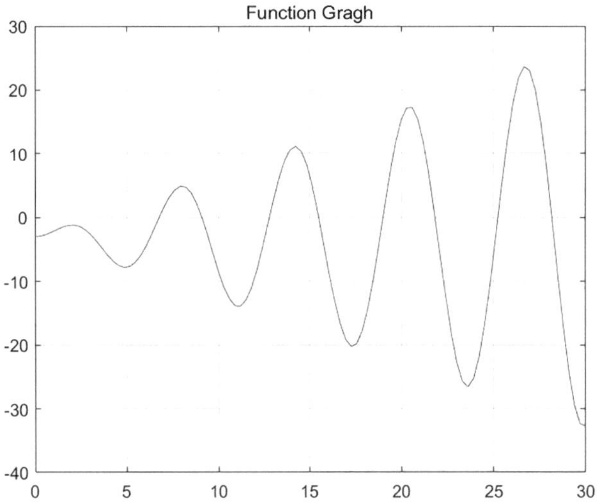

Figure 3-2. *x sin x – 3 = 0*

A function that implements `UnivariateRealFunction` works with almost all classes, functions, and utilities in NM Dev. It is the most basic building block in the NM numerical library.

3.2. Jenkins-Traub Algorithm

The Jenkins-Traub algorithm for polynomial zeros is a fast, globally convergent iterative method published by Michael A. Jenkins and Joseph F. Traub (1970). The algorithm finds the roots one at a time. After a root, r, is found, it divides the polynomial by the linear factor of r, $(x - r)$. The deflated polynomial has exactly one degree less. You repeat this process n times, where n is the degree of the polynomial. By the fundamental theorem of algebra, it guarantees that all n roots are found and each root is computed only once.

`PolyRoot` is our implementation of the Jenkins-Traub algorithm. Because our current implementation of the `Polynomial` class supports only real coefficients, it works only for polynomials with real coefficients but can solve for both real and complex roots.

For example, the roots for the polynomial in Figure 3-1 are 1, 2, 3, and 4 (as evident in the graph). To find all zeros for it, you code the following:

```
val p: Polynomial = Polynomial(1.0, -10.0, 35.0, -50.0, 24.0)
val solver = PolyRoot()
val roots: List<Number?> = solver.solve(p)
println(Arrays.toString(roots.toTypedArray()))
```

The output is as follows:

```
[3.000000-0.000000i, 4.000000+0.000000i, 1.000000-0.000000i, 2.000000+0.000000i]
```

This example solves for a polynomial with complex roots, $p(x) = x^2 + 1$. The roots are i and $-i$.

```
val p: Polynomial = Polynomial(1.0, 0.0, 1.0) // x^2 + 1 = 0
val solver = PolyRoot()

val roots0: List<Number?> = solver.solve(p)
println(Arrays.toString(roots0.toTypedArray()))

val roots1: List<Complex> = PolyRoot.getComplexRoots(roots0)
println(Arrays.toString(roots1.toTypedArray()))
```

The output is as follows:

```
[0.000000+1.000000i, 0.000000-1.000000i]
[0.000000+1.000000i, 0.000000-1.000000i]
```

3.3. The Bisection Method

The simplest root-finding algorithm is the bisection method. Let f be a continuous function, for which you know an interval $[a, b]$ contains a root. That is, $f = 0$ somewhere between a and b. Consequently, you know that $f(a)$ and $f(b)$ have opposite signs and hence a bracket. Let c be the midpoint of the interval, i.e., $c = \frac{(a+b)}{2}$. Then either $f(a)$ and $f(c)$ or $f(c)$ and $f(b)$ have opposite signs. The root will be in one of those two subintervals. Although the bisection method is robust, it gains only one bit of accuracy with each iteration. Other methods, under appropriate conditions, can be much more efficient.

Specifically, for the equation $f(x) = 0$, you need to give an interval $[a, b]$ such that $f(a)$ and $f(b)$ have opposite signs. The root in the interval can be found by the following algorithm:

1. Select values for the upper and lower bounds, $l = a$, $u = b$.
2. Calculate the midpoint $p = \frac{l+u}{2}$.
3. If $f(p) = 0$, then the root is found, $x = p$. Stop.
4. Else $f(p) \neq 0$.
   a. If $f(p) \times f(l) > 0$, $l = p$, $u = u$.
   b. If $f(p) \times f(u) > 0$, $l = l$, $u = p$.
5. Repeat Steps 2 to 4 until a prespecified tolerance is satisfied or the maximum number of iterations is reached.

The `BisectionRoot` class is our implementation of the bisection method. There are two steps to using the class. First, you need to construct a `BisectionRoot` solver, which you can use to specify its properties: the precision tolerance (or the convergence threshold) and the maximum number of iterations. The solver properties are not related to the problem it solves. The solver instance can be reused to solve many problem instances.

After you have an instance of `BisectionRoot`, you call the `solve` method to solve for a particular equation. You also need to supply an upper bound, a lower bound, and optionally an initial guess of the root. The signatures of the functions are as follows:

```
    /**
     * Construct an instance with the tolerance for convergence and the maximum
     * number of iterations.
     *
     * @param tol           the tolerance
     * @param maxIterations the maximum number of iterations
     */
public BisectionRoot(double tol, int maxIterations);
    /**
     * Search for a root, <i>x</i>, in the interval <i>[lower, upper]</i> such
     * that <i>f(x) = 0</i>.
     *
     * @param f     a univariate function
     * @param lower the lower bound of the bracketing interval
     * @param upper the upper bound of the bracketing interval
     * @param guess an initial guess of the root within <i>[lower, upper]</i>.
     *              Note that {@code guess} is a {@code double[]}.
     *              This signature allows multiple initial guesses for certain types of
     *              uniroot algorithms, e.g., Brent's algorithm.
     * @return an approximate root
     * @throws NoRootFoundException when the search fails to find a root
     */
    public double solve(
            UnivariateRealFunction f,
            double lower,
            double upper,
            double... guess
    ) throws NoRootFoundException;
```

The following code shows how to solve the function in Figure 3-2, $x \sin x - 3 = 0$, using BisectionRoot:

```
val f: UnivariateRealFunction = object: AbstractUnivariateRealFunction() {
    override fun evaluate(x: Double): Double {
        return x * Math.sin(x) - 3 // x * six(x) - 3 = 0
    }
}

val solver = BisectionRoot(1e-8, 30)
val root: Double = solver.solve(f, 12.0, 14.0)
val fx: Double = f.evaluate(root)

println(String.format("f(%f) = %f", root, fx))
```

The output is as follows:

```
f(12.802892) = -0.000000
```

You can see the bisection method in action if you print out the bracket and the approximated root in each iteration. Start with an initial bracket [12, 14] with the root somewhere in the interval, as shown in Figure 3-3.

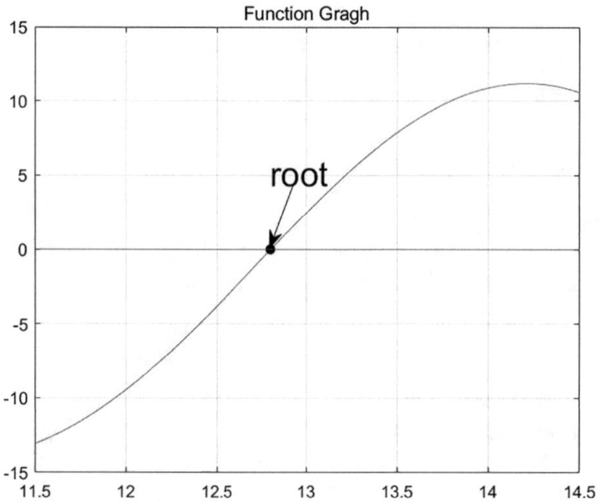

Figure 3-3. *Location of the root in [12,14]*

The midpoint is 13. You know that the root is in the left subinterval. You can therefore update the next interval to [12, 13], as shown in Figure 3-4.

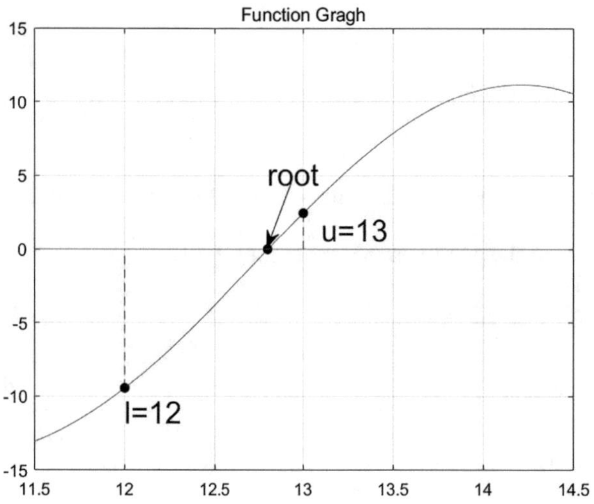

Figure 3-4. *Location of the root in [12,13]*

The midpoint is 12.5. You know that the root is in the right subinterval. You can therefore update the next interval to [12.5, 13], as shown in Figure 3-5.

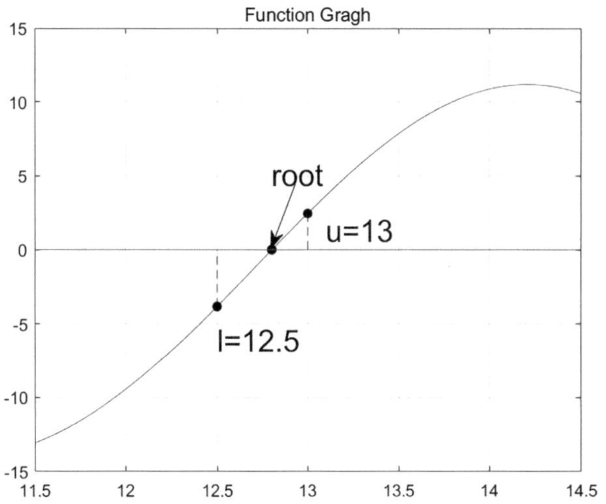

Figure 3-5. *Location of the root in [12.5,13]*

The midpoint is 12.75. You know that the root is in the right subinterval. You can therefore update the next interval to [12.75, 13], as shown in Figure 3-6.

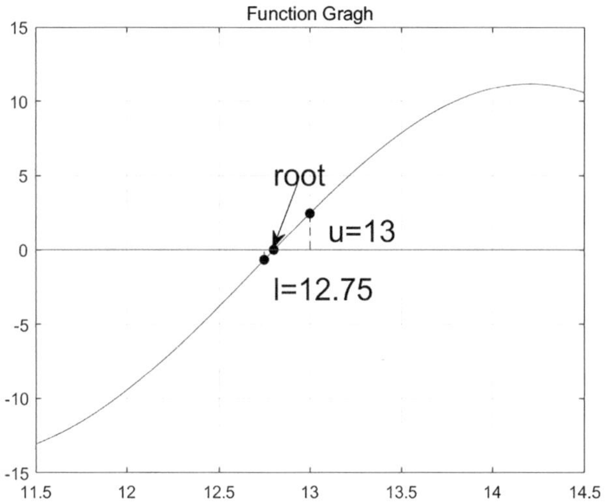

Figure 3-6. *Location of the root in [12.75,13]*

The first ten iterations are as follows:

Iterations	l	u	p
1	12	14	13
2	12	13	12.5
3	12.5	13	12.75
4	12.75	13	12.875
5	12.75	12.875	12.8125
6	12.75	12.8125	12.78125
7	12.78125	12.8125	12.796875
8	12.79688	12.8125	12.8046875
9	12.79688	12.80469	12.80078125
10	12.80078	12.80469	12.802734375

After ten times iterations, the approximated root is 12.802734375. It is worth mentioning that it takes about 30 iterations to reach a precision of eight decimal points, 12.802892. The bisection method repeatedly bisects an interval and then selects a subinterval in which a root must lie for further searching. It is a simple and robust method, but it is also relatively slow compared to other more efficient methods, such as the Newton-Raphson method. The absolute error is halved at each step, so the method converges linearly.

3.4. Brent's Method

Brent's method is a root-finding method that combines the bisection method, the secant method, and the inverse quadratic interpolation method. It uses the secant method or inverse quadratic interpolation whenever possible because they converge faster, but it falls back to the more robust bisection method if necessary. Therefore, it has the reliability of bisection, but it can be as quick as some of the less reliable methods.

3.4.1. Linear Interpolation Method, False Position Method, Secant Method

Linear interpolation uses a straight line connecting two known quantities to determine the value of an unknown quantity in between the two known quantities. The linear interpolation method to find roots is similar to the bisection method. Instead of bisecting the interval, it is an iterative method to find the roots of equations by approximating the curve with secant. A *secant* of a curve is a line that intersects the curve at a minimum of two distinct points. The intuition is as follows: Instead of solving for zero for the function (which can be complicated), you can solve for zero for the approximating straight line (which is easy). You then hope that the zero for the straight line is close to that of the function.

As illustrated in Figure 3-7, you approximate the segment of the curve using a line. The two endpoints are $(u, f(u))$ and $(l, f(l))$. Then you solve for zero for the secant by calculating its intersection with the horizontal axis $(p, f(p))$.

$$p = u - f(u)\frac{(l-u)}{f(l)-f(u)}$$

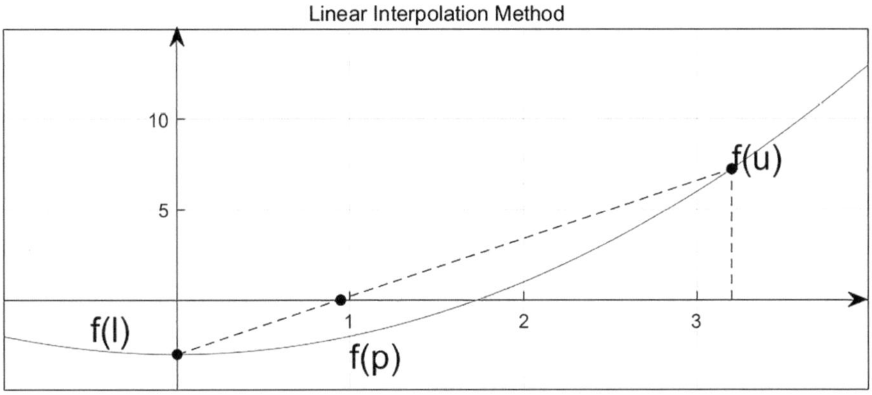

Figure 3-7. *A secant for* $f(x) = x^2 - 3$

The idea is that p should be close to the root of the function. Similar to the bisection method, you choose the bracketing subinterval depending on $f(p)$.

1. If $f(p) = 0$, the root is p.
2. If $f(p) \times f(l) > 0$, $l = p$, $u = u$.
3. If $f(p) \times f(u) > 0$, $l = l$, $u = p$.

You repeat this procedure until the precision threshold is satisfied or the maximum number of iterations is reached. See Figures 3-8 and 3-9.

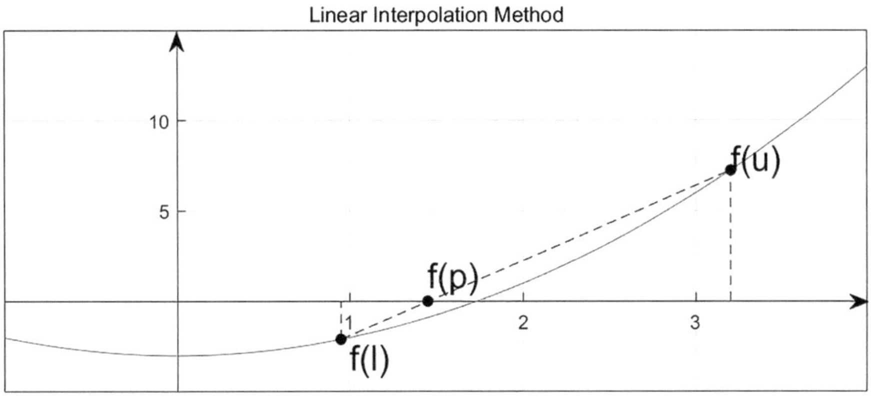

Figure 3-8. *The second iteration after setting* $l = p$

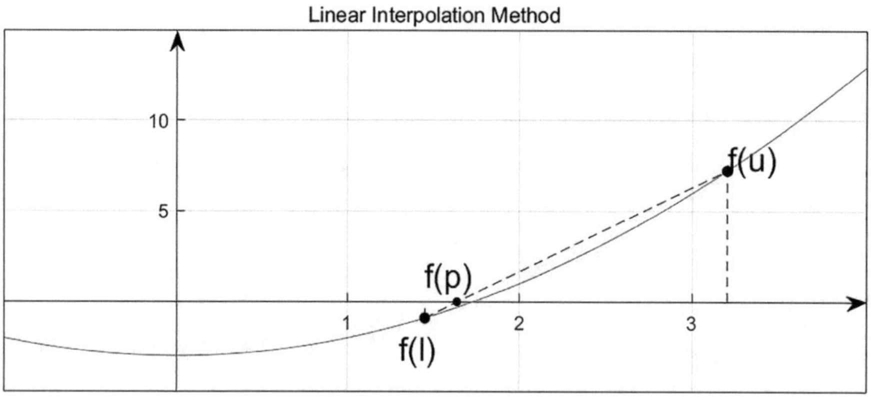

Figure 3-9. *The third iteration after setting l = p*

3.4.2. Inverse Quadratic Interpolation

The inverse quadratic interpolation method is an enhanced version of the secant method. Instead of using a line to approximate the curve, it uses a quadratic function to do so. Then, again, it solves for the root of that quadratic function easily with a closed-form solution to approximate the root of the function. When the quadratic function does not intersect the x-axis (no root), a small change is made.

It takes three points to determine a quadratic function, y: $(x_{i-2}, f(x_{i-2}))$ $(x_{i-1}, f(x_{i-1}))$ $(x_i, f(x_i))$. Then you compute the inverse: $x = y^{-1}(y)$. To solve for an (approximate) root in an iteration, you set it to 0, $y = 0$.

Specifically, the inverse function, also known as the *Lagrange polynomial,* is as follows:

$$x = \frac{\left(y-f(x_{i-1})\right)\left(y-f(x_i)\right)}{\left(f(x_{i-2})-f(x_{i-1})\right)\left(f(x_{i-2})-f(x_i)\right)} \cdot x_{i-2} + \frac{\left(y-f(x_{i-2})\right)\left(y-f(x_{i-1})\right)}{\left(f(x_i)-f(x_{i-2})\right)\left(f(x_i)-f(x_{i-1})\right)} \cdot x_i$$

$$+ \frac{\left(y-f(x_{i-2})\right)\left(y-f(x_i)\right)}{\left(f(x_{i-1})-f(x_{i-2})\right)\left(f(x_{i-1})-f(x_i)\right)} \cdot x_{i-1}$$

Setting $y = 0$, you have the root for the next iteration, shown here:

$$x_{i+1} = \frac{f(x_{i-1})f(x_i)}{\left(f(x_{i-2})-f(x_{i-1})\right)\left(f(x_{i-2})-f(x_i)\right)} \cdot x_{i-2} + \frac{f(x_{i-2})f(x_{i-1})}{\left(f(x_i)-f(x_{i-2})\right)\left(f(x_i)-f(x_{i-1})\right)} \cdot x_i$$

$$+ \frac{f(x_{i-2})f(x_i)}{\left(f(x_{i-1})-f(x_{i-2})\right)\left(f(x_{i-1})-f(x_i)\right)} \cdot x_{i-1}$$

You repeat the procedure until the precision threshold is satisfied or the maximum number of iterations is reached. See Figure 3-10.

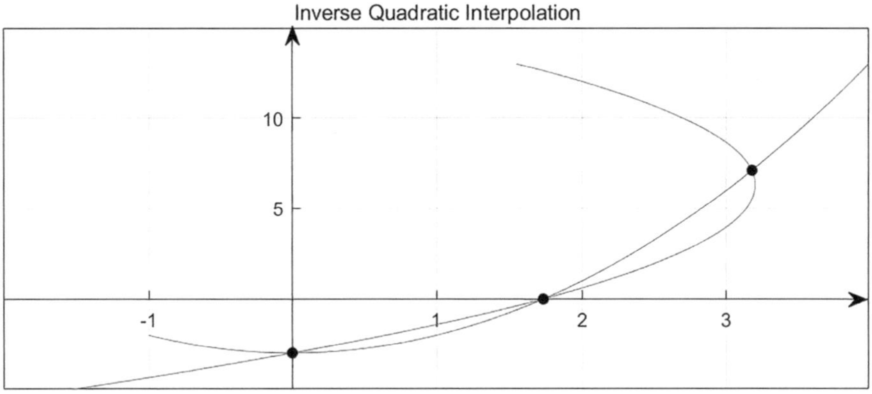

Figure 3-10. *Inverse quadratic interpolation for $f(x) = x^2 - 3$*

The asymptotic behavior is generally very good. The iterates x_i converge fast once the values get close to the actual root. However, performance is often quite poor if the initial values are not close to the root. For example, if two of the function values $f(x_i)$, $f(x_{i-1})$, and $f(x_{i-2})$ are the same, the algorithm fails. Therefore, inverse quadratic interpolation is not used as a stand-alone algorithm. It is used as part of Brent's method.

3.4.3. Brent's Method Implementation

Brent's method is a hybrid method that combines the reliability of the bracketing method and the speed of interpolation methods such as the secant or inverse quadratic interpolation method.

Again, you need to start with a bracketing interval that contains a root (a_0, b_0) such that $f(a_0)f(b_0) < 0$. You assume $|f(a_0)| < |f(b_0)|$; otherwise, switch the labeling.

Each iteration takes four points.

- a_k: Alignment points, that is, satisfy $|f(a_k)| < |f(b_k)|$ and $f(a_k)f(b_k) < 0$.
- b_k: The root estimate in the current iteration.
- b_{k-1}: The root estimate in the last iteration; the first iteration set $b_{k-1} = a_0$.
- b_{k-2}: The root estimate in the second last iteration (it does not need to be initialized).
- s: An intermediate value in this iteration; it is taken as one endpoint of the interval, a_k or b_k, both of which are taken as a_{k+1} and b_{k+1} and satisfy $|f(a_{k+1})| < |f(b_{k+1})|$ and $f(a_{k+1})f(b_{k+1}) < 0$.
- ε: A prespecified precision tolerance for convergence.

There are four inequalities that you check for conditions.

1. $|\varepsilon| < |b_k - b_{k-1}|$
2. $|\varepsilon| < |b_{k-1} - b_{k-2}|$
3. $|s - b_k| < \frac{1}{2}|b_k - b_{k-1}|$
4. $|s - b_k| < \frac{1}{2}|b_{k-1} - b_{k-2}|$

If any of the following five conditions is met, you use the bisection method to find the root in this iteration.

- The last iteration uses the bisection method and inequality 1 is false.
- The last iteration uses the interpolation method and inequality 2 is false.
- The last iteration uses the bisection method and inequality 3 is false.
- The last iteration uses the interpolation method and inequality 4 is false.
- The temporary value s calculated by interpolation is not in $\left[\frac{3a_k + b_k}{4}, b_k\right]$.

Otherwise, this iteration uses the interpolation method. The process of choosing which interpolation method is as follows: if the three points are different, then you use inverse quadratic interpolation; otherwise, you use linear interpolation.

In NM Dev, the `BrentRoot` class implements Brent's method. It is a two-step procedure: you construct the solver and then call the `solve` function. The signatures of the functions are as follows:

```
/**
 * Construct an instance of Brent's root finding algorithm.
 *
 * @param tol           the convergence tolerance
 * @param maxIterations the maximum number of iterations
 */
 public BrentRoot(double tol, int maxIterations)
/**
 * Search for a root, <i>x</i>, in the interval <i>[lower, upper]</i> such
 * that <i>f(x) = 0</i>.
 *
 * @param f     a univariate function
 * @param lower the lower bound of the bracketing interval
 * @param upper the upper bound of the bracketing interval
 * @param guess an initial guess of the root within <i>[lower, upper]</i>.
 *              Note that {@code guess} is a {@code double[]}.
 *              This signature allows multiple initial guesses for certain types of
 *              uniroot algorithms, e.g., Brent's algorithm.
 * @return an approximate root
 * @throws NoRootFoundException when the search fails to find a root
 */
public double solve(
      UnivariateRealFunction f,
      double lower,
      double upper,
      double... guess
) throws NoRootFoundException;
```

This example calls `BrentRoot` to solve the function in Figure 3-10, $f(x) = x^2 - 3$:

```
val f: UnivariateRealFunction = object : AbstractUnivariateRealFunction() {
    override fun evaluate(x: Double): Double {
        return x * x - 3 // x^2 - 3 = 0
    }
}
```

```
val solver = BrentRoot(1e-8, 10)
val root: Double = solver.solve(f, 0.0, 4.0)
val fx: Double = f.evaluate(root)

println(String.format("f(%f) = %f", root, fx))
```

The output is as follows:

```
f(1.732051) = 0.000000
```

3.5. The Newton-Raphson Method

The Newton-Raphson method is described as follows. You start with an initial guess that is reasonably close to the true root, then the function is approximated by its tangent line (which can be computed using the tools of calculus), and then you compute the x-intercept or the root of this tangent line (which is easily done with elementary algebra). This x-intercept will typically be a better approximation to the function's root than the original guess, and the procedure can be iterated. It has the following properties.

For an equation $f(x) = 0$, you choose x_i as an initial approximation of the root or the iterate from the last iteration. Then you go through the point $(x_i, f(x_i))$ to get the tangent L of the curve.

$$y = f(x_i) + f(x_i)'(x - x_i) \tag{L}$$

You calculate the abscissa of the intersection of L and x-axes.

$$x_{i+1} = x_i - \frac{f(x_i)}{f(x_i)'}$$

x_{i+1} is a better approximation of the root than x_i.

The Newton-Raphson method is an efficient way to solve for zeros for a nonlinear equation by linearizing it. It can be proved that if the function is continuous and the zero is isolated, there is a region around the zero point that, as long as the initial value is in the region, the algorithm is guaranteed to converge. The Newton-Raphson method has the performance of square convergence. Roughly speaking, this means that for each iteration, the effective precision of the result will be doubled.

In NM Dev, the `NewtonRoot` class implements the Newton-Raphson root-finding algorithm, together with a `solve` function. The signatures are as follows:

```
/**
 * Constructs an instance of Newton's root finding algorithm.
 *
 * @param tol           the convergence tolerance
 * @param maxIterations the maximum number of iterations
 */
public NewtonRoot(double tol, int maxIterations)
/**
 * Search for a root, <i>x</i>, in the interval <i>[lower, upper]</i> such
 * that <i>f(x) = 0</i>.
 *
```

```
 * @param f     a univariate function
 * @param lower the lower bound of the bracketing interval
 * @param upper the upper bound of the bracketing interval
 * @param guess an initial guess of the root within <i>[lower, upper]</i>.
 *              Note that {@code guess} is a {@code double[]}.
 *              This signature allows multiple initial guesses for certain types of
 *              uniroot algorithms, e.g., Brent's algorithm.
 * @return an approximate root
 * @throws NoRootFoundException when the search fails to find a root
 */
public double solve(
       UnivariateRealFunction f,
       double lower,
       double upper,
       double... guess
) throws NoRootFoundException;
/**
 * Searches for a root, <i>x</i>, in the interval <i>[lower, upper]</i> such
 * that <i>f(x) = 0</i>.
 *
 * @param f     a univariate function
 * @param df_   the first order derivative
 * @param guess an initial guess of the root within <i>[lower, upper]</i>
 * @return an approximate root
 * @throws NoRootFoundException when the search fails to find a root
 */
public double solve(
        UnivariateRealFunction f,
        UnivariateRealFunction df_,
        double guess
) throws NoRootFoundException
```

Note that the second `solve` function allows you to supply the derivative function f' for f. Otherwise, a derivative function computed using finite differencing is automatically generated by the code (though slower).

This example uses the Newton-Raphson method to find the root for $x^2 + 4x - 5 = 0$. First, you choose an initial guess of $x_0 = 5$. The tangent through that point is $y = 14x - 30$. Computing the intersection with x-axes gives a root approximation of x_1. You repeat the procedure until the precision threshold is satisfied or the maximum number of iterations is reached. See Figure 3-11.

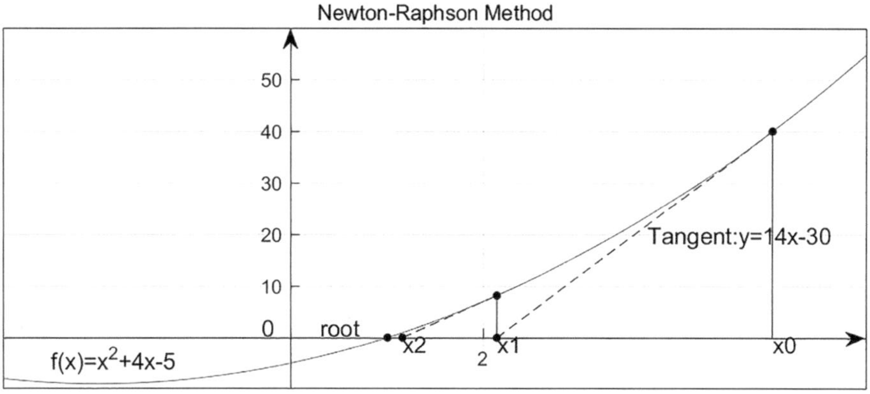

Figure 3-11. *Newton-Raphson method solving for* $f(x) = x^2 + 4x - 5$

```
val f: UnivariateRealFunction = object : AbstractUnivariateRealFunction() {
    override fun evaluate(x: Double): Double {
        return x * x + 4 * x - 5 // x^2 +4x - 5 = 0
    }
}
val df: UnivariateRealFunction = object : AbstractUnivariateRealFunction() {
    override fun evaluate(x: Double): Double {
        return 2 * x + 4 // 2x + 4
    }
}
val solver = NewtonRoot(1e-8, 5)
val root: Double = solver.solve(f, df, 5.0)
val fx: Double = f.evaluate(root)
println(String.format("f(%f) = %f", root, fx))
```

The output is as follows:

```
f(1.000000) = 0.000000
```

You can see from the following iteration results that the algorithm reaches a good result in the fourth iteration and hence is efficient.

Iterations i	x_i	ε
0	5	
1	2.142857143	1.33E+00
2	1.157635468	8.51E-01
3	1.003934739	1.53E-01
4	1.000002577	3.93E-03
5	1.000000000001107	2.58E-06
6	0.9999999999999999	1.11E-12

3.5.1. Halley's Method

Halley's method can be derived in a similar way to the Newton-Raphson method for any C^2 function. That is, it solves for zeros for a univariate function with a continuous second-order derivative. Halley's method converges to a regular zero of a function with an order of convergence that equals or exceeds 3.

In NM Dev, the `HalleyRoot` class implements Halley's method. The signatures are as follows:

```
 /**
  * Construct an instance of Halley's root finding algorithm.
  *
  * @param tol           the convergence tolerance
  * @param maxIterations the maximum number of iterations
  */
public HalleyRoot(double tol, int maxIterations)
/**
  * Search for a root, <i>x</i>, in the interval <i>[lower, upper]</i> such
  * that <i>f(x) = 0</i>.
  *
  * @param f     a univariate function
  * @param lower the lower bound of the bracketing interval
  * @param upper the upper bound of the bracketing interval
  * @param guess an initial guess of the root within <i>[lower, upper]</i>.
  *              Note that {@code guess} is a {@code double[]}.
  *              This signature allows multiple initial guesses for certain types of
  *              uniroot algorithms, e.g., Brent's algorithm.
  * @return an approximate root
  * @throws NoRootFoundException when the search fails to find a root
  */
public double solve(
        UnivariateRealFunction f,
        double lower,
        double upper,
        double... guess
) throws NoRootFoundException;
/**
  * Search for a root, <i>x</i>, in the interval <i>[lower, upper]</i> such
  * that <i>f(x) = 0</i>.
  *
  * @param f     a univariate function
  * @param guess an initial guess of the root within <i>[lower, upper]</i>
  * @return an approximate root
  * @throws NoRootFoundException when the search fails to find a root
  */
public double solve(
        UnivariateRealFunction f,
        double guess
) throws NoRootFoundException
/**
  * Search for a root, <i>x</i>, in the interval <i>[lower, upper]</i> such
  * that <i>f(x) = 0</i>.
  *
```

```
 * @param f     a univariate function
 * @param df    the first order derivative
 * @param d2f   the second order derivative
 * @param guess an initial guess of the root within <i>[lower, upper]</i>
 * @return an approximate root
 * @throws NoRootFoundException when the search fails to find a root
 */
public double solve(
        UnivariateRealFunction f,
        UnivariateRealFunction df,
        UnivariateRealFunction d2f,
        double guess
) throws NoRootFoundException
```

Note that the third solve function takes both the first-order and second-order derivate functions. If they are not supplied, the library generates them using finite differencing.

This example uses HalleyRoot to solve for $f(x) = x^2 + 4x - 5$:

```
val f: UnivariateRealFunction = object : AbstractUnivariateRealFunction() {
    override fun evaluate(x: Double): Double {
        return x * x + 4 * x - 5 // x^2 +4x - 5 = 0
    }
}

val df: UnivariateRealFunction = object : AbstractUnivariateRealFunction() {
    override fun evaluate(x: Double): Double {
        return 2 * x + 4 // 2x + 4
    }
}

val d2f: UnivariateRealFunction = object : AbstractUnivariateRealFunction() {
    override fun evaluate(x: Double): Double {
        return 2.0 // 2
    }
}

val solver = HalleyRoot(1e-8, 3)
val root: Double = solver.solve(f, df, d2f, 5.0)
val fx: Double = f.evaluate(root)

println(String.format("f(%f) = %f", root, fx))
```

The output is as follows. It converges in just three iterations.

```
f(1.000000) = 0.000000
```

CHAPTER 4

Finding Roots of System of Equations

A root-finding algorithm for a system of multivariable equations can find the values of $(x_1, x_2, \ldots, x_n)$ such that the values of the of n equations in the system equal 0.

$$\begin{cases} f_1(x_1, x_2, \ldots, x_n) = 0 \\ f_2(x_1, x_2, \ldots, x_n) = 0 \\ \vdots \\ f_n(x_1, x_2, \ldots, x_n) = 0 \end{cases}$$

There can be no solution, one unique solution, or multiple solutions for the system. Systems of nonlinear equations can be solved numerically by Newton's method, which uses the first-order derivatives or the Jacobian, an extension of the Newton-Raphson method for single variable equation. The idea is also, in each iteration, to add an increment that is proportional to the negative of the inverse of the first-order derivative, but in multivariate terms.

The source code in this chapter can be run on the S2 platform here:

```
https://s21.nm.dev/hub/user-redirect/lab/tree/s2-public/Numerical%20Methods%20Using%20
Kotlin/chapter4.ipynb
```

The source code can be found on GitHub:

```
https://github.com/apress/numerical-methods-kotlin
```

4.1. System of Equations

A multivariable equation is an equation with more than one variable. For example, $f(x_1, x_2, x_3) = 2x_1^2 + x_2^2 - x_3$ is a multivariable equation with variables (x1, x2, x3). In NM Dev, a multivariate function is constructed by implementing the `RealScalarFunction` interface. You need to specify the domain `dimensionOfDomain` in `RealScalarFunction`. To simplify implementation, you can use `AbstractRealScalarFunction`, `AbstractBiRealFunction`, and `AbstractTrivariateRealFunction`. For the latter two, the dimension is configured for you.

H. Li, PhD, *Numerical Methods Using Kotlin*, https://doi.org/10.1007/978-1-4842-8826-9_4

For example, the following implementations all represent the same function $f(x_1, x_2, x_3) = 2x_1^2 + x_2^2 - x_3$, a polynomial of degree 3:

```
val f1: RealScalarFunction = object : AbstractRealScalarFunction(3) {
    override fun evaluate(x: Vector): Double {
        val x1: Double = x.get(1)
        val x2: Double = x.get(2)
        val x3: Double = x.get(3)
        return 2 * x1 * x1 + x2 * x2 - x3
    }
}
println("f1(1,2,3) = " + f1.evaluate(DenseVector(1.0, 2.0, 3.0)))
```

The output is as follows:

```
f1(1,2,3) = 3.0
```

```
val f2: TrivariateRealFunction = object : AbstractTrivariateRealFunction() {
    override fun evaluate(x1: Double, x2: Double, x3: Double): Double {
        return 2 * x1 * x1 + x2 * x2 - x3
    }
}
println("f2(1,2,3) = " + f2.evaluate(DenseVector(1.0, 2.0, 3.0)))
```

The output is as follows:

```
f2(1,2,3) = 3.0
```

A system of n equations in n unknowns $x_1, x_2, \ldots, x_n$ is in the following form:

$$\begin{cases} f_1(x_1, x_2, \ldots, x_n) = 0 \\ f_2(x_1, x_2, \ldots, x_n) = 0 \\ \vdots \\ f_n(x_1, x_2, \ldots, x_n) = 0 \end{cases}$$

where $f(x_1, x_2, \ldots, x_n)$ are functions of $x_1, x_2, \ldots, x_n$. A system of equations can simply be represented as a `RealScalarFunction[]` array. Alternatively, you can implement it as an R^n to R^m vector function, implementing the `RealVectorFunction` interface. The two following implementations F and G are equivalent.

```
val f1: TrivariateRealFunction = object : AbstractTrivariateRealFunction() {
    override fun evaluate(x: Double, y: Double, z: Double): Double {
        return Math.pow(x, 2.0) + Math.pow(y, 3.0) - z - 6
    }
}
```

```
val f2: TrivariateRealFunction = object : AbstractTrivariateRealFunction() {
    override fun evaluate(x: Double, y: Double, z: Double): Double {
        return 2 * x + 9 * y - z - 17
    }
}

val f3: TrivariateRealFunction = object : AbstractTrivariateRealFunction() {
    override fun evaluate(x: Double, y: Double, z: Double): Double {
        return Math.pow(x, 4.0) + 5 * y + 6 * z - 29
    }
}

val x: Vector = DenseVector(1.5, 2.5, 3.5)
val f1_x: Double = f1.evaluate(x)
val f2_x: Double = f2.evaluate(x)
val f3_x: Double = f3.evaluate(x)
val F_x = doubleArrayOf(f1_x, f2_x, f3_x)
println("F(x) = " + Arrays.toString(F_x))
```

The output is as follows:

```
F(x) = [8.375, 5.0, 9.5625]
```

For G, you need to specify the domain, dimensionOfDomain, and the range, dimensionOfRange, which are both 3 in this example.

```
val G: RealVectorFunction = object : AbstractRealVectorFunction(3, 3) {
    override fun evaluate(v: Vector): Vector {
        val x: Double = v.get(1)
        val y: Double = v.get(2)
        val z: Double = v.get(3)

        val g1: Double = Math.pow(x, 2.0) + Math.pow(y, 3.0) - z - 6
        val g2: Double = 2 * x + 9 * y - z - 17
        val g3: Double = Math.pow(x, 4.0) + 5 * y + 6 * z - 29

        val g: Vector = DenseVector(g1, g2, g3)
        return g
    }
}
val Gx: Vector = G.evaluate(x)
println("G(x) = " + Gx)
```

The output is as follows:

```
G(x) = [8.375000, 5.000000, 9.562500]
```

4.2. Finding Roots of Systems of Two Nonlinear Equations

A system of two equations in two unknowns can generally be presented as follows:

$$f_1(x,y)=0$$

$$f_2(x,y)=0$$

You begin by choosing an initial guess (x_1, y_1) near the intersection of f_1 and f_2. Suppose x_2 and y_2 are the actual solution so that f_1 and f_2 equal zero. If x_1 is sufficiently close to x_2 and y_1 to y_2, then $x_2 - x_1$ and $y_2 - y_1$ are small. By Taylor series expansion, you have this:

$$f_1(x_2,y_2)=f_1(x_1,y_1)+\frac{\partial f_1}{\partial x}(x_2-x_1)+\frac{\partial f_1}{\partial y}(y_2-y_1)+\ldots$$

$$f_2(x_2,y_2)=f_2(x_1,y_1)+\frac{\partial f_2}{\partial x}(x_2-x_1)+\frac{\partial f_2}{\partial y}(y_2-y_1)+\ldots$$

where the terms involving higher powers of small quantities $x_2 - x_1$ and $y_2 - y_1$ are neglected. Letting $\Delta x = x_2 - x_1$ and $\Delta y = y_2 - y_1$ and recalling that $f_1(x_2, y_2) = 0$ and $f_2(x_2, y_2) = 0$, you can rewrite the previous equations as follows:

$$\frac{\partial f_1}{\partial x}\Delta x+\frac{\partial f_1}{\partial y}\Delta y+\ldots=-f_1(x_1,y_1)$$

$$\frac{\partial f_2}{\partial x}\Delta x+\frac{\partial f_2}{\partial y}\Delta y+\ldots=-f_2(x_1,y_1)$$

This can be expressed as follows:

$$\begin{bmatrix}\frac{\partial f_1}{\partial x} & \frac{\partial f_1}{\partial y}\\ \frac{\partial f_2}{\partial x} & \frac{\partial f_2}{\partial y}\end{bmatrix}_{(x_1,y_1)}\begin{pmatrix}\Delta x\\ \Delta y\end{pmatrix}=\begin{pmatrix}-f_1\\ -f_2\end{pmatrix}_{(x_1,y_1)}$$

This matrix:

$$J(f_1,f_2)=\begin{bmatrix}\frac{\partial f_1}{\partial x} & \frac{\partial f_1}{\partial y}\\ \frac{\partial f_2}{\partial x} & \frac{\partial f_2}{\partial y}\end{bmatrix}$$

is called the Jacobian matrix of f_1 and f_2.

This is a linear system and can be solved for Δx and Δy as long as the coefficient matrix is non-singular. Therefore, you must have the following:

$$\det\left\{\left[J(f_1,f_2)\right]_{(x_1,y_1)}\right\}\neq 0$$

Since the Jacobian matrix and $\begin{pmatrix} -f_1 \\ -f_2 \end{pmatrix}$ are known, you can solve for Δx and Δy and $x_2 = x_1 + \Delta x$ and $y_2 = y_1 + \Delta y$. (x_2, y_2) will be closer to the actual solution than (x_1, y_1) is. You use (x_2, y_2) as the new estimate to the solution. You then repeat the procedure until the precision threshold is satisfied or the maximum number of iterations is reached. Note that in each iteration step, the Jacobian matrix must be non-singular.

A reasonable terminating condition is as follows:

$$\left\| \begin{pmatrix} \Delta x \\ \Delta y \end{pmatrix} \right\| \le \varepsilon$$

$$\varepsilon(x) = \left| \frac{x_2 - x_1}{x_2} \right|$$

$$\varepsilon(y) = \left| \frac{y_2 - y_1}{y_2} \right|$$

where ε is the tolerance, $\varepsilon(x)$ is for x, and $\varepsilon(y)$, is for y.

In NM Dev, the `NewtonSystemRoot` class implements Newton's method to solve for a system of equations. If no solution is found, it throws a `NoRootFoundException` exception. The signatures are as follows:

```
/**
 * Constructs an instance of Newton's root finding algorithm for a system of
 * non-linear equations.
 *
 * @param accuracy the convergence tolerance
 * @param maxIter  the maximum number of iterations
 */
public NewtonSystemRoot(double accuracy, int maxIter) {
    this.tol = accuracy;
    this.maxIterations = maxIter;
}
/**
 * Searches for a root, <i>x</i> such that <i>f(x) = 0</i>.
 *
 * @param f     a multivariate function
 * @param guess an initial guess of the root
 * @return an approximate root
 * @throws NoRootFoundException when the search fails to find a root
 */
public Vector solve(
        RealVectorFunction f,
        Vector guess
) throws NoRootFoundException
/**
 * Searches for a root, <i>x</i> such that <i>f(x) = 0</i>.
 *
 * @param f     a system of equations
```

```
 * @param guess an initial guess of the root
 * @return an approximate root
 * @throws NoRootFoundException when the search fails to find a root
 */
public Vector solve(
        final RealScalarFunction[] f,
        Vector guess
) throws NoRootFoundException
```

See Figure 4-1.

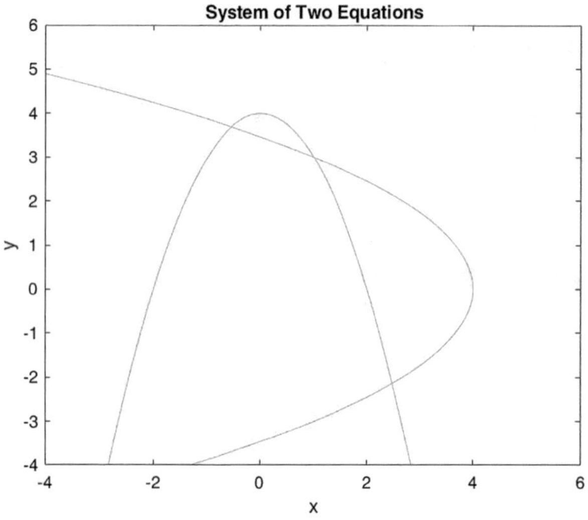

Figure 4-1. *A system of two equations and unknowns*

This example solves the root (x, y) for the following:

$$\begin{cases} 3x + y^2 = 12 \\ x^2 + y = 4 \end{cases}$$

Or equivalently, for this:

$$\begin{cases} 3x + y^2 - 12 = 0 \\ x^2 + y - 4 = 0 \end{cases}$$

By looking at the plot in Figure 4-1, you can set the initial guess (x_1, y_1) to $(0, 0)$. You can also set the accuracy to 1×10^{-8} and the maximum number of iterations to 10 (i.e., stop the loop after it runs ten times).

```
val f1: BivariateRealFunction = object : AbstractBivariateRealFunction() {
    override fun evaluate(x: Double, y: Double): Double {
        return 3 * x + y * y - 12
    }
}
```

```
val f2: BivariateRealFunction = object : AbstractBivariateRealFunction() {
    override fun evaluate(x: Double, y: Double): Double {
        return x * x + y - 4
    }
}

val solver: NewtonSystemRoot = NewtonSystemRoot(1e-8, 10)
val initial: Vector = DenseVector(arrayOf(0.0, 0.0)) // (0, 0)
val root: Vector = solver.solve(arrayOf(f1, f2), initial)

println(String.format("f(%s) = (%f, %f)", root.toString(), f1.evaluate(root),
f2.evaluate(root)))
```

Then use the solve method to find the root for the system. The root is as follows:

$$\begin{cases} x = 1 \\ y = 3 \end{cases}$$

The output is as follows:

```
f([1.000000, 3.000000] ) = (0.000000, 0.000000)
```

4.3. Finding Roots of Systems of Three or More Equations

You can extend the same math for systems of two equations to solve for systems of n equations. A system of n equations in n unknowns can in general be written as follows:

$$f_1(x_1, x_2, \ldots, x_n) = 0$$

$$f_2(x_1, x_2, \ldots, x_n) = 0$$

$$\ldots$$

$$f_n(x_1, x_2, \ldots, x_n) = 0$$

Let the initial guess be $(x_{11}, x_{21}, \ldots, x_{n1})$.

$$\begin{bmatrix} \frac{\partial f_1}{\partial x_1} & \cdots & \frac{\partial f_1}{\partial x_n} \\ \vdots & \ddots & \vdots \\ \frac{\partial f_n}{\partial x_1} & \cdots & \frac{\partial f_n}{\partial x_n} \end{bmatrix}_{(x_{11}, x_{21}, \ldots, x_{n1})} \begin{pmatrix} \Delta x_1 \\ \vdots \\ \Delta x_n \end{pmatrix} = \begin{pmatrix} -f_1 \\ \vdots \\ -f_n \end{pmatrix}_{(x_{11}, x_{21}, \ldots, x_{n1})}$$

The matrix is the Jacobian $J(f_1, f_2, \ldots, f_n)$, as shown here:

$$J(f_1, f_2, \ldots, f_n) = \begin{bmatrix} \frac{\partial f_1}{\partial x_1} & \cdots & \frac{\partial f_1}{\partial x_n} \\ \vdots & \ddots & \vdots \\ \frac{\partial f_n}{\partial x_1} & \cdots & \frac{\partial f_n}{\partial x_n} \end{bmatrix}$$

Solving for $\begin{pmatrix} \Delta x_1 \\ \vdots \\ \Delta x_n \end{pmatrix}$, you can get the next estimate by adding the increment, as shown here:

$$\begin{pmatrix} x_{12} \\ \vdots \\ x_{n2} \end{pmatrix} = \begin{pmatrix} x_{11} \\ \vdots \\ x_{n1} \end{pmatrix} + \begin{pmatrix} \Delta x_1 \\ \vdots \\ \Delta x_n \end{pmatrix}$$

The procedure for Newton's method is summarized as follows:

1. Choose an initial guess for the root of the system of n equations and n unknowns.
2. Evaluate the Jacobian at the current best solution $\boldsymbol{X}_1$, where $\boldsymbol{X}_1$ is a n-dimensional vector and $\boldsymbol{X}_1 = \begin{pmatrix} x_1 \\ \vdots \\ x_n \end{pmatrix}$.
3. Solve the linear system $J(\boldsymbol{X}_1)\Delta\boldsymbol{X} = -f(\boldsymbol{X}_1)$, where $\Delta\boldsymbol{X} = \boldsymbol{X}_2 - \boldsymbol{X}_1$.
4. Obtain $\boldsymbol{X}_2$ by adding the increment, $\boldsymbol{X}_2 = \boldsymbol{X}_1 + \Delta\boldsymbol{X}$.
5. Repeat until the precision threshold is satisfied or the maximum number of iterations is reached.
6. Return the best solution.

The following code solves for this system of three nonlinear equations (see Figure 4-2):

$$\begin{cases} x^2 + y^3 - z = 6 \\ 2x + 9y - z = 17 \\ x^4 + 5y + 6z = 29 \end{cases}$$

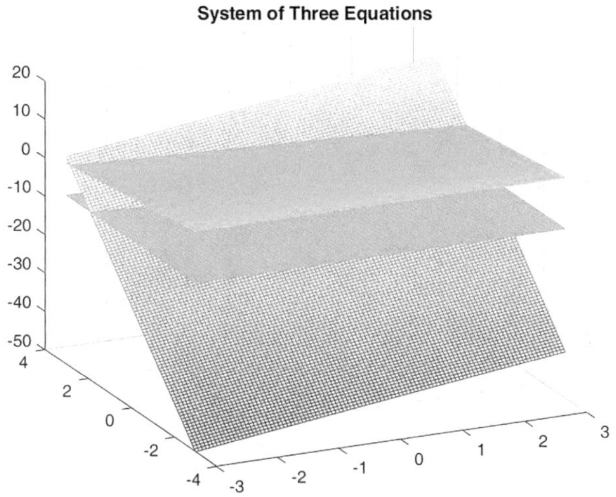

Figure 4-2. *A system of three equations and unknowns*

```
val G: RealVectorFunction = object : AbstractRealVectorFunction(3, 3) {
    override fun evaluate(v: Vector): Vector {
        val x: Double = v.get(1)
        val y: Double = v.get(2)
        val z: Double = v.get(3)

        val g1: Double = Math.pow(x, 2.0) + Math.pow(y, 3.0) - z - 6
        val g2: Double = 2 * x + 9 * y - z - 17
        val g3: Double = Math.pow(x, 4.0) + 5 * y + 6 * z - 29

        val g: Vector = DenseVector(g1, g2, g3)
        return g
    }
}

val solver: NewtonSystemRoot = NewtonSystemRoot(1e-8, 15)
val initial: Vector = DenseVector(arrayOf(0.0, 0.0, 0.0)) // (0, 0, 0)
val root: Vector = solver.solve(G, initial)

println(String.format("f(%s) = %s", root.toString(), G.evaluate(root).toString()))
```

The output is as follows:

```
f([-4.580190, -4.307120, -64.924460] ) = [0.000000, -0.000000, 0.000000]
```

CHAPTER 5

Curve Fitting and Interpolation

The data that we usually observe consists of samples from a (often unobservable) population that we usually don't have all the values for inputs. More often than not, we want to acquire values that are not directly observable or available in the samples. Techniques such as curve fitting and interpolation can help make educated guesses of the missing values to draw a line, i.e., a function, going through the data points. Values in between given data points can be estimated by evaluating the function at any inputs. See Figure 5-1.

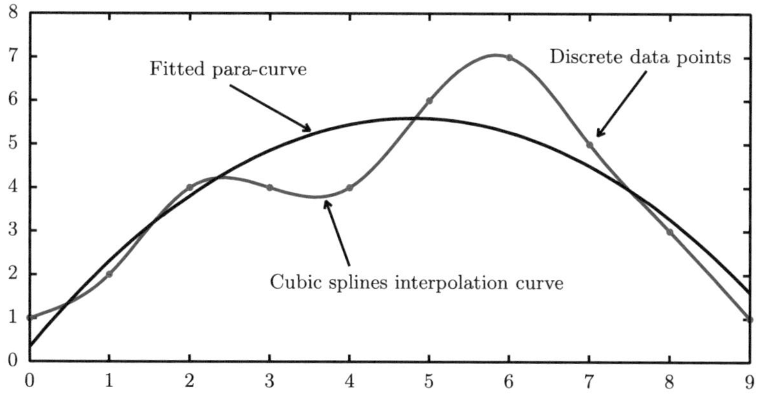

***Figure 5-1.** Curve fitting and interpolation*

The main distinction between curve fitting and interpolation is whether the fitted curve passes through all the observed data points. In the case of curve fitting, the strategy is to derive a curve that represents the general trend of the data. The fitted curve passes through the data set but does not fit precisely to every data point. The curve is intended to have the best fit to describe the data as a whole. Since it does not pass through all the points, it is normally used when the data has substantial inherent errors, such as data gathered from experimental measurements, where passing through every point precisely would otherwise inevitably capture all the undesirable noise as well. An example is linear regression, which is widely used in statistical analysis, where the data collected may contain significant errors, including systematical errors and sample errors. Curve fitting can be used to aid data visualization to perform forecasts based on the sample data and to make inference about the relationship among two or more variables.

H. Li, PhD, *Numerical Methods Using Kotlin*, https://doi.org/10.1007/978-1-4842-8826-9_5

In contrast, interpolation is used to fit a curve or a series of curves that pass precisely through all the points. It is used when the data is known to be accurate, i.e., there is no noise. An example is fitting a zero-coupon curve to discount rate data of different maturities. We often interpolate the unknown discount rates for maturities that are not directly observable in the market. We interpolate or evaluate for an unknown input between two known inputs by evaluating the fitted function. Another important use case is when we want to represent a complicated function with a relatively simpler one, often a polynomial, to avoid a huge computational cost, for example. You may use interpolation to fit a curve of a simpler function through the data points generated from the original, more complicated function.

The source code in this chapter can be run on the S2 platform here:

```
https://s21.nm.dev/hub/user-redirect/lab/tree/s2-public/Numerical%20Methods%20Using%20
Kotlin/chapter5.ipynb
```

The source code can be found on GitHub:

```
https://github.com/apress/numerical-methods-kotlin
```

5.1. Least Squares Curve Fitting

There are many ways to do curve fitting. The most basic and commonly used one is least squares. Suppose you have a set of data points like this:

$$(x_1, y_1), (x_2, y_2), \ldots, (x_n, y_n)$$

The first step in curve fitting is to choose a promising or intended function in the form $f(x)$, essentially a parameterized function, to fit the data points. NM Dev implements the most widely used form, i.e., the polynomial function form, as shown here:

$$f(x) = a_0 + a_1 x + a_2 x^2 + \ldots + a_n x^n$$

The coefficients a_0, a_1, a_2, ..., a_n in the formula are to be determined. Essentially what you do in curve fitting is find a set of these coefficients such that the function best fits the given data. There are also many possible criteria to determine what "best" means. The least squares method minimizes the root-mean-square error.

$$E(f) = \sqrt{\frac{1}{n} \sum_{i=1}^{n} \varepsilon_i^2}$$

ε_i is the error at the i-th point, that is, the distance between the data value y_i and the fitted value $\hat{y}_i = f(x_i)$ on the curve. See Figure 5-2.

$$\varepsilon_i = y_i - f(x_i)$$

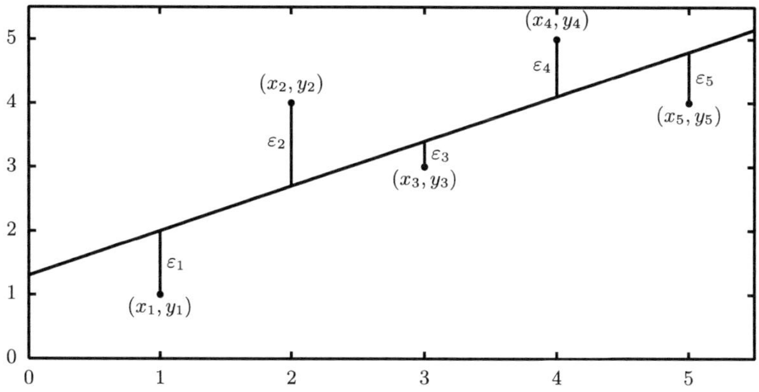

Figure 5-2. *Curve-fitting errors*

The least squares method finds the set of coefficients $\hat{a}_0, \hat{a}_1, \ldots, \hat{a}_n$ that minimizes the root-mean-square error. As a result, the fitted curve will be as follows:

$$f(x) = \hat{a}_0 + \hat{a}_1 x + \hat{a}_2 x^2 + \ldots + \hat{a}_n x^n$$

For example, say you want to fit a curve given the following set of data:

x	y
0	0.0
1	1.0
2	1.414
3	1.732
4	2.0
5	2.236

First, you need to decide the function form that you will use to fit the data. The first step in data analysis (and probably solving any problem) is to draw a picture. Plotting the data points in a picture gives you an intuitive view of the relationship between *x* and *y*. See Figure 5-3.

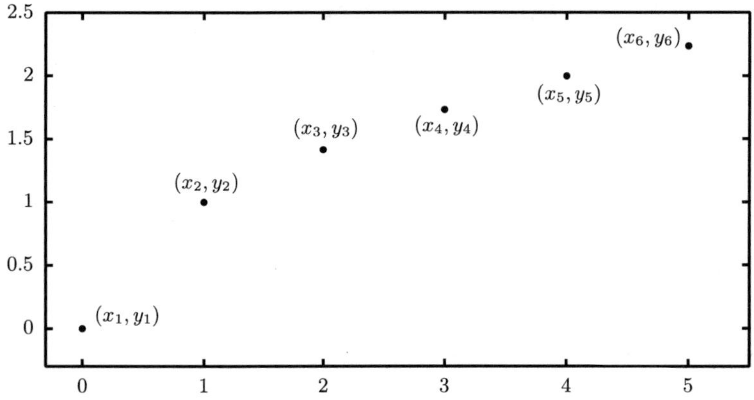

Figure 5-3. *Visualization of data points*

From Figure 5-3, you can see that the data obviously exhibits a nonlinear relationship. You may therefore use a polynomial with degree bigger than 1, say 2. It is worth pointing out that the choice of order is important. Generally speaking, you want to fit a function that is as simple as possible to avoid picking up noise from the data. In other words, you want to avoid overfitting.

Overfitting is a modeling error that occurs when a function is too closely fit to a set of data points. A data set typically has noise due to errors (recording, measuring, etc.) or randomness. Attempting to make the curve conform too closely to the data can infect the curve model with substantial error because of "fitting to the noise." Consequently, it reduces the predictive power.

Consider the comparison in Figure 5-4. A fifth-degree polynomial $f_1(x)$ and a linear polynomial $f_2(x)$ are fitted to the same set of data. Since there are six data points, the fifth-degree polynomial $f_1(x)$ can pass exactly through all the points. (In general, for n data points, an $(n - 1)$ degree polynomial can perfectly fit all the data points.) Therefore, $f_1(x)$ perfectly fits the data. However, is this perfect curve better than the simpler curve $f_2(x)$? The answer is no. Apparently, $f_2(x)$ makes a better representation of the positive relationship between x and y. That is, when x increases, y increases too. Moreover, when x goes below 0 or above 5, the fifth-degree polynomial $f_1(x)$ completely loses its prediction power. The two tails are artificial due only to the artifact of the functional form chosen rather than anything related to the data. See Figure 5-4.

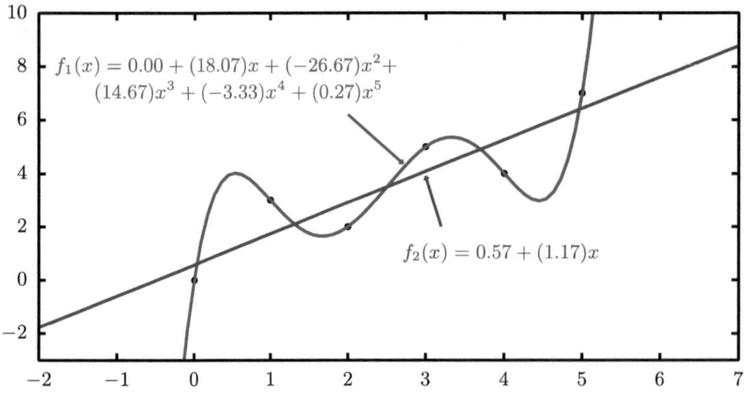

Figure 5-4. *Linear vs. high-order polynomials in curve fitting*

Now let's return to the example. The data points show a convex relationship. You can use a para-curve to fit it, as shown in Figure 5-5. The fitted curve is $f(x) = 0.1 + 0.81x - 0.08x^2$.

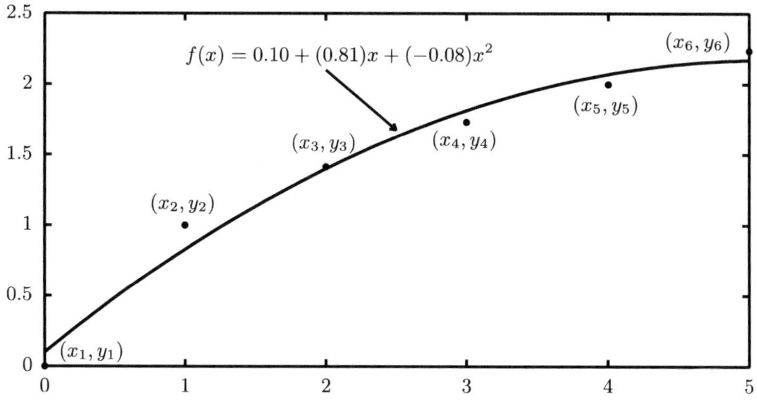

***Figure 5-5.** Parabolic curve fitting*

The fitted values $\hat{y} = f(x)$ and errors ε are shown here:

x	y	f (x)	ε
0	0.0	0.1	-0.1
1	1.0	0.83	0.17
2	1.414	1.4	0.014
3	1.732	1.81	-0.078
4	2.0	2.07	-0.07
5	2.236	2.17	0.066

The NM Dev code is as follows. You first construct a `LeastSquares` object, passing the intended order m of the polynomial function as a parameter. In this case, $m = 2$. Then you call the object's `fit` method on a set of data points to get a `UnivariateRealFunction` object that represents the fitted function curve. The function can be used to evaluate at any input.

```
// the data set
val data = SortedOrderedPairs(
        doubleArrayOf(0.0, 1.0, 2.0, 3.0, 4.0, 5.0),
        doubleArrayOf(0.0, 1.0, 1.414, 1.732, 2.0, 2.236)
)

val ls: LeastSquares = LeastSquares(2)
val f: UnivariateRealFunction = ls.fit(data)
println(String.format("f(%.0f)=%f", 0.0, f.evaluate(0.0))) // f(0) = 0.09
println(String.format("f(%.0f)=%f", 1.0, f.evaluate(1.0))) // f(1) = 0.82
println(String.format("f(%.0f)=%f", 2.0, f.evaluate(2.0))) // f(2) = 1.39
println(String.format("f(%.0f)=%f", 3.0, f.evaluate(3.0))) // f(3) = 1.81
println(String.format("f(%.0f)=%f", 4.0, f.evaluate(4.0))) // f(4) = 2.07
println(String.format("f(%.0f)=%f", 5.0, f.evaluate(5.0))) // f(5) = 2.17
```

The output is as follows:

```
f(0)=0.099286
f(1)=0.828086
f(2)=1.399600
f(3)=1.813829
f(4)=2.070771
f(5)=2.170429
```

The signatures of the constructor and the `fit` method are as follows. Note that the library allows you to give weight to each data point. If weighting is not specified, all data points are given the same weight.

```
/**
 * Construct a new instance of the algorithm 4.5.1 from Schilling & Harris,
 * which will use a weighted sum of orthogonal polynomials up to order
 * <i>n</i> (the number of points).
 *
 * @param m         the maximum degree of the orthogonal polynomials (<i>m
 *                  &le; n</i>)
 * @param weighting the function used to determine the weight for each
 *                  observation
 */
public LeastSquares(int m, Weighting weighting)
// algorithm 4.5.1 from Schilling & Harris
@Override
public UnivariateRealFunction fit(OrderedPairs f)
```

5.2. Interpolation

Interpolation is a method of constructing (finding) new data points based on the range of a discrete set of known data points. In engineering and science, we often have a number of data points, obtained by sampling or experimentation, which represent the values of a function for a limited number of values of the independent variable. It is often necessary to interpolate, that is, estimate the value of that function for an unknown intermediate value of the independent variable.

Another important application is the approximation of a complicated function by a simple function. Suppose the formula for some given function is known but is too complicated to evaluate efficiently. A few data points from the original function can be interpolated to produce a simpler function that is still fairly close to the original. The resulting gain in simplicity may outweigh the loss from interpolation error and give better performance in the computation process.

5.2.1. Linear Interpolation

One of the simplest methods is linear interpolation. The interpolation function is a piecewise function that is linear between every two adjacent data points. Given a set of data points $(x_1, y_1), (x_2, y_2), \ldots, (x_n, y_n)$, the interpolation function is as follows:

$$y = \begin{cases} y_1 + (y_2 - y_1)\dfrac{x - x_1}{x_2 - x_1}, x_1 \le x < x_2 \\ y_2 + (y_3 - y_2)\dfrac{x - x_2}{x_3 - x_2}, x_2 \le x < x_3 \\ \dots \\ \dots \\ y_{n-1} + (y_n - y_{n-1})\dfrac{x - x_{n-1}}{x_n - x_{n-1}}, x_{n-1} \le x \le x_n \end{cases}$$

The plot in Figure 5-6 shows the linearly interpolated curve for a set of data points generated using $f(x) = \sin(x)$ for range $x \in [0, 6.3]$.

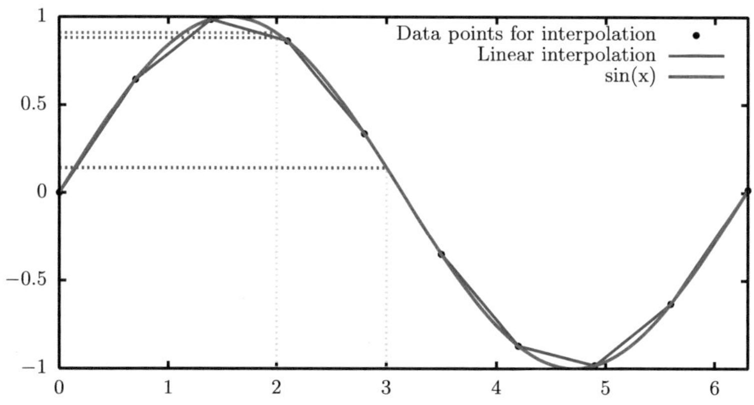

***Figure 5-6.** Linear interpolation*

As shown in the plot, linear interpolation is easy to compute. It simply connects every two adjacent points using a straight-line segment. One major drawback is that it may not perform well in predictions where the original data is far from being linear. For example, at $x = 2$, sin(2) = 0.909297, whereas the value from the interpolation is 0.880672, yielding an error that's more than 3 percent. In comparison, at $x = 3$, where the original data is close to linear (the curvature or second derivative of $f(x) = \sin(x)$ is $f''(x) = -\sin(x)$, which evaluates to about 0 around $x = 3$), sin(3) = 0.141120, whereas the value from the interpolation is 0.139053, yielding an error of only 1.5 percent.

The code to reproduce the previous example is given next. You first construct a `LinearInterpolation` object; then the member method `fit` is called to fit the data. An `UnivariateRealFunction` object that represents the interpolation curve is returned.

```
// the data set
val data = SortedOrderedPairs(
        doubleArrayOf(0.0, 0.7, 1.4, 2.1, 2.8, 3.5, 4.2, 4.9, 5.6, 6.3),
        doubleArrayOf(0.0, 0.644218, 0.98545, 0.863209, 0.334988, -0.350783, -0.871576,
        -0.982453, -0.631267, 0.0168139)
)
val li: LinearInterpolation = LinearInterpolation()
val f: UnivariateRealFunction = li.fit(data)
println(f.evaluate(2.0)) // f(2) = 0.880672
println(f.evaluate(3.0)) // f(3) = 0.139053
```

```
// plot the interpolation
val N = 100
val gridSize: Double = (6.5 - 0.0) / (N - 1)
var x: Double = 0.0

val xValues = ArrayList<Double>(N)
val yValues = ArrayList<Double>(N)

for(i in 0 until N) {
    val y = f.evaluate(x)

    xValues.add(i, x)
    yValues.add(i, y)

    x += gridSize
}

val plotData = mapOf<String, Any>(
    "x" to xValues,
    "y" to yValues,
)

val plot = ggplot(plotData) {x = "x"; y = "y"} + geomLine()
plot
```

The output is as follows:

```
0.880672
0.13905342857142847
```

Figure 5-7 shows the plot of the linear interpolation.

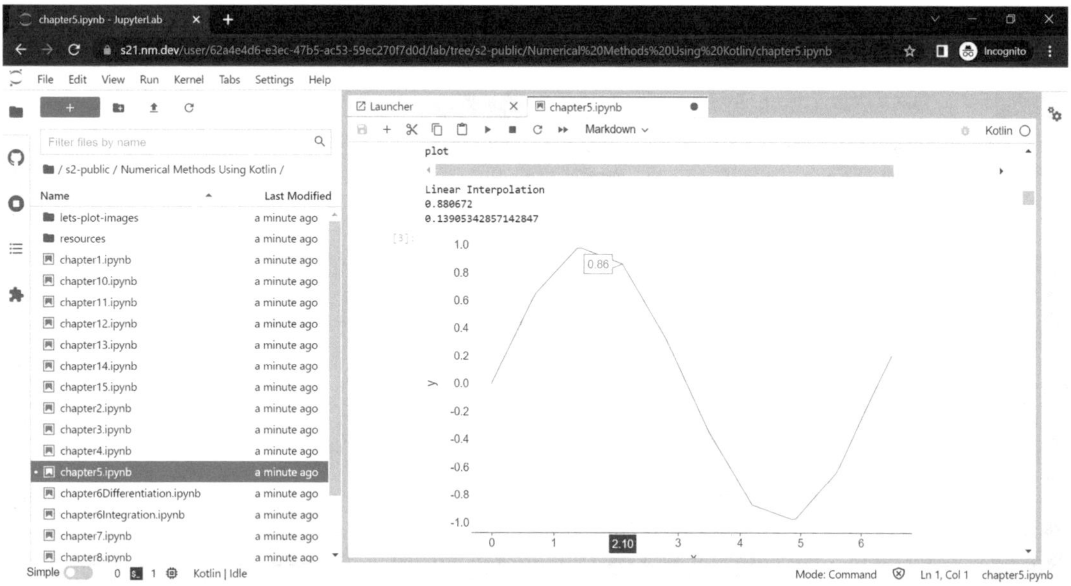

Figure 5-7. *Plot of the linear interpolation*

The class has only a default constructor that takes no argument. The `fit` function signature is as follows:

```
@Override
public UnivariateRealFunction fit(OrderedPairs f)
```

Another major drawback of linear interpolation is that an interpolated function is not smooth at the points and hence has kinks. The slopes experience sudden changes because the first derivatives of neighboring linear functions do not agree at the point they meet. This is evident in Figure 5-7. In contrast, using higher-degree polynomial splines will circumvent this problem. Quadratic splines may guarantee continuous first derivatives at the knots, but not the second derivatives. Cubic splines may guarantee continuity of both first and second derivatives at the knots and therefore are used most in practice.

5.2.2. Cubic Hermite Spline Interpolation

Cubic Hermite is a piecewise spline interpolation where each piece is a third-degree polynomial in Hermite form, that is, determined by the values and first derivatives at the two end points of the piece interval.

On a single interval $[x_1, x_2]$, given value y_1 at $x = x_1$ and y_2 at $x = x_2$ with tangent y_1' at $x = x_1$ and y_2' at $x = x_2$, the segment curve can be defined as follows:

$$f(x) = ax^3 + bx^2 + cx + d,\ x \in [x_1, x_2]$$

Plugging in the values and first derivatives at the endpoints gives the following:

$$\begin{cases} ax_1^3 + bx_1^2 + cx_1 + d = y_1, \\ ax_2^3 + bx_2^2 + cx_2 + d = y_2, \\ 3ax_1^2 + 2bx_1 + c = y_1', \\ 3ax_2^2 + 2bx_2 + c = y_2' \end{cases}$$

Solving for a, b, c, d, you can get the interpolation curve on $[x_1, x_2]$.

Take a simple case, for example. Suppose $x_1 = 0$, $x_2 = 1$. You have the following:

$$f(x) = \left(2x^3 - 3x^2 + 1\right)y_1 + \left(x^3 - 2x^2 + x\right)y_1' + \left(-2x^3 + 3x^2\right)y_2 + \left(x^3 - x^2\right)y_2'$$

where $x \in [0, 1]$. To verify it, you can check the following:

$$f(0) = y_1,\ f(1) = y_2,\ f'(0) = y_1',\ f'(1) = y_2'.$$

Repeating the previous procedure on every two adjacent points in the data set will give a piecewise interpolation that is cubic on every interval. Note that a cubic Hermite spline takes only values and tangents as inputs and no more. Therefore, it ensures the continuity of the first derivative but not second one.

When only data values $(x_1, y_1), (x_2, y_2), \ldots, (x_n, y_n)$ are available, the tangents need to be estimated from them. There are a number of ways to compute the tangents. In NM Dev, there are two methods: Catmull-Rom spline and finite-difference.

1. The Catmull-Rom spline estimates tangents as

   $$y_k' = \frac{y_{k+1} - y_{k-1}}{x_{k+1} - x_{k-1}}$$

   for internal points $k = 2, \ldots, n - 1$, and

   $$y_0' = \frac{y_1 - y_0}{x_1 - x_0},\quad y_n' = \frac{y_n - y_{n-1}}{x_n - x_{n-1}}$$

   at the endpoints.

   This method is widely used in computer graphics to get smooth, continuous motion between discrete key frames. It is popular because it's relatively easy to compute. It also ensures that every key frame position will be hit exactly and that the tangents of the generated curve are continuous over multiple segments.

2. Finite difference estimates tangents as

   $$y_k' = \frac{1}{2}\left(\frac{y_{k+1} - y_k}{x_{k+1} - x_k} + \frac{y_k - y_{k-1}}{x_k - x_{k-1}}\right)$$

   for internal points $k = 2, \ldots, n - 1$ and as this one-sided difference

   $$y_0' = \frac{y_1 - y_0}{x_1 - x_0},\quad y_n' = \frac{y_n - y_{n-1}}{x_n - x_{n-1}}$$

   at the endpoints.

Let's consider the same example as in Section 5.2.1, which is the interpolation on the data generated from $f(x) = \sin(x)$. Figure 5-8 shows the result of applying a cubic Hermite spline with a Catmull-Rom tangent. Apparently, the curve looks much smoother compared to the one from linear interpolation.

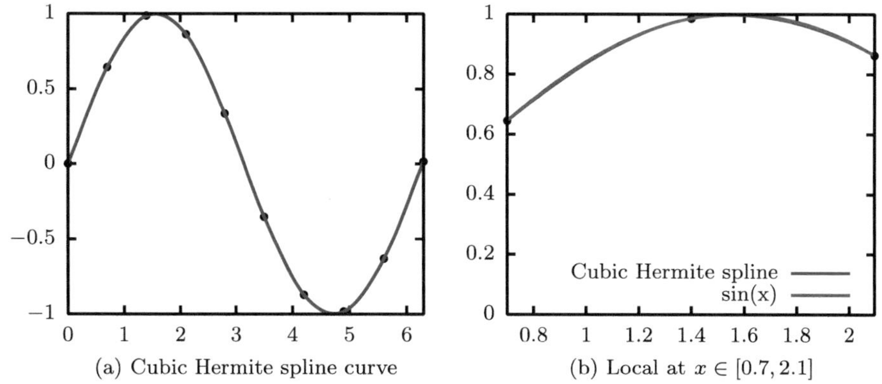

Figure 5-8. *Cubic Hermite spline on data from sin(x)*

The following code demonstrates how to do cubic Hermite spline interpolation using a Catmull-Rom tangent. To use a finite difference tangent instead, switch to the line that's commented out. The choice of tangent method makes little difference in this particular example.

```
// the data set
val data = SortedOrderedPairs(
        doubleArrayOf(0.0, 0.7, 1.4, 2.1, 2.8, 3.5, 4.2, 4.9, 5.6, 6.3),
        doubleArrayOf(0.0, 0.644218, 0.98545, 0.863209, 0.334988, -0.350783, -0.871576,
        -0.982453, -0.631267, 0.0168139)
)
val spline: CubicHermite = CubicHermite(CubicHermite.Tangents.CATMULL_ROM)
// CubicHermite spline = CubicHermite(CubicHermite.Tangents.FINITE_DIFFERENCE)
val f: UnivariateRealFunction = spline.fit(data)
println(f.evaluate(2.0)) // f(2) = 0.906030
println(f.evaluate(3.0)) // f(3) = 0.145727

val N = 100
val gridSize: Double = (2.1 - 0.7) / (N - 1)
var x: Double = 0.7

val xValues = ArrayList<Double>(N)
val yValues = ArrayList<Double>(N)

for(i in 0 until N) {
    val y = f.evaluate(x)

    xValues.add(i, x)
    yValues.add(i, y)

    x += gridSize
}
```

```
val plotData = mapOf<String, Any>(
    "x" to xValues,
    "y" to yValues,
)

val plot = ggplot(plotData) {x = "x"; y = "y"} + geom_line()
plot
```

The output is as follows:

```
0.9060307725947522
0.14572681049562664
```

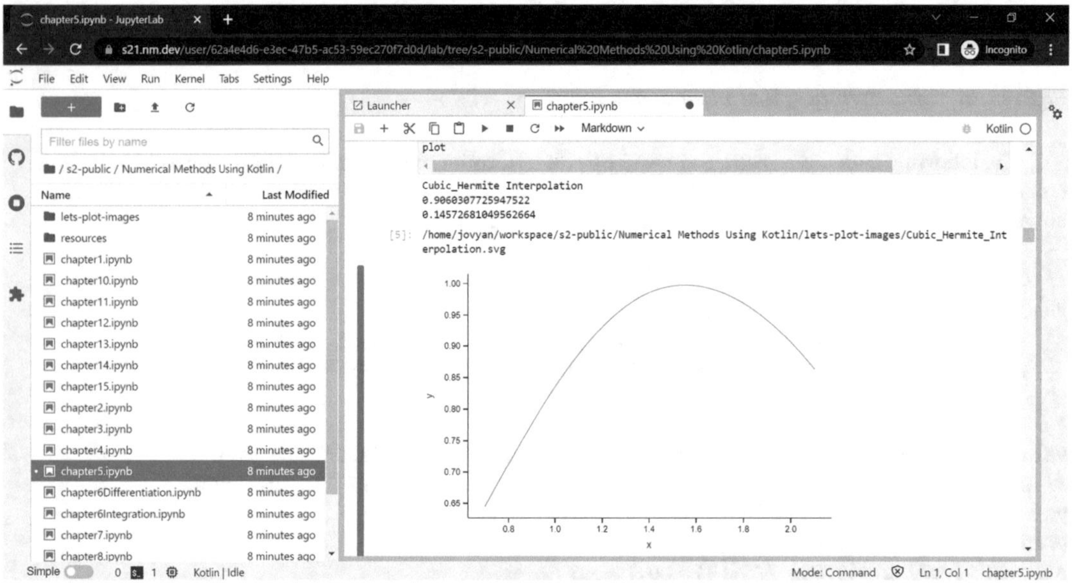

Figure 5-9. *Plot of the cubic Hermite spline on data from sin(x)*

The class and fit method signatures are as follows:

```
/**
 * Construct an instance with the given method to compute tangents.
 *
 * @param tangent computes the control tangents used for the interpolation
 */
public CubicHermite(Tangent tangent)
/**
 * The interpolated function must pass through all the given points.
 *
 * @param f {@inheritDoc }
```

```
    * @return the interpolated function
    */
   @Override
   UnivariateRealFunction fit(OrderedPairs f);
```

5.2.3. Cubic Spline Interpolation

A cubic spline is a spline composed of piecewise third-order polynomials such that the curve is continuous in both the first and second derivatives. The difference between a cubic spline and a cubic Hermite spline is discussed in Section 5.2.2. A cubic Hermite spline ensures the continuity of the first derivative, whereas a cubic spline ensures the continuity of both the first and second derivatives.

Consider the spline for a set of $n + 1$ points $(x_0, y_0), (x_1, y_1), \ldots, (x_n, y_n)$. Let the i-th piece of the spline be represented by the following:

$$Y_i(x) = a_i + b_i x + c_i x^2 + d_i x^3,$$

where $x \in [x_i, x_{i+1}]$, $i = 0, \ldots, n - 1$, as shown in Figure 5-10.

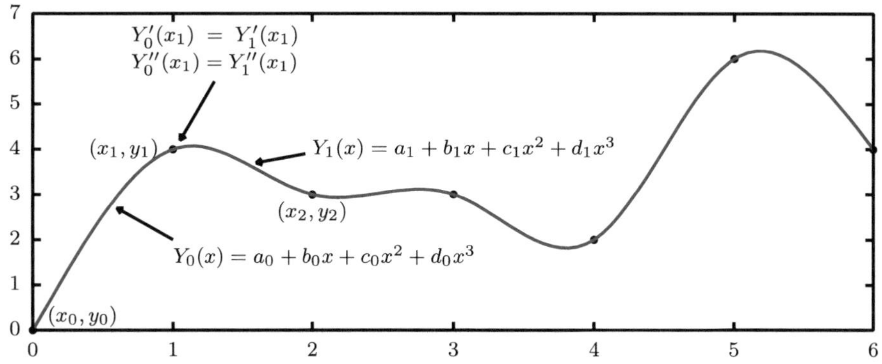

Figure 5-10. *Cubic spline interpolation*

There are $4n$ variables $(a_0, b_0, c_0, d_0, \ldots, a_{n-1}, b_{n-1}, c_{n-1}, d_{n-1})$ to solve for. Therefore, $4n$ equations are needed.

First, the spline has to satisfy these data point values:

$$Y_i(x_i) = y_i,\ Y_i(x_{i+1}) = y_{i+1} \text{ for } i = 0, \ldots, n-1$$

which gives $2n$ equations.

Second, to ensure that the curve is continuous in the first and second derivatives, another $2(n - 1)$ equations have to be satisfied.

$$Y_i'(x_{i+1}) = Y_{i+1}'(x_{i+1}),\ Y_i''(x_{i+1}) = Y_{i+1}''(x_{i+1}) \text{ for } i = 0, \ldots, n-2$$

Now there are $4n - 2$ equations. The boundary conditions give two more equations. The popular options are natural spline, clamped spline, and not-a-knot spline.

- *Natural spline*: The second derivative of the curve at the endpoints is set to be 0; that is, $Y_0''(x_0) = 0 = Y_{n-1}''(x_n)$.
- *Clamped spline*: The first derivative of the curve at the endpoints is specified; i.e., $Y_0'(x_0) = A,\ Y_{n-1}'(x_n) = B$.
- *Not-a-knot spline*: The third derivative of the spline is continuous at x_1 and xn_{-1}; i.e., $Y_0'''(x_1) = Y_1'''(x_1),\ Y_{n-2}'''(x_{n-1}) = Y_{n-1}'''(x_{n-1})$.

With the boundary condition, there are $4n$ equations in total. You can then solve for the $4n$ variables $(a_0, b_0, c_0, d_0, \ldots, a_{n-1}, b_{n-1}, c_{n-1}, d_{n-1})$ and obtain the functions $Y_0(x), Y_1(x), \ldots, Y_{n-1}(x)$. See Figure 5-11.

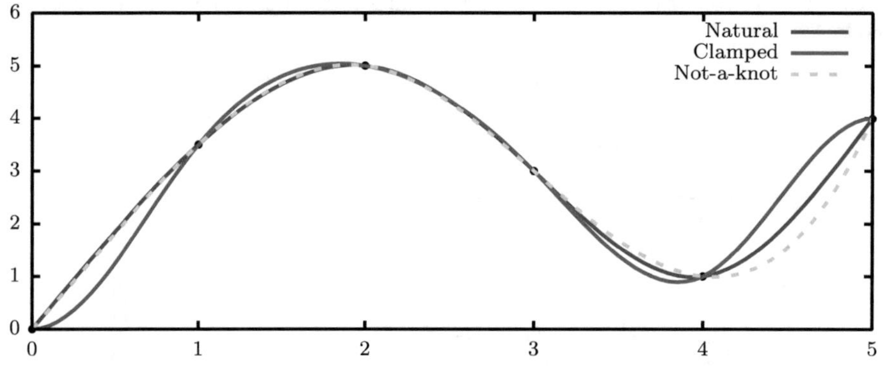

Figure 5-11. *Comparison of different boundary conditions in a cubic spline*

The following code demonstrates a cubic spline. The `f1`, `f2`, and `f3` objects are cubic spline interpolant functions using natural, clamped, and not-a-knot boundary conditions, respectively.

```
// the data set
val data = SortedOrderedPairs(
        doubleArrayOf(0.0, 1.0, 2.0, 3.0, 4.0, 5.0),
        doubleArrayOf(0.0, 3.5, 5.0, 3.0, 1.0, 4.0)
)
val cs1: CubicSpline = CubicSpline.natural()
val f1: UnivariateRealFunction = cs1.fit(data)

val cs2: CubicSpline = CubicSpline.clamped()
val f2: UnivariateRealFunction = cs2.fit(data)

val cs3: CubicSpline = CubicSpline.notAKnot()
val f3: UnivariateRealFunction = cs3.fit(data)
```

The plots are shown in Figure 5-12.

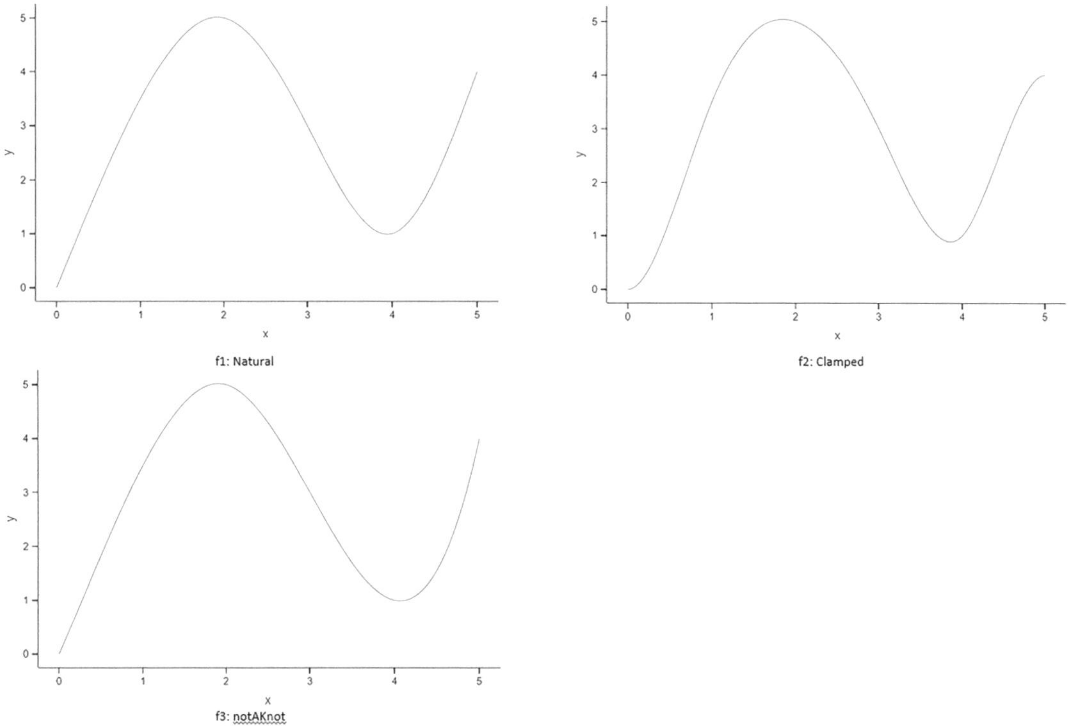

Figure 5-12. *Comparison of different cubic spline interpolations*

The signatures are as follows:

```
/**
 * Constructs an instance with end conditions which fits <em>natural</em>
 * splines, meaning that the second derivative at both ends are zero.
 *
 * @return the instance
 */
public static CubicSpline natural()
/**
 * Constructs an instance with end conditions which fits <em>clamped</em>
 * splines, and the first derivative at both ends are zero.
 *
 * @return the instance
 */
public static CubicSpline clamped()
/**
 * Constructs an instance with end conditions which fits <em>clamped</em>
 * splines, meaning that the first derivative at both ends equal to the
 * given values.
 *
```

```
 * @param df1 the first derivative at the first point
 * @param dfn the first derivative at the last point
 * @return the instance
 */
public static CubicSpline clamped(double df1, double dfn)
/**
 * The interpolated function must pass through all the given points.
 *
 * @param f {@inheritDoc }
 * @return the interpolated function
 */
@Override
UnivariateRealFunction fit(OrderedPairs f);
```

5.2.4. Newton Polynomial Interpolation

A Newton polynomial interpolation is a polynomial for interpolating a data set. It is sometimes called *Newton's divided difference interpolation polynomial* because the coefficients of a polynomial are calculated using Newton's divided difference method. In contrast to spline interpolation, a Newton polynomial is not a piecewise interpolation. Instead, it constructs an n-th-degree polynomial to interpolate a data set of $n + 1$ points. Given a set of $n + 1$ points (x_0, y_0), (x_1, y_1), ..., (x_n, y_n), the Newton interpolation polynomial is a linear combination of Newton basis polynomials.

$$N(x) := \sum_{i=0}^{n} a_i n_i(x)$$

The Newton basis polynomials are defined as follows:

$$n_i(x) := \prod_{j=0}^{i-1} (x - x_j) \text{ for } i > 0, \text{and } n_0(x) \equiv 1$$

The coefficients a_i are defined as follows:

$$a_i := [y_0, \ldots, y_i]$$

$[y_0, \ldots, y_i]$ is the notation for divided differences, which are defined as follows:

$$[y_0] = y_0$$

$$[y_0, y_1] = \frac{[y_1] - [y_0]}{x_1 - x_0} = \frac{y_1 - y_0}{x_1 - x_0}$$

$$\ldots$$

$$[y_0, \ldots y_i] = \frac{[y_1, \ldots, y_i] - [y_0, \ldots, y_{i-1}]}{x_i - x_0}$$

Linear Form

Figure 5-13 shows a Newton linear polynomial.

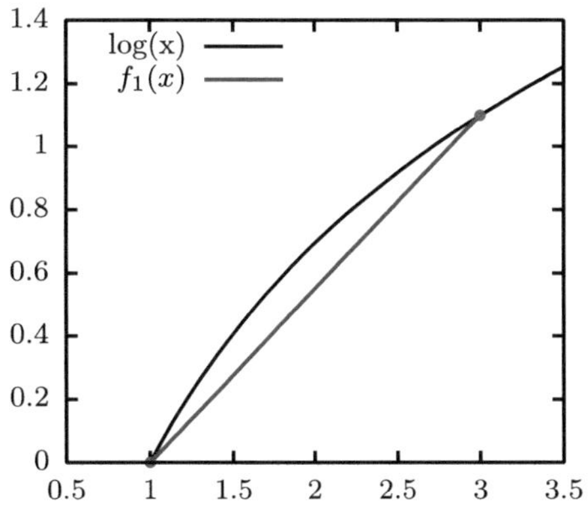

Figure 5-13. *Newton linear polynomial*

Let's start with the simplest case, the linear case. Given two points, (x_1, y_1) and (x_2, y_2), the Newton polynomial takes a linear form, as shown here:

$$f_1(x) = y_1 + \frac{y_2 - y_1}{x_2 - x_1}(x - x_1)$$

Since there are only two points, no curvature information is available. The data is interpolated simply by a straight line. Note that the coefficients y_1 and $\frac{y_2 - y_1}{x_2 - x_1}$ are the Newton's divided difference $[y_1]$ and $[y_1, y_2]$, whereas the constant 1 (in the first term) and $(x - x_1)$ are Newton's basis polynomials.

Quadratic Form

Quadratic interpolation requires three data points and introduces curvature into the function and hence improves estimation. Using the definition of a Newton polynomial provided earlier, it can be defined as a second-order polynomial of the following form:

$$f_2(x) = a_1 + a_2(x - x_1) + a_3(x - x_1)(x - x_2)$$

where the coefficients a_1, a_2, a_3 can be determined easily.
Plugging in $x = x_1$, you get this:

$$a_1 = f_2(x_1) = y_1$$

Plugging in $x = x_2$, you get this:

$$a_2 = \frac{f_2(x_2) - a_1}{x_2 - x_1} = \frac{y_2 - y_1}{x_2 - x_1}$$

See Figure 5-14.

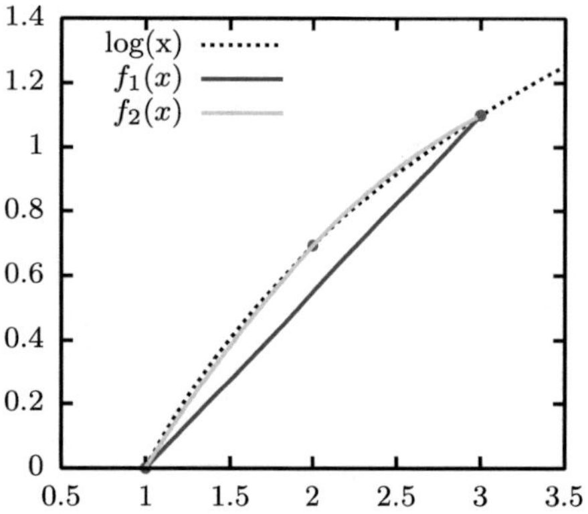

Figure 5-14. *Newton quadratic polynomial*

Plugging in $x = x_3$, you get this:

$$a_3 = \frac{f_2(x_3) - a_1 - a_2(x_3 - x_1)}{(x_3 - x_1)(x_3 - x_2)}$$

$$= \frac{y_3 - [y_2 - a_2(x_2 - x_1)] - a_2(x_3 - x_1)}{(x_3 - x_1)(x_3 - x_2)}$$

$$= \frac{y_3 - y_2 - a_2(x_3 - x_2)}{(x_3 - x_1)(x_3 - x_2)}$$

$$= \frac{\frac{y_3 - y_2}{x_3 - x_2} - \frac{y_2 - y_1}{x_2 - x_1}}{(x_3 - x_1)}$$

$f_2(x)$ has a quadratic term that $f_1(x)$ does not have, and this gives it curvature. The formulation of the coefficient a_3 in the quadratic term is actually Newton's divided difference $[y_1, y_2, y_3]$, which can be computed with $[y_3, y_2]$ and $[y_2, y_1]$.

$$[y_1, y_2, y_3] = \frac{[y_3, y_2] - [y_2, y_1]}{x_3 - x_1}$$

General Form

The interpolation in the linear and quadratic cases shown earlier can be generalized to fit a data set of $n + 1$ points, in which case the polynomial will have an order of n. The Newton's divided difference interpolation formula is therefore as follows:

$$f_n(x) = y_0 + [y_0, y_1](x - x_0) + \ldots + [y_0, \ldots, y_n](x - x_0)(x - x_1)\ldots(x - x_{n-1})$$

The divided differences are calculated in a recursive manner using the following formula:

$$[y_0,\ldots y_i]=\frac{[y_1,\ldots,y_i]-[y_0,\ldots,y_{i-1}]}{x_i-x_0}$$

To make the recursion process easier to visualize, we put the example of computing $[y_0, y_1, y_2, y_3]$ in a tabular form, as shown here:

$$\begin{array}{llllll}
(x_0,y_0) & [y_0] & & & & \\
 & & [y_0,y_1] & & & \\
(x_1,y_1) & [y_1] & & [y_0,y_1,y_2] & & \\
 & & [y_1,y_2] & & & [y_0,y_1,y_2,y_3] \\
(x_2,y_2) & [y_2] & & [y_1,y_2,y_3] & & \\
 & & [y_2,y_3] & & & \\
(x_3,y_3) & [y_3] & & & &
\end{array}$$

The table shows the relationships between the differences. For example, $[y_0, y_1]$ is computed using $[y_0]$ and $[y_1]$; $[y_0, y_1, y_2, y_3]$ is computed using $[y_0, y_1, y_2]$ and $[y_1, y_2, y_3]$.

Figure 5-15 compares Newton polynomial interpolation and natural cubic splines given a random data set of size 7. Since there are seven points, the Newton interpolant is a 6th-degree polynomial, leading to peaks and valleys in its curve that come with high-degree polynomials. This may lead to large errors. As the number of data points increases and the number of degrees of the interpolant polynomial increases, both the extent and number of peaks and valleys will go up quickly. On the other hand, a cubic spline that is a concatenation of multiple low-degree polynomials is much more stable and has a satisfying performance in this case.

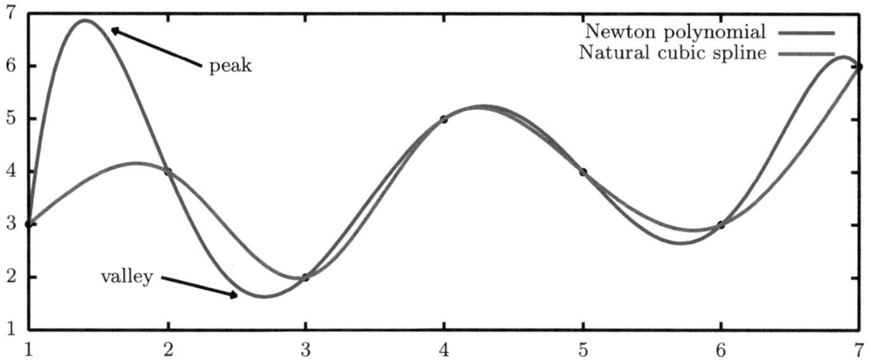

***Figure 5-15.** Comparison of Newton's polynomial and cubic spline*

The following snippet demonstrates how to use Newton polynomials interpolation:

```
// 2 data points, linear form
val data1 = SortedOrderedPairs(
        doubleArrayOf(1.0, 3.0),
        doubleArrayOf(log10(1.0), log10(3.0))
)
```

```
val np1: Interpolation = NewtonPolynomial()
val f1: UnivariateRealFunction = np1.fit(data1)
// 3 data points, quadratic form
val data2 = SortedOrderedPairs(
        doubleArrayOf(1.0, 2.0, 3.0),
        doubleArrayOf(log10(1.0), log10(2.0), log10(3.0))
)
val np2: Interpolation = NewtonPolynomial()
val f2: UnivariateRealFunction = np2.fit(data2)
```

The plots are shown in Figure 5-16.

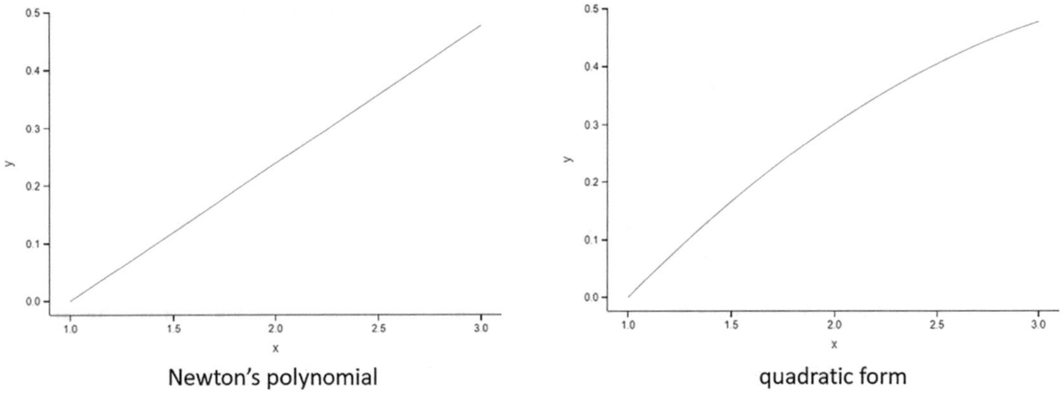

Figure 5-16. *Comparison of Newton's polynomial and quadratic form*

```
// comparison between Newton polynomial and cubic spline
val data3 = SortedOrderedPairs(
        doubleArrayOf(1.0, 2.0, 3.0, 4.0, 5.0, 6.0, 7.0),
        doubleArrayOf(3.0, 4.0, 2.0, 5.0, 4.0, 3.0, 6.0)
)
val np3: Interpolation = NewtonPolynomial()
val f3_1: UnivariateRealFunction = np3.fit(data3)
val cs: Interpolation = CubicSpline.natural()
val f3_2: UnivariateRealFunction = cs.fit(data3)
```

The plots are shown in Figure 5-17.

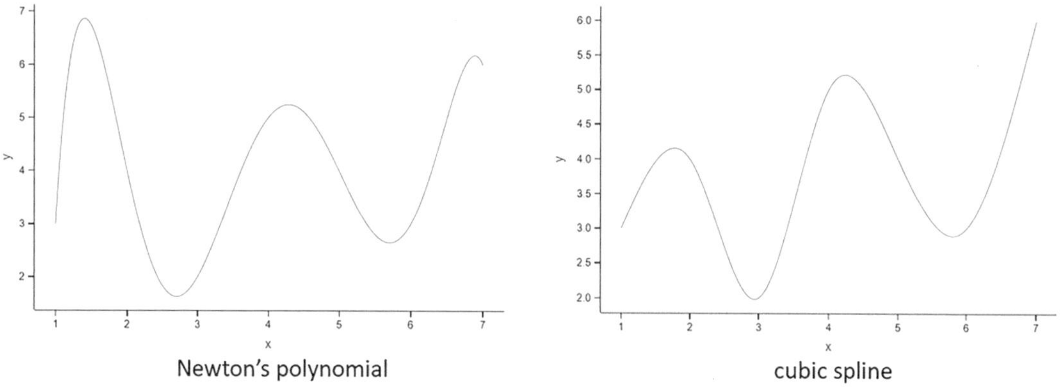

Figure 5-17. *Comparison of Newton's polynomial and cubic spline*

5.3. Multivariate Interpolation

Multivariate interpolation is interpolation of functions with more than one variable. It is an extension of the univariate case.

5.3.1. Bivariate Interpolation

Let's start with the bivariate case. Suppose you have a set of $n \times n$ data points: (x_1, y_1, z_{11}), (x_1, y_2, z_{12}), ..., (x_n, y_n, z_{nn}). Note that (x_1, y_1, z_{11}) means that the data value is z_{11} at position (x_1, y_1). That is,

$$z = f(x,y)$$

The general procedure of interpolation for a bivariate function is as follows:

1. Fix a dimension, say $y = y_1$, as a constant. For that particular slice of data (now one-dimensional), interpolate the other dimension, x.
2. For values in the other dimension x, interpolate the results from Step 1.

For example, you first fix dimension y and interpolate with respect to x. At $y = y_1$, you have (x_1, z_{11}), (x_2, z_{12}), ..., (x_n, z_{1n}). Applying any univariate interpolation algorithm such as those discussed in Section 5.2, you get $f_{y1}(x)$, which is an interpolator of x at position $y = y_1$. Repeating this process for every position in dimension y, you have $f_{y1}(x)$, $f_{y2}(x)$, ..., $f_{yn}(x)$, a set of curves parallel to the x-axis.

The second step is to interpolate on this data set $(y_1, f_{y1}(x))$, $(y_2, f_{y2}(x))$, ..., $(y_n, f_{yn}(x))$ for x-values. This can also be done by applying any univariate interpolation algorithm. Then you have $f(x, y)$.

Therefore, the properties and results of a bivariate interpolator are characterized by the (two) univariate interpolators applied inside. For example, bilinear interpolation uses linear interpolation to interpolate a single dimension twice. Bicubic spline and bicubic interpolation use cubic spline and cubic Hermite interpolation, respectively.

The interpolator $f(x, y)$ is a surface, as shown in Figure 5-18, where bicubic interpolation is applied to a data set of size 3×3. The black points are the data; the web of blue lines is the interpolator surface.

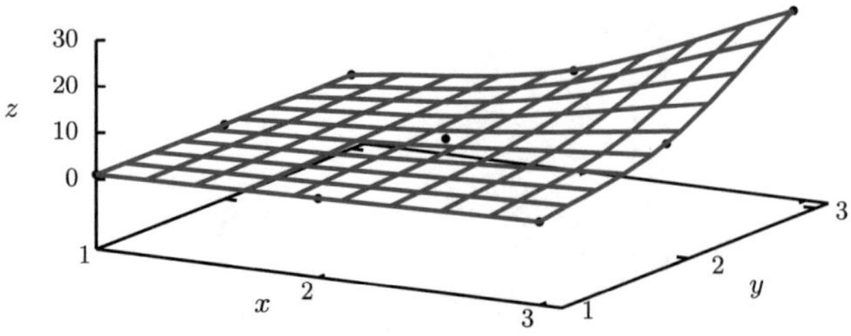

Figure 5-18. *Bicubic interpolation*

NM Dev implements bilinear interpolation, bicubic spline, and bicubic interpolation. The following code snippet shows all three methods:

```
val grids: BivariateGrid = BivariateArrayGrid(
        arrayOf(
            doubleArrayOf(1.0, 1.0, 1.0), // z(1, 1) = 1, z(1, 2) = 1, z(1, 3) = 1
            doubleArrayOf(2.0, 4.0, 8.0), // z(2, 1) = 2, z(2, 2) = 4, z(2, 3) = 8
            doubleArrayOf(3.0, 9.0, 27.0) // z(3, 1) = 3, z(3, 2) = 9, z(3, 3) = 27
        ),
        doubleArrayOf(1.0, 2.0, 3.0), // x
        doubleArrayOf(1.0, 2.0, 3.0) // y
)

val bl: BivariateGridInterpolation = BilinearInterpolation()
val f1: RealScalarFunction = bl.interpolate(grids) // f3(1.5, 1.5) = 2.0
println(f1.evaluate(DenseVector(arrayOf(1.5, 1.5))))

val bs: BivariateGridInterpolation = BicubicSpline()
val f2: RealScalarFunction = bs.interpolate(grids) // f2(1.5, 1.5) = 1.8828125
println(f2.evaluate(DenseVector(arrayOf(1.5, 1.5))))

val bi: BivariateGridInterpolation = BicubicInterpolation()
val f3: RealScalarFunction = bi.interpolate(grids) // f1(1.5, 1.5) = 1.90625
println(f3.evaluate(DenseVector(arrayOf(1.5, 1.5))))
```

The output is as follows:

```
2.0
1.8828125
1.90625
```

The `BivariateGrid` class defines a grid in a three-dimensional space, $z = f(x, y)$. The first input, z, is a two-dimensional array. It is the Cartesian product or cross product of the values in x and y, the second array, and the third array inputs. The [1, 1]th entry of z is the z-value at position $x[1]$ and $y[1]$. In this case, $x[1] = 1$, and $y[1] = 1$, so $z(1, 1) = 1$.

The BivariateArrayGrid class can define a rectilinear grid, meaning that the grid lines are not necessarily equally spaced. The BivariateRegularGrid class defines only a regular grid that has equally spaced grid lines. Their signatures are as follows:

```
/**
 * Constructs a new grid with a given two-dimensional array of grid values,
 * and values for grid line positions along the x-axis and the y-axis.
 *
 * @param z the grid values
 * @param x the grid line positions along the x-axis
 * @param y the grid line positions along the y-axis
 */
public BivariateArrayGrid(double[][] z, double[] x, double[] y)
    /**
     * Constructs a new grid where the dependent variable values are taken from
     * the given two-dimensional array and the values of the dependent variables
     * are specified by their first values and the difference between successive
     * values.
     * <p/>
     * The first index for the input array will be corresponding to <i>x</i> and
     * the second index to <i>y</i> and the size will be inferred from the size
     * of the array.
     *
     * @param z      the two-dimensional array containing the values of the
     *               dependent variable
     * @param x0     the first value of the independent variable <i>x</i>
     * @param y0     the first value of the independent variable <i>y</i>
     * @param deltaX the distance between adjacent points along the x-axis
     * @param deltaY the distance between adjacent points along the y-axis
     */
    public BivariateRegularGrid(
            double[][] z,
            double x0,
            double y0,
            double deltaX,
            double deltaY
    )
```

The constructor for the BicubicInterpolation class is as follows:

```
/**
 * Constructs a new instance which uses the given derivatives to
 * interpolate. Note that the derivatives need not necessarily be exactly
 * correct, but will be the derivatives present in the interpolated surface.
 *
 * @param derivatives the derivatives used for the interpolation
 */
public BicubicInterpolation(PartialDerivatives derivatives)
```

Note that it can take as input the partial derivatives of the function at the grid points. The `BicubicInterpolation.PartialDerivatives` interface is as follows:

```
/**
 * Specify the partial derivatives defined at points on a
 * {@link BivariateGrid}.
 */
public interface PartialDerivatives {
/**
 * Get the partial derivative \(\frac{\partial z}{\partial x}\), at the
 * given position in
 * the grid.
 *
 * @param grid the grid for which to get the partial derivative
 * @param i the index along the x-axis
 * @param j the index along the y-axis
 * @return \(\frac{\partial z}{\partial x}\) at the given point
 */
double dx(BivariateGrid grid, int i, int j);
/**
 * Get the partial derivative \(\frac{\partial z}{\partial y}\), at the
 * given position in
 * the grid.
 *
 * @param grid the grid for which to get the partial derivative
 * @param i the index along the x-axis
 * @param j the index along the y-axis
 * @return \(\frac{\partial z}{\partial y}\) at the given point
 */
double dy(BivariateGrid grid, int i, int j);
/**
 * Get the cross derivative \(\frac{\partial^2 z}{\partial x \partial
 * y}\), at the given
 * position in the grid.
 *
 * @param grid the grid for which to get the partial derivative
 * @param i the index along the x-axis
 * @param j the index along the y-axis
 * @return \(\frac{\partial^2 z}{\partial x \partial y}\) at the given
 * point
 */
double dxdy(BivariateGrid grid, int i, int j);
}
```

This example fits a bivariate data set together with the supplementary Jacobian matrix:

```
// derivatives and answers from Michael Flanagan's library
val z = arrayOf(
    doubleArrayOf(1.0, 3.0, 5.0),
    doubleArrayOf(2.0, 4.0, 8.0),
    doubleArrayOf(9.0, 10.0, 11.0),
)
```

```
val dx = arrayOf(
    doubleArrayOf(6.0, 2.0, 2.0),
    doubleArrayOf(6.0, 7.0, 8.0),
    doubleArrayOf(6.0, 12.0, 14.0),
)

val dy = arrayOf(
    doubleArrayOf(8.0, 8.0, 8.0),
    doubleArrayOf(16.0, 12.0, 8.0),
    doubleArrayOf(4.0, 4.0, 4.0),
)

val dxdy = arrayOf(
    doubleArrayOf(16.0, 8.0, 0.0),
    doubleArrayOf(-4.0, -4.0, -4.0),
    doubleArrayOf(-24.0, -16.0, -8.0),
)

val deriv: BicubicInterpolation.PartialDerivatives = object : BicubicInterpolation.
PartialDerivatives {
            override fun dx(grid: BivariateGrid, i: Int, j: Int): Double {
                return getDeriv(dx, i, j) // for some reason the y-axis is written in
                reverse...
            }

            override fun dy(grid: BivariateGrid, i: Int, j: Int): Double {
                return getDeriv(dy, i, j)
            }

            override fun dxdy(grid: BivariateGrid, i: Int, j: Int): Double {
                return getDeriv(dxdy, i, j)
            }

            private fun getDeriv(dx: Array<DoubleArray>, i: Int, j: Int): Double {
                return dx[i][2 - j]
            }
}

val interpolation: BivariateGridInterpolation = BicubicInterpolation(deriv)
val grid: BivariateGrid = BivariateRegularGrid(z, 0.0, 0.0, 0.5, 0.25)
val f: RealScalarFunction = interpolation.interpolate(grid)

println(f.evaluate(DenseVector(0.0, 0.0))) // 1.0
println(f.evaluate(DenseVector(0.0, 0.125))) // 2.0
println(f.evaluate(DenseVector(0.0, 0.25))) // 3.0
println(f.evaluate(DenseVector(0.0, 0.375))) // 4.0
println(f.evaluate(DenseVector(0.0, 0.5))) // 5.0
println(f.evaluate(DenseVector(0.25, 0.0))) // 1.125
println(f.evaluate(DenseVector(0.25, 0.125))) // 2.078125
println(f.evaluate(DenseVector(0.25, 0.25))) // 3.1875
println(f.evaluate(DenseVector(0.25, 0.375))) // 4.765625
```

```
println(f.evaluate(DenseVector(0.25, 0.5))) // 6.5
println(f.evaluate(DenseVector(0.5, 0.0))) // 2.0
println(f.evaluate(DenseVector(0.5, 0.125))) // 2.875
println(f.evaluate(DenseVector(0.5, 0.25))) // 4.0
println(f.evaluate(DenseVector(0.5, 0.375))) // 5.875
println(f.evaluate(DenseVector(0.5, 0.5))) // 8.0
println(f.evaluate(DenseVector(0.75, 0.0))) // 5.125
println(f.evaluate(DenseVector(0.75, 0.125))) // 5.828125
println(f.evaluate(DenseVector(0.75, 0.25))) // 6.6875
println(f.evaluate(DenseVector(0.75, 0.375))) // 8.015625
println(f.evaluate(DenseVector(0.75, 0.5))) // 9.5
println(f.evaluate(DenseVector(1.0, 0.0))) // 9.0
println(f.evaluate(DenseVector(1.0, 0.125))) // 9.5
println(f.evaluate(DenseVector(1.0, 0.25))) // 10.0
println(f.evaluate(DenseVector(1.0, 0.375))) // 10.5
println(f.evaluate(DenseVector(1.0, 0.5))) // 11.0
```

The output is as follows:

```
1.0
2.0
3.0
4.0
5.0
1.125
2.078125
3.1875
4.765625
6.5
2.0
2.875
4.0
5.875
8.0
5.125
5.828125
6.6875
8.015625
9.5
9.0
9.5
10.0
10.5
11.0
```

5.3.2. Multivariate Interpolation

The procedure described for the bivariate case in the previous section can also be applied to a higher-dimension case, with some modifications. You apply the procedure in a recursive way. Let's take a three-dimensional case as an example.

Suppose you have this $n \times n \times n$ data set:(x_1, y_1, z_1, w_{111}), (x_1, y_1, z_2, w_{112}), …, (x_n, y_n, z_n, w_{nnn}). First, you fix the x dimension as constant. At position $x = x_1$, you have (y_1, z_1, w_{111}), (y_1, z_2, w_{112}), …, (y_n, z_n, w_{1nn}) to interpolate upon. Now, this sliced data set is bivariate. You again fix another dimension, say y. Then at position $y = y_1$, you have (z_1, w_{111}), (z_2, w_{112}), …, (z_n, w_{11n}) to interpolate upon. This sliced data set is univariate. You can apply any univariate interpolation algorithm to get the interpolator $f_{x1y1}(z)$. Repeat this for all y values, and you will get $f_{x1y1}(z)$, $f_{x1y2}(z)$, …, $f_{x1yn}(z)$. Next, as you do in the bivariate case, you interpolate upon $(y_1, f_{x1y1}(z))$, $(y_2, f_{x1y2}(z))$, …, $(y_n, f_{x1yn}(z))$ to get the interpolator $f_{x1}(y, z)$. Repeating this process for all x values, you will get $f_{x1}(y, z)$, $f_{x2}(y, z)$, …, $f_{xn}(y, z)$. Finally, interpolating upon $(x_1, f_{x1}(y, z))$, $(x_2, f_{x2}(y, z))$, …, $(x_n, f_{xn}(y, z))$, you will get the interpolator $f(x, y, z)$.

NM Dev implements this algorithm to recursively do lower-order interpolation until a univariate algorithm can be applied to a one-dimensional sliced data set. However, the computational cost increases exponentially as the number of dimensions goes up. This is not exactly practical for high-dimensional data.

The following code example shows how to apply the algorithm to do multivariate linear interpolation:

```
// the data set
val mda: MultiDimensionalArray<Double>
        = MultiDimensionalArray<Double>(2, 2, 2)
mda.set(1.0, 0, 0, 0) // mda[0][0][0] = 1
mda.set(2.0, 1, 0, 0)
mda.set(3.0, 0, 1, 0)
mda.set(4.0, 0, 0, 1)
mda.set(5.0, 1, 1, 0)
mda.set(6.0, 1, 0, 1)
mda.set(7.0, 0, 1, 1)
mda.set(8.0, 1, 1, 1)

val mvGrid: MultivariateArrayGrid = MultivariateArrayGrid(
        mda,
        doubleArrayOf(1.0, 2.0),
        doubleArrayOf(1.0, 2.0),
        doubleArrayOf(1.0, 2.0)
)
val rgi: RecursiveGridInterpolation
        = RecursiveGridInterpolation(LinearInterpolation())
val f: RealScalarFunction = rgi.interpolate(mvGrid)
println(f.evaluate(DenseVector(arrayOf(1.5, 1.5, 1.5)))) // f(1.5, 1.5, 1.5) = 4.5
```

The output is as follows:

```
4.5
```

The signature for the RecursiveGridInterpolation class is as follows:

```
/**
 * Constructs an n-dimensional interpolation using a given univariate
 * interpolation algorithm.
 *
 * @param univariate a univariate interpolation algorithm
 */
public RecursiveGridInterpolation(Interpolation univariate)
```

It takes as input an Interpolation object. In the previous code example, you supply a LinearInterpolation object. The code will apply the linear interpolation when reducing the data set to a one-dimensional sliced data.

CHAPTER 6

■ ■ ■

Numerical Differentiation and Integration

Numerical differentiation and integration is a technique for performing differentiation and integration when you do not know the function a priori, when you treat the function as a black box, or when analytical (or symbolic or closed-form) differentiation and integration of the function is not possible. This technique approximates a function by using many linear functions, each one a tiny interval of the function domain. In fact, piecewise linear approximation of a function is the very foundation of calculus. When the intervals are small enough or when you zoom in the function enough, the function looks like a straight line (you have differentiation). When you put these "lines" together and sum the block areas (typically rectangles or trapezoids) underneath, you have integration. This concept is taken to the limit when you make the interval length infinitesimally small. On a computer, however, you cannot make the length arbitrarily small. You must be satisfied with a good enough approximation or small enough intervals, hence numerical differentiation and integration.

In Figure 6-1, the arrows are a linear approximation of the function in each interval. They look close enough to represent the slopes or the derivatives of the function in the intervals. Each block area underneath an arrow can also be easily computed (they are basically trapezoids). You can sum them to get the (definite) integral of the function. The more subintervals that you have, the more accurate the numerical derivatives and the numerical integrals are.

© Haksun Li, PhD 2023
H. Li, PhD, *Numerical Methods Using Kotlin*, https://doi.org/10.1007/978-1-4842-8826-9_6

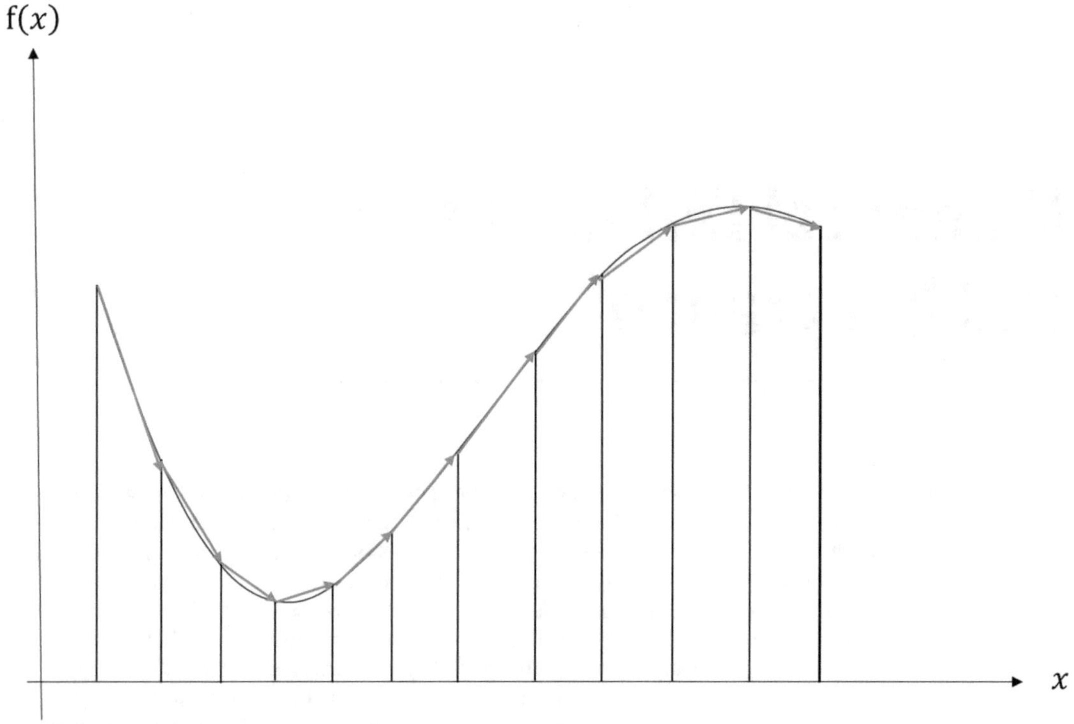

Figure 6-1. *Numerical differentiation and integration example*

The source code in this chapter can be run on the S2 platform here:

https://s21.nm.dev/hub/user-redirect/lab/tree/s2-public/Numerical%20Methods%20Using%20Kotlin/chapter6Differentiation.ipynb
https://s21.nm.dev/hub/user-redirect/lab/tree/s2-public/Numerical%20Methods%20Using%20Kotlin/chapter6Integration.ipynb

The source code can be found on GitHub:

https://github.com/apress/numerical-methods-kotlin

6.1. Numerical Differentiation

Numerical differentiation numerically estimates the derivative of a function at some point. Usually, a difference quotient is used to approximate the derivative. There are many ways to construct such a difference quotient. Taylor expansion can be used to quantify the error term of each approximation. Moreover, an extrapolation method can be used to improve accuracy to extrapolate the quotient to where the denominator is infinitesimally small. This chapter also covers some important derivatives that are used in other branches of mathematics, such as optimization theory. They are the gradient vector and Jacobian and Hessian matrices. NM Dev implements the first-order derivative of some special functions. Their derivatives cannot be computed numerically using a generic method, due to inaccuracy. They are often written as a sum of infinite series or continued fractions. Because the importance and fundamental nature of these special functions, you need special implementations for them.

6.2. Finite Difference

Finite difference is (probably) the most popular method for computing numerical derivatives. It is the foundation of numerically solving many ordinary and partial differential equations. The method discretizes the continuous function domain into a finite number of nodes to form a grid. For a one-dimensional problem, that is, computing a derivative for a univariate function, it picks a set of points along the x-axis. For a two-dimensional problem, that is, computing a partial derivative for a bivariate function, it constructs a grid or a mesh of nodes on the plane. See Figure 6-2.

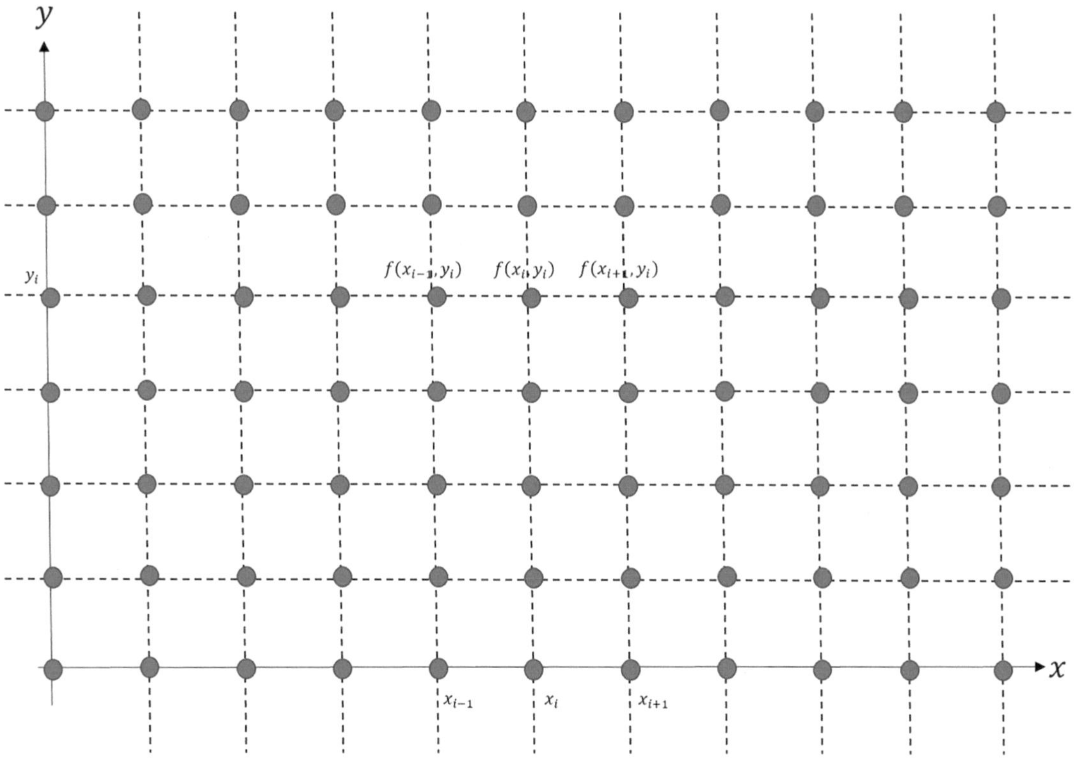

Figure 6-2. *A grid of equidistance nodes chosen for a 2D function domain*

With all the function values on the grid points known, Taylor expansion gives an expression of the derivative that you want to compute in the form of an algebraic equation (such as for an explicit method) or a system of algebraic equations (such as for an implicit method like the Crank-Nicolson method) and an error term. Finite difference is an approximate numerical solution that transforms a differential problem into an algebraic problem. The mathematical concept is intuitive, and the expression is simple.

There are many ways to construct a finite difference using Taylor expansion. The basics are first-order forward difference, first-order backward difference, first-order central difference, second-order center differential, and so on. There are also explicit methods, whereby you simply plug in numbers to get the results, and implicit methods, whereby you need to solve a system of algebraic equations to get the results. The errors of the different finite differences can be first-order, second-order, or higher-order based on the grid size.

The first-order derivative of a univariate function is the simplest and the easiest to explain. It is the slope of the function at a point. A slope between two points is the quotient, $\frac{\Delta f}{\Delta x}$, of the change in the function value between the two points, Δf, divided by the difference of the two points, Δx. The line joining these two points is called a *secant* of the function between the two points (the red line in Figure 6-3). When one of the points moves toward the other, the secant line moves. When one point completely overlaps another (i.e., the two points become the same), the secant line becomes the tangent line of the function at that point (the black line in Figure 6-3). The slope of that tangent line is defined as the slope of the function at the contact point and hence is the first-order derivative of the function at that point. In other words, the first-order derivative is the quotient of differences when the step size Δx is taken to be infinitesimally small. When Δx is small enough, the quotient is a good approximation of the first-order derivative $\frac{df}{dx}$. Depending on how you choose those two points, you'll have different finite differences.

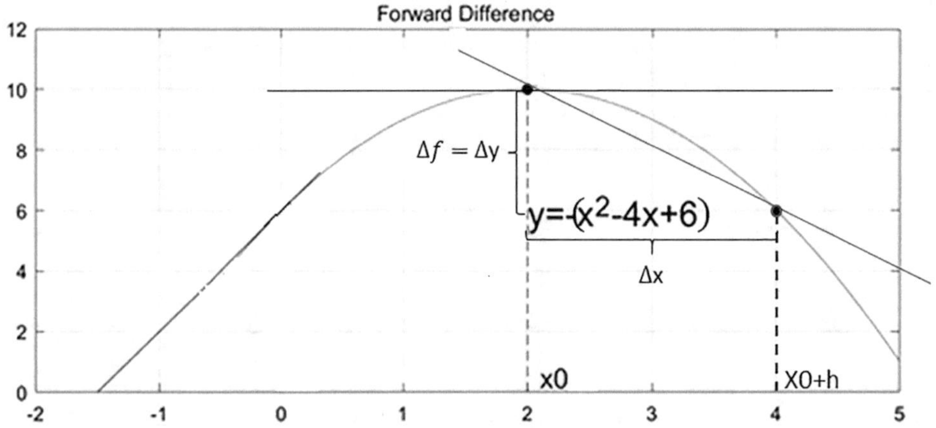

***Figure 6-3.** Forward difference*

6.2.1. Forward Difference

Suppose you want to compute the derivative of f at x_0. Consider a linear interpolation between $(x_0, f(x_0))$ and $(x_0 + h, f(x_0 + h))$. The slope of the secant line between these two points approximates the derivative by the forward (two-point) difference.

$$f'(x_0) \approx \frac{f(x_0+h)-f(x_0)}{h}$$

You can see this idea using Taylor expansion, as shown here:

$$f(x_0+h)=f(x_0)+hf'(x_0)+\frac{h^2}{2!}f''(\xi), x_0 \le \xi \le x_0+h$$

$$f'(x_0) = \frac{f(x_0+h) - f(x_0)}{h} - \frac{h}{2!} f''(\xi), x_0 \le \xi \le x_0 + h$$

$$\approx \frac{f(x_0+h) - f(x_0)}{h}$$

The error term is as follows:

$$R(x) = \left\| f'(x_0) - \frac{f(x_0+h) - f(x_0)}{h} \right\| = \frac{h}{2!} f''(\xi) = O(h)$$

The big-O notation here means that the error term is always smaller (bounded) by a constant multiplied by h, called "a big O of h." In other words, the error goes to zero faster than a constant multiplied by h. The smaller the h, the smaller the error. They both go to zero at a linear rate. The error term is of the first order. Forward difference is useful when solving ordinary differential equations using single-step predictor-corrector methods.

6.2.2. Backward Difference

Consider a different linear interpolation between $(x_0 - h, f(x_0 - h))$ and $(x_0, f(x_0))$. The slope of the secant line between these two points approximates the derivative and is given by the backward (two-point) difference. See Figure 6-4.

$$f'(x_0) \approx \frac{f(x_0) - f(x_0 - h)}{h}$$

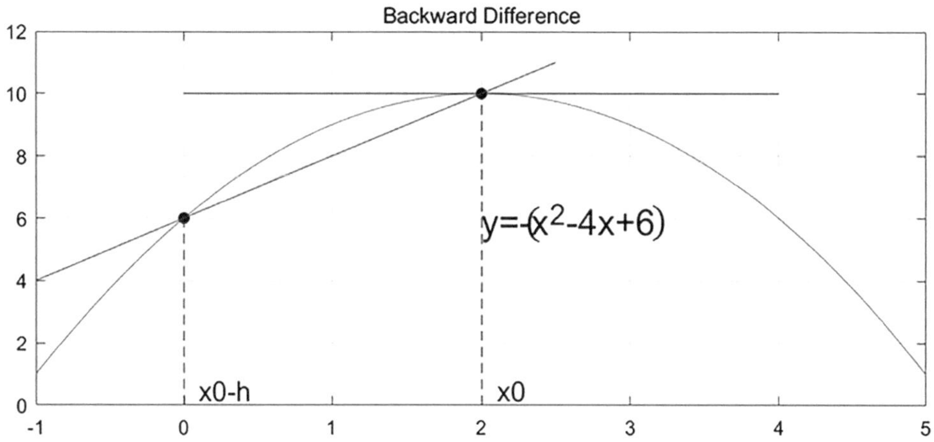

Figure 6-4. *Backward difference*

From Taylor expansion, you get this:

$$f(x_0 - h) = f(x_0) - hf'(x_0) + \frac{h^2}{2!} f''(\xi), x_0 - h \le \xi \le x_0$$

$$f'(x_0) = \frac{f(x_0) - f(x_0 - h)}{h} + \frac{h}{2!} f''(\xi), x_0 - h \le \xi \le x_0$$

The error term is the same as with the forward difference.

$$R(x) = \left\| f'(x_0) - \frac{f(x_0) - f(x_0 - h)}{h} \right\| = \frac{h}{2!} f''(\xi) = O(h)$$

Backward difference is useful when data in the future is not yet available. In certain control problems, data in the future may depend on the derivatives estimated from data in the past.

6.2.3. Central Difference

Consider a different linear interpolation between $(x_0 - h, f(x_0 - h))$ and $(x_0 + h, f(x_0 + h))$. The slope of the secant line between these two points approximates the derivative by the central (three-point) difference.

$$f'(x_0) \approx \frac{f(x_0 + h) - f(x_0 - h)}{2h}$$

See Figure 6-5.

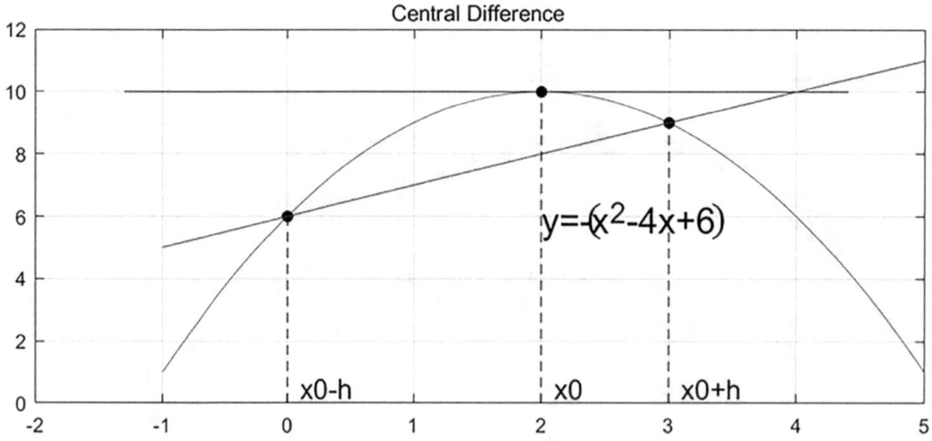

***Figure 6-5.** Central difference*

From Taylor expansion, you get this:

$$f(x_0+h)=f(x_0)+hf'(x_0)+\frac{h^2}{2!}f''(\xi)+\frac{h^3}{3!}f'''(\xi_1), x_0\le\xi_1\le x_0+h$$

$$f(x_0-h)=f(x_0)-hf'(x_0)+\frac{h^2}{2!}f''(\xi)-\frac{h^3}{3!}f'''(\xi_2), x_0-h\le\xi_2\le x_0$$

Subtracting these two equations, you get this:

$$f'(x_0)=\frac{f(x_0+h)-f(x_0-h)}{2h}-\frac{h^2}{3!}f'''(\xi_1), x_0\le\xi_1\le x_0+h$$

The error term is as follows:

$$R(x)=\left\| f'(x_0)-\frac{f(x_0+h)-f(x_0-h)}{2h}\right\|$$

$$=\frac{h^2}{3!}f'''(\xi)=O(h^2)$$

Central difference has an error of big-O of h^2. It means that the error goes to zero quadratically, faster than linearly. This error term is smaller than the forward and backward differences. Central difference is more accurate than forward and backward differences and is therefore preferable if data values are available in the past and in the future.

For the previous example, you want to compute the first-order derivative of the following function at $x = 2$:

$$f(x)=-(x^2-4x+6)$$

Forward difference gives a negative result because the secant is downward sloping; backward difference gives a positive result because the secant is upward sloping; and central difference says $\frac{df}{dx}=0$, which is the correct answer.

If the data values are equally spaced, central difference is the average of the forward and backward differences. Central difference is often used to solve partial differential equations.

6.2.4. Higher-Order Derivatives

If the first-order derivative function $f'(x)$ of the function $f(x)$ is also differentiable, the derivative of $f(x)$ is called the second-order derivative of the function fx). That is:

$$f''(x)=(f'(x))'$$

By induction, if the $(n-1)$-th order derivative of $f(x)$ exists and is differentiable, then the n-th order derivative is defined as follows:

$$f^{(n)}(x)=\left(f^{(n-1)}(x)\right)'$$

If a function, f, is continuous, you say $f \in C^0$. If f' exists and is continuous, you say f is a smooth function and $f \in C^1$. If f can be differentiated indefinitely (and hence must be continuous), you say $f \in C^\infty$. $f(x) = e^x$ is in C^∞.

Some finite difference formulas for higher-order derivatives are listed next.

Second-order derivative forward difference:

$$f''(x) = \frac{f(x+2h) - 2f(x+h) + f(x)}{h^2} + O(h^2)$$

Second-order derivative backward difference:

$$f''(x) = \frac{f(x) - 2f(x-h) + f(x-2h)}{h^2} + O(h^2)$$

Second-order derivative central difference:

$$f''(x) = \frac{f(x+h) - 2f(x) + f(x-h)}{h^2} + O(h^2)$$

Third-order derivative forward difference:

$$f'''(x) = \frac{f(x+3h) - 3f(x+2h) + 3f(x+h) - f(x)}{h^3} + O(h^3)$$

Third-order derivative backward difference:

$$f'''(x) = \frac{f(x) - 3f(x-h) + 3f(x-2h) - f(x-3h)}{h^3} + O(h^3)$$

Third-order derivative central difference:

$$f'''(x) = \frac{f(x+2h) - 2f(x+h) + 2f(x-h) - f(x-2h)}{2h^3} + O(h^3)$$

In general, you get the following.

n-th order derivative forward difference:

$$\Delta_h^n[f](x) = \sum_{i=0}^{n} (-1)^{n-i} \binom{n}{i} f(x+ih)$$

n-th order derivative backward difference:

$$\nabla_h^n[f](x) = \sum_{i=0}^{n} (-1)^{n-i} \binom{n}{i} f(x-ih)$$

n-th order derivative central difference:

$$\delta_h^n[f](x) = \sum_{i=0}^{n} (-1)^{n-i} \binom{n}{i} f\left(x + \left(\frac{n}{2} - i\right)h\right)$$

$\binom{n}{i}$ is the binomial coefficient. Each row of Pascal's triangle provides the coefficient for each value of i.

The formulas provided so far use two points for the second-order derivatives and three points for the third-order derivatives. There are formulas that use three points for the second-order derivatives and four points for the third-order derivatives. In general, using linear algebra, you can construct finite difference approximations that utilize an arbitrary number of points to the left and a (possibly different) number of points to the right of the evaluation point, for any order derivative. This involves solving a linear system such that the Taylor expansion of the sum of those points around the evaluation point best approximates the Taylor expansion of the desired derivative. This is useful for differentiating a function on a grid, whereby, as you approach the edge of the grid, you must sample fewer and fewer points on one side.

In NM Dev, the `FiniteDifference` class computes the derivative function of a given function of a given order. The following code snippet using NM Dev computes the first-order derivatives of the previous examples:

```
val f: UnivariateRealFunction = object : AbstractUnivariateRealFunction() {

    override fun evaluate(x: Double): Double {
        return -(x * x - 4 * x + 6) // -(x^2 - 4x + 6)
    }
}
val x: Double = 2.0

val df1_forward: UnivariateRealFunction
        = FiniteDifference(f, 1, FiniteDifference.Type.FORWARD)
var dfdx: Double = df1_forward.evaluate(x) // evaluate at x
println(String.format("df/dx(x=%f) = %.16f using forward difference", x, dfdx))

val df1_backward: UnivariateRealFunction
        = FiniteDifference(f, 1, FiniteDifference.Type.BACKWARD)
dfdx = df1_backward.evaluate(x) // evaluate at x
println(String.format("df/dx(x=%f) = %.16f using backward difference", x, dfdx))

val df1_central: UnivariateRealFunction
        = FiniteDifference(f, 1, FiniteDifference.Type.CENTRAL)
dfdx = df1_central.evaluate(x) // evaluate at x
println(String.format("df/dx(x=%f) = %.16f using central difference", x, dfdx))
```

Analytically, the first-order derivative function is as follows:

$$\frac{dy}{dx} = -2x + 4$$

The output is as follows:

```
df/dx(x=2.000000) = -0.0000000298023224 using forward difference
df/dx(x=2.000000) = 0.0000000298023224 using backward difference
df/dx(x=2.000000) = 0.0000000000000000 using central difference
```

Note that the forward difference result is slightly negative because the secant line is downward sloping; the backward difference result is slightly positive because the secant line is downward sloping. The central difference gives the correct answer, which is 0.

Analytically, the second-order derivative function is as follows:

$$\frac{d^2y}{dx^2} = -2$$

The following code snippet computes the second-order derivatives:

```
val f: UnivariateRealFunction = object : AbstractUnivariateRealFunction() {

    override fun evaluate(x: Double): Double {
        return -(x * x - 4 * x + 6) // -(x^2 - 4x + 6)
    }
}
val x: Double = 2.0

println("differentiate univariate functions")

val df1_forward: UnivariateRealFunction
        = FiniteDifference(f, 2, FiniteDifference.Type.FORWARD)
var dfdx: Double = df1_forward.evaluate(x) // evaluate at x
println(String.format("d2f/dx2(x=%f) = %.16f using forward difference", x, dfdx))

val df1_backward: UnivariateRealFunction
        = FiniteDifference(f, 2, FiniteDifference.Type.BACKWARD)
dfdx = df1_backward.evaluate(x) // evaluate at x
println(String.format("d2f/dx2(x=%f) = %.16f using backward difference", x, dfdx))

val df1_central: UnivariateRealFunction
        = FiniteDifference(f, 2, FiniteDifference.Type.CENTRAL)
dfdx = df1_central.evaluate(x) // evaluate at x
println(String.format("d2f/d2x(x=%f) = %.16f using central difference", x, dfdx))
```

The output is as follows:

```
d2f/dx2(x=2.000000) = -2.0000015520433827 using forward difference
d2f/dx2(x=2.000000) = -1.9999985243161564 using backward difference
d2f/d2x(x=2.000000) = -1.9999985243161564 using central difference
```

`FiniteDifference` numerically computes the derivative function of a given function of a given order. It is a function itself. It can be used to evaluate the derivative at any given point. The signature of `FiniteDifference` is as follows:

```
/**
  * Constructs an approximate derivative function for <i>f</i> using finite
  * difference.
  *
  * @param f     a univariate function
  * @param order the order of the derivative
  * @param type  the type of finite difference to use, c.f., {@link Type}
  */
```

```
public FiniteDifference(UnivariateRealFunction f, int order, Type type)
@Override
public double evaluate(double x)
  /**
   * Evaluates numerically the derivative of <i>f</i> at point <i>x</i>,
   * <i>f'(x)</i>, with step size <i>h</i>.
   * It could be challenging to automatically determine the step size
   * <i>h</i>, esp. when <i>|x|</i> is near 0.
   * It may, for example, require an analysis that involves <i>f'</i> and
   * <i>f''</i>.
   * The user may want to experiment with different <i>h</i>s by calling this
   * function.
   *
   * @param x the point to evaluate the derivative of <i>f</i> at
   * @param h step size
   * @return <i>f'(x)</i>, the numerical derivative of <i>f</i> at point
   * <i>x</i> with step size <i>h</i>
   */
public double evaluate(double x, double h)
```

The types supported are as follows:

- `FiniteDifference.FORWARD`
- `FiniteDifference.BACKWARD`
- `FiniteDifference.CENTRAL`

An important consideration in practice when calculating a derivative function using floating-point arithmetic on a computer is the choice of step size h. If h is too small, the subtraction will yield a large rounding error. On a computer, only a finite number of real numbers are representable. The two very close but different real numbers will be represented by the same floating-point representation as a finite binary. Therefore, all the finite-difference formulas are ill-conditioned and, due to cancellation, will produce a value of 0 if h is small enough. On the other hand, if h is too big, the secant and the tangent lines will not match, so the approximation will be off. For basic central differences, the optimal step is the cube root of machine epsilon, ε. For the numerical derivative formula evaluated at x and $x + h$, a choice for h that is small without producing a large rounding error is $\sqrt{\epsilon}x, x \neq 0$. The machine epsilon ε is typically of the order of 1e-16 for double precision. NM Dev chooses an h for you if you call the first `evaluate` function. Alternatively, you can have your own implementation of choosing h if you call the second `evaluate` function.

In general, for finite difference, the more points you use in computing a derivative, the more accurate will be. Also, the higher an order of a derivative, the less accurate it is. For example, approximating the second-order derivative is less accurate than approximating the first-order derivative, as you can see from the previous code examples.

6.3. Multivariate Finite Difference

A partial derivative of a multivariate function is the derivative with respect to one of the variables, with the others held constant. For example, the partial derivative of a bivariate function with respect to x is written as follows:

$$D_x f = f_x(x,y) = \frac{\partial f(x,y)}{\partial x}$$

They can be computed numerically using a finite difference just like any univariate functions in Section 6.2, except that you must impose a grid on a plane or higher-dimensional domain instead of an axis.

A second-order partial derivative with respect to x twice can be written as follows:

$$D_{xx}f = f_{xx}(x,y) = \frac{\partial^2 f(x,y)}{\partial x^2}$$

A second-order mixed partial derivative is when you first differentiate with respect to one variable and then another. For example, a second-order mixed partial derivative with respect first to x and then to y can be written as follows:

$$D_{xy}f = f_{xy}(x,y) = \frac{\partial}{\partial y}\frac{\partial f(x,y)}{\partial x}$$

A higher-order partial and mixed derivative looks like this:

$$\frac{\partial^{i+j+k} f}{\partial x^i \partial y^j \partial z^k} = \partial_x^i \partial_y^j \partial_z^k f$$

NM Dev computes these derivatives numerically by recursively applying the first-order central finite difference on the function. The class is `MultivariateFiniteDifference` and its signature is as follows:

```
/**
 * Constructs the partial derivative of a multi-variable function.
 * For example,
 * <code>varidx = new int[]{1, 2}</code> means
* \[
* f_{x_1,x_2} = {\partial^2 \over \partial x_2 \partial x_1} = {\partial
* \over \partial x_2}({\partial \over \partial x_1})
* \]
* @param f      the real multivariate function to take derivative of
 * @param varidx the variable indices of the derivative, counting from 1 up
 *               to the domain dimension of <i>f</i>
 */
public MultivariateFiniteDifference(RealScalarFunction f, int[] varidx)
```

The `varidx` argument takes the indices to the variables, and the class differentiates the function with respect to the variables in that order.

Here's an example:

$$z = f(x,y) = x^2 + xy + y^2$$

The graph of this function defines a surface in Euclidean space. To every point on this surface, there are an infinite number of tangent lines. Partial differentiation is the act of choosing one of these lines and finding its slope. Usually, the lines of most interest are those that are parallel to the xz-plane (holding y constant) and those that are parallel to the yz-plane (holding x constant). See Figure 6-6.

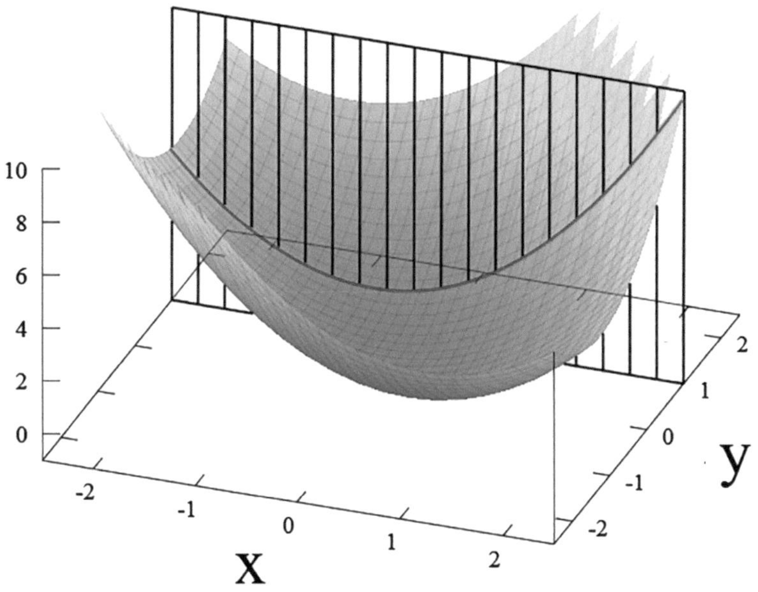

Figure 6-6. *A graph of $z = x^2 + xy + y^2$. For the partial derivative at (1, 1) that leaves y constant, the corresponding tangent line is parallel to the xz-plane*

To find the slope of the line tangent to the function at (1, 1) and parallel to the *xz*-plane, you treat *y* as a constant. By finding the derivative of the equation while assuming that *y* is a constant, you find that the slope of *f* at the point (*x*, *y*) is as follows:

$$\frac{\partial z}{\partial x} = 2x + y$$

See Figure 6-7.

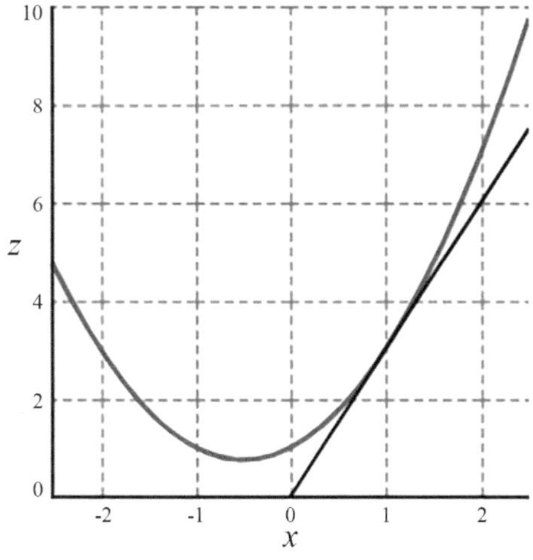

Figure 6-7. *A slice of the previous graph showing the function in the xz-plane at y = 1. Note that the two axes are shown here with different scales. The slope of the tangent line is 3*

It evaluates to 3 at point (1, 1). The following code snippet solves this problem:

```
// f = x^2 + xy + y^2
val f: RealScalarFunction = object : AbstractBivariateRealFunction() {

    override fun evaluate(x: Double, y: Double): Double {
        return x * x + x * y + y * y
    }
}

// df/dx = 2x + y
val dx: MultivariateFiniteDifference
        = MultivariateFiniteDifference(f, intArrayOf(1))
println(String.format("Dxy(1.0,1.0) %f", dx.evaluate(DenseVector(1.0, 1.0))))
```

The output is as follows:

```
Dxy(1.,1.) 3.000000
```

For another example of differentiating a multivariate function, consider the following:

$$f(x,y,z) = xy + 2xyz$$

The following code snippet computes these two mixed partial derivatives:

$$D_{xy}f = 1 + 2z$$

$$D_{yx}f = 1 + 2z$$

```
// f = xy + 2xyz
val f: RealScalarFunction = object : RealScalarFunction {

    override fun evaluate(v: Vector): Double {
        return v.get(1) * v.get(2) + 2 * v.get(1) * v.get(2) * v.get(3)
    }

    override fun dimensionOfDomain(): Int {
        return 3
    }

    override fun dimensionOfRange(): Int {
        return 1
    }
}
```

```
val dxy: MultivariateFiniteDifference // 1 + 2z
        // differentiate the first variable and then the second one
        = MultivariateFiniteDifference(f, intArrayOf(1, 2))
println(String.format("Dxy(1.0,1.0,1.0) %f", dxy.evaluate(DenseVector(1.0, 1.0, 1.0))))
println(String.format("Dxy(-100.0,0.0,-1.5) %f", dxy.evaluate(DenseVector(-100.0, 0.0, -1.5))))

//continuous function allows switching the order of differentiation by Clairaut's theorem
val dyx: MultivariateFiniteDifference // 1 + 2z
        // differentiate the second variable and then the first one
        = MultivariateFiniteDifference(f, intArrayOf(2, 1))
println(String.format("Dyx(1.0,1.0,1.0) %f", dyx.evaluate(DenseVector(1.0, 1.0, 1.0))))
println(String.format("Dyx(-100.0,0.0,-1.5) %f", dyx.evaluate(DenseVector(-100.0, 0.0, -1.5))))
```

The output is as follows:

```
Dxy(1.,1.,1.) 3.000001
Dxy(-100.,0.,-1.5) -2.000000
Dyx(1.,1.,1.) 3.000001
Dyx(-100.,0.,-1.5) -2.000000
```

6.3.1. Gradient

There are a number of important and widely used vectors and matrices of mixed partial derivatives. They are gradient vector, Jacobian matrix, and Hessian matrix.

The gradient function, ∇f, of a multivariate real-valued function, f, is a vector-valued function (or a vector field) from $\mathbb{R}^n$ to $\mathbb{R}^n$. It takes a point $\boldsymbol{x} = (x_1, \cdots, x_n)$ in $\mathbb{R}^n$ and outputs a vector in $\mathbb{R}^n$. The gradient at any point, $\nabla f(\boldsymbol{x})$, is a vector. It has components that are the partial derivatives of f at $\boldsymbol{x}$. That is:

$$\nabla f(\boldsymbol{x}) = \begin{bmatrix} \frac{\partial f}{\partial x_1}(\boldsymbol{x}) \\ \vdots \\ \frac{\partial f}{\partial x_n}(\boldsymbol{x}) \end{bmatrix}$$

Each component $\frac{\partial f}{\partial x_i}(\boldsymbol{x})$ is the partial derivative of the function along an axis and is the rate of change in that direction. So, the gradient vector is like the first-order derivative or the slope (or the tangent in the case of a univariate function). It can be interpreted as the direction and rate of fastest increase. If the gradient of a function is nonzero at point $\boldsymbol{x}$, the direction of the gradient is the direction in which the function increases most quickly from $\boldsymbol{x}$, and the magnitude of the gradient is the rate of increase in that direction, the greatest absolute directional derivative. Furthermore, the gradient is the zero vector at a point if and only if it is a stationary point (where the derivative vanishes). The gradient thus plays a fundamental role in optimization theory. You will see in Chapter 9 that many optimization algorithms such as gradient descent employ a gradient.

As an example, consider a room where the temperature is given by a scalar field, *T*. That is, the multivariate function or the field takes a point (x, y, z) and gives a temperature value $T(x, y, z)$. At each point in the room, the gradient of *T* at that point shows the direction in which the temperature rises most quickly, moving away from (x, y, z). The magnitude of the gradient determines how fast the temperature rises in that direction. More generally, if a multivariate function *f* is differentiable, the dot product between ∇f and a unit vector $\boldsymbol{v}$ is the slope or rate of change of the function in the direction of the $\boldsymbol{v}$, called the directional derivative of *f* at $\boldsymbol{v}$. The multivariate version of Taylor expansion shows that the best linear approximation of a function can be expressed in terms of the gradient.

$$f(\boldsymbol{x}) \approx f(\boldsymbol{x}_0) + \nabla f(\boldsymbol{x}_0) \bullet (\boldsymbol{x} - \boldsymbol{x}_0)$$

$\boldsymbol{x}$ and $\boldsymbol{x}_0$ are points in the $\mathbb{R}^n$ space. *f* maps $\mathbb{R}^n \to \mathbb{R}$, and ∇f: $\mathbb{R}^n \to \mathbb{R}^n$. The dot product in the last term gives a real number.

NM Dev supports computing the gradient and gradient function of a multivariate function. The classes are `Gradient` and `GradientFunction`. Their signatures are as follows:

```
/**
 * Constructs the gradient vector for a multivariate function <i>f</i> at
 * point <i>x</i>.
 *
 * @param f a multivariate function
 * @param x the point to evaluate the gradient of <i>f</i> at
 */
public Gradient(RealScalarFunction f, Vector x)
/**
 * Constructs the gradient function of a real scalar function <i>f</i>.
 *
 * @param f a real scalar function
 */
public GradientFunction(RealScalarFunction f)
```

Consider this function, for example:

$$f(x,y) = x\exp\left(-\left(x^2 + y^2\right)\right)$$

See Figure 6-8.

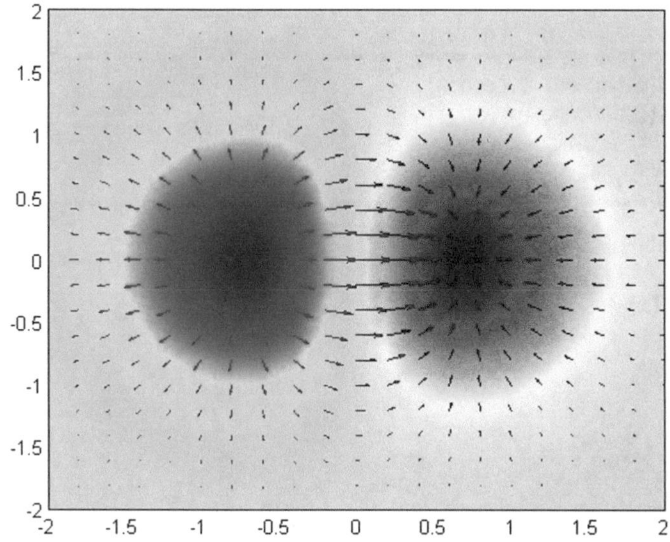

Figure 6-8. *The gradient of the 2D function $f(x, y) = xe^{-(x2 + y2)}$ is plotted as blue arrows over the pseudocolor plot of the function*

The following code computes the gradients and gradient function of the function:

```
// f = x * exp(-(x^2 + y^2))
val f: RealScalarFunction = object : AbstractBivariateRealFunction() {

    override fun evaluate(x: Double, y: Double): Double {
        return x * exp(-(x * x + y * y))
    }
}

val x1: Vector = DenseVector(0.0, 0.0)
val g1_0: Vector = Gradient(f, x1)
println(String.format("\ngradient at %s = %s", x1, g1_0))

val df: GradientFunction = GradientFunction(f)
val g1_1: Vector = df.evaluate(x1)
println(String.format("gradient at %s = %s", x1, g1_1))

val x2: Vector = DenseVector(-1.0, 0.0)
val g2: Vector = df.evaluate(x2)
println(String.format("gradient at %s = %s", x2, g2))

val x3: Vector = DenseVector(1.0, 0.0)
val g3: Vector = df.evaluate(x3)
println(String.format("gradient at %s = %s", x3, g3))
```

The output is as follows:

```
gradient at [0.000000, 0.000000]  = [1.000000, 0.000000]
gradient at [0.000000, 0.000000]  = [1.000000, 0.000000]
gradient at [-1.000000, 0.000000]  = [-0.367879, 0.000000]
gradient at [1.000000, 0.000000]  = [-0.367879, 0.000000]
```

Consider yet another function, shown here:

$$f(x,y) = -\left(\cos^2 x + \cos^2 y\right)^2$$

See Figure 6-9.

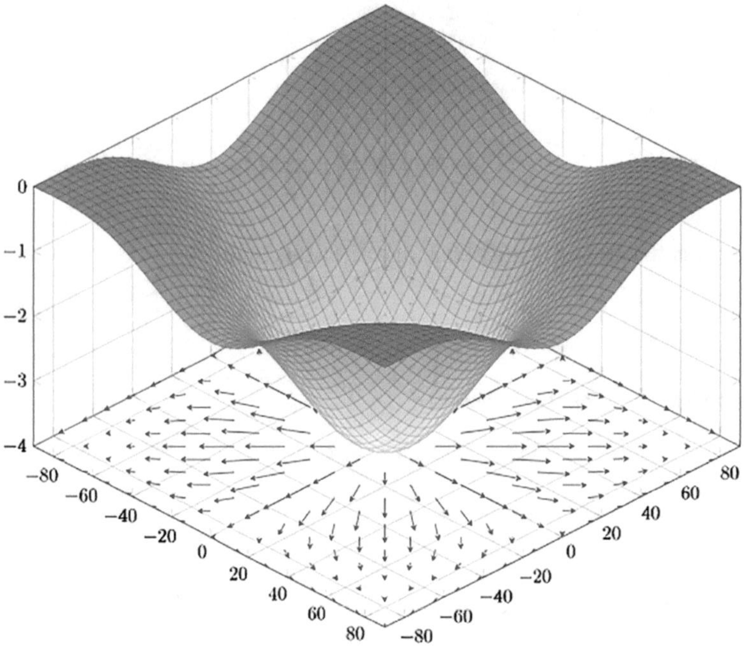

Figure 6-9. *The gradient of the function f(x,y) = −(cos²x + cos²y)² is depicted as a projected vector field on the bottom plane*

The following code computes the gradients and gradient function of the function:

```
// f = -((cos(x))^2 + (cos(y))^2)^2
val f: RealScalarFunction = object : AbstractBivariateRealFunction() {
    override fun evaluate(x: Double, y: Double): Double {
        var z: Double = cos(x) * cos(x)
        z += cos(y) * cos(y)
        z = -z * z
        return z
    }
}
```

```
val x1: Vector = DenseVector(0.0, 0.0)
val g1_0: Vector = Gradient(f, x1)
println(String.format("\ngradient at %s = %s", x1, g1_0))

val df: GradientFunction = GradientFunction(f)
val g1_1: Vector = df.evaluate(x1)
println(String.format("gradient at %s = %s", x1, g1_1))

val x2: Vector = DenseVector(-1.0, 0.0)
val g2: Vector = df.evaluate(x2)
println(String.format("gradient at %s = %s", x2, g2))

val x3: Vector = DenseVector(1.0, 0.0)
val g3: Vector = df.evaluate(x3)
println(String.format("gradient at %s = %s", x3, g3))
```

The output is as follows:

```
gradient at [0.000000, 0.000000]  = [0.000000, 0.000000]
gradient at [0.000000, 0.000000]  = [0.000000, 0.000000]
gradient at [-1.000000, 0.000000]  = [-2.349491, 0.000000]
gradient at [1.000000, 0.000000]  = [2.349491, 0.000000]
```

6.3.2. Jacobian

As you generalize the derivative of a scalar-valued function of a single variable to the gradient of a scalar-valued function in several variables, you can further generalize the concept to a vector-valued function in several variables. Suppose you have a vector-valued function $\boldsymbol{f}: \mathbb{R}^n \rightarrow \mathbb{R}^m$, which takes a point in $\mathbb{R}^n$ $\boldsymbol{x} = (x_1, \cdots, x_n)$ and outputs a vector $\boldsymbol{f}(\boldsymbol{x})$ in $\mathbb{R}^m$. The Jacobian matrix of $\boldsymbol{f}$ is defined to be an $m \times n$ matrix, denoted by $\boldsymbol{J}$, whose (i, j)-th entry is as follows:

$$\boldsymbol{J}_{ij} = \frac{\partial f_i}{\partial x_j}$$

Or explicitly:

$$\boldsymbol{J} = \begin{bmatrix} \frac{\partial \boldsymbol{f}}{\partial x_1} \cdots \frac{\partial \boldsymbol{f}}{\partial x_n} \end{bmatrix}$$

$$= \begin{bmatrix} \nabla^T f_1 \\ \vdots \\ \nabla^T f_m \end{bmatrix}$$

$$= \begin{bmatrix} \frac{\partial f_1}{\partial x_1} & \cdots & \frac{\partial f_1}{\partial x_n} \\ \vdots & \ddots & \vdots \\ \frac{\partial f_m}{\partial x_1} & \cdots & \frac{\partial f_m}{\partial x_n} \end{bmatrix}$$

$\nabla^T f_i$ is the transpose (row vector) of the gradient of the i-th component.

The Jacobian is the matrix of all its first-order partial derivatives. It represents the differential of $\boldsymbol{f}$ at every point where $\boldsymbol{f}$ is differentiable. It is the best linear approximation of the change of $\boldsymbol{f}$ in a neighborhood of $\boldsymbol{x}$. That is, the best linear approximation of $\boldsymbol{f}(\boldsymbol{y})$ for all points $\boldsymbol{y}$ close $\boldsymbol{x}$. This leads to this version of Taylor expansion:

$$\boldsymbol{f}(\boldsymbol{y}) = \boldsymbol{f}(\boldsymbol{x}) + \boldsymbol{J}_f(\boldsymbol{y} - \boldsymbol{x}) + O(\|\boldsymbol{y} - \boldsymbol{x}\|)$$

The error term approaches zero much faster than the distance between $\boldsymbol{y}$ and $\boldsymbol{x}$ does as $\boldsymbol{y}$ approaches $\boldsymbol{x}$. In this sense, the Jacobian may be regarded as a kind of "first-order derivative" of a vector-valued function of several variables.

If $m = n$, then $\boldsymbol{f}$ is a function from $\mathbb{R}^n$ to itself and the Jacobian matrix is a square matrix. You can then compute its determinant, known as the Jacobian determinant. The Jacobian determinant is sometimes simply referred to as "the Jacobian." The Jacobian determinant at a given point gives important information about the local behavior of $\boldsymbol{f}$ near that point. For instance, the inverse function theorem says that the continuously differentiable function $\boldsymbol{f}$ is invertible near a point $\boldsymbol{x} \in \mathbb{R}^n$ if the Jacobian determinant at $\boldsymbol{x}$ is nonzero. Furthermore, if the Jacobian determinant at $\boldsymbol{x}$ is positive, then $\boldsymbol{f}$ preserves orientation near $\boldsymbol{x}$; if it is negative, $\boldsymbol{f}$ reverses orientation. The absolute value of the Jacobian determinant at $\boldsymbol{x}$ gives us the factor by which the function $\boldsymbol{f}$ expands or shrinks volumes near $\boldsymbol{x}$.

NM Dev supports computing the Jacobian and Jacobian function of a multivariate vector-valued function. The classes are `Jacobian` and `JacobianFunction`. Their signatures are as follows:

```
/**
 * Constructs the Jacobian matrix for a multivariate function <i>f</i> at
 * point <i>x</i>.
 *
 * @param f a multivariate function
 * @param x the point to evaluate the Jacobian matrix at
 */
public Jacobian(RealVectorFunction f, Vector x)
/**
 * Constructs the Jacobian matrix for a multivariate function <i>f</i> at
 * point <i>x</i>.
 *
 * @param f a multivariate function in the form of an array of univariate
 *          functions
 * @param x the point to evaluate the Jacobian matrix at
 */
public Jacobian(final RealScalarFunction[] f, Vector x)
/**
 * Constructs the Jacobian matrix for a multivariate function <i>f</i> at
 * point <i>x</i>.
 *
 * @param f a multivariate function in the form of a list of univariate
 *          functions
 * @param x the point to evaluate the Jacobian matrix at
 */
public Jacobian(final List<RealScalarFunction> f, Vector x)
/**
 * Constructs the Jacobian function of a real scalar function <i>f</i>.
 *
```

```
 * @param f a real scalar function
 */
public JacobianFunction(RealVectorFunction f
```

In NM Dev, a multivariate vector-valued function can be represented by a RealVectorFunction, an array of RealScalarFunction, or a list of RealScalarFunction.

Consider this function $\boldsymbol{F}: \mathbb{R}^2 \rightarrow \mathbb{R}^2$:

$$\boldsymbol{F}\left(\begin{bmatrix} x \\ y \end{bmatrix}\right) = \begin{bmatrix} f_1(x,y) \\ f_2(x,y) \end{bmatrix} = \begin{bmatrix} x^2 y \\ 5x + \sin y \end{bmatrix}$$

The Jacobian is as follows:

$$\boldsymbol{J}_{\boldsymbol{F}}(x,y) = \begin{bmatrix} \frac{\partial f_1}{\partial x} & \frac{\partial f_1}{\partial y} \\ \frac{\partial f_2}{\partial x} & \frac{\partial f_2}{\partial y} \end{bmatrix} = \begin{bmatrix} 2xy & x^2 \\ 5 & \cos y \end{bmatrix}$$

The Jacobian determinant is as follows:

$$\left\|\boldsymbol{J}_{\boldsymbol{F}}(x,y)\right\| = 2xy\cos y - 5x^2$$

The following code solves this example:

```
val F: RealVectorFunction = object : RealVectorFunction {
    override fun evaluate(v: Vector): Vector {
        val x: Double= v.get(1)
        val y: Double= v.get(2)

        val f1: Double = x * x * y
        val f2: Double = 5.0 * x + sin(y)

        return DenseVector(f1, f2)
    }

    override fun dimensionOfDomain(): Int {
        return 2
    }

    override fun dimensionOfRange(): Int {
        return 2
    }
}

val x0: Vector = DenseVector(0.0, 0.0)
val J00: Matrix = Jacobian(F, x0)
println(String.format(
        "\nThe Jacobian at %s = %s, the det = %f",
        x0,
        J00,
        MatrixMeasure.det(J00)))
```

```
val J: RntoMatrix = JacobianFunction(F) // [2xy, x^2], [5, cosy]
val J01: Matrix = J.evaluate(x0)
println(String.format(
        "\nThe Jacobian at %s = %s, the det = %f",
        x0,
        J01,
        MatrixMeasure.det(J01)))

val x1: Vector = DenseVector(1.0, PI)
val J1: Matrix = J.evaluate(x1)
println(String.format(
        "The Jacobian at %s = %s, the det = %f",
        x1,
        J1,
        MatrixMeasure.det(J1)))
```

The output is as follows:

```
the Jacobian at [0.000000, 0.000000]  = 2x2
      [,1] [,2]
[1,] 0.000000, 0.000000,
[2,] 5.000000, 1.000000, , the det = 0.000000
the Jacobian at [0.000000, 0.000000]  = 2x2
      [,1] [,2]
[1,] 0.000000, 0.000000,
[2,] 5.000000, 1.000000, , the det = 0.000000
the Jacobian at [1.000000, 3.141593]  = 2x2
      [,1] [,2]
[1,] 6.283185, 1.000000,
[2,] 5.000000, -1.000000, , the det = -11.283185
```

Consider this function $\boldsymbol{F}$: $\mathbb{R}^3 \to \mathbb{R}^3$:

$$\boldsymbol{F}\left(\begin{bmatrix} x_1 \\ x_2 \\ x_3 \end{bmatrix}\right) = \begin{bmatrix} 5x_2 \\ 4x_1^{\ 2} - 2\sin(x_2 x_3) \\ x_2 x_3 \end{bmatrix}$$

The Jacobian is as follows:

$$\mathbf{J}_{\mathbf{F}}(x,y) = \begin{bmatrix} 0 & 5 & 0 \\ 8x_1 & -2x_3\cos(x_2 x_3) & -2x_2\cos(x_2 x_3) \\ 0 & x_3 & x_2 \end{bmatrix}$$

The Jacobian determinant is as follows:

$$\left\|\boldsymbol{J}_{\boldsymbol{F}}(x_1, x_2, x_3)\right\| = -40 x_1 x_2$$

The following code solves this example:

```
val F: RealVectorFunction = object : RealVectorFunction {
    override fun evaluate(v: Vector): Vector {
        val x1: Double = v.get(1)
        val x2: Double = v.get(2)
        val x3: Double = v.get(3)

        val f1: Double = 5.0 * x2
        val f2: Double = 4.0 * x1 * x1 - 2.0 * sin(x2 * x3)
        val f3: Double = x2 * x3

        return DenseVector(f1, f2, f3)
    }

    override fun dimensionOfDomain(): Int {
        return 3
    }

    override fun dimensionOfRange(): Int {
        return 3
    }
}

val x0: Vector = DenseVector(0.0, 0.0, 1.0)
val J: RntoMatrix = JacobianFunction(F)
val J0: Matrix = J.evaluate(x0)
println(String.format(
        "\nThe Jacobian at %s = %s, the det = %f",
        x0,
        J0,
        MatrixMeasure.det(J0)))

val x1: Vector = DenseVector(1.0, 2.0, 3.0)
val J1: Matrix = J.evaluate(x1)
println(String.format(
        "The Jacobian at %s = %s, the det = %f",
        x1,
        J1,
        MatrixMeasure.det(J1)))
```

The output is as follows:

```
the Jacobian at [0.000000, 0.000000, 1.000000]  = 3x3
        [,1] [,2] [,3]
[1,] 0.000000, 5.000000, 0.000000,
[2,] 0.000000, -2.000000, 0.000000,
[3,] 0.000000, 1.000000, 0.000000, , the det = 0.000000
```

```
the Jacobian at [1.000000, 2.000000, 3.000000]  = 3x3
        [,1] [,2] [,3]
[1,] 0.000000, 5.000000, 0.000000,
[2,] 8.000000, -5.761022, -3.840681,
[3,] 0.000000, 3.000000, 2.000000, , the det = -80.000000
```

From this, you see that $\boldsymbol{F}$ reverses orientation near those points where x_1 and x_2 have the same sign. The function is locally invertible everywhere except near points where $x_1 = 0$ or $x_2 = 0$. Intuitively, if you start with a tiny object around the point (1, 2, 3) and apply $\boldsymbol{F}$ to that object, you will get a resulting object with approximately $40 \times 1 \times 2 = 80$ times the volume of the original one, with the orientation reversed.

6.3.3. Hessian

You can generalize the concept of the second-order derivative of a univariate function to a multivariate real-valued function. First you compute the gradient of the scalar function (in a sense, taking the first-order derivative). Then you compute the Jacobian of the gradient function (in a sense, taking the second-order derivative). That Jacobian matrix is called the Hessian matrix. Hessian is a square matrix of second-order partial derivatives of a scalar-valued function or scalar field. It describes the local curvature of a multivariate function. That is:

$$\boldsymbol{H}\left(f\left(\boldsymbol{x}\right)\right) = \boldsymbol{J}\left(\nabla f\left(\boldsymbol{x}\right)\right)$$

Specifically, suppose $f\colon \mathbb{R}^n \to \mathbb{R}$. If all second partial derivatives of f exist and are continuous over the domain of the function, then the Hessian matrix $\boldsymbol{H}$ of f is a square $n \times n$ matrix, usually defined and arranged as follows:

$$\boldsymbol{H}_f = \begin{bmatrix} \dfrac{\partial^2 f}{\partial x_1^2} & \dfrac{\partial^2 f}{\partial x_1 \partial x_2} & \cdots & \dfrac{\partial^2 f}{\partial x_1 \partial x_n} \\ \dfrac{\partial^2 f}{\partial x_2 \partial x_1} & \dfrac{\partial^2 f}{\partial x_2^2} & \cdots & \dfrac{\partial^2 f}{\partial x_2 \partial x_n} \\ \vdots & \vdots & \ddots & \vdots \\ \dfrac{\partial^2 f}{\partial x_n \partial x_1} & \dfrac{\partial^2 f}{\partial x_n \partial x_2} & \cdots & \dfrac{\partial^2 f}{\partial x_n^2} \end{bmatrix}$$

In short form, you get the following:

$$\left(\boldsymbol{H}_f\right)_{i,j} = \frac{\partial^2 f}{\partial x_i \partial x_j}$$

The Hessian matrix is a symmetric matrix. The hypothesis of continuity of the second derivatives implies that the order of differentiation does not matter (by Clairaut's theorem). The determinant of the Hessian matrix is called the Hessian determinant. Hessian matrices are used to solve optimization problems within Newton-type methods because they are the coefficient of the quadratic term of a local Taylor expansion of a function. That is:

$$y = f\left(\boldsymbol{x} + \Delta\boldsymbol{x}\right) \approx f\left(\boldsymbol{x}\right) + \nabla f\left(\boldsymbol{x}\right)\Delta\boldsymbol{x} + \frac{1}{2}\Delta\boldsymbol{x}^T H\left(\boldsymbol{x}\right)\Delta\boldsymbol{x}$$

We discuss using Hessian matrix in optimization in more detail in Chapter 11.

NM Dev supports computing the Hessian and Hessian function of a multivariate real-valued function. The classes are `Hessian` and `HessianFunction`. Their signatures are as follows:

```
/**
 * Constructs the Hessian matrix for a multivariate function <i>f</i> at
 * point <i>x</i>.
 *
 * @param f a multivariate function
 * @param x the point to evaluate the Hessian of <i>f</i> at
 */
public Hessian(RealScalarFunction f, Vector x)
/**
 * Constructs the Hessian function of a real scalar function <i>f</i>.
 *
 * @param f a real scalar function
 */
public HessianFunction(RealScalarFunction f)
```

The following sample code computes the Hessian matrices and Hessian function of $f(x, y) = xy$:

```
val f: RealScalarFunction = object : AbstractBivariateRealFunction() {
    override fun evaluate(x: Double, y: Double): Double {
        return x * y // f = xy
    }
}

val x1: Vector = DenseVector(1.0, 1.0)
val H1: Hessian = Hessian(f, x1)
println(String.format(
        "\nThe Hessian at %s = %s, the det = %f",
        x1,
        H1,
        MatrixMeasure.det(H1)))

val H: RntoMatrix = HessianFunction(f)
val Hx1: Matrix = H.evaluate(x1)
println(String.format(
        "\nThe Hessian at %s = %s, the det = %f",
        x1,
        Hx1,
        MatrixMeasure.det(Hx1)))

val x2: Vector = DenseVector(0.0, 0.0)
val H2: Hessian = Hessian(f, x2)
println(String.format(
        "\nThe Hessian at %s = %s, the det = %f",
        x2,
        H2,
        MatrixMeasure.det(H2)))
```

```
val Hx2: Matrix = H.evaluate(x2)
println(String.format(
        "\nThe Hessian at %s = %s, the det = %f",
        x2,
        Hx2,
        MatrixMeasure.det(Hx2)))
```

The output is as follows:

```
the Hessian at [1.000000, 1.000000]  = 2x2
        [,1] [,2]
[1,] 0.000000, 1.000000,
[2,] 1.000000, 0.000000, , the det = -0.999999
the Hessian at [1.000000, 1.000000]  = 2x2
        [,1] [,2]
[1,] 0.000000, 1.000000,
[2,] 1.000000, 0.000000, , the det = -0.999999
the Hessian at [0.000000, 0.000000]  = 2x2
        [,1] [,2]
[1,] 0.000000, 1.000000,
[2,] 1.000000, 0.000000, , the det = -1.000000
the Hessian at [0.000000, 0.000000]  = 2x2
        [,1] [,2]
[1,] 0.000000, 1.000000,
[2,] 1.000000, 0.000000, , the det = -1.000000
```

6.4. Ridders' Method

Ridders' method improves the estimation by finite difference by extrapolating a series of approximations. To compute a numerical derivative, you must first compute a series of the approximations using a sequence of decreasing step sizes. Ridders' method then extrapolates the step size to zero using Neville's algorithm. In general, it gives a higher precision than the simple (one-time) finite differencing method.

The choice of the initial step size, h_0, is critical. If h_0 is too big, the value computed could be inaccurate. If h_0 is too small, due to rounding error, you might be computing the "same" value over and over again for different step sizes.

The following code snippet compares the first ninth-order derivatives of the log function evaluated at $x = 0.5$ calculated by the Ridders' method versus the simple finite difference.

```
val f: UnivariateRealFunction = object : AbstractUnivariateRealFunction() {
    override fun evaluate(x: Double): Double {
        return ln(x)
    }
}

val x: Double = 0.5
for (order in 1..9) {
    val fd: FiniteDifference = FiniteDifference(f, order, FiniteDifference.Type.CENTRAL)
    val ridder: Ridders = Ridders(f, order)
```

```
    println(String.format(
            "%d-nd order derivative by Ridder @ %f = %.16f", order, x, ridder.evaluate(x)))
    println(String.format(
            "%d-nd order derivative by FD @ %f = %.16f", order, x, fd.evaluate(x)))
}
```

The output is as follows:

```
1-nd order derivative by Ridder @ 0.500000 = 2.0000000000000000
1-nd order derivative by FD @ 0.500000 = 2.0000000000000000
2-nd order derivative by Ridder @ 0.500000 = -4.0000004374066640
2-nd order derivative by FD @ 0.500000 = -4.0000031040867650
3-nd order derivative by Ridder @ 0.500000 = 16.0000016378464240
3-nd order derivative by FD @ 0.500000 = 16.0002441406250000
4-nd order derivative by Ridder @ 0.500000 = -95.9999555891298100
4-nd order derivative by FD @ 0.500000 = -95.9874881885177200
5-nd order derivative by Ridder @ 0.500000 = 767.9383982440593000
5-nd order derivative by FD @ 0.500000 = 767.5675271157362000
6-nd order derivative by Ridder @ 0.500000 = -7681.9174458835320000
6-nd order derivative by FD @ 0.500000 = -7686.1197112745450000
7-nd order derivative by Ridder @ 0.500000 = 92116.9184885280300000
7-nd order derivative by FD @ 0.500000 = 92428.4022426225400000
8-nd order derivative by Ridder @ 0.500000 = -1290356.2663459945000000
8-nd order derivative by FD @ 0.500000 = -1300812.8634378603000000
9-nd order derivative by Ridder @ 0.500000 = 20941653.5495638000000000
9-nd order derivative by FD @ 0.500000 = 21347177.7802486680000000
```

The analytical results are exactly 2, -4, 16, and -96 for the first four orders. Note that the Ridders' method gives better accuracy, especially for the higher-order derivatives that are typically challenging for finite difference.

Ridders' method works for multivariate functions as well. The following example compares Ridders' method to the finite difference of the example in Section 6.3.

```
// f = xy + 2xyz
val f: RealScalarFunction = object : RealScalarFunction {

    override fun evaluate(v: Vector): Double {
        return v.get(1) * v.get(2) + 2 * v.get(1) * v.get(2) * v.get(3)
    }

    override fun dimensionOfDomain(): Int {
        return 3
    }

    override fun dimensionOfRange(): Int {
        return 1
    }
}
```

```
val dxy_ridder: Ridders = Ridders(f, intArrayOf(1, 2))
val dxy: MultivariateFiniteDifference // 1 + 2z
        // differentiate the first variable and then the second one
        = MultivariateFiniteDifference(f, intArrayOf(1, 2))
val x0: Vector = DenseVector(1.0, 1.0, 1.0)
println(String.format("Dxy(%s) by Ridder = %.16f", x0, dxy_ridder.evaluate(x0)))
println(String.format("Dxy(%s) by FD =  %.16f", x0, dxy.evaluate(x0)))
val x1: Vector = DenseVector(-100.0, 0.0, -1.5)
println(String.format("Dxy(%s) by FD = %.16f", x1, dxy_ridder.evaluate(x1)))
println(String.format("Dxy(%s) by FD = %.16f", x1, dxy.evaluate(x1)))

//continuous function allows switching the order of differentiation by Clairaut's theorem
val dyx_ridder: Ridders = Ridders(f, intArrayOf(2, 1))
val dyx: MultivariateFiniteDifference // 1 + 2z
        // differentiate the second variable and then the first one
        = MultivariateFiniteDifference(f, intArrayOf(2, 1))
println(String.format("Dyx(%s) by Ridder = %.16f", x0, dyx_ridder.evaluate(x0)))
println(String.format("Dyx(%s) by FD = %.16f", x0, dyx.evaluate(x0)))
println(String.format("Dyx(%s) by Ridder = %.16f", x1, dyx_ridder.evaluate(x1)))
println(String.format("Dyx(%s) by FD = %.16f", x1, dyx.evaluate(x1)))
```

The output is as follows:

```
Dxy([1.000000, 1.000000, 1.000000] ) by Ridder = 2.9999999941935465
Dxy([1.000000, 1.000000, 1.000000] ) by FD =  3.0000013187575885
Dxy([-100.000000, 0.000000, -1.500000] ) by FD = -2.0000000000032907
Dxy([-100.000000, 0.000000, -1.500000] ) by FD = -1.9999999999865270
Dyx([1.000000, 1.000000, 1.000000] ) by Ridder = 2.9999999941935465
Dyx([1.000000, 1.000000, 1.000000] ) by FD = 3.0000013187575885
Dyx([-100.000000, 0.000000, -1.500000] ) by Ridder = -2.0000000000044610
Dyx([-100.000000, 0.000000, -1.500000] ) by FD = -1.9999999999748960
```

The analytical results are 3 and -2, respectively. Note that the Ridders' method gives better accuracy than finite difference.

6.5. Derivative Functions of Special Functions

NM Dev supports a number of special functions and their first-order derivative functions. A special function is a function that typically cannot be computed using a finite number of elementary functions such as a sum, product, and/or composition of finitely many polynomials, rational functions, trigonometric and exponential functions, and their inverse functions. So are their derivative functions. Because of their importance in many applications, for example, the Gaussian function in statistics, you must have an accurate computation of these functions. You cannot afford such inaccuracy using finite difference. There are special techniques to compute for special functions, such as continued fractions. The special functions and their first-order derivative functions that NM Dev supports are Gaussian, Error, Beta, Regularized Incomplete Beta, and Gamma.

6.5.1. Gaussian Derivative Function

The Gaussian function is defined as follows:

$$f(x) = a\exp\left(-\frac{(x-b)^2}{2c^2}\right)$$

The class to compute the Gaussian function is `Gaussian`, and its signature is as follows:

```
/**
 * Constructs an instance of the Gaussian function.
 *
 * @param a <i>a</i>
 * @param b <i>b</i>
 * @param c <i>c</i>
 */
public Gaussian(double a, double b, double c)
```

The class to compute the derivative function of the Gaussian function is `DGaussian`, and its signature is as follows:

```
/**
 * Construct the derivative function of a Gaussian function.
 *
 * @param phi a {@link Gaussian} function
 */
public DGaussian(Gaussian phi)
```

Here's an example:

```
val G: Gaussian = Gaussian(1.0, 0.0, 1.0) // standard Gaussian
val dG: DGaussian = DGaussian(G)
var x: Double = -0.5
println(String.format("dG/dx(%f) = %f", x, dG.evaluate(x)))
x = 0.0
println(String.format("dG/dx(%f) = %f", x, dG.evaluate(x)))
x = 0.5
println(String.format("dG/dx(%f) = %f", x, dG.evaluate(x)))
```

The output is as follows:

```
dG/dx(-0.500000) = 0.176033
dG/dx(0.000000) = -0.000000
dG/dx(0.500000) = -0.176033
```

6.5.2. Error Derivative Function

The Error function is defined as follows:

$$erzz = \frac{2}{\pi}\int_0^z e^{-t^2}\,dt$$

The class to compute the Error function is `Erf`. The class to compute the derivative function of the Error function is `DErf`. Both classes inherit `evaluate(double x)` from `AbstractUnivariateRealFunction`. Their constructors do not take any arguments.

Here's an example:

```
val z: Double = 0.5
val E: Erf = Erf()
val dE: DErf = DErf()
println(String.format("erf(%f) = %f", z, E.evaluate(z)))
println(String.format("dErf/dz(%f) = %f", z, dE.evaluate(z)))
```

The output is as follows:

```
erf(0.500000) = 0.520500
dErf/dz(0.500000) = 0.878783
```

6.5.3. Beta Derivative Function

The Beta function is also called the Euler integral of the first kind. It is defined, for any real number, as $x, y > 0$.

$$B(x,y) = \int_0^1 t^{x-1}(1-t)^{y-1}\,dt$$

The class to compute the Beta function is `Beta`. The class to compute the derivative function of the Beta function is `DBeta`. Both classes inherit `evaluate(double x, double y)` from `AbstractBivariateRealFunction`. Their constructors do not take any arguments.

Here's an example:

```
val x: Double = 1.5
val y: Double = 2.5
val B: Beta = Beta()
val dB: DBeta = DBeta()
println(String.format("Beta(%f) = %f", x, B.evaluate(x, y)))
println(String.format("dBeta/dz(%f) = %f", x, dB.evaluate(x, y)))
```

The output is as follows:

```
Beta(1.500000) = 0.196350
dBeta/dz(1.500000) = -0.239473
```

6.5.4. Regularized Incomplete Beta Derivative Function

The Incomplete Beta function, a generalization of the Beta function, is defined as follows:

$$B(x,p,q)=\int_0^x t^{p-1}(1-t)^{q-1}\,dt$$

When $x = 1$, the Incomplete Beta function coincides with the complete Beta function.

The Regularized Incomplete Beta function (or Regularized Beta function for short) is defined in terms of the Incomplete Beta function and the complete Beta function.

$$I_x(p,q)=\frac{B(x,p,q)}{B(p,q)}$$

The Regularized Incomplete Beta function is the cumulative distribution function of the beta distribution.

The class to compute the Regularized Incomplete Beta function is `BetaRegularized`, and its signature is as follows:

```
/**
 * Constructs an instance of <i>I<sub>x</sub>(p,q)</i> with the parameters
 * <i>p</i> and <i>q</i>.
 *
 * @param p <i>p > 0</i>, the shape parameter
 * @param q <i>q > 0</i>, the shape parameter
 */
public BetaRegularized(final double p, final double q)
```

The class to compute the derivative function of the Regularized Incomplete Beta function is `DBetaRegularized`, and its signature is as follows:

```
/**
 * Constructs the derivative function of the Regularized Incomplete Beta
 * function, {@link BetaRegularized}.
 *
 * @param p the shape parameter
 * @param q the shape parameter
 */
public DBetaRegularized(double p, double q)
```

Here's an example:

```
val p: Double = 0.5
val q: Double = 2.5
val I: BetaRegularized = BetaRegularized(p, q)
val dI: DBetaRegularized = DBetaRegularized(p, q)

val x: Double = 1.0
println(String.format("BetaRegularized(%f) = %f", x, I.evaluate(x)))
println(String.format("dBetaRegularized/dz(%f) = %f", x, dI.evaluate(x)))
```

The output is as follows:

```
BetaRegularized(1.000000) = 1.000000
dBetaRegularized/dz(1.000000) = 0.000000
```

6.5.5. Gamma Derivative Function

The Gamma function is an extension of the factorial function to real and complex numbers, with its argument shifted down by 1. For real numbers, it is defined as follows:

$$\Gamma(z) = \int_0^{\infty} x^{z-1} e^{-x} dx$$

The class to compute the Gamma function is `Gamma`. The class to compute the derivative function of the Gamma function is `DGamma`. Both classes inherit `evaluate(double x)` from `AbstractUnivariateRealFunction`. Their constructors do not take any arguments. NM Dev has a number of implementations of the Gamma function. They have different properties in terms of accuracy and performance. The default choice is the Lanczos algorithm such that all computations are done using `double`.

Here's an example:

```
val z: Double = 0.5
// <a href="http://en.wikipedia.org/wiki/Lanczos_approximation">Wikipedia: Lanczos
approximation</a>
val G: Gamma = GammaLanczosQuick()
val dG: DGamma = DGamma()
println(String.format("Gamma(%f) = %f", z, G.evaluate(z)))
println(String.format("dGamma/dz(%f) = %f", z, dG.evaluate(z)))
```

The output is as follows:

```
Gamma(0.500000) = 1.772454
dGamma/dz(0.500000) = -3.480231
```

6.5.6. Polynomial Derivative Function

A polynomial is not exactly a special function. We include it here because NM Dev does not use finite difference to compute the derivative function of a polynomial. There is a closed-form solution to differentiate a polynomial.

$$p(x) = a_n x^n + \cdots a_1 x + a_0$$

$$\frac{dp}{dx} = n a_n x^{n-1} + \cdots a_2 x + a_1$$

The class to compute a polynomial is Polynomial, and its signature is as follows:

```
/**
 * Constructs a polynomial from an array of coefficients.
 * The first/0-th entry corresponds to the <i>x<sup>n</sup></i> term.
 * The last/n-th entry corresponds to the constant term.
 * The degree of the polynomial is <i>n</i>, the array length minus 1.
 * <p/>
 * For example,
 * <blockquote><code>
 * new Polynomial(1, -2, 3, 2)
 * </code></blockquote>
 * creates an instance of {@code Polynomial} representing <i>x<sup>3</sup> - 2x<sup>2</sup>
   + 3x + 2</i>.
 *
 * @param coefficients the polynomial coefficients
 */
public Polynomial(double... coefficients)
```

The class to compute the derivative function of a polynomial is DPolynomial, and its signature is as follows. The derivative function of a polynomial is also a polynomial.

```
/**
 * Constructs the derivative function of a {@link Polynomial}, which, again,
 * is a polynomial.
 *
 * @param polynomial a polynomial
 */
public DPolynomial(Polynomial polynomial)
```

Here's an example:

```
val p: Polynomial = Polynomial(1.0, 2.0, 1.0) // x^2 + 2x + 1
val dp: Polynomial = DPolynomial(p) // 2x + 2
val x: Double = 1.0
println(String.format("dp/dx(%f) = %f", x, dp.evaluate(x)))
```

The output is as follows:

```
dp/dx(1.000000) = 4.000000
```

6.6. Numerical Integration

A definite integral is the (signed) area under a curve or a function $f(x)$, called the *integrand*, between two points $[a, b]$ in the real line. It is defined as follows:

$$I = \int_a^b f(x)\,dx$$

The symbol *dx*, called the differential of the variable *x*, indicates that the variable of integration is *x*. It means a small change in *x* as in differentiation. Integration is the process of computing the value of a definite integral. The first fundamental theorem of calculus says that the derivative of an integral is the integrand. So, the integral is sometimes called the anti-derivative of a function. See Figure 6-10.

$$f(x)=\frac{d}{dx}\int_0^x f(t)\,dt$$

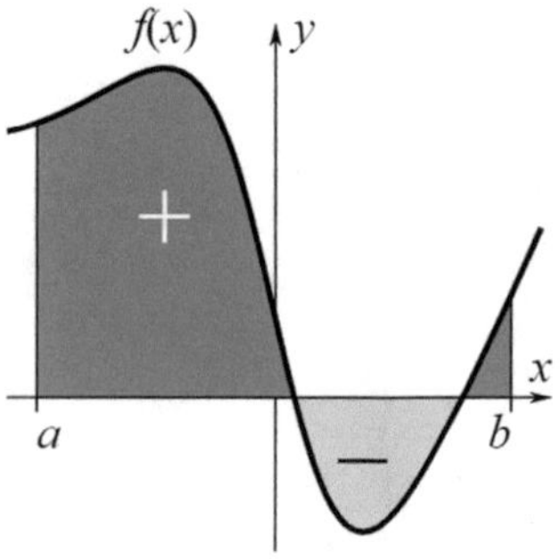

Figure 6-10. *Integral as the signed area under curve*

Riemann gave the first rigorous definition of an integral. The basic idea of the Riemann integral is to partition the area into many rectangles to approximate the area and then to sum them (hence integration). By taking better and better approximations, say infinitely many infinitesimally small rectangles, you can say that "in the limit" you get the exact area under the curve. Figure 6-11 shows a sequence of Riemann sums over a regular partition of an interval. The number on top is the total area of the rectangles, which converges to the integral of the function.

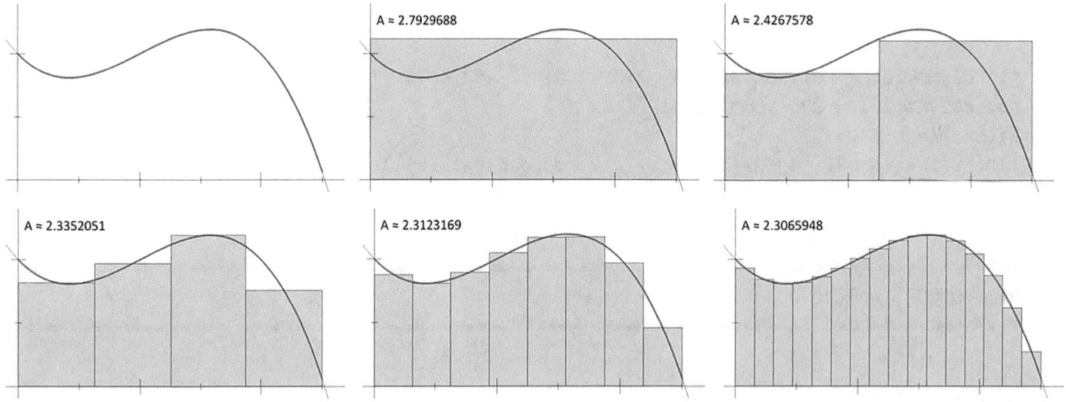

Figure 6-11. *A sequence of Riemann sums*

Mathematically, a partition of an interval [*a*, *b*] is a finite sequence of points:

$$a=x_0<x_1<\cdots x_n=b$$

There is a distinguished point $t_i \in [x_i, x_{i+1}]$ in each subinterval to determine the height of the rectangle $f(t_i)$. The rectangle area size is therefore $f(t_i)(x_{i+1} - x_i)$. The Riemann sum of *f* with respect to the partition is defined as the sum of all the rectangles.

$$S_n = \sum_{i=0}^{n-1} f(t_i)(x_{i+1} - x_i)$$

When you take the limit that *n* goes to infinity, the Riemann sum becomes the integral value:

$$I = \lim_{n \to \infty} S_n$$

Numerical integration is a technique that approximates a definite integral using a similar partitioning concept: Using a weighted average approximation of the limited sample values of the integrand to replace the value of the function. Numerical integration is important because it is (often) not possible to find the (closed-form) antiderivative analytically. Even if antiderivatives exist, they may not be easy to compute because they cannot be composed of elementary functions. It is much easier to compute a numerical approximation than the antiderivative in terms of special functions or infinite series. Moreover, the integrand may be known only at certain points, such as obtained by sampling. Some embedded systems and other computer applications may need numerical integration for this reason.

Traditionally, the mathematics of finding the size of an area is called the *quadrature*. It is now a synonym for integration but less popularly used. The numerical integration formulas are still called numerical quadrature formulas. There are many ways to do numerical integration. They differ by how many partitions they divide the interval into, whether the partitions are equally spaced, how you choose the distinguished points, whether it is open (not using endpoints) or closed (using endpoints), and how you perform extrapolation (or not). This chapter can only scratch the surface to introduce some of the most basic variants.

6.7. The Newton-Cotes Family

The Newton-Cotes formulas, also called the Newton-Cotes quadrature rules or simply Newton-Cotes rules, are a group of formulas for numerical integration (also called a quadrature) based on evaluating an integrand at equally spaced points. They are named after Isaac Newton and Roger Cotes. Newton-Cotes formulas can be useful if the values of the integrand at equally spaced points are available. If it is possible to use a different set of (possibly not equally spaced) points, then other methods such as Gaussian quadrature are probably more accurate. There are many derivations of the Newton-Cotes formulas. Two of the most famous ones are the trapezoidal quadrature and the Simpson quadrature formulas.

6.7.1. The Trapezoidal Quadrature Formula

The trapezoidal formula works by replacing the function using a straight line, essentially approximating the region under the function as a trapezoid and calculating its area. See Figure 6-12.

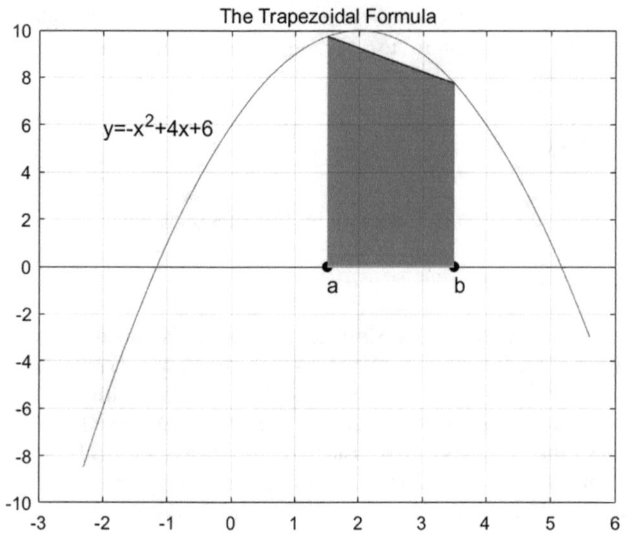

Figure 6-12. *The trapezoidal formula*

The line equation passing through the two points *a* and *b* is as follows:

$$L_1(x) = \frac{f(b) - f(a)}{b - a}(x - a) + f(a)$$

The area under the line is the area of the trapezoidal that is simply multiplying the sum of the bases (the parallel sides) by the height (the perpendicular distance between the bases) and then dividing by 2. You can also do a proper integration to get the same result.

Replacing *f*(*x*) with $L_1(x)$, you get this:

$$\int_a^b f(x)\,dx \approx \int_a^b L_1(x)\,dx$$

$$= \int_a^b \left[\frac{f(b) - f(a)}{b - a}(x - a) + f(a)\right]dx$$

$$= \frac{f(a) + f(b)}{2}(b - a)$$

For a function *f*(*x*) and an interval [*a*, *b*], you can divide the interval into *N* subintervals. Then you apply this trapezoidal rule to each subinterval and sum them.

Let

$$\Delta x = \frac{b - a}{N}$$

$$\int_a^b f(x)\,dx \approx \frac{\Delta x}{2}\sum_{k=1}^{N}\left(f(x_{k-1}) + f(x_k)\right)$$

It can be proved that, assuming $f''(x)$ exists and is continuous on $[a, b]$, the error from using the trapezoidal rule is as follows for some $\xi \in [a, b]$:

$$\varepsilon = -\frac{(b-a)^3}{12N} f''(\xi)$$

In NM Dev, the class to do the trapezoidal integration is `Trapezoidal`. The following example solves the problem in Figure 6-12:

```
val f: UnivariateRealFunction = object : AbstractUnivariateRealFunction() {

    override fun evaluate(x: Double): Double {
        return -(x * x - 4 * x - 6) // -(x^2 - 4x - 6)
    }
}

// the limit
val a: Double = 1.5
val b: Double = 3.5
// an integrator using the trapezoidal rule
val integrator: Integrator = Trapezoidal(1e-8, 20) // precision, max number of iterations
// the integration
val I: Double = integrator.integrate(f, a, b)
println(String.format("S_[%.1f,%.1f] f(x) dx = %f", a, b, I))
```

The output is as follows:

```
S_[1.5,3.5] f(x) dx = 18.833333
```

The class signature for `Trapezoidal` is as follows:

```
/**
 * Constructs an integrator that implements the Trapezoidal rule.
 *
 * @param precision     the convergence threshold
 * @param maxIterations the maximum number of iterations
 */
public Trapezoidal(double precision, int maxIterations)
```

In NM Dev, all implementations of an integrator (algorithm) inherit from the `Integrator` class. They all call `integrate` to do the job.

```
/**
 * Integrate function <i>f</i> from <i>a</i> to <i>b</i>,
 * \[
 * \int_a^b\! f(x)\, dx
 * \]
 *
 * @param f a univariate function
 * @param a the lower limit
```

```
 * @param b the upper limit
* @return \(\int_a^b\! f(x)\, dx\)
*/
public double integrate(UnivariateRealFunction f, double a, double b);
```

6.7.2. The Simpson Quadrature Formula

The Simpson formula, instead of replacing the function with a line, replaces $f(x)$ with a quadratic function or a parabola. The interval is divided into two partitions giving three points: a, b, and a midpoint $m = \frac{a+b}{2}$. The quadratic function is as follows:

$$L_2(x) =$$

$$\frac{(x-m)(x-b)}{(a-m)(a-b)} f(a) + \frac{(x-a)(x-b)}{(m-a)(m-b)} f(m) + \frac{(x-m)(x-a)}{(b-m)(b-a)} f(b)$$

From a geometrical point of view, the Simpson formula calculates the area of the curved trapezoid surrounded by a parabola to approximate the area enclosed by $f(x)$. See Figure 6-13.

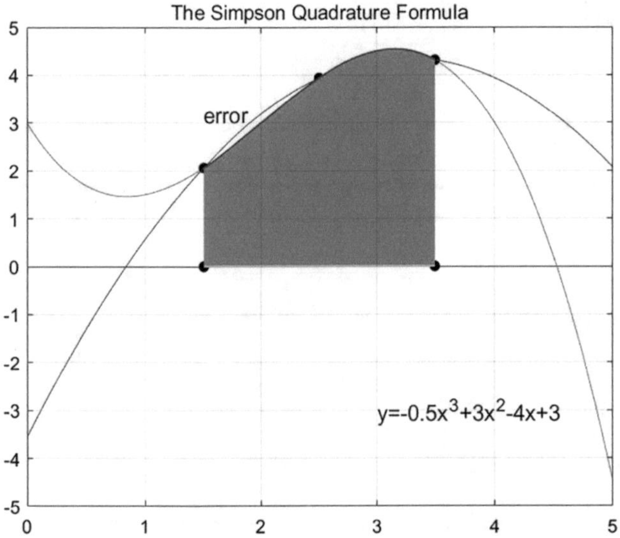

Figure 6-13. *The Simpson formula*

Replacing $f(x)$ with $L_2(x)$, you get this:

$$\int_a^b f(x)dx \approx \int_a^b L_2(x)dx$$

$$= \frac{b-a}{6}\left[f(a) + 4f\left(\frac{a+b}{2}\right) + f(b)\right]$$

$$= \frac{h}{3}\left[f(a) + 4f\left(\frac{a+b}{2}\right) + f(b)\right]$$

$h = \frac{b-a}{2}$ is the step size in each partition. Because of the $\frac{1}{3}$ in the formula, this Simpson rule is often called Simpson's 1/3 rule.

For a function $f(x)$ and an interval $[a, b]$, you can divide the interval into N subintervals. Then you apply this Simpson rule to each subinterval and sum them. You get the following:

$$\int_a^b f(x)dx \approx \frac{h}{3}\sum_{j=1}^{N/2}\left[f(x_{2j-2}) + 4f(x_{2j-1}) + f(x_{2j})\right]$$

The Simpson rule is expected to improve on the trapezoidal rule for functions that are twice continuously differentiable. However, for rougher functions, the trapezoidal rule is likely to be preferable. It can be proved that, assuming the fourth-order derivative $f^{(4)}(x)$ exists and is continuous on $[a, b]$, the error from using Simpson's 1/3 rule is as follows for some $\xi \in [a, b]$:

$$\varepsilon = -\frac{h^4}{180}(b-a)f^{(4)}(\xi)$$

In NM Dev, the class to do Simpson's 1/3 integration is `Trapezoidal`. The following example solves the problem in Figure 6-12:

```
val f: UnivariateRealFunction = object : AbstractUnivariateRealFunction() {

    override fun evaluate(x: Double): Double {
        return -(x * x - 4 * x + 6) // -(x^2 - 4x + 6)
    }
}

// the limit
val a: Double = 1.5
val b: Double = 3.5
// an integrator using the Simpson rule
val integrator: Integrator = Simpson(1e-8, 20) // precision, max number of iterations
// the integration
val I: Double = integrator.integrate(f, a, b)
println(String.format("S_[%.0f,%.0f] f(x) dx = %f", a, b, I))
```

The output is as follows:

```
S_[1.5,3.5] f(x) dx = 18.833333
```

The class signature for `Simpson` is as follows:

```
/**
 * Constructs an integrator that implements Simpson's rule.
 *
 * @param precision     the convergence threshold
 * @param maxIterations the maximum number of iterations
 */
public Simpson(double precision, int maxIterations)
```

6.7.3. The Newton-Cotes Quadrature Formulas

It is conceivable that you could divide the interval $[a, b]$ into more than one partition (as in the case of the trapezoidal rule) or more than two partitions (as in the case of the Simpson's rule). You can divide it into n intervals. You can also use a closed formula where the endpoints a and b are used, or an open formula where the endpoints are not used because $f(a)$ and $f(b)$ may not exist. The Newton-Cotes formula is such a generalization. It divides the interval $[a, b]$ into n equal partitions. For a closed formula, the equally spaced points are as follows:

$$x_i = a + ih,\ h = \frac{b-a}{n}$$

For an open formula, the equally spaced points are as follows:

$$x_i = a + (i+1)h,\ h = \frac{b-a}{n+2}$$

For the closed formula, an n-th degree difference polynomial can be constructed, as shown here:

$$L_n(x) = \sum_{k=0}^{n} \frac{w(x)}{(x-x_k)w'(x_k)} f(x_k)$$

where $w(x) = (x - x_0)(x - x_1)\cdots(x - x_n)$.
Replacing $f(x)$ with $L_n(x)$, you get the following:

$$\int_a^b f(x)dx \approx \int_a^b L_n(x)dx = \int_a^b \left(\sum_{k=0}^{n} \frac{w(x)}{(x-x_k)w'(x_k)} f(x_k) \right) dx$$

$$= \sum_{i=0}^{n} \left(\int_a^b \frac{w(x)}{(x-x_k)w'(x_k)} dx \right) f(x_k)$$

$$= \sum_{i=0}^{n} A_k f(x_k)$$

where the coefficients $A_k = \int_a^b \frac{w(x)}{(x-x_k)w'(x_k)} dx$.

This formula is called the Newton-Cotes formula. The coefficients are called the Newton-Cotes coefficients. To use the formula, you need to calculate the coefficients A_k. Substitute $x = a + th$. You get the following:

$$w(x)=w(a+th)=h^{n+1}t(t-1)\cdots(t-n)$$

$$w'(x)=h^n(-1)^{n-1}(k!)(n-k)!$$

$$A_k=\int_a^b\frac{w(x)}{(x-x_k)w'(x_k)}dx$$

$$=\int_0^n\frac{h^{n+1}t(t-1)\cdots(t-n)}{h^n(-1)^{n-1}(k!)(n-k)!h(t-k)}hdt$$

Let

$$C_k^{(n)}=\frac{(-1)^{n-k}}{n(k!)(n-k)!}\int_0^n\frac{t(t-1)\cdots(t-n)}{(t-k)}dt$$

So

$$A_k=(b-a)C_k^{(n)}$$

Note that A_k is a constant that depends only on the interval $[a, b]$ and the number of partitions n, but not on the function. The Newton-Cotes coefficients can therefore be computed in advance.

The trapezoidal formula and the Simpson formula are special cases of the Newton-Cotes formula. When $n = 1$, the Newton-Cotes formula is as follows:

$$L_1(x)=\frac{b-a}{2}\left[f(a)+f(b)\right]$$

This is the trapezoidal formula.

When $n = 2$, the Newton-Cotes formula is as follows:

$$L_2(x)=\frac{b-a}{6}\left[f(a)+4f\left(\frac{a+b}{2}\right)+f(b)\right]$$

This is the Simpson formula.

When $n = 4$, the Newton-Cotes formula is as follows:

$$C=\frac{b-a}{90}\left[7f(x_0)+32f(x_1)+12f(x_2)+32f(x_3)+7f(x_4)\right]$$

And $x_i = a + kh$ $(k = 0, 1, 2, 3, 4)$ and $h=\frac{b-a}{4}$.

See Figure 6-14.

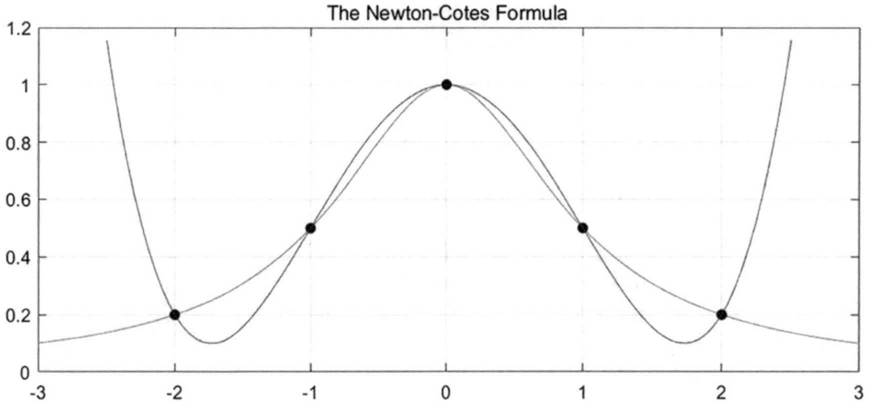

Figure 6-14. *The Newton-Cotes formula for n=2 and n = 4*

Algebraic accuracy is a way of measuring how good an approximation of a numerical integration formula is. Note that the Newton-Cotes coefficient A_k depends on n but not on the integrand function itself. For $n = 1$, the trapezoidal formula is a polynomial of degree 1. If $f(x)$ in the Newton-Cotes formula is a polynomial with a degree no higher than n, then the equals sign holds.

$$\int_a^b f(x)dx \approx \sum_{k=0}^{n} A_k f(x_k)$$

If $f(x)$ is a polynomial of degree $n + 1$, the right side is only an approximation. The quadrature formula is said to have an n-degree algebraic accuracy.

For $n = 1$, the trapezoidal quadrature rule has this error and is said to have the primary algebraic precision.

$$\varepsilon = -\frac{(b-a)^3}{12N} f''(\xi),\ a \le \xi \le b$$

For $n = 2$, the Simpson quadrature rule has this error and is said to have cubic algebraic precision.

$$\varepsilon = -\frac{h^4}{180}(b-a) f^{(4)}(\xi),\ a \le \xi \le b$$

For a general n, the error term is as follows:

$$\varepsilon = \frac{f^{(n+1)}(\xi)}{(n+1)!} w(x),\ a \le \xi \le b$$

If $f(x)$ is a polynomial of degree n, then $f^{(n+1)}(x) = 0$. So, the error $\varepsilon = 0$. The algebraic accuracy of the Newton-Cotes quadrature formula is at least n. There is a theorem that says when n is odd, the algebraic accuracy is n. When n is even, the algebraic accuracy is $n + 1$. For instance, the Simpson formula has an algebraic accuracy of 3 for $n = 2$. For $n = 4$, the algebraic accuracy is 5.

Assuming that the rounding error of $f(x_i)$ (x_i are the grid points) is $\varepsilon_i, \varepsilon_{max} = \max_{0 \le i \le n} |\varepsilon_i|$, the error of the Newton-Cotes formula is as follows:

$$\varepsilon = |b-a| \cdot \left| \sum_{i=0}^{n} C_i^{(n)} \varepsilon_i \right| \le |(b-a)| \cdot \varepsilon_{max} \cdot | \sum_{i=0}^{n} C_i^{(n)}$$

The last term, $\sum_{i=0}^{n} | C_i^{(n)}$, increases with n. This will cause the error of the approximation to increase, so the Newton-Cotes formula is unstable for big n values. Therefore, in practice, the Newton-Cotes formula is rarely used for $n \ge 8$.[1]

Consider this example of integrating the following function:

$$I = \int_0^1 y dx = \int_0^1 \frac{4}{1+x^2} dx = \pi$$

See Figure 6-15.

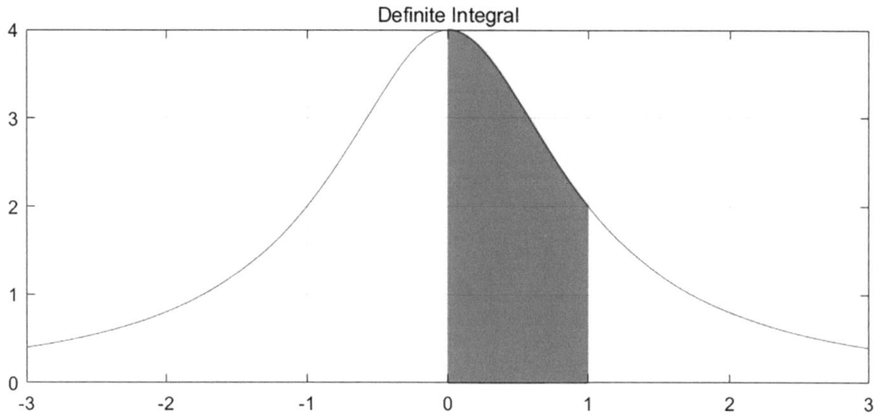

***Figure 6-15.** A definite integral for π*

Using the trapezoid formula, you get the following:

$$\int_0^1 y dx \approx \frac{1-0}{2} \left[\frac{4}{1+1} + \frac{4}{1+0} \right] = 3$$

See Figure 6-16.

[1] For higher order problems, such as n>8, you can employ the Gaussian quadrature method, which is discussed later in this chapter.

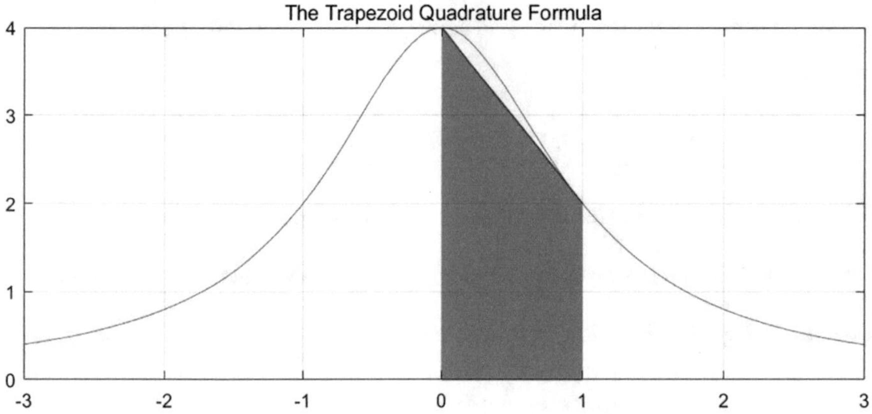

Figure 6-16. *The trapezoid formula for π*

Using the Simpson formula, you get the following:

$$\int_0^1 y dx \approx \frac{1-0}{6}\left[\frac{4}{1+1}+4\frac{4}{1+\frac{1}{4}}+\frac{4}{1+0}\right] \approx 3.1333$$

See Figure 6-17 and Figure 6-18.

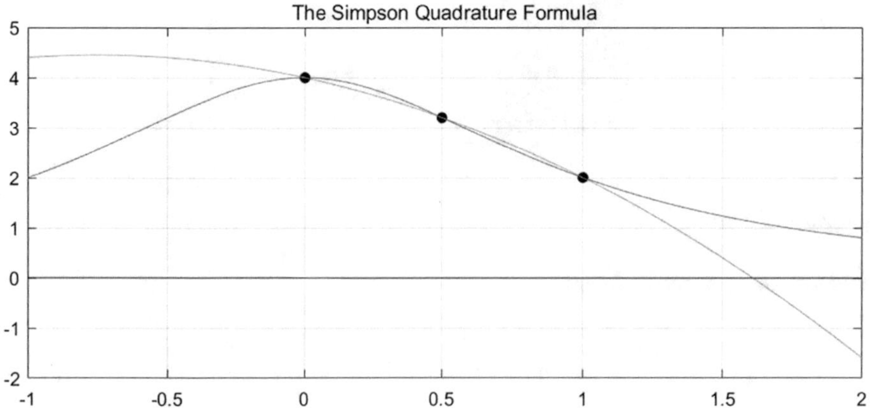

Figure 6-17. *Simpson's formula for π*

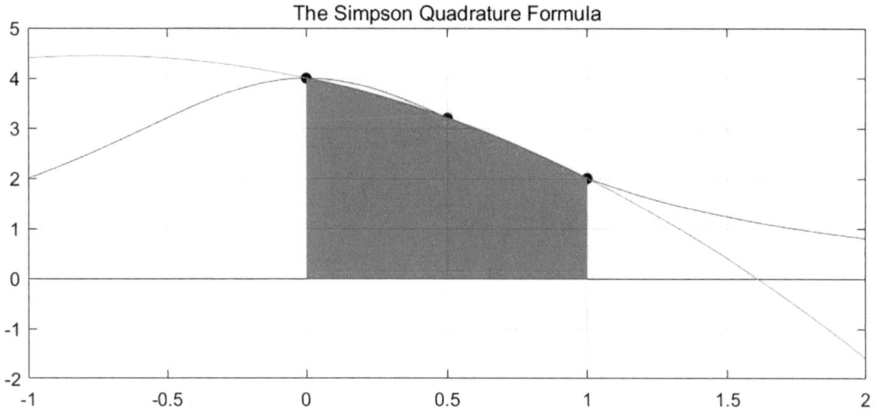

Figure 6-18. *Simpson's formula for π*

Using the Newton-Cotes formula with $n = 4$, you get the following:

$$x_0 = 0, x_1 = 0.2500, x_2 = 0.5000, x_3 = 0.7500, x_4 = 1.0000$$

$$\int_0^1 y dx \approx \frac{b-a}{90}\left[7f(x_0) + 32f(x_1) + 12f(x_2) + 32f(x_3) + 7f(x_4)\right] \approx 3.1421$$

See Figure 6-19 and Figure 6-20.

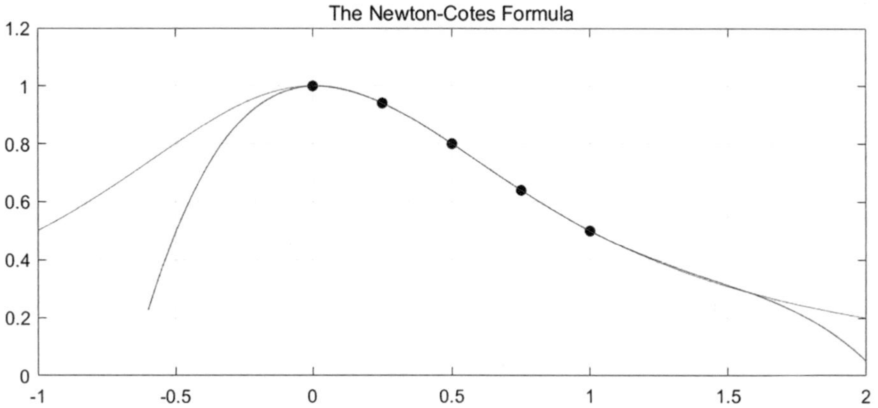

Figure 6-19. *The Newton-Cotes formula with n=4 for π*

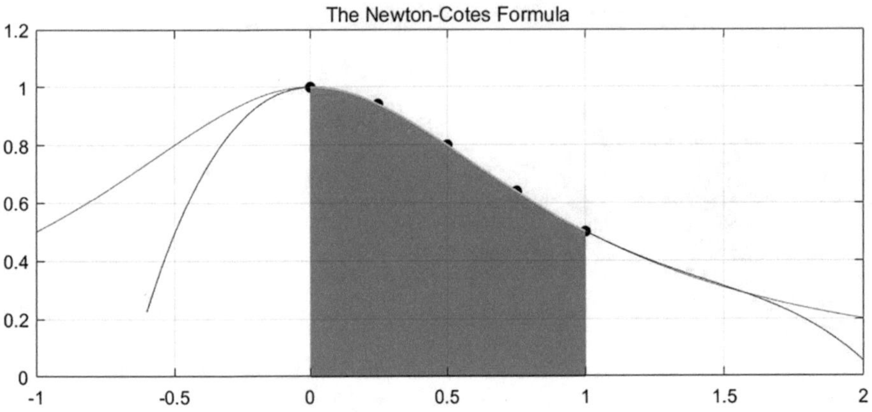

Figure 6-20. *The Newton-Cotes formula with n=4 for π*

The following NM Dev code solves this example:

```
val f: UnivariateRealFunction = object : AbstractUnivariateRealFunction() {

    override fun evaluate(x: Double): Double {
        return 4.0 / (1.0 + x * x) // 4/(1+x^2)
    }
}

// the limit
val a: Double = 0.0
val b: Double = 1.0
val integrator1: Integrator = Trapezoidal(1e-8, 20) // using the trapezoidal rule
val integrator2: Integrator = Simpson(1e-8, 20) // using the Simpson rule
val integrator3: Integrator = NewtonCotes(3, NewtonCotes.Type.CLOSED, 1e-8, 20)
// using the Newton-Cotes rule
val integrator4: Integrator = NewtonCotes(3, NewtonCotes.Type.OPEN, 1e-8, 20)
// using the Newton-Cotes rule

// the integrations
val I1: Double = integrator1.integrate(f, a, b)
println(String.format("S_[%.0f,%.0f] f(x) dx = %.16f, using the trapezoidal rule",
a, b, I1))
val I2: Double = integrator2.integrate(f, a, b)
println(String.format("S_[%.0f,%.0f] f(x) dx = %.16f, using the Simpson rule", a, b, I2))
val I3: Double = integrator3.integrate(f, a, b)
println(String.format("S_[%.0f,%.0f] f(x) dx = %.16f, using the Newton-Cotes closed rule",
a, b, I3))
val I4: Double = integrator4.integrate(f, a, b)
println(String.format("S_[%.0f,%.0f] f(x) dx = %.16f, using using the Newton-Cotes open
rule", a, b, I4))
```

The output is as follows:

```
S_[0,1] f(x) dx = 3.1415926436556850, using the trapezoidal rule
S_[0,1] f(x) dx = 3.1415926535528365, using the Simpson rule
S_[0,1] f(x) dx = 3.1415926497180000, using the Newton-Cotes closed rule
S_[0,1] f(x) dx = 3.1415926674370604, using using the Newton-Cotes open rule
```

The signature for the NewtonCotes class is as follows:

```
/**
 * Constructs an instance of the Newton-Cotes quadrature.
 *
 * @param rate          the rate of further sub-dividing an integral
 *                      interval. For example, when {@code rate = 2}, we
 *                      divide <i>[x<sub>i</sub>, x<sub>i+1</sub>]</i> into
 *                      two equal length intervals. This is equivalent to
 *                      the Trapezoidal rule.
 * @param type          specifying whether to use CLOSED or OPEN formula
 * @param precision     the precision required, e.g., {@code 1e-8}
 * @param maxIterations the maximum number of iterations
 */
public NewtonCotes(int rate, Type type, double precision, int maxIterations)
```

The accuracy and performance of an integration depend not only on which quadrature formula to use but also on the integrand function itself. In general, the trapezoidal formula is not as accurate as the Simpson formula. The low-order Newton-Cotes formulas are simple to compute, are convenient to use, and have a high degree of accuracy. On the other hand, the higher-order Newton-Cotes formulas are not only complicated to calculate but they also have poor stability. So, they are rarely used. In practice, we in general prefer low-order formulas like the Simpson rule.

6.8. Romberg Integration

The Romberg quadrature formula is also called the successive half-acceleration method. It is based on the relationship between the trapezoidal formula, the Simpson formula, and the higher-order Newton-Cotes formula to construct a method to accelerate the calculation of integral. The Romberg algorithm is an extrapolation method of combining the previous approximations to generate more accurate approximations in the process of successively dividing the integration interval into half. It improves the accuracy of the integral without increasing the amount of calculation.

According to the error estimation of the trapezoid rule, it can be seen that the truncation error of the integral (approximation) value T_n is roughly proportional to h^2. So, when the step size is divided by two, doubling the number of subintervals, the truncation error, $I - T_n$, will be reduced to $\frac{1}{4}$ of the original error. That is:

$$\frac{I - T_{2n}}{I - T_n} \approx \frac{1}{4}$$

You can rearrange the terms to get the following:

$$I - T_{2n} \approx \frac{1}{3}\left(T_{2n} - T_n\right)$$

It can be seen that as long as the two successive integral values T_n and T_{2n} before and after the further interval division are close enough, the error of the T_{2n} calculation result will be small. The error of T_{2n} is roughly equal to $\frac{1}{3}(T_{2n}-T_n)$. You can use this error to compensate for T_{2n} to get an even better estimation. That is, a more accurate approximation is as follows:

$$\bar{T}=T_{2n}+\frac{1}{3}(T_{2n}-T_n)=\frac{4}{3}T_{2n}-\frac{1}{3}T_n$$

That is to say, you linearly combine the two integral values T_n and T_{2n} computed using the trapezoid rule to get a more accurate approximation. You can go even further than this.

You can generate a Simpson sequence, $\{S_{2^k}\}$, by linearly combining the values from the trapezoidal sequence $\{T_{2^k}\}$. The Simpson sequence has a faster convergence rate than that of the trapezoidal sequence.

$$\{S_{2^k}\}: S_1, S_2, S_4 \dots$$

$$S_n=\bar{T}=\frac{4}{3}T_{2n}-\frac{1}{3}T_n=\frac{4T_{2n}-T_n}{4-1}$$

Using a similar calculation, it can be shown that:

$$I\approx S_{2n}+\frac{1}{15}(S_{2n}-S_n)$$

You can go further by linearly combining the values from the Simpson sequence to produce a Cotes sequence $\{C_{2^k}\}$ with a faster convergence rate. It can be shown that:

$$C_{2n}=\frac{16}{15}S_{2n}-\frac{1}{15}S_n=\frac{4^2 S_{2n}-S_n}{4^2-1}$$

Using a similar calculation, it can be shown that:

$$I\approx C_{2n}+\frac{1}{63}(C_{2n}-C_n)$$

You can go even further by linearly combining the values from the Cotes sequence to produce a Romberg sequence $\{R_{2^k}\}$ with an even faster convergence rate.

$$\{R_{2^k}\}: R_1, R_2, R_4 \dots$$

$$R_n=\frac{64}{63}C_{2n}-\frac{1}{63}C_n=\frac{4^3 C_{2n}-C_n}{4^3-1}$$

By using the acceleration formula in the process of variable step size, you gradually process the rough trapezoidal values T_n into the fine Simpson values S_n, then into the finer Cotes values C_n, and then into the Romberg values R_n with the highest precision. Figure 6-21 illustrates the progression sequence.

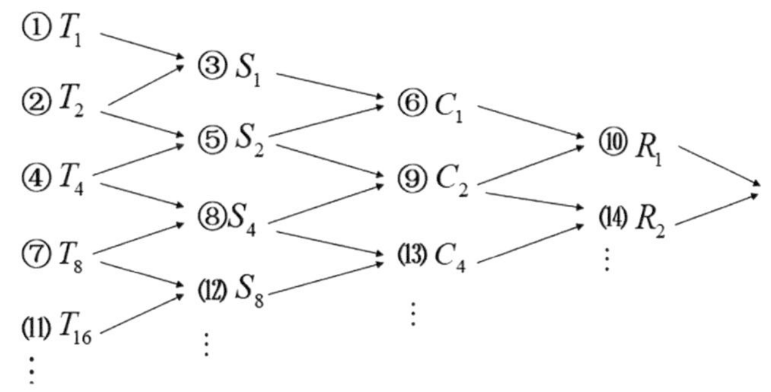

Figure 6-21. *The Romberg formula*

Let's repeat the example of calculating π using the integral in Section 6.7.3. The following is the sequence of trapezoidal values, Simpson values, Cotes values, and the Romberg values produced. See Figure 6-22.

$$I = \int_0^1 y dx = \int_0^1 \frac{4}{1+x^2} dx = \pi$$

$$f(x) = \frac{4}{1+x^2}$$

$$T_1 = \frac{1}{2}\left[f(0) + f(1)\right] = 3$$

$$T_2 = \frac{1}{2}T_1 + \frac{1}{2}f\left(\frac{1}{2}\right) = 3.1$$

$$S_1 = \frac{4}{3}T_2 - \frac{1}{3}T_1 = 3.13333$$

$$T_4 = \frac{1}{2}T_2 + \frac{1}{4}\left[f\left(\frac{1}{4}\right) + f\left(\frac{3}{4}\right)\right] = 3.131177$$

$$S_2 = \frac{4}{3}T_4 - \frac{1}{3}T_2 = 3.141569$$

$$T_8 = \frac{1}{2}T_4 + \frac{1}{8}\left[f\left(\frac{1}{8}\right) + f\left(\frac{3}{8}\right) + f\left(\frac{5}{8}\right) + f\left(\frac{7}{8}\right)\right] = 3.138989$$

$$S_4 = \frac{8}{3}T_8 - \frac{1}{3}T_4 = 3.141593$$

$$C_1 = \frac{16}{15}S_2 - \frac{1}{15}S_1 = 3.142118$$

$$C_2 = \frac{16}{15}S_4 - \frac{1}{15}S_2 = 3.1415946$$

$$R_1 = \frac{64}{63}C_2 - \frac{1}{63}C_1 = 3.141586292$$

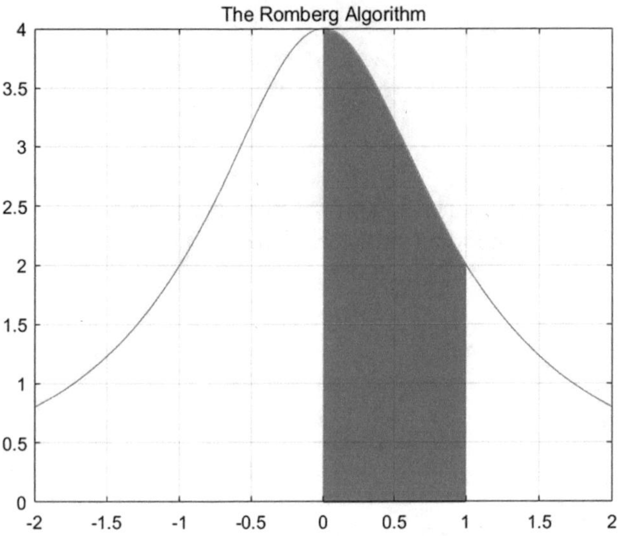

Figure 6-22. *The Romberg integral*

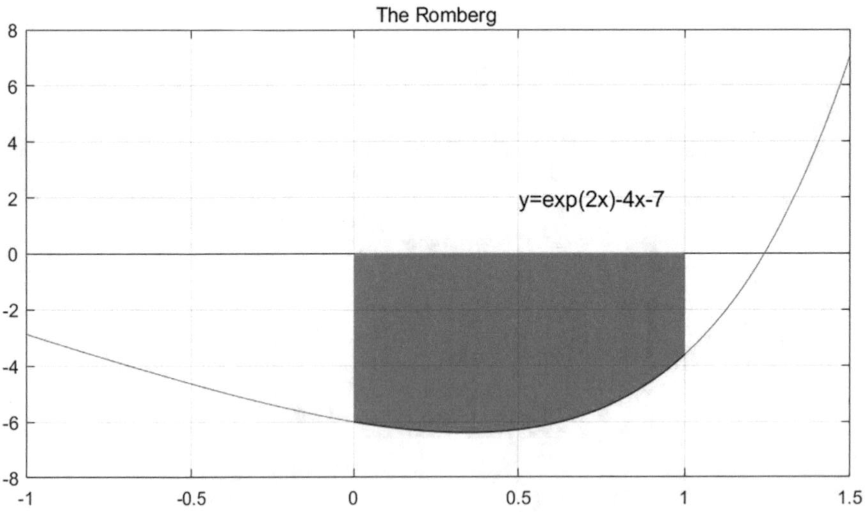

Figure 6-23. *A Romberg integral*

In NM Dev, the class to do Romberg integration is Romberg. The following code computes this integral value using Romberg integration.

```
Val f: UnivariateRealFunction = object : AbstractUnivariateRealFunction() {
    override fun evaluate(x: Double): Double {
        return exp(2.0 * x) - 4.0 * x - 7.0
    }
}
val integrator1: IterativeIntegrator = Trapezoidal(1e-8, 20) // using the trapezoidal rule
val integrator2: Integrator = Simpson(1e-8, 20) // using the Simpson rule
val integrator3: Integrator = Romberg(integrator1)
// the limit
val a: Double = 0.0
val b: Double = 1.0
// the integrations
val I1: Double = integrator1.integrate(f, a, b)
println(String.format("S_[%.0f,%.0f] f(x) dx = %.16f, using the trapezoidal rule", a, b, I1))
val I2: Double = integrator2.integrate(f, a, b)
println(String.format("S_[%.0f,%.0f] f(x) dx = %.16f, using the Simpson rule", a, b, I2))
val I3: Double = integrator3.integrate(f, a, b)
println(String.format("S_[%.0f,%.0f] f(x) dx = %.16f, using the Romberg formula", a, b, I3))
```

The output is as follows:

```
S_[0,1] f(x) dx = -5.8054719346672840, using the trapezoidal rule
S_[0,1] f(x) dx = -5.8054719494768790, using the Simpson rule
S_[0,1] f(x) dx = -5.8054719505327520, using the Romberg formula
```

The signature is as follows:

```
/**
 * Extends an integrator using Romberg's method.
 *
 * @param integrator an iterative integrator that must do at least 2
 *                   iterations
 */
public Romberg(IterativeIntegrator integrator)
```

6.9. Gauss Quadrature

The Newton-Cotes family of quadrature formulas introduced in the previous section is characterized by the $n + 1$ nodes $(x_0, x_1, \cdots, x_n)$ being equidistant or equally spaced. Consequently, their quadrature formulas are easy to construct. On the other hand, it limits the accuracy of those formulas. When n is odd, the algebraic accuracy is n. When n is even, the algebraic accuracy is $n + 1$. Can the algebraic accuracy be bigger if those $n + 1$ nodes are properly selected, i.e., not necessarily equally spaced? It can be shown that the algebraic accuracy can be up to $2n + 1$ if you choose the nodes right.

From Figure 6-24, you can see that the error of integration using the trapezoidal rule is relatively large. If you position your nodes wisely as in Figure 6-25, you can use another line approximation that balances out the positive and negative errors.

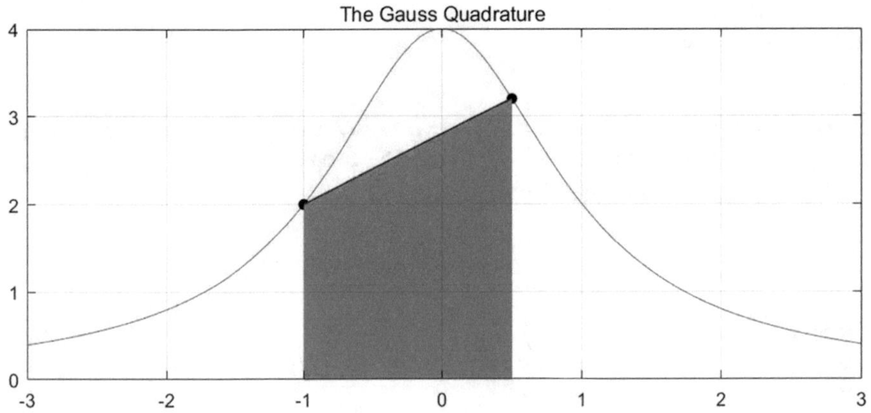

Figure 6-24. *Gauss quadrature versus trapezoidal rule*

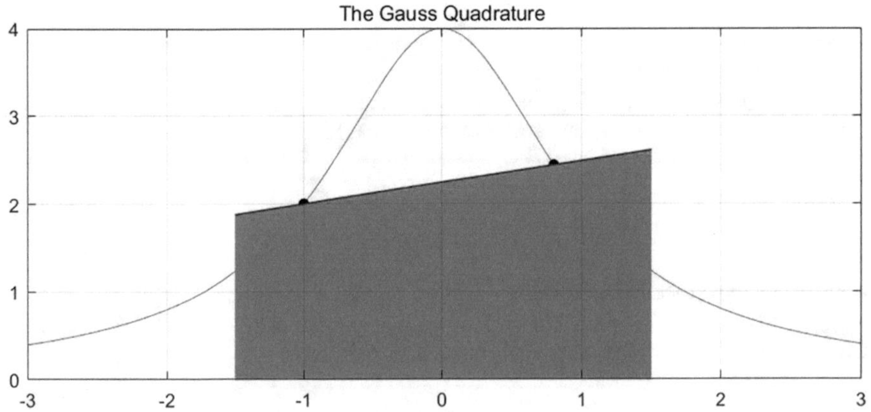

Figure 6-25. *Gauss quadrature versus trapezoidal rule*

Consider an example to integrate this polynomial:

$$f(x) = 7x^3 - 8x^2 - 3x + 3$$

The integral value is as follows:

$$\int_{-1}^{1} \left(7x^3 - 8x^2 - 3x + 3\right) dx = \frac{2}{3}$$

See Figure 6-26.

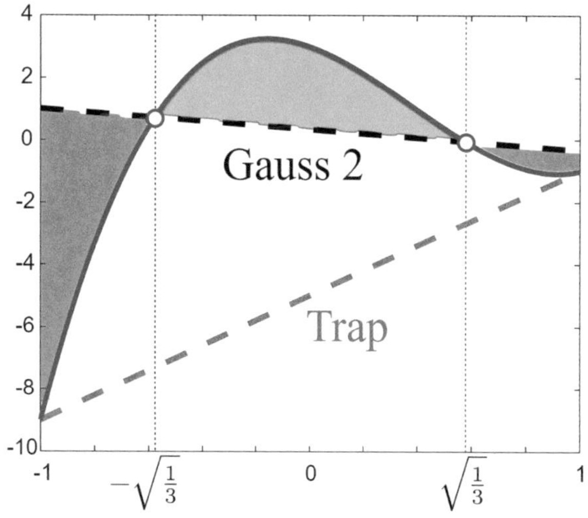

Figure 6-26. *Gauss quadrature versus trapezoidal rule*

Using the trapezoidal rule, the orange line approximates the polynomial and gives the following:

$$f(-1)+f(1)=-10$$

The two-point Gaussian quadrature rule uses the dashed black line to approximate the polynomial. It gives the exact result. The green region has the same area size as the sum of the red regions.

$$f\left(-\sqrt{\frac{1}{3}}\right)+f\left(\sqrt{\frac{1}{3}}\right)=\frac{2}{3}$$

In general, the Gauss quadrature formula (note that the symbol changes from A_k to w_k because the coefficients or weights are now computed differently) on an integral of this form is as follows:

$$\int_a^b \rho(x)f(x)dx \approx \sum_{k=0}^{n} w_k f(x_k)$$

It can achieve the algebraic accuracy of at least n and up to $2n + 1$, if you choose the right set of nodes. The nodes, $\{x_k\}$, are called the Gauss points, and the coefficients, $\{w_k\}$, are called the Gauss coefficients. Both the nodes and the coefficients do not depend on the integrand function. The nodes, $\{x_k\}$, are computed from the roots of a polynomial, depending on the form of the integrand, or $\rho(x)$.

6.9.1. Gauss-Legendre Quadrature Formula

The Gauss-Legendre quadrature formula solves the integral of the following form for $\rho(x) = 1$.

$$\int_{-1}^{1} \rho(x)f(x)dx \approx \sum_{k=0}^{n} w_k f(x_k)$$

The Gauss nodes are the roots of the Legendre polynomial $P_n(x)$.

$P_n(x)$ is a polynomial of degree n such that they are orthogonal. Two polynomials or functions are orthogonal if and only if they satisfy:

$$\int_{-1}^{1} P_m(x) P_n(x) dx = 0, \text{if } n \neq m$$

Figure 6-27 shows the first 11 Legendre polynomials (for $n = 0, \cdots, 10$).

n	$P_n(x)$
0	1
1	x
2	$\frac{1}{2}\left(3x^2 - 1\right)$
3	$\frac{1}{2}\left(5x^3 - 3x\right)$
4	$\frac{1}{8}\left(35x^4 - 30x^2 + 3\right)$
5	$\frac{1}{8}\left(63x^5 - 70x^3 + 15x\right)$
6	$\frac{1}{16}\left(231x^6 - 315x^4 + 105x^2 - 5\right)$
7	$\frac{1}{16}\left(429x^7 - 693x^5 + 315x^3 - 35x\right)$
8	$\frac{1}{128}\left(6435x^8 - 12012x^6 + 6930x^4 - 1260x^2 + 35\right)$
9	$\frac{1}{128}\left(12155x^9 - 25740x^7 + 18018x^5 - 4620x^3 + 315x\right)$
10	$\frac{1}{256}\left(46189x^{10} - 109395x^8 + 90090x^6 - 30030x^4 + 3465x^2 - 63\right)$

Figure 6-27. *The first 11 Legendre polynomials*

The first six polynomials are plotted in Figure 6-28.

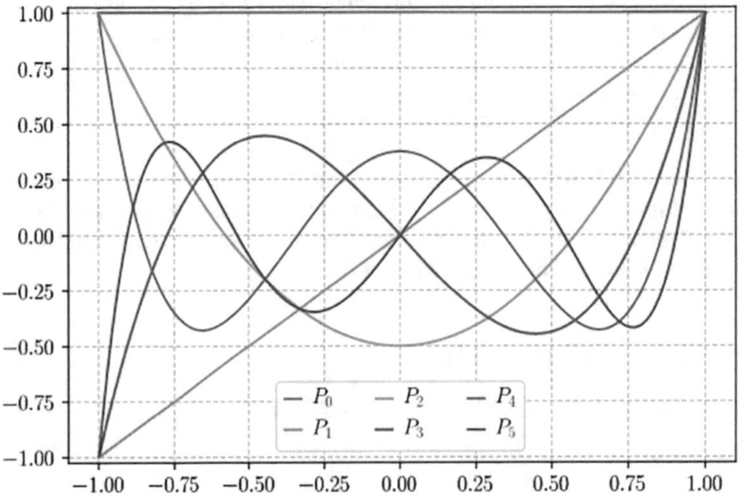

Figure 6-28. *The first six Legendre polynomials*

The weights $\{w_k\}$ are as follows:

$$w_k = \frac{2}{\left(1-x_k^2\right)\left[P_n'(x_k)\right]^2}$$

Some low-order quadrature rules are tabulated in Figure 6-29 over interval [−1, 1].

Number of points, n	Points, x_i		Weights, w_i	
1	0		2	
2	$\pm\frac{1}{\sqrt{3}}$	±0.57735...	1	
3	0		$\frac{8}{9}$	0.888889...
	$\pm\sqrt{\frac{3}{5}}$	±0.774597...	$\frac{5}{9}$	0.555556...
4	$\pm\sqrt{\frac{3}{7}-\frac{2}{7}\sqrt{\frac{6}{5}}}$	±0.339981...	$\frac{18+\sqrt{30}}{36}$	0.652145...
	$\pm\sqrt{\frac{3}{7}+\frac{2}{7}\sqrt{\frac{6}{5}}}$	±0.861136...	$\frac{18-\sqrt{30}}{36}$	0.347855...
5	0		$\frac{128}{225}$	0.568889...
	$\pm\frac{1}{3}\sqrt{5-2\sqrt{\frac{10}{7}}}$	±0.538469...	$\frac{322+13\sqrt{70}}{900}$	0.478629...
	$\pm\frac{1}{3}\sqrt{5+2\sqrt{\frac{10}{7}}}$	±0.90618...	$\frac{322-13\sqrt{70}}{900}$	0.236927...

Figure 6-29. *Low-order Gauss-Legendre quadrature rules*

With the Gauss nodes and Gauss weights, the Gauss-Legendre quadrature formula is as follows:

$$\int_{-1}^{1} f(x)dx \approx \sum_{k=0}^{n} w_k f(x_k)$$

In fact, for functions that are polynomials with a degree up to $2n + 1$, the equation is exact.

In NM Dev, the class to do Gauss-Legendre quadrature is `GaussLegendreQuadrature`. The following code computes this integral:

$$I = \int_{-1}^{1} \left(x^4 + x^2 + x\right)dx = 2$$

```
val f: UnivariateRealFunction = object : AbstractUnivariateRealFunction() {
    override fun evaluate(x: Double): Double {
        return 4 * x * x * x + 2 * x + 1 // x^4 + x^2 + x
    }
}
```

```
// the integrators
val integrator1: Integrator = Trapezoidal(1e-8, 20) // using the trapezoidal rule
val integrator2: Integrator = Simpson(1e-8, 20) // using the Simpson rule
val integrator3: Integrator = GaussLegendreQuadrature(2)
// the limits
val a: Double = -1.0
val b: Double = 1.0

// the integrations
val I1: Double = integrator1.integrate(f, a, b)
println(String.format("S_[%.0f,%.0f] f(x) dx = %.16f, using the trapezoidal rule", a, b, I1))
val I2: Double = integrator2.integrate(f, a, b)
println(String.format("S_[%.0f,%.0f] f(x) dx = %.16f, using the Sampson rule", a, b, I2))
val I3: Double = integrator3.integrate(f, a, b)
println(String.format("S_[%.0f,%.0f] f(x) dx = %.16f, using the Gauss Legendre quadrature",
a, b, I3))
```

The output is as follows:

```
S_[-1,1] f(x) dx = 2.0000000000000000, using the trapezoidal rule
S_[-1,1] f(x) dx = 2.0000000000000000, using the Simpson rule
S_[-1,1] f(x) dx = 2.0000000000000000, using the Gauss Legendre quadrature
```

The class signature of `GaussLegendreQuadrature` is as follows:

```
/**
 * Constructs an integrator of order n.
 *
 * @param n the number of points in the quadrature rule
 */
public GaussLegendreQuadrature(final int n)
```

6.9.2. Gauss-Laguerre Quadrature Formula

The Gauss-Laguerre quadrature formula numerically computes the integrals of this form:

$$\int_0^{\infty} e^{-x} f(x)\,dx$$

The Gauss nodes, $\{x_k\}$, are the roots of the Laguerre polynomials $L_n(x)$. Figure 6-30 shows the first few Laguerre polynomials.

n	$L_n(x)$
0	1
1	$-x+1$
2	$\frac{1}{2}(x^2-4x+2)$
3	$\frac{1}{6}(-x^3+9x^2-18x+6)$
4	$\frac{1}{24}(x^4-16x^3+72x^2-96x+24)$
5	$\frac{1}{120}(-x^5+25x^4-200x^3+600x^2-600x+120)$
6	$\frac{1}{720}(x^6-36x^5+450x^4-2400x^3+5400x^2-4320x+720)$
n	$\frac{1}{n!}((-x)^n+n^2(-x)^{n-1}+\ldots+n(n!)(-x)+n!)$

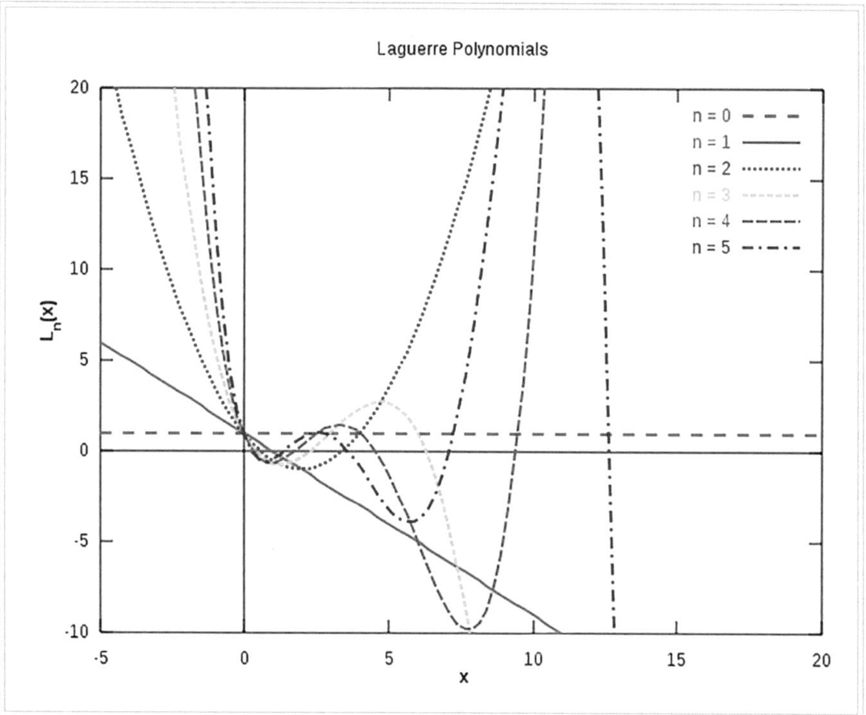

Figure 6-30. *Laguerre polynomials*

The Gauss coefficients, $\{w_k\}$, are as follows:

$$w_k = \frac{x_k}{(n+1)^2\left[L_{n+1}(x_k)\right]^2}$$

In NM Dev, the class to do Gauss-Laguerre quadrature is `GaussLaguerreQuadrature`. The following code computes this integral:

$$I = \int_0^\infty e^{-x}\left(x^2+2x+1\right)dx = 5$$

```
val poly: Polynomial = Polynomial(1.0, 2.0, 1.0) // x^2 + 2x + 1
val f: UnivariateRealFunction = object : AbstractUnivariateRealFunction() {
    override fun evaluate(x: Double): Double {
        return exp(-x) * poly.evaluate(x) // e^-x * (x^2 + 2x + 1)
    }
}

// the integrators
val integrator1: Integrator = Trapezoidal(1e-8, 20) // using the trapezoidal rule
val integrator2: Integrator = Simpson(1e-8, 20) // using the Simpson rule
val integrator3: Integrator = GaussLaguerreQuadrature(2, 1e-8)

// the limits
val a: Double = 0.0
val b: Double = Double.POSITIVE_INFINITY

// the integrations
val I1: Double = integrator1.integrate(f, a, b)
println(String.format("S_[%.0f,%.0f] f(x) dx = %.16f, using the trapezoidal rule", a, b, I1))
val I2: Double = integrator2.integrate(f, a, b)
println(String.format("S_[%.0f,%.0f] f(x) dx = %.16f, using the Sampson rule", a, b, I2))
val I3: Double = integrator3.integrate(f, a, b)
println(String.format("S_[%.0f,%.0f] f(x) dx = %.16f, using the Gauss Laguerre quadrature",
a, b, I3))
```

The output is as follows:

```
S_[0,Infinity] f(x) dx = NaN, using the trapezoidal rule
S_[0,Infinity] f(x) dx = NaN, using the Simpson rule
S_[0,Infinity] f(x) dx = 5.0000000000000000, using the Gauss Laguerre quadrature
```

It is interesting to note that neither the trapezoidal nor the Simpson rule can compute this (improper) integral, of which one limit is positive infinity.[2] You can't divide the half real-life $[0, \infty]$ into partitions.

The class signature of GaussLaguerreQuadrature is as follows:

```
/**
 * Constructs an integrator of order n.
 *
 * @param n         the number of points in the quadrature rule
 * @param precision the precision of the estimates of the coefficients
 */
public GaussLaguerreQuadrature(final int n, final double precision)
```

[2] NaN is the acronym for Not a Number.

6.9.3. Gauss-Hermite Quadrature Formula

The Gauss-Hermite quadrature formula numerically computes the integrals of this form:

$$\int_{-\infty}^{\infty} e^{-x^2} f(x)\,dx$$

The Gauss nodes, $\{x_k\}$, are the roots of the physicists' version of Hermite polynomials $H_n(x)$. Figure 6-31 and Figure 6-32 show the first few Hermite polynomials.

$$\begin{aligned}
H_0(x) &= 1,\\
H_1(x) &= 2x,\\
H_2(x) &= 4x^2 - 2,\\
H_3(x) &= 8x^3 - 12x,\\
H_4(x) &= 16x^4 - 48x^2 + 12,\\
H_5(x) &= 32x^5 - 160x^3 + 120x,\\
H_6(x) &= 64x^6 - 480x^4 + 720x^2 - 120,\\
H_7(x) &= 128x^7 - 1344x^5 + 3360x^3 - 1680x,\\
H_8(x) &= 256x^8 - 3584x^6 + 13440x^4 - 13440x^2 + 1680,\\
H_9(x) &= 512x^9 - 9216x^7 + 48384x^5 - 80640x^3 + 30240x,\\
H_{10}(x) &= 1024x^{10} - 23040x^8 + 161280x^6 - 403200x^4 + 302400x^2 - 30240.
\end{aligned}$$

Figure 6-31. *The first ten Hermite polynomials*

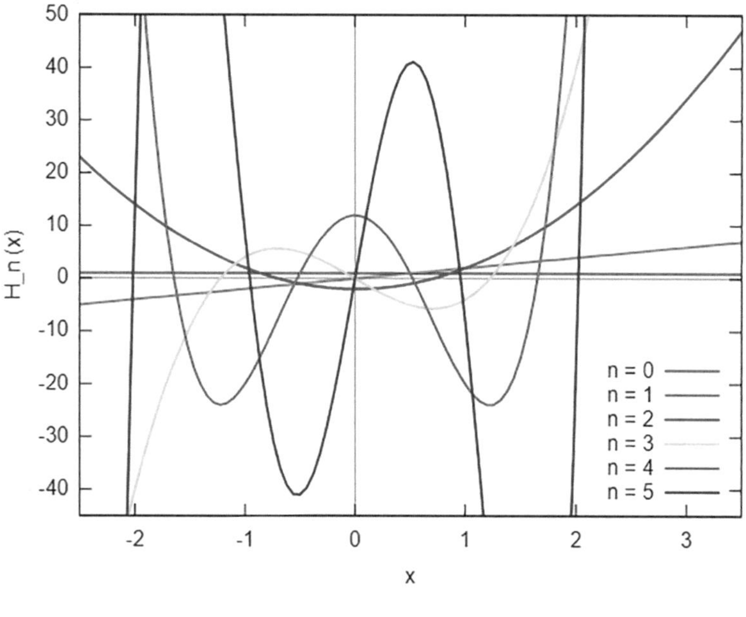

Figure 6-32. *The first six Hermite polynomials*

The Gauss coefficients, $\{w_k\}$, are as follows:

$$w_k = \frac{2^{n-1} n! \sqrt{\pi}}{n^2 \left[H_{n-1}(x_k) \right]^2}$$

In NM Dev, the class to do Gauss-Hermite quadrature is `GaussHermiteQuadrature`. The following code computes this integral:

$$I = \int_0^{\infty} e^{-x^2} \left(x^2 + 2x + 1 \right) dx = \frac{3\sqrt{\pi}}{2} \approx 2.658681$$

```
val poly: Polynomial = Polynomial(1.0, 2.0, 1.0) // x^2 + 2x + 1
val f: UnivariateRealFunction = object : AbstractUnivariateRealFunction() {
    override fun evaluate(x: Double): Double {
        return exp(-(x * x)) * poly.evaluate(x) // e^(-x^2) * (x^2 + 2x + 1)
    }
}

// the integrators
val integrator1: Integrator = Trapezoidal(1e-8, 20) // using the trapezoidal rule
val integrator2: Integrator = Simpson(1e-8, 20) // using the Simpson rule
val integrator3: Integrator = GaussHermiteQuadrature(2)

// the limits
val a: Double = Double.NEGATIVE_INFINITY
val b: Double = Double.POSITIVE_INFINITY

// the integrations
val I1: Double = integrator1.integrate(f, a, b)
println(String.format("S_[%.0f,%.0f] f(x) dx = %.16f, using the trapezoidal rule", a, b, I1))
val I2: Double = integrator2.integrate(f, a, b)
println(String.format("S_[%.0f,%.0f] f(x) dx = %.16f, using the Sampson rule", a, b, I2))
val I3: Double = integrator3.integrate(f, a, b)
println(String.format("S_[%.0f,%.0f] f(x) dx = %.16f, using the Gauss Hermite quadrature",
a, b, I3))
```

The output is as follows:

```
S_[-Infinity,Infinity] f(x) dx = NaN, using the trapezoidal rule
S_[-Infinity,Infinity] f(x) dx = NaN, using the Simpson rule
S_[-Infinity,Infinity] f(x) dx = 2.6586807763582730, using the Gauss Hermite quadrature
```

Note that neither the trapezoidal nor the Simpson rule can compute this (improper) integral, of which both limits are infinity. You can't divide the real-line $[-\infty, \infty]$ into partitions.

The class signature of GaussHermiteQuadrature is as follows:

```
/**
 * Constructs an integrator of order n.
 *
 * @param n the number of points in the quadrature rule
 */
public GaussHermiteQuadrature(final int n)
```

6.9.4. Gauss-Chebyshev Quadrature Formula

The Gauss-Chebyshev quadrature formula numerically computes the integrals of this form:

$$\int_{-1}^{1} \frac{f(x)}{\sqrt{1-x^2}} dx$$

The Gauss nodes, $\{x_k\}$, are as follows:

$$x_k = \cos\left(\frac{2i-1}{2n}\pi\right)$$

The Gauss coefficients, $\{w_k\}$, are as follows:

$$w_k = \frac{\pi}{n}$$

In NM Dev, the class to do Gauss-Chebyshev quadrature is GaussChebyshevQuadrature. The following code computes this integral:

$$I = \int_{-1}^{1} \frac{x^2+2x+1}{\sqrt{1-x^2}} dx = \frac{3\pi}{2} \approx 4.712389$$

```
val poly: Polynomial = Polynomial(1.0, 2.0, 1.0) // x^2 + 2x + 1
val f: UnivariateRealFunction = object : AbstractUnivariateRealFunction() {
    override fun evaluate(x: Double): Double {
        // second order polynomial divided by weighting can be reproduced exactly
        return poly.evaluate(x) / sqrt(1 - x * x)
    }
}

// the integrators
val integrator1: Integrator = Trapezoidal(1e-8, 20) // using the trapezoidal rule
val integrator2: Integrator = Simpson(1e-8, 20) // using the Simpson rule
val integrator3: Integrator = GaussChebyshevQuadrature(2)

// the limits
val a: Double = -1.0
val b: Double = 1.0
```

```
// the integrations
val I1: Double = integrator1.integrate(f, a, b)
println(String.format("S_[%.0f,%.0f] f(x) dx = %.16f, using the trapezoidal rule", a, b, I1))
val I2: Double = integrator2.integrate(f, a, b)
println(String.format("S_[%.0f,%.0f] f(x) dx = %.16f, using the Sampson rule", a, b, I2))
val  I3: Double = integrator3.integrate(f, a, b)
println(String.format("S_[%.0f,%.0f] f(x) dx = %.16f, using the Gauss Hermite quadrature",
a, b, I3))
```

The output is as follows:

```
S_[-1,1] f(x) dx = NaN, using the trapezoidal rule
S_[-1,1] f(x) dx = NaN, using the Simpson rule
S_[-1,1] f(x) dx = 4.7123889803846900, using the Gauss Hermite quadrature
```

Note that neither the trapezoidal nor the Simpson rule can compute this integral.

6.10. Integration by Substitution

The functional forms in Section 6.9 are restrictive. For example, the interval to apply the Gauss-Legendre formula is [−1, 1]. Often, you'll want more flexibility in the interval. The other forms integrate from and/or until infinity, which makes it infeasible to apply simpler quadrature rules like trapezoidal or Simpson's. Many integrands are difficult to calculate because they are complicated. There are also functions that cannot be evaluated at certain points due to singularity. Integration by substitution writes an integral in a simpler form so it is easier to compute, for example, by avoiding singularity. It can transform the interval to a desired range and to avoid infinity. Moreover, it speeds up computation by reducing the number of iterations needed for convergence. The substitution rule says that you find a change of variable, as shown here:

$$x = \varphi(t)$$

such that

$$dx = \varphi'(t)dt$$

You can then replace the integral in *t* with an integral in *x*.

$$\int_a^b f(\varphi(t))\varphi'(t)dx = \int_{\varphi(a)}^{\varphi(b)} f(x)du$$

An example will make it easier to understand. Suppose you want to calculate the following:

$$I = \int_0^2 t\cos\left(t^2+1\right)dt$$

Note that if you set this:

$$x = t^2 + 1$$

You get the following:

$$dx = 2tdt$$

Or the following:

$$\frac{1}{2}dx = tdt$$

Plugging these into the original integral and getting rid of *t*, you get the following:

$$I = \int_0^2 t\cos\left(t^2+1\right)dx = \int_{x=1}^{x=5} \frac{1}{2}\cos x dx$$

The new integral in *x* is much less intimidating.

$$I = \frac{1}{2}\int_1^5 \cos x dx = \frac{1}{2}(\sin 5 - \sin 1)$$

To do integration by substitution in NM Dev, you need to specify the change of variable by inheriting the `SubstitutionRule` interface.

```
public interface SubstitutionRule {
    /**
     * the transformation: <i>x(t)</i>
     *
     * @return <i>x(t)</i>
     */
    public UnivariateRealFunction x();
    /**
     * the first order derivative of the transformation: <i>x'(t) = dx(t)/dt</i>
     *
     * @return <i>x'(t) = dx(t)/dt</i>
     */
    public UnivariateRealFunction dx();
    /**
     * the lower limit of the integral.
     *
     * @return the lower limit
     */
    public double ta();
    /**
     * the upper limit of the integral.
     *
     * @return the upper limit
     */
    public double tb();
}
```

The change of variable is specified in `x()`. You also need to specify the differential of the change of variable in `dx()`, as well as the limits `ta()` and `tb()`.

NM Dev has a suite of substitution rules ready to be used out of the box.

6.10.1. Standard Interval

This transformation maps the integral interval from $[a, b]$ to $[-1, 1]$. The substitution rule is as follows:

$$x(t)=\frac{(b-a)t+(a+b)}{2}$$

$$x'(t)=\frac{(b-a)}{2}$$

$$\int_a^b f(x)dx=\int_{-1}^{1}\frac{(b-a)}{2}f\left(\frac{(b-a)t+(a+b)}{2}\right)dt$$

Here's an example:

```
val a: Double = 0.0
val b: Double = 10.0 // the limits
val integrator1: Integrator
        = NewtonCotes(3, NewtonCotes.Type.OPEN, 1e-8, 10)
val integrator2: Integrator
        = ChangeOfVariable(StandardInterval(a, b), integrator1)

val f: UnivariateRealFunction = object : AbstractUnivariateRealFunction() {
    override fun evaluate(t: Double): Double {
        return t // the original integrand
    }
}

val I: Double = integrator2.integrate(
        f,
        a,
        b // the original limits
)

println(String.format("S_[%.0f,%.0f] f(x) dx = %f", a, b, I))
```

The output is as follows:

```
S_[0,10] f(x) dx = 50.000000
```

6.10.2. Inverting Variable

This transformation is useful when the following happens:

1. $b \to \infty, a > 0$
2. $a \to -\infty, b < 0$
3. Any function that decreases toward infinity faster than $\frac{1}{x^2}$

The integrator for this substitution should use an open formula to avoid computing for the endpoint where $t = 0$. The substitution is as follows:

$$x(t) = \frac{1}{t}$$

$$x'(t) = -\frac{1}{t^2}$$

$$\int_a^b f(x)dx = \int_{1/b}^{1/a} \frac{1}{t^2} f(t)dt, ab > 0$$

Here's an example:

```
val a: Double = 1.0
val b: Double = Double.POSITIVE_INFINITY // the limits
val integrator1: NewtonCotes
        = NewtonCotes(3, NewtonCotes.Type.OPEN, 1e-15, 10)
val integrator2: ChangeOfVariable
        = ChangeOfVariable(InvertingVariable(a, b), integrator1)

val f: UnivariateRealFunction = object : AbstractUnivariateRealFunction() {
    override fun evaluate(x: Double): Double {
        return 1 / x / x // the original integrand
    }
}

val  I: Double = integrator2.integrate( // I = 1
        f,
        a,
        b // the original limits
)

println(String.format("S_[%.0f,%.0f] f(x) dx = %f", a, b, I))
```

The output is as follows:

```
S_[1,Infinity] f(x) dx = 1.000000
```

6.10.3. Exponential

This transformation is useful when the lower limit is finite, the upper limit is infinite, and the integrand falls off exponentially. The integrator for this substitution should use an open formula to avoid computing for the endpoint where $t = 0$. The substitution is as follows:

$$x(t) = -\log t$$

$$x'(t) = -\frac{1}{t}$$

$$\int_a^{\infty} f(x)dx = \int_0^{e^a} \frac{f(-\log t)}{t} dt$$

Here's an example:

```
val a: Double = 0.0
val b: Double = Double.POSITIVE_INFINITY // the limits
val integrator1: NewtonCotes
        = NewtonCotes(3, NewtonCotes.Type.OPEN, 1e-15, 15)
val integrator2: ChangeOfVariable
        = ChangeOfVariable(Exponential(a), integrator1)

val f: UnivariateRealFunction = object :  AbstractUnivariateRealFunction() {
    override fun evaluate(x: Double): Double {
        return sqrt(x) * exp(-x) // the original integrand
    }
}

val I: Double = integrator2.integrate( // I = sqrt(PI)/2
        f,
        a,
        b // the original limits
)

println(String.format("S_[%.0f,%.0f] f(x) dx = %f", a, b, I))
```

The output is as follows:

```
S_[0,Infinity] f(x) dx = 0.886227
```

6.10.4. Mixed Rule

The mixed rule is good for functions that fall off rapidly at infinity, e.g., e^x or e^{x^2}. The integral interval is [0, ∞). The tricky part of using this transformation is to figure out a good range for *t*. If there is information about the integrand available, `SubstitutionRule.ta()` and `SubstitutionRule.tb()` should be overridden. The substitution is as follows:

$$x(t) = e^{t-e^{-t}}$$

Here's an example:

```
val f: UnivariateRealFunction = object : AbstractUnivariateRealFunction() {
    override fun evaluate(x: Double): Double {
        return exp(-x) * x.pow(-1.5) * sin(x / 2)
    }
}

val a: Double = 0.0
val b: Double = Double.POSITIVE_INFINITY // the limits
val integrator1: NewtonCotes
        = NewtonCotes(2, NewtonCotes.Type.CLOSED, 1e-15, 7) // only 7 iteration!
val integrator2: ChangeOfVariable
        = ChangeOfVariable(MixedRule(f, a, b, 1.0), integrator1)
val I: Double = integrator2.integrate(f, a, b) // I = sqrt(PI * (sqrt(5) - 2))

println(String.format("S_[%.0f,%.0f] f(x) dx = %f", a, b, I))
```

The output is as follows:

```
S_[0,Infinity] f(x) dx = 0.861179
```

6.10.5. Double Exponential

This transformation speeds up the convergence of the trapezoidal rule exponentially. It applies to a finite integral interval $[a, b]$. The tricky part of using this transformation is to figure out a good range for t. If there is information about the integrand available, `SubstitutionRule.ta()` and `SubstitutionRule.tb()` should be overridden. The substitution is as follows:

$$x(t) = \frac{b+a}{2} + \frac{b-a}{2}\tanh(c \sinh t)$$

Here's an example:

```
val f: UnivariateRealFunction = object : AbstractUnivariateRealFunction() {
    override fun evaluate(x: Double): Double {
        return ln(x) * ln(1 - x)
    }
}

val a: Double = 0.0
val b: Double = 1.0 // the limits
val integrator1: NewtonCotes
        = NewtonCotes(2, NewtonCotes.Type.CLOSED, 1e-15, 6) // only 6 iterations!
val integrator2: ChangeOfVariable
        = ChangeOfVariable(DoubleExponential(f, a, b, 1.0), integrator1)
val I: Double = integrator2.integrate(f, a, b) // I = 2 - PI * PI / 6

println(String.format("S_[%.0f,%.0f] f(x) dx = %f", a, b, I))
```

The output is as follows:

```
S_[0,1] f(x) dx = 0.355066
```

6.10.6. Double Exponential for Real Line

This transformation is good for the interval $(-\infty, \infty)$. The tricky part of using this transformation is to figure out a good range for t. If there is information about the integrand available, `SubstitutionRule.ta()` and `SubstitutionRule.tb()` should be overridden. The substitution is as follows:

$$x(t) = \sinh(c \sinh t)$$

Here's an example:

```
val f: UnivariateRealFunction = object : AbstractUnivariateRealFunction() {
    override fun evaluate(x: Double): Double {
        return exp(-x * x)
    }
}

val a: Double = Double.NEGATIVE_INFINITY
val b: Double = Double.POSITIVE_INFINITY // the limits
val integrator1: NewtonCotes
        = NewtonCotes(3, NewtonCotes.Type.CLOSED, 1e-15, 6)//only 6 iterations!
val integrator2: ChangeOfVariable
        = ChangeOfVariable(DoubleExponential4RealLine(f, a, b, 1.0), integrator1)
val I: Double = integrator2.integrate(f, a, b) // sqrt(PI)

println(String.format("S_[%.0f,%.0f] f(x) dx = %f", a, b, I))
```

The output is as follows:

```
S_[-Infinity,Infinity] f(x) dx = 1.772454
```

6.10.7. Double Exponential for Half Real Line

This transformation is good for the interval $(0, \infty)$. The tricky part of using this transformation is to figure out a good range for t. If there is information about the integrand available, `SubstitutionRule.ta()` and `SubstitutionRule.tb()` should be overridden. The substitution is as follows:

$$x(t) = \exp(2c \sinh t)$$

Here's an example:

```
val f: UnivariateRealFunction = object :  AbstractUnivariateRealFunction() {
    override fun evaluate(x: Double): Double {
        return x / (exp(x) - 1)
    }
}
```

```
val a: Double = Double.NEGATIVE_INFINITY
val b: Double = Double.POSITIVE_INFINITY // the limits
val integrator: NewtonCotes
        = NewtonCotes(3, NewtonCotes.Type.OPEN, 1e-15, 15)
val instance: ChangeOfVariable
        = ChangeOfVariable(DoubleExponential4HalfRealLine(f, a, b, 1.0), integrator)
val I: Double = instance.integrate(f, a, b) // PI * PI / 6

println(String.format("S_[%.0f,%.0f] f(x) dx = %f", a, b, I))
```

The output is as follows:

```
S_[-Infinity,Infinity] f(x) dx = 1.644936
```

6.10.8. Power Law Singularity

This transformation is good for an integral that diverges at one of the end points.

For singularity at the lower limit, you get $(x - a)^{-\gamma}$ diverging near $x = a$. $0 \le \gamma \le 1$. The substitution rule is as follows:

$$\int_a^b f(x)dx = \int_0^{(b-a)^{1-\gamma}} \frac{t^{\frac{\gamma}{1-\gamma}} f\left(t^{\frac{1}{1-\gamma}} + a\right)}{1-\gamma} dt, b > a$$

For singularity at the upper limit, you get $(x - b)^{-\gamma}$ diverging near $x = b$. $0 \le \gamma \le 1$. The substitution rule is as follows:

$$\int_a^b f(x)dx = \int_0^{(b-a)^{1-\gamma}} \frac{t^{\frac{\gamma}{1-\gamma}} f\left(b - t^{\frac{1}{1-\gamma}}\right)}{1-\gamma} dt, b > a$$

A common case is when $\gamma = 0.5$.

Here's an example:

```
val a: Double = 1.0
val b: Double = 2.0 // the limits
val integrator1: NewtonCotes
       = NewtonCotes(3, NewtonCotes.Type.OPEN, 1e-15, 15)
val integrator2 = ChangeOfVariable(
               PowerLawSingularity(
                       PowerLawSingularity.PowerLawSingularityType.LOWER,
                       0.5, // gamma = 0.5
                       a, b),
               integrator1)
```

```
val f: UnivariateRealFunction = object : AbstractUnivariateRealFunction() {
    override fun evaluate(x: Double): Double {
        return 1 / sqrt(x - 1)
    }
}

val I: Double = integrator2.integrate( // I = 2
        f,
        a,
        b
)

println(String.format("S_[%.0f,%.0f] f(x) dx = %f", a, b, I))
```

The output is as follows:

```
S_[1,2] f(x) dx = 2.000000
```

CHAPTER 7

■ ■ ■

Ordinary Differential Equations

An ordinary differential equation (ODE) is an equation that involves the derivatives of one independent variable. The term "ordinary" is used in contrast to the term partial differential equation (PDE), which involves more than one independent variable. Differential equations arise in many contexts of mathematics and sciences. More often than not, it is easier to describe the changes, dynamics, or variations of a system than the system itself. The system itself can be complex, but its dynamics may be simple (or simpler). For instance, it is not always easy (or even feasible) to determine the trajectory of an object to start with. By contrast, Newton's famous second law of motion can describe the trajectory of any object, from a football to a planet, in a simple expression using an ODE.

$$F\left(x\left(t\right)\right) = ma^2 = m\frac{d^2 x\left(t\right)}{dt^2}$$

Moreover, many phenomena fundamentally relate different differential quantities together, for example, the rate of change or gradient, or curvature. For example, the previous ODE connects these quantities: position (or displacement) over time $x(t)$, force F, time t, and mass m. The first derivative of a position function with respect to time is velocity; the second derivative is acceleration, a. Ordinary differential equations are ubiquitous in almost all sciences, such as physics and astronomy (celestial mechanics), meteorology (weather modeling), chemistry (reaction rates), biology (infectious diseases, genetic variation), ecology and population modeling (population competition), and economics (stock trends, interest rates, and market equilibrium price changes).

The numerical solution of ordinary differential equations is a branch of computational mathematics that solves ordinary differential equation problems. That is, you find a function that satisfies the ODE. The numerical solution is important because many ODEs cannot be solved analytically. Even if they can be, the solutions cannot be expressed in terms of elementary functions. In these cases, you can resort only to numerically solving them. The numerical solution is an approximation of the true solution of an ODE at certain discrete points. We need to study the existence, uniqueness, and stability of such a numerical solution.

7.1. Single-Step Method

Initial value problems are one class of ODE problem. An initial value problem (IVP) is an ordinary differential equation together with an initial condition that specifies the value of the unknown function at a given point in the domain. Modeling a system in physics or other sciences frequently amounts to solving an IVP. In that context, the differential equation is an equation that specifies how the system evolves with time given the initial conditions of the system at time zero. Mathematically, an initial value problem is a differential equation, as shown here:

$$y'\left(t\right) = f\left(t, y\left(t\right)\right)$$

© Haksun Li, PhD 2023
H. Li, PhD, *Numerical Methods Using Kotlin*, https://doi.org/10.1007/978-1-4842-8826-9_7

This is together with the initial condition, as shown here:

$$y_0 = y(t_0)$$

The solution to the IVP is a function y that is a solution to the differential equation and satisfies the initial condition. The concept can be extended to higher orders by treating the derivatives in the same way as an independent function. For a second-order ODE, you have this:

$$y''(t) = f(t, y(t), y'(t))$$

In general, it is assumed that the function $f(x, y)$ satisfies the Lipschitz condition, as shown here:

$$|f(x,y) - f(x,\bar{y})| \le L|y - \bar{y}|$$

L is a constant. The condition is basically saying that the function f cannot change too fast. This condition guarantees that the ODE has one and only one solution.

For example, you can find the solution of the following ODE:

$$\begin{cases} y' = 1 - 2xy \\ y(0) = 0 \end{cases}$$

A numerical solution gives the approximation values, $y_1, y_2, \ldots, y_n, y_{n+1}$, of $y(x)$ at a set of discrete points, as shown here:

$$x_0 < x_1 < x_2 < \cdots < x_n < x_{n+1} < \cdots$$

$h_i = x_{i+1} - x_i$ is called the *step size*. Unless it's otherwise specified, you assume that the step size is equal and equally spaced.

Conceptually, you can solve an ODE in the following manner. You already know the value $y(x_0) = y_0$ from the initial condition. To find $y(x_1) = y(x_0 + h)$, you can use an approximation: $\Delta y(x) \approx y'(x)h$. So, you get this:

$$\begin{aligned} y(x_1) &= y(x_0 + h) \\ &= y(x_0) + \Delta y(x_0) \\ &= y(x_0) + y'(x_0)h \end{aligned}$$

You can repeat this to iterate for $y(x_2) = y(x_1) + y'(x_1)h$ and $y(x_3) = y(x_2) + y'(x_2)h$, and so on and so forth, step-by-step. This is the general idea of how to solve an ODE numerically. This family of methods is called the step-by-step method. Figure 7-1 shows a numerical solution to this problem.

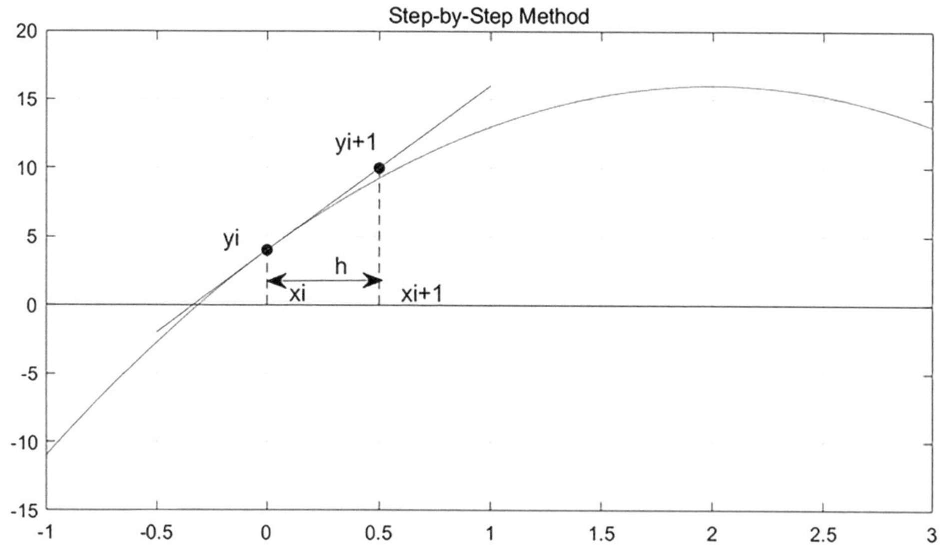

Figure 7-1. *A numerical solution to the IVP using the step-by-step method*

7.1.1. Euler's Method (Polygon Method)

Euler's method (polygon method) is a first-order numerical procedure for solving ordinary differential equations with a given initial value. It is the most basic explicit method for the numerical integration of ordinary differential equations and is the simplest Runge-Kutta method (discussed in Section 7.1.2). Being a first-order method, its local error (error per step) is proportional to the square of the step size, and the global error (error at a given time or value) is proportional to the step size. The accuracy is not high. It also suffers from a stability problem. For these reasons, Euler's method is not often used in practice. It, however, illustrates some basic ideas in numerical integration. Euler's method serves as the basis to construct more complicated methods.

Euler's Formula

You can use Taylor expansion to derive Euler's formula.

$$y(x_{n+1}) = y(x_n + h) = y(x_n) + y'(x_n)h + \frac{h^2}{2!}y''(\xi_n)\text{, } \xi_n \in (x_n, x_{n+1})$$

$$y(x_{n+1}) = y(x_n) + hf\left[x_n, y(x_n)\right] + \frac{h^2}{2!}y''(\xi_n)\text{, } n = 0, 1, 2, \cdots$$

When h is sufficiently small, you can ignore the higher-order term $\frac{h^2}{2!}y''(\xi_n)$ and get an approximation, as shown here:

$$y(x_{n+1}) \approx y(x_n) + hf\left[x_n, y(x_n)\right]$$

Using the notation that $y_{n+1} \approx y(x_{n+1})$, Euler's formula is as follows:

$$y_{n+1} = y_n + hf(x_n, y_n),\ n = 0, 1, 2, \cdots$$

The local truncation error for this formula is the error in the n-th step, which is given by $\frac{h^2}{2!}y''(\xi_n)$, which is proportional to the square of the step size h^2. The global error, on the other hand, is the error accumulated from the beginning to the current step. See Figure 7-2.

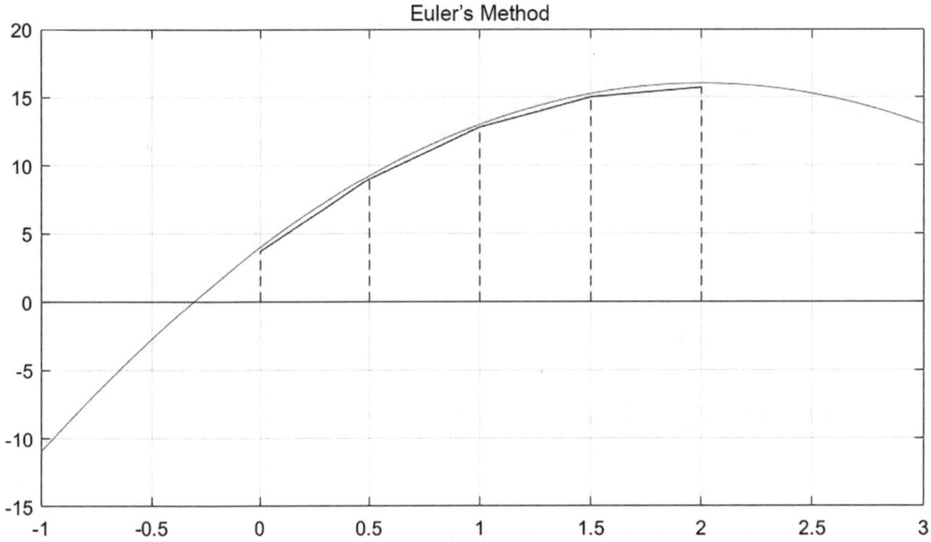

Figure 7-2. *Euler's method and the approximation errors*

Euler's method is a polyline method rather than a tangent method. Except for the first point, which is a tangent on the curve, the function is approximated by a piecewise polyline.

Implicit Euler Formula

You can derive an implicit formula or a backward formula for Euler's method. The difference quotient is as follows:

$$y'(x_{n+1}) \approx \frac{y(x_{n+1}) - y(x_n)}{x_{n+1} - x_n} = \frac{y(x_{n+1}) - y(x_n)}{h_n}$$

Assuming that $y_n = y(x_n)$ and you already know that $y'(x_{n+1}) = f(x_{n+1}, y(x_{n+1}))$, the implicit (backward) Euler formula is as follows:

$$y_{n+1} = y_n + hf(x_{n+1}, y_{n+1}),\ n = 0, 1, 2, \cdots$$

This formula is called an implicit formula because it has y_{n+1} on both the left and right sides. Unlike an explicit formula, where you just need to plug in the numbers to compute y_{n+1}, computing using an implicit formula involves solving equations for y_{n+1}.

One way to solve the equation is to use an iterative method. You start with an initial guess of what y_{n+1} may be, $y_{n+1}^{(0)}$. Then you plug it into the right side to compute the next guesstimate $y_{n+1}^{(1)}$. You repeat until it converges. Specifically, the iteration formula is as follows:

$$\begin{cases} y_{n+1}^{(0)} = y_n + hf(x_n, y_n) \\ y_{n+1}^{(k+1)} = y_n + hf\left(x_{n+1}, y_{n+1}^{(k)}\right) \end{cases}, k = 0, 1, \cdots$$

$$\left|y_{n+1}^{(k+1)} - y_{n+1}^{(k)}\right| < \varepsilon$$

We study the local truncation error of the implicit formula. Given this:

$$y_{n+1} = y_n + hf(x_{n+1}, y_{n+1}) = y_n + hy'(x_{n+1})$$

$$y'(x_{n+1}) = y'(x_n + h) = y'(x_n) + y''(\xi_n)h$$

and substituting the second equation into the first one, you get the following:

$$y_{n+1} = y_n + hy'(x_n) + h^2 y''(\xi_n)$$

You also get this:

$$y(x_{n+1}) = y(x_n) + hf(x_n, y(x_n)) + \frac{h^2}{2!} y''(\xi_n)$$

Assuming that $y_n = y(x_n)$ and subtracting the first equation from the second one, you get the local truncation error, as shown here:

$$y(x_{n+1}) - y_{n+1} = -\frac{h^2}{2} y''(\xi_n)$$

Alternatively, the local truncation error of the implicit Euler formula is approximately the following:

$$-\frac{h^2}{2!} y''(x_n)$$

Trapezoidal Formula

Note that the local truncation errors of the explicit and implicit methods differ by only a negative sign. That is:

$$y_{n+1} = y_n + hf(x_n, y_n) + \frac{h^2}{2!} y''(x_n) + o(h^3)$$

$$y_{n+1} = y_n + hf(x_{n+1}, y_{n+1}) - \frac{h^2}{2!} y''(x_n) + o(h^3)$$

Adding these two equations together and dividing by 2, you eliminate $\frac{h^2}{2!} y''(x_n)$ and get this:

$$y_{n+1} = y_n + \frac{h}{2}\left[f(x_n, y_n) + f(x_{n+1}, y_{n+1})\right] + o(h^3)$$

The trapezoidal formula is as follows (by ignoring $o(h^3)$):

$$y_{n+1} = y_n + \frac{h}{2}\left[f(x_n, y_n) + f(x_{n+1}, y_{n+1})\right]$$

The trapezoidal formula is also an implicit formula. It can be solved by using an iterative method as follows:

$$\begin{cases} y_{n+1}^{(0)} = y_n + hf(x_n, y_n) \\ y_{n+1}^{(k+1)} = y_n + \frac{h}{2}\left[f(x_n, y_n) + f\left(x_{n+1}, y_{n+1}^{(k)}\right)\right] \end{cases}, k = 0, 1, \cdots$$

This iteration method will converge because:

$$\left|y_{n+1} - y_{n+1}^{(k+1)}\right| = \frac{h}{2}\left|f(x_{n+1}, y_{n+1}) - f\left(x_{n+1}, y_{n+1}^{(k)}\right)\right|$$

It has been assumed that $f(x, y)$ satisfies the Lipschitz condition.

$$\left|f(x,y) - f(x,\bar{y})\right| \le L\left|y - \bar{y}\right|$$

That is:

$$\left|y_{n+1} - y_{n+1}^{(k+1)}\right| \le \frac{Lh}{2}\left|y_{n+1} - y_{n+1}^{(k)}\right|$$

Take $\frac{Lh}{2} < 1$ and then the following:

$$\left|y_{n+1} - y_{n+1}^{(k+1)}\right| \le \left|y_{n+1} - y_{n+1}^{(k)}\right|$$

Hence, you get (conditional) convergence. The trapezoidal formula is more accurate than either the explicit Euler method or the implicit backward Euler formula (first-order accuracy $o(h^2)$), and it has the second-order accuracy $o(h^3)$.

Prediction-Correction Method

While the trapezoid formula gives good accuracy $o(h^3)$, the workload is too large. The prediction-correction method improves upon Euler's formula by using the trapezoidal formula, but doing only one round of iteration. Specifically, you get this:

- Prediction: $\bar{y}_{n+1} = y_n + hf(x_n, y_n)$
- Correction: $y_{n+1} = y_n + \frac{h}{2}\left[f(x_n, y_n) + f(x_{n+1}, \bar{y}_{n+1})\right]$

This formula is also known as the improved Euler's formula.

In general, the prediction-correction system uses the explicit formula to do a prediction and combines the results from both the explicit and implicit formulas to give a better result.

$$\begin{cases} y_p = y_n + hf(x_n, y_n) \\ y_c = y_n + hf(x_{n+1}, y_p) \\ y_{n+1} = \frac{1}{2}(y_p + y_c) \end{cases}$$

Here is another example of using the prediction-correction system. It uses the central difference quotient to rederive the implicit Euler's formula.

$$\frac{y(x_{n+1})-y(x_{n-1})}{2h}\approx y'(x_n)$$

Take out the approximation and rearrange the terms, as shown here:

$$y(x_{n+1})-y(x_{n-1})=2hf(x_n,y_n)$$

Thus, you get the following:

$$y_{n+1}=y_{n-1}+2hf(x_n,y_n)$$

This explicit formula gives the prediction value. Combining it with the implicit trapezoidal formula, you get the following prediction-correction system:

Prediction: $\bar{y}_{n+1}=y_{n-1}+2hf(x_n,y_n)$

Correction: $y_{n+1}=y_n+\frac{h}{2}\left[f(x_n,y_n)+f(x_{n+1},\bar{y}_{n+1})\right]$

This is an example of a two-step formula that involves both y_{n-1} and y_n. (All the previous formulas are single-step formulas.) A two-step, or more generally a multistep, formula needs a single-step formula to kick-start the computation from the beginning for $n = 1$.

The NM Dev library supports a wide range of ordinary differential equation solvers. An ODE can be constructed by implementing the `DerivativeFunction` interface. The signature is as follows:

```
public interface DerivativeFunction {
    /**
     * Computes the derivative at the given point, <i>x</i>.
     *
     * @param x the independent variable, <i>x</i>
     * @param y the dependent variable, <i>y</i>
     * @return the derivative <i>F(x, y)</i>
     */
    Vector evaluate(double x, Vector y);
    /**
     * Gets the dimension of <i>y</i>.
     *
     * @return the dimension of <i>y</i>
     */
    int dimension();
}
```

Using the ODE definition together with the initial condition and the integrating interval, you can construct an initial value problem. The `ODE1stOrder` class constructs an IVP.

```
/**
 * Constructs a first order ODE with the given vector-valued function and
 * its initial values. Solves
 * \[
 * y' = F(x, y) \\
 * y(x_0) = y_0
```

```
 * \]
 *
 * @param dy the first order derivative function <i>y' = F(x, y)</i>
 * @param y0 <i>y<sub>0</sub></i>
 * @param x0 the start point of the integrating interval <i>[x<sub>0</sub>,
 *           x<sub>1</sub>]</i>
 * @param x1 the end point of the integrating interval <i>[x<sub>0</sub>,
 *           x<sub>1</sub>]</i>
 */
public ODE1stOrder(DerivativeFunction dy, Vector y0, double x0, double x1)
```

The following sample code solves this IVP using Euler's method:

$$\begin{cases} y' = 1 - 2xy \\ y(0) = 0 \end{cases}, x \in [0, 1]$$

```
// define the ODE to solve
val dy: DerivativeFunction = object : DerivativeFunction {

    override fun evaluate(x: Double, y: Vector): Vector {

    val dy: Vector = y.scaled(-2.0 * x)
        return dy.add(1.0) // y' = 1 - 2xy
    }

    override fun dimension(): Int {
        return 1
    }
}
// initial condition, y0=0
val y0: Vector = DenseVector(0.0)

val x0: Double = 0.0
val x1: Double = 1.0 // solution domain
val h: Double = 0.1 // step size

// define an IVP
val ivp: ODE1stOrder = ODE1stOrder(dy, y0, x0, x1)
// construct an ODE solver using Euler's method
val solver: ODESolver = EulerMethod(h)
// solve the ODE
val soln: ODESolution = solver.solve(ivp)
// print out the solution function, y, at discrete points
val x: DoubleArray = soln.x()
val y: Array<Vector> = soln.y()
for (i in x.indices) {
    println(String.format("y(%f) = %s", x[i], y[i]))
}
```

The output is as follows (see Figure 7-3):

```
y(0.000000) = [0.000000]
y(0.100000) = [0.100000]
y(0.200000) = [0.198000]
y(0.300000) = [0.290080]
y(0.400000) = [0.372675]
y(0.500000) = [0.442861]
y(0.600000) = [0.498575]
y(0.700000) = [0.538746]
y(0.800000) = [0.563322]
y(0.900000) = [0.573190]
y(1.000000) = [0.570016]
```

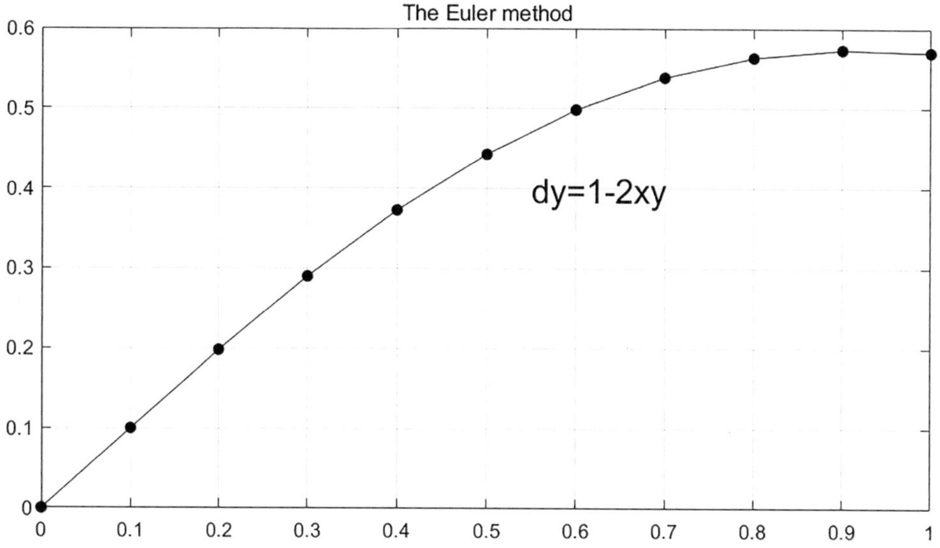

Figure 7-3. *Solution to an IVP using Euler's method*

The `ODESolver` class solves a first-order IVP. The signature is as follows:

```
public interface ODESolver {
    /**
     * Solves an IVP problem.
     *
     * @param ivp an IVP problem
     * @return a solution
     */
    ODESolution solve(ODE1stOrder ivp);
}
```

7.1.2. Runge-Kutta Family

In deriving Euler's formula Runge-Kutta methods, we left out the $o(h^2)$ term in the Taylor expansion. In general, the more (higher-order) terms that you include in the integrating formula, the more accurate the formula is. Suppose you construct an explicit formula using the first p derivatives.

$$y_{n+1} = y_n + hy'_n + \frac{h^2}{2!}y''_n + \cdots + \frac{h^p}{p!}y_n^{(p)}$$

The local truncation error, of order $o(h^{p+1})$, is as follows:

$$y(x_{n+1}) - y_{n+1} = \frac{h^{p+1}}{(p+1)!}y^{(p+1)}(\xi_n),\ \xi_n \in (x_n, x_{n+1})$$

This integrating formula has the order accuracy p. The explicit Euler's formula has the order accuracy 1; the implicit Euler's formula is also 1. The trapezoidal formula has the second-order accuracy. In practice, however, this formulation is seldom used because it is not always easy to find the higher-order derivatives of y.

The Runge-Kutta methods take a different approach. According to the mean value theorem, there is $0 < \theta < 1$ such that you get this:

$$\frac{y(x_{n+1}) - y(x_n)}{h} = y'(x_n + \theta h)$$

$$y'(x_n + \theta h) = f\left(x_n + \theta h, y(x_n + \theta h)\right)$$

So, you get this:

$$y(x_{n+1}) = y(x_n) + hf\left(x_n + \theta h, y(x_n + \theta h)\right) = y(x_n) + hK^*$$

Let $K^* = f(x_n + \theta h, y(x_n + \theta h))$ be called the average slope in the interval $[x_n, x_{n+1}]$. Using different definitions of K^*, you can construct different integrating formulas. If $\theta = 0$, the slope at the point (x_n, y_n) is taken as the average slope of the entire interval $[x_n, x_{n+1}]$. Then $K^* = f(x_n, y_n)$, and the integrating formula is $y_{n+1} = y_n + hf(x_n, y_n)$. This is Euler's formula. If $\theta = 1$, the slope at point (x_{n+1}, y_{n+1}) is taken as the average slope of the whole interval $[x_n, x_{n+1}]$. Then $K^* = f(x_{n+1}, y_{n+1})$, and the integrating formula is $y_{n+1} = y_n + hf(x_{n+1}, y_{n+1})$. This is the implicit/backward Euler's formula. Let $K_1 = f(x_n, y_n)$ and $K_2 = f(x_{n+1}, y_n + hf(x_n, y_n))$. Define $K^* = \frac{1}{2}(K_1 + K_2)$. K^* is the arithmetic average of the slopes at (x_n, y_n) and (x_{n+1}, y_{n+1}). You use it as the average slope of the entire interval $[x_n, x_{n+1}]$. Then the integrating formula is the trapezoidal formula, $y_{n+1} = y_n + \frac{h}{2}(K_1 + K_2)$. You know that the trapezoidal formula has second-order accuracy, while the explicit and implicit Euler's formulas have only first-order accuracy. It can be seen that using the arithmetic average of the slopes at two points as the average slope of the integrating interval is more accurate than using the slope at either endpoint. It is therefore conceivable that, if you are using a weighted average of the slopes at multiple points in $[x_n, x_{n+1}]$ as the average slope K^*, it is possible to construct an integrating formula with a higher accuracy. This is the basic idea of the Runge-Kutta methods.

Second-Order Runge-Kutta Method

The trapezoidal formula is a special case of the second-order Runge-Kutta method. It uses the slope values at the two endpoints x_n and x_{n+1} and lets the average slope of the interval K^* be a linear combination of them. You don't have to use the endpoint x_{n+1}. Suppose $0 < p \le 1$, $K_1 = f(x_n, y_n)$, and $K_2 = f(x_{n+p}, y_{n+p})$, where $x_{n+p} \in (x_n, x_{n+1}]$ and $y_{n+p} = y_n + phf(x_n, y_n)$. The integrating formula is as follows:

$$\begin{cases} K_1 = f(x_n, y_n) = f_n \\ K_2 = f(x_{n+p}, y_n + phK_1) \\ y_{n+1} = y_n + h(\lambda_1 K_1 + \lambda_2 K_2) \end{cases}$$

This system has three undetermined parameters: λ_1, λ_2, p. You want to find a set of parameters to make the integrating formula the second-order accuracy. You first expand K_2 at (x_n, y_n) as a bivariate function using Taylor expansion.

$$K_2 = f(x_n, y_n) + ph(f_x + f_y) + \cdots$$

Substituting K_1 and K_2 into the integrating formula, you get this:

$$y_{n+1} = y_n + h(\lambda_1 K_1 + \lambda_2 K_2)$$

$$= y_n + h\left[\lambda_1 f_n + \lambda_2 f_n + \lambda_2 ph(f_x + f_y) + \cdots\right]$$

$$= y_n + (\lambda_1 + \lambda_2)hf_n + \lambda_2 ph^2(f_x + f_y) + \cdots$$

Comparing coefficients to the second-order Taylor expansion, you get this:

$$y_{n+1} = y_n + hy_n' + \frac{h^2}{2!}y_n''$$

You can see that the three undetermined parameters λ_1, λ_2, and p must satisfy the following:

$$\begin{cases} \lambda_1 + \lambda_2 = 1 \\ \lambda_2 p = \dfrac{1}{2} \end{cases}$$

Any integrating formulas that satisfy the previous conditions are called the *second-order* Runge-Kutta formulas. The trapezoidal formula is a special case when $\lambda_1 = \lambda_2 = \frac{1}{2}$ and $p = 1$.

Third-Order Runge-Kutta Method

You can further improve the accuracy using three points instead of two. Let the three points be x_n, x_{n+p}, and x_{n+q} in $[x_n, x_{n+1}]$ where $0 < p < q \le 1$. Let the slopes at these three points be K_1, K_2, and K_3. The average slope K^* is a liner combination of them. Then define the following:

$$\begin{cases} K_1 = f(x_n, y_n) \\ K_2 = f(x_{n+p}, y_n + phK_1) \\ K_3 = f(x_{n+q}, y_{n+q}) = f(x_n + qh, y_n + qh(rK_1 + sK_2)) \end{cases}$$

Note that for K_3, y_{n+q} is defined in terms of the average slope of K_1 and K_2. The third-order integrating formula is as follows:

$$y_{n+1} = y_n + h(\lambda_1 K_1 + \lambda_2 K_2 + \lambda_3 K_3)$$

The undetermined parameters are λ_1, λ_2, λ_3, p, q, r, and s. You can repeat a similar procedure used to derive the second-order formula to derive the third-order formula. You first do Taylor expansion of K_1, K_2, and K_3 and substitute them into y_{n+1}. By comparing the coefficients to the third-order Taylor expansion of y_{n+1}, you can derive the system of equations that the parameters must satisfy.

$$\begin{cases} r + s = 1 \\ \lambda_1 + \lambda_2 + \lambda_3 = 1 \\ \lambda_2 p + \lambda_3 q = \dfrac{1}{2} \\ \lambda_2 p^2 + \lambda_3 q^2 = \dfrac{1}{3} \\ \lambda_3 pqs = \dfrac{1}{6} \end{cases}$$

Any integrating formulas that satisfy these conditions are called *third-order Runge-Kutta formulas.*

Higher-Order Runge-Kutta Method

In general, the Runge-Kutta integrating formula of any order is in terms of a linear combination of the slopes at multiple chosen points.

$$\begin{cases} y_{n+1} = y_n + h\sum_{i=1}^{r} \lambda_i K_i \\ K_1 = f(x_n, y_n) \\ K_i = f\left(x_n + p_i h, y_n + h\sum_{j=1}^{i-1} r_{ij} K_j\right), i = 2,3,\cdots,r \end{cases}$$

For instance, when $r = 4$, the fourth-order Runge-Kutta formula is as follows:

$$\begin{cases} y_{n+1} = y_n + \dfrac{h}{6}(K_1 + 2K_2 + 2K_3 + K_4) \\ K_1 = f(x_n, y_n) \\ K_2 = f\left(x_n + \dfrac{h}{2}, y_n + \dfrac{h}{2}K_1\right) \\ K_3 = f\left(x_n + \dfrac{h}{2}, y_n + \dfrac{h}{2}K_2\right) \\ K_4 = f(x_n + h, y_n + hK_3) \end{cases}$$

It can be proved that the truncation error is $o(h^5)$.

It is important to note that because the Runge-Kutta formulas are derived from Taylor expansion, they assume that the solution function $y(x)$ is sufficiently smooth and that the higher-order derivatives exist. Otherwise, using a higher-order Runge-Kutta formula may not be as effective as using a lower-order Runge-Kutta formula.

NM Dev supports a suite of Runge-Kutta formulas to solve ordinary differential equations, from the first order to the tenth order. The `RungeKutta` class takes a `RungeKuttaStepper` object that implements a Runge-Kutta formula. For example, `RungeKutta2` implements the second-order Runge-Kutta integrating formula. The signature of `RungeKutta` is as follows:

```
/**
 * Constructs a Runge-Kutta algorithm with the given integrator and the
 * constant step size.
 *
 * @param stepper the integrator algorithm
 * @param h       constant step size
 */
public RungeKutta(RungeKuttaStepper stepper, final double h)
```

The following code numerically solves this IVP for $x \in [0, 1]$ using a number of Runge-Kutta formulas:

$$\begin{cases} y' = y - x + 1 \\ y(0) = 1 \end{cases}$$

The analytical solution is as follows:

$$y = e^x + x$$

```
// define the ODE to solve
val dy: DerivativeFunction = object : DerivativeFunction {

    override fun evaluate(x: Double, v: Vector): Vector {
        val y: Double = v.get(1)
        val dy: Double = y - x + 1
        return DenseVector(dy)
    }

    override fun dimension(): Int {
        return 1
    }
}
// initial condition, y0=1
val y0: Vector = DenseVector(1.0)

val x0: Double = 0.0
val x1: Double = 1.0 // solution domain
val h: Double = 0.1 // step size
```

```
// the analytical solution
val y: UnivariateRealFunction = object : AbstractUnivariateRealFunction() {

    override fun evaluate(x: Double): Double {
        val y: Double = exp(x) + x
        return y
    }
}

// define an IVP
val ivp: ODE1stOrder = ODE1stOrder(dy, y0, x0, x1)

// using first order Runge-Kutta formula
val stepper1: RungeKuttaStepper = RungeKutta1()
val solver1: ODESolver = RungeKutta(stepper1, h)
val soln1: ODESolution = solver1.solve(ivp)

// using second order Runge-Kutta formula
val stepper2: RungeKuttaStepper = RungeKutta2()
val solver2: ODESolver = RungeKutta(stepper2, h)
val soln2: ODESolution = solver2.solve(ivp)

// using third order Runge-Kutta formula
val stepper3: RungeKuttaStepper = RungeKutta3()
val solver3: ODESolver = RungeKutta(stepper3, h)
val soln3: ODESolution = solver3.solve(ivp)

val x: DoubleArray = soln1.x()
val y1: Array<Vector> = soln1.y()
val y2: Array<Vector> = soln2.y()
val y3: Array<Vector> = soln3.y()
for (i in x.indices) {
    val yx: Double = y.evaluate(x[i]) // the analytical solution
    val diff1: Double = yx - y1[i].get(1) // the first order error
    val diff2: Double = yx - y2[i].get(1) // the second order error
    val diff3: Double = yx - y3[i].get(1) // the third order error
    println(
            String.format("y(%f) = %s (%.16f) = %s (%.16f) = %s (%.16f)",
                    x[i], y1[i], diff1,
                    y2[i], diff2,
                    y3[i], diff3
            ))
}
```

The output is as follows:

```
y(0.000000) = [1.000000]  (0.0000000000000000); = [1.000000]  (0.0000000000000000); =
[1.000000]  (0.0000000000000000)
y(0.100000) = [1.200000]  (0.0051709180756478); = [1.205000]  (0.0001709180756477); =
[1.205167]  (0.0000042514089811)
```

```
y(0.200000) = [1.410000] (0.0114027581601699); = [1.421025] (0.0003777581601696); =
[1.421393] (0.0000093970490587)
y(0.300000) = [1.631000] (0.0188588075760032); = [1.649233] (0.0006261825760030); =
[1.649843] (0.0000155779880402)
y(0.400000) = [1.864100] (0.0277246976412704); = [1.890902] (0.0009226470162702); =
[1.891802] (0.0000229550749731)
y(0.500000) = [2.110510] (0.0382112707001285); = [2.147447] (0.0012745047595035); =
[2.148690] (0.0000317115406090)
y(0.600000) = [2.371561] (0.0505578003905094); = [2.420429] (0.0016901240261187); =
[2.422077] (0.0000420559260470)
y(0.700000) = [2.648717] (0.0650356074704770); = [2.711574] (0.0021790200878256); =
[2.713698] (0.0000542253798352)
y(0.800000) = [2.943589] (0.0819521184924685); = [3.022789] (0.0027520039346389); =
[3.025472] (0.0000684893686271)
y(0.900000) = [3.257948] (0.1016554201569502); = [3.356182] (0.0034213495205484); =
[3.359518] (0.0000851538519182)
y(1.000000) = [3.593742] (0.1245393683590454); = [3.714081] (0.0042009818508215); =
[3.718177] (0.0001045659774346)
```

The output displays the approximation values using the first-, second-, and third-order Runge-Kutta formulas. The approximation values are in brackets, and the errors are in parentheses. Note that a higher-order formula gives more accurate results (smaller errors).

Figure 7-4 compares the results of the analytical solution versus the first-order Runge-Kutta approximation.

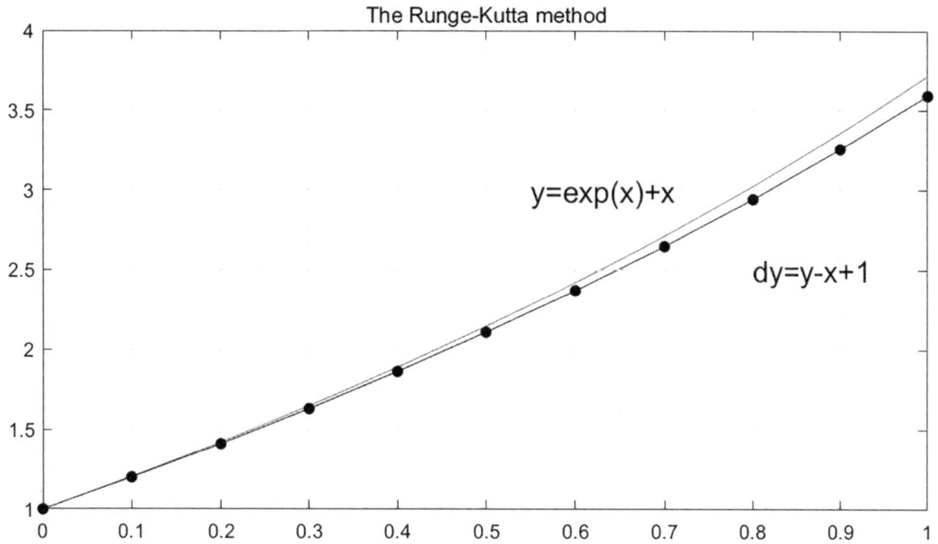

Figure 7-4. *Comparing the analytical solution versus first-order Runge-Kutta*

Figure 7-5 compares the results of the analytical solution (blue) versus the first-order (black), second-order (red), and third-order (green) Runge-Kutta approximations. The second- and third-order results are very good. You can barely see the lines because they almost overlap with the exact solution (blue line).

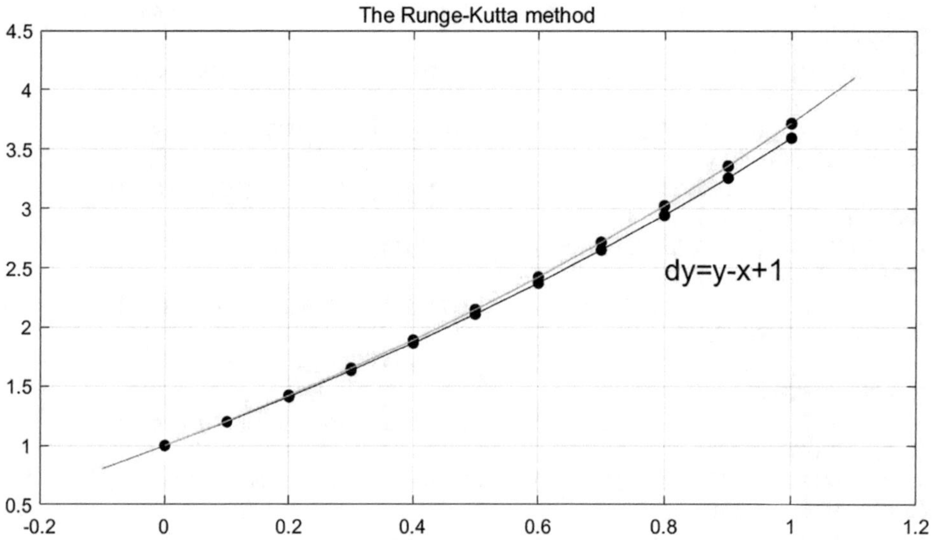

Figure 7-5. *Comparing analytical solution versus Runge-Kutta*

7.1.3. Convergence

For a single-step method, an integrating formula, $y_{n+1} = y_n + h\phi(x_n, y_n, h)$, converges if, for a fixed $x_n = x_0 + nh$, the following is true:

$$\lim_{h \to 0 (n \to \infty)} y_n = y(x_n)$$

Consider, for example, the following:

$$\begin{cases} y' = \lambda y \\ y(0) = y_0 \end{cases}$$

Euler's formula for this ODE is as follows:

$$y_{n+1} = y_n + h\lambda y_n = (1 + \lambda h)y_n$$

So, you get this:

$$y_n = (1 + \lambda h)^n y_0$$

Let $x_0 = 0$ and $x_n = nh$, as shown here:

$$y_n = \left[(1+\lambda h)^{\frac{1}{\lambda h}}\right]^{\lambda h n} y_0 = \left[(1+\lambda h)^{\frac{1}{\lambda h}}\right]^{\lambda x_n} y_0$$

$$\lim_{h \to 0} y_n = y_0 e^{\lambda x_n} = y(x_n)$$

So, Euler's formula converges for this ODE.

Suppose a single-step method has the p-th order accuracy. Suppose also that the incremental function $\phi(x, y, h)$ satisfies the Lipschitz condition with respect to y. That is, for any y and $\bar{y}$, there is a constant $L > 0$ such that the following is true:

$$\left|\phi(x,y,h)-\phi(x,\bar{y},h)\right| \le L\left|y-\bar{y}\right|$$

It can be proven that this single-step method converges and that the overall truncation error is as follows:

$$y(x_n)-y_n = o\left(h^p\right)$$

You can apply this theorem to prove the convergence of the trapezoidal formula. The incremental function of the trapezoidal formula is as follows:

$$\phi(x,y,h)=\frac{1}{2}\left[f(x,y)+f\left(x+h,y+hf(x,y)\right)\right]$$

And as follows:

$$\phi(x,\bar{y},h)=\frac{1}{2}\left[f(x,\bar{y})+f\left(x+h,\bar{y}+hf(x,\bar{y})\right)\right]$$

Subtracting the two equations, you get this:

$$\left|\phi(x,y,h)-\phi(x,\bar{y},h)\right| \le \frac{1}{2}\left|f(x,y)-f(x,\bar{y})\right|+\frac{1}{2}\left|f\left(x+h,y+hf(x,y)\right)-f(x+h,\bar{y}+hf(x,\bar{y}))\right|$$

Because the function $f(x, y)$ satisfies the Lipschitz condition with respect to y, the inequality becomes the following:

$$\left|\phi(x,y,h)-\phi(x,\bar{y},h)\right|$$

$$\le \frac{L}{2}\left|y-\bar{y}\right|+\frac{L}{2}\left|y+hf(x,y)-\bar{y}-hf(x,\bar{y}))\right|$$

Rearrange the terms to get this:

$$\left|\phi(x,y,h)-\phi(x,\bar{y},h)\right| \le \left\{\frac{L}{2}+\frac{L}{2}+\frac{hL^2}{2}\right\}\left|y-\bar{y}\right| = L_\phi\left|y-\bar{y}\right|$$

Therefore, the incremental function of the trapezoidal formula satisfies the Lipschitz condition with respect to y, and hence there is convergence.

7.1.4. Stability

A solution to an ordinary differential equation is said to be stable if the errors, the differences between the real solutions and the approximated solutions, do not increase.

Consider this simple ODE, for example:

$$y = \lambda y,\ \lambda < 0$$

The analytical solution is as follows:

$$y^*_{n+1} = (1 + \lambda h) y^*_n$$

Using Euler's formula, the numerical solution is as follows:

$$y_{n+1} = y_n + h\lambda y_n = (1 + \lambda h) y_n$$

Define the errors as follows:

$$\varepsilon_n = y^*_n - y_n$$

The recurrent relationship for errors is as follows:

$$\varepsilon_{n+1} = (1 + \lambda h)\varepsilon_n$$

The condition to ensure stability is as follows:

$$|\varepsilon_{n+1}| \le |\varepsilon_n|$$

That is:

$$|1 + \lambda h| \le 1$$

Therefore, the stable region of the (explicit) Euler's formula is as follows:

$$-2 \le \lambda h \le 0$$

You can apply a similar analysis to the implicit Euler's formula.
The analytical solution is as follows:

$$y^*_{n+1} = y^*_n + h\lambda y^*_{n+1}$$

Using the implicit Euler's formula, the numerical solution is as follows:

$$y_{n+1} = y_n + h\lambda y_{n+1}$$

The stability equation (obtained by subtraction of the two equations) is as follows:

$$\varepsilon_{n+1} = \varepsilon_n + h\lambda\varepsilon_{n+1}$$

Rearranging terms, you get this:

$$\varepsilon_{n+1} = \frac{1}{1 - \lambda h}\varepsilon_n$$

Because $\lambda < 0$, $\frac{1}{1 - \lambda h} \le 1$ for any step size $h > 0$. That is, the stable region is $-\infty < \lambda h \le 0$ or $h > 0$. The implicit Euler formula is unconditionally stable. Both the explicit and implicit Euler's formula have the first order of accuracy. The latter is preferred because it is unconditionally stable regardless of the step size, while the former is stable only over certain values of h. In fact, many implicit methods in a numerical solution of (ordinary and partial) differential equations are unconditionally stable. For example, the Crank-Nicolson method for solving partial differential equations is an implicit method and is unconditionally stable. Thus, implicit methods are generally preferred to explicit methods.

7.2. Linear Multistep Method

The limitation of a single-step method, such as Euler's method, is that it uses the information (value and derivatives) only at the last node to compute for the current node. Although methods like the Runge-Kutta formulas use multiple points, they use those points only as intermediaries and discard them before proceeding to the next node. In contrast, a multistep method attempts to improve the accuracy by retaining and using the information (values and derivatives) computed for the previous nodes. In the case of a linear multistep method, a linear combination of the values and derivatives at a number of previous nodes is used to determine the value of the current node. The integrating formula of a general linear multistep method is as follows:

$$y_{n+1} = \sum_{k=0}^{r} \alpha_k y_{n-k} + h \sum_{k=-0}^{r} \beta_k y'_{n-k}$$

$$y'_{n-k} = f\left(x_{n-k}, y_{n-k}\right)$$

If $\beta_{-1} = 0$, the integrating formula is an explicit formula (y_{n+1} not on the right-hand side); if $\beta_{-1} \neq 0$, the formula is an implicit formula. By properly selecting the undetermined parameters, a family of linear multistep formulas can be constructed. Similar to deriving the Runge-Kutta family of formulas, you can determine the parameters by comparing coefficients to Taylor expansion. Let

$$y_{n-k} = y\left(x_{n-k}\right) = y\left(x_n - kh\right)$$

$$y'_{n-k} = y'\left(x_{n-k}\right) = y'\left(x_n - kh\right)$$

Do Taylor expansion at x_n for both y_{n-k} and y'_{n-k}.

$$y_{n-k} = \sum_{j=0}^{p} \frac{(-kh)^j}{j!} y_n^{(j)} + \frac{(-kh)^{p+1}}{(p+1)!} y_n^{(p+1)} + \cdots$$

$$y'_{n-k} = \sum_{j=0}^{p} \frac{(-kh)^{j-1}}{(j-1)!} y_n^{(j)} + \frac{(-kh)^{p}}{p!} y_n^{(p+1)} + \cdots$$

Plug them into the integrating formula and rearrange the terms, as shown here:

$$\begin{aligned} y_{n+1} = &\left(\sum_{k=0}^{r} \alpha_k\right) y_n + \sum_{j=1}^{p} \frac{h^j}{j!} \left[\sum_{k=1}^{r} (-k)^j \alpha_k + j \sum_{k=-1}^{r} (-k)^{j-1} \beta_k\right] \\ & y_n^{(j)} + \frac{h^{p+1}}{(p+1)!} \left[\sum_{k=1}^{r} (-k)^{p+1} \alpha_k + (p+1) \sum_{k=-1}^{r} (-k)^{p} \beta_k\right] y_n^{(p+1)} + \cdots \end{aligned}$$

You can also do Taylor expansion of $y(x_{n+1})$ at x_n and will get the following:

$$y\left(x_{n+1}\right) = \sum_{j=0}^{p} \frac{h^j}{j!} y_n^{(j)} + \frac{h^{p+1}}{(p+1)!} y_n^{(p+1)} + \cdots$$

To make the integrating formula have p-order accuracy, that is, the local truncation error would be $O(h^{p+1})$, you match the coefficients of y_{n+1} and $y(x_{n+1})$ for up to the h^p term. The following system of equations of parameters must hold:

$$\begin{cases} \sum_{k=0}^{r} \alpha_k = 1 \\ \sum_{k=1}^{r} (-k)^j \alpha_k + j \sum_{k=-1}^{r} (-k)^{j-1} \beta_k = 1 \end{cases}$$

The local truncation error is as follows:

$$y(x_{n+1}) - y_{n+1} = \frac{h^{p+1}}{(p+1)!} \left[1 - \sum_{k=1}^{r} (-k)^{p+1} \alpha_k - (p+1) \sum_{k=-1}^{r} (-k)^p \beta_k \right] y_n^{(p+1)} + \cdots$$

7.2.1. Adams-Bashforth Method

The Adams-Bashforth methods are a family of linear multistep methods. Let's consider an explicit formula (i.e., not having y_{n+1} on the right side of the formula) using four steps (i.e., using the last four nodes). The integrating formula (with parameters still undetermined) is as follows:

$$y_{n+1} = \alpha_0 y_n + \alpha_1 y_{n-1} + \alpha_2 y_{n-2} + h\left(\beta_0 y_n' + \beta_1 y_{n-1}' + \beta_2 y_{n-2}' + \beta_3 y_{n-3}'\right)$$

To make this formula be of the fourth-order accuracy (setting $r = 3$ in the linear multistep framework), the coefficients must satisfy the following:

$$\begin{cases} \alpha_0 + \alpha_1 + \alpha_2 = 1 \\ -\alpha_1 - 2\alpha_2 + \beta_0 + \beta_1 + \beta_2 + \beta_3 = 1 \\ \alpha_1 + 4\alpha_2 - 2\beta_1 - 4\beta_2 - 6\beta_3 = 1 \\ -\alpha_1 - 8\alpha_2 + 3\beta_1 + 12\beta_2 + 27\beta_3 = 1 \\ \alpha_1 + 16\alpha_2 - 4\beta_1 - 32\beta_2 - 108\beta_3 = 1 \end{cases}$$

As there are seven unknowns and only five equations, the solution to the system of equations is not unique. One convention is to set $\alpha_1 = \alpha_2 = 0$. Then you get this:

$$\alpha_0 = 1, \beta_0 = \frac{55}{24}, \beta_1 = -\frac{59}{24}, \beta_2 = \frac{37}{24}, \beta_3 = -\frac{9}{24}$$

The integrating formula becomes the following:

$$y_{n+1} = y_n + \frac{h}{24}\left(55 f_n - 59 f_{n-1} + 37 f_{n-2} - 9 f_{n-3}\right)$$

$$f_{n-k} = f\left(x_{n-k}, y_{n-k}\right)$$

This is the four-step Adams-Bashforth explicit formula of the fourth order.

The first-order formula is the same as Euler's formula:

$$y_{k+1} = y_k + hf_k$$

The second-order formula is as follows:

$$y_{k+1} = y_k + \frac{h}{2}[3f_k - f_{k-1}]$$

The third-order formula is as follows:

$$y_{k+1} = y_k + \frac{h}{12}[23f_k - 16f_{k-1} + 5f_{k-2}]$$

Although these formulas are explicit and thus easy to calculate, they suffer from poor stability.

Adams-Bashforth Implicit Formulas

Consider the following four-step implicit formula (basically replacing y'_{n-3} with y'_{n+1}):

$$y_{n+1} = \alpha_0 y_n + \alpha_1 y_{n-1} + \alpha_2 y_{n-2} + h\left(\beta_{-1} y'_{n+1} + \beta_0 y'_n + \beta_1 y'_{n-1} + \beta_2 y'_{n-2}\right)$$

To make this integrating formula have fourth-order accuracy, the coefficients should satisfy the following:

$$\begin{cases} \alpha_0 + \alpha_1 + \alpha_2 = 1 \\ -\alpha_1 - 2\alpha_2 + \beta_{-1} + \beta_0 + \beta_1 + \beta_2 = 1 \\ \alpha_1 + 4\alpha_2 + 2\beta_{-1} - 2\beta_1 - 4\beta_2 = 1 \\ -\alpha_1 - 8\alpha_2 + +3\beta_{-1} + 3\beta_1 + 12\beta_2 = 1 \\ \alpha_1 + 16\alpha_2 + 4\beta_{-1} - 4\beta_1 - 32\beta_2 = 1 \end{cases}$$

There are seven unknowns and only five equations, so the solution is not unique. A typical convention is to set $\alpha_1 = \alpha_2 = 0$. Then you get this:

$$\alpha_0 = 1, \beta_{-1} = \frac{9}{24}, \beta_0 = \frac{19}{24}, \beta_1 = -\frac{5}{24}, \beta_2 = \frac{1}{24}$$

The integrating formula becomes as follows:

$$y_{n+1} = y_n + \frac{h}{24}\left(9f_{n+1} + 19f_n - 5f_{n-1} + f_{n-2}\right)$$

$$f_{n-k} = f\left(x_{n-k}, y_{n-k}\right)$$

The first-order Adams-Bashforth implicit formula is the same as the implicit Euler's formula:

$$y_{k+1} = y_k + hf_{k+1}$$

The second-order is the same as the trapezoidal formula:

$$y_{k+1} = y_k + \frac{h}{2}[f_{k+1} + f_k]$$

The third-order formula is as follows:

$$y_{k+1} = y_k + \frac{h}{12}[5f_{k+1} + 8f_k - f_{k-1}]$$

Note that the Adams-Bashforth formulas are not self-starting. A single-step method such as a Runge-Kutta formula is used to compute the first few points.

NM Dev supports the first five orders of the Adams-Bashforth formulas. The following code solves the same IVP given in Section 7.1.2.3:

```
// define the ODE to solve
val dy: DerivativeFunction = object : DerivativeFunction {

    override fun evaluate(x: Double, v: Vector): Vector {
        val y: Double= v.get(1)
        val dy: Double = y - x + 1
        return DenseVector(dy)
    }

    override fun dimension(): Int {
        return 1
    }
}
// initial condition, y0=1
val y0: Vector = DenseVector(1.0)

val x0: Double = 0.0
val x1: Double = 1.0 // solution domain
val h: Double = 0.1 // step size

// the analytical solution
val y: UnivariateRealFunction = object : AbstractUnivariateRealFunction() {

    override fun evaluate(x: Double): Double {
        val y: Double = exp(x) + x
        return y
    }
}

// define an IVP
val ivp: ODE1stOrder = ODE1stOrder(dy, y0, x0, x1)

// using first order Adams-Bashforth formula
val solver1: ODESolver = AdamsBashforthMoulton(ABMPredictorCorrector1(), h)
val soln1: ODESolution = solver1.solve(ivp)
```

```
// using second order Adams-Bashforth formula
val solver2: ODESolver = AdamsBashforthMoulton(ABMPredictorCorrector2(), h)
val soln2: ODESolution = solver2.solve(ivp)

// using third order Adams-Bashforth formula
val solver3: ODESolver = AdamsBashforthMoulton(ABMPredictorCorrector3(), h)
val soln3: ODESolution = solver3.solve(ivp)

// using forth order Adams-Bashforth formula
val solver4: ODESolver = AdamsBashforthMoulton(ABMPredictorCorrector4(), h)
val soln4: ODESolution = solver4.solve(ivp)

// using fifth order Adams-Bashforth formula
val solver5: ODESolver = AdamsBashforthMoulton(ABMPredictorCorrector5(), h)
val soln5: ODESolution = solver5.solve(ivp)

val x: DoubleArray = soln1.x()
val y1: Array<Vector> = soln1.y()
val y2: Array<Vector> = soln2.y()
val y3: Array<Vector> = soln3.y()
val y4: Array<Vector> = soln4.y()
val y5: Array<Vector> = soln5.y()
for (i in x.indices) {
    val yx: Double = y.evaluate(x[i]) // the analytical solution
    val diff1: Double = yx - y1[i].get(1) // the first order error
    val diff2: Double = yx - y2[i].get(1) // the second order error
    val diff3: Double = yx - y3[i].get(1) // the third order error
    val diff4: Double = yx - y4[i].get(1) // the forth order error
    val diff5: Double = yx - y5[i].get(1) // the fifth order error
    println(
            String.format("y(%f) = %s (%.16f) = %s (%.16f) = %s (%.16f) = %s (%.16f) = %s
            (%.16f)",
                    x[i], y1[i], diff1,
                    y2[i], diff2,
                    y3[i], diff3,
                    y4[i], diff4,
                    y5[i], diff5
            ))
}
```

The output is as follows:

```
y(0.000000) = [1.000000]  (0.0000000000000000); = [1.000000]  (0.0000000000000000); =
[1.000000]  (0.0000000000000000); = [1.000000]  (0.0000000000000000); = [1.000000]
(0.0000000000000000)
y(0.100000) = [1.210000]  (-0.0048290819243522); = [1.205000]  (0.0001709180756477); =
[1.205000]  (0.0001709180756477); = [1.205000]  (0.0001709180756477); = [1.205000]
(0.0001709180756477)
y(0.200000) = [1.432100]  (-0.0106972418398301); = [1.421288]  (0.0001152581601698); =
[1.421025]  (0.0003777581601696); = [1.421025]  (0.0003777581601696); = [1.421025]  (
0.0003777581601696)
```

```
y(0.300000) = [1.667631] (-0.0177721924239969); = [1.649813] (0.0000454013260032); =
[1.649443] (0.0004159690343364); = [1.649443] (0.0004159690343364); = [1.649443]
(0.0004159690343364)
y(0.400000) = [1.918070] (-0.0262457123587299); = [1.891865] (-0.0000404310306048); =
[1.891369]
(0.0004556955886803); = [1.891369] (0.0004556955886803); = [1.891369] (0.0004556955886803)
y(0.500000) = [2.185058] (-0.0363368843998719); = [2.148866] (-0.0001448257883485); =
[2.148222] (0.0004994814440833); = [2.148222] (0.0004994814440833); = [2.148222]
(0.0004994814440833)
y(0.600000) = [2.470415] (-0.0482957517704916); = [2.422390] (-0.0002707386487995); =
[2.421571] (0.0005474439430126); = [2.421571] (0.0005474439430126); = [2.421571]
(0.0005474439430126)
y(0.700000) = [2.776160] (-0.0624074454282342); = [2.714174] (-0.0004215417743363); =
[2.713153] (0.0005999698250871); = [2.713153] (0.0005999698250871); = [2.713153]
(0.0005999698250871)
y(0.800000) = [3.104538] (-0.0789968412251016); = [3.026142] (-0.0006010786985646); =
[3.024883] (0.0006574888333333); = [3.024883] (0.0006574888333333); = [3.024883]
(0.0006574888333333)
y(0.900000) = [3.458037] (-0.0984338132295521); = [3.360417] (-0.0008137261840067); =
[3.358883] (0.0007204702609296); = [3.358883] (0.0007204702609296); = [3.358883]
(0.0007204702609296)
y(1.000000) = [3.839421] (-0.1211391576099716); = [3.719346] (-0.0010644638780861); =
[3.717492] (0.0007894268678772); = [3.717492] (0.0007894268678772); = [3.717492]
(0.0007894268678772)
```

The output displays the approximation values using the first-, second-, third-, fourth-, and fifth-order Adams-Bashforth formulas. The approximation values are in brackets, and the errors are in parentheses. Note that a higher-order formula gives more accurate results (smaller errors). For this example, the third-, fourth-, and fifth-order formulas produce the same results.

7.3. Comparison of Different Methods

This section summarizes the results of solving the following initial value problem using the different methods covered in this chapter. The IVP is as follows:

$$\begin{cases} y' = -y + x + 1, 0 < x \leq 0.6 \\ y(0) = 1 \end{cases}$$

The analytical solution is as follows:

$$y = e^{-x} + x$$

We use step size $h = 0.1$, so $x_k = kh$ ($k = 0, 1, \ldots, 6$). The calculation results and absolute errors of each method are shown in the following tables.

	Euler's Method		Trapezoidal Formula		Fourth-Order Runge-Kutta Formula	
x_n	y_n	ε	y_n	ε	y_n	ε
0	1	0	1	0	1	0
0.1	1	4.80e-03	1.005	1.60e-04	1.0048375	8.00e-08
0.2	1.01	8.70e-03	1.019025	2.90e-04	1.0187309	1.50e-07
0.3	1.029	1.20e-03	1.041218	4.00e-04	1.04081842	2.00e-07
0.4	1.0561	1.40e-03	1.070802	4.80e-04	1.07032029	2.40e-07
0.5	1.09049	1.60e-03	1.107076	5.50e-04	1.10653093	2.70e-07
0.6	1.131441	1.80e-03	1.149404	5.90e-04	1.14881193	2.90e-07

Four-Step Adams-Bashforth Formulas

n	*xn*	**Explicit Formula**		**Implicit Formula**	
		y_n	ε	y_n	ε
4	0.4	1.070323	2.90e-06	1.07032	3.90e-07
5	0.5	1.106535	4.80e-06	1.10653	5.20e-07
6	0.6	1.148815	6.80e-06	1.148811	6.50e-07

In general, the higher the order of the method, the higher the accuracy of the solution. The first-order Euler's formula has the lowest accuracy, while the fourth-order Runge-Kutta formula has the highest accuracy, in fact much better (1e-7 versus 1e-3). For the fourth-order Adams-Bashforth method, the implicit formula is slightly more accurate than the explicit formula.

In terms of computation workload, the fourth-order Runge-Kutta method has the biggest computation workload. The function *f* is evaluated four times in each step. In contrast, the Adams-Bashforth method, of similar accuracy, evaluates the function only twice. Therefore, the latter is preferable. However, it is a four-step method, so the starting value must be provided by another method. The computation procedure is slightly more complicated.

Consider solving the following IVP using Euler's formula:

$$\begin{cases} y' = -1000\left(y - x^2\right) + 2x \\ y(0) = 1 \end{cases}$$

Note that the exact solution says $y(1) = 1$.

Take these step sizes: $h = 10^{-1}$, $h = 10^{-2}$, $h = 10^{-3}$, and $h = 10^{-4}$. The results are shown in the following table. First, for $h = 10^{-1}$ and $h = 10^{-2}$, the results are completely distorted. Second, from $h = 10^{-3}$ to $h = 10^{-4}$, the calculation workload increases by tenfold, but the accuracy does not improve. $h = 10^{-4}$ and finer steps are a waste of computation.

h	y
10^{-1}	0.904382×10^{16}
10^{-2}	$>10^{38}$
10^{-3}	0.999999000001
10^{-4}	0.999999000000

The reason for the rubbish results for $h = 10^{-1}$ and $h = 10^{-2}$ is because of the stability region. As discussed in Section 7.1.4, h needs to satisfy the following:

$$-2 < -1000h < 0$$

Or equivalently:

$$0 < h < 2 \times 10^{-3}$$

The first two step sizes fall outside the stability region.

These examples show that there are a number of considerations when choosing the appropriate method and parameters to solve a differential equation. The choices affect the accuracy, computation workload, and stability. When the step size is too big, the solution may be distorted; when it is too small, it unnecessarily increases the amount of computation. The good choices depend not only on the numerical method used but also on the characteristics of the differential equation to be solved.

7.4. System of ODEs and Higher-Order ODEs

Consider a system of N first-order ordinary differential equations and their initial conditions, as shown here:

$$\begin{cases} y_1' = f_1(x, y_1, \cdots, y_N) \\ y_2' = f_2(x, y_1, \cdots, y_N) \\ \vdots \\ y_N' = f_N(x, y_1, \cdots, y_N) \\ y_1(x_0) = y_1^0 \\ y_2(x_0) = y_2^0 \\ \vdots \\ y_N(x_0) = y_N^0 \end{cases}$$

To solve this system of ODEs, you write the following:

$$\mathbf{Y} = \begin{pmatrix} y_1 \\ \vdots \\ y_N \end{pmatrix}$$

$$\mathbf{F} = \begin{pmatrix} f_1 \\ \vdots \\ f_N \end{pmatrix}$$

Then the system of ODEs can be written in vector form:

$$\begin{cases} \boldsymbol{Y}' = \boldsymbol{F}(x,\boldsymbol{Y}) \\ \boldsymbol{Y}(x_0) = \boldsymbol{Y_0} \end{cases}$$

Note that this IVP has the same form as the other ODEs discussed in this chapter except that the variables and functions are now vectors. The NM Dev classes `DerivativeFunction` and `ODE1stOrder` support vector form. Therefore, you can apply all the methods to solve systems of ODEs. For example, the Euler's formula in vector form is as follows:

$$\boldsymbol{Y_{n+1}} = \boldsymbol{Y_n} + h\boldsymbol{F}(x_n, \boldsymbol{Y_n})$$

The components are as follows:

$$\begin{cases} y_{1,n+1} = y_{1,n} + hf_1(x_n, y_{1,n}, \cdots, y_{N,n}) \\ y_{2,n+1} = y_{2,n} + hf_2(x_n, y_{1,n}, \cdots, y_{N,n}) \\ \vdots \\ y_{N,n+1} = y_{N,n} + hf_N(x_n, y_{1,n}, \cdots, y_{N,n}) \end{cases}$$

For example, the following code solves this system of ODEs:

$$\begin{cases} \dfrac{dx}{dt} = 3x - 4y \\ \dfrac{dy}{dt} = 4x - 7y \\ x(0) = y(0) = 1 \end{cases}$$

The analytical solution is as follows:

$$\begin{cases} x = \dfrac{2}{3}e^t + \dfrac{1}{3}e^{-5t} \\ y = \dfrac{1}{3}e^t + \dfrac{2}{3}e^{-5t} \end{cases}$$

```
// define the system of ODEs to solve
val dY: DerivativeFunction = object : DerivativeFunction {

    override fun evaluate(t: Double, v: Vector): Vector {
        val x: Double = v.get(1)
        val y: Double = v.get(2)

        val dx: Double  = 3.0 * x - 4.0 * y
        val dy: Double  = 4.0 * x - 7.0 * y
        return DenseVector(dx, dy)
    }
```

```
    override fun dimension(): Int {
        return 2
    }
}
// initial condition, x0=y0=1
val Y0: Vector = DenseVector(1.0, 1.0)

val x0: Double = 0.0
val x1: Double = 1.0 // solution domain
val h: Double = 0.1 // step size

// the analytical solution
val F: RealVectorFunction = object : AbstractRealVectorFunction(1, 2) {

    override fun evaluate(v: Vector): Vector {
        val t: Double = v.get(1)
        val x: Double = 2.0 / 3 * exp(t) + 1.0 / 3 * exp(-5.0 * t)
        val y: Double = 1.0 / 3 * exp(t) + 2.0 / 3 * exp(-5.0 * t)
        return DenseVector(x, y)
    }
}

// define an IVP
val ivp: ODE1stOrder = ODE1stOrder(dY, Y0, x0, x1)
// construct an ODE solver using Euler's method
val solver: ODESolver = EulerMethod(h)
// solve the ODE
val soln: ODESolution = solver.solve(ivp)
// print out the solution function, y, at discrete points
val t: DoubleArray = soln.x()
val v: Array<Vector> = soln.y()
for (i in t.indices) {
    println(String.format(
            "y(%f) = %s vs %s",
            t[i],
            v[i],
            F.evaluate(DenseVector(t[i]))
    ))
}
```

The output is as follows:

```
y(0.000000) = [1.000000, 1.000000]  vs [1.000000, 1.000000]
y(0.100000) = [0.900000, 0.700000]  vs [0.938957, 0.772744]
y(0.200000) = [0.890000, 0.570000]  vs [0.936895, 0.652387]
y(0.300000) = [0.929000, 0.527000]  vs [0.974283, 0.598706]
y(0.400000) = [0.996900, 0.529700]  vs [1.039662, 0.587498]
y(0.500000) = [1.084090, 0.557670]  vs [1.126509, 0.604297]
y(0.600000) = [1.186249, 0.600937]  vs [1.231342, 0.640564]
y(0.700000) = [1.301749, 0.654781]  vs [1.352568, 0.691382]
```

```
y(0.800000) = [1.430361, 0.717134]  vs [1.489799, 0.754057]
y(0.900000) = [1.572616, 0.787285]  vs [1.643438, 0.827274]
y(1.000000) = [1.729487, 0.865232]  vs [1.814434, 0.910586]
```

The first column of vectors consists of the numerical solutions, and the second column contains the analytical solutions. You could potentially improve the accuracy using other, more advanced methods.

Consider an ordinary differential equation that involves higher-order derivatives, shown here:

$$\begin{cases} y^{(m)} = f\left(x, y, y', \cdots, y^{(m-1)}\right) \\ y(x_0) = y_0 \\ y'(x_0) = y_0' \\ \vdots \\ y^{(m-1)}(x_0) = y_0^{(m-1)} \end{cases}$$

You can convert this m-th order ODE into a system of first-order ODEs by setting $y_1 = y$, $y_2 = y''$, $\cdots$, $y_m = y^{(m-1)}$. Specifically, here's an example:

$$y = y_1$$

$$\begin{cases} y_1' = y_2 \\ y_2' = y_3 \\ \vdots \\ y_{m-1}' = y_m \\ y_m' = f\left(x, y_1, y_2, \cdots, y_m\right) \end{cases}$$

You can solve a system of first-order ODEs using `DerivativeFunction` and `ODE1stOrder` together with any NM Dev ODE solvers.

For example, the following code solves this second-order ODE:

$$\begin{cases} y'' - y' - 6y = 0 \\ y(0) = 1 \\ y'(0) = 2 \end{cases}$$

The analytic solution is as follows:

$$y = \frac{4}{5}e^{3t} + \frac{1}{5}e^{-2t}$$

You can rewrite the IVP in terms of a system of first-order ODEs.

Letting $y_1 = y$ and $y_2 = y'$, you get the following:

$$\begin{cases} \dfrac{dy_1}{dt} = y_2 \\ \dfrac{dy_2}{dt} = y_2 + 6y_1 \\ y_1(0) = 1 \\ y_2(0) = 2 \end{cases}$$

Let's first solve this system using Euler's method.

```
// define the equivalent system of ODEs to solve
val dY: DerivativeFunction = object : DerivativeFunction {

    override fun evaluate(t: Double, v: Vector): Vector {
        val y_1: Double= v.get(1)
        val y_2: Double= v.get(2)

        val dy_1: Double = y_2
        val dy_2: Double = y_2 + 6.0 * y_1
        return DenseVector(dy_1, dy_2)
    }

    override fun dimension(): Int {
        return 2
    }
}
// initial condition, y1(0) = 1, y2(0) = 2
val Y0: Vector = DenseVector(1.0, 2.0)

val t0: Double = 0.0
val t1: Double = 1.0 // solution domain
val h: Double = 0.1 // step size

// the analytical solution
val f: UnivariateRealFunction = object : AbstractUnivariateRealFunction() {
    override fun evaluate(t: Double): Double {
        var f: Double = 0.8 * exp(3.0 * t)
        f += 0.2 * exp(-2.0 * t)
        return f
    }
}

// define an IVP
val ivp: ODE1stOrder = ODE1stOrder(dY, Y0, t0, t1)
// construct an ODE solver using Euler's method
val solver: ODESolver = EulerMethod(h)
// construct an ODE solver using the third order Runge-Kutta formula
// val stepper3: RungeKuttaStepper = RungeKutta3()
// val solver: ODESolver = RungeKutta(stepper3, h)

// solve the ODE
val soln: ODESolution = solver.solve(ivp)
// print out the solution function, y, at discrete points
val t: DoubleArray = soln.x()
val v: Array<Vector> = soln.y()
for (i in t.indices) {
    val y1: Double = v[i].get(1) // the numerical solution
    println(String.format(
            "y(%f) = %f vs %f",
```

```
            t[i],
            y1,
            f.evaluate(t[i])
        ))
}
```

The output is as follows:

```
y(0.000000) = 1.000000 vs 1.000000
y(0.100000) = 1.200000 vs 1.243633
y(0.200000) = 1.480000 vs 1.591759
y(0.300000) = 1.860000 vs 2.077445
y(0.400000) = 2.366800 vs 2.745959
y(0.500000) = 3.035880 vs 3.658927
y(0.600000) = 3.913876 vs 4.899957
y(0.700000) = 5.061824 vs 6.582255
y(0.800000) = 6.559400 vs 8.858920
y(0.900000) = 8.510443 vs 11.936845
y(1.000000) = 11.050154 vs 16.095497
```

Note that the accuracy using Euler's formula is pretty bad. (I thought it was a bug in my code but I could not find any problems.)

Let's try this again using the third-order Runge-Kutta formula.

```
// define the equivalent system of ODEs to solve
val dY: DerivativeFunction = object : DerivativeFunction {

    override fun evaluate(t: Double, v: Vector): Vector {
        val y_1: Double= v.get(1)
        val y_2: Double= v.get(2)

        val dy_1: Double = y_2
        val dy_2: Double = y_2 + 6.0 * y_1
        return DenseVector(dy_1, dy_2)
    }

    override fun dimension(): Int {
        return 2
    }
}
// initial condition, y1(0) = 1, y2(0) = 2
val Y0: Vector = DenseVector(1.0, 2.0)

val t0: Double = 0.0
val t1: Double = 1.0 // solution domain
val h: Double = 0.1 // step size
```

```
// the analytical solution
val f: UnivariateRealFunction = object : AbstractUnivariateRealFunction() {
    override fun evaluate(t: Double): Double {
        var f: Double = 0.8 * exp(3.0 * t)
        f += 0.2 * exp(-2.0 * t)
        return f
    }
}

// define an IVP
val ivp: ODE1stOrder = ODE1stOrder(dY, Y0, t0, t1)
// construct an ODE solver using Euler's method
// ODESolver solver = EulerMethod(h)
// construct an ODE solver using the third order Runge-Kutta formula
val stepper3: RungeKuttaStepper = RungeKutta3()
val solver: ODESolver = RungeKutta(stepper3, h)

// solve the ODE
val soln: ODESolution = solver.solve(ivp)
// print out the solution function, y, at discrete points
val t: DoubleArray = soln.x()
val v: Array<Vector> = soln.y()
for (i in t.indices) {
    val y1: Double = v[i].get(1) // the numerical solution
    println(String.format(
            "y(%f) = %f vs %f",
            t[i],
            y1,
            f.evaluate(t[i])
    ))
}
```

The output is as follows:

```
y(0.000000) = 1.000000 vs 1.000000
y(0.100000) = 1.243333 vs 1.243633
y(0.200000) = 1.590963 vs 1.591759
y(0.300000) = 2.075850 vs 2.077445
y(0.400000) = 2.743108 vs 2.745959
y(0.500000) = 3.654136 vs 3.658927
y(0.600000) = 4.892215 vs 4.899957
y(0.700000) = 6.570082 vs 6.582255
y(0.800000) = 8.840160 vs 8.858920
y(0.900000) = 11.908375 vs 11.936845
y(1.000000) = 16.052815 vs 16.095497
```

The result from using the Runge-Kutta method is satisfactory.

CHAPTER 8

■ ■ ■

Partial Differential Equations

A partial differential equation (PDE) relates the quantities of a multivariate function and its various partial derivatives in an equation. An ordinary partial differential, as discussed in the previous chapter, is a subclass of partial differential equations because ordinary partial differential equations deal with functions with one variable. Partial differential equations are significantly more difficult to solve than ordinary partial differentials because a simple PDE can admit a large class of solutions. For example, for this simple PDE:

$$\frac{\partial^2 v}{\partial x \partial y} = 0$$

Any function $v(x, y) = f(x) + g(y)$ for any univariate functions f and g will satisfy the equation. This is far beyond the choices available in ODE solution formulas, which typically allow the free choice of some numbers or coefficients. In the study of PDE, one generally has a free choice of functions.

In general, a partial differential equation is rarely solved analytically except for a few classes of problems. There is no general formula to most PDEs. Therefore, there is a vast amount of modern mathematical and scientific research on methods to numerically approximate solutions of certain partial differential equations. Partial differential equations are ubiquitous in mathematics, the sciences, and engineering. For instance, they are foundational in the modern scientific understanding of sound, heat, diffusion, electrostatics, electrodynamics, fluid dynamics, aero dynamics, elasticity, general relativity, and quantum mechanics. They also arise from many purely mathematical considerations, such as differential geometry and the calculus of variations. One of the millennium problems[1] is to prove the existence and uniqueness of the Navier-Stokes equation, which is a famous partial differential equation. Partial differential equations are a very big topic. We cannot even scratch the surface in this chapter. We briefly discuss one small subclass of partial differential equations (namely, second-order linear PDEs) and explain how to solve them using one particular numerical method (namely, finite difference).

---

[1] You get a million dollars for being the first person to solve each of those six millennium problems. So, you can theoretically earn US$6 million by building a career solving math problems.

© Haksun Li, PhD 2023
H. Li, PhD, *Numerical Methods Using Kotlin*, https://doi.org/10.1007/978-1-4842-8826-9_8

8.1. Second-Order Linear PDE

A second-order PDE has this form:

$$a(*)\frac{\partial^2 u}{\partial x^2}+b(*)\frac{\partial^2 u}{\partial x\partial y}+c(*)\frac{\partial^2 u}{\partial y^2}+d(*)\frac{\partial u}{\partial x}+e(*)\frac{\partial u}{\partial y}+f(*)u+g(*)=0$$

Depending on the functional forms of the coefficients *a*(*), *b*(*), *c*(*), *d*(*), *e*(*), *f*(*), and g(*), you classify them into three different categories.

This PDE is a linear partial differential equation if the coefficient depends only on the variables and not the derivatives. That is:

$$*=x,y$$

This PDE is a quasilinear partial differential equation if the coefficient depends on the variables and the lower-order derivatives. That is:

$$*=x,y,\frac{\partial u^{n-1}}{\partial x},\frac{\partial u^{n-1}}{\partial y},\ldots$$

This PDE is a nonlinear partial differential equation if the coefficient depends on the highest-order derivatives. That is:

$$*=x,y,\frac{\partial u^{n}}{\partial x},\frac{\partial u^{n}}{\partial y},\ldots$$

8.1.1. Parabolic Equation

A second-order PDE is in the parabolic form if the following is true:

$$b^2(*)-a(*)c(*)=0$$

One of the simplest yet most popular examples of a parabolic PDE is the one-dimensional heat equation, as shown here:

$$u_t=\frac{\partial u}{\partial t}=\alpha\frac{\partial^2 u}{\partial x^2}=\alpha u_{xx}$$

$u(t, x)$ is the temperature at time t and at position x along a thin rod. α is the thermal diffusivity, a positive constant. The heat equation roughly states the second law of thermodynamics: Heat will flow from hotter bodies to adjacent colder bodies in proportion to the difference of temperature and of the thermal conductivity of the material between them. When heat flows into (out of) a material, its temperature increases (decreases) in proportion to the amount of heat divided by the amount (mass) of material, with a proportionality factor called the specific thermal diffusivity of the material. Simply put, the temperature at a given time and point rises or falls at a rate proportional to the difference between the temperature at that point and the average temperature near that point. This concept can be generalized using the three-dimensional heat equation, shown here:

$$u_t=\frac{\partial u}{\partial t}=\alpha\left(\frac{\partial^2 u}{\partial x^2}+\frac{\partial^2 u}{\partial y^2}+\frac{\partial^2 u}{\partial z^2}\right)=\alpha\Delta u$$

Δ is the Laplace operator, which is a second-order differential operator in the n-dimensional Euclidean space, defined as the divergence of the gradient of a twice-differentiable real-valued function. It gives the difference between the average value of a function in the neighborhood of a point. In the current example, it measures how far off the temperature is from satisfying the mean value property of harmonic functions.

A PDE can represent a large of class of equations or phenomena. The heat equation has a very wide range of applicability. The Black-Scholes equation of financial mathematics, which started in the trillion-dollar market of options and derivatives, is a variant of the heat equation. The Schrödinger equation of quantum mechanics can be regarded as a heat equation in imaginary time. In image analysis, the heat equation is used to resolve pixelation and identify edges. Solutions of heat equations are useful in the mathematical formulation of hydrodynamical shocks.

As when solving an ordinary differential equation, you need certain initial conditions or boundary conditions or constraints to narrow the scope to solve a partial differential equation. There are three typical types of boundary conditions that correspond to three boundary value problems.

The first type of boundary value problem has a boundary condition that specifies the value of the function itself on the boundary of a function domain. It is called a Dirichlet boundary condition. For example, if one end of an iron rod is held at a constant temperature, then the value of the problem (computing the heat or temperature in an area) is known at that point in space. See Figure 8-1.

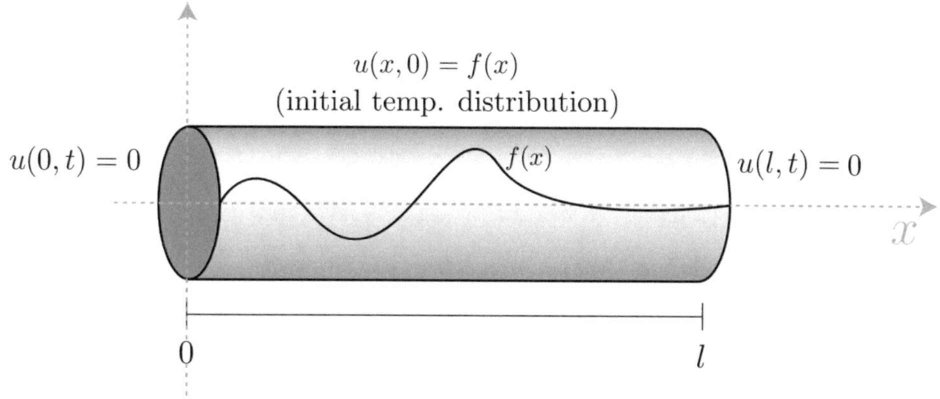

Figure 8-1. *Initial boundary value problem for heat equation*

Mathematically, you write this:

$$\begin{cases} \dfrac{\partial u}{\partial t} - a\dfrac{\partial^2 u}{\partial x^2} = 0, 0 < t < T, 0 < x < l \\ u(x,0) = \phi(x), 0 \le x \le l \\ u(0,t) = g_1(t), u(l,t) = g_2(t), 0 \le t \le T \end{cases}$$

The first (differential) equation describes the dynamics of the system of heat. The second equation is the initial condition and describes the initial temperature anywhere in the rod. The third equation is the boundary condition and specifies the temperatures of the two ends of the rod at any time. The boundary condition $u(0, t) = g_1(t)$, $u(l, t) = g_2(t)$ is called the first-type boundary condition. $\phi(x)$, $g_1(t)$ and $g_2(t)$ are known functions. They also meet the connection conditions.

$$\begin{cases} \phi(0) = g_1(0) \\ \phi(l) = g_2(0) \end{cases}$$

The second type of boundary condition is called the Neumann boundary condition. It specifies the values of the normal derivative of the function on the boundary. A normal derivative is a directional derivative taken in the direction normal (that is, orthogonal) to some surface in space. If the normal direction, that is, the direction of the outer normal of the boundary Γ, is denoted by $\boldsymbol{n}$, then the directional derivative of a function f is sometimes denoted as follows:

$$\frac{\partial f}{\partial \boldsymbol{n}} = \nabla f(x) \cdot \boldsymbol{n} = \frac{\partial f}{\partial \boldsymbol{x}} \cdot \boldsymbol{n}$$

An example is that if there is a heater at one end of an iron rod, then energy would be added at a constant rate, but the actual temperature is not known.

The third type of boundary condition is also known as the Cauchy boundary condition. It specifies both the function value and normal derivative on the boundary of the domain. This corresponds to imposing a Dirichlet and a Neumann boundary condition.

Formally, the second and third types of boundary conditions can be expressed as follows:

$$\begin{cases} \left[\frac{\partial u}{\partial x} - \lambda_1(t)u\right]_{x=0} = g_1(t) \\ \left[\frac{\partial u}{\partial x} - \lambda_2(t)u\right]_{x=l} = g_1(t) \end{cases}$$

When $\lambda_1(t) = \lambda_2(t) = 0$, it is the second type of boundary condition. When $\lambda_1(t) \geq 0$ and $\lambda_2(t) \geq 0$, it is the third type of boundary condition.

8.1.2. Hyperbolic Equation

A second-order PDE is in the hyperbolic form if the following is true:

$$b^2(*) - a(*)c(*) > 0$$

The simplest yet most popular example of a hyperbolic PDE is the one-dimensional wave equation.

$$u_{tt} = \frac{\partial^2 u}{\partial t^2} = c^2 \frac{\partial^2 u}{\partial x^2} = c^2 \nabla^2 u$$

The solutions of hyperbolic equations are “wave-like.” If a disturbance is made in the initial data of a hyperbolic differential equation, then not every point of space feels the disturbance at once. Relative to a fixed time coordinate, disturbances have a finite propagation speed. They travel along the characteristics of the equation. This feature qualitatively distinguishes hyperbolic equations from parabolic partial differential equations and elliptic partial differential equations. A perturbation of the initial (or boundary) data of an elliptic or parabolic equation is felt at once by essentially all points in the domain. See Figure 8-2.

Figure 8-2. *A traveling pulse can be modeled by the wave equation*

The wave equation alone does not specify a physical solution; a unique solution is usually obtained by setting a problem with further conditions, such as initial conditions that prescribe the amplitude and phase of the wave. Another important class of problems occurs in enclosed spaces specified by boundary conditions, for which the solutions represent standing waves, or harmonics, analogous to the harmonics of musical instruments.

The initial value problem of a hyperbolic equation is as follows:

$$\begin{cases} \frac{\partial^2 u}{\partial t^2} = c^2 \frac{\partial^2 u}{\partial x^2}, t > 0 \\ u(x,0) = \phi(x) \\ \left.\frac{\partial u}{\partial t}\right|_{t=0} = \psi(x) \end{cases}$$

It can be shown that this equation has the property that, if u and its first-time derivative are arbitrarily specified by initial data on the line $t = 0$ (with sufficient smoothness properties), then there exists a solution for all time t.

The boundary value problems are as follows:

$$\begin{cases} \frac{\partial^2 u}{\partial t^2} = c^2 \frac{\partial^2 u}{\partial x^2}, t > 0 \\ u(x,0) = \phi(x), \left.\frac{\partial u}{\partial t}\right|_{t=0} = \psi(x) \\ u(0,t) = g_1(t), u(l,t) = g_2(t) \end{cases}$$

The last set of boundary conditions are the first-type boundary conditions.

8.1.3. Elliptic Equation

A second-order PDE is in the elliptic form if the following is true:

$$b^2(*) - a(*)c(*) < 0$$

The simplest form is the Poisson equation:

$$\Delta u = \nabla^2 u = \frac{\partial^2 u}{\partial x^2} + \frac{\partial^2 u}{\partial y^2} = f(x,y)$$

In particular, when $f(x, y) = 0$, it is the Laplace equation, also known as the harmonic equation:

$$\Delta u = \frac{\partial^2 u}{\partial x^2} + \frac{\partial^2 u}{\partial y^2} = 0$$

For example, the Poisson equation for gravity relating a scalar potential ϕ and an attracting mass ρ is as follows:

$$\nabla^2 \phi = 4\pi G \rho$$

The first-type boundary value problem of the Poisson equation is as follows:

$$\begin{cases} \frac{\partial^2 u}{\partial x^2} + \frac{\partial^2 u}{\partial y^2} = f(x,y), (x,y) \in \Omega \\ u(x,y)\big|_{(x,y)\in\Gamma} = \phi(x,y), \Gamma = \partial\Omega \end{cases}$$

Ω is the solution domain or a region; Γ is the boundary (or edge) of Ω. $f(x, y)$ and $\phi(x, y)$ are known, continuous functions on $\Omega \cup \Gamma$. $u(x, y)$ is the solution function that you want to solve for.

The second and third types of boundary conditions can be expressed as follows:

$$\left(\frac{\partial u}{\partial n} + \alpha u\right)\bigg|_{(x,y)\in\Gamma} = \phi(x,y)$$

When $\alpha = 0$, it is the second-type of boundary condition. When $\alpha \neq 0$, it is the third-type of boundary condition.

8.2. Finite Difference Method

There are three main numerical methods for computing numerical solutions for partial differential equations. They are the finite element method, the finite volume method, and the finite difference method. As of this writing, NM Dev supports only the finite difference method, also known as the grid method.

We covered the basic concepts of finite difference method in Chapters 6 and 7. The idea is the same except that you extend it to the higher dimension for multiple variables for partial differential equations. Here is a summary of the steps:

1. Impose a mesh or a grid on the solution domain.
2. Replace the continuous variable domain of the independent variables with a set of finite, discrete nodes (grid nodes).
3. Define the function values at the grid nodes.
4. Replace the derivative values at the grid nodes with their difference quotients.
5. The partial differential equation is now reduced to a system of algebraic equations, the difference equations, with a limited number of unknowns.
6. Analyze the convergence and estimate the errors.
7. If the system of difference equations has a solution and the solution converges to the solution of the original differential equation when the grid is infinitely small, then the solution of the difference equations is an approximate solution (or numerical solution) for the original problem.

8.2.1. Numerical Solution for Hyperbolic Equation

Consider this one-dimensional wave equation:

$$\frac{\partial^2 u}{\partial t^2} = c^2 \frac{\partial^2 u}{\partial x^2}$$

Both boundary ends are fixed at 0. That is:

$$u(t,0)=u(t,a)=0$$

The two initial conditions, namely u and its first-time derivative u_t at $t = 0$, are as follows:

$$\begin{cases} u(0,x)=f(x), 0<x<a \\ u_t(0,x)=g(x), 0<x<a \end{cases}$$

In NM Dev, the WaveEquation1D class can be used to construct such a one-dimensional wave equation. The signature is as follows:

```
/**
 * Constructs an one-dimensional wave equation.
 *
 * @param c2 the wave coefficient <i>&c^2;</i> in the equation
 * @param T   the time period of interest <i>(0, T)</i>
 * @param a   the region of interest <i>(0, a)</i>
 * @param f   the initial condition of <i>u</i>, i.e., <i>u(0, x)</i>
 * @param g   the initial condition of the time-derivative of <i>u</i>, i.e.,
 * <i>u<sub>t</sub>(0,x)</i>
 */
public WaveEquation1D(
    double c2,
    double T,
    double a,
    UnivariateRealFunction f,
    UnivariateRealFunction g)
```

Since both time and space derivatives are of second order, you use central differences to approximate them. Let the time step size be Δt and the space step size be Δx. Denote $u_j^k = u(t_k, x_j)$ as the approximate value at (k, j) in the grid. The difference formula is as follows:

$$\frac{u_j^{k+1} - 2u_j^k + u_j^{k-1}}{(\Delta t)^2} = c^2 \frac{u_{j+1}^k - 2u_j^k + u_{j-1}^k}{(\Delta x)^2}$$

Let

$$s = c^2 \frac{(\Delta t)^2}{(\Delta x)^2}$$

Solving u_j^{k+1} gives you the following:

$$u_j^{k+1} = s\left(u_{j+1}^k + u_{j-1}^k\right) + 2(1-s)u_j^k - u_j^{k-1}$$

Note that to compute each u_j^{k+1} you use four nodes from two previous time steps. Therefore, this is an explicit scheme for finding a numerical solution for $u_j^k = u(t_k, x_j)$.

As an explicit scheme, it is not unconditionally stable. It can be shown that the scheme is stable only when this is true.

$$s = c^2 \frac{(\Delta t)^2}{(\Delta x)^2} \le 1$$

If you define $\Delta t / \Delta x$ as the speed of the scheme, then the stability condition implies that the speed of the scheme must be at least as big as c, which is the speed of the wave (exact solution).

$$\Delta x \ge c\Delta t$$

This method is called the central difference method and is a second-order method with a truncation error of order $O((\Delta t)^2 + (\Delta x)^2)$. See Figure 8-3.

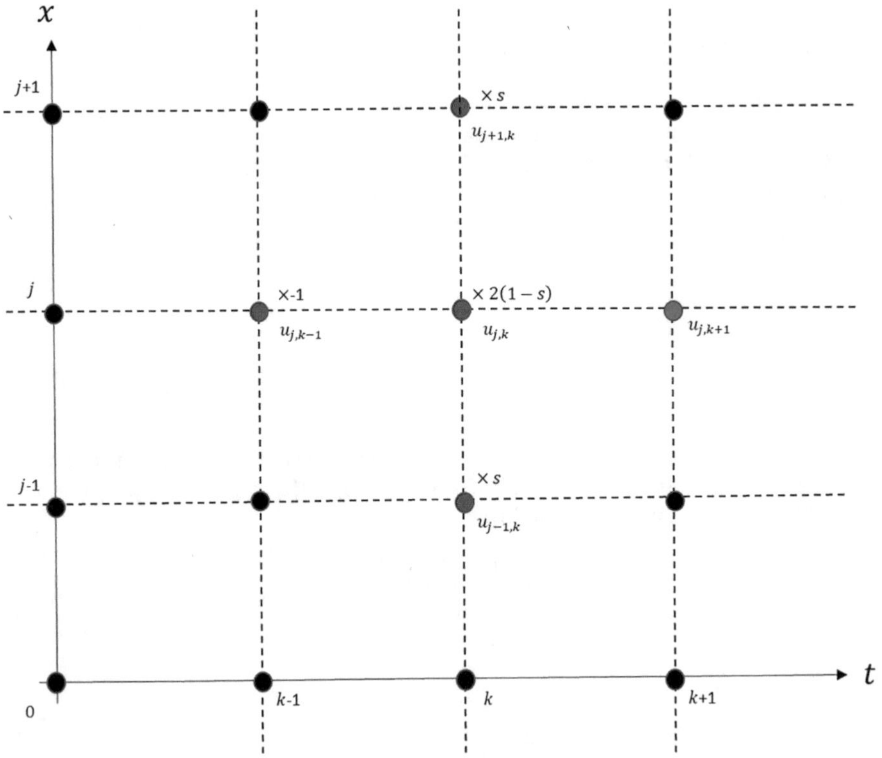

***Figure 8-3.** The explicit scheme to solve the one-dimensional wave equation*

The following NM Dev code solves the wave equation in the region [0, 1] × [0, 2] with $c^2 = 4$ and with these initial conditions:

$$\begin{cases} u(0,x) = 0.1\sin(\pi x) \\ u_t(0,x) = 0.2\pi\sin(\pi x) \end{cases}$$

```
val f1: UnivariateRealFunction = object : AbstractUnivariateRealFunction() {
    override fun evaluate(x: Double): Double {
        return 0.1 * sin(PI * x) // 0.1 * sin(π x)
    }
}

val f2: UnivariateRealFunction = object : AbstractUnivariateRealFunction() {
    override fun evaluate(x: Double): Double {
        return 0.2 * PI * sin(PI * x) // 0.2π * sin(π x)
    }
}

val c2:  Double = 4.0 // c^2
val T:  Double = 1.0 // time upper bond
val a:  Double = 2.0 // x upper bound
val pde: WaveEquation1D = WaveEquation1D(c2, T, a, f1, f2)

val m: Int = 80 // dt = T/m
val n: Int = 39 // dx = a/n
val soln: PDESolutionTimeSpaceGrid1D = ExplicitCentralDifference1D().solve(pde, m, n)

var t: Int = 0 // time index
var x: Int = 1 // x index
println(String.format("u(%d,%d) = %f", t, x, soln.u(t, x)))
t = 0
x = 16
println(String.format("u(%d,%d) = %f", t, x, soln.u(t, x)))
t = 0
x = 31
println(String.format("u(%d,%d) = %f", t, x, soln.u(t, x)))
t = 20
x = 1
println(String.format("u(%d,%d) = %f", t, x, soln.u(t, x)))
t = 20
x = 16
println(String.format("u(%d,%d) = %f", t, x, soln.u(t, x)))
t = 20
x = 31
println(String.format("u(%d,%d) = %f", t, x, soln.u(t, x)))
t = 40
x = 1
println(String.format("u(%d,%d) = %f", t, x, soln.u(t, x)))
t = 40
x = 16
println(String.format("u(%d,%d) = %f", t, x, soln.u(t, x)))
t = 40
x = 31
println(String.format("u(%d,%d) = %f", t, x, soln.u(t, x)))
t = 60
x = 1
println(String.format("u(%d,%d) = %f", t, x, soln.u(t, x)))
```

```
t = 60
x = 16
println(String.format("u(%d,%d) = %f", t, x, soln.u(t, x)))
t = 60
x = 31
println(String.format("u(%d,%d) = %f", t, x, soln.u(t, x)))
```

The output is as follows:

```
u(0,1) = 0.015643
u(0,16) = 0.058779
u(0,31) = -0.098769
u(20,1) = 0.015691
u(20,16) = 0.058956
u(20,31) = -0.099066
u(40,1) = -0.015605
u(40,16) = -0.058636
u(40,31) = 0.098529
u(60,1) = -0.015728
u(60,16) = -0.059098
u(60,31) = 0.099305
```

The `WaveEquation1D` class constructs a one-dimensional wave equation PDE. You need to specify the solution domain and the initial boundary conditions. The signature is as follows:

```
/**
 * Constructs an one-dimensional wave equation.
 *
 * @param beta the wave coefficient <i>&beta;</i> in the equation
 * @param T    the time period of interest <i>(0, T)</i>
 * @param a    the region of interest <i>(0, a)</i>
 * @param f    the initial condition of <i>u</i>, i.e., <i>u(0, x)</i>
 * @param g    the initial condition of the time-derivative of <i>u</i>,
 *             i.e.,
 * <i>u<sub>t</sub>(0,x)</i>
 */
public WaveEquation1D(
        double beta,
        double T,
        double a,
        UnivariateRealFunction f,
        UnivariateRealFunction g)
```

`ExplicitCentralDifference1D` is a PDE solver that solves the one-dimensional wave equation using the central difference method. The signature is as follows:

```
/**
 * Solves a one-dimensional wave equation, with the resolution parameters of
 * the solution grid.
 *
```

```
 * @param pde the wave equation problem
 * @param m   the number of grid points along the time-axis
 * @param n   the number of grid points along the space-axis
 * @return the solution grid
 */
public PDESolutionTimeSpaceGrid1D solve(
        WaveEquation1D pde,
        final int m,
        final int n
)
```

The solution is represented in the PDESolutionTimeSpaceGrid1D object. It is applicable to methods that produce the solution as a grid of time and space. The signature is as follows:

```
public interface PDESolutionTimeSpaceGrid1D {
    /**
     * Gets the value of the grid point at <i>(t<sub>m</sub>,
     * x<sub>n</sub>)</i>.
     *
     * @param m the index along the time axis
     * @param n the index along the space axis
     * @return the value at that point
     */
    double u(int m, int n);
    /**
     * Gets the value on the time axis at index {@code k}.
     *
     * @param m the index of the grid point
     * @return <i>t<sub>m</sub></i>
     */
    double t(int m);
    /**
     * Gets the value on the space axis at index {@code j}.
     *
     * @param n the index of the grid point
     * @return <i>x<sub>n</sub></i>
     */
    double x(int n);
    /**
     * Gets the number of interior time-axis grid points in the solution.
     *
     * @return the number of solution grid points along the time-axis
     */
    int M();
    /**
     * Gets the number of interior space-axis grid points in the solution.
     *
     * @return the number of solution grid points along the space-axis
     */
    int N();
}
```

NM Dev supports solving wave equations up to the second dimension. The two-dimensional wave equation problem is defined as follows:

$$\frac{\partial^2 u}{\partial t^2} = c^2 \left(\frac{\partial^2 u}{\partial x^2} + \frac{\partial^2 u}{\partial y^2} \right)$$

Both boundary ends are fixed at 0. That is,

$$u(t,0,0) = u(t,a,0) = u(t,0,b) = u(t,a,b) = 0$$

The two initial conditions, namely u and its first time derivative u_t at $t = 0$, are as follows:

$$\begin{cases} u(0,x,y) = f(x,y), 0 < x < a, 0 < y < b \\ u_t(0,x,y) = g(x,y), 0 < x < a, 0 < y < b \end{cases}$$

In NM Dev, the `WaveEquation2D` class can be used to construct such a two-dimensional wave equation. The signature is as follows:

```
/**
 * Constructs a two-dimensional wave equation.
 *
 * @param c2 the c^2 in the equation
 * @param T  the time period of interest <i>(0, T)</i>
 * @param a  the size of the region along the x-axis, <i>x &isin; (0,
 *           a)</i>
 * @param b  the size of the region along the y-axis <i>y &isin; (0,
 *           b)</i>
 * @param f  the initial condition of <i>u</i>, i.e., <i>u(0, x, y)</i>
 * @param g  the initial condition of the time-derivative of <i>u</i>,
 *           i.e.,
 * <i>u<sub>t</sub>(0,x,y)</i>
 */
public WaveEquation2D(
        double c2,
        double T,
        double a,
        double b,
        BivariateRealFunction f,
        BivariateRealFunction g
)
```

The two-dimensional central difference scheme is as follows:

$$\frac{u_{ij}^{k+1} - 2u_{ij}^{k} + u_{ij}^{k-1}}{(\Delta t)^2} = c^2 \left(\frac{u_{i+1j}^{k} - 2u_{ij}^{k} + u_{i-1j}^{k}}{(\Delta x)^2} + \frac{u_{ij+1}^{k} - 2u_{ij}^{k} + u_{ij-1}^{k}}{(\Delta y)^2} \right)$$

This scheme is stable when the following is true:

$$\frac{(\Delta x)^2 + (\Delta y)^2}{(\Delta t)^2} \geq 4c^2$$

The truncation error is of order $O((\Delta t)^2 + (\Delta x)^2 + (\Delta y)^2)$.

As an example, the following NM Dev code solves the two-dimensional wave equation in the region $[0, 2] \times [0, 2] \times [0, 2]$ with $c^2 = \frac{1}{4}$ and with these initial conditions:

```
println("Solve a 2-dimensional wave equation")

val f1: BivariateRealFunction = object : AbstractBivariateRealFunction() {
    override fun evaluate(x: Double,y: Double): Double {
        return 0.1 * sin(PI * x) * sin(PI * y / 2.0)
    }
}

val f2: BivariateRealFunction = object : AbstractBivariateRealFunction() {
    override fun evaluate(x: Double, y: Double): Double {
        return 0.0
    }
}

val c2: Double = 1.0 / 4 // wave speed squared
val T: Double = 2.0
val a: Double = 2.0
val b: Double = 2.0 // the solution domain bounds
val pde: WaveEquation2D = WaveEquation2D(
        c2, T, a, b, f1, f2)

val m: Int = 40 // dt = T/m
val n: Int = 39 // dx = a/n
val p: Int = 39 // dy = b/p
val soln: PDESolutionTimeSpaceGrid2D = ExplicitCentralDifference2D().solve(pde, m, n, p)

var t: Int = 40 // t index
var x: Int = 1 // x index
var y: Int = 1 // y index
println(String.format("u(%d,%d,%d) = %f", t, x, y, soln.u(t, x, y)))
t = 40 // t index
x = 1 // x index
y = 16 // y index
println(String.format("u(%d,%d,%d) = %f", t, x, y, soln.u(t, x, y)))
t = 40 // t index
x = 1 // x index
y = 31 // y index
println(String.format("u(%d,%d,%d) = %f", t, x, y, soln.u(t, x, y)))
t = 40 // t index
x = 16 // x index
```

```
y = 1 // y index
println(String.format("u(%d,%d,%d) = %f", t, x, y, soln.u(t, x, y)))
t = 40 // t index
x = 16 // x index
y = 16 // y index
println(String.format("u(%d,%d,%d) = %f", t, x, y, soln.u(t, x, y)))
t = 40 // t index
x = 16 // x index
y = 31 // y index
println(String.format("u(%d,%d,%d) = %f", t, x, y, soln.u(t, x, y)))
t = 40 // t index
x = 31 // x index
y = 1 // y index
println(String.format("u(%d,%d,%d) = %f", t, x, y, soln.u(t, x, y)))
t = 40 // t index
x = 31 // x index
y = 16 // y index
println(String.format("u(%d,%d,%d) = %f", t, x, y, soln.u(t, x, y)))
t = 40 // t index
x = 31 // x index
y = 31 // y index
println(String.format("u(%d,%d,%d) = %f", t, x, y, soln.u(t, x, y)))
```

The output is as follows:

```
u(40,1,1) = -0.001145
u(40,1,16) = -0.013877
u(40,1,31) = -0.009476
u(40,16,1) = -0.004302
u(40,16,16) = -0.052141
u(40,16,31) = -0.035606
u(40,31,1) = 0.007228
u(40,31,16) = 0.087616
u(40,31,31) = 0.059830
```

`ExplicitCentralDifference2D` is a PDE solver that solves the two-dimensional wave equation using the central difference method. The signature is as follows:

```
/**
 * Solves a two-dimensional wave equation, with the resolution parameters of
 * the solution grid.
 *
 * @param pde the wave equation problem
 * @param m   the number of grid points along the time-axis (excluding the
 *            initial condition)
 * @param n   the number of grid points along the x-axis (excluding the two
 *            boundaries)
 * @param p   the number of grid points along the y-axis (excluding the two
 *            boundaries)
 * @return the solution grid
 */
```

```
public PDESolutionTimeSpaceGrid2D solve(
        WaveEquation2D pde,
        final int m,
        final int n,
        final int p
)
```

The solution is represented in the PDESolutionTimeSpaceGrid2D object. It is applicable to methods that produce the solution as a grid of time and space. The signature is as follows:

```
public interface PDESolutionTimeSpaceGrid2D {
    /**
     * Gets the value of the grid point at <i>(t<sub>k</sub>, x<sub>i</sub>,
     * y<sub>j</sub>)</i>.
     *
     * @param k the index along the time-axis
     * @param i the index along the x-axis
     * @param j the index along the y-axis
     * @return the value at the grid point
     */
    double u(int k, int i, int j);
    /**
     * Gets the value on the time-axis at index {@code k}.
     *
     * @param k the index of the grid point
     * @return <i>t<sub>k</sub></i>
     */
    double t(int k);
    /**
     * Gets the value on the x-axis at index {@code i}.
     *
     * @param i the index of the grid point
     * @return <i>x<sub>i</sub></i>
     */
    double x(int i);
    /**
     * Gets the value on the y-axis at index {@code j}.
     *
     * @param j the index of the grid point
     * @return <i>y<sub>j</sub></i>
     */
    double y(int j);
    /**
     * Gets the number of interior time-axis grid points in the solution.
     *
     * @return the number of solution grid points along the time-axis
     */
    int m();
    /**
     * Gets the number of interior x-axis grid points in the solution.
```

```
         *
         * @return the number of solution grid points along the x-axis
         */
        int n();
        /**
         * Gets the number of interior y-axis grid points in the solution.
         *
         * @return the number of solution grid points along the y-axis
         */
        int p();
}
```

8.2.2. Numerical Solution for Elliptic Equation

Consider the first-type boundary value problem of a Poisson equation (see Figure 8-4), as shown here:

$$\begin{cases} \frac{\partial^2 u}{\partial x^2}+\frac{\partial^2 u}{\partial y^2}=f(x,y),(x,y)\in\Omega \\ u(x,y)\big|_{(x,y)\in\Gamma}=\phi(x,y),\Gamma=\partial\Omega \end{cases}$$

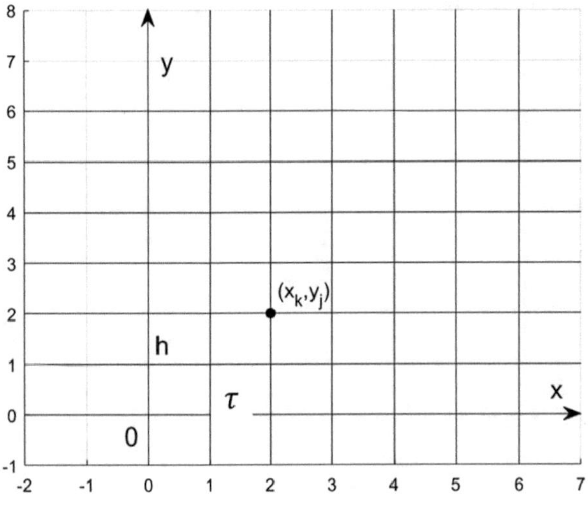

Figure 8-4. *A grid on a two-dimensional domain*

Take h and τ as the step sizes in the x and y directions, respectively. The nodes inside the grid are denoted as $\{(x_k, y_j) \mid x_k = kh, y_j = j\tau, k, j \in Z\}$, $(k, j = 0, \pm1, \pm2, \cdots)$. The nodes inside the solution domain are called the interior nodes. They belong to $\Omega \cup \Gamma$. For each node, there are four adjacent nodes that are only one step away in both the x and y directions, $(k, j = \pm 1, \pm2)$. If all four adjacent nodes of a node are interior nodes, the node is called a regular interior node. The set of regular interior nodes is denoted as $\Omega^{(1)}$. If one of the adjacent nodes is not interior, the node is a nonregular interior node. The set of nonregular interior nodes is denoted as $\Omega^{(2)}$. The intersection of the boundary Γ and the grid lines is called the boundary node. A numerical solution of a partial differential equation determines the value of the function u at all the interior nodes.

To simplify the notation, denote $f_j^k = f\left(x_k, y_j\right)$. For a regular interior node $(k, j) \in \Omega^{(1)}$, the second-order central difference quotient formulas are as follows:

$$\left.\frac{\partial^2 u}{\partial x^2}\right|_{(k,j)} = \frac{\dfrac{u_j^{k+1} - u_j^k}{h} - \dfrac{u_j^k - u_j^{k-1}}{h}}{h} - \frac{h^2}{12} u_{x^4}^{(4)}\left(x_k + \theta_1 h, y_j\right) = \frac{u_j^{k+1} - 2u_j^k + u_j^{k-1}}{h^2} - \frac{h^2}{12} u_{x^4}^{(4)}\left(x_k + \theta_1 h, y_j\right)$$

$$\left.\frac{\partial^2 u}{\partial y^2}\right|_{(k,j)} = \frac{u_{j+1}^k - 2u_j^k + u_{j-1}^k}{\tau^2} - \frac{\tau^2}{12} u_{y^4}^{(4)}\left(x_k, y_j + \theta_2 \tau\right)$$

where $0 < \theta_1, \theta_2 < 1$.

The Poisson equation $\dfrac{\partial^2 u}{\partial x^2} + \dfrac{\partial^2 u}{\partial y^2} = f(x, y)$ at node (k, j) can be expressed as follows:

$$\frac{u_j^{k+1} - 2u_j^k + u_j^{k-1}}{h^2} + \frac{u_{j+1}^k - 2u_j^k + u_{j-1}^k}{\tau^2} = f_j^k + R(k, j)$$

The truncation error is as follows:

$$R(k, j) = \frac{h^2}{12} u_{x^4}^{(4)}\left(x_k + \theta_1 h, y_j\right) + \frac{\tau^2}{12} u_{x^4}^{(4)}\left(x_k, y_j + \theta_2 \tau\right) = O\left(h^2 + \tau^2\right)$$

The difference equation approximation to the Poisson equation, by ignoring the error term $R(k, j)$, is as follows:

$$\frac{u_j^{k+1} - 2u_j^k + u_j^{k-1}}{h^2} + \frac{u_{j+1}^k - 2u_j^k + u_{j-1}^k}{\tau^2} = f_j^k$$

The number of difference equations is equal to the number of regular interior nodes $u_{k,j}$. Each difference equation contains not only the approximate value of the solution $u_{k,j}$ at regular interior nodes but also those for nonregular interior nodes. Thus, the number of equations is smaller than that of unknowns to be solved for. The approximate values at the nonregular interior nodes are given by the boundary conditions. There are various schemes to handle the boundary conditions. We describe the two simpler ones next.

Direct Transfer

The u value in the set of boundary nodes closest to the nonregular interior node is used as an approximation of the $u_{k,j}$ value at the node. We call this the direct transfer of the boundary conditions.

For example, suppose the node $P(k, j)$ is a nonregular interior node and the closest boundary node is the Q node; then you have the following:

$$u_j^k = u(Q) = \phi(Q), (k, j) \in \Omega^{(2)}$$

This formula can be seen as the zero-order interpolation of the nodes. It is easy, and the truncation error is $O(h + \tau)$. Using the previous substitution, the number of equations is equal to the number of unknowns. You can now solve the system of linear equations.

Linear Interpolation

This scheme is to approximate the value of $u_{k,j}$ at a nonregular interior node $P(k, j)$ by linearly interpolating a boundary node Q and an interior node R adjacent to node P on the same grid line. That is:

$$u_j^k = \frac{h}{h+d}\phi(Q) + \frac{d}{h+d}\phi(R)$$

$d = |QR|$, and the truncation error is $O(h^2)$. Using the previous substitution, the number of equations is equal to the number of unknowns. You can now solve the system of linear equations.

Note that there are five nodes involved in each difference equation: $\left\{u_j^{k+1}, 2u_j^k, u_j^{k-1}, u_{j+1}^k, u_{j-1}^k\right\}$. This is called a five-point stencil of a node in a grid or the five-point diamond scheme.

$$\frac{u_j^{k+1} - 2u_j^k + u_j^{k-1}}{h^2} + \frac{u_{j+1}^k - 2u_j^k + u_{j-1}^k}{\tau^2} = f_j^k$$

In practice, you'll often set $h = \tau$. The five-point diamond scheme is then simplified to the following:

$$\frac{1}{h^2}\left(u_j^{k+1} + u_j^{k-1} + u_{j+1}^k + u_{j-1}^k - 4u_j^k\right) = f_j^k$$

It is abbreviated as follows:

$$\frac{1}{h^2}\Diamond u_j^k = f_j^k$$

where $\Diamond u_j^k = u_j^{k+1} + u_j^{k-1} + u_{j+1}^k + u_{j-1}^k - 4u_j^k$. See Figure 8-5.

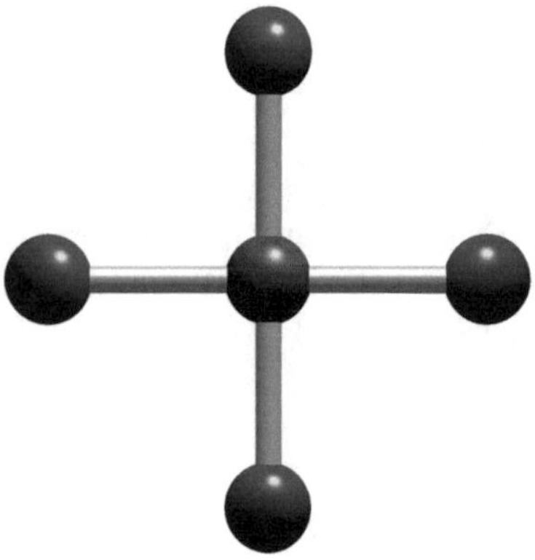

Figure 8-5. *A five-point stencil of a node in a grid*

As an example, consider solving the following first-type boundary value problem of the Laplace equation using the five-point diamond scheme, as shown here:

$$\begin{cases} \dfrac{\partial^2 u}{\partial x^2}+\dfrac{\partial^2 u}{\partial y^2}=0 \\ u(x,y)\big|_{\Gamma}=\log\left[(1+x)^2+y^2\right] \end{cases}$$

$$\Omega=\left\{(x,y)\middle|0\le x,y\le 1\right\}$$

You take $h=\tau=\dfrac{1}{3}$. There are four interior nodes (red) in the grid, all of which are regular interior nodes. From the five-point diamond scheme, the system of linear equations is as follows:

$$\begin{cases} \dfrac{1}{h^2}\left(u_1^2+u_1^0+u_2^1+u_0^1-4u_1^1\right)=0 \\ \dfrac{1}{h^2}\left(u_1^3+u_1^1+u_2^2+u_0^2-4u_1^2\right)=0 \\ \dfrac{1}{h^2}\left(u_2^2+u_2^0+u_3^1+u_1^1-4u_2^1\right)=0 \\ \dfrac{1}{h^2}\left(u_2^3+u_2^1+u_3^2+u_1^2-4u_2^2\right)=0 \end{cases}$$

The boundary values (blue), which can be directly computed from $u(x, y)|_{\Gamma}$, are as follows:

$$\begin{cases} u_0^1=\log\dfrac{16}{9},\ u_0^2=\log\dfrac{25}{9} \\ u_1^0=\log\dfrac{10}{9},\ u_2^0=\log\dfrac{13}{9} \\ u_3^1=\log\dfrac{25}{9},\ u_3^2=\log\dfrac{34}{9} \\ u_1^3=\log\dfrac{37}{9},\ u_2^3=\log\dfrac{40}{9} \end{cases}$$

The solutions to the system of linear equation are as follows (see Figure 8-6):

$$\begin{cases} u_1^1=0.634804 \\ u_1^2=1.059992 \\ u_2^1=0.798500 \\ u_2^2=1.169821 \end{cases}$$

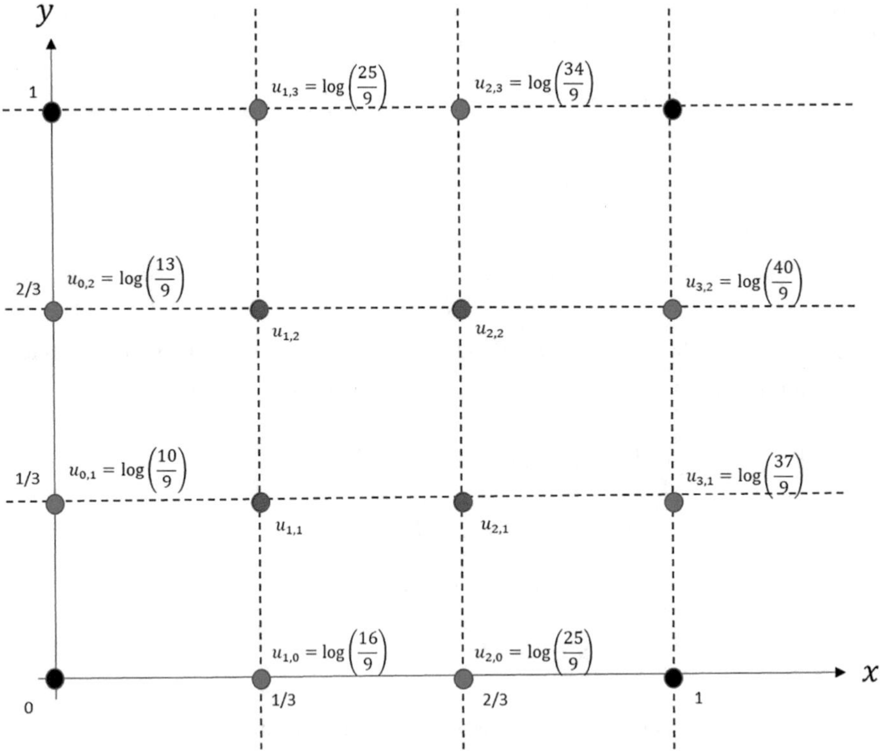

Figure 8-6. *The grid and solutions for the Laplace equation*

The following NM Dev code solves this example:

```
val ZERO: BivariateRealFunction // a constant zero function, f = 0
        = object : AbstractBivariateRealFunction() {
    override fun evaluate(x: Double, y: Double): Double {
        return 0.0
    }

    override fun evaluate(x: Vector): Double {
        return 0.0
    }
}

// the boundary conditions
val g: BivariateRealFunction = object : AbstractBivariateRealFunction() {
    override fun evaluate(x: Double, y: Double): Double {
        return ln((1.0 + x) * (1.0 + x) + y * y)
    }
}

val a: Double = 1.0 // width of the x-dimension
val b: Double = 1.0 // height of the y-dimension
```

```
val pde: PoissonEquation2D = PoissonEquation2D(a, b, ZERO, g)
val solver: IterativeCentralDifference = IterativeCentralDifference(
        1e-8, // precision
        40) // max number of iterations
val soln: PDESolutionGrid2D = solver.solve(pde, 2, 2)
var k: Int = 1
var j: Int = 1 // node indices
val u_11: Double = soln.u(k, j) // x = 0.3, y = 0.3
println(String.format("u_%d,%d = u(%f,%f): %f", k, j, soln.x(k), soln.y(j), u_11))
k = 1
j = 2
val u_12: Double = soln.u(k, j) // x = 0.3, y = 0.6
println(String.format("u_%d,%d = u(%f,%f): %f", k, j, soln.x(k), soln.y(j), u_12))
k = 2
j = 1
val u_21: Double = soln.u(k, j) // x = 0.6, y = 0.3
println(String.format("u_%d,%d = u(%f,%f): %f", k, j, soln.x(k), soln.y(j), u_21))
k = 2
j = 2
val u_22: Double = soln.u(k, j) // x = 0.6, y = 0.6
println(String.format("u_%d,%d = u(%f,%f): %f", k, j, soln.x(k), soln.y(j), u_22))
```

The output is as follows:

```
u_1,1 = u(0.333333,0.333333): 0.634804
u_1,2 = u(0.333333,0.666667): 0.798500
u_2,1 = u(0.666667,0.333333): 1.059992
u_2,2 = u(0.666667,0.666667): 1.169821
```

To set up a Poisson PDE problem, you first need to set up a PoissonEquation2D object. Its signature is as follows:

```
/**
 * Constructs a Poisson's equation problem.
 *
 * @param a the region of interest <i>[0, a]</i>
 * @param b the region of interest <i>[0, b]</i>
 * @param f the forcing term in the equation <i>f(x, y)</i>
 * @param g the Dirichlet boundary condition <i>g(x, y)</i>
 */
public PoissonEquation2D(
    double a,
    double b,
    BivariateRealFunction f,
    BivariateRealFunction g)
```

f is the term on the right side of the Poisson equation. When $f = 0$, it becomes the Laplace equation. g specifies the first-type boundary condition of the PDE problem. The domain solution for the PoissonEquation2D class is $[0, a] \times [0, b]$. To solve for another domain range, the user needs to do a transformation before coding.

IterativeCentralDifference is a PDE solver to solve Poisson equation problems using the central difference formula. Its signature is as follows:

```
/**
 * Constructs an instance of this method with the given precision as the
 * convergence criterion, and the maximum number of iterations allowed. The
 * iteration stops when the difference between successive iterations is
 * within the given precision.
 *
 * @param precision     the convergence threshold
 * @param maxIterations the maximum number of iterations allowed
 */
public IterativeCentralDifference(
        double precision,
        int maxIterations
) {
/**
 * Solves a Poisson's equation problem, with the given grid resolution
 * parameters.
 *
 * {@link UnsatisfiableErrorCriterionException} is thrown when the iteration
 * cannot converge to the specified error bound within the maximum allowed
 * number of iterations.
 *
 * @param pde the Poisson's equation
 * @param m   the number of interior points along the x-axis of the grid
 * @param n   the number of interior points along the y-axis of the grid
 * @return the solution grid
 */
public PDESolutionGrid2D solve(
        final PoissonEquation2D pde,
        final int m,
        final int n
)
```

In NM Dev, solving a two-dimensional PDE problem using a finite difference method will generate an PDESolutionGrid2D object. It contains all the information about the grid, the nodes, and the approximate values at each node. The signature is as follows:

```
/**
 * A solution to a bivariate PDE, which is applicable to methods which produce
 * the solution as a two-dimensional grid. The indices are within ranges 0 <= k <= (m+1),
   where the boundaries
 * lie at <i>0</i> and <i>(m+1)</i> and <i>0</i> and <i>(n+1)</i> respectively.
 *
*/
public interface PDESolutionGrid2D {
    /**
     * Gets the value of the grid point at <i>(x<sub>k</sub>,
     * y<sub>j</sub>)</i>.
     *
```

```
     * @param k the index along the x-axis
     * @param j the index along the y-axis
     * @return the value at that point
     */
    double u(int k, int j);
    /**
     * Gets the value on the x-axis at index {@code k}.
     *
     * @param k the index of the grid point
     * @return <i>x<sub>k</sub></i>
     */
    double x(int k);
    /**
     * Gets the value on the y-axis at index {@code j}.
     *
     * @param j the index of the grid point
     * @return <i>y<sub>j</sub></i>
     */
    double y(int j);
    /**
     * Gets the number of interior x-axis grid points in the solution.
     *
     * @return the number of solution grid points along the x-axis
     */
    int m();
    /**
     * Gets the number of interior y-axis grid points in the solution.
     *
     * @return the number of solution grid points along the y-axis
     */
    int n();
}
```

Note that the double `u(int k, int j)` function takes the node indices as inputs, not as domain values. `PDESolutionGrid2D` contains information only at the grid nodes. If you need the approximate values of the function not at the grid nodes, some interpolation will be needed.

As another example, the following NM Dev code solves the Laplace equation with the initial and boundary conditions for $0 \le x \le 0.5$, $0 \le y \le 0.5$:

$$\begin{cases} u(0,y) = u(x,0) = 0 \\ u(x,0.5) = 200x \\ u(0.5,y) = 200y \end{cases}$$

```
val ZERO: BivariateRealFunction // a constant zero function, f = 0
        = object : AbstractBivariateRealFunction() {
    override fun evaluate(x: Double, y: Double): Double {
        return 0.0
    }
```

```
    override fun evaluate(x: Vector): Double {
        return 0.0
    }
}

// the boundary conditions
val EPSION: Double = 1e-8
val g: BivariateRealFunction = object : AbstractBivariateRealFunction() {
    override fun evaluate(x: Double, y: Double): Double {
        if (DoubleUtils.isZero(x, EPSION) || DoubleUtils.isZero(y, EPSION)) {
            return 0.0
        } else if (DoubleUtils.equal(x, 0.5, EPSION)) {
            return 200.0 * y
        } else if (DoubleUtils.equal(y, 0.5, EPSION)) {
            return 200.0 * x
        }

        // not reachable don't matter
        return Double.NaN
    }
}

val a: Double = 0.5 // width of the x-dimension
val b: Double = 0.5 // height of the y-dimension
val pde: PoissonEquation2D = PoissonEquation2D(a, b, ZERO, g)
val solver: IterativeCentralDifference = IterativeCentralDifference(
        EPSION, // precision
        40) // max number of iterations
val soln: PDESolutionGrid2D = solver.solve(pde, 4, 4)
var k: Int = 1
var j: Int = 1 // node indices
val u_11: Double = soln.u(k, j)
println(String.format("u_%d,%d = u(%f,%f): %f", k, j, soln.x(k), soln.y(j), u_11))
k = 1
j = 2
val u_12: Double = soln.u(k, j)
println(String.format("u_%d,%d = u(%f,%f): %f", k, j, soln.x(k), soln.y(j), u_12))
k = 2
j = 1
val u_21: Double = soln.u(k, j)
println(String.format("u_%d,%d = u(%f,%f): %f", k, j, soln.x(k), soln.y(j), u_21))
k = 2
j = 2
val u_22: Double = soln.u(k, j)
println(String.format("u_%d,%d = u(%f,%f): %f", k, j, soln.x(k), soln.y(j), u_22))
k = 3
j = 3
val u_33: Double = soln.u(k, j)
println(String.format("u_%d,%d = u(%f,%f): %f", k, j, soln.x(k), soln.y(j), u_33))
k = 4
j = 4
```

```
val u_44: Double = soln.u(k, j)
println(String.format("u_%d,%d = u(%f,%f): %f", k, j, soln.x(k), soln.y(j), u_44))
k = 5
j = 5
val u_55: Double = soln.u(k, j)
println(String.format("u_%d,%d = u(%f,%f): %f", k, j, soln.x(k), soln.y(j), u_55))
```

The output is as follows (see Figure 8-7):

```
u_1,1 = u(0.100000,0.100000): 4.000000
u_1,2 = u(0.100000,0.200000): 8.000000
u_2,1 = u(0.200000,0.100000): 8.000000
u_2,2 = u(0.200000,0.200000): 16.000000
u_3,3 = u(0.300000,0.300000): 36.000000
u_4,4 = u(0.400000,0.400000): 64.000000
u_5,5 = u(0.500000,0.500000): 100.000000
```

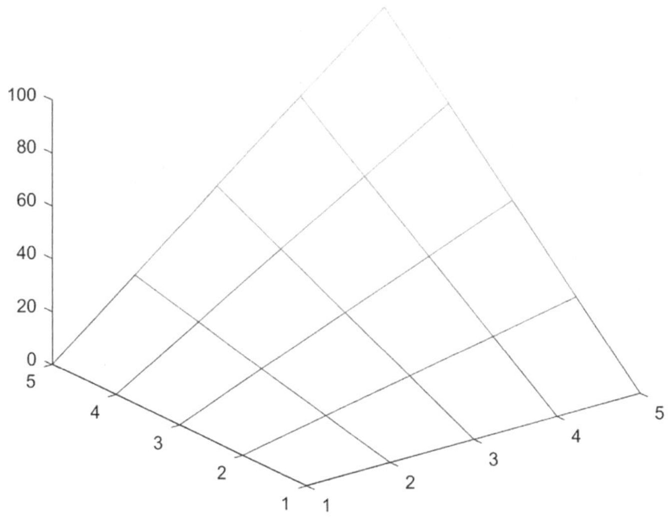

Figure 8-7. *The 5×5 solution grid*

8.2.3. Numerical Solution for Parabolic Equation

Consider this one-dimensional heat equation:

$$\frac{\partial u}{\partial t} = a\frac{\partial^2 u}{\partial x^2}, a > 0$$

The most famous application of this PDE that changed the course of history is probably the Black-Scholes equation, which is used to determine the price of a European option. The Black-Scholes equation gave birth to the trillion-dollar derivative business on Wall Street. After changing the variables, the Black-Scholes equation can be written in the following form:

$$\frac{\partial u}{\partial \tau} = \frac{\partial^2 u}{\partial x^2}$$

τ is the option's time to maturity. The option expires at $\tau = 0$. x is the price of the underlying stock that the option references. The initial condition (E is the strike price of the option) is simply the payoff function, as shown here:

$$u(0,x) = \max(x - E, 0)$$

The boundary condition says that when the stock becomes worthless, so does the option.

$$u(\tau,0) = 0$$

When the stock price is way above the strike price, the option behaves just like the stock.

$$\lim_{x \to \infty} u(\tau,x) = x$$

One straightforward way to approximate the PDE is to replace the time derivative using forward difference and the second-order derivative using central difference. That is:

$$\frac{u_j^{k+1} - u_j^k}{\Delta\tau} = \frac{u_{j+1}^k - 2u_j^k + u_{j-1}^k}{(\Delta x)^2}$$

Solving for u_j^{k+1}, you get this (see Figure 8-8):

$$u_j^{k+1} = \alpha u_{j+1}^k + (1 - 2\alpha) u_j^k + \alpha u_{j-1}^k$$

$$\alpha = \frac{\Delta\tau}{(\Delta x)^2}$$

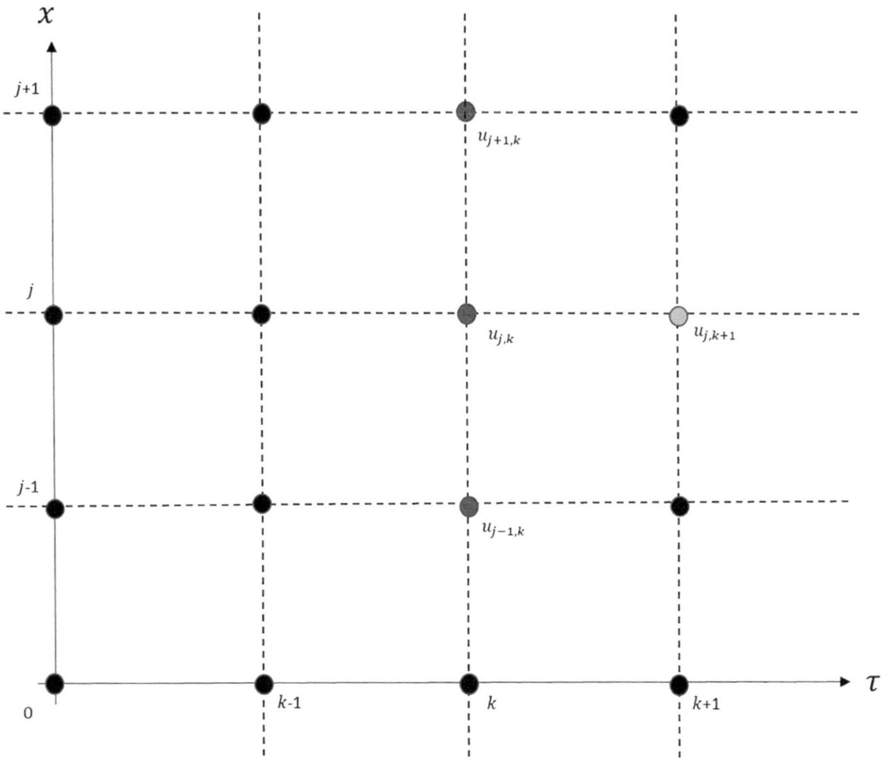

***Figure 8-8.** Explicit scheme for heat equation*

This is an explicit formula because at time-step *k*, you know all u_j^k for all *j*. You can use the three nodes (red) to explicitly compute u_j^{k+1} (blue) using this formula. This explicit scheme is not conditionally stable. It can be proven that it is stable only when the following is true:

$$0 < \alpha \leq \frac{1}{2}$$

Or, this works:

$$2\Delta\tau \leq (\Delta x)^2$$

Consequently, if you want to double the number of nodes in *x*, you need to quarter the time-step. Each time-step takes twice as long (twice as many nodes in *x*) and there are four times as many time-steps. Doubling the number of nodes in *x* means that it takes eight times as long to find a solution.

Alternatively, you can use the backward difference to approximate the time derivative. The difference equation approximation is as follows:

$$\frac{u_j^k - u_j^{k-1}}{\Delta\tau} = \frac{u_{j+1}^k - 2u_j^k + u_{j-1}^k}{(\Delta x)^2}$$

Rearranging the terms of time k on the left side, you get this (see Figure 8-9):

$$-\alpha u_{j-1}^{k}+(1+2\alpha)u_{j}^{k}-\alpha u_{j+1}^{k}=u_{j}^{k-1}$$

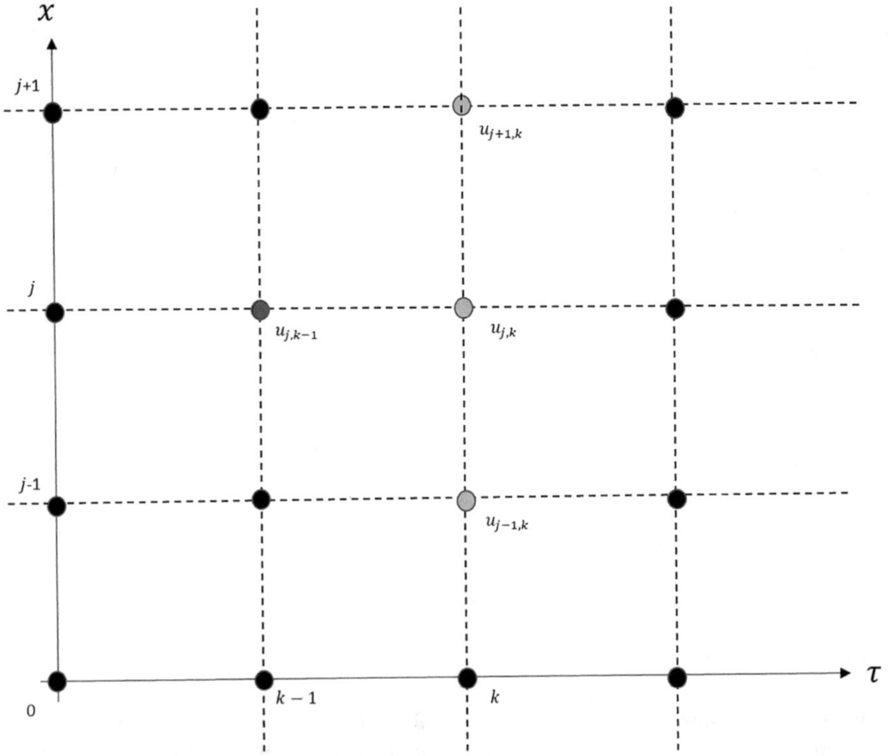

Figure 8-9. *Implicit scheme for heat equation*

The (three) values at the next time step k cannot be immediately computed in terms of the old values at $k-1$. You can collect the values at time steps k and $k+1$ and write them in a system of linear equations.

$$\begin{bmatrix} 1+2\alpha & -\alpha & 0 & \cdots & 0 \\ -\alpha & 1+2\alpha & -\alpha & & 0 \\ 0 & -\alpha & \ddots & \ddots & \\ \vdots & & \ddots & \ddots & -\alpha \\ 0 & 0 & & -\alpha & 1+2\alpha \end{bmatrix} \begin{bmatrix} u_{N^{-}+1}^{k} \\ \vdots \\ u_{0}^{k} \\ \vdots \\ u_{N^{+}-1}^{k} \end{bmatrix}$$

$$=\begin{bmatrix} u_{N^-+1}^{k-1} \\ \vdots \\ u_0^{k-1} \\ \vdots \\ u_{N^+-1}^{k-1} \end{bmatrix} + \alpha \begin{bmatrix} u_{N^-}^{k} \\ 0 \\ \vdots \\ 0 \\ u_{N^+}^{k} \end{bmatrix} = \begin{bmatrix} b_{N^-+1}^{k} \\ \vdots \\ b_0^{k} \\ \vdots \\ b_{N^+-1}^{k} \end{bmatrix}$$

$u_{N^-+1}^k$, $u_{N^+-1}^k$, $u_{N^-+1}^{k-1}$, $u_{N^+-1}^{k-1}$, $u_{N^-}^k$, and $u_{N^+}^k$ come from the boundary conditions. In matrix form, you can write this:

$$\boldsymbol{M}\boldsymbol{u}^k = \boldsymbol{b}^m$$

Or you can write this:

$$\boldsymbol{u}^k = \boldsymbol{M}^{-1}\boldsymbol{b}^m$$

In practice, you'll almost never compute the inverse because inverting a matrix is very computationally expensive and is subject to rounding errors. More efficient methods, in terms of the amount of computation and storage—such as LU decomposition, successive over-relaxation (SOR), and the Gauss-Seidel method—are used. The NM Dev library has implemented all these methods. The implicit finite-difference algorithm is unconditionally stable.

The Crank-Nicolson finite difference method further improves both the explicit and implicit methods so that it is unconditionally stable and has a truncation error of order $O((\Delta\tau)^2)$ (instead of $O(\Delta\tau)$ for the other two methods). The Crank-Nicolson finite difference method takes an average of the forward-difference and back-difference approximations. The average of those two equations is as follows:

$$\frac{u_j^{k+1} - u_j^k}{\Delta\tau} = \frac{1}{2}\left(\frac{u_{j+1}^k - 2u_j^k + u_{j-1}^k}{(\Delta x)^2} + \frac{u_{j+1}^{k+1} - 2u_j^{k+1} + u_{j-1}^{k+1}}{(\Delta x)^2}\right)$$

Rearranging so that the terms of time step $k + 1$ are on the left side and those of time-step k are on the right side, you get this:

$$u_j^{k+1} - \frac{1}{2}\alpha\left(u_{j+1}^{k+1} - 2u_j^{k+1} + u_{j-1}^{k+1}\right) = u_j^k + \frac{1}{2}\alpha\left(u_{j+1}^k - 2u_j^k + u_{j-1}^k\right)$$

You can again write this system of linear equations in matrix form:

$$\begin{bmatrix} 1+\alpha & -\frac{1}{2}\alpha & 0 & \cdots & 0 \\ -\frac{1}{2}\alpha & 1+\alpha & -\frac{1}{2}\alpha & & 0 \\ 0 & -\frac{1}{2}\alpha & \ddots & \ddots & \\ \vdots & & \ddots & \ddots & -\frac{1}{2}\alpha \\ 0 & 0 & & -\frac{1}{2}\alpha & 1+\alpha \end{bmatrix} \begin{bmatrix} u_{N^-+1}^{k+1} \\ \vdots \\ u_0^{k+1} \\ \vdots \\ u_{N^+-1}^{k+1} \end{bmatrix}$$

$$= \begin{bmatrix} Z_{N^-+1}^k \\ \vdots \\ Z_0^k \\ \vdots \\ Z_{N^+-1}^k \end{bmatrix} + \frac{1}{2}\alpha \begin{bmatrix} u_{N^-}^{k+1} \\ 0 \\ \vdots \\ 0 \\ u_{N^+}^{k+1} \end{bmatrix}$$

$$Z_j^k = (1-\alpha)u_j^k + \frac{1}{2}\alpha\left(u_{j-1}^k + u_{j+1}^k\right)$$

The system can then be solved by SOR (the default in NM Dev).

As an example, the following NM Dev code solves this heat equation on the region [0, 6000] × [0, 1] using Crank-Nicolson:

$$\begin{cases} \dfrac{\partial u}{\partial t} = 10^{-5}\dfrac{\partial^2 u}{\partial x^2} \\ u(0,x) = 2x + \sin(2\pi x) \\ u(t,0) = 0 \\ u(t,1) = 2 \end{cases}$$

```
val f1: UnivariateRealFunction = object : AbstractUnivariateRealFunction() {
    override fun evaluate(x: Double): Double {
        return 2.0 * x + sin(2.0 * PI * x) // initial condition
    }
}

val f2: UnivariateRealFunction = object : AbstractUnivariateRealFunction() {
    override fun evaluate(t: Double): Double {
        return 0.0 // boundary condition at x = 0
    }
}

val f3: UnivariateRealFunction = object :  AbstractUnivariateRealFunction() {
    override fun evaluate(t: Double): Double {
        return 2.0 // boundary condition at x = 6000
    }
}

val pde: HeatEquation1D = HeatEquation1D(
        1e-5, // heat equation coefficient
        1.0, 6000.0, // solution domain bounds
        f1,
        0.0,
        f2,
        0.0,
        f3
)
```

```
// c_k are 0 for Dirichlet boundary conditions
val m: Int = 50
val n: Int = 39

val soln: PDESolutionTimeSpaceGrid1D
        = CrankNicolsonHeatEquation1D().solve(pde, m, n)

var t: Int = 0
var x: Int = 1
println(String.format("u(%d,%d) = %f", t, x, soln.u(t, x)))
t = 0
x = 16
println(String.format("u(%d,%d) = %f", t, x, soln.u(t, x)))
t = 0
x = 31
println(String.format("u(%d,%d) = %f", t, x, soln.u(t, x)))
t = 15
x = 1
println(String.format("u(%d,%d) = %f", t, x, soln.u(t, x)))
t = 15
x = 16
println(String.format("u(%d,%d) = %f", t, x, soln.u(t, x)))
t = 15
x = 31
println(String.format("u(%d,%d) = %f", t, x, soln.u(t, x)))
t = 30
x = 1
println(String.format("u(%d,%d) = %f", t, x, soln.u(t, x)))
t = 30
x = 16
println(String.format("u(%d,%d) = %f", t, x, soln.u(t, x)))
t = 30
x = 31
println(String.format("u(%d,%d) = %f", t, x, soln.u(t, x)))
t = 45
x = 1
println(String.format("u(%d,%d) = %f", t, x, soln.u(t, x)))
t = 45
x = 16
println(String.format("u(%d,%d) = %f", t, x, soln.u(t, x)))
t = 45
x = 31
println(String.format("u(%d,%d) = %f", t, x, soln.u(t, x)))
```

The output is as follows:

```
u(0,1) = 0.206434
u(0,16) = 1.387785
u(0,31) = 0.562312
u(15,1) = 0.126965
u(15,16) = 1.089188
u(15,31) = 1.064061
u(30,1) = 0.087867
u(30,16) = 0.942280
u(30,31) = 1.310920
u(45,1) = 0.068630
u(45,16) = 0.870001
u(45,31) = 1.432373
```

The HeatEquation1D class constructs such a heat equation problem. The signature is as follows:

```
/**
 * Constructs a heat equation problem.
 *
 * @param beta the beta in the equation
 * @param a    the region of interest <i>(0, a)</i>
 * @param T    the time period of interest <i>(0, T)</i>
 * @param f    the initial condition of <i>u</i>, i.e., <i>u(0,x)</i>
 * @param c1   the coefficient in the mixed boundary condition at <i>x =
 *             0</i>
 * @param g1   the mixed boundary condition at <i>x = 0</i>
 * @param c2   the coefficient in the mixed boundary condition at <i>x =
 *             a</i>
 * @param g2   the mixed boundary condition at <i>x = a</i>
 */
public HeatEquation1D(
        double beta,
        double a,
        double T,
        UnivariateRealFunction f,
        double c1,
        UnivariateRealFunction g1,
        double c2,
        UnivariateRealFunction g2)
```

The CrankNicolsonHeatEquation1D class solves the one-dimensional heat equation using the Crank-Nicolson finite difference algorithm. The signature is as follows:

```
/**
 * Solves the given one-dimensional heat equation.
 *
 * @param pde the PDE problem
 * @param M   the number of grid points along the time-axis (excluding the
 *            initial condition)
```

```
 * @param N   the number of grid points along the space-axis (excluding the
 *            two boundaries)
 * @return the solution \(u(t,x)\) at the grid points
 */
public PDESolutionTimeSpaceGrid1D solve(
        final HeatEquation1D pde,
        final int M,
        final int N
)
```

Furthermore, NM Dev library supports solving a two-dimensional heat equation. It has this form:

$$\frac{\partial u}{\partial t} = \beta\left(\frac{\partial^2 u}{\partial x^2} + \frac{\partial^2 u}{\partial y^2}\right)$$

The initial condition is as follows:

$$u(0,x,y) = f(x,y)$$

The boundary condition is as follows:

$$u(t,x,y) = g(t,x,y)$$

$(x, y) \in \delta R$, where δR is the boundary of the surface R.

The NM Dev class `HeatEquation2D` constructs such an object. The signature is as follows:

```
/**
 * Constructs a two-dimensional heat equation problem.
 *
 * @param beta the beta in the equation
 * @param T    the time period of interest <i>(0, T)</i>
 * @param a    the size of the region along the x-axis, <i>x &isin; (0, a)</i>
 * @param b    the size of the region along the y-axis <i>y &isin; (0, b)</i>
 * @param f    the initial condition of <i>u</i>, i.e., <i>u(0,x,y)</i>
 * @param g    the boundary condition at <i>x = 0, a</i> and <i>y = 0, b</i>
 */
public HeatEquation2D(
    double beta,
    double T,
    double a,
    double b,
    BivariateRealFunction f,
    TrivariateRealFunction g
)
```

The NM Dev class `AlternatingDirectionImplicitMethod` solves the two-dimensional heat equation using the alternating direction implicit (ADI) method. The idea behind the ADI method is to split the finite difference equations into two, one with the x-derivative taken implicitly and the other with the y-derivative taken implicitly. That allows you to solve the symmetric and tridiagonal systems of linear equations by using LU decomposition, at each step. Solutions are computed on a three-dimensional grid (time and x- and y-coordinates). ADI is an implicit method and is unconditionally stable; it is a second-order method with a truncation error of order $O(\Delta t^2 + \Delta x^2 + \Delta y^2)$.

The following code solves this example PDE problem:

$$\begin{cases} \frac{\partial u}{\partial t} = 10^{-4}\left(\frac{\partial^2 u}{\partial x^2} + \frac{\partial^2 u}{\partial y^2}\right) \\ u(0,x,y) = 0 \\ u(t,x,y) = e^y \cos x - e^x \cos y \\ \end{cases}$$

```
println("Solve a 2-dimensional heat equation")

// solution domain
val a: Double = 4.0
val b: Double = 4.0
// time domain
val T: Double = 5000.0

// heat equation coefficient
val beta: Double = 1e-4

// initial condition
val f: BivariateRealFunction = object : AbstractBivariateRealFunction() {
    override fun evaluate(x1: Double, x2: Double): Double {
        return 0.0
    }
}

// boundary condition
val g: TrivariateRealFunction = object : AbstractTrivariateRealFunction() {
    override fun evaluate(t: Double, x: Double, y: Double): Double {
        return exp(y) * cos(x) - exp(x) * cos(y)
    }
}
val PDE: HeatEquation2D = HeatEquation2D(beta, T, a, b, f, g)

val adi: AlternatingDirectionImplicitMethod
        = AlternatingDirectionImplicitMethod(1e-5)
val soln: PDESolutionTimeSpaceGrid2D = adi.solve(PDE, 50, 39, 39)

var t: Int = 50
var x: Int = 1
var y: Int = 1
println(String.format("u(%d,%d,%d) = %f", t, x, y, soln.u(t, x, y)))
t = 50
x = 1
y = 16
println(String.format("u(%d,%d,%d) = %f", t, x, y, soln.u(t, x, y)))
t = 50
x = 1
y = 31
```

```
println(String.format("u(%d,%d,%d) = %f", t, x, y, soln.u(t, x, y)))
t = 50
x = 16
y = 1
println(String.format("u(%d,%d,%d) = %f", t, x, y, soln.u(t, x, y)))
t = 50
x = 16
y = 16
println(String.format("u(%d,%d,%d) = %f", t, x, y, soln.u(t, x, y)))
t = 50
x = 16
y = 31
println(String.format("u(%d,%d,%d) = %f", t, x, y, soln.u(t, x, y)))
t = 50
x = 31
y = 1
println(String.format("u(%d,%d,%d) = %f", t, x, y, soln.u(t, x, y)))
t = 50
x = 31
y = 16
println(String.format("u(%d,%d,%d) = %f", t, x, y, soln.u(t, x, y)))
t = 50
x = 31
y = 31
println(String.format("u(%d,%d,%d) = %f", t, x, y, soln.u(t, x, y)))
```

The output is as follows:

```
u(50,1,1) = -0.000000
u(50,1,16) = 4.771024
u(50,1,31) = 22.814937
u(50,16,1) = -4.771024
u(50,16,16) = -0.000000
u(50,16,31) = 2.415165
u(50,31,1) = -22.814937
u(50,31,16) = -2.415165
u(50,31,31) = -0.000000
```

The signature for the AlternatingDirectionImplicitMethod class is as follows:

```
/**
 * Constructs an ADI method with the given precision parameter. By default,
 * multi-core parallel computation is used for higher performance.
 *
 * @param epsilon the precision parameter
 */
public AlternatingDirectionImplicitMethod(double epsilon)
/**
 * Solves the given two-dimensional heat equation problem, with the given
 * numbers of points along the three axes in the grid (time, x, and y).
```

```
 *
 * @param pde the heat equation problem
 * @param m   the number of grid points along the time-axis (excluding the
 *            initial condition)
 * @param n   the number of grid points along the x-axis (excluding the
 *            boundary)
 * @param p   the number of grid points along the y-axis (excluding the
 *            boundary)
 * @return the solution grid
 */
public PDESolutionTimeSpaceGrid2D solve(
        HeatEquation2D pde,
        final int m,
        final int n,
        final int p
)
```

CHAPTER 9

■ ■ ■

Unconstrained Optimization

Unconstrained optimization finds a variable (or a set of variables) that minimize or maximize an objective function without restrictions on their values. Mathematically, it says, find x^* such that function $f(x^*)$ takes the smallest value.

$$x^* = \min_x f(x)$$

x may be a scalar (in $\mathbb{R}^1$) or a vector (in $\mathbb{R}^n$). $f(x)$ is always a scalar (in $\mathbb{R}^1$). Unconstrained optimization has applications in many branches of science. In finance, constructing a yield curve involves finding a set of parameters to minimize the difference between the theoretical prices and the market prices of bonds. A constrained optimization problem may also be formulated as an unconstrained optimization problem by converting the constraints of the constrained optimization problem into penalty terms in the objective function of an equivalent unconstrained optimization problem. Moreover, many constrained optimization solvers or algorithms involve solving unconstrained optimization problems as subproblems. NM Dev has a suite of optimizers or minimizers that solve unconstrained optimization problems, for both univariate and multivariate problems, with and without derivative information. This implementation and hence discussion is by and large based on Antoniou & Lu (2007).

9.1. Brute-Force Search

The simplest and probably easiest-to-understand solver is the brute-force search. That is, you simply go through all possible values, x, in the domain of the function to enumerate all possible values of $f(x)$. Then you pick the x that corresponds to the smallest $f(x)$. There may be more than one solution. However, this method is rarely used because it is not practical. One requirement is that the domain must be enumerable. Most practical optimization problems solve over a continuous domain such as the real numbers. You cannot enumerate an infinite number of numbers. One way to circumvent the problem is discretization. You choose a finite number of points from the infinite domain. For example, you can discretize the unit interval $[0, 1]$ into 11 discrete values, $0, 0.1, 0.2, ..., 1.0$. The most obvious drawback of discretization is that you may (likely) get a suboptimal solution when the chosen points do not contain the optimal answer. In fact, if the domain is unbounded, $(-\infty, +\infty)$, it is not obvious how to choose the points to contain a solution. Moreover, the performance is very slow for any but tiny problems. Suppose you have ten variables to solve for; then the dimension of the problem is n^{10}, where n is the number of discretized points chosen for each dimension. The complexity of the problem grows exponentially. Nonetheless, the brute-force search is easy to understand. We therefore start with it first.

© Haksun Li, PhD 2023
H. Li, PhD, *Numerical Methods Using Kotlin*, https://doi.org/10.1007/978-1-4842-8826-9_9

The following NM Dev code illustrates in general how to solve an optimization problem using the library. Suppose you want to minimize the function $f(x) = x^2 - 4$.

```
// define the optimization problem using an objective function
val problem: OptimProblem = object : OptimProblem {

    override fun dimension(): Int {
        return 1
    }

    override fun f(): RealScalarFunction {
        return object : RealScalarFunction {

            // the objective function
            override fun evaluate(v: Vector): Double {
                val x: Double = v.get(1)
                val polynomial: Polynomial = Polynomial(1.0, 0.0, -4.0) // f(x) = x^2 - 4
                val fx: Double = polynomial.evaluate(x)
                return fx
            }

            override fun dimensionOfDomain(): Int {
                return 1
            }

            override fun dimensionOfRange(): Int {
                return 1
            }
        }
    }
}

// set up the solver to use and the solution
val solver: DoubleBruteForceMinimizer = DoubleBruteForceMinimizer(false)
val soln = solver.solve(problem)

// for brute force search, we need to explicitly enumerate the values in the domain
val domain = mutableListOf<Vector>(
    DenseVector(-2.0),
    DenseVector(-1.0),
    DenseVector(0.0), // the minimizer
    DenseVector(1.0),
    DenseVector(2.0)
)
soln.setDomain(domain)

println(String.format("f(%s) = %f", soln.minimizer(), soln.min()))
```

The output is as follows:

```
f([0.000000] ) = -4.000000
```

There are a number of steps to follow to use a solver in NM Dev to solve an optimization problem:

1. Define an optimization problem by implementing the `OptimProblem` interface. You give the objective function in the implementation.
2. Construct a solver to use, such as `DoubleBruteForceMinimizer`.
3. Call the `solve` function to construct a `Solution` object from the solver using the optimization problem. In other words, the solver object is a factory that creates a solution called `Solution` for an optimization problem, called `OptimProblem`. While the solver may be reused for other problems, a solution corresponds to only one problem.
4. Supply any problem-related information to the `Solution` object. In this case, for a brute-force search, you need to list the possible values, i.e., the domain, to search.
5. Call the `minimizer` function to run the algorithm to compute the minimizer x^*, or the `min` function to return the minimum value of the function $f(x^*)$.

The previous procedure works for all solvers in the NM Dev library. All NM solvers do minimization. To do maximization, you simply negate the objective function by multiplying it by -1. In general, the signatures for `OptimProblem`, solvers, and `Solution` are as follows:

```
public interface OptimProblem {
    /**
     * Get the number of variables.
     *
     * @return the number of variables.
     */
    public int dimension();
    /**
     * Get the objective function.
     *
     * @return the objective function
     */
    public RealScalarFunction f();
}
public interface MultivariateMinimizer<P extends OptimProblem, S extends
MinimizationSolution<Vector>> extends Minimizer<P, S> {
    /**
     * Solve an optimization problem, e.g., {@link OptimProblem}.
     *
     * @param problem an optimization problem
     * @return a solution to the optimization problem
     * @throws Exception when there is an error solving the problem
     */
    public S solve(P problem) throws Exception;
}
public interface MinimizationSolution<T> {
    /**
     * Get the (approximate) minimum found.
     *
     * @return the (approximate) minimum found
     */
```

```
    public double minimum();
    /**
     * Get the minimizer (solution) to the minimization problem.
     *
     * @return the minimizer
     */
    public T minimizer();
}
```

DoubleBruteForceMinimizer has the following signature:

```
public DoubleBruteForceMinimizer(boolean isParallel);
@Override
public BruteForceMinimizer.Solution solve(OptimProblem problem) throws Exception
```

When the isParallel flag is set to true, the code runs the search in parallel using multithreaded code to search all supplied domain values on all available threads.

The brute-force search can be used to solve univariate optimization problems, as in the previous example, as well as multivariate optimization problems. Here is an example of solving for:

$$f(x, y) = x^2 + y^2$$

```
val problem = object : OptimProblem {
    override fun dimension(): Int {
        return 2
    }
    override fun f(): RealScalarFunction {
        return object : RealScalarFunction {
            override fun evaluate(v: Vector): Double {
                val x: Double= v.get(1)
                val y: Double= v.get(2)
                val fx: Double = x * x + y * y
                return fx
            }
            override fun dimensionOfDomain(): Int {
                return 2
            }
            override fun dimensionOfRange(): Int {
                return 1
            }
        }
    }
}
val bf = DoubleBruteForceMinimizer(true)
val soln = bf.solve(problem)
val domain = mutableListOf<Vector>(
    DenseVector(-2.0, -2.0),
    DenseVector(-1.0, -1.0),
    DenseVector(0.0, 0.0), // the minimizer
    DenseVector(1.0, 1.0),
    DenseVector(2.0, 2.0)
)
```

```
soln.setDomain(domain)
println(String.format("f(%s) = %f", soln.minimizer(), soln.min()))
```

The output is as follows:

```
f([0.000000, 0.000000] ) = 0.000000
```

As shown in this example, unless you magically know the solution, (0, 0) in this case, and put it in the domain list, the brute-force search will not find the solution. In such cases, if you had known the answer, you would not need an optimizer.

9.2. C²OptimProblem

The `OptimProblem` class is somewhat difficult to set up and is inconvenient to use in most cases. A C^0 function is a continuous function. A C^1 function is a smooth function. A C^2 function is a function that is continuous, is smooth, and has a second derivative. It is also called a twice differentiable function. If you are to optimize such a function, `C2OptimProblemImpl` provides a convenient wrapper to create an `OptimProblem` object. Its signature is as follows:

```
/**
 * Construct an optimization problem with an objective function.
 * This uses a numerical gradient and a numerical Hessian, if needed.
 *
 * @param f the objective function to be minimized
 */
public C2OptimProblemImpl(RealScalarFunction f)
```

You can rewrite the previous examples using simplified code.

For the univariate function $f(x) = x^2 - 4$, you get this:

```
// set up the solver to use and the solution
val solver = DoubleBruteForceMinimizer(false)
val soln = solver.solve(C2OptimProblemImpl(Polynomial(1.0, 0.0, -4.0))) // f(x) = x^2 - 4
// for brute force search, we need to explicitly enumerate the values in the domain
val domain = mutableListOf<Vector>(
    DenseVector(-2.0),
    DenseVector(-1.0),
    DenseVector(0.0), // the minimizer
    DenseVector(1.0),
    DenseVector(2.0)
)
soln.setDomain(domain)
println(String.format("f(%s) = %f", soln.minimizer(), soln.min()))
```

The output is as follows:

```
f([0.000000] ) = -4.000000
```

For a multivariate function $f(x, y) = x^2 + y^2$, you get this:

```
val bf = DoubleBruteForceMinimizer(true)
val soln = bf.solve(
        C2OptimProblemImpl(
            object : AbstractBivariateRealFunction() {

            override fun evaluate(x: Double, y: Double): Double {
                val fx: Double  = x * x + y * y
                return fx
            }
        }))

val domain = mutableListOf<Vector>(
    DenseVector(-2.0, -2.0),
    DenseVector(-1.0, -1.0),
    DenseVector(0.0, 0.0), // the minimizer
    DenseVector(1.0, 1.0),
    DenseVector(2.0, 2.0)
)
soln.setDomain(domain)
println(String.format("f(%s) = %f", soln.minimizer(), soln.min()))
```

The output is as follows:

```
f([0.000000, 0.000000] ) = 0.000000
```

9.3. Bracketing Methods

A univariate bracketing method solves a univariate unconstrained optimization problem. A fast univariate method is crucial in optimization. A multivariate constrained optimization problem can often be cast into an equivalent multivariate unconstrained optimization problem. Solving a multivariate unconstrained optimization problem often involves solving multiple univariate unconstrained optimization problems, such as line searches. Many multivariate unconstrained optimization algorithms discussed in the later sections use a line search.

The simplest univariate algorithm is the bracket search method. Suppose you have a three-point bracketing interval containing a minimum, $x_L < x_a < x_U$, and suppose $[x_L, x_U]$ contains a minimum. You compute a fourth point, x_b, according to an interval dividing schedule, to form two overlapping subintervals, $[x_L, x_a]$ and $[x_b, x_U]$. The smaller subinterval that contains the new minimum is chosen. Repeat the procedure to divide the interval until convergence, that is, when the chosen subinterval is sufficiently small. This algorithm is most effective with a unimodal function in interval $[x_L, x_U]$. A unimodal function is a function that increases (or decreases) from x_L until a certain point, and then it decreases (or increases) toward x_U. It contains exactly one minimum (or maximum) in the interval.

Consider a unimodal function that has a minimum in $[x_L, x_U]$. This interval is called the range of uncertainty. With four points, $f(x_L)$, $f(x_a)$, $f(x_b)$, and $f(x_U)$, you can determine where the one minimum is. A dichotomous search says that if $f(x_a) < f(x_b)$, x^* is located in $x_L < x^* < x_b$. There are two possibilities: either $x_L < x^* < x_b$ (as in the blue curve) or $x_a < x^* < x_b$ (as in the orange curve). Combining them gives $x_L < x^* < x_b$. See Figure 9-1.

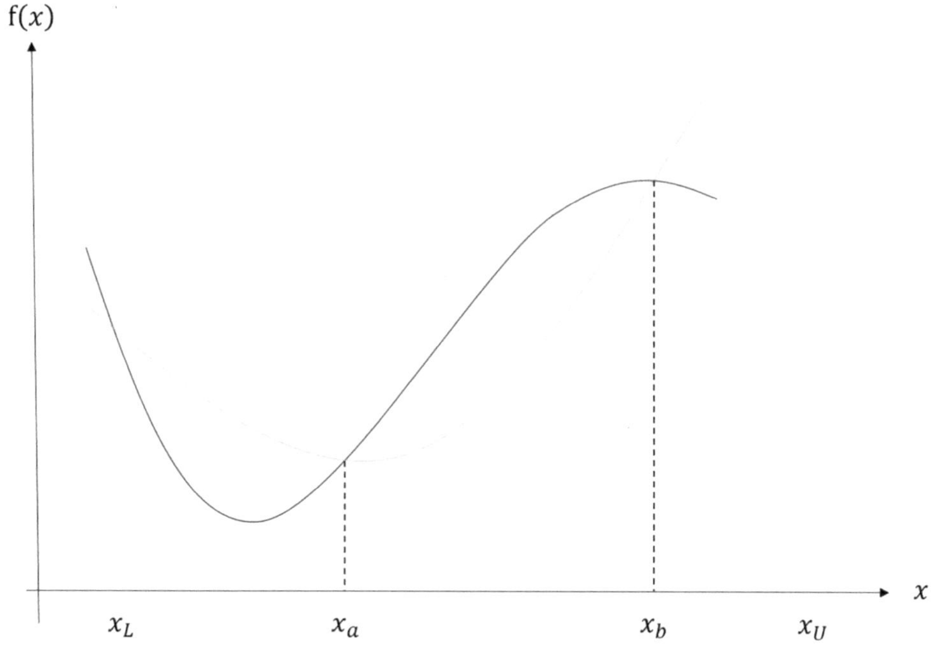

Figure 9-1. *x^* in the left interval*

Similarly, if $f(x_a) > f(x_b)$, you get $x_a < x^* < x_U$, as shown in Figure 9-2.

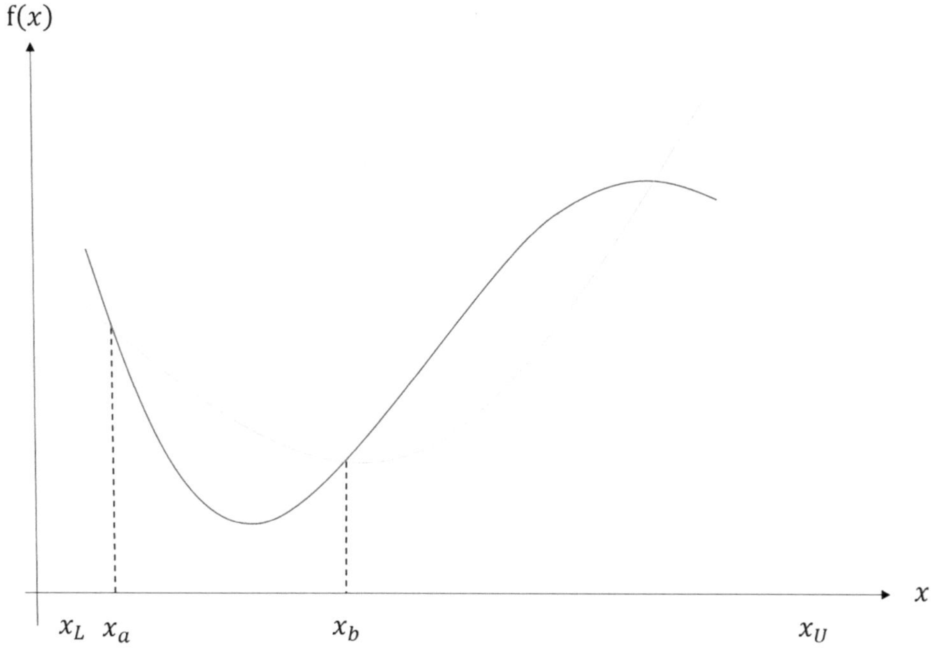

Figure 9-2. *x^* in the right interval*

If $f(x_a) = f(x_b)$, you get $x_a < x^* < x_b$. See Figure 9-3.

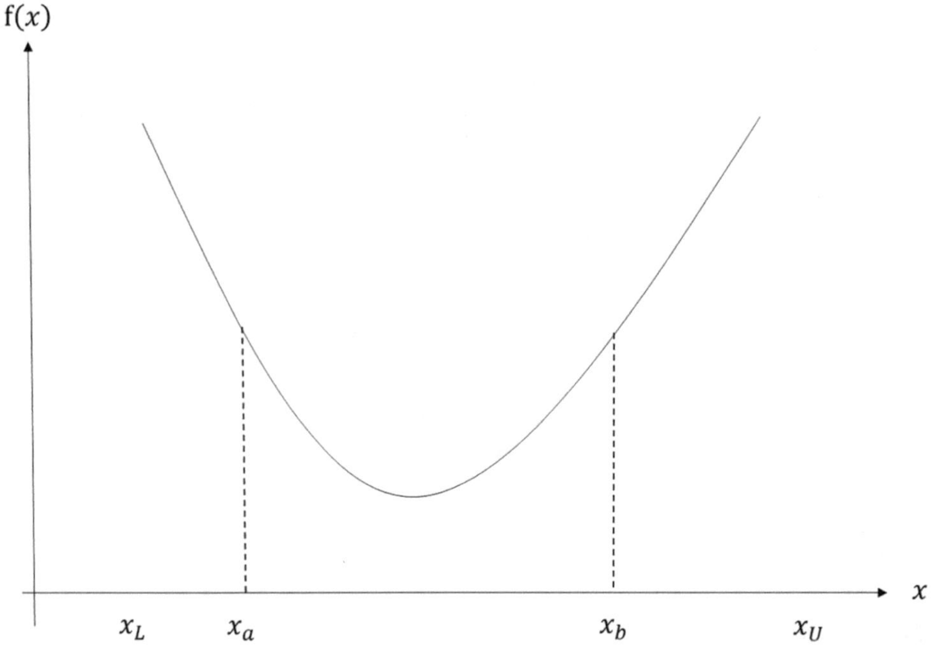

Figure 9-3. $x_a < x^* < x_b$

A naïve dichotomous search can simply divide the interval roughly into two each time. The size of the subintervals decreases exponentially (halved each iteration). After about seven iterations, the interval size is less than 1 percent of the initial interval. There are a total of 14 evaluations of the function, as each iteration requires two computations, $f(x_a)$ and $f(x_b)$. NM Dev implements two more sophisticated interval-dividing schedules.

9.3.1. Fibonacci Search Method

Let's start by analyzing interval sizes. For the sake of simplicity, assume that the left and right subintervals are the same length. See Figure 9-4.

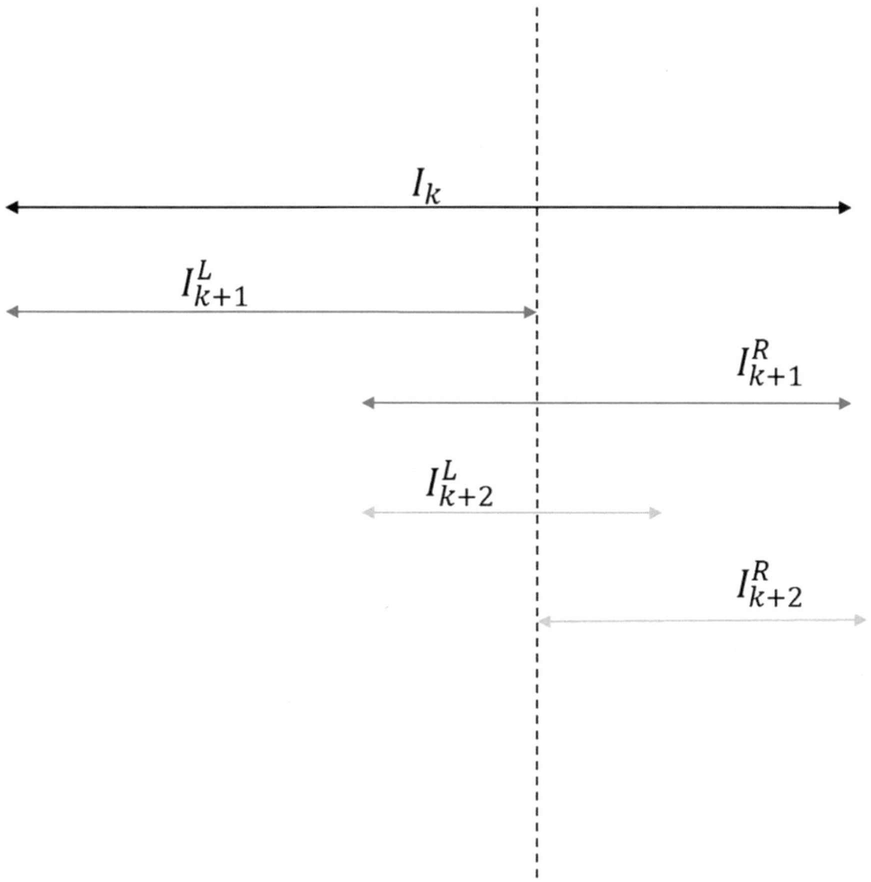

Figure 9-4. *Subintervals in iterations k, k+1, k+2*

You get the following:

$$I_{k+1} = I_{k+1}^L = I_{k+1}^R$$

$$I_k = I_{k+1}^L + I_{k+2}^R = I_{k+1} + I_{k+2}$$

For n iterations, you get the following recurrence relationship:

$$I_1 = I_2 + I_3$$

$$I_2 = I_3 + I_4$$

$$\ldots$$

$$I_n = I_{n+1} + I_{n+2}$$

There are n equations, and you assume I_1 is known. There are $n + 2$ variables. You can impose one additional condition to generate a sequence of intervals.

In particular, the Fibonacci sequence is generated if you assume that the interval in the last iteration vanishes. That is, $I_{n+2} = 0$.

Solving the previous system of equations gives the following:

$$I_{n+1} = F_0 I_n$$

$$I_n = F_0 I_n$$

$$I_k = F_{n-k+1} I_n$$

$$I_1 = F_n I_n$$

where

$$F_k = F_{k-1} + F_{k-2}, k \geq 2$$

F_k is the definition of the Fibonacci sequence, {1, 1, 2, 3, 5, 8, 13, ...}.

For example, if $n = 11$, $F_n = 144$. $I_n = I_1/F_n$. I_n is reduced to 0.69 percent of I_1. Moreover, by choosing either the left or right subinterval, you already have two endpoints and one point in between, $\{x_L, x_a, x_b\}$ or $\{x_a, x_b, x_U\}$. You need only one more point and hence one computation of the function. For 11 iterations, you need 14 computations in total, compared to 22 in the naïve dichotomous search.

One major drawback of using the Fibonacci sequence is that it requires foreknowledge of n. It is okay if you want x^* to be within a prespecified precision. You use $I_n = I_1/F_n$ to determine n. However, if you make $f(x^*)$ within a certain precision, you do not know what n is to start with.

9.3.2. Golden-Section Search

In contrast to the Fibonacci section, the golden-section search carries out iterations until the function accuracy is achieved. The recursive relation is the same as the Fibonacci method: $I_k = I_{k-1} + I_{k-2}$. The additional condition is to keep the ratio of two adjacent intervals constant.

$$\frac{I_k}{I_{k+1}} = K, \forall k$$

Using these two equations, you can solve for K, as shown here:

$$K^2 = K + 1$$

$$K = \frac{1+\sqrt{5}}{2} \approx 1.618034$$

This number is known as the golden ratio. The interval sequence is as follows:

$$\left\{ I_1, \frac{I_1}{K}, \frac{I_1}{K^2}, \ldots\ldots, \frac{I_1}{K^{n-1}} \right\}$$

Here's an example: {100, 61.8, 38.2, 23.6, 14.6, 9, ...}. This can go on without a predetermined n.

Let's compare the efficiencies of the golden-section search and the Fibonacci search. The relationship between F_n and K is $F_n \approx \frac{K^{n+1}}{\sqrt{5}}$. The region of uncertainty in the Fibonacci search is as follows:

$$\Lambda_F = I_n = \frac{I_1}{F_n} \approx \frac{\sqrt{5}}{K^{n+1}} I_1$$

For the golden-section search, it is as follows:

$$\Lambda_G = I_n = \frac{I_1}{K^{n+1}}$$

Hence, you get the following:

$$\frac{\Lambda_G}{\Lambda_F} = \frac{K^2}{\sqrt{5}} = 1.17$$

Therefore, the golden-section search needs more iterations to achieve the same accuracy as the Fibonacci search. The Fibonacci search is more efficient, but the golden-section search does not require knowing n a priori.

9.3.3. Brent's Search

The golden-section search has a linear convergence rate. The parabolic search we are about to discuss has a convergence rate of 1.325; hence, it's more efficient. In each bracketing interval, you again choose three points: $x_L < x_m < x_U$. You approximate the function in this interval by a quadratic polynomial (aka, a parabola).

$$p(x) = a_0 + a_1 x + a_2 x^2$$

With the three points, you can determine the polynomial coefficients by solving a system of three linear equations. The minimum of the $p(x)$, $\bar{x}$, can be easily determined by solving its first derivative equal to zero:

$$\bar{x} = -\frac{a_1}{2a_2}$$

By virtue of Taylor's expansion, $\bar{x}$ will be sufficiently close to x^*; in fact, it will be exact if the function is quadratic. By examining $\bar{x}$, you can choose a new interval by rejecting either x_L or x_U and keeping $\bar{x}$. You repeat the process until all three points are sufficiently close (to x^*). See Figure 9-5.

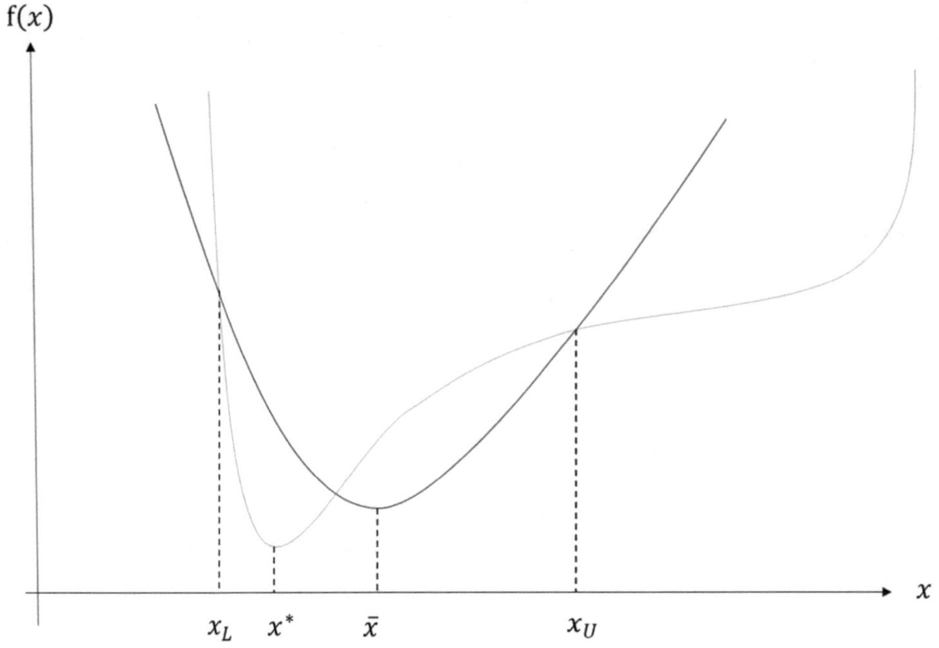

Figure 9-5. *Parabolic approximation of a curve segment*

While the parabolic search has a super-linear convergence rate, it does not always converge (even to a local minima). For example, if the three points are collinear, the resulting parabola is degenerate and thus does not provide a new candidate point. This method is therefore seldom used alone.

Brent's method combines both the parabolic search and the golden-section search. Brent's method uses the parabolic search whenever applicable (e.g., no two points are the same). When the conditions fail, it switches to use the golden-section search. In other words, Brent's method combines the best of both worlds: super-linear convergence and the guarantee of finding the minimum. Therefore, in practice, you should almost always use Brent's search as the default for univariate optimization. See Figure 9-6.

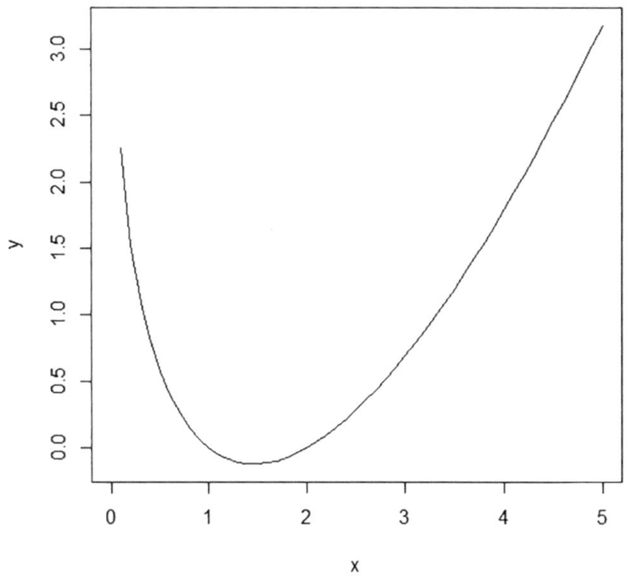

Figure 9-6. *Log-gamma function*

The following NM Dev code solves for the log-gamma function using the Fibonacci search, the golden-section search, and Brent's search:

```
val logGamma = LogGamma() // the log-gamma function

// Using the Fibonacc method
val solver1 = FibonaccMinimizer(1e-8, 15)
val soln1: UnivariateMinimizer.Solution = solver1.solve(logGamma)
val x_min_1: Double = soln1.search(0.0, 5.0)
println(String.format("f(%f) = %f", x_min_1, logGamma.evaluate(x_min_1)))
```

The output is as follows:

```
f(1.463682) = -0.121484

// Using the Golden section method
val solver2 = GoldenMinimizer(1e-8, 15)
val soln2: UnivariateMinimizer.Solution = solver2.solve(logGamma)
val x_min_2: Double = soln2.search(0.0, 5.0)
println(String.format("f(%f) = %f", x_min_2, logGamma.evaluate(x_min_2)))
```

The output is as follows:

```
f(1.460813) = -0.121486
```

```
// Using Brent's method
val solver3 = BrentMinimizer(1e-8, 10) // fewer itertaions than that of Fibonacci or
                                          golden search
val soln3: UnivariateMinimizer.Solution = solver3.solve(logGamma)
val x_min_3: Double = soln3.search(0.0, 5.0)
println(String.format("f(%f) = %f", x_min_3, logGamma.evaluate(x_min_3)))
```

The output is as follows:

```
f(1.461632) = -0.121486
```

Their signatures are as follows:

```
/**
 * Construct a univariate minimizer using the Fibonacci method.
 *
 * @param epsilon       a precision parameter: when a number |x| &le;
 *                      &epsilon;, it is considered 0
 * @param maxIterations the maximum number of iterations
 */
public FibonaccMinimizer(double epsilon, int maxIterations)
/**
 * Construct a univariate minimizer using the Golden method.
 *
 * @param epsilon       a precision parameter: when a number |x| &le;
 *                      &epsilon;, it is considered 0
 * @param maxIterations the maximum number of iterations
 */
public GoldenMinimizer(double epsilon, int maxIterations)
/**
 * Construct a univariate minimizer using Brent's algorithm.
 *
 * @param epsilon       a precision parameter: when a number |x| &le;
 *                      &epsilon;, it is considered 0
 * @param maxIterations the maximum number of iterations
 */
public BrentMinimizer(double epsilon, int maxIterations)
/**
 * This is the solution to a univariate minimization problem.
 */
public static interface Solution extends MinimizationSolution<Double> {
    /**
     * Search for a minimum within the interval <i>[lower, upper]</i>.
     *
     * @param lower   the lower bound for the bracketing interval which
     *                contains a minimum
     * @param initial an initial guess
     * @param upper   the upper bound for the bracketing interval which
     *                contains a minimum
     * @return an approximate minimizer
     */
```

```
    public double search(double lower, double initial, double upper);
    /**
     * Search for a minimum within the interval <i>[lower, upper]</i>.
     *
     * @param lower the lower bound for the bracketing interval which
     *              contains a minimum
     * @param upper the upper bound for the bracketing interval which
     *              contains a minimum
     * @return an approximate minimizer
     */
    public double search(double lower, double upper);
}
```

You call the search method to find a minimizer for univariate function minimization.

9.4. Steepest Descent Methods

The general idea of searching for minimization usually starts with an initial point and then modifies some parameters to find the next point that (hopefully) gives a smaller function value. If you have no information, a blind search would not be efficient. Two pieces of information are useful: the gradient $\boldsymbol{g}$ and the Hessian $\boldsymbol{H}$.

Steepest-descent algorithms are a family of algorithms that use the gradient and Hessian information to search in a direction that gives that biggest reduction in function value. We first discuss the first-order methods in which only gradient information is used. Consider the following optimization problem:

$$\min F = f\left(\boldsymbol{x}\right) for \;\; \boldsymbol{x} \in E^n$$

Taylor expansion gives the following:

$$F + \Delta F = f(\boldsymbol{x} + \boldsymbol{\delta}) \approx f(\boldsymbol{x}) + \boldsymbol{g}^T\boldsymbol{\delta} + O(\boldsymbol{\delta}^T\boldsymbol{\delta}) \text{ as } \|\boldsymbol{\delta}\| \to 0,\ \Delta F \approx \boldsymbol{g}^T\boldsymbol{\delta}$$

$$\Delta F \approx \sum_{i=1}^{n} \boldsymbol{g}_i \delta_i = \| \boldsymbol{g} \| \, \| \delta \| \, cos\theta$$

For any vector $\boldsymbol{\delta}$, ΔF is the maximum when $\boldsymbol{\theta} = 0$, which means that $\boldsymbol{\delta}$ is in the same direction as $\boldsymbol{g}$. ΔF is the minimum when $\boldsymbol{\theta} = \pi$, which means that $\boldsymbol{\delta}$ is in the opposite direction of $\boldsymbol{g}$ or in the direction of $-\boldsymbol{g}$. They are said to be the steepest-ascent and steepest-descent directions, respectively, and they are shown in Figure 9-7.

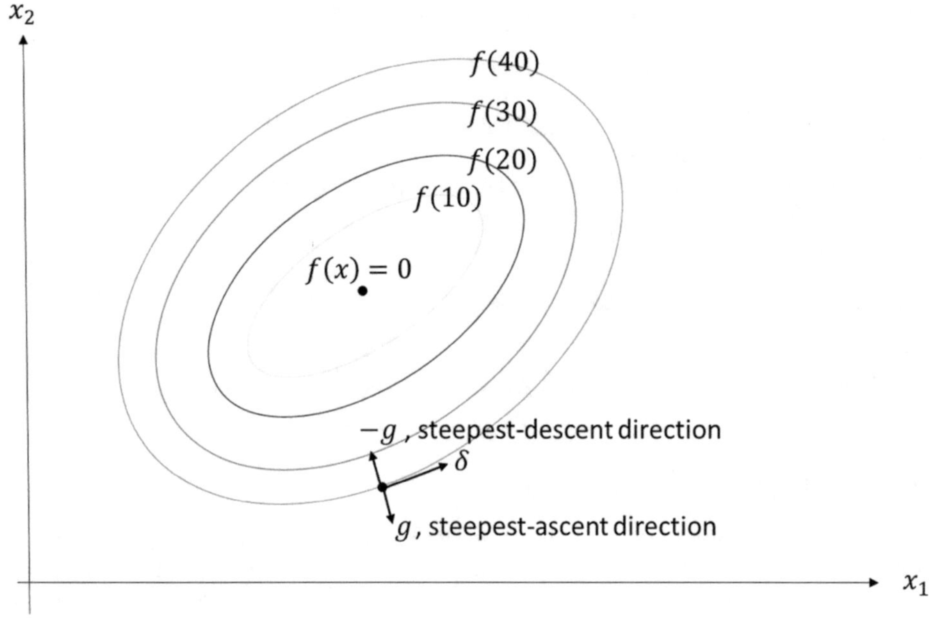

Figure 9-7. *Steepest-descent and steepest-ascent directions*

The general framework of a steepest-descent algorithm is as follows:

1. Specify an initial point $\boldsymbol{x}_0$ and the tolerance ε.
2. Calculate the gradient $\boldsymbol{g}_k$ and set the Newton direction vector $\boldsymbol{d}_k = -\boldsymbol{g}_k$.
3. Minimize $f(\boldsymbol{x}_k + \alpha \boldsymbol{d}_k)$ with respect to α to compute the increment α_k.
4. Set the next point $\boldsymbol{x}_{k+1} = \boldsymbol{x}_k + \alpha_k \boldsymbol{d}_k$ and compute the next function value $f_{k+1} = f(\boldsymbol{x}_{k+1})$.
5. If $\|\alpha_k \boldsymbol{d}_k\| < \varepsilon$, then
   a. Done. $\boldsymbol{x}^* = \boldsymbol{x}_{k+1}$ and $f(\boldsymbol{x}^*) = f_{k+1}$.
   b. Otherwise, repeat Step 2.

In Step 3, α_k can be computed by using a line search for univariate optimization algorithm. In this implementation, we use Fletcher's inexact line search method. A lot of optimization algorithms are shown to be quite tolerant of line search imprecision. Alternatively, α_k can be computed analytically.

The following NM Dev code minimizes this function using the first-order steepest-descent method:

$$f(x_1,x_2,x_3,x_4) = (x_1 - 4x_2)^4 + 12(x_3 - x_4)^4 + 3(x_2 - 10x_3)^2 + 55(x_1 - 2x_4)^2$$

```
// the objective function
// the global minimizer is at x = [0,0,0,0]
val f = object : RealScalarFunction {
```

```
    override fun evaluate(x: Vector): Double {
        val x1: Double = x.get(1)
        val x2: Double = x.get(2)
        val x3: Double = x.get(3)
        val x4: Double = x.get(4)

        var result: Double = (x1 - 4 * x2).pow(4)
        result += 12 * (x3 - x4).pow(4)
        result += 3 * (x2 - 10 * x3).pow(2)
        result += 55 * (x1 - 2 * x4).pow(2)

        return result
    }

    override fun dimensionOfDomain(): Int {
        return 4
    }

    override fun dimensionOfRange(): Int {
        return 1
    }
}

// the gradient function
val g = object : RealVectorFunction {

    override fun evaluate(x: Vector): Vector {
        val x1 = x.get(1)
        val x2 = x.get(2)
        val x3 = x.get(3)
        val x4 = x.get(4)

        var result = ArrayList<Double>(4)
        result.add(0, 4 * (x1 - 4 * x2).pow(3) + 110 * (x1 - 2 * x4))
        result.add(1, -16 * (x1 - 4 * x2).pow(3) + 6 * (x2 - 10 * x3))
        result.add(2, 48 * (x3 - x4).pow(3) - 60 * (x2 - 10 * x3))
        result.add(3, -48 * (x3 - x4).pow(3) - 220 * (x1 - 2 * x4))
        return DenseVector(result)
    }

    override fun dimensionOfDomain(): Int {
        return 4
    }

    override fun dimensionOfRange(): Int {
        return 4
    }
}
```

```
val problem = C2OptimProblemImpl(f, g) // only gradient information
val firstOrderMinimizer: SteepestDescentMinimizer
        = FirstOrderMinimizer(
                FirstOrderMinimizer.Method.IN_EXACT_LINE_SEARCH,
// FirstOrderMinimizer.Method.ANALYTIC
                1e-8,
                40000
        )
val soln: IterativeSolution<Vector> = firstOrderMinimizer.solve(problem)

val xmin: Vector = soln.search(DenseVector(1.0, -1.0, -1.0, 1.0))
val f_xmin: Double = f.evaluate(xmin)
println(String.format("f(%s) = %f", xmin.toString(), f_xmin))
```

The output is as follows:

```
f([0.046380, 0.016330, 0.001634, 0.023189] ) = 0.000003
```

It takes about 40,000 iterations, which is way too slow.

```
The signature of FirstOrderMinimizer is as follows.
/**
 * Construct a multivariate minimizer using the First-Order method.
 *
 * @param method        the method to do line search
 * @param epsilon       a precision parameter: when a number |x| &le;
 *                      &epsilon;, it is considered 0
 * @param maxIterations the maximum number of iterations
 */
public FirstOrderMinimizer(Method method, double epsilon, int maxIterations)
```

`Method` specifies whether you use line search or an analytical expression to compute α_k.

9.4.1. Newton-Raphson Method

The second-order methods use (a nonsingular) Hessian in additional to a gradient to determine the direction vector $\boldsymbol{d}_k$ and the increment α_k in the steepest-descent framework to speed up the convergence. The Newton-Raphson method expands the Taylor series to the second order. Letting $\boldsymbol{\delta}$ be the change in $\boldsymbol{x}$, you get the following:

$$f(\boldsymbol{x}+\delta) \approx f(\boldsymbol{x}) + \sum_{j=1}^{n} \frac{\partial f}{\partial x_i}\delta_i + \frac{1}{2}\sum_{i=1}^{n}\sum_{j=1}^{n} \frac{\partial^2 f}{\partial x_i \partial x_j}\delta_i\delta_j$$

Differentiating $f(\boldsymbol{x} + \delta)$ with respect to δ_k to minimize $f(\boldsymbol{x} + \delta)$, you get the following:

$$\frac{\partial f}{\partial x_k} + \sum_{i=1}^{n} \frac{\partial^2 f}{\partial x_i \partial x_j}\delta_i = 0 \quad for \;\; k = 1, 2, \ldots, n$$

Rewrite it in matrix form as follows:

$$\boldsymbol{g} = -\boldsymbol{H}\delta$$

The optimal change in $\boldsymbol{x}$ is as follows:

$$\delta = -\boldsymbol{H}^{-1}\boldsymbol{g}$$

A line search is used to compute the maximum reduction in $f(\boldsymbol{x})$ along the direction. The next point $\boldsymbol{x}_{k+1}$ is as follows:

$$\boldsymbol{x}_{k+1} = \boldsymbol{x}_k + \delta_k = \boldsymbol{x}_k + \alpha_k \boldsymbol{d}_k$$

where the following is true:

$$\boldsymbol{d}_k = -\boldsymbol{H}_k^{-1}\boldsymbol{g}_k$$

α_k is the α that minimizes $f(x_k + \alpha \boldsymbol{d}_k)$.

The Newton-Raphson method, compared to the first-order method, uses Hessian information to speed up convergence, especially when it is close to the solution. The following NM Dev code minimizes the same function using the Newton-Raphson method:

```
// the objective function
// the global minimizer is at x = [0,0,0,0]
val f = object : RealScalarFunction {

    override fun evaluate(x: Vector): Double {
        val x1: Double = x.get(1)
        val x2: Double = x.get(2)
        val x3: Double = x.get(3)
        val x4: Double = x.get(4)

        var result: Double = (x1 - 4 * x2).pow(4)
        result += 12 * (x3 - x4).pow(4)
        result += 3 * (x2 - 10 * x3).pow(2)
        result += 55 * (x1 - 2 * x4).pow(2)

        return result
    }

    override fun dimensionOfDomain(): Int {
        return 4
    }

    override fun dimensionOfRange(): Int {
        return 1
    }
}
```

```
// the gradient function
val g =  object : RealVectorFunction {

    override fun evaluate(x: Vector): Vector {
        val x1: Double = x.get(1)
        val x2: Double = x.get(2)
        val x3: Double = x.get(3)
        val x4: Double = x.get(4)

        var result = ArrayList<Double>(4)
        result.add(0, 4 * (x1 - 4 * x2).pow(3) + 110 * (x1 - 2 * x4))
        result.add(1, -16 * (x1 - 4 * x2).pow(3) + 6 * (x2 - 10 * x3))
        result.add(2, 48 * (x3 - x4).pow(3) - 60 * (x2 - 10 * x3))
        result.add(3, -48 * (x3 - x4).pow(3) - 220 * (x1 - 2 * x4))
        return DenseVector(result)
    }

    override fun dimensionOfDomain(): Int {
        return 4
    }

    override fun dimensionOfRange(): Int {
        return 4
    }
}

val problem = C2OptimProblemImpl(f, g) // use numerical Hessian
val newtonRaphsonMinimizer: SteepestDescentMinimizer
        = NewtonRaphsonMinimizer(
                1e-8,
                20
        )
val soln: IterativeSolution<Vector> = newtonRaphsonMinimizer.solve(problem)

val xmin: Vector = soln.search(DenseVector(1.0, -1.0, -1.0, 1.0))
val f_xmin: Double = f.evaluate(xmin)
println(String.format("f(%s) = %f", xmin.toString(), f_xmin))
```

The output is as follows:

```
f([0.000134, -0.000009, -0.000001, 0.000067] ) = 0.000000
```

It is worth pointing out that the Newton-Raphson method converges much faster than the first-order method. It uses only 20 iterations to attain much better accuracy versus 40,000 iterations.

The signature of NewtonRaphsonMinimizer is as follows:

```
/**
 * Construct a multivariate minimizer using the Newton-Raphson method.
 *
 * @param epsilon       a precision parameter: when a number |x| &le;
```

```
 *                         &epsilon;, it is considered 0
 * @param maxIterations the maximum number of iterations
 */
public NewtonRaphsonMinimizer(double epsilon, int maxIterations)
```

9.4.2. Gauss-Newton Method

The Gauss-Newton method minimizes an objective function in this form:

$$\boldsymbol{f} = \left[f_1(x) f_2(x) \ldots\ldots f_m(x)\right]^T$$

The solution is a point $\boldsymbol{x}$ such that all $f_p(\boldsymbol{x})$ are reduced to zero simultaneously.

You can construct a real-valued function F such that if F is minimized, and so are functions $f_p(\boldsymbol{x})$ in the least-square sense.

$$F = \sum_{p=1}^{m} f_p(\boldsymbol{x})^2 = \boldsymbol{f}\boldsymbol{f}^T$$

The Jacobian matrix of gradients is as follows:

$$\mathbf{J} = \begin{bmatrix} \frac{\partial f_1}{\partial x_1} & \cdots & \frac{\partial f_m}{\partial x_1} \\ \vdots & \ddots & \vdots \\ \frac{\partial f_1}{\partial x_n} & \cdots & \frac{\partial f_m}{\partial x_n} \end{bmatrix}$$

Differentiating F with respect to x_i, you get the following:

$$\frac{\partial F}{\partial x_i} = \sum_{p=1}^{m} 2 f_p(\boldsymbol{x}) \frac{\partial f_p}{\partial x_i}$$

Or, in matrix form, you get the gradient vector as follows:

$$\mathbf{g}_F = 2\mathbf{J}^T \boldsymbol{f}$$

Differentiating again, you get the following:

$$\frac{\partial^2 F}{\partial x_i \partial x_j} \approx 2 \sum_{p=1}^{m} \frac{\partial f_p}{\partial x_i} \frac{\partial f_p}{\partial x_j}$$

The Hessian $\mathbf{H}_F$ is as follows. It needs to be nonsingular and positive definite:

$$\mathbf{H}_F \approx 2\mathbf{J}^T \mathbf{J}$$

The next point is given by the recursive relation:

$$\boldsymbol{x}_{k+1} = \boldsymbol{x}_k - \alpha_k \left(2\mathbf{J}^T\mathbf{J}\right)^{-1} \left(2\mathbf{J}^T\mathbf{f}\right)$$

The following code solves the same minimization problem using the Gauss-Newton method:

```
// the objective function
//  the global minimizer is at x = [0,0,0,0]
val f = object : RealVectorFunction {

    override fun evaluate(x: Vector): Vector {
        val x1: Double = x.get(1)
        val x2: Double = x.get(2)
        val x3: Double = x.get(3)
        val x4: Double = x.get(4)

        var fx = ArrayList<Double>(4)
        fx.add(0, (x1 - 4 * x2).pow(2))
        fx.add(1, sqrt(12.0) * (x3 - x4).pow(2))
        fx.add(2, sqrt(3.0) * (x2 - 10 * x3))
        fx.add(3, sqrt(55.0) * (x1 - 2 * x4))

        return DenseVector(fx)
    }

    override fun dimensionOfDomain(): Int {
        return 4
    }

    override fun dimensionOfRange(): Int {
        return 4
    }
}

// the Jacobian
val J = object : RntoMatrix {

    override fun evaluate(x: Vector): Matrix {
        val x1: Double = x.get(1)
        val x2: Double = x.get(2)
        val x3: Double = x.get(3)
        val x4: Double = x.get(4)

        var Jx: Matrix = DenseMatrix(4, 4)

        var value: Double = 2 * (x1 - 4 * x2)
        Jx.set(1, 1, value)

        value = -8 * (x1 - 4 * x2)
        Jx.set(1, 2, value)

        value = 2 * sqrt(12.0) * (x3 - x4)
        Jx.set(2, 3, value)
        Jx.set(2, 4, -value)
```

```
        Jx.set(3, 2, sqrt(3.0))
        Jx.set(3, 3, -10 * sqrt(3.0))

        Jx.set(4, 1, sqrt(55.0))
        Jx.set(4, 4, -2 * sqrt(55.0))

        return Jx
    }

    override fun dimensionOfDomain(): Int {
        return 4
    }

    override fun dimensionOfRange(): Int {
        return 1
    }
}

val optim1 = GaussNewtonMinimizer(1e-8, 10)

val soln: IterativeSolution<Vector> = optim1.solve(f, J)//analytical gradient

val xmin: Vector = soln.search(DenseVector(1.0, -1.0, -1.0, 1.0))
println(String.format("f(%s) = %s", xmin.toString(), f.evaluate(xmin).toString()))
```

The output is as follows:

```
f([0.000007, -0.000000, -0.000000, 0.000003] ) = [0.000000, 0.000000, -0.000000,
-0.000000]
```

The Gauss-Newton method is more efficient than the Newton-Raphson method. It takes about ten iterations for the previous problem versus 20.

The signature for GaussNewtonMinimizer is as follows:

```
/**
 * Construct a multivariate minimizer using the Gauss-Newton method.
 *
 * @param epsilon       a precision parameter: when a number |x| &le;
 *                      &epsilon;, it is considered 0
 * @param maxIterations the maximum number of iterations
 */
public GaussNewtonMinimizer(double epsilon, int maxIterations)
```

9.5. Conjugate Direction Methods

The successive search directions in the steepest-descent methods may or may not relate to each other. Also, they are determined entirely by the local properties of the objective function, namely, gradient and Hessian (Hestenes & Stiefel, 1952). On the other hand, there is a strict mathematical relationship between successive search directions in the conjugate direction methods. Conjugate methods were developed for solving quadratic optimization problems with the following objective function:

$$\min \boldsymbol{x}^{\mathrm{T}}\mathbf{b} + \frac{1}{2}\mathbf{x}^{T}\boldsymbol{H}\mathbf{X}$$

where $\boldsymbol{H}$ is an $n * n$ symmetric positive definite matrix for a n-variable function.

For a quadratic problem, the search will converge to a minimum in a finite number of iterations. The conjugate methods have since been extended to solve more general optimization problems.

9.5.1. Conjugate Directions

For a symmetric matrix $\boldsymbol{H}$, a finite set of vectors $\{\boldsymbol{d}_0, \boldsymbol{d}_1, \cdots, \boldsymbol{d}_k\}$ are said to be conjugate with respect to $\boldsymbol{H}$ or $\boldsymbol{H}$-orthogonal if $\boldsymbol{d}_i^T\boldsymbol{Q}\boldsymbol{d}_j = 0$ for all $i \neq j$. If $\boldsymbol{H}$ is positive definite, the vectors are linearly independent. If $\boldsymbol{H} = \boldsymbol{I}$, the vectors are orthogonal.

For the quadratic minimization problem shown previously and when $\boldsymbol{H}$ is positive definite, simple calculus shows that the solution is unique and can be computed analytically by solving a system of linear equations:

$$\boldsymbol{H}\mathbf{x}^* = \mathbf{b}$$

Because the set of conjugate vectors are linearly independent and thus span the n-dimensional space E^n, $\boldsymbol{x}^*$ can be written as a linear combination of those vectors:

$$\boldsymbol{x}^* = \alpha_0\boldsymbol{d}_0 + \ldots + \alpha_{n-1}\boldsymbol{d}_{n-1}$$

Multiplying by $\boldsymbol{H}$ on both sides and taking the scalar product with $\boldsymbol{d}_i$ gives the following:

$$\alpha_i = -\frac{\boldsymbol{d}_i^T\boldsymbol{H}\boldsymbol{x}^*}{\boldsymbol{d}_i^T\boldsymbol{H}\boldsymbol{d}_i} = -\frac{\boldsymbol{d}_i^T\boldsymbol{b}}{\boldsymbol{d}_i^T\boldsymbol{H}\boldsymbol{d}_i}$$

Or equivalently:

$$\boldsymbol{x}^* = \sum_{i=0}^{n-1}\frac{\boldsymbol{d}_i^T\boldsymbol{b}}{\boldsymbol{d}_i^T\boldsymbol{H}\boldsymbol{d}_i}\boldsymbol{d}_i$$

This expansion of $\boldsymbol{x}^*$ can be considered as a sum or an n-step iterative process of adding $\alpha_i\boldsymbol{d}_i$.

Conjugate Direction Theorem

Let $\{\boldsymbol{d}_i\}_{i=0}^{n-1}$ be a set of nonzero $\boldsymbol{H}$-orthogonal vectors. For any $\boldsymbol{x}_0 \in E^n$, the sequence $\{\boldsymbol{x}_i\}$ generated according to the following:

$$\boldsymbol{x}_{k+1} = \boldsymbol{x}_k + \alpha_k\boldsymbol{d}_k, k \geq 0$$

with the following:

$$\alpha_k = -\frac{\boldsymbol{g}_k^T \boldsymbol{d}_k}{\boldsymbol{d}_k^T \boldsymbol{H} \boldsymbol{d}_k}$$

and the following:

$$\boldsymbol{g}_k = \boldsymbol{b} + \boldsymbol{H}\boldsymbol{x}_k$$

This converges to the unique solution **x*** of **HX** = **b** after n steps, that is, $\mathbf{x}_n = \mathbf{x}^*$.

Using this theorem and a number of ways to generate conjugate vectors, a number of conjugate-direction methods can be devised. You also need to extend the theorem to solve nonquadratic problems. The conjugate-direction methods fit well in the steepest-descent framework. They differ only by how the direction vectors $\boldsymbol{d}_k$ and consequently the magnitude α_k are computed. Here, we use the conjugate directions instead of the steepest descent directions. The idea of iteratively adding an increment $\alpha_k \boldsymbol{d}_k$ to an $\boldsymbol{x}_k$ to generate $\boldsymbol{x}_{k+1}$ is the same.

9.5.2. Conjugate Gradient Method

Hestenes & Stiefel (1952) proposed the conjugate-gradient method. In this method, the new direction is a weighted sum of the last direction and the negative of the gradient.

$$\boldsymbol{d}_0 = -\boldsymbol{g}_0 = -(\boldsymbol{b} + \boldsymbol{H}\boldsymbol{x}_0)$$

$$\boldsymbol{d}_k = -\boldsymbol{g}_k + \beta_k \boldsymbol{d}_{k-1}$$

$$\boldsymbol{g}_k = \boldsymbol{b} + \boldsymbol{H}\boldsymbol{x}_k$$

$$\beta_k = \frac{\boldsymbol{g}_k^T H d_k}{\boldsymbol{d}_k^T H d_k}$$

$$\alpha_k = -\frac{\boldsymbol{g}_k^T d_k}{\boldsymbol{d}_k^T H d_k}$$

The following are the advantages of this method:

- The gradient is finite and is linearly independent of all previous direction vectors, except when the solution is found.
- It is relatively easy to compute a new direction vector.
- There is no line search.
- It converges in n steps for quadratic problems.
- The first direction is the same as in steepest-descent, $\boldsymbol{d}_0 = -\mathbf{g}_0$, and it gives a first good reduction.
- There is no inversion of Hessian.

The following are the disadvantages:

- Hessian must be supplied, stored, and manipulated.
- Convergence is not guaranteed for nonquadratic problems. In fact, if the initial point is far from a solution, the search may wander in some suboptimal area because unreliable directions build up over iterations. As you will see from the code example later, the conjugate-gradient method takes the biggest number of iterations to converge for the Himmelblau function.

9.5.3. Fletcher-Reeves Method

The Fletcher-Reeves method is a variant of the conjugate-gradient method. The main difference is that α_k is computed using a line search by minimizing $f(\boldsymbol{X} + \alpha_k \boldsymbol{d}_k)$ and that $\boldsymbol{d}_k$ is a conjugate direction with respect to $\{\boldsymbol{d}_0, \boldsymbol{d}_1, \cdots, \boldsymbol{d}_k\}$ rather than the steepest-descent or Newton directions. Consequently, this algorithm is similar to the conjugate-gradient method but requires more computations due to the line search, which is a disadvantage. There are, however, two advantages.

- The modification works better for minimization of nonquadratic functions because a larger reduction can be achieved in $f(\boldsymbol{x})$ along $\boldsymbol{d}_k$ at points outside the neighborhood of a solution.
- This algorithm does not need the Hessian.

9.5.4. Powell Method

Powell's algorithm generates a series of conjugate directions using line search.

Let $\boldsymbol{x}_a^*$ and $\boldsymbol{x}_b^*$ be the minimizers obtained if the following convex quadratic function:

$$f(\boldsymbol{x}) = \boldsymbol{x}^T b + \frac{1}{2}\boldsymbol{x}^T \boldsymbol{H}\boldsymbol{x}$$

is minimized with respect to α on lines $\boldsymbol{d}_a$ and $\boldsymbol{d}_b$:

$$\boldsymbol{x} = \boldsymbol{x}_a + \alpha \boldsymbol{d}_a$$

and the following:

$$\boldsymbol{x} = \boldsymbol{x}_b + \alpha \boldsymbol{d}_b$$

If $\boldsymbol{d}_a = \boldsymbol{d}_b$, then vector $\boldsymbol{x}_b^* - \boldsymbol{x}_a^*$ is conjugate with respect to $\boldsymbol{d}_a$. See Figure 9-8.

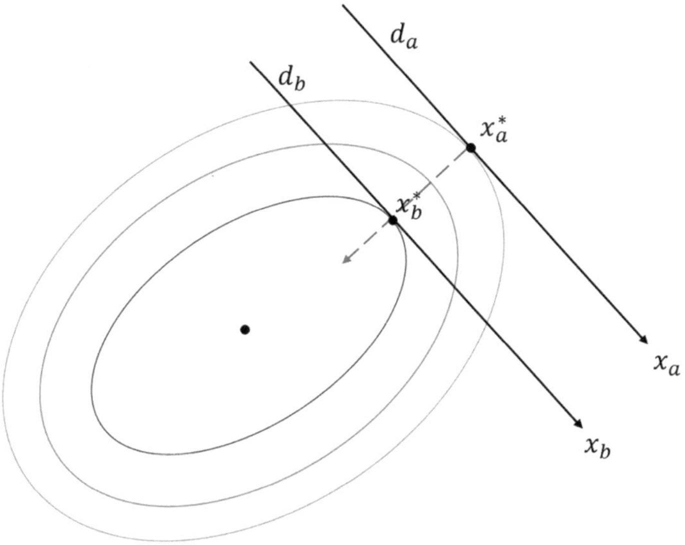

***Figure 9-8.** Generation of a conjugate direction*

In this algorithm, an initial point of $\boldsymbol{x}_{00}$ and the n linearly independent directions $\{\boldsymbol{d}_0, \boldsymbol{d}_1, \cdots, \boldsymbol{d}_n\}$, conveniently taking the coordinate directions, are assumed, and a series of line searches is performed in each iteration. In the first iteration, $f(\boldsymbol{x})$ is minimized sequentially in the directions $\{\boldsymbol{d}_0, \boldsymbol{d}_1, \cdots, \boldsymbol{d}_n\}$ starting from point $\boldsymbol{x}_{00}$ to yield points $\boldsymbol{x}_{01}, \boldsymbol{x}_{02}, \ldots, \boldsymbol{x}_{0n}$. Then a new direction $\boldsymbol{d}_{0(n+1)}$ is generated as follows:

$$\boldsymbol{d}_{0(n+1)} = \boldsymbol{x}_{0n} - \boldsymbol{x}_{00}$$

and $f(\boldsymbol{x})$ is minimized in this direction to yield a new point $\boldsymbol{x}_{0(n+1)}$. Directions are updated by setting the following (see Figure 9-9):

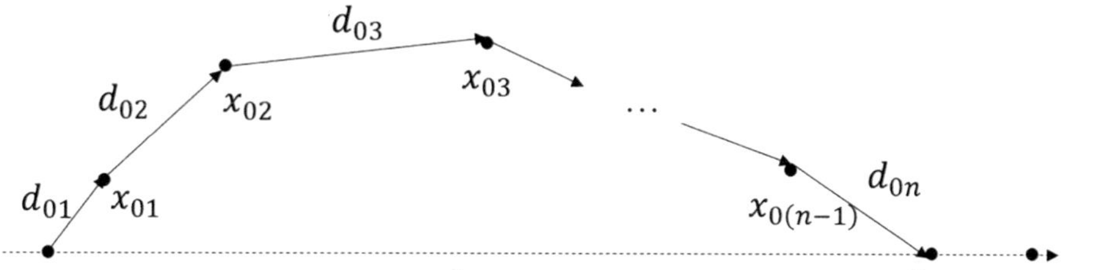

***Figure 9-9.** First iteration in Powell's algorithm*

$$\boldsymbol{d}_{11} = \boldsymbol{d}_{02}$$

$$\boldsymbol{d}_{12} = \boldsymbol{d}_{03}$$

$$\ldots$$

$$\boldsymbol{d}_{1(n-1)} = \boldsymbol{d}_{0n}$$

$$\boldsymbol{d}_{1n} = \boldsymbol{d}_{0(n+1)}$$

The same process repeats in the second iteration that starts with point $\boldsymbol{x}_{10} = \boldsymbol{x}_{0(n+1)}$. $f(\boldsymbol{x})$ is minimized sequentially in directions $\{\boldsymbol{d}_{11}, \boldsymbol{d}_{12}, \cdots, \boldsymbol{d}_{1n}\}$ to yield points $\boldsymbol{x}_{11}, \boldsymbol{x}_{12}, \ldots, \boldsymbol{x}_{1n}$. Then a new direction $\boldsymbol{d}_{1(n+1)}$ is generated as follows (see Figure 9-10):

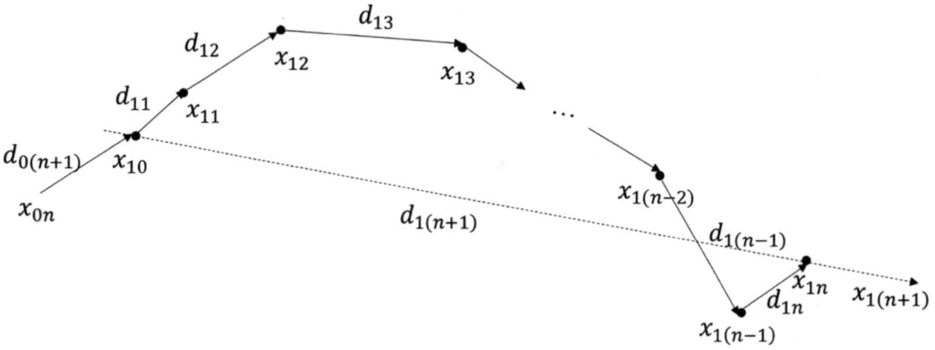

Figure 9-10. *Second iteration in Powell's algorithm*

$$\boldsymbol{d}_{1(n+1)} = \boldsymbol{x}_{1n} - \boldsymbol{x}_{10}$$

Proceeding in the same way, each new iteration will increase one conjugate direction and remove one other and hence be a substitution. Since each iteration requires $(n + 1)$ line searches, Powell's method performs $n(n + 1)$ line searches in n iterations.

The advantage of Powell's method is that it does not need to supply, store, or manipulate Hessian. It does not even need a gradient. However, it may not generate a set of linearly independent directions spanning E^n, and the algorithm may not converge to a solution.

9.5.5. Zangwill Method

Zangwill's algorithm is an improved version of Powell's algorithm. Its modifications generate a set of conjugate directions that are always linearly independent. Therefore, it eliminates the disadvantage in Powell's algorithm.

The modifications are as follows: First, the set of coordinate directions was chosen such that the determinant is 1. Second, the new direction is normalized to unit length. Third, the direction substation must maintain that the determinant of the matrix of the direction vectors is positive and still less than or equal to 1. The last item ensures that the direction vectors are always linearly independent.

The following code minimizes the Himmelblau function (see Figure 9-11):

$$f(x_1, x_2) = (x_1^2 + x_2 - 11)^2 + (x_1 + x_2^2 - 7)^2$$

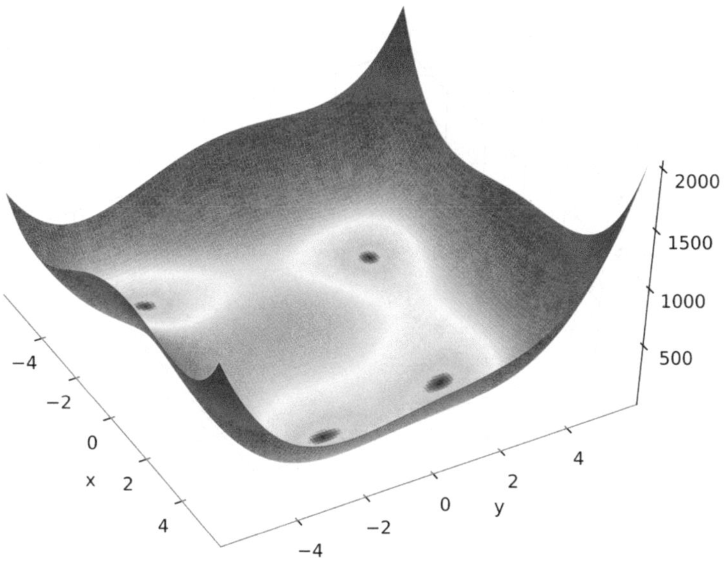

Figure 9-11. *The Himmelblau function with four minimums*

There are four minimums. They are:

$$\begin{cases} f(3.0, 2.0) = 0 \\ f(-2.805118, 3.131312) = 0 \\ f(-3.779310, -3.283186) = 0 \\ f(3.584428, -1.848126) = 0 \end{cases}$$

```
/**
* The Himmelblau function: f(x) = (x1^2 + x2 - 11)^2 + (x1 + x2^2 -
* 7)^2
*/
val f = object : RealScalarFunction {

    override fun evaluate(x: Vector): Double {
        val x1: Double = x.get(1)
        val x2: Double = x.get(2)

        var result: Double = (x1 * x1 + x2 - 11).pow(2)
        result += (x1 + x2 * x2 - 7).pow(2)

        return result
    }
```

```
    override fun dimensionOfDomain(): Int {
        return 2
    }

    override fun dimensionOfRange(): Int {
        return 1
    }
}

val g = object : RealVectorFunction {

    override fun evaluate(x: Vector): Vector {
        val x1: Double = x.get(1)
        val x2: Double = x.get(2)

        val w1: Double = x1 * x1 + x2 - 11
        val w2: Double = x1 + x2 * x2 - 7

        var result = ArrayList<Double>(2)
        result.add(0, 4 * w1 * x1 + 2 * w2)
        result.add(1, 2 * w1 + 4 * w2 * x2)
        return DenseVector(result)
    }

    override fun dimensionOfDomain(): Int {
        return 2
    }

    override fun dimensionOfRange(): Int {
        return 2
    }
}
val problem = C2OptimProblemImpl(f, g)

// Using the Conjugate Gradient method
val ConjugateGradientMinimizer
        = ConjugateGradientMinimizer(1e-16, 40)
val soln1: IterativeSolution<Vector> = ConjugateGradientMinimizer.solve(problem)
val xmin1: Vector = soln1.search(DenseVector(6.0, 6.0))
val f_xmin1: Double = f.evaluate(xmin1)
println(String.format("f(%s) = %.16f", xmin1.toString(), f_xmin1))
```

The output is as follows:

```
f([3.000000, 2.000000] ) = 0.0000000000013999
```

```
// Using the Fletcher Reeves method
val fletcherReevesMinimizer
        = FletcherReevesMinimizer(1e-16, 20)
val soln2: IterativeSolution<Vector> = fletcherReevesMinimizer.solve(problem)
```

```
val xmin2: Vector = soln2.search(DenseVector(6.0, 6.0))
val f_xmin2: Double = f.evaluate(xmin2)
println(String.format("f(%s) = %.16f", xmin2.toString(), f_xmin2))
```

The output is as follows:

```
f([3.000002, 1.999998] ) = 0.0000000001278725
```

```
// Using the Powell method
val powellMinimizer: SteepestDescentMinimizer
        = PowellMinimizer(1e-16, 20)
val soln3: IterativeSolution<Vector> = powellMinimizer.solve(problem)
val xmin3: Vector = soln3.search(DenseVector(6.0, 6.0))
val f_xmin3: Double = f.evaluate(xmin3)
println(String.format("f(%s) = %.16f", xmin3.toString(), f_xmin3))
```

The output is as follows:

```
f([-2.805114, 3.131310] ) = 0.0000000007791914
```

```
// Using the Zangwill method
val zangwillMinimizer: SteepestDescentMinimizer
        = ZangwillMinimizer(1e-16, 1e-16, 20)
val soln4: IterativeSolution<Vector> = zangwillMinimizer.solve(problem)
val xmin4: Vector = soln4.search(DenseVector(6.0, 6.0))
val f_xmin4: Double = f.evaluate(xmin4)
println(String.format("f(%s) = %.16f", xmin4.toString(), f_xmin4))
```

The output is as follows:

```
f([-2.805117, 3.131311] ) = 0.0000000001359077
```

The two minimums found are (3, 2) and (–2.805118,3.131312).

The signatures of these minimizers are as follows:

```
/**
 * Construct a multivariate minimizer using the Conjugate-Gradient method.
 *
 * @param epsilon       a precision parameter: when a number |x| &le;
 *                      &epsilon;, it is considered 0
 * @param maxIterations the maximum number of iterations
 */
public ConjugateGradientMinimizer(double epsilon, int maxIterations)
/**
 * Construct a multivariate minimizer using the Fletcher-Reeves method.
 *
 * @param epsilon       a precision parameter: when a number |x| &le;
 *                      &epsilon;, it is considered 0
```

```
 * @param maxIterations the maximum number of iterations
 */
public FletcherReevesMinimizer(double epsilon, int maxIterations)
/**
 * Construct a multivariate minimizer using the Powell method.
 *
 * @param epsilon       a precision parameter: when a number |x| &le;
 *                      &epsilon;, it is
 *                      considered 0
 * @param maxIterations the maximum number of iterations
 */
public PowellMinimizer(double epsilon, int maxIterations)
/**
 * Construct a multivariate minimizer using the Zangwill method.
 *
 * @param epsilon       a precision parameter: when a number |x| &le;
 *                      &epsilon;, it is considered 0
 * @param epsilon2      a precision parameter to decide whether there is a
 *                      linear dependence among the conjugate directions
 * @param maxIterations the maximum number of iterations
 */
public ZangwillMinimizer(double epsilon, double epsilon2, int maxIterations)
```

9.6. Quasi-Newton Methods

Quasi-Newton methods is another framework of algorithms that do not require the explicit expression of Hessian. It is built on the Newton method in Section 9.4.1, except that the search direction is based on an $n * n$ matrix **S**, which serves the same purpose as the inverse Hessian matrix in the Newton method. That is,

$$\boldsymbol{x}_{k+1} = \boldsymbol{x}_k - \alpha_k \boldsymbol{S}_k \boldsymbol{g}_k$$

When $\boldsymbol{S}_k = \boldsymbol{I}$, it is the steepest-descent algorithm. When $\boldsymbol{S}_k = \mathbf{H}^{-1}$, it is the Newton's method. When the Hessian is not available, **S** is derived from available data and is meant to be an approximation of $\mathbf{H}^{-1}$. In fact, it can be shown that the previous algorithm to update $\boldsymbol{x}_{k+1}$ converges the fastest when $\boldsymbol{S}_k = \mathbf{H}^{-1}$. Quasi-Newton methods combine the advantages of steepest-descent and conjugate-direction methods with effective direction-updating rules. They are the most efficient among all methods that we discuss in this chapter and are extensively used in many applications.

Assume that the difference in successive $\boldsymbol{x}_k$ is as follows:

$$\delta_k = \boldsymbol{x}_{k+1} - \boldsymbol{x}_k$$

The difference in successive gradient g_k is as follows:

$$\gamma_k = \boldsymbol{g}_{k+1} - \boldsymbol{g}_k$$

Then you get this:

$$\gamma_k = \boldsymbol{H} \delta_k$$

Newton's method determines the direction vector as follows:

$$\boldsymbol{d}_k = -\mathbf{S}_k \boldsymbol{g}_k$$

The magnitude α_k can be determined by a line search minimizing the function:

$$f(\boldsymbol{x}_k + \alpha \boldsymbol{d}_k)$$

We want to avoid inverting a matrix such as computing $\mathbf{S}_k = \mathbf{H}^{-1}$ and checking that $\mathbf{S}_k$ is positive definite in each iteration. We want a simple updating rule for $\mathbf{S}_{k+1}$.

$$\mathbf{S}_{k+1} = \mathbf{S}_k + \boldsymbol{C}_k$$

$\mathbf{C}_k$ is an $n * n$ correction matrix that can be computed from available data. In any definition of $\boldsymbol{C}_k$, $\boldsymbol{S}_{k+1}$ must satisfy these three properties:

- $\mathbf{S}_{k+1}\gamma_k = \boldsymbol{\delta}_k$.
- The vectors $\{\boldsymbol{\delta}_0, \boldsymbol{\delta}_1, \cdots, \boldsymbol{\delta}_{n-1}\}$ must be conjugate directions.
- A positive definite $\boldsymbol{S}_k$ must produce a positive definite $\boldsymbol{S}_{k+1}$.

The second property ensures that the excellent properties of conjugate-direction search apply to Quasi-Newton search as well. The third property ensures that the direction vector is valid in each iteration. There are many ways to define $\boldsymbol{C}_k$, and they give rise to different variants of Quasi-Newton methods. In this chapter, we introduce several variants depending on how they compute $\boldsymbol{C}_k$ or how they update $\boldsymbol{S}_k$.

9.6.1. Rank-One Method

The rank-one method is featured by that the correction matrix $\mathbf{C}_k$ has a rank of unity.

Assume the following:

$$\mathbf{S}_{k+1}\gamma_k = \delta_k$$

Let

$$\mathbf{S}_{k+1} = \mathbf{S}_k + \beta \xi_k \xi_k^T$$

$\boldsymbol{\xi}_k$ is a column vector, and β_k is a constant. The correction matrix $\beta \xi_k \xi_k^T$ is symmetric and has a rank of one. Combining the two equations, you get the following:

$$\delta_k = \mathbf{S}_k \gamma_k + \beta \xi_k \xi_k^T \gamma_k$$

And you get the following:

$$\gamma_k^T (\delta_k - \mathbf{S}_k \gamma_k) = \beta_k \gamma_k^T \xi_k \xi_k^T \gamma_k = \beta_k (\xi_k^T \gamma_k)^2$$

$$(\delta_k - \mathbf{S}_k \gamma_k)(\delta_k - \mathbf{S}_k \gamma_k)^T = \beta_k (\xi_k^T \gamma_k)^2 \beta_k \xi_k \xi_k^T$$

Then you get the following:

$$\beta_k \xi_k \xi_k^T = \frac{(\delta_k - \mathbf{S}_k \gamma_k)(\delta_k - \mathbf{S}_k \gamma_k)^T}{\gamma_k^T (\delta_k - \mathbf{S}_k \gamma_k)}$$

Therefore, you get the following:

$$\mathbf{S}_{k+1} = \mathbf{S}_k + \frac{(\delta_k - \mathbf{S}_k \gamma_k)(\delta_k - \mathbf{S}_k \gamma_k)^T}{\gamma_k^T (\delta_k - \mathbf{S}_k \gamma_k)}$$

There are two serious problems for this method. First, a positive definite $\mathbf{S}_k$ may not give a positive definite $\mathbf{S}_{k+1}$. If that happens, the next direction is not a good direction. Second, the denominator in the correction formula may approach zero or equal zero. If that happens, the method breaks down because $\mathbf{S}_{k+1}$ is undefined.

9.6.2. Davidon-Fletcher-Powell Method

The Davidon-Fletcher-Powell (DPF) method is similar to the rank one method, but it has one important advantage: if initial matrix $\mathbf{S}_0$ is positive definite, the subsequent matrices are always positive definite. Unlike the rank one method, every new direction is a descent direction.

The DPF-updating formula is as follows:

$$\mathbf{S}_{k+1} = \mathbf{S}_k + \frac{\delta_k \delta_k^T}{\delta_k^T \gamma_k} - \frac{\mathbf{S}_k \gamma_k \gamma_k^T \mathbf{S}_k}{\gamma_k^T \mathbf{S}_k \gamma_k}$$

The correction is an $n * n$ symmetric matrix of rank two.

9.6.3. Broyden-Fletcher-Goldfarb-Shanno Method

The BFGS updating formula is as follows:

$$\mathbf{S}_{k+1} = \mathbf{S}_k + \left(1 + \frac{\gamma_k^T \mathbf{S}_k \gamma_k}{\gamma_k^T \delta_k}\right) \frac{\delta_k \delta_k^T}{\gamma_k^T \delta_k} - \frac{\delta_k \gamma_k^T \mathbf{S}_k + \mathbf{S}_k \gamma_k \delta_k^T}{\gamma_k^T \delta_k}$$

The BFGS method has the following properties:

1. $\mathbf{S}_{k+1}$ becomes identical to $\mathbf{H}^{-1}$ for $k = n - 1$.
2. Directions $\{\delta i\} i_{= 1, 2, \dots,} n_{-1}$ form a conjugate set.
3. $\mathbf{S}_{k+1}$ is the positive definite if $\mathbf{S}_k$ is positive definite.
4. $\delta_k^T \gamma_k = \delta_k^T \mathbf{g}_{k+1} - \delta_k^T \mathbf{g}_k > 0$.

The BFGS solver is the best solver among all. It is used by default in many of the NM unconstrained optimization applications.

9.6.4. Huang Family (Rank One, DFP, BFGS, Pearson, McCormick)

The Huang updating formula is a general formula that encompasses the rank one, DFP, BFGS, Pearson, and McCormick methods. It has this form:

$$\mathbf{S}_{k+1} = \mathbf{S}_k + \frac{\delta_k\left(\theta\delta_k + \phi\mathbf{S}_k^T\gamma_k\right)^T}{\left(\theta\delta_k + \phi\mathbf{S}_k^T\gamma_k\right)^T\gamma_k} - \frac{\mathbf{S}_k\gamma_k\left(\varphi\delta_k + \omega\mathbf{S}_k^T\gamma_k\right)^T}{\left(\varphi\delta_k + \omega\mathbf{S}_k^T\gamma_k\right)^T\gamma_k}$$

θ, ϕ, φ, and ω are independent parameters.

By letting $\theta = 1$, $\phi = -1$, $\psi = 1$, $\omega = -1$, you get the rank one formula.

By letting $\theta = 1$, $\phi = 0$, $\psi = 0$, $\omega = 1$, you get the DFP formula.

By letting $\frac{\phi}{\theta} = \frac{-\gamma_k\delta_k^T}{\gamma_k\delta_k^T + \gamma_k^T\mathbf{S}_k\gamma_k}$, $\psi = 1$, and $\omega = 0$ you get the BFGS formula.

By letting $\theta = 1$, $\phi = 0$, $\psi = 1$, and $\omega = 0$, you get the McCormick formula.

$$\mathbf{S}_{k+1} = \mathbf{S}_k + \frac{\left(\delta_k - \mathbf{S}_k\gamma_k\right)\delta_k^T}{\delta_k^T\gamma_k}$$

By letting $\theta = 0$, $\phi = 1$, $\psi = 0$, $\omega = 1$, you get the Pearson formula.

$$\mathbf{S}_{k+1} = \mathbf{S}_k + \frac{\left(\delta_k - \mathbf{S}_k\gamma_k\right)\gamma_k^T\mathbf{S}_k}{\gamma_k^T\mathbf{S}_k\gamma_k}$$

NM Dev has a suite of Quasi-Newton methods. The following code solves a Himmelblau function in Figure 9-11 using different Quasi-Newton methods:

```
/**
* The Himmelblau function: f(x) = (x1^2 + x2 - 11)^2 + (x1 + x2^2 -
* 7)^2
*/
val f = object : RealScalarFunction {

    override fun evaluate(x: Vector): Double {
        val x1: Double = x.get(1)
        val x2: Double = x.get(2)

        var result: Double = (x1 * x1 + x2 - 11).pow(2)
        result += (x1 + x2 * x2 - 7).pow(2)

        return result
    }

    override fun dimensionOfDomain(): Int {
        return 2
    }

    override fun dimensionOfRange(): Int {
        return 1
    }
}
```

```
val g = object : RealVectorFunction {

    override fun evaluate(x: Vector): Vector {
        val x1: Double = x.get(1)
        val x2: Double = x.get(2)

        val w1: Double = x1 * x1 + x2 - 11
        val w2: Double = x1 + x2 * x2 - 7

        var result = ArrayList<Double>(2)
        result.add(0, 4 * w1 * x1 + 2 * w2)
        result.add(1, 2 * w1 + 4 * w2 * x2)
        return DenseVector(result)
    }

    override fun dimensionOfDomain(): Int {
        return 2
    }

    override fun dimensionOfRange(): Int {
        return 2
    }
}
val problem = C2OptimProblemImpl(f, g)

// Using the Rank One method
val rankOneMinimizer: QuasiNewtonMinimizer = RankOneMinimizer(1e-16, 15)
val soln1: IterativeSolution<Vector> = rankOneMinimizer.solve(problem)
var xmin: Vector = soln1.search(DenseVector(6.0, 6.0))
var f_xmin: Double = f.evaluate(xmin)
println(String.format("f(%s) = %.16f", xmin.toString(), f_xmin))
```

The output is as follows:

```
f([3.000000, 2.000000] ) = 0.0000000000000000
```

```
// Using the DFP method
val dfpMinimizer: QuasiNewtonMinimizer = DFPMinimizer(1e-16, 15)
val soln2: IterativeSolution<Vector> = dfpMinimizer.solve(problem)
xmin = soln2.search(DenseVector(6.0, 6.0))
f_xmin = f.evaluate(xmin)
println(String.format("f(%s) = %.16f", xmin.toString(), f_xmin))
```

The output is as follows:

```
f([3.000000, 2.000000] ) = 0.0000000000000000
```

```
// Using the BFGS method
val bfgsMinimizer: QuasiNewtonMinimizer = BFGSMinimizer(false, 1e-16, 15)
```

```
val soln3: IterativeSolution<Vector> = bfgsMinimizer.solve(problem)
xmin = soln3.search(DenseVector(6.0, 6.0))
f_xmin = f.evaluate(xmin)
println(String.format("f(%s) = %.16f", xmin.toString(), f_xmin))
```

The output is as follows:

```
f([3.000000, 2.000000] ) = 0.0000000000000000
```

```
// Using the Huang method
val huangMinimizer: QuasiNewtonMinimizer = HuangMinimizer(0.0, 1.0, 0.0, 1.0, 1e-16, 15)
val soln4: IterativeSolution<Vector> = huangMinimizer.solve(problem)
xmin = soln4.search(DenseVector(6.0, 6.0))
f_xmin = f.evaluate(xmin)
println(String.format("f(%s) = %.16f", xmin.toString(), f_xmin))
```

The output is as follows:

```
f([3.000000, 2.000000] ) = 0.0000000000000000
```

```
// Using the Pearson method
val pearsonMinimizer: QuasiNewtonMinimizer = PearsonMinimizer(1e-16, 15)
val soln5: IterativeSolution<Vector> = pearsonMinimizer.solve(problem)
xmin = soln5.search(DenseVector(6.0, 6.0))
f_xmin = f.evaluate(xmin)
println(String.format("f(%s) = %.16f", xmin.toString(), f_xmin))
```

The output is as follows:

```
f([3.000000, 2.000000] ) = 0.0000000000000000
```

The Quasi-Newton methods seem much more efficient than any of the conjugate-direction methods. They take far fewer iterations, 15 versus 20, and give better precision.

The signatures of these solvers are as follows:

```
/**
 * Construct a multivariate minimizer using the Rank One method.
 *
 * @param epsilon       a precision parameter: when a number |x| &le;
 *                      &epsilon;, it is considered 0
 * @param maxIterations the maximum number of iterations
 */
public RankOneMinimizer(double epsilon, int maxIterations)
/**
 * Construct a multivariate minimizer using the DFP method.
 *
 * @param epsilon       a precision parameter: when a number |x| &le;
 *                      &epsilon;, it is considered 0
```

```
 * @param maxIterations the maximum number of iterations
 */
public DFPMinimizer(double epsilon, int maxIterations)
/**
 * Construct a multivariate minimizer using the BFGS method.
 *
 * @param epsilon          a precision parameter: when a number |x| &le;
 *                         &epsilon;, it is considered 0
 * @param maxIterations    the maximum number of iterations
 * @param isFletcherSwitch indicate whether to use the Fletcher switch
 */
public BFGSMinimizer(boolean isFletcherSwitch, double epsilon, int maxIterations)
/**
 * Construct a multivariate minimizer using Huang's method.
 *
 * @param theta         &theta; in Huang's formula
 * @param phi           &phi; in Huang's formula
 * @param psi           &psi; in Huang's formula
 * @param omega         &omega; in Huang's formula
 * @param epsilon       a precision parameter: when a number |x| &le;
 *                      &epsilon;, it is considered 0
 * @param maxIterations the maximum number of iterations
 */
public HuangMinimizer(
        double theta,
        double phi,
        double psi,
        double omega,
        double epsilon,
        int maxIterations
)
/**
 * Construct a multivariate minimizer using the Pearson method.
 *
 * @param epsilon       a precision parameter: when a number |x| &le;
 *                      &epsilon;, it is considered 0
 * @param maxIterations the maximum number of iterations
 */
public PearsonMinimizer(double epsilon, int maxIterations)
```

CHAPTER 10

Constrained Optimization

Optimization is ubiquitous in many branches of mathematics and industrial applications. For example, many statistical theories such as regression and maximum likelihood are formulated into optimization problems. Quantitative finance maximizes the reward-risk ratio of a portfolio to allocate assets. In our company, NM Limited, we build data-driven decision-making systems to assist management in making scientific rather than ad hoc business decisions. Examples include a resource allocation system for a steel manufacturing plant to optimize use of raw materials, machines, and manpower; a route planner to find the best routes to pick up and deliver mail; and a scheduling system to arrange vehicles and their shifts.

The source code in this chapter can be run on the S2 platform here:

```
https://s21.nm.dev/hub/user-redirect/lab/tree/s2-public/Numerical%20Methods%20Using%20
Kotlin/chapter10.ipynb
```

The source code can be found on GitHub:

```
https://github.com/apress/numerical-methods-kotlin
```

10.1. The Optimization Problem

In general, a constrained optimization problem finds a vector $\boldsymbol{x}^*$ that satisfies the following:

$$\min_{\boldsymbol{x}} f(\boldsymbol{x})$$

Subject to the following:

$$a_i(\boldsymbol{x}) = 0, i = 1,2,\ldots p$$

$$c_j(\boldsymbol{x}) \geq 0, j = 1,2,\ldots q$$

Assume that $a_i(x)$ and $c_j(x)$ are twice differentiable continuous functions. The constraints together define the feasible region, R, for the optimization problem. That is, $\boldsymbol{x}^* \in R$. The feasible region is assumed to be convex.

H. Li, PhD, *Numerical Methods Using Kotlin*, https://doi.org/10.1007/978-1-4842-8826-9_10

A convex set is a set that, for any two points $\boldsymbol{x}$ and $\boldsymbol{y}$ in the set, any line segment joining the two points, $(1 - t)\boldsymbol{x} + t\boldsymbol{y}$, lies in the set. Figure 10-1 shows an example of a convex set.

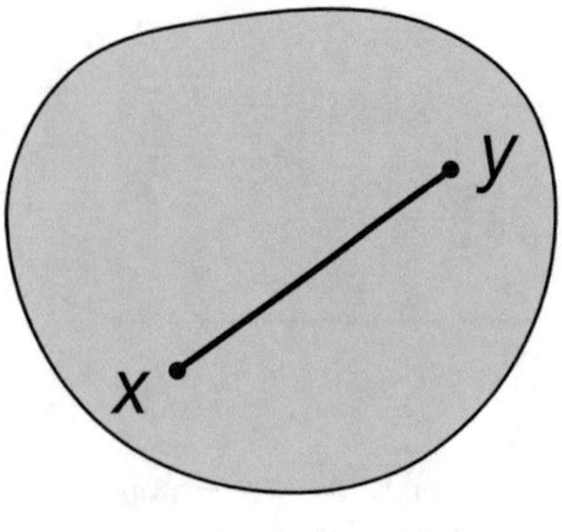

Figure 10-1. *A convex set*

Figure 10-2 shows an example of a nonconvex set.

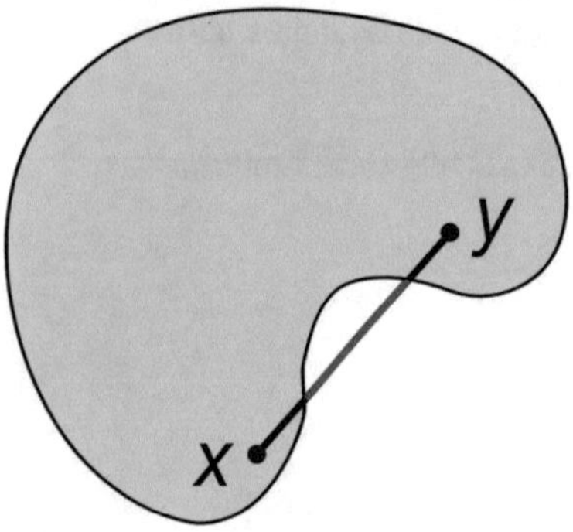

Figure 10-2. *A nonconvex set*

The following is an example of a constrained optimization problem:

$$\min_{\boldsymbol{x}} f(\boldsymbol{x}) = \min_{\boldsymbol{x}} \left((x_1 - 1.5)^2 + 2x_2^2 \right)$$

Subject to the following:

$$\begin{cases} x_1^2 + x_2^2 = 0 \\ x_1^2 - x_2 \le 0 \end{cases}$$

Figure 10-3 shows the feasible region defined by the intersection of the two curves in the constraints.

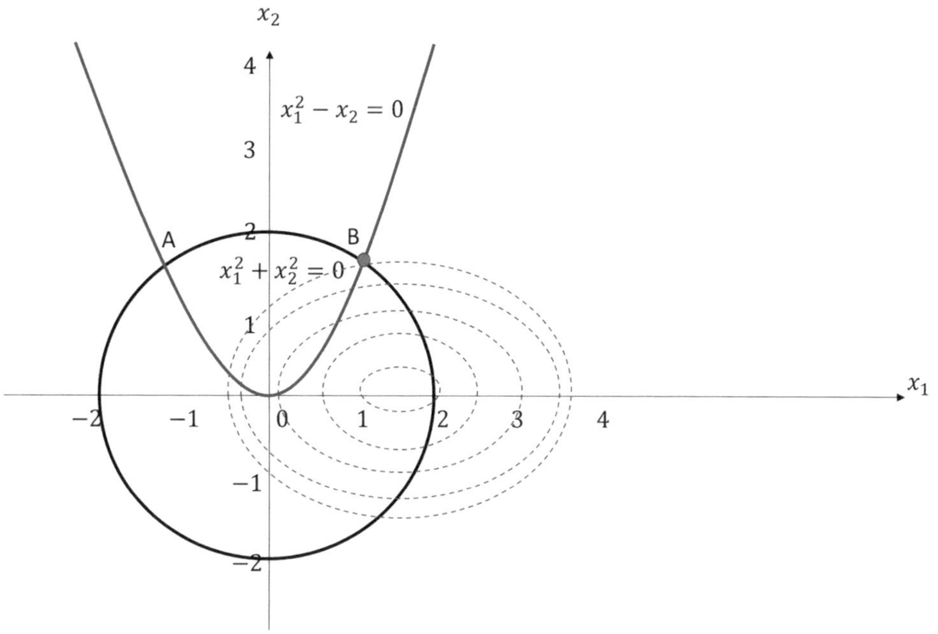

Figure 10-3. *Feasible region defined by the constraints*

The contour plots (the dashed lines) are the (same) values that the objective function can take. The inequality (less-than) constraint restricts the solution to be above the parabolic curve. The equality constraint requires the solution to be on the circumference of the circle. The feasible region is therefore only the AB arc of the circle inside the parabolic curve. The dot at point B shows the solution where the objective function is the smallest on the arc.

10.1.1. General Optimization Algorithm

In general, searching for a solution to an optimization problem is an iterative process (unless you have an analytical expression for it, which you usually don't). So, you start with an initial point or guess and try it. If it does not work, you try another one. The core component in any numerical optimization algorithm is how you choose the next point to try. There are two factors that determine the search point in the *k*-th iteration. They are the direction $\boldsymbol{d}_k$ and the magnitude of change α_k in that direction. The next search point is therefore as follows:

$$\boldsymbol{x}_k = \boldsymbol{x}_{k-1} + \alpha_k \boldsymbol{d}_k$$

You repeat this process until the convergence criterion is met. The criterion can be that the change in the objective function value is too small.

$$\left| f(\boldsymbol{x}_k) - f(\boldsymbol{x}_{k-1}) \right| < \varepsilon_f$$

Or it can be that the change in $\boldsymbol{x}_k$ is too small.

$$\left| \Delta \boldsymbol{x}_k \right| = \left| \boldsymbol{x}_k - \boldsymbol{x}_{k-1} \right| < \varepsilon_x$$

10.1.2. Constraints

In NM Dev, a set of equality or inequality constraints is represented by a list of real-valued multivariate functions. The interface is called Constraints. The class signature is as follows:

```
public interface Constraints {
    /**
     * Get the list of constraint functions.
     *
     * @return the list of constraint functions
     */
    public List<RealScalarFunction> getConstraints();
    /**
     * Get the number of variables.
     *
     * @return the number of variables
     */
    public int dimension();
    /**
     * Get the number of constraints.
     *
     * @return the number of constraints
     */
    public int size();
}
```

Equality Constraints

The set of equality constraints is shown here:

$$a_i(\boldsymbol{x}) = 0, i = 1, 2, \ldots p$$

Or in vector form, it is as follows:

$$a(\boldsymbol{x}) = \left[a_1(\boldsymbol{x}), a_2(\boldsymbol{x}), \ldots, a_p(\boldsymbol{x})\right]^T = 0$$

This defines a hypersurface in R^n.

A point $\boldsymbol{x}$ is called a regular point of the equality constraints if $\boldsymbol{x}$ satisfies the constraints and the column vectors $\nabla a_1(\boldsymbol{x})$, $\nabla a_2(\boldsymbol{x})$, ..., $\nabla a_p(\boldsymbol{x})$ are linearly independent. That is, $\boldsymbol{x}$ is a solution:

$$\boldsymbol{a}(\boldsymbol{x}) = \boldsymbol{0}$$

And the Jacobian matrix looks like this:

$$\mathbf{J_e}(\boldsymbol{x}) = \left[\nabla a_1(\boldsymbol{x}), \nabla a_2(\boldsymbol{x}), \ldots, \nabla a_p(\boldsymbol{x})\right]$$

$$
= \begin{bmatrix} \frac{da_1}{dx_1} & \cdots & \frac{da_1}{dx_n} \\ & \ddots & \\ \frac{da_p}{dx_1} & & \frac{da_p}{dx_n} \end{bmatrix}
$$

It has full-row rank p.

If $p > n$, then $\mathbf{J}_e$ cannot be full-row rank. There is no regular point. If $p = n$, then there are only a finite number of regular points, and the optimization problem becomes trivial. You can therefore usually assume that $p < n$. If $\boldsymbol{x}$ is a regular point for a set of equality constraints, it defines a tangent plane of the hypersurface of constraints.

Antoniou & Lu (2007) provide the following example:

$$
\begin{cases} -x_1 + x_3 - 1 = 0 \\ x_1^2 + x_2^2 - 2x_1 = 0 \end{cases}
$$

The Jacobian matrix is as follows:

$$
\mathbf{J}_e(\boldsymbol{x}) = \begin{bmatrix} -1 & 0 & 1 \\ 2x_1 - 2 & 2x_2 & 0 \end{bmatrix}
$$

It has rank 2 except at $\boldsymbol{x} = [1\ \ 0\ \ x_3]^T$ because it does not satisfy the constraints. Any other point is regular.

In NM Dev, the `EqualityConstraints` interface is a marker to denote a set of equality constraints. Its signature is as follows:

```
public interface EqualityConstraints extends Constraints {
}
```

The `GeneralEqualityConstraints` class implements a set of equality constraints. The class signature is as follows:

```
public class GeneralEqualityConstraints extends GeneralConstraints implements
EqualityConstraints {
    /**
     * Constructs an instance of equality constraints from a collection of
     * real-valued functions.
     *
     * @param constraints the equality constraints
     */
    public GeneralEqualityConstraints(Collection<RealScalarFunction> constraints) {
        super(constraints);
    }
    /**
     * Constructs an instance of equality constraints from an array of
     * real-valued functions.
     *
     * @param constraints the equality constraints
     */
```

```
    public GeneralEqualityConstraints(RealScalarFunction... constraints) {
        super(constraints);
    }
}
```

The following code snippet represents the previous example:

```
// non-linear constraints
val a = GeneralEqualityConstraints(
                // the first equality constraint
        object : AbstractRealScalarFunction(3) { // the domain dimension

            override fun evaluate(x: Vector): Double {
                val x1: Double = x.get(1)
                val x3: Double = x.get(3)

                val a1: Double = -x1 + x3 + 1
                return a1
            }
        },
                // the second equality constraint
        object : AbstractRealScalarFunction(3) { // the domain dimension

            override fun evaluate(x: Vector): Double {
                val x1: Double = x.get(1)
                val x2: Double = x.get(2)

                val a2: Double = x1 * x1 + x2 * x2 - 2.0 * x1
                return a2
            }
        }
)
```

If all equality constraints are linear, they can be written as follows:

$$\mathbf{A}\boldsymbol{x} = \mathbf{b}$$

A is a $p \times n$ matrix. $\boldsymbol{b}$ is a $p \times 1$ vector. The Jacobian matrix $\mathbf{J}_e$ is the same as the constant matrix **A**. Therefore, if rank(**A**) = p, then any solution to the linear system $\mathbf{A}\boldsymbol{x} = \boldsymbol{b}$ is a regular point. Otherwise, there are two possibilities for rank(**A**) = $p' < p$.

If $rank([\mathbf{A} \quad \mathbf{b}]) > p$, then there is no solution to the linear system. A careful examination is needed to remove the contradictions. If $rank([\mathbf{A} \quad \mathbf{b}]) = rank(\mathbf{A}) = p' < p$, then you can reduce the constraints to a smaller and equivalent set of equality constraints.

$$\hat{\mathbf{A}}\boldsymbol{x} = \hat{\mathbf{b}}$$

where $\hat{\mathbf{A}}$ is a $p' \times n$ matrix and $\hat{\boldsymbol{b}}$ a $p' \times 1$ vector.

One way to do this is to apply singular value decomposition (SVD) to **A**. See Chapter 2 for more information. You can decompose **A** as follows:

$$\mathbf{A} = \mathbf{UD}\boldsymbol{V}^T$$

where **U** is a $p \times p$ orthogonal matrix and **V** is an $n \times n$ orthogonal matrix.

$$\mathbf{D} = \begin{bmatrix} \hat{\boldsymbol{D}} & \mathbf{0} \\ \mathbf{0} & \mathbf{0} \end{bmatrix}$$

where $\hat{\boldsymbol{D}}$ has all the positive singular values.

$$\mathbf{A} = \mathbf{U}\mathbf{D}\boldsymbol{V}^T = \boldsymbol{U}\begin{bmatrix} \hat{\boldsymbol{A}} \\ \mathbf{0} \end{bmatrix}$$

$$\hat{\boldsymbol{A}} = \hat{\boldsymbol{D}}\left[\boldsymbol{v}_1, \ldots, \boldsymbol{v}_{p'}\right]^T$$

$\boldsymbol{v}_i$ are the columns in $\boldsymbol{V}^T$. $\hat{\boldsymbol{A}}$ is a $p' \times n$ matrix.

$$\begin{bmatrix} \hat{\boldsymbol{A}} \\ \mathbf{0} \end{bmatrix} \boldsymbol{x} = \begin{bmatrix} \hat{\boldsymbol{b}} \\ \mathbf{0} \end{bmatrix}$$

$\hat{\boldsymbol{b}}$ is the first p' entries of $\mathbf{U}^T\boldsymbol{b}$.
The following code snippet reproduces Example 10.2 in Antoniou & Lu (2007):

$$\begin{cases} x_1 - 2x_2 + 3x_3 + 2x_4 = 4 \\ 2x_2 - x_3 = 1 \\ 2x_1 - 10x_2 + 9x_3 + 4x_4 = 5 \end{cases}$$

The rank of this linear system is 2 and hence reducible. The reduced set of equality constraints is as follows:

$$\begin{cases} 2.177001x_1 - 10.342933x_2 + 9.525469x_3 + 4.354003x_4 = 5.713540 \\ 0.510554x_1 + 1.011800x_2 + 0.515208x_3 + 1.021108x_4 = 3.058670 \end{cases}$$

```
/** Example 10.2, p. 270. Practical Optimization: Algorithms and
 * Engineering Applications. Andreas Antoniou, Wu-Sheng Lu */
// linear constraints
val A: Matrix = DenseMatrix(
    arrayOf(
        doubleArrayOf(1.0, -2.0, 3.0, 2.0),
        doubleArrayOf(0.0, 2.0, -1.0, 0.0),
        doubleArrayOf(2.0, -10.0, 9.0, 4.0)
    )
)

val b: Vector = DenseVector(4.0, 1.0, 5.0)
val A_eq = LinearEqualityConstraints(A, b)
println("original equality constraints: ")
println(A_eq)

// do SVD decomposition to reduce the equality constraints
```

```
val svd: SVD = SVD(A, true)
val U: Matrix = svd.U()
println("\nU = ")
println(U)
val D: Matrix = svd.D()
println("\nD = ")
println(D)
val V: Matrix = svd.V()
println("\nV = ")
println(V)

// check if the original equality constraints are reducible
val epsilon: Double = 1e-8 // the precision parameter under which is considered 0
val isReducible: Boolean = A_eq.isReducible()
println(isReducible)
val r: Int = MatrixMeasure.rank(
        A,
        epsilon
)
println(String.format("rank of A = %d%n", r))
```

The output is as follows:

```
original equality constraints:
3x4
         [,1] [,2] [,3] [,4]
[1,] 1.000000, -2.000000, 3.000000, 2.000000,
[2,] 0.000000, 2.000000, -1.000000, 0.000000,
[3,] 2.000000, -10.000000, 9.000000, 4.000000,  * x =
[4.000000, 1.000000, 5.000000]
U =
3x3
         [,1] [,2] [,3]
[1,] 0.271659, 0.800304, -0.534522,
[2,] -0.136451, 0.581828, 0.801784,
[3,] 0.952671, -0.144875, 0.267261,
D =
3x3
         [,1] [,2] [,3]
[1,] 14.879768, 0.000000, 0.000000,
[2,] 0.000000, 1.610126, 0.000000,
[3,] 0.000000, 0.000000, 0.000000,
V =
4x3
         [,1] [,2] [,3]
[1,] 0.146306, 0.317089, -0.936741,
[2,] -0.695100, 0.628398, 0.112540,
[3,] 0.640162, 0.319980, 0.225081,
[4,] 0.292612, 0.634179, 0.243290,
true
rank of A = 2
```

Inequality Constraints

Inequality constraints are in this form:

$$c_j(\boldsymbol{x}) \geq 0, j = 1, 2, \ldots q$$

Unlike equality constraints, the number of inequality constraints, q, are not required to be less than n. There are two classes of inequality constraints for any feasible point $\bar{\boldsymbol{x}}$. The set of constraints with $c_j(\boldsymbol{x}) > 0$ are called inactive constraints such as $c_1(\bar{\boldsymbol{x}})$ and $c_2(\bar{\boldsymbol{x}})$ in Figure 10-2. Because $\bar{\boldsymbol{x}}$ is on their boundaries, the next search point cannot move in a direction that violates the constraints. These active constraints therefore restrict the feasible region in the neighborhood of $\bar{\boldsymbol{x}}$. On the other hand, inactive constraints such as $c_3(\bar{\boldsymbol{x}})$ are far away from $\bar{\boldsymbol{x}}$ so they have no effect on the feasible region in a sufficiently small neighborhood of $\bar{\boldsymbol{x}}$. See Figure 10-4.

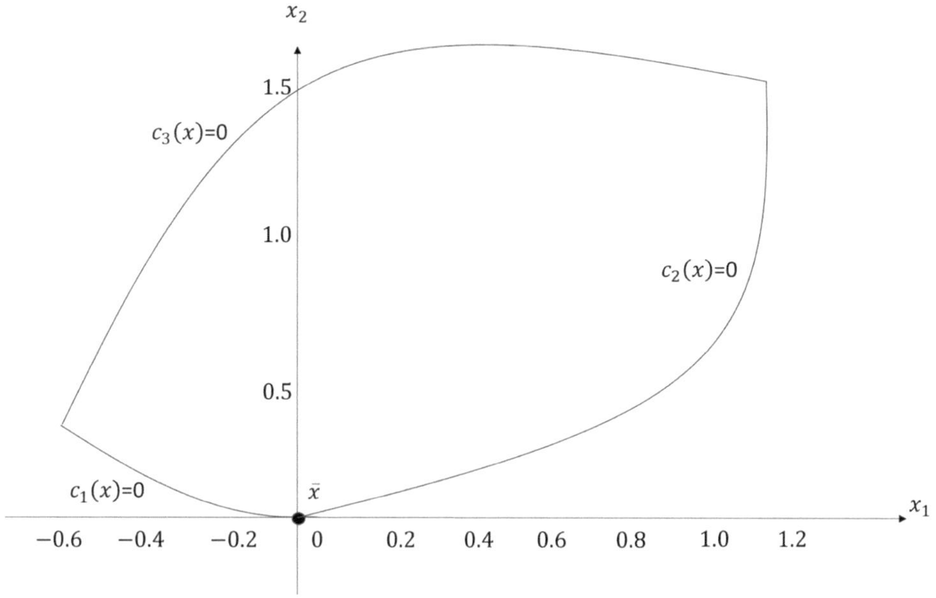

***Figure 10-4.** Inequality constraints*

In NM Dev, the `GreaterThanConstraints` interface is a marker to denote a set of (greater-than) inequality constraints. Its signature is as follows:

```
public interface GreaterThanConstraints extends Constraints {
    /**
     * Convert the greater-than or equal-to constraints to less-than or equal-to
     * constraints.
     *
     * @return the equivalent less-than or equal-to constraints
     */
    public LessThanConstraints toLessThanConstraints();
}
```

Equivalently, you can write the inequality constraints as less-than inequality constraints by changing the sign. That is:

$$c_j(\boldsymbol{x}) \le 0, j = 1,2,\ldots q$$

The LessThanConstraints interface is a marker to denote a set of less-than inequality constraints. Its signature is as follows:

```
public interface LessThanConstraints extends Constraints {
    /**
     * Convert the less-than or equal-to constraints to greater-than or equal-to
     * constraints.
     *
     * @return the equivalent greater-than or equal-to constraints
     */
    public GreaterThanConstraints toGreaterThanConstraints();
}
```

The GeneralGreaterThanConstraints class implements a set of greater-than equality constraints. The class signature is as follows:

```
public class GeneralGreaterThanConstraints
        extends GeneralConstraints
        implements GreaterThanConstraints {
    /**
     * Construct an instance of greater-than-or-equal-to inequality constraints
     * from a collection of real-valued functions.
     *
     * @param constraints the greater-than-or-equal-to inequality constraints
     */
    public GeneralGreaterThanConstraints(Collection<RealScalarFunction> constraints) {
        super(constraints);
    }
    /**
     * Construct an instance of greater-than-or-equal-to inequality constraints
     * from an array of real-valued functions.
     *
     * @param constraints the greater-than-or-equal-to inequality constraints
     */
    public GeneralGreaterThanConstraints(RealScalarFunction... constraints) {
        super(constraints);
}
...
}
```

For example, the following code snippet constructs this greater-than inequality constraint:

$$x_2 - x_1^2 \ge 0$$

```
val c_gr = GeneralGreaterThanConstraints(
            object : AbstractBivariateRealFunction() {
```

```
        override fun evaluate(x1: Double, x2: Double): Double {
            val c: Double = x2 - x1 * x1
            return c
        }
    })
```

Alternatively, you can construct the same constraint using the GeneralLessThanConstraints class. The class signature is as follows:

```
public class GeneralLessThanConstraints
        extends GeneralConstraints
        implements LessThanConstraints {
    /**
     * Construct an instance of less-than or equal-to inequality constraints
     * from a collection of real-valued functions.
     *
     * @param constraints the less-than or equal-to inequality constraints
     */
    public GeneralLessThanConstraints(Collection<RealScalarFunction> constraints) {
        super(constraints);
    }
    /**
     * Construct an instance of less-than or equal-to inequality constraints
     * from an array of real-valued functions.
     *
     * @param constraints the less-than or equal-to inequality constraints
     */
    public GeneralLessThanConstraints(RealScalarFunction... constraints) {
        super(constraints);
}
...
}
```

For instance, the same constraint can be written as follows:

$$x_1^2 - x_2 \leq 0$$

The code is as follows:

```
val c_less = GeneralLessThanConstraints(
    object : AbstractBivariateRealFunction() {

    override fun evaluate(x1: Double, x2: Double): Double {
        val c: Double = x1 * x1 - x2
        return c
    }
})
```

If all the inequality constraints are linear, as shown here:

$$\boldsymbol{Ax} \geq \boldsymbol{b}$$

then you can use the LinearGreaterThanConstraints class . The class signature is as follows:

```
public class LinearGreaterThanConstraints
        extends LinearConstraints
        implements GreaterThanConstraints {
    /**
     * Construct a collection of linear greater-than or equal-to constraints.
     *
     * @param A the inequality coefficients
     * @param b the inequality values
     */
    public LinearGreaterThanConstraints(Matrix A, Vector b);
    @Override
    public LinearLessThanConstraints toLessThanConstraints();
    /**
     * Given a collection of linear greater-than-or-equal-to constraints as well
     * as a collection of equality constraints,
     * find a feasible initial point that satisfy the constraints.
     * This implementation solves eq. 11.25 in the reference.
     * The first (n-1) entries consist of a feasible initial point.
     * The last entry is the single point perturbation.
     *
     * @param equal a collection of linear equality constraints
     * @return a feasible initial point, and the single point perturbation (in
     *         one vector)
     * @see
     * <ul>
     * <li>"Jorge Nocedal, Stephen Wright, "p. 473," Numerical
     * Optimization."</li>
     * <li>"Andreas Antoniou, Wu-Sheng Lu, "Eq 11.25, Quadratic and Convex
     * Programming," Practical
     * Optimization: Algorithms and Engineering Applications."</li>
     * </ul>
     */
    public Vector getFeasibleInitialPoint(LinearEqualityConstraints equal);
    /**
     * Given a collection of linear greater-than-or-equal-to constraints,
     * find a feasible initial point that satisfy the constraints.
     * This implementation solves eq. 11.25 in the reference.
     * The first (n-1) entries consist of a feasible initial point.
     * The last entry is the single point perturbation.
     *
     * @return a feasible initial point, and the single point perturbation (in
     *         one vector)
     * @see "Andreas Antoniou, Wu-Sheng Lu, "Eq 11.25, Quadratic and Convex
     * Programming," Practical
     * Optimization: Algorithms and Engineering Applications."
     */
    public Vector getFeasibleInitialPoint();
}
```

For example, in modern portfolio optimization, you'll often impose a minimum weight for each stock at, for example, 0 percent. This is saying that no short selling is allowed. This inequality constraints can be written as follows:

$$w \geq 0$$

The following code represents this set of constraints:

```
// w_i >= 0 mean no short selling
val A: Matrix = DenseMatrix(
    arrayOf(
        doubleArrayOf(1.0, 0.0, 0.0),
        doubleArrayOf(0.0, 1.0, 0.0),
        doubleArrayOf(0.0, 0.0, 1.0),
    )
)
val b1: Vector = DenseVector(0.0, 0.0, 0.0) // 3 stocks
val no_short_selling1 = LinearGreaterThanConstraints(A, b1)// w >= 0
println(no_short_selling1)
```

The output is as follows:

```
3x3
         [,1] [,2] [,3]
[1,] 1.000000, 0.000000, 0.000000,
[2,] 0.000000, 1.000000, 0.000000,
[3,] 0.000000, 0.000000, 1.000000,   * x >=
[0.000000, 0.000000, 0.000000]
```

Alternatively, you can use the wrapper class `LowerBoundConstraints` to construct a set of lower bound constraints.

```
val no_short_selling2 = LowerBoundConstraints(3, 0.0);
println(no_short_selling2);
```

The output is as follows:

```
3x3
         [,1] [,2] [,3]
[1,] 1.000000, 0.000000, 0.000000,
[2,] 0.000000, 1.000000, 0.000000,
[3,] 0.000000, 0.000000, 1.000000,   * x >=
[0.000000, 0.000000, 0.000000]
```

If the lower bounds for all variables are all 0, you can simply use the `NonNegativityConstraints` class . For instance, the following code snippet constructs exactly the same no short selling constraint:

```
val no_short_selling3 = NonNegativityConstraints(3);
println(no_short_selling3);
```

The output is as follows:

```
3x3
         [,1] [,2] [,3]
[1,] 1.000000, 0.000000, 0.000000,
[2,] 0.000000, 1.000000, 0.000000,
[3,] 0.000000, 0.000000, 1.000000,   * x >=
[0.000000, 0.000000, 0.000000]
```

Similarly, the LinearLessThanConstraints class represents linear less-than constraints.

$$Ax \leq b$$

The class signature is as follows:

```
public class LinearLessThanConstraints
        extends LinearConstraints
        implements LessThanConstraints {
    /**
     * Construct a collection of linear less-than or equal-to constraints.
     *
     * @param A the less-than inequality constraints
     * @param b the less-than inequality values
     */
    public LinearLessThanConstraints(Matrix A, Vector b) {
        super(A, b);
    }
    @Override
    public LinearGreaterThanConstraints toGreaterThanConstraints() {
        return new LinearGreaterThanConstraints(A().scaled(-1), b().scaled(-1));
    }
    /**
     * Given a collection of linear less-than-or-equal-to constraints as well as
     * a collection of equality constraints,
     * find a feasible initial point that satisfy the constraints.
     * This implementation solves eq. 11.25 in the reference.
     * The first (n-1) entries consist of a feasible initial point.
     * The last entry is the single point perturbation.
     *
     * @param equal a collection of linear equality constraints
     * @return a feasible initial point, and the single point perturbation (in
     *         one vector)
     * @see "Andreas Antoniou, Wu-Sheng Lu, "Eq 11.25, Quadratic and Convex
     * Programming," Practical Optimization: Algorithms and Engineering
     * Applications."
     */
    public Vector getFeasibleInitialPoint(LinearEqualityConstraints equal) {
        return this.toGreaterThanConstraints().getFeasibleInitialPoint(equal);
    }
    /**
     * Given a collection of linear less-than-or-equal-to constraints,
```

```
     * find a feasible initial point that satisfy the constraints.
     * This implementation solves eq. 11.25 in the reference.
     * The first (n-1) entries consist of a feasible initial point.
     * The last entry is the single point perturbation.
     *
     * @return a feasible initial point, and the single point perturbation (in
     *         one vector)
     * @see "Andreas Antoniou, Wu-Sheng Lu, "Eq 11.25, Quadratic and Convex
     * Programming," Practical Optimization: Algorithms and Engineering
     * Applications."
     */
    public Vector getFeasibleInitialPoint() {
        return getFeasibleInitialPoint(null);
    }
}
```

For example, you may want to impose a maximum weight to each stock in the portfolio to avoid over-concentration. The following inequality constraint ensures that no stock is more than 20 percent of the portfolio:

$$\boldsymbol{w} \le 0.2$$

The corresponding code snippet is as follows:

```
// w_i <= 0.2
val A: Matrix = DenseMatrix(
    arrayOf(
        doubleArrayOf(1.0, 0.0, 0.0),
        doubleArrayOf(0.0, 1.0, 0.0),
        doubleArrayOf(0.0, 0.0, 1.0),
    )
)
val b2: Vector = DenseVector(0.2, 0.2, 0.2) // 3 stocks
val maximum_exposure = LinearLessThanConstraints(A, b2)// w <= 0.2
println(maximum_exposure)
```

The output is as follows:

```
3x3
         [,1] [,2] [,3]
[1,] 1.000000, 0.000000, 0.000000,
[2,] 0.000000, 1.000000, 0.000000,
[3,] 0.000000, 0.000000, 1.000000,    * x <=
[0.200000, 0.200000, 0.200000]
```

10.2. Linear Programming

Linear programming (LP) is important in mathematical optimization. A number of algorithms for other types of optimization problems work by solving LP problems as subproblems. It is widely used in business, economics, and engineering. Industries that use LP models include transportation, energy, telecommunications, and manufacturing. It has been proven useful in modeling diverse types of problems in planning, routing, scheduling, assignment, and design. For example, management uses LP to maximize profits and minimize costs with limited resources. YouTube uses LP to stabilize videos. It is known that the optimal solution to an LP problem must be one of the vertices of the feasible region. Although you can use a brute-force approach to check all the vertices one by one and compare them in theory, it is not a practical approach. Some large-scale LP problems can involve as many as 12 million variables. There are many efficient algorithms to solve an LP problem. In this section, we introduce the basic simplex method, which is the primary method for solving LP problems.

10.2.1. Linear Programming Problems

The standard-form LP problem is stated as follows:

$$\min_{\boldsymbol{x}} f(\boldsymbol{x}) = \boldsymbol{c}^T \boldsymbol{x}$$

which is subject to the following:

$$\boldsymbol{A}\boldsymbol{x} = \boldsymbol{b}$$

$$\boldsymbol{x} \geq 0$$

where $\boldsymbol{c} \neq \boldsymbol{0}$ is an $n \times 1$ vector, n is the number of variables, $\boldsymbol{A}$ is a $p \times n$ matrix, p is the number of constraints, and $\boldsymbol{b}$ is a $p \times 1$ vector. It assumes that $\boldsymbol{A}$ is of full rank, that is, rank($\boldsymbol{A}$) = $p < n$. The objective function f and all constraints are linear functions.

For a fixed scalar β, $\boldsymbol{c}^T\boldsymbol{x} = \beta$ defines an affine (linear) manifold in the n-dimensional Euclidean space. When $n = 2$, it is a line. $\boldsymbol{c}^T\boldsymbol{x} = \beta_i$ for different β_i represents a family of parallel lines. The normal of these lines is $\boldsymbol{c}$, and therefore $\boldsymbol{c}$ is often referred to as the normal vector of the objective function.

In NM Dev, you can construct a standard-form LP problem using the `LPStandardProblem` class. The class signature is as follows:

```
public class LPStandardProblem extends LPProblemImpl1 {
    /**
     * Construct a linear programming problem in the standard form.
     *
     * @param c     the objective function
     * @param equal the equality constraints
     */
    public LPStandardProblem(Vector c, LinearEqualityConstraints equal);
}
```

For example, the following code snippet constructs this LP problem:

$$\min_{\boldsymbol{x}} f(\boldsymbol{x}) = -x_1 - x_2$$

Subject to the following:

$$\begin{bmatrix} 7 & 1 & 1 & 0 \\ -1 & 1 & 0 & 1 \end{bmatrix} \begin{bmatrix} x_1 \\ x_2 \\ x_3 \\ x_4 \end{bmatrix} = \begin{bmatrix} 15 \\ 1 \end{bmatrix}$$

$$\boldsymbol{x} \geq 0$$

```
// construct an LP problem in standard form
val problem1 = LPStandardProblem(
        DenseVector(-1.0, -1.0, 0.0, 0.0), // c
        LinearEqualityConstraints(
                DenseMatrix(
                    arrayOf(
                        doubleArrayOf(7.0, 1.0, 1.0, 0.0),
                        doubleArrayOf(-1.0, 1.0, 0.0, 1.0)
                    )
                ),
                DenseVector(15.0, 1.0) // b
        ))
println(problem1)
```

The output is as follows:

```
min. objective:
[-1.000000, -1.000000, 0.000000, 0.000000]
less-than-or-equal-to inequalities:
4x4
         [,1] [,2] [,3] [,4]
[1,] -7.000000, -1.000000, -1.000000, -0.000000,
[2,] 1.000000, -1.000000, -0.000000, -1.000000,
[3,] 7.000000, 1.000000, 1.000000, 0.000000,
[4,] -1.000000, 1.000000, 0.000000, 1.000000,  * x <=
[-15.000000, -1.000000, 15.000000, 1.000000]
equalities:
free variables:
```

Note that the output is actually in the canonical form of LP problem. The canonical form is stated as follows:

$$\min_{\boldsymbol{x}} f(\boldsymbol{x}) = \boldsymbol{c}^T \boldsymbol{x}$$

It's subject to inequality constraints:

$$\boldsymbol{A}\boldsymbol{x} \geq \boldsymbol{b}$$

$$\boldsymbol{x} \geq \boldsymbol{0}$$

A standard form, which has equality constraints, can be converted into a canonical form by writing the equality constraints into inequality constraints.

$$\boldsymbol{Ax} = \boldsymbol{b}$$

The previous is equivalent to this:

$$\begin{cases} \boldsymbol{Ax} \geq \boldsymbol{b} \\ \boldsymbol{Ax} \leq \boldsymbol{b} \end{cases}$$

The inequality constraints in the canonical form are therefore as follows:

$$\begin{bmatrix} \boldsymbol{A} \\ -\boldsymbol{A} \end{bmatrix} \boldsymbol{x} \geq \begin{bmatrix} \boldsymbol{b} \\ -\boldsymbol{b} \end{bmatrix}$$

Likewise, a canonical form can be converted into a standard form by introducing a p-dimensional slack vector variable $\boldsymbol{y}$ such that:

$$\boldsymbol{y} = \boldsymbol{Ax} - \boldsymbol{b} \geq 0$$

The original vector variable $\boldsymbol{x}$ can be decomposed into the positive part $\boldsymbol{x}^{+} \geq 0$ and the negative part $\boldsymbol{x}^{-} \geq 0$.

$$\boldsymbol{x} = \boldsymbol{x}^{+} - \boldsymbol{x}^{-}$$

Let:

$$\hat{\boldsymbol{x}} = \begin{bmatrix} \boldsymbol{x}^{+} \\ \boldsymbol{x}^{-} \\ \boldsymbol{y} \end{bmatrix},\ \hat{\boldsymbol{c}} = \begin{bmatrix} \boldsymbol{c} \\ -\boldsymbol{c} \\ \boldsymbol{0} \end{bmatrix},\ \hat{\boldsymbol{A}} = \begin{bmatrix} \boldsymbol{A} - \boldsymbol{A} - \boldsymbol{I}_p \end{bmatrix}$$

Then the equivalent LP problem in standard form is as follows:

$$\min_{\boldsymbol{x}} f(\boldsymbol{x}) = \hat{\boldsymbol{c}}^T \boldsymbol{x}$$

Subject to the following:

$$\hat{\boldsymbol{A}}\hat{\boldsymbol{x}} = \boldsymbol{b}$$

$$\hat{\boldsymbol{x}} \geq 0$$

The NM Dev class `LPCanonicalProblem1` constructs the canonical-form LP problem. The class signature is as follows:

```
public class LPCanonicalProblem1 extends LPProblemImpl1 {
    /**
     * Construct a linear programming problem in the canonical form.
     *
     * @param c the objective function
     * @param A the coefficients, <i>A</i>, of the greater-than-or-equal-to
     *          constraints <i>A * x &ge; b</i>
```

```
     * @param b the values, <i>b</i>, of the greater-than-or-equal-to
     *          constraints <i>A * x &ge; b</i>
     */
    public LPCanonicalProblem1(
            Vector c,
            Matrix A,
            Vector b
    );
    /**
     * Construct a linear programming problem in the canonical form.
     *
     * @param cost    the objective function
     * @param greater a collection of greater-than-or-equal-to constraints
     */
    public LPCanonicalProblem1(
            Vector cost,
            LinearGreaterThanConstraints greater
    );
    /**
     * Convert a linear programming problem from the 2nd canonical form to the
     * 1st canonical form.
     *
     * @param problem a linear programming problem in the 2nd canonical form
     */
    public LPCanonicalProblem1(LPCanonicalProblem2 problem);
    /**
     * Get the greater-than-or-equal-to constraints of the linear programming
     * problem.
     *
     * @return the greater-than-or-equal-to constraints
     */
    public LinearGreaterThanConstraints getGreaterThanConstraints();
}
```

The following code snippet constructs the same LP problem in canonical form:

```
// construct an LP problem in canonical form 1
val problem2 = LPCanonicalProblem1(
                DenseVector(-1.0, -1.0, 0.0, 0.0), // c
                DenseMatrix(
                    arrayOf(
                        doubleArrayOf(7.0, 1.0, 1.0, 0.0),
                        doubleArrayOf(-1.0, 1.0, 0.0, 1.0),
                        doubleArrayOf(-7.0, -1.0, -1.0, 0.0),
                        doubleArrayOf(1.0, -1.0, 0.0, -1.0),
                    )
                ),
                DenseVector(15.0, 1.0, -15.0, -1.0) // b
        )
println(problem2)
```

The output is as follows:

```
min. objective:
[-1.000000, -1.000000, 0.000000, 0.000000]
less-than-or-equal-to inequalities:
4x4
         [,1] [,2] [,3] [,4]
[1,] -7.000000, -1.000000, -1.000000, -0.000000,
[2,] 1.000000, -1.000000, -0.000000, -1.000000,
[3,] 7.000000, 1.000000, 1.000000, -0.000000,
[4,] -1.000000, 1.000000, -0.000000, 1.000000,   * x <=
[-15.000000, -1.000000, 15.000000, 1.000000]
equalities:
free variables:
```

It is the same as the last output constructed in standard form.

NM Dev provides another class, called `LPCanonicalProblem2`, to construct an LP problem in canonical form using less-than inequality constraints.

$$\min_{x} f(\boldsymbol{x}) = \boldsymbol{c}^T \boldsymbol{x}$$

This is subject to the following:

$$\boldsymbol{Ax} \leq \boldsymbol{b}$$

$$\boldsymbol{x} \geq \boldsymbol{0}$$

The following code snippet constructs the same LP problem shown previously:

```
// construct an LP problem in canonical form 2
// construct an LP problem in canonical form 2
val problem3 = LPCanonicalProblem2(
                DenseVector(-1.0, -1.0, 0.0, 0.0), // c
                DenseMatrix(
                    arrayOf(
                        doubleArrayOf(-7.0, -1.0, -1.0, 0.0),
                        doubleArrayOf(1.0, -1.0, 0.0, -1.0),
                        doubleArrayOf(7.0, 1.0, 1.0, 0.0),
                        doubleArrayOf(-1.0, 1.0, 0.0, 1.0),
                    )
                ),
                DenseVector(-15.0, -1.0, 15.0, 1.0) // b
        )
println(problem3)
```

The output is as follows:

```
min. objective:
[-1.000000, -1.000000, 0.000000, 0.000000]
less-than-or-equal-to inequalities:
4x4
          [,1] [,2] [,3] [,4]
[1,] -7.000000, -1.000000, -1.000000, 0.000000,
[2,] 1.000000, -1.000000, 0.000000, -1.000000,
[3,] 7.000000, 1.000000, 1.000000, 0.000000,
[4,] -1.000000, 1.000000, 0.000000, 1.000000,  * x <=
[-15.000000, -1.000000, 15.000000, 1.000000]
equalities:
free variables:
```

As another example, the following code snippet constructs this LP problem:

$$\min_{\boldsymbol{x}} f(\boldsymbol{x}) = x_1 + x_2$$

Subject to the following:

$$\begin{bmatrix} 1 & 1 \\ 1 & 2 \\ 0 & 3 \end{bmatrix} \begin{bmatrix} x_1 \\ x_2 \end{bmatrix} \le \begin{bmatrix} 150 \\ 170 \\ 180 \end{bmatrix}$$

$$\boldsymbol{x} \ge 0$$

```
// construct an LP problem in canonical form 2
val problem4 = LPCanonicalProblem2(
                DenseVector(1.0, 1.0), // c
                DenseMatrix(
                    arrayOf(
                        doubleArrayOf(1.0, 1.0),
                        doubleArrayOf(1.0, 2.0),
                        doubleArrayOf(0.0, 3.0)
                    )
                ),
                DenseVector(150.0, 170.0, 180.0) // b
        )
println(problem4)
```

The output is as follows:

```
min. objective:
[1.000000, 1.000000]
less-than-or-equal-to inequalities:
3x2
        [,1] [,2]
```

```
[1,] 1.000000, 1.000000,
[2,] 1.000000, 2.000000,
[3,] 0.000000, 3.000000,   * x <=
[150.000000, 170.000000, 180.000000]
equalities:
free variables:
```

Figure 10-5 plots the constraints. The feasible region is shaded.

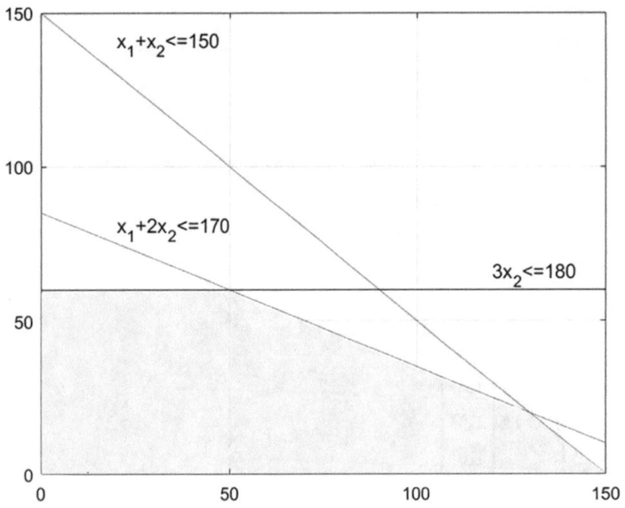

Figure 10-5. *A linear programming problem in canonical form*

10.2.2. First-Order Necessary Conditions

In mathematical optimization, the method of Lagrange multipliers is a strategy for finding the local maxima and minima of a function subject to equality constraints. It is a first-order derivative test for extrema. It relates the gradient of the objective function to the gradient of the equality constraints.

Suppose you want to solve this:

$$\min_{\boldsymbol{x}} f(\boldsymbol{x})$$

Subject to the following:

$$g(\boldsymbol{x}) = 0$$

You construct the Lagrangian function, a function of $\boldsymbol{x}$ and λ:

$$\mathcal{L}(\boldsymbol{x}, \lambda) = f(\boldsymbol{x}) - \lambda g(\boldsymbol{x})$$

The solution $\boldsymbol{x}^*$ corresponding to the original constrained optimization is always a saddle point[1] of the Lagrangian function. So, you get this:

$$\nabla \mathcal{L}\left(\boldsymbol{x}^*,\lambda^*\right)=\nabla f\left(\boldsymbol{x}^*\right)-\lambda^*\nabla g\left(\boldsymbol{x}^*\right)=0$$

$$\nabla f\left(\boldsymbol{x}^*\right)=\lambda^*\nabla g\left(\boldsymbol{x}^*\right)$$

For example, suppose you want to solve this:

$$\min_{x,y} f\left(x,y\right)=x+y$$

Subject to the following:

$$g\left(x,y\right)=x^2+y^2-1=0$$

The feasible set is the unit circle, and the level sets of f are diagonal lines (with slope −1). Figure 10-6 graphically shows that the minimum occurs at $\left(-\frac{\sqrt{2}}{2},-\frac{\sqrt{2}}{2}\right)$.

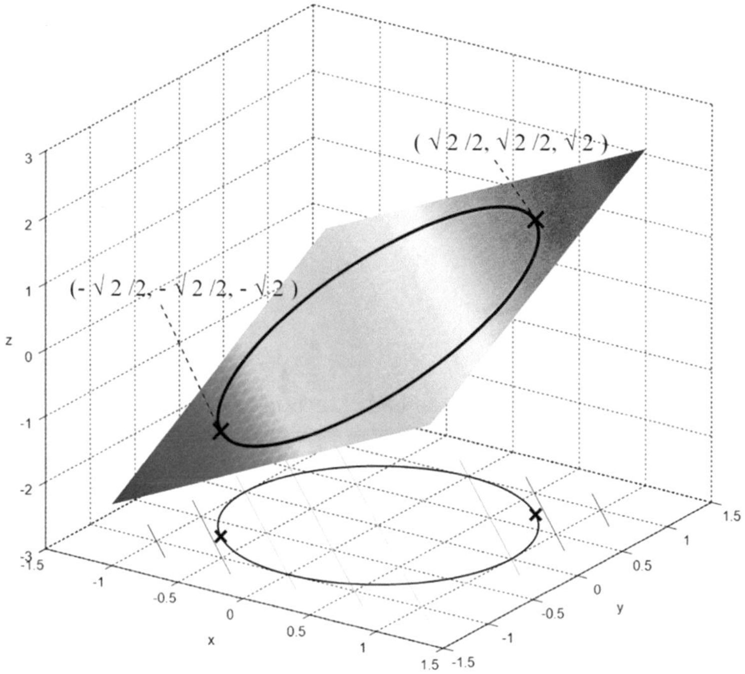

Figure 10-6. *A minimization problem with an equality constraint*

[1] A saddle point or minimax point is a point on the surface of the graph of a function where the slopes (derivatives) in orthogonal directions are all zero (a critical point), but which is not a local extremum of the function.

Applying the Lagrange multipliers, you get the following:

$$\mathcal{L}(x,y,\lambda) = f(x,y) + \lambda g(x,y)$$

$$= x + y + \lambda\left(x^2 + y^2 - 1\right)$$

The gradient is as follows:

$$\nabla\mathcal{L}(x,y,\lambda) = \left(\frac{\partial\mathcal{L}}{\partial x}, \frac{\partial\mathcal{L}}{\partial y}, \frac{\partial\mathcal{L}}{\partial\lambda},\right)$$

$$= \left(1 + 2\lambda x, 1 + 2\lambda y, x^2 + y^2 - 1\right)$$

Solving $\nabla L(x, y, \lambda) = 0$ gives the following:

$$\begin{cases} 1 + 2\lambda x = 0 \\ 1 + 2\lambda y = 0 \\ x^2 + y^2 - 1 = 0 \end{cases}$$

Or equivalently:

$$\begin{cases} x = -\frac{\sqrt{2}}{2} \\ y = -\frac{\sqrt{2}}{2} \\ \lambda = \frac{1}{\sqrt{2}} \end{cases}$$

Therefore, $f\left(-\frac{\sqrt{2}}{2}, -\frac{\sqrt{2}}{2}\right) = -\sqrt{2}$ is the minimum.

The Karush-Kuhn-Tucker (KKT) conditions generalize the method of Lagrange multipliers to account for also inequality constraints. Similar to the Lagrange approach, the constrained minimization (maximization) problem is rewritten as a Lagrange function whose optimal point is a saddle point, that is, a global minimum (maximum) over the domain of the choice variables and a global minimum (maximum) over the multipliers. The KKT conditions state that if $\boldsymbol{x}^*$ is a local minimizer to the following problem:

$$\min_{\boldsymbol{x}} f(\boldsymbol{x})$$

Subject to the following:

$$a_i(\boldsymbol{x}) = 0, i = 1,2,\ldots p$$

$$c_j(\boldsymbol{x}) \geq 0, j = 1,2,\ldots q$$

then there exist Lagrange multipliers $\boldsymbol{\lambda}^*$ and $\boldsymbol{\mu}^*$ such that the following Lagrangian function:

$$\mathcal{L}(\boldsymbol{x},\lambda,\mu) = f(\boldsymbol{x}) - \lambda a(\boldsymbol{x}) - \mu c(\boldsymbol{x})$$

has a saddle point at $\boldsymbol{x}^*$. That is:

$$\nabla \mathcal{L}\left(\boldsymbol{x}^*, \lambda^*, \mu^*\right) = \nabla f\left(\boldsymbol{x}^*\right) - \lambda^* \nabla a\left(\boldsymbol{x}^*\right) - \mu^* \nabla c\left(\boldsymbol{x}^*\right) = 0$$

Or:

$$\nabla f\left(\boldsymbol{x}^*\right) = \lambda^* \nabla a\left(\boldsymbol{x}^*\right) + \mu^* \nabla c\left(\boldsymbol{x}^*\right)$$

Moreover:

$$\lambda^* a\left(\boldsymbol{x}^*\right) = 0$$

$$\mu^* c\left(\boldsymbol{x}^*\right) = 0$$

And:

$$\mu_j^* \geq 0, j = 1,2,\ldots q$$

Consequently, for the inactive constraints $c_j(\boldsymbol{x}^*) > 0$, μ_j^* needs to be 0.

For example, suppose, for simplicity, that the optimization problem has no equality constraint and only one inequality constraint. If the minimizer $\boldsymbol{x}^*$ is inside the feasible region, R, defined by c_1, then c_1 is an inactive constraint. $\mu_1^* = 0$. Otherwise, if the minimizer is on the boundary of c_1, that is, $c_1(\boldsymbol{x}^*) = 0$, then $\mu_1^* > 0$. $\nabla f\left(\mathbf{x}^*\right) = \mu_1^* \nabla c_1\left(\mathbf{x}^*\right)$. The gradient of f and c must be pointing the same direction toward the interior of R, as in Figure 10-7.

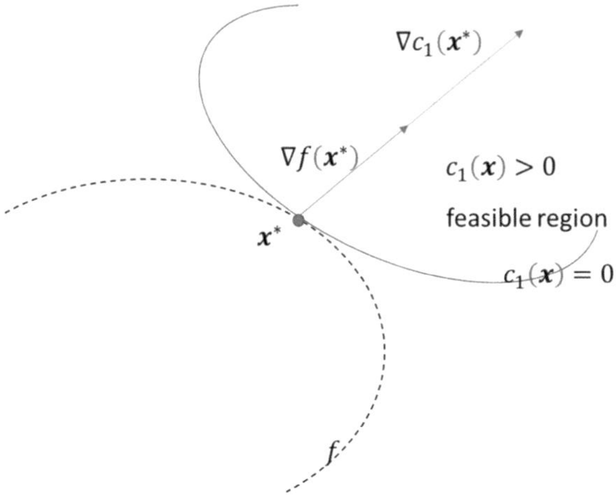

Figure 10-7. *x^* is a minimizer on the boundary of an inequality constraint*

10.2.3. Simplex Method

When you apply the KKT conditions to the standard form of LP problem, as follows:

$$\min_{x} f(\boldsymbol{x}) = \boldsymbol{c}^T \boldsymbol{x}$$

Subject to the following:

$$\boldsymbol{Ax} = \boldsymbol{b}$$

$$\boldsymbol{x} \geq 0$$

You get this:

$$\boldsymbol{c} = \boldsymbol{A}^T \lambda^* + \mu^*$$

And:

$$\mu_i^* x_i^* = 0, 1 \leq i \leq n$$

An immediate observation is that a solution $\boldsymbol{x}^*$ cannot be in the interior of the feasible region. If it were, then there would be no active constraint, $\boldsymbol{\mu}^* = \mathbf{0}$. Then you would have the following:

$$\boldsymbol{c} = \boldsymbol{A}^T \lambda^*$$

The n-dimensional vector $\boldsymbol{c}$ would lie in the p-dimensional subspace spanned by the p columns of $\boldsymbol{A}^T$. Since $p < n$, this is highly unlikely unless the solution is on the boundary. Therefore, any solutions of an LP problem are likely to be located on the boundary of feasible region, that is, on those edges defined by the inequality constraints.

Furthermore, if a candidate solution is on the boundary of the feasible region, you can simply move along the boundary to decrease the objective function value. In other words, starting with a candidate solution on the boundary, you can slide down the edge to find a smaller value until you reach the end of the edge, namely, a vertex. See Figure 10-8.

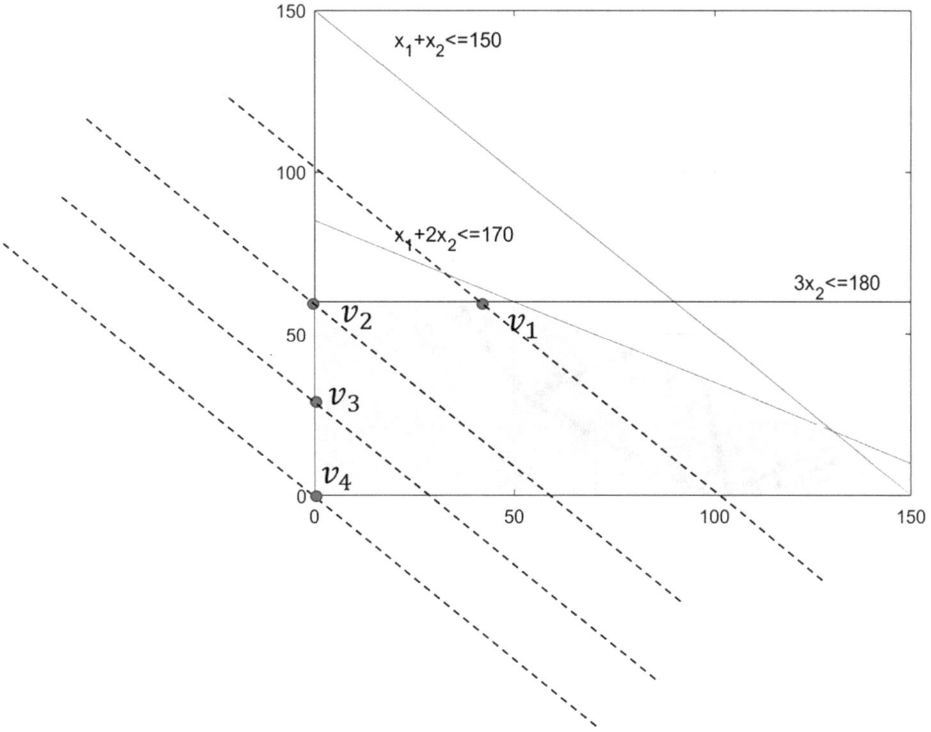

Figure 10-8. *A solution to an LP problem must be on a vertex*

For the example in Figure 10-8, suppose you start at v_1. You can move (left) in the direction that the function is decreasing in value. When you reach a vertex v_2, you switch to another edge and continue to slide down in the direction that the function is decreasing in value to v_3 and then finally v_4. v_4 is a vertex where the edge ends. Moving to another edge from this vertex no longer decreases the function value. Indeed, you have found the minimizer $v_4 = (0, 0)$. It is easy to see that $x_1 + x_2 = 0 + 0 = 0$ is the solution to this problem.

It can be shown that for a linear problem in standard form, if the objective function has a minimum value in the feasible region, then it has this value on (at least) one of the vertices. This reduces the problem to a finite computation since there are a finite number of vertices. You could, in principle, check all the values at all the vertices to find the minimum. See Figure 10-9.

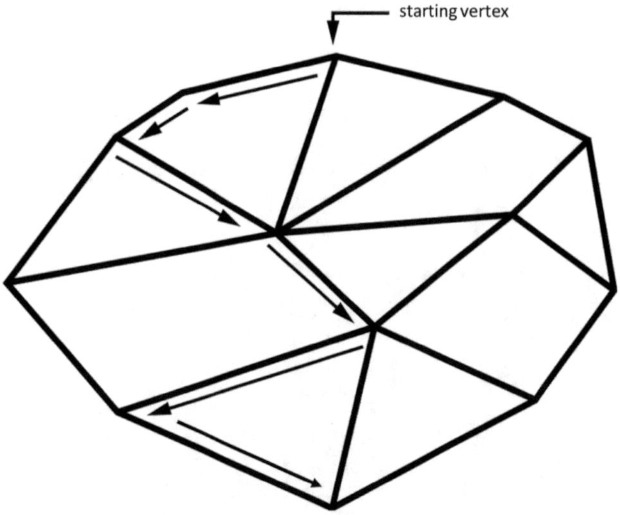

Figure 10-9. *A system of linear inequalities defines a polytope as a feasible region. The simplex algorithm begins at a starting vertex and moves along the edges of the polytope until it reaches the vertex of the optimal solution*

It can also be shown that, if a vertex is not a minimum point of the objective function, then there is an edge containing the vertex so that the value of the objective function is strictly decreasing on the edge moving away from the vertex. If the edge is finite, then the edge connects to another vertex where the objective function has a smaller value; otherwise, the objective function is unbounded below on the edge and the linear problem has no solution. The simplex method applies this insight by walking along edges of the polytope (the feasible region defined by the constraints) to vertices with smaller and smaller objective values. This continues until the minimum value is reached or an unbounded edge is visited (concluding that the problem has no solution). The algorithm always terminates because the number of vertices in the polytope is finite. Moreover, since you jump between vertices always in the same direction (that of the objective function), you hope that the number of vertices visited will be small.

For an LP problem in canonical form, as shown here:

$$\min_{\boldsymbol{x}} f(\boldsymbol{x}) = \boldsymbol{c}^T \boldsymbol{x}$$

Subject to the following:

$$\boldsymbol{Ax} \geq \boldsymbol{b}$$

$$\mathbf{x} \geq \mathbf{0}$$

It can be converted into the standard form by introducing slack variables $\boldsymbol{x}_B$, as shown here:

$$\boldsymbol{x}_B = \boldsymbol{Ax}_N - \boldsymbol{b}$$

(Here we write the original variables $\boldsymbol{x}$ as $\boldsymbol{x}_N$.)

The equivalent LP problem in standard form is as follows:

$$\min_{\boldsymbol{x}_N, \boldsymbol{x}_B} \boldsymbol{c}^T \boldsymbol{x}_N + \boldsymbol{0}^T \boldsymbol{x}_B$$

Subject to the following:

$$\boldsymbol{x}_B = \boldsymbol{A}\boldsymbol{x}_N - \boldsymbol{b}$$

$$\boldsymbol{x}_N, \boldsymbol{x}_B \geq \boldsymbol{0}$$

Here, $\boldsymbol{N} = \{1, 2, \ldots, n\}$ is the set of indices for the original variables and $\boldsymbol{B} = \{n + 1, \ldots, n + m\}$ is the set of indices for the slack variables.

We will represent the standard LP problem using the following tableau:

$$\begin{array}{ccccccc} & & x_1 & \cdots & x_n & 1 \\ x_{n+1} & = & A_{11} & & A_{1n} & -b_1 \\ \vdots & & & & & \\ x_{n+m} & = & A_{m1} & & A_{mn} & -b_m \\ f & = & c_1 & & c_n & 0 \end{array}$$

The way to read this tableau is that the leftmost column has the dependent variables (or basic variables), and the topmost row has the independent variables (or nonbasic variables). Here's an example:

$$x_{n+i} = A_{i1}x_1 + \ldots + A_{in}x_n - b_i$$

$$f = c_1x_1 + \ldots + c_nx_n + 0$$

In condensed form, the tableau is as follows:

$$\begin{array}{cccc} & & \boldsymbol{x}_N & \boldsymbol{1} \\ \boldsymbol{x}_B & = & \boldsymbol{A} & -\boldsymbol{b} \\ f & = & \mathbf{c}^T & \boldsymbol{0} \end{array}$$

Ferris, Mangasarian, & Wright (2007) provide the following example:

$$\min_{x_1, x_2} 3x_1 - 6x_2$$

Subject to the following:

$$\begin{cases} x_1 + 2x_2 \geq -1 \\ 2x_1 + x_2 \geq 0 \\ x_1 - x_2 \geq -1 \\ x_1 - 4x_2 \geq -13 \\ -4x_1 + x_2 \geq -23 \\ x_1, x_2 \geq 0 \end{cases}$$

The slack variables for the constraints are as follows:

$$\begin{cases} x_3 = x_1 + 2x_2 + 1 \\ x_4 = 2x_1 + x_2 \\ x_5 = x_1 - x_2 + 1 \\ x_6 = x_1 - 4x_2 + 13 \\ x_7 = -4x_1 + x_2 + 23 \end{cases}$$

The NM Dev class called `SimplexTable` constructs the simplex tableau for an LP problem. Here's an example:

```
// construct an LP problem
val problem = LPCanonicalProblem1(
        DenseVector(3.0, -6.0), // c
        DenseMatrix(
            arrayOf(
                doubleArrayOf(1.0, 2.0),
                doubleArrayOf(2.0, 1.0),
                doubleArrayOf(1.0, -1.0),
                doubleArrayOf(1.0, -4.0),
                doubleArrayOf(-4.0, 1.0)
            )
        ),
        DenseVector(-1.0, 0.0, -1.0, -13.0, -23.0) // b
)

var tableau = SimplexTable(problem)
println(tableau)
```

The output is as follows:

	x,1	x,2	B,2147483647
x_slack,1	1.000000	2.000000	1.000000
x_slack,2	2.000000	1.000000	-0.000000
x_slack,3	1.000000	-1.000000	1.000000
x_slack,4	1.000000	-4.000000	13.000000
x_slack,5	-4.000000	1.000000	23.000000
COST,2147483647	3.000000	-6.000000	0.000000

In this initial tableau, `x,1` is x_1, and `x,2` is x_2. The five `x_slack` variables are the slack variables for the five inequality constraints. See Figure 10-10.

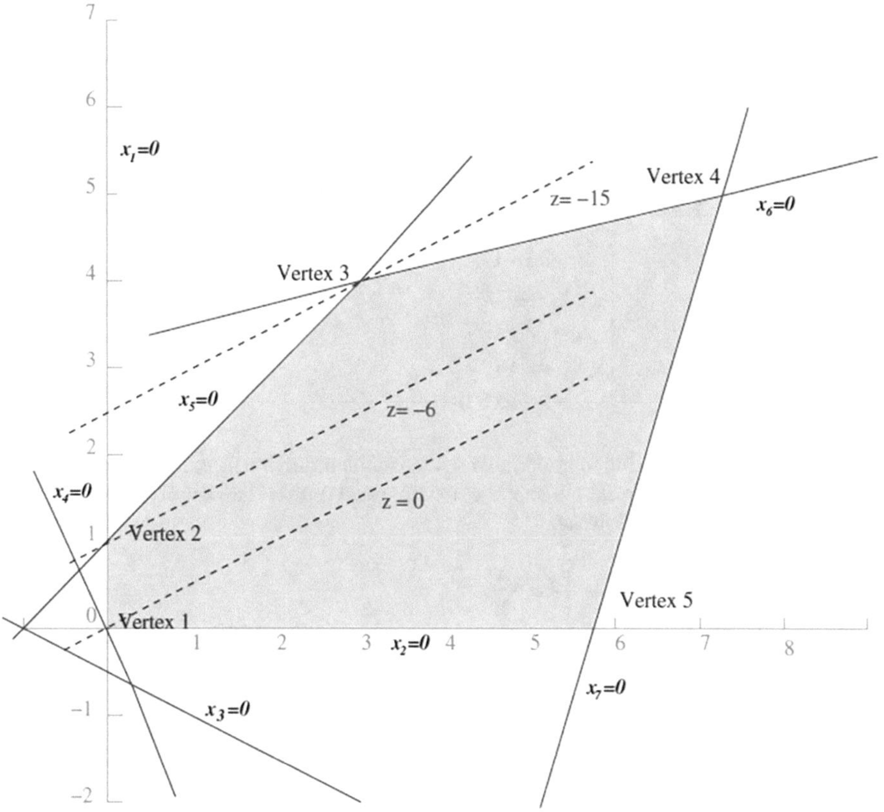

Figure 10-10. *The vertices are intersections of constraints (Ferris, Mangasarian, & Wright, 2007)*

Each vertex in the polytope of the feasible region is the intersection of n hyperplanes defined by the n corresponding constraints. Figure 10-8 shows the vertices as intersections of the constraints. It can be proved that this is equivalent to setting all n nonbasic variables to 0, that is, $\boldsymbol{x}_N = \mathbf{0}$. For example, the initial tableau shown earlier corresponds to the vertex at the origin of the coordinate system such that all original variables are 0, that is, $\boldsymbol{x} = \boldsymbol{x}_N = \mathbf{0}$. For this $\boldsymbol{x}$ to be feasible (not violating any constraints), the slack variables in $\boldsymbol{x}_B = -\boldsymbol{b}$ must be non-negative. That is, $\boldsymbol{b} \le \mathbf{0}$. In this case, the objective value $f(\mathbf{0}) = 0$.

To examine another (adjacent) vertex, you can swap a nonbasic variable with a basic variable, effectively increasing the value of a nonbasic variable from 0 to a positive value and at the same time setting a basic variable to 0. For example, say you need to move away from $\boldsymbol{x} = (x_1, x_2) = (0, 0)$ to the next vertex. You can increase the values of the variables only because of the non-negativity constraints of them in a standard LP problem. For example, you can try to increase x_1.

$$x_1 = \lambda > 0$$

Then, the objective value becomes as follows:

$$f = 3\lambda - 6(0) = 3\lambda > 0$$

Increasing x_1 actually increases f, which is exactly the opposite of what you want. So, you can try this:

$$x_2 = \lambda > 0$$

For this choice, you get the following:

$$f = 3(0) - 6\lambda = -6\lambda < 0$$

The process of choosing a nonbasic variable or a pivot column is called *pricing*. The pivot column is called the entering variable because it is "entering" the basic variables.

To determine which basic variable to swap out with the entering variable, you need to examine the effect of increasing the entering variable on each basic variable. For this example, you get the following:

$$\begin{cases} x_3 = 2\lambda + 1 \geq 0 \\ x_4 = \lambda \geq 0 \\ x_5 = -\lambda + 1 \geq 0 \\ x_6 = -4\lambda + 13 \geq 0 \\ x_7 = \lambda + 23 \geq 0 \end{cases}$$

You should try to make λ as big as possible to maximally decrease the objective function value, but it cannot be too big so that some of the basic variables become negative and thus violate the constraints. The non-negativity constraints translate to the following:

$$\begin{cases} \lambda \geq -\frac{1}{2} \\ \lambda \geq 0 \\ \lambda \leq 1 \\ \lambda \leq \frac{13}{4} \\ \lambda \geq -23 \end{cases}$$

The largest non-negative value that λ can take without violating any of these constraints is $\lambda = 1$. Moreover, observe that the blocking variable, namely, the one that will become negative if you increase λ above its limit of 1, is x_5. Therefore, you should choose x_5 as the pivot row.

The process of choosing a basic variable or a pivot row is called a *ratio test*. The pivot row is called the leaving variable because it is "leaving" the basic variables to become a nonbasic variable and to take value 0.

You use Jordan exchange to swap x_5 (row 3) and x_2 (column 2) in the tableau. For a linear system, Jordan exchange is an operation that swaps one of the independent variables with one of the dependent variables. Consider this simple example:

$$y = ax$$

To reverse the role of x and y, write the following:

$$x = \tilde{a}y, \tilde{a} = \frac{1}{a}$$

You can generalize this idea to the multivariate case where the independent variables $\boldsymbol{x} \in \mathbb{R}^n$ and the dependent variables $\boldsymbol{y} \in \mathbb{R}^m$. To be more specific, suppose you have this:

$$y_i = A_{i1}x_1 + A_{i2}x_2 + \ldots + A_{in}x_n, i = 1, \ldots, m$$

Equivalently, in tableau form, suppose you have this:

$$\begin{array}{ccccccc} & & x_1 & \cdots & x_s & \cdots & x_n \\ y_1 & = & A_{11} & \cdots & A_{1s} & \cdots & A_{1n} \\ \vdots & & \vdots & & \vdots & & \vdots \\ y_r & = & A_{r1} & & A_{rs} & & A_{rn} \\ \vdots & & \vdots & & \vdots & & \vdots \\ y_m & = & A_{m1} & & A_{ms} & & A_{mn} \end{array}$$

Swapping row r (y_r) with column s (x_s) means that you write x_s in terms of y_r and leave the other x_i unchanged. This can be done by solving a system of linear equations for x_s. The resultant tableau looks like this:

$$\begin{array}{ccccccccc} & & x_1 & \cdots & x_{s-1} & y_r & x_{s+1} & \cdots & x_n \\ y_1 & = & B_{11} & \cdots & & B_{1s} & & \cdots & B_{1n} \\ \vdots & & \vdots & & & \vdots & & & \vdots \\ y_{r-1} & & & & & & & & \\ x_s & = & B_{r1} & & & B_{rs} & & & B_{rn} \\ y_{r+1} & & & & & & & & \\ \vdots & & \vdots & & & \vdots & & & \vdots \\ y_m & = & B_{m1} & & & B_{ms} & & & B_{mn} \end{array}$$

This code performs the Jordan exchange to swap row 3 (x_5) with column 2 (x_2) in this example.

```
tableau = tableau.swap(3, 2)
println(tableau)
```

The output is as follows:

```
6x3
                    x,1                 x_slack,3           B,2147483647
x_slack,1           3.000000            -2.000000           3.000000
x_slack,2           3.000000            -1.000000           1.000000
x,2                 1.000000            -1.000000           1.000000
x_slack,4           -3.000000           4.000000            9.000000
x_slack,5           -3.000000           -1.000000           24.000000
COST,2147483647     -3.000000           6.000000            -6.000000
```

The objective function value has decreased from 0 to -6.

By repeating the processes of pricing and ratio test, you test the next vertices until the optimal solution is found (or proved no solution). Note that the bottom row of the tableau contains the coefficients of the current nonbasic variables. It is the decrease in f per unit increase in the variable. A rule of thumb is therefore to choose the column with the most negative coefficient in the pricing process. In this example, it will be x_1 next (with the coefficient -3).

This code performs the swapping row 4 (x_6) with column 1 (x_1).

```
tableau = tableau.swap(4, 1)
println(tableau)
```

The output is as follows:

```
6x3
                    x_slack,4       x_slack,3       B,2147483647
x_slack,1           -1.000000       2.000000        12.000000
x_slack,2           -1.000000       3.000000        10.000000
x,2                 3.000000        0.333333        4.000000
x,1                 3.000000        1.333333        3.000000
x_slack,5           1.000000        -5.000000       15.000000
COST,2147483647     1.000000        2.000000        -15.000000
```

Now that all coefficients in the bottom rows are positive, you can read the solution of the LP problem from the last column in the tableau.

$$f(3,4) = 3(3) - 6(4) = -15$$

This simplex algorithm is efficient to solve LP problems. It is an iterative method that updates a feasible point (a vertex in feasible region) until an optimum is reached. It finds the next vertex by performing a linear transformation on the matrix corresponding to the linear system of constraint equations. Therefore, it usually involves two phases to solve an LP problem. The first phase is to find a feasible starting point that satisfies all constraints. That is, it finds a tableau such that the last column is non-negative. In the previous example, if the LP problem is in standard form, it means that the origin ($\boldsymbol{x} = \boldsymbol{0}$) satisfies all constraints. The second phase starts with a feasible tableau and applies a sequence of linear transformations until the optimal tableau is found.

To find a feasible starting point, you will see how to solve a related LP problem, called the Phase 1 LP problem. It should be easy to identify an initial feasible point for this Phase 1 problem, and its solution should give you a feasible point to the original problem. Specifically, given a standard LP problem, as shown here:

$$\min_{\boldsymbol{x}} f(\boldsymbol{x}) = \boldsymbol{c}^T \boldsymbol{x}$$

Subject to the following:

$$\boldsymbol{A}\boldsymbol{x} = \boldsymbol{b}$$

$$\boldsymbol{x} \geq 0$$

You can construct the Phase 1 LP problem by introducing one additional artificial variable x_0 and slack variables x_{n+i} as such:

$$\min_{x_0, \boldsymbol{x}} f(\boldsymbol{x}) = x_0$$

Subject to the following:

$$x_{n+i} = \boldsymbol{A_i x} - b_i + x_0, b_i > 0$$

$$x_{n+i} = \boldsymbol{A_i x} - b_i, b_i \le 0$$

$$x_0, x_{n+i}, \mathbf{x} \ge 0$$

First, the objective function is bounded below, so the minimum solution is $f = x_0 = 0$. Second, there is an obvious feasible point for the Phase 1 LP problem, as shown here:

$$x_0 = \max\left(\max_{1 \le i \le m} b_i, 0\right)$$

And here:

$$\boldsymbol{x_N} = \boldsymbol{x} = \boldsymbol{0}$$

The slack variables are then as follows:

$$b_i > 0 \Rightarrow x_{n+i} = \boldsymbol{A_i x} - b_i + x_0 = -b_i + \max_{1 \le i \le m} b_i \ge 0$$

$$b_i \le 0 \Rightarrow x_{n+i} = \boldsymbol{A_i x} - b_i = -b_i \ge 0$$

So, $\boldsymbol{x_B} \ge \boldsymbol{0}$, satisfying all constraints.

Third, if there exists a feasible point $\bar{\boldsymbol{x}}$ for the original problem, then the point $(x_0, \boldsymbol{x}) = (0, \bar{\boldsymbol{x}})$ is feasible for the Phase 1 problem because $\boldsymbol{x_B} \ge \boldsymbol{0}$.

Fourth, if $(0, \bar{\boldsymbol{x}})$ is a solution to the Phase 1 problem, then $\bar{\boldsymbol{x}}$ is a feasible point for the original problem. Because this is true:

$$b_i > 0 \Rightarrow 0 \le x_{n+i} = \boldsymbol{A_i x} - b_i + x_0 = \boldsymbol{A_i x} - b_i$$

$$b_i \le 0 \Rightarrow 0 \le x_{n+i} = \boldsymbol{A_i x} - b_i$$

You get this:

$$\boldsymbol{Ax} \ge \boldsymbol{b}$$

which satisfies all the constraints in the original problem.

Finally, if $(x_0, \boldsymbol{x})$ is a solution to the Phase 1 problem and $x_0 > 0$, then the original problem must be infeasible.

You can solve the Phase 1 problem using the simplex method described earlier. The NM Dev class called `FerrisMangasarianWrightPhase1` implements this Phase 1 procedure to find a feasible table from an infeasible one by pivoting the simplex table of the related Phase 1 problem. Here's an example:

$$\min 4x_1 + 5x_2$$

Subject to the following:

$$\begin{cases} x_1 + x_2 \geq -1 \\ x_1 + 2x_2 \geq 1 \\ 4x_1 + 2x_2 \geq 8 \\ -x_1 - x_2 \geq -3 \\ -x_1 + x_2 \geq 1 \\ x_1, x_2 \geq 0 \end{cases}$$

```
// construct an LP problem
problem = LPProblemImpl1(
        DenseVector(4.0, 5.0), // c
        LinearGreaterThanConstraints(
                DenseMatrix(
                    arrayOf(
                        doubleArrayOf(1.0, 1.0),
                        doubleArrayOf(1.0, 2.0),
                        doubleArrayOf(4.0, 2.0),
                        doubleArrayOf(-1.0, -1.0),
                        doubleArrayOf(-1.0, 1.0)
                    )
                ),
                DenseVector(-1.0, 1.0, 8.0, -3.0, 1.0)), // b
        null, // less-than constraints
        null, // equality constraints
        null) // box constraints
table0 = SimplexTable(problem)
println("tableau for the original problem:")
println(table0)

val phase1 = FerrisMangasarianWrightPhase1(table0)
val table1 = phase1.process()
println("tableau for the phase 1 problem:")
println(table1)

println(String.format("minimum = %f%n", table1.minimum()))
println(String.format("minimizer = %s%n", table1.minimizer()))
```

The output is as follows:

```
tableau for the original problem:

6x3
                    x,1                x,2                B,2147483647
x_slack,1           1.000000           1.000000           1.000000
x_slack,2           1.000000           2.000000           -1.000000
x_slack,3           4.000000           2.000000           -8.000000
x_slack,4           -1.000000          -1.000000          3.000000
x_slack,5           -1.000000          1.000000           -1.000000
                    4.000000           5.000000           0.000000

tableau for the original problem:
6x3
                          x_slack,3          x_slack,5          B,2147483647
x_slack,1                 0.333333           0.333333           4.000000
x_slack,2                 0.500000           1.000000           4.000000
x,2                       0.166667           0.666667           2.000000
x_slack,4                 -0.333333          -0.333333          0.000000
x,1                       0.166667           -0.333333          1.000000
COST,2147483647           1.500000           2.000000           14.000000

minimum = 14.000000
minimizer = [1.000000, 2.000000]
```

You have found a feasible point to the original problem, $\boldsymbol{x} = (1, 2)$. The minimum $f(\boldsymbol{x}) = 14$ for the original problem.

In NM Dev, a simplex solver implements the `LPSimplexSolver` interface.

```
public interface LPSimplexSolver<P extends LPProblem>
        extends LPSolver<P, LPSimplexSolution> {
    /**
     * Solve an LP problem by a simplex algorithm on a simplex table
     *
     * @param table the initial simplex table corresponding to the LP problem
     * @return an LP solution
     * @throws Exception when there is an error
     */
    public LPSimplexSolution solve(SimplexTable table) throws Exception;
}
```

The `LPTwoPhaseSolver` class implements the two-phase algorithm described in this section. It takes an LP problem in the form of `LPProblem` and outputs a solution in the form of `LPSimplexSolution`. The class signature is as follows:

```
public class LPTwoPhaseSolver implements LPSimplexSolver<LPProblem> {
    private class Solution implements LPSimplexSolution {
......
    }
    private final LPSimplexSolver<LPCanonicalProblem1> solver;//a canonical LP solver
    /**
     * Construct an LP solver to solve LP problems.
     *
     * @param solver a canonical LP solver
     */
    public LPTwoPhaseSolver(LPSimplexSolver<LPCanonicalProblem1> solver) {
        this.solver = solver;
    }
    /**
     * Construct an LP solver to solve LP problems.
     */
    public LPTwoPhaseSolver() {
        this(new LPCanonicalSolver());
    }
    @Override
    public LPSimplexSolution solve(SimplexTable table) throws LPInfeasible, Exception {
        return new Solution(table);
    }
    @Override
    public LPSimplexSolution solve(LPProblem problem) throws LPInfeasible, Exception {
        return solve(new SimplexTable(problem));
    }
}
```

Continuing with the earlier example, the following code solves the LP problem using the two-phase algorithm:

```
// construct an LP problem
var problem = LPProblemImpl1(
        DenseVector(4.0, 5.0), // c
        LinearGreaterThanConstraints(
                DenseMatrix(
                    arrayOf(
                        doubleArrayOf(1.0, 1.0),
                        doubleArrayOf(1.0, 2.0),
                        doubleArrayOf(4.0, 2.0),
                        doubleArrayOf(-1.0, -1.0),
                        doubleArrayOf(-1.0, 1.0)
                    )
                ),
                DenseVector(-1.0, 1.0, 8.0, -3.0, 1.0)), // b
        null, // less-than constraints
        null, // equality constraints
        null) // box constraints
```

```
// construct the simplex tableau for the LP problem
var table0 = SimplexTable(problem)
println("simplex tableau for the problem:")
println(table0)

// solve the LP problem using the 2-phase algorithm
val solver = LPTwoPhaseSolver()
val solution = solver.solve(problem).minimizer() as LPBoundedMinimizer

println(String.format("minimum = %f%n", solution.minimum()))
println(String.format("minimizer = %s%n", solution.minimizer()))
```

The output is as follows:

```
simplex tableau for the problem:
6x3

                        x,1             x,2             B,2147483647
x_slack,1               1.000000        1.000000        1.000000
x_slack,2               1.000000        2.000000        -1.000000
x_slack,3               4.000000        2.000000        -8.000000
x_slack,4               -1.000000       -1.000000       3.000000
x_slack,5               -1.000000       1.000000        -1.000000
COST,2147483647         4.000000        5.000000        0.000000

minimum = 14.000000
minimizer = [1.000000, 2.000000]
```

It turns out that $f(1, 2) = 14$ is indeed the solution to the original problem.

As another example, the following code solves this LP problem in Chen, Batson, & Dang (2009):

$$\min_{x_1,x_2} -5x_1 + 2x_2$$

Subject to the following:

$$\begin{cases} x_1 + 3x_2 \geq 9 \\ -x_1 + 2x_2 \leq 5 \\ 3x_1 + 2x_2 \geq 19 \end{cases}$$

```
// construct an LP problem
val problem = LPProblemImpl1(
        DenseVector(-5.0, 2.0), // c
        LinearGreaterThanConstraints(
                DenseMatrix(
```

```
                arrayOf(
                    doubleArrayOf(1.0, 3.0)
                )
            ),
            DenseVector(9.0)), // b1
        LinearLessThanConstraints(
            DenseMatrix(
                arrayOf(
                    doubleArrayOf(-1.0, 2.0),
                    doubleArrayOf(3.0, 2.0)
                )
            ),
            DenseVector(5.0, 19.0)), // b2
        null,
        null)

// construct the simplex tableau for the LP problem
val table0 = SimplexTable(problem)
println("simplex tableau for the problem:")
println(table0)

// solve the LP problem using the 2-phase algorithm
val solver = LPTwoPhaseSolver()
val solution: LPMinimizer = solver.solve(problem).minimizer()

println(String.format("minimum = %f%n", solution.minimum()))
println(String.format("minimizer = %s%n", solution.minimizer()))
```

The output is as follows:

```
simplex tableau for the problem:
4x3

                            x,1             x,2             B,2147483647
x_slack,1                   1.000000        3.000000        -9.000000
x_slack,2                   1.000000        -2.000000       5.000000
x_slack,3                   -3.000000       -2.000000       19.000000
COST,2147483647             -5.000000       2.000000        0.000000

minimum = -25.571429
minimizer = [5.571429, 1.142857]
```

The optimal solution is $f\left(\frac{39}{7},\frac{8}{7}\right)=-25.57$.

As another example, the following code solves this LP problem in Ferris, Mangasarian, & Wright (2007).

$$\min_{x_1,x_2} 2x_1 - x_2$$

Subject to the following:

$$\begin{cases} x_1 \geq -6 \\ -x_1 = -4 \\ x_1 \geq 0 \end{cases}$$

```
// construct an LP problem
fun problem(): LPProblem {
    // min c'x
    val c: Vector = DenseVector(2.0, -1.0)

    // the constraints
    // Ax >= b
    val greaterThanConstraints = LinearGreaterThanConstraints(
        DenseMatrix(arrayOf(doubleArrayOf(1.0, 0.0))), // A
        DenseVector(-6.0)) // b
    val lessThanConstraints: LinearLessThanConstraints? = null // no less than constraints
    // Ax = b
    val equalityConstraints = LinearEqualityConstraints(
        DenseMatrix(arrayOf(doubleArrayOf(-1.0, 0.0))), // A
        DenseVector(-4.0)) // b
    // the whole plane
    val boxConstraints = BoxConstraints(
        2,
        BoxConstraints.Bound(2, Double.NEGATIVE_INFINITY, Double.POSITIVE_INFINITY)
    )

    // construct an LP problem with constraints
    val problem: LPProblem = LPProblemImpl1(
        c,
        greaterThanConstraints,
        lessThanConstraints,
        equalityConstraints,
        boxConstraints
    ) // x2 is free
    return problem
}

// construct the simplex tableau for the LP problem
val table0 = SimplexTable(problem())
println("simplex tableau for the problem:")
println(table0)

// solve the LP problem using the 2-phase algorithm
val solver = LPTwoPhaseSolver()
val solution: LPMinimizer = solver.solve(problem()).minimizer()

println(String.format("minimum = %f%n", solution.minimum()))
println(String.format("minimizer = %s%n", solution.minimizer()))
```

The output is as follows:

```
simplex tableau for the problem:
3x3

                            x,1                 FREE,2              B,2147483647
x_slack,1                   1.000000            0.000000            6.000000

EQUALITY,1                  -1.000000           0.000000            4.000000

COST,2147483647             2.000000            -1.000000           0.000000

minimum = -Infinity
minimizer = [0.000000, 1.000000]
```

It turns out that this problem is unbounded below.

In yet another example, the following code solves this LP problem in Ferris, Mangasarian, & Wright (2007):

$$\min_{x_1, x_2} 2x_1 - x_2$$

Subject to the following:

$$\begin{cases} x_1 - 2x_2 \geq -2 \\ x_1 = 4 \\ 2x_1 = 6 \\ x_1 \geq 0 \end{cases}$$

```
// construct an LP problem
fun problem(): LPProblem {
    // min c'x
    val c: Vector = DenseVector(2.0, -1.0)

    // the constraints
    // Ax >= b
    val greaterThanConstraints = LinearGreaterThanConstraints(
        DenseMatrix(arrayOf(doubleArrayOf(1.0, 0.0))), // A
        DenseVector(6.0)) // b
    val lessThanConstraints: LinearLessThanConstraints? = null // no less than constraints
    // Ax = b
    val equalityConstraints = LinearEqualityConstraints(
        DenseMatrix(arrayOf(doubleArrayOf(-1.0, 0.0))), // A
        DenseVector(-4.0)) // b
    // the whole plane
    val boxConstraints = BoxConstraints(
        2,
        BoxConstraints.Bound(2, Double.NEGATIVE_INFINITY, Double.POSITIVE_INFINITY)
    )
```

```
    // construct an LP problem with constraints
    val problem: LPProblem = LPProblemImpl1(
        c,
        greaterThanConstraints,
        lessThanConstraints,
        equalityConstraints,
        boxConstraints
    ) // x2 is free
    return problem
}

// construct the simplex tableau for the LP problem
val table0 = SimplexTable(problem())
println("simplex tableau for the problem:")
println(table0)

// solve the LP problem using the 2-phase algorithm
val solver = LPTwoPhaseSolver()
val solution: LPMinimizer = solver.solve(problem()).minimizer()
```

The output is as follows:

```
simplex tableau for the problem:
3x3

                        x,1             FREE,2          B,2147483647
x_slack,1               1.000000        0.000000        -6.000000

EQUALITY,1              -1.000000       0.000000        4.000000

COST,2147483647         2.000000        -1.000000       0.000000
```

```
Exception in thread "main" dev.nm.solver.multivariate.constrained.convex.sdp.socp.qp.lp.
exception.LPInfeasible
        at dev.nm.solver.multivariate.constrained.convex.sdp.socp.qp.lp.simplex.
FerrisMangasarianWrightPhase1.process(FerrisMangasarianWrightPhase1.java:81)
        at dev.nm.solver.multivariate.constrained.convex.sdp.socp.qp.lp.simplex.solver.LPTw
oPhaseSolver$Solution.<init>(LPTwoPhaseSolver.java:64)
        at dev.nm.solver.multivariate.constrained.convex.sdp.socp.qp.lp.simplex.solver.LPTw
oPhaseSolver$Solution.<init>(LPTwoPhaseSolver.java:45)
        at dev.nm.solver.multivariate.constrained.convex.sdp.socp.qp.lp.simplex.solver.
LPTwoPhaseSolver.solve(LPTwoPhaseSolver.java:104)
        at dev.nm.solver.multivariate.constrained.convex.sdp.socp.qp.lp.simplex.solver.
LPTwoPhaseSolver.solve(LPTwoPhaseSolver.java:109)
        at dev.nm.nmj.Chapter10.lp_solver_3(Chapter10.java:108)
        at dev.nm.nmj.Chapter10.main(Chapter10.java:75)
```

Note that this program throws an `LPInfeasible` exception. It is detected in Phase 1 that this problem is infeasible.

10.2.4. The Algebra of the Simplex Method

The previous section discussed the geometry of the simplex method. You can also cast the algorithm in the general optimization framework in Section 10.1.1. Given a vertex $\boldsymbol{x}_k$ (nondegenerate, meaning that it has exactly n edges or active constraints), a vertex $\boldsymbol{x}_{k+1}$ is said to be adjacent to $\boldsymbol{x}_k$ if $\boldsymbol{A}_{ak+1}$ differs from $\boldsymbol{A}_{ak}$ by exactly one row:

$$\boldsymbol{A}_{ak} = \begin{bmatrix} \boldsymbol{a}_{j1}^T \\ \boldsymbol{a}_{j2}^T \\ \vdots \\ \boldsymbol{a}_{jn}^T \end{bmatrix}$$

where $\boldsymbol{a}_{ji}^T$ are the coefficients of the ji-th constraint. Associated with $\boldsymbol{A}_{ak}$ is the set of indices of active constraints:

$$\Im_k = \{j1, j2, \ldots jn\}$$

where ji stands for an index in the original variable.

In other words, if I_k and I_{k+1} have exactly $(n-1)$ same members, $\boldsymbol{x}_k$ and $\boldsymbol{x}_{k+1}$ are adjacent. As vertex $\boldsymbol{x}_k$, the simplex algorithm checks if $\boldsymbol{x}_k$ is a minimizer. If it is not, it finds an adjacent $\boldsymbol{x}_{k+1}$ that gives a smaller objective function value. If a minimizer exists and there are a finite number of vertices, the simplex algorithm will always find a solution in a finite number of iterations.

The KKT conditions say that there exists a $\boldsymbol{\lambda}_k \in \mathbb{R}^n$ such that:

$$\boldsymbol{c} = \boldsymbol{A}_{ak}^T \boldsymbol{\lambda}_k$$

And that $\boldsymbol{x}_k$ is a minimizer if this is true:

$$\boldsymbol{\lambda}_k \geq \boldsymbol{0}$$

In other words, $\boldsymbol{x}_k$ is not a minimizer if and only if at least one component of $\boldsymbol{\lambda}_k$, say the l-th component $(\boldsymbol{\lambda}_k)_l$, is negative. That is:

$$(\lambda_k)_l < 0$$

In the general optimization algorithm, the next (and adjacent) vertex is given by the following:

$$\boldsymbol{x}_{k+1} = \boldsymbol{x}_k + \alpha_k \boldsymbol{d}_k$$

It can be shown that a feasible descent direction $\boldsymbol{d}_k$ is characterized by the following:

$$\boldsymbol{A}_{ak}\boldsymbol{d}_k \geq \boldsymbol{0},\ \boldsymbol{c}^T\boldsymbol{d}_k < 0$$

To find the edge $\boldsymbol{d}_k$, solve for the following:

$$\boldsymbol{A}_{ak}\boldsymbol{d}_k = \boldsymbol{e}_l \geq \boldsymbol{0}$$

where $\boldsymbol{e}_l$ is l-th coordinate vector (i.e., the l-th column of the $n \times n$ identity matrix).

Then, you get the following:

$$\boldsymbol{c}^T\boldsymbol{d}_k = \boldsymbol{\lambda}_k^T \boldsymbol{A}_{ak}\boldsymbol{d}_k = \boldsymbol{\lambda}_k^T \boldsymbol{e}_l = (\lambda_k)_l < 0$$

Therefore, $\boldsymbol{d}_k$ is a feasible descent direction.

Moreover, for $i \neq l$, you get this:

$$\boldsymbol{a}_{ji}^T\left(\boldsymbol{x}_k+\alpha_k\boldsymbol{d}_k\right)=\boldsymbol{a}_{ji}^T\boldsymbol{x}_k+\alpha_k\boldsymbol{a}_{ji}^T\boldsymbol{d}_k=b_{ji}$$

You can solve α_i for each i in the index set I_k of the inactive constraints at $\boldsymbol{x}_k$ and with $\mathbf{a}_{ji}^T\mathbf{d}_k<0$

$$\mathcal{I}_k=\left\{i:\boldsymbol{a}_{ji}^T\boldsymbol{x}_k-b_{ji}>0,\boldsymbol{a}_{ji}^T\boldsymbol{d}_k<0\ \right\}$$

$$\alpha_k=\min_{i\in\mathcal{I}_k}\left\{\alpha_i\right\}=\min_{i\in\mathcal{I}_k}\left(\frac{b_i-\boldsymbol{a}_i^T\boldsymbol{x}_k}{\boldsymbol{a}_i^T\boldsymbol{d}_k}\right)$$

The NM Dev class called `LPRevisedSimplexSolver` implements this algebraic form of simplex algorithm as described in Antoniou & Lu (2007). You can use this solver to solve the same LP problem in Chen, Batson, & Dang (2009) that you solved in the previous section.

You need to change this one line from this:

```
LPTwoPhaseSolver solver = new LPTwoPhaseSolver();
```

to this:

```
LPRevisedSimplexSolver solver = new LPRevisedSimplexSolver(1e-8);
```

to use a different solver.

$$\min_{x_1,x_2} -5x_1+2x_2$$

Subject to the following:

$$\begin{cases} x_1+3x_2\geq 9\\ -x_1+2x_2\leq 5\\ 3x_1+2x_2\geq 19\end{cases}$$

```
// construct an LP problem
val problem = LPProblemImpl1(
        DenseVector(-5.0, 2.0), // c
        LinearGreaterThanConstraints(
                DenseMatrix(
                    arrayOf(
                        doubleArrayOf(1.0, 3.0)
                    )
                ),
                DenseVector(9.0)), // b1
        LinearLessThanConstraints(
                DenseMatrix(
                    arrayOf(
                        doubleArrayOf(-1.0, 2.0),
                        doubleArrayOf(3.0, 2.0)
                    )
                ),
                DenseVector(5.0, 19.0)), // b2
        null,
        null)
```

```
// solve the LP problem using the algebraic LP solver
val solver = LPRevisedSimplexSolver(1e-8)
val solution: LPMinimizer = solver.solve(problem).minimizer()

println(String.format("minimum = %f%n", solution.minimum()))
println(String.format("minimizer = %s%n", solution.minimizer()))
```

The output is as follows:

```
minimum = -25.571429
minimizer = [5.571429, 1.142857]
```

This is exactly the same result as from the two-phase solver.

10.3. Quadratic Programming

Quadratic programming (QP) is used to minimize a quadratic objective function subject to linear constraints. It has important applications such as in quantitative finance. Also, it is often used to solve subproblems in other more general, nonlinear constrained optimization, such as sequential quadratic programming. The problem is often stated as follows:

$$\min_{\mathbf{x}} f(\boldsymbol{x}) = \frac{1}{2}\boldsymbol{x}^T \boldsymbol{H}\boldsymbol{x} + \boldsymbol{x}^T \boldsymbol{p}$$

Subject to the following:

$$\boldsymbol{A}x \geq \boldsymbol{b}$$

where $\boldsymbol{A} \in \mathbb{R}^{p \times n}$ for p linear constraints for n variables. You should usually assume that the matrix $\boldsymbol{A}$ is symmetric, of full rank, and positive semidefinite $\boldsymbol{A} \succcurlyeq 0$.

If the Hessian matrix $\boldsymbol{H} \succcurlyeq 0$ is positive semidefinite, then the problem is a convex optimization problem. The problem can be solved in (weakly) polynomial time. Otherwise, the problem is NP-hard. There can be several stationary points and local minima for a nonconvex problem. In fact, even if $\boldsymbol{H}$ has only one negative eigenvalue, the problem is strongly NP-hard.

An important application of QP is modern portfolio theory. Suppose you want to allocate a pool of money to buy n stocks and hold the portfolio for one year. Although the exact return for a stock one year later is unknown, you can model the annual return, r_i, for stock i as a random variable, say normal distribution. That is:

$$r_i \sim N(\mu_i, \sigma_i)$$

Because stocks are not exactly independent, they tend to move up and down in tandem. They are correlated. The correlation between stock i and stock j is as follows:

$$\rho_{ij} = \frac{\mathrm{E}\left[(r_i - \mu_i)(r_j - \mu_j)\right]}{\sigma_i \sigma_j}$$

The investor's decision is to decide what portion or weight, w_i, of the pool of money to put into each stock to construct their portfolio. The expected return of the portfolio is then as follows:

$$\mathrm{E}[R] = \mathrm{E}\left[\sum_{i=1}^{n} w_i r_i\right] = \sum_{i=1}^{n} w_i \mathrm{E}[r_i] = \sum_{i=1}^{n} w_i \mu_i = \boldsymbol{w}^T \mu$$

The variance of the portfolio is as follows:

$$Var[R] = \mathrm{E}\left[\left(R - \mathrm{E}[R]\right)^2\right] = \sum_{i=1}^{n}\sum_{j=1}^{n} w_i w_j \sigma_i \sigma_j \rho_{ij} = \boldsymbol{w}^T \Sigma \boldsymbol{w}$$

where $\sum$ is the $n \times n$ symmetric positive semidefinite covariance matrix defined as follows:

$$\Sigma_{ij} = \rho_{ij} \sigma_i \sigma_j$$

Markowitz proposed that the investor should find a weighting so that the expected return of the portfolio is maximized while the risk (measured by portfolio variance) is minimized. This essentially sets up the following QP problem:

$$\min_{\mathbf{w}} \lambda \boldsymbol{w}^T \Sigma \boldsymbol{w} - \boldsymbol{w}^T \mu$$

Subject to the following:

$$\sum_{i=1}^{n} w_i = 1$$

The sum of all weights is equal to 100 percent. You can impose other constraints such as a minimum weight for each stock at, for example, 0 percent. This is saying that no short selling is allowed. This inequality constraints can be written as follows:

$$\boldsymbol{w} \geq 0$$

$\lambda > 0$ is called the *risk-averse coefficient*. An investor who is more conservative and wants to minimize risk will choose a smaller λ. On the other hand, a more aggressive investor, who aims for a bigger expected return and can sustain a possible bigger drawdown, will choose a bigger λ. Changing λ gives different portfolios (different weightings) that satisfy the condition that no other portfolio exists with a higher expected return but with the same standard deviation of return (i.e., the risk) for that λ. The set of these optimal portfolios (for different λs) together draw what is called the *efficient frontier*. See Figure 10-11.

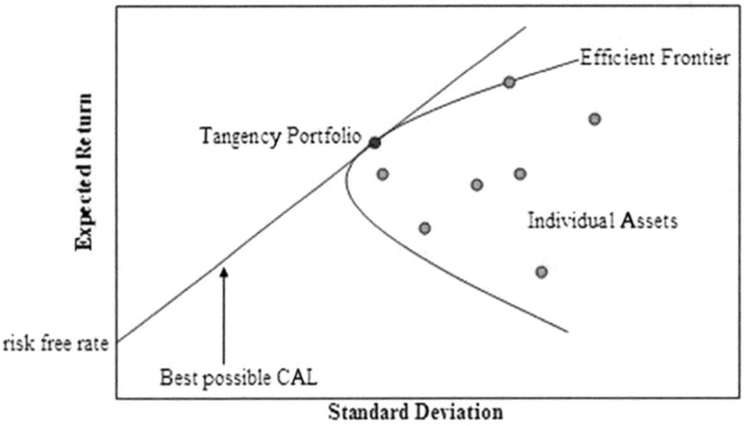

Figure 10-11. *Efficient frontier of portfolios*

10.3.1. Convex QP Problems with Only Equality Constraints

Let's start with an easy convex QP problem that you can solve analytically. A convex QP problem with only equality constraints is stated as follows:

$$\min_{x} f(\boldsymbol{x}) = \frac{1}{2}\boldsymbol{x}^T \boldsymbol{H}\boldsymbol{x} + \boldsymbol{x}^T \boldsymbol{p}$$

Subject to the following:

$$\boldsymbol{A}x = \boldsymbol{b}$$

where $\boldsymbol{H} \succcurlyeq 0, \boldsymbol{A} \succcurlyeq 0, \boldsymbol{A} \in \mathbb{R}^{p \times n}$, $\boldsymbol{A}$ is symmetric and of full rank with $p < n$.

It can be shown that the solution $\boldsymbol{x}$ takes this form:

$$\boldsymbol{x} = \boldsymbol{V}_r \phi + \boldsymbol{A}^+ \boldsymbol{b}$$

where $\boldsymbol{V}_r$ is composed of the last $n - p$ columns of $\boldsymbol{V}$. $\boldsymbol{V}$ is from a singular-value decomposition of $\boldsymbol{A} = \boldsymbol{U}\Sigma\boldsymbol{V}^T$. $\boldsymbol{A}^+$ is the Moore-Penrose inverse of $\boldsymbol{A}$.

Using this solution form, the problem can be reformulated as an equivalent unconstrained minimization problem, as shown here:

$$\min_{\phi} \hat{f}(\phi) = \frac{1}{2}\phi^T \hat{\boldsymbol{H}}\phi + \phi^T \hat{\boldsymbol{p}}$$

where

$$\hat{\boldsymbol{H}} = \boldsymbol{V}_r^T \boldsymbol{H} \boldsymbol{V}_r$$

$$\hat{\boldsymbol{p}} = \boldsymbol{V}_r^T \left(\boldsymbol{H}\boldsymbol{A}^+ \boldsymbol{b} + \boldsymbol{p} \right)$$

If $H \succ 0$ is positive definite, then so is $\hat{H} \succ 0$ The unique global minimizer of the problem is as follows:

$$x^* = V_r \phi^* + A^+ b$$

where ϕ^* is the solution of the linear system:

$$\hat{H}\phi = -\hat{p}$$

If $H \succcurlyeq 0$ is positive semidefinite, then $\hat{H}$ is either positive definite or positive semidefinite. If $\hat{H} \succ 0$ is positive definite, then x^* is the unique global minimizer of the problem. If $\hat{H} \succeq 0 \succcurlyeq 0$ is positive semidefinite, then there are two possibilities. If $\hat{p}$ can be expressed as a linear combination of columns of $\hat{H}$, then $f(x)$ has infinitely many global minimizers. Otherwise, there is no minimizer.

Let's illustrate this method using the following QP problem in Antoniou & Lu (2007):

$$\min_{x_1, x_2, x_3} f(x_1, x_2, x_3) = \frac{1}{2}\left(x_1^2 + x_2^2\right) + 2x_1 + x_2 - x_3$$

Subject to the following:

$$Ax = b$$

$$A = [0\ 1\ 1],\ b = 1$$

The objective function in matrix form is as follows:

$$\min_x f(x) = \frac{1}{2} x^T H x + x^T p$$

$$H = \begin{bmatrix} 1 & 0 & 0 \\ 0 & 1 & 0 \\ 0 & 0 & 0 \end{bmatrix} \succeq 0$$

$$p = \begin{bmatrix} 2 \\ 1 \\ -1 \end{bmatrix}$$

The singular-value decomposition of A gives the following:

$$\mathbf{V_r} = \begin{bmatrix} 1 & 0 \\ 0 & \frac{\sqrt{2}}{2} \\ 0 & -\frac{\sqrt{2}}{2} \end{bmatrix}$$

$$\mathbf{A}^+ = \begin{bmatrix} 0 \\ 0.5 \\ 0.5 \end{bmatrix}$$

Therefore, you get the following:

$$\hat{H} = V_r^T H V_r = \begin{bmatrix} 1 & 0 \\ 0 & \frac{\sqrt{2}}{2} \end{bmatrix} \succ 0$$

The unique global minimizer is as follows:

$$x^* = V_r \phi^* + A^+ b$$

$$= \begin{bmatrix} 1 & 0 \\ 0 & \frac{\sqrt{2}}{2} \\ 0 & -\frac{\sqrt{2}}{2} \end{bmatrix} \times \begin{bmatrix} -2 \\ -3.5355 \end{bmatrix} + \begin{bmatrix} 0 \\ 0.5 \\ 0.5 \end{bmatrix} [1] = \begin{bmatrix} -2 \\ -2 \\ 3 \end{bmatrix}$$

In NM Dev, the `QuadraticFunction` class constructs a quadratic function of this form:

$$f(x) = \frac{1}{2} x^T H x + x^T p + c$$

The class signature is as follows:

```
public class QuadraticFunction extends AbstractRealScalarFunction {
    /**
* Construct a quadratic function of this form: \(f(x) = \frac{1}{2} \times
     * x'Hx + x'p + c\).
     * @param H a symmetric, positive semi-definite matrix
     * @param p a vector
     * @param c a constant
     */
    public QuadraticFunction(Matrix H, Vector p, double c);
    /**
* Construct a quadratic function of this form: \(f(x) = \frac{1}{2} \times
 x'Hx + x'p\).
     *
     * @param H a symmetric, positive semi-definite matrix
     * @param p a vector
     */
    public QuadraticFunction(Matrix H, Vector p);
    /**
     * Copy constructor.
     *
     * @param f a quadratic function
     */
    public QuadraticFunction(QuadraticFunction f);
    public ImmutableMatrix Hessian();
    public ImmutableVector p();
    @Override
```

```
    public Double evaluate(Vector z);
    @Override
    public String toString();
}
```

The QPSimpleMinimizer class is a utility class that has a collection of utility functions to solve unconstrained QP problems and QP problems with only equality constraints. Both these problems can be solved analytically. The following code reproduces the previous example:

```
//construct the QP problem with only equality constraints
val H: DenseMatrix = DenseMatrix(
    arrayOf(
        doubleArrayOf(1.0, 0.0, 0.0),
        doubleArrayOf(0.0, 1.0, 0.0),
        doubleArrayOf(0.0, 0.0, 0.0)
    )
)

val p: DenseVector = DenseVector(2.0, 1.0, -1.0)
val f = QuadraticFunction(H, p)
println("minimizing:")
println(f)

// equality constraints
val A: DenseMatrix = DenseMatrix(
        arrayOf(
            doubleArrayOf(0.0, 1.0, 1.0)
        ))
val b: DenseVector = DenseVector(1.0)
val Aeq = LinearEqualityConstraints(A, b)

// solve a QP problem with only equality constraints
val soln = QPSimpleMinimizer.solve(f, Aeq)
val x: Vector = soln.minimizer()
val fx: Double = f.evaluate(x)
println(String.format("f(%s) = %f%n", x, fx))
println(String.format("is unique = %b%n", soln.isUnique()))
```

The output is as follows:

```
minimizing:
1/2 * x'3x3
         [,1] [,2] [,3]
[1,] 1.000000, 0.000000, 0.000000,
[2,] 0.000000, 1.000000, 0.000000,
[3,] 0.000000, 0.000000, 0.000000, x + x'[2.000000, 1.000000, -1.000000]
f([-2.000000, -2.000000, 3.000000] ) = -5.000000
is unique = true
```

NM Dev computes the same optimal solution $\boldsymbol{x}^* = \begin{bmatrix} -2 \\ -2 \\ 3 \end{bmatrix}$ and the minimum value –5.

10.3.2. Active-Set Methods for Strictly Convex QP Problems

In general, a QP problem can be stated as follows:

$$\min_{\mathbf{x}} f(\boldsymbol{x}) = \frac{1}{2}\boldsymbol{x}^T \boldsymbol{H}\boldsymbol{x} + \boldsymbol{x}^T \boldsymbol{p}$$

Subject to the following:

$$\boldsymbol{A}\boldsymbol{x} \ge \boldsymbol{b}$$

where $\boldsymbol{A} \in \mathbb{R}^{p \times n}$.

Without loss of generality, you can skip the equality constraints because they can be eliminated, as in Section 10.3.1.

The Karush-Kuhn-Tucker (KKT) conditions at a minimizer $\boldsymbol{x}$ are given by the following:

$$\boldsymbol{H}\boldsymbol{x} + \boldsymbol{p} - \boldsymbol{A}^T \mu = \mathbf{0}$$

$$\left(\boldsymbol{a}_i^T \boldsymbol{x} - b_i\right)\mu_i = 0, i = 1,2,\ldots,p$$

$$\mu_i \ge 0, i = 1,2,\ldots,p$$

Suppose solution $\boldsymbol{x}^*$ is in the interior of the feasible region. (Unlike LP, where a solution must be on the boundary, the solution for a QP problem can be inside the feasible region.) Then you have this:

$$\boldsymbol{A}\boldsymbol{x}^* - \boldsymbol{b} > 0$$

This implies the following:

$$\mu^* = \mathbf{0}$$

Then you have this:

$$\boldsymbol{H}\boldsymbol{x}^* + \boldsymbol{p} = \mathbf{0}$$

The unique global minimizer $\boldsymbol{x}^*$ is the solution to this linear system, as shown here:

$$\boldsymbol{x}^* = -\boldsymbol{H}^{-1}\boldsymbol{p}$$

Primal Active-Set Method

If the solution $\boldsymbol{x}^*$ is not an interior point but on the boundary of feasible region, the next search direction is to consider the active constraints at the current iterate point $\boldsymbol{x}$ as a set of equality constraints while ignoring the other constraints. This is the active-set method to solve a general convex QP problem.

Let $\boldsymbol{x}_k$ be a feasible iterate point in the k-th iterations. Let J_k be the index set of active constraints, namely, those constraints with $\boldsymbol{a}_i^T \boldsymbol{x} - b_i = \mathbf{0}$, which is called an active set. The next iteration, as in the general optimization algorithm in Section 10.1.1, is as follows:

$$\boldsymbol{x}_{\mathbf{k+1}} = \boldsymbol{x}_k + \boldsymbol{d} = \boldsymbol{x}_{\mathbf{k}} + \alpha_k \boldsymbol{d}_{\boldsymbol{k}}$$

Constraints that are active at $\boldsymbol{x}_k$ remain active at $\boldsymbol{x}_{k+1}$ if the following is true:

$$\boldsymbol{a}_j^T \boldsymbol{x}_{k+1} - b_j = 0 , j \in J_k$$

Multiplying $\boldsymbol{a}_j^T$ on both sides of the next iterate equation, you get this:

$$\boldsymbol{a}_j^T \boldsymbol{d}_k = 0 , j \in J_k$$

The objective function at $\boldsymbol{xk} + \boldsymbol{d}$ is as follows:

$$f_k(\boldsymbol{d}) = \frac{1}{2}\boldsymbol{d}^T \boldsymbol{H}\boldsymbol{d} + \boldsymbol{d}^T \boldsymbol{g}_k + c_k$$

where

$$\boldsymbol{g}_k = \boldsymbol{p} + \boldsymbol{H}\boldsymbol{x}_k$$

and c_k is a constant.

A major step in the active set method is to solve this following QP subproblem with only equality constraints, as shown here:

$$\min_{\boldsymbol{d}} \hat{f}(\boldsymbol{d}) = \frac{1}{2}\boldsymbol{d}^T \boldsymbol{H}\boldsymbol{d} + \boldsymbol{d}^T \boldsymbol{g}_k$$

Subject to the following:

$$\boldsymbol{a}_j^T \boldsymbol{d}_k = 0 , j \in J_k$$

This can be solved using the method in Section 10.3.1. The primal active-set algorithm is as follows:

Primal Active-Set Algorithm

Step 1

Start with a feasible initial point $\boldsymbol{x}_0$.
Identify the initial active set J_0.
Form matrix $\boldsymbol{Aa}_0$ as a submatrix of $\boldsymbol{A}$ using only the active constraints in J_0.
Set $k = 0$.

Step 2

Compute $\boldsymbol{g}_k = \boldsymbol{p} + \boldsymbol{H}\boldsymbol{x}_k$.
Use $\boldsymbol{g}_k$ to check whether $\boldsymbol{d}_k$ will be zero. If $\boldsymbol{d}_k$ is not zero, go to Step 4.

Step 3

$$(\boldsymbol{d}_k = \boldsymbol{0})$$

Solve for $\hat{\mu}$ using $\mathbf{A}_{\mathbf{ak}}^{\mathbf{T}} \hat{\mu} = \mathbf{g}_{\mathbf{k}}$.
If $\hat{\mu} \geq \mathbf{0}$, output $\boldsymbol{x}_k$ as the solution and terminate.
Otherwise, remove the index that is associated with the most negative Lagrange multiplier from $\boldsymbol{J}_k$.

Step 4

$$(\boldsymbol{d}_k \neq \boldsymbol{0})$$

Solve for $\boldsymbol{d}_k$ using the sub-QP problem with only equality constraints.

Step 5
Compute a_k.

$$\alpha_k = \min\left\{1, \min_{i \notin J_k, \boldsymbol{a}_i^T \boldsymbol{d}_k < 0} \frac{b_i - \boldsymbol{a}_i^T \boldsymbol{x}_k}{\boldsymbol{a}_i^T \boldsymbol{d}_k}\right\}$$

Set $\boldsymbol{x}_{k+1} = \boldsymbol{x}_k + \alpha_k \boldsymbol{d}_k$.
Step 6
If $\alpha_k < 1$, build J_{k+1} by adding the index that yields the minimum to J_k in Step 5.
Otherwise, let $J_k = J_{k+1}$.
Step 7
Set $k = k + 1$.
Repeat from Step 2.
Consider this example problem in Nocedal & Wright (2006):

$$\min_{\mathbf{x}} q(\mathbf{x}) = (x_1 - 1)^2 + (x_2 - 2.5)^2$$

The constraints are as follows:

$$\begin{cases} x_1 - 2x_2 + 2 \geq 0 \\ -x_1 - 2x_2 + 6 \geq 0 \\ -x_1 + 2x_2 + 2 \geq 0 \\ x_1 \geq 0 \\ x_2 \geq 0 \end{cases}$$

You can write the problem in matrix form.

$$\min_{\boldsymbol{x}} f(\boldsymbol{x}) = \frac{1}{2}\boldsymbol{x}^T \boldsymbol{H} \boldsymbol{x} + \boldsymbol{x}^T \boldsymbol{p}$$

Subject to the following:

$$\boldsymbol{A}\boldsymbol{x} \geq \boldsymbol{b}$$

where:

$$\boldsymbol{H} = \begin{bmatrix} 2 & 0 \\ 0 & 2 \end{bmatrix}$$

$$\boldsymbol{p} = \begin{bmatrix} -2 \\ -5 \end{bmatrix}$$

$$\boldsymbol{A} = \begin{bmatrix} 1 & -2 \\ -1 & -2 \\ -1 & 2 \\ 1 & 0 \\ 0 & 1 \end{bmatrix}$$

$$\boldsymbol{b} = \begin{bmatrix} -2 \\ -6 \\ -2 \\ 0 \\ 0 \end{bmatrix}$$

(Note that these two formulations have different constant terms, but they are irrelevant to the solution.) This is shown in Figure 10-12.

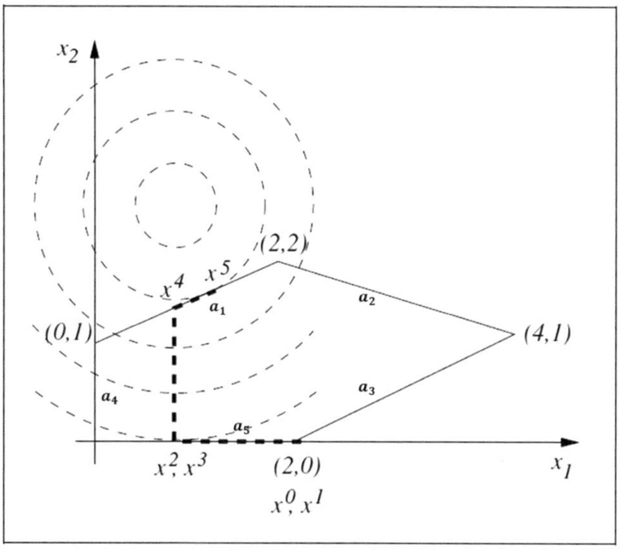

***Figure 10-12.** A quadratic programming problem*

Figure 10-12 shows the feasible region, the boundary, the contour of the objective function, and the constraint labels $\boldsymbol{a}_i$.

Suppose the initial iterate point is $\boldsymbol{x}^0 = [2, 0]^T$ (here a superscript indicates the number of iterations, and a subscript indicates the component). There are two active constraints for this vertex, $\boldsymbol{a}_3$ and $\boldsymbol{a}_5$. $\boldsymbol{a}_3\boldsymbol{x}^0 = \boldsymbol{a}_5\boldsymbol{x}^0 = \boldsymbol{0}$. The working set is $J_0 = \{3, 5\}$. The solution to the QP subproblem is $\boldsymbol{d}^0 = \boldsymbol{0}$. You need to solve for the Lagrange multipliers in the KKT conditions to check if it is a minimum point.

$$\begin{bmatrix} -1 & 2 \\ 0 & 1 \end{bmatrix} \begin{bmatrix} \hat{\mu}_1 \\ \hat{\mu}_2 \end{bmatrix} = \begin{bmatrix} 2 \\ -5 \end{bmatrix}$$

That is, you get this:

$$\begin{bmatrix} \hat{\mu}_3 \\ \hat{\mu}_5 \end{bmatrix} = \begin{bmatrix} -2 \\ -1 \end{bmatrix}$$

This does not meet the non-negativity requirement, meaning that the minimum has not been found. You remove constraint 3, $\boldsymbol{a}_3$, from the working set because it has the biggest absolute value of the Lagrange multipliers.

In the next iteration $k = 1$, the active working set is now $J_1 = \{5\}$. $\boldsymbol{x}^1 = \boldsymbol{x}^0 = [2, 0]^T$ because the last iteration does not move the search point. $\boldsymbol{d}^1 = [-1, 0]^T$. The step-length formula yields $\alpha_1 = 1$. The new iterate is $\boldsymbol{x}^2 = [1, 0]^T$.

In the next iteration $k = 2$, $\boldsymbol{x}^2 = [1, 0]^T$. $\boldsymbol{d}^2 = \mathbf{0}$. $\hat{\mu}_5 = -5$. You drop $\boldsymbol{a}_5$ from the working set. It is now empty, $J_1 = \{\}$.

In the next iteration $k = 3$, $\boldsymbol{x}^3 = [1, 0]^T$ because $\boldsymbol{d}^2 = \mathbf{0}$. Because the working set is empty, the QP subproblem is unconstrained. Solving it gives $\boldsymbol{d}^3 = [0, 2.5]^T$. The step-length formula yields $\alpha_3 = 0.6$. The new iterate is $\boldsymbol{x}^4 = [1, 1.5]^T$.

In the next iteration $k = 4$, $\boldsymbol{x}^4 = [1, 1.5]^T$. There is a single blocking constraint $\boldsymbol{a}_1$. The first constraint is added to the working set, $J_4 = \{1\}$. $\boldsymbol{d}^4 = [0.4, 0.2]^T$. $\alpha_4 = 1$. The new iterate is $\boldsymbol{x}^5 = [1.4, 1.7]^T$. The working set remains unchanged.

In the next iteration $k = 5$, $\boldsymbol{x}^5 = [1.4, 1.7]^T$. $\boldsymbol{d}^5 = \mathbf{0}$. Checking the KKT conditions gives $\hat{\mu}_1 = 0.8 > 0$. The minimizer has been found. You have the following:

$$\boldsymbol{x}^* = \begin{bmatrix} 1.4 \\ 1.7 \end{bmatrix}$$

The following NM Dev code solves this QP problem:

```
// construct a quadratic function
val H: Matrix = DenseMatrix(
    arrayOf(
        doubleArrayOf(2.0, 0.0),
        doubleArrayOf(0.0, 2.0),
    )
)

val p: Vector = DenseVector(-2.0, -5.0)
val f = QuadraticFunction(H, p)

// construct the linear inequality constraints

val A: Matrix = DenseMatrix(
    arrayOf(
        doubleArrayOf(1.0, -2.0),
        doubleArrayOf(-1.0, -2.0),
        doubleArrayOf(-1.0, 2.0),
        doubleArrayOf(1.0, 0.0),
        doubleArrayOf(0.0, 1.0),
    )
)

val b: Vector = DenseVector(-2.0, -6.0, -2.0, 0.0, 0.0)
val greater = LinearGreaterThanConstraints(A, b)// x >= 0
// construct the QP problem
val problem = QPProblem(f, null, greater)

// construct a primal active set solver
val epsion: Double = Math.sqrt(PrecisionUtils.autoEpsilon(problem.f().Hessian()))
val solver1 = QPPrimalActiveSetMinimizer(
                epsion, // precision
```

```
                Integer.MAX_VALUE // max number of iterations
        )
// solve the QP problem using the primal active set method
val solution1: QPPrimalActiveSetMinimizer.Solution = solver1.solve(problem)
solution1.search(DenseVector(2.0, 0.0))
// print out the solution
println("minimizer = " + solution1.minimizer().minimizer())
println("minimum = " + solution1.minimum())
```

The output is as follows:

```
x_0 = [2.000000, 0.000000]
J_0
 = active: [3, 5]; inactive: []
g_0 = [2.000000, -5.000000]
d_0 = [0.000000, 0.000000]
mu = [-2.000000, -1.000000]
x_1 = [2.000000, 0.000000]
J_1
 = active: [5]; inactive: [3]
g_1 = [2.000000, -5.000000]
d_1 = [-1.000000, 0.000000]
a = 1.000000
x_2 = [1.000000, 0.000000]
J_2
 = active: [5]; inactive: [3]
g_2 = [0.000000, -5.000000]
d_2 = [0.000000, 0.000000]
mu = [-5.000000]
x_3 = [1.000000, 0.000000]
J_3
 = active: []; inactive: [3, 5]
g_3 = [0.000000, -5.000000]
d_3 = [-0.000000, 2.500000]
a = 0.600000
x_4 = [1.000000, 1.500000]
J_4
 = active: [1]; inactive: [3, 5]
g_4 = [0.000000, -2.000000]
d_4 = [0.400000, 0.200000]
a = 1.000000
x_5 = [1.400000, 1.700000]
J_5
 = active: [1]; inactive: [3, 5]
g_5 = [0.800000, -1.600000]
d_5 = [0.000000, 0.000000]
mu = [0.800000]
minimizer = [1.400000, 1.700000]
minimum = -6.450000000000001
```

Again, you have $f(1.4, 1.7) = -6.45$. You are encouraged to compare the output to the trace of iterations discussed earlier.

Dual Active-Set Method

The concept of duality is a technique to solve a problem related to the original problem, referred to as the *primal* problem. The related problem is called the *dual* problem. The dual problem is one in which the parameters are the Lagrange multipliers of the primal. In the case where the number of inequality constraints is much greater than the dimension of $\boldsymbol{x}$, solving the dual problem to find the Lagrange multipliers and then finding $\boldsymbol{x}^*$ for the primal problem can be easier. Specifically, let $\boldsymbol{x}^*, \boldsymbol{\lambda}^*, \boldsymbol{\mu}^*$ be the minimizer, the two Lagrange multipliers of a constrained optimization problem as in the KKT conditions. They solve the dual problem, as shown here:

$$\max_{\boldsymbol{x},\lambda,\mu} \mathcal{L}(\boldsymbol{x},\lambda,\mu)$$

Subject to the following:

$$\begin{cases} \nabla\mathcal{L}(\boldsymbol{x},\lambda,\mu) = \mathbf{0} \\ \mu \geq \mathbf{0} \end{cases}$$

In addition, you get this:

$$f(\mathbf{x}^*) = \mathcal{L}(\mathbf{x}^*, \lambda^*, \mu^*)$$

The dual active-set method to solve the QP problem is essentially the active-set method in the previous section but applies to the dual of the QP problem. The dual of a QP problem is as follows:

$$\min_{\mu} h(\mu) = \frac{1}{2}\mu^T A H^{-1} A^T \mu - \mu^T \left(\boldsymbol{A}\boldsymbol{H}^{-1}\boldsymbol{p} + \boldsymbol{b}\right)$$

Subject to the following:

$$\mu \geq \mathbf{0}$$

After its minimizer $\boldsymbol{\mu}^*$ is determined, the minimizer of the primal problem can be obtained from the KKT conditions, as shown here:

$$\boldsymbol{H}\boldsymbol{x} + \boldsymbol{p} - \boldsymbol{A}^T \mu = \mathbf{0}$$

That is:

$$\boldsymbol{x}^* = \boldsymbol{H}^{-1}\left(\boldsymbol{A}^T \mu^* - \boldsymbol{p}\right)$$

There are some advantages of solving the dual problem instead of the primal problem:

- A feasible initial point can be readily identified as any vector with non-negative entries, for example, $\boldsymbol{\mu}_0 = \mathbf{0}$.
- The constraint matrix in the problem is the $p \times p$ identity matrix. Therefore, the dual problem always satisfies the nondegeneracy assumption.
- The problem involves only bounded inequality constraints that significantly reduce the computation cost required in the algorithm.

In NM Dev, the `QPDualActiveSetMinimizer` class transforms a QP problem into its dual problem and then applies the active-set method. The following code uses the dual active-set method to solve the same problem:

```
// construct a quadratic function
val H: Matrix = DenseMatrix(
    arrayOf(
        doubleArrayOf(2.0, 0.0),
        doubleArrayOf(0.0, 2.0),
    )
)

val p: Vector = DenseVector(-2.0, -5.0)
val f = QuadraticFunction(H, p)

// construct the linear inequality constraints

val A: Matrix = DenseMatrix(
    arrayOf(
        doubleArrayOf(1.0, -2.0),
        doubleArrayOf(-1.0, -2.0),
        doubleArrayOf(-1.0, 2.0),
        doubleArrayOf(1.0, 0.0),
        doubleArrayOf(0.0, 1.0),
    )
)

val b: Vector = DenseVector(-2.0, -6.0, -2.0, 0.0, 0.0)
val greater = LinearGreaterThanConstraints(A, b)// x >= 0
// construct the QP problem
val problem = QPProblem(f, null, greater)

// construct a dual active set solver
val epsion: Double = Math.sqrt(PrecisionUtils.autoEpsilon(problem.f().Hessian()))
// solve the QP problem using the dual active set method
val solver2 = QPDualActiveSetMinimizer(
                epsion, // precision
                Integer.MAX_VALUE) // max number of iterations
val solution2: QPDualActiveSetMinimizer.Solution = solver2.solve(problem)
solution2.search()
// print out the solution
println("minimizer = " + solution2.minimizer().minimizer())
println("minimum = " + solution2.minimum())
```

We changed only the solver from this:

```
val solver1 = QPPrimalActiveSetMinimizer(
                epsion, // precision
                Integer.MAX_VALUE // max number of iterations
        )
```

```
// solve the QP problem using the primal active set method
val solution1: QPPrimalActiveSetMinimizer.Solution = solver1.solve(problem)
to
// solve the QP problem using the dual active set method
val solver2 = QPDualActiveSetMinimizer(
                epsion, // precision
                Integer.MAX_VALUE) // max number of iterations
val solution2: QPDualActiveSetMinimizer.Solution = solver2.solve(problem)
```

You do not even need to provide an initial guess for the dual active-set solver.

The output is as follows:

```
x_0 = [0.000000, 0.000000, 0.000000, 0.000000, 0.000000]
J_0
 = active: [1, 2, 3, 4, 5]; inactive: []
g_0 = [-2.000000, 0.000000, 6.000000, 1.000000, 2.500000]
d_0 = [0.000000, 0.000000, 0.000000, 0.000000, 0.000000]
mu = [-2.000000, 0.000000, 6.000000, 1.000000, 2.500000]
x_1 = [0.000000, 0.000000, 0.000000, 0.000000, 0.000000]
J_1
 = active: [2, 3, 4, 5]; inactive: [1]
g_1 = [-2.000000, 0.000000, 6.000000, 1.000000, 2.500000]
d_1 = [0.800000, 0.000000, 0.000000, 0.000000, 0.000000]
a = 1.000000
x_2 = [0.800000, 0.000000, 0.000000, 0.000000, 0.000000]
J_2
 = active: [2, 3, 4, 5]; inactive: [1]
g_2 = [0.000000, 1.200000, 4.000000, 1.400000, 1.700000]
d_2 = [0.000000, 0.000000, 0.000000, 0.000000, 0.000000]
mu = [1.200000, 4.000000, 1.400000, 1.700000]
minimizer = [1.400000, 1.700000]
minimum = -6.450000000000001
```

The result is the same as when using the primal active-set method.

10.4. Semidefinite Programming

Semidefinite programming (SDP) is a subfield of convex optimization concerned with the optimization of a linear objective function over the intersection of the cone of positive semidefinite matrices with an affine space. Positive semidefinite matrices are symmetric matrices whose eigenvalues are non-negative. SDP is a field of growing interest for several reasons. Many practical problems in operations research and combinatorial optimization can be modeled or approximated as SDP problems. In automatic control theory, SDP is used in the context of linear matrix inequalities. Some quantum query complexity problems have been formulated in terms of SDP. Moreover, all linear programs such as LP and QP can be reformulated as SDPs. The vector inequality constraints are replaced by matrix inequality constraints. Figure 10-13 shows the hierarchy of convex programming and subfields.

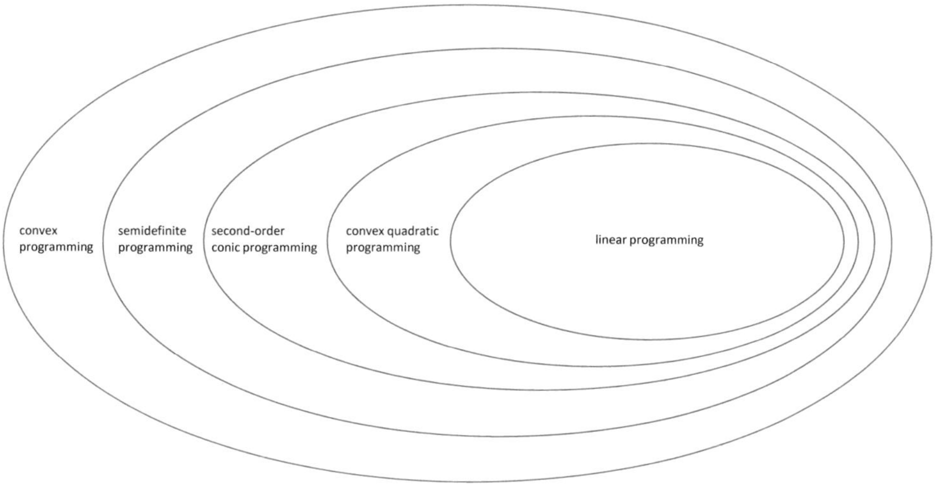

Figure 10-13. *Hierarchy of convex programming*

10.4.1. Primal and Dual SDP Problems

Let $\boldsymbol{S}^n$ be the space of real symmetric $n \times n$ matrices. The standard inner product on $\boldsymbol{S}^n$ is defined as follows:

$$\boldsymbol{A} \cdot \boldsymbol{B} = \text{trace}(\boldsymbol{AB}) = \sum_{i=1}^{n}\sum_{j=1}^{n} a_{ij} b_{ij}$$

The primal SDP problem is defined as follows:

$$\min \boldsymbol{C} \cdot \boldsymbol{X}$$

Subject to the following:

$$\boldsymbol{A}_i \cdot \boldsymbol{X} = \boldsymbol{b}_i, \text{ for } i = 1, 2, \ldots, p$$
$$\boldsymbol{X} \succcurlyeq \boldsymbol{0}$$

where $\boldsymbol{C},\boldsymbol{X},\boldsymbol{A}_i$ are in $\boldsymbol{S}^n$. $\boldsymbol{X}$ is positive semidefinite.
A sample SDP problem looks like this:

$$\min_{\boldsymbol{X}} x_{11} + 2x_{12} + 3x_{13} + 2x_{21} + 9x_{22} + 0x_{23} + 3x_{31} + 0x_{32} + 7x_{33} = x_{11} + 4x_{12} + 6x_{13} + 9x_{22} + 7x_{33}$$

Subject to the following:

$$\begin{cases} x_{11} + 2x_{13} + 3x_{22} + 14x_{23} + 5x_{33} = 11 \\ 4x_{12} + 16x_{13} + 6x_{22} + 4x_{33} = 19 \end{cases}$$

$$\boldsymbol{X} = \begin{bmatrix} x_{11} & x_{12} & x_{13} \\ x_{21} & x_{22} & x_{23} \\ x_{31} & x_{32} & x_{33} \end{bmatrix} \pm 0$$

In matrix form, the problem is written as follows:

$$\min_{X} \begin{bmatrix} 1 & 2 & 3 \\ 2 & 9 & 0 \\ 3 & 0 & 7 \end{bmatrix} \cdot \begin{bmatrix} x_{11} & x_{12} & x_{13} \\ x_{12} & x_{22} & x_{23} \\ x_{13} & x_{23} & x_{33} \end{bmatrix}$$

Subject to the following:

$$\begin{cases} \begin{bmatrix} 1 & 0 & 1 \\ 0 & 3 & 7 \\ 1 & 7 & 5 \end{bmatrix} \cdot \begin{bmatrix} x_{11} & x_{12} & x_{13} \\ x_{12} & x_{22} & x_{23} \\ x_{13} & x_{23} & x_{33} \end{bmatrix} = 11 \\ \begin{bmatrix} 0 & 2 & 8 \\ 2 & 6 & 0 \\ 8 & 0 & 4 \end{bmatrix} \cdot \begin{bmatrix} x_{11} & x_{12} & x_{13} \\ x_{12} & x_{22} & x_{23} \\ x_{13} & x_{23} & x_{33} \end{bmatrix} = 19 \end{cases}$$

This SDP problem looks remarkably similar to an LP problem. Note that the decision variable involved now is a matrix $\boldsymbol{X}$ rather than a vector. Also, just as $\boldsymbol{x} \geq \boldsymbol{0}$ means that each of the n components must be non-negative, $\boldsymbol{X} \succcurlyeq \boldsymbol{0}$ means that each of the n eigenvalues must be non-negative.

In NM Dev, the `SDPPrimalProblem` class constructs an SDP problem in primal form. The class signature is as follows:

```
public class SDPPrimalProblem { // TODO: convert to SDPDualProblem; implement
ConstrainedOptimProblem
    /**
     * Constructs a primal SDP problem.
     * \[
     * \min_x \mathbf{c'x} \textrm{, s.t., } \\
     * \mathbf{Ax} = \mathbf{b}, \mathbf{x} \geq \mathbf{0}
     * \]
     *
* @param C \(C\)
* @param A \(A\)
     */
    public SDPPrimalProblem(SymmetricMatrix C, SymmetricMatrix[] A);
    /**
     * Gets the dimension of the system, i.e., the dimension of <i>x</i>, the
     * number of variables.
     *
     * @return the dimension of the system
     */
    public int n();
    /**
     * Gets the size of <i>b</i>.
     *
     * @return the size of <i>b</i>
     */
    public int p();
```

```
    /**
     * Gets <i>C</i>.
     *
     * @return <i>C</i>
     */
    public SymmetricMatrix C();
    /**
     * Gets <i>A<sub>i</sub></i>.
     *
     * @param i an index to the A's, counting from 1
     * @return <i>A<sub>i</sub></i>
     */
    public SymmetricMatrix A(int i);
}
```

The following code constructs the primal problem in the previous example:

```
// the primal SDP matrices
val C: SymmetricMatrix = SymmetricMatrix(
    arrayOf(
        doubleArrayOf(1.0),
        doubleArrayOf(2.0, 9.0),
        doubleArrayOf(3.0, 0.0, 7.0)
    )
)

val A1: SymmetricMatrix = SymmetricMatrix(
    arrayOf(
        doubleArrayOf(1.0),
        doubleArrayOf(0.0, 3.0),
        doubleArrayOf(1.0, 7.0, 5.0)
    )
)

val A2: SymmetricMatrix = SymmetricMatrix(
    arrayOf(
        doubleArrayOf(0.0),
        doubleArrayOf(2.0, 6.0),
        doubleArrayOf(8.0, 0.0, 4.0)
    )
)

// construct the primal SDP problem
val primal = SDPPrimalProblem(
                C,
                arrayOf<SymmetricMatrix>(A1, A2))
```

If $\boldsymbol{C} = \text{diag}\,(\boldsymbol{c})$ and $\boldsymbol{Ai} = \text{diag}\,(\boldsymbol{ai})$ are all diagonal matrices, then the problem can be immediately reduced to a standard-form LP problem. The dual problem of a standard-form LP problem is as follows:

$$\max \boldsymbol{b}^t \boldsymbol{y}$$

Subject to the following:

$$\boldsymbol{A}^T \boldsymbol{y} + \boldsymbol{s} = \boldsymbol{c}$$

$$\mathbf{s} \geq \mathbf{0}$$

where $\boldsymbol{s}$ is a slack variable.

Similarly, the dual SDP problem with respect to the primal SDP problem is as follows:

$$\max \boldsymbol{b}^t \boldsymbol{y}$$

Subject to the following:

$$\sum_{i=1}^{p} y_i \boldsymbol{A}_i + \boldsymbol{S} = \boldsymbol{C}$$

$$\boldsymbol{S} \succcurlyeq \mathbf{0}$$

where $\boldsymbol{S}$ is a slack variable.

The dual problem of the example is as follows:

$$\max 11y_1 + 19y_2$$

Subject to the following:

$$y_1 \begin{bmatrix} 1 & 0 & 1 \\ 0 & 3 & 7 \\ 1 & 7 & 5 \end{bmatrix} + y_2 \begin{bmatrix} 0 & 2 & 8 \\ 2 & 6 & 0 \\ 8 & 0 & 4 \end{bmatrix} + \boldsymbol{S} = \begin{bmatrix} 1 & 2 & 3 \\ 2 & 9 & 0 \\ 3 & 0 & 7 \end{bmatrix}$$

$$\boldsymbol{S} \succcurlyeq \mathbf{0}$$

Alternatively, it is as follows:

$$\max 11y_1 + 19y_2$$

Subject to the following:

$$\begin{bmatrix} 1 - 1y_1 - 0y_2 & 2 - 0y_1 - 2y_2 & 3 - 1y_1 - 8y_2 \\ 2 - 0y_1 - 2y_2 & 9 - 3y_1 - 6y_2 & 0 - 7y_1 - 0y_2 \\ 3 - 1y_1 - 8y_2 & 0 - 7y_1 - 0y_2 & 7 - 5y_1 - 4y_2 \end{bmatrix} \succeq \mathbf{0}$$

It is often easier to see and work with the dual form because the variables are the p multipliers, y_is.

The NM Dev `SDPPrimalProblem` class constructs an SDP problem in dual form. The class signature is as follows:

```
public class SDPDualProblem extends ConstrainedOptimProblemImpl1 {
    /**
     * Constructs a dual SDP problem.
     *
* @param b \(b\)
* @param C \(C\)
* @param A \(A\)
     */
```

```
    public SDPDualProblem(
            final Vector b,
            final SymmetricMatrix C,
            final SymmetricMatrix[] A
    );
    /**
     * Gets the dimension of the square matrices <i>C</i> and <i>A</i>s.
     *
     * @return the dimension of the matrices
     */
    public int n();
    /**
     * Gets the dimension of the system, i.e., <i>p</i> = the dimension of
     * <i>y</i>, the number of
     * variables.
     *
     * @return the dimension of the system
     */
    public int p();
    /**
     * Gets <i>b</i>.
     *
     * @return <i>b</i>
     */
    public ImmutableVector b();
    /**
     * Gets <i>C</i>.
     *
     * @return <i>C</i>
     */
    public SymmetricMatrix C();
    /**
     * Gets <i>A<sub>i</sub></i>.
     *
     * @param i an index to the A's, counting from 1
     * @return <i>A<sub>i</sub></i>
     */
    public SymmetricMatrix A(int i);
}
```

Continuing with this example, the following code constructs the dual problem:

```
// the dual SDP vector and matrices
val b: Vector = DenseVector(11.0, 19.0)
// construct the primal SDP problem
val dual = SDPDualProblem(
                b,
                C,
                arrayOf<SymmetricMatrix>(A1, A2))

println(dual)
```

10.4.2. Central Path

The Karush-Kuhn-Tucker (KKT) conditions for an SDP problem say that matrix $\boldsymbol{X}^*$ is a minimizer of the primal problem if and only if there exists a matrix $\boldsymbol{S}^* \in \boldsymbol{S}^n$ and a vector $\boldsymbol{y}^* \in R^p$ such that the following system holds:

$$\sum_{i=1}^{p} \boldsymbol{y}_i^* \boldsymbol{A}_i + \boldsymbol{S}^* = \boldsymbol{C}$$

$$\boldsymbol{A}_i \cdot \boldsymbol{X}^* = b_i$$

$$\boldsymbol{S}^* \boldsymbol{X}^* = \boldsymbol{0}$$

$$X^* \succcurlyeq 0, S^* \succcurlyeq 0,$$

It can be shown that a solution to the KKT conditions exists. The primal solution is $\left\{\boldsymbol{X}^*, \boldsymbol{y}_i^*, \boldsymbol{S}^*\right\}$. It can also be shown that $\left\{\boldsymbol{y}_i^*, \boldsymbol{S}^*\right\}$ is then a maximizer, and hence a solution, for the dual problem. Therefore, this solution is called a primal-dual solution.

The central path plays an essential role in the construction of interior-point algorithms. For SDP problems, the central path consists of a set $\{\boldsymbol{X}(\tau), \boldsymbol{y}(\tau), \boldsymbol{S}(\tau)\}$ such that the following system holds:

$$\sum_{i=1}^{p} \boldsymbol{y}(\tau) \boldsymbol{A}_i + \boldsymbol{S}(\tau) = \boldsymbol{C}$$

$$\boldsymbol{A}_i \cdot \boldsymbol{X}(\tau) = b_i$$

$$\boldsymbol{S}(\tau) \boldsymbol{X}(\tau) = \tau \boldsymbol{I}$$

$$\boldsymbol{X}(\tau) \succcurlyeq \boldsymbol{0}, \boldsymbol{S}(\tau) \succcurlyeq \boldsymbol{0}$$

It is almost a solution to the KKT conditions except for the $\tau \boldsymbol{I}$.

This difference or duality gap, δ, along the central path can be evaluated as follows:

$$\delta\left[\boldsymbol{X}(\tau), \boldsymbol{y}(\tau)\right] = \boldsymbol{C} \cdot \boldsymbol{X}(\tau) - \boldsymbol{b}^T \boldsymbol{y}(\tau)$$

$$= \left[\sum_{i=1}^{p} \boldsymbol{y}(\tau) \boldsymbol{A}_i + \boldsymbol{S}(\tau)\right] \cdot \boldsymbol{X}(\tau) - \boldsymbol{b}^T \boldsymbol{y}(\tau)$$

$$= \boldsymbol{S}(\tau) \boldsymbol{X}(\tau) = \text{trace}\left(\boldsymbol{S}(\tau) \boldsymbol{X}(\tau)\right) = \text{trace}(\tau \boldsymbol{I})$$

$$= n\tau$$

If you can close the gap by tracing τ to 0, the central path approaches a solution to the SDP problem. See Figure 10-14.

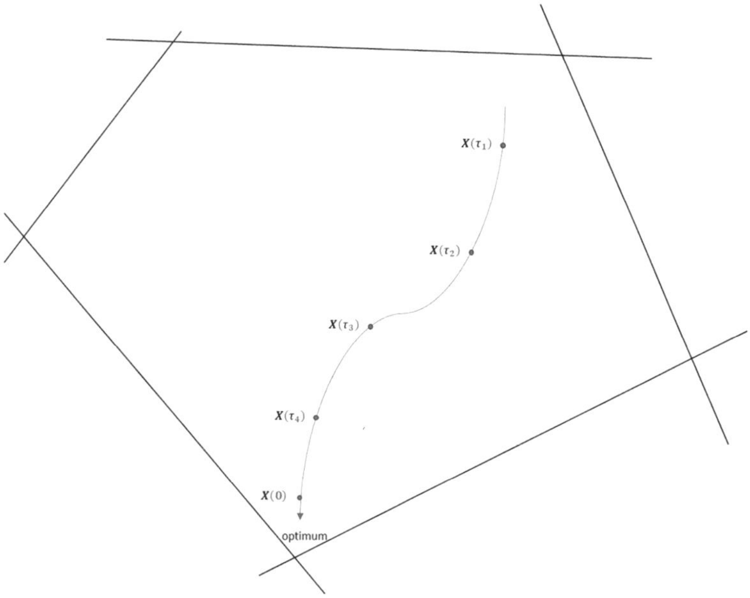

Figure 10-14. *A central path for interior point algorithm*

In other words:

$$\lim_{\tau \to 0} \delta\left[\boldsymbol{X}(\tau), \boldsymbol{y}(\tau)\right] = 0$$

Also, you have this:

$$\lim_{\tau \to 0} \boldsymbol{X}(\tau) = \boldsymbol{X}^*$$

$$\lim_{\tau \to 0} \boldsymbol{y}(\tau) = \boldsymbol{y}^*$$

$$\lim_{\tau \to 0} \boldsymbol{S}(\tau) = \boldsymbol{S}^*$$

The primal-dual solution is $\left\{\boldsymbol{X}^*, \boldsymbol{y}_i^*, \boldsymbol{S}^*\right\}$.

Interior-point algorithms are developed to generate iterates that converge to a primal-dual solution by following the central path of the problem. For each $\tau > 0$, $\boldsymbol{X}(\tau)$ and $\{\boldsymbol{y}(\tau), \boldsymbol{S}(\tau)\}$ are in the interior of the feasible region for the primal problem and the dual problem, respectively. Such is a path-following algorithm.

10.4.3. Primal-Dual Path-Following Method

You first define some operations and notations. Given matrices $\boldsymbol{K}, \boldsymbol{M}, \boldsymbol{N}$ in $\mathbb{R}^{n \times n}$, the general asymmetric Kronecker product is defined as follows:

$$\boldsymbol{M} \otimes \boldsymbol{N} = \begin{bmatrix} m_{11}\boldsymbol{N} & \dots & m_{1n}\boldsymbol{N} \\ \vdots & \ddots & \vdots \\ m_{n1}\boldsymbol{N} & \dots & m_{nn}\boldsymbol{N} \end{bmatrix}$$

The svec(***K***) operation converts a symmetric matrix $\boldsymbol{K} = \{k_{ij}\}$ into a vector of dimension $n(n+1)/2$ as follows:

$$\text{svec}(\boldsymbol{K}) = \left[k_{11}, \sqrt{2}k_{12}, \ldots, \sqrt{2}k_{1n}, k_{22}, \sqrt{2}k_{23}, \ldots, \sqrt{2}k_{2n}, \ldots, k_{nn}\right]^T$$

The symmetric Kronecker product is defined by the identity, as shown here:

$$(\boldsymbol{M} \odot \boldsymbol{N})\text{svec}(\boldsymbol{K}) = \text{svec}\left[\frac{1}{2}\left(\boldsymbol{NKM}^T + \boldsymbol{MKN}^T\right)\right]$$

For matrix variables, it is sometimes easier to represent and work with a matrix as a vector. The nevc(***K***) operation stacks the columns in ***K*** to create a vector.

In the Newton method, you start with a given set {***X***, ***y***, ***S***} and find increments $\Delta\boldsymbol{X}$, $\Delta\boldsymbol{y}$, $\Delta\boldsymbol{S}$, where $\Delta\boldsymbol{X}$ and $\Delta\boldsymbol{S}$ are symmetric, such that $\{\Delta\boldsymbol{X}, \Delta\boldsymbol{y}, \Delta\boldsymbol{S}\}$ satisfies the following linearized equations:

$$\sum_{i=1}^{p} \Delta \boldsymbol{y}_i \boldsymbol{A}_i + \Delta\boldsymbol{S} = \boldsymbol{C} - \boldsymbol{S} - \sum_{i=1}^{p} \boldsymbol{y}_i \boldsymbol{A}_i$$

$$\boldsymbol{A}_i \cdot \Delta\boldsymbol{X} = b_i - \boldsymbol{A}_i \bullet \boldsymbol{X}$$

$$\boldsymbol{X}\Delta\boldsymbol{S} + \Delta\boldsymbol{S}\boldsymbol{X} + \Delta\boldsymbol{X}\boldsymbol{S} + \boldsymbol{S}\Delta\boldsymbol{X} = 2\tau\boldsymbol{I} - \boldsymbol{XS} - \boldsymbol{SX}$$

The last equation can be expressed in terms of a symmetric Kronecker product:

$$(\boldsymbol{X} \odot \mathbf{I})\text{svec}(\Delta\boldsymbol{S}) + (\boldsymbol{S} \odot \boldsymbol{I})\text{svec}(\Delta\boldsymbol{X}) = \text{svec}\left[\tau\boldsymbol{I} - \frac{1}{2}(\boldsymbol{XS} + \boldsymbol{SX})\right]$$

For simplicity, let's denote the following:

$$\text{svec}(\Delta\boldsymbol{X}) = \Delta\mathbf{x}$$

$$\text{svec}(\Delta\boldsymbol{S}) = \Delta\boldsymbol{s}$$

$$\boldsymbol{S} \odot \boldsymbol{I} = \boldsymbol{E}$$

$$\boldsymbol{X} \odot \boldsymbol{I} = \boldsymbol{F}$$

$$\text{svec}\left[\tau\boldsymbol{I} - \frac{1}{2}(\boldsymbol{XS} + \boldsymbol{SX})\right] = \boldsymbol{r}_c$$

The last equation in these notations becomes as follows:

$$\boldsymbol{E}\Delta\mathbf{x} + \mathbf{F}\Delta\mathbf{s} = \boldsymbol{r}_c$$

Furthermore, let:

$$\boldsymbol{A} = \begin{bmatrix} \left[\text{svec}\left(\boldsymbol{A}_1\right)\right]^T \\ \left[\text{svec}\left(\boldsymbol{A}_2\right)\right]^T \\ \vdots \\ \left[\text{svec}\left(\boldsymbol{A}_p\right)\right]^T \end{bmatrix}$$

$$\boldsymbol{x} = \text{svec}\left(\boldsymbol{X}\right)$$

$$\boldsymbol{y} = \left[y_1, y_2, \ldots, y_p\right]^T$$

$$\Delta\boldsymbol{y} = \left[\Delta y_1, \Delta y_2, \ldots, \Delta y_p\right]^T$$

$$\boldsymbol{r}_p = \boldsymbol{b} - \boldsymbol{A}\boldsymbol{x}$$

$$\boldsymbol{r}_d = \text{svec}\left(\boldsymbol{C} - \boldsymbol{S} - \text{mat}\left(\boldsymbol{A}^T\boldsymbol{y}\right)\right)$$

where `mat( )` is the inverse of `svec( )`.

With these notations, the linearized system can be written as follows:

$$\begin{cases} \boldsymbol{A}^T\Delta\boldsymbol{y} + \Delta\boldsymbol{s} = \boldsymbol{r}_d \\ \boldsymbol{A}\Delta\boldsymbol{x} = \boldsymbol{r}_p \end{cases}$$

Or in succent form, you get this:

$$\boldsymbol{J}\begin{bmatrix} \Delta\boldsymbol{x} \\ \Delta\boldsymbol{y} \\ \Delta\boldsymbol{s} \end{bmatrix} = \begin{bmatrix} \boldsymbol{r}_d \\ \boldsymbol{r}_p \\ \boldsymbol{r}_c \end{bmatrix}$$

where:

$$\boldsymbol{J} = \begin{bmatrix} \boldsymbol{0} & \boldsymbol{A}^T & \boldsymbol{I} \\ \boldsymbol{A} & \boldsymbol{0} & \boldsymbol{0} \\ \boldsymbol{E} & \boldsymbol{0} & \boldsymbol{F} \end{bmatrix}$$

Antoniou & Lu (2007) provide the details of the interior point algorithm to solve the SDP problem as follows:

Primal-Dual Path-Following Algorithm for SDP Problem

Step 1

Input the problem as $\boldsymbol{A}i$ for $1 \le i \le p$, $\boldsymbol{b} \in \mathbb{R}p$, $\boldsymbol{C} \in \mathbb{R}n^{\times} n$, and a strictly feasible set $\{\boldsymbol{X}_0, \boldsymbol{y}_0, \boldsymbol{S}_0\}$ that satisfies feasibility constraints and that $\boldsymbol{X}_0 \succ 0$, $\boldsymbol{S}_0 \succ 0$.

Choose a scalar $\sigma \in [0, 1)$.

Set iteration counter $k = 0$ and initialize the tolerance ε for the duality gap δ_k.

Step 2

Compute the following:

$$\delta_k = \frac{\boldsymbol{X}_k \cdot \boldsymbol{S}_k}{n}$$

Step 3

If $\delta_k \le \varepsilon$, output the solution $\{\boldsymbol{X}_k, \boldsymbol{y}_k, \boldsymbol{S}_k\}$ and stop.

Otherwise, set the following:

$$\tau_k = \sigma \frac{\boldsymbol{X}_k \cdot \boldsymbol{S}_k}{n}$$

Step 4

Solve the following:

$$\boldsymbol{J} \begin{bmatrix} \Delta \boldsymbol{x} \\ \Delta \boldsymbol{y} \\ \Delta \boldsymbol{s} \end{bmatrix} = \begin{bmatrix} \boldsymbol{r}_d \\ \boldsymbol{r}_p \\ \boldsymbol{r}_c \end{bmatrix}$$

The solution is as follows:

$$\Delta \boldsymbol{x} = -\boldsymbol{E}^{-1}\left[\boldsymbol{F}\left(\boldsymbol{r}_d - \boldsymbol{A}^{\mathrm{T}}\Delta \boldsymbol{y}\right) - \boldsymbol{r}_c\right]$$

$$\Delta \boldsymbol{s} = \boldsymbol{r}_d - \boldsymbol{A}^T \Delta \boldsymbol{y}$$

$$\boldsymbol{M}\Delta \boldsymbol{y} = \boldsymbol{r}_p + \boldsymbol{A}\boldsymbol{E}^{-1}\left(\boldsymbol{F}\boldsymbol{r}_d - \boldsymbol{r}_c\right)$$

where $\boldsymbol{M}$ is the Schur complement matrix given by the following:

$$\boldsymbol{M} = \boldsymbol{A}\boldsymbol{E}^{-1}\boldsymbol{F}\boldsymbol{A}^T$$

Convert the solution $\{\Delta \mathbf{x}, \Delta \boldsymbol{y}, \Delta \mathbf{s}\}$ into $\{\Delta \boldsymbol{X}, \Delta \boldsymbol{y}, \Delta \boldsymbol{S}\}$ with $\Delta \boldsymbol{X} = \mathrm{mat}(\Delta \mathbf{x})$ and $\Delta \boldsymbol{S} = \mathrm{mat}(\Delta \mathbf{s})$.

Step 5

Choose a parameter $\gamma \in (0, 1)$ and determine parameters α and β as follows:

$$\alpha = \min\left(1, \gamma\hat{\alpha}\right)$$

$$\beta = \min\left(1, \gamma\hat{\beta}\right)$$

where:

$$\hat{\alpha} = \max_{X_k + \bar{\alpha}\Delta X \geq 0} \bar{\alpha}$$

$$\hat{\beta} = \max_{S_k + \bar{\beta}\Delta S \geq 0} \bar{\beta}$$

Step 6
Set the following:

$$\boldsymbol{X}_{k+1} = \boldsymbol{X}_k + \alpha \Delta \boldsymbol{X}$$

$$\boldsymbol{y}_{k+1} = \boldsymbol{y}_k + \beta \Delta \boldsymbol{y}$$

$$\boldsymbol{S}_{k+1} = \boldsymbol{S}_k + \beta \Delta \boldsymbol{S}$$

Set $k = k + 1$ and repeat from Step 2.

Antoniou & Lu (2007) provide the following example. Find scalars y_1, y_2, y_3 such that the maximum eigenvalue of the following:

$$\boldsymbol{F} = \boldsymbol{A_0} + y_1 \boldsymbol{A_1} + y_2 \boldsymbol{A_2} + y_3 \boldsymbol{A_3}$$

is minimized.

$$\boldsymbol{A}_0 = \begin{bmatrix} 2 & -0.5 & -0.6 \\ -0.5 & 2 & 0.4 \\ -0.6 & 0.4 & 3 \end{bmatrix}$$

$$\boldsymbol{A}_1 = \begin{bmatrix} 0 & 1 & 0 \\ 1 & 0 & 0 \\ 0 & 0 & 0 \end{bmatrix}$$

$$\boldsymbol{A}_2 = \begin{bmatrix} 0 & 0 & 1 \\ 0 & 0 & 0 \\ 1 & 0 & 0 \end{bmatrix}$$

$$\boldsymbol{A}_3 = \begin{bmatrix} 0 & 0 & 0 \\ 0 & 0 & 1 \\ 0 & 1 & 0 \end{bmatrix}$$

This problem can be formulated as a (dual) SDP problem.

$$\max_{y} \boldsymbol{b}^T \boldsymbol{y}$$

Subject to the following:

$$\sum_{i=1}^{4} y_i \boldsymbol{A}_i + \boldsymbol{S} = \boldsymbol{C}$$

$$S \succcurlyeq 0$$

And:

$$\boldsymbol{b} = \begin{bmatrix} 0 & 0 & 0 & 1 \end{bmatrix}^T$$

$$\boldsymbol{y} = \begin{bmatrix} y_1 & y_2 & y_3 & y_4 \end{bmatrix}^T$$

$$\boldsymbol{C} = -\boldsymbol{A}_0$$

$$\boldsymbol{A}_4 = \boldsymbol{I}$$

$-y_4$ is the maximum eigenvalue of matrix $\boldsymbol{F}$.
It is easy to verify that the initial set $\{\boldsymbol{X}_0, \boldsymbol{y}_0, \boldsymbol{S}_0\}$:

$$\boldsymbol{X}_0 = \frac{1}{3}\boldsymbol{I}$$

$$\boldsymbol{y}_0 = \begin{bmatrix} 0.2 & 0.2 & 0.2 - 4 \end{bmatrix}^T$$

$$\boldsymbol{S}_0 = \begin{bmatrix} 2 & 0.3 & 0.4 \\ 0.3 & 2 & -0.6 \\ 0.4 & -0.6 & 1 \end{bmatrix}$$

is strictly feasible for this primal-dual problem.
The matrix $\boldsymbol{A}$ is as follows:

$$\boldsymbol{A} = \begin{bmatrix} 0 & \sqrt{2} & 0 & 0 & 0 & 0 \\ 0 & 0 & \sqrt{2} & 0 & 0 & 0 \\ 0 & 0 & 0 & 0 & \sqrt{2} & 0 \\ 1 & 0 & 0 & 1 & 0 & 1 \end{bmatrix}$$

Set $\sigma = \dfrac{n}{15\sqrt{n} + n} = 0.1035$, $\gamma = 0.9$, $\varepsilon = 0.001$.

The algorithm, after four iterations, returns the solution $\{\boldsymbol{X}^*, \boldsymbol{y}^*, \boldsymbol{S}^*\}$ where you get this:

$$\boldsymbol{y}^* = \begin{bmatrix} 0.392921 \\ 0.599995 \\ -0.399992 \\ -3.000469 \end{bmatrix}$$

The maximum eigenvalue of ***F*** is 3.

In NM Dev, the `PrimalDualPathFollowingMinimizer` class implements this primal-dual path-following algorithm. The following code solves the previous SDP problem:

```
/**
* p.465 in
* Andreas Antoniou, Wu-Sheng Lu
*/

println("Solving an SDP problem")

// define an SDP problem with matrices and vectors
val A0: SymmetricMatrix = SymmetricMatrix(
    arrayOf(
        doubleArrayOf(2.0),
        doubleArrayOf(-0.5, 2.0),
        doubleArrayOf(-0.6, 0.4, 3.0)
    )
)

val A1: SymmetricMatrix = SymmetricMatrix(
    arrayOf(
        doubleArrayOf(0.0),
        doubleArrayOf(1.0, 0.0),
        doubleArrayOf(0.0, 0.0, 0.0)
    )
)

val A2: SymmetricMatrix = SymmetricMatrix(
    arrayOf(
        doubleArrayOf(0.0),
        doubleArrayOf(0.0, 0.0),
        doubleArrayOf(1.0, 0.0, 0.0)
    )
)

val A3: SymmetricMatrix = SymmetricMatrix(
    arrayOf(
        doubleArrayOf(0.0),
        doubleArrayOf(0.0, 0.0),
        doubleArrayOf(0.0, 1.0, 0.0)
    )
)

val A4: SymmetricMatrix = A3.ONE()
val C: SymmetricMatrix = A0.scaled(-1.0)
val b: Vector = DenseVector(0.0, 0.0, 0.0, 1.0)
// construct an SDP problem
val problem = SDPDualProblem(
        b,
        C,
        arrayOf<SymmetricMatrix>(A1, A2, A3, A4))
```

```
// the initial feasible point
val X0: DenseMatrix = DenseMatrix(
    arrayOf(
        doubleArrayOf(1.0 / 3.0, 0.0, 0.0),
        doubleArrayOf(0.0, 1.0 / 3.0, 0.0),
        doubleArrayOf(0.0, 0.0, 1.0 / 3.0)
    )
)

val y0: Vector = DenseVector(0.2, 0.2, 0.2, -4.0)

val S0: DenseMatrix = DenseMatrix(
    arrayOf(
        doubleArrayOf(2.0, 0.3, 0.4),
        doubleArrayOf(0.3, 2.0, -0.6),
        doubleArrayOf(0.4, -0.6, 1.0)
    )
)

// the initial central path
val path0: CentralPath = CentralPath(X0, y0, S0)

// solving SDP problem
val solver = PrimalDualPathFollowingMinimizer(
                0.9, // γ
                0.001) // ε
val solution: IterativeSolution<CentralPath> = solver.solve(problem)
val path: CentralPath = solution.search(path0)

//the solution from the textbook is accurate up to epsilon
//changing epsilon will change the answers
// primal solution
println("X = ")
println(path.X)
// dual solution
println("Y = ")
println(path.y)
println("S = ")
println(path.S)
```

The output is as follows:

```
X =
3x3
         [,1] [,2] [,3]
[1,] 0.000552, -0.000000, -0.000000,
[2,] -0.000000, 0.000552, 0.000000,
[3,] -0.000000, 0.000000, 0.998896,
y =
[0.392921, 0.599995, -0.399992, -3.000469]
```

```
S =
3x3
         [,1] [,2] [,3]
[1,] 1.000469, 0.107079, 0.000005,
[2,] 0.107079, 1.000469, -0.000008,
[3,] 0.000005, -0.000008, 0.000469,
```

10.5. Second-Order Cone Programming

Second-order cone programming (SOCP) problems are convex optimization problems in which a linear function is minimized over the intersection of an affine linear manifold with the Cartesian product of second-order cones. SOCP is widely applied in robust optimization and combinatorial optimization in engineering, control, and finance. LP, convex QP, and many other linear problems can be formulated as SOCP problems. On the other hand, SDP includes SOCP as a special case. Like LP, QP, and SDP problems, SOCP problems can be solved in polynomial time by interior point methods. The computational effort per iteration required by these methods to solve SOCP problems is greater than that required to solve LP and QP problems, but less than that required to solve SDPs of similar size and structure. While SOCP problems can be solved as SDP problems, you will usually do not do that because of numerical stability and computational complexity.

10.5.1. SOCP Problems

A cone $\mathbb{C}$ is a set such that $x \in \mathbb{C}$ implies that $\alpha x \in \mathbb{C}$ for any scalar $\alpha \geq 0$. By definition, a cone is always unbounded. A convex cone $\mathcal{K}$ is a convex set such that $\mathbf{x} \in \mathcal{K}$. This implies that $\alpha \mathbf{x} \in \mathcal{K}$ for any scalar $\alpha \geq 0$. Figure 10-15 shows a convex cone in $\mathbb{R}^3$.

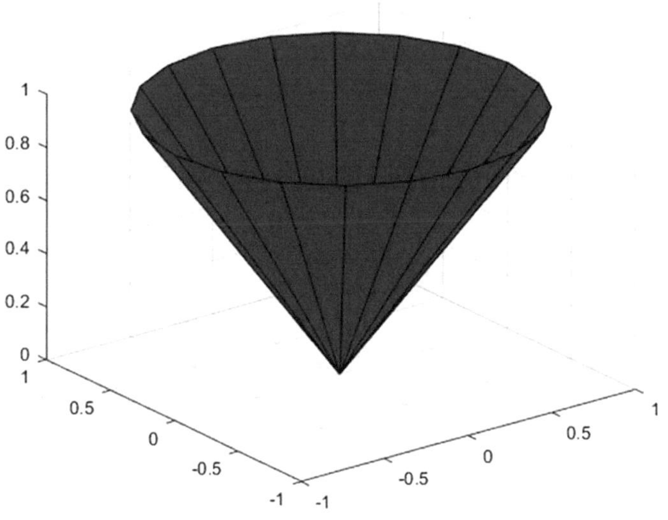

***Figure 10-15.** A convex cone*

Not all cones are convex. For example, the following one-dimensional cone is not convex (see Figure 10-16):

$$y = |x|$$

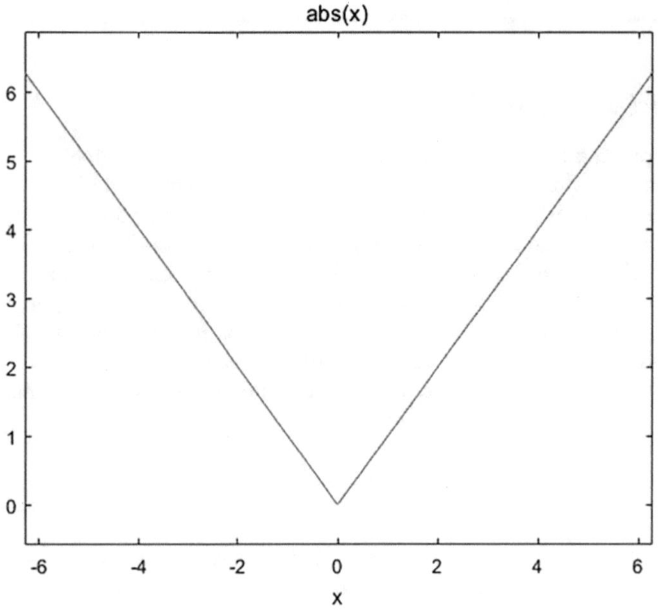

Figure 10-16. *A nonconvex cone*

The midpoint, (0, 2), of the two points, (−2, 2) and (2, 2), is not on the curve.

A *norm cone* is defined as follows:

$$C = \{(\boldsymbol{x}, t) \mid \|\boldsymbol{x}\| \le t, \boldsymbol{x} \in \mathbb{R}^{n-1}, t \in \mathbb{R}\}$$

A second-order cone is the norm cone for Euclidean space. It is defined as follows:

$$\mathcal{K} = \left\{ \begin{bmatrix} t \\ \boldsymbol{u} \end{bmatrix} \mid \|\boldsymbol{u}\| \le t, \boldsymbol{u} \in \mathbb{R}^{n-1}, t \in \mathbb{R} \right\}$$

Figure 10-17 shows the second-order cones for dimensions 1, 2, and 3.

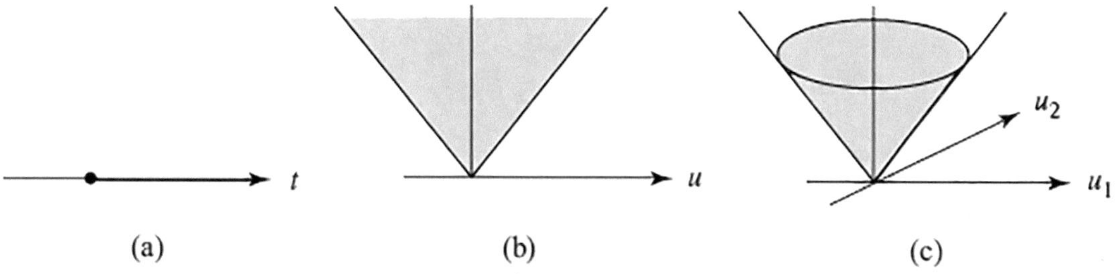

Figure 10-17. *Second-order cones of dimensions 1, 2, and 3 (Antoniou & Lu, 2007)*

The primal SOCP problem is stated as follows:

$$\min \sum_{i=1}^{q} \hat{\boldsymbol{c}}_i^T \boldsymbol{x}_i$$

Subject to the following:

$$\sum_{i=1}^{q} \hat{\boldsymbol{A}}_i^T \boldsymbol{x}_i = \boldsymbol{b}$$

$$\boldsymbol{x}_i \in \mathcal{K}_i \text{ , } i = 1, \ldots, q$$

where $\hat{\boldsymbol{c}}_i \in \mathbb{R}^{n_i}$, $\boldsymbol{x}_i \in \mathbb{R}^{n_i}$, $\hat{\boldsymbol{A}}_i \in \mathbb{R}^{m \times n_i}$, $\boldsymbol{b} \in R^m$.

$\mathcal{K}_i$ is a second-order cone of dimension n_i. Each variable vector $\boldsymbol{x}_i$ in an SOCP problem is constrained to a second-order cone $\mathcal{K}_i$.

The dual of SOCP problem is stated as follows:

$$\max \boldsymbol{b}^T \boldsymbol{y}$$

Subject to the following:

$$\hat{\boldsymbol{A}}_i^T \boldsymbol{y} + \boldsymbol{s}_i = \hat{\boldsymbol{c}}_i$$

$$\boldsymbol{s}_i \in \mathcal{K}_i \text{ , } i = 1, \ldots, q$$

where $\boldsymbol{y} \in \mathbb{R}^m$ and $\boldsymbol{s}_i \in \mathbb{R}^{n_i}$.

If you let

$$\boldsymbol{x} = -\boldsymbol{y}$$

$$\hat{\boldsymbol{A}}_i^T = \begin{bmatrix} \boldsymbol{b}_i^T \\ \boldsymbol{A}_i^T \end{bmatrix}$$

$$\hat{\boldsymbol{c}}_i = \begin{bmatrix} d_i \\ \boldsymbol{c}_i \end{bmatrix}$$

where $\boldsymbol{b}_i \in \mathbb{R}^m$ and d_i is a scalar, then the dual of SOCP problem can be written in the standard form, as shown here:

$$\min \boldsymbol{b}^T \boldsymbol{x}$$

Subject to the following:

$$\| \boldsymbol{A}_i^T \boldsymbol{x} + \boldsymbol{c}_i \| \leq \boldsymbol{b}_i^T \boldsymbol{x} + d_i$$

The NM Dev class called `SOCPGeneralConstraint` implements the constraints in standard form. The class signature is as follows:

```
public class SOCPGeneralConstraint {
    private final Matrix A;
    private final Vector c;
    private final Vector b;
    private final double d;
    /**
     * Constructs a SOCP general constraint.
     *
     * @param A <i>A</i>
     * @param c <i>c</i>
     * @param b <i>b</i>
     * @param d <i>d</i>
     */
    public SOCPGeneralConstraint(
            Matrix A,
            Vector c,
            Vector b,
            double d
    ) {
        this.A = A;
        this.c = c;
        this.b = b;
        this.d = d;
    }
    /**
     * Gets <i>A</i>.
     *
     * @return <i>A</i>
     */
    public Matrix A() {
        return A;
    }
    /**
     * Gets <i>c</i>.
     *
     * @return <i>c</i>
     */
    public Vector c() {
        return c;
    }
```

```
    /**
     * Gets <i>b</i>.
     *
     * @return <i>b</i>
     */
    public Vector b() {
        return b;
    }
    /**
     * Gets <i>d</i>.
     *
     * @return <i>d</i>
     */
    public double d() {
        return d;
    }
}
```

NM Dev also supports SOCP equality constraints with the `SOCPLinearEquality` class.

$$\boldsymbol{A}^T \boldsymbol{x} = \boldsymbol{c}$$

The class signature is as follows:

```
public class SOCPLinearEquality {
    private final Matrix A;
    private final Vector c;
    public SOCPLinearEquality(Matrix A, Vector c) {
        assertTrue(
            A.nCols() == c.size(),
            "A.nCols() (%d) == c.size() (%d)",
            A.nCols(), c.size()
        );
        this.A = A;
        this.c = c;
    }
    /**
     * @return the matrix A
     */
    public Matrix A() {
        return A;
    }
    /**
     * @return the vector c
     */
    public Vector c() {
        return c;
    }
}
```

The NM Dev class called SOCPGeneralProblem constructs an SOCP problem in standard form. The class signature is as follows:

```
public class SOCPGeneralProblem extends SOCPDualProblem {
    /**
     * Copy constructor.
     *
     * @param that another {@linkplain  SOCPGeneralProblem}
     */
    public SOCPGeneralProblem(SOCPGeneralProblem that);
    /**
     * Construct a general Second Order Conic Programming problem. Minimize
     **\[
     **f^' x
    *\]
     * subject to the SOCP constraints
     * \[
    * \lVert A_i x + b_i \rVert_2 \leq c_i^T x + d_i,\quad i = 1,\dots,m
    *\]
     * @param f           <i>f</i>
     * @param constraints the SOCP constraints
     */
    public SOCPGeneralProblem(
            Vector f,
            SOCPGeneralConstraint[] constraints
    );
    /**
     * Construct a general Second Order Conic Programming problem. Minimize
    * \[
    * f^' x
    * \]
     * subject to the SOCP constraints
    * \[
    * \lVert A_i x + b_i \rVert_2 \leq c_i^T x + d_i,\quad i = 1,\dots,m
* \]
     *
     * @param f           <i>f</i>
     * @param constraints the SOCP constraints
     */
    public SOCPGeneralProblem(
            Vector f,
            List<SOCPGeneralConstraint> constraints
    );
}
```

This standard-form SOCP turns out to have a direct connection to many convex-programming problems in engineering and sciences such as quantitative finance.

Portfolio Optimization

We formulated the classic modern portfolio theory as a quadratic programming problem in Section 10.3.

$$\min_{\boldsymbol{x}} \lambda \boldsymbol{x}^T \Sigma \boldsymbol{x} - \boldsymbol{x}^T \mu$$

Subject to the following:

$$\sum_{i=1}^{n} x_i = 1$$

$$\boldsymbol{x} \geq 0$$

In practice, you can add other constraints to match real trading scenarios. Suppose you are a large bank that wants to sell a large block of stocks. You do not want to just dump the stocks to the market, which will cause a sharp drop in prices, which in turn is bad for your selling. You would want to minimize the market impact when rebalancing a large portfolio of stocks. The market impact of a stock is usually modeled as proportional to the volume of the stock to the power of 3/2. The constraint to minimize market impact is often stated as follows:

$$\sum_{j=1}^{n} \left(m_j \left| x_j \right|^{\frac{3}{2}} \right) \leq t_2$$

where m_j is the market impact coefficient for a stock; x_j is the stock volume, position, or weight; and t_2 is a constant of acceptable tolerance.

This is not a linear constraint because of the term with power 3/2. It can be formulated as an SOCP constraint, however, and the portfolio optimization problem can be formulated and solved as an SOCP problem.

Letting $\bar{x} = |\boldsymbol{x}|$, the market impact term is transformed into the following:

$$\sum_{j=1}^{n} \left(m_j \bar{x}_j^{\frac{3}{2}} \right) \leq t_2$$

By introducing variables $\boldsymbol{y} = \boldsymbol{x} + \boldsymbol{w}^0$ ($\boldsymbol{w}^0$ represents the last or original stock positions, $\boldsymbol{x}$ represents the adjustments or the trading volumes, and $\boldsymbol{y}$ represents the new stock positions), α, and β, the previous inequality is equivalent to the following:

$$\begin{cases} \sum_{j=1}^{n} \beta_j \leq t_2 \\ \left| y_j - w_j^0 \right| \leq \bar{x}_j \\ m_j \bar{x}_j^{\frac{3}{2}} \leq \beta_j \end{cases}$$

These constraints can be further transformed into the following:

$$\begin{cases} \sum_{j=1}^{n} \beta_j \le t_2 \\ y_j - w_j^0 \le \bar{x}_j \\ -y_j + w_j^0 \le \bar{x}_j \\ \bar{x}_j^{\frac{3}{2}} \le \dfrac{\beta_j}{m_j} \end{cases}$$

Therefore, you get the following:

$$\begin{cases} \|0\|_2 \le t_2 - \sum_{j=1}^{n} \beta_j \\ \|0\|_2 \le \bar{x}_j - \left(y_j - w_j^0\right) \\ \|0\|_2 \le \bar{x}_j - \left(-y_j + w_j^0\right) \\ \bar{x}_j^{\frac{3}{2}} \le \dfrac{\beta_j}{m_j} \end{cases}$$

The last inequality, $\bar{x}_j^{\frac{3}{2}} \le \frac{\beta_j}{m_j}$, is equivalent to the following:

$$\bar{x}_j^{\frac{3}{2}} \le \frac{\beta_j}{m_j}, \bar{x}_j \ge 0$$

$$\Leftrightarrow \bar{x}_j^2 \le s_j \frac{\beta_j}{m_j}, s_j \le \sqrt{\bar{x}_j}, \bar{x}_j \ge 0, s_j \ge 0, \frac{\beta_j}{m_j} \ge 0$$

$$\Leftrightarrow \bar{x}_j^2 \le s_j \frac{\beta_j}{m_j}, s_j^2 \le \bar{x}_j, \bar{x}_j \ge 0, s_j \ge 0, \frac{\beta_j}{m_j} \ge 0$$

$$\Leftrightarrow \bar{x}_j^2 + \left(\frac{\beta_j}{2m_j} - \frac{s_j}{2}\right)^2 \le \left(\frac{\beta_j}{2m_j} + \frac{s_j}{2}\right)^2, s_j^2 + \left(\frac{1-\bar{x}_j}{2}\right)^2 \le \left(\frac{1+\bar{x}_j}{2}\right)^2, \bar{x}_j \ge 0, s_j \ge 0, \frac{\beta_j}{m_j} \ge 0$$

Because $\bar{x}_j \ge 0, s_j \ge 0, \frac{\beta_j}{m_j} \ge 0$ can be deduced from other constraints, and they can be deleted from the system of constraints. The previous constraints can be written as follows:

$$\begin{cases} \left\| \begin{pmatrix} \bar{x}_j \\ \dfrac{\beta_j}{2m_j} - \dfrac{s_j}{2} \end{pmatrix} \right\|_2 \le \dfrac{\beta_j}{2m_j} + \dfrac{s_j}{2} \\ \left\| \begin{pmatrix} s_j \\ \dfrac{1-\bar{x}_j}{2} \end{pmatrix} \right\|_2 \le \dfrac{1+\bar{x}_j}{2} \end{cases}$$

Combining all the constraints, the system of constraints for market impact is as follows:

$$\begin{cases} \|0\|_2 \leqslant t_2 - \sum_{j=1}^{n} \beta_j \\ \|0\|_2 \leqslant \bar{x}_j - \left(y_j - w_j^0\right) \\ \|0\|_2 \leqslant \bar{x}_j - \left(-y_j + w_j^0\right) \\ \left\| \begin{pmatrix} \bar{x}_j \\ \dfrac{\beta_j}{2m_j} - \dfrac{s_j}{2} \end{pmatrix} \right\|_2 \leqslant \dfrac{\beta_j}{2m_j} + \dfrac{s_j}{2} \\ \left\| \begin{pmatrix} s_j \\ \dfrac{1-\bar{x}_j}{2} \end{pmatrix} \right\|_2 \leqslant \dfrac{1+\bar{x}_j}{2} \end{cases}$$

Then, the SOCP constraints in standard form are as follows:

$$\begin{cases} \|0\|_2 \le t_2 - \sum_{j=1}^{n} \beta_j \Leftrightarrow \| \boldsymbol{A}_1^T \boldsymbol{z} + \boldsymbol{C}_1 \|_2 \le \boldsymbol{b}_1^T \boldsymbol{z} + d_1 \\ \boldsymbol{A}_1^T = \boldsymbol{0}_{1\times n}, \boldsymbol{C}_1 = \boldsymbol{0}, \boldsymbol{b}_1 = \begin{pmatrix} -\boldsymbol{1}_{n\times 1} \\ \boldsymbol{1} \end{pmatrix}, d_1 = 0, \boldsymbol{z} = \begin{pmatrix} \beta \\ t_2 \end{pmatrix} \end{cases}$$

And as follows:

$$\begin{cases} \|0\|_2 \le \bar{x}_j - \left(y_j - w_j^0\right) \Leftrightarrow \| \boldsymbol{A}_{2,j}^T \boldsymbol{z} + \boldsymbol{C}_{2,\mathbf{j}} \|_2 \le \boldsymbol{b}_{2,\mathbf{j}}^T \boldsymbol{z} + d_{2,j} \\ \boldsymbol{A}_{2,j}^T = \boldsymbol{0}_{1\times 2n}, \boldsymbol{C}_{2,j} = \boldsymbol{0}, \boldsymbol{b}_{2,j} = \begin{pmatrix} -\boldsymbol{e}_j \\ \boldsymbol{e}_j \end{pmatrix}, d_{2,j} = w_j^0, \boldsymbol{z} = \begin{pmatrix} \boldsymbol{y} \\ x \end{pmatrix} \end{cases}$$

$$\begin{cases} \|0\|_2 \le \bar{x}_j - \left(-y_j + w_j^0\right) \Leftrightarrow \| \boldsymbol{A}_{3,j}^T \boldsymbol{z} + \boldsymbol{C}_{3,j} \|_2 \le \boldsymbol{b}_{3,j}^T \boldsymbol{z} + d_{3,j} \\ \boldsymbol{A}_{3,j}^T = \boldsymbol{0}_{1\times 2n}, \boldsymbol{C}_{3,j} = \boldsymbol{0}, \boldsymbol{b}_{3,j} = \begin{pmatrix} \boldsymbol{e}_j \\ \boldsymbol{e}_j \end{pmatrix}, d_{3,j} = -w_j^0, \boldsymbol{z} = \begin{pmatrix} \boldsymbol{y} \\ x \end{pmatrix} \end{cases}$$

where $\boldsymbol{e}_j$ is an n-dimensional vector whose j-th entry is 1 and all the other entries are 0. Also, you get the following:

$$\begin{cases} \left\| \begin{pmatrix} \bar{x}_j \\ \dfrac{\beta_j}{2m_j} - \dfrac{s_j}{2} \end{pmatrix} \right\|_2 \leqslant \dfrac{\beta_j}{2m_j} + \dfrac{s_j}{2} \Leftrightarrow \| A_{4,j}^T z + C_{4,j} \|_2 \leqslant b_{4,j}^T z + d_{4,j} \\ A_{4,j}^T = \begin{pmatrix} e_j^T & \boldsymbol{0}_{1\times n} & \boldsymbol{0}_{1\times n} \\ \boldsymbol{0}_{1\times n} & \dfrac{1}{2m_j} e_j^T & -\dfrac{1}{2} e_j^T \end{pmatrix}, C_{4,j} = \boldsymbol{0}_{2\times 1}, b_{4,j} = \begin{pmatrix} \boldsymbol{0}_{n\times 1} \\ \dfrac{1}{2m_j} e_j \\ \dfrac{1}{2} e_j \end{pmatrix}, d_{4,j} = 0, z = \begin{pmatrix} \bar{x} \\ \beta_j \\ s \end{pmatrix} \end{cases}$$

$$\begin{cases} \left\| \begin{pmatrix} s_j \\ \dfrac{1-\overline{x}_j}{2} \end{pmatrix} \right\|_2 \leqslant \dfrac{1+\overline{x}_j}{2} \Leftrightarrow \| A_{5,j}^T z + C_{5,j} \|_2 \leqslant b_{5,j}^T z + d_{5,j} \\ A_{5,j}^T = \begin{pmatrix} \mathbf{0}_{1\times n} & e_j^T \\ -\dfrac{1}{2} e_j^T & \mathbf{0}_{1\times n} \end{pmatrix}, C_{5,j} = \begin{pmatrix} \mathbf{0} \\ \dfrac{1}{2} \end{pmatrix}, b_{5,j} = \begin{pmatrix} \dfrac{1}{2} e_j \\ \mathbf{0}_{n\times 1} \end{pmatrix}, d_{5,j} = \dfrac{1}{2}, z = \begin{pmatrix} \overline{x} \\ s \end{pmatrix} \end{cases}$$

The NM Dev class called `MarketImpact1` implements this SOCP constraint for advanced portfolio optimization. The class signature is as follows:

```
public class MarketImpact1 extends SOCPPortfolioConstraint {
    /**
     * Constructs a market impact term.
     *
     * @param w_0 the initial position
     * @param m   the market impact parameter
     */
    public MarketImpact1(Vector w_0, Vector m);
}
```

The previous example shows how to transform a nonlinear constraint into a set of SOCP constraints in standard form. Similar techniques can be applied to other nonlinear constraints as well. The other `SOCPPortfolioConstraint` constraints that NM FinTech currently supports are as follows:

- `SOCPMaximumLoan`: Maximum allowed borrowing for stocks
- `SOCPNoTradingList1`: Black list for stocks that are not allowed to trade
- `SOCPSectorExposure`: Maximum exposure allowed for sectors
- `SOCPSectorNeutrality`: Sector-neutral portfolio
- `SOCPSelfFinancing`: Self-financing portfolio
- `SOCPZeroValue`: Zero-cost portfolio

You can find more information in the NM FinTech package:

```
tech.nmfin.portfoliooptimization
```

Or, check out the website :
`https://nmfin.tech/`

10.5.2. Primal-Dual Method for SOCP Problems

Let:

$$\boldsymbol{c} = \left[\hat{\boldsymbol{c}}_1 \ \hat{\boldsymbol{c}}_2 \ldots \hat{\boldsymbol{c}}_q \right]^T$$

$$\boldsymbol{x} = \left[\boldsymbol{x}_1 \ \boldsymbol{x}_2 \ldots \boldsymbol{x}_q \right]^T$$

$$\boldsymbol{s} = \begin{bmatrix} \boldsymbol{s}_1 & \boldsymbol{s}_2 \ldots \boldsymbol{s}_q \end{bmatrix}^T$$

$$\boldsymbol{A} = \begin{bmatrix} \hat{\boldsymbol{A}}_1 \hat{\boldsymbol{A}}_2 \ldots \hat{\boldsymbol{A}}_q \end{bmatrix}^T$$

$$\mathcal{K} = \mathcal{K}_1 * \mathcal{K}_2 * \ldots * \mathcal{K}_q$$

where $\mathcal{K}_1\ \mathcal{K}_2 \ldots \mathcal{K}_q$ are second-order cones and $\mathcal{K}$ represents a second-order cone whose elements are $\boldsymbol{x} = [\boldsymbol{x}_1\, \boldsymbol{x}_2 \ldots \boldsymbol{x}_q]^T$ with $\boldsymbol{x}_i \in \mathcal{K}_i$. Then, the primal SOCP problem can be written as follows:

$$\min \boldsymbol{c}^T \boldsymbol{x}$$

Subject to the following:

$$\boldsymbol{Ax} = \boldsymbol{b}, \boldsymbol{x} \in \mathcal{K}$$

Or, in dual form, you get this:

$$\max \boldsymbol{b}^T \boldsymbol{y}$$

Subject to the following:

$$\boldsymbol{A}^T \boldsymbol{y} + \boldsymbol{s} = \boldsymbol{c}, \boldsymbol{s} \in \mathcal{K}$$

Therefore, the duality gap between $\boldsymbol{x}$ and ($\boldsymbol{s}$, $\boldsymbol{y}$) is as follows:

$$\delta(\boldsymbol{x},\boldsymbol{s},\boldsymbol{y}) = \boldsymbol{c}^T \boldsymbol{x} - \boldsymbol{b}^T \boldsymbol{y} = \left(\mathbf{A}^T\ \ \mathbf{y} + \boldsymbol{s}\right)^T \boldsymbol{x} - \boldsymbol{b}^T \boldsymbol{y} = \boldsymbol{s}^T \boldsymbol{x}$$

The KKT conditions, for a primal-dual solution $(\mathbf{x},\mathbf{s},\mathbf{y}) \in \mathcal{K} * \mathcal{K} * \mathbb{R}^m$, are as follows:

$$\boldsymbol{Ax} = \boldsymbol{b}$$

$$\boldsymbol{A}^T \boldsymbol{y} + \boldsymbol{s} = \boldsymbol{c}$$

$$\boldsymbol{x}^T \boldsymbol{s} = 0$$

Suppose after the k-th iterations, the vector set is ($\boldsymbol{x}_k$, $\boldsymbol{s}_k$, $\boldsymbol{y}_k$). The next update is as follows:

$$(\boldsymbol{x}_{k+1}, \boldsymbol{s}_{k+1}, \boldsymbol{y}_{k+1}) = (\boldsymbol{x}_k, \boldsymbol{s}_k, \boldsymbol{y}_k) + \alpha_k (\Delta \boldsymbol{x}, \Delta \boldsymbol{s}, \Delta \boldsymbol{y})$$

where α_k is a positive scalar.
($\Delta\boldsymbol{x}$, $\Delta\boldsymbol{s}$, $\Delta\boldsymbol{y}$) is obtained by solving the system of equations, as shown here:

$$\boldsymbol{A}\Delta\boldsymbol{x} = \boldsymbol{b} - \boldsymbol{Ax}$$

$$\boldsymbol{A}^T \Delta\boldsymbol{y} + \Delta\boldsymbol{s} = \boldsymbol{c} - \boldsymbol{s} - \boldsymbol{A}^T \boldsymbol{y}$$

$$\boldsymbol{S}\Delta\boldsymbol{x} + \boldsymbol{X}\Delta\boldsymbol{s} = \sigma\mu\boldsymbol{e} - \boldsymbol{Xs}$$

where

$$e = [1\ 1 \ldots 1]^T$$

$$X = \text{diag}\,\{X_1, \ldots, X_q\},\ X_1 = \begin{bmatrix} t_i & u_i^T \\ u_i & t_i I_i \end{bmatrix}$$

$$S = diag\{S_1, \ldots, S_q\}$$

$$\mu = x^T s / q$$

σ is a small positive scalar. I_i is an $n_i - 1$ identity matrix. It can be shown that the vector set (x_k, s_k, y_k) is updated so that the new vector set $(x_k +{}_1, s_{k+1}, y_{k+1})$ better approximates KKT conditions and hence creates a smaller duality gap.

Antoniou & Lu (2007) provide the details of the interior point algorithm to solve SOCP problems as follows.

Primal-Dual Interior-Point Algorithm for SOCP Problems

Step 1

Input the problem specification $\{A, b, c\}$, parameters q and $\{n_i\}$ for $i = 1, 2, \ldots, q$, and tolerance ε.

Input an initial vector set (x_0, s_0, y_0) in the interior of the feasible region.

Set $\delta_0 = \frac{x_0^T s_0}{q}$, $\sigma = 10^{-5}$.

Se the iteration counter $k = 0$.

Step 2

Solve for $(\Delta x, \Delta s, \Delta y)$.

Step 3

Choose α_k.

Step 4

Update $(x_{k+1}, s_{k+1}, y_{k+1}) = (x_k, s_k, y_k) + \alpha_k(\Delta x, \Delta s, \Delta y)$.

Step 5

Compute the following:

$$\delta_{k+1} = \frac{x_{k+1}^T s_{k+1}}{q}$$

If $\delta_{k+1} \le \varepsilon$, output the solution $(x^*, s^*, y^*) = (x_{k+1}, s_{k+1}, y_{k+1})$ and stop.

Otherwise, set $k = k + 1$ and repeat from Step 2.

Antoniou & Lu (2007) provide the following example to demonstrate the algorithm:

$$\min \delta$$

Subject to the following:

$$\left[(x_1 - x_3)^2 + (x_2 - x_4)^2\right]^{1/2} \le \delta$$

$$\begin{bmatrix} x_1 & x_2 \end{bmatrix} \begin{bmatrix} 0.25 & 0 \\ 0 & 1 \end{bmatrix} \begin{bmatrix} x_1 \\ x_2 \end{bmatrix} - \begin{bmatrix} x_1 & x_2 \end{bmatrix} \begin{bmatrix} 0.5 \\ 0 \end{bmatrix} \le 0.75$$

$$\begin{bmatrix} x_3 & x_4 \end{bmatrix} \begin{bmatrix} 0.625 & 0.375 \\ 0.375 & 0.625 \end{bmatrix} \begin{bmatrix} x_3 \\ x_4 \end{bmatrix} - \begin{bmatrix} x_3 & x_4 \end{bmatrix} \begin{bmatrix} 5.5 \\ 6.5 \end{bmatrix} \leq -17.5$$

First write the problem in standard form. Let:

$$\boldsymbol{x} = \begin{bmatrix} \delta x_1 & x_2 & x_3 & x_4 \end{bmatrix}^T$$

The SOCP problem can be written as follows:

$$\min \boldsymbol{b}^T \boldsymbol{x}$$

Subject to the following:

$$\| \boldsymbol{A}_i^T \boldsymbol{x} + \boldsymbol{c}_i \| \leq \boldsymbol{b}_i^T \boldsymbol{x} + d_i$$

where:

$$\boldsymbol{b} = \begin{bmatrix} 1 & 0 & 0 & 0 & 0 \end{bmatrix}^T$$

$$\boldsymbol{A}_1^T = \begin{bmatrix} 0 & -1 & 0 & 1 & 0 \\ 0 & 0 & 1 & 0 & -1 \end{bmatrix}$$

$$\boldsymbol{A}_2^T = \begin{bmatrix} 0 & 0.5 & 0 & 0 & 0 \\ 0 & 0 & 1 & 0 & -0 \end{bmatrix}$$

$$\boldsymbol{A}_3^T = \begin{bmatrix} 0 & 0 & 0 & -0.7071 & -0.7071 \\ 0 & 0 & 0 & -0.3536 & 0.3536 \end{bmatrix}$$

$$\boldsymbol{b}_1 = \boldsymbol{b}, \boldsymbol{b}_2 = \boldsymbol{0}, \boldsymbol{b}_3 = \boldsymbol{0}$$

$$\boldsymbol{c}_1 = \boldsymbol{0}, \boldsymbol{c}_2 = \begin{bmatrix} -0.5 \\ 0 \end{bmatrix}, \boldsymbol{c}_3 = \begin{bmatrix} 4.2426 \\ -0.7071 \end{bmatrix}$$

$$d_1 = 0, d_2 = 1, d_3 = 1$$

To generate an initial strictly feasible vector set ($\boldsymbol{x}_0$, $\boldsymbol{s}_0$, $\boldsymbol{y}_0$), try the following:

$$\begin{bmatrix} x_1 & x_2 & x_3 & x_4 \end{bmatrix} = \begin{bmatrix} 1.5 & 0.5 & 2.5 & 4 \end{bmatrix}$$

$$\boldsymbol{y}_0 = \begin{bmatrix} \beta & -1.5 & -0.5 & -2.5 & -4 \end{bmatrix}^T$$

where β is a scalar to ensure that $\boldsymbol{s}_0$ is an interior point.

$$\boldsymbol{s}_0 = \boldsymbol{c} - \boldsymbol{A}^T \boldsymbol{y} = \begin{bmatrix} \beta & 1 & 3.5 & 0 & 0 & 1 & 0.25 & 0.5 & -0.3535 & -0.1767 \end{bmatrix}^T$$

When $n_1 = 5$, $n_2 = 3$, $n_3 = 3$, choosing $\beta = 3.7$ can guarantee that $\boldsymbol{s}_0$ is an interior point. This gives the following:

$$\mathbf{y}_0 = \begin{bmatrix} 3.7 & -1.5 & -0.5 & -2.5 & -4 \end{bmatrix}^T$$

$$\boldsymbol{s}_0 = \begin{bmatrix} 3.7 & 1 & 3.5 & 0 & 0 & 1 & 0.25 & 0.5 & 1 & -0.3535 & -0.1767 \end{bmatrix}^T$$

$$\boldsymbol{x}_0 = \begin{bmatrix} 1 & 0 & 0 & 0 & 0 & 0.1 & 0 & 0 & 0.1 & 0 & 0 \end{bmatrix}^T$$

Setting $\varepsilon = 10^{-4}$, the algorithm returns a solution after 15 iterations.

$$\boldsymbol{y}^* = \begin{bmatrix} -1.707791 & -2.044005 & -0.852730 & -2.544838 & -2.485646 \end{bmatrix}^T$$

The NM Dev class called `PrimalDualInteriorPointMinimizer` implements this algorithm. The following code solves the previous example problem:

```
fun problem() : SOCPGeneralProblem {
    // min f'x
    val f: Vector = DenseVector(1.0, 0.0, 0.0, 0.0, 0.0)

    // The A's in the conic constraints.
    val A1t: Matrix = DenseMatrix(arrayOf(doubleArrayOf(0.0, -1.0, 0.0, 1.0, 0.0),
    doubleArrayOf(0.0, 0.0, 1.0, 0.0, -1.0)))
    val A2t: Matrix = DenseMatrix(arrayOf(doubleArrayOf(0.0, 0.5, 0.0, 0.0, 0.0),
    doubleArrayOf(0.0, 0.0, 1.0, 0.0, 0.0)))
    val A3t: Matrix = DenseMatrix(arrayOf(doubleArrayOf(0.0, 0.0, 0.0, -0.7071, -0.7071),
    doubleArrayOf(0.0, 0.0, 0.0, -0.3536, 0.3536)))

    // The b's in the conic constraints.
    val b1: Vector = f
    val b2: Vector = f.ZERO()
    val b3: Vector = f.ZERO()

    // The c's in the conic constraints.
    val c1: Vector = DenseVector(2) // zero
    val c2: Vector = DenseVector(-0.5, 0.0)
    val c3: Vector = DenseVector(4.2426, -0.7071)

    // The d's in the conic constraints.
    val d = doubleArrayOf(0.0, 1.0, 1.0)
    val constraints: kotlin.collections.List<SOCPGeneralConstraint> = java.util.Arrays.
    asList<SOCPGeneralConstraint>(
        SOCPGeneralConstraint(A1t.t(), c1, b1, d[0]),
        SOCPGeneralConstraint(A2t.t(), c2, b2, d[1]),
        SOCPGeneralConstraint(A3t.t(), c3, b3, d[2])
    )
```

```
    // The SOCP problem to be solved.
    val problem: SOCPGeneralProblem = SOCPGeneralProblem(
        f,
        constraints) // ||Ax + b|| <= c'x + d
    return problem
}

// Uses interior point method to solve the given problem from a given starting point.
val x0: Vector = DenseVector(1.0, 0.0, 0.0, 0.1, 0.0, 0.0, 0.1, 0.0, 0.0)
val s0: Vector = DenseVector(3.7, 1.0, -3.5, 1.0, 0.25, 0.5, 1.0, -0.35355, -0.1767)
val y0: Vector = DenseVector(-3.7, -1.5, -0.5, -2.5, -4.0)
// an initial guess
val soln0 = PrimalDualSolution(x0, s0, y0)

// construct an SOCP solver
val solver = PrimalDualInteriorPointMinimizer(
    1e-8,
    20) // max number of iterations

// solve the SOCP problem
val p = problem()
val soln: IterativeSolution<PrimalDualSolution> = solver.solve(p)
soln.search(soln0)

// primal solution
println("X = ")
println(soln.minimizer().x)
// dual solution
println("Y = ")
println(soln.minimizer().y)
println("S = ")
println(soln.minimizer().s)
println("minimum = " + soln.minimum())
```

The output is as follows:

```
X =
[1.000000, -0.292607, 0.956232, 1.121095, -0.585213, -0.956232, 1.288558, -0.883070,
0.938384]
y =
[-1.707796, -2.043378, -0.853136, -2.544339, -2.485799]
S =
[1.707796, 0.500961, -1.632663, 1.000000, 0.521689, 0.853136, 1.000000, 0.685789, -0.727800]
minimum = -1.7077862121401681
```

As of January 9, 2014, this SOCP solver tested up to 6,000 variables and 26,000 constraints in solving a large portfolio optimization problem. It took five minutes to return the results.

10.6. General Nonlinear Optimization Problems

The most general class of optimization problems is when both the objective function and constraints are nonlinear. There are a number of methods to solve these problems, such as the penalty method covered in Chapter 11. In this section, we introduce the sequential quadratic programming (SQP) method. It is one of the most effective methods for solving general constrained problems when both the objective function and constraints are twice continuously differentiable. SQP is appropriate for small and large problems, and it is well-suited to solving problems with significant nonlinearities. The SQP method can be viewed as a generalization of Newton's method for unconstrained optimization in that it finds a step away from the current point by minimizing a quadratic model of the problem.

10.6.1. SQP Problems with Only Equality Constraints

Consider the following optimization problem:

$$\min_{\boldsymbol{x}} f(\boldsymbol{x})$$

Subject to the following:

$$a_i(\boldsymbol{x}) = 0,\ i = 1, \ldots, p$$

where f and a_i's are continuous functions and have continuous first and second partial derivatives. Assume that the feasible region is nonempty and that $p \le n$. The first-order necessary condition for minimization is given by the Lagrange multiplier method, as shown here:

$$\mathcal{L}(\boldsymbol{x},\lambda) = f(\boldsymbol{x}) - \sum_{i=1}^{p} \lambda_i a_i(\boldsymbol{x})$$

$$\nabla\mathcal{L}(\boldsymbol{x}^*,\lambda^*) = 0$$

Suppose you have the k-th iterate set $\{\boldsymbol{x}_k, \lambda_k\}$, which is assumed to be sufficiently close to the solution $\{\boldsymbol{x}^*, \lambda^*\}$, and you want to find an increment $\{\delta_x, \delta_\lambda\}$ such that the next iteration is closer to the optimum. Using Taylor series, you get the following:

$$\nabla\mathcal{L}(\boldsymbol{x}_{k+1},\lambda_{k+1}) \approx \nabla\mathcal{L}(\boldsymbol{x}_k,\lambda_k) + \nabla^2\mathcal{L}(\boldsymbol{x}_k,\lambda_k)\begin{bmatrix}\delta_x \\ \delta_\lambda\end{bmatrix}$$

$\{\boldsymbol{x}_{k+1}, \lambda_{k+1}\}$ is a better approximation of $\{\boldsymbol{x}^*, \lambda^*\}$ if $\nabla L(\boldsymbol{x}_{k+1}, \lambda_{k+1}) = 0$ That is, you get the following:

$$\nabla^2\mathcal{L}(\boldsymbol{x}_k,\lambda_k)\begin{bmatrix}\delta_x \\ \delta_\lambda\end{bmatrix} = -\nabla\mathcal{L}(\boldsymbol{x}_k,\lambda_k)$$

You can rewrite this equation in terms of the Hessian matrix of the Lagrangian $\boldsymbol{W}$ for $\{\boldsymbol{x}, \lambda\} = \{\boldsymbol{x}_k, \lambda_k\}$ and the Jacobian $\boldsymbol{A}$ for $\boldsymbol{x} = \boldsymbol{x}_k$:

$$\begin{bmatrix}\boldsymbol{W}_k & -\boldsymbol{A}_k^T \\ -\boldsymbol{A}_k & \boldsymbol{0}\end{bmatrix}\begin{bmatrix}\delta_x \\ \delta_\lambda\end{bmatrix} = \begin{bmatrix}\boldsymbol{A}_k^T\lambda_k - \boldsymbol{g}_k \\ \boldsymbol{a}_k\end{bmatrix}$$

where:

$$\boldsymbol{W}_k = \nabla_x^2 f(\boldsymbol{x}_k) - \sum_{i=1}^{p} (\lambda_k)_i \nabla_{\boldsymbol{x}}^2 a_i(\boldsymbol{x}_k)$$

$$\boldsymbol{A}_k = \begin{bmatrix} \nabla_{\mathbf{x}}^T a_1(\boldsymbol{x}_k) \\ \nabla_{\mathbf{x}}^T a_2(\boldsymbol{x}_k) \\ \vdots \\ \nabla_{\mathbf{x}}^T a_p(\boldsymbol{x}_k) \end{bmatrix}$$

$$\boldsymbol{g}_k = \nabla_{\boldsymbol{x}} f(\boldsymbol{x}_k)$$

$$\boldsymbol{a}_k = \begin{bmatrix} a_1(\mathbf{x}_k) & a_2(\boldsymbol{x}_k) & \dots & a_p(\boldsymbol{x}_k) \end{bmatrix}$$

If $\boldsymbol{W}_k \succ 0$ and $\boldsymbol{A}_k$ is of full rank, the solution to the equation, namely, $\begin{bmatrix} \delta_x \\ \delta_\lambda \end{bmatrix}$, exists. To compute $\delta\boldsymbol{x}$, you can expand the matrix equation into this:

$$\begin{cases} \boldsymbol{W}_k \delta_{\boldsymbol{x}} + \boldsymbol{g}_k = \boldsymbol{A}_k^T \lambda_k + \boldsymbol{A}_k^T \delta_k = \boldsymbol{A}_k^T \lambda_{k+1} \\ \boldsymbol{A}_k \delta_{\boldsymbol{x}} = -\boldsymbol{a}_k \end{cases}$$

These two equations are essentially the first-order necessary conditions for a QP problem for $\delta\boldsymbol{x}$. That is, you get this:

$$\min_{\delta_{\mathbf{x}}} \frac{1}{2} \delta_{\boldsymbol{x}}^T \boldsymbol{W}_k \delta_{\boldsymbol{x}} + \delta_{\boldsymbol{x}}^T \boldsymbol{g}_k$$

Subject to the following:

$$\mathbf{A}_k \delta_{\boldsymbol{x}} = -\mathbf{a}_k$$

This is a QP problem with only equality constraints. It can be solved using the algorithm in Section 10.3.1. Once $\delta\boldsymbol{x}$ is found, the next iterate is as follows:

$$\boldsymbol{x}_{k+1} = \boldsymbol{x}_k + \delta_{\mathbf{x}}$$

$\boldsymbol{\lambda}_{k+1}, \boldsymbol{W}_{k+1}, \boldsymbol{g}_{k+1}, \boldsymbol{A}_{k+1}$ can be evaluated from the previous equations. You continue this process until the algorithm converges when $\|\delta\boldsymbol{x}\|$ is sufficiently small. This iterative method of repeatedly solving QP subproblems is called sequential quadratic programming (SQP). Essentially, what SQP is doing is trying to iteratively minimize the second-order approximation of the Lagrangian $L(\boldsymbol{x}, \boldsymbol{\lambda})$ rather than the function $f(\boldsymbol{x})$ itself.

Antoniou & Lu (2007) discuss the following examples:

$$\min_{\boldsymbol{x}} -x_1^4 - 2x_2^4 - x_3^4 - x_1^2 x_2^2 - x_1^2 x_3^2$$

Subject to the following:

$$\begin{cases} a_1(\boldsymbol{x}) = x_1^4 + x_2^4 + x_3^4 - 25 = 0 \\ a_2(\boldsymbol{x}) = 8x_1^2 + 14x_2^2 + 7x_3^2 - 56 = 0 \end{cases}$$

With $\mathbf{x_k} = [x_1 \quad x_2 \quad x_3]^T$ and $\lambda_k = [\lambda_1 \quad \lambda_2]^T$, you have the following:

$$g_k = \begin{bmatrix} -4x_1^3 - 2x_1x_2^2 - 2x_1x_3^2 \\ -8x_2^3 - 2x_1^2x_2 \\ -4x_3^3 - 2x_1^2x_3 \end{bmatrix}$$

$$A_k = \begin{bmatrix} 4x_1^3 & 4x_2^3 & 4x_3^3 \\ 16x_1 & 28x_2 & 14x_3 \end{bmatrix}$$

$$a_k = \begin{bmatrix} x_1^4 + x_2^4 + x_3^4 - 25 \\ 8x_1^2 + 14x_2^2 + 7x_3^2 - 56 \end{bmatrix}$$

With $x_k = [3 \quad 1.5 \quad 3]^T$ and $\lambda_k = [-1 \quad -1]^T$, the algorithm finds the solution:

$$x^* = \begin{bmatrix} 1.874065 \\ -0.465820 \\ 1.884720 \end{bmatrix}$$

$$f(x) = -38.384828$$

The NM Dev class called `SQPActiveSetOnlyEqualityConstraint1Minimizer` implements this algorithm to solve SDP problems with only equality constraints. The following sample code solves the previous example:

```
// objective function
val f: RealScalarFunction = object : RealScalarFunction {

        override fun evaluate(x: Vector): Double {
            val x1: Double = x.get(1)
            val x2: Double = x.get(2)
            val x3: Double = x.get(3)

            var fx: Double = -x1.pow(4.0)
            fx -= 2.0 * x2.pow(4.0)
            fx -= x3.pow(4.0)
            fx -= (x1 * x2).pow(2.0)
            fx -= (x1 * x3).pow(2.0)

            return fx
        }

        override fun dimensionOfDomain(): Int {
            return 3
        }
```

```
        override fun dimensionOfRange(): Int {
            return 1
        }
}

// equality constraints
val equality_constraints: EqualityConstraints = GeneralEqualityConstraints(
    object : RealScalarFunction {

        override fun evaluate(x: Vector): Double {
            val x1: Double = x.get(1)
            val x2: Double = x.get(2)
            val x3: Double = x.get(3)

            var fx: Double = x1.pow(4.0)
            fx += x2.pow(4.0)
            fx += x3.pow(4.0)
            fx -= 25.0

            return fx // a1
        }

        override fun dimensionOfDomain(): Int {
            return 3
        }

        override fun dimensionOfRange(): Int {
            return 1
        }
    },
    object : RealScalarFunction {

        override fun evaluate(x: Vector): Double {
            val x1: Double = x.get(1)
            val x2: Double = x.get(2)
            val x3: Double = x.get(3)

            var fx: Double = 8.0 * x1.pow(2.0)
            fx += 14.0 * x2.pow(2.0)
            fx += 7.0 * x3.pow(2.0)
            fx -= 56.0

            return fx // a2
        }

        override fun dimensionOfDomain(): Int {
            return 3
        }
```

```
        override fun dimensionOfRange(): Int {
            return 1
        }
})

// construct an SQP solver
val solver = SQPActiveSetOnlyEqualityConstraint1Minimizer(
    object : SQPActiveSetOnlyEqualityConstraint1Minimizer.VariationFactory {
        override fun newVariation(
        f: RealScalarFunction?,
        equal: EqualityConstraints?
        ): SQPASEVariation {
            val impl = SQPASEVariation2(100.0, 0.01, 10)
            impl.set(f, equal)
            return impl
        }
    },
    1e-8, // epsilon, threshold
    20) // max number of iterations
// solving an SQP problem
val solution: IterativeSolution<Vector>
        = solver.solve(f, equality_constraints)
val x: Vector = solution.search(
        DenseVector(3.0, 1.5, 3.0), // x0
        DenseVector(-1.0, -1.0)) // λ0
val fx: Double = f.evaluate(x)
// print out the solution
println("x = " + x)
println("fx = " + fx)
```

The output is as follows:

```
x = [1.874065, -0.465820, 1.884720]
fx = -38.28482786994784
```

Note that there are multiple solutions to this problem. Changing the parameters such as x0 will lead to a different solution. Another solution is as follows:

$$\boldsymbol{x}^* = \begin{bmatrix} 1.874065 \\ 0.465820 \\ 1.884720 \end{bmatrix}$$

10.6.2. SQP Problems with Inequality Constraints

You can extend the previous algorithm to the case of inequality constraints. Consider the general optimization problem:

$$\min_{\boldsymbol{x}} f(\boldsymbol{x})$$

Subject to the following:

$$c_j(\boldsymbol{x}) \geq 0,\ i = 1, 2, \ldots q$$

Assume that f and $\{c_j\}$ are twice differentiable. Using the same idea, you again, for the k-th iterate $\{\boldsymbol{x}_k, \boldsymbol{\mu}_k\}$, find an increment $\{\delta_{\boldsymbol{x}}, \delta_{\boldsymbol{\mu}}\}$ for the next iterate, as shown here:

$$\{\boldsymbol{x}_{k+1}, \mu_{k+1}\} = \{\boldsymbol{x}_k + \delta_{\boldsymbol{x}}, \mu_k + \delta_\mu\}$$

Such that it satisfies the approximate KKT conditions:

$$\nabla_{\boldsymbol{x}} \mathcal{L}(\boldsymbol{x}, \mu) = 0$$

$$c_j(\boldsymbol{x}) \geq 0$$

$$\mu \geq 0$$

$$\mu_i c_i = 0$$

Using Taylor expansion, you get the following:

$$\nabla_{\boldsymbol{x}} \mathcal{L}(\boldsymbol{x}_{k+1}, \mu_{k+1}) \approx \nabla_{\boldsymbol{x}} \mathcal{L}(\boldsymbol{x}_k, \mu_k) + \nabla^2_{\boldsymbol{x}} \mathcal{L}(\boldsymbol{x}_k, \mu_k)\delta_{\boldsymbol{x}} + \nabla^2_{\boldsymbol{x}\mu} \mathcal{L}(\boldsymbol{x}_k, \mu_k)\delta_\mu = 0$$

$$c_j(\boldsymbol{x}_k + \delta_{\boldsymbol{x}}) \approx c_j(\boldsymbol{x}_k) + \delta^T_{\boldsymbol{x}} \nabla_{\boldsymbol{x}} c_j(\boldsymbol{x}_k) \geq 0$$

$$\mu_{k+1} \geq 0$$

Combining the last two equations gives the following:

$$\mu_{k+1}\left[c_j(\boldsymbol{x}_k) + \delta^T_{\boldsymbol{x}} \nabla_{\boldsymbol{x}} c_j(\boldsymbol{x}_k)\right] = 0$$

The Lagrangian is defined as follows:

$$\mathcal{L}(\boldsymbol{x}, \mu) = f(\boldsymbol{x}) - \sum_{i=1}^{q} \mu_j c_j(\boldsymbol{x})$$

Therefore, you get the following:

$$\nabla_{\boldsymbol{x}} \mathcal{L}(\boldsymbol{x}_k, \mu_k) = \nabla_{\boldsymbol{x}} f(\boldsymbol{x}_k) - \sum_{i=1}^{q} (\mu_k)_j \nabla_{\boldsymbol{x}} c_j(\boldsymbol{x}_k) = \boldsymbol{g}_k - \boldsymbol{A}_k^T \mu_k$$

$$\nabla^2_{\boldsymbol{x}} \mathcal{L}(\boldsymbol{x}_k, \mu_k) = \nabla^2_{\boldsymbol{x}} f(\boldsymbol{x}_k) - \sum_{i=1}^{q} (\mu_k)_j \nabla^2_{\boldsymbol{x}} c_j(\boldsymbol{x}_k) = \boldsymbol{Y}_k$$

$$\nabla^2_{\boldsymbol{x}\mu} \mathcal{L}(\boldsymbol{x}_k, \mu_k) = -\boldsymbol{A}_k^T$$

Where $\boldsymbol{A}_k$ is the Jacobian of the constraints at $\boldsymbol{x}_k$, that is:

$$\boldsymbol{A}_k = \begin{bmatrix} \nabla_{\boldsymbol{x}}^T c_1(\boldsymbol{x}_k) \\ \vdots \\ \nabla_{\boldsymbol{x}}^T c_q(\boldsymbol{x}_k) \end{bmatrix}$$

Using these notations, the approximate KKT conditions can be written as follows:

$$\boldsymbol{Y}_k \delta_{\boldsymbol{x}} + \boldsymbol{g}_k - \boldsymbol{A}_k^T \mu_{k+1} = 0$$

$$\boldsymbol{A}_k \delta_{\boldsymbol{x}} \geq -\boldsymbol{c}_k$$

$$\mu_{k+1} \geq 0$$

$$(\mu_{k+1})_j (\boldsymbol{A}_k \delta_{\boldsymbol{x}} + \boldsymbol{c}_k)_j = 0$$

Where you have this:

$$\boldsymbol{c}_k = \left[c_1(\boldsymbol{x}_k) \quad c_2(\mathbf{x}_k) \quad \ldots \quad c_q(\mathbf{x}_k) \right]^T$$

These approximate KKT conditions are the exact KKT conditions of this QP problem:

$$\min \frac{1}{2} \delta_{\boldsymbol{x}}^T \boldsymbol{Y}_k \delta_{\boldsymbol{x}} + \delta_{\boldsymbol{x}}^T \boldsymbol{g}_k$$

Subject to the following:

$$\boldsymbol{A}_k \delta_{\boldsymbol{x}} \geq -\mathbf{c}_k$$

Then, after solving the QP subproblem for $\delta_{\boldsymbol{x}}$, you get the following:

$$\boldsymbol{x}_{k+1} = \boldsymbol{x}_k + \delta_{\boldsymbol{x}}$$

The SQP algorithm iteratively solves QP subproblems until the solution converges. Antoniou & Lu (2007) discuss this SQP example.

$$\min_{\boldsymbol{x}} f(\boldsymbol{x}) = \frac{1}{2}\left[(x_1 - x_3)^2 + (x_2 - x_4)^2 \right]$$

Subject to the following:

$$\begin{cases} c_1(\boldsymbol{x}) = -\begin{bmatrix} x_1 & x_2 \end{bmatrix} \begin{bmatrix} \frac{1}{4} & 0 \\ 0 & 1 \end{bmatrix} \begin{bmatrix} x_1 \\ x_2 \end{bmatrix} + \begin{bmatrix} x_1 & x_2 \end{bmatrix} \begin{bmatrix} \frac{1}{2} \\ 0 \end{bmatrix} + \frac{3}{4} \geq 0 \\ c_2(\boldsymbol{x}) = -\frac{1}{8}\begin{bmatrix} x_3 & x_4 \end{bmatrix} \begin{bmatrix} 5 & 3 \\ 3 & 5 \end{bmatrix} \begin{bmatrix} x_3 \\ x_4 \end{bmatrix} + \begin{bmatrix} x_3 & x_4 \end{bmatrix} \begin{bmatrix} \frac{11}{2} \\ \frac{13}{2} \end{bmatrix} - \frac{35}{2} \geq 0 \end{cases}$$

where:

$$\boldsymbol{x} = \begin{bmatrix} x_1 \\ x_2 \\ x_3 \\ x_4 \end{bmatrix}$$

Since both the objective function and constraints are quadratic, the Hessian $\boldsymbol{Y}_k$ is independent of $\boldsymbol{x}_k$ and is given as follows:

$$\boldsymbol{Y}_k = \begin{bmatrix} 1+\frac{\mu_1}{2} & 0 & -1 & 0 \\ 0 & 1+2\mu_1 & 0 & -1 \\ -1 & 0 & 1+\frac{5\mu_2}{4} & \frac{3\mu_2}{4} \\ 0 & -1 & \frac{3\mu_2}{4} & 1+\frac{5\mu_2}{4} \end{bmatrix} \succ 0$$

Use these initials:

$$\boldsymbol{x}_0 = \begin{bmatrix} 1.0 \\ 0.5 \\ 2.0 \\ 3.0 \end{bmatrix}$$

And this:

$$\mu_0 = \begin{bmatrix} 1 \\ 1 \end{bmatrix}$$

The solution is as follows:

$$\boldsymbol{x}^* = \begin{bmatrix} 2.044750 \\ 0.852716 \\ 2.544913 \\ 2.485633 \end{bmatrix}$$

And:

$$\mu^* = \begin{bmatrix} 0.957480 \\ 1.100145 \end{bmatrix}$$

The NM Dev class called `SQPActiveSetOnlyInequalityConstraintMinimizer` implements this algorithm for solving the SQP problem with only inequality constraints. The following code solves the previous example problem:

```
// objective function
val f: RealScalarFunction = object : RealScalarFunction {

    override fun evaluate(x: Vector): Double {
        val x1: Double = x.get(1)
        val x2: Double = x.get(2)
        val x3: Double = x.get(3)
        val x4: Double = x.get(4)

        var fx: Double = (x1 - x3) * (x1 - x3)
        fx += (x2 - x4) * (x2 - x4)
        fx /= 2

        return fx
    }

    override fun dimensionOfDomain(): Int {
        return 4
    }

    override fun dimensionOfRange(): Int {
        return 1
    }
}

// inequality constraints
val greater = GeneralGreaterThanConstraints(
                        // c1
            object : RealScalarFunction {

            override fun evaluate(x: Vector): Double {
                val x1: Double = x.get(1)
                val x2: Double = x.get(2)

                val x12: Matrix = DenseMatrix(
                    arrayOf(
                        doubleArrayOf(x1, x2),
                        doubleArrayOf(2.0, 1.0)
                    )
                )

                val A: Matrix = DenseMatrix(
                    arrayOf(
                        doubleArrayOf(0.25, 0.0),
                        doubleArrayOf(0.0, 1.0)
                    )
                )

                val B: Matrix = DenseMatrix(
                    arrayOf(
                        doubleArrayOf(0.5, 0.0),
```

```
                doubleArrayOf(2.0, 1.0)
            )
        )

        var FX: Matrix = x12.t().multiply(A).multiply(x12)
        FX = FX.scaled(-1.0)
        FX = FX.add(x12.t().multiply(B))

        var fx: Double = FX.get(1, 1)
        fx += 0.75

        return fx
    }

    override fun dimensionOfDomain(): Int {
        return 4
    }

    override fun dimensionOfRange(): Int {
        return 1
    }
},
                // c2
    object : RealScalarFunction {

    override fun evaluate(x: Vector): Double {
        val x3: Double = x.get(3)
        val x4: Double = x.get(4)

        val x34: Matrix = DenseMatrix(
            arrayOf(
                doubleArrayOf(x3, x4),
                doubleArrayOf(2.0, 1.0)
            )
        )

        val A: Matrix = DenseMatrix(
            arrayOf(
                doubleArrayOf(5.0, 3.0),
                doubleArrayOf(3.0, 5.0)
            )
        )

        val B: Matrix = DenseMatrix(
            arrayOf(
                doubleArrayOf(11.0 / 2.0, 13.0 / 2.0),
                doubleArrayOf(2.0, 1.0)
            )
        )
```

```
                var FX: Matrix = x34.t().multiply(A).multiply(x34)
                FX = FX.scaled(-1.0 / 8.0)
                FX = FX.add(x34.t().multiply(B))

                var fx: Double = FX.get(1, 1)
                fx += -35.0 / 2.0

                return fx
            }

            override fun dimensionOfDomain(): Int {
                return 4
            }

            override fun dimensionOfRange(): Int {
                return 1
            }
        })

/**
* TODO: making the 2nd precision parameter 0 gives a better minimizer
* how to choose the precision parameters in general?
*/
// construct an SQP solver
val solver = SQPActiveSetOnlyInequalityConstraintMinimizer(
        1e-7, // epsilon1
        1e-3, // epsilon2
        10 // max number of iterations
)
// solving the SQP problem
val solution: IterativeSolution<Vector> = solver.solve(f, greater)
val x: Vector = solution.search(
        DenseVector(1.0, 0.5, 2.0, 3.0), // x0
        DenseVector(1.0, 1.0)) // μ0
val fx: Double = f.evaluate(x)
// print out the solution
println("x = " + x)
println("fx = " + fx)
```

The output is as follows:

```
x = [2.044833, 0.852724, 2.545007, 2.485578]
fx = 1.4581925507489448
```

CHAPTER 11

■ ■ ■

Heuristics

In computer science and mathematical optimization, a *heuristic* is a procedure designed to find a good enough solution to an optimization problem when the classical methods (LP, QP, SOCP, SDP, and SQP) discussed in the past few chapters fail, are too slow, are infeasible, or are not applicable. This is especially true when the problem is too big (e.g., beyond the limited computation capacity), has incomplete or imperfect information (e.g., lack of structure for pruning), has a complex objective function (e.g., nondifferentiable), or has difficult constraints (rule-based constraints, exceptions). A heuristic often speeds up the computation by eliminating a large subset of the solution candidates using ad hoc rules. Equivalently, it searches only a subset of the solution space that is otherwise too large to be completely enumerated or otherwise explored. Those ad hoc rules often make assumptions about the problem being solved and hence also the solution space. They may or may not eliminate the true solutions. Although these ad hoc rules are often not proven or given their properties, in practice heuristics often return good, usable solutions to many otherwise unsolvable problems, such as the whole class of NP-Complete problems like the traveling salesman problem.

The classical optimization algorithms are designed to find globally optimal solutions, and they are often iterative and deterministic in nature. In contrast, the ad hoc rules for heuristics are often experimental in nature. They are designed to efficiently explore the search space in order to find good enough solutions. They often employ some randomness to explore the search space, so the solutions found are dependent on the set of random variables generated. These ad hoc algorithms range from simple local search procedures (e.g., hill-climbing algorithm) to complex learning processes (e.g., genetic algorithm). Figure 11-1 shows the Euler diagram of the different classifications of *metaheuristics*.

© Haksun Li, PhD 2023
H. Li, PhD, *Numerical Methods Using Kotlin*, https://doi.org/10.1007/978-1-4842-8826-9_11

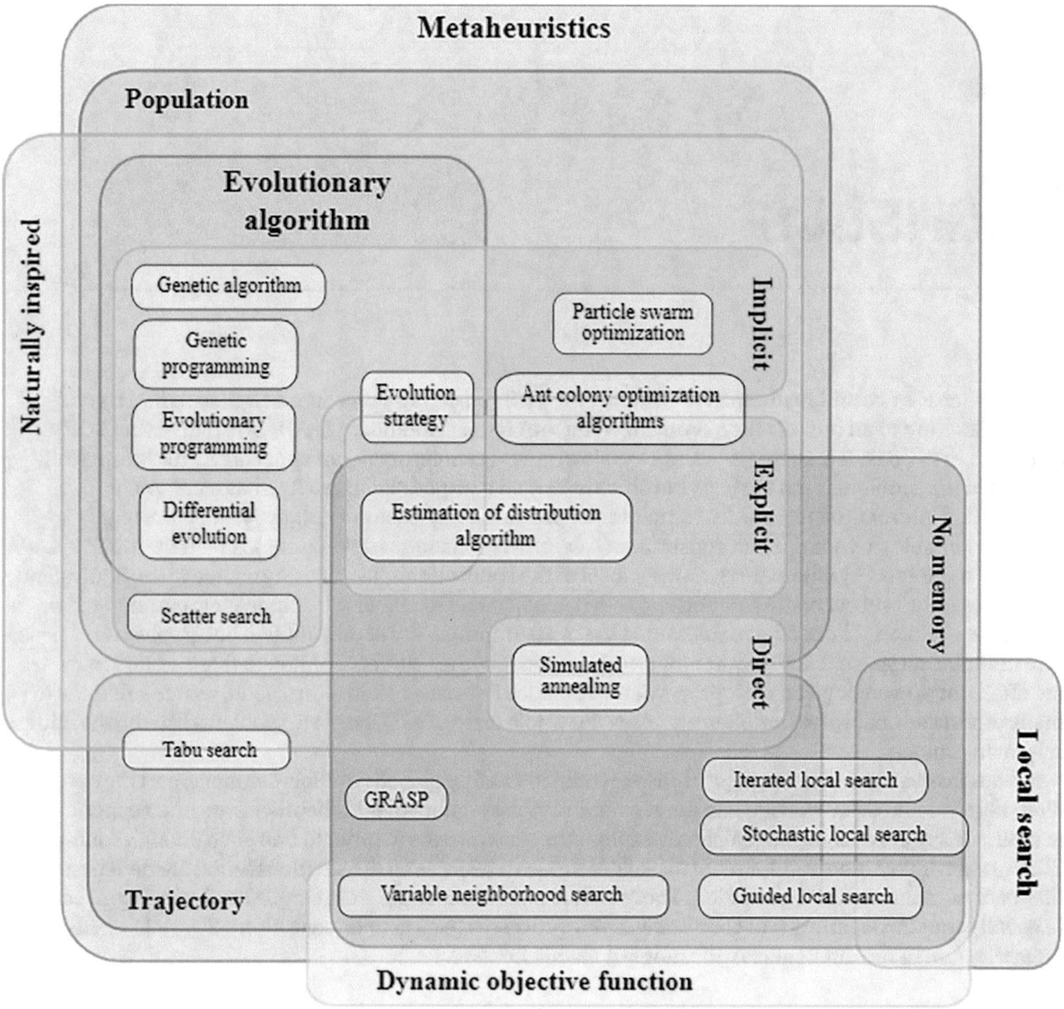

Figure 11-1. *Euler diagram of the different classifications of metaheuristics*

In combinatorial optimization, such as the traveling salesman problem, the search space of candidate solutions grows faster than exponentially as the size of the problem increases. Similarly, high-dimensional problems suffer from the curse of dimensionality. An exhaustive search or analytical method for the optimal solution for these problems is infeasible. A heuristic can search over a large set of feasible solutions to find approximate solutions with less computational effort than other exhaustive optimization algorithms, such as simulated annealing.

The source code in this chapter can be run on the S2 platform here:

```
https://s21.nm.dev/hub/user-redirect/lab/tree/s2-public/Numerical%20Methods%20Using%20
Kotlin/chapter11.ipynb
```

The source code can be found on GitHub:

```
https://github.com/apress/numerical-methods-kotlin
```

11.1. Penalty Function Method

The penalty function method is a way of transforming a constrained optimization problem to an unconstrained optimization problem by converting the constraints to a penalty term. The idea is that when the solution is in the feasible region, the penalty term is zero. When the solution is outside the feasible region, the penalty term is positive. You would usually assign a large positive number M as the coefficient, called the penalty factor, to the penalty term to ensure that the constraints of the original problem will be satisfied. This method is to search in the interior of the feasible region with the constraint boundaries acting like a wall. If the current solution is far from the constraint boundaries, the penalty term value is small, signaling that the solution is in the feasible region. The unconstrained optimization problem, $F(\boldsymbol{x}, M)$, is the same as the original constrained optimization problem $f(\boldsymbol{x})$. Otherwise, the penalty term value approaches infinity, signaling that the solution violates some constraints. The equivalent unconstrained optimization problem can, in principle, be solved by any unconstrained optimizers, like those discussed in Chapter 9. NM Dev uses the BFGS minimizer, `BFGSMinimizer`, by default. See Figure 11-2.

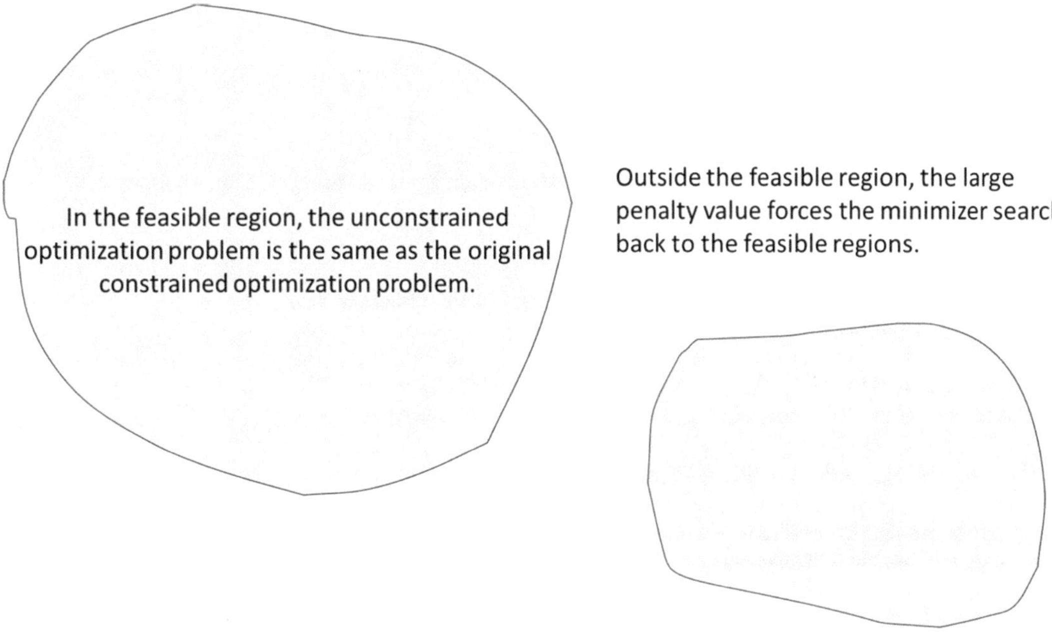

In the feasible region, the unconstrained optimization problem is the same as the original constrained optimization problem.
Outside the feasible region, the large penalty value forces the minimizer search back to the feasible regions.

Figure 11-2. *The penalty function method*

To search for the optimal solution x^*, you can start with an initial guess in the feasible or infeasible region. If you start in the feasible region, the constraint boundaries act like walls, and you do not get out of the feasible region. When the current solution is far from the constraint boundaries, the penalty function value is very small; otherwise, the penalty function value is close to infinity, preventing the solution from leaving the feasible region. However, finding a feasible solution to a large-scale problem instance can be NP-hard (a fancy way of saying they are the hardest problems to solve for computers), thus making this method impossible to apply. Alternatively, you can start the search anywhere or in the infeasible region and then gradually move to the feasible region. Then there is no prerequisite of an initial feasible solution.

Consider a general constrained optimization problem, as shown here:

$$\min_{x} f(\boldsymbol{x}), \text{ s.t.,}$$

$$hi(x) = 0, i \in E = \{1, 2, \ldots, m\}$$

$$gj(x) \le 0, j \in I = \{1, 2, \ldots, n\}$$

$\{h_i(\boldsymbol{x})\}$ is the equality constraints, and $\{g_j(\boldsymbol{x})\}$ is the inequality constraints.

You can convert the problem into an equivalent unconstrained optimization problem by penalizing any violation of any constraints. The general form of a penalty function method is as follows:

$$F(\boldsymbol{x}) = f(\boldsymbol{x}) + M(H + G)$$

$F(\boldsymbol{x})$ is the new objective function. H and G are the penalty terms, which are functions of the constraints $\{h_i(\boldsymbol{x})\}$ and $\{g_j(\boldsymbol{x})\}$, respectively. M is the penalty factor.

One way to convert equality constraints $\{h_i(\boldsymbol{x})\}$ into a penalty term H is to sum their absolute values. Specifically, you get this:

$$H = \sum_{i=1}^{m} p_i \left| h_i(\boldsymbol{x}) \right|$$

$\{p_i\}$ are the weights to each equality constraint.

The NM Dev class `AbsoluteErrorPenalty` constructs such a penalty function from a collection of equality constraints. The signature is as follows:

```
/**
 * Construct an absolute value penalty function from a collection of
 * equality constraints.
 *
 * @param constraints a collection of equality constraints
 * @param weights     the weights assigned to the constraints
 */
public AbsoluteErrorPenalty(EqualityConstraints constraints, double[] weights)
```

Courant penalty is another way to convert equality constraints $\{h_i(\boldsymbol{x})\}$ into a penalty term H. It sums up the squared values. Specifically, you get this:

$$H = \sum_{i=1}^{m} p_i \left| h_i(\boldsymbol{x}) \right|^2$$

$\{p_i\}$ are the weights to each equality constraint.

The NM Dev class `CourantPenalty` constructs a Courant penalty function from a collection of equality constraints. The signature is as follows:

```
/**
 * Construct a CourantPenalty penalty function from a collection of equality
 * constraints.
 *
 * @param constraints a collection of equality constraints
 * @param weights     the weights assigned to the constraints
 */
public CourantPenalty(EqualityConstraints constraints, double[] weights)
```

The Fletcher penalty is one way to convert inequality constraints $\{g_j(\boldsymbol{x})\}$ into a penalty term G. It sums up the squared errors greater than 0. Specifically, you get this:

$$H = \sum_{j=1}^{n} q_j \max\left(g_j(x), 0\right)^2$$

$\{q_j\}$ consists of the weights to each inequality constraint.

The NM Dev class `FletcherPenalty` constructs a Fletcher penalty function from a collection of less-than constraints. (A greater-than constraint can also be converted into a less-than constraint by inverting the sign.) The signature is as follows:

```
/**
 * Construct a Fletcher penalty function from a collection of less-than inequality constraints.
 *
 * @param constraints a collection of less-than inequality constraints
 * @param weights     the weights assigned to the constraints
 */
public FletcherPenalty(LessThanConstraints constraints, double[] weights)
```

Although the penalty function method is theoretically feasible, it suffers from the disadvantage that the value of the penalty factor M is difficult to estimate. If it is too small, the solution returned may be infeasible and violate the constraints. If it is too big and the optimal solution is at (or close to) the boundary of a feasible region, the search will soon be pushed into the feasible region and will not return close to the boundary of the feasible region. A big penalty factor will hinder the search of infeasible regions at the beginning of the search process. It will also cause severe numerical errors, and a solution may not be found even if it exists.

This shortcoming can be improved by the following iterative process. First, start with a smaller but still big positive number M and find the optimal solution $\boldsymbol{x}^*$ to $F(x, M)$. If $\boldsymbol{x}^*$ fails to satisfy the constraints of the original constrained optimization problem, increase M (for example, multiply it by 10). Repeat the process until $\boldsymbol{x}^*$ meets the constraints of the original constrained optimization problem.

In NM Dev, the `PenaltyMethodMinimizer` class implements the penalty function method. The following code solves this constrained optimization problem:

$$\min_{x,y} (x+1)^2 + (y+1)^2 \text{, s.t.,}$$

$$y = 0$$

$$x \geq 1$$

```
val f: RealScalarFunction = object : AbstractBivariateRealFunction() {
    override fun evaluate(x: Double, y: Double): Double {
        // f = (x+1)^2 + (y+1)^2
        return (x + 1) * (x + 1) + (y + 1) * (y + 1)
    }
}
val c1: RealScalarFunction = object : AbstractBivariateRealFunction() {
    override fun evaluate(x: Double, y: Double): Double {
        // y = 0
        return y
    }
}
```

```
val c2: RealScalarFunction = object : AbstractBivariateRealFunction() {
    override fun evaluate(x: Double, y: Double): Double {
        // x >= 1
        return 1 - x
    }
}
val problem: ConstrainedOptimProblemImpl1
        = ConstrainedOptimProblemImpl1(
                f,
                GeneralEqualityConstraints(c1), // y = 0
                GeneralLessThanConstraints(c2)) // x >= 1
val M: Double = 1e30 // the penalty factor
val optim: PenaltyMethodMinimizer
        = PenaltyMethodMinimizer(                PenaltyMethodMinimizer.DEFAULT_PENALTY_
          FUNCTION_FACTORY,
                M,
                // the solver to solve the equivalent unconstrained optimization problem
                BFGSMinimizer(false, 1e-8, 200)
        )
val soln: IterativeSolution<Vector> =
optim.solve(problem)
val xmin: Vector = soln.search( // the minimizer
        DenseVector(arrayOf(0.0, 0.0)) // an initial guess
)
val fxmin: Double = f.evaluate(xmin) // the minimum
println(String.format("f(%s) = %f", xmin, fxmin))
// alternatively
println(String.format("f(%s) = %f", soln.minimizer(), soln.minimum()))
```

The output is as follows:

```
f([1.000000, 0.000000] ) = 5.000000
f([1.000000, 0.000000] ) = 5.000000
```

The PenaltyFunctionFactory DEFAULT_PENALTY_FUNCTION_FACTORY constructs the penalty term from the equality and inequality constraints. It uses CourantPenalty for equality constraints and FletcherPenalty for inequality constraints. You can use a customized PenaltyFunctionFactory if you want to construct the penalty term differently from the default implementation.

11.2. Genetic Algorithm

Genetic algorithm (GA) is a metaheuristic that mirrors the evolutionary law of organisms in the nature. It is a computational model that simulates Darwin's biological evolution process of natural selection and genetic variation. The algorithm transforms the search for an optimal solution to an optimization problem into a process similar to the crossover, mutation, and selection of chromosomal genes in biological evolution by means of mathematics and computer simulation operations. Compared to classic optimization algorithms when solving a large-scale and complex problem, GA may return a solution in less time. GA has been widely used in the fields of combinatorial optimization, machine learning, signal processing, adaptive control, and so on. Genetic algorithm was made popular by Professor John Holland and his students at the University of Michigan, Ann Arbor, in the early 1970s. He also introduced a formalized framework for predicting the quality of the next generation, known as Holland's schema theorem.

A classic application of genetic algorithm is function optimization. GA has been tested on many complex functions: continuous and discrete, convex and concave, low-dimensional and high-dimensional, unimodal and multimodal. For some nonlinear, nondifferentiable, multimodel, multi-objective function optimization problems with many complex constraints that are difficult to solve using other optimization methods, GA may give better results. In addition, with the modern rapid increase in problem scale and hence search space of combinatorial optimization problem, it is difficult to find optimal solution by enumeration. For such complex problems, practitioners are often happy with satisfactory solutions instead of optimal solutions. GA turns out to be one of the most effective tools for seeking satisfactory solutions, especially for NP-hard combinatorial optimization problems. For example, GA has been successfully applied in solving the traveling salesman problem, the knapsack problem, the packing problem, the graph partition problem, Sudoku puzzles, and so on. Notably, NM Optim Limited (`https://nmoptim.com/`), an industrial optimization company, built a job-shop scheduling system that handles many complex and ad hoc constraints using genetic algorithm for steel manufacturing factories.

Mathematically, a genetic algorithm starts with a population of candidate solutions to an optimization problem. Each candidate solution is encoded such that its fitness (value to the optimization problem) can be evaluated and that the encoding can be altered (mutation) or mixed with another candidate (crossover) to produce a new candidate solution (new encoding). Iteratively, a population evolves to produce the next generation of candidate solutions until a satisfactory fitness level has been reached or a maximum number of generations has been produced. The basic GA framework is as follows.

11.2.1. Encoding

Genetic algorithm cannot work directly with or manipulate candidate solutions of a problem, such as schedule of jobs. You must first design a representation of a solution, called an encoding or chromosome, that GA can operate with. A standard representation or chromosome of each candidate solution is as an array or a string of bits, 0s and 1s. The encoding strategy needs to fulfil these requirements to make the GA search effective.

- **Completeness**: All candidate solutions in the problem space can be represented as chromosomes in the GA space.
- **Soundness**: The chromosomes in the GA space correspond to all candidate solutions in the problem space.
- **Non-redundancy**: The chromosomes corresponding to candidate solutions is a one-to-one relationship.

11.2.2. Fitness Function

Survival fitness in the theory of evolution refers to how well an organism adapts to its environment and its ability to reproduce offspring. It is the measurement of how good a candidate solution is. In terms of optimization, it is the value that indicates how well you optimize the objective function of a problem. Note that the fitness function (value) is not the same as the objective function (value), although they are positively related. Often, you need to have a map between the objective function value and the fitness function value. The fitness values of the candidates need to be compared and ranked. It is also the basis for being selected (randomly) for mutation and crossover and thus needs to be a positive number (for computing the probability of being selected) and bounded. Genetic algorithm generally does not require other external information in the process of search and evolution and uses only the fitness function to evaluate the pros and cons of a candidate solution. The design of fitness function is critical to the success of running a GA. It should meet the following conditions:

- Single value, continuous, non-negative, bounded
- Reasonable and consistent
- Easy to compute
- Strong versatility

11.2.3. Initial Population

GA starts with an initial population of individual candidate solutions for iteration. The population size depends on the nature of the problem but typically contains several hundreds or thousands of possible individuals. Often, the initial population is generated randomly and should reasonably cover the entire range of possible solutions (the search space). Occasionally, the solutions may be "seeded" in areas where optimal solutions are likely to be found. The typical initial setup strategies are as follows:

1. Using some knowledge about the problem, you can try to get a rough idea of the distribution or range of the solution space. The initial population should be distributed according to this a priori distribution of where the optimal solution lies.
2. First randomly generate a certain number of individuals; then select the best individuals from them and add them to the initial population. Repeat the process until the number of individuals in the initial population reaches a predetermined size.

11.2.4. The Operation Process

The basic genetic algorithm operation process is as follows:

1. **Initialization**: Set the evolution counter `t=0`, the maximum number of evolution `T`, and randomly generate `M` individuals as the initial population `P(0)`.
2. **Evaluation**: Calculate the fitness of each individual in the group `P(t)`.
3. **Selection**: Apply the selection operator to the group. The purpose of selection is to pass on the good chromosomes (genes) to the next generation through crossover and mutation.
4. **Crossover**: Apply the crossover operator to the group to generate new candidate solutions for the next generation by pairing two selected individuals.
5. **Mutation**: Apply the mutation operator to the group to generate new candidate solutions for the next generation by changing the genes at some loci of the representations of the selected individuals. The next generation is `P(t+1)`.
6. **Termination condition**: If `t=T`, the individual with the best fitness obtained in the evolution process is returned as the optimal solution; the calculation is terminated. Alternatively, when the fitness of the best individual reaches a given threshold or when the fitness of the group no longer improves, the calculation stops. The number of generations is generally set to 100 to 500.

The three main basic genetic operations are selection, crossover, and mutation.

11.2.5. Selection

The selection operation is to pick the superior individuals and to eliminate the inferior ones from the group. The operation ensures the next generation will inherit the good genes and will not have the bad ones. It is a kind of hill-climbing search. The selection is based on the fitness of the individuals. The better the fitness of an individual, the higher the probability (but not guaranteed) that it will be selected. Note that even less fit individuals may be selected albeit with a lower chance. This is to ensure diversity in the population and to get out of local optimums. The commonly used selection operators are fitness ratio method, random traversal sampling method, and local selection method.

11.2.6. Crossover

The reorganization (also mutation) of biological genes plays a central role in the evolution of natural organisms. Similarly, the key operation in genetic algorithm is the crossover operator of the representation or encoding of candidate solutions. The crossover operator replaces and recombines the (random) partial structures of two parent individuals to generate two new individuals. The popular crossover methods for arrays of bits are single-point crossover, two-point and k-point crossover, and uniform crossover.

In single-point crossover, a point on both parents' chromosomes is picked randomly and designated a "crossover point." Bits to the right of that point are swapped between the two parent chromosomes. This results in two offspring, each carrying some genetic information from both parents. See Figure 11-3.

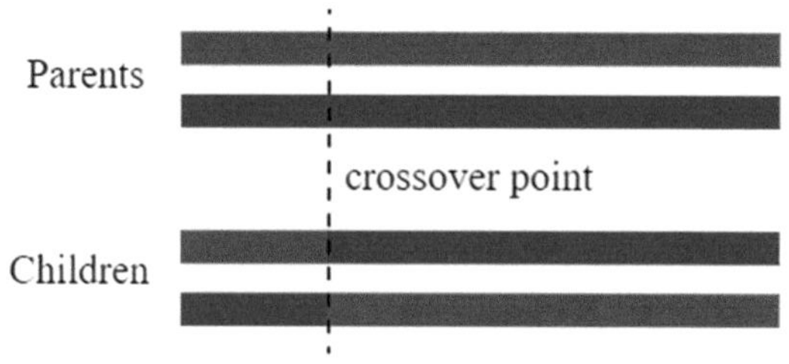

Figure 11-3. *Single-point crossover*

In two-point crossover, two crossover points are picked randomly from the parent chromosomes. The bits in between the two points are swapped between the parent organisms. It is equivalent to performing two single-point crossovers with different crossover points. This strategy can be generalized to k-point crossover for any positive integer k, picking k crossover points. See Figure 11-4.

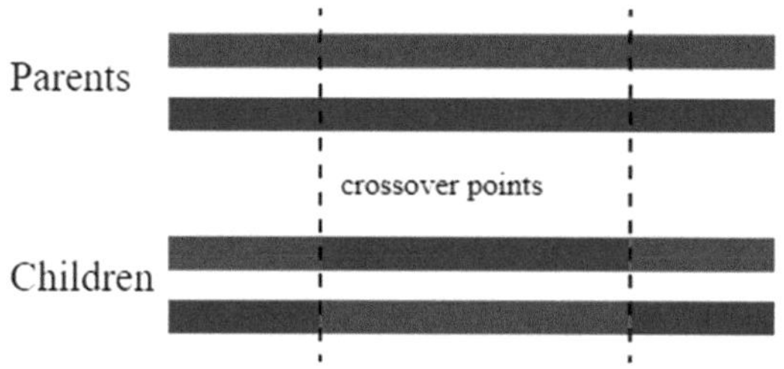

Figure 11-4. *Two-point crossover*

In uniform crossover, typically each bit is chosen from either parent with equal probability. Other mixing ratios are sometimes used, resulting in offspring that inherit more genetic information from one parent than the other.

11.2.7. Mutation

Genetic algorithm introduces mutation for two purposes. The first reason is to ensure genetic diversity from one generation of a population of genetic algorithm chromosomes to the next. Mutation alters one or more gene values in a chromosome from its initial state. The solution may change entirely from its parent, so GA may come to a better solution. Mutation occurs during evolution according to a predetermined mutation probability. This probability should be set low. If it is set too high, the search will turn into a primitive random search.

The second reason is to control the local search when close to the optimal solution. When the GA is in the neighborhood of the optimal solution through the crossover operator, the local random search due to the mutation operator can accelerate the convergence to the optimal solution. In such a case, the mutation probability should be small; otherwise, the building blocks close to the optimal solution would be destroyed due to mutation. On the other hand, to escape the local optimums and to maintain group diversity, the mutation probability should take a bigger value to prevent the chromosomes from becoming too similar to each other, thus slowing or even stopping convergence to the global optimum.

There are many ways to define a mutation operator depending on the encoding. One classic example involves a probability that an arbitrary bit in a genetic sequence will be flipped from its original state. A common method of implementing the mutation operator involves generating a random variable for each bit in a sequence. This random variable tells whether a particular bit will be flipped. This mutation procedure, based on the biological point mutation, is called single-point mutation. Other types are inversion and floating-point mutation. When the gene encoding is restrictive as in permutation problems, mutations are swaps, inversions, and scrambles. See Figure 11-5.

```
1 0 1 0 0 1 0
      ↓
1 0 1 0 1 1 0
```

Figure 11-5. *Bit string mutation. Bit flips at random positions*

In NM Dev, the `GeneticAlgorithm` class and the `Chromosome` interface provide a framework to implement a customized genetic algorithm. `GeneticAlgorithm` allows the user to define how the first population is initialized and the termination condition. In fact, most of the methods in the class are protected, meaning that the user can override them to provide a different implementation. The signature is as follows:

```
public abstract class GeneticAlgorithm {
    /**
     * Initialize the first population.
     *
     * @return the first population
     */
    protected abstract List<? extends Chromosome> getFirstGeneration();
    /**
     * This is the convergence criterion.
     *
     * @return {@code true} if the search has converged
```

```
 */
protected abstract boolean isConverged();
/**
 * Run the genetic algorithm.
 */
public void run() {
    population.addAll(getFirstGeneration());
    for (; !isConverged();) {
        step();
    }
}
/**
 * Run a step in genetic algorithm: produce the next generation of chromosome pool.
 *
 * @return true
 */
protected Object step();
/**
 * Produce a child chromosome.
 * <p/>
 * This implementation first applies the crossover and then the mutation operators.
 *
 * @param i an index that ranges from 0 to (population size - 1)
 * @return a child chromosome
 */
protected Chromosome getChild(int i);
/**
 * Pick a chromosome for mutation/crossover.
 * <p/>
 * This implementation uniformly and randomly chooses from the population.
 *
 * @return a chromosome
 */
protected Chromosome getOne();
/**
 * Populate the next generation using the parent and children chromosome pools.
 * <p/>
 * This implementation chooses the best chromosomes among the parents and children.
 *
 * @param parents  the parent chromosome pool
 * @param children the children chromosome pool
 * @return the next generation population
 */
protected List<Chromosome> getNextGeneration(List<Chromosome> parents, List<Chromosome>
children);
/**
 * Get the size of the population pool, that is the number of chromosomes.
 *
 * @return the population size
 */
protected int nPopulation();
```

```
    /**
     * Get the number of children before populating the next generation.
     * <p/>
     * In this implementation, it is the same as the population size (same as the number of
     * parents).
     *
     * @return the number of children
     */
    protected int nChildren();
    /**
     * Get the <i>i</i>-th best chromosome.
     *
     * @param i an index
     * @return the <i>i</i>-th best chromosome
     */
    protected Chromosome getBest(int i);
    /**
     * Allocate space for a population pool.
     *
     * @param size the population size
     * @return a population pool
     */
    protected static ArrayList<Chromosome> getNewPool(int size);
}
```

For any specific optimization problem, the user will need to define the encoding, the associated crossover operator, and the mutation operator by implementing the Chromosome interface . As a genetic algorithm implementation usually runs in a multicore environment for performance, it is important to ensure that an implementation of the chromosome operations is thread-safe and can run in parallel. The signature is as follows:

```
public interface Chromosome extends Comparable<Chromosome> {
    /**
     * This is the fitness to determine how good this chromosome is.
     *
     * @return the fitness
     */
    public double fitness();
    /**
     * Construct a {@code Chromosome} by mutation.
     *
     * @return a mutated chromosome
     */
    public Chromosome mutate();
    /**
     * Construct a {@code Chromosome} by crossing over a pair of chromosomes.
     *
     * @param that another chromosome
     * @return a crossed over chromosome
     */
    public Chromosome crossover(Chromosome that);
}
```

For instance, NM Dev implements the SimpleGridMinimizer solver to minimize a multivariate real-valued function (from $\mathbb{R}^n$ to $\mathbb{R}^1$) using this genetic algorithm framework. This optimizer does not use the gradient of the function being optimized, which means that it does not require the optimization problem to be differentiable, as is required by classic optimization methods such as gradient descent and quasi-Newton methods. It can therefore also be used on optimization problems that are not even continuous, are noisy, change over time, change with ad hoc constraints, and so on.

SimpleGridMinimizer starts with a population of initial guesses distributed over the solution space. Then it pairs them to do crossovers and mutations to search for the optimal solution. Specifically, the encoding of the solution candidates is simply a vector in $\mathbb{R}^n$.

```
public abstract class RealScalarFunctionChromosome implements Chromosome {
    private Double fx = null;
    private final RealScalarFunction f;
private final ImmutableVector x; // the encoding
}
```

The crossover operator is to take the midpoint between two individuals. The mutation operator is to add a small random disturbance to the vector. That is, you get this:

```
/**
 * A {@code SimpleCell} implements the two genetic operations.
 * <ul>
 * <li>Mutation by disturbing (scaling) the fitness by a percentage;</li>
 * <li>Crossover by taking the midpoint (average) of two cells.</li>
 * </ul>
 */
public class SimpleCell extends RealScalarFunctionChromosome {
    protected SimpleCell(RealScalarFunction f, Vector x) {
        super(f, x);
    }
    /**
     * Mutate by random disturbs in a neighborhood.
     *
     * @return a mutant chromosome
     */
    @Override
    public Chromosome mutate() {
        final double offset = 1 - rate;
        final double width = 2 * rate;
        Vector z = new DenseVector(x());
        for (int i = 1; i <= z.size(); ++i) {
            double rand = uniform.nextDouble();
            double u = offset + rand * width;
            z.set(i, z.get(i) * u);
        }
        return getSimpleCell(f(), z);
    }
    /**
     * Crossover by taking the midpoint.
     *
     * @param other another chromosome
```

```
     * @return a hybrid chromosome
     */
    @Override
    public Chromosome crossover(Chromosome other) {
        SimpleCell that = (SimpleCell) other;
        Vector z = this.x().add(that.x()).scaled(0.5);
        return getSimpleCell(f(), z);
    }
}
```

The following code minimizes the following function using this particular implementation of genetic algorithm:

$$\min_{x,y}\left(x^2+y^2\right)$$

```
// the objective function to minimize
val f: RealScalarFunction = object : AbstractBivariateRealFunction() {
    override fun evaluate(x: Double, y: Double): Double {
        return x * x + y * y // x^2 + y^2
    }
}

// a uniform random number generator
val rng: RandomLongGenerator = UniformRNG()
rng.seed(123456798L)

// construct an instance of the genetic algorithm solver
val solver = SimpleGridMinimizer(
                // define the encoding, crossover and mutation operator
                object : SimpleGridMinimizer.NewCellFactoryCtor {
                    override fun newCellFactory() : SimpleCellFactory {
                        return SimpleCellFactory(0.1, rng)
                    }
                },
                rng, // source of randomness for the GA
                1e-15, // a precision parameter
                500, // the maximum number of iterations
                500 // the maximum number of iterations of no improvement
        )

// run the solver to solve the optimization problem
val soln: IterativeSolution<Vector>
        = solver.solve(C2OptimProblemImpl(f))
val xmin: Vector = soln.search(
        // the boundaries: [-10, 10], [-10, 10]
    DenseVector(-10.0, 10.0),
    DenseVector(10.0, -10.0),
    DenseVector(10.0, 10.0),
    DenseVector(-10.0, -10.0)
)
```

```
val fxmin: Double = f.evaluate(xmin) // the minimum
println(String.format("f(%s) = %f", xmin, fxmin))
```

The output is as follows:

```
f([0.000000, 0.000000] ) = 0.000000
```

11.2.8. Differential Evolution

The differential evolution (DE) algorithm is a particular implementation of the genetic algorithm to optimize a multivariate real-valued function. The main innovation is its differential mutation operator. Let $CR \in [0, 1]$ be the crossover probability and $F \in [0, 2]$ the differential weight. The differential mutation operator, for each individual $\boldsymbol{x}$, picks three random and distinct candidate solutions, $\boldsymbol{a}$, $\boldsymbol{b}$, $\boldsymbol{c}$, and does the following:

1. Picks a random index $R \in \{1, \ldots, n\}$, where n is the dimensionality of the objective function.
2. Computes a new individual $\boldsymbol{y} = (y_1, \ldots, y_n)$ as follows:

    a. For each index $i \in \{1, \ldots, n\}$, picks a uniformly distributed random number $ri \sim U(0, 1)$.

    b. If $r_i < CR$ or $i = R$, then $y_i = a_i + F \times (b_i - c_i)$. Otherwise, $y_i = x_i$.

The new candidate, at each index if mutated, is the weighted sum of a random vector and the differential of two random vectors ***b-c***, which is why it's called differential evolution. Note that the index position at R is always replaced with the linear combination. See Figure 11-6.

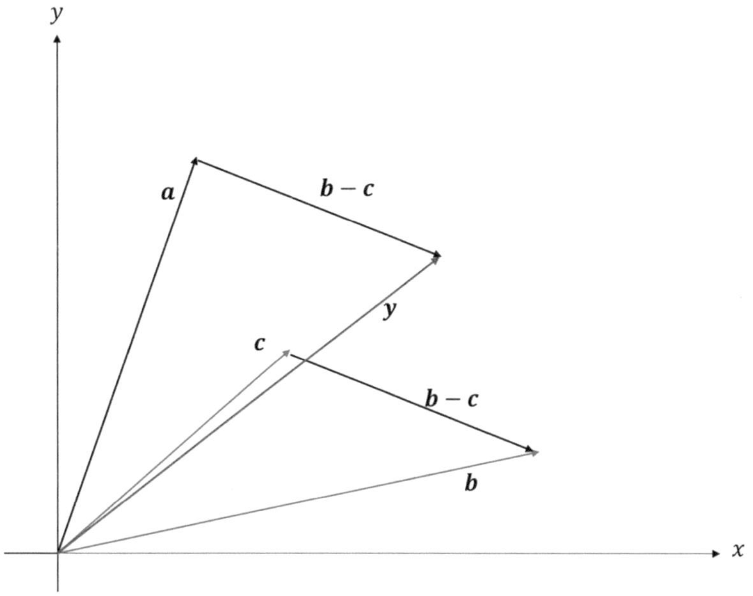

Figure 11-6. *Differential mutation*

The choice of DE parameters *CR* and *F* and the population size can have a large impact on optimization performance. Selecting the DE parameters that yield good performance has therefore been the subject of much research. A rule of thumb suggests that $CR = 0.9$ and $F = 0.8$.

The following NM Dev code solves an integer-constrained optimization problem. Integer programming problems are in general difficult to solve by classic algorithms and are the subject of much active research. This example shows the strong versatility of GA and how it handles difficult constraints.

$$\min_{x,y}(x-1)^2+(y-3)^2$$

```
// the objective function to minimize
val f: RealScalarFunction = object : AbstractBivariateRealFunction() {
    override fun evaluate(x: Double, y: Double): Double {
        return (x - 1) * (x - 1) + (y - 3) * (y - 3) // (x - 1)^2 + (y - 3)^2
    }
}

// construct an integer programming problem
val problem: IPProblem
        // both x and y need to be integers
        = IPProblemImpl1(f, null, null, intArrayOf(1, 2), 0.0)

// a uniform random number generator
val rng: RandomLongGenerator = UniformRNG()
rng.seed(123456798L)

// construct an instance of a genetic algorithm solver
val solver = DEOptim(
        object : DEOptim.NewCellFactory {
            override fun newCellFactory() : DEOptimCellFactory {
                return IntegralConstrainedCellFactory(
                        Rand1Bin(0.5, 0.5, rng), // the DE operator
                        IntegralConstrainedCellFactory.SomeIntegers(problem))
            }
        },
        rng, // a uniform random number generator
        1e-15, // a precision parameter
        100, // the maximum number of iterations
        20 // the maximum number of iterations of no improvement
)

val soln: IterativeSolution<Vector> = solver.solve(problem)
val xmin: Vector = soln.search(
        // the boundaries: [-10, 10], [-10, 10]
    DenseVector(-10.0, 10.0),
    DenseVector(10.0, -10.0),
    DenseVector(10.0, 10.0),
    DenseVector(-10.0, -10.0)
)

val fxmin: Double = f.evaluate(xmin) // the minimum
println(String.format("f(%s) = %f", xmin, fxmin))
```

The output is as follows:

```
f([1.000000, 3.000000] ) = 0.000000
```

The `Rand1Bin` class is an implementation of the DE operators proposed by Price, Storn, & Lampinen (2005). They are as follows:

- Differential mutation by adding a scaled, randomly sampled vector difference to a third vector
- Crossover by performing a uniform crossover (discrete recombination)

11.3. Simulated Annealing

Simulated annealing (SA) is a metaheuristic for finding a global optimum and is inspired by annealing in metallurgy. Annealing involves heating materials to a high temperature and then letting them cool slowly. This allows the particles to move freely to align at high temperature and to settle down at low temperature. Simulated annealing can be used for hard computational optimization problems where classic algorithms fail. Even though it usually achieves an approximate solution to the global minimum, it is usually enough for many practical problems.

The core idea in SA is a cooling schedule or annealing schedule of temperature. When the temperature is high in the beginning of the search, SA is more likely to accept a worse solution as the next solution candidate. When the temperature slowly decreases, the probability of accepting a worse solution decreases as well. Accepting worse solutions allows for a more extensive search for the global optimal solution, such as escaping local minima.

Figure 11-7 shows how simulated annealing searches for a maximum. The objective here is to get to the highest point. However, it is not enough to use a simple hill climbing algorithm, as there are many local maxima. By cooling the temperature slowly, the global maximum is found. Note that how the search can move widely in the beginning of the search and stays more or less in the neighborhood of the maximum when the temperature approaches 0.

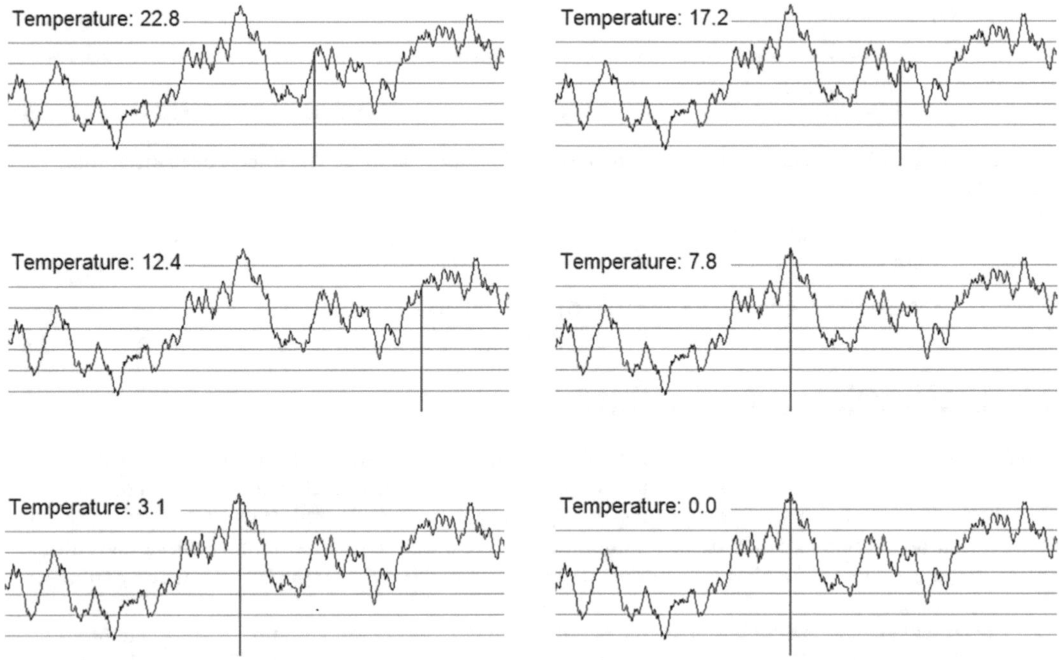

Figure 11-7. *Simulated annealing*

In general, the basic version of an SA algorithm work as follows. The temperature progressively decreases from an initial positive value to zero. At each time step, the algorithm randomly selects a solution close to the current one, measures its quality, and moves to/accept it according to the temperature-dependent probabilities of selecting better or worse solutions, which respectively remain positive and decrease toward zero. The algorithm asymptotically tends toward a hill-climb search when the temperature approaches 0. Algorithmically, to minimize a function f, it is as follows:

1. Let $s = s_0$ be the initial state.
2. For $k = 0$ through k_{max}, the maximum number of iterations:
   a. Temperature $T = T(k)$ is a function of k according to the cooling or annealing schedule.
   b. Pick a random neighbor s_{new} of s.
   c. Decide whether to accept s_{new} based on the acceptance probability $P(f(s), f(s_{new}), T)$, which is a function of $f(s)$, $f(s_{new})$, and T. If $f(s_{new}) < f(s)$, you always accept the new, better solution.
3. Output the final step state s.

In NM Dev, the `SimulatedAnnealingMinimizer` class provides a framework to implement a customized simulated annealing algorithm. The signature is as follows:

```
/**
 * Construct a new instance.
 *
 * @param temperatureFunction a function that for a given iteration i gives
 *                            T_i, the temperature_levels. The function must be
                              monotonically
```

```
 *                              increasing with
 * @param probabilityFunction gives the acceptance probability for a state
 *                              transition at a given temperature
 * @param annealingFunction   proposes next states
 * @param markovLength        the number of times we attempt a state change
 *                              per iteration (per temperature)
 * @param stopCondition       the {@linkplain StopCondition}
 * @param uniform             the rlg to be used to control the stochastic
 *                              element of the algorithm
 */
public SimulatedAnnealingMinimizer(
        TemperatureFunction,
        AnnealingFunction,
        TemperedAcceptanceProbabilityFunction probabilityFunction,
        int markovLength,
        StopCondition stopCondition,
        RandomLongGenerator uniform
)
```

A temperature function, TemperatureFunction, defines a temperature schedule used in simulated annealing. In general, the temperature for the visiting distribution (proposal generation) may not be equal to the temperature for determining the acceptance probability. The signature is as follows:

```
public interface TemperatureFunction {
    /**
     * Gets the acceptance temperature \(T^A_t\) at time t.
     *
     * @param t the time at which to get a temperature, or the annealing
     *          parameter, same as the iteration number until re-annealing
     * @return the acceptance temperature at time t
     */
    public double acceptanceTemperature(int t);
    /**
     * Gets the visiting temperature \(T^V_t\) at time t.
     *
     * @param t the time at which to get a temperature, or the annealing
     *          parameter, same as the iteration number until re-annealing
     * @return the visiting temperature at time t
     */
    public double visitingTemperature(int t);
}
```

The physical analogy used to justify simulated annealing assumes that the cooling rate is low enough for the probability distribution of the current state to be near thermodynamic equilibrium at all times. Unfortunately, the relaxation time, the time you must wait for the equilibrium to be restored after a change in temperature, strongly depends on the "topography" of the energy/objective function and on the current temperature. In the simulated annealing algorithm, the relaxation time also depends on how the next candidate is generated, in a very complicated way. Therefore, the ideal cooling rate cannot be determined beforehand and should be empirically adjusted for each problem. NM Dev has implemented a number of temperature functions. They are as follows:

- BoltzTemperatureFunction, $Tk = T_0 / \ln k$
- ExpTemperatureFunction, $Tk = 0.95kT_0$
- FastTemperatureFunction, $Tk = T_0 / k$
- GSATemperatureFunction

An annealing function, AnnealingFunction, or a tempered proposal function gives the next proposal or next state from the current state and temperature. The signature is as follows:

```
public interface AnnealingFunction {
    /**
     * Gets the next proposal, given the current state and the temperature.
     *
     * @param currentState the current state of the system
     * @param temperature  the current temperature of the system
     * @return the next proposal
     */
    public Vector nextProposal(Vector currentState, double temperature);
}
```

You must consider that after a few iterations of the simulated annealing algorithm, the current state is expected to have much lower energy than a random state. Therefore, as a general rule, you should skew the generator toward candidate moves where the energy of the destination state is likely to be similar to that of the current state. This heuristic tends to exclude "very good" candidate moves as well as "very bad" ones. However, the former is usually much less common than the latter, so the heuristic is generally quite effective. NM Dev has implemented a number of annealing functions. They are as follows:

- BoltzAnnealingFunction: The step has length square root of temperature, with direction uniformly at random.
- FastAnnealingFunction: The step has length temperature, with direction uniformly at random. The square size is equal to the temperature.
- GSAAnnealingFunction
- BoxGSAAnnealingFunction

A tempered acceptance probability function, called TemperedAcceptanceProbabilityFunction, computes the probability that the next state transition will be accepted. The signature is as follows:

```
public interface TemperedAcceptanceProbabilityFunction {
    /**
     * Compute the probability that the next state transition will be accepted.
     *
     * @param currentState   the current state of the system
     * @param energyCurrent  the energy in the current state
     * @param proposedState  the proposed next state of the system
     * @param energyProposed the energy in the proposed state
     * @param temperature    the current temperature
     * @return the acceptance probability
     */
```

```
    public double acceptanceProbability(
            Vector currentState,
            double energyCurrent,
            Vector proposedState,
            double energyProposed,
            double temperature);
}
```

The following code demonstrates using a simulated annealing solver to minimize a complex function:

```
// the objective function to minimize
val f: RealScalarFunction = object : AbstractRealScalarFunction(2) {

    override fun evaluate(x: Vector): Double {
        val x1: Double = x.get(1)
        val x2: Double = x.get(2)
        // (4 - 2.1*x(1)^2 + x(1)^4/3)*x(1)^2
        val term1: Double
                    = (4.0 - 2.1 * x1.pow(2.0) + x1.pow(4.0) / 3.0) * x1.pow(2.0)
        // x(1)*x(2)
        val term2: Double = x1 * x2
        // (-4 + 4*x(2)^2)*x(2)^2
        val term3: Double = (-4.0 + 4.0 * x2.pow(2.0)) * x2.pow(2.0)
        return term1 + term2 + term3
    }
}

// construct an optimization problem
val problem = object : OptimProblem {
    override fun f(): RealScalarFunction {
        return f
    }

    override fun dimension(): Int {
        return 2
    }
}

// stop after 5000 iterations
val stopCondition: StopCondition = AfterIterations(5000)
// an instance of a simulated annealing solver
val solver: IterativeMinimizer<OptimProblem> = GeneralizedSimulatedAnnealingMinimizer(
                2, // dimension of the objective function
                stopCondition
        )
val soln: IterativeSolution<Vector> = solver.solve(problem)
val x0: Vector = DenseVector(0.5, 0.5) // the initial guess
val xmin: Vector = soln.search(x0)
val fxmin: Double = f.evaluate(xmin) // the minimum
println(String.format("f(%s) = %f", xmin, fxmin))
```

The output is as follows:

```
f([-0.089836, 0.712655] ) = -1.031628
```

Sometimes it is better to move back to a solution that was significantly better rather than always moving from the current state. This process is called the restarting of simulated annealing. The decision to restart could be based on several criteria. Notable among these include restarting based on a fixed number of steps, based on whether the current energy is too high compared to the best energy obtained so far, restarting randomly, and so on.

CHAPTER 12

■ ■ ■

Basic Statistics

Statistics is a branch of mathematics that studies the collection, organization, analysis, interpretation, and presentation of data. There are two major statistical methods used in the study. The field of descriptive statistics summarizes and describes the properties of the data for a sample. The field of inferential statistics draws conclusions and makes predictions about the population. A population is the entire set of data, known and unknown, observable and unobservable, that we want to study and draw conclusions about. A set of samples of a population is a subset of the population that we have the (observed) data of. Population does not change. A sample set varies depending on how we collect the data. A sample set can be different each time we collect the data. The size of the samples is always less than the size of the population and is always finite. The population size can be very big or even infinite. The field of inferential statistics draws conclusions about the population from the descriptive statistics of the sample. For instance, to estimate the number of galaxies in the entire universe, we take the portion of sky imaged by the telescope, say the Hubble. Then, using the ratio of the sliver of sky to the entire universe, we estimate the number of galaxies in the universe. This sampling and making inference process is central to statistics analysis. This is how we estimate the number of atoms in the universe, the number of cows on the planet (we normally don't count and name 1.5 billion of them), and many other measurements even if we do not see (meaning have the data for) all of them. Statistics are used in virtually all scientific disciplines such as the physical and social sciences, as well as in business, humanities, government, and manufacturing.

The NM Dev library has a large suite of statistical tools to do data analysis. It covers descriptive statistics, many univariate and multivariate probability distributions, regression analysis, time-series analysis, multivariate analysis, data filtering, hypothesis testing, random number generation, simulation, and more. These are the topics that we are going to cover in the next few chapters.

The source code in this chapter can be run on the S2 platform here:

```
https://s21.nm.dev/hub/user-redirect/lab/tree/s2-public/Numerical%20Methods%20Using%20
Kotlin/chapter12.ipynb
```

The source code can be found on github:

```
https://github.com/apress/numerical-methods-kotlin
```

© Haksun Li, PhD 2023
H. Li, PhD, *Numerical Methods Using Kotlin*, https://doi.org/10.1007/978-1-4842-8826-9_12

12.1. Random Variables

The concept of random variables is fundamental to statistics. It is (probably) not too wrong to say that the mathematics of statistics is all about studying random variables. A nonrandom variable, e.g., $x = 1$, is a variable that takes the same value, 1 in this example, every time we look at it. It is always the same. A random variable, in contrast, may take a different value each time we make an observation or take a sample. We do not know the value that it will take until we look at it. Suppose we label the heads (H) of a coin toss as 1 and the tails (T) as 0. Then a random variable, X, representing the coin toss can be either 1 or 0 each time we toss a coin (or take a sample). Suppose we toss the coin five times and we get $\{H, H, T, T, H\}$. Then the samples of X from this experiment are $\{x_1 = 1, x_2 = 1, x_3 = 0, x_4 = 0, x_5 = 1\}$. Each sample or observation can give a different value depending on the outcome of the experiment.

More formally, a random variable X is a function that maps the outcomes in a domain (called sample space Ω) to some real numbers (range E). The outcomes $\omega \in \Omega$, for example, can depend on some physical process that is not predictable. In the case of coin tossing, the outcomes are $\Omega = \{H, T\}$, and the random variable X maps it to $E = \{1, 0\}$.

Moreover, a random variable has a probability distribution P, which specifies the probability of the random variable taking a certain value or values. It is equal to the likelihood of the outcome turning out to be the events corresponding to the values. For example, for a fair coin toss, these three quantities have the same value: the probability that $X = 1$ denoted as $P(X = 1)$, or the likelihood that the outcome is H, or 50 percent. A discrete random variable takes on only a finite number of or countably many values, e.g., $\{1, 0\}$ in the coin toss example. The probability distribution for a discrete random variable is called the probability mass function. The random variable and the probability mass function of a fair coin toss are as follows:

$$\begin{cases} X(\omega = H) = 1 \\ X(\omega = T) = 0 \end{cases}$$

and as follows:

$$\begin{cases} P(X = 1) = P(\omega = H) = 0.5 \\ P(X = 0) = P(\omega = T) = 0.5 \end{cases}$$

Figure 12-1 shows the relationships between sample space Ω, range of random variable E (which is the same as the domain for the probability function), random variable X, and the probability P.

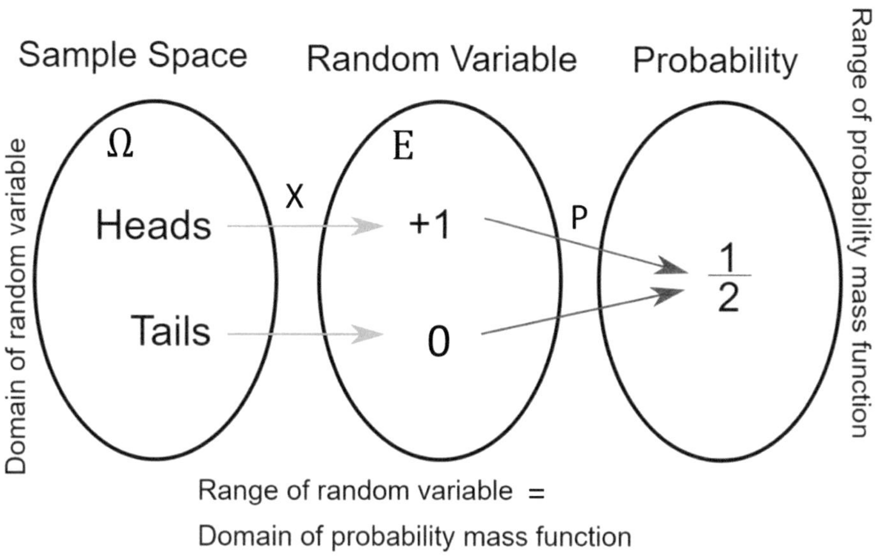

Figure 12-1. *Random variable for fair coin toss*

12.2. Sample Statistics

Given a set of samples $(x_1, x_2, \ldots, x_n)$ of a random variable X, we can describe the statistical properties of the set using sample statistics or descriptive statistics. Some of them measure the central tendency (or location) of the data, such as mean. Some measure the variability (or spread) of the sample, such as variance. Some highlight potential relationships between variables, such as covariance. There are others. It is important to note that sample statistics do not necessarily equal the corresponding statistics of the underlying population. They may be good approximations if the sample size, n, is big enough.

In NM Dev, all classes computing statistics from a data set or a sample inherit from the `Statistic` interface. The signature is as follows:

```
/**
 * A statistic (singular) is a single measure of some attribute of a sample
 * (e.g., its arithmetic mean value). It is calculated by applying a function
 * (statistical algorithm) to a sample, i.e., a set of data.
 *
 * @author Haksun Li
 * @see <a href="http://en.wikipedia.org/wiki/Statistic">Wikipedia:
 * Statistic</a>
 */
public interface Statistic {
    /**
     * Get the value of the statistic.
     *
     * @return the statistic
     */
    public double value();
```

```
    /**
     * Get the size of the sample.
     *
     * @return the sample size
     */
    public long N();
    /**
     * Recompute the statistic with more data, incrementally if possible.
     *
     * @param data an array of new items
     */
    public void addData(double... data);
}
```

The function `value()` computes the statistic. The function `N()` returns the sample size.

12.2.1. Mean

The simplest sample statistics is the sample mean or arithmetic mean or average of the data, denoted as $\bar{x}$. It measures the central location of the data set. It is the sum of all samples and divides the sum by the sample size or count. Mathematically, the sample mean is defined as follows:

$$\bar{x} = \frac{\sum_{i=1}^{n} x_i}{n}$$

The law of large numbers says that if the samples are randomly drawn from a population X with a population mean or expectation of $E(X) = \mu$ (and with a finite variance), then the sample mean converges to the population mean. That is:

$$\lim_{n \to \infty} \bar{x} = \mu$$

For example, for the sample $X = \{2, 3, 3, 1\}$, the sample mean is as follows:

$$\bar{x} = \frac{\sum_{i=1}^{4} x_i}{4} = \frac{2+3+3+1}{4} = 2.25$$

In NM Dev, the class `Mean` computes the sample mean for a data set. The following code computes for the previous example:

```
// the sample data set
val X1: DoubleArray = doubleArrayOf(2.0, 3.0, 3.0, 1.0)

// compute the mean of the data set
val mean: Mean = Mean(X1)
println("sample size = " + mean.N())
println("sample mean = " + mean.value())
```

The output is as follows:

```
sample size = 4
sample mean = 2.25
```

12.2.2. Weighted Mean

The sample mean assumes that each of the data points contributes equally to the final average. A weighted sample mean allows some data points to contribute more than others. That is, each data point can have a different weight, w_i. Mathematically, the weighted sample mean is defined as follows:

$$\bar{x}^* = \frac{\sum_{i=1}^{n} w_i x_i}{\sum_{i=1}^{n} w_i}$$

Suppose that the grades of a student in each course are $X = \{82, 94, 90, 83, 87\}$ and that the credit for each course is $W = \{1, 4, 8, 4, 4\}$, respectively. Then the overall grade, which is the weighted sample mean, is as follows:

$$\bar{x}^* = \frac{1\times 82 + 4\times 94 + 8\times 90 + 4\times 83 + 4\times 87}{1+4+8+4+4} = 88.48.$$

In NM Dev, the class `WeightedMean` computes the weighted sample mean for a data set. The following code computes the weighted sample mean for the previous example:

```
// the sample data set
val X2: DoubleArray = doubleArrayOf(82.0, 94.0, 90.0, 83.0, 87.0)
val W2: DoubleArray = doubleArrayOf(1.0, 4.0, 8.0, 4.0, 4.0)

// compute the mean of the data set
val weighted_mean: WeightedMean = WeightedMean(
        X2, // the data
        W2 // the weights
)
println("sample size = " + mean.N())
println("sample weighted mean = " + weighted_mean.value())
```

The output is as follows:

```
sample size = 4
sample weighted mean = 88.47619047619048
```

12.2.3. Variance

The sample variance measures how far a set of numbers is spread out from their average value. In other words, it is the degree of dispersion or how much the data is spread out. In the context of estimation, an estimator can be viewed as a random variable. The sample mean of the estimator is the estimation value. Then, the sample variance of the estimator is how uncertain the estimation is. For instance, if we take five readings of the temperature, then the sample mean is the measurement of the temperature; the sample variance is how uncertain our measurement is. See Figure 12-2.

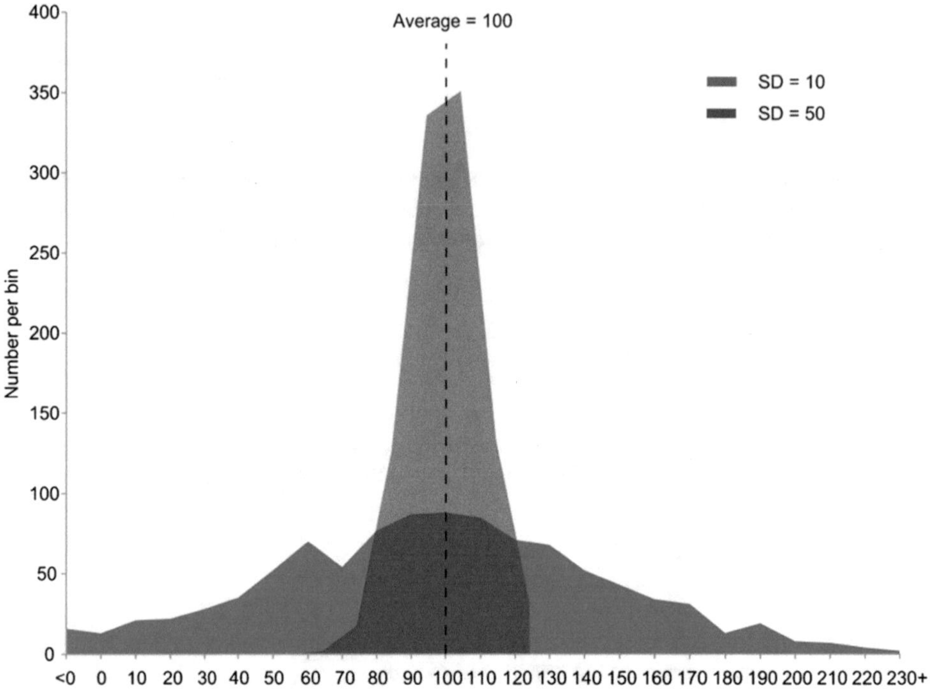

Figure 12-2. *Two samples with the same mean but different variances*

Figure 12-2 shows two samples with the same sample mean but different sample variances. The red sample has mean 100 and variance 100 (standard deviation = 10), while the blue sample has mean 100 and variance 2500 (standard deviation = 50). It is clear that the data in the blue sample spreads out much more than the red one. The blue data is further away from the mean.

Mathematically, sample variance is defined as follows:

$$s^2 = \frac{\sum_{i=1}^{n}(x_i - \bar{x})^2}{n}$$

Alternatively, the unbiased version is as follows:

$$s^2 = \frac{\sum_{i=1}^{n}(x_i - \bar{x})^2}{n-1}$$

The sample standard deviation, *s*, is the square root of the sample variance. From the formula, it is easy to see that sample variance is the average of the squared distance of the data from the sample mean.

For the sample $X = \{2, 3, 3, 1\}$, the sample variance is as follows:

$$s^2 = \frac{\sum_{i=1}^{4}(x_i - \bar{x})^2}{4-1} = \frac{(2-2.25)^2 + (3-2.25)^2 \times 2 + (1-2.25)^2}{3} = 0.9167$$

The sample standard deviation is as follows:

$$s = \sqrt{0.9167} = 0.9574$$

In NM Dev, the class `Variance` computes the sample variance for a data set. The following code computes the sample variance for the previous example:

```
// the sample data set
val X3: DoubleArray = doubleArrayOf(2.0, 3.0, 3.0, 1.0)

// compute the biased and unbiased variances and standard deviations
val var1: Variance = Variance(X3, false) // biased
println("sample standard deviation (biased) = " + var1.standardDeviation())
println("sample variance (biased) = " + var1.value())
val var2: Variance = Variance(X3, true) // unbiased
println("sample standard deviation (unbiased) = " + var2.standardDeviation())
println("sample variance (unbiased) = " + var2.value())
```

The output is as follows:

```
sample standard deviation (biased) = 0.82915619758885
sample variance (biased) = 0.6875
sample standard deviation (unbiased) = 0.9574271077563381
sample variance (unbiased) = 0.9166666666666666
```

12.2.4. Weighted Variance

Similarly, the weighted sample variance of a sample set can be defined as follows:

$$s^2 = \frac{\sum_{i=1}^{n} w_i (x_i - \bar{x}^*)^2}{V_1}$$

The unbiased version is as follows:

$$s^2 = \frac{V_1}{V_1^2 - V_2} \sum_{i=1}^{n} w_i (x_i - \bar{x}^*)^2$$

where:

$$V_2 = \sum_{i=1}^{n} w_i^2$$

In NM Dev, the class WeightedVariance computes the weighted sample variance for a data set. The following code computes the weighted sample variance for the student grade example in Section 12.2.2:

```
// the sample data set
val X2: DoubleArray = doubleArrayOf(82.0, 94.0, 90.0, 83.0, 87.0)
val W2: DoubleArray = doubleArrayOf(1.0, 4.0, 8.0, 4.0, 4.0)

// compute the biased and unbiased vairances and standard deviations
val wvar1: WeightedVariance = WeightedVariance(
        X2, // the data
        W2, // the weights
        false) // biased
println("sample weighted standard deviation (biased) = " + wvar1.stdev())
println("sample weighted variance (biased) = " + wvar1.value())
val wvar2: WeightedVariance = WeightedVariance(
        X2, // the data
        W2, // the weights
        false) // unbiased
println("sample standard deviation (unbiased) = " + wvar2.stdev())
println("sample variance (unbiased) = " + wvar2.value())
```

The output is as follows:

```
sample weighted standard deviation (biased) = 3.849787225030045
sample weighted variance (biased) = 14.820861678004535
sample standard deviation (unbiased) = 3.849787225030045
sample variance (unbiased) = 14.820861678004535
```

12.2.5. Skewness

The sample skewness is a measure of the asymmetry of the distribution of the data about its mean. The skewness value can be positive, zero, or negative. For a unimodal distribution (a distribution that has a single peak), negative skew commonly indicates that the tail is on the left side of the distribution, and positive skew indicates that the tail is on the right. A zero skew value means that the tails on both sides of the mean balance out overall. A symmetric distribution always has zero skewness. But this can also be true for an asymmetric distribution where one tail is long and thin, and the other is short but fat. See Figure 12-3.

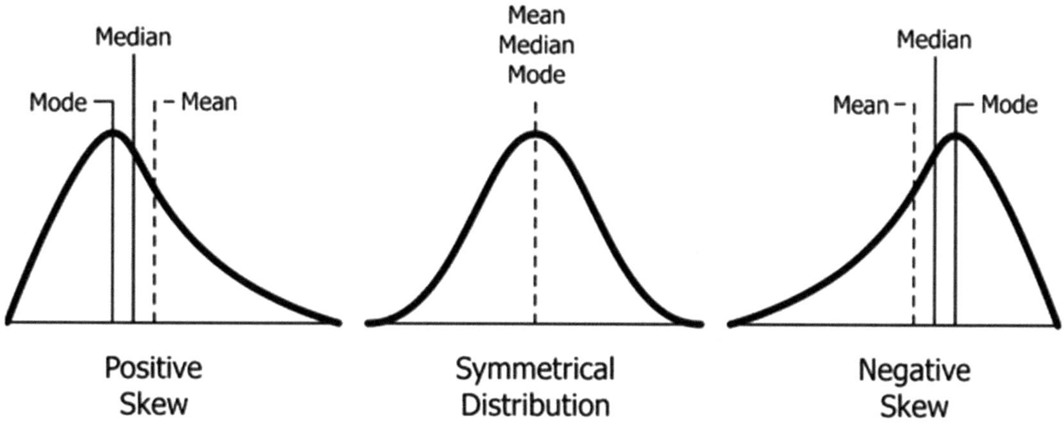

Figure 12-3. *Examples of skewness related to the mean/median/mode of a unimodal distribution*

Mathematically, sample skewness (or the Fisher-Pearson coefficient of skewness) is defined as follows:

$$g_1 = \frac{\frac{1}{n}\sum_{i=1}^{n}(x_i - \bar{x})^3}{\left(\frac{1}{n-1}\sum_{i=1}^{n}(x_i - \bar{x})^2\right)^{\frac{3}{2}}}$$

$$= \frac{\frac{1}{n}\sum_{i=1}^{n}(x_i - \bar{x})^3}{s^3}$$

where s is the sample standard deviation computed using n rather than $(n - 1)$.

$$s = \sqrt{\frac{\sum_{i=1}^{n}(x_i - \bar{x})^2}{n}}$$

The adjusted Fisher-Pearson coefficient of skewness is defined as follows:

$$G_1 = \frac{\sqrt{n(n-1)}}{n-2} g_1$$

For the sample $X = \{1, 1, 2, 1, 2, 3, 2, 1, 0\}$ and the sample mean $\bar{x} = 1.4444$, the sample skewness is as follows:

$$g_1 = \frac{\frac{1}{9}\sum_{i=1}^{9}(x_i - 1.4444)^3}{\left(\frac{1}{8}\sum_{i=1}^{9}(x_i - 1.4444)^2\right)^{3/2}} = 0.147986$$

In NM Dev, the class Skewness computes the sample skewness for a data set. The following code computes the sample skewness for the previous example:

```
// Skewness of the sample data
val X3: DoubleArray = doubleArrayOf(1.0, 1.0, 1.0, 1.0, 2.0, 2.0, 2.0, 3.0, 0.0)
val skew: Skewness = Skewness(X3)
println("sample skewness = " + skew.value())
```

The output is as follows:

```
sample skewness = 0.14798608996128484
```

12.2.6. Kurtosis

Sample kurtosis is a measure of the "tailedness" of a distribution. The kurtosis of the standard normal distribution is 3. It is common to compare the kurtosis of a distribution to this value. Distributions with kurtosis less than 3 are said to be thin-tailed. It means that the distribution produces fewer and less extreme outliers than does the normal distribution. An example of a thin-tailed distribution is the uniform distribution, which does not produce outliers. Distributions with kurtosis greater than 3 are said to be heavy-tailed or fat-tailed. An example of a fat-tailed distribution is the Laplace distribution, which has tails that asymptotically approach zero more slowly than a Gaussian and therefore produces more outliers than the normal distribution. Often, we use excess kurtosis, which is defined as the kurtosis κ minus 3, to provide comparison to the standard normal distribution. Mathematically, sample excess kurtosis is defined as follows:

$$g_2 = \kappa - 3 = \frac{\frac{1}{n}\sum_{i=1}^{n}(x_i - \overline{x})^4}{\left(\frac{1}{n-1}\sum_{i=1}^{n}(x_i - \overline{x})^2\right)^2} - 3$$

$$= \frac{\frac{1}{n}\sum_{i=1}^{n}(x_i - \overline{x})^4}{s^4} - 3$$

In 1986, Moors gave an interpretation of kurtosis. Define z-score as follows:

$$Z = \frac{X - \mu}{\sigma}$$

where X is a random variable, μ the mean, and σ the standard deviation. The z-score normalizes the random variable or data to be in the unit of numbers of σ. The z-score is often used to compare random variables of different distributions so they have the "same" unit.

By definition of the kurtosis and the identity, we have this:

$$E\left(Z^2\right) = \text{var}\left(Z\right) + \left(E\left(Z\right)\right)^2$$

$$\kappa = E\left(Z^4\right) = \text{var}\left(Z^2\right) + \left[E\left(Z^2\right)\right]^2$$

$$= \text{var}\left(Z^2\right) + \left(\text{var}\left(Z\right)\right)^2$$

$$= \text{var}\left(Z^2\right) + 1$$

The kurtosis can now be seen as a measure of the dispersion of Z^2 around its expectation. Alternatively, it can be seen to be a measure of the dispersion of Z around +1 and −1. κ attains its minimal value in a symmetric two-point distribution. In terms of the original variable X, the kurtosis is a measure of the dispersion of X around the two values $\mu \pm \sigma$.

κ has high values in these two circumstances:

- The probability mass is concentrated around the mean, and the distribution produces occasional values far from the mean.
- The probability mass is concentrated in the tails of the distribution.

Figure 12-4 shows the difference of low kurtosis and high kurtosis. The kurtosis of the distribution on the left is bigger than that on the right because the data in the left distribution spreads out (or disperses) more to a wider range, i.e., more outliers and extreme samples.

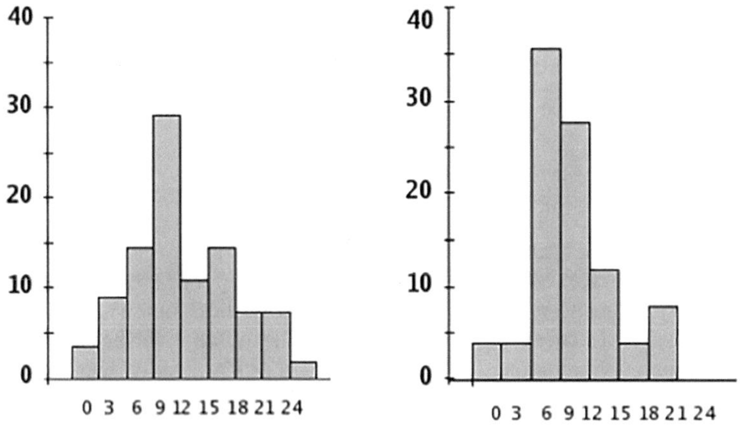

Figure 12-4. *Fat-tailed versus thin-tail distributions*

For the sample $X = \{1, 1, 2, 1, 2, 3, 2, 1, 0\}$, the sample kurtosis is as follows:

$$g_2 = \frac{\frac{1}{9}\sum_{i=1}^{9}\left(x_i - 1.4444\right)^4}{\left(\frac{1}{8}\sum_{i=1}^{9}\left(x_i - 1.4444\right)^2\right)^2} - 3 = -1.04384$$

In NM Dev, the class `Kurtosis` computes the sample kurtosis for a data set. The following code computes the sample kurtosis for the previous example:

```
// Kurtosis of the sample data
val X3: DoubleArray = doubleArrayOf(1.0, 1.0, 1.0, 1.0, 2.0, 2.0, 2.0, 3.0, 0.0)
val kur: Kurtosis = Kurtosis(X3)
println("sample kurtosis = " + kur.value())
```

The output is as follows:

```
sample kurtosis = -1.043839758125472
```

12.2.7. Moments

Mean, variance, skewness, and kurtosis are ways of looking at the data by combining the data in certain (nonlinear) ways. We can generalize these concepts to higher moments. Mathematically, for all k, the k-th raw sample moment is defined as follows:

$$\overline{x}_n^k = \frac{1}{n}\sum_{i=1}^{n} x_i^k$$

It is easy to see that the first sample moment is simply the sample mean.

It can be shown that the expected value of the raw sample moment is equal to the k-th raw moment of the population, if that moment exists, for any sample size n. It is thus an unbiased estimator.

The k-th central sample moment is defined as follows:

$$M_n^k = \frac{1}{n}\sum_{i=1}^{n}\left(x_i - \overline{x}_n^1\right)^k$$

where $\overline{x}_n^1$ or simply $\overline{x}_n$ is the average or the first raw sample moment.

It is easy to see that the first sample central moment $M_n^1 = 0$.

Also, $M_n^2 = s^2$, the unadjusted sample variance.

High-order moments are moments beyond the fourth moments. As with variance, skewness, and kurtosis, these are higher-order statistics that are nonlinear combinations of the data. They can be used for description or estimation of shape parameters. The higher the moment, the harder it is to estimate, in the sense that larger samples are required to obtain estimates of similar quality. This is due to the excess degrees of freedom consumed by the higher orders. Moreover, they can be difficult to understand. One way to interpret the higher orders is to discuss them in terms of lower orders. For example, the fourth moment (kurtosis) can be interpreted as "relative importance of tails versus shoulders in causing dispersion" (for a given dispersion, high kurtosis corresponds to heavy tails, while low kurtosis corresponds to broad shoulders). The fifth moment can be interpreted as measuring "relative importance of tails versus center (mode, shoulders) in causing skew." (For a given skew, a high fifth moment corresponds to heavy tail and little movement of mode, while a low fifth moment corresponds to more change in shoulders.)

In NM Dev, the class `Moments` computes the sample moments for a data set. Here's an example:

```
// the sample data set
val X4: DoubleArray = doubleArrayOf(1.0, 1.0, 1.0, 1.0, 2.0, 2.0, 2.0, 3.0, 0.0)
// compute moments of a data set
val moments: Moments = Moments(6) // up to the 6th moments
```

```
// data generated using rexp in R with λ = 1

val values: DoubleArray = doubleArrayOf(
    1.050339964176429, 0.906121669295144, 0.116647826876888,
    4.579895872370673, 1.714264543643022, 0.436467861756682,
    0.860735191921604, 1.771233864044571, 0.623149028640023,
    1.058291583279980
)
for (i in 0 until values.size) {
    moments.addData(values[i])
}

println("sample size = " + moments.N())
println("1st central moment = " + moments.centralMoment(1)) // ok
println("2nd central moment = " + moments.centralMoment(2)) // ok
println("3rd central moment = " + moments.centralMoment(3)) // off, // not enough data
println("4th central moment = " + moments.centralMoment(4)) // way off, // not enough data
println("5th central moment = " + moments.centralMoment(5)) // meaningless, not enough data
println("6th central moment = " + moments.centralMoment(6)) // meaningless, not enough data
```

The output is as follows:

```
sample size = 10
1st central moment = 1.3117147406005016
2nd central moment = 1.422300520892388
3rd central moment = 3.217342528890056
4th central moment = 11.708334307448762
5th central moment = 36.97401011137275
6th central moment = 122.20276981014138
```

12.2.8. Rank

A ranking is an ordering Ranking between a set of items such that, for any two items, the first is either "ranked higher than," "ranked lower than," or "ranked equal to" the second. If there can be ties in the ranking, the ranking is called a weak order. Otherwise, if there is no tie, it is called a total order. By reducing detailed measures to a sequence of ordinal numbers, rankings make it possible to evaluate complex information according to certain criteria. For example, an Internet search engine may rank the pages it finds according to an estimation of their relevance, making it possible for the user to quickly select the pages they are likely to want to see. In statistics, ranking is the transformation of data such that numerical or ordinal values are assigned to the data when they are sorted. For example, suppose the numerical data 3.4, 5.1, 2.6, and 7.3 are observed. The ranks of these data items, after sorting them, would be 2, 3, 1, and 4, respectively. For another example, the ordinal data hot, cold, warm would be replaced by 3, 1, 2. In these examples, the ranks are assigned to values in ascending order. (In some other cases, descending ranks are used.)

In NM Dev, the class `Rank` is used to rank a set of data. It returns the sample ranks of the values. Ties (i.e., equal values) and missing values can be handled in several ways. The `FIRST` method results in a permutation with increasing values at each index set of ties and analogously `LAST` with decreasing values. The `RANDOM` method puts these in random order, whereas the default, `AVERAGE`, replaces them by their mean, and `MAX` and `MIN` replace them by their maximum and minimum, respectively, with the latter being the typical sports ranking. The method `AS_26` breaks a tie by following Freeman (1970). It adds 0.5 to the rank of each duplicated items. This is our default implementation.

Here's an example:

```
val x: DoubleArray = doubleArrayOf(3.0, 1.0, 4.0, 1.0, 5.0, 9.0, 2.0, 6.0, 5.0, 3.0, 5.0)
println("Ranking data: " + Arrays.toString(x))

var rank: Rank = Rank(x, Rank.TiesMethod.AS_26) // default implementation
println("AS_26 rank: " + Arrays.toString(rank.ranks()))

rank = Rank(x, Rank.TiesMethod.AVERAGE)
println("AVERAGE rank: " + Arrays.toString(rank.ranks()))

rank = Rank(x, Rank.TiesMethod.FIRST)
println("FIRST rank: " + Arrays.toString(rank.ranks()))

rank = Rank(x, Rank.TiesMethod.LAST)
println("LAST rank: " + Arrays.toString(rank.ranks()))

rank = Rank(x, Rank.TiesMethod.MAX)
println("MAX rank: " + Arrays.toString(rank.ranks()))

rank = Rank(x, Rank.TiesMethod.MIN)
println("MIN rank: " + Arrays.toString(rank.ranks()))

rank = Rank(x, Rank.TiesMethod.RANDOM)
println("RANDOM rank: " + Arrays.toString(rank.ranks()))
```

The output is as follows:

```
Ranking data: [3.0, 1.0, 4.0, 1.0, 5.0, 9.0, 2.0, 6.0, 5.0, 3.0, 5.0]
AS_26 rank: [4.5, 1.5, 6.0, 1.5, 8.0, 11.0, 3.0, 10.0, 8.0, 4.5, 8.0]
AVERAGE rank: [4.5, 1.5, 6.0, 1.5, 8.0, 11.0, 3.0, 10.0, 8.0, 4.5, 8.0]
FIRST rank: [4.0, 1.0, 6.0, 2.0, 7.0, 11.0, 3.0, 10.0, 8.0, 5.0, 9.0]
LAST rank: [5.0, 2.0, 6.0, 1.0, 9.0, 11.0, 3.0, 10.0, 8.0, 4.0, 7.0]
MAX rank: [5.0, 2.0, 6.0, 2.0, 9.0, 11.0, 3.0, 10.0, 9.0, 5.0, 9.0]
MIN rank: [4.0, 1.0, 6.0, 1.0, 7.0, 11.0, 3.0, 10.0, 7.0, 4.0, 7.0]
RANDOM rank: [4.0, 1.0, 6.0, 2.0, 9.0, 11.0, 3.0, 10.0, 7.0, 5.0, 8.0]
```

Quantile

q-quantiles are values that partition a finite and ordered set of data into q subsets of (nearly) equal sizes. The quantiles are the data values marking the boundaries between consecutive subsets. There are $q - 1$ of the q-quantiles, one for each integer k satisfying $0 < k < q$. Considering the data as samples from a random variable, the k-th q-quantile of a random variable is the value x such that the probability that a sample or the random variable will be less than x is at most $\frac{k}{q}$ and the probability that a sample or the random variable will be more than x is at most $\frac{q-k}{q}$. The smallest observation corresponds to probability 0 and the largest probability 1.

Quantiles can also be applied to continuous distributions (see Sections 12.3 and 12.3.1), providing a way to generalize rank statistics to continuous variables. When the cumulative distribution function of a random variable is known, the q-quantiles are the application of the quantile function (the inverse function of the cumulative distribution function, CDF) to the values $\left\{\frac{1}{q}, \frac{2}{q}, \ldots, \frac{q-1}{q}\right\}$.

In NM Dev, the class `Quantile` computes the quantiles for a data set. There are nine different quantile definitions and implementations as described in Hyndman & Fan (1996). Briefly, they are as follows. The default implementation is `APPROXIMATELY_MEDIAN_UNBIASED`.

1. `INVERSE_OF_EMPIRICAL_CDF`: The inverse of empirical distribution function.
2. `INVERSE_OF_EMPIRICAL_CDF_WITH_AVERAGING_AT_DISCONTINUITIES`: The inverse of empirical distribution function with averaging at discontinuities.
3. `NEAREST_EVEN_ORDER_STATISTICS`: The nearest even-order statistic as in SAS.
4. `LINEAR_INTERPOLATION_OF_EMPIRICAL_CDF`: The linear interpolation of the empirical CDF.
5. `MIDWAY_THROUGH_STEPS_OF_EMPIRICAL_CDF`: A piecewise linear function where the knots are the values midway through the steps of the empirical CDF.
6. `MINITAB_SPSS`: The definition in Minitab and SPSS.
7. `S`: The definition in S.
8. `APPROXIMATELY_MEDIAN_UNBIASED`: The resulting quantile estimates are approximately median-unbiased regardless of the distribution of the sample.
9. `APPROXIMATELY_UNBIASED_IF_DATA_IS_NORMAL`: The resulting quantile estimates are approximately unbiased for the expected order statistics if the sample is normally distributed.

Here's an example:

```
println("Quantiles")

val x: DoubleArray = doubleArrayOf(0.0, 1.0, 2.0, 3.0, 3.0, 3.0, 6.0, 7.0, 8.0, 9.0) // with
repeated observations
val qs: DoubleArray = doubleArrayOf(1e-10, 0.1, 0.15, 0.2, 0.3, 0.4, 0.5, 0.6, 0.7, 0.8,
0.9, 0.95, 1.0) // qu

println("APPROXIMATELY_MEDIAN_UNBIASED")
val stat1: Quantile = Quantile(
        x,
        Quantile.QuantileType.APPROXIMATELY_MEDIAN_UNBIASED
)

println("\nnumber of samples = " + stat1.N())
for (q in qs) {
    println(String.format("Q(%f) = %f", q, stat1.value(q)))
}

println("\nthe median = " + stat1.value(0.5))
println("the 100% quantile = " + stat1.value(1.0))
println("the maximum = " + Max(x).value())
```

The output is as follows:

```
APPROXIMATELY_MEDIAN_UNBIASED
number of samples = 10
Q(0.000000) = 0.000000
Q(0.100000) = 0.366667
Q(0.150000) = 0.883333
Q(0.200000) = 1.400000
Q(0.300000) = 2.433333
Q(0.400000) = 3.000000
Q(0.500000) = 3.000000
Q(0.600000) = 4.600000
Q(0.700000) = 6.566667
Q(0.800000) = 7.600000
Q(0.900000) = 8.633333
Q(0.950000) = 9.000000
Q(1.000000) = 9.000000

the median = 3.0
the 100% quantile = 9.0
the maximum = 9.0
```

```
println("NEAREST_EVEN_ORDER_STATISTICS")
val stat2: Quantile = Quantile(
        x,
        Quantile.QuantileType.NEAREST_EVEN_ORDER_STATISTICS)
println("\nnumber of samples = " + stat2.N())

for (q in qs) {
    println(String.format("Q(%f) = %f", q, stat2.value(q)))
}

println("\nthe median = " + stat2.value(0.5))
println("the 1e-10 quantile = " + stat2.value(1e-10))
println("the minimun = " + Min(x).value())
```

The output is as follows:

```
NEAREST_EVEN_ORDER_STATISTICS
number of samples = 10
Q(0.000000) = 0.000000
Q(0.100000) = 0.000000
Q(0.150000) = 1.000000
Q(0.200000) = 1.000000
Q(0.300000) = 2.000000
Q(0.400000) = 3.000000
Q(0.500000) = 3.000000
Q(0.600000) = 3.000000
Q(0.700000) = 6.000000
Q(0.800000) = 7.000000
```

```
Q(0.900000) = 8.000000
Q(0.950000) = 9.000000
Q(1.000000) = 9.000000

the median = 3.0
the 1e-10 quantile = 0.0
the minimun = 0.0
```

Median

The median of a data set is defined such that no more than half the data values are larger than, and no more than half are smaller than, the median. While the arithmetic mean is often used to report central tendencies, it is not a robust statistic, meaning that it is greatly influenced by outliers (values that are very much larger or smaller than most of the values). For skewed distributions, such as the distribution of income for which a few people's incomes are substantially greater than most people's, the arithmetic mean may not coincide with one's notion of "middle," and robust statistics, such as the median, may provide better description of central tendency. Mathematically, it is the 50 percent quantile, i.e., $Q(0.5)$. See Figure 12-5.

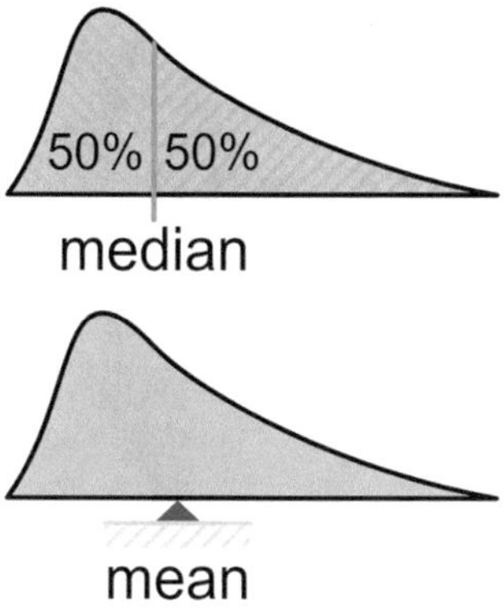

Figure 12-5. *Comparing median and mean for a probability distribution*

Here's an example:

```
val x: DoubleArray = doubleArrayOf(0.0, 1.0, 2.0, 3.0, 3.0, 3.0, 6.0, 7.0, 8.0, 9.0) // with
repeated observations

println("APPROXIMATELY_MEDIAN_UNBIASED")
val stat1: Quantile = Quantile(
        x,
        Quantile.QuantileType.APPROXIMATELY_MEDIAN_UNBIASED
);
println("the median = " + stat1.value(0.5));
```

```
println("NEAREST_EVEN_ORDER_STATISTICS");
val stat2: Quantile = Quantile(
        x,
        Quantile.QuantileType.NEAREST_EVEN_ORDER_STATISTICS
);
println("the median = " + stat2.value(0.5));
```

The output is as follows:

```
APPROXIMATELY_MEDIAN_UNBIASED
the median = 3.0
NEAREST_EVEN_ORDER_STATISTICS
the median = 3.0
```

Maximum and Minimum

Maximum is the largest value in a data set, while minimum is the smallest value in the data set. Mathematically, they are equivalent to the 100 percent quantile and smallest quantile, say 1e-10 percent quantile, $Q(1)$ and $Q(1e - 10)$. But the results may be subject to the interpolation method used. In NM Dev, the classes Max and Min are used to compute the maximum and minimum, respectively. Here's an example:

```
val x: DoubleArray = doubleArrayOf(0.0, 1.0, 2.0, 3.0, 3.0, 3.0, 6.0, 7.0, 8.0, 9.0)
// with repeated observations

println("APPROXIMATELY_MEDIAN_UNBIASED");
val stat1: Quantile = Quantile(
        x,
        Quantile.QuantileType.APPROXIMATELY_MEDIAN_UNBIASED
);
println("the 100% quantile = " + stat1.value(1.0));
println("the maximum = " + Max(x).value());

println("NEAREST_EVEN_ORDER_STATISTICS");
val stat2: Quantile = Quantile(
        x,
        Quantile.QuantileType.NEAREST_EVEN_ORDER_STATISTICS
);
println("the 1e-10 quantile = " + stat2.value(1e-10));
println("the minimun = " + Min(x).value());
```

The output is as follows:

```
APPROXIMATELY_MEDIAN_UNBIASED
the 100% quantile = 9.0
the maximum = 9.0
NEAREST_EVEN_ORDER_STATISTICS
the 1e-10 quantile = 0.0
the minimun = 0.0
```

12.2.9. Covariance

CovarianceCovariance is a measure of the joint variability of two samples or two random variables. If big values of one sample/variable correspond to big values in the other sample/variable and the same holds for the smaller values (that is, the variables tend to show similar behavior), the covariance is positive. See Figure 12-6.

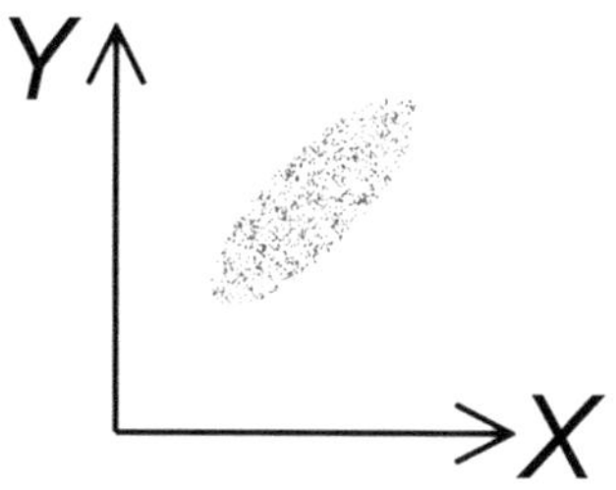

Figure 12-6. *positive covariance*

In the opposite case, when the big values of one sample/variable usually correspond to the smaller values of the other (that is, the variables tend to show opposite behavior), the covariance is negative. See Figure 12-7.

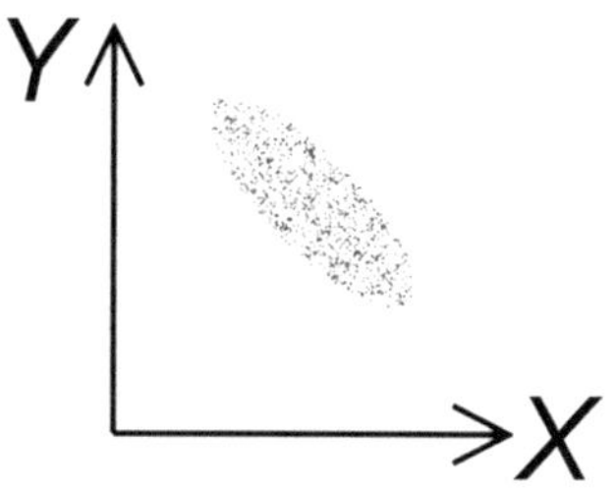

Figure 12-7. *negative covariance*

Similarly, if the values in of the one sample/variable do not predict the values in the other sample/variable, the covariance is zero. See Figure 12-8.

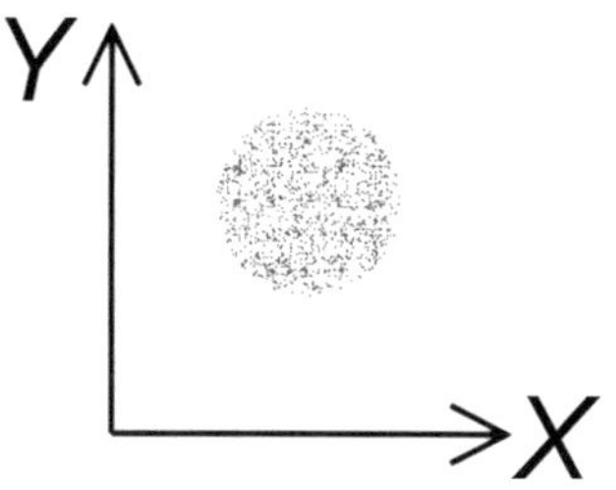

Figure 12-8. *zero covariance*

The sign of the covariance therefore shows the tendency in the linear relationship between the variables. The magnitude of the covariance is not easy to interpret because it is not normalized and hence depends on the magnitudes of the variables. The normalized version of the covariance, called the correlation coefficient, however, shows by its magnitude the strength of the linear relation.

Sample Covariance

Mathematically, the sample covariance of two samples *X* and *Y* are as follows:

$$\mathrm{cov}(X,Y)=\mathrm{E}(X-\mathrm{E}(X))\mathrm{E}(Y-\mathrm{E}(Y))$$

$$=\frac{1}{N-1}\sum_{i=1}^{N}(X_i-\bar{X})(Y_i-\bar{Y})$$

$\bar{X}$ is the sample mean of *X*. $\bar{Y}$ is the sample mean of *Y*. Here we use as the denominator $N-1$ instead of *N* to make the estimator unbiased because we use the sample mean instead of the population mean in the computation. If the population mean is known, then the unbiased estimator is as follows:

$$\mathrm{cov}(X,Y)=\frac{1}{N}\sum_{i=1}^{N}(X_i-\mathrm{E}(X))(Y_i-\mathrm{E}(Y))$$

The sample variance is a special case of the covariance in which the two samples/variables are identical (that is, in which one variable always takes the same value as the other):

$$\mathrm{var}(X)=\mathrm{cov}(X,X)=\sigma^2(X)=\sigma_X^2$$

The sample standard deviation is the square root of var(*X*).

$$\sigma_X=\sqrt{\sigma_X^2}$$

Correlation

The correlation coefficient of two samples is defined as the covariance divided by the product of their standard deviations. The sample correlation is also called the Spearman rank correlation. It is essentially a normalized measurement of the covariance, such that the result always has a value between –1 and 1. As with covariance itself, the measure can only reflect a linear correlation of variables and ignores many other types of relationship or correlation. See Figure 12-9.

$$\mathrm{corr}(X,Y)=\rho_{XY}=\frac{\mathrm{cov}(X,Y)}{\sigma_X\sigma_Y}$$

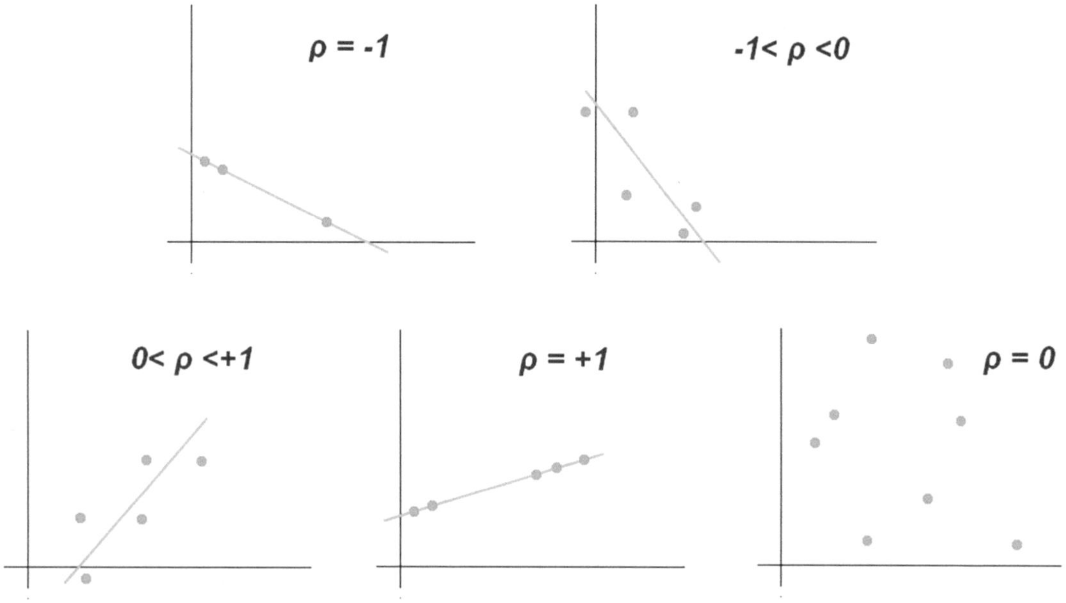

Figure 12-9. *Examples of scatter diagrams with different values of correlation coefficient*

In NM Dev, the class `SpearmanRankCorrelation` computes the sample correlation between two sample sets. Here's an example:

```
// the sample data sets
val X5: DoubleArray = doubleArrayOf(106.0, 86.0, 100.0, 101.0, 99.0, 103.0, 97.0, 113.0,
112.0, 110.0)
val X6: DoubleArray = doubleArrayOf(7.0, 0.0, 27.0, 50.0, 28.0, 29.0, 20.0, 12.0, 6.0, 17.0)
// compute the sample correlation of the data sets
println("the sample correlation = " + SpearmanRankCorrelation(X5, X6).value())
```

The output is as follows:

```
the sample correlation = -0.17575757575757575
```

Covariance Matrix and Correlation Matrix

For more than two samples, a covariance matrix is a square matrix giving the covariance between each pair of samples. Any covariance matrix is symmetric and positive semi-definite. The entries on the main diagonal are variances of the samples. Intuitively, the covariance matrix generalizes the notion of variance to multiple dimensions. As an example, the variation in a collection of random samples in two-dimensional space cannot be characterized fully by a single number, nor would the variances in the x and y directions contain all the necessary information; a 2×2 matrix containing both covariances and variances would be necessary to fully characterize the two-dimensional variation.

Mathematically, for a column vector of random samples of multiple variables $\boldsymbol{X} = (X_1, X_2, \cdots, X_n)^T$, each with finite variance and expected value $E(X_i)$, then the covariance matrix Σ^X is a matrix whose (i, j) entry is the covariance $\text{cov}(X_i, X_j)$. That is,

$$(\Sigma_\mathbf{X})_{ij} = \text{cov}(X_i, X_j)$$

$$= E(X_i - E(X_i))E(X_j - E(X_j))$$

The diagonal entries are $\sigma^2_{X_i}$.

Likewise, the correlation matrix is a matrix whose (i, j) entry is the correlation coefficient $\rho_{X_i X_j}$. The diagonal entries are all 1. The correlation matrix is necessarily a symmetric and positive-semidefinite matrix. Moreover, the correlation matrix is strictly positive definite if no variable can have all its values exactly generated as a linear function of the values of the others.

For example, suppose we have five data sets.

X_1 = {1.4022225, -0.2230975,0.6939930,0.6939930,0.6939930, -2.5275280}

X_2 = {-0.04625344,0.91561987,1.94611387,0.18818663, -0.10749210,0.64942255}

X_3 = {1.26176112,1.17086252, -0.82939259, -0.29040783,3.27376532,0.07506224}

X_4 = {-1.8394428,0.2282348,1.0905923,0.6937185,0.5141217, -1.0787524}

X_5 = {0.7182637,0.0690674,0.1458883,0.4664052,0.7691778,1.6217606}

The sample covariance is as follows:

$$£_X = \begin{bmatrix} 1.891462 & -0.094053 & 0.665669 & 0.176962 & -0.487023 \\ -0.094053 & 0.600273 & -0.742584 & 0.404512 & -0.173547 \\ 0.665669 & -0.742584 & 2.167306 & -0.250672 & 0.085099 \\ 0.176962 & 0.404512 & -0.250672 & 1.301751 & -0.385892 \\ -0.487023 & -0.173547 & 0.085099 & -0.385892 & 0.317301 \end{bmatrix}$$

Note that each sample set (or each variable) is arranged in columns. There are five columns that correspond to five variables. Each set has six samples/observations/values. Each row is one observation of five variables. For instance, the numbers in a row, e.g., {1.4022225, –0.04625344, 1.26176112, –1.8394428, 0.7182637}, are supposed to be observed together. So, the order of the numbers matters. The resultant covariance matrix is thus a 5 × 5 matrix.

In NM Dev, the class `SampleCovariance` computes the sample covariance of a data set. The following code reproduces the previous example:

```
// each column is a sample set there are 5 data sets
val X7: Matrix = DenseMatrix(
    arrayOf(
        doubleArrayOf(1.4022225, -0.04625344, 1.26176112, -1.8394428, 0.7182637),
        doubleArrayOf(-0.2230975, 0.91561987, 1.17086252, 0.2282348, 0.0690674),
        doubleArrayOf(0.6939930, 1.94611387, -0.82939259, 1.0905923, 0.1458883),
        doubleArrayOf(-0.4050039, 0.18818663, -0.29040783, 0.6937185, 0.4664052),
        doubleArrayOf(0.6587918, -0.10749210, 3.27376532, 0.5141217, 0.7691778),
        doubleArrayOf(-2.5275280, 0.64942255, 0.07506224, -1.0787524, 1.6217606)
    )
)
```

```
// compute the sample covariance of the data sets
val cov: Matrix = SampleCovariance(X7) // a 5x5 matrix
println("\nsample covariance =")
println(cov)
```

The output is as follows:

```
sample covariance =
5x5
        [,1] [,2] [,3] [,4] [,5]
[1,] 1.891462, -0.094053, 0.665669, 0.176962, -0.487023,
[2,] -0.094053, 0.600273, -0.742584, 0.404512, -0.173547,
[3,] 0.665669, -0.742584, 2.167306, -0.250672, 0.085099,
[4,] 0.176962, 0.404512, -0.250672, 1.301751, -0.385892,
[5,] -0.487023, -0.173547, 0.085099, -0.385892, 0.317301,
```

Ledoit-Wolf Linear Shrinkage

This section follows Ledoit & Wolf (2004), which proposes a better estimator than sample covariance for a covariance matrix. Many real-life (not textbook) problems require an estimate of a covariance matrix and/or of its inverse, where the matrix dimension p is large compared to the sample size n. Examples include selecting a mean-variance efficient portfolio from a large universe of stocks, running generalized least squares (GLS) regressions on large cross-sections, and choosing an optimal weighting matrix in the general method of moments where the number of moment restrictions is large. In such situations, the usual estimator, namely, the sample covariance matrix, is known to perform poorly. When the matrix dimension p is larger than the number n of observations available $\frac{p}{n} > 1$, the sample covariance matrix is not even invertible. This happens often when estimating the covariance matrix for, say, 3,000 stocks and we do not have enough data for the estimation. Ten years' worth of data is only 2,500 trading day or worse only 120 months. The estimated daily or monthly covariance matrix is not invertible. All portfolio optimization algorithms that require computing the inverse matrix fail.

When the ratio $\frac{p}{n} < 1$ is not negligible, the sample covariance matrix is invertible but maybe numerically ill-conditioned. (A matrix is said to be ill-conditioned if its condition number is very large. Practically, such a matrix is almost singular, and the computation of its inverse, or solution of a linear system of equations is prone to large numerical errors. A matrix that is not invertible has condition number equal to infinity.) It means that inverting it amplifies estimation error dramatically. For large p, it is difficult to find enough observations, big n, to make $\frac{p}{n}$ close to 0, and therefore it is important to develop a well-conditioned estimator for large-dimensional covariance matrices.

If we want a well-conditioned estimator at any cost, we can always impose some ad hoc structure on the covariance matrix to force it to be well-conditioned, such as diagonality, sparseness, a graph model, or a factor model. But, in the absence of prior information about the true structure of the matrix, this ad hoc structure will be in general mis-specified, and the resulting estimator may be so biased that it bears little resemblance to the true covariance matrix. There was no estimator that was both well-conditioned and more accurate than the sample covariance matrix before (Ledoit & Wolf, 2004).

In 2003, Ledoit &Wolf (2003, 2004) proposed an estimator that possesses both these properties asymptotically. One way to get a well-conditioned structured estimator is to impose the condition that all variances are the same and all covariances are zero. The estimator they recommend is a weighted average of this structured estimator and the sample covariance matrix. This estimator ensures that the weighted average of the sample covariance matrix and the structured estimator is more accurate than either of them. This new estimation method tends to pull the most extreme coefficients toward more central values (thus so called shrinkage), thereby systematically reducing estimation error where it matters most.

Extensive studies indicate that (i) the new estimator is more accurate than the sample covariance matrix, even for very small numbers of observations and variables and usually by a lot; (ii) it is essentially as accurate or substantially more accurate than some estimators proposed in finite sample decision theory, as soon as there are at least ten variables and observations; (iii) it is better conditioned than the true covariance matrix; and (iv) general asymptotics are a good approximation of finite sample behavior when there are at least 20 observations and variables. Figure 12-10 compares the condition number (how unstable a matrix is with respect to small changes in data; the smaller the better) of S^* the linearly shrunk covariance matrix versus σ the sample covariance matrix.

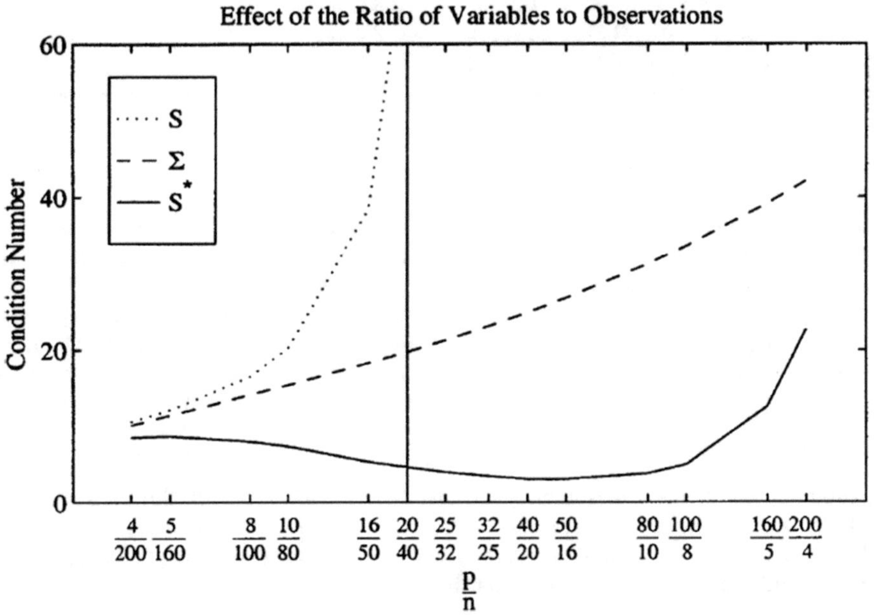

Figure 12-10. *Comparing the condition numbers of matrices given by Ledoit-Wolf 2004 and sample covariance matrices (credit Ledoit & Wolf, 2004)*

In NM Dev, the class `LedoitWolf2004` computes this linear shrinkage covariance matrix estimator. Here's an example:

```
//          * These are the stock returns for MSFT, YHOO, GOOG, AAPL, MS, XOM from
//          * Aug 20, 2012 to Jan 15, 2013 (i.e., returns for 100 days).

val X: Matrix = DenseMatrix(
    arrayOf(
        doubleArrayOf(0.001968, 0.000668, -0.008926, -0.013668, 0.004057, -0.005492),
        doubleArrayOf(-0.008511, -0.003340, 0.011456, 0.019523, -0.002020, 0.002991),
        doubleArrayOf(-0.009244, -0.003351, -0.000561, -0.009327, -0.024291, -0.004703),
        doubleArrayOf(0.009997, 0.003362, 0.002704, 0.000879, 0.004149, 0.008413),
        doubleArrayOf(0.004289, -0.004692, -0.013866, 0.018797, -0.002066, -0.003543),
```

```
doubleArrayOf(-0.001971, -0.008754, 0.011999, -0.001308, 0.004831, 0.004129),
doubleArrayOf(0.000658, 0.008152, 0.015888, -0.001965, 0.014423, -0.002284),
doubleArrayOf(-0.010855, -0.011456, -0.009200, -0.014260, 0.006093, -0.007899),
doubleArrayOf(0.016628, -0.001363, 0.005002, 0.002073, 0.006729, 0.001154),
doubleArrayOf(-0.014066, 0.016382, -0.005912, 0.014617, 0.033422, -0.002075),
doubleArrayOf(0.000000, 0.013432, -0.000470, -0.007025, 0.010996, 0.002426),
doubleArrayOf(0.031520, 0.001325, 0.027442, 0.009023, 0.036468, 0.019011),
doubleArrayOf(-0.012544, 0.007280, 0.009651, 0.006165, 0.051235, 0.010403),
doubleArrayOf(-0.007492, -0.007227, -0.007619, -0.026013, -0.027598, -0.004924),
doubleArrayOf(0.002297, 0.003309, -0.012244, -0.003244, 0.038647, 0.001574),
doubleArrayOf(-0.000327, 0.015831, -0.001893, 0.013914, 0.009884, -0.000786),
doubleArrayOf(0.005241, 0.012987, 0.021943, 0.019693, 0.027634, 0.018766),
doubleArrayOf(0.008798, 0.010897, 0.005156, 0.012164, 0.019048, 0.011802),
doubleArrayOf(0.000000, -0.005707, 0.000423, 0.012294, -0.024189, -0.004252),
doubleArrayOf(-0.000969, 0.014668, 0.011690, 0.003043, -0.009577, -0.002847),
doubleArrayOf(-0.004203, -0.003143, 0.012836, 0.000272, -0.003413, -0.011748),
doubleArrayOf(0.012662, -0.004414, 0.000852, -0.004850, -0.020548, 0.010443),
doubleArrayOf(-0.008015, -0.003167, 0.008062, 0.001999, -0.007576, 0.004398),
doubleArrayOf(-0.013251, 0.016518, 0.020968, -0.013287, -0.002349, -0.000438),
doubleArrayOf(-0.012774, -0.020000, -0.000294, -0.024969, -0.025898, -0.001533),
doubleArrayOf(-0.007299, -0.004464, 0.005740, -0.012409, -0.010272, -0.005594),
doubleArrayOf(-0.000334, 0.027546, 0.004035, 0.024254, 0.025031, 0.006287),
doubleArrayOf(-0.013039, -0.003741, -0.002644, -0.020863, -0.005956, -0.003836),
doubleArrayOf(-0.009146, -0.009387, 0.009649, -0.011565, 0.002996, 0.003851),
doubleArrayOf(0.005812, 0.006949, -0.006288, 0.002910, 0.007168, -0.000877),
doubleArrayOf(0.006798, 0.016939, 0.007279, 0.015343, 0.007117, -0.000219),
doubleArrayOf(0.005739, 0.003701, 0.007279, -0.006927, 0.025913, 0.005706),
doubleArrayOf(-0.006042, -0.011063, -0.000521, -0.021318, 0.001722, 0.003492),
doubleArrayOf(-0.002364, -0.003729, -0.012779, -0.022090, -0.002865, 0.001414),
doubleArrayOf(-0.016926, -0.011229, -0.018144, -0.003636, -0.005747, -0.005863),
doubleArrayOf(-0.010331, -0.001262, 0.000632, 0.007963, 0.002890, -0.012014),
doubleArrayOf(-0.001044, 0.005685, 0.009294, -0.020000, 0.026513, 0.001548),
doubleArrayOf(0.008708, -0.002513, -0.008956, 0.002575, -0.030882, -0.001545),
doubleArrayOf(0.010704, -0.012594, -0.005062, 0.008008, 0.025492, 0.005306),
doubleArrayOf(-0.000683, 0.015306, 0.005020, 0.023692, 0.006780, 0.009567),
doubleArrayOf(0.003419, 0.010678, 0.014489, -0.007977, 0.034792, 0.010892),
doubleArrayOf(-0.003066, -0.005594, -0.080067, -0.018576, -0.037961, 0.000970),
doubleArrayOf(-0.029050, -0.010000, -0.019007, -0.036030, -0.014656, -0.014209),
doubleArrayOf(-0.022527, -0.004419, -0.004576, 0.039666, -0.004577, 0.000437),
doubleArrayOf(0.001801, 0.057070, 0.002475, -0.032607, -0.019540, -0.021829),
doubleArrayOf(-0.005392, -0.007199, -0.004483, 0.005667, 0.004103, -0.003347),
doubleArrayOf(-0.000723, 0.003625, 0.000679, -0.011824, -0.004670, 0.006158),
doubleArrayOf(0.011935, 0.010837, -0.003851, -0.009097, -0.003519, 0.002114),
doubleArrayOf(0.011794, 0.002978, 0.007628, -0.014370, 0.022955, 0.005996),
doubleArrayOf(0.034264, 0.006532, 0.010716, 0.002059, 0.013234, 0.004746),
doubleArrayOf(-0.000683, 0.009440, 0.000480, -0.033090, 0.009654, -0.014501),
doubleArrayOf(0.004443, 0.015196, -0.007210, 0.013550, -0.001687, 0.004013),
doubleArrayOf(0.007826, 0.005181, -0.001816, -0.003024, 0.024789, 0.010769),
doubleArrayOf(-0.026334, -0.004009, -0.021416, -0.038263, -0.085761, -0.031415),
doubleArrayOf(-0.009015, -0.008626, -0.022230, -0.036290, -0.006615, -0.012588),
doubleArrayOf(0.000700, 0.001160, 0.016465, 0.017313, 0.005448, 0.001608),
```

```
        doubleArrayOf(-0.021329, 0.014484, 0.004329, -0.007732, 0.009633, 0.001261),
        doubleArrayOf(-0.032154, 0.019417, -0.010287, 0.000129, -0.014908, -0.009734),
        doubleArrayOf(-0.009228, -0.001120, -0.009863, -0.011089, -0.026029, -0.004626),
        doubleArrayOf(-0.006706, 0.003365, -0.008107, -0.020973, 0.010566, 0.000813),
        doubleArrayOf(-0.005251, -0.001677, -0.000124, 0.003919, -0.004920, 0.003599),
        doubleArrayOf(0.007919, 0.027996, 0.032495, 0.072108, 0.021014, 0.014112),
        doubleArrayOf(-0.000748, -0.006536, 0.002634, -0.008520, -0.010291, -0.001939),
        doubleArrayOf(0.008985, 0.008772, -0.006120, 0.001408, -0.006116, 0.005829),
        doubleArrayOf(0.027829, 0.009239, 0.003154, 0.017447, 0.011077, 0.012271),
        doubleArrayOf(-0.011191, 0.010232, -0.010210, 0.031549, 0.010956, -0.005276),
        doubleArrayOf(-0.011318, 0.009062, 0.014460, -0.008057, 0.001204, -0.014331),
        doubleArrayOf(0.010340, -0.001057, 0.019323, -0.003146, 0.015033, 0.008586),
        doubleArrayOf(-0.014985, -0.002115, 0.012023, 0.011013, -0.001185, 0.000227),
        doubleArrayOf(-0.012245, -0.005299, 0.009366, -0.006923, 0.000593, 0.000227),
        doubleArrayOf(-0.007137, -0.011721, -0.004468, 0.001555, -0.023711, -0.006013),
        doubleArrayOf(-0.002270, 0.020485, -0.006070, -0.017639, 0.008500, -0.004794),
        doubleArrayOf(0.011377, -0.002113, -0.004645, -0.064357, 0.022276, 0.006193),
        doubleArrayOf(0.002250, 0.016411, 0.004812, 0.015683, -0.014134, 0.003078),
        doubleArrayOf(-0.010101, 0.000000, -0.010013, -0.025565, 0.013740, 0.006818),
        doubleArrayOf(0.018141, 0.011979, 0.001768, -0.006432, 0.002357, -0.002144),
        doubleArrayOf(0.014105, 0.004632, 0.016720, 0.021838, 0.043504, 0.006560),
        doubleArrayOf(-0.002928, -0.007172, 0.000976, -0.004415, -0.002817, 0.005169),
        doubleArrayOf(-0.004772, -0.001548, 0.007369, -0.017273, 0.005650, -0.009726),
        doubleArrayOf(-0.011066, 0.014987, -0.001053, -0.037569, 0.014045, -0.005645),
        doubleArrayOf(0.010817, 0.002546, 0.026811, 0.017733, 0.026593, 0.008969),
        doubleArrayOf(0.016974, -0.003555, 0.000402, 0.029046, 0.031840, 0.007764),
        doubleArrayOf(-0.009071, -0.001019, -0.001331, -0.014216, -0.001569, -0.012506),
        doubleArrayOf(0.013548, 0.004592, 0.003125, -0.008702, 0.009429, 0.005088),
        doubleArrayOf(-0.008309, -0.017268, -0.009317, -0.004600, -0.018163, -0.018675),
        doubleArrayOf(-0.014208, 0.015504, -0.008566, 0.001617, 0.001586, -0.003554),
        doubleArrayOf(-0.007391, -0.004071, -0.000888, -0.013784, -0.003694, 0.001726),
        doubleArrayOf(0.003723, 0.001533, -0.003640, 0.004016, -0.005826, -0.002412),
        doubleArrayOf(-0.015208, -0.005102, -0.008892, -0.010620, -0.007991, -0.020262),
        doubleArrayOf(0.006026, 0.020513, 0.010528, 0.044310, 0.026853, 0.017039),
        doubleArrayOf(0.034070, 0.009045, 0.022435, 0.031682, 0.026151, 0.024957),
        doubleArrayOf(-0.013396, -0.014940, 0.000581, -0.012622, -0.002039, -0.001804),
        doubleArrayOf(-0.018716, 0.004044, 0.019760, -0.027855, 0.031154, 0.004630),
        doubleArrayOf(-0.001870, -0.023162, -0.004363, -0.005882, -0.019316, -0.011578),
        doubleArrayOf(-0.005245, 0.013402, -0.001973, 0.002691, -0.007576, 0.006255),
        doubleArrayOf(0.005650, -0.017294, 0.006573, -0.015629, -0.001527, -0.003843),
        doubleArrayOf(-0.008989, -0.017081, 0.004552, 0.012396, 0.036697, 0.010892),
        doubleArrayOf(0.013983, 0.015798, -0.002009, -0.006132, -0.008358, 0.005724),
        doubleArrayOf(0.002236, 0.007258, -0.022622, -0.035653, -0.004958, -0.000335),
        doubleArrayOf(0.011900, 0.004632, 0.002323, -0.031550, 0.017937, -0.000558)
))

//          * From Wolf's implementation (http://www.econ.uzh.ch/faculty/wolf/publications.
html#9):
//          * phi = 4.11918014563813e-06
//          * rho = 2.59272437810913e-06
//          * gamma = 1.64807384775746e-08
```

```
//          * kappa = 9.26205927972248e+01
//          * shrinkage = 9.26205927972248e-01
//          * sigma =
//          * 1e-4 *
//          * 1.515632920116000 0.485389976957753 0.569819071905581 0.832527350192132
0.847148840587289
//          * 0.397609074332363
//          * 0.485389976957753 1.385321425539000 0.536232629487419 0.789078831932216
0.788206205379818
//          * 0.348026133393798
//          * 0.569819071905581 0.536232629487419 1.821791453675000 0.934388133855881
0.952823814063320
//          * 0.422051935833047
//          * 0.832527350192132 0.789078831932216 0.934388133855881 3.948763689179000
1.349588317003072
//          * 0.628591706535889
//          * 0.847148840587289 0.788206205379818 0.952823814063320 1.349588317003072
3.907173836600000
//          * 0.644231481562656
//          * 0.397609074332363 0.348026133393798 0.422051935833047 0.628591706535889
0.644231481562656
//          * 0.792958306075000

val result: LedoitWolf2004.Result
= LedoitWolf2004(false).compute(X) // use biased sample (as Wolf's code)
// the Ledoi-Wolf linearly-shrunk covariance matrix
val S_lshrunk: Matrix = result.getCovarianceMatrix()
println("Ledoit-Wolf-2004 linearly shrunk covariance matrix is:")
println(S_lshrunk)

// the same covariance matrix
val S: Matrix = SampleCovariance(X)
println("\nsample covariance =")
println(S)
```

The output is as follows:

```
Ledoit-Wolf-2004 shrunk covariance matrix is:
6x6
        [,1] [,2] [,3] [,4] [,5] [,6]
[1,] 0.000152, 0.000049, 0.000057, 0.000083, 0.000085, 0.000040,
[2,] 0.000049, 0.000139, 0.000054, 0.000079, 0.000079, 0.000035,
[3,] 0.000057, 0.000054, 0.000182, 0.000093, 0.000095, 0.000042,
[4,] 0.000083, 0.000079, 0.000093, 0.000395, 0.000135, 0.000063,
[5,] 0.000085, 0.000079, 0.000095, 0.000135, 0.000391, 0.000064,
[6,] 0.000040, 0.000035, 0.000042, 0.000063, 0.000064, 0.000079,
```

```
sample covariance =
6x6
        [,1] [,2] [,3] [,4] [,5] [,6]
[1,] 0.000153, 0.000028, 0.000050, 0.000065, 0.000091, 0.000063,
[2,] 0.000028, 0.000140, 0.000036, 0.000053, 0.000057, 0.000016,
[3,] 0.000050, 0.000036, 0.000184, 0.000101, 0.000132, 0.000050,
[4,] 0.000065, 0.000053, 0.000101, 0.000399, 0.000122, 0.000083,
[5,] 0.000091, 0.000057, 0.000132, 0.000122, 0.000395, 0.000109,
[6,] 0.000063, 0.000016, 0.000050, 0.000083, 0.000109, 0.000080,
```

We can see that the Ledoit-Wolf linearly shrunk covariance matrix is very different from the sample covariance matrix.

Ledoit-Wolf Nonlinear Shrinkage

This section follows Ledoit & Wolf (2012). In the absence of further knowledge about the structure of the true covariance matrix, the most successful approach so far, arguably, has been shrinkage estimation. Shrinking the sample covariance matrix to a multiple of the identity, by taking a weighted average of the two, turns out to be equivalent to linearly shrinking the sample eigenvalues to their group mean, while retaining the sample eigenvectors. This approach works because the sample eigenvalues in a sample covariance matrix are such that the largest sample eigenvalues are systematically biased upward and the smallest ones downward. The linear shrinkage approach corrects this bias by pulling down the largest eigenvalues and pushing up the smallest ones, toward the group mean of all sample eigenvalues. In other words, it applies the same shrinkage intensity to all sample eigenvalues, regardless of their positions. For example, if the linear shrinkage intensity is 0.5, then every sample eigenvalue is moved halfway toward the group mean of all sample eigenvalues.

Depending on the situation at hand, the improvement over the sample covariance matrix can be either gigantic or minuscule. When $\frac{p}{n}$ is large and/or the population eigenvalues are close to one another, linear shrinkage captures most of the potential improvement over the sample covariance matrix. In the opposite case, that is, when $\frac{p}{n}$ is small and/or the population eigenvalues are dispersed, linear shrinkage hardly improves at all over the sample covariance matrix.

The intuition behind in Ledoit & Wolf (2016, 2015, 2012) is that the first-order approximation does not deliver a sufficient improvement when higher-order effects are too pronounced. The improvement is to upgrade to nonlinear shrinkage estimation of the covariance matrix. Instead of giving all sample eigenvalue the same shrinkage intensity, we give individualized shrinkage intensity to each sample eigenvalue. Such an estimator has the potential to asymptotically at least match the linear shrinkage estimator of Ledoit & Wolf (2004) and often do a lot better, especially when linear shrinkage does not deliver a sufficient improvement over the sample covariance matrix. In fact, in terms of finite-sample performance, the linear shrinkage estimator rarely performs better than the nonlinear shrinkage estimator. This happens only when the linear shrinkage estimator is (nearly) optimal already. However, as shown in simulations, the outperformance over the nonlinear shrinkage estimator is very small in such cases. Most of the time, the linear shrinkage estimator is far from optimal, and nonlinear shrinkage then offers a considerable amount of finite-sample improvement, even for matrix dimensions as low as $p = 30$. Since the magnitude of higher-order effects depends on the population covariance matrix, which is unobservable, it is always safer a priori to use nonlinear shrinkage by default. See Figure 12-11.

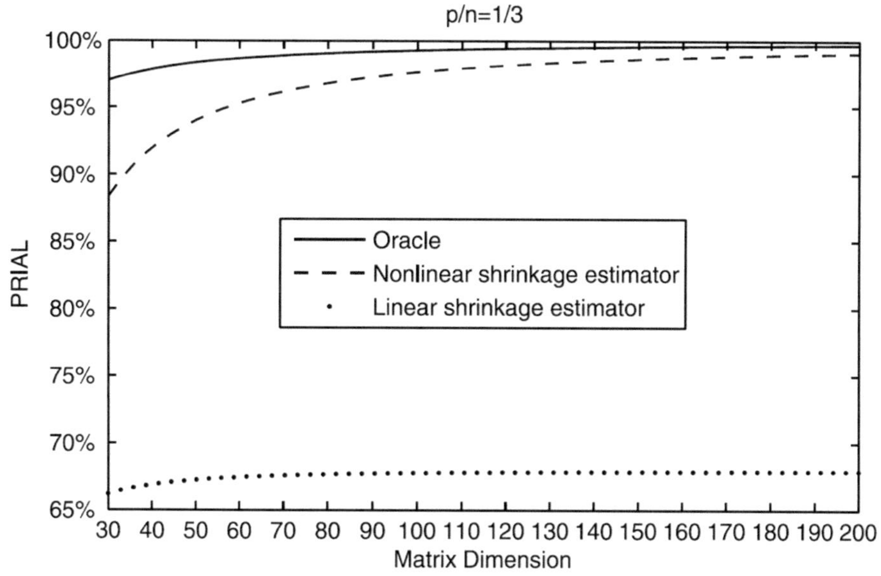

Figure 12-11. *Comparison of the nonlinear versus linear shrinkage estimators of covariance matrix*

Figure 12-11 compares the performance of the nonlinear and linear shrinkage estimators of covariance matrix in terms of percentage relative improvement in average loss (PRIAL). Not only does the nonlinear shrinkage estimator improve significantly over the linear one and over the sample covariance matrix, but the nonlinear shrinkage estimator is asymptotically equivalent to an oracle estimator (one that would be observable only if we had all the information about the true population).

In NM Dev, the class `LedoitWolf2016` computes this nonlinear shrinkage covariance matrix estimator. Here's an example:

```
/*
* These are the stock returns for MSFT, YHOO, GOOG, AAPL, MS, XOM from
* Aug 20, 2012 to Jan 15, 2013 (i.e., returns for 100 days).
*
* Case1 n>>p
* n=100,p=6
*/
val X: Matrix = DenseMatrix(
    arrayOf(
        doubleArrayOf(0.001968, 0.000668, -0.008926, -0.013668, 0.004057, -0.005492),
        doubleArrayOf(-0.008511, -0.003340, 0.011456, 0.019523, -0.002020, 0.002991),
        doubleArrayOf(-0.009244, -0.003351, -0.000561, -0.009327, -0.024291, -0.004703),
        doubleArrayOf(0.009997, 0.003362, 0.002704, 0.000879, 0.004149, 0.008413),
        doubleArrayOf(0.004289, -0.004692, -0.013866, 0.018797, -0.002066, -0.003543),
        doubleArrayOf(-0.001971, -0.008754, 0.011999, -0.001308, 0.004831, 0.004129),
        doubleArrayOf(0.000658, 0.008152, 0.015888, -0.001965, 0.014423, -0.002284),
        doubleArrayOf(-0.010855, -0.011456, -0.009200, -0.014260, 0.006093, -0.007899),
        doubleArrayOf(0.016628, -0.001363, 0.005002, 0.002073, 0.006729, 0.001154),
        doubleArrayOf(-0.014066, 0.016382, -0.005912, 0.014617, 0.033422, -0.002075),
        doubleArrayOf(0.000000, 0.013432, -0.000470, -0.007025, 0.010996, 0.002426),
        doubleArrayOf(0.031520, 0.001325, 0.027442, 0.009023, 0.036468, 0.019011),
```

```
doubleArrayOf(-0.012544, 0.007280, 0.009651, 0.006165, 0.051235, 0.010403),
doubleArrayOf(-0.007492, -0.007227, -0.007619, -0.026013, -0.027598, -0.004924),
doubleArrayOf(0.002297, 0.003309, -0.012244, -0.003244, 0.038647, 0.001574),
doubleArrayOf(-0.000327, 0.015831, -0.001893, 0.013914, 0.009884, -0.000786),
doubleArrayOf(0.005241, 0.012987, 0.021943, 0.019693, 0.027634, 0.018766),
doubleArrayOf(0.008798, 0.010897, 0.005156, 0.012164, 0.019048, 0.011802),
doubleArrayOf(0.000000, -0.005707, 0.000423, 0.012294, -0.024189, -0.004252),
doubleArrayOf(-0.000969, 0.014668, 0.011690, 0.003043, -0.009577, -0.002847),
doubleArrayOf(-0.004203, -0.003143, 0.012836, 0.000272, -0.003413, -0.011748),
doubleArrayOf(0.012662, -0.004414, 0.000852, -0.004850, -0.020548, 0.010443),
doubleArrayOf(-0.008015, -0.003167, 0.008062, 0.001999, -0.007576, 0.004398),
doubleArrayOf(-0.013251, 0.016518, 0.020968, -0.013287, -0.002349, -0.000438),
doubleArrayOf(-0.012774, -0.020000, -0.000294, -0.024969, -0.025898, -0.001533),
doubleArrayOf(-0.007299, -0.004464, 0.005740, -0.012409, -0.010272, -0.005594),
doubleArrayOf(-0.000334, 0.027546, 0.004035, 0.024254, 0.025031, 0.006287),
doubleArrayOf(-0.013039, -0.003741, -0.002644, -0.020863, -0.005956, -0.003836),
doubleArrayOf(-0.009146, -0.009387, 0.009649, -0.011565, 0.002996, 0.003851),
doubleArrayOf(0.005812, 0.006949, -0.006288, 0.002910, 0.007168, -0.000877),
doubleArrayOf(0.006798, 0.016939, 0.007279, 0.015343, 0.007117, -0.000219),
doubleArrayOf(0.005739, 0.003701, 0.007279, -0.006927, 0.025913, 0.005706),
doubleArrayOf(-0.006042, -0.011063, -0.000521, -0.021318, 0.001722, 0.003492),
doubleArrayOf(-0.002364, -0.003729, -0.012779, -0.022090, -0.002865, 0.001414),
doubleArrayOf(-0.016926, -0.011229, -0.018144, -0.003636, -0.005747, -0.005863),
doubleArrayOf(-0.010331, -0.001262, 0.000632, 0.007963, 0.002890, -0.012014),
doubleArrayOf(-0.001044, 0.005685, 0.009294, -0.020000, 0.026513, 0.001548),
doubleArrayOf(0.008708, -0.002513, -0.008956, 0.002575, -0.030882, -0.001545),
doubleArrayOf(0.010704, -0.012594, -0.005062, 0.008008, 0.025492, 0.005306),
doubleArrayOf(-0.000683, 0.015306, 0.005020, 0.023692, 0.006780, 0.009567),
doubleArrayOf(0.003419, 0.010678, 0.014489, -0.007977, 0.034792, 0.010892),
doubleArrayOf(-0.003066, -0.005594, -0.080067, -0.018576, -0.037961, 0.000970),
doubleArrayOf(-0.029050, -0.010000, -0.019007, -0.036030, -0.014656, -0.014209),
doubleArrayOf(-0.022527, -0.004419, -0.004576, 0.039666, -0.004577, 0.000437),
doubleArrayOf(0.001801, 0.057070, 0.002475, -0.032607, -0.019540, -0.021829),
doubleArrayOf(-0.005392, -0.007199, -0.004483, 0.005667, 0.004103, -0.003347),
doubleArrayOf(-0.000723, 0.003625, 0.000679, -0.011824, -0.004670, 0.006158),
doubleArrayOf(0.011935, 0.010837, -0.003851, -0.009097, -0.003519, 0.002114),
doubleArrayOf(0.011794, 0.002978, 0.007628, -0.014370, 0.022955, 0.005996),
doubleArrayOf(0.034264, 0.006532, 0.010716, 0.002059, 0.013234, 0.004746),
doubleArrayOf(-0.000683, 0.009440, 0.000480, -0.033090, 0.009654, -0.014501),
doubleArrayOf(0.004443, 0.015196, -0.007210, 0.013550, -0.001687, 0.004013),
doubleArrayOf(0.007826, 0.005181, -0.001816, -0.003024, 0.024789, 0.010769),
doubleArrayOf(-0.026334, -0.004009, -0.021416, -0.038263, -0.085761, -0.031415),
doubleArrayOf(-0.009015, -0.008626, -0.022230, -0.036290, -0.006615, -0.012588),
doubleArrayOf(0.000700, 0.001160, 0.016465, 0.017313, 0.005448, 0.001608),
doubleArrayOf(-0.021329, 0.014484, 0.004329, -0.007732, 0.009633, 0.001261),
doubleArrayOf(-0.032154, 0.019417, -0.010287, 0.000129, -0.014908, -0.009734),
doubleArrayOf(-0.009228, -0.001120, -0.009863, -0.011089, -0.026029, -0.004626),
doubleArrayOf(-0.006706, 0.003365, -0.008107, -0.020973, 0.010566, 0.000813),
doubleArrayOf(-0.005251, -0.001677, -0.000124, 0.003919, -0.004920, 0.003599),
doubleArrayOf(0.007919, 0.027996, 0.032495, 0.072108, 0.021014, 0.014112),
doubleArrayOf(-0.000748, -0.006536, 0.002634, -0.008520, -0.010291, -0.001939),
```

```
        doubleArrayOf(0.008985, 0.008772, -0.006120, 0.001408, -0.006116, 0.005829),
        doubleArrayOf(0.027829, 0.009239, 0.003154, 0.017447, 0.011077, 0.012271),
        doubleArrayOf(-0.011191, 0.010232, -0.010210, 0.031549, 0.010956, -0.005276),
        doubleArrayOf(-0.011318, 0.009062, 0.014460, -0.008057, 0.001204, -0.014331),
        doubleArrayOf(0.010340, -0.001057, 0.019323, -0.003146, 0.015033, 0.008586),
        doubleArrayOf(-0.014985, -0.002115, 0.012023, 0.011013, -0.001185, 0.000227),
        doubleArrayOf(-0.012245, -0.005299, 0.009366, -0.006923, 0.000593, 0.000227),
        doubleArrayOf(-0.007137, -0.011721, -0.004468, 0.001555, -0.023711, -0.006013),
        doubleArrayOf(-0.002270, 0.020485, -0.006070, -0.017639, 0.008500, -0.004794),
        doubleArrayOf(0.011377, -0.002113, -0.004645, -0.064357, 0.022276, 0.006193),
        doubleArrayOf(0.002250, 0.016411, 0.004812, 0.015683, -0.014134, 0.003078),
        doubleArrayOf(-0.010101, 0.000000, -0.010013, -0.025565, 0.013740, 0.006818),
        doubleArrayOf(0.018141, 0.011979, 0.001768, -0.006432, 0.002357, -0.002144),
        doubleArrayOf(0.014105, 0.004632, 0.016720, 0.021838, 0.043504, 0.006560),
        doubleArrayOf(-0.002928, -0.007172, 0.000976, -0.004415, -0.002817, 0.005169),
        doubleArrayOf(-0.004772, -0.001548, 0.007369, -0.017273, 0.005650, -0.009726),
        doubleArrayOf(-0.011066, 0.014987, -0.001053, -0.037569, 0.014045, -0.005645),
        doubleArrayOf(0.010817, 0.002546, 0.026811, 0.017733, 0.026593, 0.008969),
        doubleArrayOf(0.016974, -0.003555, 0.000402, 0.029046, 0.031840, 0.007764),
        doubleArrayOf(-0.009071, -0.001019, -0.001331, -0.014216, -0.001569, -0.012506),
        doubleArrayOf(0.013548, 0.004592, 0.003125, -0.008702, 0.009429, 0.005088),
        doubleArrayOf(-0.008309, -0.017268, -0.009317, -0.004600, -0.018163, -0.018675),
        doubleArrayOf(-0.014208, 0.015504, -0.008566, 0.001617, 0.001586, -0.003554),
        doubleArrayOf(-0.007391, -0.004071, -0.000888, -0.013784, -0.003694, 0.001726),
        doubleArrayOf(0.003723, 0.001533, -0.003640, 0.004016, -0.005826, -0.002412),
        doubleArrayOf(-0.015208, -0.005102, -0.008892, -0.010620, -0.007991, -0.020262),
        doubleArrayOf(0.006026, 0.020513, 0.010528, 0.044310, 0.026853, 0.017039),
        doubleArrayOf(0.034070, 0.009045, 0.022435, 0.031682, 0.026151, 0.024957),
        doubleArrayOf(-0.013396, -0.014940, 0.000581, -0.012622, -0.002039, -0.001804),
        doubleArrayOf(-0.018716, 0.004044, 0.019760, -0.027855, 0.031154, 0.004630),
        doubleArrayOf(-0.001870, -0.023162, -0.004363, -0.005882, -0.019316, -0.011578),
        doubleArrayOf(-0.005245, 0.013402, -0.001973, 0.002691, -0.007576, 0.006255),
        doubleArrayOf(0.005650, -0.017294, 0.006573, -0.015629, -0.001527, -0.003843),
        doubleArrayOf(-0.008989, -0.017081, 0.004552, 0.012396, 0.036697, 0.010892),
        doubleArrayOf(0.013983, 0.015798, -0.002009, -0.006132, -0.008358, 0.005724),
        doubleArrayOf(0.002236, 0.007258, -0.022622, -0.035653, -0.004958, -0.000335),
        doubleArrayOf(0.011900, 0.004632, 0.002323, -0.031550, 0.017937, -0.000558)
    )
)

val result1: LedoitWolf2016.Result = LedoitWolf2016().estimate(X)
// the Ledoi-Wolf nonlinearly-shrunk covariance matrix
val S_nlShrunk: Matrix = result1.getShrunkCovarianceMatrix()
println("Ledoit-Wolf-2016 non-linearly shrunk covariance matrix is:")
println(S_nlShrunk)

val result2: LedoitWolf2004.Result
        = LedoitWolf2004(false).compute(X) // use biased sample (as Wolf's code)
// the Ledoi-Wolf linearly-shrunk covariance matrix
val S_lshrunk: Matrix = result2.getCovarianceMatrix()
println("Ledoit-Wolf-2004 linearly shrunk covariance matrix is:")
println(S_lshrunk)
```

```
// the same covariance matrix
val S: Matrix = SampleCovariance(X)
println("\nsample covariance =")
println(S)
```

The output is as follows:

```
Ledoit-Wolf-2016 non-linearly shrunk covariance matrix is:
6x6
         [,1] [,2] [,3] [,4] [,5] [,6]
[1,] 0.000153, 0.000025, 0.000048, 0.000063, 0.000088, 0.000061,
[2,] 0.000025, 0.000141, 0.000031, 0.000052, 0.000057, 0.000015,
[3,] 0.000048, 0.000031, 0.000192, 0.000096, 0.000125, 0.000048,
[4,] 0.000063, 0.000052, 0.000096, 0.000390, 0.000118, 0.000080,
[5,] 0.000088, 0.000057, 0.000125, 0.000118, 0.000386, 0.000105,
[6,] 0.000061, 0.000015, 0.000048, 0.000080, 0.000105, 0.000083,
Ledoit-Wolf-2004 linearly shrunk covariance matrix is:
6x6
         [,1] [,2] [,3] [,4] [,5] [,6]
[1,] 0.000152, 0.000049, 0.000057, 0.000083, 0.000085, 0.000040,
[2,] 0.000049, 0.000139, 0.000054, 0.000079, 0.000079, 0.000035,
[3,] 0.000057, 0.000054, 0.000182, 0.000093, 0.000095, 0.000042,
[4,] 0.000083, 0.000079, 0.000093, 0.000395, 0.000135, 0.000063,
[5,] 0.000085, 0.000079, 0.000095, 0.000135, 0.000391, 0.000064,
[6,] 0.000040, 0.000035, 0.000042, 0.000063, 0.000064, 0.000079,
sample covariance =
6x6
         [,1] [,2] [,3] [,4] [,5] [,6]
[1,] 0.000153, 0.000028, 0.000050, 0.000065, 0.000091, 0.000063,
[2,] 0.000028, 0.000140, 0.000036, 0.000053, 0.000057, 0.000016,
[3,] 0.000050, 0.000036, 0.000184, 0.000101, 0.000132, 0.000050,
[4,] 0.000065, 0.000053, 0.000101, 0.000399, 0.000122, 0.000083,
[5,] 0.000091, 0.000057, 0.000132, 0.000122, 0.000395, 0.000109,
[6,] 0.000063, 0.000016, 0.000050, 0.000083, 0.000109, 0.000080,
```

12.3. Probability Distribution

A probability distribution is a mathematical function that gives the probabilities of occurrence of different possible outcomes for an experiment. For example, the probability distribution of tossing a fair coin assigns 0.5 (50 percent) to heads and 0.5 (50 percent) to tails, respectively. A probability distribution is formally defined by a cumulative distribution function. The cumulative distribution function (CDF) of a real-valued random variable *X*, evaluated at *x*, is the probability that *X* will take a value less than or equal to *x*. Mathematically, it is:

$$F_X(x) = P(X \leq x)$$

The CDF for tossing a fair coin, labeling heads as 0 and tails as 1, is a step-function, as shown here:

$$F_X(x) = \begin{cases} 0.5, x = 0 \\ 1, x = 1 \end{cases}$$

See Figure 12-12.

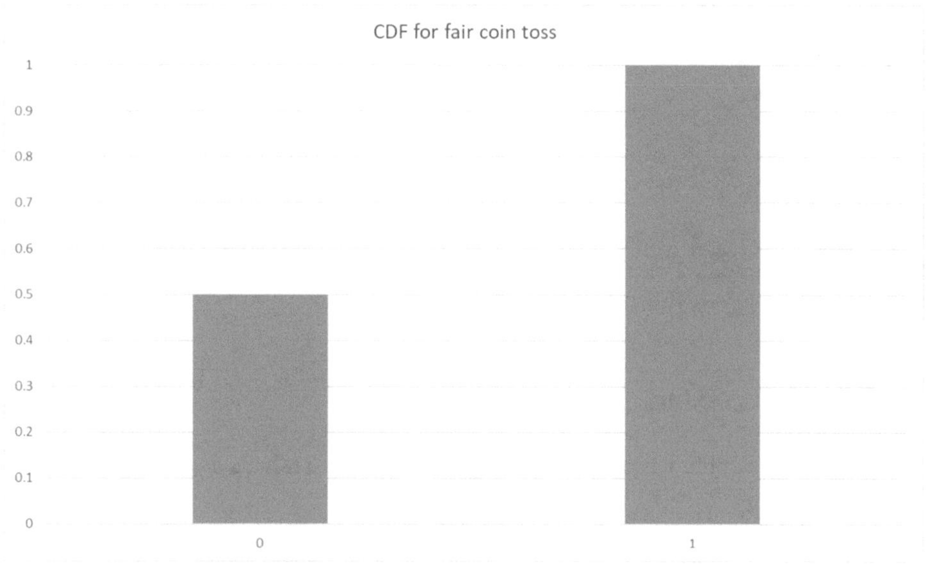

***Figure 12-12.** Cumulative distribution function for fair coin toss*

A random variable can be continuous, taking any numerical value in an interval or collection of intervals on the real line (having an uncountable range). Figure 12-13 shows a few CDFs for normal distributions. We see that for a normal distribution with $\mu = 0$ (mean is 0), the chance of getting one sample from the probability distribution with a value smaller (or bigger) than 0 is 0.5.

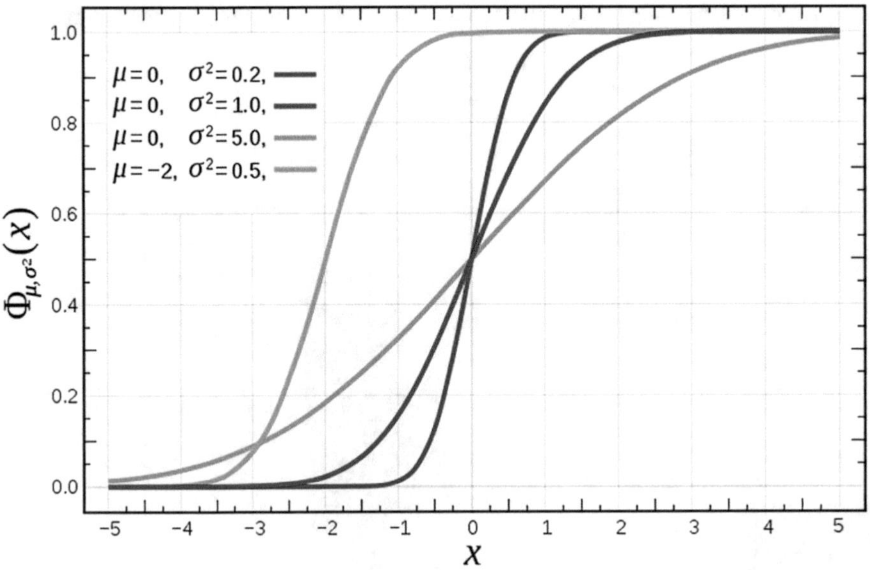

Figure 12-13. *Cumulative distribution functions for the normal distributions*

For a continuous random variable, it is often more intuitive to describe it using a probability density function (PDF).

$$f_X(x) = \frac{d}{dx} F_X(x)$$

$f_X(x)$ is the relative likelihood that the random variable equals a sample value x. The bigger the relative likelihood, the more likely that we see this sample over another. The absolute likelihood is always 0 for a continuous random variable. Figure 12-14 shows the probability density functions for the cumulative distribution functions in Figure 12-13.

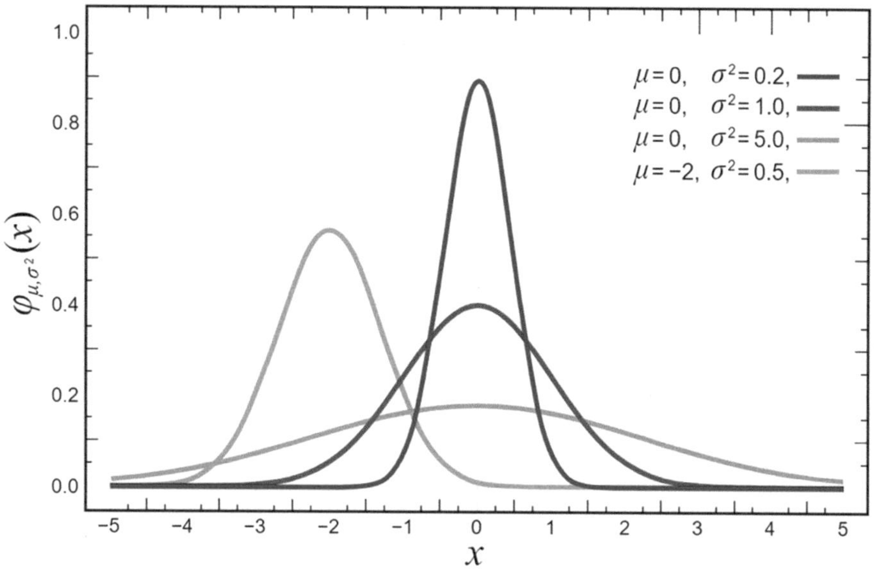

***Figure 12-14.** Probability density functions for the normal distributions*

The probability that the value of a random variable falls within a certain region is the area of the region under the PDF, i.e., the integral of the PDF in the region. Mathematically, it is:

$$P(a \le X \le b) = \int_a^b f(x)\,dx$$

In particular, we have this (see Figure 12-15):

$$F_X(x) = P(-\infty < X \le b) = \int_{-\infty}^{b} f(x)\,dx$$

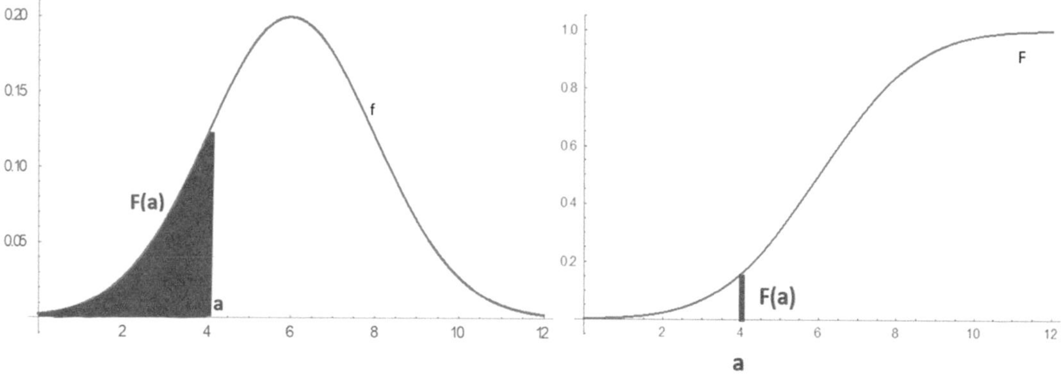

***Figure 12-15.** The area under the probability density curve (left) is the value of the cumulative distribution function (right)*

The quantile function of a probability distribution of a random variable specifies the value of the random variable such that the probability of the variable being less than or equal to that value equals the given probability. It is also called the inverse cumulative distribution function. Mathematically, the quantile function Q returns the value x such that:

$$F_X(x) = \mathrm{P}(X \leq x) = u$$

Or equivalently,

$$Q(p) = \inf\{x \in \mathbb{R} \mid u \leq F(x)\}$$

inf is the infimum operator that gives the biggest element in the set that is smaller than or equal to all elements in the set, aka the greatest lower bound.

In general, almost surely, we have this:

$$Q(F(X)) = X$$

Hence, we have the inverse cumulative distribution function. Here we capture the fact that the quantile function returns the minimum value of x from among all those values whose CDF value exceeds u (for continuous distributions).

In NM Dev, an implementation for a univariate probability function inherits from the `ProbabilityDistribution` interface. Such an implementation specifies not only the CDF and the PDF but also the descriptive statistics, e.g., mean and variance, of the distribution, among other information. The signature is as follows:

```
public interface ProbabilityDistribution {
    /**
     * Gets the mean of this distribution.
     *
     * @return the mean
     * @see <a href="http://en.wikipedia.org/wiki/Expected_value">Wikipedia:
     * Expected value</a>
     */
    public double mean();
    /**
     * Gets the median of this distribution.
     *
     * @return the media
     * @see <a href="http://en.wikipedia.org/wiki/Median">Wikipedia: Median</a>
     */
    public double median();
    /**
     * Gets the variance of this distribution.
     *
     * @return the variance
     * @see <a href="http://en.wikipedia.org/wiki/Variance">Wikipedia:
     * Variance</a>
     */
    public double variance();
    /**
     * Gets the skewness of this distribution.
     *
```

```
     * @return the skewness
     * @see <a href="http://en.wikipedia.org/wiki/Skewness">Wikipedia:
     * Skewness</a>
     */
    public double skew();
    /**
     * Gets the excess kurtosis of this distribution.
     *
     * @return the excess kurtosis
     * @see <a href="http://en.wikipedia.org/wiki/Kurtosis">Wikipedia:
     * Kurtosis</a>
     */
    public double kurtosis();
    /**
     * Gets the entropy of this distribution.
     *
     * @return the entropy
     * @see
     * <a href="http://en.wikipedia.org/wiki/Information_entropy">Wikipedia:
     * Entropy
     * (information theory)</a>
     */
    public double entropy();
    /**
     * Gets the cumulative probability <i>F(x) = Pr(X &le; x)</i>.
     *
     * @param x <i>x</i>
     * @return <i>F(x) = Pr(X &le; x)</i>
     * @see
     * <a href="http://en.wikipedia.org/wiki/Cumulative_distribution_function">Wikipedia:
     * Cumulative distribution function</a>
     */
    public double cdf(double x);
    /**
     * Gets the quantile, the inverse of the cumulative distribution function.
     * It is the value below which random draws from the distribution would fall
     * <i>u&times;100</i> percent of the time.
     * <blockquote><pre><i>
     * F<sup>-1</sup>(u) = x, such that
     * Pr(X &le; x) = u
     * </i></pre></blockquote>
     * <em>This may not always exist.</em>
     *
     * @param u {@code u}, a quantile
     * @return <i>F<sup>-1</sup>(u)</i>
     * @see <a href="http://en.wikipedia.org/wiki/Quantile_function">Wikipedia:
     * Quantile function</a>
     */
    public double quantile(double u);
```

```
    /**
     * The density function, which, if exists, is the derivative of <i>F</i>.
     * It describes the density of probability at each point in the sample
     * space.
     * <blockquote><i>
     * f(x) = dF(X) / dx
     * </i></blockquote>
     * <em>This may not always exist.</em>
     * <p/>
     * For the discrete cases, this is the probability mass function. It gives
     * the probability that a discrete random variable is exactly equal to some
     * value.
     *
     * @param x <i>x</i>
     * @return <i>f(x)</i>
     * @see
     * <ul>
     * <li><a href="http://en.wikipedia.org/wiki/Probability_density_function">Wikipedia:
     * Probability density function</a></li>
     * <li><a href="http://en.wikipedia.org/wiki/Probability_mass_function">Wikipedia:
     * Probability
     * mass function</a></li>
     * </ul>
     */
    public double density(double x);
    /**
     * The moment generating function is the expected value of
     * <i>e<sup>tX</sup></i>. That is,
     * <blockquote><i>
     * E(e<sup>tX</sup>)
     * </i></blockquote>
     * <em>This may not always exist.</em>
     *
     * @param t <i>t</i>
     * @return <i>E(exp(tX))</i>
     * @see
     * <a href="http://en.wikipedia.org/wiki/Moment_generating_function">Wikipedia:
     * Moment-generating function</a>
     */
    public double moment(double t);
}
```

12.3.1. Moments

The mean or expected value of a probability distribution of a random variable *X*, denoted as E(*X*), is a generalization of the weighted sample mean or weighted average. For a discrete probability distribution, it is the weighted average with weights equal to the probability mass of the values.

$$\mathrm{E}(X)=\sum_{-\infty}^{\infty}x\mathrm{P}(x)$$

It is intuitively the arithmetic mean of a large number of independent realizations of X. The mean for a continuous probability distribution with PDF $f(x)$ is defined as follows:

$$E(X) = \mu = \int_{-\infty}^{\infty} x f(x) dx$$

The mean may not exist or be finite. For some probability distributions, the mean is infinite (∞ or $-\infty$), while for others the mean is undefined.

The variance of a probability distribution is defined as follows:

$$\mathrm{Var}(X) = \sigma^2 = \int_{-\infty}^{\infty} (x-\mu)^2 f(x) dx$$

$$= \int_{-\infty}^{\infty} x^2 f(x) dx - \mu^2$$

In general, a standardized moment of a probability distribution is a moment (normally a higher-degree central moment) that is normalized. The normalization is typically a division by an expression of the standard deviation that renders the moment scale invariant. This has the advantage that such normalized moments differ only in other properties than variability so that the comparison of shape of different probability distributions is made easy. Mathematically, the standardized moment of degree k is defined as follows:

$$\tilde{\mu}_k = \frac{\mu_k}{\sigma^k}$$

where

$$\mu_k = E\left[(X-\mu)^k\right] = \int_{-\infty}^{\infty} (x-\mu)^k f(x) dx$$

and

$$\sigma^k = \left(\sqrt{E\left[(X-\mu)^2\right]}\right)^k$$

Standardized moments are dimensionless numbers. The first standardized moment is zero, because the first moment about the mean is always zero. The second standardized moment is one, because the second moment about the mean is equal to the variance σ^2.

Skewness of a probability distribution, $\gamma = \tilde{\mu}_3$, is the third standardized moment. It is a measure of the lopsidedness of the distribution. Any symmetric distribution will have a third central moment, if defined, of zero. A distribution that is skewed to the left (the tail of the distribution is longer on the left) will have a negative skewness. A distribution that is skewed to the right (the tail of the distribution is longer on the right) will have a positive skewness.

Kurtosis of a probability distribution, $\kappa = \tilde{\mu}_4$, is the fourth standardized moment. It is a measure of the heaviness of the tail of the distribution, compared to the normal distribution of the same variance. Since it is the expectation of a fourth power, the fourth central moment, where defined, is always nonnegative; and except for a point distribution, it is always strictly positive and can be unbounded. If a distribution has heavy tails, the kurtosis will be high (called leptokurtic); conversely, thin-tailed distributions (for example, bounded distributions such as the uniform) have low kurtosis (called platykurtic).

The moment-generating function of a real-valued random variable is an alternative specification of its probability distribution. Like a probability density function or a cumulative distribution function, a moment-generating function, if it exists, also uniquely defines a probability distribution. As its name implies, the moment-generating function can be used to compute a distribution's moments: the n-th moment about 0 is the n-th derivative of the moment-generating function, evaluated at 0. Mathematically, the moment-generating function of a random variable X is defined as follows:

$$M_x(t) = \mathrm{E}\left[e^{tX}\right]$$

That is, the function is an expectation of the random variable e^{tX} for $t \in \mathbb{R}$. The moment generation function does not exist if the integrals do not converge.

The moment-generating function is so named because it can be used to compute the moments of the distribution. Taylor's expansion of e^{tX} gives the following:

$$e^{tX} = 1 + tX + \frac{t^2X^2}{2!} + \frac{t^3X^3}{3!} + \cdots + + \frac{t^nX^n}{n!} + \cdots$$

So, we have this:

$$M_x(t) = \mathrm{E}\left[e^{tX}\right]$$

$$= 1 + t\mathrm{E}(X) + \frac{t^2\mathrm{E}(X^2)}{2!} + \frac{t^3\mathrm{E}(X^3)}{3!} + \cdots + + \frac{t^n\mathrm{E}(X^n)}{n!} + \cdots$$

$$= 1 + tm_1 + \frac{t^2m_2}{2!} + \frac{t^3m_3}{3!} + \cdots$$

where m_n is the n-th moment. Differentiating $M_x(t)$ i times with respect to t and setting $t = 0$ gives the i-th moment about the origin m_i.

There are particularly simple results for the moment-generating functions of distributions defined by a linear transformation of random variables, if they exist. Specifically, if a random variable X has a moment-generating function $M_X(t)$, then $\alpha X + \beta$ has the following moment-generating function:

$$M_{\alpha X+\beta}(t) = \mathrm{E}\left[e^{t(\alpha X+\beta)}\right] = e^{\beta t}M_X(\alpha t)$$

Moreover, if S_n is a linear combination of random variables $\{X_i\}$ weighted by $\{a_i\}$, as shown here:

$$S_n = \sum_{i=1}^{n} a_i X_i$$

then the moment-generating function for S_n is as follows:

$$M_{S_n}(t) = M_{X_1}(a_1t)M_{X_2}(a_2t)\cdots M_{X_n}(a_nt)$$

12.3.2. Normal Distribution

The most important distribution is (probably) the normal distribution or Gaussian distribution. Many natural processes such as heat diffusion are normally distributed. Moreover, the central limit theorem says that the average of many samples (observations) of a random variable with finite mean and variance is itself a random variable whose distribution converges to a normal distribution as the number of samples increases. Therefore, physical quantities that are the sum of many independent measurements, such as measurement errors, often have distributions that are nearly normal.

Mathematically, suppose $\{X_1, \cdots, X_n\}$ is a sequence of independent and identically distributed (i.i.d.) random variables with $E(X_i) = \mu$ and $Var(X_i) = \sigma^2 < \infty$. Then as n goes to infinity, the random variable $\sqrt{n}\left(\bar{X}_n - \mu\right)$ converges in distribution to a normal distribution with mean 0 and variance σ^2, i.e., $N(0, \sigma^2)$.

$$\sqrt{n}\left(\bar{X}_n - \mu\right) \rightarrow N\left(0, \sigma^2\right)$$

A normal distribution mean μ and variance σ^2, denoted as $N(\mu, \sigma^2)$, has a PDF as follows:

$$f(x) = \frac{1}{\sigma\sqrt{2\pi}} \exp\left(-\frac{1}{2}\left(\frac{x-\mu}{\sigma}\right)^2\right)$$

Figure 12-16 shows an example.

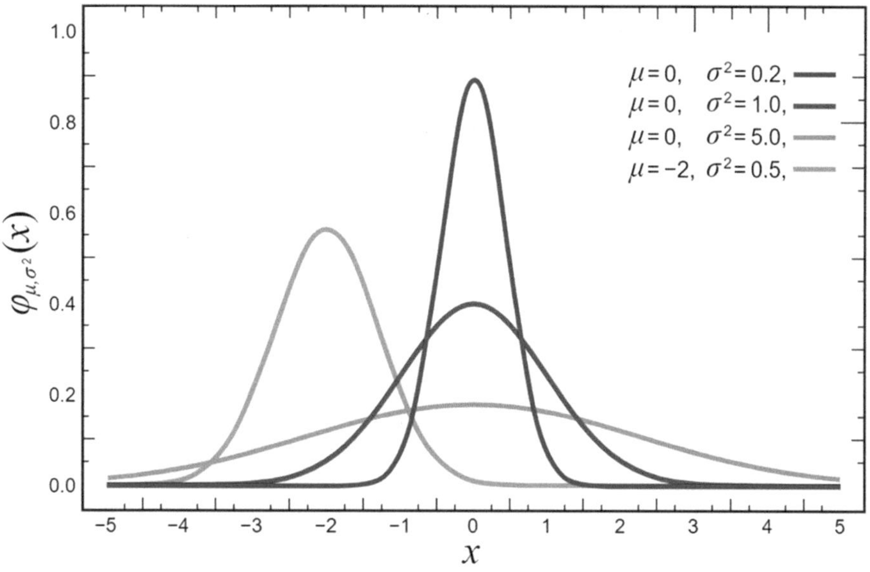

Figure 12-16. *Probability density functions for normal distributions*

The CDF is as follows:

$$F(x) = \frac{1}{2}\left[1 + erf\left(\frac{x-\mu}{\sigma\sqrt{2}}\right)\right]$$

Figure 12-17 shows an example.

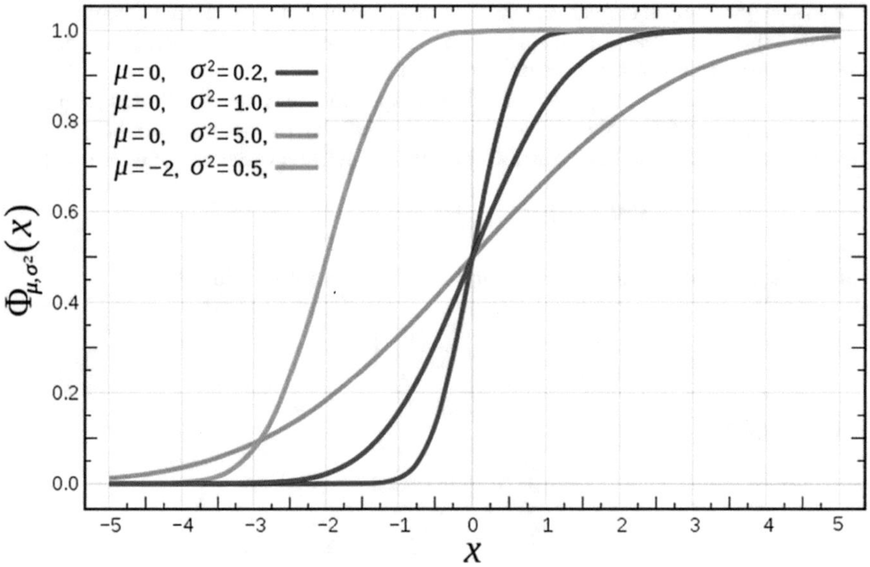

Figure 12-17. *Cumulative distribution functions for normal distributions*

The quantile function is as follows:

$$Q(q) = \mu + \sigma\sqrt{2} erf^{-1}(2q-1)$$

The mean is as follows:

$$\mathrm{E}(X) = \mu$$

The variance is as follows:

$$\mathrm{Var}(X) = \mu$$

The skewness is as follows:

$$\gamma = 0$$

The excess kurtosis is as follows:

$$\kappa = 0$$

The moment-generating function is as follows:

$$M_X(t) = \exp\left(\mu t + \frac{\sigma^2 t^2}{2}\right)$$

The NM Dev class `NormalDistribution` implements normal distribution. Here's an example:

```
val dist = NormalDistribution(
        0.0, // mean
        1.0 // variance
)

println("mean = " + dist.mean())
println("median = " + dist.median())
println("variance = " + dist.variance())
println("skew = " + dist.skew())
println("kurtosis = " + dist.kurtosis())
println("entropy = " + dist.entropy()) // Math.log(2 * Math.PI * Math.E)

println("")
val xs: DoubleArray = doubleArrayOf(
    -1000000.0, -10000.0, -1000.0, -100.0, -10.0, -1.0, -0.1, -0.01, -0.001, -0.0001,
    0.0, 0.0001, 0.001, 0.01, 0.1, 1.0, 2.0, 3.0, 10.0, 100.0, 1000.0)
for (x in xs) {
    println(String.format("F(%f) = %f", x, dist.cdf(x)))
}
println("")
for (x in xs) {
    println(String.format("f(%f) = %f", x, dist.density(x)))
}

var allEquals: Boolean = true
var u: Double = 0.000001
while(u < 0.1) {
    val x: Double = dist.quantile(u)
    val y: Double = dist.cdf(x)
    if (abs(u - y) > 1e-9) {
        allEquals = false
    }

    u += 0.000001
}

println("\nF(Q(u)) = u for all u = " + allEquals)
```

The output is as follows:

```
mean = 0.0
median = 0.0
variance = 1.0
skew = 0.0
kurtosis = 0.0
entropy = 2.8378770664093453
F(-1000000.000000) = 0.000000
F(-10000.000000) = 0.000000
F(-1000.000000) = 0.000000
F(-100.000000) = 0.000000
F(-10.000000) = 0.000000
```

```
F(-1.000000) = 0.158655
F(-0.100000) = 0.460172
F(-0.010000) = 0.496011
F(-0.001000) = 0.499601
F(-0.000100) = 0.499960
F(0.000000) = 0.500000
F(0.000100) = 0.500040
F(0.001000) = 0.500399
F(0.010000) = 0.503989
F(0.100000) = 0.539828
F(1.000000) = 0.841345
F(2.000000) = 0.977250
F(3.000000) = 0.998650
F(10.000000) = 1.000000
F(100.000000) = 1.000000
F(1000.000000) = 1.000000
f(-1000000.000000) = 0.000000
f(-10000.000000) = 0.000000
f(-1000.000000) = 0.000000
f(-100.000000) = 0.000000
f(-10.000000) = 0.000000
f(-1.000000) = 0.241971
f(-0.100000) = 0.396953
f(-0.010000) = 0.398922
f(-0.001000) = 0.398942
f(-0.000100) = 0.398942
f(0.000000) = 0.398942
f(0.000100) = 0.398942
f(0.001000) = 0.398942
f(0.010000) = 0.398922
f(0.100000) = 0.396953
f(1.000000) = 0.241971
f(2.000000) = 0.053991
f(3.000000) = 0.004432
f(10.000000) = 0.000000
f(100.000000) = 0.000000
f(1000.000000) = 0.000000
F(Q(u)) = u for all u = true
```

12.3.3. Log-Normal Distribution

A log-normal (or lognormal) distribution is a continuous probability distribution of a random variable whose logarithm is normally distributed. Thus, if the random variable X is log-normally distributed, then $Y = \ln X$ has a normal distribution. Equivalently, if Y has a normal distribution, then the exponential function of Y, $X = \exp(Y)$ has a log-normal distribution. A random variable that is log-normally distributed takes only positive real values. It is a convenient and useful model for measurements in exact and engineering sciences, as well as medicine, economics, and finance. The famous Black-Scholes model assumes that the stock returns are log-normally distributed.

Mathematically, a positive random variable X is log-normally distributed $X \sim \text{Lognormal}(\mu, \sigma^2)$, if $\ln X \sim N(\mu, \sigma^2)$.

Let $\varphi(x)$ and $\varphi(x)$ be the probability density function and the cumulative probability distribution function of the standard normal distribution $N(0, 1)$. Then the PDF of X~Lognormal(μ, σ^2) is as follows:

$$f_X(x) = \frac{d}{dx}\Pr(X \le x) = \frac{d}{dx}\Pr(\ln X \le \ln x)$$
$$= \frac{d}{dx}\Phi\left(\frac{\ln x - \mu}{\sigma}\right)$$

$$= \frac{1}{x\sigma\sqrt{2\pi}}\exp\left(-\frac{(\ln x - \mu)^2}{2\sigma^2}\right)$$

Figure 12-18 shows an example.

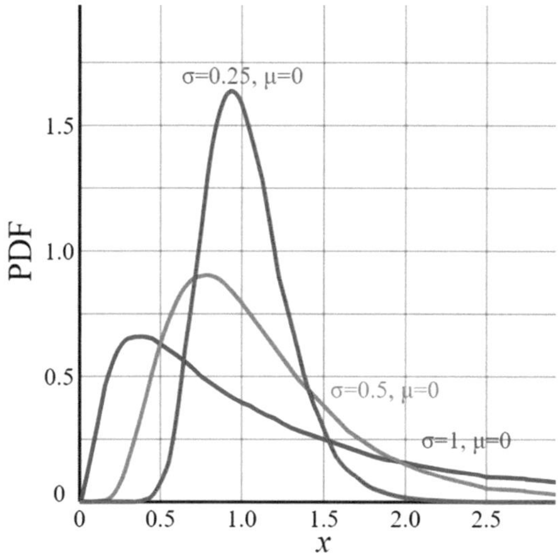

***Figure 12-18.** Probability density functions for lognormal distributions; same μ but different σ*

The CDF is as follows:

$$F_X(x) = \Phi\left(\frac{\ln x - \mu}{\sigma}\right) = \frac{1}{2}erfc\left(-\frac{\ln x - \mu}{\sigma\sqrt{2}}\right)$$

erfc is a special function called the complementary error function.
Figure 12-19 shows an example.

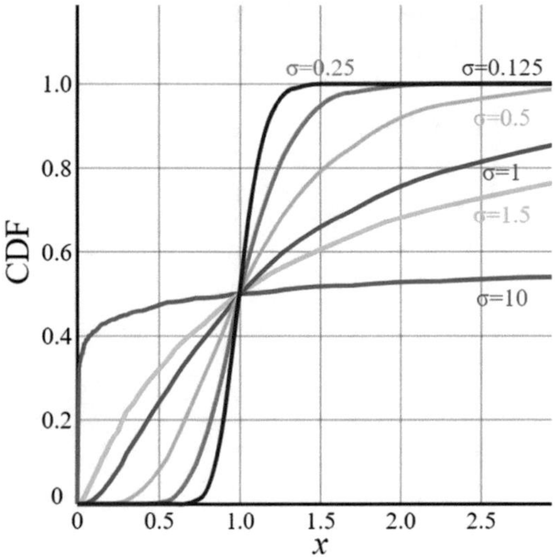

***Figure 12-19.** Cumulative distribution functions for lognormal distributions; same μ but different σ*

The quantile function is as follows:

$$Q(q) = \exp(q + \sigma Q_\Phi(q))$$

$Q_\Phi(q)$ is the quantile function of the standard normal distribution.
The mean is as follows:

$$E(X) = \exp\left(\mu + \frac{\sigma^2}{2}\right)$$

The variance is as follows:

$$\text{Var}(X) = \left[\exp(\sigma^2) - 1\right]\exp(2\mu + \sigma^2)$$

The skewness is as follows:

$$\gamma = \left[\exp(\sigma^2) + 2\right]\sqrt{\exp(\sigma^2) - 1}$$

The excess kurtosis is as follows:

$$\kappa = \exp(4\sigma^2) + 2\exp(3\sigma^2) + 3\exp(2\sigma^2) - 6$$

The moment-generating function is as follows:

$$M_X(t) = \exp\left(\mu t + \frac{\sigma^2 t^2}{2}\right)$$

The NM Dev class `LogNormalDistribution` implements log-normal distribution. Here's an example:

```
val dist = LogNormalDistribution(
        1.0, // mean
        2.0 // variance
)

println("mean = " + dist.mean())
println("median = " + dist.median())
println("variance = " + dist.variance())
println("skew = " + dist.skew())
println("kurtosis = " + dist.kurtosis())
println("entropy = " + dist.entropy())

println("")
val xs: DoubleArray = doubleArrayOf(
    -1000000.0, -10000.0, -1000.0, -100.0, -10.0, -1.0, -0.1, -0.01, -0.001, -0.0001,
    0.0, 0.0001, 0.001, 0.01, 0.1, 1.0, 2.0, 3.0, 10.0, 100.0, 1000.0)
for (x in xs) {
    println(String.format("F(%f) = %f", x, dist.cdf(x)))
}
println("")
for (x in xs) {
    println(String.format("f(%f) = %f", x, dist.density(x)))
}

var allEquals: Boolean = true
var u: Double = 0.000001
while(u < 0.1) {
    val x: Double = dist.quantile(u)
    val y: Double = dist.cdf(x)
    if (abs(u - y) > 1e-9) {
        allEquals = false
    }

    u += 0.000001
}

println("\nF(Q(u)) = u for all u = " + allEquals)
```

The output is as follows:

```
mean = 20.085536923187668
median = 2.718281828459045
variance = 21623.03700131398
skew = 414.359343300147
kurtosis = 9220556.977307005
entropy = 3.112085713764618
F(-1000000.000000) = 0.000000
F(-10000.000000) = 0.000000
F(-1000.000000) = 0.000000
F(-100.000000) = 0.000000
F(-10.000000) = 0.000000
```

```
F(-1.000000) = 0.000000
F(-0.100000) = 0.000000
F(-0.010000) = 0.000000
F(-0.001000) = 0.000000
F(-0.000100) = 0.000000
F(0.000000) = 0.000000
F(0.000100) = 0.000000
F(0.001000) = 0.000038
F(0.010000) = 0.002535
F(0.100000) = 0.049339
F(1.000000) = 0.308538
F(2.000000) = 0.439031
F(3.000000) = 0.519662
F(10.000000) = 0.742571
F(100.000000) = 0.964273
F(1000.000000) = 0.998431
f(-1000000.000000) = 0.000000
f(-10000.000000) = 0.000000
f(-1000.000000) = 0.000000
f(-100.000000) = 0.000000
f(-10.000000) = 0.000000
f(-1.000000) = 0.000000
f(-0.100000) = 0.000000
f(-0.010000) = 0.000000
f(-0.001000) = 0.000000
f(-0.000100) = 0.000000
f(0.000000) = 0.000000
f(0.000100) = 0.004369
f(0.001000) = 0.080387
f(0.010000) = 0.392917
f(0.100000) = 0.510235
f(1.000000) = 0.176033
f(2.000000) = 0.098569
f(3.000000) = 0.066410
f(10.000000) = 0.016135
f(100.000000) = 0.000393
f(1000.000000) = 0.000003
F(Q(u)) = u for all u = true
```

12.3.4. Exponential Distribution

A Poisson process is a model for a series of discrete events where the probability of an event happening is the same at any time or during any equal length time interval, but the exact timing of events is random. The arrival of an event, and hence the waiting time before the event happens, is independent of all the events and information before. The process is therefore said to be memoryless. For example, from historical data we know that the arrival of new customers is on average $\lambda = 10$ people per hour, but the timing of the next customer is completely random and is independent of any previous customers. The customer arrival process can be modeled as a Poisson process.

More abstractly, in Figure 12-20, a process starting at state 0 can jump to the next incremental state at a random time. We do not know when exactly it will happen as it is random. But we know that it can happen at any time with equal probability.

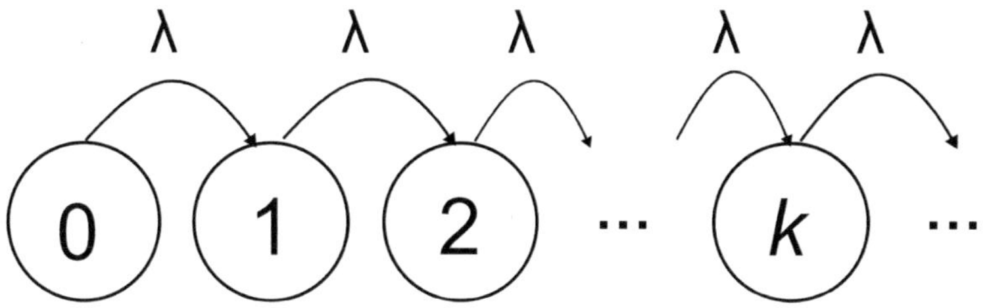

***Figure 12-20.** A Poisson point process starting from 0, in which increments occur continuously and independently at rate λ*

A Poisson process is defined as a random process such that the following holds:

1. $N(0) = 0$.
2. The increments $\{N(t_{n+1}) - N(t_n)\}$ are independent random variables.
3. The mean of the i.i.d. random increments is $E(N(t_{n+1}) - N(t_n)) = \lambda(t_{n+1} - t_n)$.

λ, called the intensity, is the expected number of arrivals that occurs per unit of time.

The random time between events or the random time before the next jump is called the waiting time. Its distribution is governed by the exponential distribution with the rate parameter λ.

Mathematically, a non-negative random variable X has exponential distribution $X \sim \text{Exp}(\lambda)$ if and only if it has the following PDF:

$$f(x \mid \lambda) = \begin{cases} \lambda e^{-\lambda x}, x \geq 0 \\ 0, x < 0 \end{cases}$$

Figure 12-21 shows an example.

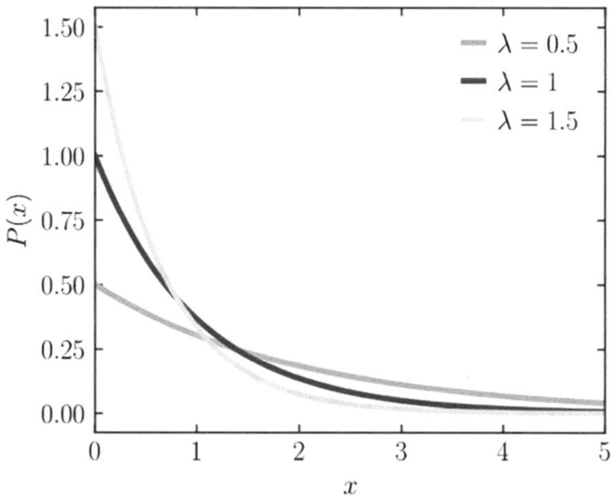

***Figure 12-21.** Probability density functions for exponential distributions*

The CDF is as follows:

$$F(x \mid \lambda) = \begin{cases} 1 - e^{-\lambda x}, x \geq 0 \\ 0, x < 0 \end{cases}$$

Figure 12-22 shows an example.

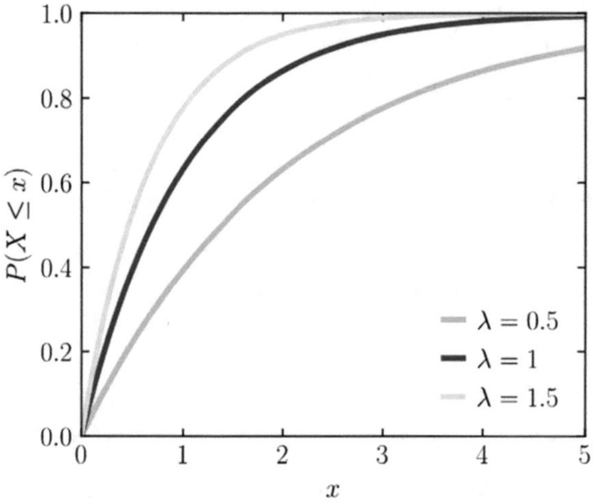

Figure 12-22. *Cumulative distribution functions for exponential distributions*

We can derive an important property of the exponential distribution called the memoryless property from the CDF. Specifically, here's an example:

$$\Pr(T > s + t \mid T > s) = \frac{\Pr(T > s + t \cap T > s)}{\Pr(T > s)}$$

$$= \frac{\Pr(T > s + t\ )}{\Pr(T > s)}$$

$$= \frac{e^{-\lambda(s+t)}}{e^{-\lambda s}} = e^{-\lambda t}$$

$$= \Pr(T > t)$$

s is irrelevant. When *T* is interpreted as the waiting time for an event to occur relative to some initial time, this relation implies that if *T* is conditioned on a failure to observe the event over some initial period of time *s*, the distribution of the remaining waiting time is the same as the original unconditional distribution. For example, if an event has not occurred after 30 seconds, the conditional probability that occurrence will take at least 10 more seconds is equal to the unconditional probability of observing the event more than 10 seconds after the initial time.

The quantile function is as follows:

$$Q(q) = -\frac{\ln(1-q)}{\lambda}$$

The mean is as follows:

$$\mathrm{E}(X) = \frac{1}{\lambda}$$

The variance is as follows:

$$\mathrm{Var}(X) = \frac{1}{\lambda^2}$$

The skewness is as follows:

$$\gamma = 2$$

The excess kurtosis is as follows:

$$\kappa = 6$$

The moment-generating function is as follows:

$$M_X(t) = \frac{\lambda}{\lambda - t}, t < \lambda$$

The NM Dev class `ExponentialDistribution` implements the exponential distribution. Here's an example:

```
val dist = ExponentialDistribution(
        1.0 // lambda = 1.
)

println("mean = " + dist.mean())
println("median = " + dist.median())
println("variance = " + dist.variance())
println("skew = " + dist.skew())
println("kurtosis = " + dist.kurtosis())
println("entropy = " + dist.entropy())

println("")
val xs: DoubleArray = doubleArrayOf(
    -1000000.0, -10000.0, -1000.0, -100.0, -10.0, -1.0, -0.1, -0.01, -0.001, -0.0001,
    0.0, 0.0001, 0.001, 0.01, 0.1, 1.0, 2.0, 3.0, 10.0, 100.0, 1000.0)
for (x in xs) {
    println(String.format("F(%f) = %f", x, dist.cdf(x)))
}
println("")
for (x in xs) {
    println(String.format("f(%f) = %f", x, dist.density(x)))
}
```

```
var allEquals: Boolean = true
var u: Double = 0.000001
while(u < 1.0) {
    val x: Double = dist.quantile(u)
    val y: Double = dist.cdf(x)
    if (abs(u - y) > 1e-9) {
        allEquals = false
    }

    u += 0.000001
}

println("\nF(Q(u)) = u for all u = " + allEquals)
```

The output is as follows:

```
mean = 1.0
median = 0.6931471805599453
variance = 1.0
skew = 2.0
kurtosis = 6.0
entropy = 1.0
F(-1000000.000000) = 0.000000
F(-10000.000000) = 0.000000
F(-1000.000000) = 0.000000
F(-100.000000) = 0.000000
F(-10.000000) = 0.000000
F(-1.000000) = 0.000000
F(-0.100000) = 0.000000
F(-0.010000) = 0.000000
F(-0.001000) = 0.000000
F(-0.000100) = 0.000000
F(0.000000) = 0.000000
F(0.000100) = 0.000100
F(0.001000) = 0.001000
F(0.010000) = 0.009950
F(0.100000) = 0.095163
F(1.000000) = 0.632121
F(2.000000) = 0.864665
F(3.000000) = 0.950213
F(10.000000) = 0.999955
F(100.000000) = 1.000000
F(1000.000000) = 1.000000
f(-1000000.000000) = 0.000000
f(-10000.000000) = 0.000000
f(-1000.000000) = 0.000000
f(-100.000000) = 0.000000
f(-10.000000) = 0.000000
f(-1.000000) = 0.000000
f(-0.100000) = 0.000000
f(-0.010000) = 0.000000
```

```
f(-0.001000) = 0.000000
f(-0.000100) = 0.000000
f(0.000000) = 1.000000
f(0.000100) = 0.999900
f(0.001000) = 0.999000
f(0.010000) = 0.990050
f(0.100000) = 0.904837
f(1.000000) = 0.367879
f(2.000000) = 0.135335
f(3.000000) = 0.049787
f(10.000000) = 0.000045
f(100.000000) = 0.000000
f(1000.000000) = 0.000000
F(Q(u)) = u for all u = true
```

12.3.5. Poisson Distribution

While the waiting time between events of a Poisson process is governed by the exponential distribution, the number of events is governed by the Poisson distribution. In other words, a Poisson distribution is a discrete probability distribution that expresses the probability of a given number of events occurring in a fixed interval of time if these events occur with a known constant mean rate and independently of the time since the last event. Note that unlike the other continuous probability distributions that we have discussed so far, Poisson distribution is a discrete probability distribution. It "counts" the number of event occurrences.

For instance, a call center receives an average of 180 calls per hour, 24 hours a day. The calls are independent; receiving one does not change the probability of when the next one will arrive. The number of calls received during any minute has a Poisson distribution: the most likely numbers are 2 and 3, but 1 and 4 are also likely, and there is a small probability of it being as low as zero and a very small probability it could be 10. Another example is the number of decay events that occur from a radioactive source in a given observation period.

A discrete random variable X is said to have a Poisson distribution, with parameter $\lambda > 0$, if it has a probability mass function (PMF) given by the following:

$$f(k \mid \lambda) = \Pr(X = k) = \frac{\lambda^k e^{-\lambda}}{k!}$$

where $k = 0, 1, 2, \ldots$ is the number of occurrences.

For the example in Figure 12-23, k is the number of occurrences. λ is the expected rate of occurrences. The vertical axis is the probability of k occurrences given λ. The function is defined only at integer values of k; the connecting lines are only guides for the eye.

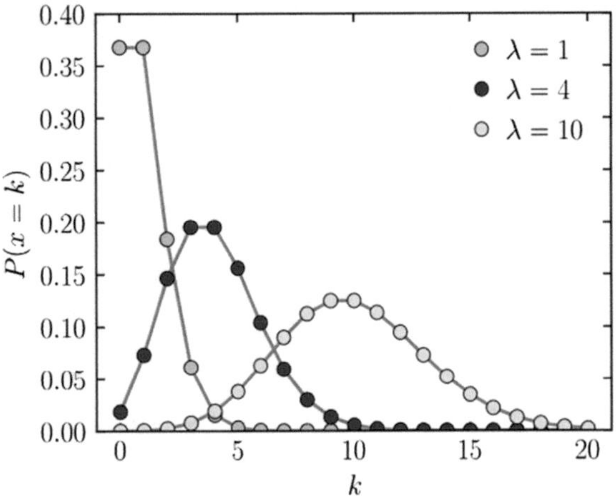

Figure 12-23. *Probability mass functions for Poisson distributions*

The CDF is as follows:

$$F(k) = e^{-\lambda} \sum_{i=0}^{\underline{k}} \frac{\lambda^i}{i!}$$

$\underline{k}$ is the floor function, the smallest integer smaller than or equal to k.

For the example in Figure 12-23, the horizontal axis is the index k, which is the number of occurrences. The CDF is discontinuous at the integers of k and flat everywhere else because a variable that is Poisson distributed takes on only integer values. See Figure 12-24.

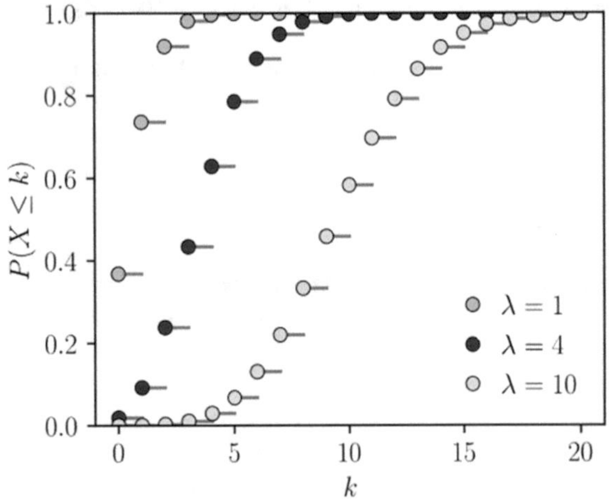

Figure 12-24. *Cumulative probability functions for Poisson distributions*

There is no closed form for the quantile function, but it can be computed by a search for the biggest k using the CDF such that $F(k) < q$.

The mean is as follows:

$$\mathrm{E}(X) = \lambda$$

The variance is as follows:

$$\mathrm{Var}(X) = \lambda$$

The skewness is as follows:

$$\gamma = \lambda^{-\frac{1}{2}}$$

The excess kurtosis is as follows:

$$\kappa = \lambda^{-1}$$

The moment-generating function is as follows:

$$M_X(t) = \exp\lambda\left(e^t - 1\right)$$

The NM Dev class `PoissonDistribution` implements the Poisson distribution. Here's an example:

```
val dist = PoissonDistribution(
        2.0 // lambda = 2.0
)

println("mean = " + dist.mean())
println("median = " + dist.median())
println("variance = " + dist.variance())
println("skew = " + dist.skew())
println("kurtosis = " + dist.kurtosis())
println("entropy = " + dist.entropy())

println("")
val ks: DoubleArray = doubleArrayOf(0.0, 1.0, 2.0, 3.0, 4.0, 5.0)
for (k in ks) {
    println(String.format("F(%f) = %f", k, dist.cdf(k)))
}
println("")
for (k in ks) {
    println(String.format("f(%f) = %f", k, dist.density(k)))
}
println("")
var u: Double = 0.1
while(u < 1.0) {
    val x: Double = dist.quantile(u)
    println(String.format("Q(%f) = %f", u, x))

    u += 0.1
}
```

The output is as follows:

```
mean = 2.0
median = 2.0
variance = 2.0
skew = 0.7071067811865475
kurtosis = 0.5
entropy = 1.7048826437056113
F(0.000000) = 0.135335
F(1.000000) = 0.406006
F(2.000000) = 0.676676
F(3.000000) = 0.857123
F(4.000000) = 0.947347
F(5.000000) = 0.983436
f(0.000000) = 0.135335
f(1.000000) = 0.270671
f(2.000000) = 0.270671
f(3.000000) = 0.180447
f(4.000000) = 0.090224
f(5.000000) = 0.036089
Q(0.100000) = 0.000000
Q(0.200000) = 1.000000
Q(0.300000) = 1.000000
Q(0.400000) = 1.000000
Q(0.500000) = 2.000000
Q(0.600000) = 2.000000
Q(0.700000) = 3.000000
Q(0.800000) = 3.000000
Q(0.900000) = 4.000000
Q(1.000000) = 22.000000
```

12.3.6. Binomial Distribution

The binomial distribution with parameters n and p is the discrete probability distribution of the number of successes in a sequence of n independent experiments, each with its own yes or no outcome: yes/success (with probability p) or no/failure (with probability $q = 1 - p$). A single success/failure experiment is also called a Bernoulli trial or Bernoulli experiment, and a sequence of Boolean outcomes is called a Bernoulli process. For a single trial, i.e., $n = 1$, the binomial distribution is a Bernoulli distribution. For one fair coin toss, $n = 1, p = 0.5$.

The binomial distribution is frequently used to model the number of successes in a sample of size n drawn with replacement from a population of size N. If the sampling is carried out without replacement, the draws are not independent and so the resulting distribution is a hypergeometric distribution, not a binomial one. However, for N much larger than n, the binomial distribution remains a good approximation and is widely used.

The binomial and Poisson distributions are similar in the sense that they both measure the number of certain random events (or "successes") within a certain frame. However, they are different because the binomial distribution counts discrete occurrences among discrete trials, while the Poisson distribution counts discrete occurrences among a continuous domain. That is, with a binomial distribution you have a certain number, n, of "attempts," each of which has probability of success p. With a Poisson distribution, you essentially have infinite attempts, with infinitesimal chance of success. That is, given a binomial distribution with parameters n and p, if you let $n \to \infty$ and $p \to 0$ in such a way that $np \to \lambda$, then that distribution approaches a Poisson distribution with parameter λ. The Poisson distribution can therefore be derived as a limit of the binomial distribution.

Because of this limiting behavior, Poisson distributions are used to model rare occurrences of events that could happen a large number of times, but happen with a small probability. That is, they are used in situations that would be more properly represented by a binomial distribution with a very large n and small p, especially when the exact values of n and p are unknown, for example, a once-in-100-year flood.

In summary, if a mean or average probability of an event happening per unit time is given and you are asked to calculate a probability of n events happening in a given time, then the Poisson distribution is used. If, on the other hand, an exact probability of an event happening is given and you are asked to calculate the probability of this event happening k times out of n, then the binomial distribution should be used.

Moreover, if n is big enough, then the binomial random variable X can be well approximated by a normal distribution. That is, $X \sim N(np, np(1-p))$. Equivalently, the normalized random variable $z = \frac{x-\mu}{\sigma}$ has a standard normal distribution $N(0, 1)$.

If the random variable X follows the binomial distribution with parameters $n \in \mathbb{N}$ and $p \in [0, 1]$, we write $X \sim B(n, p)$. The probability of getting exactly k successes in n independent Bernoulli trials is given by the PMF:

$$f(k|n,p) = \Pr(k|n,p) = \Pr(X = k) = \binom{n}{k} p^k (1-p)^{n-k}$$

for $k = 0, 1, 2, \ldots, n$.

$\binom{n}{k} = \frac{n!}{k!(n-k)!}$ is the binomial coefficient, which is the reason for the name of the distribution. The formula can be understood as follows: k successes occur with probability p^k, and $n - k$ failures occur with probability $(1-p)^{n-k}$. However, the k successes can occur anywhere among the n trials, and there are $\binom{n}{k}$ different ways of distributing k successes in a sequence of k trials.

Figure 12-25 shows an example.

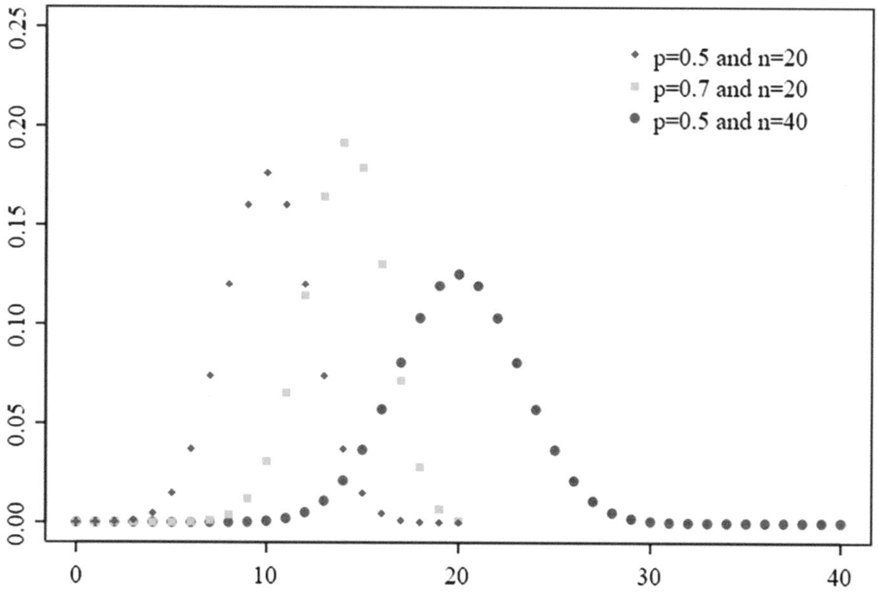

***Figure 12-25.** Probability mass functions for binomial distributions*

The CDF is as follows:

$$F(k \mid n,p) = \Pr(X \leq k) = \sum_{i=0}^{k} \binom{n}{i} p^i (1-p)^{n-i}$$

Figure 12-26 shows an example.

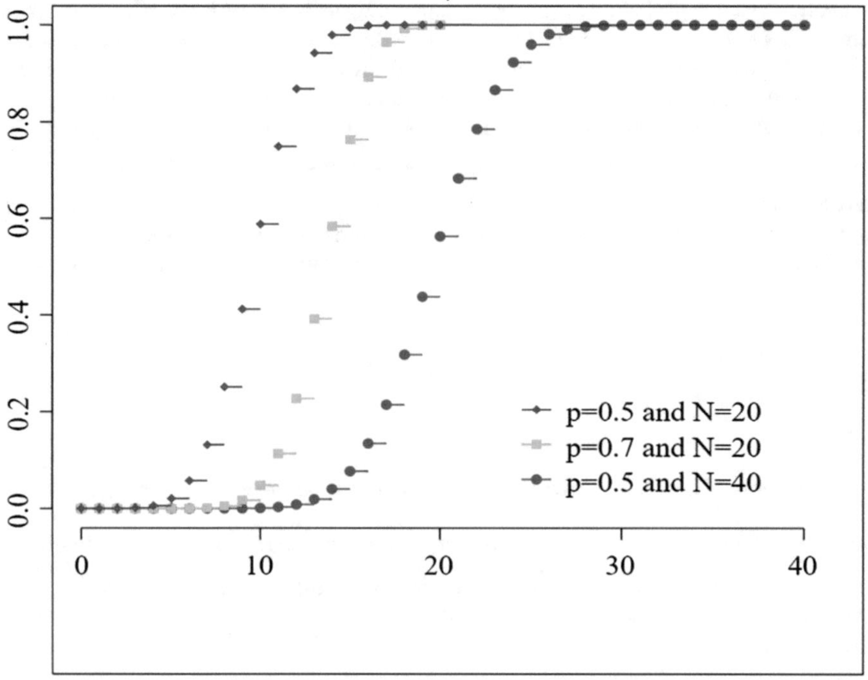

Figure 12-26. *Cumulative probability functions for binomial distributions*

There is no closed form for the quantile function, but it can be computed by a search for the biggest k using the CDF such that $F(k) < q$.

The mean is as follows:

$$\mathrm{E}(X) = np$$

The variance is as follows:

$$\mathrm{Var}(X) = npq$$

The skewness is as follows:

$$\gamma = \frac{q-p}{\sqrt{npq}}$$

The excess kurtosis is as follows:

$$\kappa = \frac{1-6pq}{npq}$$

The moment-generating function is as follows:

$$M_X(t) = \left(q + pe^t\right)^n$$

The NM Dev class `BinomialDistribution` implements the binomial distribution. Here's an example:

```
val dist1 = BinomialDistribution(
        20, // n
        0.7 // p
)

println("mean = " + dist1.mean())
println("median = " + dist1.median())
println("variance = " + dist1.variance())
println("skew = " + dist1.skew())
println("kurtosis = " + dist1.kurtosis())
println("entropy = " + dist1.entropy())

println("")
val ks: DoubleArray = DoubleUtils.seq(0.0, 20.0, 1.0) // a sequence of numbers from 0 to 20
for (k in ks) {
    println(String.format("F(%f) = %f", k, dist1.cdf(k)))
}
println("")
for (k in ks) {
    println(String.format("f(%f) = %f", k, dist1.density(k)))
}
println("")
var u: Double = 0.1
while(u < 1.0) {
    val x: Double = dist1.quantile(u)
    println(String.format("Q(%f) = %f", u, x))

    u += 0.1
}
```

The output is as follows:

```
mean = 14.0
median = 14.0
variance = 4.200000000000001
skew = -0.19518001458970657
kurtosis = -0.06190476190476189
entropy = 3.0822902491263404
F(0.000000) = 0.000000
F(1.000000) = 0.000000
```

```
F(2.000000) = 0.000000
F(3.000000) = 0.000001
F(4.000000) = 0.000006
F(5.000000) = 0.000043
F(6.000000) = 0.000261
F(7.000000) = 0.001279
F(8.000000) = 0.005138
F(9.000000) = 0.017145
F(10.000000) = 0.047962
F(11.000000) = 0.113331
F(12.000000) = 0.227728
F(13.000000) = 0.391990
F(14.000000) = 0.583629
F(15.000000) = 0.762492
F(16.000000) = 0.892913
F(17.000000) = 0.964517
F(18.000000) = 0.992363
F(19.000000) = 0.999202
F(20.000000) = 1.000000
f(0.000000) = 0.000000
f(1.000000) = 0.000000
f(2.000000) = 0.000000
f(3.000000) = 0.000001
f(4.000000) = 0.000005
f(5.000000) = 0.000037
f(6.000000) = 0.000218
f(7.000000) = 0.001018
f(8.000000) = 0.003859
f(9.000000) = 0.012007
f(10.000000) = 0.030817
f(11.000000) = 0.065370
f(12.000000) = 0.114397
f(13.000000) = 0.164262
f(14.000000) = 0.191639
f(15.000000) = 0.178863
f(16.000000) = 0.130421
f(17.000000) = 0.071604
f(18.000000) = 0.027846
f(19.000000) = 0.006839
f(20.000000) = 0.000798
Q(0.100000) = 11.000000
Q(0.200000) = 12.000000
Q(0.300000) = 13.000000
Q(0.400000) = 14.000000
Q(0.500000) = 14.000000
Q(0.600000) = 15.000000
Q(0.700000) = 15.000000
Q(0.800000) = 16.000000
Q(0.900000) = 17.000000
Q(1.000000) = 20.000000
```

12.3.7. T-Distribution

The student's t-distribution (or simply the t-distribution) is the probability distribution of the sample mean relative to the true mean of a sample of i.i.d. normally distributed population when the sample size is small and the population's standard deviation is unknown. Specifically, suppose the set $\{x_1, \ldots, x_n\}$ is drawn from a normal distribution with known mean μ and unknown variance; then the t-value, a standardized value, of such a sample is defined as follows:

$$t = \frac{\bar{x} - \mu}{s / \sqrt{n}}$$

where $\bar{x}$ is the sample mean and s is the unbiased sample standard deviation (with the denominator $n - 1$) in place of the true population standard deviation σ. t is random because $\bar{x}$ and s are random. The random variable t has the t-distribution with $\upsilon = n - 1$ degrees of freedom.

The t-distribution plays a role in a number of widely used statistical analyses including student's t-test for assessing the statistical significance of the difference between two sample means (whether two means are significantly different statistically), in the construction of confidence intervals for the difference between two population means, and in linear regression analysis. The student's t-distribution also arises in the Bayesian analysis of data from a normal family.

Mathematically, a random variable X has the t-distribution if and only if it has the PDF as shown here:

$$f(t) = \frac{\Gamma\left(\frac{\upsilon+1}{2}\right)}{\sqrt{\upsilon\pi}\,\Gamma\left(\frac{\upsilon}{2}\right)} \left(1 + \frac{t^2}{\upsilon}\right)^{-\frac{\upsilon+1}{2}}$$

where υ is the number of degree of freedom and Γ the gamma function.

Figure 12-27 shows an example.

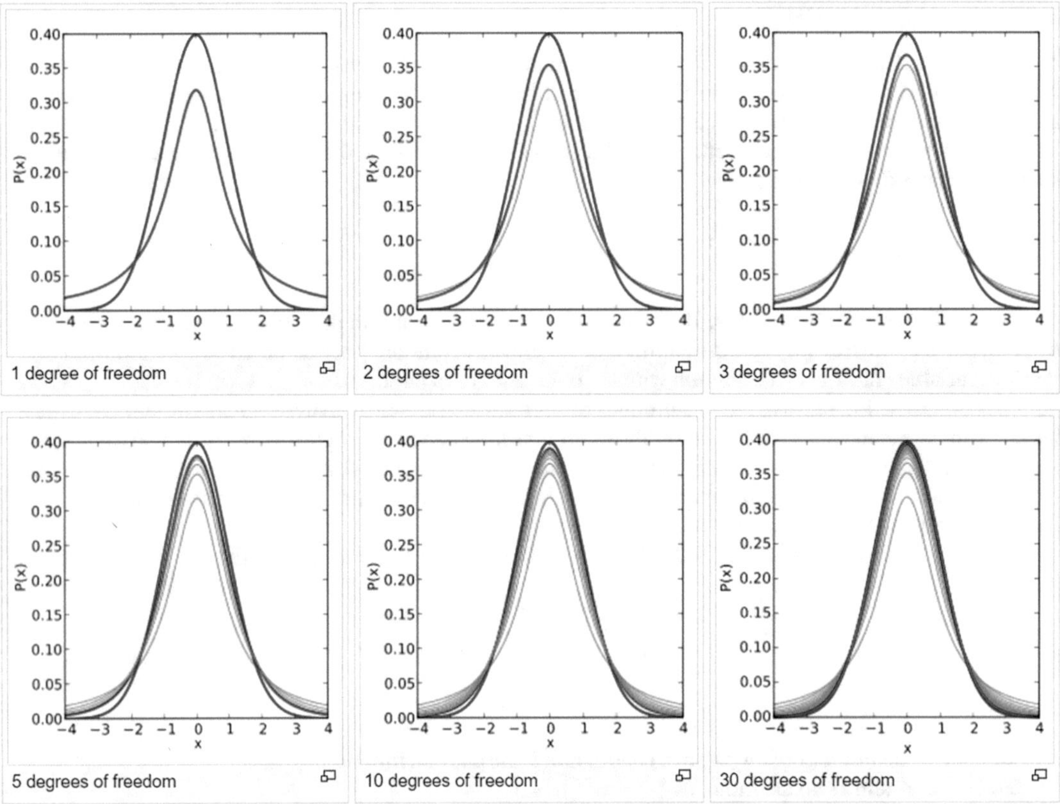

Figure 12-27. *T-distributions (red) versus normal distributions (blue)*

The t-distribution is symmetric and bell-shaped, like the normal distribution. However, the t-distribution has heavier tails, meaning that it is more prone to producing values that fall far from its mean. When the degree of freedom goes to infinity, the t-distribution converges to normal distribution. That is,

$$\lim_{\upsilon \to \infty} t = \frac{\overline{x} - \mu}{\sigma / \sqrt{n}}$$

This has a standard normal distribution with mean 0 and variance 1.

The CDF is as follows:

$$F(t) = 1 - \frac{1}{2} I_{x(t)}\left(\frac{v}{2}, \frac{1}{2}\right)$$

where I is the the regularized incomplete beta function, $t > 0$, and we have this:

$$x(t) = \frac{v}{t^2 + v}$$

Figure 12-28 shows an example.

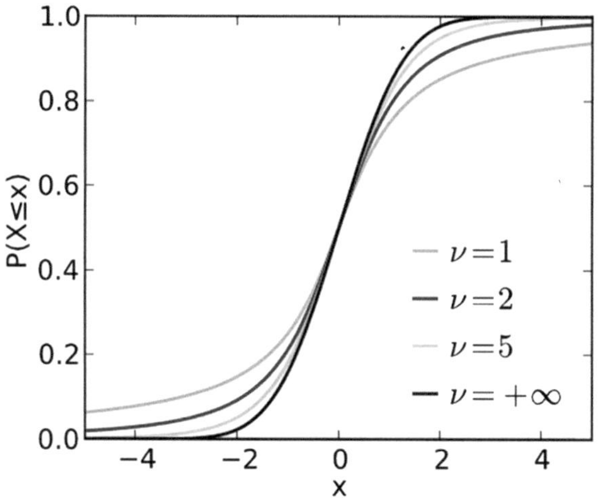

Figure 12-28. *Cumulative probability functions for t-distributions*

The quantile function for the t-distribution has simple formulas when the degree of freedom $\upsilon = 1, 2, 4$. They are as follows:

$$\upsilon = 1,$$
$$Q(q) = \tan\left(\pi\left(q - \frac{1}{2}\right)\right)$$

$$\upsilon = 2,$$

$$Q(q) = 2\left(q - \frac{1}{2}\right)\sqrt{\frac{2}{\alpha}}$$

$$\alpha = 4q(1-q)$$

$$\upsilon = 4,$$

$$Q(q) = sign\left(q - \frac{1}{2}\right)2\sqrt{u-1}$$

$$u = \frac{\cos\left(\frac{1}{3}\cos^{-1}\sqrt{\alpha}\right)}{\sqrt{\alpha}}$$

The sign function returns 1 for a positive number, -1 for a negative number, and 0 otherwise. In general, the quantile function is as follows:

$$Q(q) = sign\left(I^{-1} - \frac{1}{2}\right) \frac{1}{\sqrt{\frac{1}{4\nu\left(I^{-1} - \frac{1}{2}\right)^2} - \frac{1}{\nu}}}$$

$I^{-1} = I^{-1}_{\left(\frac{\nu}{2},\frac{\nu}{2}\right)}(q)$ is the inverse of the regularized incomplete Beta function with both shape parameters being $\frac{\nu}{2}$.

The mean is as follows:

$$\mathrm{E}(X) = 0$$

The variance is as follows:

$$Var(X) = \begin{cases} \infty, 1 < \nu \le 2 \\ \frac{\nu}{\nu - 2}, \nu > 2 \end{cases}, \text{ otherwise undefined}$$

The skewness is as follows:

$$\gamma = 0,\ \nu > 3, \text{ otherwise undefined}$$

The excess kurtosis is as follows:

$$\kappa = \begin{cases} \infty, 2 < \nu \le 4 \\ \frac{6}{\nu - 4}, \nu > 4 \end{cases}, \text{ otherwise undefined}$$

The moment-generating function is undefined.

The NM Dev class `TDistribution` implements the t-distribution. Here's an example:

```
val dist = TDistribution(4.5) // degree of freedom = 4.5

println("mean = " + dist.mean())
println("median = " + dist.median())
println("variance = " + dist.variance())
println("skew = " + dist.skew())
println("kurtosis = " + dist.kurtosis())
println("entropy = " + dist.entropy())

println("")
val ks: DoubleArray = DoubleUtils.seq(0.0, 20.0, 1.0) // a sequence of numbers from 0 to 20
for (k in ks) {
    println(String.format("F(%f) = %f", k, dist.cdf(k)))
}
println("")
for (k in ks) {
    println(String.format("f(%f) = %f", k, dist.density(k)))
}

var allEquals: Boolean = true
```

```
var u: Double = 0.1
while(u < 1.0) {
    val x: Double = dist.quantile(u)
    val y: Double = dist.cdf(x)
    if (abs(u - y) > 1e-9) {
        allEquals = false
    }

    u += 0.1
}

println("\nF(Q(u)) = u for all u = " + allEquals)
```

The output is as follows:

```
mean = 0.0
median = 0.0
variance = 1.8
skew = 0.0
kurtosis = 12.0
entropy = 1.6515357247574647
F(0.000000) = 0.500000
F(1.000000) = 0.815997
F(2.000000) = 0.945871
F(3.000000) = 0.982810
F(4.000000) = 0.993618
F(5.000000) = 0.997262
F(6.000000) = 0.998679
F(7.000000) = 0.999301
F(8.000000) = 0.999602
F(9.000000) = 0.999759
F(10.000000) = 0.999847
F(11.000000) = 0.999899
F(12.000000) = 0.999931
F(13.000000) = 0.999952
F(14.000000) = 0.999965
F(15.000000) = 0.999974
F(16.000000) = 0.999981
F(17.000000) = 0.999985
F(18.000000) = 0.999989
F(19.000000) = 0.999991
F(20.000000) = 0.999993
f(0.000000) = 0.000000
f(1.000000) = 0.217424
f(2.000000) = 0.065675
f(3.000000) = 0.018403
f(4.000000) = 0.005834
f(5.000000) = 0.002144
f(6.000000) = 0.000897
f(7.000000) = 0.000417
f(8.000000) = 0.000211
```

```
f(9.000000) = 0.000115
f(10.000000) = 0.000066
f(11.000000) = 0.000040
f(12.000000) = 0.000025
f(13.000000) = 0.000016
f(14.000000) = 0.000011
f(15.000000) = 0.000008
f(16.000000) = 0.000005
f(17.000000) = 0.000004
f(18.000000) = 0.000003
f(19.000000) = 0.000002
f(20.000000) = 0.000002
F(Q(u)) = u for all u = true
```

12.3.8. Chi-Square Distribution

While the scaled sample mean, a sum of *k* independent normal random variables, follows the t-distribution, a sum of the squares of *k* independent standard normal random variables follows the Chi-square distribution (also χ^2-distribution). This distribution is sometimes called the central Chi-square distribution, a special case of the more general noncentral Chi-square distribution. The Chi-square distribution is one of the most widely used probability distributions in inferential statistics, notably in hypothesis testing and in the construction of confidence intervals. It is also used in the common Chi-square tests for goodness of fit of an observed distribution to a theoretical one. See Section 12.4.

Mathematically, if each variable in $\{Z_1, \ldots, Z_k\}$ is an independent, standard normal random variable, then the sum of their squares, as shown here:

$$Q = \sum_{i=1}^{k} Z_i^2$$

has the Chi-square distribution *k* degrees of freedom. This is usually denoted as $Q \sim \chi^2(k)$ or $Q \sim \chi_k^2$. The Chi-square distribution has one parameter: a positive integer *k* that specifies the degree of freedom (the number of random variables being summed, Z_i s).

Moreover, the sample variance S^2 has the scaled Chi-square distribution.

$$S^2 = \frac{1}{n-1} \sum_{i=1}^{n} (x_i - \bar{x})^2$$

$$S^2 \sim \frac{\sigma^2}{n-1} \chi_{n-1}^2$$

Equivalently, we have this:

$$\frac{S^2}{\sigma^2} \sim \frac{\chi^2_{n-1}}{n-1}$$

The PDF of the Chi-square distribution is as follows:

$$f(x \mid k) = \frac{x^{\frac{k}{2}-1} e^{-\frac{x}{2}}}{2^{\frac{k}{2}} \Gamma\left(\frac{k}{2}\right)}, x > 0$$

where $\Gamma\left(\frac{k}{2}\right)$ is the gamma function.

Figure 12-29 shows an example.

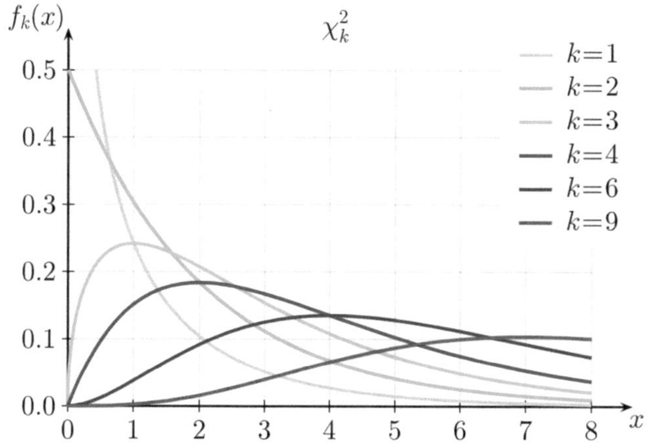

***Figure 12-29.** Probability density functions for Chi-square distributions*

The CDF is as follows:

$$F(x \mid k) = \frac{\gamma\left(\frac{k}{2}, \frac{x}{2}\right)}{\Gamma\left(\frac{k}{2}\right)} = P\left(\frac{k}{2}, \frac{x}{2}\right)$$

where $\gamma(s, t)$ is the lower incomplete gamma function, and $P(s, t)$ is the regularized incomplete gamma function.

Figure 12-30 shows an example.

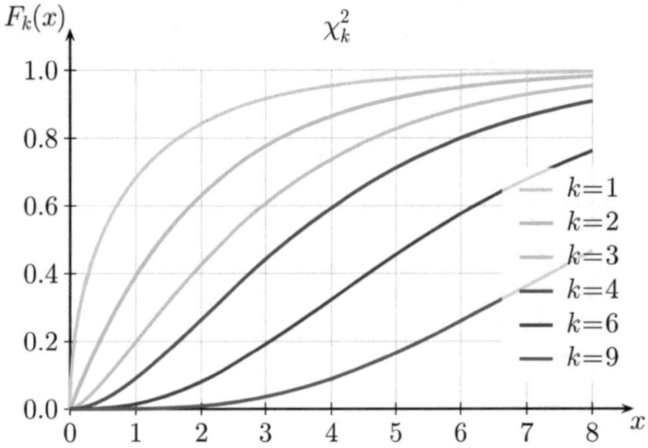

***Figure 12-30.** Cumulative distribution functions for Chi-square distributions*

The quantile function is the inverse of the regularized incomplete gamma function.

$$Q(q) = P^{-1}\left(\frac{k}{2}, \frac{q}{2}\right) = 2P^{-1}\left(\frac{k}{2}, q\right)$$

The mean is as follows:

$$\mathrm{E}(X) = k$$

The variance is as follows:

$$\mathrm{Var}(X) = 2k$$

The skewness is as follows:

$$\gamma = \sqrt{\frac{8}{k}}$$

The excess kurtosis is as follows:

$$\kappa = \frac{12}{k}$$

The moment-generating function is as follows:

$$M_X(t) = (1-2t)^{-\frac{k}{2}}, t < \frac{1}{2}$$

The NM Dev class ChiSquareDistribution implements the Chi-square distribution. Here's an example:

```
val dist = ChiSquareDistribution(
        1.5 // degree of freedom
)

println("mean = " + dist.mean())
println("median = " + dist.median())
println("variance = " + dist.variance())
println("skew = " + dist.skew())
println("kurtosis = " + dist.kurtosis())
println("entropy = " + dist.entropy())

println("")
val xs: DoubleArray = doubleArrayOf(0.0, 0.0001, 0.001, 0.01, 0.1, 1.0, 2.0, 3.0, 10.0,
100.0, 1000.0)
for (x in xs) {
    println(String.format("F(%f) = %f", x, dist.cdf(x)))
}
println("")
for (x in xs) {
    println(String.format("f(%f) = %f", x, dist.density(x)))
}

var allEquals: Boolean = true
var u: Double = 0.1
while(u < 1.0) {
    val x: Double = dist.quantile(u)
    val y: Double = dist.cdf(x)
    if (abs(u - y) > 1e-9) {
        allEquals = false
    }

    u += 0.1
}

println("\nF(Q(u)) = u for all u = " + allEquals)
```

The output is as follows:

```
mean = 1.5
median = 1.5
variance = 3.0
skew = 2.309401076758503
kurtosis = 8.0
entropy = 1.3749629120446232
F(0.000000) = 0.000000
F(0.000100) = 0.000647
```

```
F(0.001000) = 0.003637
F(0.010000) = 0.020415
F(0.100000) = 0.112622
F(1.000000) = 0.527937
F(2.000000) = 0.739980
F(3.000000) = 0.852400
F(10.000000) = 0.996474
F(100.000000) = 1.000000
F(1000.000000) = 1.000000
f(0.000000) = Infinity
f(0.000100) = 4.852013
f(0.001000) = 2.727260
f(0.010000) = 1.526765
f(0.100000) = 0.820784
f(1.000000) = 0.294304
f(2.000000) = 0.150104
f(3.000000) = 0.082266
f(10.000000) = 0.001839
f(100.000000) = 0.000000
f(1000.000000) = 0.000000
F(Q(u)) = u for all u = true
```

12.3.9. F-Distribution

While the scaled sample mean, namely, the t-value, has the t-distribution, the ratio of the scaled sample variances has the F-distribution. In fact, the ratio of a random variable that has a Chi-square distribution with the degree of freedom d_1 over another random variable that has a Chi-square distribution with the degree of freedom d_2 follows the F-distribution with the degrees of freedom (d_1, d_2), $F(d_1, d_2)$. That is,

$$\frac{\chi^2_{d_1}}{\chi^2_{d_2}} \sim F(d_1, d_2)$$

Moreover, the sample variance S^2 has Chi-square distribution.

$$S^2 = \frac{1}{n-1}\sum_{i=1}^{n}(x_i - \bar{x})^2 \sim \frac{\sigma^2}{n-1}\chi^2_{n-1}$$

Then the ratio of the sample variances of two samples $\frac{S_1^2}{S_2^2}$ and the ratio of the scaled sample variances $\frac{S_1^2/\sigma_1^2}{S_2^2/\sigma_2^2}$ follow the F-distribution. Moreover, for the random variable t with the degree of freedom ν, t^2 has the F-distribution $F(1, \nu)$.

If a random variable X has an F-distribution with parameters $d_1 > 0$ and $d_2 > 0$, we write $X \sim F(d_1, d_2)$. The PDF is as follows:

$$f(x \mid d_1, d_2) = \frac{\sqrt{\frac{(d_1 x)^{d_1} d_2^{d_2}}{(d_1 x + d_2)^{d_1 + d_2}}}}{x B\left(\frac{d_1}{2}, \frac{d_2}{2}\right)}$$

B is the beta function.
Figure 12-31 shows an example.

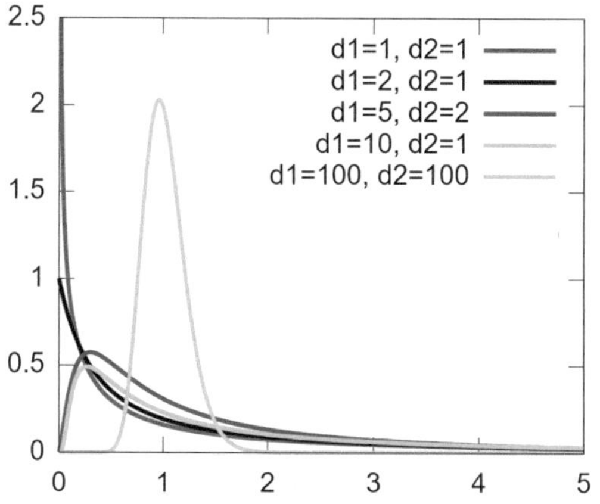

***Figure 12-31.** Probability density functions for F-distributions*

The CDF is as follows:

$$F\left(x \mid d_1, d_2\right) = I_{\frac{d_1 x}{d_1 x + d_2}}\left(\frac{d_1}{2}, \frac{d_2}{2}\right)$$

I is the regularized incomplete beta function.
Figure 12-32 shows an example.

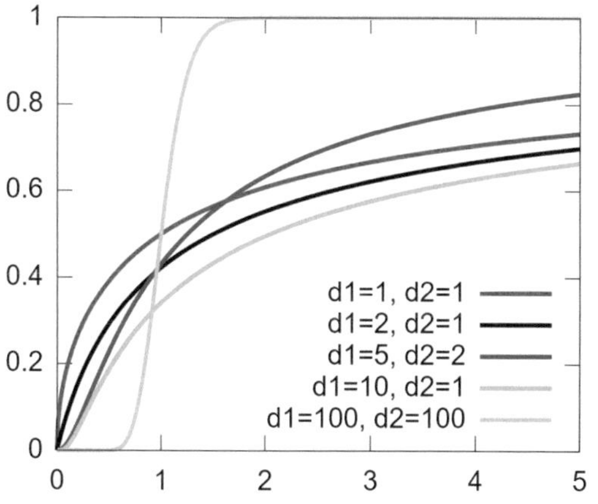

***Figure 12-32.** Cumulative distribution functions for F-distributions*

The quantile function is as follows:

$$Q(q) = \frac{d_2 I^{-1}}{d_1 - d_1 I^{-1}}$$

$I^{-1} = I^{-1}_{\left(\frac{d_1}{2}, \frac{d_2}{2}\right)}(q)$ is the inverse of the regularized incomplete Beta functions with the shape parameters $\frac{d_1}{2}$ and $\frac{d_2}{2}$.

The mean is as follows:

$$E(X) = \frac{d_2}{d_2 - 2}, d_2 > 2$$

The variance is as follows:

$$\text{Var}(X) = \frac{2d_2^2(d_1 + d_2 - 2)}{d_1(d_2 - 2)^2(d_2 - 4)}, d_2 > 4$$

The skewness is as follows:

$$\gamma = \frac{(2d_1 + d_2 - 2)\sqrt{8(d_2 - 4)}}{(d_2 - 6)\sqrt{d_1(d_1 + d_2 - 2)}}, d_2 > 6$$

The excess kurtosis is as follows:

$$\kappa = 12\frac{d_1(5d_2 - 22)(d_1 + d_2 - 2) + (d_2 - 4)(d_2 - 2)^2}{d_1(d_2 - 6)(d_2 - 8)(d_1 + d_2 - 2)}$$

The moment-generating function for F-distribution does not exist.
The NM Dev class `FDistribution` implements F-distribution. Here's an example:

```
val dist = FDistribution(100.5, 10.0) // degrees of freedom = {100.5, 10}

println("mean = " + dist.mean())
println("variance = " + dist.variance())
println("skew = " + dist.skew())
println("kurtosis = " + dist.kurtosis())

println("")
val ks: DoubleArray = DoubleUtils.seq(0.0, 20.0, 1.0) // a sequence of numbers from 0 to 20
for (k in ks) {
    println(String.format("F(%f) = %f", k, dist.cdf(k)))
}
println("")
for (k in ks) {
    println(String.format("f(%f) = %f", k, dist.density(k)))
}

var allEquals: Boolean = true
var u: Double = 0.1
while(u < 1.0) {
    val x: Double = dist.quantile(u)
    val y: Double = dist.cdf(x)
    if (abs(u - y) > 1e-9) {
        allEquals = false
    }

    u += 0.1
}
```

```
println("\nF(Q(u)) = u for all u = " + allEquals)
```

The output is as follows:

```
mean = 1.25
variance = 0.5622927031509121
skew = 3.4666421524967395
kurtosis = 39.05282344040168
F(0.000000) = 0.000000
F(1.000000) = 0.448778
F(2.000000) = 0.886374
F(3.000000) = 0.970125
F(4.000000) = 0.989870
F(5.000000) = 0.995874
F(6.000000) = 0.998080
F(7.000000) = 0.999013
F(8.000000) = 0.999452
F(9.000000) = 0.999676
F(10.000000) = 0.999799
F(11.000000) = 0.999870
F(12.000000) = 0.999913
F(13.000000) = 0.999940
F(14.000000) = 0.999958
F(15.000000) = 0.999969
F(16.000000) = 0.999977
F(17.000000) = 0.999983
F(18.000000) = 0.999987
F(19.000000) = 0.999990
F(20.000000) = 0.999992
f(0.000000) = 0.000000
f(1.000000) = 0.836572
f(2.000000) = 0.168807
f(3.000000) = 0.035722
f(4.000000) = 0.009923
f(5.000000) = 0.003404
f(6.000000) = 0.001365
f(7.000000) = 0.000616
f(8.000000) = 0.000304
f(9.000000) = 0.000162
f(10.000000) = 0.000091
f(11.000000) = 0.000054
f(12.000000) = 0.000034
f(13.000000) = 0.000021
f(14.000000) = 0.000014
f(15.000000) = 0.000010
f(16.000000) = 0.000007
f(17.000000) = 0.000005
f(18.000000) = 0.000003
f(19.000000) = 0.000003
f(20.000000) = 0.000002
F(Q(u)) = u for all u = true
```

12.3.10. Rayleigh Distribution

The Rayleigh distribution is a continuous probability distribution for non-negative-valued random variables. It is essentially a Chi-square distribution with two degrees of freedom. For example, $X = \sqrt{X_1^2 + X_2^2}$ follows the Rayleigh distribution, where X_1 and X_2 are two normal distributions, and X_1^2 and X_2^2 are two Chi-square distributions.

A Rayleigh distribution is often observed when the overall magnitude of a vector is related to its directional components. One example where the Rayleigh distribution naturally arises is when wind velocity is analyzed in two dimensions. Assuming that each component is uncorrelated, normally distributed with equal variance, and zero mean, then the overall wind speed (vector magnitude) will be characterized by a Rayleigh distribution. A second example of the distribution arises in the case of random complex numbers whose real and imaginary components are independently and identically normally distributed with equal variance and zero mean. In that case, the absolute value of the complex number is Rayleigh-distributed.

Another possibility is that $X = \sigma\sqrt{-2\ln U}$, where U is a uniform distributed random variable, has a Rayleigh distribution with parameters σ.

The PDF is as follows:

$$f(x \mid \sigma) = \frac{x}{\sigma^2}\exp\left(-\frac{x^2}{2\sigma^2}\right), x \geq 0$$

where σ is the scale parameter of the distribution.

Figure 12-33 shows an example.

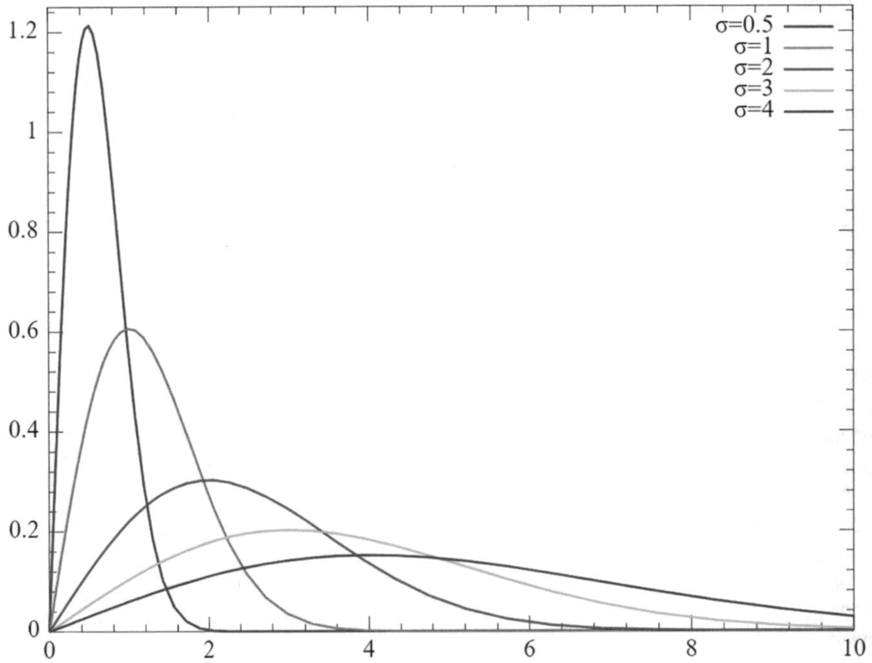

***Figure 12-33.** Probability density functions for Rayleigh distributions*

The CDF is as follows:

$$F(x \mid \sigma) = 1 - \exp\left(-\frac{x^2}{2\sigma^2}\right), x \geq 0$$

Figure 12-34 shows an example.

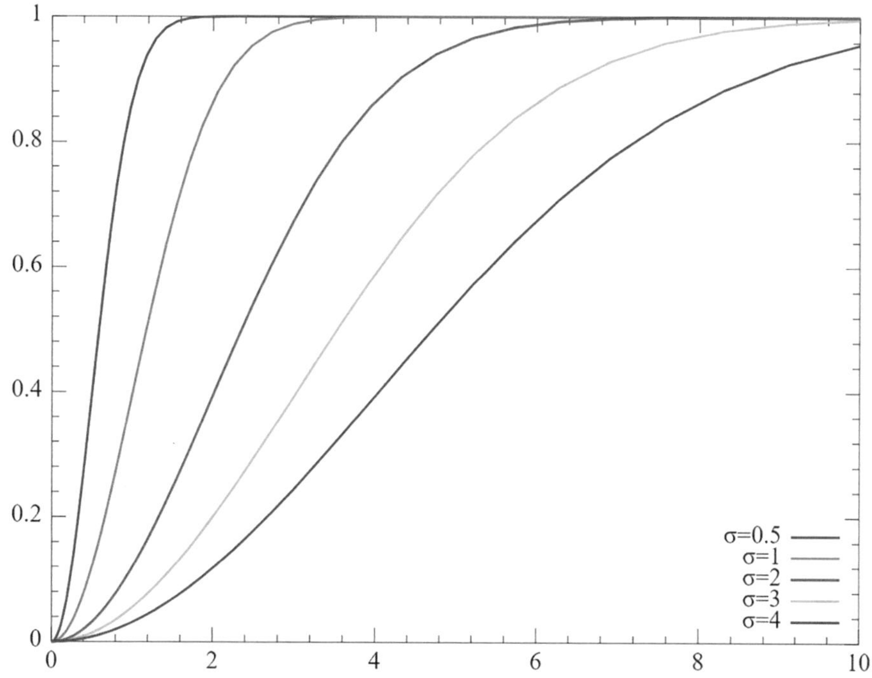

Figure 12-34. *Cumulative distribution functions for Rayleigh distributions*

The quantile function is as follows:

$$Q(q) = \sigma\sqrt{-2\ln(1-q)}$$

The mean is as follows:

$$\mathrm{E}(X) = \sigma\sqrt{\frac{\pi}{2}}$$

The variance is as follows:

$$\mathrm{Var}(X) = \frac{4-\pi}{2}\sigma^2$$

The skewness is as follows:

$$\gamma = \frac{2\sqrt{\pi}(\pi-3)}{(4-\pi)^{\frac{3}{2}}}$$

The excess kurtosis is as follows:

$$\kappa = -\frac{6\pi^2 - 24\pi + 16}{(4-\pi)^2}$$

The moment-generating function is as follows:

$$M_X(t) = 1 + \sigma t \exp\left(\frac{\sigma^2 t^2}{2}\right)\sqrt{\frac{\pi}{2}}\left(erf\left(\frac{\sigma t}{\sqrt{2}}\right)+1\right)$$

The NM Dev class `RayleighDistribution` implements the Rayleigh distribution. Here's an example:

```
val dist = RayleighDistribution(
        2.0 // sigma = 2
)

println("mean = " + dist.mean())
println("median = " + dist.median())
println("variance = " + dist.variance())
println("skew = " + dist.skew())
println("kurtosis = " + dist.kurtosis())
println("entropy = " + dist.entropy())

println("")
val xs: DoubleArray = doubleArrayOf(0.0, 0.0001, 0.001, 0.01, 0.1, 1.0, 2.0, 3.0, 10.0,
100.0, 1000.0)
for (x in xs) {
    println(String.format("F(%f) = %f", x, dist.cdf(x)))
}
println("")
for (x in xs) {
    println(String.format("f(%f) = %f", x, dist.density(x)))
}

var allEquals: Boolean = true
var u: Double = 0.000001
while(u < 1.0) {
    val x: Double = dist.quantile(u)
    val y: Double = dist.cdf(x)
    if (abs(u - y) > 1e-9) {
        allEquals = false
    }

    u += 0.000001
}

println("\nF(Q(u)) = u for all u = " + allEquals)
```

The output is as follows:

```
mean = 2.5066282746310002
median = 2.3548200450309493
variance = 1.7168146928204138
skew = 0.6311106578189364
kurtosis = 0.2450893006876391
entropy = 1.635181422730739
F(0.000000) = 0.000000
F(0.000100) = 0.000000
F(0.001000) = 0.000000
F(0.010000) = 0.000012
F(0.100000) = 0.001249
F(1.000000) = 0.117503
F(2.000000) = 0.393469
F(3.000000) = 0.675348
F(10.000000) = 0.999996
F(100.000000) = 1.000000
F(1000.000000) = 1.000000
f(0.000000) = 0.000000
f(0.000100) = 0.000025
f(0.001000) = 0.000250
f(0.010000) = 0.002500
f(0.100000) = 0.024969
f(1.000000) = 0.220624
f(2.000000) = 0.303265
f(3.000000) = 0.243489
f(10.000000) = 0.000009
f(100.000000) = 0.000000
f(1000.000000) = 0.000000
F(Q(u)) = u for all u = true
```

12.3.11. Gamma Distribution

The gamma distribution is a two-parameter family of continuous probability distributions. The exponential distribution and Chi-square distribution are special cases of the gamma distribution. There are two different parameterizations in common use:

- With a shape parameter $k > 0$ and a scale parameter $\theta > 0$
- With a shape parameter $\alpha = k > 0$ and an inverse scale parameter $\beta = \frac{1}{\theta} > 0$, called a rate parameter

The parameterization with k and θ appears to be more common in econometrics and certain other applied fields, where for example the gamma distribution is frequently used to model waiting times. For instance, the waiting time until failure is a random variable that is frequently modeled with a gamma distribution. NM Dev uses this parameterization with k and θ.

The parameterization with α and β is more common in Bayesian statistics, where the gamma distribution is used as a conjugate prior distribution for various types of inverse scale (rate) parameters, such as the λ of an exponential distribution or a Poisson distribution or, for that matter, the β of the gamma distribution itself.

A random variable X has the gamma distribution with shape k, and scale θ is denoted by the following:

$$X \sim \Gamma(k,\theta)$$

The PDF is as follows:

$$f(x|k,\theta)=\frac{x^{k-1}\exp\left(-\frac{x}{\theta}\right)}{\Gamma(k)}$$

where $\gamma(k)$ is the Gamma function evaluated at k.
Figure 12-35 shows an example.

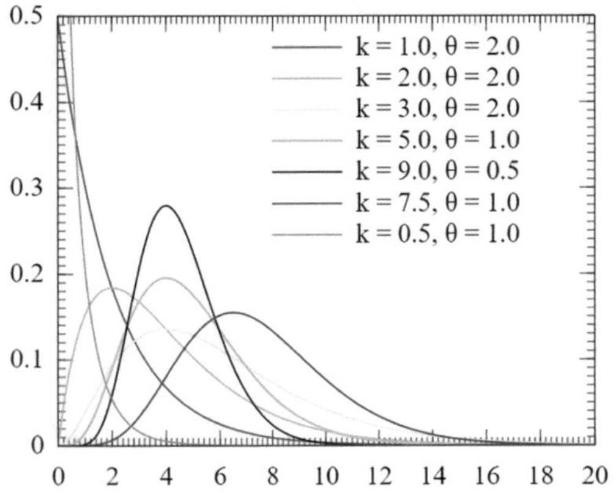

Figure 12-35. *Probability density functions for Gamma distributions*

The CDF is as follows:

$$f(x|k,\theta)=\frac{\gamma\left(k,\frac{x}{\theta}\right)}{\Gamma(k)}$$

Figure 12-36 shows an example.

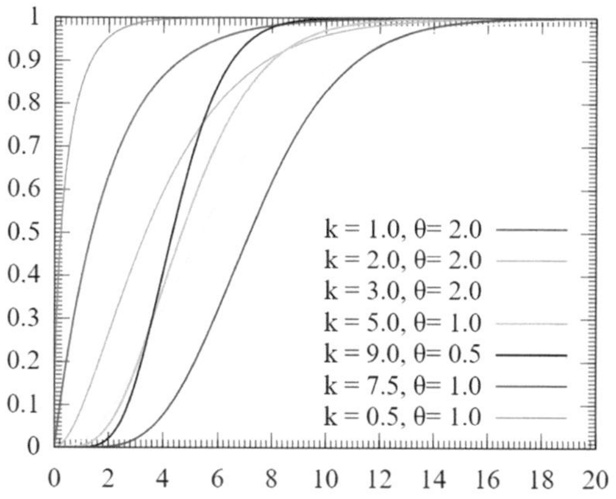

Figure 12-36. *Cumulative distribution functions for Gamma distributions*

The quantile function is as follows:

$$Q(q) = \theta P^{-1}(k, q)$$

where P^{-1} is the inverse of the regularized incomplete gamma function.
The mean is as follows:

$$\mathrm{E}(X) = k\theta$$

The variance is as follows:

$$\mathrm{Var}(X) = k\theta^2$$

The skewness is as follows:

$$\gamma = \frac{2}{k}$$

The excess kurtosis is as follows:

$$\kappa = \frac{6}{k}$$

The moment-generating function is as follows:

$$M_X(t) = (1 - \theta t)^{-k}, t < \frac{1}{\theta}$$

The NM Dev class `GammaDistribution` implements the Gamma distribution. Here's an example:

```
val dist = GammaDistribution(
        1.0, // k = 1
        2.0 // theta = 2
)

println("mean = " + dist.mean())
```

```
println("variance = " + dist.variance())
println("skew = " + dist.skew())
println("kurtosis = " + dist.kurtosis())

println("")
val xs: DoubleArray = doubleArrayOf(0.0, 0.0001, 0.001, 0.01, 0.1, 1.0, 2.0, 3.0, 10.0,
100.0, 1000.0)
for (x in xs) {
    println(String.format("F(%f) = %f", x, dist.cdf(x)))
}
println("")
for (x in xs) {
    println(String.format("f(%f) = %f", x, dist.density(x)))
}

var allEquals: Boolean = true
var u: Double = 0.001
while(u < 1.0) {
    val x: Double = dist.quantile(u)
    val y: Double = dist.cdf(x)
    if (abs(u - y) > 1e-9) {
        allEquals = false
    }

    u += 0.001
}

println("\nF(Q(u)) = u for all u = " + allEquals)
```

The output is as follows:

```
mean = 2.0
variance = 4.0
skew = 2.0
kurtosis = 6.0
F(0.000000) = 0.000000
F(0.000100) = 0.000050
F(0.001000) = 0.000500
F(0.010000) = 0.004988
F(0.100000) = 0.048771
F(1.000000) = 0.393469
F(2.000000) = 0.632121
F(3.000000) = 0.776870
F(10.000000) = 0.993262
F(100.000000) = 1.000000
F(1000.000000) = 1.000000
f(0.000000) = 0.500000
f(0.000100) = 0.499975
f(0.001000) = 0.499750
f(0.010000) = 0.497506
f(0.100000) = 0.475615
```

```
f(1.000000) = 0.303265
f(2.000000) = 0.183940
f(3.000000) = 0.111565
f(10.000000) = 0.003369
f(100.000000) = 0.000000
f(1000.000000) = 0.000000
F(Q(u)) = u for all u = true
```

12.3.12. Beta Distribution

The beta distribution is a family of continuous probability distributions defined on the unit interval [0, 1] parameterized by two positive shape parameters α and β, which appear as exponents of the random variable and control the shape of the distribution. The beta distribution has been applied to model the behavior of random variables limited to intervals of finite length in a wide variety of disciplines. In Bayesian inference, the beta distribution is the conjugate prior probability distribution for the Bernoulli, binomial, negative binomial, and geometric distributions. The beta distribution is a suitable model for the random behavior of percentages and proportions.

A random variable X that has the beta distribution with parameters α and β is denoted by the following:

$$X \sim \mathrm{Beta}(\alpha,\beta)$$

The PDF is as follows:

$$f(x|\alpha,\beta)=\frac{1}{\mathrm{B}(\alpha,\beta)}x^{\alpha-1}(1-x)^{\beta-1}$$

where $\mathrm{B}(\alpha, \beta)$ is the beta function.

Figure 12-37 shows an example.

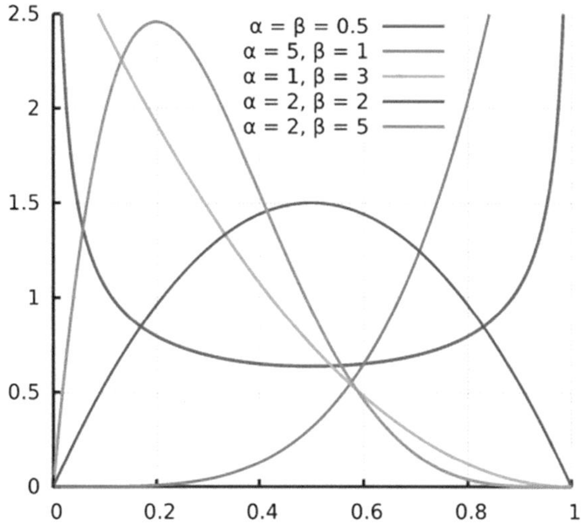

Figure 12-37. *Probability density functions for Beta distributions*

The CDF is as follows:

$$f(x|\alpha,\beta)=\frac{\mathrm{B}(x|\alpha,\beta)}{\mathrm{B}(\alpha,\beta)}=I_x(\alpha,\beta)$$

where $\mathrm{B}(x \mid \alpha, \beta)$ is the incomplete beta function and $I_x(\alpha, \beta)$ is the regularized incomplete beta function. Figure 12-38 shows an example.

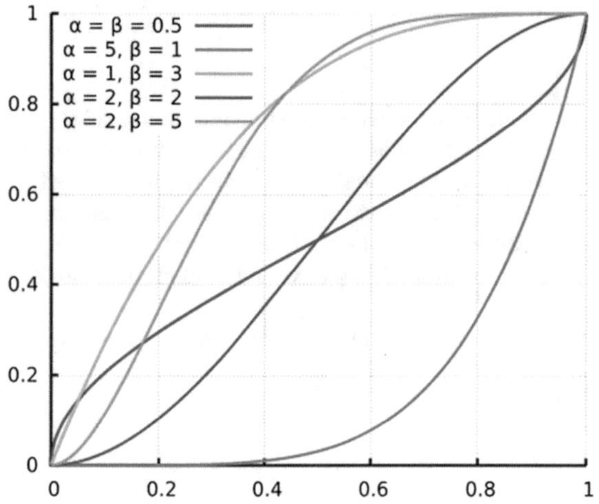

Figure 12-38. *Cumulative distribution functions for Beta distributions*

The quantile function is the inverse of regularized incomplete beta function.

$$Q(q)=I_q^{-1}(\alpha,\beta)$$

The mean is as follows:

$$\mathrm{E}(X)=\frac{\alpha}{\alpha+\beta}$$

The variance is as follows:

$$\mathrm{Var}(X)=\frac{\alpha\beta}{(\alpha+\beta)^2(\alpha+\beta+1)}$$

The skewness is as follows:

$$\gamma=\frac{2(\beta-\alpha)\sqrt{\alpha+\beta+1}}{(\alpha+\beta+2)\sqrt{\alpha\beta}}$$

The excess kurtosis is as follows:

$$\kappa=\frac{6\left[(\alpha-\beta)^2(\alpha+\beta+1)-\alpha\beta(\alpha+\beta+2)\right]}{\alpha\beta(\alpha+\beta+1)(\alpha+\beta+3)}$$

The moment-generating function is as follows:

$$M_X(t) = 1 + \sum_{k=1}^{\infty} \left(\prod_{r=0}^{k-1} \frac{\alpha + r}{a + \beta + r} \right) \frac{t^k}{k!}$$

The NM Dev class BetaDistribution implements the Beta distribution. Here's an example:

```
val dist = BetaDistribution(
        0.5, // alpha = 0.5
        1.5 // beta = 1.5
)

println("mean = " + dist.mean())
println("variance = " + dist.variance())
println("skew = " + dist.skew())
println("kurtosis = " + dist.kurtosis())

println("")
val xs: DoubleArray = doubleArrayOf(0.0, 0.0001, 0.001, 0.01, 0.1, 1.0, 2.0, 3.0)
for (x in xs) {
    println(String.format("F(%f) = %f", x, dist.cdf(x)))
}
println("")
for (x in xs) {
    println(String.format("f(%f) = %f", x, dist.density(x)))
}

var allEquals: Boolean = true
var u: Double = 0.001

while(u < 1.0) {
    val x: Double = dist.quantile(u)
    val y: Double = dist.cdf(x)
    if (abs(u - y) > 1e-9) {
        allEquals = false
    }

    u += 0.001
}

println("\nF(Q(u)) = u for all u = " + allEquals)
```

The output is as follows:

```
mean = 0.25
variance = 0.0625
skew = 1.0
kurtosis = 0.0
F(0.000000) = 0.000000
F(0.000100) = 0.012732
F(0.001000) = 0.040257
```

```
F(0.010000) = 0.127111
F(0.100000) = 0.395819
F(1.000000) = 1.000000
F(2.000000) = NaN
F(3.000000) = NaN
f(0.000000) = Infinity
f(0.000100) = 63.658794
f(0.001000) = 20.121616
f(0.010000) = 6.334287
f(0.100000) = 1.909859
f(1.000000) = 0.000000
f(2.000000) = NaN
f(3.000000) = NaN
F(Q(u)) = u for all u = true
```

Notice that the distribution is not defined outside the unit interval [0, 1] and that the probability density goes to infinity at $x = 0$.

12.3.13. Weibull Distribution

A non-negative random variable has the Weibull distribution with shape parameters $\lambda > 0$ and $k > 0$ if it has the following PDF:

$$f(x|\lambda,k)=\frac{k}{\lambda}\left(\frac{x}{\lambda}\right)^{k-1}\exp\left(-\left(\frac{x}{\lambda}\right)^{k}\right)$$

Figure 12-39 shows an example.

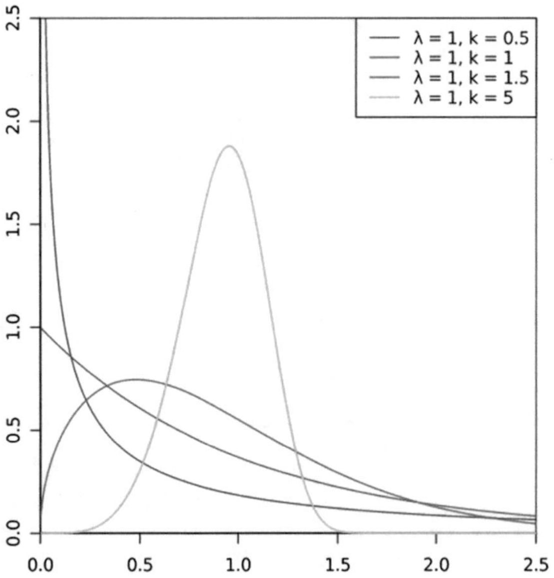

Figure 12-39. *Probability density functions for Weibull distributions*

The CDF is as follows:

$$F(x\,|\,\lambda,k) = 1 - \exp\left(-\left(\frac{x}{\lambda}\right)^k\right)$$

Figure 12-40 shows an example.

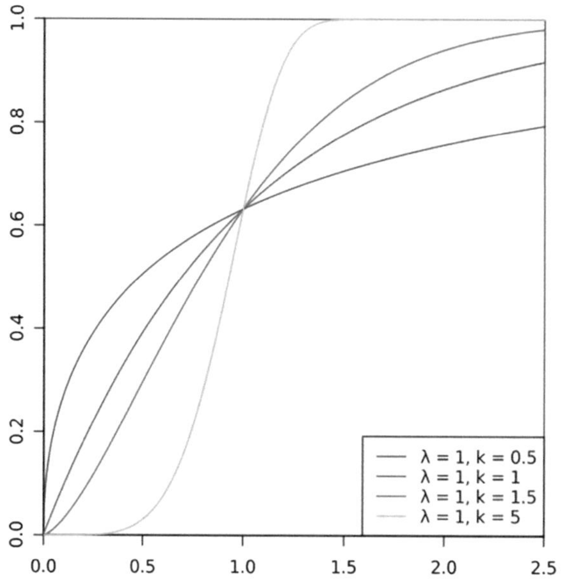

Figure 12-40. *Cumulative distribution functions for Weibull distributions*

The quantile function is as follows:

$$Q(q) = \lambda\left(-\ln(1-q)\right)^{\frac{1}{k}}$$

The mean is as follows:

$$\mathrm{E}(X) = \lambda\Gamma\left(1+\frac{1}{k}\right)$$

Γ is the gamma function.
The variance is as follows:

$$\mathrm{Var}(X) = \lambda^2\Gamma\left(1+\frac{1}{2}\right) - \left(\Gamma\left(1+\frac{1}{k}\right)\right)^2$$

The skewness is as follows:

$$\gamma = \frac{\lambda^3\Gamma\left(1+\frac{3}{k}\right) - 3\mu\sigma^2 - \mu^3}{\sigma^3}$$

The excess kurtosis is as follows:

$$\kappa = \frac{\lambda^4 \Gamma\left(1+\frac{4}{k}\right) - 4\gamma\sigma^3\mu - 6\mu^2\sigma^2 - \mu^4}{\sigma^4} - 3$$

The moment-generating function is as follows:

$$M_X(t) = \sum_{n=0}^{\infty} \frac{t^n \lambda^n}{n!} \Gamma\left(1+\frac{n}{k}\right), k \geq 1$$

The NM Dev class `WeibullDistribution` implements the Weibull distribution. Here's an example:

```
val dist = WeibullDistribution(
        1.0, // lambda, the scale parameter = 1
        1.0 // the shape parameter = 1
)

println("mean = " + dist.mean())
println("variance = " + dist.variance())
println("skew = " + dist.skew())
println("kurtosis = " + dist.kurtosis())
println("entropy = " + dist.entropy())

println("")
val xs: DoubleArray = doubleArrayOf(0.0, 0.0001, 0.001, 0.01, 0.1, 1.0, 2.0, 3.0)
for (x in xs) {
    println(String.format("F(%f) = %f", x, dist.cdf(x)))
}
println("")
for (x in xs) {
    println(String.format("f(%f) = %f", x, dist.density(x)))
}

var allEquals: Boolean = true
var u: Double = 0.001
while(u < 1.0) {
    val x: Double = dist.quantile(u)
    val y: Double = dist.cdf(x)
    if (abs(u - y) > 1e-9) {
        allEquals = false
    }

    u += 0.001
}

println("\nF(Q(u)) = u for all u = " + allEquals)
```

The output is as follows:

```
mean = 1.0
variance = 1.0
skew = 1.9999999999999973
kurtosis = 6.0000000000000036
entropy = 1.0
F(0.000000) = 0.000000
F(0.000100) = 0.000100
F(0.001000) = 0.001000
F(0.010000) = 0.009950
F(0.100000) = 0.095163
F(1.000000) = 0.632121
F(2.000000) = 0.864665
F(3.000000) = 0.950213
f(0.000000) = 1.000000
f(0.000100) = 0.999900
f(0.001000) = 0.999000
f(0.010000) = 0.990050
f(0.100000) = 0.904837
f(1.000000) = 0.367879
f(2.000000) = 0.135335
f(3.000000) = 0.049787
F(Q(u)) = u for all u = true
```

12.3.14. Empirical Distribution

The probability distributions that we have discussed so far are all model-based parametric distributions. The shapes of those distributions are determined by a few (shape) parameters. Model-based or parametric distributions require a knowledge or an assumption of the underlying statistical nature of the data set or generating process. For example, we may assume that the rate of atomic decay follows exponential distribution and that stock prices follow log-normal distribution. However, it is sometimes difficult to justify such an assumption or even to find a parametric distribution to describe the data.

Empirical distribution, on the other hand, requires no prior knowledge of the statistical nature of the data set. Its shape is entirely determined by the data set itself. They are useful when we cannot justify or fit a parametric distribution reasonably accurate enough. This may be the case when there are not enough samples or there lacks a theoretical underpinning for the data.

Specifically, an empirical cumulative distribution function is a step function that jumps up by $\frac{1}{n}$ at each of the n data points. Its value at any specified value of the random variable is the fraction of observations of the variable that are less than or equal to the specified value. The empirical distribution function is an estimate of the cumulative distribution function that generates the points in the sample. It converges with probability 1 to that underlying distribution, according to the Glivenko-Cantelli theorem.

Mathematically, let $\{X_1, \ldots, X_n\}$ be independent, identically distributed real random variables with the same cumulative distribution function $F(x)$. Then the empirical cumulative distribution function is defined as follows:

$$\hat{F}_n(x) = \frac{1}{n}\sum_{i=1}^{n}\mathbf{1}_{X_i \le x}$$

where $\mathbf{1}_A$ is the indicator of event A. It equals 1 when the condition or event is satisfied. In this case, the condition is $X_i \le x$. $\hat{F}_n(x)$ is an unbiased estimator for $F(x)$.

For example, in Figure 12-41, the smooth curve, which asymptotically approaches heights of 0 and 1 without reaching them, is the true cumulative distribution function of the standard normal distribution. The hash marks at the bottom represent the observations in a particular sample drawn from that distribution. The horizontal steps of the step function (including the leftmost point in each step but not including the rightmost point) form the empirical distribution function of that sample.

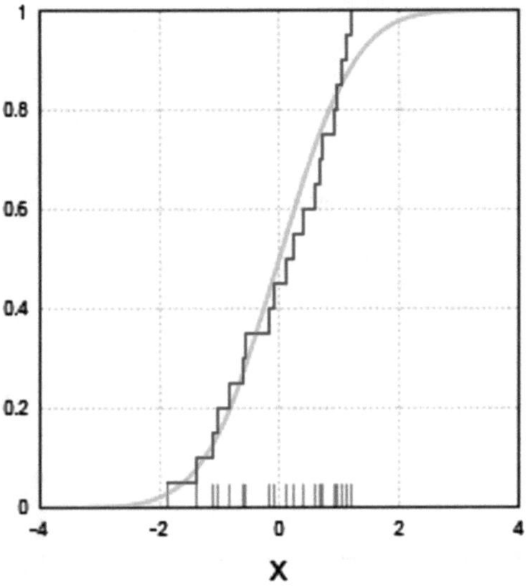

Figure 12-41. *An empirical distribution versus normal distribution*

The quantile function of an empirical distribution of sample size n is such that if nq is not an integer, then the q-th quantile is unique and is equal to the $\overline{nq}$ -th sample, where $\overline{nq}$ is the biggest integer less than or equal to nq.

$$Q(q) = x_{\overline{nq}}$$

If nq is an integer, then the q-th quantile is not unique and is any real number x such that:

$$x_{nq} < x < x_{nq+1}$$

The mean is an unbiased estimator of the mean of the population distribution:

$$\mathrm{E}_n(X) = \bar{x} = \frac{1}{n}\left(\sum_{i=1}^{n} x_i\right)$$

The variance is as follows:

$$\mathrm{Var}(X) = \frac{1}{n}\left(\sum_{i=1}^{n} (x_i - \bar{x})^2\right)$$

The skewness is the sample skewness.

The excess kurtosis is the sample excess kurtosis.

The NM Dev class EmpiricalDistribution computes the empirical distribution for a data set. Here's an example:

```
// the data set
val X: DoubleArray = doubleArrayOf(0.0, 1.0, 2.0, 3.0, 4.0, 5.0, 6.0, 7.0, 8.0, 99.0)
// construct the empirical distribution from the data set
val dist = EmpiricalDistribution(X)

println("mean = " + dist.mean())
println("variance = " + dist.variance())
println("skew = " + dist.skew())
println("kurtosis = " + dist.kurtosis())

println("")
val xs: DoubleArray = doubleArrayOf(0.0, 0.0001, 0.001, 0.01, 0.1, 1.0, 2.0, 3.0)
for (x in xs) {
    println(String.format("F(%f) = %f", x, dist.cdf(x)))
}
for (x in xs) {
    println(String.format("f(%f) = %f", x, dist.density(x)))
}

var allEquals: Boolean = true
var u: Double = 0.1
while(u < 1.0) {
    val x: Double = dist.quantile(u)
    val y: Double = dist.cdf(x)
    if (abs(u - y) > 1e-9) {
        allEquals = false
    }

    u += 0.1
}

println("\nF(Q(u)) = u for all u = " + allEquals)
```

The output is as follows:

```
mean = 13.5
variance = 909.1666666666666
skew = 2.2456049365721427
kurtosis = 3.478017579042259
F(0.000000) = 0.100000
F(0.000100) = 0.100000
F(0.001000) = 0.100000
F(0.010000) = 0.100000
F(0.100000) = 0.100000
F(1.000000) = 0.200000
F(2.000000) = 0.300000
F(3.000000) = 0.400000
f(0.000000) = 0.100000
```

```
f(0.000100) = 0.000000
f(0.001000) = 0.000000
f(0.010000) = 0.000000
f(0.100000) = 0.000000
f(1.000000) = 0.100000
f(2.000000) = 0.100000
f(3.000000) = 0.100000
F(Q(u)) = u for all u = true
```

12.4. Multivariate Probability Distributions

Given multiple random variables $\{X_1, \cdots, X_n\}$ that are defined on a probability space, the joint probability distribution for them is a probability distribution that gives the probability that each of X_i falls in any particular range or discrete set of values specified for that variable, $P(X_1 \in x_1, \cdots, X_n \in x_n)$. In the case of only two discrete random variables X and Y, it is the probability that $X = x_1$ taking a certain value and $Y = y_1$ taking a certain value at the same time. This is called a bivariate distribution, but the concept generalizes to any number of random variables and continuous variables, giving a multivariate probability distribution.

The joint probability distribution can be expressed either in terms of a joint cumulative distribution function or in terms of a joint probability density function (in the case of continuous variables) or a joint probability mass function (in the case of discrete variables, see Section 12.3.3.4).

These in turn can be used to find two other types of distributions. The marginal distribution gives the probabilities for any one variable in a specific range while the others can take any values. The conditional probability distribution gives the probabilities for any subset of the variables conditional on the other variables taking particular values.

For example, suppose that each of two urns contains twice as many red balls as blue balls. Suppose also that one ball is randomly selected from each urn, with the two draws being independent of each other. Let A and B be discrete random variables associated with the outcomes of the draw from the first urn and second urn, respectively. The probability of drawing a red ball from either of the urns is 2/3, and the probability of drawing a blue ball is 1/3. The joint probability distribution is presented in the following table:

	A = Red	A = Blue	P(B), marginal
B = Red	(2/3) (2/3)=4/9	(1/3) (2/3)=2/9	4/9+2/9=2/3
B = Blue	(2/3) (1/3)=2/9	(1/3) (1/3)=1/9	2/9+1/9=1/3
P(A), marginal	4/9+2/9=2/3	2/9+1/9=1/3	

Each of the four inner cells shows the probability of a particular combination of results from the two draws. The joint probability distribution is composed of these probabilities. In any one cell, the probability of a particular combination occurring is (since the draws are independent) the product of the probability of the specified result for A and the probability of the specified result for B. The probabilities in these four cells sum to 1, as it is always true for probability distribution.

Moreover, the final row and the final column give the marginal probability distribution for A and the marginal probability distribution for B, respectively. For example, for A the first of these cells gives the sum of the probabilities for A being red, regardless of what value B takes, as 2/3. Thus, the marginal probability distribution for A gives A's probabilities unconditional on B, in a margin of the table. Likewise, the marginal probability distribution for B being blue is 1/3 across over all values of A.

Mathematically, for n random variables $\{X_1, \cdots, X_n\}$ as a random vector $\boldsymbol{X} = (X_1, \cdots, X_n)^T$, the joint CDF is as follows:

$$F_{\boldsymbol{x}}(\boldsymbol{x}) = \mathrm{P}(X_1 \le x_1, \ldots, X_n \le x_n)$$

In the case of two random variables X and Y, the joint CDF simplifies to the following:

$$F_{X,Y}(x,y) = \mathrm{P}(X \le x, Y \le y)$$

The right-hand side represents the probability that the random variable X takes on a value less than or equal to x and that Y takes on a value less than or equal to y.

The joint probability density function for continuous random variables is defined as the partial derivative of the joint CDF with respect to all of the variables each once, as shown here:

$$f_{\boldsymbol{x}}(\boldsymbol{x}) = \frac{\partial^n F_{\boldsymbol{x}}(\boldsymbol{x})}{\partial x_1 \ldots \partial x_n}$$

In the case of two random variables X and Y, the joint PDF simplifies to the following:

$$f_{X,Y}(x,y) = \frac{\partial^2 F_{X,Y}(x,y)}{\partial x \partial y}$$

This equals the following:

$$f_{X,Y}(x,y) = f_{Y|X}(y \mid x) f_X(x) = f_{X|Y}(x \mid y) f_Y(y)$$

$f_{Y|X}(y \mid x)$ is the conditional PDF of Y given X. $f_X(x)$ is the marginal PDF of X. $f_{X|Y}(x \mid y)$ is the conditional PDF of X given Y. $f_Y(y)$ is the marginal PDF of Y.

It is important to distinguish between the joint probability distribution of X and Y (multivariate distribution) and the probability distribution of each variable individually (univariate distribution). The individual probability distribution of a random variable is referred to as its marginal probability distribution. In general, the marginal probability distribution of X can be determined from the joint probability distribution of X and other random variables. For example, if the joint probability density function of random variable X and Y is $f_{X,Y}(x, y)$, the marginal probability density function of X and Y, which defines the marginal distribution, is given by the following:

$$f_X(x) = \int f_{X,Y}(x,y)dy$$

$$f_Y(y) = \int f_{X,Y}(x,y)dx$$

The first integral is over all points in the range of (X, Y) for a particular $X = x$ summing up over all y. The second integral is over all points in the range of (X, Y) for which $Y = y$ summing up over all x.

For example, Figure 12-42 shows the random samples (black dots) drawn from a bivariate normal distribution. The marginal probability density functions are shown as well.

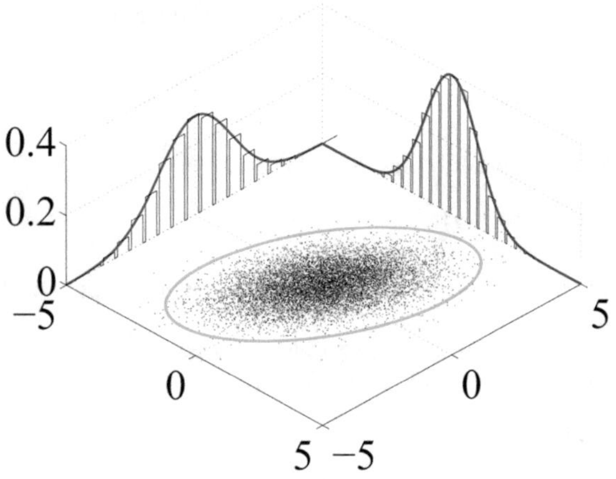

Figure 12-42. *Random samples from a bivariate normal distribution*

In NM Dev, an implementation for a univariate probability function inherits from the MultivariateProbabilityDistribution interface. Such an implementation specifies not only the CDF and the PDF but also the descriptive statistics, e.g., mean and variance, of the distribution, among other information. The signature is as follows:

```
public interface MultivariateProbabilityDistribution {
    /**
     * Gets the cumulative probability <i>F(x) = Pr(X &le; x)</i>.
     *
     * @param x <i>x</i>
     * @return <i>F(x) = Pr(X &le; x)</i>
     */
    public double cdf(Vector x);
    /**
     * The density function, which, if exists, is the derivative of <i>F</i>. It
     * describes the density of probability at each point in the sample space.
     * <blockquote><i>
     * f(x) = dF(X) / dx
     * </i></blockquote>
     * <em>This may not always exist.</em>
     * <p/>
     * For the discrete cases, this is the probability mass function. It gives
     * the probability that a discrete random variable is exactly equal to some
     * value.
     *
     * @param x <i>x</i>
     * @return <i>f(x)</i>
     */
    public double density(Vector x);
    /**
     * Gets the mean of this distribution.
     *
     * @return the mean
```

```
     */
    public Vector mean();
    /**
     * Gets the mode of this distribution.
     *
     * @return the mean
     */
    public Vector mode();
    /**
     * Gets the covariance matrix of this distribution.
     *
     * @return the covariance
     */
    public Matrix covariance();
    /**
     * Gets the entropy of this distribution.
     *
     * @return the entropy
     * @see
     * <a href="http://en.wikipedia.org/wiki/Information_entropy">Wikipedia:
     * Entropy
     * (information theory)</a>
     */
    public double entropy();
    /**
     * The moment generating function is the expected value of
     * <i>e<sup>tX</sup></i>. That is,
     * <blockquote><i>
     * E(e<sup>tX</sup>)
     * </i></blockquote>
     * <em>This may not always exist.</em>
     *
     * @param t <i>t</i>
     * @return <i>E(exp(tX))</i>
     * @see
     * <a href="http://en.wikipedia.org/wiki/Moment_generating_function">Wikipedia:
     * Moment-generating function</a>
     */
    public double moment(Vector t);
}
```

Note that for a multivariate distribution some member functions may not be supported.

12.4.1. Multivariate Normal Distribution

The multivariate normal distribution, multivariate Gaussian distribution, or joint normal distribution is a generalization of the one-dimensional (univariate) normal distribution to higher dimensions. It is often used to describe, at least approximately, any set of (possibly) correlated real-valued random variables, each of which clusters around a mean value.

A k-dimensional random vector $\boldsymbol{X} = (X_1, \cdots, X_k)^T$ is called a standard normal random vector if all of its components are independent standard normal with a zero mean and unit variance. That is, $X_i \sim N(0, 1)$ for all i.

A k-dimensional random vector $\boldsymbol{X} = (X_1, \cdots, X_k)^T$ has a multivariate normal distribution, denoted as $\boldsymbol{X} \sim N(\boldsymbol{\mu}, \Sigma)$, if and only if there exists a standard normal random vector $\boldsymbol{Z} \in \mathbb{R}^l$, a vector $\boldsymbol{\mu} \in \mathbb{R}^k$, and a matrix $\boldsymbol{A} \in \mathbb{R}^{k \times l}$ such that we have this:

$$\boldsymbol{X} = \boldsymbol{AZ} + \mu$$

The matrix $\Sigma = \boldsymbol{AA}^T$ is the covariance matrix of the random variables $\{X_i\}$.

It can be proven that if $\boldsymbol{X} \sim N(\boldsymbol{\mu}, \sigma)$, then every linear combination of its components, $Y = a_1 X_1 + \ldots + a_k X_k$, is normally distributed. That is, for any constant vector $\boldsymbol{a} \in \mathbb{R}^k$, the random variable $Y = \boldsymbol{a}^T \boldsymbol{X}$ has a univariate normal distribution.

The probability density function for a multivariate normal distribution, given the mean $\boldsymbol{\mu}$ and the positive-definite covariance matrix σ, is as follows:

$$f_X(\boldsymbol{x}) = \frac{1}{\sqrt{(2\pi)^k |\Sigma|}} \exp\left(-\frac{1}{2}(\boldsymbol{x} - \mu)^T \Sigma^{-1} (\boldsymbol{x} - \mu)\right)$$

The previous equation reduces to that of the univariate normal distribution if $\sum$ is a 1×1 matrix (i.e., a single real number).

In the case of two random variables X and Y, the joint PDF of a vector $[XY]^T$ is as follows:

$$f(x,y) = \frac{1}{2\pi\sigma_X\sigma_Y\sqrt{1-\rho^2}} \exp\left(-\frac{1}{2(1-\rho^2)}\left[\left(\frac{x-\mu_X}{\sigma_X}\right)^2 - 2\rho\left(\frac{x-\mu_X}{\sigma_X}\right)\left(\frac{y-\mu_Y}{\sigma_Y}\right) + \left(\frac{y-\mu_Y}{\sigma_Y}\right)^2\right]\right) \quad \text{(V)}$$

where ρ is the correlation between X and Y and where $\sigma_X > 0$ and $\sigma_Y > 0$. In terms of the more general multivariate normal PDF, we have this:

$$\mu = \begin{pmatrix} \mu_X \\ \mu_Y \end{pmatrix} \text{ and } \Sigma = \begin{pmatrix} \sigma_X^2 & \rho\sigma_X\sigma_Y \\ \rho\sigma_X\sigma_Y & \sigma_Y^2 \end{pmatrix}$$

For example, Figure 12-43 shows sample points from a bivariate normal distribution with the following:

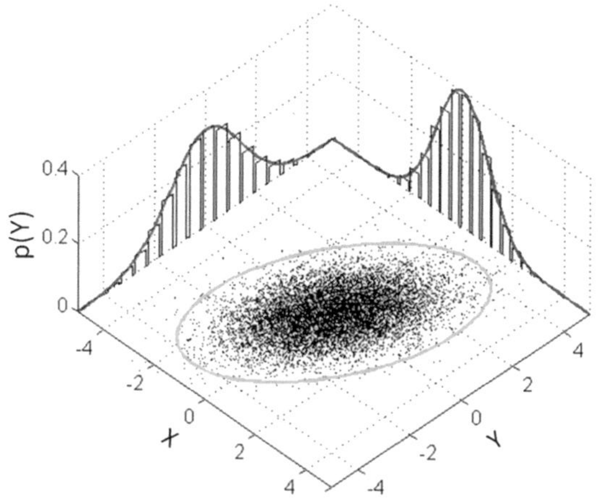

***Figure 12-43.** A bivariate normal distribution*

$$\mu = \begin{pmatrix} 0 \\ 0 \end{pmatrix} \text{ and } \Sigma = \begin{pmatrix} 1 & 0.6 \\ 0.6 & 1 \end{pmatrix}$$

The two marginal distributions, the one-dimensional histograms, and the three-sigma ellipse are also shown.

The mean is as follows:

$$\mathrm{E}(\boldsymbol{X}) = \mu$$

The variance is as follows:

$$\mathrm{Var}(\boldsymbol{X}) = \Sigma$$

The moment-generating function is as follows:

$$M_X(t) = \exp\left(\mu^T \boldsymbol{t} + \frac{1}{2}\boldsymbol{t}^T \Sigma \boldsymbol{t}\right)$$

The NM Dev class `MultivariateNormalDistribution` implements the multivariate normal distribution. Here's an example:

```
println("Construct a 3-dimensional multivariate standard normal distribution")
val mvnorm1 = MultivariateNormalDistribution(
            3 // dimension
    )
println("mean = " + mvnorm1.mean())
println("variance = " + mvnorm1.covariance())

println("")
var x1: Vector = DenseVector(0.0, 0.0, 0.0)
println(String.format("f(%s) = %f", x1, mvnorm1.density(x1)))
x1 = DenseVector(1.0, 0.0, 0.0)
println(String.format("f(%s) = %f", x1, mvnorm1.density(x1)))
```

```
x1 = DenseVector(0.0, 0.5, 0.0)
println(String.format("f(%s) = %f", x1, mvnorm1.density(x1)))
x1 = DenseVector(0.0, 0.0, 0.3)
println(String.format("f(%s) = %f", x1, mvnorm1.density(x1)))
x1 = DenseVector(1.0, 0.5, 0.0)
println(String.format("f(%s) = %f", x1, mvnorm1.density(x1)))
x1 = DenseVector(0.0, 0.5, 0.3)
println(String.format("f(%s) = %f", x1, mvnorm1.density(x1)))
x1 = DenseVector(1.0, 0.0, 0.3)
println(String.format("f(%s) = %f", x1, mvnorm1.density(x1)))
x1 = DenseVector(1.0, 0.5, 0.3)
println(String.format("f(%s) = %f", x1, mvnorm1.density(x1)))
```

The output is as follows:

```
mean = [0.000000, 0.000000, 0.000000]
variance = 3x3
        [,1] [,2] [,3]
[1,] 1.000000, 0.000000, 0.000000,
[2,] 0.000000, 1.000000, 0.000000,
[3,] 0.000000, 0.000000, 1.000000,
f([0.000000, 0.000000, 0.000000] ) = 0.063494
f([1.000000, 0.000000, 0.000000] ) = 0.038511
f([0.000000, 0.500000, 0.000000] ) = 0.056033
f([0.000000, 0.000000, 0.300000] ) = 0.060700
f([1.000000, 0.500000, 0.000000] ) = 0.033986
f([0.000000, 0.500000, 0.300000] ) = 0.053567
f([1.000000, 0.000000, 0.300000] ) = 0.036816
f([1.000000, 0.500000, 0.300000] ) = 0.032490
```

```
println("Construct a 2-dimensional multivariate normal distribution")
val mu: DenseVector = DenseVector(1.0, 2.0)
val sigma: DenseMatrix = DenseMatrix(arrayOf(doubleArrayOf(4.0, 2.0),
doubleArrayOf(2.0, 3.0)))
val mvnorm2 = MultivariateNormalDistribution(mu, sigma)

println("\nmean = " + mvnorm2.mean()) // same as mu
println("\nvariance = " + mvnorm2.covariance()) // same as sigma

var x2: Vector = DenseVector(0.3, 0.4)
println(String.format("f(%s) = %f", x2, mvnorm2.density(x2)))
x2 = DenseVector(0.4, 0.3)
println(String.format("f(%s) = %f", x2, mvnorm2.density(x2)))
```

The output is as follows:

```
construct a 2-dimensional multivariate normal distribution
mean = [1.000000, 2.000000]
variance = 2x2
        [,1] [,2]
```

```
[1,] 4.000000, 2.000000,
[2,] 2.000000, 3.000000,
f([0.300000, 0.400000] ) = 0.035812
f([0.400000, 0.300000] ) = 0.032955
```

12.4.2. Multivariate T-Distribution

The multivariate t-distribution is a generalization of the one-dimensional (univariate) t-distribution to higher dimensions. For a p dimension t-distribution, suppose $\boldsymbol{y} \sim N(\mathbf{0}, \Sigma)$ is a multivariate normal, $u \sim \chi^2_\upsilon$ is a Chi-square of υ degrees of freedom, and we have a $p \times p$ positive-definite scale matrix Σ such that $\frac{\boldsymbol{y}}{\sqrt{u/\upsilon}} = \boldsymbol{x} - \mu$, then the random vector $\boldsymbol{x}$ has a multivariate t-distribution.

The PDF is as follows:

$$f(\boldsymbol{x}|\upsilon,\mu,\Sigma) = \frac{\Gamma\left(\frac{\upsilon+p}{2}\right)}{\Gamma\left(\frac{\upsilon}{2}\right)\upsilon^{\frac{p}{2}}\pi^{\frac{p}{2}}|\Sigma|^{\frac{1}{2}}}\left[1+\frac{1}{\upsilon}(\boldsymbol{x}-\mu)^T\Sigma^{-1}(\boldsymbol{x}-\mu)\right]^{-\frac{\upsilon+p}{2}}$$

The mean is as follows:

$$E(\boldsymbol{X}) = \boldsymbol{\mu},\ \upsilon > 1;\ \text{else undefined}$$

The variance is as follows:

$$\text{Var}(\boldsymbol{X}) = \frac{\upsilon}{\upsilon-2}\Sigma,\ \upsilon > 2;\ \text{else undefined}$$

The skewness is 0.

The NM Dev class `MultivariateTDistribution` implements the multivariate t-distribution. Here's an example:

```
val p = 2 // dimension
val mu: Vector = DenseVector(1.0, 2.0) // mean
val Sigma: Matrix = DenseMatrix(p, p).ONE() // scale matrix

var v = 1 // degree of freedom
var t = MultivariateTDistribution(v, mu, Sigma)
var x: Vector = DenseVector(1.23, 4.56)
println(String.format("f(%s) = %f", x, t.density(x)))

v = 2
t = MultivariateTDistribution(v, mu, Sigma)
x = DenseVector(1.23, 4.56)
println(String.format("f(%s) = %f", x, t.density(x)))

v = 3
t = MultivariateTDistribution(v, mu, Sigma)
x = DenseVector(1.23, 4.56)
println(String.format("f(%s) = %f", x, t.density(x)))
```

```
v = 4
t = MultivariateTDistribution(v, mu, Sigma)
x = DenseVector(1.23, 4.56)
println(String.format("f(%s) = %f", x, t.density(x)))

v = 5
t = MultivariateTDistribution(v, mu, Sigma)
x = DenseVector(1.23, 4.56)
println(String.format("f(%s) = %f", x, t.density(x)))

v = 6
t = MultivariateTDistribution(v, mu, Sigma)
x = DenseVector(1.23, 4.56)
println(String.format("f(%s) = %f", x, t.density(x)))
```

The output is as follows:

```
f([1.230000, 4.560000] ) = 0.007587
f([1.230000, 4.560000] ) = 0.008595
f([1.230000, 4.560000] ) = 0.008674
f([1.230000, 4.560000] ) = 0.008537
f([1.230000, 4.560000] ) = 0.008351
f([1.230000, 4.560000] ) = 0.008167
```

12.4.3. Multivariate Beta Distribution

The multivariate beta distribution, often known as Dirichlet distribution, is a generalization of the one-dimensional (univariate) beta distribution to higher dimensions. Its probability density function returns the belief that the probabilities of K rival events are x_i given that each event has been observed a_i times.

The Dirichlet distribution of order $K \geq 2$ with parameters $a_1, \ldots, a_K$ has a probability density function, as shown here:

$$f\left(x_1,\ldots|x_K, a_1,\ldots,a_K\right) = \frac{1}{B(\boldsymbol{a})}\prod_{i=1}^{K} x_i^{a_i - 1}$$

with $\sum_{i=1}^{K} x_i = 1$ and $x_i \geq 0$ for all i.

The normalizing constant is the multivariate beta function, which can be expressed in terms of the gamma function, as shown here:

$$B(\boldsymbol{a}) = \frac{\prod_{i=1}^{K}\Gamma(a_i)}{\Gamma\left(\sum_{i=1}^{K} a_i\right)}$$

Figure 12-44 shows an example.

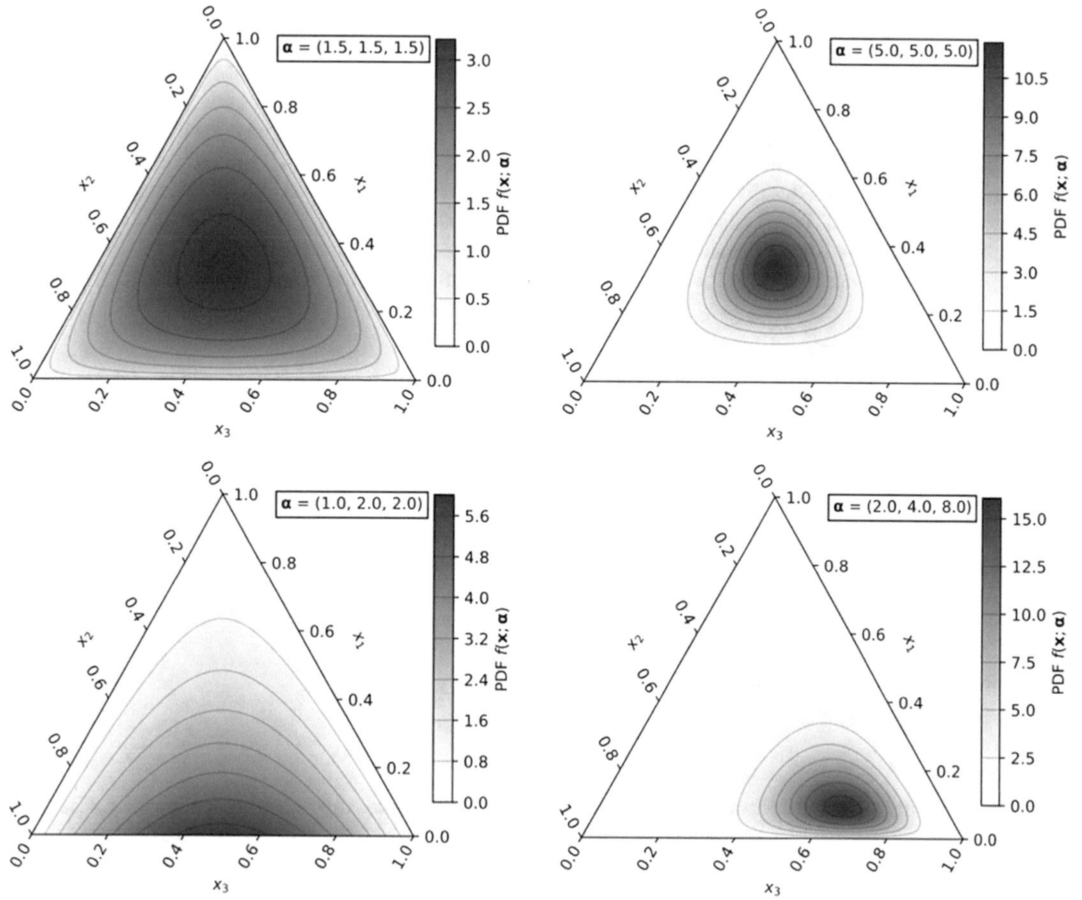

***Figure 12-44.** Probability density functions for Dirichlet distributions*

The NM Dev class `DirichletDistribution` implements the Dirichlet distribution. Here's an example:

```
// the parameters
val a: DoubleArray = doubleArrayOf(1.0, 2.0, 3.0, 4.0, 5.0)
val dist = DirichletDistribution(a)
val x: Vector = DenseVector(0.1, 0.2, 0.3, 0.2, 0.2)
println(String.format("f(%s) = %f", x, dist.density(x)))
```

The output is as follows:

```
f([0.100000, 0.200000, 0.300000, 0.200000, 0.200000] ) = 69.742633
```

12.4.4. Multinomial Distribution

The multinomial distribution is a generalization of the binomial distribution to higher dimensions. While the binomial distribution gives the probabilities of numbers of successes (and failures) in a series of binary outcome experiments, the multinomial distribution gives the probabilities of counts for each of the k-sided die rolled n times. In other words, for n independent trials each of which leads to a success for exactly one of k categories, with each category having a given fixed success probability, the multinomial distribution gives the probability of any particular combination of numbers of successes for the various categories. When k is 2 and n is 1, the multinomial distribution is the Bernoulli distribution. When k is 2 and n is bigger than 1, it is the binomial distribution. When k is bigger than 2 and n is 1, it is the categorical distribution.

Mathematically, we have k possible mutually exclusive outcomes, with corresponding probabilities $p_1, \ldots, p_k$ and n independent trials. Since the k outcomes are mutually exclusive and one must occur, we have $p_i \geq 0$ for $i = 1, \ldots, k$ and $\sum_{i=1}^{k} p_i = 1$.

If the random variables $\{X_i\}$ indicate the number of times the i-th outcome is observed over the n trials, the random vector $X = (X_1, \ldots, X_k)^T$ follows a multinomial distribution with parameters n and p, where $p = (p_1, \ldots, p_k)$. While the trials are independent, their outcomes X are dependent because they must be summed to n, $\sum_{i=1}^{k} x_i = n$.

The multinomial distribution is a discrete probability distribution. The probability mass function describes the joint probability of the k events happening at the same time.

$$p_{X_1,\ldots,X_k}(x_1,\ldots,x_k) = \mathrm{P}(X_1 = x_1 \wedge \ldots \wedge X_k = x_k)$$

The sum of all outcomes equals 1.

$$\sum_i \sum_j \ldots \sum_n \mathrm{P}(X_1 = x_{1i},\ldots,X_k = x_{kn}) = 1$$

The probability mass function of this multinomial distribution gives the probability of picking n balls of k different colors from a bag, replacing the extracted balls after each draw. Balls of the same color are equivalent.

$$f(x_1,\ldots|x_k,n,p_1,\ldots,p_k) = \mathrm{P}(X_1 = x_1,\ldots,X_k = x_k)$$

$$= \frac{n!}{x_1!\ldots x_k!} p_1^{x_1} \times \ldots \times p_k^{x_k}$$

The mean is as follows:

$$\mathrm{E}(X_i) = np_i$$

The variances and covariances are as follows:

$$\mathrm{Var}(X_i) = np_i(1 - p_i)$$

$$\mathrm{cov}(X_i,X_j) = -np_i p_j, i \neq j$$

The moment-generating function is as follows:

$$M_X(t) = \left(\sum_{i=1}^{k} p_i e^{t_i}\right)^n$$

Suppose we drop 100 balls into 3 bins, each bin with a probability of success of 0.1, 0.2, and 0.7, respectively. The probability of having 10, 20, and 70 in each bin is 0.013279. See Figure 12-45.

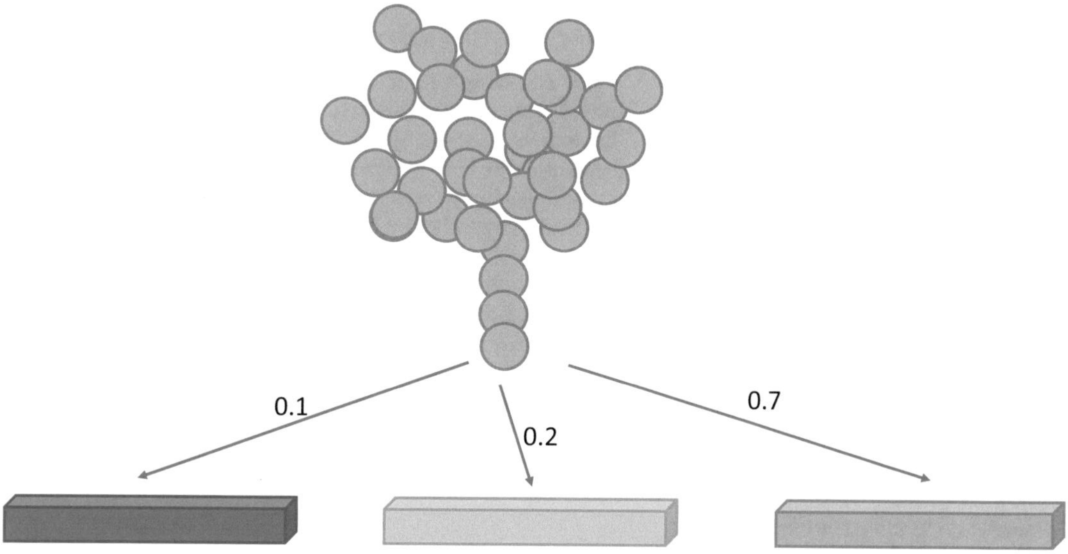

Figure 12-45. *Multinomial distribution, k = 3, n = 100*

The NM Dev class `MultinomialDistribution` implements the multinomial distribution. The following code implements the previous example:

```
// k = 3, each of the 3 probabilities of success
val prob: DoubleArray = doubleArrayOf(0.1, 0.2, 0.7)
val n = 100
var dist = MultinomialDistribution(n, prob[0])

// an outcome of the n trials
val x: Vector = DenseVector(10.0, 20.0, 70.0)
println(String.format("f(%s) = %f", x, dist.density(x)))
```

The output is as follows:

```
f([10.000000, 20.000000, 70.000000] ) = 0.013279
```

12.5. Hypothesis Testing

A statistical hypothesis test is a method of statistical inference. Hypothesis testing is used to assess whether the sample data supports an interpretation of the data that we call a hypothesis. A hypothesis is Boolean, either yes or no. For example, we may want to test the following:

- The data has a normal distribution.
- An assumption regarding a population parameter is true.
- Two samples were drawn from the same underlying population distribution.

The idea behind hypothesis testing is to assess, assuming that the (null) hypothesis is true, how likely we are to observe the data. If that likelihood is low, we say that the results are statistically significant enough to "reject the null hypothesis." Otherwise, we "fail to reject the null hypothesis." Statistical inference provides an alternative method to "prove" something. We may not be able to prove the existence of God using deductive logic step by step from a set of axioms until reaching a conclusion. We can prove the existence of God statistically. At the least, we can fail to reject the null hypothesis of the existence of God.

Passing a hypothesis test does not mean that the null hypothesis is true. It only means that there is not sufficient evidence to say that it is likely false. The results are not statistically significant. In fact, there are two types of inference errors that we can make using hypothesis testing. A Type I error is when the null hypothesis is indeed true but we reject it. It is also known as a false positive. That would be the case if our observations are extreme (unlikely but yet happened). A Type II error is when the null hypothesis is false, but we fail to reject it. It is also known as a false negative. For example, a medicine is ineffective, but we consider it OK according to the data.

For another example, suppose we suspect that a coin is biased, landing fewer heads than a 50 percent chance when spinning. To test this suspicion, we run an experiment to spin the coin 100 times to get 37 heads and 63 tails. The observed proportion of heads is $\frac{37}{100} = 37 \text{ percent}$. We have two possible explanations for the data.

- Null hypothesis (H_0): The data is merely a reflection of chance variation. The probability of heads when spinning the coin is really $p = 0.5$.
- Alternative hypothesis (H_1) as follows: The probability of heads when the coin is spun is really $p < 0.5$.

Note that the null hypothesis and the alternative hypothesis must be mutually exclusive. If we fail to reject the null hypothesis, we will accept the alternative to explain the data.

Let's answer the question "Does the null hypothesis support a reasonable explanation of the data?" First, we need to design a test statistic to measure the difference between the data and what is expected assuming that the null hypothesis is true. In our example, if the null hypothesis is true, the number of heads (and hence the proportion of heads) has the binomial distribution with $p = 0.5$ and $\upsilon = 100$. The standard deviation of this distribution equals 0.05. It can be computed using the following code:

```
val n = 100
val dist2 = BinomialDistribution(
        n,
        0.5 // p
)
val stdev: Double = sqrt(dist2.variance()) / n
println("standard deviation = " + stdev)
```

The output is as follows:

```
standard deviation = 0.05
```

The standardized z-score of the difference in the observed proportion (37 percent) and the true proportion (50 percent) is therefore as follows:

$$z = \frac{0.37 - 0.5}{0.05} = -2.6$$

We can see that if the null hypothesis is true, then this z-score is unusually negative, on the extreme side of the normal distribution. Reading off the standard normal CDF, the probability of the z-score being –2.6 is 0.004661188023718749 (p-value), less than a 0.5 percent chance of happening. This code computes the z-score and p-value.

```
val z_score: Double = (0.37 - 0.5) / stdev
println("z-score = " + z_score)
val p_value: Double = NormalDistribution() // default ctor for standard normal distribution
        .cdf(z_score)
println("p-value = " + p_value)
```

The output is as follows:

```
z-score = -2.6
p-value = 0.004661188023718749
```

In other words, if the null hypothesis is true, the probability of us observing the data (37 percent of heads) is unlikely to happen. The null hypothesis provides a poor explanation for our data. Therefore, we reject the null hypothesis and accept the alternative hypothesis. It may actually be the case that this coin is a biased coin and spinning it has less than a 50 percent chance of landing heads. See Figure 12-46.

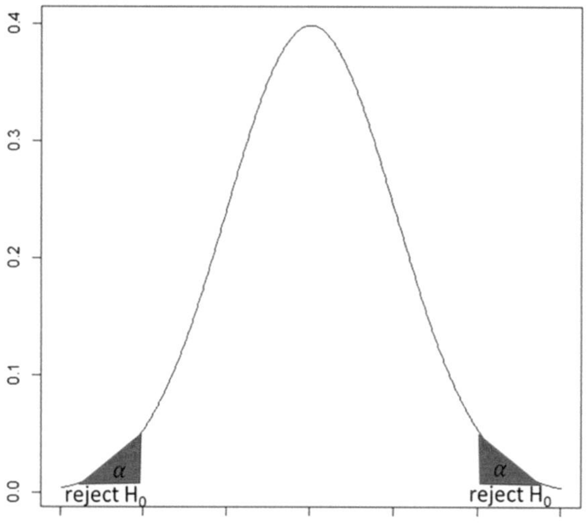

Figure 12-46. *Hypothesis testing rejection regions*

This example illustrates the general procedure of doing hypothesis testing. The six steps are as follows:

1. Collect data and/or run experiments.
2. State the null hypothesis (H_0) and alternative hypothesis (H_1). The null hypothesis itself does not involve the data. It is a statement about a parameter or numerical characteristic of the population. We test for the validity of that parameter. The alternative hypothesis is the mutually exclusive negated version of the null hypothesis.
3. Design an appropriate test and the test statistic T. Derive the distribution of the test statistic under the null hypothesis and the assumptions. Normal distribution and t-distribution are commonly used.
4. Select a significance level, α, which is a probability threshold below which the null hypothesis will be rejected. Common values are 5 percent (statistically significant) and 1 percent (statistically very significant).
5. Compute from the observations the observed value $\hat{t}$ of the test statistic T. Calculate the p-value. This is the probability, under the null hypothesis, of sampling a test statistic at least as extreme as that which was observed (the maximal probability of that event).
6. Reject the null hypothesis, in favor of the alternative hypothesis, if and only if the p-value is less than (or equal to) the significance level threshold α. See Figure 12-47.

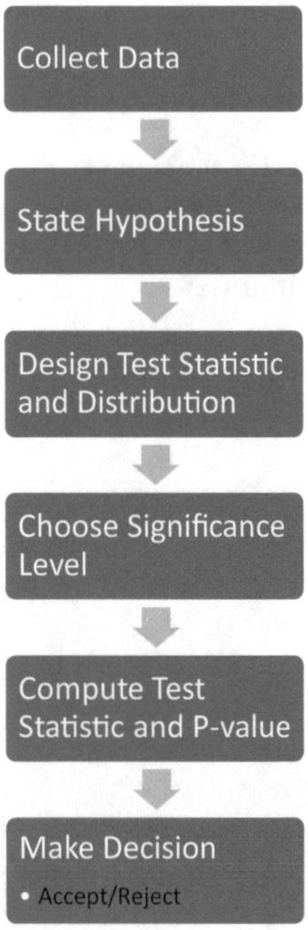

Figure 12-47. *Hypothesis testing steps*

NM Dev provides a wide range of hypothesis tests for testing population distribution, testing population parameters, and comparing underlying population distributions. All hypothesis test implementations extend this abstract class `HypothesisTest`. The signature is as follows:

```
public abstract class HypothesisTest {
    /**
     * Get the test statistics.
     *
     * @return the test statistics
     * @see <a href="http://en.wikipedia.org/wiki/Test_statistic">Wikipedia:
     * Test statistic</a>
     */
    public abstract double statistics();
    /**
     * Get the p-value for the test statistics.
     *
     * @return the p-value
     * @see <a href="http://en.wikipedia.org/wiki/P-value">Wikipedia:
     * P-value</a>
     */
    public abstract double pValue();
    /**
     * Get a description of the null hypothesis.
     *
     * @see <a href="http://en.wikipedia.org/wiki/Null_hypothesis">Wikipedia:
     * Null hypothesis</a>
     *
     * @return the null hypothesis description
     */
    public abstract String getNullHypothesis();
    /**
     * Get the description of the alternative hypothesis.
     *
     * @return the alternative hypothesis description
     * @see
     * <a href="http://en.wikipedia.org/wiki/Alternative_hypothesis">Wikipedia:
     * Alternative hypothesis</a>
     */
    public abstract String getAlternativeHypothesis();
    /**
     * Get the number of groups of observations.
     *
     * @return the number of groups of observations
     */
    public int nGroups() {
        return k;
    }
    /**
     * Get the total number of observations.
     *
     * @return the total number of observations
```

```
     */
    public int nObs() {
        return N;
    }
    /**
     * Use the p-value to check whether the null hypothesis can be rejected for
     * a given significance level. That is, the probability of making the
     * observations under the null is small.
     *
     * @param alpha a significance level of test
     * @return {@code true} if the hypothesis is rejected due to <i>p-value <
     *         &alpha;</i>
     */
    public boolean isNullRejected(double alpha) {
        return pValue() < alpha;
    }
    /**
     * The one-sided p-value is the probability of observing a test statistic
     * <em>at least</em> as extreme as the one observed. For a continuous
     * distribution, it is given by the complementary cumulative distribution
     * function (survival function). For a discrete distribution, we need to add
     * also the probability of observing the critical value.
     *
     * @param F a univariate distribution
     * @param x the critical value
     * @return the p-value for the critical value
     */
    public static double oneSidedPvalue(ProbabilityDistribution F, double x) {
        if (F instanceof EmpiricalDistribution) {
            return 1.0 - F.cdf(x) + F.density(x);
        }
        return 1.0 - F.cdf(x);
    }
}
```

12.5.1. Distribution Tests

NM Dev supports a large range of hypothesis tests to assess whether a data sample comes from a particular distribution, e.g., normal distribution, or whether two samples have the same underlying population distribution.

Normality Test

There are a number of hypothesis tests to assess whether a sample has the normal distribution. They have different powers and limitations such as upper sample size.

Shapiro-Wilk Test

The best test of normality is the Shapiro-Wilk test for a sample size up to 5,000 data point and not to have too many identical values. The Shapiro-Wilk test tests the null hypothesis that a sample $\{x_1, \ldots, x_n\}$ comes from a normally distributed population. The test statistic is as follows:

$$W = \frac{\left(\sum_{i=i}^{n} a_i x_{(i)}\right)^2}{\sum_{i=1}^{n} (x_i - \overline{x})^2}$$

where $x_{(i)}$ (with parentheses enclosing the subscript index i; not to be confused with x_i) is the i-th order statistics. To find the order statistics, we need to sort the samples and find the i-th smallest number in the samples. $\overline{x}$ is the sample mean.

The coefficients a_i are given as follows:

$$(a_1, \ldots, a_n) = \frac{m^T V^{-1}}{C}$$

where C is a vector norm, as shown here:

$$C = \| V^{-1} m \| = \left(m^T V^{-1} V^{-1} m\right)^{\frac{1}{2}}$$

The vector m is made of the expected values of the order statistics of independent and identically distributed random variables sampled from the standard normal distribution. V is the covariance matrix of those normal order statistics.

W follows the Shapiro-Wilk distribution as implemented in ALGORITHM AS R94 (Anon., 1995).

The NM Dev class `ShapiroWilk` implements the Shapiro-Wilk test. Here's an example:

```
val sample: DoubleArray = doubleArrayOf(-1.7, -1.0, -1.0, -0.73, -0.61, -0.5, -0.24, 0.45,
0.62, 0.81, 1.0, 5.0)
val test = ShapiroWilk(sample)
println("H0: " + test.getNullHypothesis())
println("H1: " + test.getAlternativeHypothesis())
println("test statistics = " + test.statistics())
println("p-value = " + test.pValue())
println("is null rejected at 5% = " + test.isNullRejected(0.05))
```

The output is as follows:

```
H0: the samples come from a normally distributed population
H1: the samples do not come from a normally distributed population
test statistics = 0.7818521311977514
p-value = 0.005868730248429044
is null rejected at 5% = true
```

The null hypothesis is rejected at 5 percent for this sample. The alternative hypothesis that the sample does not have a normal distribution is accepted instead.

Jarque-Bera Test

The Jarque-Bera test is a goodness-of-fit test of whether sample data has the skewness and kurtosis matching a normal distribution. The normal distribution has both skewness and excess kurtosis equal to zero. If either is far from zero, it signals that the data does not have a normal distribution.

The test statistic *JB* is defined as follows:

$$JB = \frac{n}{6}\left(S^2 + \frac{1}{4}(K-3)^2\right)$$

where n is the number of observations (or degrees of freedom in general), S is the sample skewness, and K is the sample kurtosis.

If the data comes from a normal distribution, the *JB* statistic asymptotically has a Chi-square distribution with two degrees of freedom, so the statistic can be used to test the hypothesis that the data is from a normal distribution. The null hypothesis is a joint hypothesis of the skewness being zero, and the excess kurtosis is zero. As the definition of *JB* shows, any deviation from this increases the JB statistic.

For small samples the Chi-square approximation is overly sensitive, often rejecting the null hypothesis when it is true. Furthermore, the distribution of p-values departs from a uniform distribution and becomes a right-skewed unimodal distribution, especially for small p-values. This leads to a large Type I error rate. There are more powerful tests for normality.

The NM Dev class `JarqueBera` implements the Jarque-Bera test. Here's an example:

```
val samples: DoubleArray = doubleArrayOf(
    39.0, 35.0, 33.0, 33.0, 32.0, 30.0, 30.0, 30.0, 28.0, 28.0,
    27.0, 27.0, 27.0, 27.0, 27.0, 26.0, 26.0, 26.0, 26.0, 26.0,
    26.0, 25.0, 25.0, 25.0, 25.0, 25.0, 25.0, 24.0, 24.0, 24.0,
    24.0, 24.0, 23.0, 23.0, 23.0, 23.0, 23.0, 23.0, 23.0, 23.0,
    23.0, 23.0, 23.0, 23.0, 23.0, 22.0, 22.0, 22.0, 22.0, 21.0,
    21.0, 21.0, 21.0, 21.0, 21.0, 21.0, 20.0, 20.0, 19.0, 19.0,
    18.0, 16.0
)
val test = JarqueBera(
        samples,
        false // not using the exact Jarque-Bera distribution
)
println("H0: " + test.getNullHypothesis())
println("H1: " + test.getAlternativeHypothesis())
println("test statistics = " + test.statistics())
println("p-value = " + test.pValue())
println("is null rejected at 5% = " + test.isNullRejected(0.05))
```

The output is as follows:

```
H0: both the skewness and the excess kurtosis are 0
H1: either the skewness or the excess kurtosis is non-zero
test statistics = 18.957211215941424
p-value = 7.647049269299266E-5
is null rejected at 5% = true
```

D'Agostino Test

The D'Agostino test is a more powerful test than Jarque-Bera to test for normality. It is also a goodness-of-fit measure of departure from normality. The test is based on transformations of the sample kurtosis and skewness. It combines a skewness test and a kurtosis test. The skewness test determines whether the skewness of the data is statistically different from zero. The test statistics is z_s^2. Likewise, this kurtosis test determines whether the excess kurtosis of the data is statistically different from zero. The test statistics is z_k^2. The D'Agostino test is based on the fact that when the data is normally distributed the test statistic $T = z_s^2 + z_k^2$ has a Chi-square distribution with 2 degrees of freedom. This test should generally not be used for data sets with less than 20 elements. The null hypothesis is as follows: both the skewness and the excess kurtosis are 0. The alternative hypothesis is as follows: either the skewness or the excess kurtosis is nonzero.

The NM Dev class DAgostino implements the D'Agostino test. Here's an example:

```
val samples: DoubleArray = doubleArrayOf(
    39.0, 35.0, 33.0, 33.0, 32.0, 30.0, 30.0, 30.0, 28.0, 28.0,
    27.0, 27.0, 27.0, 27.0, 27.0, 26.0, 26.0, 26.0, 26.0, 26.0,
    26.0, 25.0, 25.0, 25.0, 25.0, 25.0, 25.0, 24.0, 24.0, 24.0,
    24.0, 24.0, 23.0, 23.0, 23.0, 23.0, 23.0, 23.0, 23.0, 23.0,
    23.0, 23.0, 23.0, 23.0, 23.0, 22.0, 22.0, 22.0, 22.0, 21.0,
    21.0, 21.0, 21.0, 21.0, 21.0, 21.0, 20.0, 20.0, 19.0, 19.0,
    18.0, 16.0
)
val test = DAgostino(samples)
println("H0: " + test.getNullHypothesis())
println("H1: " + test.getAlternativeHypothesis())
println("skewness test statistics " + test.Z1())
println("p-value for skewness test = " + test.pvalueZ1())
println("kurtosis test statistics " + test.Z2())
println("test statistics = " + test.statistics())
println("p-value = " + test.pValue())
println("is null rejected at 5% = " + test.isNullRejected(0.05))
```

The output is as follows:

```
H0: both the skewness and the excess kurtosis are 0
H1: either the skewness or the excess kurtosis is non-zero
skewness test statistics 3.1816798934083783
p-value for skewness test = 0.001464235568704897
kurtosis test statistics 2.328055257751046
test statistics = 15.542928227261438
p-value = 4.2159555092358136E-4
is null rejected at 5% = true
```

Lilliefors Test

The Lilliefors test tests the null hypothesis that data comes from a normally distributed population with an estimated sample mean and variance. The test statistic is the maximal absolute difference between an empirical distribution and a hypothetical normal distribution. Since the hypothesized CDF is using the mean and variance estimations based on the data, the "null distribution" of the test statistic, i.e., its probability distribution assuming the null hypothesis is true, is stochastically smaller than it would have been if the null hypothesis had singled out just one normal distribution (the reason for the Lilliefors distribution).

The test proceeds as follows:

1. First, estimate the population mean and population variance based on the data.
2. Then, find the maximum discrepancy between the empirical distribution function and the cumulative distribution function of the normal distribution with the estimated mean and estimated variance.
3. Finally, assess whether the maximum discrepancy is large enough to be statistically significant, thus rejecting the null hypothesis. We use the Lilliefors distribution for the cutoff regions.

The NM Dev class `Lilliefors` implements the Lilliefors test. In this implementation, we first compute the p-value using the formula in Dallal & Wilkinson (1986), which is claimed reliable only when the p-value is smaller than 0.1. When this p-value is bigger than 0.1, we compute again the p-value using the distribution of the modified statistic (Stephens, 1974). Here's an example:

```
val sample: DoubleArray = doubleArrayOf(-1.7, -1.0, -1.0, -0.73, -0.61, -0.5, -0.24, 0.45,
0.62, 0.81, 1.0, 5.0)
val test = Lilliefors(sample)
println("H0: " + test.getNullHypothesis())
println("H1: " + test.getAlternativeHypothesis())
println("test statistics = " + test.statistics())
println("p-value = " + test.pValue())
println("is null rejected at 5% = " + test.isNullRejected(0.05))
```

The output is as follows:

```
H0: the samples come from a normally distributed population
H1: the samples do not come from a normally distributed population
test statistics = 0.23353570622938402
p-value = 0.0696831488554199
is null rejected at 5% = false
```

Kolmogorov Test

There are two versions of the Kolmogorov-Smirnov test (K-S test or KS test). The one-sample KS test compares the distance between the empirical distribution function of the sample and the cumulative distribution function of the reference distribution (as in the Lilliefors test). The two-sample KS test compares the distance between the empirical distribution functions of two samples. The null distribution of this statistic is calculated under the null hypothesis that the sample is drawn from the reference distribution (in the one-sample case) or that the samples are drawn from the same distribution (in the two-sample case). See Figure 12-48.

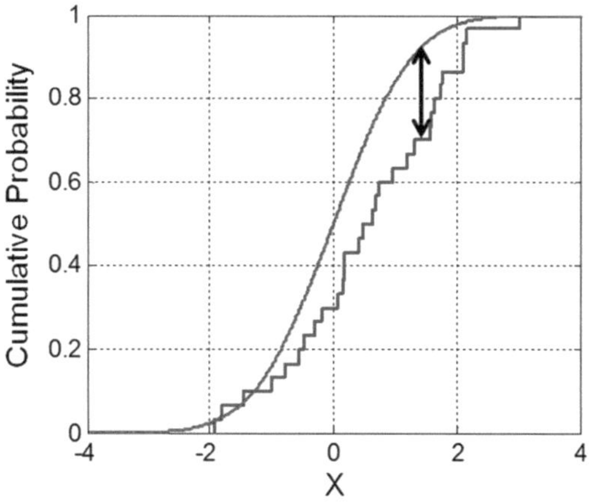

Figure 12-48. *Illustration of the one-sample Kolmogorov-Smirnov statistic. The smooth line is a reference CDF, the step line is an empirical CDF, and the black arrow is the K-S statistic*

The one-sample Kolmogorov-Smirnov statistic is as follows:

$$D_n = \sup_x \left| F_n(x) - F(x) \right|$$

where $\sup_x$ is the supremum of the set of distances between the empirical distribution function $F_n(x)$ and the cumulative distribution function $F(x)$. Intuitively, the statistic takes the largest absolute difference between the two distribution functions across all x values. By the Glivenko-Cantelli theorem, if the sample comes from distribution $F(x)$, then D_n converges to 0 almost surely in the limit when n goes to infinity. In practice, the statistic requires a relatively large number of data points (in comparison to other goodness-of-fit criteria such as the Anderson-Darling test statistic) to properly reject the null hypothesis. If the parameters of $F(x)$ are determined from the data, for example, sample mean and sample variance as in the Lilliefors test, the critical values determined using the Kolmogorov-Smirnov distribution are invalid.

The two-sample Kolmogorov-Smirnov test assesses whether two underlying one-dimensional probability distributions differ. The two-sample KS statistic is as follows:

$$D_{n,m} = \sup_x \left| F_{1,n}(x) - F_{2,m}(x) \right|$$

where $F_{1,n}(x)$ and $F_{2,m}(x)$ are the empirical distribution functions of the first and second samples, respectively, and $\sup_x$ is the supremum function.

The two-sample KS test is one of the most useful and general nonparametric methods for comparing two samples, as it is sensitive to differences in both location and shape of the empirical cumulative distribution functions of the two samples. See Figure 12-49.

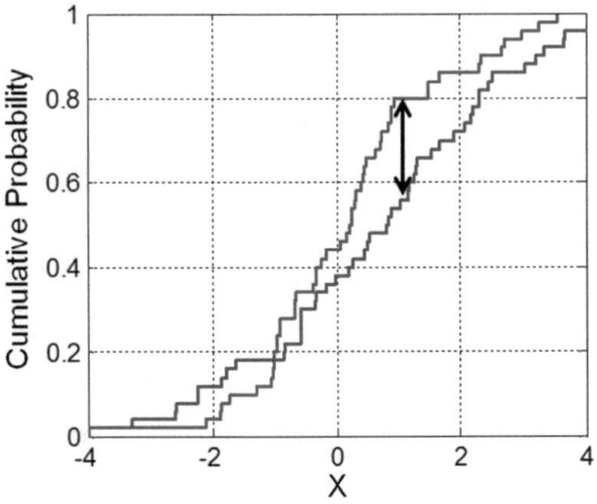

Figure 12-49. *Illustration of the two-sample Kolmogorov-Smirnov statistic. Smooth and step lines each correspond to an empirical distribution function, and the black arrow is the two-sample KS statistic*

The Kolmogorov-Smirnov test can be modified to serve as a goodness-of-fit test. In the special case of testing for normality of the distribution, samples are standardized and compared with a standard normal distribution. This is equivalent to setting the mean and variance of the reference distribution equal to the sample estimates, and it is known that using these to define the specific reference distribution changes the null distribution of the test statistic (see the Lilliefors Test). Various studies have found that, even in this corrected form, the test is less powerful for testing normality than the Shapiro-Wilk test or Anderson-Darling test. However, these other tests have their own disadvantages. For instance, the Shapiro-Wilk test is known not to work well in large samples or samples with many identical values.

The NM Dev class `KolmogorovSmirnov1Sample` and `KolmogorovSmirnov2Samples` implement the one-sample and two-sample Kolmogorov-Smirnov test. Following are examples for both the one-sample and two-sample KS tests:

```
// one-sample KS test
val test1 = KolmogorovSmirnov1Sample(
        doubleArrayOf( // with duplicates
            1.2142038235675114, 0.8271665834857130, -2.2786245743283295, 0.8414895245471727,
            -1.4327682855296735, -0.2501807766164897, -1.9512765152306415,
0.6963626117638846,
            0.4741320101265005, 1.2142038235675114
        ),
        NormalDistribution(),
        KolmogorovSmirnov.Side.TWO_SIDED // options are: TWO_SIDED, GREATER, LESS
)
println("H0: " + test1.getNullHypothesis())
println("test statistics = " + test1.statistics())
println("p-value = " + test1.pValue())
println("is null rejected at 5% = " + test1.isNullRejected(0.05))
```

The output is as follows:

```
H0: the true distribution function of sample is equal to the hypothesized distribution
function
test statistics = 0.2822971133259847
p-value = 0.4028859117233684
is null rejected at 5% = false
```

```
// two-sample KS test
val test2 = KolmogorovSmirnov2Samples(
        doubleArrayOf( // x = rnorm(10)
            1.2142038235675114, 0.8271665834857130, -2.2786245743283295, 0.8414895245471727,
            -1.4327682855296735, -0.2501807766164897, -1.9512765152306415,
0.6963626117638846,
            0.4741320101265005, -1.2340784297133520
        ),
        doubleArrayOf( // x = rnorm(15)
            1.7996197748754565, -1.1371109188816089, 0.8179707525071304, 0.3809791236763478,
            0.1644848304811257, 0.3397412780581336, -2.2571685407244795, 0.4137315314876659,
            0.7318687611171864, 0.9905218801425318, -0.4748590846019594, 0.8882674167954235,
            1.0534065683777052, 0.2553123235884622, -2.3172807717538038),
        KolmogorovSmirnov.Side.GREATER // options are: TWO_SIDED, GREATER, LESS
)
println("H0: " + test2.getNullHypothesis())
println("test statistics = " + test2.statistics())
println("p-value = " + test2.pValue())
println("is null rejected at 5% = " + test2.isNullRejected(0.05))
```

The output is as follows:

```
H0: the true distribution function of sample is greater than the distribution function of
the other sample
test statistics = 0.2666666666666667
p-value = 0.4259925874001307
is null rejected at 5% = false
```

Anderson-Darling Test

The Anderson-Darling K-sample test tests whether the K samples are from the same distribution, which needs not be specified. The test produces two statistics and two p-values. T_{kN} and p_{kN} are the statistic and p-value when there are no tied observations. T_{akN} and p_{akN} are the alternative statistic and p-value for ties when the distribution is discrete or when the continuous data is grouped. Under these two circumstances there may be tied observations.

The NM Dev class `AndersonDarling` implements the Anderson-Darling K-sample test. Here's an example:

```
// the samples
val x1: DoubleArray = doubleArrayOf(38.7, 41.5, 43.8, 44.5, 45.5, 46.0, 47.7, 58.0)
```

```
val x2: DoubleArray = doubleArrayOf(39.2, 39.3, 39.7, 41.4, 41.8, 42.9, 43.3, 45.8)
val x3: DoubleArray = doubleArrayOf(34.0, 35.0, 39.0, 40.0, 43.0, 43.0, 44.0, 45.0)
val x4: DoubleArray = doubleArrayOf(34.0, 34.8, 34.8, 35.4, 37.2, 37.8, 41.2, 42.8)

val test = AndersonDarling(x1, x2, x3, x4)
println("H0: " + test.getNullHypothesis())
println("H1: " + test.getAlternativeHypothesis())
println("test statistics = " + test.statistics())
println("p-value = " + test.pValue())
println("alternative test statistics = " + test.statisticsAlternative())
println("alternative p-value = " + test.pValueAlternative())
println("is null rejected at 5% = " + test.isNullRejected(0.05))
```

The output is as follows:

```
H0: all samples come from a common distribution
H1: not all samples come from a common distribution
test statistics = 4.449262232403152
p-value = 0.0023633128630889486
alternative test statistics = 4.479780627135353
alternative p-value = 0.0022781660876509324
is null rejected at 5% = true
```

Cramer Von Mises Test

The two-sample Cramer Von Mises test is another test to compare two samples to assess whether they come from the same underlying population distribution.

The NM Dev class `CramerVonMises2Samples` implements the two-sample Cramer Von Mises test. Here's an example:

```
// the samples
val x1: DoubleArray = doubleArrayOf(-0.54289848, 0.08999578, -1.77719573, -0.67991860,
-0.65741590, -0.25776164, 1.02024626, 1.26434300, 0.51068476, -0.23998229)
val x2: DoubleArray = doubleArrayOf(1.7053818, 1.0260726, 1.7695157, 1.5650577, 1.4945107,
1.8593791, 2.1760302, -0.9728721, 1.4208313, 1.5892663)
val test = CramerVonMises2Samples(x1, x2)
println("H0: " + test.getNullHypothesis())
println("H1: " + test.getAlternativeHypothesis())
println("test statistics = " + test.statistics())
println("p-value = " + test.pValue())
println("is null rejected at 5% = " + test.isNullRejected(0.05))
```

The output is as follows:

```
H0: the two samples are drawn from the same distribution
H1: the two samples are not drawn from the same distribution
test statistics = 1.1450000000000002
p-value = 0.0010713596423332916
is null rejected at 5% = true
```

Pearson's Chi-Square Test

Pearson's Chi-square test of independence assesses whether paired observations on two variables, expressed in a contingency table (a matrix), are independent of each other. The null hypothesis is that the two variables are statistically independent of each other.

For example, suppose we want to find out whether attending class helps pass an exam, like those tests for the opportunity class in Australia. We would record the attendance/absence versus pass/fail relationship in a contingency table like the following:

	Pass	Fail	Total
Attended	25	6	31
Absent	8	15	23
Total	33	21	54

If the variables are truly independent, we would expect a fair outcome like the following:

	Pass	Fail	Total
Attended	31*33/54 = 18.94	31*21/54 = 12.06	31
Absent	23*33/54 = 14.06	23*21/54 = 8.94	23
Total	33	21	54

The test statistic is as follows:

$$\chi^2 = \sum_{i=1}^{r}\sum_{j=1}^{c}\frac{\left(O_{ij} - E_{ij}\right)^2}{E_{ij}}$$

where O_{ij} is the observed frequency in a cell, and E_{ij} is the expected frequency assuming the null hypothesis of independence. The test statistic is summing up over all rows (r) and columns (c). It is basically a sum of squared deviations scaled by the expected frequency to normalize big and small counts in all cells. Note that $\chi^2 = 0$ if and only if $O_{ij} = E_{ij}$ for all cells.

When the sample size is small and the contingency table unbalanced, χ^2 has the Fisher's exact distribution. Otherwise, when the sample size is large and the contingency table balanced, we use the Chi-square distribution, which is the asymptotic distribution of Fisher's exact distribution.

The NM Dev class `ChiSquareIndependenceTest` implements Pearson's Chi-square test of independence. The following code computes for the previous example:

```
// the attendance/absence vs. pass/fail counts
val counts: Matrix = DenseMatrix(
    arrayOf(
        doubleArrayOf(25.0, 6.0),
        doubleArrayOf(8.0, 15.0)
    )
)
val test1 = ChiSquareIndependenceTest(
            counts,
            0,
```

```
                // the asymptotic distribution is the Chi-square distribution
                ChiSquareIndependenceTest.Type.ASYMPTOTIC
        )

val expected: Matrix = ChiSquareIndependenceTest.getExpectedContingencyTable(
        intArrayOf(31, 23), // row sums
        intArrayOf(33, 21) // column sums
)
println("the expected frequencies:")
println(expected)

println("H0: " + test1.getNullHypothesis())
println("H1: " + test1.getAlternativeHypothesis())
println("test statistics = " + test1.statistics())
println("p-value = " + test1.pValue())
println("is null rejected at 5% = " + test1.isNullRejected(0.05))

val test2 = ChiSquareIndependenceTest(
                counts,
                100000,// number of simulation to compute the Fisher exact distribution
                ChiSquareIndependenceTest.Type.EXACT // use the Fisher exact distribution
        )
println("p-value = " + test2.pValue())
println("is null rejected at 5% = " + test2.isNullRejected(0.05))
```

The output is as follows:

```
the expected frequencies:
2x2
         [,1] [,2]
[1,] 18.944444, 12.055556,
[2,] 14.055556, 8.944444,
H0: the two random variables in the contingency table are independent
H1: the two random variables in the contingency table are not independent
test statistics = 9.835886413726527
p-value = 0.0017113979062570728
is null rejected at 5% = true
p-value = 6.500000000000436E-4
is null rejected at 5% = true
```

Using the Chi-square distribution as the asymptotic distribution, we have the p-value as 0.0017. Using the Fisher exact distribution, we have the p-value as 0.0006. In any case, the null hypothesis is safely rejected at 5 percent. We conclude that attending class having no influence on passing exam is very unlikely. Or equivalently, attending class and passing exam are probably related. So, don't skip classes!

12.5.2. Rank Test

NM DevRank test supports a suite of hypothesis tests that assess whether two samples have the same population mean, median, and variability.

T-Test

The t-test provides an exact test for the equality of the means of two i.i.d. normal populations with unknown, but equal, variances. Welch's t-test is a nearly exact test for the case where the data is normal but the variances may be different. When used for one sample, the tests can be used to compare the sample mean to a hypothetical mean. For moderately large samples and a one tailed test, the t-test is relatively robust to moderate violations of the normality assumption. In large enough samples, the t-test asymptotically approaches the z-test and becomes robust even to large deviations from normality. However, if the data is substantially non-normal and the sample size is small, the t-test can give misleading results.

The NM Dev class T implements both the t-test for equal variance and Welch's t-test for possibly unequal variance. Here's an example:

```
// The t-test
val test1: T = T(
        doubleArrayOf(1.0, 3.0, 5.0, 2.0, 3.0, 5.0),
        doubleArrayOf(2.0, 5.0, 6.0, 4.0, 9.0, 8.0),
        true, // assume variances are equal
        4.0 // the hypothetical mean-difference = 4 in the null hypothesis
)
println("H0: " + test1.getNullHypothesis())
println("H1: " + test1.getAlternativeHypothesis())
println("test statistics = " + test1.statistics())
println("1st mean = " + test1.mean1())
println("2nd mean = " + test1.mean2())
println("p-value = " + test1.pValue())
println("p-value, right sided = " + test1.rightOneSidedPvalue())
println("p-value, left sided = " + test1.leftOneSidedPvalue())
println(String.format("95%% confidence interval = (%f, %f)", test1.
leftConfidenceInterval(0.95), test1.rightConfidenceInterval(0.95)))
println("97.5%% confidence interval = " + Arrays.toString(test1.confidenceInterval(0.975)))
println("is null rejected at 5% = " + test1.isNullRejected(0.05))
```

The output is as follows:

```
H0: the means are equal
H1: the means are different
test statistics = -5.239739845279477
1st mean = 3.1666666666666665
2nd mean = 5.666666666666667
p-value = 3.7894052596908147E-4
p-value, right sided = 0.9998105297370155
p-value, left sided = 1.8947026298454073E-4
95% confidence interval = (-0.251606, -4.748394)
97.5%% confidence interval = [-5.26404992720365, 0.26404992720364895]
is null rejected at 5% = true
```

The mean of the first group is 3.17 and that of the second group is 5.67. The t-test, assuming equal variance, rejects the null hypothesis that the mean difference is 4 at 5 percent significance level.

```
// Welch's t-test
val test2: T = T(
        doubleArrayOf(1.0, 3.0, 5.0, 2.0, 3.0, 5.0),
        doubleArrayOf(2.0, 5.0, 6.0, 4.0, 9.0, 8.0),
        false, // assume variances are different
        4.0 // the hypothetical mean-difference = 4 in the null hypothesis
)
println("test statistics = " + test2.statistics())
println("p-value = " + test2.pValue())
println("p-value, right sided = " + test2.rightOneSidedPvalue())
println("p-value, left sided = " + test2.leftOneSidedPvalue())
println(String.format("95%% confidence interval = (%f, %f)", test2.
leftConfidenceInterval(0.95), test2.rightConfidenceInterval(0.95)))
println("97.5%% confidence interval = " + Arrays.toString(test2.confidenceInterval(0.975)))
println("is null rejected at 5% = " + test2.isNullRejected(0.05))
```

The output is as follows:

```
test statistics = -5.239739845279477
p-value = 6.816159267755681E-4
p-value, right sided = 0.9996591920366122
p-value, left sided = 3.4080796338778404E-4
95% confidence interval = (-0.205769, -4.794231)
97.5%% confidence interval = [-5.339736444764696, 0.33973644476469556]
is null rejected at 5% = true
```

Welch's t-test, assuming unequal variance, also rejects the null hypothesis.

One-Way ANOVA Test

The one-way ANOVA test tests for the equality of the means of several groups. ANOVAs are helpful because they possess an advantage over a two-sample t-test. Doing multiple two-sample t-tests would result in an increased chance of committing a Type I error (false positive error). For this reason, ANOVAs are useful in comparing three or more means. The NM Dev class `OneWayANOVA` implements the one-way ANOVA test.

Kruskal-Wallis Test

The Kruskal-Wallis test is a nonparametric method for testing the equality of population medians among groups. It is identical to a one-way ANOVA with the data replaced by their ranks. Since it is a nonparametric method, the Kruskal-Wallis test does not assume a normal population, unlike the analogous one-way ANOVA. However, the test does assume an identically shaped and scaled distribution for each group, except for any difference in medians. The NM Dev class `KruskalWallis` implements the one-way ANOVA test.

Wilcoxon Signed Rank Test

The Wilcoxon signed rank test tests, for the one-sample case, the median of the distribution against a hypothetical median and, for the two-sample case, the equality of medians of groups. Unlike the t-test, the Wilcoxon signed rank test does not assume any distribution of the population. The Wilcoxon rank sum statistic is the number of all pairs $\{(x, y) \mid y \leq x\}$ for which y is not bigger than x. This statistic takes values between 0 and MN, where M is the number of observations in group 1 and N is the number of observations in group 2. The test statistic has the Wilcoxon rank sum distribution, see class `WilcoxonRankSumDistribution`.

The NM Dev class `WilcoxonSignedRank` implements the Wilcoxon signed rank test. Here's an example:

```
val sample1: DoubleArray = doubleArrayOf(1.3, 5.4, 7.6, 7.2, 3.5)
val sample2: DoubleArray = doubleArrayOf(2.7, 5.2, 6.3, 4.4, 9.8)

val test = WilcoxonSignedRank(
        sample1, sample2,
        2.0, // the hypothetical median that the distribution is symmetric about
        true // use the exact Wilcoxon rank sum distribution rather than normal distribution
)
println("H0: " + test.getNullHypothesis())
println("H1: " + test.getAlternativeHypothesis())
println("test statistics = " + test.statistics())
println("p-value = " + test.pValue())
println("p-value, right sided = " + test.rightOneSidedPvalue())
println("p-value, left sided = " + test.leftOneSidedPvalue())
println("is null rejected at 5% = " + test.isNullRejected(0.05))
```

The output is as follows:

```
H0: the medians are equal (by offset mu)
H1: the medians are different (not by mu)
test statistics = 2.0
p-value = 0.1875
p-value, right sided = 0.9375
p-value, left sided = 0.09375
is null rejected at 5% = false
```

Siegel-Tukey Test

The Siegel-Tukey test tests if one of two groups of data tends to have more widely dispersed values than the other. In other words, the test determines whether one of the two groups tends to move, sometimes to the right, sometimes to the left, but away from the center (of the ordinal scale). The null hypothesis is that both groups have the same variance and median. The alternative hypothesis is that one group has a bigger variance than the other.

Suppose there are two groups A and B with n observations for the first group and m observations for the second (so there are $N = n + m$ total observations). If all N observations are arranged in ascending order, it can be expected that the values of the two groups will be mixed or sorted randomly if there are no differences between the two groups (following the null hypothesis H_0). This would mean that among the ranks of extreme (high and low) scores, there would be similar values from Group A and Group B. If, say, Group A were more inclined to extreme values (the alternative hypothesis H_1), then there will be a higher proportion of observations from group A with low or high values and a reduced proportion of values at the center. The test statistic has the Wilcoxon rank sum distribution, see class `WilcoxonRankSumDistribution`.

The NM Dev class `SiegelTukey` implements the Siegel-Tukey test. Here's an example:

```
val sample1: DoubleArray = doubleArrayOf(4.0, 16.0, 48.0, 51.0, 66.0, 98.0)
val sample2: DoubleArray = doubleArrayOf(33.0, 62.0, 84.0, 85.0, 88.0, 93.0, 97.0)

val test: SiegelTukey = SiegelTukey(
        sample1,
        sample2,
        0.0, // the hypothetical mean difference
        true // use the exact Wilcoxon Rank Sum distribution rather than normal distribution
)
println("H0: " + test.getNullHypothesis())
println("H1: " + test.getAlternativeHypothesis())
println("test statistics = " + test.statistics())
println("p-value = " + test.pValue())
println("p-value, right sided = " + test.rightOneSidedPvalue())
println("p-value, left sided = " + test.leftOneSidedPvalue())
println("is null rejected at 5% = " + test.isNullRejected(0.05))
```

The output is as follows:

```
H0: the two samples have the same variability and median
H1: the two samples have different variabilities
test statistics = 16.0
p-value = 0.5337995337995338
p-value, right sided = 0.7773892773892773
p-value, left sided = 0.2668997668997669
is null rejected at 5% = false
```

Van der Waerden Test

The Van der Waerden test converts the ranks from a standard Kruskal-Wallis one-way analysis of variance to quantiles of the standard normal distribution. These are called normal scores, and the test is computed from these normal scores. The most common nonparametric test for the one-factor model is the Kruskal-Wallis test. The Kruskal-Wallis test is based on the ranks of the data. The advantage of the Van der Waerden test is that it provides the high efficiency of the standard ANOVA analysis when the normality assumptions are in fact satisfied, but it also provides the robustness of the Kruskal-Wallis test when the normality assumptions are not satisfied. The NM Dev class `VanDerWaerden` implements the Van der Waerden test.

12.6. Markov Models

A Markov model is a stochastic model describing a sequence of possible states in which the probability of the next state depends only on the current state and not on the history and is hence memoryless (don't remember anything in the past). There are a wide range of applications in Bayesian statistics, thermodynamics, statistical mechanics, physics, chemistry, economics, finance, signal processing, information theory, and speech processing. Markov processes are the basis for general stochastic simulation methods known as Markov chain Monte Carlo (MCMC), which are used for simulating sampling from complex probability distributions.

12.6.1. Discrete-Time Markov Chain

The simplest type of a Markov model is a discrete-time Markov chain (DTMC). It moves state at discrete time steps, and there are a finite or countable number of states. The probability of the next state depends only on the current state and not any information in the past. Mathematically, suppose a sequence of random variables $X_0, X_1, X_2, \ldots$ with the Markov property, then we have this (see Figure 12-50):

$$\Pr\left(X_{n+1}=x \mid X_1=x_1, X_2=x_2, \ldots, X_n=x_n\right)=\Pr\left(X_{n+1}=x \mid X_n=x_n\right)$$

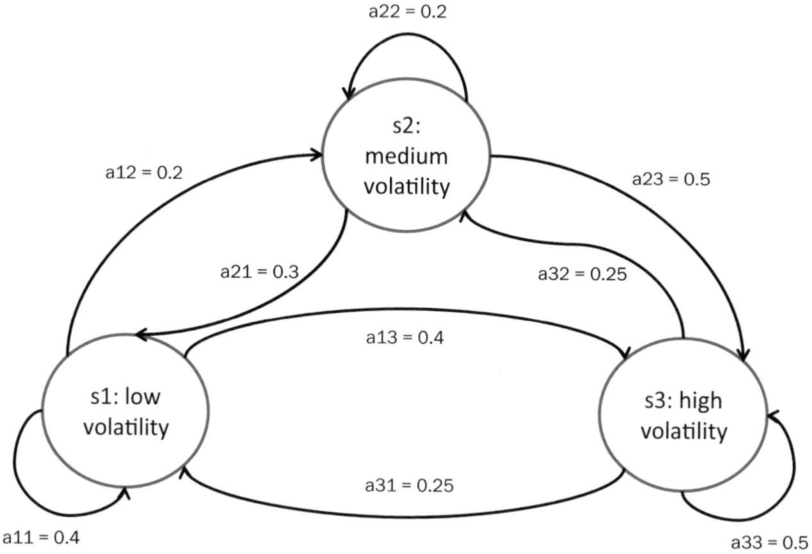

Figure 12-50. *A discrete-time Markov chain with three states*

For example, in Figure 12-50, we may classify the stock market into three different states: low, medium, and high volatility. It is possible that the market may stay in the same (low volatility) state tomorrow (40 percent chance), but it may also move to another state, such as medium volatility state (20 percent chance) or high volatility state (40 percent chance). The transition probabilities (represented by the arrows and the numbers) are the probabilities that the process may go from one state to another. Note that the sum of the transition probabilities leaving one state and staying in the same state (the arrow pointing to itself) must sum to 1. The transition probabilities are usually described by a stochastic matrix, which lists the probabilities of moving from any individual state (row) to each state (column). The stochastic matrix for the DTMC in Figure 12-50 is as follows:

$$A=\begin{bmatrix} 0.4 & 0.2 & 0.4 \\ 0.3 & 0.2 & 0.5 \\ 0.25 & 0.25 & 0.5 \end{bmatrix}$$

From this matrix and together with the initial probabilities of the initial states completely characterize a time-homogeneous DTMC. The probability of the system being in a particular state n steps in the future can be calculated. For example, we can calculate the probability of observing this sequence of states $Q = \{s_3, s_1, s_1, s_1\}$. The system starts in state s_3 (with probability 1).

$$\Pr(Q \mid A) = \mathrm{P}(s_1, s_1 | s_1 | s_3 | A)$$

$$= \Pr(s_3 \mid A) \times \Pr(s_1 | s_3, A) \times \Pr(s_1 | s_1, s_3, A) \times \Pr(s_1 | s_1, s_1, s_3, A)$$

$$= \Pr(s_3 \mid A) \times \Pr(s_1 | s_3, A) \times \Pr(s_1 | s_1, A) \times \Pr(s_1 | s_1, A)$$

$$= 1 \times 0.25 \times 0.4 \times 0.4 = 0.04$$

We used the Markov property in step 3 to simply the conditional probabilities. Specifically, the Markov property says the following:

$$\Pr(q_t | q_{t-1}, \cdots, q_1) = \Pr(q_t | q_{t-1})$$

In quantitative finance, the Markov property is consistent with the weak form of the efficient market hypothesis that says the future price of the market depends not on any historical prices. They don't predict the future.

A DTMC can move from state to state forever. The sequence of states that it generates is a sequence of random numbers (integers). A DTMC with stochastic matrix, A, has a stationary distribution, π, if and only if $\pi A = \pi$. The stationary distribution is the probability that we find the system in each state when time goes to infinity.

The NM Dev class `SimpleMC` implements a time-homogeneous DTMC. For example, the following code implements the previous three-state Markov chain:

```
// the stochastic matrix of transition probabilities
val A: Matrix = DenseMatrix(
    arrayOf(
        doubleArrayOf(0.4, 0.2, 0.4),
        doubleArrayOf(0.3, 0.2, 0.5),
        doubleArrayOf(0.25, 0.25, 0.5)
    )
)
// start in state 3
val I: Vector = DenseVector(0.0, 0.0, 1.0)

val MC: SimpleMC = SimpleMC(I, A)
val PI: Vector = SimpleMC.getStationaryProbabilities(A)
println("The stationary distribution = " + PI)

// simulate the next 9 steps
println("time 0 = " + 3)
for (i in 1 until 10) {
    val state: Int = MC.nextState()
    println(String.format("time %d = %d", i, state))
}
```

The output is as follows:

```
the stationary distribution = [0.307263, 0.223464, 0.469274]
time 0 = 3
time 1 = 3
time 2 = 3
time 3 = 3
time 4 = 3
time 5 = 3
time 6 = 1
time 7 = 2
time 8 = 2
time 9 = 1
```

The stationary distribution is in which state we will find the system when time goes to infinity. In this case, we will find the system 47 percent of the time in state 3 of this Markov chain.

12.6.2. Hidden Markov Model

A hidden Markov model (HMM) is a stochastic process that the underlying process is a Markov chain of states but you do not see which state the system is in, and hence it is hidden. What you do see are the observations. There is a (different) probability distribution of the observations that is associated with each of the hidden states. See Figure 12-51.

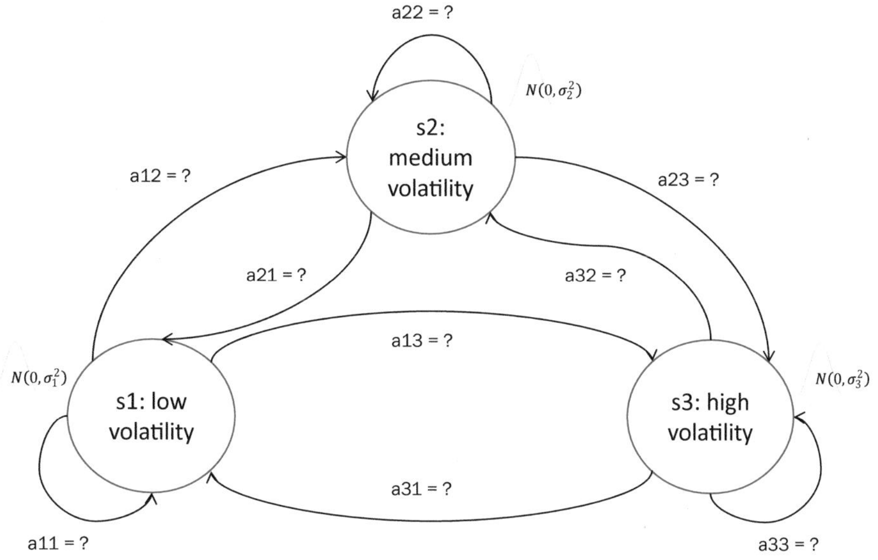

***Figure 12-51.** A hidden Markov model of a stock market*

For example, extending the example in Figure 12-51, the market can be in each of the three states: low, medium, and high volatility. The daily returns of the stock in each of the state are normally distributed with zero mean but different volatilities, $\sigma_1^2 \le \sigma_2^2 \le \sigma_3^2$. Notice that each state generates the same set of returns

(−∞, +∞) but with different probabilities. We do not and cannot tell exactly which state the market is in at any point in time. Not only do we not know the (hidden) states, we also do not know the parameters of the model, λ, such as the transition probabilities and the $\{\sigma_i^2\}$. All we observe and all the information that we have are the historical returns, the sequence of observations Ω (and the HMM structure).

There are three questions that we may ask about an HMM. First, the likelihood question. Given the parameters, λ, and an observation sequence, Ω, can we compute the likelihood of observing this particular sequence $\Pr(\Omega \mid \lambda)$? Second, the decoding question. Given the parameters, λ, and an observation sequence, Ω, can we determine the most likely hidden sequence of states Q? Third, the learning question. Given an observation sequence, Ω, and the HMM structure, can we learn λ?

The Likelihood Question

Given the parameters of model λ, we want to compute the probability of a particular observed or output sequence Ω. The conceptually easiest way is just to sum up the probabilities of observing Ω over all possible sequences of states. That is,

$$\Pr(\Omega|\lambda) = \sum_{\{q\}'s} \Pr(\Omega, Q|\lambda) = \sum_{\{q\}'s} \Pr(\Omega|Q,\lambda) \times \Pr(Q|\lambda)$$

The first term is the probability of observing Ω given the hidden sequence of states Q; the second term is the probability of that hidden sequence of states given the HMM parameters λ. For the first term, we have this:

$$\Pr(\Omega|Q,\lambda) = \prod_{t=1}^{T} \Pr(\omega_t|q_t,\lambda)$$

$\Pr(\omega_t| q_t, \lambda)$ is the probability of observing ω_t in state q_t at time t. This is given by the probability distribution associated with each of the states. In our example in Figure 12-51, it is given by the normal distribution in the state q_t (the state that the system is in at time t).

For the second term, we have this:

$$\Pr(Q|\lambda) = \pi_{q_1} \times a_{q_1 q_2} \times a_{q_2 q_3} \times \cdots \times a_{q_{T-1} q_T}$$

which is simply a product of the initial state probability π_{q_1} (starting in state q_1) and the transition probabilities.

However, this naïve method is not computationally feasible because the number of paths grows exponentially. We will need a more efficient method.

Define the forward probability $\alpha_t(i)$ as the probability of the partial observation sequence until time t and the system in state s_i at time t. That is,

$$\alpha_t(i) = \Pr(\omega_1, \omega_2 | \cdots | \omega_t | q_t = s_i \mid \lambda)$$

This can be computed using forward induction. Initialize the first-time step, as shown here:

$$\alpha_1(i) = \pi_i b_i(\omega_1)$$

where $b_i(\omega_1)$ is the probability of observing ω_1 in state i. It is given by the probability distribution in the state. In our example, it is given by the normal distribution. (It is probably easier to work with a discrete probability distribution that has a probability mass function here because the ωs are discrete in our math. The idea is the same.) See Figure 12-52.

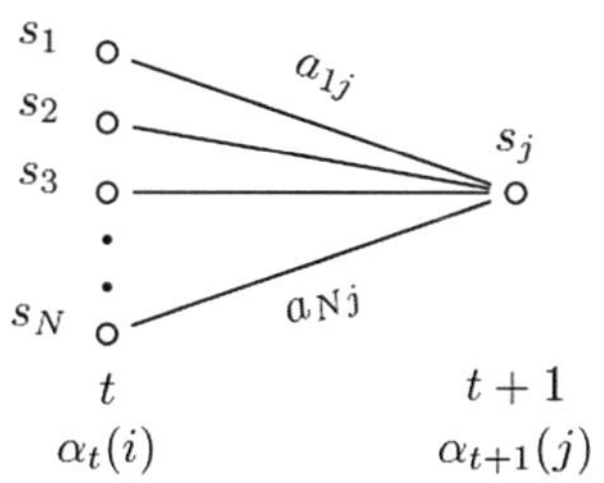

Figure 12-52. *The forward algorithm*

The induction step says that $\alpha_{t+1}(i)$ is the sum of all previous $\alpha_t(j)$ and then reaching state j. That is,

$$\alpha_{t+1}(i)=\left[\sum_{j=1}^{N}\alpha_t(i)a_{ij}\right]b_i(\omega_{t+1})$$

where N is the number of states in the HMM and a_{ij} is the transition probability from state i to state j. Finally, the probability of observing Ω given λ is simply the sum of all α_T across all states.

$$\Pr(\Omega|\lambda)=\sum_{j=1}^{N}\alpha_T(j)$$

For example, consider a village where all villagers either are healthy or have a fever and only the village doctor can determine whether each has a fever. The doctor diagnoses a fever by asking patients how they feel. The villagers may only answer that they feel normal, dizzy, or cold.

The doctor believes that the health condition of his patients operates as a discrete Markov chain. There are two states, Healthy and Fever, but the doctor cannot observe them directly; they are hidden from him. On each day, there is a certain chance that the patient will tell the doctor he is normal, cold, or dizzy, depending on his health condition.

The observations (normal, cold, or dizzy) along with a hidden state (healthy, fever) form a hidden Markov model (HMM) and can be represented as shown in Figure 12-53.

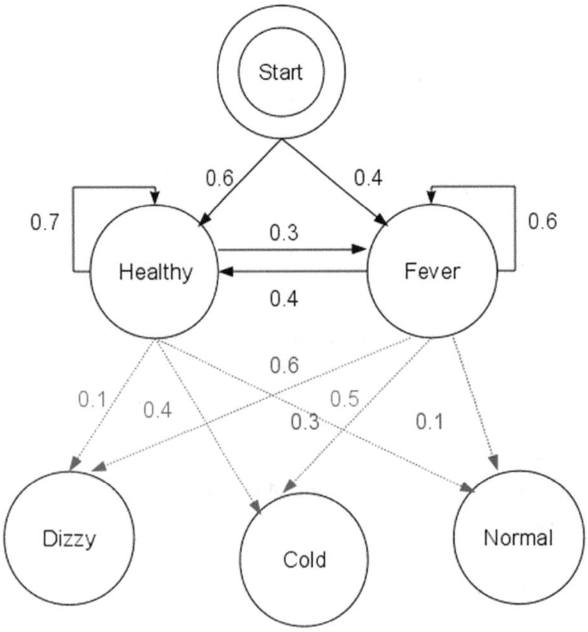

Figure 12-53. *A hidden Markov model of a villager's health*

The NM Dev class DiscreteHMM implements a discrete hidden Markov model, and the class ForwardBackwardProcedure performs the forward-back algorithm to compute the forward and backward probabilities. For example, the following code implements the previous two-state HMM:

```
// the initial probabilities for 2 states
val PI: DenseVector = DenseVector(0.6, 0.4)
// the transition probabilities
val A: DenseMatrix = DenseMatrix(
    arrayOf(
        doubleArrayOf(0.7, 0.3),
        doubleArrayOf(0.4, 0.6)
    )
)
// the observation probabilities 3 possible outcomes for 2 states
val B: DenseMatrix = DenseMatrix(
    arrayOf(
        doubleArrayOf(0.5, 0.4, 0.1),
        doubleArrayOf(0.1, 0.3, 0.6)
    )
)
// construct an HMM1
val hmm: DiscreteHMM = DiscreteHMM(PI, A, B)

// the realized observations
val observations: DoubleArray = doubleArrayOf(1.0, 2.0, 3.0)
```

```
// run the forward-backward algorithm
val fb = ForwardBackwardProcedure(hmm, observations)
for (t in 1 until observations.size) {
    println(String.format(
            "The *scaled* forward probability, alpha, in each state at time %d: %s",
            t,
            fb.scaledAlpha(t)
    ))
}
```

The output is as follows:

```
the *scaled* forward probability, alpha, in each state at time 1: [0.882353, 0.117647]
the *scaled* forward probability, alpha, in each state at time 2: [0.725522, 0.274478]
```

The Decoding Question

Given the model parameters λ and a sequence of observations Ω, the filtering problem is to compute the probability of the system in a state at the end of the sequence, i.e., $\Pr(q_T = s_i | \lambda, \Omega)$. This problem can be solved efficiently using the forward algorithm shown previously.

The smoothing problem is similar to the filtering problem, but it computes the probability of the system in a state in the middle of a sequence, in other words, $\Pr(q_t = s_i | \lambda, \Omega)$.

Define the backward probability $\beta_t(i)$ as the probability of the system in state s_i at time t, and the partial observations from then onward until time t. That is,

$$\beta_t(i) = \Pr(\omega_{t+1}, \omega_{t+2} | \cdots, \omega_T, \lambda, q_t = s_i)$$

This can be computed using backward induction. Initialize the last-time step, as shown in Figure 12-54.

$$\beta_T(i) = 1$$

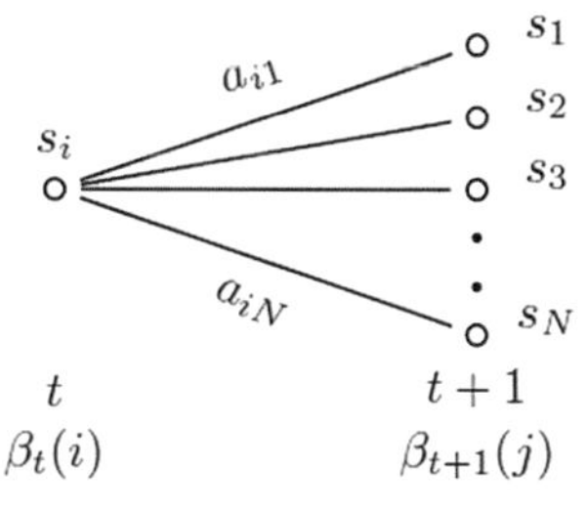

Figure 12-54. *The backward algorithm*

The induction step says that $\beta_t(i)$ is the sum of all possible paths to the next time step $\beta_{t+1}(j)$ from state i and makes the observation ω_{t+1} in all the paths. That is,

$$\beta_t(i) = \sum_{j=1}^{N} a_{ij} b_j(\omega_{t+1}) \beta_{t+1}(j)$$

Finally, the probability of the system in state *i* at time *t* given the observations Ω and the parameters *λ* is as follows:

$$\gamma_t(i) = \Pr(q_t = s_i | \Omega, \lambda)$$

$$= \frac{\Pr(q_t = s_i \Omega | \lambda)}{\Pr(\Omega | \lambda)}$$

$$= \frac{\alpha_t(i)\beta_t(i)}{\Pr(\Omega | \lambda)}$$

$$= \frac{\alpha_t(i)\beta_t(i)}{\sum_{j=1}^{N} \alpha_t(j)\beta_t(j)}$$

The most likely state at every instant *t*, without regard to the probability of occurrence of sequences of states, is as follows:

$$q_t = \underset{1 \le i \le N}{\operatorname{argmax}} \left[\gamma_t(i) \right]$$

The most likely sequence of hidden states, i.e., finding a maximum over all possible state sequences, can be solved using the Viterbi algorithm. Define the maximal probability of the system traveling these states, landing state s_i at time *t* and generating the observations:

$$\delta_t(i) = \max\left[\Pr(q_1, q_2 | \cdots | q_t = s_i | \omega_0 | \cdots | \omega_t | \lambda) \right]$$

Initialization:

$$\delta_1(i) = \pi_i b_i(\omega_1)$$

$$\psi_1 = 0$$

Recursion:

$$\delta_t(j) = \max_i \left[\delta_{t-1}(i) a_{ij} b_j(\omega_t) \right]$$

Here $\delta_t(i)$ is the probability of the most probable state sequence $q_1, q_2, \cdots, q_t$ responsible for the first *t* observations that have *j* as its final state.

$$\psi_t = \underset{i}{\operatorname{argmax}} \left[\delta_{t-1}(i) a_{ij} \right]$$

where ψ_t is the state chosen at time *t* to maximize $\delta_t(j)$.
Termination:

$$\delta_T^* = \max_i \delta_T(i)$$

$$q_T = \underset{i}{\operatorname{argmax}} \, \delta_T$$

The NM Dev class Viterbi implements the Viterbi algorithm. The following code continues the example in Figure 12-54:

```
// run the Viterbi algorithm to find the most likely sequence of hidden states
val viterbi = Viterbi(hmm)
val viterbi_states: IntArray = viterbi.getViterbiStates(observations)
println("The Viterbi states: " + Arrays.toString(viterbi_states))
```

The output is as follows:

```
the Viterbi states: [1, 1, 2]
```

The Learning Question

The parameter learning task in HMM is to find, given an output sequence Ω, the best set of state transition probabilities A and probability distribution parameters λ. The task is usually to derive the maximum likelihood estimate of the parameters of the HMM given the set of output sequences. That is, our objective is to find λ that maximizes $\Pr(\Omega|\lambda)$. For any λ, we can compute $\Pr(\Omega|\lambda)$. The problem becomes a multivariate unconstrained optimization problem. Any optimization algorithm, such as Nelder-Mead, can in principle solve it. In practice, however, there are convergence and efficiency problems. No tractable algorithm is known for solving this problem exactly, but a local maximum likelihood can be derived efficiently using the Baum-Welch algorithm. The Baum-Welch algorithm is a special case of the expectation-maximization algorithm (EM algorithm). It makes use of the forward-backward algorithm to compute the statistics in the expectation step. See Figure 12-55.

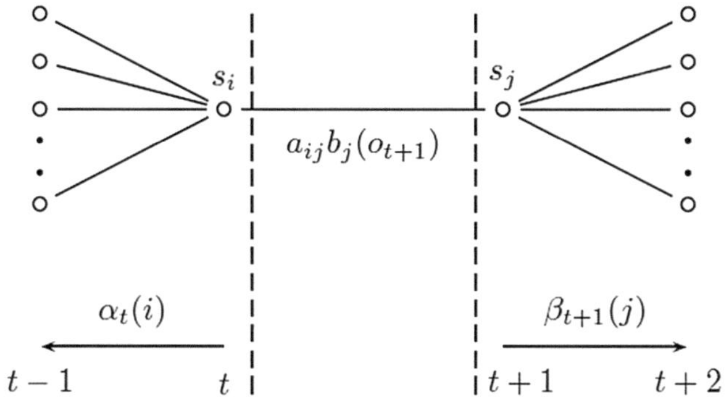

Figure 12-55. *The Baum-Welch algorithm, $\xi_t(i, j)$*

Define $\xi_t(i, j)$ as the probability of being in state s_i at time t, and state s_j at time $t + 1$, given the model λ and the observation sequence Ω. That is,

$$\xi_t(i,j) = \Pr\left(q_t = s_i, q_{t+1} = s_j | \Omega, \lambda\right)$$

We can write this in terms of forward and backward probabilities.

$$\xi_t(i,j) = \Pr\left(q_t = s_i, q_{t+1} = s_j | \Omega, \lambda\right)$$

$$= \frac{\Pr\left(q_t = s_i, q_{t+1} = s_j | \Omega | \lambda\right)}{\Pr(\Omega|\lambda)}$$

$$= \frac{\alpha_t(i) a_{ij} b_j(\omega_{t+1}) \beta_{t+1}(j)}{\Pr(\Omega|\lambda)}$$

Therefore, we have this:

$$\gamma_t(i) = \Pr(q_t = s_i | \Omega, \lambda)$$

$$= \sum_{j=1}^{N} \xi_t(i,j)$$

Summing $\gamma_t(i)$ over time is the number of times that state s_i is visited. Summing $\xi_t(i, j)$ over time is the number of times the system goes from state s_i to state s_j. We can now estimate the model parameters λ as follows:

$\hat{\pi}_i = \gamma_1(i)$, the initial state probabilities

$$\hat{a}_{ij} = \frac{\sum_{t=1}^{T-1} \xi_t(i,j)}{\sum_{t=1}^{T-1} \gamma_t(i)}$$, the transition probabilities

$$\widehat{b_{j(v_k)}} = \frac{\sum_{t=1,\omega_t=v_k}^{T-1} \gamma_t(j)}{\sum_{t=1}^{T-1} \gamma_t(i)}$$, the conditional probabilities for observations in state s_j, for discrete observations

The NM Dev class BaumWelch implements the Baum-Welch algorithm. The following code learns the HMM in Figure 12-53 from some randomly generated samples from the original HMM:

```
// generate a sequence of observations from a HMM
// the initial probabilities for 2 states
val PI: DenseVector = DenseVector(0.6, 0.4)
// the transition probabilities
val A: DenseMatrix = DenseMatrix(
    arrayOf(
        doubleArrayOf(0.7, 0.3),
        doubleArrayOf(0.4, 0.6)
))
// the observation probabilities 3 possible outcomes for 2 states
val B: DenseMatrix = DenseMatrix(
    arrayOf(
        doubleArrayOf(0.5, 0.4, 0.1),
        doubleArrayOf(0.1, 0.3, 0.6)
))
// construct an HMM1
```

```
val model: DiscreteHMM = DiscreteHMM(PI, A, B)
model.seed(1234507890L, 1234507891L)

// generate the observations
val T = 10000
var innovations = ArrayList<HmmInnovation>(T)
println(innovations)
var states: IntArray = IntArray(T)
val observations: IntArray = IntArray(T)
for (t in 0 until T) {
    innovations.add(t, model.next())
    states[t] = innovations.get(t).state()
    observations[t] = innovations.get(t).observation().toInt()
}
println("\nObservations: ")
for (t in 1 until 100) {
    print(observations[t].toString() + ", ")
    if (t % 20 == 0) {
        println("")
    }
}
```

The output is as follows:

```
observations:
2, 3, 3, 3, 3, 2, 1, 3, 2, 2, 2, 1, 2, 3, 3, 2, 2, 2, 2, 3,
1, 2, 3, 2, 2, 3, 2, 1, 3, 1, 1, 2, 2, 1, 2, 2, 2, 3, 1, 1,
3, 3, 1, 1, 3, 2, 3, 1, 3, 3, 2, 2, 2, 1, 3, 3, 1, 1, 2, 3,
3, 3, 3, 2, 1, 1, 1, 2, 1, 1, 3, 2, 3, 1, 1, 2, 1, 1, 3, 3,
1, 1, 1, 2, 2, 2, 1, 3, 2, 3, 2, 1, 1, 1, 3, 3, 1, 2, 2, 1,
```

```
// learn the HMM from observations
val PI_0: DenseVector = DenseVector(0.5, 0.5) // initial guesses
val A_0: DenseMatrix = DenseMatrix( // initial guesses
    arrayOf(
        doubleArrayOf(0.5, 0.5),
        doubleArrayOf(0.5, 0.5)
    )
)
val B_0: DenseMatrix = DenseMatrix( // initial guesses
    arrayOf(
        doubleArrayOf(0.60, 0.20, 0.20),
        doubleArrayOf(0.20, 0.20, 0.60)
))
var model_0: DiscreteHMM = DiscreteHMM(PI_0, A_0, B_0)  // initial guesses

// training
val nIterations = 40
for (i in 1 until nIterations) {
    model_0 = BaumWelch.train(observations, model_0)
}
```

```
// training results
println("Estimated transition probabilities: ")
println(model_0.A()) // should be close to A

println("(Observation) Conditional probabilities: ")
println(model_0.B())  // should be close to B
```

The output is as follows:

```
estimated transition probabilities:
2x2
        [,1] [,2]
[1,] 0.701488, 0.298512,
[2,] 0.336808, 0.663192,
(observation) conditional probabilities:
2x3
        [,1] [,2] [,3]
[1,] 0.500569, 0.428947, 0.070485,
[2,] 0.130704, 0.271811, 0.597485,
```

The trained HMM has parameters close to the original one, up to the first two decimal digits.

Our formulation so far assumes discrete conditional probabilities. The formulations that take continuous probability density functions, e.g., normal distribution, are similar, but the computations are more complicated. Those are called the mixture hidden Markov model (mixture HMM). The observations are continuous and follow a continuous distribution. The NM Dev class `MixtureHMM` implements mixture HMM. To learn their parameters, we need to derive their respective maximum likelihood function to be used in the EM algorithm. The E-step computes the conditional expectations given the observations and the current estimates of the parameters. The M-step maximizes the log-likelihood function with respect to the estimated parameters and the data set. These two steps are repeated until some convergence criterion is satisfied. However, their solutions may not even be analytical, e.g., the t-distribution. NM Dev supports a suite of mixture distributions, such as the following:

- `NormalMixtureDistribution`
- `LogNormalMixtureDistribution`
- `ExponentialMixtureDistribution`
- `PoissonMixtureDistribution`
- `GammaMixtureDistribution`
- `BetaMixtureDistribution`
- `BinomialMixtureDistribution`

The NM Dev class `MixtureHMMEM` implements the EM algorithm to learn a mixture HMM. The following code demonstrates learning an HMM with normal mixture distribution, which is the model for daily stock returns in three regimes in Figure 12-50:

```
println("Learning hidden Markov model with normal distribution")

// the initial probabilities
val PI0: Vector = DenseVector(0.0, 0.0, 1.0)
```

```
// the transition probabilities
val A0: Matrix = DenseMatrix(
    arrayOf(
        doubleArrayOf(0.4, 0.2, 0.4),
        doubleArrayOf(0.3, 0.2, 0.5),
        doubleArrayOf(0.25, 0.25, 0.5)
))
// the conditional normal distributions
val lambda0: Array<NormalMixtureDistribution.Lambda> = arrayOf<NormalMixtureDistribution.
Lambda>(
    NormalMixtureDistribution.Lambda(0.0, 0.5), // (mu, sigma)
    NormalMixtureDistribution.Lambda(0.0, 1.0), // medium volatility
    NormalMixtureDistribution.Lambda(0.0, 2.5) // high volatility
)
// the original HMM: a model of daily stock returns in 3 regimes
val model0: MixtureHMM = MixtureHMM(PI0, A0, NormalMixtureDistribution(lambda0))
model0.seed(1234567890L)

// generate a sequence of observations from the HMM
val T = 10000
var innovations = ArrayList<HmmInnovation>(T)
var observations: DoubleArray = DoubleArray(T)
for (t in 0 until T) {
    innovations.add(t, model0.next())
    observations[t] = innovations.get(t).observation()
}
println("\nObservations: ")
for (t in 1 until 100) {
    print(observations[t].toString() + ", ")
    if (t % 20 == 0) {
        println("")
    }
}
println("")
```

The output is as follows:

```
observations:
0.6667426768019611, -0.32352325221978717, 3.694903034165229, -1.3008707225256613,
0.07691232606090105, -1.0668653899699068, 1.2547831047356035, -0.3246773249494731,
-3.1233208370458296, 0.07292920944831502, -0.11620867976390438, -0.09177918144492855,
1.061260530481548, 3.7632206619139903, 0.8109245344429039, -1.0456473967986801,
0.023362246470829524, 0.7787930654317092, -2.576397166364735, -0.0467834253483496,
3.503162408902286, 1.1028762361945696, 0.18432457538929753, -0.1560288586724O143,
0.2860555006413944, 0.5199262544700902, 3.289672039992487, 0.3423964725249409,
1.4075325491240163, 4.10317186600716, 0.4828282434224251, 0.25452361143844454,
0.5712599275796462, -2.5704804292527013, 0.33450861675375654, -2.8531667206093934,
-3.0936506692640764, -0.15973644756612507, -0.47277685283533033, 0.0707131186690788,
-1.7796825533737028, 0.9864117126346634, 0.2939922129246895, -2.5399726513271608,
-2.6290623371098096, 0.25314785052888766, -0.18575291314328318, -0.7946029274675578,
0.23552969611536276, 2.9897693796241063, 0.5660684741804526, -0.6527078440547278,
```

```
-0.5004832349155411, -0.2704637817979793, -0.6025767412479524, 0.5771268464391458,
-0.24208449949682542, -0.02819954652010102, -2.486386056973469, -3.441724309397634,
-0.4133398692983409, 0.31129502315376223, -0.04193184097521976, -1.0182212276190052,
-0.3671837409753249, 0.536533989621346, 3.462093125207502, -2.461234362203126,
-2.3392296163644772, -0.47516934718702636, -0.11730581631252934, -0.4265784970780354,
-0.8615577291928018, 6.920251345713026, 1.76323228509548, -2.6811368060909544,
-1.5171036957836417, -4.899485440536609, -3.610116084182736, 0.33601950735980296,
-0.5835341423322717, 2.6648103130978678, 0.10317758590238832, 0.19254522009732306,
-2.2919311524559345, -2.7407736539634344, 0.17291860725525898, 0.18227164156727216,
-0.5643594075632472, -0.035583544387142646, -0.09409631532976256, -0.025219030831549336,
0.4529864965098783, -0.8837144318482597, -0.12251468831918433, -0.31744262647741256,
5.209863176061461, -2.474241618649255, 0.1755140184813729, 0.2368171868332689,
```

```
// learn an HMM from the observations
val model1: MixtureHMM
        = MixtureHMMEM(observations, model0, 1e-5, 20) // using true parameters as initial
estimates
val A1: Matrix = model1.A()
val lambda1: Array<NormalMixtureDistribution.Lambda>
        = (model1.getDistribution() as NormalMixtureDistribution).getParams()

println("Original transition probabilities")
println(A0)

println("Learned transition probabilities")
println(A1)

for (i in 0 until lambda0.size) {
    println(String.format("Compare mu: %f vs %f", lambda0[i].mu, lambda1[i].mu))
    println(String.format("Compare sigma: %f vs %f", lambda0[i].sigma, lambda1[i].sigma))
}
```

The output is as follows:

```
original transition probabilities
3x3
         [,1] [,2] [,3]
[1,] 0.400000, 0.200000, 0.400000,
[2,] 0.300000, 0.200000, 0.500000,
[3,] 0.250000, 0.250000, 0.500000,
learned transition probabilities
3x3
         [,1] [,2] [,3]
[1,] 0.413363, 0.192624, 0.394012,
[2,] 0.291749, 0.191727, 0.516524,
[3,] 0.262275, 0.245234, 0.492491,
compare mu: 0.000000 vs -0.006115
```

```
compare sigma: 0.500000 vs 0.509837
compare mu: 0.000000 vs 0.036859
compare sigma: 1.000000 vs 0.952345
compare mu: 0.000000 vs 0.000615
compare sigma: 2.500000 vs 2.559295
```

We can see from the output that the EM algorithm learns the true HMM pretty well from the daily stock returns, matching the variances of the three regimes.

12.7. Principal Component Analysis

Consider a motivating example of plotting (say, experimental) data on the XY-plane as in Figure 12-56. We see that the two variables X and Y are quite correlated. When X is big, Y tends to be big. Likewise, when X is small, Y tends to be small. In fact, Y can be approximated by a linear function of X. If we record only X, we have good enough estimation of Y. There is no need to record both; recording only X is sufficient. We essentially "compress" a two-dimensional data to a one-dimensional space. This is the very basis of dimension reduction.

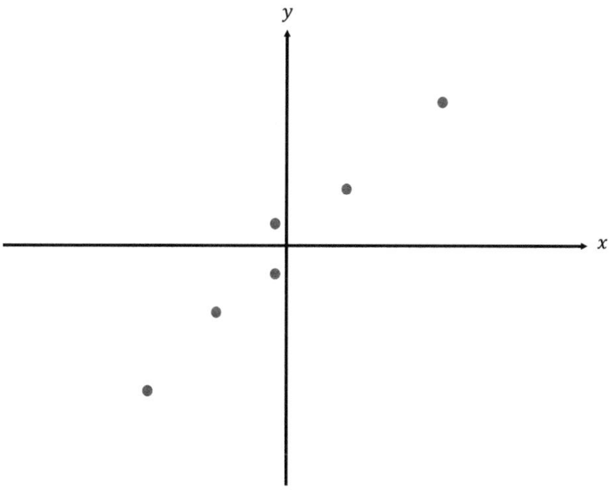

Figure 12-56. *Data on the XY-plane*

We can see this dimension reduction even better if we rotate the XY-plane's axis so that most of the points lie on or close to the new x-axis, x', as in Figure 12-57. We do not really need to record y' because they are all close to 0 within a narrow band. We need to record only x' because they can take many values of a wide range. The data is mostly spread out on x', and that is where most of the variance is. Finding a new coordinate system so that most of the variance is on only a small subset of the axes helps reduce the dimension, filter out noise, identify the important parts of the data, and recognize patterns. This is the very principle of Principal Component Analysis (PCA).

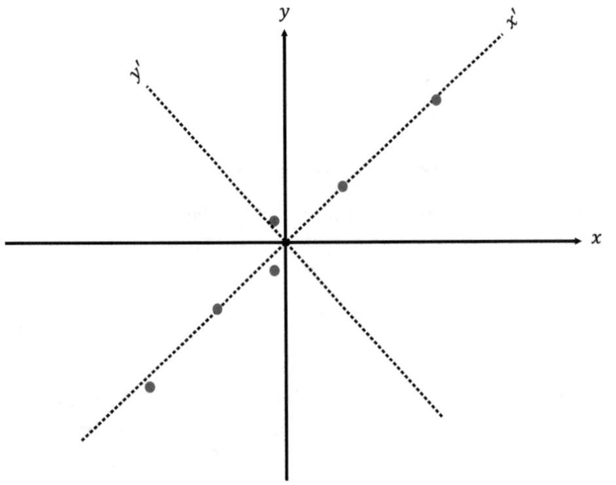

***Figure 12-57.** Data on a rotated XY-plane*

Jon (2003) gives another real-life example to illustrate why and how we do PCA. As often in experimental physics, we need to take many measurements for a phenomenon. Figure 12-58 shows that we use three cameras to capture the motion of a ball attached to a spring. Before we understand a phenomenon, we do not necessarily know how to do the measurements. We may simply place the cameras where it is convenient and where space is available. Each camera records a sequence of *x*s and *y*s from their perspective. There are a total of six coordinates in each snapshot.

$$\boldsymbol{X} = \begin{bmatrix} x_A \\ y_A \\ x_B \\ y_B \\ x_C \\ y_C \end{bmatrix}$$

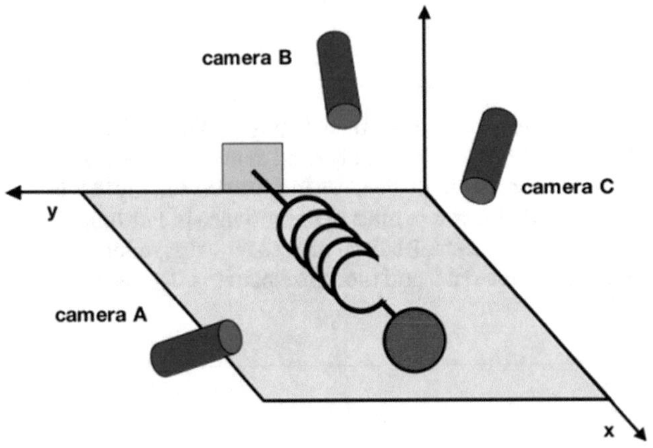

***Figure 12-58.** Taking measurements of the motion of a ball attached to a spring*

We can collect thousands of these coordinates for analysis. However, we know that, with hindsight of how a spring works, this data of six coordinates is difficult to analyze, and they hide the big picture of spring motion, which really moves in only one direction. Is it possible to "transform" the data so that the main component is easy to visualize? Mathematically, we want to find a change of coordinates or change of basis so that the new coordinates reflect the one dimension that the spring bounces back and forth. That is, a change of basis matrix $\boldsymbol{P}$ such that:

$$\boldsymbol{PX} = \boldsymbol{Y}$$

where $\boldsymbol{X}$ is the demeaned data (in PCA, we always first subtract off the mean for every factor or row $\boldsymbol{x}_i$); $\boldsymbol{Y}$ is the new coordinate in the new basis. See Chapter 2 for more details.

To find $\boldsymbol{P}$, we need to impose some properties to justify that $\boldsymbol{P}$ is a good change of basis. For example, we would want $\boldsymbol{Y}$ in the new coordinate system so that

- The variance in each new axis is maximized.
- The covariance between any pair of variables is minimized, say, 0.

These two properties are basically saying that the covariance matrix of $\boldsymbol{Y}$ should be a diagonal matrix. That is, the diagonal elements (variances) are maximized and the off-diagonal elements (covariances) are 0. Mathematically, we have this:

$$\boldsymbol{S}_Y = \frac{1}{n-1}\boldsymbol{YY}^T$$

$$= \frac{1}{n-1}(\boldsymbol{PX})(\boldsymbol{PX})^T$$

$$= \frac{1}{n-1}\boldsymbol{PXX}^T\boldsymbol{P}$$

Note that $\boldsymbol{A} = \boldsymbol{XX}^T$ is the covariance matrix of $\boldsymbol{X}$ (after removing the sample mean and scaling factor). It is symmetric and thus diagonalizable. There exists a matrix of eigenvectors $\boldsymbol{E}$ and a diagonal matrix $\boldsymbol{D}$ such that:

$$\boldsymbol{A} = \boldsymbol{EDE}^T$$

Suppose we select the change of basis $\boldsymbol{P} = \boldsymbol{E}^T$; we have the following:

$$\boldsymbol{S}_Y = \frac{1}{n-1}\boldsymbol{PP}^T\boldsymbol{DP}^T\boldsymbol{P}$$

$= \frac{1}{n-1}\boldsymbol{PP}^{-1}\boldsymbol{DP}^{-1}\boldsymbol{P}$, because $\boldsymbol{P}$ is orthonormal

$$= \frac{1}{n-1}\boldsymbol{D}$$

Evidently, $\boldsymbol{P} = \boldsymbol{E}^T$ diagonalizes $\boldsymbol{S}_Y$. This is the PCA of $\boldsymbol{X}$ to produce a change of coordinates $\boldsymbol{P}$ to have $\boldsymbol{Y}$.

We can also do PCA using SVD. For demeaned data (data subtracting the sample mean) $\boldsymbol{X}$, there exist the orthonormal basis $\boldsymbol{U}$ and $\boldsymbol{V}$ and a diagonal matrix σ such that:

$$\boldsymbol{X} = \boldsymbol{U}\Sigma\boldsymbol{V}^T$$

Equivalently,

$$\boldsymbol{U}^T\boldsymbol{X} = \Sigma\boldsymbol{V}^T$$

Here again, we have the change of basis as follows:

$$\boldsymbol{P} = \boldsymbol{U}^T$$

and the new coordinates as follows:

$$\boldsymbol{Y} = \Sigma\boldsymbol{V}^T$$

U are orthonormal sets of vectors that span an n-dimensional space; ***V*** are orthonormal sets of vectors that span an m-dimensional space. This SVD or PCA projects the n-dimensional space to an m-dimensional space and hence dimension reduction. We usually sort in descending order the diagonal elements in σ so that we may choose to truncate the insignificant singular values. This will further reduce the dimension in the projection space. Going back to the spring example in Figure 12-58, we want to find ***P*** that rotates the coordinates so that most of the data lies on one (new) x-axis. Furthermore, we keep only one most significant singular value and truncate the other five to remove noise. This reduces the dimension of the data from 6 to 1. We can then easily visualize and analyze the spring moving back and forth along a straight line.

NM Dev supports both eigen decomposition and SVD to do PCA. All implementations inherit from the interface PCA. The signature is as follows:

```
public interface PCA {
    /**
     * Gets the number of observations in the original data; sample size.
     *
     * @return <i>nObs</i>, the number of observations in the original data
     */
    public int nObs();
    /**
     * Gets the number of variables in the original data.
     *
     * @return <i>nFactors</i>, the number of variables in the original data
     */
    public int nFactors();
    /**
     * Gets the sample means that were subtracted.
     *
     * @return the sample means of each variable in the original data
     */
    public Vector mean();
    /**
     * Gets the scalings applied to each variable.
     *
     * @return the scalings applied to each variable in the original data
     */
    public Vector scale();
    /**
     * Gets the (possibly centered and/or scaled) data matrix <i>X</i> used for
     * the PCA.
     *
     * @return the (possibly centered and/or scaled) data matrix <i>X</i>
```

```
 */
public Matrix X();
/**
 * Gets the standard deviations of the principal components (i.e., the
 * square roots of the eigenvalues of the correlation (or covariance)
 * matrix).
 *
 * @return the standard deviations of the principal components
 */
public Vector sdPrincipalComponents();
/**
 * Gets the standard deviation of the <i>i</i>-th principal component.
 *
 * @param i an index, counting from 1
 * @return the standard deviation of the <i>i</i>-th principal component.
 */
public double sdPrincipalComponent(int i);
/**
 * Gets the matrix of variable loadings.
 * The signs of the columns of the loading are arbitrary.
 *
 * @return the matrix of variable loadings
 */
public Matrix loadings();
/**
 * Gets the loading vector of the <i>i</i>-th principal component.
 *
 * @param i an index, counting from 1
 * @return the loading vector of the <i>i</i>-th principal component
 */
public Vector loading(int i);
/**
 * Gets the proportion of overall variance explained by each of the
 * principal components.
 *
 * @return the proportion of overall variance explained by each of the
 *         principal components
 */
public Vector proportionVar();
/**
 * Gets the proportion of overall variance explained by the <i>i</i>-th
 * principal component.
 *
 * @param i an index, counting from 1
 * @return the proportion of overall variance explained by the <i>i</i>-th
 *         principal component
 */
public double proportionVar(int i);
/**
 * Gets the cumulative proportion of overall variance explained by the
 * principal components
```

```
     *
     * @return the cumulative proportion of overall variance explained by the
     *         principal components
     */
    public Vector cumulativeProportionVar();
    /**
     * Gets the scores of supplied data on the principal components.
     * The signs of the columns of the scores are arbitrary.
     *
     * @return the scores of supplied data on the principal components
     */
    public Matrix scores();
}
```

For example, the following code runs PCA of the USA arrest data in R. (The data set is given in the source code with this book.)

```
// run PCA on the data using eigen decomposition
val pca: PCA = PCAbyEigen(
        USArrests, // the data set in matrix form
        false // use covariance matrix instead of correlation matrix
)

// number of factors
val p: Int = pca.nFactors()
// number of observations
val n: Int = pca.nObs()

val mean: Vector = pca.mean()
val scale: Vector = pca.scale()
val sdev: Vector = pca.sdPrincipalComponents()
val loadings: Matrix = pca.loadings()
val proportion: Vector = pca.proportionVar()
val cumprop: Vector = pca.cumulativeProportionVar()
val scores: Matrix = pca.scores()

println("Number of factors = " + p)
println("Number of observations = " + n)
```

The output is as follows:

```
number of factors = 4
number of observations = 50
```

```
println("Mean: " + mean)

println("Scale: " + scale)

// The standard deviations differ by a factor of sqrt(50 / 49),
// since we use divisor (nObs - 1) for the sample covariance matrix
```

```
println("Standard deviation: " + sdev)

// The signs of the columns of the loading are arbitrary.
println("Loading: ")
println(loadings)

// the proportion of variance in each dimension
println("Proportion of variance: " + proportion)
println("Cumulative proportion of variance: " + cumprop)

println("Score: ")
println(scores)
```

The output is as follows:

```
mean: [7.788000, 170.760000, 65.540000, 21.232000]
scale: [1.000000, 1.000000, 1.000000, 1.000000]
standard deviation: [83.732400, 14.212402, 6.489426, 2.482790]
loading:
4x4
         [,1] [,2] [,3] [,4]
[1,] -0.041704, 0.044822, 0.079891, 0.994922,
[2,] -0.995221, 0.058760, -0.067570, -0.038938,
[3,] -0.046336, -0.976857, -0.200546, 0.058169,
[4,] -0.075156, -0.200718, 0.974081, -0.072325,
proportion of variance: [0.965534, 0.027817, 0.005800, 0.000849]
cumulative proportion of variance: [0.965534, 0.993352, 0.999151, 1.000000]
```

The PCA reduces the dimension of the data from 4 to 1 or 2. The first principal component accounts for 96.6 percent of the data variability. The first two principal components account for 99 percent of the data variability. We can safely truncate the last two components.

The following code solves the same problem using SVD:

```
// run PCA on the data using SVD
val pca: PCA = PCAbySVD(
        USArrests // the data set in matrix form
)

// number of factors
val p: Int = pca.nFactors()
// number of observations
val n: Int = pca.nObs()

val mean: Vector = pca.mean()
val scale: Vector = pca.scale()
val sdev: Vector = pca.sdPrincipalComponents()
val loadings: Matrix = pca.loadings()
val proportion: Vector = pca.proportionVar()
val cumprop: Vector = pca.cumulativeProportionVar()
```

```
println("Number of factors = " + p)
println("Number of observations = " + n)
```

The output is as follows:

```
number of factors = 4
number of observations = 50
```

```
println("Mean: " + mean)

println("Scale: " + scale)

// The standard deviations differ by a factor of sqrt(50 / 49),
// since we use divisor (nObs - 1) for the sample covariance matrix
println("Standard deviation: " + sdev)

// The signs of the columns of the loading are arbitrary.
println("Loading: ")
println(loadings)

// the proportion of variance in each dimension
println("Proportion of variance: " + proportion)
println("Cumulative proportion of variance: " + cumprop)
```

The output is as follows:

```
mean: [7.788000, 170.760000, 65.540000, 21.232000]
scale: [4.355510, 83.337661, 14.474763, 9.366385]
standard deviation: [1.574878, 0.994869, 0.597129, 0.416449]
loading:
4x4
         [,1] [,2] [,3] [,4]
[1,] 0.535899, -0.418181, -0.341233, 0.649228,
[2,] 0.583184, -0.187986, -0.268148, -0.743407,
[3,] 0.278191, 0.872806, -0.378016, 0.133878,
[4,] 0.543432, 0.167319, 0.817778, 0.089024,
proportion of variance: [0.620060, 0.247441, 0.089141, 0.043358]
cumulative proportion of variance: [0.620060, 0.867502, 0.956642, 1.000000]
```

12.8. Factor Analysis

Factor analysis is used to explain a set of correlated variables or observations in terms of a smaller number of unobserved variables called factors. For example, it may be possible that variations in ten observed variables mainly reflect the variations in two unobserved (underlying) variables. The observed variables are modeled as linear combinations of the unobserved factors plus "error" terms. Similar to PCA, it helps reduce the dimensionality of the data. Factor analysis is commonly used in biology, psychometrics, personality theories, marketing, product management, operations research, and finance when dealing with large data sets.

The concept is best illustrated with an example. Suppose a psychologist has the hypothesis that there are two kinds of intelligence, verbal intelligence and mathematical intelligence, neither of which is directly observed. Evidence for the hypothesis is sought in the examination scores from each of 10 different academic fields of 1,000 students. The psychologist's hypothesis says that for each of the 10 academic fields, the score for a student is a linear combination of his verbal intelligence and mathematical intelligence. While each student has their verbal intelligence and mathematical intelligence, the coefficients for the two factors are the same for everyone. The coefficients are called factor loadings. The factor loading of a factor quantifies the extent (weight) to which an observed variable is related with a given factor. For example, the hypothesis may predict that a student's score in astronomy is as follows:

{10 × the student's verbal intelligence} + {6 × the student's mathematical intelligence}

The numbers 10 and 6 are the factor loadings associated with astronomy. Other academic subjects may have different factor loadings.

Two students assumed to have identical verbal and mathematical intelligence, and hence the same predicted scores, may achieve different scores in astronomy and other subjects. Such differences between the predicted values and the actual values (observations) are called errors.

The observable data are the 10 scores of the 1,000 students for a total of 10,000 numbers. The unobserved factor values (2 for each student for a total of 2,000 numbers) and the factor loadings are estimated from the data using factor analysis.

We can write out the relationships in mathematics. For a student *i*, his standardized z-scores (we work with z-scores so that the magnitudes of all variables are comparable) in the 10 subjects can be modeled as follows:

$$z_{1,i} = l_{1,1}F_{1,i} + l_{1,2}F_{2,i} + \varepsilon_{1,i}$$
$$\vdots$$
$$z_{10,i} = l_{10,1}F_{1,i} + l_{10,2}F_{2,i} + \varepsilon_{10,i}$$

Or, more succinctly, it can be written as follows:

$$z_{a,i} = \sum_{p=1}^{2} l_{a,1}F_{p,i} + \varepsilon_{a,i}$$

where $F_{1,i}$ is student *i*'s verbal intelligence, $F_{2,i}$ is student *i*'s mathematical intelligence, and $l_{a,p}$ are the factor loadings for the *a*-th subject for $p = 1, 2$. See Figure 12-59.

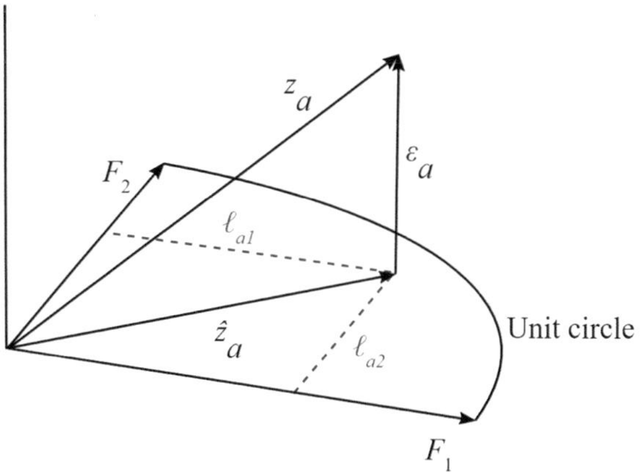

Figure 12-59. *Geometrical interpretation of factor analysis*

Geometrically, the data ($z_{a,i}$), the factors ($F_{p,i}$), and the errors ($\varepsilon_{a,i}$) can be viewed as vectors in an N-dimensional Euclidean space (sample space), represented as $\boldsymbol{z}_a$, $\boldsymbol{F}_j$, and $\boldsymbol{\varepsilon}_a$, respectively. Since the data is standardized, the data vectors are of unit length ($\|\boldsymbol{z}_a\| = 1$). The factor vectors define an k-dimensional linear subspace (i.e., a hyperplane) in this space, upon which the data vectors are projected orthogonally. In the previous example, the hyperplane is a two-dimensional plane defined by the two factor vectors as in Figure 12-59. The goal of factor analysis is to find a hyperplane that is a "best fit" to the data in some sense, so it doesn't matter how the factor vectors that define this hyperplane are chosen, as long as they are independent and lie in the hyperplane.

In general, for all students all subjects, in matrix notation, we have this:

$$Z = LF + \varepsilon$$

The NM Dev class `FactorAnalysis` implements the factor analysis procedure to find L, F, and ε given Z (or X). Here's an example:

```
// number of hidden factors
val nFactors = 3
val factor_analysis
        = FactorAnalysis(
                R_data,
                nFactors,
                FactorAnalysis.ScoringRule.THOMSON // specify the scoring rule
        )

println("Number of observations = " + factor_analysis.nObs())
println("Number of variables = " + factor_analysis.nVariables())
println("Number of factors = " + factor_analysis.nFactors())

// covariance matrix
val S = factor_analysis.S()
println("\nCovariance matrix: ")
println(S)
```

The output is as follows:

```
number of observations = 18
number of variables = 6
number of factors = 3
covariance matrix:
6x6
         [,1] [,2] [,3] [,4] [,5] [,6]
[1,] 1.000000, 0.939308, 0.512887, 0.432031, 0.466495, 0.408608,
[2,] 0.939308, 1.000000, 0.412444, 0.408428, 0.436393, 0.432611,
[3,] 0.512887, 0.412444, 1.000000, 0.877075, 0.512887, 0.432031,
[4,] 0.432031, 0.408428, 0.877075, 1.000000, 0.432031, 0.432326,
[5,] 0.466495, 0.436393, 0.512887, 0.432031, 1.000000, 0.947345,
[6,] 0.408608, 0.432611, 0.432031, 0.432326, 0.947345, 1.000000,
```

```
val estimators: FAEstimator = factor_analysis.getEstimators(700)
val fitted: Double = estimators.logLikelihood()
println("Log-likelihood of the fitting = " + fitted)
```

```
val uniqueness: Vector = estimators.psi()
println("Uniqueness = " + uniqueness)

val dof: Int = estimators.dof()
println("Degree of freedom = " + dof)

// the factor loadings
val loadings: Matrix = estimators.loadings()
println("Factor loadings:")
println(loadings)

val testStats: Double = estimators.statistics()
println("Test statistics = " + testStats)

val pValue: Double = estimators.pValue()
println("P-value = " + pValue)

val scores: Matrix = estimators.scores()
println("Scores:")
println(scores)
```

The output is as follows:

```
log-likelihood of the fitting = 0.475515649954116
```

```
uniqueness = [0.005000, 0.100900, 0.005000, 0.224053, 0.084290, 0.005000]
degree of freedom = 0
factor loadings:
6x3
         [,1] [,2] [,3]
[1,] 0.943840, 0.181926, 0.266614,
[2,] 0.904720, 0.234836, 0.159479,
[3,] 0.235639, 0.209603, 0.946344,
[4,] 0.179976, 0.242255, 0.827568,
[5,] 0.242107, 0.880640, 0.285599,
[6,] 0.192766, 0.958837, 0.196209,
test statistics = 5.785440407775078
p-value = -1.0
scores:
18x3
         [,1] [,2] [,3]
[1,] -0.896511, -0.924689, 0.936376,
[2,] -0.861396, -0.926617, 0.924255,
[3,] -0.900730, -0.925772, 0.950364,
[4,] -0.993305, -0.251413, 0.808659,
[5,] -0.896511, -0.924689, 0.936376,
[6,] -0.741151, 0.720108, -0.783533,
[7,] -0.706036, 0.718180, -0.795654,
[8,] -0.745370, 0.719025, -0.769545,
[9,] -0.802830, 1.391456, -0.923371,
[10,] -0.741151, 0.720108, -0.783533,
```

```
[11,] 0.916893, -0.925056, -0.830334,
[12,] 0.952008, -0.926984, -0.842455,
[13,] 0.912674, -0.926140, -0.816346,
[14,] 0.820099, -0.251780, -0.958051,
[15,] 0.916893, -0.925056, -0.830334,
[16,] 0.426454, 2.035689, 1.282442,
[17,] 1.464788, 1.290102, 0.547953,
[18,] 1.875185, 0.313530, 1.946731,
```

12.9. Covariance Selection

This section follows d'Aspremont (2011). The covariance matrix is fundamental in modeling covariates and understanding the relationship among variables. It is a piece of critical information in many algorithms, such as portfolio optimization (that needs the inverse of the covariance matrix). To get insight into why estimating covariance matrix is difficult, we look at the case where we want to estimate the covariance matrix for 3,000 stocks (about the number of stocks listed on NYSE). The covariance matrix is a 3000×3000 matrix. Because of symmetry, the number of free elements is as follows:

$$\frac{3000^2 + 3000}{2} = 4{,}504{,}500$$

In other words, we would need to estimate about 4.5 million parameters! That seems to be way beyond feasibility given a limited data set. For 10 years of data, there are only 2,500 trading days. For 100 years of data (not sure if we actually have that much recording so far back), there are only 25,000 trading days, and that's assuming (wrongly) that the covariances of the stocks do not change in the last 100 years.

Estimating covariance matrix from real data is in general difficult. There has been a lot of research in this topic. The shrinkage methods in Sections 12.2.9.4 and 12.2.9.5 are one way to do it. Another popular way to do it is to impose structure on the covariance matrix such as setting elements in the inverse of the covariance matrix to zeros. The latter method is called covariance selection.

Zeros in the inverse covariance matrix correspond to conditionally independent variables in the model, and this approach can be used to simultaneously obtain a robust estimate of the covariance matrix while, perhaps more importantly, discovering structure in the underlying graphical model. This trade-off is between log-likelihood of the solution matrix $\boldsymbol{X}$ and number of zeros in its inverse (i.e., model structure), which can be formalized in the following problem:

$$\max_{\mathbf{X}} \left\{ \log\det(\boldsymbol{X}) - Tr(\Sigma \boldsymbol{X}) - \rho \operatorname{Card}(\boldsymbol{X}) \right\}$$

where we are choosing a covariance matrix $\boldsymbol{X}$. Card($\boldsymbol{X}$) is the cardinality of $\boldsymbol{X}$, i.e., the number of nonzero coefficients in $\boldsymbol{X}$ and $\rho > 0$ is a parameter controlling the trade-off between likelihood and structure.

Solving this penalized maximum likelihood estimation problem both improves the stability of this estimation procedure by implicitly reducing the number of parameters and directly highlights structure in the underlying model. Unfortunately, the cardinality penalty makes this problem very hard to solve numerically. d'Aspremont (2011) describes a solution. It is to relax the Card($\boldsymbol{X}$) penalty and replace it by the (convex) L1 norm of the coefficients of $\boldsymbol{X}$ to solve instead.

$$\max_{X} \left(\log\det(\boldsymbol{X}) - Tr(\Sigma \boldsymbol{X}) - \rho \sum_{i,j=1}^{n} \left| X_{ij} \right| \right)$$

The penalty term involving the sum of absolute values of the entries of ***X*** acts as a proxy for the cardinality: the function $\sum_{i,j=1}^{n} |X_{ij}|$ can be seen as the largest convex lower bound on Card(***X***) on the hypercube for rank minimization. It is also often used in regression and variable selection procedures, such as the LASSO.

In a multivariate Gaussian distribution, zeros in the inverse covariance matrix point to variables that are conditionally independent, conditioned on all the remaining variables. This has a clear financial interpretation: the inverse covariance matrix reflects independence relationships between the idiosyncratic components of asset price dynamics.

Figure 12-60 shows the resulting network of dependence, or graphical model for U.S. swap rates. In this graph, variables (nodes) are joined by a link if and only if they are conditionally dependent. This is the graphical model inferred from the pattern of zeros in the inverse sample covariance matrix.

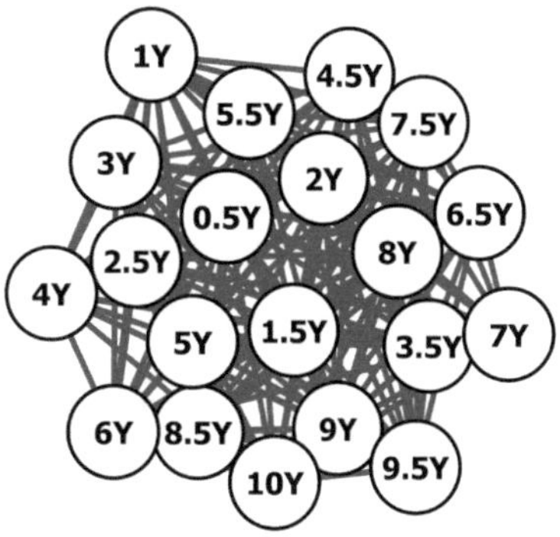

Figure 12-60. *Conditional dependence network inferred from the pattern of zeros in the inverse sample covariance matrix*

Figure 12-61 shows the same graph, using this time the penalized covariance estimate with penalty parameter $\rho = 0.1$. Notice that in the penalized estimate, rates are clustered by maturity. The graph clearly reveals that swap rates are moving as a curve.

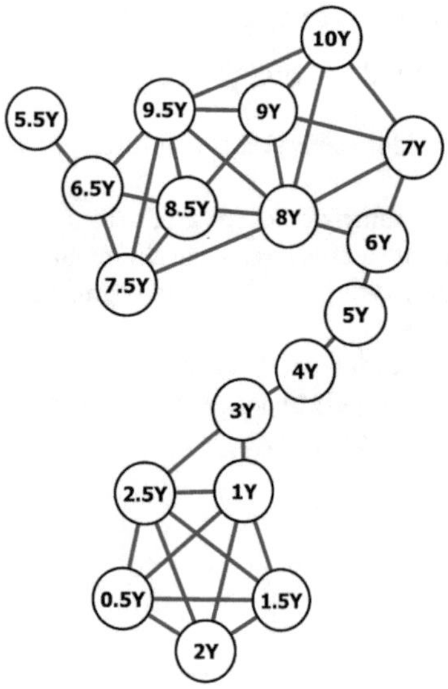

Figure 12-61. *Conditional dependence network using the penalized covariance estimate*

The NM Dev class CovarianceSelectionLASSO implements this LASSO approach of covariance selection. Here's an example:

```
// generate random samples from standard normal distribution
val rnorm = StandardNormalRNG()
rnorm.seed(1234567890L)
val nRows = 50
val nCols = 10
val X = DenseMatrix(nRows, nCols)
for (i in 1 until nRows) {
    for (j in 1 until nCols) {
        X.set(i, j, rnorm.nextDouble())
    }
}

// sample covariance matrix
val S = SampleCovariance(X)
println("sample covariance: \n")
println(S)

// the penalty parameter
val rho = 0.03
val problem = CovarianceSelectionProblem(S, rho)

var time1: Long = System.currentTimeMillis()
val lasso = CovarianceSelectionLASSO(problem, 1e-5)
val sigma: Matrix = lasso.covariance()
time1 = System.currentTimeMillis() - time1
```

```
println("Estimated sigma: \n")
println(sigma)

println("Inverse sigma: \n")
val sigma_inv = lasso.inverseCovariance()
println(sigma_inv)
```

The output is as follows:

```
sample covariance:
10x10
     [,1] [,2] [,3] [,4] [,5] [,6] [,7] [,8] [,9] [,10]
[1,] 0.925475, 0.004218, 0.036085, -0.056795, 0.173294, -0.352947, 0.047752, -0.086790,
0.129483, 0.000000,
[2,] 0.004218, 1.044569, 0.028598, -0.103705, -0.084960, -0.176651, 0.308747, -0.138218,
0.127196, 0.000000,
[3,] 0.036085, 0.028598, 0.767803, 0.057206, -0.088929, 0.002309, -0.016617, -0.208669,
-0.120564, 0.000000,
[4,] -0.056795, -0.103705, 0.057206, 1.174416, -0.150165, 0.199965, -0.165554, 0.002550,
0.074200, 0.000000,
[5,] 0.173294, -0.084960, -0.088929, -0.150165, 0.977483, -0.207569, -0.124171, -0.076252,
0.235514, 0.000000,
[6,] -0.352947, -0.176651, 0.002309, 0.199965, -0.207569, 1.242628, -0.096799, 0.047458,
-0.014898, 0.000000,
[7,] 0.047752, 0.308747, -0.016617, -0.165554, -0.124171, -0.096799, 1.120136, 0.048563,
-0.187201, 0.000000,
[8,] -0.086790, -0.138218, -0.208669, 0.002550, -0.076252, 0.047458, 0.048563, 1.154475,
0.036975, 0.000000,
[9,] 0.129483, 0.127196, -0.120564, 0.074200, 0.235514, -0.014898, -0.187201, 0.036975,
0.838084, 0.000000,
[10,] 0.000000, 0.000000, 0.000000, 0.000000, 0.000000, 0.000000, 0.000000, 0.000000,
0.000000, 0.000000,
Estimated sigma:

10x10
     [,1] [,2] [,3] [,4] [,5] [,6] [,7] [,8] [,9] [,10]
[1,] 0.925475, 0.000000, 0.000000, -0.000833, -0.000000, -0.027764, 0.000000, -0.000000,
0.000000, 0.000000,
[2,] 0.000000, 1.044569, 0.000000, -0.000000, -0.000015, -0.000000, 0.031337, -0.000000,
-0.000495, 0.000000,
[3,] 0.000000, 0.000000, 0.767803, -0.000000, -0.000000, -0.000000, 0.000000, -0.023034,
-0.000000, 0.000000,
[4,] -0.000833, -0.000000, -0.000000, 1.174416, 0.000000, 0.000025, -0.000000, 0.000000,
0.000000, 0.000000,
[5,] -0.000000, -0.000015, -0.000000, 0.000000, 0.977483, -0.000000, -0.000000, 0.000000,
0.013875, 0.000000,
[6,] -0.027764, -0.000000, -0.000000, 0.000025, -0.000000, 1.242628, -0.000000, 0.000000,
0.000000, 0.000000,
[7,] 0.000000, 0.031337, 0.000000, -0.000000, -0.000000, -0.000000, 1.120136, -0.000000,
-0.017704, 0.000000,
```

```
[8,] -0.000000, -0.000000, -0.023034, 0.000000, 0.000000, 0.000000, -0.000000, 1.154475,
0.000000, 0.000000,
[9,] 0.000000, -0.000495, -0.000000, 0.000000, 0.013875, 0.000000, -0.017704, 0.000000,
0.838084, 0.000000,
[10,] 0.000000, 0.000000, 0.000000, 0.000000, 0.000000, 0.000000, 0.000000, 0.000000,
0.000000, 0.000000,
Inverse sigma:

10x10
     [,1] [,2] [,3] [,4] [,5] [,6] [,7] [,8] [,9] [,10]
[1,] 1.081252, 0.000000, -0.000000, 0.000766, 0.000000, 0.024159, -0.000000, 0.000000,
-0.000000, 0.000000,
[2,] 0.000000, 0.958137, -0.000000, 0.000000, 0.000015, 0.000000, -0.026805, 0.000000,
-0.000000, 0.000000,
[3,] -0.000000, -0.000000, 1.303197, 0.000000, 0.000000, 0.000000, -0.000000, 0.026001,
0.000000, 0.000000,
[4,] 0.000766, 0.000000, 0.000000, 0.851487, -0.000000, -0.000000, 0.000000, -0.000000,
-0.000000, 0.000000,
[5,] 0.000000, 0.000015, 0.000000, -0.000000, 1.023276, 0.000000, -0.000268, -0.000000,
-0.016947, 0.000000,
[6,] 0.024159, 0.000000, 0.000000, -0.000000, 0.000000, 0.805286, -0.000000, -0.000000,
-0.000000, 0.000000,
[7,] -0.000000, -0.026805, -0.000000, 0.000000, -0.000268, -0.000000, 0.893797, 0.000000,
0.018870, 0.000000,
[8,] 0.000000, 0.000000, 0.026001, -0.000000, -0.000000, -0.000000, 0.000000, 0.866713,
-0.000000, 0.000000,
[9,] -0.000000, -0.000000, 0.000000, -0.000000, -0.016947, -0.000000, 0.018870, -0.000000,
1.193877, 0.000000,
[10,] 0.000000, 0.000000, 0.000000, 0.000000, 0.000000, 0.000000, 0.000000, 0.000000,
0.000000, 100000000.000000,
```

We see that the penalized covariance matrix (and its inverse) is much closer to the identity matrix (as they should be because the data are i.i.d. standard normal) than the sample covariance matrix (and its inverse), highlighting the problem with sample covariance matrix and the effectiveness of the LASSO covariance selection approach.

Sustik & Ben (2012) develops an implementation that is magnitude faster than the original LASSO implementation. Figure 12-62 shows the benchmark comparison between various LASSO implementations.

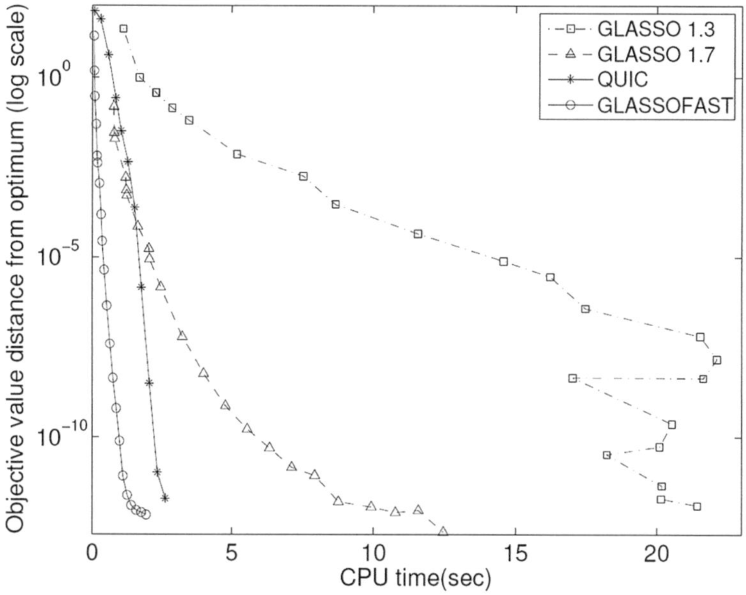

***Figure 12-62.** Comparing GLASSOFAST versus GLASSO*

The NM Dev class CovarianceSelectionGLASSOFAST implements this fast LASSO algorithm of covariance selection. Here's an example:

```
// generate random samples from standard normal distribution
val rnorm = StandardNormalRNG()
rnorm.seed(1234567890L)
val nRows = 50
val nCols = 10
val X = DenseMatrix(nRows, nCols)
for (i in 1 until nRows) {
    for (j in 1 until nCols) {
        X.set(i, j, rnorm.nextDouble())
    }
}

// sample covariance matrix
// val S = SampleCovariance(X)
// println("Sample covariance: \n")
// println(S)

// the penalty parameter
val rho = 0.03
val problem = CovarianceSelectionProblem(S, rho)

var time2: Long = System.currentTimeMillis()
val lasso2 = CovarianceSelectionGLASSOFAST(problem)
val sigma2 = lasso2.covariance()
time2 = System.currentTimeMillis() - time2
```

```
println("Estimated sigma: \n")
println(sigma2)

 println("CovarianceSelectionLASSO took " + time1 + " millisecs")
println("CovarianceSelectionGLASSOFAST took " + time2 + " millisecs")
```

The output is as follows:

```
covariance selection using GLASSOFAST
Estimated sigma:

10x10
     [,1] [,2] [,3] [,4] [,5] [,6] [,7] [,8] [,9] [,10]
[1,] 0.955475, 0.034218, 0.006085, -0.048451, 0.143294, -0.322947, 0.017752, -0.056790,
0.099483, 0.000000,
[2,] 0.034218, 1.074569, 0.008399, -0.073705, -0.054960, -0.146651, 0.278747, -0.108218,
0.097196, 0.000000,
[3,] 0.006085, 0.008399, 0.797803, 0.027206, -0.058929, 0.005653, 0.013383, -0.178669,
-0.090564, 0.000000,
[4,] -0.048451, -0.073705, 0.027206, 1.204416, -0.120165, 0.169965, -0.135554, 0.006710,
0.044200, 0.000000,
[5,] 0.143294, -0.054960, -0.058929, -0.120165, 1.007483, -0.177569, -0.094172, -0.046252,
0.205514, 0.000000,
[6,] -0.322947, -0.146651, 0.005653, 0.169965, -0.177569, 1.272628, -0.066798, 0.037528,
-0.044898, 0.000000,
[7,] 0.017752, 0.278747, 0.013383, -0.135554, -0.094172, -0.066798, 1.150136, 0.018563,
-0.157201, 0.000000,
[8,] -0.056790, -0.108218, -0.178669, 0.006710, -0.046252, 0.037528, 0.018563, 1.184475,
0.006975, 0.000000,
[9,] 0.099483, 0.097196, -0.090564, 0.044200, 0.205514, -0.044898, -0.157201, 0.006975,
0.868084, 0.000000,
[10,] 0.000000, 0.000000, 0.000000, 0.000000, 0.000000, 0.000000, 0.000000, 0.000000,
0.000000, 0.030000,

CovarianceSelectionLASSO took 542 millisecs
CovarianceSelectionGLASSOFAST took 9 millisecs
```

Clearly, GLASSOFAST is orders of magnitude faster than the classical LASSO implementation.

CHAPTER 13

■ ■ ■

Random Numbers and Simulation

A random number or random variable is the result of a random process whereby the result is not deterministic. We can only know the exact value of the variable *a posteriori,* meaning after the fact. For example, the next roll of the dice is random. We only know the result after we roll them. A coin toss is also random. We only know which side it lands on after it is tossed. Another way to look at random variables is to consider the information they reveal. For example, while a student's test score is fixed, it is random because it is unknown or uncertain to us before we look at it. We only know the test score after the information becomes available. Many applications and physical phenomena are therefore random, because of their nature, because of uncertainty, or because the information is unavailable. The study of random numbers is central to statistics.

There are many ways to generate random numbers. These methods are called *random number generators* (RNGs). The most important characteristic of an RNG is that it generates independent and identically distributed (i.i.d.) random numbers. That is, the next random number that's generated has nothing to do with any previously generated numbers, except that they come from the same probability distribution.

True random numbers are generated using physical phenomena, such as coin tosses, dice rolls, noise from electronic components, nuclear fission, and radioactive decay. Such RNGs are called physical random number generators. They are expensive and difficult to integrate into a computer. To generate true random numbers using a computer, we count the number of calculations over a period of time, the error of the system time, and the noise of the sound card. In practice, we do not use true random numbers because they are expensive to produce. More importantly, they are not repeatable. Often, we must repeat the same sequence of random numbers in a simulation to make our computations and experiments repeatable. It is also much easier to debug a problem that we can reproduce rather than one that keeps changing each time.

A *pseudorandom* number generator is an algorithm designed to generate a sequence of pseudorandom numbers that lack a pattern. It is important to know that the sequence is not random at all and that it is completely determined by a relatively small set of initial values. Knowing the generation algorithm and the states, the computer can predict the next value. The "seemingly" random values are generated in a deterministic way. On the other hand, they have a long periodicity, meaning that they don't repeat the same pattern until after a very long sequence. They have statistical properties similar to those of their true counterparts. A good pseudo-RNG or simply RNG implementation must be fast, because we often need to generate millions or billions of random numbers in an application. In addition, we can assess the quality of an RNG by checking the uniformity, randomness, and independence of the random numbers that it generates.

The source code in this chapter can be run on the S2 platform here:

```
https://s21.nm.dev/hub/user-redirect/lab/tree/s2-public/Numerical%20Methods%20Using%20
Kotlin/chapter13.ipynb
```

© Haksun Li, PhD 2023
H. Li, PhD, *Numerical Methods Using Kotlin*, https://doi.org/10.1007/978-1-4842-8826-9_13

The source code can be found on GitHub:

https://github.com/apress/numerical-methods-kotlin

13.1. Uniform Random Number Generators

The simplest RNGs are a class of uniform RNGs. They produce random numbers between 0 and 1, inclusively, according to uniform distribution. That is, any number between 0 and 1 inclusively is chosen with equal chance. They are the building blocks for all other more complicated RNGs such as those sampling from probability distributions like Gaussian, beta, and gamma RNGs. The more complicated distributions often do a transformation on the uniform distribution.

13.1.1. Linear Congruential Methods

A classic and best-known pseudorandom number generator algorithm for uniform distribution is the family of linear congruential generators (LCGs). They produce integers and then scale them to be within the unit interval. The theory is relatively easy to understand. They are easily implemented and fast, especially on computer hardware that supports modular arithmetic by storage-bit truncation.

Two integers A and B are said to be congruent with respect to modulo M if and only if they have the same remainder when divided by a natural number M. Here's an example:

$$55 = 7 \times 7 + 6$$

$$461 = 65 \times 7 + 6$$

461 divided by 7 has a remainder 6; 55 divided by 7 has also a remainder 6. Therefore, 461 and 55 are congruent with respect to modulo 7. We write the following:

$$461 \equiv 55 \bmod 7$$

An LCG is defined by the following recurrence relation:

$$X_{n+1} = (aX_n + c) \bmod m$$

X_n is a random number sequence.
m, $0 < m$, which is the modulus.
a, $0 < a < m$, which is the multiplier.
$0 \le c < m$, which is the increment, also called the offset.
X_0, $0 \le X_0 < m$, which is the starting value.

Given a starting value X_0, you can keep running the recurrence relation to produce a sequence of random numbers. Assuming that the parameters are properly chosen, the quality of randomness is good. All possible integers will appear eventually. The maximum period of the sequence is m. However, the quality of the LCG depends heavily on the parameters you choose. It may produce a short period or even nonrandom numbers (highly serially correlated). You do not usually hand-pick those parameters.

The Lehmer random number generator is another popular choice of parameters. It sets m to a prime number or a power of a prime number and $c = 0$. For example, NM Dev by default uses $m = 2147483563$ and $a = 40014$.

One problem with an LCG is that the period may be too small for applications. One way to create an LCG with a bigger period is to combine several LCGs. The output of the composite LCG is equivalent to the output of a single LCG with a modulus the same as the product of the component generators' moduli and with a period that's the least common multiple of the component periods.

In NM Dev, we provide a few dozen random number generators. A complete list can be found here:

https://nm.dev/html/javadoc/nmdev/dev/nm/stat/random/rng/univariate/RandomNumberGenerator.html

The signature of a random number generator is as follows. The seed method initializes the RNG to the beginning of a random sequence. The nextDouble method produces the next random number based on the property of that particular RNG.

```
public interface Seedable {
    /**
     * Seed the random number/vector/scenario generator to produce repeatable experiments.
     *
     * @param seeds the seeds
     */
    public void seed(long... seeds);
}
public interface RandomNumberGenerator extends Seedable {
    /**
     * Get the next random {@code double}.
     *
     * @return the next random number
     */
    public double nextDouble();
}
```

The following code produces a number of sequences of random numbers using various LCGs. The nextLong method for LCG produces integers; the nextDouble method produces doubles between 0 and 1.[1]

```
println("Generate random numbers using an Lehmer RNG:")
val rng1 = Lehmer()
rng1.seed(1234567890L)
generateIntAndPrint(rng1, 10)
var arr: DoubleArray = generate(rng1, 10)
print(arr)
```

The output is as follows:

```
generate random numbers using an Lehmer RNG:
[1435150771, 264992611, 1287986023, 14695885, 1778129691, 1803529921, 261124279, 1119365911,
242889263, 1607847107]

[0.9693015489683634, 0.6321804200929291, 0.06732959846175084, 0.12655284849786763,
0.8856797936757945, 0.591264143240383, 0.8434276206844243, 0.9128140665540452,
0.34205909356243114, 0.15256980711986945]
```

[1] Some auxiliary functions such as generateIntAndPrint, generate, match, print, and printStats are not listed in the text. They can be found in the source code on S2.

```
println("Generate random numbers using an LEcuyer RNG:")
val rng2 = LEcuyer()
rng2.seed(1234567890L)
generateIntAndPrint(rng2, 10)
arr = generate(rng2, 10)
print(arr)
```

The output is as follows:

```
Generate random numbers using an LEcuyer RNG:
[931800788, 1315300572, 50110053, 1984090886, 1233048435, 1852047791, 1666959172, 802962765,
288962461, 1436549801]

[0.5579439720874392, 0.8760583083499495, 0.27437038918694967, 0.8951008789684162,
0.9749086084658786, 0.5236797712387888, 0.5190309786792058, 0.07284812912011898,
0.947280622528531, 0.9903890099331686]
```

```
println("Generate random numbers using a composite LCG:")
val rng3 = CompositeLinearCongruentialGenerator(
                arrayOf<LinearCongruentialGenerator>(
                    rng1 as LinearCongruentialGenerator,
                    rng2 as LinearCongruentialGenerator
                )
        )
rng3.seed(1234567890L)
generateIntAndPrint(rng3, 10)
arr = generate(rng3, 10)
print(arr)
```

The output is as follows:

```
Generate random numbers using a composite LCG:

[1435150771, 264992611, 1287986023, 14695885, 1778129691, 1803529921, 261124279, 1119365911,
242889263, 1607847107]

[0.9693015115049681, 0.6321803956592273, 0.06732959585946947, 0.12655284360661437,
0.8856797594443706, 0.5912641203880907, 0.8434275880860421, 0.9128140312738847,
0.34205908034188587, 0.15256980122306366]
```

Note that the LCGs produce integers. To sample from uniform distribution, they scale the integers to be within the unit interval.

By using the same seed, 1234567890L in this example, the code always produces the same sequences of random numbers. This is important when you want to repeat the same random experiment over and over, such as when debugging or getting the same value computing π. In general, in an application where there are multiple RNGs, they should all share the same underlying uniform RNG. In other words, an application should have one and only one uniform RNG regardless of how many RNGs it may use. That uniform RNG takes one seed and should be seeded only once in the beginning of the application throughout the lifetime of the application.

The signature of a CompositeLinearCongruentialGenerator is as follows:

```
/**
 * Constructs a linear congruential generator from some simpler and shorter
 * modulus generators.
 *
 * @param rng simpler and shorter modulus linear congruential generators
 */
public CompositeLinearCongruentialGenerator(LinearCongruentialGenerator[] rng)
```

13.1.2. Mersenne Twister

One problem with the linear congruential methods is that the period may be too small for applications. For example, 2^{32} is still small even when you use a composite LCG. Therefore, an LCG is good for a small application that needs only a few thousand random numbers, not millions. In contrast, a commonly used Mersenne Twister (MT) RNG, known as MT19937, has period of $2^{19937} - 1$ (Matsumoto & Nishimura, 1998). Also, an MT RNG has good statistical randomness. MT19937 is the most widely used, general-purpose RNG.

The following code produces 1 million random numbers using MT19937 in 38.72 milliseconds:

```
val rng = MersenneTwister()

val startTime: Long = System.nanoTime()
val N = 1_000_000
for (i in 0 until N) {
    rng.nextDouble()
}
val endTime: Long = System.nanoTime()

val duration: Long = (endTime - startTime)
val ms: Double = duration.toDouble() / 1_000_000.0 // divide by 1000000 to get milliseconds
println(String.format("Took MT19937 %f milliseconds to generate %d random numbers", ms, N))
```

The output is as follows:

```
Took MT19937 38.72 milliseconds to generate 1000000 random numbers
```

13.2. Sampling from Probability Distributions

Random number generation is widely used in gaming, gambling, cryptography, simulation, and many other areas where producing an unpredictable result is desirable. Some physical phenomena are fundamentally *stochastic* (a fancy word for random) in nature, such as coin tosses, radioactive decay, particle positions, and everything in the quantum realm. Simulation and Monte Carlo methods have been proven effective for solving difficult problems where there is no other known solution. They are widely applied in every branch of science and are based on random number generation. Therefore, you'll often need to model the stochastic nature of a process or a system. In other words, you want to generate random numbers that mimic the probabilistic properties of a system. For example, say you want to write a program to simulate an experiment of tossing 100 coins and count the number of heads in each experiment. You need to generate a lot of random numbers (heads = 0, tails = 1) according to the 50-50 probability distribution. This is called random number generation sampling from a probability distribution.

A random variable, X, is a variable that can take different values. You do not know what value it takes until you look at it (information revealed). This is in contrast to a (deterministic) variable, such as $x = 1$, which can always take only one value. Each time you "look at" a random variable, it is a sampling from that random variable. For example, the outcome of a coin toss is a random variable. You do not know whether it is heads or tails until you toss the coin. Tossing the coin ten times gives you ten observations or samples, for example, $\{x_1 = 1, x_2 = 1, x_3 = 0, \cdots, x_{10} = 0\}$. Each sample comes from the probability distribution of a fair coin.

A probability distribution is a mathematical function that gives the probabilities of occurrences of different possible outcomes of an experiment. For example, the probability distribution of tossing a fair coin assigns 0.5 (50 percent) to heads and 0.5 (50 percent) to tails, respectively. A probability distribution is formally defined by a cumulative distribution function. The cumulative distribution function (CDF) of a real-valued random variable X, evaluated at x, and it is the probability that X will take a value less than or equal to x. Mathematically, you get this (see Figure 13-1):

$$F_X(x) = P(X \le x)$$

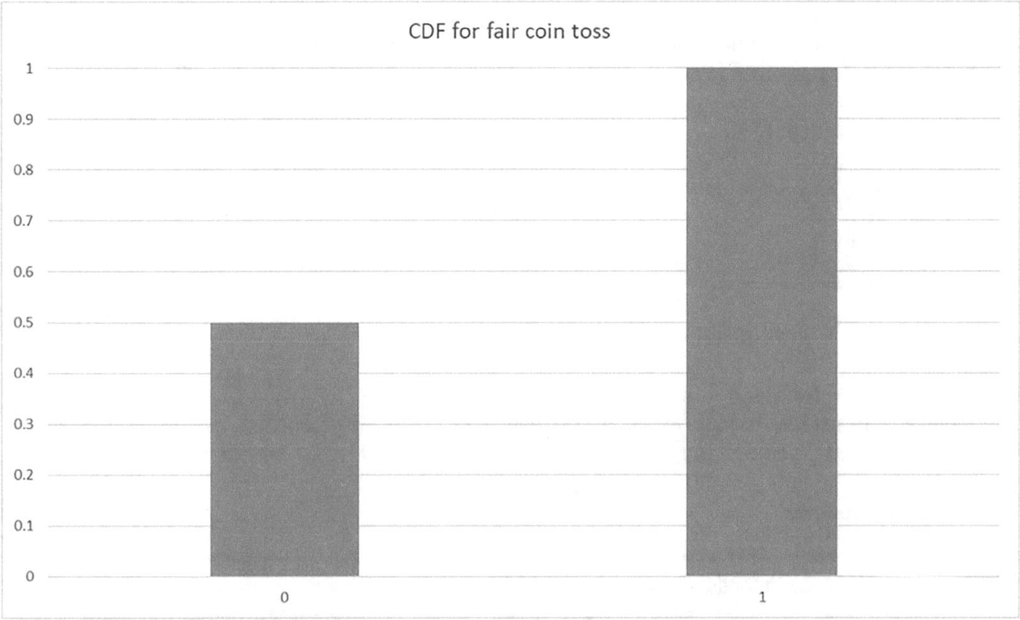

Figure 13-1. *Cumulative distribution function for fair coin toss*

The CDF for tossing a fair coin, labeling heads as 0 and tails as 1, is as follows:

$$F_X(x) = \begin{cases} 0.5, x = 0 \\ 1, x = 1 \end{cases}$$

Figure 13-2 shows a few CDFs for normal distributions. Note that for a normal distribution with $\mu = 0$ (mean is 0), the chance of getting one sample from the probability distribution with a value that's smaller (or bigger) than 0 is 0.5.

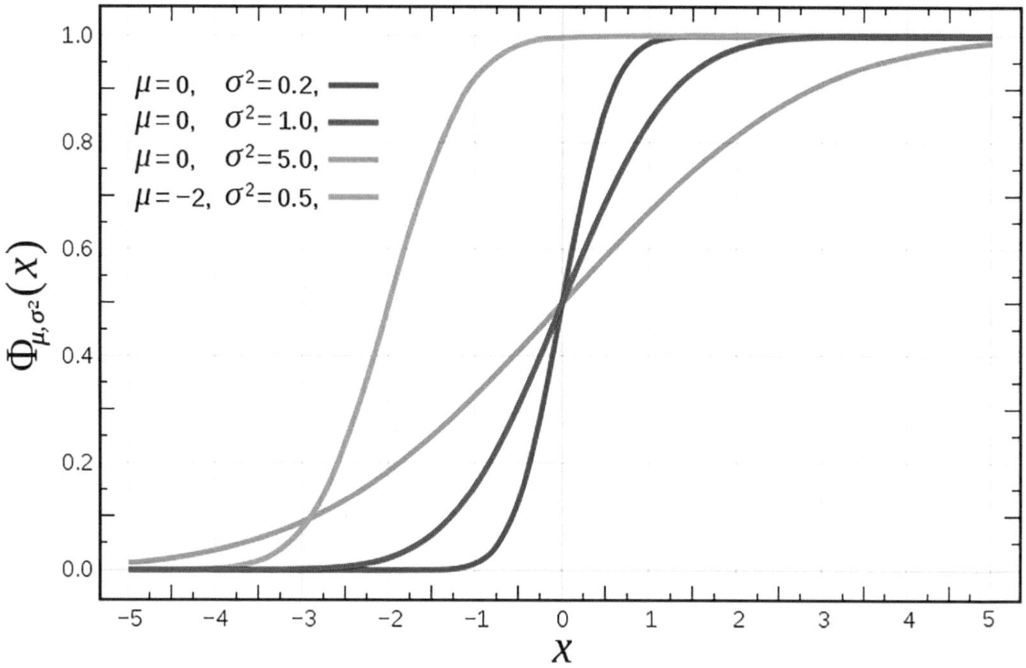

Figure 13-2. *Cumulative distribution functions for the normal distributions*

For a continuous random variable, it is often more intuitive to describe it using a probability density function (PDF).

$$f_X(x) = \frac{d}{dx} F_X(x)$$

$f_X(x)$ is the relative likelihood that the random variable equals a sample value x. The bigger the relative likelihood, the more likely that you'll see this sample over another. The absolute likelihood is always 0 for a continuous random variable. The probability that the value of a random variable will fall within a certain region is the area of the region under the PDF, that is, the integral of the PDF in the region.

We discussed sampling from a uniform distribution in Section 13.1. This section discusses methods to sample from an arbitrary probability distribution.

13.2.1. Inverse Transform Sampling

Inverse transform sampling is a method to generate samples at random from any probability distribution given its cumulative distribution function. It takes a random number from the uniform distribution y between 0 and 1, interpreted as a probability, and then returns the largest number x from the domain of the distribution $F_X(x)$ such that $F_X(x) \le y$. In other words, it computes the inverse $F_X^{-1}(y) = \inf\{x | F_X(x) \ge y\}$. For the example in Figure 13-3, a uniform random number produces four samples, U_1, U_2^a, U_2^b, U_2^c. The corresponding samples from the probability distribution $F_X(x)$ are $F_X^{-1}(U_1)$ and three $F_X^{-1}(U_2)$ s.

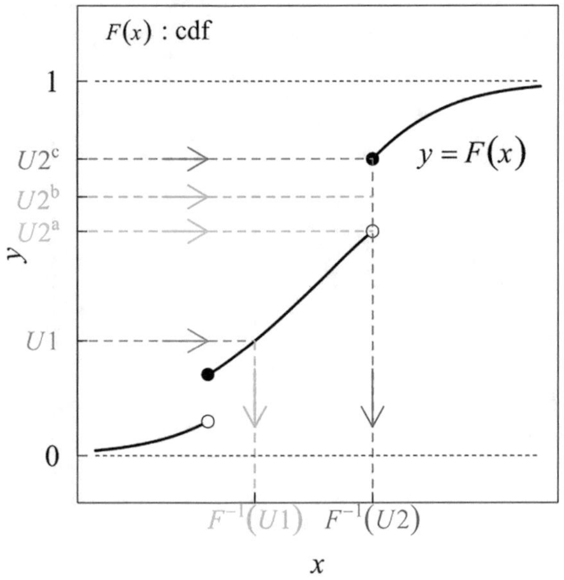

Figure 13-3. *Schematic of the inverse transform sampling*

NM Dev has a class to do inverse transform sampling. The signature is as follows:

```
/**
 * Constructs a random number generator to sample from a distribution.
 *
 * @param distribution the distribution to sample from
 * @param uniform      a uniform random number generator
 */
public InverseTransformSampling(
                                ProbabilityDistribution distribution,
                                RandomLongGenerator uniform)
```

The Rayleigh distribution has the following CDF:

$$F(x|\sigma) = 1 - \exp\left(-\frac{x^2}{2\sigma^2}\right), x \in [0, \infty)$$

To construct an RNG for the Rayleigh distribution, you simply pass its probability distribution to `InverseTransformSampling` (see Figure 13-4).

```
/**
 * Constructs a random number generator to sample from the Rayleigh
 * distribution.
 *
 * @param sigma the standard deviation
 */
public RayleighRNG(double sigma) {
    super(new dev.nm.stat.distribution.univariate.RayleighDistribution(sigma));
}
```

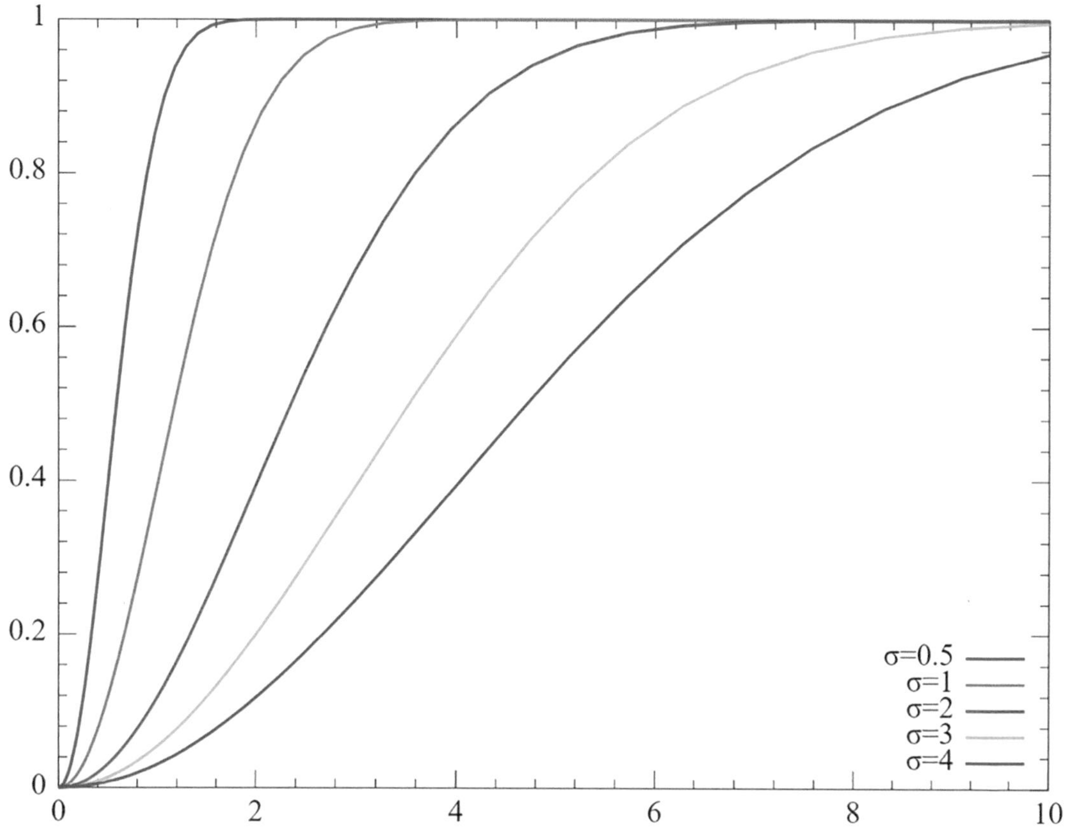

Figure 13-4. *CDF for the Rayleigh distribution*

Computationally, this method involves computing the quantile function of the distribution, that is, the inverse of the cumulative distribution function. That's why the term *inverse* is in the name for this method. Unfortunately, this method is computationally inefficient or infeasible for many distributions when it is difficult or impossible to integrate the PDF of a distribution or to compute the inverse of the CDF. Inverse transform sampling is inefficient for rare events. For those events that have probability close to 0, $P(X \in A) \approx 0$, it would take close to an infinite number of uniform samples, $\frac{1}{P(X \in A)}$, to get to them.

13.2.2. Acceptance-Rejection Sampling

Suppose you want to sample from a PDF $f_X(x)$. You draw the PDF on a large rectangle board. You randomly and uniformly throw darts to the board. You then remove the darts that are outside the area under the curve. The remaining darts will be distributed uniformly within the area under the curve, and the x-positions of these darts will be distributed according to the random variable's density. This is because there is the most room for the darts to land where the curve is highest and thus the probability density is the greatest (see Figure 13-5).

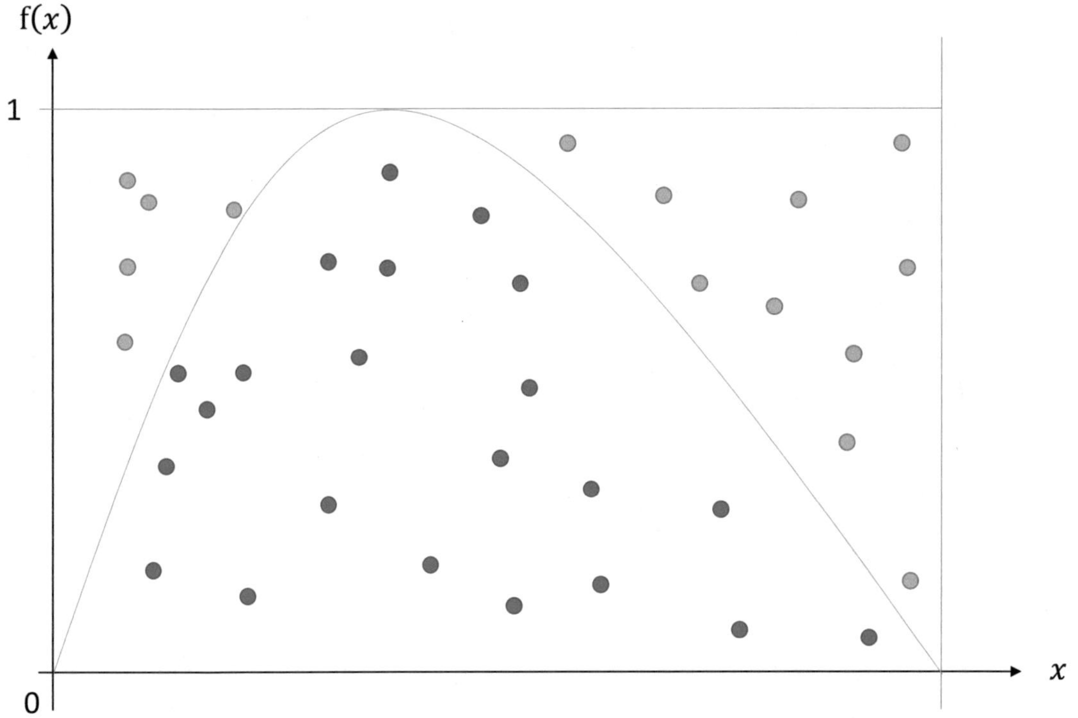

Figure 13-5. *Conceptual diagram for acceptance-rejection; accept the dots below the curve and reject the dots above the curve*

This idea can be extended to where the proposal distribution is not uniform (i.e., the rectangle board) but also any distribution that you know how to sample from. The proposal distribution needs to be at least as high as the target distribution to completely enclose the latter. Otherwise, there would be parts of the curved area that you want to sample from that could never be reached. This acceptance-rejection algorithm also works for higher-dimension PDFs.

Suppose you want to sample from a target PDF $f(x)$. You want to propose a PDF $g(x)$ such that:

- For any x, $f(x) <= M \times g(x)$.
- $g(x)$ is easy to sample from.
- $g(x)$ should be similar to $f(x)$ in shape.

The rejection method is as follows:

1. Sample from the proposal distribution $g(x)$ to get x_i, $x_i \sim g(x)$.
2. Sample from the uniform distribution to get $u_i \sim U(a, b)$.
3. If $u_i \le \frac{f(x_i)}{M \times g(x_i)}$, then accept x_i as a valid sample; otherwise, reject it.
4. Repeat Steps 1 to 3 until you are happy with the sample set.

One drawback of the algorithm is that it may take a lot of unwanted samples before finding a valid one. The problem is worse in high dimensions, making it inefficient and impractical in such situations.

13.2.3. Sampling from Univariate Distributions

Inverse transform sampling and acceptance-rejection sampling are generic methods that work with (almost) all probability distributions, but they are slow. For some specific probability distribution, there are specialized and faster methods to sample from it. NM Dev has a large suite of RNGs that sample from some most popular probability distributions: Gaussian/normal, beta, gamma, exponential, Poisson, Bernoulli, binomial, Rayleigh, Weibull, and so on. There are multiple implementations for some of them, for example, normal distribution.

Gaussian or Normal Distribution

The most important probability distribution is probably the Gaussian or normal distribution. There are many natural phenomena that are either exactly, approximately, or assumed normal. The position of a diffusing particle after an elapsed time is exactly normal. The number of heads in a series of coin tosses is approximately normal. The changes in the logarithm of stock returns are assumed to be normal. Its applications are ubiquitous in finance, physics, biology, statistics, and so on.

Mathematically, the normal distribution has many nice properties. They are symmetric, unimodal, infinitely differentiable, completely characterized by the first two moments (mean and variance), maximal entropy, no correlation implying independence, and additive. Perhaps what makes the normal distribution central to statistics is the central limit theorem that says the distribution of the average of a sample set is normally distributed as the sample size goes to infinity. In other words, everything that is the average (or sum) of sample values, for example, measurements and errors, is approximately normally distributed. See Figure 13-6.

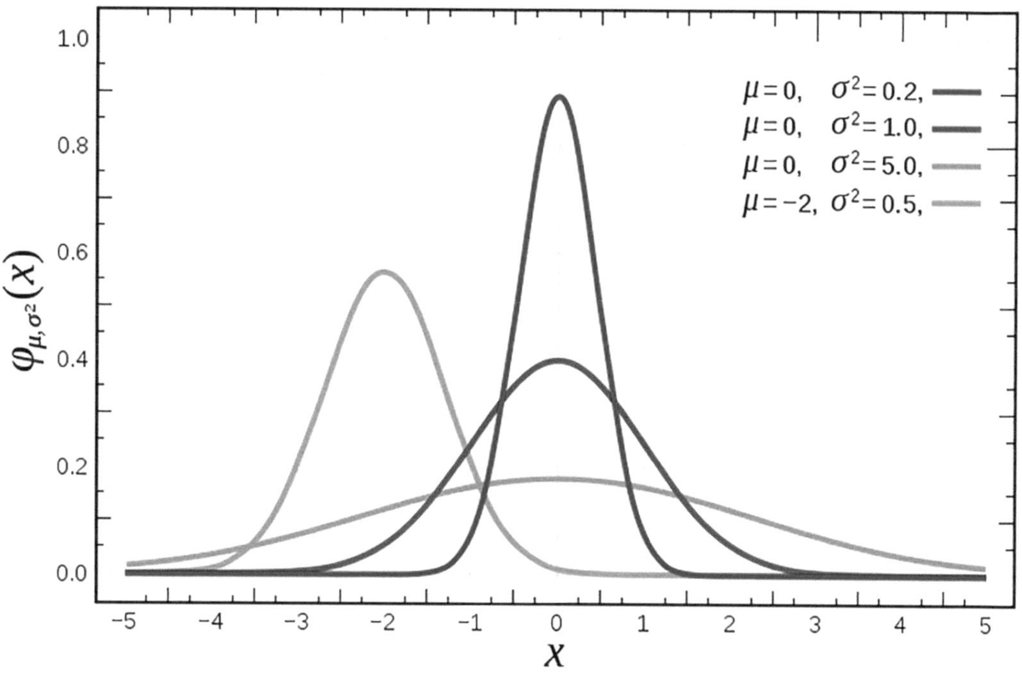

Figure 13-6. *Probability density functions for the normal distributions*

The probability density function of a normal distribution is as follows:

$$f(x|\mu,\sigma)=\frac{1}{\sqrt{2\pi}\sigma}\exp\left(-\frac{1}{2}\left(\frac{x-\mu}{\sigma}\right)^2\right)$$

The parameter μ is the mean or expectation of the distribution, and the parameter σ is the standard deviation. The variance of the distribution is σ^2. A random variable X with a Gaussian distribution is said to be normally distributed and is denoted as $X\text{\textasciitilde}N(\mu, \sigma^2)$. The mean μ of a normal distribution determines its location, and the standard deviation σ determines the magnitude of the distribution. When $\mu = 0$ and $\sigma = 1$, the normal distribution is the standard normal distribution.

NM Dev has a number of implementations to generate random normal samples. They are `Zignor2005` (Doornik, 2005), `Ziggurat2000` (Marsaglia & Tsang, 2000), `MarsagliaBray1964` (G. & Bray), and `BoxMuller` (Box & Muller, 1958). By default, we use `Zignor2005`.

The following code snippets are examples to generate standard normal samples and normal samples:

```
val uniform = MersenneTwister()
uniform.seed(1234567890L)

val rng1 = Zignor2005(uniform) // mean = 0, stdev = 1
val N = 1000
var arr1: DoubleArray = DoubleArray(N)
for (i in 0 until N) {
    arr1[i] = rng1.nextDouble()
}

// check the statistics of the random samples
val var1 = Variance(arr1)
println(
        String.format(
                "mean = %f, stdev = %f",
                var1.mean(),
                var1.standardDeviation()))

val rng2 = NormalRNG(1.0, 2.0, rng1) // mean = 1, stdev = 2
var arr2: DoubleArray = DoubleArray(N)
for (i in 0 until N) {
    arr2[i] = rng2.nextDouble()
}

// check the statistics of the random samples
val var2 = Variance(arr2)
println(
        String.format(
                "mean = %f, stdev = %f",
                var2.mean(),
                var2.standardDeviation()))
```

The output is as follows:

```
mean = 0.011830, stdev = 1.009379

mean = 0.940225, stdev = 2.037228
```

The statistics of the sample match the parameters of the distribution passed to the RNG constructors. The signatures are as follows:

```
/**
 * Constructs an improved Ziggurat random normal generator.
 *
 * @param uniform a uniform random number generator
 */
public Zignor2005(RandomLongGenerator uniform)
/**
 * Construct a random number generator to sample from the Normal distribution.
 *
 * @param mean  the mean
 * @param sigma the standard deviation
 * @param rnorm a standard random normal number generator
 */
public NormalRNG(double mean, double sigma, RandomStandardNormalGenerator rnorm)
```

The standard normal RNG `Zignor2005` takes as input a uniform RNG, which is `MersenneTwister` in this example. Then the normal RNG takes a standard normal RNG and the distribution parameters as inputs. Note that you only seed the uniform RNG once in an application.

Beta Distribution

The beta distribution is a family of continuous probability distributions defined on the unit interval [0, 1] parameterized by two positive shape parameters, denoted by α and β, that control the shape of the distribution. The beta distribution has been applied to model the behavior of random variables limited to intervals of finite length in a wide variety of disciplines. The probability density function of the beta distribution is as follows:

$$f(x|\alpha,\beta)=\frac{1}{B(\alpha,\beta)}x^{\alpha-1}(1-x)^{\beta-1}$$

$B(\alpha, \beta)$ is the beta function. The random variable X that obeys the beta distribution with parameters α and β is written as $X\sim Be(\alpha, \beta)$. See Figure 13-7.

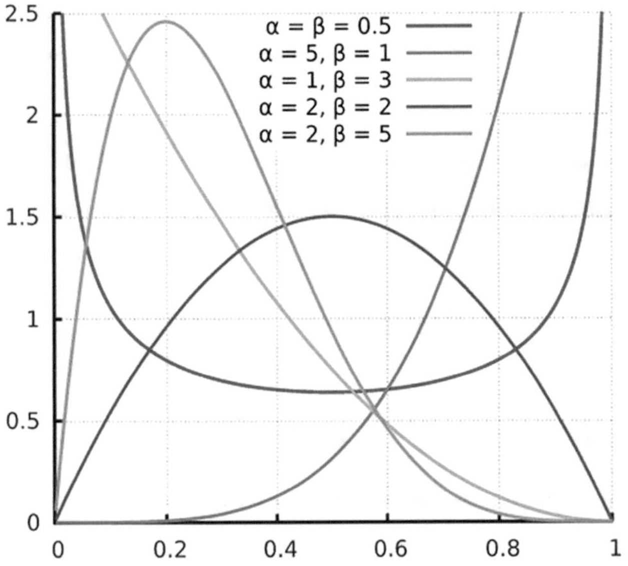

Figure 13-7. *Probability density functions for the beta distributions*

NM Dev has a number of implementations to generate random beta samples. They are `Cheng1978` (Cheng, 1978) and `VanDerWaerden1969` (van der Waerden). By default, we use `Cheng1978`. The `Cheng1978` class is a new rejection method for generating beta variates. The method is compared with previously published methods, both theoretically and through computer timings. It is suggested that the method has advantages in both speed and programming simplicity over previous methods, especially for "difficult" combinations of parameter values. Specifically, if X and Y are independent of $X \sim \Gamma(\alpha, \theta)$ and $Y \sim \Gamma(\beta, \theta)$, then $\frac{X}{X+Y} \sim \mathrm{Beta}(\alpha, \theta)$. To sample from the beta distribution, you can generate $\frac{X}{X+Y}$ where X is a gamma variate with parameter $\Gamma(\alpha, 1)$ and Y is an independent gamma variate with parameter $\Gamma(\beta, 1)$.

The following code snippet generates beta variates with $\alpha = 0.1,\ \beta = 0.2$:

```
val size = 1_000_000

val alpha : Double = 0.1
val beta : Double= 0.2

val rng = Cheng1978(alpha, beta, UniformRNG())
rng.seed(1234567890L)

var x: DoubleArray = DoubleArray(size)
for (i in 0 until size) {
    x[i] = rng.nextDouble()
}

// compute the sample statistics
val mean = Mean(x)
val variance = Variance(x)
val skew = Skewness(x)
val kurtosis = Kurtosis(x)
```

```
// compute the theoretical statistics
val dist: ProbabilityDistribution = BetaDistribution(alpha, beta)

// compare sample vs theoretical statistics
printStats(dist, mean, variance, skew, kurtosis)
```

The output is as follows:

```
theoretical mean = 0.333333, sample mean = 0.333402
theoretical var = 0.170940, sample var = 0.171025
theoretical skew = 0.701066, sample skew = 0.700741
theoretical kurtosis = -1.304348, sample kurtosis = -1.305287
```

You can see that the sample statistics match the theoretical values computed analytically from the probability distribution function.

The constructor signature is as follows:

```
/**
 * Constructs a random number generator to sample from the beta
 * distribution.
 *
 * @param aa      the degree of freedom
 * @param bb      the degree of freedom
 * @param uniform a uniform random number generator
 */
public Cheng1978(double aa, double bb, RandomLongGenerator uniform)
```

Gamma Distribution

The gamma distribution is a two-parameter family of continuous probability distributions. The exponential distribution, Erlang distribution, and Chi-square distribution are special cases of the gamma distribution. The two parameters are a shape parameter k and a scale parameter θ. The gamma distribution is frequently used to model waiting times. For instance, in life testing, the waiting time until death is a random variable that is frequently modeled with a gamma distribution. The gamma distribution is also used to model the size of insurance claims and rainfalls. This means that aggregate insurance claims and the amount of rainfall accumulated in a reservoir are modeled by a gamma process.

In oncology, the age distribution of cancer incidence often follows the gamma distribution, whereas the shape and scale parameters predict, respectively, the number of driver events and the time interval between them. In neuroscience, the gamma distribution is often used to describe the distribution of inter-spike intervals. In bacterial gene expression, the copy number of a constitutively expressed protein often follows the gamma distribution, where the scale and shape parameter are, respectively, the mean number of bursts per cell cycle and the mean number of protein molecules produced by a single mRNA during its lifetime.

The parameter $\alpha = k$ is called the shape parameter, and $\beta = \frac{1}{\theta}$ is called the inverse scale parameter. The probability density function of the gamma distribution is as follows:

$$f(x|\beta,\alpha) = \frac{\beta^{\alpha} x^{\alpha-1} e^{-\beta x}}{\Gamma(\alpha)}, x > 0$$

$\Gamma(\alpha)$ is the gamma function. The random variable X that obeys the gamma distribution with parameters α and β is written as $X \sim \Gamma(\alpha, \beta)$. See Figure 13-8.

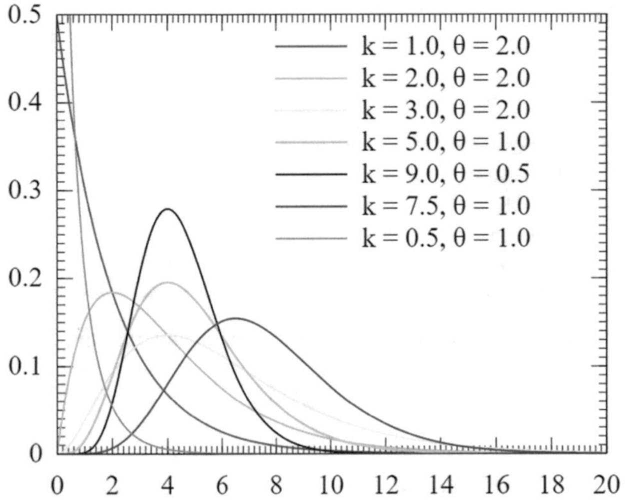

Figure 13-8. *Probability density functions for the gamma distributions*

NM Dev has a number of implementations to generate random gamma samples. They are `InverseTransformSamplingGammaRNG` inverse transform sampling (which is inefficient), `MarsagliaTsang2000` (Marsaglia & Tsang, 2000), `XiTanLiu2010a` and `XiTanLiu2010b` (Xi, Tan, & Liu), and `KunduGupta2007` (Kundu & Gupta, 2007). By default, we use `KunduGupta2007`. It uses a convenient way to generate gamma variates using generalized exponential distribution, when the shape parameter lies between 0 and 1.

The following code snippet generates gamma variates with $k = 0.1,\ \theta = 1$:

```
val size = 1_000_000

val k: Double = 0.1
val theta: Double = 1.0

val rng = KunduGupta2007(k, theta, UniformRNG())
rng.seed(1234567895L)

val x: DoubleArray = DoubleArray(size)
for (i in 0 until size) {
    x[i] = rng.nextDouble()
}

// compute the sample statistics
val mean = Mean(x)
val variance = Variance(x)
val skew = Skewness(x)
val kurtosis = Kurtosis(x)

// compute the theoretical statistics
```

```
val dist: ProbabilityDistribution = GammaDistribution(k, theta)

// compute the theoretical statistics
printStats(dist, mean, variance, skew, kurtosis)
```

The output is as follows:

```
theoretical mean = 0.100000, sample mean = 0.102555
theoretical var = 0.100000, sample var = 0.102297
theoretical skew = 6.324555, sample skew = 6.303562
theoretical kurtosis = 60.000000, sample kurtosis = 60.330271
```

Note that the sample statistics match the theoretical values computed analytically from the probability distribution function.

The constructor signature is as follows:

```
/**
 * Constructs a random number generator to sample from the gamma
 * distribution.
 *
 * @param k       the shape parameter
 * @param theta   the scale parameter
 * @param uniform a uniform random number generator
 */
public KunduGupta2007(double k, double theta, RandomLongGenerator uniform)
```

Poisson Distribution

A *Poisson* process is a series of discrete events where the average time between events is known, but the exact timing of the next event is random. The arrival of an event is independent of the events before it; that is, the waiting time between events is Markovian or memoryless. For example, a call center receives an average of 180 calls per hour, 24 hours a day. The calls are independent; receiving one does not change the probability of when the next one will arrive. The number of calls received during any minute has a Poisson probability distribution: the most likely numbers are 2 and 3, but 1 and 4 are also likely and there is a small probability of it being 0, and a very small probability it could be 10. Another example is the number of decay events that occur from a radioactive source in a given observation period. The Poisson distribution probability mass function gives the probability of observing *k* random events in a fixed time interval if the number of events has a known average per interval and is independent of the time since the last event. The probability mass function has this form:

$$P(X=k)=\frac{\lambda^k e^{-\lambda}}{k!}, k=0,1,\ldots$$

The parameter λ of the Poisson distribution is the average number of random events in a unit time. The expectation and variance of the Poisson distribution are both λ. Note that unlike all previous distributions that you have seen, the Poisson distribution is a discrete distribution. X takes integer values. See Figure 13-9.

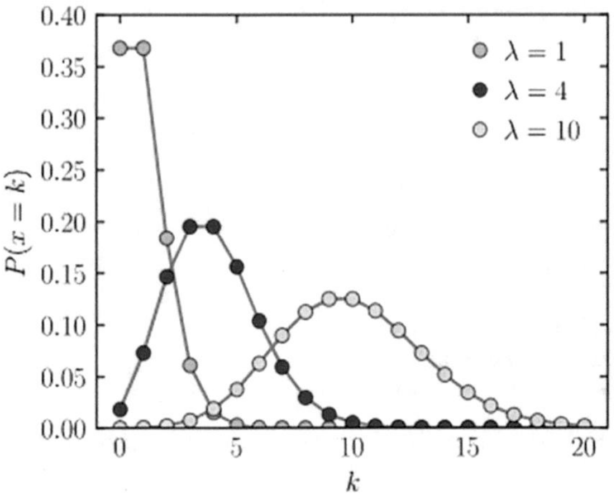

Figure 13-9. *Probability mass functions for the Poisson distributions*

In NM Dev, the Poisson RNG class is `Knuth1969`. The following code snippet generates Poisson variates with $\lambda = 1$:

```
val N = 10_000
val lambda: Double = 1.0

val rng = Knuth1969(lambda)
rng.seed(123456789L)

var x: DoubleArray = DoubleArray(N)
for (i in 0 until N) {
    x[i] = rng.nextDouble()
}

// compute the sample statistics
val mean = Mean(x)
val variance = Variance(x)
val skew = Skewness(x)
val kurtosis = Kurtosis(x)

// compute the theoretical statistics
val dist: PoissonDistribution = PoissonDistribution(lambda)

// compute the theoretical statistics
printStats(dist, mean, variance, skew, kurtosis)
```

The output is as follows:

```
theoretical mean = 1.000000, sample mean = 1.013300
theoretical var = 1.000000, sample var = 1.022225
theoretical skew = 1.000000, sample skew = 1.000960
theoretical kurtosis = 1.000000, sample kurtosis = 0.990813
```

Note that the sample statistics match the theoretical values computed analytically from the probability distribution function.

The constructor signature is as follows:

```
/**
 * Constructs a random number generator to sample from the Poisson
 * distribution.
 *
 * @param lambda  the shape parameter
 * @param uniform a uniform random number generator
 */
public Knuth1969(double lambda, RandomLongGenerator uniform)
```

Exponential Distribution

While the Poisson distribution describes the number of events in an interval, the exponential distribution describes the times between events in a Poisson process. It is the distribution for the random times. It is a special case of the gamma distribution. There are many examples of the exponential distribution, such as the time until a radioactive particle decays, the time before your next telephone call, and the time until you default on a loan payment in credit risk modeling.

$\lambda > 0$ is called the rate parameter. It is the average number of occurrences of events per unit time. The random time range is $[0, \infty)$. If a random variable X is exponentially distributed, it is denoted as $X \sim E(\lambda)$. The probability density function is as follows (Figure 13-10):

$$f(x|\lambda) = \begin{cases} \lambda e^{-\lambda x} & x > 0 \\ 0 & x \le 0 \end{cases}$$

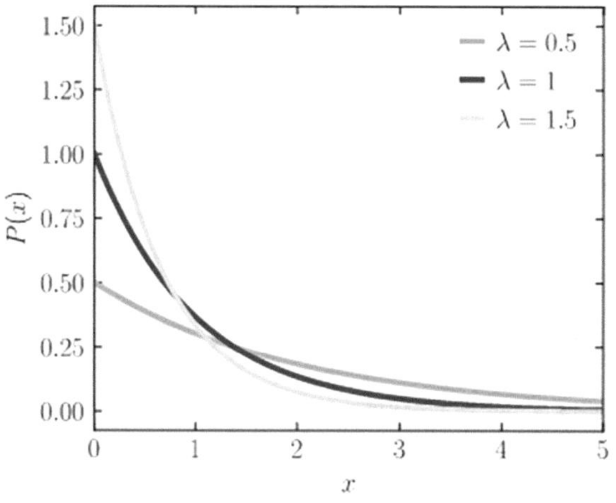

Figure 13-10. *Probability density functions for the exponential distributions*

You can generate exponential variates by using inverse transform sampling. NM Dev implements a more efficient algorithm, called Ziggurat2000Exp (Marsaglia & Tsang, 2000). The following code snippet generates standard exponential variates with $\lambda = 1$. Note that Ziggurat2000Exp uses a default constructor and does not take an argument.

```
val size = 500_000

val rng = Ziggurat2000Exp()
rng.seed(634641070L)

var x: DoubleArray = DoubleArray(size)
for (i in 0 until size) {
    x[i] = rng.nextDouble()
}

// compute the sample statistics
val mean = Mean(x)
val variance = Variance(x)
val skew = Skewness(x)
val kurtosis = Kurtosis(x)

// compute the theoretical statistics
val dist: ProbabilityDistribution = ExponentialDistribution()

// compute the theoretical statistics
printStats(dist, mean, variance, skew, kurtosis)
```

The output is as follows:

```
theoretical mean = 1.000000, sample mean = 1.000983
theoretical var = 1.000000, sample var = 0.996058
theoretical skew = 2.000000, sample skew = 1.958222
theoretical kurtosis = 6.000000, sample kurtosis = 5.489008
```

Note that the sample statistics match the theoretical values computed analytically from the probability distribution function.

To generate nonstandard exponential variance, you can first generate the standard exponential variates and then scale them. Alternatively, you can directly use InverseTransformSamplingExpRNG, which takes λ as an argument. The signature is as follows:

```
/**
 * Constructs a random number generator to sample from the exponential
 * distribution using the inverse transform sampling method.
 *
 * @param lambda the rate parameter
 */
public InverseTransformSamplingExpRNG(double lambda)
```

13.2.4. Sampling from Multivariate Distributions

NM Dev supports random vector generation for some multivariate distributions for higher dimensions. Each sample is a vector of numbers instead of just one number. They include, but are not limited to, the following:

- Multivariate uniform distribution over a high-dimension box region
- Multivariate uniform distribution over a high-dimension unit hypersphere
- Multivariate normal distribution
- Multinomial distribution

The signature for a random vector RNG, `RandomVectorGenerator`, is as follows:

```
public interface RandomVectorGenerator extends Seedable {
    /**
     * Gets the next random vector.
     *
     * @return the next random vector
     */
    public double[] nextVector();
}
```

Each call to `nextVector` generates a vector sample in the form of a `double[]`.

Multivariate Uniform Distribution Over Box

The `UniformDistributionOverBox` class is a random vector RNG that produces samples uniformly over a high-dimensional hypercube, or a box. It takes as inputs a one-dimensional uniform RNG and the dimensions of the box (see Figure 13-11). The signature is as follows:

```
/**
 * Constructs a random vector generator to uniformly sample points over a
 * box region.
 *
 * @param uniform a uniform random number generator
 * @param bounds  the feasible box region
 */
public UniformDistributionOverBox(
        RandomLongGenerator uniform,
        RealInterval... bounds
)
```

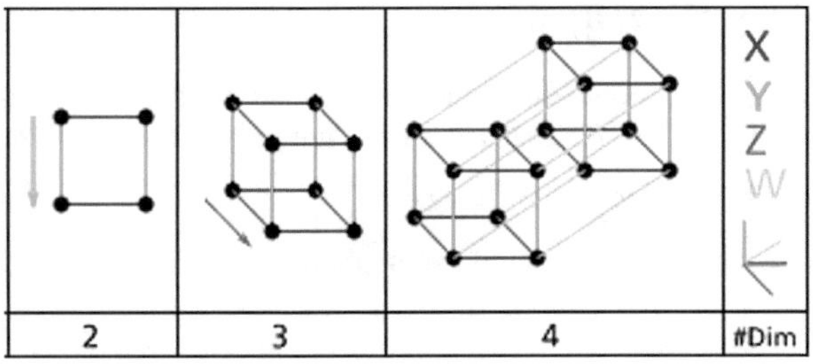

Figure 13-11. *Cubes in different dimensions*

The following shows how to use random sampling to compute the ratio of a circle's circumference to the diameter, which is π. The idea is to throw random darts at a unit board, $x \in [-1, 1]$, $y \in [-1, 1]$, with a circle in it. The area of the square is 1, the area of the circle is $\frac{\pi}{4}$ because the radius is $\frac{1}{2}$. That is, the number of darts inside the circle, N_0, versus those in the whole board, N, has this ratio:

$$\frac{N_0}{N} = \frac{\pi}{4}$$

Solve for π. The following code implements the procedure:

```
val N = 1_000_000

val rvg = UniformDistributionOverBox(
            RealInterval(-1.0, 1.0), // a unit square box
            RealInterval(-1.0, 1.0))

var NO = 0
for (i in 0 until N) {
    val xy: DoubleArray = rvg.nextVector()
    val x: Double = xy[0]
    val y: Double = xy[1]
    if (x * x + y * y <= 1.0) { // check if the dot is inside a circle
        NO++
    }
}
val pi: Double = 4.0 * NO / N
println("pi = " + pi)
```

The output is as follows:

```
pi = 3.139588
```

Multivariate Uniform Distribution Over Hypersphere

The HypersphereRVG class is a random vector RNG that produces samples uniformly over the surface of a high-dimensional hypersphere. It takes as inputs the sphere dimension and a one-dimensional standard normal RNG. The signature is as follows:

```
/**
 * Constructs a hypersphere RVG to generate random uniform points.
 *
 * @param dimension the dimension of the hypersphere
 * @param rnorm     the standard Normal RNG to be used
 */
public HypersphereRVG(int dimension, RandomStandardNormalGenerator rnorm)
```

Multivariate Normal Distribution

The multivariate normal distribution, multivariate Gaussian distribution, or joint normal distribution is a generalization of the one-dimensional (univariate) normal distribution to higher dimensions. One definition is that a random vector is said to be k-variate normally distributed if every linear combination of its k components has a univariate normal distribution. The multivariate normal distribution is often used to describe, at least approximately, any set of (possibly) correlated real-valued random variables, each of which clusters around a mean value, by the multidimensional central limit theorem.

A real random vector $\boldsymbol{X} = (X_1, \cdots, X_k)T$ is called a (multivariate) standard normal random vector if each of its components X_i is itself a univariate standard normal and if they are independent. That is, $X_i \sim N(0, 1)$ for all i. It can be proved that any multivariate normal vector can be written as a sum of a k-vector μ and a scaled multivariate standard normal. That is, $\boldsymbol{X} \sim N(\boldsymbol{\mu}, \sigma)$ if and only if there exists $\boldsymbol{\mu} \in \mathbb{R}_k$ and $\boldsymbol{A} \in \mathbb{R}^{kxl}$ such that $\boldsymbol{X} = \boldsymbol{AZ} + \boldsymbol{\mu}$, where Z is a multivariate standard normal. $\boldsymbol{\mu}$ is the k-dimensional mean vector, and σ is the $k \times k$ covariance matrix of the components. See Figure 13-12.

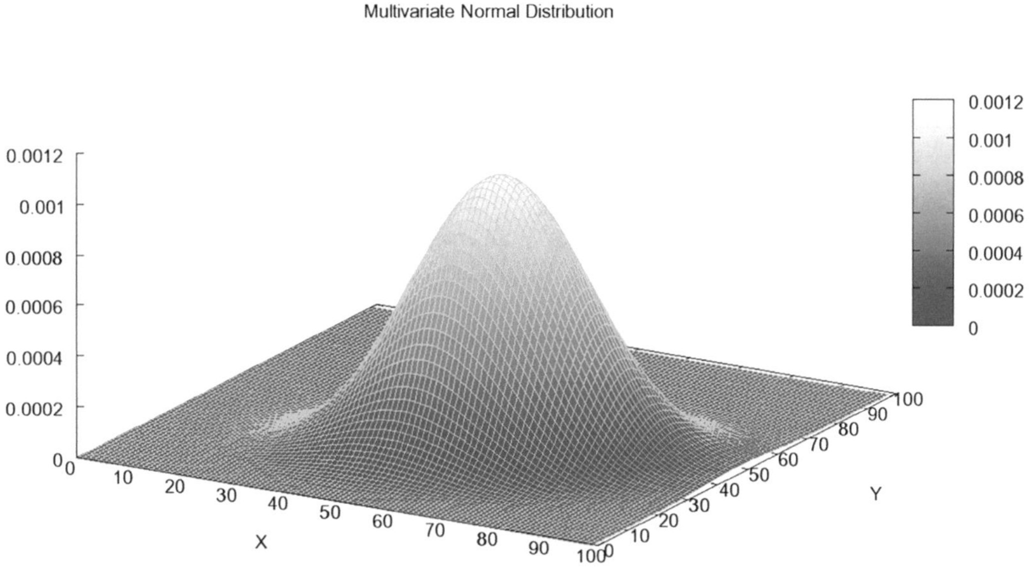

***Figure 13-12.** Probability density functions for a two-dimensional normal distribution*

The probability density function of a multivariate normal distribution is as follows:

$$f_X(x_1,\cdots,x_k)=\frac{1}{\sqrt{(2\pi)^k|\Sigma|}}\exp\left(-\frac{1}{2}(\boldsymbol{x}-\mu)^T\Sigma^{-1}(\boldsymbol{x}-\mu)\right)$$

In NM Dev, the NormalRVG class samples from multivariate normal distribution. The following code snippet produces correlated multivariate normal variates:

```
// mean
val mu: Vector = DenseVector(arrayOf(-2.0, 2.0))
// covariance matrix
val sigma: Matrix = DenseMatrix(
    arrayOf(
        doubleArrayOf(1.0, 0.5),
        doubleArrayOf(0.5, 1.0)
    )
)

val rvg = NormalRVG(mu, sigma)
rvg.seed(1234567890L)
val size = 10_000
var mean1 = Mean()
var mean2 = Mean()
val X: Matrix = DenseMatrix(size, 2)

for (i in 0 until size) {
    val v: DoubleArray = rvg.nextVector()
    mean1.addData(v[0])
    mean2.addData(v[1])

    X.set(i+1, 1, v[0])
    X.set(i+1, 2, v[1])
}

println(String.format("mean of X_1 = %f", mean1.value()))
println(String.format("mean of X_2 = %f", mean2.value()))

val cov: SampleCovariance = SampleCovariance(X)
println(String.format("sample covariance = %s", cov.toString()))
```

The output is as follows:

```
mean of X_1 = -2.007342
mean of X_2 = 1.995800
sample covariance = 2x2
        [,1] [,2]
[1,] 1.003598, 0.496158,
[2,] 0.496158, 1.012381,
```

Both the sample means and the sample covariance matrix match the inputs reasonably well.

The NormalRVG constructor signature is as follows:

```
/**
 * Constructs a multivariate normal random vector generator.
 *
 * @param mu      the mean
 * @param sigma   the covariance matrix
 * @param epsilon a precision parameter: when a number |x| &le; &epsilon;,
 *                it is considered 0
 * @param rnorm   a random standard normal number generator
 */
public NormalRVG(
        final Vector mu,
        final Matrix sigma,
        final double epsilon,
        final RandomStandardNormalGenerator rnorm
)
```

Multinomial Distribution

A multinomial distribution puts n items into k bins according to the bins' probabilities. An output random vector counts the number of objects in each bin, making a total of n. When $k = 2$ and $n = 1$ (putting one object into two bins), it is the Bernoulli distribution. The output is either (0, 1) or (1, 0). It is like flipping a (not necessarily a fair) coin once, and you get either heads or tails. When $k = 2$ and $n > 1$ (putting n objects into two bins), it is the binomial distribution. It is like flipping the same coin n times and counting the number of heads (or tails). For a fixed finite k, the i-th component in $\boldsymbol{X}$ indicates the number of items in the i-th bin out of the total of n items.

The probability mass function of a multinomial distribution is as follows:

$$f\left(x_1,\cdots|x_k,n,p_1,\cdots,p_k\right)=\Pr\left(X_1=x_1,\cdots,X_k=x_k\right)$$

$$=\begin{cases}\dfrac{n!}{x_1!\cdots x_k!}p_1^{x_1}\times\cdots\times p_k^{x_k}\\ 0,\text{otherwise}\end{cases}$$

In NM Dev, the MultinomialRVG class samples from multinomial distribution. The following code snippet puts 10,000 items into two bins, a 70 percent chance and a 30 percent chance:

```
val rvg = MultinomialRVG(100_000, doubleArrayOf(0.7, 0.3)) // bin0 is 70% chance, bin1
30% chance
val bin: DoubleArray = rvg.nextVector()
var total: Double = 0.0
for (i in 0 until bin.size) {
    total += bin[i]
}
val bin0: Double = bin[0] / total // bin0 percentage
val bin1: Double = bin[1] / total // bin0 percentage
println(String.format("bin0 %% = %f, bin1 %% = %f", bin0, bin1))
```

The output is as follows:

```
bin0 % = 0.702410, bin1 % = 0.297590
```

The sample percentages match the individual probability of each bin in the input reasonably well.
The MultinomialRVG constructor signature is as follows:

```
/**
 * Constructs a multinomial random vector generator.
 *
 * @param N       an integer, say <i>N</i>, specifying the total number of
 *                objects that are put into <i>K</i> boxes in a typical multinomial
 *                experiment
 * @param prob    a numeric non-negative vector of length <i>K</i>,
 *                specifying the probability for the <i>K</i> boxes
 * @param uniform a uniform random number generator
 */
public MultinomialRVG(int N, double[] prob, RandomLongGenerator uniform)
```

13.2.5. Resampling Method

One way to visualize the empirical distribution method is the following. Given a set of samples, the empirical distribution assigns the probability of $1/N$ to each sample. Then, with the probability of $1/N$, it randomly draws a sample from the set to be the next random variate. The items that appear more often in the set are more likely to be drawn and therefore have higher probability masses. The rare items are less likely to be drawn and will appear less often in the output. Essentially, you sample from the sample set to generate new samples. You can generalize this resampling idea to draw more than one item at a time. One important advantage of drawing multiple items at one time over the empirical distribution method is that the former accounts also for the serial correlation between the samples, whereas the latter assumes all samples in the data set are independent and identically distributed. In other words, the variates generated by a resampling method not only have a similar probability distribution to the true distribution, but they also have a similar serial correlation (time dependency between the samples). The resampling method is a common nonparametric method of making statistical estimation and statistical inference when the true probability distribution of the system is unknown.

In NM Dev, a resampling class extends this interface. Each call to the newResample() method generates a block of new samples based on the original sample set.

```
public interface Resampler extends Seedable {
    /**
     * Gets a resample from the original sample.
     *
     * <em>It is very important this method is thread-safe so resampling can be
     * run in parallel.</em>
     *
     * @return a resample, e.g., a bootstrap sample
     */
    public double[] newResample();
}
```

Bootstrapping Methods

Bootstrapping is a uniform sampling with replacement from a given sample set, often called a training set. When a block of samples is selected, it is the output of the RNG. The same samples are "put back" into the training set and are available for reselection. The basic idea of bootstrapping is that inference about a population of the true probability distribution *J* can be approximated by computing the inference using the empirical distribution $\hat{J}$. The accuracy of the inferences regarding $\hat{J}$ using the resampled data can be measured because you know $\hat{J}$. If $\hat{J}$ is a reasonable approximation to J, then the quality of inference on J can in turn be inferred.

To be more specific, suppose you want to estimate the average (or mean) height of people worldwide. You cannot measure all the people in the global population. Instead, you sample only a tiny part and measure that. Assume the sample is of size *N*; that is, you measure the heights of *N* individuals. From that single sample, only one estimate of the mean can be obtained. To reason about the population, you need some sense of the variability of the mean that you have computed. The simplest bootstrap method involves taking the original data set of heights (the training set) and sampling from it to form a new sample (called a resample or bootstrap sample) that is also of size *N*. The bootstrap sample is taken from the original by using sampling with replacement (e.g., you might "resample" five times from [150,155,160,165,170] and get [155,170,165,165,150]). If *N* is sufficiently large, for all practical purposes there is virtually zero probability that it will be identical to the training set. This process is repeated a large number of times (typically 1,000 or 10,000 times). For each of these bootstrap samples, you compute its mean (each of these is called a bootstrap estimate). You now can create a histogram of bootstrap means, as shown in Figure 13-13. This histogram provides an estimate of the shape of the distribution of the sample mean from which you can answer questions about how much the mean varies across different resamples. The method here, described for the mean, can be applied to almost any statistic or estimator.

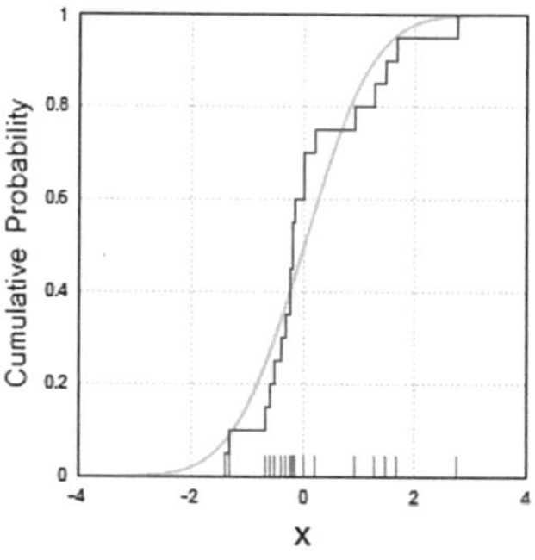

Figure 13-13. *A histogram of bootstrap means*

The following code snippet implements the previous example of estimating the average height:

```
// sample from true population
val sample: DoubleArray = doubleArrayOf(150.0, 155.0, 160.0, 165.0, 170.0)
val boot = CaseResamplingReplacement(sample)
boot.seed(1234567890L)
val B = 1000
var means = DoubleArray(B)
for (i in 0 until B) {
    val resample: DoubleArray = boot.newResample()
    means[i] = Mean(resample).value()
}
```

```
// estimator of population mean
val mean: Double = Mean(means).value()
// variance of estimator limited by sample size (regardless of how big B is)
val variance: Double = Variance(means, true).value()
println(
        String.format("mean = %f, variance of the estimated mean = %f",
                mean,
                variance))
```

Alternatively, BootstrapEstimator provides a convenient wrapper to rewrite this example, as shown here:

```
// sample from true population
val sample = doubleArrayOf(150.0, 155.0, 160.0, 165.0, 170.0)
val boot = CaseResamplingReplacement(sample)
boot.seed(1234567890L)

val B = 1000
val estimator = BootstrapEstimator(
    boot,
    object : StatisticFactory {
        override fun getStatistic(): Statistic {
            return Mean()
        }
    },
    B
)

println(
        String.format("mean = %f, variance of the estimated mean = %f",
                estimator.value(),
                estimator.variance()))
```

The output is as follows:

```
mean = 159.976000, variance of the estimated mean = 9.286711
```

The estimated mean of the population height is 159.976 with an accuracy (measured in term of variance of the estimated mean) of 9.2867. Note that this is the variance of the estimation, not the variance of the population height.

The bootstrap resampler used in this example is the CaseResamplingReplacement class. The signature is as follows:

```
/**
 * Constructs a bootstrap sample generator. This is the classical bootstrap
 * with replacement.
 *
 * @param sample the original sample.
 */
public CaseResamplingReplacement(double[] sample)
```

The BootstrapEstimator signature is as follows:

```
    /**
     * Constructs a bootstrap estimator.
     *
     * @param bootstrap the bootstrap method and the sample
     * @param factory   the statistic
     * @param B         the number of bootstrap replicas
     */
    public BootstrapEstimator(
            Resampler bootstrap,
            StatisticFactory factory,
            int B
    )
```

In general, increasing the size of the training set, the *N*, improves the accuracy for the same number of bootstrap resamples. Increasing the number of bootstrap resamples, the *B*, improves the estimator estimation but not the accuracy. The probability of a sample being selected in each resampling is $\frac{1}{N}$, so the probability of not being selected is $1-\frac{1}{N}$. The probability of not being selected for all *B* times, that is, not appearing in any resample set, is $\left(1-\frac{1}{N}\right)^B$. When both the training set size and the number of resampling go to infinity, that probability will approach $e^{-1} = 0.368$.[2] In other words, using the naïve case resampling with replacement method, only about 63.2 percent of the original data set in the training set will appear in the resamples.

The Politis-White-Patton Method

NM Dev has also implemented the bootstrapping method according to Automatic Block-Length Selection for the Dependent Bootstrap (Politis & White, 2004) and the CORRECTION TO Automatic Block-Length Selection for the Dependent Bootstrap (Politis, White, & Patton, 2009). The Politis-White-Patton bootstrap method generates resamples of sequences, that is, data series that are serially or time dependent, that resemble the training data better than the simple case resampling with a replacement method. For example, the number of occurrences of any given pattern is closer to that in the original sequence. The following code example constructs a serially dependent sequence (consisting of 0 and 1) by retaining the last value with probability q while changing the last value with probability $(1 - q)$. Then, for a given pattern such as {1, 0, 1, 0, 1}, it compares the number of occurrences in the training sequence with those in different bootstrapped resampled sequences.

```
/**
 * Constructs a dependent sequence (consisting of 0 and 1) by retaining the
 * last value with probability <i>q</i> while changing the last value with
 * probability <i>1-q</i>.
 * <p/>
 * The simple bootstrapping method {@linkplain CaseResamplingReplacement}
 * will severely overestimate the occurrences of certain pattern, while
 * block bootstrapping method {@linkplain BlockBootstrap} gives a good
 * estimation of the occurrences in the original sample. All estimators over
 * estimate.
 */
```

[2] $e \approx 2.71828182846$, which is Euler's number.

```
val N: Int = 10000
val q: Double = 0.70 // the probability of retaining last value

val uniformRNG = UniformRNG()
uniformRNG.seed(1234567890L)

// generate a random series of 0s and 1s with serial correlation
var sample: DoubleArray = DoubleArray(N)
sample[0] = if(uniformRNG.nextDouble() > 0.5) 1.0 else 0.0
for (i in 1 until N) {
    sample[i] = if(uniformRNG.nextDouble() < q) sample[i - 1] else 1 - sample[i - 1]
}

// simple case resampling with replacement method
val simpleBoot = CaseResamplingReplacement(sample, uniformRNG)
val countInSimpleBootstrap = Mean()

val rlg: RandomNumberGenerator = Ziggurat2000Exp()
rlg.seed(1234567890L)

// Patton-Politis-White method using stationary blocks
val stationaryBlock = PattonPolitisWhite2009(
                sample,
                PattonPolitisWhite2009ForObject.Type.STATIONARY,
                uniformRNG,
                rlg)
val countInStationaryBlockBootstrap = Mean()

// Patton-Politis-White method using circular blocks
val circularBlock = PattonPolitisWhite2009(
                sample,
                PattonPolitisWhite2009ForObject.Type.CIRCULAR,
                uniformRNG,
                rlg)
val countInCircularBlockBootstrap= Mean()

// change this line to use a different pattern
val pattern: DoubleArray = doubleArrayOf(1.0, 0.0, 1.0, 0.0, 1.0)

val B: Int = 10000
for (i in 0 until B) {
    // count the number of occurrences for the pattern in the series
    var numberOfMatches = match(simpleBoot.newResample(), pattern)
    countInSimpleBootstrap.addData(numberOfMatches)

    // count the number of occurrences for the pattern in the series
    numberOfMatches = match(stationaryBlock.newResample(), pattern)
    countInStationaryBlockBootstrap.addData(numberOfMatches)
```

```
    // count the number of occurrences for the pattern in the series
    numberOfMatches = match(circularBlock.newResample(), pattern)
    countInCircularBlockBootstrap.addData(numberOfMatches)
}

// compare the numbers of occurrences of the pattern using different bootstrap methods
val countInSample = match(sample, pattern).toInt()
println("matched patterns in sample: " + countInSample)
println("matched patterns in simple bootstrap: " + countInSimpleBootstrap.value())
println("matched patterns in stationary block bootstrap: " +
countInStationaryBlockBootstrap.value())
println("matched patterns in circular block bootstrap: " + countInCircularBlockBootstrap.
value())
```

The output is as follows:

```
matched patterns in sample: 39
matched patterns in simple bootstrap: 316.8101000000013
matched patterns in stationary block bootstrap: 45.09940000000004
matched patterns in circular block bootstrap: 44.1490999999999
```

There are 39 occurrences of the pattern {1, 0, 1, 0, 1} in the original training sequence. The bootstrapped sequences from using simple case resampling with a replacement method is way off (316). The bootstrapped sequences from using the Politis-White-Patton methods are close to the original training sequence, 45 and 44, respectively.

The `PattonPolitisWhite2009` class has the following signature:

```
/**
 * Constructs a block bootstrap sample generator. The block length is
 * automatically selected.
 *
 * @param sample  the original sample
 * @param type    the type of block bootstrap, either
 *                {@linkplain Type#STATIONARY} or
 *                {@linkplain Type#CIRCULAR}
 * @param uniform a concurrent random long generator
 * @param rng     a concurrent random exponential generator
 */
public PattonPolitisWhite2009(
        double[] sample,
        PattonPolitisWhite2009ForObject.Type type,
        RandomLongGenerator uniform,
        RandomNumberGenerator rng
)
```

13.3. Variance Reduction

Suppose you want to estimate a statistics Z for a random variable X. You need to generate a lot of $X_1, \cdots, X_n$ and then compute for each X_i the statistics Z_i to get $Z_1, \cdots, Z_n$. The estimator is then as follows:

$$\hat{z} = \frac{1}{n}\sum_{i=1}^{n} Z_i$$

This method is called the Monte Carlo simulation. By the very nature of this computation based on randomness, every random sample is associated with a variance that limits the precision of the result. The central limit theorem says that $\hat{z}$ converges to a normal distribution with the true mean z and a standard error $\frac{\sigma}{\sqrt{n}}$ when $n \to \infty$. That means the standard error (the inverse accuracy) goes to 0 at the rate $\sqrt{n}$. To make the estimator double in accuracy, you need four times the number of random samples. For instance, for the `compute_Pi` code in Section 13.2.4.1, with 1,000,000 samples, the accuracy is two decimal points. To double that precision, you would need 4,000,000 samples. That is a lot of points to generate.

Variance reduction helps to improve the accuracy of an estimator given the same amount of computational effort, such as the number of random samples used. NM Dev has a suite of variance reduction techniques out of the box that you can use to improve estimator accuracy.

13.3.1. Common Random Numbers

Common random numbers (CRNs) are popular and useful variance reduction techniques to use when you want to compare two or more estimators. To be more specific, say you want to estimate the following:

$$d = \mathrm{E}(f) - \mathrm{E}(g)$$

If you use two sequences of independent streams for f and g separately, as shown here:

$$\mathrm{E}(f) = \frac{1}{n}\sum_{i=1}^{n} f(X_{1,i})$$

$$\mathrm{E}(g) = \frac{1}{n}\sum_{i=1}^{n} f(X_{2,i})$$

You get this:

$$\mathrm{Var}(M_2 - M_1) = \mathrm{Var}\left(\frac{1}{n}\sum_{i=1}^{n} f(X_{1,i}) - \frac{1}{n}\sum_{i=1}^{n} g(X_{2,i})\right)$$

$$= \frac{1}{n}\mathrm{Var}(f(X_1)) + \frac{1}{n}\mathrm{Var}(g(X_2))$$

Suppose $X_{1,i}$ and $X_{2,i}$ are positively correlated; then you would have this:

$$M_3 = \mathrm{Var}\left(\frac{1}{n}\sum_{i=1}^{n} f(X_{1,i}) - \frac{1}{n}\sum_{i=1}^{n} g(X_{2,i})\right)$$

$$= \frac{1}{n}\mathrm{Var}(f(X_1)) + \frac{1}{n}\mathrm{Var}(g(X_2)) - \mathrm{cov}(f(X_1), g(X_2))$$

If you further assume that both *f* and *g* are monotonically nondecreasing, then positive Cov(X_1, X_2) implies positive Cov($f(X_1)$, $g(X_2)$). Consequently, you get a reduction in variance of the estimator.

$$M_3 < \mathrm{Var}\left(M_2 - M_1\right)$$

The following code computes this:

$$d = \int_0^1 \left(2 - \frac{\sin x}{x}\right)dx - \int_0^1 \left(e^{x^2} - \frac{1}{2}\right)dx$$

```
val f: UnivariateRealFunction = object : AbstractUnivariateRealFunction() {
    override fun evaluate(x: Double): Double {
        val fx: Double = 2.0 - Math.sin(x) / x
        return fx
    }
}
val g: UnivariateRealFunction = object : AbstractUnivariateRealFunction() {
    override fun evaluate(x: Double): Double {
        val gx: Double = Math.exp(x * x) - 0.5
        return gx
    }
}
val X1: RandomLongGenerator = UniformRNG()
X1.seed(1234567890L)
val crn0: CommonRandomNumbers
        = CommonRandomNumbers(
                f,
                g,
                X1,
                object : AbstractUnivariateRealFunction() { // another independent
                uniform RNG
                    override fun evaluate(x: Double): Double {
                        var X2: RandomLongGenerator = UniformRNG()
                        X2.seed(246890123L)
                        return X2.nextDouble()
                    }
        })
val estimator0: Estimator = crn0.estimate(100_000)
println(
        String.format("d = %f, Variance = %f",
                estimator0.mean(),
                estimator0.variance()))

val crn1: CommonRandomNumbers
        = CommonRandomNumbers(f, g, X1) // use X1 for both f and g
val estimator1: Estimator = crn1.estimate(100_000)
println(
        String.format("d = %f, variance = %f",
                estimator1.mean(),
                estimator1.variance()))
```

The output is as follows:

```
d = 0.091698, variance = 0.227836

d = 0.090606, variance = 0.182244
```

$d \approx 0.091$ in both CRN estimators. The second CRN estimator, whioch uses a correlated (actually the same) sequence of random numbers X_1, has better accuracy (smaller variance) than the first CRN estimator, which uses two independent streams of random numbers X_1 and X_2. Note that CRN may not apply in some situations or it may perform worse if $\text{Cov}(f(X_1), g(X_2)) < 0$.

The signature of a constructor of the CommonRandomNumbers class is as follows:

```
/**
 * Estimates \(E(f(X_1) - g(X_2))\),, where <i>f</i> and <i>g</i> are
 * functions of uniform random variables. We set <i>X<sub>2</sub> =
 * X<sub>1</sub></i>.
 *
 * @param f  the first system
 * @param g  the second system
 * @param X1 a uniform random number generator
 */
public CommonRandomNumbers(
        UnivariateRealFunction f,
        UnivariateRealFunction g,
        RandomLongGenerator X1
)
```

13.3.2. Antithetic Variates

The method of antithetic variates is a technique that reduces variance by introducing negative correlation between pairs of observations. In general, you have this:

$$\text{Var}(X+Y) = \text{Var}(X) + \text{Var}(Y) + 2\text{cov}(X,Y)$$

$$= \text{Var}(X) + \text{Var}(Y) + 2\rho_{XY}\sigma_X\sigma_Y$$

If the correlation ρ_{XY} between X and Y is negative, the variance of $(X + Y)$ is smaller than the sum of their variances, hence achieving variance reduction. One way to do it is that for every sample path obtained, $\{\varepsilon_1, \cdots, \varepsilon_n\}$, you make the antithetic path be $\{-\varepsilon_1, \cdots, -\varepsilon_n\}$. This effectively doubles the number of samples and reduces the variance of the sample paths to improve the precision.

The following code computes the integral $I = \int_0^1 \frac{1}{1+x} dx = \ln 2$:

```
val f: UnivariateRealFunction = object : AbstractUnivariateRealFunction() {
    override fun evaluate(x: Double): Double {
        val fx: Double = 1.0 / (1.0 + x)
        return fx
    }
}
```

```
val uniform: RandomLongGenerator = UniformRNG()
uniform.seed(1234567894L)
val av: AntitheticVariates = AntitheticVariates(
                f,
                uniform,
                AntitheticVariates.REFLECTION)
val estimator: Estimator = av.estimate(1500)
println(
        String.format(
                "mean = %f, variance = %f",
                estimator.mean(),
                estimator.variance()))
```

The output is as follows:

```
mean = 0.693158, variance = 0.000595
```

The variance is 0.0006. It would otherwise be 0.00255 using a naïve method.
The signature of a constructor of the AntitheticVariates class is as follows:

```
/**
 * Estimates \(E(f(X_1))\), where <i>f</i> is a function of a random
 * variable.
 *
 * @param f  the random function to evaluate the expectation of
 * @param X1 a random number generator
 * @param X2 the antithetic function, given {@code X}
 */
public AntitheticVariates(
        UnivariateRealFunction f,
        RandomNumberGenerator X1,
        UnivariateRealFunction X2
)
```

13.3.3. Control Variates

The control variates method is a variance reduction technique that exploits information about errors in estimates of known quantities to reduce the error of an estimate of an unknown quantity. To be more specific, suppose you want to estimate μ and the statistic is m, so $E(m) = \mu$. Suppose you have another statistic t that you know is $E(t) = \tau$. You can use t to help estimate μ. Say you have this:

$$m^* = m + c(t - \tau)$$

Then m^* is also an estimator of μ for any c because $E(m^*) = E(m) = \mu$. The variance of m^* is as follows:

$$\mathrm{Var}(m^*) = \mathrm{Var}(m) + c^2\mathrm{Var}(t) + 2c\mathrm{Cov}(m,t)$$

The variance of m^* is minimized, as shown here:

$$c^* = -\frac{\text{Cov}(m,t)}{\text{Var}(t)}$$

$$\text{Var}(m^*) = \text{Var}(m) - \frac{\text{cov}(m,t)^2}{\text{Var}(t)}$$

$$= (1 - \rho_{m,t}^2)\text{Var}(m)$$

$\rho_{m,t}^2 = \text{Corr}(m,t)$, which is the correlation between m and t. The bigger the value of $\rho_{m,t}^2$, the more variance reduction is achieved.

The following code example computes the same integral from the previous example:

$$f(x) = \frac{1}{1+x}$$

It uses this known integral shown here:

$$\text{E}(g(U)) = \int_0^1 (1+x)dx = \frac{3}{2}$$

You get the following:

$$I \approx \frac{1}{n}\sum_i f(u_i) + c\left(\frac{1}{n}\sum_i g(u_i) - \frac{3}{2}\right)$$

u_i are samples from the uniform distribution.

```
val f: UnivariateRealFunction = object : AbstractUnivariateRealFunction() {
    override fun evaluate(x: Double): Double {
        val fx: Double = 1.0 / (1.0 + x)
        return fx
    }
}

val g: UnivariateRealFunction = object : AbstractUnivariateRealFunction() {
    override fun evaluate(x: Double): Double {
        val gx: Double = 1.0 + x
        return gx
    }
}

val uniform: RandomLongGenerator = UniformRNG()
uniform.seed(1234567891L)

val cv: ControlVariates = ControlVariates(f, g, 1.5, -0.4773, uniform)
val estimator: ControlVariates.Estimator = cv.estimate(1500)
println(
        String.format(
```

```
                "mean = %f, variance = %f, b = %f",
                estimator.mean(),
                estimator.variance(),
                estimator.b()))
```

The output is as follows:

```
mean = 0.692015, variance = 0.000601, b = -0.472669
```

The variance is 0.0006. It would otherwise be 0.00255 using a naïve method. The result of using control variates is similar to using antithetic variates for this problem.

The signature of a constructor of the ControlVariates class is as follows:

```
/**
 * Estimates \(E(f(X_1))\), where <i>f</i> is a function of a random
 * variable.
 *
 * @param f  the random function to evaluate the expectation of
 * @param g  the random function with known value
 * @param Eg the expectation of g
 * @param c  a coefficient
 * @param X  a random number generator
 */
public ControlVariates(
        UnivariateRealFunction f,
        UnivariateRealFunction g,
        double Eg,
        double c,
        RandomNumberGenerator X
)
```

13.3.4. Importance Sampling

Importance sampling is an important strategy in using Monte Carlo simulation that estimates the property of a probability distribution while using samples generated from a different distribution than the one of interest. The idea behind importance sampling is that certain values of the input random variables in a simulation have more impact on the integral (or the average) being computed than others. If these "important" values are emphasized by sampling more frequently, then the estimator variance can be reduced. Hence, the basic methodology in importance sampling is to choose a distribution that "encourages" the important values. This use of a "biased" distribution will result in a biased estimator if it is applied directly to the simulation. However, the simulation outputs are weighted to correct for the use of the biased distribution. This ensures that the new importance sampling estimator is unbiased.

Suppose you want to compute the expectation of the function $f(x)$ under the target distribution P. If you sample from P, using the Monte Carlo method leads to the following calculations:

$$E_{x\text{-}P}\left[f(x)\right] = \int_x^N P(x)f(x)dx \approx \frac{1}{N}\sum_{x_i\text{-}P,i=1}^{N} f(x_i)$$

However, if you cannot sample from P easily or efficiently, this summing cannot be performed. You can try to find another distribution P' that you know how to sample from to do the integration. The change of measure or probability distribution formula is as follows:

$$E_{x \sim P}\left[f(x)\right] = \int_x^N f(x)P(x)dx$$

$$= \int_x^N f(x)\frac{P(x)}{P'(x)}P'(x)dx$$

$$= E_{x \sim P'}\left[\frac{P}{P'}f(x)\right]$$

$$\approx \frac{1}{N}\sum_{x_i \sim P', i=1}^{N}\frac{P(x)}{P'(x)}f(x_i)$$

The mathematics says that you now sample x_is from P', and for each $f(x_i)$, you need to scale the output by $\frac{P(x)}{P'(x)}$ to correct the bias.

Here is a simple example. Suppose you want to compute the integral of the identity function $f(x) = x$ under the normal distribution (mean = 1 and standard deviation = 1), $N_0 = N(0, 1)$. Instead of sampling from the standard normal, you sample from another normal distribution with mean = 1 and standard deviation = 0.5, $N_1 = N(0, 0.5)$. For each sample x_i you draw from N_1, you compute the corrected output and take the average.

$$\frac{N_0(x)}{N_1(x)}x_i$$

To be more specific, let's say you draw from N_1 twice and get 1.09 and 2.36. The calculations are as follows:

$$\frac{1}{2}\left(\frac{0.3973}{0.7851}1.09 + \frac{0.1582}{0.0197}2.36\right) = 9.7517$$

You can further develop this example to compute the integral of the standard normal function, $\phi(x)$, between 0 and 1. That is:

$$I = \int_0^1 \phi(x)dx$$

One way to do this is to sample x^s from the standard normal distribution N_0 and keep only the samples where $x^s \in [0, 1]$ and reject the samples otherwise. This mean is as follows:

$$I_0 = \frac{\sum_{s=1}^{S} x^s \cdot \mathbf{1}\left(x^s \in [0,1]\right)}{\mathbf{1}\left(x^s \in [0,1]\right)}$$

This computation is inefficient if you reject a lot of the samples, that is, $\mathbf{1}(x^s \in [0, 1]) \ll S$.

Alternatively, you can draw from the uniform distribution and let $g(x) = 1$ if $x^s \in [0, 1]$. The weight is as follows:

$$w^s = \frac{\phi(x^s)}{\int_0^1 \phi(z)dz}$$

The mean is as follows:

$$I_1 = \frac{1}{S}\sum_{s=1}^{S} x^s \cdot w^s$$

No samples are rejected. The following code snippet solves this example:

```
val h: UnivariateRealFunction = object : AbstractUnivariateRealFunction() {
    override fun evaluate(x: Double): Double {
        return x // the identity function
    }
}

val w: UnivariateRealFunction = object : AbstractUnivariateRealFunction() {
    val phi: Gaussian = Gaussian()
    val N: StandardCumulativeNormal = CumulativeNormalMarsaglia()
    val I: Double = N.evaluate(1.0) - N.evaluate(0.0)

    override fun evaluate(x: Double): Double {
        val w: Double = phi.evaluate(x) / I // the weight
        return w
    }
}

val rng: RandomNumberGenerator = UniformRNG()
rng.seed(1234567892L)

val imortsampl: ImportanceSampling = ImportanceSampling(h, w, rng)
val estimator: Estimator = imortsampl.estimate(100000)
println(
        String.format(
                "mean = %f, variance = %f",
                estimator.mean(),
                estimator.variance()))
```

The output is as follows:

```
mean = 0.459671, variance = 0.047314
```

The signature of a constructor of the ImportanceSampling class is as follows:

```
/**
 * Uses importance sample to do Monte Carlo integration.
 *
 * @param h the function to integrate
 * @param w the weight function or the change of measure
 * @param G a uniform random number generator
 */
public ImportanceSampling(
        UnivariateRealFunction h,
        UnivariateRealFunction w,
        RandomNumberGenerator G
)
```

This example is from Scratchapixel and it shows the effectiveness of importance sampling. It is efficient if you can use a "matching" distribution rather than a uniform distribution. Suppose you want to use Monte Carlo simulation to compute this integration. See Figure 13-14.

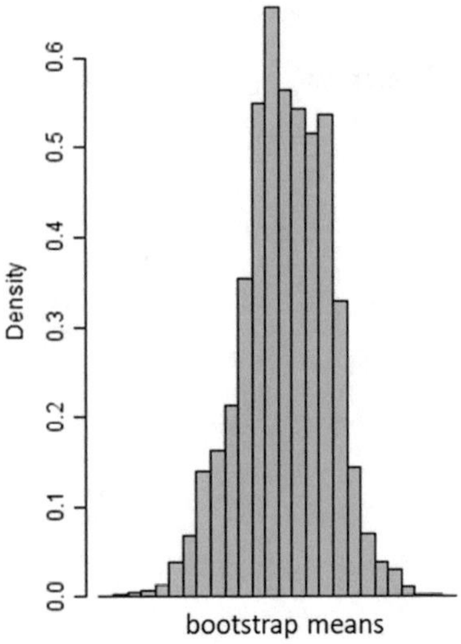

Figure 13-14. *Importance sampling using two different PDFs*

$$I = \int_0^{\frac{\pi}{2}} \sin(x)\,dx$$

$$= \left[-\cos(x)\right]_0^{\frac{\pi}{2}}$$

$$= -\cos\left(\frac{\pi}{2}\right) - -\cos(0)$$

$$= 1$$

You have a choice of two distributions:

- A uniform distribution like you normally would use: $f_0(x) = \frac{1}{\frac{\pi}{2}} = \frac{2}{\pi}$
- A distribution with PDF close to the integrand: $f_1(x) = \frac{8x}{\pi^2}$

Using the uniform distribution, you first invert the CDF.

$$\xi_0 = F_0(x) = \int_0^x f_0(z)dz = \frac{2}{\pi}x$$

$$x = \frac{\pi}{2}\xi_0$$

ξ_0 has a uniform distribution on the unit interval. The Monte Carlo sum is as follows:

$$\int_0^{\frac{\pi}{2}} f(x)dx \approx \frac{1}{N}\sum_{i=1}^{N}\frac{f(x_i)}{f_0(x_i)} = \frac{\pi}{2N}\sum_{i=1}^{N}\sin x_i$$

Using the second distribution, you again first invest the CDF.

$$\xi_1 = F_1(x) = \int_0^x f_0(z)dz = \frac{4}{\pi^2}x^2$$

$$x = \frac{\pi}{2}\sqrt{\xi_1}$$

ξ_1 has a uniform distribution on the unit interval. The Monte Carlo sum is as follows:

$$\int_0^{\frac{\pi}{2}} f(x)dx \approx \frac{1}{N}\sum_{i=1}^{N}\frac{f(x_i)}{f_1(x_i)} = \frac{\pi^2}{8N}\sum_{i=1}^{N}\frac{\sin x_i}{x_i}$$

The following code compares the two sums:

```
val rng: RandomNumberGenerator = UniformRNG()
rng.seed(1234567892L)
val N: Int = 16
for (n in 0 until 10) {
    var sumUniform: Double = 0.0
    var sumImportance: Double = 0.0
    for (i in 0 until N) {
        val r: Double = rng.nextDouble()
        sumUniform += sin(r * PI * 0.5)
        val xi: Double = sqrt(r) * PI * 0.5
        sumImportance += sin(xi) / ((8 * xi) / (PI * PI))
    }
```

```
    sumUniform *= (PI * 0.5) / N
    sumImportance *= 1.0 / N
    println(String.format("%f %f\n", sumUniform, sumImportance))
}
```

The output is as follows:

```
1.016777 1.000049
0.984924 1.000781
1.075695 0.981736
0.910973 1.023657
0.908362 1.030897
0.841806 1.048676
1.007154 0.993348
1.133367 0.955110
1.182259 0.947664
1.085175 0.984744
```

You can see that, for the same number of random samples and the same random values $\xi_0 = \xi_1$, the importance sampling technique significantly reduces variance and converges faster.

CHAPTER 14

Linear Regression

In statistics, linear regression is a linear method to model the relationship between a scalar response (dependent variable), *y*, and one or more explanatory variables (independent variables), $\boldsymbol{x}$, a vector. When there is only one explanatory variable, it is called *simple linear regression*. When there is more than one explanatory variable, it is called *multiple linear regression*. The parameters of such a linear model, $\boldsymbol{\beta}$, are the coefficients for the explanatory variables. The parameters are estimated from the data. When such a linear model is used to predict the outcome of the response given the values of the explanatory variables, it is assumed that the conditional mean of the response or a transformation, *g*, of that is a linear function of the explanatory variables, namely, $g\left(\hat{y}\right)=g\left(\mathrm{E}\left(y\right)\right)=\boldsymbol{x}\beta$. When the transformation is the identify function, it simplifies to $\hat{y}=\mathrm{E}\left(y\right)=\boldsymbol{x}\beta$.

Linear regression is widely used in many applications and sciences because it is simple to visualize. For simple linear regression, as in Figure 14-1, the model is just a line in the *xy*-plane. For multiple linear regression, it is a hyper-plane. The parameters are easy to determine. Moreover, there is a large body of work that studies linear regression extensively and rigorously. The model and its properties are well understood.

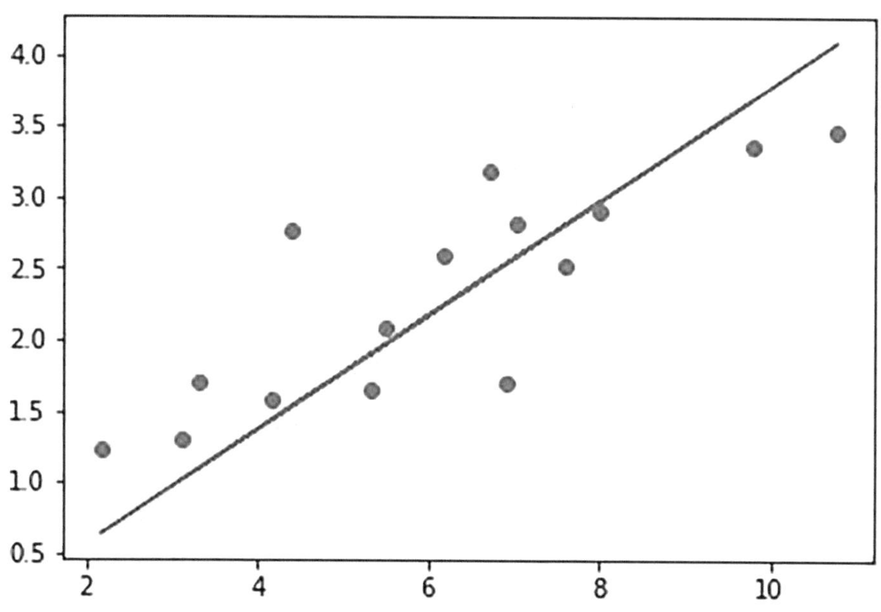

Figure 14-1. *Simple linear regression*

H. Li, PhD, *Numerical Methods Using Kotlin*, https://doi.org/10.1007/978-1-4842-8826-9_14

For example, in finance, the famous capital asset pricing model (CAPM) is a simple linear regression between the fair/expected excess return of a stock, $E(R_i) - R_f$, and the expected excess return of the market, $E(R_M) - R_f$. Because the return of a stock or the market is unknown or random, we put an expectation operator E() around it. Excess return of an asset is the return above a risk-free rate R_f, like the interest rate from a government guaranteed treasury bond. The simple linear regression model is as follows: $E(R_i) = R_f + \beta_i(E(R_M) - R_f)$. The coefficient β_i, called the beta of the stock *i*, measures the sensitivity of the expected excess asset returns to the expected excess market returns. This is one of the most important ways to describe a stock in finance.

In economics, linear regression is the predominant empirical tool. It is used to predict consumption spending, fixed investment spending, inventory investment, purchases of a country's exports, spending on imports, the demand to hold liquid assets, and labor demand and supply. Linear regression can be applied to construct a trend line that represents the long-term movement in time-series data. It tells whether a particular data set (say GDP, oil prices or stock prices) has increased or decreased over the period of time. A trend line could simply be drawn by eye through a set of data points, but more properly their position and slope are calculated using statistical techniques such as linear regression. Linear regression is also extensively used in biology, behavioral science, social science, and so on, to describe possible relationships between variables in experiments and surveys. It is one of the most important tools used in these disciplines. See Figure 14-2.

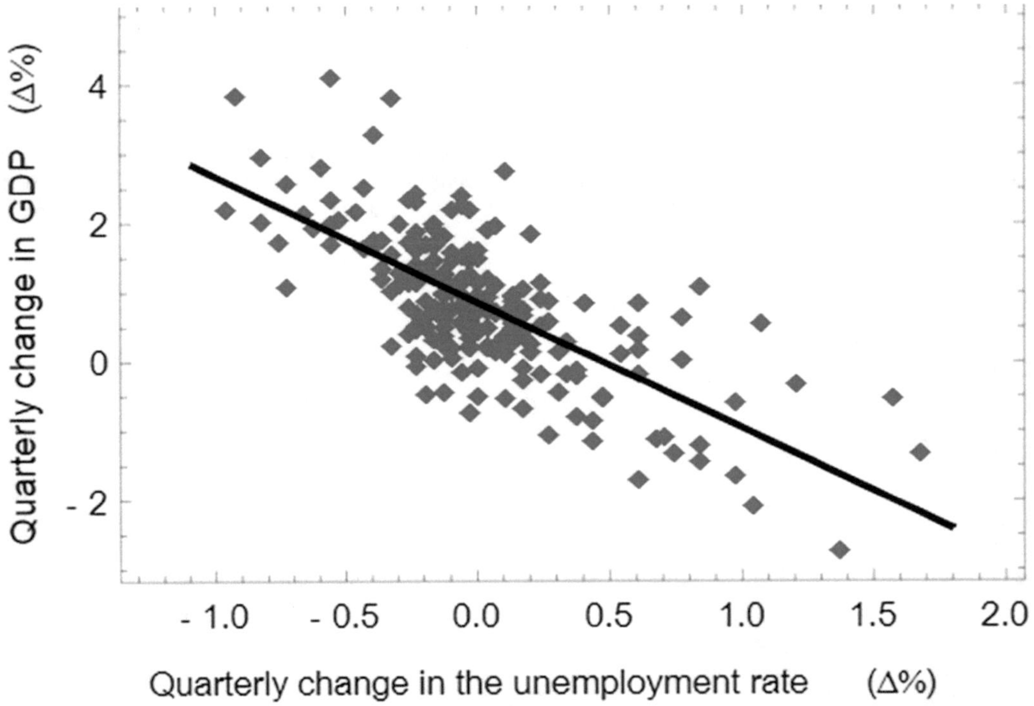

***Figure 14-2.** In economics, Okun's law states that GDP growth depends linearly on the changes in the unemployment rate*

Suppose your data consists of n observations, $\{\boldsymbol{x}_i, y_i\}_{i=1}^n$. Each observation includes one response y_i and p explanatory variables $\boldsymbol{x}_i = (x_{i1}, x_{i2}, \ldots, x_{ip})T$. The data can be tabulated as shown here:

Obs.	y	x_1	x_2	...	x_p
1	y_1	x_{11}	x_{12}	...	x_{1p}
2	y_2	x_{21}	x_{22}	...	x_{2p}
3	y_3	x_{31}	x_{32}	...	x_{3p}
⋮	⋮	⋮	⋮	...	⋮
n	y_n	x_{n1}	x_{n2}	...	x_{np}

In a linear model, the response y_i is a linear function of the explanatory variables $\boldsymbol{x}_i$. That is:

$$y_1 = \beta_1 x_{11} + \cdots + \beta_p x_{1p} + \varepsilon_1$$

$$y_2 = \beta_1 x_{21} + \cdots + \beta_p x_{2p} + \varepsilon_2$$

$$\vdots$$

$$y_n = \beta_1 x_{n1} + \cdots + \beta_p x_{np} + \varepsilon_n$$

Or, in vector form, it looks like this:

$$y_i = \boldsymbol{x}_i^T \beta + \varepsilon_i$$

$\boldsymbol{x}_i$ is the column vector of the explanatory variables in the i-th observation, $\boldsymbol{\beta}$ is the $p \times 1$ vector of the model parameters that you need to estimate from the data, and ε_i is called the *residual* and it accounts for the randomness of y_i that may be due to measurement error or influence unexplained by $\boldsymbol{x}_i$. ε_i is a random variable and thus so is y_i. The response value is a particular realization of the random variable y_i.

In matrix form, you write the following:

$$\mathbf{y} = \boldsymbol{X}\beta + \varepsilon$$

$$\text{where } \mathbf{y} = \begin{bmatrix} y_1 \\ y_2 \\ \vdots \\ y_n \end{bmatrix}, \mathbf{X} = \begin{bmatrix} x_{11} & x_{12} & \cdots & x_{1p} \\ x_{21} & x_{22} & \cdots & x_{2p} \\ & & \ddots & \\ x_{n1} & x_{n2} & \cdots & x_{np} \end{bmatrix}, \beta = \begin{bmatrix} \beta_1 \\ \beta_2 \\ \vdots \\ \beta_p \end{bmatrix} \text{ and } \varepsilon = \begin{bmatrix} \varepsilon_1 \\ \varepsilon_2 \\ \vdots \\ \varepsilon_p \end{bmatrix}.$$

Explanatory variables do not have to be independent. There can be any relationship between them (so long as it is not a linear relationship). For instance, when tossing a small ball up in the air, the height follows this relationship with time:

$$h_i = \beta_1 t_i + \beta_2 t_i^2 + \varepsilon_i$$

β_1 is related to the initial velocity of the ball, and β_2 is proportional to the earth's gravity (de/acceleration). ε_i is the measurement error. This model is nonlinear (quadratic) in the time variable t_i, but it is linear in the parameters β_1 and β_2. It is still a linear model in the standard form.

The source code in this chapter can be run on the S2 platform here:

```
https://s21.nm.dev/hub/user-redirect/lab/tree/s2-public/Numerical%20Methods%20Using%20
Kotlin/chapter14.ipynb
```

The source code can be found on GitHub:

https://github.com/apress/numerical-methods-kotlin

14.1. Ordinary Least Squares

There are many ways to choose the model parameters, $\boldsymbol{\beta}$, depending on the objective function and assumptions. One of the most commonly used methods is ordinary least squares (OLS). OLS minimizes the sum of the squares of the differences between the observed response (values of the variable being observed) in the given data set, y_i, and the fitted values predicted by the linear function of the explanatory variable, $\hat{y}_i$. That is, the objective function is given as follows:

$$S(\beta) = \sum_{i=1}^{n} \left| y_i - \hat{y}_i \right|^2 = \sum_{i=1}^{n} \left| y_i - \sum_{j=1}^{p} X_{ij}\beta_j \right|^2 = \mathbf{y} - \mathbf{X}\beta^2$$

The OLS beta is chosen such that you have this (see Figure 14-3):

$$\hat{\beta} = \underset{\beta}{\operatorname{argmin}}\, S(\beta)$$

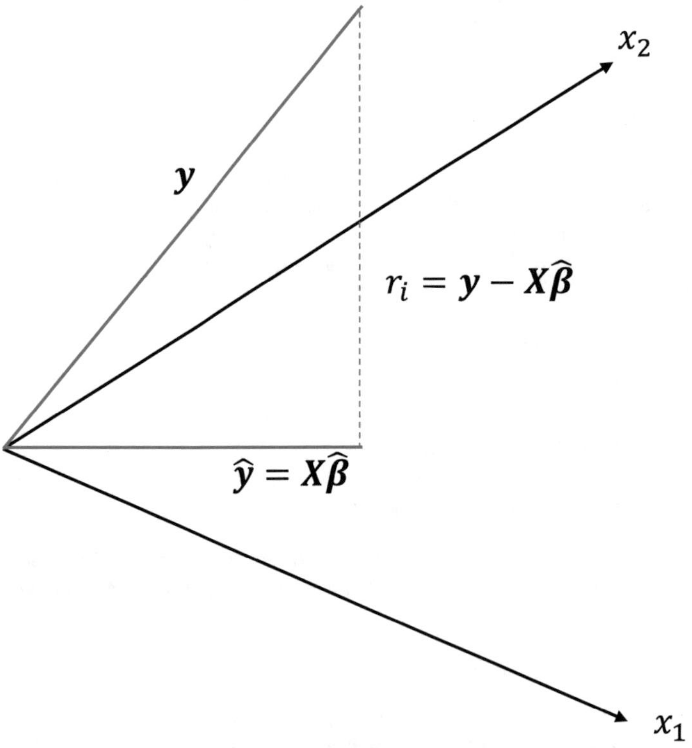

Figure 14-3. *Normal equation*

It can be proven that the solution to the normal equation is as follows (see Figure 14-4). (It is called a normal equation because the residuals $\boldsymbol{y} - \boldsymbol{X\beta}$ are perpendicular to the space spanned by $\boldsymbol{X}$.)

$$\hat{\beta} = \left(\boldsymbol{X}^{\mathrm{T}}\boldsymbol{X}\right)^{-1}\boldsymbol{X}^{\mathrm{T}}\boldsymbol{y}$$

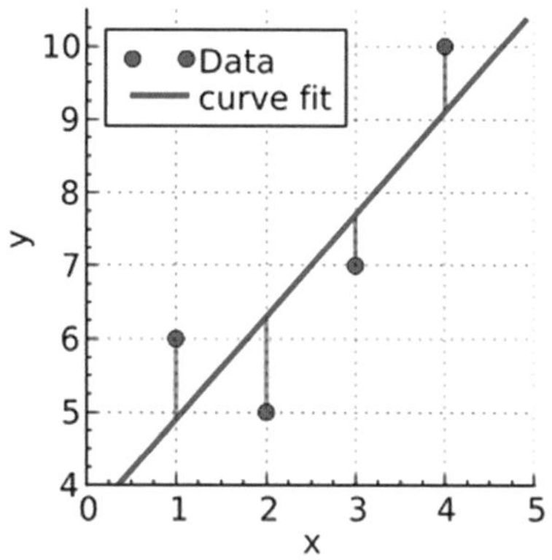

Figure 14-4. *Least square estimation to minimize the sum of squared errors*

Therefore, you get this:

$$\hat{\boldsymbol{y}} = \boldsymbol{X}\hat{\beta} = \boldsymbol{X}\left(\boldsymbol{X}^{T}\boldsymbol{X}\right)^{-1}\boldsymbol{X}^{T}\boldsymbol{y} = \boldsymbol{H}\boldsymbol{y}$$

$\boldsymbol{H} = \boldsymbol{X}(\boldsymbol{X}^T\boldsymbol{X})^{-1}\boldsymbol{X}^T$ is called the hat matrix because it is this matrix that puts the hat, ^, on the observed response vector $\boldsymbol{y}$ to get the fitted response vector $\hat{\mathbf{y}}$.

14.1.1. Assumptions

The OLS theory makes a number of assumptions.

Correct Specification

The linear functional form must coincide with the form of the actual data-generating process. Some linear data generating processes include home runs in a season, fan attendance, and quarterly revenue trends. Some nonlinear examples include the Earth's population, radioactive particles over time, and YouTube channel user growth.

Exogeneity

Exogeneity means that the explanatory variables are uncorrelated with the errors, that is, $\mathrm{E}(\boldsymbol{X}^T\epsilon) = 0$. Otherwise, you have *endogeneity*. In addition, the errors in the regression model should have conditional means of zero.

$$\mathrm{E}\left(\epsilon \mid \boldsymbol{X}\right) = 0$$

The immediate consequence of the exogeneity assumption is that the errors have mean zero: $\mathrm{E}(\epsilon) = 0$.

No Linear Dependence

The explanatory variables or the design matrix $\boldsymbol{X}$ must all be linearly independent. Mathematically, this means that the matrix $\boldsymbol{X}$ must have full column rank almost surely.

$$\Pr\left(\text{rank}(\boldsymbol{X}) = p\right) = 1$$

Usually, it is also assumed that $\boldsymbol{X}$ has finite moments up to at least the second moment. Then the matrix $\boldsymbol{Q}^{XX} = \text{E}(\boldsymbol{X}^T\boldsymbol{X}/n)$ is finite and positive semidefinite. When this assumption is violated, the design matrix is said to be linearly dependent or perfectly multicollinear.

Homoscedasticity

$\text{E}\left(\epsilon_i^2 \mid \boldsymbol{X}\right) = \sigma^2$ means that the error term has the same variance σ^2 in each observation. This is often not the case, as a variable whose mean is big will typically have a bigger variance than one whose mean is small. For example, a person whose income is predicted to be \$100,000 may easily have an actual income of \$80,000 or \$120,000, that is, a standard deviation of around \$20,000. In contrast, another person with a predicted income of \$10,000 is unlikely to have the same \$20,000 standard deviation, since that would imply their actual income could vary anywhere between -\$10,000 and \$30,000. When this requirement is violated, this is called heteroscedasticity. In such cases, a more efficient estimator (an estimator that has a lower variance) is weighted least squares (see Section 14.2), where you can assign a different weight to each observation in the data.

No Autocorrelation

The errors are uncorrelated between observations, that is, $\text{E}(\epsilon_i\epsilon_j \mid \boldsymbol{X}) = 0$ for $i \neq j$. This assumption may be violated in the context of time-series data, panel data, cluster samples, hierarchical data, repeated measures data, longitudinal data, and other data with dependencies. In such cases, generalized least squares provides a better alternative than the OLS (see Section 14.3).

Normality

It is sometimes additionally assumed that the errors have normal distribution, conditional on the explanatory variables.

$$\varepsilon \mid \boldsymbol{X} \sim N\left(0, \sigma^2 \boldsymbol{I}_n\right)$$

This assumption is not needed for the validity of the OLS method, although certain additional finite-sample properties (size of the data set n is finite) can be established in cases when it does (especially in the area of hypotheses testing). Also, when the errors are normal, the OLS estimator is equivalent to the maximum likelihood estimator (MLE), and therefore it is asymptotically efficient (having the smallest variance when $n \to \infty$) in the class of all regular estimators. Importantly, the normality assumption applies only to the error terms; contrary to a popular misconception, the response, y, is not required to be normally distributed.

14.1.2. Model Properties

The OLS estimators $\hat{\beta}$ and s^2 are unbiased under the assumption of exogeneity, meaning that their expected values coincide with their true values.

$$\text{E}(\beta \mid \boldsymbol{X}) = \hat{\beta} \text{ and } \text{E}(s^2 \mid \boldsymbol{X}) = \sigma^2$$

s^2 is called the standard error of the regression and is defined as the sum of squared errors divided by the degree of freedom of the problem.

$$s^2 = \frac{\varepsilon^T \varepsilon}{n-p}$$

Under the assumption that the errors are uncorrelated and homoscedastic, the estimator $\hat{\beta}$ is efficient in the class of linear unbiased estimators. This is called the best linear unbiased estimator (BLUE). It means that the variance of $\hat{\beta}$ is smaller than the variance of any other estimator that is a linear combination of observations. In this sense, the OLS estimator is the best, or optimal, estimator of the parameters. Note particularly that this property is independent of the statistical distribution of the errors. In other words, the distribution function of the errors need not be a normal distribution.

If, however, you are to assume that the errors are indeed normally distributed, $\varepsilon \sim N(0, \sigma^2 \boldsymbol{I}_n)$, then $\hat{\beta}$ is also normally distributed.

$$\hat{\beta} \sim N\left(\beta, \sigma^2 \left(\boldsymbol{X}^T \boldsymbol{X}\right)^{-1}\right)$$

Moreover, this estimator reaches the Cramér-Rao bound for the model and thus is optimal in the class of all unbiased estimators.

The higher the absolute value of the beta coefficient for an explanatory variable, the stronger the effect of the variable. For example, a beta of -0.9 has a stronger effect than a beta of +0.8 for the same variable. However, the magnitudes of beta coefficients do not let us compare the significance between variables. For example, the unit of x_1 may be in dollars and the unit of x_2 in cents. 0.1 beta for x_1 versus 1.0 for x_2 does not imply that the beta for x_1 is more significant than that of x_2 because when expressing x_1 in cents, its beta would become 10.

Standardized beta coefficients have standard deviations as their units. This means the variables can be easily compared. In other words, standardized beta coefficients are the coefficients that you would get if the variables in the regression were all converted to z-scores before running the analysis. A coefficient divided by its standard error is also called the t-statistics and follows the student t's distribution. You can use the student t's distribution to compute the p-value of a standardized beta coefficient to determine its significance. As a rule of thumb, a beta/variable/t-statistic is significant if its t-statistic is bigger than 2.0 or equivalently p-value smaller than 0.05. This corresponds to a significance level of 5 percent. There is 95 percent probability of being correct that the variable is having some effect, assuming your model is specified correctly.

14.1.3. Residual Analysis

Residual analysis, OLS, is defined as the difference between the observed value and the fitted value for given values of the explanatory variables. Note that, in statistics, residual and error are two different concepts. Residual is the difference between the observed value and the model value $\varepsilon_i = y_i - \hat{y}_i$; error is the difference between the observed value and the true (unobservable) value. Residual is an estimation of the error.

Because the regression assumptions are not always satisfied, residual analysis is important to assess the appropriateness of a linear regression model (not just OLS). For simple linear regression, a residual graph plots the residuals versus the one explanatory variable. Ideally, the residual plot should be like random noise around zero without patterns. If the data exhibits a trend, the regression model is likely incorrect; for example, the true function may be a quadratic or higher-order polynomial. If they are random or have no trend but "fan out," they exhibit heteroscedasticity. See Figure 14-5.

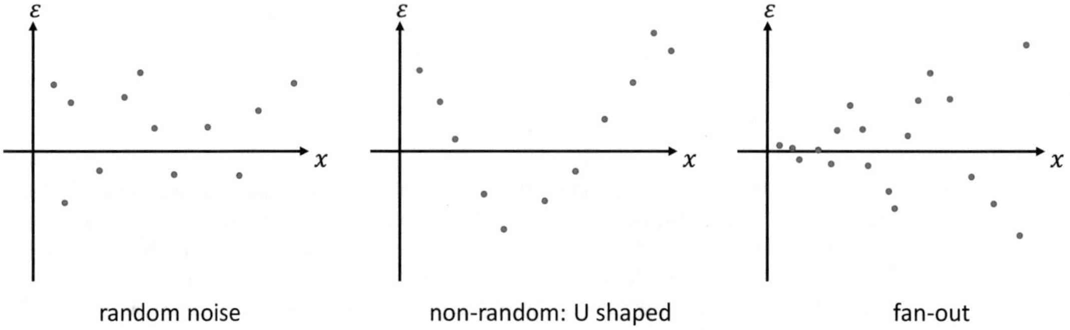

Figure 14-5. *Residual plots*

RSS

There are a number of statistics associated with the residuals that you can use to assess how fit the resultant linear regression model is. As OLS aims at minimizing the sum of square errors, residual sum of squares (RSS) measures the amount of variance in the data that is not explained by the regression. That is, RSS is the amount of derivation of the data from the model expectation.

$$RSS = \sum_{i=1}^{n} \left(y_i - \hat{y}_i\right)^2$$

RMSE

The average error or deviation is called the root mean square error (RMSE).

$$RMSE = \sqrt{\frac{\sum_{i=1}^{n} \left(y_i - \hat{y}_i\right)^2}{n}}$$

RSE

You could also divide the sum by the degree of freedom, which is the sample size of data minus the number of parameters, to get an unbiased estimator of the standard deviation of the error term σ. In such cases, you have the residual standard error (RSE).

$$RSE = \sqrt{\frac{\sum_{i=1}^{n} \left(y_i - \hat{y}_i\right)^2}{n-p}}$$

Under the assumption that the error ε is normally distributed, the model expectation $\hat{y}_i$ and RSE give the normal distribution of the model forecast for y_i. The distribution can be used to find a confidence interval. The true value for y_i has a 68 percent chance of landing in the interval $\left(\hat{y}_i - \sigma, \hat{y}_i + \sigma\right)$. See Figure 14-6.

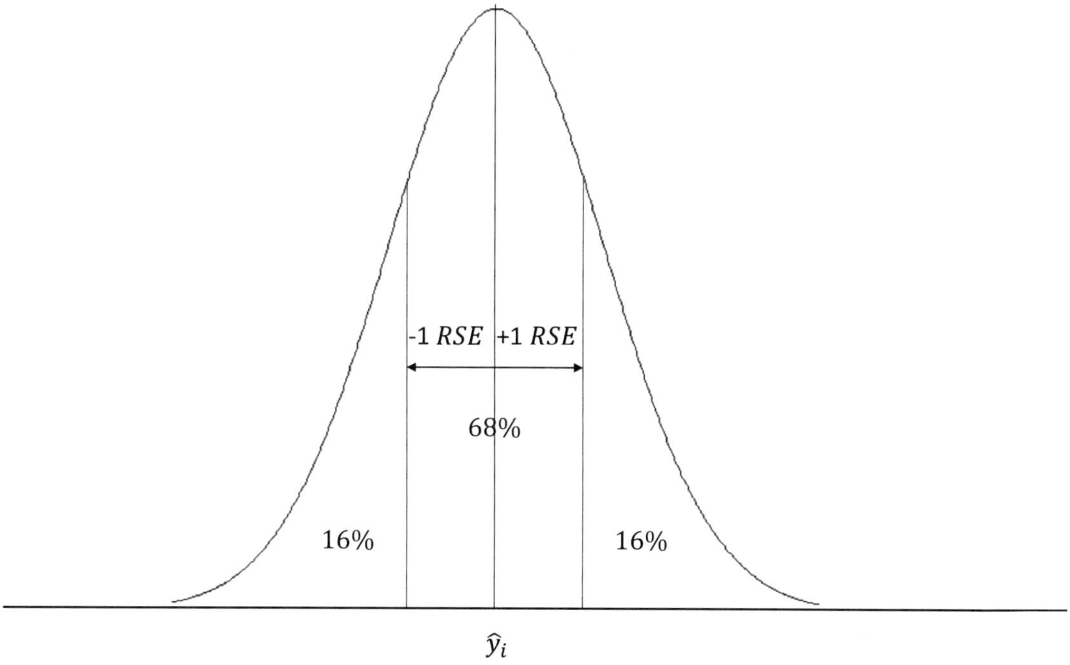

Figure 14-6. *Confidence interval of a model prediction*

ESS

Let $\bar{y}$ be the sample mean of the response. Then the explained sum of squares (ESS) measures how much variation there is in the modeled values.

$$ESS = \sum_{i=1}^{n} \left(\hat{y}_i - \bar{y}\right)^2$$

TSS

The total sum of squares (TSS) is the sum of ESS and RRS. It measures how much variation there is in the observed data.

$$TSS = ESS + RSS = \sum_{i=1}^{n} \left(\hat{y}_i - \bar{y}\right)^2 + \sum_{i=1}^{n} \left(y_i - \hat{y}_i\right)^2$$

R-squared

An important measure of goodness of fit is the coefficient of determination or R^2. R^2 is defined as the proportion of variation in the data explained by the model. The value is always between 0 (0 percent) and 1 (100 percent). The more the amount of explanation of variation a model can provide, the higher its value of R^2.

$$R^2 = \frac{ESS}{TSS} = 1 - \frac{RSS}{TSS}$$

Adjusted R-squared

R^2 by itself does not tell whether a model is good or bad. You can have a low R^2 for a good model. For instance, models to predict human behavior, such as psychology, typically have an R^2 value smaller than 50 percent. It is simply much more difficult to predict humans than physical processes. On the other hand, you can have a high R^2 for a bad model. For example, if a model could explain 100 percent of the variance, $R^2 = 1$, the fitted values would always equal the observed values. All the data points would fall on the fitted regression line/plane. In fact, you can arbitrarily increase R^2 by keep adding explanatory variables. R^2 always increases and never decreases even if the new variable is by chance correlated with the response. This is a typical case of over-fitting. Your high R^2 model may not be finding any meaningful pattern but is simply connecting the dots in the data.

Adjusted R^2, R^2_{adj}, is a modified version of R^2 that has been adjusted for the number of explanatory variables in the model. The adjusted R^2_{adj} increases only if you add useful variables that will actually improve the model. It decreases if you add useless variables to the model. The adjusted R^2_{adj} can be negative, but it is usually not. It is always lower than the R^2.

$$R^2_{adj} = 1 - \frac{\left(1-R^2\right)\left(n-1\right)}{n-p-1}$$

F-statistic

The t-statistic or the p-value of a beta coefficient tells whether the coefficient/variable is significant (see Section 14.1.2) at 5 percent significance level. That means there is a 5 percent chance that it is a false positive result (beta actually not significant). As all these t-statistics are independent, the more variables you have in your model, the more likely it will have (at least) one p-value < 0.05 just by chance. With four explanatory variables, there is a $1 - (1 - 0.05)^4 = 18.5$ percent chance of having at least one significant beta with p-value < 0.05. Or, there is a 18.5 percent chance that you will falsely conclude that the model is useful. With more than 100 variables, it will be likely (99.4 percent) to have one significant beta with a p-value < 0.05, and thus you will likely conclude the model is useful whether or not this is actually the case. Therefore, you need another way to determine whether a linear regression model is useful, that is, if it really has at least one significant explanatory variable not by chance.

The F-statistic tests for the overall significance of a linear regression model. The null hypothesis states that there is no relationship between any of the explanatory variables and the response. The alternative hypothesis says that there is at least one significant variable. At a significance level of 5 percent, if the p-value of the F-statistics is smaller than 0.05, you can reject the null hypothesis and conclude that the model is useful. It is possible that the F-statistics is insignificant, but some of the beta t-statistics are significant; in this case, you would accept the null hypothesis and reject the model. On the other hand, it is possible that the F-statistics is significant but none of the beta t-statistics are significant (all are insignificant, or less than 2); in this case, you reject the null hypothesis and accept the model. The bottom line is that when it comes to the overall significance of the linear regression model, you always trust the statistical significance of the p-value associated with the F-statistic over that of each explanatory variable. The following example is when F-statistics are insignificant but some of the beta t-statistics are significant:

```
beta hat
beta^ = [3.055264, -0.347572, 0.019219, -4.357924]
beta^ standard error = [0.491998, 0.194540, 0.299207, 3.958854]
beta^ t = [6.209908, -1.786633, 0.064232, -1.100804]
residual F-stat = 0.528805679720477
```

The following example is when F-statistics are significant but none of the beta t-statistics are significant:

```
beta^ = [0.055264, -0.347572, 0.019219, -4.357924]
beta^ standard error = [0.491998, 0.194540, 0.299207, 3.958854]
beta^ t = [0.112326, -1.786633, 0.064232, -1.100804]
residual F-stat = 13.528805679720477
```

14.1.4. Influential Point

Recall that for the hat matrix $\boldsymbol{H} = \boldsymbol{X}(\boldsymbol{X}^T\boldsymbol{X})^{-1}\boldsymbol{X}^T$, the model parameters are linear combinations of the observations, but each observation has a different influence on the hat matrix and hence beta hat $\hat{\beta}$ and the fitted values $\hat{\boldsymbol{y}}$. An observation may have undue influence on the regression and may give a different result depending on whether this particular observation is present. See Figure 14-7.

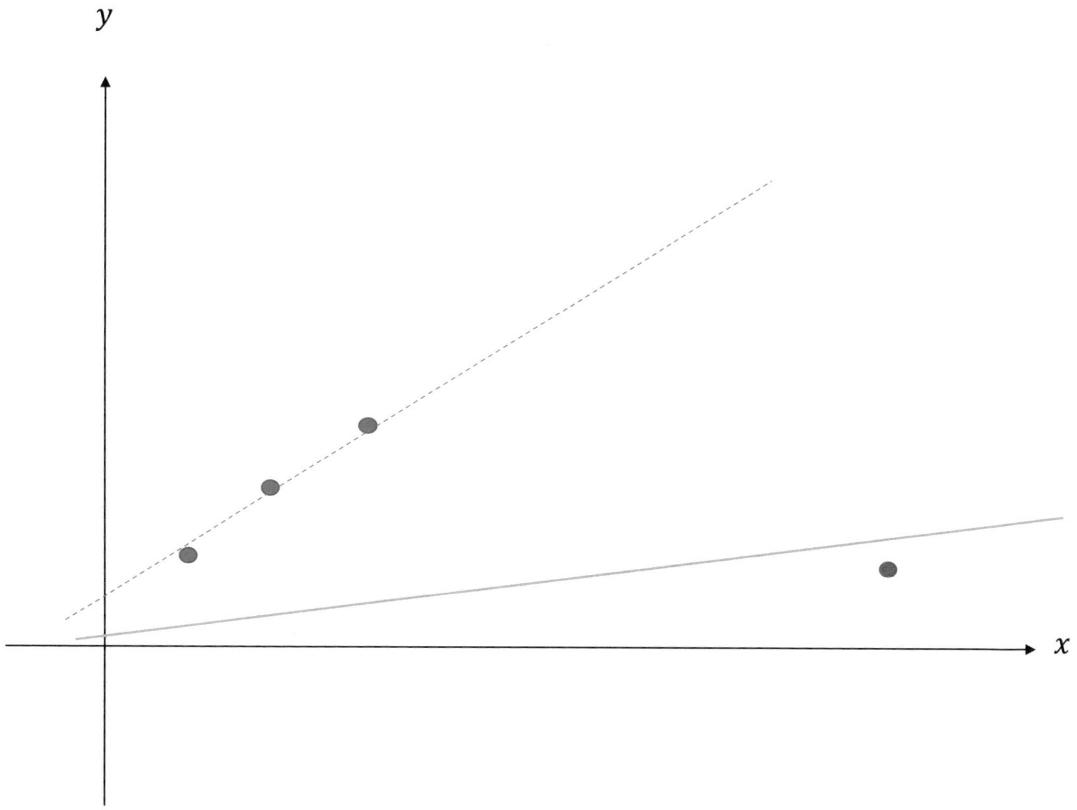

Figure 14-7. *Heavy influence of the red dot on the regression*

For instance, in Figure 14-7, if without the red dot (the dot furthest on the right), the linear regression model would go through the three blue dots (the dashed line). The presence of the red dot "pulls" the regression line toward the x-axis by a lot. The red dot is said to have a heavy influence on the regression result. One drawback of OLS is that it is easily influenced by a few influential points in the data set.

There are two types of influential point. The first type is called an *outlier*. An outlier is a data point whose response *y* does not follow the general trend of the rest of the data. For example, the red dot in Figure 14-8 is an outlier because it has an extreme *y*-value. It does not follow the general trend constructed by the other three blue dots.

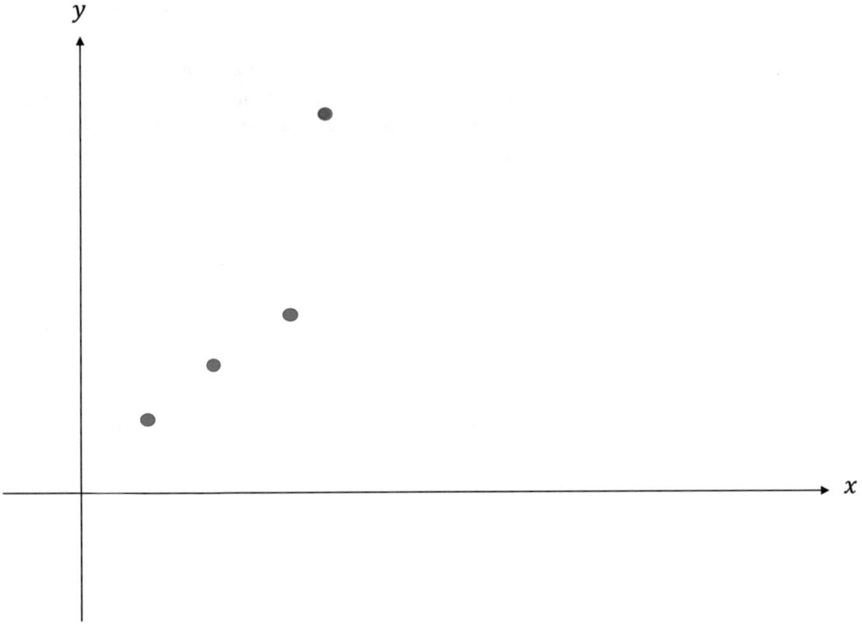

Figure 14-8. *An outlier*

The second type of influential point is called the *high leverage point*. A data point is said to have high leverage if it has extreme values in the explanatory variables or a linear combination of the explanatory variables. For example, the red dot in Figure 14-9 has a much larger *x*-value compared to the other three blue dots.

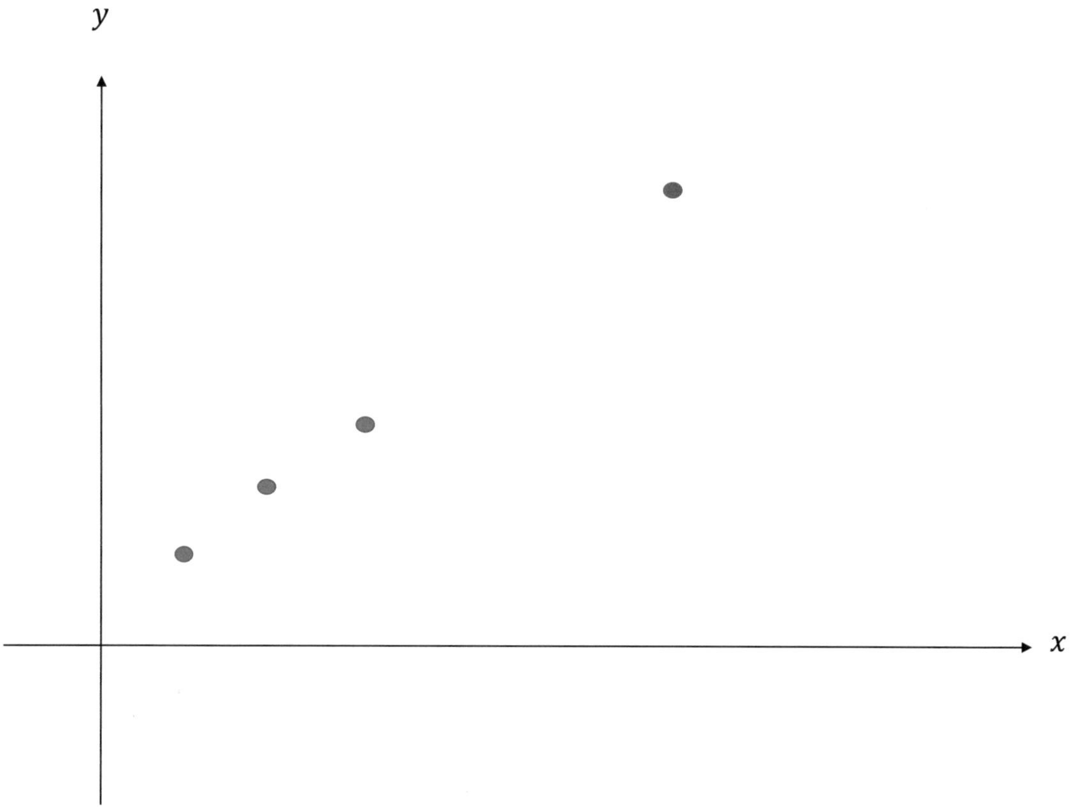

Figure 14-9. *A high leverage point*

A data point can both be an outlier and have a high leverage. For example, the red dot in Figure 14-9 has both an extreme *y* value and an extreme *x* value. The way to assess whether an influential point has any impact (and how much) on a regression is to run the regression twice: one with the point included and another one with the point excluded. You can then compare the results, such as the fitted responses, hypothesis test results, confidence, and prediction intervals, of the two regressions.

Leverage

Expanding $\hat{\boldsymbol{y}} = \boldsymbol{H}\boldsymbol{y}$ gives the following:

$$\hat{y}_1 = h_{11}y_1 + h_{12}y_2 + \ldots + h_{1n}y_n$$

$$\hat{y}_2 = h_{21}y_1 + h_{22}y_2 + \ldots + h_{2n}y_n$$

$$\vdots$$

$$\hat{y}_i = h_{i1}y_1 + h_{i2}y_2 + \ldots + h_{in}y_n$$

The leverage, h_{ii}, quantifies the influence that the observed response y_i has on its fitted value $\hat{y}_i$. That is, if h_{ii} is small, then the observed response y_i plays only a small role in the value of the fitted response $\hat{y}_i$. On the other hand, if h_{ii} is large, then the observed response y_i plays a large role in the value of the fitted response $\hat{y}_i$. This is why it has the name *leverage*.

A high leverage data point can potentially have undue influence on the regression result. As a rule of thumb, a data point *i* is said to have a high leverage if its leverage is three times more than the average leverage.

$$h_{ii} > 3\bar{h} = 3\frac{p}{n}$$

As h_{ii} is a linear combination of the explanatory variables $\boldsymbol{X}$, an extreme h_{ii} implies a large linear combination in the *x*-values. Whether the data point is actually influential or not depends also on the observed response y_i.

Studentized Residuals

An extreme *y* value indicates an outlier, but the ordinary residual $\varepsilon_i = y_i - \hat{y}_i$ is not a good way to quantify an outlier because its magnitude depends on the unit of measurement, for example, dollar versus cents. One way to eliminate the unit is to divide the residuals by an estimate of their standard deviation, thereby obtaining what are known as standardized residuals.

Standardized residuals (aka internally studentized residuals) are defined for each observation, $i = 1, \ldots, n$, as an ordinary residual divided by an estimate of its standard deviation:

$$r_i = \frac{\varepsilon_i}{s(\varepsilon_i)} = \frac{\varepsilon_i}{RMSE\sqrt{1-h_{ii}}}$$

The standardized residual for a given data point depends not only on the ordinary residual ε_i but also the root mean square error (RMSE) and its leverage h_{ii}.

One problem with standardized residuals is that the presence of a potential outlier may "pull" the regression toward it so much that this particular data point is not "flagged" as an outlier. To address this issue, you can delete one observation at a time, and each time you fit a new regression on the remaining $n - 1$ observations. Then compare the observed responses y_i to the fitted responses $\hat{y}_{(i)}$ based on the regression model with the *i*-th observation deleted. The *i*-th deleted residual is defined as follows:

$$d_i = y_i - \hat{y}_{(i)}$$

A data point having a large, deleted residual suggests that the data point is influential because its presence "moves" the regression line.

An externally studentized residual or simply studentized residual is a deleted residual divided by its estimated standard deviation. It can be proven that it is equal to the ordinary residual divided by the root mean square error based on the regression model with the *i*-th observation deleted, $RMSE_{(i)}$, and by the leverage, h_{ii}. That is:

$$t_i = \frac{d_i}{s(d_i)} = \frac{\varepsilon_i}{RMSE_{(i)}\sqrt{1-h_{ii}}}$$

As a rule of thumb, you should consider a data point an outlier if $|t_i| > 3$.

DFFITS

To evaluate the impact of an influential point, say the i-th data point, the idea is to run two regressions, one with the i-th data point included and one with the i-th data point deleted; then you compare the fitted responses of the two models. This is the idea behind difference in fits (DFFITS).

$$DFFITS_i = \frac{\hat{y}_i - \hat{y}_{(i)}}{RMSE_{(i)}\sqrt{h_{ii}}}$$

The numerator is the difference between the fitted responses when running the regression with and without the i-th data point. The denominator is the estimated standard deviation of the numerator/difference. In other words, $DFFITS_i$ measures the change in the number of standard deviations when the i-th data point is removed.

As a rule of thumb, a data point i is considered influential if:

$$|DFFITS_i| > 2\sqrt{\frac{p+1}{n-p-1}}$$

Cook's Distance

Cook's distance is defined as follows:

$$D_i = \frac{1}{p}\left(\frac{\varepsilon_i}{RMSE}\right)^2 \frac{h_{ii}}{(1-h_{ii})^2}$$

The definition depends on both the residual (for extreme y value) and leverage (for extreme x value). It measures how much all of the fitted values change when the i-th observation is deleted. As a rule of thumb, if $D_i > 0.5$, the data point may be influential; if $D_i > 1$, the data point is likely to be influential; if D_i is much bigger than other Cook's distance, then the data point is almost certainly influential. In Figure 14-10, there is one data point that has its Cook's distance (the red dashed line) barely above 0.5. It is worth considering whether to include it in the regression, as it carries some leverage.

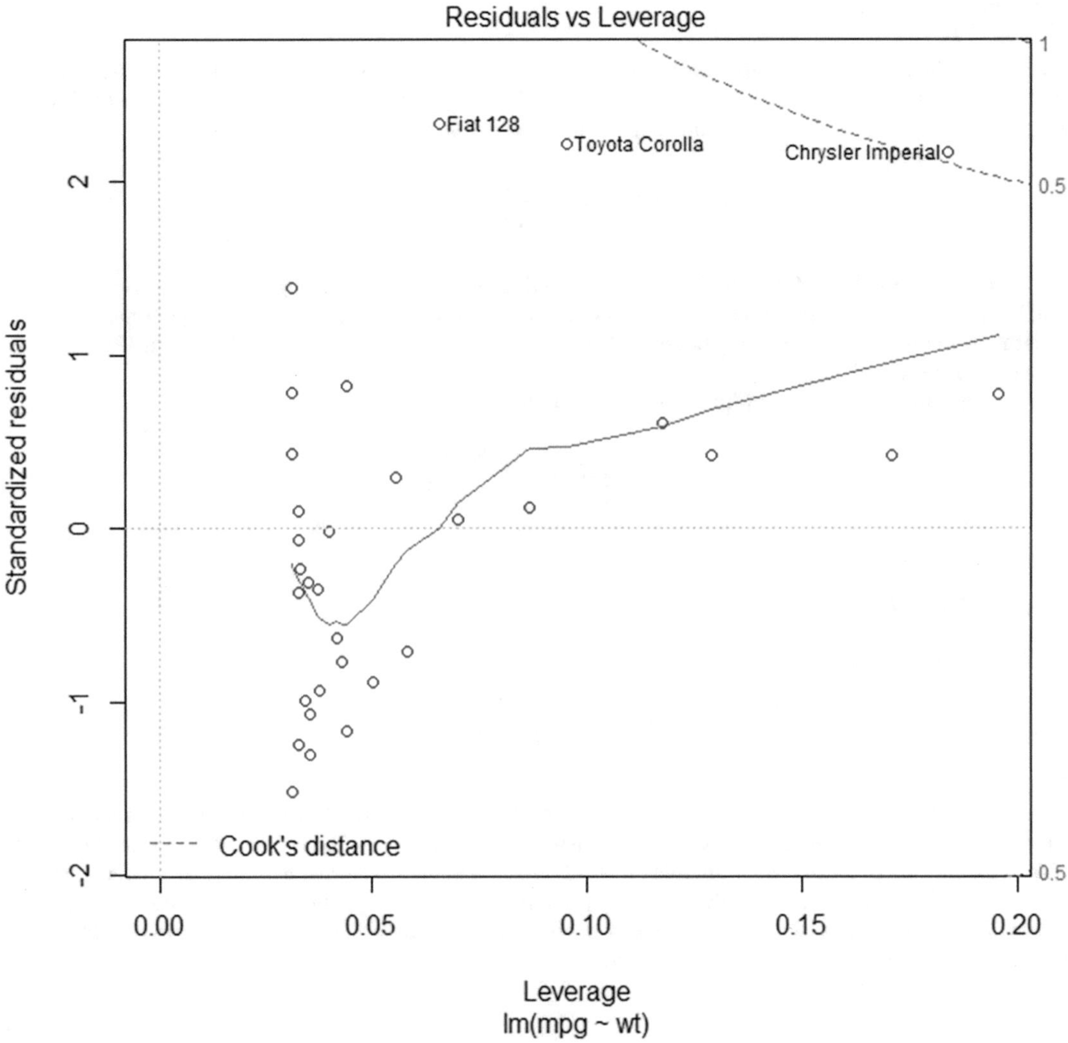

Figure 14-10. Influence of each data point in the mtcars data set

14.1.5. Information Criteria

Given a number of competing models for a set of data, an information criterion (IC) estimates the quality of each model relative to each of the other models and ranks them by the IC values. This provides a mean of model selection. For example, the one with the lowest IC may be chosen as the best model. Using the IC values, you may infer that the top three models are in a tier, and the rest are far worse. However, it would be rather arbitrary to assign a value above which a given model is "rejected." Note that an IC value tells nothing about the absolute quality of a model, but only the quality relative to other models. If all candidate models fit poorly, an IC will not give any warning of that. Therefore, after selecting a model using an IC, it is usually a good practice to validate the absolute quality of the model. Such validation commonly includes checks of the model's residuals (to determine whether the residuals seem like white noise) and tests of the model's predictions.

AIC

In general, when using a statistical model to represent the true process that generates the data, the model is almost never an exact representation. Information will be lost by using a model representation. Akaike information criterion (AIC) estimates the relative amount of information lost by a given model: the less information a model loses, the higher the quality of that model. In estimating the amount of information lost for a model, AIC deals with the trade-off between the goodness of fit of the model and the simplicity of the model. In other words, AIC deals with both the risk of overfitting and the risk of underfitting. AIC rewards goodness of fit (as assessed by the likelihood function, or *RSS* in case of linear regression model), and it also includes a penalty that is an increasing function of the number of estimated parameters to discourage overfitting. Specifically, the mathematical definition is as follows:

$$AIC = n\ln\left(\frac{RSS}{n}\right) + 2(p+1)$$

BIC

The formula for the Bayesian information criterion (BIC) is similar to that for AIC, but with a different penalty for the number of parameters. While the AIC penalty coefficient is 2, the BIC penalty coefficient is ln n. In general, BIC penalizes free parameters more strongly than AIC.

$$BIC = n\ln\left(\frac{RSS}{n}\right) + \ln n(p+1)$$

It has been pointed out that AIC and BIC are appropriate for different tasks. In particular, BIC is argued to be appropriate for selecting the "true model" (i.e., the process that generates the data) from a set of candidate models if the "true model" is in the set, whereas AIC is not appropriate. To be specific, if the "true model" is in the set of candidates, then BIC will select the "true model" with a probability of 1 as $n \to \infty$. In contrast, when the selection is done via AIC, the probability can be less than 1. However, it is argued that this issue is irrelevant, because the "true model" is practically never in the candidate set. Indeed, it is a common aphorism in statistics that "all models are wrong"; hence, the "true model" (i.e., reality) cannot be in the candidate set.

Another study presents a simulation study that allows the "true model" to be in the candidate set. The simulation demonstrates, in particular, that AIC sometimes selects a much better model than BIC even when the "true model" is in the candidate set. The reason is that, for finite n, BIC can have a substantial risk of selecting a bad model from the candidate set. This reason can arise even when n is much larger than p^2. With AIC, the risk of selecting a very bad model is minimized. If the "true model" is not in the candidate set, then the most that you can hope to do is select the model that best approximates the "true model." AIC is appropriate for finding the best approximating model, under certain assumptions. In regression, AIC is asymptotically optimal for selecting the model with the least mean squared error under the assumption that the "true model" is not in the candidate set. BIC is not asymptotically optimal under the assumption.

14.1.6. NM Dev Linear Regression Package

NM Dev has an extensive package to solve many types of linear model problems using a wide range of regression methods: ordinary least squares (unweighted, Section 14.1; and weighted, Section 14.2), logistic regression (Section 14.3), generalized linear model (Section 14.4), stepwise regression (Section 14.5), and LASSO (Section 14.6). To build and analyze a linear model, you must first construct an `LMProblem`. The class signature is as follows:

```
/**
 * Construct a linear regression problem.
 *
 * @param y         the dependent variables
 * @param X         the factors
 * @param intercept {@code true} if to additionally add an intercept term to
 *                  the linear regression
 * @param weights   the weights assigned to each observation
 */
public LMProblem(Vector y, Matrix X, boolean intercept, Vector weights)
```

Applying any of the regression methods in the NM Dev package will generate a `LinearModel` object. The interface signature is as follows:

```
public interface LinearModel {
    /**
     * Gets \(\hat{\beta}\) and statistics.
     *
     * @return \(\hat{\beta}\) and statistics
     */
    public LMBeta beta();
    /**
     * Gets the residual analysis of an OLS regression.
     *
     * @return the residual analysis
     */
    public LMResiduals residuals();
    /**
     * Computes the expectation \(E(y(x))\) given an input.
     *
     * @param x an input
     * @return \(E(y(x))\)
     */
    public double Ey(Vector x); // TODO: confidence intervals, prediction intervals
}
```

This `LinearModel` object contains the results for the estimated beta hat `LMBeta`, the prediction method `Ey`, and the residuals `LMResiduals`. The `Ey` function can be used to compute the model-fitted values. `LMBeta` contains the expectation of a beta hat, the covariance matrix of the estimated betas, their standard errors, and the t-statistics. The class signature is as follows:

```
public abstract class LMBeta {
    /**
     * Gets the coefficient estimates, <i>&beta;^</i>.
     *
     * @return the coefficient estimates, <i>&beta;^</i>
     */
    public ImmutableVector betaHat();
    /**
     * Gets the covariance matrix of the coefficient estimates, <i>&beta;^</i>.
     *
```

```
     * @return the covariance matrix of the coefficient estimates,
     *         <i>&beta;^</i>
     */
    public abstract ImmutableMatrix covariance();
    /**
     * Gets the standard errors of the coefficients <i>&beta;^</i>.
     *
     * @return the standard errors of the coefficients <i>&beta;^</i>
     */
    public ImmutableVector stderr();
    /**
     * Gets the t- or z- value of the regression coefficients <i>&beta;^</i>.
     *
     * @return the t- or z- value of the regression coefficients <i>&beta;^</i>
     */
    public ImmutableVector t();
}
```

The LMResiduals class contains a lot of information about the residuals and their analysis. The class signature is as follows:

```
public class LMResiduals {
    /**
     * Gets the fitted values, <i>y^</i>.
     *
     * @return the fitted values, <i>y^</i>
     */
    public ImmutableVector fitted();
    /**
     * Gets the residuals, <i>&epsilon;</i>, the differences between sample and
     * fitted values.
     *
     * @return the residuals, <i>&epsilon;</i>
     */
    public ImmutableVector residuals();
    /**
     * Gets the weighted, fitted values.
     *
     * @return the weighted, fitted values
     */
    public ImmutableVector weightedFittedValues();
    /**
     * Gets the weighted residuals.
     *
     * @return the weighted residuals
     */
    public ImmutableVector weightedResiduals();
    /**
     * Gets the diagnostic measure: sum of squared residuals, \(\sum
     * \epsilon^2\).
     * @return sum of squared residuals, \(\sum \epsilon^2\)
     */
```

```
public double RSS();
/**
 * Gets the diagnostic measure: total sum of squares, , \(\sum (y-y_mean)^2
 * \).
 * @return total sum of squares, \(\sum (y-y_mean)^2 \)
 */
public double TSS();
/**
 * Gets the diagnostic measure: R-squared.
 *
 * @return R-squared
 */
public double R2();
/**
 * Gets the diagnostic measure: adjusted R-squared
 *
 * @return adjusted R-squared
 */
public double AR2();
/**
 * Gets the standard error of the residuals.
 *
 * @return the standard error of the residuals
 */
public double stderr();
/**
 * Gets the diagnostic measure: F statistics
 * <blockquote><pre><i>
 * mean of regression / mean squared error =
 * sum((y_i_hat-y_mean)^2) / mean squared error =
 * [(TSS-RSS)/n] / [RSS/(m-n)]
 * </i></pre></blockquote>
 * <i>y_i_hat</i> are the fitted values of the regression.
 *
 * @return F statistics
 * @see "Kutner, Nachtsheim and Neter, "p.69, equation (2.60)," Applied
 * linear regression
 * models. 4th edition."
 */
public double Fstat();
/**
 * Gets the projection matrix, H-hat.
 *
 * @return the projection matrix
 * @see "Sanford Weisberg, "p.168, Section 8.1, Chapter 8," Applied Linear
 * Regression, 3rd
 * edition, 2005. Wiley-Interscience."
 */
public ImmutableMatrix hHat();
/**
 * Gets the leverage.
```

```
     * The bigger the leverage for an observation, the bigger influence on the
     * prediction.
     *
     * @return the leverage
     */
    public ImmutableVector leverage();
    /**
     * <i>standard residual = residual / v1 / sqrt(RSS / (n-m))</i>
     *
     * @return standardized residuals
     */
    public ImmutableVector standardized();
    /**
     * <i>studentized residual = standardized * sqrt((n-m-1) /
     * (n-m-standardized^2))</i>
     *
     * @return studentized residuals
     * @see
     * <ul>
     * <li>"Chatterjee, Hadi and Price, "p.90 (4.15), Section 4.3," Regression
     * Analysis by Example,
     * 3rd edition, 2000. Wiley Series in Probability and Statistics."</li>
     * <li>@see
     * <a href="http://en.wikipedia.org/wiki/Studentized_residual">Wikipedia:
     * Studentized
     * residual</a></li>
     * </ul>
     */
    public ImmutableVector studentized();
    /**
     * Gets the degree of freedom.
     * <p/>
     * TODO: User should be able to modify this method for a different
     * regression.
     *
     * @return the degree of freedom
     */
    public int df();
```

The LMDiagnostics class computes the influential points. The class signature is as follows:

```
public class LMDiagnostics {
    /**
     * DFFITS, Welsch and Kuh Measure.
     *
     * @return DFFITS
     * @see
     * <ul>
     * <li>"Chatterjee, Hadi and Price, "p.105 (4.23), Section 4.9.2, Regression
     * Analysis by Example," 3rd edition, 2000. Wiley Series in Probability and
     * Statistics."</li>
```

```
     * <li>"David A. Belsley, Edwin Kuh, Roy E. Welsch, Regression diagnostics:
     * identifying influential data and sources of collinearity. Wiley series in
     * probability and mathematical statistics. New York: John Wiley & Sons.
     * ISBN 0471058564. 1980."</li>
     * </ul>
     */
    public ImmutableVector DFFITS;
    /**
     * Cook distances.
     *
     * @return Cook distances
     * @see "Sanford Weisberg, "p.200," Applied Linear Regression, 3rd edition,
     * 2005.
     * Wiley-Interscience."
     */
    public ImmutableVector cookDistances();
    /**
     * Hadi's influence measure.
     *
     * @return Hadi's influence measure
     * @see "Chatterjee, Hadi and Price, "p.105 (4.24), Section 4.9.2,"
     * Regression Analysis by Example, 3rd edition, 2000. Wiley Series in
     * Probability and Statistics."
     */
    public ImmutableVector Hadi();
```

The `LMInformationCriteria` class computes the AIC and BIC for the model.

The `OLSRegression` class, taking an `LMProblem` as input, runs the OLS regression and produces a `LinearModel`. The class signature is as follows:

```
public class OLSRegression implements LinearModel {
    /**
     * Constructs an <tt>OLSRegression</tt> instance.
     *
     * @param problem the linear regression problem to be solved
     * @param epsilon a precision parameter: when a number |x| &le; &epsilon;,
     *                it is considered 0
     */
    public OLSRegression(LMProblem problem, double epsilon;
}
```

The following is an example that solves an OLS problem.

The response vector is as follows:

$$\boldsymbol{y} = \begin{bmatrix} 2.32 \\ 0.452 \\ 4.53 \\ 12.34 \\ 32.2 \end{bmatrix}$$

The design matrix of explanatory variables is as follows:

$$X = \begin{bmatrix} 1.52 & 2.23 & 4.31 \\ 3.22 & 6.34 & 3.46 \\ 4.32 & 12.2 & 23.1 \\ 10.1034 & 43.2 & 22.3 \\ 12.1 & 2.12 & 3.27 \end{bmatrix}$$

```
// construct a linear model problem
val problem = LMProblem(
        // the independent variable, y
        DenseVector(2.32, 0.452, 4.53, 12.34, 32.2),
        // the design matrix of dependent variable, X
        DenseMatrix(
            arrayOf(
                doubleArrayOf(1.52, 2.23, 4.31),
                doubleArrayOf(3.22, 6.34, 3.46),
                doubleArrayOf(4.32, 12.2, 23.1),
                doubleArrayOf(10.1034, 43.2, 22.3),
                doubleArrayOf(12.1, 2.12, 3.27)
            )
        ),
        true // with intercept
)

// solve an OLS problem
val ols = OLSRegression(problem)

println("beta hat")
// the means of betas
println("beta^ = " + ols.beta().betaHat())
// the standard errors of betas
println("beta^ standard error = " + ols.beta().stderr())
// a beta/variable is significant if its t-stat is bigger than 2
println("beta^ t = " + ols.beta().t())
```

The output has all the results and statistics covered in the past few sections:

```
beta hat
beta^ = [3.055264, -0.347572, 0.019219, -4.357924]
beta^ standard error = [0.491998, 0.194540, 0.299207, 3.958854]
beta^ t = [6.209908, -1.786633, 0.064232, -1.100804]
```

```
println("residuals")
println("residual F-stat = " + ols.residuals().Fstat())
println("fitted values: " + ols.residuals().fitted())
println("residuals: " + ols.residuals().residuals())
println("residual standard error = " + ols.residuals().stderr())
```

```
println("RSS = " + ols.residuals().RSS())
println("TSS = " + ols.residuals().TSS())
println("R2 = " + ols.residuals().R2())
println("AR2 = " + ols.residuals().AR2())
```

The output is as follows:

```
residuals
residual F-stat = 13.528805679720477
fitted values: [-0.406176, 3.342917, 5.044391, 11.924108, 31.936759]
residuals: [2.726176, -2.890917, -0.514391, 0.415892, 0.263241]
residual standard error = 4.036867249675668
RSS = 16.29629719150399
TSS = 677.7046112
R2 = 0.9759536870161641
AR2 = 0.9038147480646566
```

```
println("influential points")
println("standardized residuals: " + ols.residuals().standardized())
println("studentized residuals: " + ols.residuals().studentized())
println("leverage/hat values: " + ols.residuals().leverage())
println("DFFITS: " + ols.diagnostics().DFFITS())
println("cook distances: " + ols.diagnostics().cookDistances())
println("Hadi: " + ols.diagnostics().Hadi())
```

The output is as follows:

```
influential points
standardized residuals: [1.000000, -1.000000, -1.000000, 1.000000, 1.000000]
studentized residuals: [0.000000, 0.000000, 0.000000, 0.000000, 0.000000]
leverage/hat values: [0.543943, 0.487159, 0.983763, 0.989386, 0.995748]
DFFITS: [0.000000, 0.000000, 0.000000, 0.000000, 0.000000]
cook distances: [0.298178, 0.237481, 15.147200, 23.304136, 58.542696]
Hadi: [8.546417, 9.160788, 64.654821, 97.259457, 238.187865]
```

```
println("information criteria")
println("AIC = " + ols.informationCriteria().AIC())
println("BIC = " + ols.informationCriteria().BIC())
```

The output is as follows:

```
information criteria
AIC = 30.096885349082104
BIC = 28.144074911252606
```

14.2. Weighted Least Squares

One important assumption in OLS is homoscedasticity, meaning that all errors or residuals have the same constant variance. This assumption is often invalid in many real applications. As illustrated by the example of incomes, high-income earners tend to have a bigger variance than lower-income earners. The size of variance often depends on the size of the value. Weighted least squares (WLS) is an extension of OLS to solve the problem of heteroscedasticity, meaning that all errors or residuals have different variances. Mathematically, for the regression model shown here:

$$\boldsymbol{y} = \boldsymbol{X}\beta + \varepsilon$$

Suppose you can scale each observation by the standard deviation of its error.

$$\frac{y_1}{\sigma_1} = \beta_0 \frac{1}{\sigma_1} + \beta_1 \frac{x_{11}}{\sigma_1} + \cdots + \beta_p \frac{x_{1p}}{\sigma_1} + \varepsilon_1$$

$$\frac{y_2}{\sigma_2} = \beta_0 \frac{1}{\sigma_2} + \beta_1 \frac{x_{21}}{\sigma_2} + \cdots + \beta_p \frac{x_{2p}}{\sigma_2} + \varepsilon_2$$

$$\vdots$$

$$\frac{y}{\sigma_n} = \beta_0 \frac{1}{\sigma_n} + \beta_1 \frac{x_{n1}}{\sigma_n} + \cdots + \beta_p \frac{x_{np}}{\sigma_n} + \varepsilon_n$$

Then this scaled model has a constant error variance. The sum of squared errors is as follows:

$$S(\beta_0,\ldots,\beta_p) = \sum_{i=1}^{n}\left[\frac{y_i}{\sigma_i} - \left(\beta_0 \frac{1}{\sigma_i} + \beta_1 \frac{x_{i1}}{\sigma_i} + \cdots + \beta_p \frac{x_{ip}}{\sigma_i}\right)\right]^2 = \sum_{i=1}^{n} \sigma_i^{-2}\left[y_i - \left(\beta_0 + \beta_1 x_{i1} + \cdots + \beta_p x_{ip}\right)\right]^2$$

The coefficients $w_i = \sigma_i^{-2}$ are essentially weights assigned to the observations.
The normal equation is as follows:

$$\boldsymbol{X}^T \boldsymbol{W} \boldsymbol{X} \beta = \boldsymbol{X}^T \boldsymbol{W} \boldsymbol{y}$$

Where $\boldsymbol{W}$ is an $n \times n$ diagonal matrix of weights.

$$W = \begin{pmatrix} w_1 & 0 & \cdots & 0 \\ 0 & w_2 & \cdots & 0 \\ \vdots & \vdots & \ddots & \vdots \\ 0 & 0 & \cdots & w_n \end{pmatrix}$$

The weights can be extended to more general cases when you want to assign a different significance to observations. For example, you may want to focus the regression model on certain parts of the data (or experiments) that are difficult, expensive, or time-consuming to reproduce. You may want to give more preference to data that is more accurately measured and reliable and lower preference to data that is estimated and unreliable. It is important to note that the weight of each observation is given relative to the weights of the other observations, so different sets of absolute weights can have the same effects. The weights do not necessarily sum to 1.

To solve the normal equations, find a $\hat{\beta}$ that minimizes this objective function.

$$\underset{\beta}{\operatorname{argmin}} \sum_{i=1}^{n} w_i \left| y_i - \sum_{j=1}^{m} X_{ij}\beta_j \right|^2 = \underset{\beta}{\operatorname{argmin}} \| \boldsymbol{W}^{\frac{1}{2}} (\mathbf{y} - \boldsymbol{X}\beta) \|^2$$

The WLS estimator of the beta hat is as follows:

$$\hat{\beta} = \left(\boldsymbol{X}^T \boldsymbol{W} \boldsymbol{X} \right)^{-1} \boldsymbol{X}^T \boldsymbol{W} \boldsymbol{y}$$

In practice, you may not know exactly the weights and variances. Using estimated weights may produce bad results, especially when the weights are estimated from small samples. WLS is also subject to the problem of outliers. The problem is more pronounced when you unwittingly increase the influence of an outlier by giving it a big weight.

In NM Dev, the `OLSRegression` class can take weights as input to perform WLS. Here is an example:

```
// construct a linear model problem
val problem = LMProblem(
        // the independent variable, y
        DenseVector(2.32, 0.452, 4.53, 12.34, 32.2),
        // the design matrix of dependent variable, X
        DenseMatrix(
            arrayOf(
                doubleArrayOf(1.52, 2.23, 4.31),
                doubleArrayOf(3.22, 6.34, 3.46),
                doubleArrayOf(4.32, 12.2, 23.1),
                doubleArrayOf(10.1034, 43.2, 22.3),
                doubleArrayOf(12.1, 2.12, 3.27)
            )
        ),
        // with intercept
        true,
        // the weights assigned to each observation
        DenseVector(0.2, 0.4, 0.1, 0.3, 0.1)) // do not sum to 1

// solve a weighted OLS problem
val ols = OLSRegression(problem)

println("beta hat")
// the means of betas
println("beta^ = " + ols.beta().betaHat())
// the standard errors of betas
println("beta^ standard error = " + ols.beta().stderr())
// a beta/variable is significant if its t-stat is bigger than 2
println("beta^ t = " + ols.beta().t())
```

The output is as follows:

```
beta hat
beta^ = [3.105333, -0.379722, 0.119115, -5.651285]
beta^ standard error = [0.707175, 0.257982, 0.428017, 3.876511]
beta^ t = [4.391181, -1.471895, 0.278296, -1.457828]
```

```
println("residuals")
println("residual F-stat = " + ols.residuals().Fstat())
println("fitted values: " + ols.residuals().fitted())
println("weighted residuals: " + ols.residuals().weightedResiduals())
println("residuals: " + ols.residuals().residuals())
println("residual standard error = " + ols.residuals().stderr())
println("RSS = " + ols.residuals().RSS())
println("TSS = " + ols.residuals().TSS())
println("R2 = " + ols.residuals().R2())
println("AR2 = " + ols.residuals().AR2())
```

The output is as follows:

```
residuals
residual F-stat = 6.986438687095603
fitted values: [-1.264570, 2.352592, 5.882717, 11.975437, 31.507745]
weighted residuals: [1.603069, -1.202040, -0.427767, 0.199680, 0.218910]
residuals: [3.584570, -1.900592, -1.352717, 0.364563, 0.692255]
residual standard error = 2.070146550717054
RSS = 4.285506741445716
TSS = 94.10679701818182
R2 = 0.9544612410874239
AR2 = 0.8178449643496957
```

```
println("influential points")
println("standardized residuals: " + ols.residuals().standardized())
println("studentized residuals: " + ols.residuals().studentized())
println("leverage/hat values: " + ols.residuals().leverage())
println("DFFITS: " + ols.diagnostics().DFFITS())
println("cook distances: " + ols.diagnostics().cookDistances())
println("Hadi: " + ols.diagnostics().Hadi())
```

The output is as follows:

```
influential points
standardized residuals: [1.000000, -1.000000, -1.000000, 1.000000, 1.000000]
studentized residuals: [-0.000000, -0.000000, -0.000000, -0.000000, 0.000000]
leverage/hat values: [0.400344, 0.662840, 0.957302, 0.990696, 0.988818]
DFFITS: [-0.000000, -0.000000, -0.000000, -0.000000, 0.000000]
cook distances: [0.166906, 0.491488, 5.605022, 26.620466, 22.106825]
Hadi: [10.659025, 8.000590, 26.598499, 110.519428, 92.472535]
```

```
println("information criteria")
println("AIC = " + ols.informationCriteria().AIC())
println("BIC = " + ols.informationCriteria().BIC())
```

The output is as follows:

```
information criteria
AIC = 31.753261426689598
BIC = 29.8004509888601
```

14.3. Logistic Regression

Consider this problem: a group of 20 students spends between zero and five and a half hours studying for an exam. How does the number of hours spent studying affect the probability of the student passing the exam? The data is given in the following table. It shows the number of hours each student spent studying and whether they passed (1) or failed (0). Note that 1 and 0 are nominal responses, meaning that 1 and 0 are merely labels or categories. There is no meaning to say $\frac{1+0}{2}$ or $1 > 0$.

Hours	0.5	0.75	1.00	1.25	1.50	1.75	1.75	2.00	2.25	2.50	2.75	3.00	3.25	3.50	4.00	4.25	4.50	4.75	5.00	5.50
Pass	0	0	0	0	0	0	1	0	1	0	1	0	1	0	1	1	1	1	1	1

You cannot use OLS mainly because the responses, *y*, are not numbers but labels. Suppose you instead use the probability of passing, $p = \Pr(y = 1)$, as the dependent variable. You still cannot use OLS because the range of p is $[0, 1]$ rather than $(-\infty, \infty)$. You can transform the range using the logit function. It is also called the log-odds because it is the logarithm of the odds ratio, $\frac{p}{1-p}$. See Figure 14-11.

$$\text{logit}(p) = \sigma^{-1}(p) = \log\left(\frac{p}{1-p}\right)$$

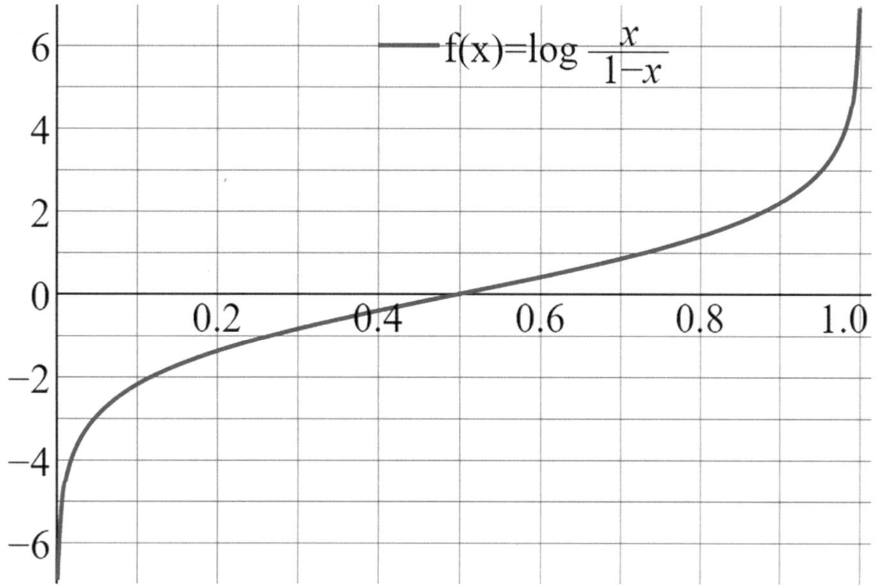

Figure 14-11. *The logit or log-odd function*

These transformations set up a linear regression problem such that a function (logit) of the response (p) is a linear model of the independent variable (hours). That is:

$$l = \log\left(\frac{p}{1-p}\right) = \beta_0 + \beta_1 h$$

You can recover the probability of passing by exponentiating the log-odds, as shown here:

$$\frac{p}{1-p} = e^{\beta_0 + \beta_1 h}$$

Or equivalently:

$$p = \frac{1}{1 - e^{-(\beta_0 + \beta_1 h)}} = S(\beta_0 + \beta_1 h)$$

Where S is the sigmoid function. See Figure 14-12.

$$S(x) = \frac{1}{1+e^{-x}} = \frac{e^x}{e^x+1} = 1 - S(-x)$$

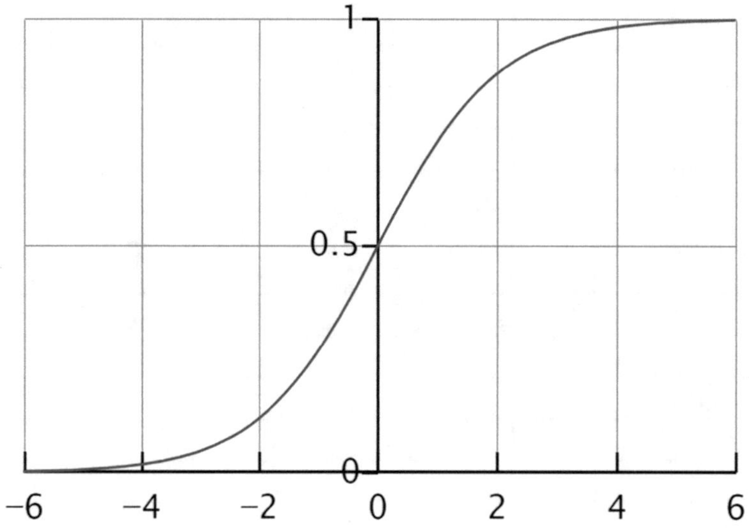

Figure 14-12. *The sigmoid function*

Running the OLS regression on the transformed problem, or running the logistic regression, gives the following results:

	Beta Hat	Standard Error	T-stat	P-value
Intercept	-4.0777	1.7610	-2.316	0.0206
Hours	1.5046	0.6287	2.393	0.0167

The output indicates that hours studying is significantly associated with the probability of passing the exam with p-value $0.0167 < 5$ percent. You can compute the probability of a passing exam ($y = 1$) as a function of the number of hours of study (h):

$$\Pr(y=1) = \frac{1}{1+\exp(-(1.5046 \times h - 4.0777))}$$

Figure 14-13 shows this probability function of passing an exam as a function of the number of hours you studied.

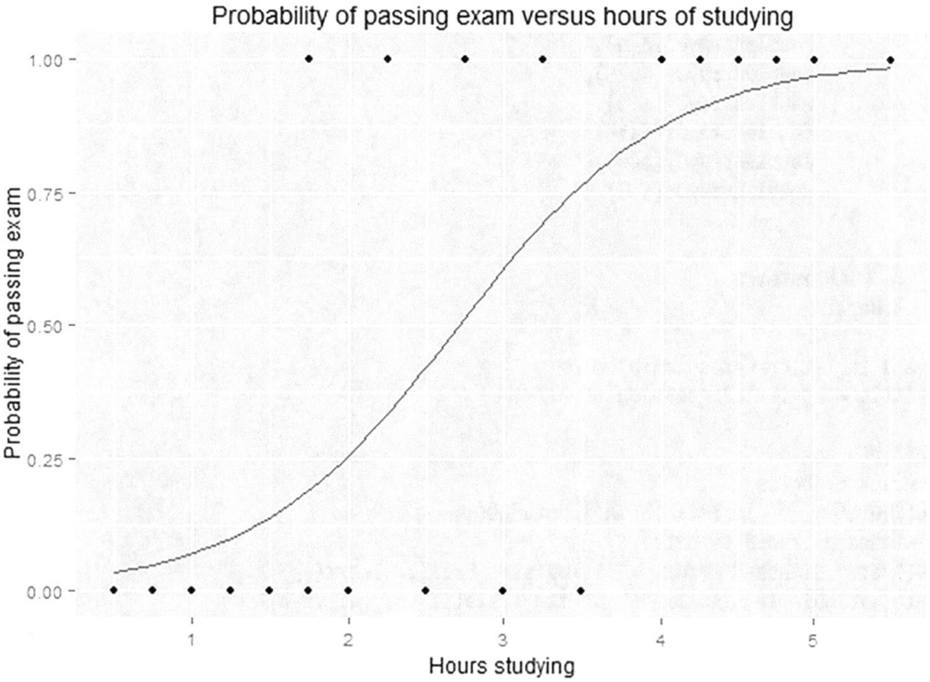

Figure 14-13. *The logistic regression result showing the relationship between the probability of passing exam and the number of hours studying*

The NM Dev class called `LogisticRegression` performs logistic regression on an `LMProblem`. The following code snippet solves the problem discussed earlier:

```
// construct a linear model problem
val problem = LMProblem(
        // the independent variable, y, {pass, fail}
        DenseVector(0.0, 0.0, 0.0, 0.0, 0.0, 0.0, 1.0, 0.0, 1.0, 0.0, 1.0, 0.0, 1.0, 0.0,
        1.0, 1.0, 1.0, 1.0, 1.0, 1.0),
        // the design matrix of dependent variable, X, number of hours of study
        DenseMatrix(
            arrayOf(
                doubleArrayOf(0.5),
                doubleArrayOf(0.75),
                doubleArrayOf(1.0),
                doubleArrayOf(1.25),
                doubleArrayOf(1.5),
                doubleArrayOf(1.75),
                doubleArrayOf(1.75),
                doubleArrayOf(2.0),
                doubleArrayOf(2.25),
                doubleArrayOf(2.5),
                doubleArrayOf(2.75),
                doubleArrayOf(3.0),
                doubleArrayOf(3.25),
```

```
                doubleArrayOf(3.5),
                doubleArrayOf(4.0),
                doubleArrayOf(4.25),
                doubleArrayOf(4.5),
                doubleArrayOf(4.75),
                doubleArrayOf(5.0),
                doubleArrayOf(5.5)
            )
        ),
        // with intercept
        true)

// solve a logistic regression problem
val logistic = LogisticRegression(problem)

println("beta hat")
// the means of betas
println("beta^ = " + logistic.beta().betaHat())
// the standard errors of betas
println("beta^ standard error = " + logistic.beta().stderr())
// a beta/variable is significant if its t-stat is bigger than 2
println("beta^ t = " + logistic.beta().t())

println("residuals")
println("fitted values: " + logistic.residuals().fitted())
println("deviance residuals: " + logistic.residuals().devianceResiduals())
println("deviance: " + logistic.residuals().deviance())
println("null deviance: " + logistic.residuals().nullDeviance())

println("information criteria")
println("AIC = " + logistic.AIC())
```

The output is as follows:

```
beta hat
beta^ = [1.504645, -4.077713]
beta^ standard error = [0.628721, 1.760994]
beta^ t = [2.393185, -2.315574]
residuals
fitted values: [0.034710, 0.049773, 0.070892, 0.100029, 0.139344, 0.190837, 0.190837,
0.255703, 0.333530, 0.421627, 0.515011, 0.607359, 0.692617, 0.766481, 0.874448, 0.910278,
0.936624, 0.955611, 0.969097, 0.985194]
deviance residuals: [-0.265808, -0.319544, -0.383485, -0.459113, -0.547834, -0.650775,
1.820076, -0.768525, 1.481905, -1.046456, 1.152013, -1.367376, 0.857062, -1.705574,
0.518002, 0.433603, 0.361867, 0.301346, 0.250561, 0.172721]
deviance: 16.059756928689346
null deviance: 27.725887222397812
information criteria
AIC = 20.059756928689346
```

14.4. Generalized Linear Model

There are a number of situations that OLS fails to address (you have already seen two), such as heteroskedasticity; discrete, binary, or categorical responses; responses in a restricted range—for example [0, 1], instead of the whole real line $(-\infty, \infty)$; and a probability distribution that is not normal. (Note that there is no restriction on the explanatory variables.) The generalized linear model (GLM) relaxes many of OLS's restrictive assumptions in order to provide a framework to perform linear regression for a much wider range of problems.

Consider the case of simple linear regression. It is best applied to data like that in Figure 14-14: continuous data clustered on a trend line, responses and errors are normally distributed, and errors in a constant variance.

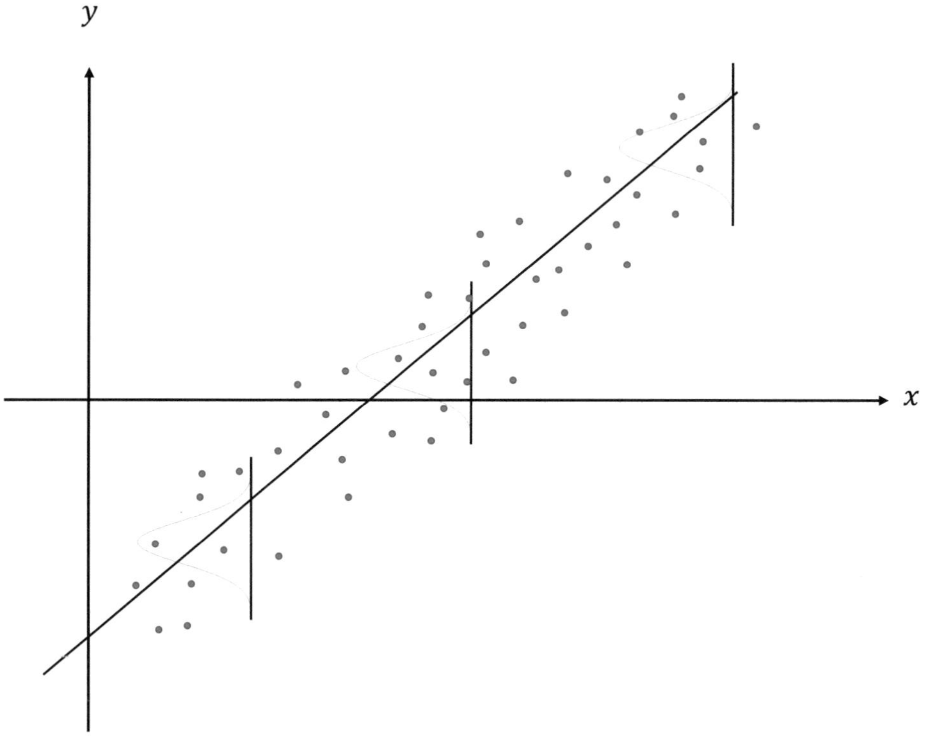

Figure 14-14. *OLS regression*

Mathematically, the linear predictor, $b_0 + b_1x$, predicts the mean of the response y_i. Then y_i is determined by a prior distribution, in this case, normal distribution with constant variance ε in this case.

$$\begin{cases} \mathrm{E}(y_i) = \mu_i = b_0 + b_1 x \\ y_i \sim N(\mu_i, \varepsilon) \end{cases}$$

Consider another data set, say, the number of rabbits living in the backyard versus time, as shown in Figure 14-15. The population is random because their birth and death is uncertain. If you draw a line across the dots, the curve looks more like exponential than a straight line (nonlinear). The dots spread out more as t gets bigger (heteroskedasticity). The rabbit population is a positive integer (discrete, restricted range). Clearly, OLS does not apply to this data set, as it violates pretty much every assumption.

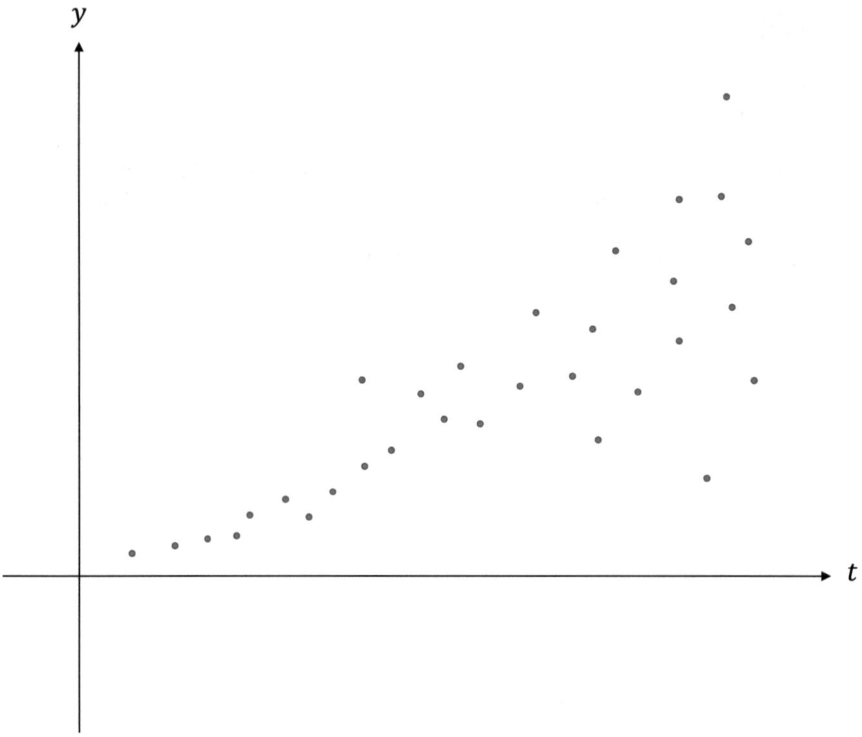

Figure 14-15. *Rabbit population versus time*

To fix the probability distribution, and hence range, of responses, instead of using normal distribution, you can use Poisson distribution. Poisson distribution is a discrete probability distribution that gives the probability of counts. It has only one parameter, λ, which happens to be the mean and the variance of the distribution. See Section 12.3.5. Once you determine the mean using the predictor function, the variance and the Poisson distribution are completely determined. You can use a bigger λ for a bigger t to model the increasing variance over time. See Figure 14-16.

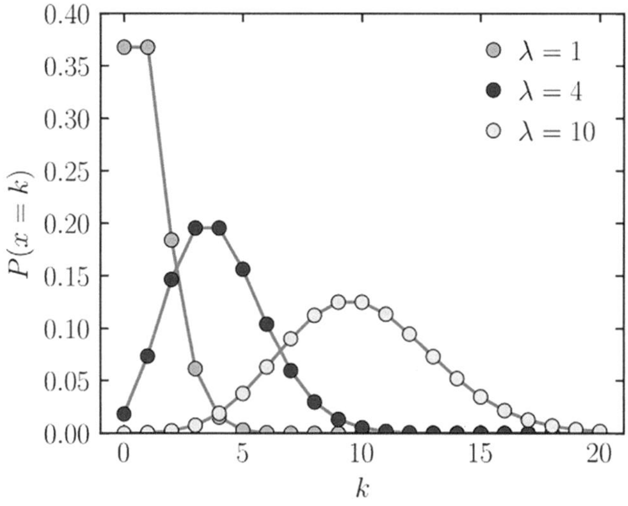

Figure 14-16. *Probability mass functions of Poisson distributions*

To fix the regression line across the dots, you may do a transformation on the predictor value to match the expectation of the distribution. In OLS, the predictor value is the expectation. The straight regression line is a result of using the identity function to "link" the predictor value and the expectation. To model an exponential curve, you may use an exponential function instead. That is:

$$\lambda_i = \exp(b_0 + b_1 x)$$

Or equivalently:

$$\ln \lambda_i = b_0 + b_1 x$$

This regression (Poisson distribution, linear predictor, exponential function) is called the Poisson regression. The result looks like something in Figure 14-17. The Poisson distributions of different variances are overlaid on the exponential regression line.

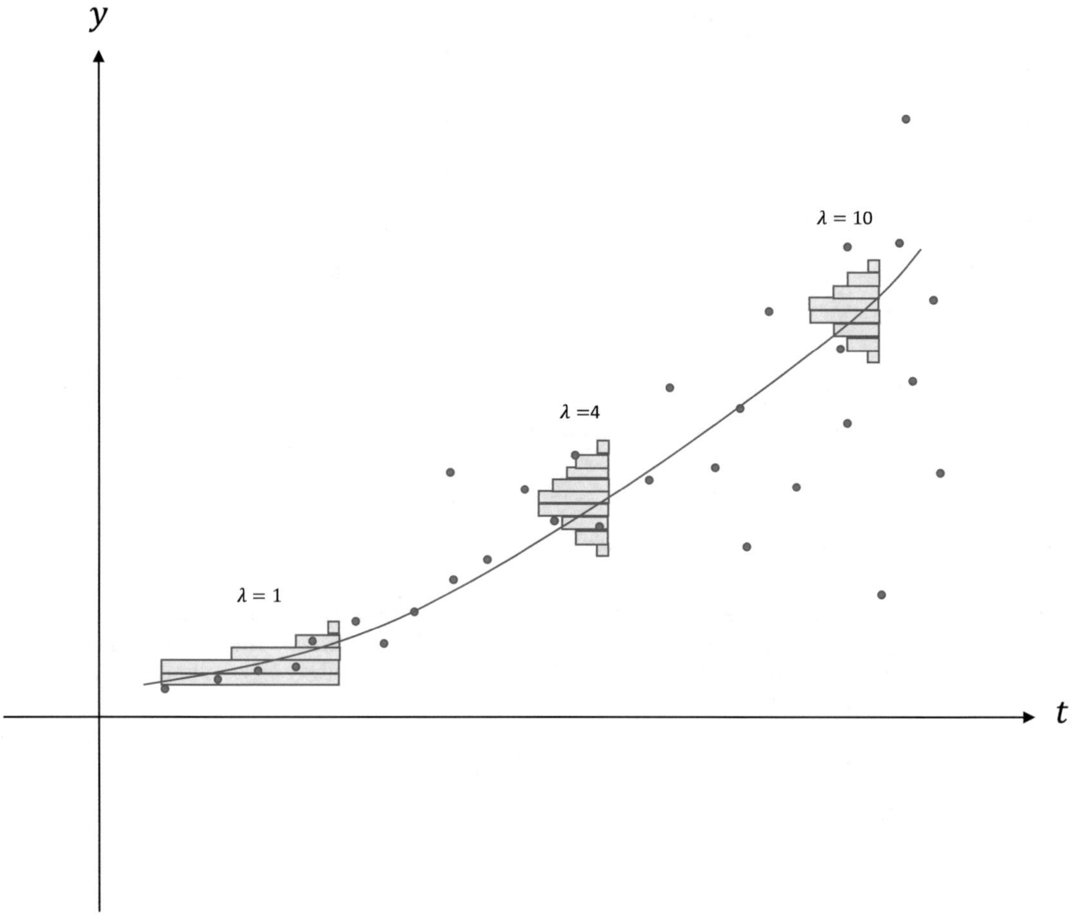

***Figure 14-17.** Poisson regression*

Generalized linear models (GLM) extend the application range of linear modeling by accommodating varying variances as well as alternative distributions for residuals and hence responses. GLM unifies many other statistical models. WLS, logistic regression, and Poisson regression are all special cases in the GLM framework. There are three common elements in all GLM regressions. First, the systematic and deterministic component is the predictor function, which is a linear combination of the explanatory variables, $\boldsymbol{X\beta}$. Second, the random component is the specification of the probability distribution of the residuals/responses. The distributions all come from the family of exponential distributions, which are characterized by some function of the mean (canonical or location parameter) and a function of the variance (dispersion parameter). The general form of the probability density function of a probability distribution from the exponential family is as follows:

$$f_Y(y|\theta,\phi)=\exp\left(\frac{y\theta-b(\theta)}{a(\phi)}+c(y,\phi)\right)$$

where the parameter θ is the canonical parameter, $b(\theta)$ is the cumulant function, and ϕ is the dispersion parameter. The NM Dev interface called `GLMExponentialDistribution` represents this family of exponential probability distributions.

Third, the link function, often denoted as *g*, links the systematic component and the random component. Its inverse transforms the predictor value to the mean of the probability distribution. Mathematically, you get this:

$$\mathrm{E}(\boldsymbol{Y} \mid \boldsymbol{X}) = \mu = g^{-1}(\boldsymbol{X}\beta)$$

The following table summarizes these three components for various GLM regressions and their support in NM Dev:

Regression Model	Response Variable	Probability Distribution	Canonical Link Function	NM Dev Class
Linear regression	Continuous measurements	Normal	Identity	`GLMGaussian`
Logistic regression	Binary	Binomial	Logit	`GLMBinomial`
Poisson regression	Counts	Poisson	Log	`GLMPoisson`
Gamma regression	Survival	Gamma	Log	`GLMGamma`
				`GLMInverseGaussian`

In NM Dev, to run a GLM regression, you first need to construct a problem instance using the `GLMProblem` class. The class signature is as follows:

```
/**
 * Construct a GLM problem.
 *
 * @param y         the dependent variables
 * @param X         the factors
 * @param intercept {@code true} if to add an additional intercept term to
 *                  the linear regression
 * @param family    the exponential family distribution of the mean
 */
public GLMProblem(
        Vector y,
        Matrix X,
        boolean intercept,
        GLMFamily family
)
```

The `GeneralizedLinearModel` class runs the GLM regression. The class signature is as follows:

```
/**
 * Construct a {@code GeneralizedLinearModel} instance.
 *
 * @param problem the generalized linear regression problem to be solved
 * @param fitting the fitting method, c.f., {@link GLMFitting}
 */
public GeneralizedLinearModel(GLMProblem problem, GLMFitting fitting)
```

The parameter `fitting` specifies the method to use to estimate the regression parameters. The default estimation method is the iteratively reweighted least squares algorithm (IWLS). It is a maximum likelihood algorithm.

The following example runs a GLM regression using the binomial distribution and the logit link function:

```
// construct a linear model problem
val problem = GLMProblem(
        // the independent variable, y
        DenseVector(1.0, 1.0, 0.0, 1.0, 1.0),
        // the design matrix of dependent variable, X
        DenseMatrix(
            arrayOf(
                doubleArrayOf(1.52),
                doubleArrayOf(3.22),
                doubleArrayOf(4.32),
                doubleArrayOf(10.1034),
                doubleArrayOf(12.1)
            )
        ),
        // with intercept
        true,
        // use the binomial distribution
        GLMFamily(GLMBinomial()))

// solve a GLM regression problem
val glm = GeneralizedLinearModel(problem)

println("beta hat")
// the means of betas
println("beta^ = " + glm.beta().betaHat())
// the standard errors of betas
println("beta^ standard error = " + glm.beta().stderr())
// a beta/variable is significant if its t-stat is bigger than 2
println("beta^ t = " + glm.beta().t())

println("residuals")
println("fitted values: " + glm.residuals().fitted())
println("deviance residuals: " + glm.residuals().devianceResiduals())
println("deviance: " + glm.residuals().deviance())
println("over dispersion: " + glm.residuals().overdispersion())

println("information criteria")
println("AIC = " + glm.AIC())
```

The output is as follows:

```
beta hat
beta^ = [0.165250, 0.487592]
beta^ standard error = [0.328662, 1.917517]
beta^ t = [0.502798, 0.254283]
residuals
fitted values: [0.676727, 0.734914, 0.768787, 0.896338, 0.923234]
deviance residuals: [0.883727, 0.784859, -1.711383, 0.467841, 0.399681]
deviance: 4.704428247887891
over dispersion: 1.0
information criteria
AIC = 8.70442824788789
```

The following example runs a GLM regression using the Poisson distribution and the log link function:

```
// construct a linear model problem
val problem = GLMProblem(
        // the independent variable, y
        DenseVector(4.0, 1.0, 4.0, 5.0, 7.0),
        // the design matrix of dependent variable, X
        DenseMatrix(
            arrayOf(
                doubleArrayOf(1.52, 2.11),
                doubleArrayOf(3.22, 4.32),
                doubleArrayOf(4.32, 1.23),
                doubleArrayOf(10.1034, 8.43),
                doubleArrayOf(12.1, 7.31),
            )
        ),
        // with intercept
        true,
        // use the binomial distribution
        GLMFamily(GLMPoisson()))

// solve a GLM regression problem
val glm = GeneralizedLinearModel(problem)

println("beta hat")
// the means of betas
println("beta^ = " + glm.beta().betaHat())
// the standard errors of betas
println("beta^ standard error = " + glm.beta().stderr())
// a beta/variable is significant if its t-stat is bigger than 2
println("beta^ t = " + glm.beta().t())

println("residuals")
println("fitted values: " + glm.residuals().fitted())
println("deviance residuals: " + glm.residuals().devianceResiduals())
println("deviance: " + glm.residuals().deviance())
```

```
println("over dispersion: " + glm.residuals().overdispersion())

println("information criteria")
println("AIC = " + glm.AIC())
```

The output is as follows:

```
beta hat
beta^ = [0.159667, -0.126816, 0.952348]
beta^ standard error = [0.107230, 0.154416, 0.470909]
beta^ t = [1.489023, -0.821261, 2.022359]
residuals
fitted values: [2.528082, 2.505862, 4.419947, 4.465919, 7.080190]
deviance residuals: [0.852544, -1.083724, -0.203045, 0.247925, -0.030194]
deviance: 2.0048958300580386
over dispersion: 1.0
information criteria
AIC = 23.8245863701111
```

14.4.1. Quasi-family

Overdispersion is the presence of greater variability or variance in a data set than would be expected under a given statistical model. This is especially common when using GLM to model discrete data because exponential distribution stipulates a particular relationship between the mean and the variance. For example, for Poisson distribution, the mean is equal to the variance, which are both λ. The discrete data set may have mean λ but exhibit a variability bigger than λ.

One way to fix this is to introduce a dispersion parameter, σ^2, into the Poisson model so that the modified conditional variance of the response is as follows:

$$V(y_i \mid \lambda_i) = \sigma^2 \lambda_i$$

If $\sigma^2 > 1$, then the conditional variance of response increases more rapidly than its mean. There is no distribution from the exponential family that corresponds to this specification to use with GLM. Instead, you specify the conditional mean and conditional variance directly like the previous scaled variance equation. Although there is no likelihood function (due to no probability density function), the usual procedure for maximum likelihood estimation of a GLM yields the so-called quasi-likelihood estimators of the regression coefficients, which share many of the properties of maximum-likelihood estimators. In fact, this method for overdispersion gives the same $\hat{\beta}$ estimation. The estimated standard errors, however, must be multiplied by the factor $\sigma = \sqrt{\sigma^2}$.

The NM Dev library supports a number of quasi-distributions. The interface is `QuasiDistribution`. The class signature is as follows:

```
public interface QuasiDistribution extends GLMExponentialDistribution {
    /**
     * the quasi-likelihood function corresponding to a single observation
     * <i>Q(&mu;; y)</i>
     *
     * @param mu <i>&mu;</i>
```

```
     * @param y  <i>y</i>
     * @return <i>Q(&mu;; y)</i>
     *
     * @see "P. J. MacCullagh and J. A. Nelder, <i>Generalized Linear
     * Models,</i> 2nd ed. Chapter 9. Table 9.1. p.326."
     */
    public double quasiLikelihood(double mu, double y);
    /**
     * the quasi-deviance function corresponding to a single observation
     *
     * @param y  <i>y</i>
     * @param mu <i>&mu;</i>
     * @return <i>D(y; &mu;;)</i>
     *
     * @see "P. J. MacCullagh and J. A. Nelder, <i>Generalized Linear
     * Models,</i> 2nd ed. Chapter 9. Eq. 9.4., the integral form, p.327."
     */
    public double quasiDeviance(double y, double mu);
}
```

The quasi-distributions that NM Dev supports are as follows:

- `QuasiBinomial`
- `QuasiGamma`
- `QuasiGaussian`
- `QuasiInverseGaussian`
- `QuasiPoisson`

The following example runs OLS regression using the quasi-binomial distribution and logit link function:

```
// construct a linear model problem
val problem = QuasiGLMProblem(
        // the independent variable, y
        DenseVector(1.0, 1.0, 0.0, 1.0, 1.0),
        // the design matrix of dependent variable, X
        DenseMatrix(
            arrayOf(
                doubleArrayOf(1.52),
                doubleArrayOf(3.22),
                doubleArrayOf(4.32),
                doubleArrayOf(10.1034),
                doubleArrayOf(12.1)
            )
        ),
        // with intercept
        true,
```

```
        QuasiFamily(
                QuasiBinomial(), // the quasi-binomial distribution
                LinkLogit() // logit link function
        ))

// solve a GLM regression problem
val glm = GeneralizedLinearModelQuasiFamily(problem)

println("beta hat")
// the means of betas
println("beta^ = " + glm.beta().betaHat())
// the standard errors of betas
println("beta^ standard error = " + glm.beta().stderr())
// a beta/variable is significant if its t-stat is bigger than 2
println("beta^ t = " + glm.beta().t())

println("residuals")
println("fitted values: " + glm.residuals().fitted())
println("deviance residuals: " + glm.residuals().devianceResiduals())
println("deviance: " + glm.residuals().deviance())
println("over dispersion: " + glm.residuals().overdispersion())
```

The output is as follows:

```
beta hat
beta^ = [0.165250, 0.487592]
beta^ standard error = [0.396316, 2.312236]
beta^ t = [0.416966, 0.210875]
residuals
fitted values: [0.676727, 0.734914, 0.768787, 0.896338, 0.923234]
deviance residuals: [0.883727, 0.784859, -1.711383, 0.467841, 0.399681]
deviance: 4.704428247887892
over dispersion: 1.4540719510495013
```

Note that the overdispersion is 1.454 > 1. This data set would otherwise be poorly fit using the regular Poisson distribution.

The following example runs OLS regression using the quasi-normal distribution and inverse link function:

```
// construct a linear model problem
val problem = QuasiGLMProblem(
        // the independent variable, y
        DenseVector(1.0, 1.0, 0.0, 1.0, 1.0),
        // the design matrix of dependent variable, X
        DenseMatrix(
            arrayOf(
                doubleArrayOf(1.52),
                doubleArrayOf(3.22),
                doubleArrayOf(4.32),
                doubleArrayOf(10.1034),
```

```
                doubleArrayOf(12.1)
            )
        ),
        // with intercept
        true,
        QuasiFamily(
                QuasiGaussian(), // the quasi-normal distribution
                LinkInverse() // inverse link function
        ))

// solve a GLM regression problem
val glm = GeneralizedLinearModelQuasiFamily(problem)

println("beta hat")
// the means of betas
println("beta^ = " + glm.beta().betaHat())
// the standard errors of betas
println("beta^ standard error = " + glm.beta().stderr())
// a beta/variable is significant if its t-stat is bigger than 2
println("beta^ t = " + glm.beta().t())

println("residuals")
println("fitted values: " + glm.residuals().fitted())
println("deviance residuals: " + glm.residuals().devianceResiduals())
println("deviance: " + glm.residuals().deviance())
println("over dispersion: " + glm.residuals().overdispersion())
```

The output is as follows:

```
beta hat
beta^ = [-0.045443, 1.566066]
beta^ standard error = [0.083658, 0.800455]
beta^ t = [-0.543192, 1.956470]
residuals
fitted values: [0.668008, 0.704356, 0.730060, 0.903390, 0.984046]
deviance residuals: [0.331992, 0.295644, -0.730060, 0.096610, 0.015954]
deviance: 0.7401995829806532
over dispersion: 0.24673319432688443
```

Note that the overdispersion is 0.2467 < 1, indicating that the data set exhibits underdispersion.

14.5. Stepwise Regression

For a high-dimensional data set that has many possible explanatory variables, you may not know which subset should be included in the regression model. A systematic way to select explanatory variables is stepwise regression. In each step, a variable is considered for addition to or subtraction from the set of explanatory variables based on some specified criterion. Usually, this takes the form of a sequence of F-tests or t-tests, but other techniques are possible, such as adjusted R^2, AIC, BIC, and so on.

There are three main approaches. Forward selection involves starting with no variables in the model, testing the addition of each variable using a chosen model fit criterion, adding the variable (if any) whose inclusion gives the most statistically significant improvement of the fit, and repeating this process until none improves the model to a statistically significant extent. The NM Dev class called `ForwardSelection` implements such a procedure. The following example runs a step-wise forward selection on a GLM model using AIC as the selection criterion:

```
// read the birth weight data from a csv file
val birthwt = DataFrame.readCSV("https://raw.githubusercontent.com/nmltd/s2-public/main/
Data/linear-reg-data.csv")

// construct a linear model problem
val problem = GLMProblem(
        DenseVector(birthwt["y"].asDoubles()), // Y, the dependent variables
        DenseMatrix(DenseVector(birthwt["x"].asDoubles())), // X, the independent variables
        true, // with intercept
        GLMFamily(GLMBinomial()) // GLM with binomial distribution
)

// run a step-wise forward selection on covariates
val forwardSelection = ForwardSelection(problem, SelectionByAIC())

println("selection sequence:")
println(Arrays.toString(forwardSelection.getFlags()))
```

The output is the selection sequence of adding a covariate one at a time:

```
selection sequence:
[0, 2, 3, 4, 5, 6, 7, 0]
```

Backward elimination involves starting with all candidate variables, testing the deletion of each variable using a chosen model fit criterion, deleting the variable (if any) whose loss gives the most statistically insignificant deterioration of the model fit, and repeating this process until no further variables can be deleted without a statistically insignificant loss of fit. The NM Dev class called `BackwardElimination` implements such a procedure. The following example runs a step-wise backward elimination on a GLM model using AIC as the elimination criterion:

```
// read the birth weight data from a csv file
val birthwt = DataFrame.readCSV("https://raw.githubusercontent.com/nmltd/s2-public/main/
Data/linear-reg-data.csv")

// construct a linear model problem
val problem = GLMProblem(
        DenseVector(birthwt["y"].asDoubles()), // Y, the dependent variables
        DenseMatrix(DenseVector(birthwt["x"].asDoubles())), // X, the independent variables
        true, // with intercept
        GLMFamily(GLMBinomial()) // GLM with binomial distribution
)
```

```
val backwardElimination = BackwardElimination(problem, EliminationByAIC())

println("elimination sequence:")
println(Arrays.toString(backwardElimination.getFlags()))
```

The output is the elimination sequence of removing a covariate one at a time:

```
elimination sequence:
[0, 2, 3, 4, 5, 6, 7, 0]
```

Bidirectional elimination is a combination of the two, testing at each step for variables to be included or excluded. The principal drawbacks of stepwise regression include bias in parameter estimation, inconsistencies among model selection algorithms, an inherent (but often overlooked) problem of multiple hypothesis testing, and an inappropriate focus or reliance on a single best model. These approaches only improve prediction accuracy in certain cases, such as when only a few covariates have a strong relationship with the outcome. However, in other cases, they can increase prediction error.

14.6. LASSO

Least absolute shrinkage and selection operator (LASSO) is another automatic/systematic method that does variable selection. It uses regularization or penalty to the size of the sum of the beta coefficients to force some of them to zero, effectively excluding them from the model. In contrast to stepwise regression, which is a greedy algorithm to consider one variable at a time, LASSO chooses all significant variables simultaneously and globally. Mathematically, LASSO solves a residual sum of squared errors (RSS) problem with ℓ_1 regularization as a constraint.

$$\min_{\beta} \| \boldsymbol{X}\beta - \boldsymbol{y} \|_2^2 \text{, s.t., } \|\boldsymbol{\beta}\|_1 \le t$$

The NM Dev class called `ConstrainedLASSOProblem` constructs such a problem. The class signature is as follows:

```
/**
 * Constructs a LASSO problem in the constrained form.
 *
 * @param y the vector of response variable <i>(n * 1)</i>, properly
 *          demeaned and scaled
 * @param X the design matrix of factors <i>(n * m)</i>, properly demeaned
 *          and scaled
 * @param t the penalization parameter
 */
public ConstrainedLASSOProblem(Vector y, Matrix X, double t)
```

Equivalently, you can write the constrained problem in the Lagrangian form as an unconstrained minimization problem.

$$\min_{\beta} \| \boldsymbol{X}\beta - \boldsymbol{y} + \lambda \| \beta_1 \|_2^2$$

where $\|\boldsymbol{u}\|_p = \left(\sum_{i=1}^{n} |u_i|^p \right)^{\frac{1}{p}}$ is the standard ℓ_p-norm.

The NM Dev class called UnconstrainedLASSOProblem constructs such a problem. The class signature is as follows:

```
/**
 * Constructs a LASSO problem.
 *
 * @param y      the vector of response variable <i>(n * 1)</i>, properly
 *               demeaned and scaled
 * @param X      the design matrix of factors <i>(n * m)</i>, properly
 *               demeaned and scaled
 * @param lambda the penalization parameter
 */
public UnconstrainedLASSOProblem(Vector y, Matrix X, double lambda)
```

There are two ways to solve a LASSO problem: quadratic programming (QP) or least-angle regression (LARS).

The QP approach transforms the problem into a single quadratic programming problem with $2p$ constraints, where p is the number of columns in the design matrix or number of explanatory variables.

The following code example builds a linear model by selecting a subset of explanatory variables in the diabetes data set[1] by solving a LASSO problem using the QP approach, ConstrainedLASSObyQP.

```
// the regularization penalty
var t = 0.0

// construct a constrained LASSO problem
var problem = ConstrainedLASSOProblem(diabetes_y, diabetes_X, t)
// run LASSO regression
var betaHat: Vector = ConstrainedLASSObyQP(problem).beta().betaHat()
println("beta^ = " + betaHat)

t = 1500.0
problem = ConstrainedLASSOProblem(diabetes_y, diabetes_X, t)
betaHat = ConstrainedLASSObyQP(problem).beta().betaHat()
println("beta^ = " + betaHat)

// relaxing the constraint essentially the same as the OLS solution
t = 10000.0
problem = ConstrainedLASSOProblem(diabetes_y, diabetes_X, t)
betaHat = ConstrainedLASSObyQP(problem).beta().betaHat()
println("beta^ = " + betaHat)
```

[1] This data set is available on S2. Load it first before executing this code.

The output is as follows:

```
beta^ = [0.000000, 0.000000, 0.000000, 0.000000, 0.000000, 0.000000, 0.000000, 0.000000,
0.000000, 0.000000]
beta^ = [0.000000, -96.348737, 508.285354, 243.727200, 0.000000, 0.000000, -186.148813,
0.000000, 455.180652, 10.309244]
beta^ = [-18.448399, -235.622288, 516.365580, 323.720107, -798.129152, 477.715312,
112.248720, 189.372882, 754.619923, 70.468112]
```

The last result is for a very big *t* so the beta coefficients are not constrained. The result will be equivalent running an OLS.

Least-angle regression (LARS) is an algorithm for fitting linear regression models to high-dimensional data by selecting a subset of covariates. Instead of just giving a vector result, the LARS solution consists of a curve denoting the solution for each value of the ℓ_1-norm of the parameter vector. The algorithm is similar to forward stepwise regression, but instead of including variables at each step, the estimated parameters are increased in a direction equiangular to each one's correlations with the residual.

The following code solves the same LASSO problem using the LARS method, `ConstrainedLASSObyLARS`:

```
// the regularization penalty
var t = 0.0

// construct a constrained LASSO problem
var problem = ConstrainedLASSOProblem(diabetes_y, diabetes_X, t)
// run LASSO regression
var betaHat: Vector = ConstrainedLASSObyLARS(problem).beta().betaHat()
println("beta^ = " + betaHat)

t = 1500.0
problem = ConstrainedLASSOProblem(diabetes_y, diabetes_X, t)
betaHat = ConstrainedLASSObyLARS(problem).beta().betaHat()
println("beta^ = " + betaHat)

// relaxing the constraint essentially the same as the OLS solution
t = 10000.0
problem = ConstrainedLASSOProblem(diabetes_y, diabetes_X, t)
betaHat = ConstrainedLASSObyLARS(problem).beta().betaHat()
println("beta^ = " + betaHat)
```

The output is similar to the previous result:

```
beta^ = [0.000000, 0.000000, 0.000000, 0.000000, 0.000000, 0.000000, 0.000000, 0.000000,
0.000000, 0.000000]
beta^ = [0.000000, -96.348697, 508.285327, 243.727190, 0.000000, 0.000000, -186.148803,
0.000000, 455.180663, 10.309320]
beta^ = [-18.448420, -235.622167, 516.365552, 323.720053, -798.128410, 477.714962,
112.248151, 189.372251, 754.619805, 70.468203]
```

`ConstrainedLASSObyLARS` actually calls another NM Dev class, called `LARSFitting`, to compute all the selection steps. The following code repeats the LARS computation shown previously and shows the selection steps:

```
// construct a LARS problem
val problem = LARSProblem(
        diabetes_y,
        diabetes_X,
        true) // use LASSO variation

// run the LARS fitting algorithm
val fit = LARSFitting(problem, 1e-8, 100)

val estimators: LARSFitting.Estimators = fit.getEstimators()
// The sequence of actions taken: they are the variables added or dropped in each iteration.
println("action sequence: " + estimators.actions())
// The entire sequence of estimated LARS regression coefficients, scaled by the L2 norm of
each row.
println("sequence of estimated LARS regression coefficients:")
println(estimators.scaledBetas())
```

The output is as follows:

```
action sequence: [3, 9, 4, 7, 2, 10, 5, 8, 1, 6, -7, 7]
sequence of estimated LARS regression coefficients:
13x10
     [,1] [,2] [,3] [,4] [,5] [,6] [,7] [,8] [,9] [,10]
[1,] 0.000000, 0.000000, 0.000000, 0.000000, 0.000000, 0.000000, 0.000000, 0.000000,
0.000000, 0.000000,
[2,] 0.000000, 0.000000, 52.609314, 0.000000, 0.000000, 0.000000, 0.000000, 0.000000,
0.000000, 0.000000,
[3,] 0.000000, 0.000000, 359.691510, 0.000000, 0.000000, 0.000000, 0.000000, 0.000000,
307.082199, 0.000000,
[4,] 0.000000, 0.000000, 430.923197, 77.462073, 0.000000, 0.000000, 0.000000, 0.000000,
378.584828, 0.000000,
[5,] 0.000000, 0.000000, 502.777391, 191.000733, 0.000000, 0.000000, -115.633979, 0.000000,
444.203866, 0.000000,
[6,] 0.000000, -64.714355, 507.691240, 228.045408, 0.000000, 0.000000, -163.671347,
0.000000, 453.708049, 0.000000,
[7,] 0.000000, -109.231911, 508.527271, 250.113659, 0.000000, 0.000000, -195.302838,
0.000000, 455.780391, 14.507832,
[8,] 0.000000, -191.033013, 518.274174, 292.677114, -99.127088, 0.000000, -221.890826,
0.000000, 515.246160, 55.218187,
[9,] 0.000000, -211.502913, 521.607265, 305.105662, -164.885174, 0.000000, -170.351154,
76.710531, 526.186572, 62.229531,
[10,] -7.654507, -221.991725, 523.427831, 313.543043, -199.964577, 0.000000, -141.794223,
118.564050, 532.755032, 67.213806,
[11,] -13.679150, -229.599582, 519.486007, 319.223360, -533.830831, 266.637493, 0.000000,
158.085779, 656.589267, 69.030254,
[12,] -15.114733, -232.602466, 517.737868, 320.563603, -562.905016, 296.771112, 0.000000,
148.040585, 669.812407, 69.972772,
[13,] -18.448420, -235.622167, 516.365552, 323.720053, -798.128410, 477.714962,
112.248151, 189.372251, 754.619805, 70.468203,
```

CHAPTER 15

■ ■ ■

Time-Series Analysis

Time-series analysis is a statistical technique that studies time-series data. A time series is a sequence of data points indexed in a discrete-time order. In general, a time series is a sequence taken at successive equally spaced points in time (but not necessarily). Examples of time series are daily closing values of the S&P 500 (SPX), the population in the last 100 years, and monthly sales figures. Time-series analyses extract meaningful statistics and other characteristics from time-series data. Time-series forecasting predicts future values based on observed values.

In regression, you analyze the relationship between the response and the (other) explanatory variables. In time-series analysis, you are interested in not only the relationship between the observed values and the explanatory variable, namely time, but more importantly the relationship between the observed values themselves, say the value at time t and the two last values before it. For example, regression analysis computes the correlations between response and explanatory variables. Time-series analysis computes the correlations between the observed values themselves. Regression does not assume ordering of observations. Time-series data has a natural temporal ordering, namely, time. A time-series model will generally reflect the fact that observations close together in time will be more closely related than observations farther apart. In both simple linear regression (one explanatory variable) and time-series analysis, you draw a line across the data points to best fit the sequence. Time-series analysis often uses linear regression to study the data.

Time-series analysis can be applied to real-valued, continuous data, discrete numeric data, or even discrete symbolic data (e.g., sequences of characters, such as letters and words in the English language). Time-series analysis (and forecasting) is a big subject. There are many methods to study time series: parametric versus nonparametric, linear versus nonlinear, and frequency-domain versus time-domain. In this chapter, we briefly discuss only one important class: linear parametric time-domain methods.

Time series as a major statistical tool is widely applied to many applications and fields. In statistics, econometrics, quantitative finance, seismology, meteorology, and geophysics, the primary goal of time-series analysis is forecasting. In signal processing, control engineering, and communication engineering, it is used for signal detection. In machine learning, data mining, and pattern recognition, it is used for clustering, classification, query by content, anomaly detection, and forecasting.

The first step in any time-series analysis is to plot the data. Visualization is important to discover patterns to gain insight into a data set, such as identifying trends, detecting anomalies, and finding clusters. Before you build a model, you need to have some idea of what the data looks like. For example, Figure 15-1 shows a plot of the SPX daily prices from January 2015 to December 2019. You can see that the SPX in general goes up (which is exactly why Warren Buffet suggests that passive investors buy SPX stocks). In addition, notice the few big drawdowns where the index could drop by more than 40 percent but would eventually recover (which is exactly why Warren Buffet suggests that passive investors hold SPX index for years and ignore all the ups and downs however volatile the market is). Another finding is that the SPX has multiple regimes: up, down, and sideways. Also, small volatility periods are usually followed by small volatility periods, and big volatility periods are followed by big volatility periods; hence, this is volatility clustering.

© Haksun Li, PhD 2023
H. Li, PhD, *Numerical Methods Using Kotlin*, https://doi.org/10.1007/978-1-4842-8826-9_15

Figure 15-1. *Time series of the daily closing prices of the S&P 500 index*

It is important to understand that a time series is a stochastic process. The observed value at a time point is a realization of the random variable at that time point. (It could take another value.) A time series is often denoted as follows:

$$X = \{X_1, X_2, \ldots\}$$

where the indices are natural numbers.

Alternatively, you have this:

$$X = \{X_t \mid t \in T\}$$

Where T is the index set.

Each X_t is a random variable. A time series is therefore a sequence of indexed random variables that are related.

There are three broad classes of models that represent a linear time series, that is, values depending linearly only on past values: the autoregressive (AR) models, the moving-average (MA) models, and the integrated (I) models. Combinations of these ideas produce autoregressive moving-average (ARMA) and autoregressive integrated moving-average (ARIMA) models. Extensions of these classes to deal with vector-valued data are available under the heading of multivariate time-series models, and sometimes the preceding acronyms are extended by including an initial *V* for "vector," as in VAR for vector autoregression. These models describe the first-order effect, namely, the mean or level of a time series. To describe the second-order effect of a (nonlinear) time series, namely volatility, you use models such as autoregressive conditional heteroskedasticity (ARCH) and generalized autoregressive conditional heteroskedasticity (GARCH).

In the NM Dev library, there is a large number of classes that represent the models and forecasts for single-variable and multiple-variable time series. There is also a collection of utility functions and classes that manipulate, transform, and compute properties for time series. The interface for a generic time series is `TimeSeries`. The signature is as follows:

```
public interface TimeSeries<T extends Comparable<? super T>, V, E extends TimeSeries.
Entry<T, V>> extends Iterable<E> {
    /**
     * A time series is composed of a sequence of {@code Entry}s.
     * <p/>
```

```
     * An {@code TimeSeries.Entry} is immutable.
     *
     * @param <T> the time type
     * @param <V> the value type
     */
    public static interface Entry<T, V> {
        /**
         * Get the timestamp.
         *
         * @return the timestamp
         */
        public T getTime();
        /**
         * Get the entry value.
         *
         * @return the entry value
         */
        public V getValue();
    }
    /**
     * Get the length of the time series.
     *
     * @return the time series length
     */
    public int size();
}
```

This implementation represents the data point and its timestamp as a pair of value and index often called time. The entries (pairs) are sorted in ascending order by their timestamps. This is a generic interface where the generic type T can be any class that admits an ordering or is comparable. For example, T can be an actual timestamp implemented by LocalDateTime. Here's an example:

```
public class DateTimeGenericTimeSeries<V>
    implements TimeSeries<LocalDateTime, V, DateTimeGenericTimeSeries.Entry<V>> {...}
```

On the other hand, the generic type V can represent any value type. When V is a vector, it can represent a multivariate time series. In the case of univariate time series, you most often want to study a time series of real numbers, which are represented by double. The UnivariateTimeSeries interface extends TimeSeries and implements such a time series. The index is some notion of time, and the values are double.

```
public interface UnivariateTimeSeries<T extends Comparable<? super T>, E extends
UnivariateTimeSeries.Entry<T>> extends dev.nm.stat.timeseries.datastructure.TimeSeries<T,
Double, E> {...}
```

In most applications, the index set consists of natural numbers. The IntTimeTimeSeries interface, extending UnivariateTimeSeries, is indexed by integers, and the value type is double.

```
public interface IntTimeTimeSeries extends dev.nm.stat.timeseries.datastructure.univariate.
UnivariateTimeSeries<Integer, IntTimeTimeSeries.Entry> {...}
```

To simplify coding and usage, NM Dev uses the `SimpleTimeSeries` class , implementing `IntTimeTimeSeries`, to represent a time series that is indexed by natural numbers and takes real number values. This class also supports a number of common operations to manipulate such a time series. Its signature is as follows:

```
public class SimpleTimeSeries implements IntTimeTimeSeries {
    /**
     * Construct an instance of {@code SimpleTimeSeries}.
     *
     * @param values an array of values
     */
    public SimpleTimeSeries(double[] values);
    @Override
    public int size();
    @Override
    public Iterator<Entry> iterator();
    @Override
    public double[] toArray();
    @Override
    public double get(int t);
    /**
     * Constructs an instance of {@code SimpleTimeSeries} by dropping the
     * first {@code nItems} entries.
     *
     * @param nItems the number of leading entries to be dropped
     * @return a {@code SimpleTimeSeries}
     */
    public SimpleTimeSeries drop(int nItems);
    /**
     * Constructs an instance of {@code SimpleTimeSeries} by taking the first
     * difference {@code d} times.
     *
     * @param d the number of differences
     * @return {@code diff(x, lag = 1, differences = d)} as in DoubleUtils
     */
    public SimpleTimeSeries diff(int d);
    /**
     * Constructs an instance of {@code SimpleTimeSeries} by lagging the time
     * series. This operation makes sense only for equidistant data points.
     *
     * @param nLags  the number of lags
     * @param length the length of the lagged time series
     * @return a lagged time series
     */
    public SimpleTimeSeries lag(int nLags, int length);
    /**
     * Constructs an instance of {@code SimpleTimeSeries} by lagging the time
     * series. This operation makes sense only for equidistant data points.
     *
     * @param nLags the number of lags
     * @return a lagged time series
```

```
     */
    public SimpleTimeSeries lag(int nLags);
    @Override
    public String toString();
}
```

Figure 15-2 charts the hierarchy of classes to represent different univariate time series depending on their time or index type and value type.

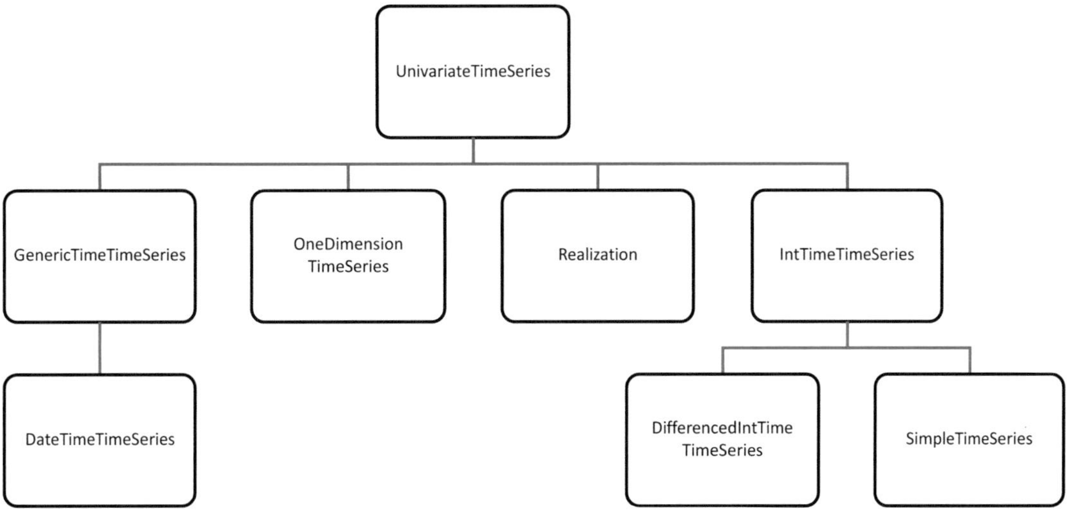

***Figure 15-2.** The hierarchy of classes to represent univariate time series*

The following example constructs a univariate time series and demonstrates a few operations on it:

```
// construct a time series
var ts1 = SimpleTimeSeries(doubleArrayOf(1.0, 2.0, 3.0, 4.0, 5.0, 6.0, 7.0, 8.0, 9.0, 10.0))
println("ts1:" + ts1)

// construct a time series by taking the first difference of another one
// each term is the difference between two successive terms in the original time series
val ts2 = ts1.diff(1)
println("ts2:" + ts2)

// construct a time series by dropping the first two terms of another one
val ts3 = ts1.drop(2)
println("ts3:" + ts3)

// construct a time series by lagging another one
// This operation makes sense only for equidistant data points.
val ts4 = ts1.lag(2)
println("ts4:" + ts4)
```

The output is as follows:

```
ts1:length = 10
[1,] 1.000000, [2,] 2.000000, [3,] 3.000000, [4,] 4.000000, [5,] 5.000000, [6,] 6.000000,
[7,] 7.000000, [8,] 8.000000, [9,] 9.000000, [10,] 10.000000,
ts2:length = 9
[1,] 1.000000, [2,] 1.000000, [3,] 1.000000, [4,] 1.000000, [5,] 1.000000, [6,] 1.000000,
[7,] 1.000000, [8,] 1.000000, [9,] 1.000000,
ts3:length = 8
[1,] 3.000000, [2,] 4.000000, [3,] 5.000000, [4,] 6.000000, [5,] 7.000000, [6,] 8.000000,
[7,] 9.000000, [8,] 10.000000,
ts4:length = 8
[1,] 1.000000, [2,] 2.000000, [3,] 3.000000, [4,] 4.000000, [5,] 5.000000, [6,] 6.000000,
[7,] 7.000000, [8,] 8.000000,
```

A lead or a drop operation (the `drop` function) shifts a time series to the left. Note that a time series lists the oldest observations (left) to the newest observations (right). Dropping the first or leading observations mean dropping the oldest observations. For example, for the following:

$$\{X_{0,t}\} = \{1,2,3,4,5,6,7,8,9,10\}$$

The oldest observation is 1, and the most recent one is 10. You may predict the next item to be 11. So, leading or dropping two observations gives the following:

$$\{X_{1,t}\} = \{2,3,4,5,6,7,8,9,10\}$$

$$\{X_{2,t}\} = \{3,4,5,6,7,8,9,10\}$$

In contrast, the lag operation (the `lag` function) shifts the sequence to the right so that the most recent observations are oldest.

$$\{X_{0,t}\} = \{1,2,3,4,5,6,7,8,9,10\}$$

Lagging by one means that the most recent observation is from one time unit (e.g., year, month, or day) before.

$$\{X_{1,t}\} = \{NA,1,2,3,4,5,6,7,8,9\}$$

Lagging by two means that the most recent observation is from two time units before.

$$\{X_{2,t}\} = \{NA,NA,1,2,3,4,5,6,7,8\}$$

NM Dev does not output `NaN` in the array or time series. The users may need to add padding if needed. The source code in this chapter can be run on the S2 platform here:

```
https://s21.nm.dev/hub/user-redirect/lab/tree/s2-public/Numerical%20Methods%20Using%20
Kotlin/chapter15.ipynb
```

The source code can be found on GitHub:

```
https://github.com/apress/numerical-methods-kotlin
```

15.1. Univariate Time Series

A univariate time series is a *stochastic* (a fancy word for "random") process that consists of a sequence of time-indexed random variables $X_t = \{X_1, X_2, ...\}$, where X_1 denotes the random variable at time $t = 1$, X_2 represents the random variable at time $t = 2$, and so on. The observed values of such a stochastic process, $X_1 = x_1, X_2 = x_2$, and so on, is called a *realization* of the stochastic process. This sequence $\{X_t\} = \{x_1, x_2, ...\}$ is also called a time series. It will be clear from the context whether we are referring to the stochastic process or a particular realization of the process.

The following NM Dev code reads in the SPX data to create a univariate time series using the adjusted daily close prices of the index from January 2, 2015 to December 30, 2019. The adjusted close prices are not exactly the same as the close prices of the index published each day. Because the stocks can split and distribute dividends in the past, you must adjust the data using the appropriate split and dividend multipliers according to the Center for Research in Security Prices (CRSP) standards. We usually analyze an equity asset price using the adjusted prices instead of raw prices.

```
// read the daily S&P 500 data from a csv file
val spx_arr = DoubleUtils.readCSV2d("./resources/sp500_daily.csv", true, true)
// convert the csv file into a matrix for manipulation
val spx_M: Matrix = DenseMatrix(spx_arr)
// extract the column of adjusted close prices
val spx_v: Vector = spx_M.getColumn(5) // adjusted closes
// construct a univariate time series from the data
val spx = SimpleTimeSeries(spx_v.toArray())
println(spx)
```

The (abridged) output is as follows:

```
length = 1257
[1,] 2058.199951, [2,] 2020.579956, [3,] 2002.609985, [4,] 2025.900024, [5,] 2062.139893,
[6,] 2044.810059, [7,] 2028.260010, [8,] 2023.030029, [9,] 2011.270020, [10,] 1992.670044,
[11,] 2019.420044, [12,] 2022.550049, [13,] 2032.119995, [14,] 2063.149902, [15,]
2051.820068, [16,] 2057.090088, [17,] 2029.550049, [18,] 2002.160034, [19,] 2021.250000,
[20,] 1994.989990,
[21,] 2020.849976, [22,] 2050.030029, [23,] 2041.510010, [24,] 2062.520020, [25,]
2055.469971, [26,] 2046.739990, [27,] 2068.590088, [28,] 2068.530029, [29,] 2088.479980,
[30,] 2096.989990, [31,] 2100.340088, [32,] 2099.679932, [33,] 2097.449951, [34,]
2110.300049, [35,] 2109.659912, [36,] 2115.479980, [37,] 2113.860107, [38,] 2110.739990,
[39,] 2104.500000, [40,] 2117.389893,
[41,] 2107.780029, [42,] 2098.530029, [43,] 2101.040039, [44,] 2071.260010, [45,]
2079.429932, [46,] 2044.160034, [47,] 2040.239990, [48,] 2065.949951, [49,] 2053.399902,
[50,] 2081.189941, [51,] 2074.280029, [52,] 2099.500000, [53,] 2089.270020, [54,]
2108.100098, [55,] 2104.419922, [56,] 2091.500000, [57,] 2061.050049, [58,] 2056.149902,
[59,] 2061.020020, [60,] 2086.239990,
```

Again, the first step in any data analysis is visualization, in this case, plotting the data (after data collection, data cleaning, etc.). The SPX data is plotted in Figure 15-3.

Figure 15-3. *Time series of the daily close prices of S&P 500 index*

The (daily) price of the SPX (or a stock) has different statistical properties at different times. For example, in 2015 the levels/means of the prices were around 2,000 (yet still different in each day); in 2019 they ranged from 2,500 to 3,000. You cannot work on the price data because statistical analysis usually works on stationary data, meaning that the data shares the same probability distribution, same mean, same variance, and so on.

One way to get around this problem is to convert prices P_t into simple returns R_t. This normalization measures all stocks in a comparable metric, namely, a percentage. This allows the evaluation of relationships, for example, a covariance matrix, among two or more stocks despite their prices possibly having different magnitudes. (As of today, the SPX is at $4370.04, GOOG is at $2619.38, AAPL is at $145.62, and SRNE is at $8.25.)

$$R_t = \frac{P_t - P_{t-1}}{P_{t-1}}$$

Continuing with the previous example, the following code computes simple returns from prices:

```
// compute simple returns from prices
val diff: DoubleArray = spx.diff(1).toArray()
val p0: DoubleArray = spx.lag(1).toArray()
var simple_returns: DoubleArray = DoubleArray(diff.size)
for (i in 0 until diff.size) {
    simple_returns[i] = diff[i] / p0[i]
}
println(Arrays.toString(simple_returns))
```

The (abridged) output is as follows:

```
[-0.01827810508970322, -0.008893471870112912, 0.011629842642575248, 0.01788828104579755,
-0.008403811040573337, -0.008093685243358803, -0.002578555497921567,
-0.005813066949783809, -0.00924787612555373, 0.013424199395451945, 0.0015499524278268393,
0.0047316238254433785, 0.015269721805970466, -0.0054915224477955155, 0.002568461085935695,
-0.013387862379316457, -0.013495609538427277, 0.009534685377702431, -0.01299196536796535,
```

```
0.012962464037225537, 0.014439494938539686, -0.004156045950290833, 0.010291406800400634,
-0.003418172396697485, -0.0042471946188310196, 0.010675561188404731,
-2.903378506370865E-5, 0.009644506350069552, 0.004074738604868008, 0.001597574626476824,
-3.14309098689124E-4,
```

In quantitative finance, we often use log returns r_t instead of simple returns for a number of reasons:

$$r_t = \ln\left(\frac{P_t}{P_{t-1}}\right) = \ln(P_t) - \ln(P_{t-1})$$

First, you should usually assume that prices are log-normally distributed instead of normally distributed. Log-normal distribution is always positive, but normal distribution may give a negative price. Then the log returns are conveniently normally distributed, as classical statistics mostly assume normality. The relationship between prices, simple returns, and log returns is as follows:

$$1 + R_t = \frac{P_t}{P_{t-1}} = \exp(r_t)$$

Second, when returns are very small (common for price changes for a short duration but not too short like with high-frequency trading), simple return and log return are close to each other:

$$r_t = \log\exp(r_t) = \log(1 + R_t) \approx R_t$$

Third, simple returns are not time-additive, but log returns are. Specifically, the compounding return for a sequence of simple returns is as follows:

$$\frac{P_t}{P_0} = \frac{P_t}{P_{t-1}}\frac{P_{t-1}}{P_{t-2}} \times \cdots \times \frac{P_1}{P_0} = (1+R_1)(1+R_2)\cdots(1+R_n) = \prod_{i=1}^{n}(1+R_i)$$

This compounding return is a product of (independent) normal variables and is not normally distributed.

In contrast, the log of compounding return is a sum of a sequence of log returns:

$$\ln\left(\frac{P_t}{P_0}\right) = \ln(P_t) - \ln(P_0) = \ln(P_t) - \ln(P_{t-1}) + \ln(P_{t-1}) - \ln(P_{t-2}) + \ln(P_{t-2}) + \ldots$$

$$-\ln(P_0) = \ln\left(\frac{P_t}{P_{t-1}}\right) + \ln\left(\frac{P_{t-1}}{P_{t-2}}\right) + \ldots + \ln\left(\frac{P_1}{P_0}\right) = r_t + r_{t-1} + \ldots + r_1$$

The log of a compounding return is normally distributed as the sum of (independent) normal variables and so is normally distributed. Even if the log returns are not normal, their sum (and average) approximately is when t is big enough because of the central limit theorem.

Fourth, much of financial mathematics is built on continuous time stochastic processes that rely heavily on integration and differentiation. The exponents of log returns, that is, prices, are easy to work with in calculus:

$$e^x = \int e^x dx = \frac{de^x}{dx} = e^x$$

Fifth, adding small numbers is numerically more stable, but multiplying small numbers is not, as it is subject to arithmetic underflow. This can be a serious problem, especially for long computation. To solve this, either the algorithm needs to be modified to be numerically robust or it can be transformed into a numerically safe summation via logs.

Continuing with the previous example, the following code computes log returns from prices:

```
// compute log returns from prices
val p1: DoubleArray = spx.drop(1).toArray()
val p: DoubleArray = spx.toArray()
var log_returns: DoubleArray = DoubleArray(p1.size)
for (i in 0 until p1.size) {
    log_returns[i] = log10(p1[i]) - log10(p[i])
}
println(Arrays.toString(log_returns))
```

The (abridged) output is as follows:

```
[-0.008011523019181066, -0.0038796632820945476, 0.0050216323606129265,
0.0077001143584523035, -0.003665151042045789, -0.003529344887759578,
-0.001121298711597607, -0.002531949245178744, -0.004034987996080819, 0.005791270527407466,
6.726146608051486E-4, 0.002050071849203139, 0.006581434496294225, -0.002391510439545552,
0.0011140384061145703, -0.005853546010243349, -0.0059009775694272015,
0.004121244933307455, -0.005679311988768365, 0.005593352602593971, 0.006226149153559124,
-0.001808708970410855, 0.0044466590418430485, -0.0014870363336996206,
-0.00184846135865957, 0.004611764296467147, -1.2609395692031455E-5, 0.004168486547660777,
0.0017660408524449167, 6.932642213732798E-4, -1.3652416369014375E-4,
-4.614908574080978E-4, 0.002652602461047149, -1.3175858134362173E-4, 0.001196469267293221,
-3.3267693078009586E-4, -6.415044317846785E-4, -0.0012858082624620515,
0.002651905633783258, -0.00197555041841
```

Figure 15-4 plots this output, which is the time series of log returns of the SPX.

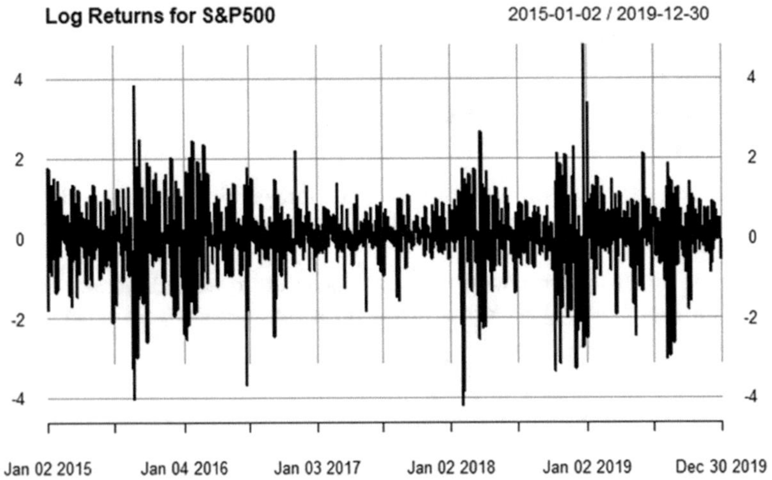

***Figure 15-4.** Time series of the log returns of the S&P 500 index*

15.1.1. Stationarity

A stationary time series is one whose statistical properties do not depend on the time at which the series is observed. Thus, a time series with trend or seasonality is not stationary. The trend and seasonality will affect the value, such as the level/mean, of the time series at different times. On the other hand, a white noise series is stationary. Every point looks like it was drawn from the same (normal) distribution at all times. Comparing Figure 15-3 and Figure 15-4, you can see that the SPX price is not stationary, as it increases over time; the log returns (or simply returns) are stationary, as they simply oscillate around 0 like white noise. It is much easier to predict where the future returns will be (probably around 0) than to guess where the SPX will be in the future (the smartest in Wall Street have tried and many have failed!). You can make predictions for stationary time series because their statistical properties do not change over time, but not for nonstationary ones. Moreover, sample statistics such as means, variances, and correlations with other variables are meaningful only when the data is stationary. *First differencing*—taking the difference between successive observations or taking the difference between successive log of the observations—is a popular technique to transform a nonstationary time series into a stationary one. If once is not enough, you can do twice, meaning second-order differencing. It is almost never necessary to go beyond second-order differences in practice.

Mathematically, a time series $\{X_t\}$ is first-order strongly stationary if all random variables X_t for all $t = 1, \ldots, T$ have the same probability density function. A time series $\{X_t\}$ is first-order weakly stationary if all random variables X_t for all $t = 1, \ldots, T$ have the same finite mean. It is second-order weakly stationary if all random variables X_t for all $t = 1, \ldots, T$ have the same finite mean and finite variance and the covariances do not depend on t and only on the number of lags between the variables. A (second-order) weakly stationary process $\{X_t\}$ satisfies the following:

- $E(X_t) = \mu < \infty$
- $E(|X_t|^2) = \sigma^2 < \infty$
- $\text{cov}(X_t, X_s) = f(|t - s|)$ and is independent of t and s

15.1.2. Autocovariance

The third condition defines a function called the *autocovariance function*. Mathematically, given a time series $\{X_t\}$ and the autocovariance function (ACVF), $\text{cov}(X_t, X_s)$ gives the covariance of the process with itself at pairs of time points (t, s). For a stationary process, the function depends only on the distance or lag $k = |t - s|$ between t and s and not on t and s themselves. That is, for all $k = 0, 1, 2, \ldots$:

$$\gamma(k) = \text{cov}(X_t, X_{t+k})$$

Note that because of the symmetry property of the autocovariance function (because only the distance matters, not the indices), you get:

$$\gamma(k) = \text{cov}(X_t, X_{t+k}) = \text{cov}(X_{t-k}, X_t) = \text{cov}(X_t, X_{t-k}) = \gamma(-k)$$

Specifically, you have this:

$$\gamma(0) = \text{cov}(X_t, X_t) = \text{var}(X_t)$$

The sample autocovariance coefficient (ACVF) of order k for $k = 0, 1, 2, \ldots$ is defined as follows:

$$\hat{\gamma}(k) = \sum_{t=1}^{n-k} (X_t - \bar{X})(X_{t+k} - \bar{X})$$

where $\bar{X} = \sum_{t=1}^{n} X_t / n$ is the sample mean of the time series.

In NM Dev, the `SampleAutoCovariance` class computes the sample ACVF at each lag. For example, the following code computes $\hat{\gamma}(k)$ for the first 25 lags for the monthly S&P 500 adjusted closes from January 1981 to December 2019:

```
// read the monthly S&P 500 data from a csv file
val spx_arr = DoubleUtils.readCSV2d("./resources/sp500_monthly.csv", true, true)
// convert the csv file into a matrix for manipulation
val spx_M: Matrix = DenseMatrix(spx_arr)
// extract the column of adjusted close prices
val spx_v: Vector = spx_M.getColumn(5) // adjusted closes
// construct a univariate time series from the data
val spx = SimpleTimeSeries(spx_v.toArray())
//      println(spx)

// ACVF for lags 0, 1, 2, ..., 24
val acvf = SampleAutoCovariance(spx)
for (i in 0 until 25) {
    println(String.format("acvf(%d) = %f", i, acvf.evaluate(i)))
}
```

The output is as follows:

```
acvf(0) = 551182.987070
acvf(1) = 543953.818490
acvf(2) = 537216.947501
acvf(3) = 530958.035823
acvf(4) = 524883.334938
acvf(5) = 519097.358346
acvf(6) = 512715.454348
acvf(7) = 506618.687345
acvf(8) = 501222.083894
acvf(9) = 494564.151860
acvf(10) = 488414.476447
acvf(11) = 482362.807657
acvf(12) = 476667.617979
acvf(13) = 471903.185864
acvf(14) = 465878.602696
acvf(15) = 460072.984734
acvf(16) = 453220.603768
acvf(17) = 446307.958179
acvf(18) = 439721.402860
acvf(19) = 433499.577238
acvf(20) = 427157.843522
acvf(21) = 421179.456775
acvf(22) = 415192.648687
acvf(23) = 409011.565601
acvf(24) = 402280.844734
```

15.1.3. Autocorrelation

The autocorrelation function (ACF), normalizing the ACVF, of order k is defined as follows:

$$\rho(k)=\frac{\gamma(k)}{\gamma(0)}=\frac{\operatorname{cov}(X_t,X_{t+k})}{\sqrt{\operatorname{var}(X_t)}\sqrt{\operatorname{var}(X_{t+k})}}$$

Note the following:

$$\rho(0)=\frac{\gamma(0)}{\gamma(0)}=1$$

The ACF has the symmetry property $\rho(k) = \rho(-k)$.

The sample autocorrelation coefficient (ACF) of order k for $k = 0, 1, 2, \ldots$ is defined as follows:

$$\hat{\rho}(k)=\frac{\sum_{t=1}^{n-k}(X_t-\bar{X})(X_{t+k}-\bar{X})}{\sum_{t=1}^{n}(X_t-\bar{X})^2}$$

where $\bar{X}=\sum_{t=1}^{n}X_t/n$ is the sample mean of the time series.

When the time series has a trend, the ACF for small lags tend to be big and positive; the successive terms are more correlated. When time series has seasonality, the ACF will be bigger at seasonal lags or at multiples of the seasonal frequency; the terms at the seasons are more correlated. When the time series has both properties, the ACF will show a combination of these features.

In NM Dev, the `SampleAutoCorrelation` class computes the sample ACF at each lag. Continuing with the previous example, the following code computes $\hat{p}_k$ for the first 25 lags for monthly S&P 500 adjusted closes from January 1981 to December 2019:

```
// ACF for lags 0, 1, 2, ..., 24
val acf = SampleAutoCorrelation(spx)
for (i in 0 until 25) {
    println(String.format("acf(%d) = %f", i, acf.evaluate(i)))
}
```

The output is as follows:

```
acvf(0) = 1.000000
acvf(1) = 0.986884
acvf(2) = 0.974662
acvf(3) = 0.963306
acvf(4) = 0.952285
acvf(5) = 0.941788
acvf(6) = 0.930209
acvf(7) = 0.919148
acvf(8) = 0.909357
acvf(9) = 0.897278
acvf(10) = 0.886120
acvf(11) = 0.875141
acvf(12) = 0.864808
```

```
acvf(13) = 0.856164
acvf(14) = 0.845234
acvf(15) = 0.834701
acvf(16) = 0.822269
acvf(17) = 0.809727
acvf(18) = 0.797778
acvf(19) = 0.786489
acvf(20) = 0.774984
acvf(21) = 0.764137
acvf(22) = 0.753276
acvf(23) = 0.742061
acvf(24) = 0.729850
```

Figure 15-5 plots the results.[1] You can see that the sample ACF for the monthly S&P 500 drops from positive to negative after lag 22.

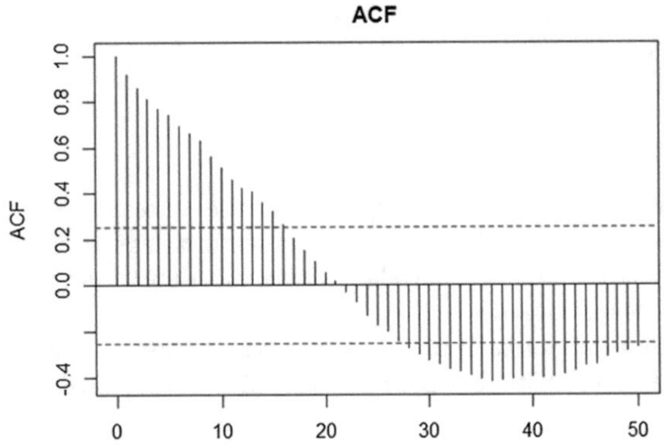

Figure 15-5. *ACF of monthly S&P 500 returns*

15.1.4. Partial Autocorrelation

The partial autocorrelation coefficient (PACF) ϕ_k measures the correlation between two variables X_{t-k} and X_t with the influence of all intermediary variables between them removed. It is the autocorrelation between X_{t-k} and X_t that is not accounted for by lags $t-k+1$ through $t-1$, inclusive for a total of $k-1$ terms. Mathematically, you get this:

$$\phi_k = \frac{\operatorname{cov}\left(X_t, X_{t+k} | X_{t+1}, X_{t+2}, \ldots, X_{t+k-1}\right)}{\sqrt{\operatorname{var}\left(X_t | X_{t+1}\ X_{t+2}, \ldots, X_{t+k-1}\right)}\sqrt{\operatorname{var}\left(X_{t+k} | X_{t+1}, X_{t+2}, \ldots, X_{t+k-1}\right)}}$$

For a mean-zero stationary time series, you need to run two regressions to remove the linear dependency of the intermediary variables. (There is no intercept because the mean of X_t is zero.)

$$\hat{X}_{t+k} = \beta_{11} X_{t+k-1} + \beta_{12} X_{t+k-2} + \ldots + \beta_{1,k+1} X_{t+1}$$

[1] Values between the blue upper and lower bounds are considered insignificant.

$$\hat{X}_t = \beta_{21}X_{t+1} + \beta_{22}X_{t+2} + \ldots + \beta_{2,k-1}X_{t+k-1}$$

Then, you get this:

$$\phi_1 = cor\left(X_{t+1}, X_t\right) = \rho_1$$

$$\phi_k = cor\left(X_{t+k} - \hat{X}_{t+k}, X_t - \hat{X}_t\right) = \frac{\operatorname{cov}\left(X_{t+k} - \hat{X}_{t+k}, X_t - \hat{X}_t\right)}{\sqrt{\operatorname{var}\left(X_{t+k} - \hat{X}_{t+k}\right)}\sqrt{\operatorname{var}\left(X_t - \hat{X}_t\right)}}, k \geq 2$$

The sample PACF can be computed recursively in terms of sample ACF $\hat{\rho}(k)$:

$$\hat{\phi}_k = \hat{\phi}_{k+1,k+1} = \frac{\hat{\rho}(k+1) - \sum_{j=1}^{k} \hat{\phi}_{kj}\hat{\rho}(k+1-j)}{1 - \sum_{j=1}^{k} \hat{\phi}_{kj}\hat{\rho}(j)}$$

and

$$\hat{\phi}_{k+1,j} = \hat{\phi}_{k,j} + \hat{\phi}_{k+1,k+1}\hat{\phi}_{k,k+1-j}$$

$$\hat{\phi}_1 = \hat{\phi}_{1,1} = \hat{\rho}(1)$$

for $j = 1, \ldots, k$.

In NM Dev, the `SamplePartialAutoCorrelation` class computes the sample PACF at each lag. Continuing with the previous example, the following code computes the $\hat{\phi}_k$ for the first 24 lags, starting from 1 and not 0, for monthly S&P 500 adjusted closes from January 1981 to December 2019:

```
// PACF for lags 1, 2, ..., 24
val pacf = SamplePartialAutoCorrelation(spx)
for (i in 1 until 25) {
    println(String.format("pacf(%d) = %f", i, pacf.evaluate(i)))
}
```

The output is as follows:

```
pacf(1) = 0.986884
pacf(2) = 0.027673
pacf(3) = 0.028265
pacf(4) = 0.009367
pacf(5) = 0.016586
pacf(6) = -0.044565
pacf(7) = 0.012763
pacf(8) = 0.042335
pacf(9) = -0.089551
pacf(10) = 0.025976
pacf(11) = 0.001272
pacf(12) = 0.019560
pacf(13) = 0.056418
pacf(14) = -0.078582
```

```
pacf(15) = 0.006884
pacf(16) = -0.089247
pacf(17) = -0.005869
pacf(18) = 0.000041
pacf(19) = 0.028124
pacf(20) = -0.015747
pacf(21) = 0.010677
pacf(22) = 0.012282
pacf(23) = -0.032621
pacf(24) = -0.031604
```

Figure 15-6 plots the output.

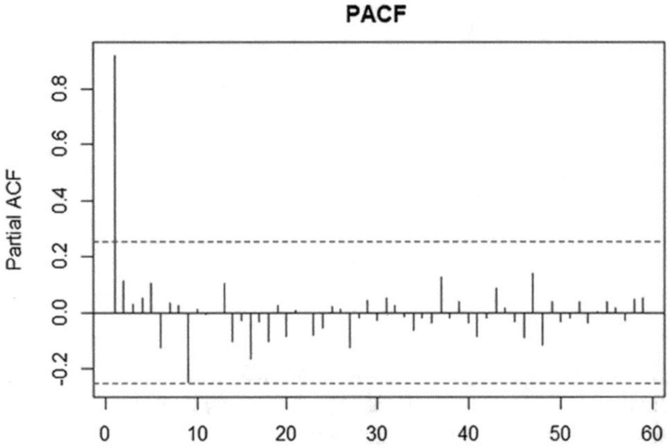

Figure 15-6. *PACF of monthly S&P 500 returns*

15.1.5. White Noise Process and Random Walk

There is a special time series called white noise. Let $\{\varepsilon_t\}$ be a white noise process, and then ε_t satisfies the following:

- $E(\varepsilon_t) = \mu < \infty, \forall t$
- $var(\varepsilon_t) = \sigma^2 < \infty, \forall t$
- $cov(\varepsilon_t, \varepsilon_s) = 0, \forall t \neq s$

The ACF and PACF for a white noise process are all zero for all lags because $\rho(k) = \frac{\gamma(k)}{\gamma(0)} = 0$ for all $k = 1, 2, \ldots$ by its definition.

A random walk is a stochastic process that is a sum of random steps. A summation of ε_t, $W_t = \sum_{i=1}^{t} \varepsilon_i$, is a random walk. Each next value W_{t+1} is a random step away from the previous value. When $E(\varepsilon_t) = 0$, W_t is called a random-walk-without-drift model. A random walk down Wall Street suggests that the market is a random walk. This is consistent with the efficient-market hypothesis that past information does not help in predicting the future. My personal (and purely my own) opinion is that technical analysis is as illusory as astrology. There is no science or proof or mathematics behind it. In contrast, quantitative trading is based on solid mathematics and proofs. Quantitative trading is to technical analysis as astronomy is to astrology. As luck has it, astrology may sometimes get it right, as a broken clock is also right twice a day.

For instance, if you simulate a random walk process (say by summing up 100 standard normal variables), you will find that many of them have significant-looking trends, as shown in Figure 15-7. In fact, the same model will usually yield both upward and downward trends in repeated iterations, as well as interesting-looking curves that seem to demand some sort of complex model. This is just a statistical illusion. Our brain tries hard to find patterns, even when they are not there. Figure 15-7 looks like a good stock to buy because of the strong upward trend. However, this time series is purely a random-walk-without-drift model that was generated by summing 100 standard normal variables, mean 0, and variance 1. Buying this stock is likely to yield nothing over the long term. Trying to predict its future price, say using technical analysis, is deceptive.

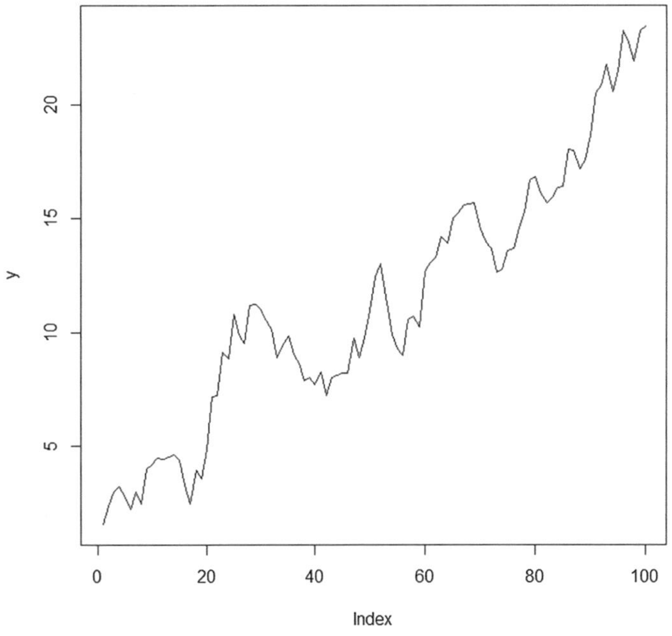

Figure 15-7. *A random walk of the sum of standard normal variables*

15.1.6. Ljung-Box Test for White Noise

One way (there are many ways, as you will see in this chapter) to check whether a time series is a random walk is to check if its first difference is white noise. The theoretical ACF of white noise is 0. However, the sample ACF values that you compute from the data are small but unlikely to be exactly 0. The question is how small these values must be to be deemed numerically 0 so you can conclude with high confidence (but never be absolutely sure) that the process is white noise.

The Ljung-Box test is a hypothesis test for zero autocorrelations for a time series or a series of residuals. It tests whether any autocorrelations for any number of lags in a time series are different from zero. The sample ACF $\hat{\rho}$ values are calculated for a number of lags that you want to test for. The null hypothesis is that the first m autocorrelations are jointly zero.

$$H_0 : \hat{\rho}(1) = \hat{\rho}(2) = \ldots = \hat{\rho}(m) = 0$$

Rejecting the null means that there are some autocorrelations up to order m that are different from zero. The Ljung-Box test statistic is as follows:

$$Q(m) = n(n+2)\sum_{k=1}^{m}\frac{\hat{\rho}(k)^2}{n-k}$$

Where n is the sample size.

Under the null hypothesis, this statistic follows a Chi-squared distribution with a degree of freedom m, χ_m^2. If this test statistic is bigger than the critical value (a p-value smaller than the threshold), you reject the null and conclude that this time series is not a white noise process. Otherwise, you accept the null (or technically, fail to reject the null) and conclude that this time series is a white noise process.

You can check whether the daily returns of the S&P 500 are white noise using the Ljung-Box test. First, you plot the ACF to check how many lags are insignificant. Figure 15-8 shows that the first 14 lags are likely insignificant ($\hat{\rho}(1) = 1$ always). Thus, you test this null hypothesis as follows:

$$H_0 : \hat{\rho}(1) = \hat{\rho}(2) = \ldots = \hat{\rho}(14) = 0$$

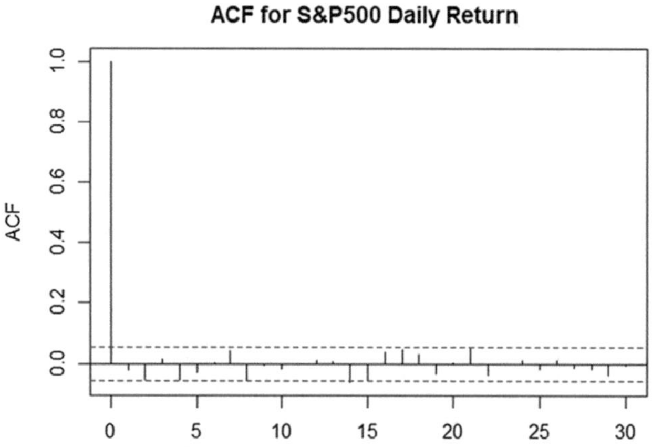

Figure 15-8. *ACF of daily S&P 500 returns*

Rejecting the null means that there are some autocorrelations up to the 14th lag that are different from zero. Here the degree of freedom is $m = 14$. The NM Dev class called `LjungBox` implements the Ljung-Box test. The following code solves this example:

```
// run the Ljung-Box test
val lb_test = LjungBox(log_returns, 14, 0)
println(String.format("The null hypothesis is: %s%n", lb_test.getNullHypothesis()))
println(String.format("The alternative hypothesis is: %s%n", lb_test.
getAlternativeHypothesis()))
println(String.format("The test statistic = %f%n", lb_test.statistics()))
println(String.format("The p-value = %f", lb_test.pValue()))
```

The output is as follows:

```
The null hypothesis is: none of the autocorrelation coefficients up to lag 14 are
different from zero; the data is random
The alternative hypothesis is: at least one value of autocorrelation coefficient is
statistically different from zero at the specified significance level; the data is
not random
The test statistic = 20.203475
The p-value = 0.123856
```

The test statistic is 20.20. The p-value is 0.124, which is bigger than the 5 percent significance level. Thus, you fail to reject the null that none of the autocorrelation coefficients up to lag 14 is different from zero. You conclude that the returns are white noise.

15.1.7. Model Decomposition

The white noise process is important in time-series analysis. It is a fundamental building block of any time series. The Wold decomposition theorem says that for any covariance stationary stochastic process $\{X_t\}$, it can be written as the sum of a deterministic time series and a stochastic time series. Mathematically, if $\{X_t\}$ is a covariance stationary process and $\{\varepsilon_t\}$ is a white noise zero-mean process, then there exists a unique linear representation, as shown here:

$$X_t = \mu + V_t + \varepsilon_t + \psi_1 \varepsilon_{t-1} + \psi_2 \varepsilon_{t-2} + \ldots = \mu + V_t + \sum_{j=0}^{\infty} \psi_j \varepsilon_{t-j}$$

Where V_t is the deterministic component, $\sum_{j=0}^{\infty} \psi_j \varepsilon_{t-j}$ is the stochastic component with $\psi_0 = 1$, and $\sum_{j=0}^{\infty} \psi_j^2 < \infty$. Since $\sum_{j=0}^{\infty} \psi_j^2 < \infty$, there should be a time j such that ψ_i for $i = j + 1, j + 2, \ldots$ will get smaller and smaller.

If there is no deterministic component, then $\{X_t\}$ is a random walk with drift μ:

$$X_t = \mu + \sum_{j=0}^{\infty} \psi_j \varepsilon_{t-j}$$

And:

$$\mathrm{E}(X_t) = \mu$$

$$\mathrm{var}(X_t) = \sigma^2 \sum_{j=0}^{\infty} \psi_j^2$$

$$\gamma(k) = \mathrm{cov}(X_t, X_{t+k}) = \sigma^2 \sum_{j=0}^{\infty} \psi_j \psi_{j+k}$$

$$\rho(k) = \frac{\gamma(k)}{\gamma(0)} = \frac{\sigma^2 \sum_{j=0}^{\infty} \psi_j \psi_{j+k}}{\sigma^2 \sum_{j=0}^{\infty} \psi_j^2} = \frac{\sum_{j=0}^{\infty} \psi_j \psi_{j+k}}{1 + \sum_{j=1}^{\infty} \psi_j^2}$$

Where μ is a constant and ε_t is the white noise.

The determinist component can be a trend or a seasonal component, or both. In general, a time series can be decomposed into these three components:

- Trend component
- Seasonal component
- Irregular random component

A trend component exists when there is a long-term increase or decrease in the data. For instance, the S&P 500 increases with time. The seasonal component exists when the data exhibits patterns with seasons such as months or quarters. For instance, the number of visitors to Disneyland changes with the seasons (more people in the summer and fewer in the winter). An irregular random component, aka stochastic component or white noise, consists of the innovations with time. That is the source of uncertainty of a time series. For instance, the return of the S&P 500 is an irregular process.

This decomposition is called the *classical decomposition model*. There are two forms of decomposition: additive and multiplicative. They combine the trend component T_t, the seasonal component S_t, and the random component ε_t to build a time-series model.

The additive model adds these components:

$$X_t = T_t + S_t + \varepsilon_t$$

In NM Dev, the `AdditiveModel` class constructs such an additive model. The trend, seasonal, and random components are given in arrays. Here's an example:

```
val rng = StandardNormalRNG()

// construct an additive model
val additive_model = AdditiveModel(
        // the trend
        doubleArrayOf(
            1.0, 3.0, 5.0, 7.0, 9.0, 11.0, 13.0, 15.0, 17.0, 19.0
        ),
        // the seasonal component
        doubleArrayOf(
            0.0, 1.0
        ),
        // the source of randomness
        rng
)
println(additive_model)
```

The output is as follows:

```
length = 10
[1,] 0.657586, [2,] 3.794529, [3,] 5.718166, [4,] 6.634372, [5,] 9.802750, [6,] 10.789668,
[7,] 12.700581, [8,] 16.614644, [9,] 15.694052, [10,] 20.973963,
```

Note that the length of the seasonal component array is only 2 rather than 10. This is because the elements in the array are used repeatedly to represent a cycle of a seasonal pattern.

The multiplicative model multiplies these components:

$$X_t = T_t \times S_t \times \varepsilon_t$$

In NM Dev, the `MultiplicativeModel` class constructs such a multiplicative model. The trend, seasonal, and random components are given in arrays. Here's an example:

```
// construct a multiplicative model
val multiplicative_model = MultiplicativeModel(
        // the trend
        doubleArrayOf(
            1.0, 3.0, 5.0, 7.0, 9.0, 11.0, 13.0, 15.0, 17.0, 19.0
        ),
        // the seasonal component
        doubleArrayOf(
            -1.0, 1.0
        ),
        // the source of randomness
        rng
)
println(multiplicative_model)
```

The output is as follows:

```
length = 10
[1,] 0.035056, [2,] 4.531332, [3,] -5.732130, [4,] -1.103154, [5,] 0.125291, [6,]
4.601235, [7,] -35.735400, [8,] -8.219343, [9,] -14.441234, [10,] -11.707299,
```

On the other hand, the NM Dev class called `MADecomposition` decomposes a time series into the trend, seasonal, and random components using the moving average estimation method with a symmetric window. The class first determines the trend component using a moving average (using a symmetric window with equal weights) and removes it from the time series. Then, the seasonal figure is computed by averaging, for each time unit, over all periods. The seasonal figure is then centered. Finally, the error component is determined by removing trend and seasonal figures (recycled as needed) from the original time series. It builds a time-series model as follows:

$$X_t = T_t \times S_t \times \varepsilon_t$$

Such that you get this:

- $E(\varepsilon_t) = 0$
- $var(\varepsilon_t) = \sigma^2$
- $cov(\varepsilon_t, \varepsilon_s) = 0$
- $S_{t+d} = S_t$; d is the length of one season

The following code decomposes the monthly returns of the S&P 500 into three components. The length of the seasonality is set to 12.

```
// decompose the S&P 500 monthly returns into a classical additive model
val spx_model = MADecomposition(
                spx.toArray(), // the SP 500 monthly returns
                12 // the length of seasonality
        )
println(String.format("The trend component: %s", Arrays.toString(spx_model.getTrend())))
```

The (abridged) output is as follows:

```
The trend component: [NaN, NaN, NaN, NaN, NaN, NaN, 127.46125054166667,
126.32333370833332, 124.56500020833334, 122.88125033333331, 121.33625054166666,
119.57333366666664, 117.68041666666666, 116.55083329166666, 116.59083325,
117.26041658333331, 118.26083337499999, 119.52208324999998, 121.313333125,
123.80708304166664, 126.97166658333332, 130.67958320833333, 134.7837495833333,
139.30624958333334, 144.03541625000003, 148.21708266666667, 151.98958270833333,
155.13458316666663, 157.53874970833334, 159.7120825833333, 161.47874904166665,
162.60833241666666, 163.24249849999998, 163.31916499999997, 162.64333225,
161.54749883333332, 160.4491655, 160.04833237499997, 160.14458229166664,
160.25166529166668, 160.23999866666668, 160.2187495, 160.990833375, 162.67166654166667,
164.5716667916667, 166.29083387500003, 168.74000050000004, 171.97625104166664,
175.26500133333332, 177.85708491666668, 179.4375019166667, 181.09208554166668,
183.6887525, 187.13166875000002, 190.30625158333334, 193.55166820833333, 197.884168,
202.631251, 207.36000120833333, 212.22625091666666, 216.56750037499998, 221.12999975,
225.86083279166667, 230.16916587499998, 234.38624887499998, 237.63374895833334,
241.51666508333332, 246.49916516666661, 251.0858331666666, 255.48749979166666,
259.47041566666667, 263.4666658333333, 269.12083304166663, 275.7629165416667,
282.73708216666665, 286.83374787500003, 286.3708311666667, 285.78708141666664,
285.28291575, 283.891666375, 281.8420829583333, 279.34874983333333, 277.05833316666667,
274.62333308333336, 271.4091657916667, 266.62083187499996, 261.695832625,
260.74833366666667, 263.68916770833334, 266.77416804166666, 269.7341677499999,
272.2941665833334, 274.6699981666667, 278.1820818333334, 282.6266657083334,
286.9116655416667, 291.8508325833334, 298.6837501250001, 305.64916733333337, 311.42541625,
316.9954
```

```
println(String.format("The seasonal component: %s", Arrays.toString(spx_model.
getSeasonal())))
```

The (abridged) output is as follows:

```
The seasonal component: [-0.5639809618055622, -3.041018432200329, 3.4700367717470804,
13.175939164290902, 7.950252372624271, 4.350280714729547, 7.173618380299682,
-3.484653234831845, -13.151856919042393, -10.369815636147619, -3.732548819261692,
-1.7762534004020436, -0.5639809618055622, -3.041018432200329, 3.4700367717470804,
13.175939164290902, 7.950252372624271, 4.350280714729547, 7.173618380299682,
-3.484653234831845, -13.151856919042393, -10.369815636147619, -3.732548819261692,
-1.7762534004020436, -0.5639809618055622, -3.041018432200329, 3.4700367717470804,
13.175939164290902, 7.950252372624271, 4.350280714729547, 7.173618380299682,
```

```
-3.484653234831845, -13.151856919042393, -10.369815636147619, -3.732548819261692,
-1.7762534004020436, -0.5639809618055622, -3.041018432200329, 3.4700367717470804,
13.175939164290902, 7.950252372624271, 4.350280714729547, 7.173618380299682,
-3.484653234831845, -13.151856919042393, -10.369815636147619, -3.732548819261692,
-1.7762534004020436, -0.5639809618055622, -3.041018432200329, 3.4700367717470804,
13.175939164290902, 7.950252372624271, 4.350280714729547, 7.173618380299682,
-3.484653234831845, -13.151856919042393, -10.369815636147619, -3.732548819261692,
-1.7762534004020436, -0.5639809618055622, -3.041018432200329, 3.4700367717470804,
13.175939164290902, 7.950252372624271, 4.350280714729547, 7.173618380299682,
-3.484653234831845, -13.151856919042393, -10.369815636147619, -3.732548819261692,
-1.7762534004020436, -0.5639809618055622, -3.041018432200329, 3.4700367717470804,
13.175939164290902, 7.950252372624271,
```

```
println(String.format("The random component: %s", Arrays.toString(spx_model.getRandom())))
```

The (abridged) output is as follows:

```
The random component: [NaN, NaN, NaN, NaN, NaN, NaN, -3.714870921966366,
-0.04867947350147972, 4.76685671070905, 9.378564302814297, 8.746296277595036,
4.752922733735403, 3.283566295138897, -0.3998138594663345, -8.100871021747082,
-13.996353747624212, -14.331088747624264, -14.262362964729533, -21.396955505299687,
-0.8124278068348048, 6.600188335709092, 13.41023342781429, 7.478798235928394,
3.110002817068704, 1.8285677118055332, 2.883933765533669, -2.4996124800804296,
-3.880529330957529, -3.0990030809576297, 3.5776357019371403, -6.0923694219663105,
5.27631481816519, 15.97936541904241, 10.600653636147655, 7.489210569261701,
5.15874756706873, 3.5248194618055493, 0.052684057200366397, -4.434626063413731,
-13.377601455957574, -17.640248039290952, -11.389037214729541, -17.50444775529968,
7.492979693165182, 14.680196127375694, 10.168977761147602, -1.4274496807383343,
-2.9599926412645914, 4.92898462847225, 6.363926515533649, -2.2475346884137934,
-14.438022705957565, -2.089001872624266, 0.3680565352704548, -6.5598719636330145,
-1.4370099735014605, -2.6523090809575933, -2.441428363852367, -1.4574543890716427,
0.8300014837354013,
```

Figure 15-9 plots the three-component time series. It confirms the expectations. The trend time series is upward trending. The seasonal time series exhibits a cyclical pattern. The random time series is a white noise process.

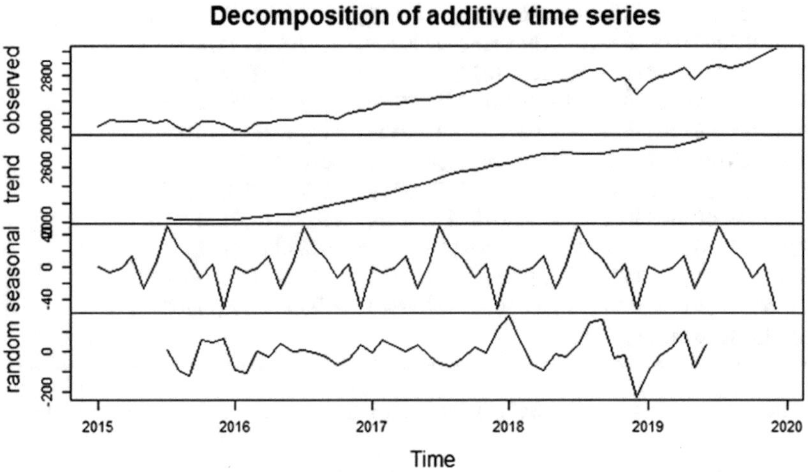

Figure 15-9. *Decomposition of the S&P 500 monthly returns using an additive model*

15.2. Time-Series Models

In general, you can use a function of time or a smoothing method (like a moving average) to model the trend component. You can use a function of a dummy variable to model the seasonal component. After removing the trend and seasonal components, you are left with the random residuals. The following list summarizes the general steps of time-series modeling:

1. Plot the time series to check for nonstationary behavior, such as trend and seasonal components.
2. Remove the nonstationary components by subtracting trend and seasonality, taking the first difference, and so on, to obtain a stationary time series of random residuals.
3. Choose an appropriate time-series model to fit the residuals.
4. Check the goodness of fit of the model.
5. Invert the operations in Step 2, such as adding the trend and seasonal components back in, integrating the residuals, and so on, to build a model for the original time series.

There are a number of important time-series models to model the random residuals. They are the subjects of this section.

15.2.1. AR Models

Given a time series X_t, the lag operator or backshift operator B is such that it shifts the time series to the right. Mathematically, you get this:

$$BX_t = X_{t-1}$$

$$B^k X_t = X_{t-k}$$

$$Bc = c$$

Where k is a positive integer that represents the number of lags and c is a constant.

For example, suppose you have this:

$$\{X_t\} = \{1,2,3,4,5,6,7,8,9,10\}$$

Then, you have this:

$$BX_t = \{1,2,3,4,5,6,7,8,9\}$$

$$B^2 X_t = \{1,2,3,4,5,6,7,8\}$$

The NM Dev function called `lag` implements the backshift operator.

You can write the first difference operator Δ applied to X_t in terms of the backshift operator:

$$\Delta X_t = X_t - X_{t-1}$$

$$= X_t - BX_t$$

The backshift operator is used ubiquitously in time-series models because many time-series models depend on past values.

AR(1)

An autoregressive (AR) model specifies that the output variable depends linearly on its own previous values (or lagged values) and on a stochastic term. The simplest AR model is AR(1), an autoregressive model with order 1. Its output depends on a constant (level), the last value, and a white noise. Specifically, you have this:

$$X_t = \phi_0 + \phi_1 X_{t-1} + \varepsilon_t$$

Where ϕ_0 is a constant, ϕ_1 is the autoregressive coefficient, and ε_t is the stochastic or random or error term. It is white noise with the following:

- Zero mean, $\mathrm{E}[\varepsilon_t] = 0$
- Constant variance σ^2, $\mathrm{var}[\varepsilon_t] = \mathrm{E}[\varepsilon_t \varepsilon_t] = \sigma^2$
- Independently distributed, $\mathrm{E}[\varepsilon_t \varepsilon_{t-1}] = 0$

AR(1) is said to be of order 1 because it has only one past value as a dependent variable.

In terms of the backshift operator, you have this:

$$X_t = \phi_0 + BX_t + \varepsilon_t$$

Rearranging the terms and using the polynomial notation, you get this:

$$(1-B)X_t = \phi_0 + \varepsilon_t$$

$$X_t = \frac{1}{(1-B)}(\phi_0 + \varepsilon_t)$$

The conditional expectation and conditional variance are as follows:

$$\mathrm{E}(X_t \mid X_{t-1}) = \phi_0 + \phi_1 X_{t-1}$$

$$\mathrm{var}(X_t \mid X_{t-1}) = \mathrm{var}(\varepsilon_t) = \sigma^2$$

If $\{X_t\}$ is a stationary process (i.e., X_t has a constant mean and variance), then the unconditional expectation is as follows:

$$\mathrm{E}(X_t) = \mathrm{E}(\phi_0 + \phi_1 X_{t-1} + \varepsilon_t) = \phi_0 + \phi_1 \mathrm{E}(X_{t-1}) + \mathrm{E}(\varepsilon_t) = \phi_0 + \phi_1 \mathrm{E}(X_t)$$

$$(1+\phi_1)\mathrm{E}(X_t) = \phi_0$$

$$\mathrm{E}(X_t) = \frac{\phi_0}{(1+\phi_1)}$$

The unconditional variance is as follows (note that X_{t-1} and ε_t are independent, so their covariance is 0):

$$\mathrm{var}(X_t) = \mathrm{var}(\phi_0 + \phi_1 X_{t-1} + \varepsilon_t)$$

$$= \mathrm{var}(\phi_1 X_{t-1}) + \mathrm{var}(\varepsilon_t)$$

$$= \phi_1^2\,\mathrm{var}(X_{t-1}) + \mathrm{var}(\varepsilon_t)$$

$$= \phi_1^2\,\mathrm{var}(X_t) + \sigma^2$$

$$(1-\phi_1^2)\mathrm{var}(X_t) = \sigma^2$$

$$\mathrm{var}(X_t) = \frac{\sigma^2}{(1-\phi_1^2)}$$

It can be seen from the last expression of the variance formula that AR(1) is stationary only when $|\phi_1|$ < 1. A necessary (and can be proven also sufficient) condition for AR(1) to be covariance stationary is that $|\phi| < 1$. This condition prevents the series from "blowing up." ϕ_1 measures the persistence of the model. The smaller ϕ_1 is, the smaller the variance is.

Assume that AR(1) is a stationary process having a constant mean μ, then the demeaned process is as follows:

$$X_t - \mu = \phi_1 (X_{t-1} - \mu) + \varepsilon_t$$

Or, with $\tilde{X}_t = X_t - \mu$,

$$\tilde{X}_t = \phi_1 \tilde{X}_{t-1} + \varepsilon_t$$

Then, the covariance between the demeaned variable and the error is as follows:

$$\mathrm{E}\left[\tilde{X}_t \varepsilon_t\right] = \mathrm{E}\left[\left(\phi_1 \tilde{X}_{t-1} + \varepsilon_t\right)\varepsilon_t\right] = \phi_1 \mathrm{E}\left[\tilde{X}_{t-1}\varepsilon_t\right] + \sigma^2 = \sigma^2$$

The variance is as follows:

$$\gamma(0) = \mathrm{E}\left[\tilde{X}_t \tilde{X}_t\right] = \mathrm{E}\left[\left(\phi_1 \tilde{X}_{t-1} + \varepsilon_t\right)\left(\phi_1 \tilde{X}_{t-1} + \varepsilon_t\right)\right]$$

$$= \mathrm{E}\left[\left(\phi_1^2 \tilde{X}_{t-1}\tilde{X}_{t-1} + 2\phi_1 \tilde{X}_{t-1}\varepsilon_t + \varepsilon_t^2\right)\right]$$

$$= \phi_1^2 \mathrm{E}\left[\tilde{X}_{t-1}\tilde{X}_{t-1}\right] + 2\phi_1 \mathrm{E}\left[\tilde{X}_{t-1}\varepsilon_t\right] + \mathrm{E}\left[\varepsilon_t^2\right]$$

That is:

$$\gamma(0) = \phi_1^2 \gamma(0) + \sigma^2$$

$$\gamma(0) = \frac{\sigma^2}{1 - \phi_1^2}$$

The ACVF for AR(1) is as follows:

$$\mathrm{E}\left[\tilde{X}_t \tilde{X}_{t-j}\right] = \mathrm{E}\left[\left(\phi_1 \tilde{X}_{t-1} + \varepsilon_t\right)\tilde{X}_{t-j}\right]$$

$$= \phi_1 \mathrm{E}\left[\tilde{X}_{t-1}\tilde{X}_{t-j}\right] + \mathrm{E}\left[\varepsilon_t \tilde{X}_{t-j}\right]$$

$$= \phi_1 \mathrm{E}\left[\tilde{X}_{t-1}\tilde{X}_{t-j}\right]$$

That is, you have this:

$$\gamma(j) = \phi_1 \gamma(j-1), j = 1, 2, \ldots$$

The ACF for AR(1) is as follows:

$$\rho(j) = \frac{\gamma(j)}{\gamma(0)} = \phi_1^j, j = 1, 2, \ldots$$

When $|\phi_1| < 1$, the magnitude of ACF $|\rho(j)|$ for AR(1) decreases exponentially.

The AR(1) model is the discrete time analogy of the continuous time mean-reverting process called the Ornstein-Uhlenbeck process. It is therefore sometimes useful to understand the properties of the AR(1) model cast in an equivalent form. In this form, the AR(1) model, with the mean reversion parameter θ, is given by the following:

$$X_{t+1} = X_t + (1-\theta)(\mu - X_t) + \varepsilon_{t+1}$$

The following can be proven:

$$\mathrm{E}[X_{t+n} \mid X_t] = \mu(1-\theta^n) + X_t\theta^n$$

$$\mathrm{var}[X_{t+n} \mid X_t] = \sigma^2 \frac{1-\theta^{2n}}{1-\theta^2}$$

In NM Dev, the ARModel class constructs an AR model. The class signature is as follows:

```
public class ARModel extends ARMAModel {
    /**
     * Construct a univariate AR model.
     *
     * @param mu    the intercept (constant) term
     * @param AR    the AR coefficients (excluding the initial 1)
     * @param sigma the white noise variance
     */
    public ARModel(double mu, double[] AR, double sigma) {
        super(mu, AR, null, sigma);
    }
    /**
     * Construct a univariate AR model with unit variance.
     *
     * @param mu the intercept (constant) term
     * @param AR the AR coefficients (excluding the initial 1)
     */
    public ARModel(double mu, double[] AR) {
        this(mu, AR, 1);
    }
    /**
     * Construct a univariate AR model with zero-intercept (mu).
     *
     * @param AR    the AR coefficients (excluding the initial 1)
     * @param sigma the white noise variance
     */
    public ARModel(double[] AR, double sigma) {
        this(0, AR, sigma);
    }
    /**
     * Construct a univariate AR model with unit variance and zero-intercept
     * (mu).
     *
     * @param AR the AR coefficients (excluding the initial 1)
     */
```

```
    public ARModel(double[] AR) {
        this(AR, 1);
    }
    /**
     * Copy constructor.
     *
     * @param that a univariate AR model
     */
    public ARModel(ARModel that) {
        super(that);
    }
}
```

For example, the following code constructs this AR(1) model and computes the ACVF and ACF for it:

$$X_t = 0.6X_{t-1} + \varepsilon_t$$

```
// define an AR(1) model
val ar1 = ARModel(
        doubleArrayOf(0.6) // phi_1 = 0.6
)
val nLags = 10
// compute the autocovariance function for the model
val acvf1 = AutoCovariance(ar1)
for (i in 0 until nLags) {
    println(String.format("The acvf of the AR(1) model at lag%d = %f", i, acvf1.evaluate(i.
    toDouble())))
}
```

The output is as follows:

```
the acvf of the AR(1) model at lag0 = 1.562500
the acvf of the AR(1) model at lag1 = 0.937500
the acvf of the AR(1) model at lag2 = 0.562500
the acvf of the AR(1) model at lag3 = 0.337500
the acvf of the AR(1) model at lag4 = 0.202500
the acvf of the AR(1) model at lag5 = 0.121500
the acvf of the AR(1) model at lag6 = 0.072900
the acvf of the AR(1) model at lag7 = 0.043740
the acvf of the AR(1) model at lag8 = 0.026244
the acvf of the AR(1) model at lag9 = 0.015746
```

The following code computes the autocorrelation function for the model.

```
val acf1 = AutoCorrelation(ar1, nLags)
for (i in 0 until nLags) {
    println(String.format("The acf of the AR(1) model at lag%d = %f", i, acf1.evaluate(i.
    toDouble())))
}
```

The output is as follows:

```
the acf of the AR(1) model at lag0 = 1.000000
the acf of the AR(1) model at lag1 = 0.600000
the acf of the AR(1) model at lag2 = 0.360000
the acf of the AR(1) model at lag3 = 0.216000
the acf of the AR(1) model at lag4 = 0.129600
the acf of the AR(1) model at lag5 = 0.077760
the acf of the AR(1) model at lag6 = 0.046656
the acf of the AR(1) model at lag7 = 0.027994
the acf of the AR(1) model at lag8 = 0.016796
the acf of the AR(1) model at lag9 = 0.010078
```

You can see that ACVF and ACF both exponentially decay to 0. Figure 15-10 plots the ACF values.

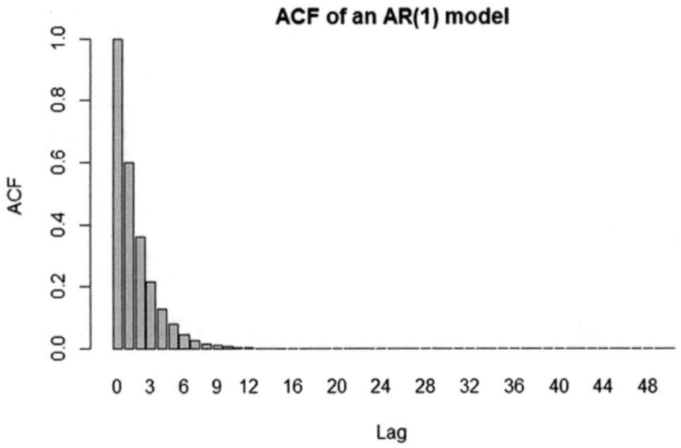

Figure 15-10. *ACF of the AR(1) process when* $\boldsymbol{\phi 1 = 0.6}$

AR(2)

An AR(2) model is as follows:

$$X_t = \phi_0 + \phi_1 X_{t-1} + \phi_2 X_{t-2} + \varepsilon_t$$

where ϕ_1 and ϕ_2 are the autoregressive coefficients. ε_t is the error term or white noise with zero mean and constant variance σ^2. AR(2) is said to have an order 2 because it has X_{t-1} and X_{t-2} as its dependent variables.

In terms of the backshift operator, you have this:

$$X_t = \phi_0 + \phi_1 B X_t + \phi_2 B^2 X_t + \varepsilon_t$$

Rearranging the terms and using the polynomial notation, you get this:

$$\left(1-\phi_1 B-\phi_2 B^2\right)X_t=\phi_0+\varepsilon_t$$

$$X_t=\frac{1}{\left(1-\phi_1 B-\phi_2 B^2\right)}\left(\phi_0+\varepsilon_t\right)$$

The conditional mean and variance of AR(2), taking X_{t-1} and X_{t-2} as constants, are as follows:

$$\mathrm{E}\left[X_t \mid X_{t-1},X_{t-2}\right]=\phi_0+\phi_1 X_{t-1}+\phi_2 X_{t-2}$$

$$\mathrm{var}\left[X_t \mid X_{t-1},X_{t-2}\right]=\sigma^2$$

Assuming $\{X_t\}$ is stationary, then the unconditional expectation is as follows:

$$\mathrm{E}\left[X_t\ \right]=\mathrm{E}\left[\phi_0+\phi_1 X_{t-1}+\phi_2 X_{t-2}+\varepsilon_t\right]$$

$$=\phi_0+\phi_1\mathrm{E}\left[X_{t-1}\right]+\phi_2\mathrm{E}\left[X_{t-2}\right]$$

$$=\phi_0+\phi_1\mathrm{E}\left[X_t\right]+\phi_2\mathrm{E}\left[X_t\right]$$

That is:

$$(1-\phi_1-\phi_2)\mathrm{E}\left[X_t\right]=\phi_0$$

$$\mathrm{E}\left[X_t\right]=\frac{\phi_0}{1-\phi_1-\phi_2}$$

The unconditional variance is a bit more complicated to compute because you need to account for the covariance between X_{t-1} and X_{t-2}, which is nonzero. You can use the ACVF to compute the variance, which is the same as autocovariance at lag 0, $\gamma(0)$.

Assume that AR(2) is a stationary process having a constant mean μ; then the demeaned process is as follows:

$$X_t-\mu=\phi_1\left(X_{t-1}-\mu\right)+\phi_2\left(X_{t-2}-\mu\right)+\varepsilon_t$$

Or equivalently:

$$\tilde{X}_t=\phi_1\tilde{X}_{t-1}+\phi_2\tilde{X}_{t-2}+\varepsilon_t$$

Then, the covariance between the demeaned variable and the error is as follows:

$$\mathrm{E}\left[\varepsilon_t\tilde{X}_t\right]=\mathrm{E}\left[\varepsilon_t\left(\phi_1\tilde{X}_{t-1}+\phi_2\tilde{X}_{t-2}+\varepsilon_t\right)\right]$$

$$=\phi_1\mathrm{E}\left[\varepsilon_t\tilde{X}_{t-1}\right]+\phi_2\mathrm{E}\left[\varepsilon_t\tilde{X}_{t-2}\right]+E\left[\varepsilon_t^2\right]=\sigma^2$$

The ACVF for AR(2) is as follows:

$$E\left[\tilde{X}_t\tilde{X}_{t-j}\right]=E\left[\left(\phi_1\tilde{X}_{t-1}+\phi_2\tilde{X}_{t-2}+\varepsilon_t\right)\tilde{X}_{t-j}\right]$$

$$=E\left[\phi_1\tilde{X}_{t-1}\tilde{X}_{t-j}+\phi_2\tilde{X}_{t-2}\tilde{X}_{t-j}+\varepsilon_t\tilde{X}_{t-j}\right]$$

$$=\phi_1E\left[\tilde{X}_{t-1}\tilde{X}_{t-j}\right]+\phi_2E\left[\tilde{X}_{t-2}\tilde{X}_{t-j}\right]$$

That is:

$$\gamma(j)=\phi_1\gamma(j-1)+\phi_2\gamma(j-2)$$

The initial conditions are given by the following:

$$\gamma(0)=E\left[\tilde{X}_t\tilde{X}_t\right]=E\left[\tilde{X}_t\left(\phi_1\tilde{X}_{t-1}+\phi_2\tilde{X}_{t-2}+\varepsilon_t\right)\right]$$

$$=E\left[\phi_1\tilde{X}_t\tilde{X}_{t-1}+\phi_2\tilde{X}_t\tilde{X}_{t-2}+\tilde{X}_t\varepsilon_t\right]$$

$$=\phi_1E\left[\tilde{X}_t\tilde{X}_{t-1}\right]+\phi_2E\left[\tilde{X}_t\tilde{X}_{t-2}\right]+E\left[\tilde{X}_t\varepsilon_t\right]$$

$$=\phi_1\gamma(1)+\phi_2\gamma(2)+\sigma^2$$

$$\gamma(1)=\phi_1\gamma(0)+\phi_2\gamma(-2)=\phi_1\gamma(0)+\phi_2\gamma(2)$$

$$\gamma(2)=\phi_1\gamma(1)+\phi_2\gamma(0)$$

The system of linear equations is as follows:

$$\left\{\begin{array}{c}\gamma(0)=\phi_1\gamma(1)+\phi_2\gamma(2)+\sigma^2\\ \gamma(1)=\phi_1\gamma(0)+\phi_2\gamma(2)\\ \gamma(2)=\phi_1\gamma(1)+\phi_2\gamma(0)\end{array}\right\}$$

You can solve for $\gamma(0)=E\left[\tilde{X}_t\tilde{X}_t\right]$, $\gamma(1)$ and $\gamma(2)$, and then you can use the recursive relationship to compute $\gamma(j)$ for $j = 1, 2, ...$

The ACF is as follows:

$$\rho(j)=\phi_1\rho(j-1)+\phi_2\rho(j-2),\ j=1,2,\ldots$$

Likewise, the initial conditions are given by the following:

$$\rho(0)=1$$

$$\rho(1)=\phi_1\rho(0)+\phi_2\rho(-1)=\phi_1\rho(0)+\phi_2\rho(1)$$

$$\rho(1)=\frac{\phi_1}{1-\phi_2}$$

Doing more algebra, you get the variance of the variable as follows:

$$\mathrm{E}\left[\tilde{X}_t\tilde{X}_t\right]=\gamma(0)=\frac{1}{1-\phi_1\rho(1)-\phi_2\rho(2)}\sigma^2$$

The following code constructs this AR(2) model and computes the ACVF and ACF for it:

$$X_t = 1.2X_{t-1} - 0.35X_{t-2} + \varepsilon_t$$

```
// define an AR(2) model
val ar2 = ARModel(
        doubleArrayOf(1.2, -0.35)
)
// compute the autocovariance function for the model
val acvf2 = AutoCovariance(ar2)
for (i in 1 until nLags) {
    println(String.format("The acvf of the AR(2) model at lag%d = %f", i, acvf2.evaluate(i.
toDouble())))
}
println("")
// compute the autocorrelation function for the model
val acf2 = AutoCorrelation(ar2, 10)
for (i in 0 until nLags) {
    println(String.format("The acf of the AR(2) model at lag%d = %f", i, acf2.evaluate(i.
toDouble())))
}
```

The output is as follows:

```
the acvf of the AR(2) model at lag1 = 4.826546
the acvf of the AR(2) model at lag2 = 3.891403
the acvf of the AR(2) model at lag3 = 2.980392
the acvf of the AR(2) model at lag4 = 2.214480
the acvf of the AR(2) model at lag5 = 1.614238
the acvf of the AR(2) model at lag6 = 1.162018
the acvf of the AR(2) model at lag7 = 0.829438
the acvf of the AR(2) model at lag8 = 0.588620
the acvf of the AR(2) model at lag9 = 0.416040
the acf of the AR(2) model at lag0 = 1.000000
the acf of the AR(2) model at lag1 = 0.888889
the acf of the AR(2) model at lag2 = 0.716667
the acf of the AR(2) model at lag3 = 0.548889
the acf of the AR(2) model at lag4 = 0.407833
the acf of the AR(2) model at lag5 = 0.297289
the acf of the AR(2) model at lag6 = 0.214005
the acf of the AR(2) model at lag7 = 0.152755
the acf of the AR(2) model at lag8 = 0.108404
the acf of the AR(2) model at lag9 = 0.076621
```

Figure 15-11 plots the ACF of the model. The values exponentially decay to 0.

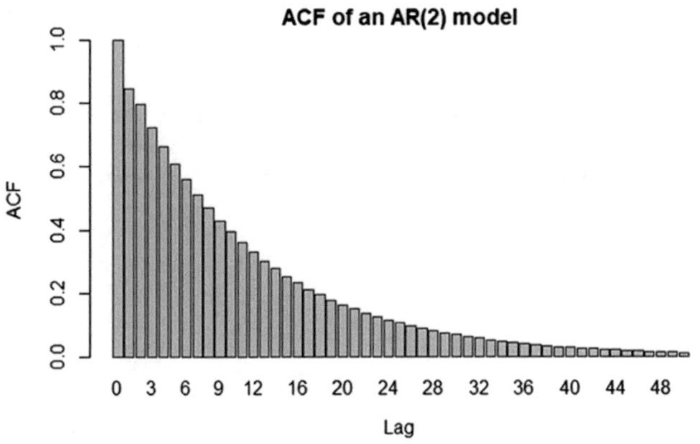

Figure 15-11. *ACF of the AR(2) process when $\phi_1 = 1.2$, $\phi_2 = -0.35$*

AR(p)

AR(1) and AR(2) are important special cases of the more general AP(p) model of order *p*. It is defined as follows:

$$X_t = \phi_0 + \phi_1 X_{t-1} + \phi_2 X_{t-2} + \ldots + \phi_p X_{t-p} + \varepsilon_t$$

Where $\{\phi_i\}$ are the autoregressive coefficients and ε_t is the white noise.

In terms of the backshift operator, you write the following:

$$X_t = \phi_0 + \phi_1 B X_t + \phi_2 B^2 X_t + \ldots + \phi_p B^p X_t + \varepsilon_t$$

$$X_t - \phi_1 B X_t - \phi_2 B^2 X_t - \ldots - \phi_p B^p X_t = \phi_0 + \varepsilon_t$$

$$\underbrace{\left(1 - \phi_1 B - \phi_2 B^2 - \ldots - \phi_p L^p\right)}_{\phi(B)} X_t = \phi_0 + \varepsilon_t$$

$$\phi(B) X_t = \phi_0 + \varepsilon_t$$

$$X_t = \frac{\phi_0 + \varepsilon_t}{\phi(B)}$$

When the polynomial division on the right side is carried out, the polynomial in the backshift operator applied to ε_t has an infinite order, meaning that an infinite number of ε_t, ε_{t-1}, ε_{t-2}, ... appear on the right side of the equation. So, an AR model can be considered a sum of an infinite number of past error terms. Consequently, a one-time shock affects values of the evolving variable permanently and infinitely far into the future. For example, consider the AR(1) model $X_t = \phi_0 + \phi_1 X_{t-1} + \varepsilon_t$. A nonzero value for ε_t at, say, time $t = 1$ affects X_1 by the amount ε_1. Then by the AR equation for X_2 in terms of X_1, this affects X_2 by the amount $\phi_1 \varepsilon_1$. Then by the AR equation for X_3 in terms of X_2, this affects X_3 by the amount $\phi_1^2 \varepsilon_1$. Continuing this process shows that the effect of ε_1 never ends, although if the process is stationary, then the effect diminishes toward zero in the limit.

The simplest AR process is AR(0), which has no dependence between the terms. Only the error term contributes to the output of the process. AR(0) corresponds to white noise in Figure 15-12. For an AR(1) process with a positive ϕ_1, only the previous term in the process and the noise term contribute to the output. If ϕ_1 is close to 0, then the process still looks like white noise, but as ϕ_1 approaches 1, the output gets a larger contribution from the previous term relative to the noise. This results in a "smoothing" or integration of the output, similar to a low pass filter in Figure 15-12. For an AR(2) process, the previous two terms and the noise term contribute to the output. If both ϕ_1 and ϕ_2 are positive, the output will resemble a low-pass filter, with the high frequency part of the noise decreased. If ϕ_1 is positive while ϕ_2 is negative, the process favors changes in sign between terms of the process. The output oscillates. This can be likened to edge detection or detection of changes in direction, as shown in Figure 15-12.

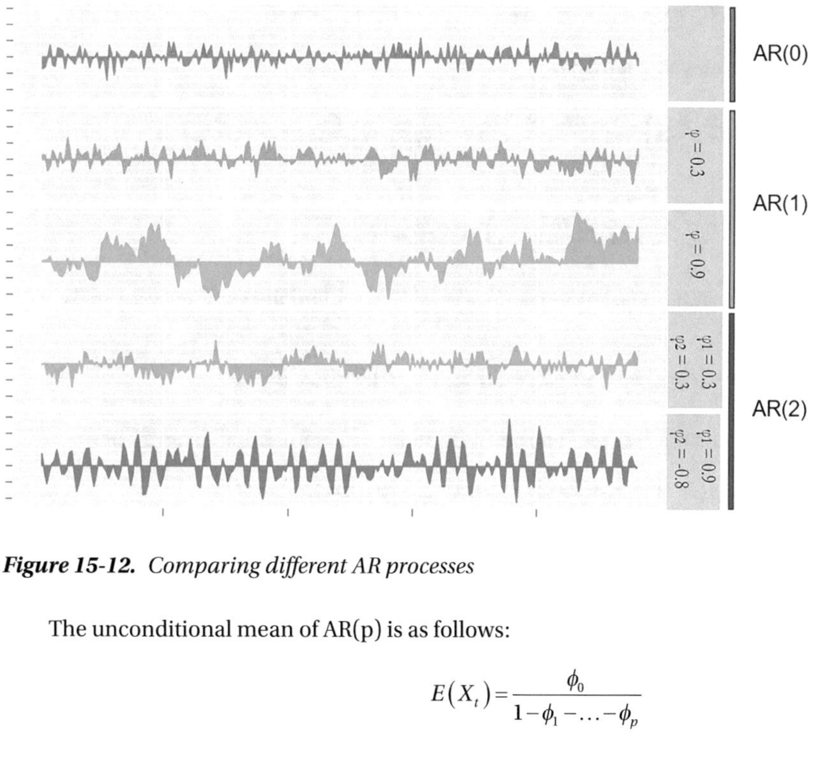

***Figure 15-12.** Comparing different AR processes*

The unconditional mean of AR(p) is as follows:

$$E(X_t) = \frac{\phi_0}{1 - \phi_1 - \ldots - \phi_p}$$

Estimation

Given a time series of data, you may want to construct an AR(p) model for it. The first thing you need to do is identify the order of lags, p. This determines the specification of an AR model. You then only need to determine the autoregressive coefficients ϕ_i, $0 \le I \le p$.

Consider an AR(p) model:

$$X_t = \phi_0 + \phi_1 X_{t-1} + \phi_2 X_{t-2} + \ldots + \phi_p X_{t-p} + \varepsilon_t$$

Intuitively, as X_t is a linear combination of X_{t-i}, $1 \le i \le p$, then X_{t-i} for $i \ge p + 1$ has no influence on X_t after accounting for the variables in between, namely, X_{t-i}, $1 \le i \le p$. $X_t - \mathrm{E}[X_t \mid X_{t-i}, 1 \le i \le p] = \varepsilon_t$ is just white noise and is thus not correlated with anything before t, such as X_{t-i} for $i \ge p + 1$. It can be proven that the PACF, that is, the correlation between X_t and X_{t+k} after removing the influence of the intermediate variables X_{t-i}, $i \ge p + 1$

of an AR(p) model vanishes (equals 0) after lag p. You can use this fact to determine the appropriate lag of an AR model using a PACF plot such as the one for the monthly S&P 500 returns. Put another way, the number of nonzero partial autocorrelations tells the order of the AR model.

After fixing a p, there are many ways to estimate the coefficients. One way is the Yule-Walker equations. NM Dev does not use the Yule-Walker equations for AR estimation, but we include the discussion here for completeness. Starting with the demeaned AR model ($\phi_0 = 0$), you have this:

$$\tilde{X}_t = \phi_1 \tilde{X}_{t-1} + \phi_2 \tilde{X}_{t-2} + \ldots + \phi_p \tilde{X}_{t-p} + \varepsilon_t$$

Multiplying X_{t-k} on both sides, you get this:

$$\tilde{X}_t \tilde{X}_{t-k} = \phi_1 \tilde{X}_{t-1} \tilde{X}_{t-k} + \phi_2 \tilde{X}_{t-2} \tilde{X}_{t-k} + \ldots + \phi_p \tilde{X}_{t-p} \tilde{X}_{t-k} + \varepsilon_t \tilde{X}_{t-k}$$

Taking expectation on both sides, you get this:

$$E\left(\tilde{X}_t \tilde{X}_{t-k}\right) = \phi_1 E\left(\tilde{X}_{t-1} \tilde{X}_{t-k}\right) + \phi_2 E\left(\tilde{X}_{t-2} \tilde{X}_{t-k}\right) + \ldots + \phi_p E\left(\tilde{X}_{t-p} \tilde{X}_{t-k}\right) + E\left(\varepsilon_t \tilde{X}_{t-k}\right)$$

$$= \phi_1 E\left(\tilde{X}_{t-1} \tilde{X}_{t-k}\right) + \phi_2 E\left(\tilde{X}_{t-2} \tilde{X}_{t-k}\right) + \ldots + \phi_p E\left(\tilde{X}_{t-p} \tilde{X}_{t-k}\right)$$

If you rewrite it using autocovariance $\gamma(k) = \text{cov}\left(\tilde{X}_t, \tilde{X}_{t+k}\right) = \text{E}\left(\tilde{X}_t \tilde{X}_{t+k}\right)$ and the symmetry property $\gamma(k) = \gamma(-k)$, you get this:

$$\gamma(k) = \phi_1 \gamma(k-1) + \phi_2 \gamma(k-2) + \ldots + \phi_p \gamma(k-p), k = 1, \ldots, p$$

Dividing by the variance gives the equivalent in terms of the autocorrelation function as follows:

$$\rho(k) = \phi_1 \rho(k-1) + \phi_2 \rho(k-2) + \ldots + \phi_p \rho(k-p), k = 1, \ldots, p$$

Expanding it (note that $\rho(0) = 1$ and $\rho(k) = \rho(-k)$), you get this:

$$\begin{cases} \rho(1) = \phi_1 \rho(0) + \phi_2 \rho(-1) + \ldots + \phi_p \rho(1-p) = \phi_1 + \phi_2 \rho(1) + \ldots + \phi_p \rho(p-1) \\ \rho(2) = \phi_1 \rho(1) + \phi_2 \rho(0) + \ldots + \phi_p \rho(2-p) = \phi_1 \rho(1) + \phi_2 + \ldots + \phi_p \rho(p-2) \\ \vdots \end{cases}$$

Or in matrix form, you get this:

$$\begin{bmatrix} 1 & \rho(1) & \cdots & \rho(p-1) \\ \rho(1) & 1 & \cdots & \rho(p-2) \\ \vdots & \vdots & \vdots & \vdots \\ \rho(p-1) & \rho(p-2) & \cdots & 1 \end{bmatrix} \begin{bmatrix} \phi_1 \\ \phi_2 \\ \vdots \\ \phi_p \end{bmatrix} = \begin{bmatrix} \rho(1) \\ \rho(2) \\ \vdots \\ \rho(p) \end{bmatrix}$$

This is known as the Yule-Walker equation.

In the case of AR(2), you get this:

$$\begin{bmatrix} 1 & \rho(1) \\ \rho(1) & 1 \end{bmatrix} \begin{bmatrix} \phi_1 \\ \phi_2 \end{bmatrix} = \begin{bmatrix} \rho(1) \\ \rho(2) \end{bmatrix}$$

Solving this system of linear equation gives the following:

$$\begin{cases} \phi_1 = \dfrac{\rho(1)(1-\rho(2))}{1-\rho^2(1)} \\ \phi_2 = \dfrac{\rho(2)-\rho^2(1)}{1-\rho^2(1)} \end{cases}$$

To estimate $\hat{\phi}_i$, you simply replace $\rho(i)$ in the formulas by the estimated autocorrelations $\hat{\rho}(i)$ from the data.

NM Dev uses the method of maximum likelihood to estimate the coefficients. The `ConditionalSumOfSquares` class implements this estimation algorithm. The following code demonstrates the estimation of coefficients from data. It first defines an AR(2) model. The `ARIMASim` class takes an AR model and generates a time series of random numbers according to the model. Then, you estimate another AR(2) model by first identifying the order of the lag (which is 2) using PACF and then fitting the time series. The estimated coefficients should match the coefficients in the original model.

```
// create a random number generator from the AR model
val sim = ARIMASim(ar2)
sim.seed(1234567890L)

// generate a random time series
val T = 500 // length of the time series
var x: DoubleArray = DoubleArray(T)
for (i in 0 until T) {
    // call the RNG to generate random numbers according to the specification
    x[i] = sim.nextDouble()
}
// determine the cutoff lag using partial autocorrelation
val acf2_hat = SamplePartialAutoCorrelation(SimpleTimeSeries(x))
for (i in 1 until 5) {
    println(String.format("The empirical pacf of a time series at lag%d: %f", i, acf2_hat.
    evaluate(i)))
}
// fit an AR(2) model using the data
val fit = ConditionalSumOfSquares(
                x,
                2, // the AR order
                0,
                0)
println(String.format("phi: %s", Arrays.toString(fit.getARMAModel().phi())))
println(String.format("var of error term: %s", fit.`var`()))
```

The output is as follows:

```
the empirical pacf of a time series at lag1: 0.870717
the empirical pacf of a time series at lag2: -0.361752
the empirical pacf of a time series at lag3: 0.006046
the empirical pacf of a time series at lag4: 0.050507
phi: [1.0, 1.1861775215396104, -0.3622433585852758]
var of error term: 1.0322854887339732
```

The original model used to generate the random time series is $\begin{cases} \phi_1 = 1.2 \\ \phi_2 = -0.35 \\ \sigma^2 = 1 \end{cases}$.

The estimated coefficients and estimated variance are $\begin{cases} \hat{\phi}_1 = 1.19 \\ \hat{\phi}_2 = -0.36 \\ \hat{\sigma}^2 = 1.03 \end{cases}$. They are reasonably close enough.

Forecast

Given an AR(p) model, as shown here:

$$X_t = \phi_0 + \phi_1 X_{t-1} + \phi_2 X_{t-2} + \ldots + \phi_p X_{t-p} + \varepsilon_t$$

The one-step forecast f_{t+1} is the conditional expectation of X_{t+1}, which is a linear combination of the last p observations.

$$f_{t+1} = E(X_{t+1} | X_1, \ldots, X_t) = \phi_0 + \phi_1 X_t + \phi_2 X_{t-1} + \ldots + \phi_p X_{t+1-p}$$

For the two-step forecast f_{t+2}, you do not have the observation at time $t + 1$, but you have the forecast f_{t+1} in lieu of it. That is, you have this:

$$f_{t+2} = E(X_{t+2} | X_1, \ldots, X_t) = E(\phi_0 + \phi_1 X_{t+1} + \phi_2 X_t + \ldots + \phi_p X_{t+2-p} + \varepsilon_{t+2} | X_1, \ldots X_t)$$

$$= \phi_0 + \phi_1 E(X_{t+1} | X_1, \ldots, X_t) + \phi_2 X_t + \ldots + \phi_p X_{t+2-p}$$

$$= \phi_0 + \phi_1 f_{t+1} + \phi_2 X_t + \ldots + \phi_p X_{t+2-p}$$

It is important to differentiate between a two-step forecast, f_{t+2}, and a one-step forecast at one step later, $f_{t+2|t+1}$. The former one is made without the observation at time $t + 1$, while the latter incorporates the information because the forecast is made in the future after that information comes out. Let's compare them. This one:

$$f_{t+2} = E(X_{t+2} | X_1, \ldots, X_t)$$

versus the following:

$$f_{t+2|t+1} = E(X_{t+2} | X_1, \ldots, X_t, X_{t+1})$$

In general, first, you use t to refer to the first period for which data is not yet available. You substitute the known preceding values X_{t-i}, $1 \le i \le p$ into the autoregressive equation while setting the error term ε_t equal to zero (because you forecast X_t to equal its expected value and the expected value of the unobserved error term is zero). The output of the autoregressive equation is the forecast for the first unobserved period. Next, you use the autoregressive equation to make the forecast, with one difference: the value of X_{t+1} one period prior to the one now being forecast is not known, so its expected value, that is, the predicted value arising from the previous forecasting step, is used instead. Then for future periods the same procedure is used, each time using one more forecast value on the right side of the predictive equation until, after p predictions, all p right-side values are predicted values from preceding steps. You get this:

$$f_{t+3} = \phi_0 + \phi_1 f_{t+2} + \phi_2 f_{t+1} + \ldots + \phi_p X_{t+3-p}$$

$$\vdots$$

$$f_{t+s} = \phi_0 + \phi_1 f_{t+(s-1)} + \phi_2 f_{t+(s-2)} + \ldots + \phi_p X_{t+(s-p)}, s > p$$

In NM Dev, the ARMAForecast class takes a model specification and computes the next n-step forecasts. The class signature is as follows:

```
/**
 * Constructs a forecaster for a time series assuming ARMA model.
 *
 * @param xt   a time series
 * @param arma the ARMA specification
 */
public ARMAForecast(IntTimeTimeSeries xt, ARMAModel arma);
/**
 * Gets the next forecast.
 *
 * @return the next forecast
 */
public Forecast next();
/**
 * Gets the next n-step forecasts.
 *
 * @param nSteps the number of steps to forecast
 * @return all the n-step forecasts
 */
public List<Forecast> next(int nSteps);
```

The following code snippet continues the previous example and computes the next ten n-step forecasts:

```
// make forecast
val forecast_ar2 = ARMAForecast(SimpleTimeSeries(x), ar2)
println("The forecasts for the AR(2) model are")
for (j in 0 until 10) {
    println(forecast_ar2.next())
}
```

The output is as follows:

```
The forecasts for the AR(2) model are
[501]: 0.355169 (1.000000)
[502]: 0.370225 (2.440000)
[503]: 0.319961 (3.628100)
[504]: 0.254374 (4.416644)
[505]: 0.193263 (4.884637)
[506]: 0.142884 (5.144859)
[507]: 0.103819 (5.283771)
```

```
[508]: 0.074574 (5.355976)
[509]: 0.053152 (5.392841)
[510]: 0.037681 (5.411433)
```

15.2.2. MA Model

The moving-average model specifies that the output variable depends linearly on the current and various past values of an error term, random shocks, or white noise. Contrary to the AR model, which is stationary only when the autoregressive coefficients satisfy certain conditions, the finite MA model is always stationary.

The moving-average model should not be confused with the moving average function or method, a distinct concept. When people say moving average of data, as in financial application or technical analysis, they actually mean a (weighted) average of the data rather than a (weighted) average of the unobservable error terms. Even more confusing, a moving average (or weighted average) of data is actually an autoregressive process. For example, a simple moving average (SMA) is the unweighted mean of the previous k data points.

$$SMA_k = \frac{x_t + x_{t-1} + \ldots + x_{t-k+1}}{k}$$

This is an AR process of order k with all coefficients equal to $\frac{1}{k}$.

In fact, a large class of the technical indicators or technical rules consists of different moving averages of past prices. They are simply finite linear combinations of past prices or returns, and hence they are AR models. Emmanual & Stephen (2002) analyze these trading rules and prove mathematically the condition under which they would be profitable. One necessary condition is that the stock traded needs to have autocorrelation. However, there is no serial dependency in stocks. Both theoretical (the efficient market hypothesis) and empirical (no significant serial correlation) evidence, as far as I am aware of, suggests no scientific reason for why trading using technical analysis would be profitable other than luck. When enough people are doing it, some are bound to make money, just like a competition of flipping coins where the winner is the one who gets 20 heads in a row. It is even easier considering that the U.S. market has been going up since I was born. Interested readers may find more details in my other book, *Numerical Methods in Quantitative Trading.*

MA(1)

A moving-average model of the order 1, MA(1), model is as follows:

$$X_t = \theta_0 + \theta_1\varepsilon_{t-1} + \varepsilon_t$$

Where θ_0 is a constant and θ_1 is the autoregressive coefficient, and ε_t is the stochastic or random or error term. It is white noise with the following:

- Zero mean, $E[\varepsilon_t] = 0$
- Constant variance σ^2, $\text{var}[\varepsilon_t] = E[\varepsilon_t\varepsilon_t] = \sigma^2$
- Independently distributed, $E[\varepsilon_t\varepsilon_{t-1}] = 0$

The unconditional mean of X_t is as follows:

$$E(X_t) = E(\theta_0 + \theta_1\varepsilon_{t-1} + \varepsilon_t) = E(\theta_0) + \theta_1 E(\varepsilon_{t-1}) + E(\varepsilon_t) = \theta_0$$

The unconditional variance of X_t is as follows:

$$\gamma(0) = \text{var}(X_t) = \text{E}(X_t^2) - [\text{E}(X_t)]^2 = \text{E}(X_t^2)$$

$$= \text{E}\left((\theta_0 + \theta_1\varepsilon_{t-1} + \varepsilon_t)^2\right)$$

$$= \text{E}\left(\theta_0^2 + \theta_1^2\varepsilon_{t-1}^2 + \varepsilon_t^2\right)$$

$$= \theta_1^2\text{E}(\varepsilon_{t-1}^2) + \text{E}(\varepsilon_t^2)$$

$$= \theta_1^2\sigma^2 + \sigma^2$$

$$= (1 + \theta_1^2)\sigma^2$$

The demeaned time series is as follows:

$$\tilde{X}_t = X_t - \theta_0$$

The ACVF for X_t is as follows:

$$\gamma(1) = \text{E}(\tilde{X}_t\tilde{X}_t) = \text{E}\left((\varepsilon_t + \theta_1\varepsilon_{t-1})(\varepsilon_{t-1} + \theta_1\varepsilon_{t-2})\right) = \theta_1\text{E}(\varepsilon_{t-1}^2) = \theta_1\sigma^2$$

$$\gamma(k) = \text{E}(\tilde{X}_t\tilde{X}_{t-k}) = \text{E}\left((\varepsilon_t + \theta_1\varepsilon_{t-1})(\varepsilon_{t-k} + \theta_1\varepsilon_{t-k-1})\right) = 0 \text{, k} > 1$$

The ACF for X_t is as follows:

$$\rho(0) = \frac{\gamma(0)}{\gamma(0)} = 1$$

$$\rho(1) = \frac{\gamma(1)}{\gamma(0)} = \frac{\theta_1\sigma^2}{(1 + \theta_1^2)\sigma^2} = \frac{\theta_1}{1 + \theta_1^2}$$

$$\rho(k) = \frac{\gamma(k)}{\gamma(0)} = \frac{0}{(1 + \theta_1^2)\sigma^2} = 0, k > 1$$

An example of an MA(1) model is as follows:

$$X_t = 0.8\varepsilon_{t-1} + \varepsilon_t$$

In NM Dev, an MA model can be constructed using the MAModel class. The following code snippet constructs the previous model:

```
// define an MA(1) model
val ma1 = MAModel(
        doubleArrayOf(0.8) // theta_1 = 0.8
)
```

```
val nLags = 10
// compute the autocovariance function for the model
val acvf1 = AutoCovariance(ma1)
for (i in 0 until nLags) {
    println(String.format("the acvf of the MA(1) model at lag%d = %f", i, acvf1.evaluate(i.
    toDouble())))
}
println("")
// compute the autocorrelation function for the model
val acf1 = AutoCorrelation(ma1, nLags)
for (i in 0 until nLags) {
    println(String.format("the acf of the MA(1) model at lag%d = %f", i, acf1.evaluate(i.
    toDouble())))
}
```

The output is as follows:

```
the acvf of the MA(1) model at lag0 = 1.640000
the acvf of the MA(1) model at lag1 = 0.800000
the acvf of the MA(1) model at lag2 = 0.000000
the acvf of the MA(1) model at lag3 = 0.000000
the acvf of the MA(1) model at lag4 = 0.000000
the acvf of the MA(1) model at lag5 = 0.000000
the acvf of the MA(1) model at lag6 = 0.000000
the acvf of the MA(1) model at lag7 = 0.000000
the acvf of the MA(1) model at lag8 = 0.000000
the acvf of the MA(1) model at lag9 = 0.000000
the acf of the MA(1) model at lag0 = 1.000000
the acf of the MA(1) model at lag1 = 0.487805
the acf of the MA(1) model at lag2 = 0.000000
the acf of the MA(1) model at lag3 = 0.000000
the acf of the MA(1) model at lag4 = 0.000000
the acf of the MA(1) model at lag5 = 0.000000
the acf of the MA(1) model at lag6 = 0.000000
the acf of the MA(1) model at lag7 = 0.000000
the acf of the MA(1) model at lag8 = 0.000000
the acf of the MA(1) model at lag9 = 0.000000
```

Note that all the ACVF and ACF are 0 after lag 1, $\gamma(k) = 0$, $k > 1$. This is a useful property that you can use to identify the order for an MA model. See Figure 15-13.

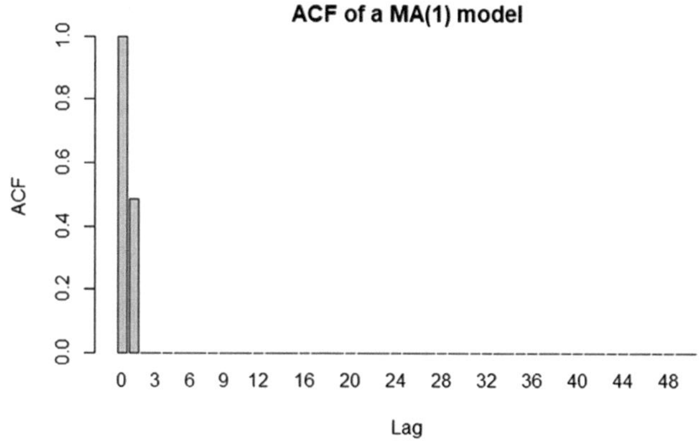

Figure 15-13. *ACF of the MA(1) process when $\theta_1 = 0.8$*

MA(p)

In general, an MA(q) model with order q is as follows:

$$X_t = \theta_0 + \theta_1 \varepsilon_{t-1} + \theta_2 \varepsilon_{t-2} + \ldots + \theta_q \varepsilon_{t-q} + \varepsilon_t$$

Where θ_t are the moving-average coefficients.
Equivalently, you can write this using the backshift operator:

$$X_t = \theta_0 + \varepsilon_t + \theta_1 B \varepsilon_t + \theta_2 B^2 \varepsilon_t + \ldots + \theta_q B^q \varepsilon_t$$

$$X_t = \theta_0 + \underbrace{\left(1 + \theta_1 B + \theta_2 B^2 + \ldots + \theta_q B^q\right)}_{\theta(L)} \varepsilon_t$$

$$X_t = \theta_0 + \theta(B) \varepsilon_t$$

Where θ_0 is where the process is at time 0, and ε_t is the white noise.
The mean of X_t is as follows:

$$\mathrm{E}(X_t) = \mathrm{E}\left(\theta_0 + \theta_1 \varepsilon_{t-1} + \theta_2 \varepsilon_{t-2} + \ldots + \theta_q \varepsilon_{t-q} + \varepsilon_t\right) = \mathrm{E}(\theta_0) = \theta_0$$

The variance of X_t is as follows:

$$\mathrm{var}(X_t) = \mathrm{var}\left(\theta_0 + \theta_1 \varepsilon_{t-1} + \theta_2 \varepsilon_{t-2} + \ldots + \theta_q \varepsilon_{t-q} + \varepsilon_t\right)$$

$$= \mathrm{E}\left(\left(\theta_0 + \theta_1 \varepsilon_{t-1} + \theta_2 \varepsilon_{t-2} + \ldots + \theta_q \varepsilon_{t-q} + \varepsilon_t\right)^2\right)$$

$$= \left(1 + \theta_1^2 + \ldots + \theta_q^2\right)\sigma^2$$

Combining both, this is saying that an MA process over time is just bouncing up and down around where it starts off θ_0 with a constant variance, $\left(1+\theta_1^2+\ldots+\theta_q^2\right)\sigma^2$. The moving-average model is essentially a finite impulse response filter applied to white noise, with some additional interpretation placed on it. The role of the random shocks in the MA model differs from their role in the AR model in two ways. First, they are propagated to future values of the time series directly; for example, in an MA model, past shocks like ε_{t-1} appear directly on the right side of the equation for X_t. In contrast, in an AR model, ε_{t-1} does not appear on the right side of the X_t equation. It does appear on the right side of the X_{t-1} equation, and X_{t-1} appears on the right side of the X_t equation, giving only an indirect effect of ε_{t-1} on X_{t-1}. Second, in the MA model, a shock affects the time series only for the current period and q periods into the future; in contrast, in the AR model a shock affects the time-series values permanently and infinitely far into the future, because ε_t affects X_t, which affects X_{t+1}, which in turn affects X_{t+2}, and so on forever.

The ACVF is as follows:

$$\gamma(k)=\begin{cases}\sigma^2\sum_{i=0}^{q-k}\theta_i\theta_{i+k}, k\le q\\ 0, k>q\end{cases}$$

Where $\theta_0 = 1$.

For example, for MA(2), you have the ACVF as follows:

$$\begin{cases}\gamma(0)=\left(1+\theta_1^2+\theta_2^2\right)\sigma^2\\ \gamma(1)=\left(\theta_1+\theta_1\theta_2\right)\sigma^2\\ \gamma(2)=\theta_2^2\sigma^2\end{cases}$$

And the ACF is as follows:

$$\begin{cases}\rho(0)=1\\ \rho(1)=\dfrac{\left(\theta_1+\theta_1\theta_2\right)}{1+\theta_1^2+\theta_2^2}\\ \rho(2)=\dfrac{\theta_2^2\sigma^2}{1+\theta_1^2+\theta_2^2}\end{cases}$$

The following code constructs this MA(2) mode and computes the ACVF and ACF, as shown here:

$$X_t=\varepsilon_t-0.2\varepsilon_{t-1}+0.01\varepsilon_{t-2}$$

```
// define an MA(2) model
val ma2 = MAModel(
        doubleArrayOf(-0.2, 0.01) // the moving-average coefficients
)
val acvf2 = AutoCovariance(ma2)
for (i in 1 until 10) {
    println(String.format("The acvf of the MA(2) model at lag%d: %f", i, acvf2.evaluate(i.
    toDouble())))
}
val acf2 = AutoCorrelation(ma2, 10)
```

```
for (i in 0 until 10) {
    println(String.format("The acf of the MA(2) model at lag%d: %f", i, acf2.evaluate(i.
    toDouble())))
}
```

The output is as follows:

```
the acvf of the MA(2) model at lag1: -0.202000
the acvf of the MA(2) model at lag2: 0.010000
the acvf of the MA(2) model at lag3: 0.000000
the acvf of the MA(2) model at lag4: 0.000000
the acvf of the MA(2) model at lag5: 0.000000
the acvf of the MA(2) model at lag6: 0.000000
the acvf of the MA(2) model at lag7: 0.000000
the acvf of the MA(2) model at lag8: 0.000000
the acvf of the MA(2) model at lag9: 0.000000
the acf of the MA(2) model at lag0: 1.000000
the acf of the MA(2) model at lag1: -0.194212
the acf of the MA(2) model at lag2: 0.009614
the acf of the MA(2) model at lag3: 0.000000
the acf of the MA(2) model at lag4: 0.000000
the acf of the MA(2) model at lag5: 0.000000
the acf of the MA(2) model at lag6: 0.000000
the acf of the MA(2) model at lag7: 0.000000
the acf of the MA(2) model at lag8: 0.000000
the acf of the MA(2) model at lag9: 0.000000
```

Note that the PACF and ACF of an MA(2) model with lags bigger than 2 are all zero. See Figure 15-14.

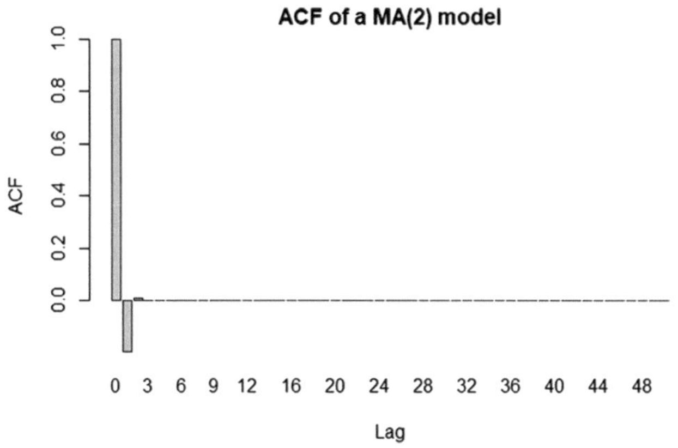

Figure 15-14. *ACF of the MA(2) process when* $\theta_1 = -0.2, \theta_2 = 0.01$

Invertibility and Causality

Consider an MA(1) model:

$$X_t = \theta_0 + \theta_1 \varepsilon_{t-1} + \varepsilon_t$$

Written using the backshift operator, you have this:

$$X_t = \theta_0 + \theta_1 \varepsilon_{t-1} + \varepsilon_t = \theta_0 + \theta_1 B \varepsilon_t + \varepsilon_t = \theta_0 + (1 + \theta_1 B)\varepsilon_t$$

Or equivalently:

$$\varepsilon_t = \frac{X_t - \theta_0}{1 - (-\theta_1 B)}$$

You can write the polynomial division as a sum of an infinite series.

$$\sum_{i=0}^{\infty} a^i = \frac{1}{1-a}, |a| < 1$$

The series converges when $|a| < 1$.
Here $a = (-\theta_1 L)$. When $|\theta_1| < 1$, then you get this:

$$\begin{aligned}\varepsilon_t &= (X_t - \theta_0)\sum_{i=0}^{\infty}(-\theta_1 B)^i = (X_t - \theta_0)(1 - \theta_1 B + \theta_1^2 B^2 - \theta_1^3 B^3 + \ldots)\\ &= (X_t - \theta_0) - \theta_1 B (X_t - \theta_0) + \theta_1^2 B^2 (X_t - \theta_0) - \theta_1^3 B^3 (X_t - \theta_0) + \ldots\\ &= (X_t - \theta_0) - \theta_1 (X_{t-1} - \theta_0) + \theta_1^2 (X_{t-2} - \theta_0) - \theta_1^3 (X_{t-3} - \theta_0) + \ldots\end{aligned}$$

Note that this is an AR process with infinity order, AR(∞).

An MA model is said to be invertible if it is algebraically equivalent to a converging infinite-order AR model. By converging, we mean that the AR coefficients is absolutely summable $\sum_{i=0}^{\infty}|\theta_1^i| < \infty$. This is true for MA(1) when $|\theta_1| < 1$. You should impose the invertibility condition to ensure that there is a unique MA process for a given autocorrelation function. This is a constraint in estimating the moving-average coefficients from data.

On the other hand, consider an AR(1) process (with zero mean for simplicity):

$$X_t = \phi_1 X_{t-1} + \varepsilon_t$$

You can expand it by recursively substituting the past error terms:

$$X_t = \phi_1 X_{t-1} + \varepsilon_t = \phi_1 (\phi_1 X_{t-2} + \varepsilon_{t-1}) + \varepsilon_t = \phi_1^2 X_{t-2} + \phi_1 \varepsilon_{t-1} + \varepsilon_t == \phi_1^3 X_{t-3} + \phi_1^2 \varepsilon_{t-2} + \phi_1 \varepsilon_{t-1} + \varepsilon_t = \ldots \sum_{i=0}^{\infty} \phi_1^i \varepsilon_{t-i}$$

The AR(1) process is called *causal* if it can be written as a sum of infinitely many past error terms and the sequence of MA coefficients is absolutely summable $\sum_{i=0}^{\infty}|\phi_1^i| < \infty$. Causality means that a process is expressible in terms of a linear process of shocks, ε_t. In general, a finite-order MA is an infinite-order AR, and a finite-order AR is an infinite-order MA.

Estimation

To fit a set of data to an MA model, you first determine the order q by looking at the ACF. The ACF of an MA(q) process is zero at lag $q + 1$ and greater. Therefore, you determine the appropriate maximum lag for the estimation by examining the sample autocorrelation function to see where it becomes insignificantly different from zero for all lags beyond a certain lag, which is designated as the maximum lag q.

Finding the MA coefficients is not as easy because the lagged error terms are not observable. In NM Dev, we use the method of maximum likelihood to estimate the coefficients. The `ConditionalSumOfSquares` class implements this estimation algorithm. The following code demonstrates the estimation of coefficients from data. It first defines an MA(2) model. The `ARIMASim` class takes an MA model and generates a time series of random numbers according to the model. Then, you estimate another MA(2) model by first identifying the order of lag (which is 2) using ACF and then fitting the time series. The estimated coefficients should match the coefficients in the original model.

```
// define an MA(2) model
val ma3 = MAModel(
        0.1, // the mean
        doubleArrayOf(-0.5, 0.01), // the moving-average coefficients
        10.0 // the standard deviation
)

// create a random number generator from the MA model
val sim = ARIMASim(ma3)
sim.seed(1234567890L)

// generate a random time series
val T = 500 // length of the time series
var x: DoubleArray = DoubleArray(T)
for (i in 0 until T) {
    // call the RNG to generate random numbers according to the specification
    x[i] = sim.nextDouble()
}

// determine the cutoff lag using autocorrelation
val acf3_hat = SampleAutoCorrelation(SimpleTimeSeries(x))
for (i in 0 until 5) {
    println(String.format("The empirical acf of a time series at lag%d: %f", i, acf3_hat.
    evaluate(i)))
}
// fit an MA(2) model using the data
val fit = ConditionalSumOfSquares(
                x,
                0,
                0,
                2) // the MA order
println(String.format("Theta: %s", Arrays.toString(fit.getARMAModel().theta())))
println(String.format("Var of error term: %s", fit.`var`()))
```

The output is as follows:

```
the empirical acf of a time series at lag0: 1.000000
the empirical acf of a time series at lag1: -0.400610
the empirical acf of a time series at lag2: 0.021983
the empirical acf of a time series at lag3: -0.056620
the empirical acf of a time series at lag4: 0.034655
theta: [1.0, -0.4990165791512235, -0.00881872629264049]
var of error term: 98.13651792771375
```

The original model used to generate the random time series is $\begin{cases} \phi_1 = -0.5 \\ \phi_2 = 0.01 \\ \sigma^2 = 100 \end{cases}$.

The estimated coefficients and estimated variance are $\begin{cases} \hat{\phi}_1 = -0.4990 \\ \hat{\phi}_2 = -0.0088 \\ \hat{\sigma}^2 = 98.1365 \end{cases}$. They are reasonably close.

Forecast

Given an MA(q) process:

$$X_t = \theta_0 + \theta_1 \varepsilon_{t-1} + \theta_2 \varepsilon_{t-2} + \ldots + \theta_q \varepsilon_{t-q} + \varepsilon_t$$

The one-step forecast is as follows:

$$f_{t+1} = E(X_{t+1} | X_1, \ldots, X_t)$$

$$= E\left(\theta_0 + \theta_1 \varepsilon_t + \theta_2 \varepsilon_{t-1} + \ldots + \theta_q \varepsilon_{t-q+1} + \varepsilon_{t+1} \,|\, X_1, \ldots, X_t\right)$$

$$= \theta_0 + \theta_1 \varepsilon_t + \theta_2 \varepsilon_{t-1} + \ldots + \theta_q \varepsilon_{t-q+1}$$

Similarly, for the two-step forecast f_{t+2}, you have this:

$$f_{t+2} = E(X_{t+2} \,|\, X_1, \ldots, X_t)$$

$$= E\left(\theta_0 + \theta_1 \varepsilon_{t+1} + \theta_2 \varepsilon_t + \ldots + \theta_q \varepsilon_{t-q+2} + \varepsilon_{t+2} \,|\, X_1, \ldots X_t\right)$$

$$= \theta_0 + \theta_2 \varepsilon_t + \ldots + \varepsilon_q \varepsilon_{t-q+2}$$

You need to compute the past error terms (innovations). The expectation of any future error term is 0. Therefore, for an n-step forecast where $n > q$, the forecast is the mean of the process θ_0:

$$f_{t+n} = \theta_0, n > p$$

In NM Dev, the `ARMAForecast` class takes a model specification and computes the next n-step forecasts. The following code snippet continues the previous example and computes the next ten n-step forecasts:

```
// make forecast
val forecast_ma3 = ARMAForecast(SimpleTimeSeries(x), ma3)
println("The forecasts for the MA(2) model are")
for (j in 0 until 10) {
    println(forecast_ma3.next())
}
```

The output is as follows:

```
The forecasts for the MA(2) model are
[1001]: -3.918696 (1.000000)
[1002]: 0.180772 (1.250000)
[1003]: 0.100000 (1.250100)
[1004]: 0.100000 (1.250100)
[1005]: 0.100000 (1.250100)
[1006]: 0.100000 (1.250100)
[1007]: 0.100000 (1.250100)
[1008]: 0.100000 (1.250100)
[1009]: 0.100000 (1.250100)
[1010]: 0.100000 (1.250100)
```

Note that all forecasts beyond the next two are simply the mean $\theta_0 = 0.1$.

15.2.3. ARMA Model

The ARMA model combines the AR model and the MA model, where the future values depend on both the past observations and the past innovations (error terms).

ARMA(1,1)

The simplest case is the ARMA(1, 1) model, which combines AR(1) and MA(1). The model structure is as follows (assume $\mu = 0$ or demeaned $X_t - \mu$):

$$X_t = \phi_1 X_{t-1} + \theta_1 \varepsilon_{t-1} + \varepsilon_t$$

Or, it is often written so that AR terms are on the left side of the equation and MA terms are on the right side:

$$X_t - \phi_1 X_{t-1} = \theta_1 \varepsilon_{t-1} + \varepsilon_t$$

Where ε_t is i.i.d. white noise.

When $-\phi_1 \neq \theta_1$, you can write the model in terms of the backshift operator:

$$(1 - \phi_1 B) X_t = (1 + \theta_1 B) \varepsilon_t$$

Or equivalently:

$$X_t = \frac{(1 + \theta_1 B)}{(1 - \phi_1 B)} \varepsilon_t$$

Otherwise, the model becomes just white noise by dividing either $(1 - \phi_1 B)$ or $(1 + \theta_1 B)$ on both sides. Expand the following:

$$\frac{(1+\theta_1 B)}{(1-\phi_1 B)} = \left(1+\phi_1 B+\phi_1^2 B^2+\phi_1^3 B^3+\ldots\right)(1+\theta_1 B)$$

$$=1+\phi_1 B+\phi_1^2 B^2+\phi_1^3 B^3+\ldots+\theta_1 B+\phi_1\theta_1 B^2+\phi_1^2\theta_1 B^3+\phi_1^3\theta_1 B^4+\ldots$$

$$=1+(\phi_1+\theta_1)B+\left(\phi_1^2+\phi_1\theta_1\right)B^2+\left(\phi_1^3+\phi_1^2\theta_1\right)B^3+\ldots$$

$$=1+(\phi_1+\theta_1)B+(\phi_1+\theta_1)\phi_1 B^2+(\phi_1+\theta_1)\phi_1^2 B^3+\ldots$$

$$=\sum_{i=0}^{\infty}\psi_i B^i$$

where $\psi_0 = 1$ and $\psi_i = (\phi_1+\theta_1)\phi_1^{i-1}$.
The MA(∞) representation is therefore as follows:

$$X_t = \varepsilon_t + (\phi_1+\theta_1)\sum_{i=1}^{\infty}\phi_1^{i-1}\varepsilon_{t-i}$$

This representation is valid only when $|\phi_1| < 1$, so ψ_i will not blow up for big i. That is, the causality condition (hence stationarity) for ARMA(1, 1) is that $|\phi_1| < 1$.

In addition, you can write the following:

$$\varepsilon_t = \frac{(1-\phi_1 B)}{(1+\theta_1 B)}X_t$$

Consider this power series expansion:

$$\frac{1}{1+\theta_1 x} = \sum_{i=0}^{\infty}(-\theta_1)^i x^i$$

Combining these two equations, you get the following:

$$\varepsilon_t = \sum_{i=0}^{\infty}(-\theta_1)^i B^i(1-\phi_1 B)X_t = X_t - (\phi_1+\theta_1)\sum_{i=1}^{\infty}(-\theta_1)^{i-1}X_{t-i}$$

This expression is valid only when $|\theta_1| < 1$ so the AR coefficients do not blow up. This is the invertible condition for ARMA(1, 1). Figure 15-15 summarizes the causality and invertibility conditions for an ARMA(1, 1) process and the admissible parameters for it.

$$\begin{cases}-1<\phi_1<1\\-1<\theta_1<1\end{cases}$$

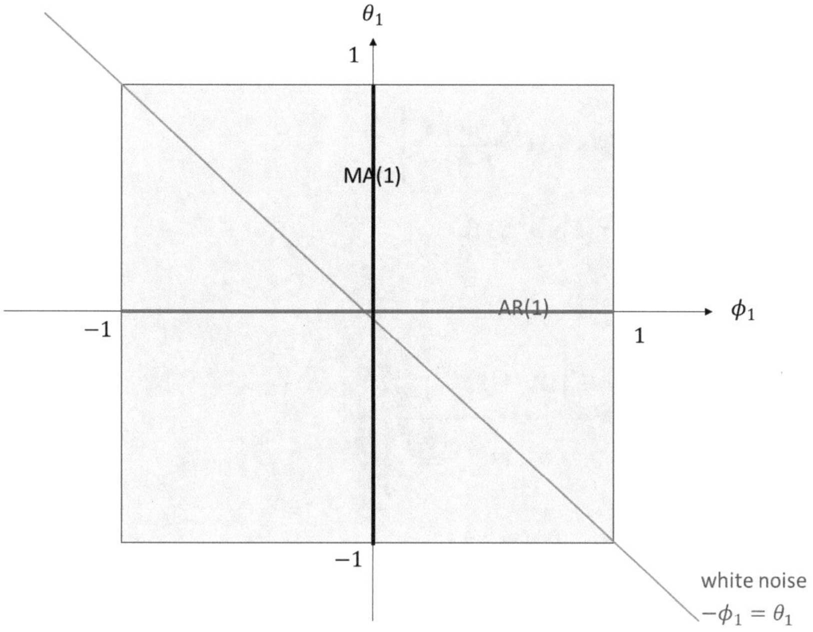

Figure 15-15. *Admissible parameter region for ARMA(1,1)*

You can usually assume an ARMA process to be stationary, causal, and invertible, so you can switch between the AR and MA representations of the time series.

You can compute the ACVF for ARMA(1,1) using the MA form:

$$X_t = \sum_{i=0}^{\infty} \psi_i \varepsilon_{t-i}$$

Then the ACVF is as follows:

$$\gamma(k) = \mathrm{E}(X_t X_{t-k}) = \mathrm{E}\left(\sum_{i=0}^{\infty} \psi_i \varepsilon_{t-i} \sum_{i=0}^{\infty} \psi_i \varepsilon_{t-k-i} \right) = \sigma^2 \sum_{i=o}^{\infty} \psi_i \psi_{i+k}$$

$$\gamma(0) = \sigma^2 \sum_{i=o}^{\infty} \psi_i^2 = \sigma^2 \left[1 + (\phi_1 + \theta_1)^2 \sum_{i=1}^{\infty} \phi_1^{2(i-1)} \right]$$

$$= \sigma^2 \left[1 + \frac{(\phi_1 + \theta_1)^2}{1 - \phi_1^2} \right]$$

$$\gamma(1) = \sigma^2 \sum_{i=o}^{\infty} \psi_i \psi_{i+1}$$

$$= \sigma^2 \left[(\phi_1 + \theta_1) + (\phi_1 + \theta_1)(\phi_1 + \theta_1)\phi_1 + (\phi_1 + \theta_1)\phi_1 (\phi_1 + \theta_1)\phi_1^2 + (\phi_1 + \theta_1)\phi_1^2 (\phi_1 + \theta_1)\phi_1^3 + \ldots \right]$$

$$= \sigma^2\left[(\phi_1+\theta_1)+(\phi_1+\theta_1)^2\phi_1\left(1+\phi_1^2+\phi_1^4+\ldots\right)\right] = \sigma^2\left[(\phi_1+\theta_1)+(\phi_1+\theta_1)^2\phi_1\sum_{i=0}^{\infty}\phi_1^{2i}\right]$$

$$= \sigma^2\left[(\phi_1+\theta_1)+\frac{(\phi_1+\theta_1)^2\phi_1}{1-\phi_1^2}\right]$$

$$\gamma(k) = \phi_1^{k-1}\gamma(1)$$

The ACF is to divide $\gamma(k)$ by $\gamma(0)$.

$$\rho(1) = \frac{\gamma(1)}{\gamma(0)} = \frac{\sigma^2\left[(\phi_1+\theta_1)+\frac{(\phi_1+\theta_1)^2\phi_1}{1-\phi_1^2}\right]}{\sigma^2\left[1+\frac{(\phi_1+\theta_1)^2}{1-\phi_1^2}\right]}$$

$$= \frac{(\phi_1+\theta_1)(1+\phi_1\theta_1)}{1+2\phi_1\theta_1+\theta_1^2}$$

$$\rho(k) = \phi_1^{k-1}\rho(1)$$

Note that when $-\phi_1 = \theta_1$, $\gamma(1) = \gamma(k) = \rho(1) = \rho(k) = 0$. The process is just white noise.

NM Dev uses the ARMAModel class to construct an ARMA process. The class signature is as follows:

```
public class ARMAModel extends ARIMAModel {
    /**
     * Construct a univariate ARMA model.
     *
     * @param mu    the intercept (constant) term
     * @param AR    the AR coefficients (excluding the initial 1); {@code null}
     *              if no AR coefficients
     * @param MA    the MA coefficients (excluding the initial 1); {@code null}
     *              if no MA coefficients
     * @param sigma the white noise variance
     */
    public ARMAModel(double mu, double[] AR, double[] MA, double sigma) {
        super(mu, AR, 0, MA, sigma);
    }
    /**
     * Construct a univariate ARMA model with unit variance.
     *
     * @param mu the intercept (constant) term
     * @param AR the AR coefficients (excluding the initial 1); {@code null} if
     *           no AR coefficients
     * @param MA the MA coefficients (excluding the initial 1); {@code null} if
     *           no MA coefficients
     */
```

```
public ARMAModel(double mu, double[] AR, double[] MA) {
    this(mu, AR, MA, 1);
}
/**
 * Construct a univariate ARMA model with zero-intercept (mu).
 *
 * @param AR    the AR coefficients (excluding the initial 1); {@code null}
 *              if no AR coefficients
 * @param MA    the MA coefficients (excluding the initial 1); {@code null}
 *              if no MA coefficients
 * @param sigma the white noise variance
 */
public ARMAModel(double[] AR, double[] MA, double sigma) {
    this(0, AR, MA, sigma);
}
/**
 * Construct a univariate ARMA model with unit variance and zero-intercept
 * (mu).
 *
 * @param AR the AR coefficients (excluding the initial 1); {@code null} if
 *           no AR coefficients
 * @param MA the MA coefficients (excluding the initial 1); {@code null} if
 *           no MA coefficients
 */
public ARMAModel(double[] AR, double[] MA) {
    this(AR, MA, 1);
}
/**
 * Copy constructor.
 *
 * @param that a univariate ARMA model
 */
public ARMAModel(ARMAModel that) {
    super(that);
}
/**
 * Compute the univariate ARMA conditional mean, given all the lags.
 *
 * @param arLags the AR lags
 * @param maLags the MA lags
 * @return the conditional mean
 */
public double conditionalMean(double[] arLags, double[] maLags);
/**
 * Compute the multivariate ARMA unconditional mean.
 *
 * @return the unconditional mean
 */
public double unconditionalMean();
/**
```

```
     * Get the demeaned version of the time series model.
     * \[
     * Y_t = (X_t - \mu) = \sum_{i=1}^p \phi_i (X_{t-i} - \mu) + \sum_
       {i=1}^q
       * \theta_j
     * \epsilon_{t-j} + \epsilon_t
* \]

     * &mu; is the unconditional mean.
     *
     * @return the demeaned time series
     */
    public ARMAModel getDemeanedModel();
```

The following code constructs an instance for the following ARMA(1,1) model and computes its ACVF and ACF:

$$X_t = 0.2X_{t-1} + \varepsilon_t + 1.1\varepsilon_{t-1}$$

```
// build an ARMA(1, 1)
val arma11 = ARMAModel(
        doubleArrayOf(0.2), // the AR coefficients
        doubleArrayOf(1.1) // the MA coefficients
)
// compute the autocovariance function for the model
val acvf = AutoCovariance(arma11)
for (i in 1 until 10) {
    println(String.format("The acvf of the ARMA(1,1) model at lag%d: %f", i, acvf.
    evaluate(i.toDouble())))
}
// compute the autocorrelation function for the model
val acf = AutoCorrelation(arma11, 10)
for (i in 0 until 10) {
    println(String.format("The acf of the ARMA(1,1) model at lag%d: %f", i, acf.evaluate(i.
    toDouble())))
}
```

The output is as follows:

```
the acvf of the ARMA(1,1) model at lag1: 1.652083
the acvf of the ARMA(1,1) model at lag2: 0.330417
the acvf of the ARMA(1,1) model at lag3: 0.066083
the acvf of the ARMA(1,1) model at lag4: 0.013217
the acvf of the ARMA(1,1) model at lag5: 0.002643
the acvf of the ARMA(1,1) model at lag6: 0.000529
the acvf of the ARMA(1,1) model at lag7: 0.000106
the acvf of the ARMA(1,1) model at lag8: 0.000021
the acvf of the ARMA(1,1) model at lag9: 0.000004
the acf of the ARMA(1,1) model at lag0: 1.000000
the acf of the ARMA(1,1) model at lag1: 0.598491
```

```
the acf of the ARMA(1,1) model at lag2: 0.119698
the acf of the ARMA(1,1) model at lag3: 0.023940
the acf of the ARMA(1,1) model at lag4: 0.004788
the acf of the ARMA(1,1) model at lag5: 0.000958
the acf of the ARMA(1,1) model at lag6: 0.000192
the acf of the ARMA(1,1) model at lag7: 0.000038
the acf of the ARMA(1,1) model at lag8: 0.000008
the acf of the ARMA(1,1) model at lag9: 0.000002
```

Figure 15-16 plots the ACF of the model from the output. Note that the ACF (and PACF) do not vanish after lag 1 although they decay to 0. For the ARMA model, there is no cutoff lag for ACF and PACF. They are indicative only of what the AR and MA orders may be.

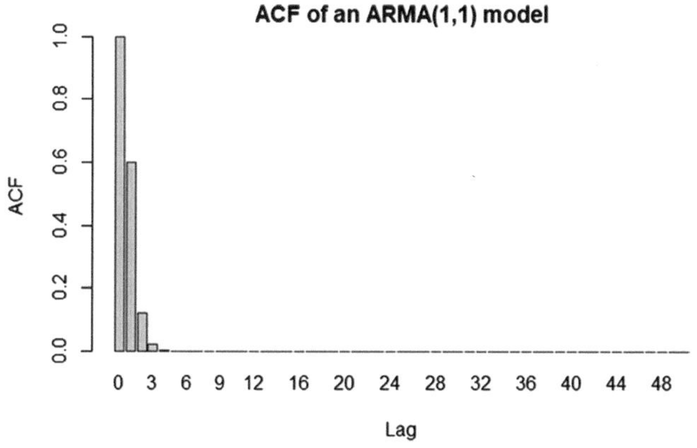

Figure 15-16. *ACF for the ARMA(1,1) process with $\phi 1 = 0.2$, $\theta 1 = 1.1$*

ARMA(p, q)

An ARMA(p, q) model combines an AR(p) model and an MA(q) model. The former considers its own past behavior as inputs for the model to explain, for example, the momentum and mean reversion effects often observed in financial trading market. The latter incorporates the shock effect such as unexpected events affecting the process (such as surprise earnings announcements, wars, and COVID-19). Hence, an ARMA model attempts to capture both of these aspects when modeling a time series. Note that AR, MA, and ARMA all model the first order (level) of a process and not the second order (volatility), such as volatility clustering, a key empirical phenomenon of many financial time series. That is the subject of Section 15.2.5.

An ARMA(p, q) model, where *p* is the order of the AR model and *q* is the order of the MA model, is defined as the sum of an AR(p) model and an MA(q) model. The model structure is as follows (assume $\mu = 0$ or demeaned $X_{t-\mu}$):

$$X_t = \phi_1 X_{t-1} + \ldots + \phi_p X_{t-p} + \theta_1 \varepsilon_{t-1} + \ldots + \theta_q \varepsilon_{t-q} + \varepsilon_t$$

Or, it is often written so that AR terms are on the left side of the equation and MA terms on the right side:

$$X_t - \phi_1 X_{t-1} - \ldots - \phi_p X_{t-p} = \varepsilon_t + \theta_1 \varepsilon_{t-1} + \ldots + \theta_q \varepsilon_{t-q}$$

Where ε_t is i.i.d. white noise.

You can write the model in terms of the backshift operator:

$$\left(1-\sum_{i=1}^{p}\phi_i B^i\right)X_t=\left(1+\sum_{i=1}^{q}\theta_i B^i\right)\varepsilon_t$$

Or equivalently:

$$X_t=\frac{\left(1+\sum_{i=1}^{q}\theta_i B^i\right)}{\left(1-\sum_{i=1}^{p}\phi_i B^i\right)}\varepsilon_t=\frac{\theta(B)}{\phi(B)}\varepsilon_t$$

Where B is the lag operator, ε_t are the error terms, ϕ_t are the autoregressive coefficients, and θ_t are the moving-average coefficients.

This model requires a number of conditions imposed on $\theta(B)$ and $\phi(B)$. They are as follows:

- Identifiability condition that the polynomials $\phi(B)$ and $\theta(B)$ have no zeros in common; otherwise, you would have $\frac{0}{0}$ dividing the two polynomials.
- Normalization condition that $\phi(0) = \theta(0) = 1$.
- $\{X_t\}$ is stationary.
- $\{X_t\}$ is invertible.
- $\{X_t\}$ is causal.

The last causality condition means that there exists an absolutely summable sequence of coefficients $\{\psi_i\}$ such that X_t can be written as an infinite sum of MA terms. This infinite linear combination of white noise is called the linear representation of a time series.

$$X_t=\sum_{i=0}^{\infty}\psi_i\varepsilon_{t-i}=\underbrace{\left(\sum_{i=0}^{\infty}\psi_i B^i\right)}_{\psi(B)}\varepsilon_t=\psi(B)\varepsilon_t$$

Let:

$$\psi(B)=\frac{\theta(B)}{\phi(B)}=\sum_{i=0}^{\infty}\psi_i B^i$$

You can solve for the values of ψ_i using this equation:

$$\psi(B)\phi(B)=\theta(B)$$

That is:

$$\left(\psi_0+\psi_1 B+\psi_2 B^2+\ldots\right)\left(1-\phi_1 B-\ldots\right)=\left(1+\theta_1 B+\theta_2 B^2+\ldots\right)$$

$$\psi_0-\psi_0\phi_1 B+\psi_1 B+\psi_2 B^2-\psi_1\phi_1 B^2+\ldots=1+\theta_1 B+\theta_2 B^2+\ldots$$

$$\psi_0+\left(-\psi_0\phi_1+\psi_1\right)B+\left(\psi_2-\psi_1\phi_1\right)B^2+\ldots=1+\theta_1 B+\theta_2 B^2+\ldots$$

By matching the coefficients of B, you have the following.
For lag 0, you have this:

$$\psi_0 = 1$$

For lag 1:

$$-\psi_0 \phi_1 + \psi_1 = \theta_1$$

$$\psi_1 = \theta_1 + \psi_0 \phi_1 = \theta_1 + \phi_1$$

For an ARMA(1, 1) process where $\psi_i = \theta_i = 0$, $i \geq 2$, you have the following.
For lag 2, you have this:

$$\psi_2 - \psi_1 \phi_1 = 0$$

$$\psi_2 = \phi_1 \psi_1 = \phi_1 (\theta_1 + \phi_1)$$

For lag k where $k \geq 2$, you have this:

$$\psi_k - \psi_{k-1} \phi = 0$$

$$\psi_k = \phi_1 \psi_{k-1} = \psi_1 \phi_1^{k-1} = (\theta_1 + \phi_1) \phi_1^{k-1}$$

In NM Dev, the `LinearRepresentation` class computes the linear representation of an ARMA process and calculates the values for ψ_k. Suppose you have this:

$$X_t - 0.2 X_{t-1} = \varepsilon_t + 1.1 \varepsilon_{t-1}$$

$$\phi_1 = 0.2, \theta_1 = 1.1.$$

The following code solves ψ_k for the first 20 lags:

```
// build an ARMA(1, 1)
val arma11 = ARMAModel(
        doubleArrayOf(0.2), // the AR coefficients
        doubleArrayOf(1.1) // the MA coefficients
)
// compute the linear representation
val ma = LinearRepresentation(arma11)
for (i in 1..20) {
    println(String.format("The coefficients of the linear representation at lag %d = %f", i,
    ma.AR(i)))
}
```

The output is as follows:

```
the coefficients of the linear representation at lag 1 = 1.300000
the coefficients of the linear representation at lag 2 = 0.260000
the coefficients of the linear representation at lag 3 = 0.052000
the coefficients of the linear representation at lag 4 = 0.010400
the coefficients of the linear representation at lag 5 = 0.002080
the coefficients of the linear representation at lag 6 = 0.000416
the coefficients of the linear representation at lag 7 = 0.000083
the coefficients of the linear representation at lag 8 = 0.000017
the coefficients of the linear representation at lag 9 = 0.000003
the coefficients of the linear representation at lag 10 = 0.000001
the coefficients of the linear representation at lag 11 = 0.000000
the coefficients of the linear representation at lag 12 = 0.000000
the coefficients of the linear representation at lag 13 = 0.000000
the coefficients of the linear representation at lag 14 = 0.000000
the coefficients of the linear representation at lag 15 = 0.000000
the coefficients of the linear representation at lag 16 = 0.000000
the coefficients of the linear representation at lag 17 = 0.000000
the coefficients of the linear representation at lag 18 = 0.000000
the coefficients of the linear representation at lag 19 = 0.000000
the coefficients of the linear representation at lag 20 = 0.000000
```

Because the coefficients are absolutely summable, they will eventually converge to 0.

The linear representation of an ARMA is an infinite sum of the moving-average terms. Using the result from Section 15.2.3.2, you can compute the autocovariance function for ARMA.

$$\gamma\left(|k|\right)=\sum_{i=0}^{\infty}\psi_i\psi_{i+|k|}$$

The autocorrelation is as follows:

$$\rho(k)=\frac{\gamma(k)}{\gamma(0)}$$

It can be shown that the sequence $\{\gamma(k)\}$ is also absolutely summable. In other words, you have this:

$$\sum_{k=-\infty}^{\infty}\left|\gamma(k)\right|<\infty$$

Consequently, the autocovariance converges to 0 as the lag number gets bigger. In other words, you have this:

$$\lim_{k\to\infty}\gamma(k)=0$$

The following code computes the linear representation, autocovariance, and autocorrelation for an ARMA(2, 3) model:

$$X_t=0.6X_{t-1}-0.23X_{t-2}+0.1\varepsilon_{t-1}+0.2\varepsilon_{t-2}+0.4\varepsilon_{t-3}+\varepsilon_t$$

```
// build an ARMA(2, 3)
val arma23 = ARMAModel(
        doubleArrayOf(0.6, -0.23), // the AR coefficients
        doubleArrayOf(0.1, 0.2, 0.4) // the MA coefficients
)

// compute the linear representation
val ma = LinearRepresentation(arma23)
for (i in 1..20) {
    println(String.format("The coefficients of the linear representation at lag %d = %f", i,
    ma.AR(i)))
}
```

The output is as follows:

```
the coefficients of the linear representation at lag 1 = 0.700000
the coefficients of the linear representation at lag 2 = 0.390000
the coefficients of the linear representation at lag 3 = 0.473000
the coefficients of the linear representation at lag 4 = 0.194100
the coefficients of the linear representation at lag 5 = 0.007670
the coefficients of the linear representation at lag 6 = -0.040041
the coefficients of the linear representation at lag 7 = -0.025789
the coefficients of the linear representation at lag 8 = -0.006264
the coefficients of the linear representation at lag 9 = 0.002173
the coefficients of the linear representation at lag 10 = 0.002745
the coefficients of the linear representation at lag 11 = 0.001147
the coefficients of the linear representation at lag 12 = 0.000057
the coefficients of the linear representation at lag 13 = -0.000230
the coefficients of the linear representation at lag 14 = -0.000151
the coefficients of the linear representation at lag 15 = -0.000038
the coefficients of the linear representation at lag 16 = 0.000000
the coefficients of the linear representation at lag 17 = 0.000000
the coefficients of the linear representation at lag 18 = 0.000000
the coefficients of the linear representation at lag 19 = 0.000000
the coefficients of the linear representation at lag 20 = 0.000000
```

```
// compute the autocovariance function for the model
val acvf = AutoCovariance(arma23)
for (i in 1 until 10) {
    println(String.format("The acvf of the ARMA(2,3) model at lag%d: %f", i, acvf.
    evaluate(i.toDouble())))
}
```

The output is as follows:

```
the acvf of the ARMA(2,3) model at lag1: 1.251651
the acvf of the ARMA(2,3) model at lag2: 0.792637
the acvf of the ARMA(2,3) model at lag3: 0.587703
the acvf of the ARMA(2,3) model at lag4: 0.170315
the acvf of the ARMA(2,3) model at lag5: -0.032983
```

```
the acvf of the ARMA(2,3) model at lag6: -0.058962
the acvf of the ARMA(2,3) model at lag7: -0.027791
the acvf of the ARMA(2,3) model at lag8: -0.003113
the acvf of the ARMA(2,3) model at lag9: 0.004524
```

The following code computes the autocorrelation function for the model.

```
// compute the autocorrelation function for the model
val acf = AutoCorrelation(arma23, 10)
for (i in 0 until 10) {
    println(String.format("The acf of the ARMA(2,3) model at lag%d: %f", i, acf.evaluate(i.
    toDouble())))
}
```

The output is as follows:

```
the acf of the ARMA(2,3) model at lag0: 1.000000
the acf of the ARMA(2,3) model at lag1: 0.656730
the acf of the ARMA(2,3) model at lag2: 0.415890
the acf of the ARMA(2,3) model at lag3: 0.308362
the acf of the ARMA(2,3) model at lag4: 0.089363
the acf of the ARMA(2,3) model at lag5: -0.017306
the acf of the ARMA(2,3) model at lag6: -0.030937
the acf of the ARMA(2,3) model at lag7: -0.014582
the acf of the ARMA(2,3) model at lag8: -0.001634
the acf of the ARMA(2,3) model at lag9: 0.002374
```

Figure 15-17 plots the ACF for this ARMA(2, 3) process. Although the ACF (and PACF) converges to 0 exponentially after lag q (and p), there is no clear cutoff lag for ARMA to determine p or q, unlike the plots for the AR and MA models.

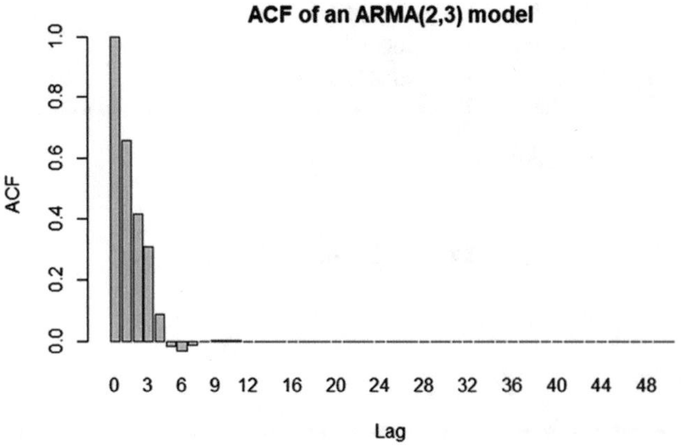

Figure 15-17. *ACF of the ARMA(2, 3) process*

Forecast

Making a forecast for the next step $\hat{X}_{n+1}$ given all the observations $\{X_1, X_2, ..., X_n\}$ for a (zero mean or demeaned) ARMA model is the same as computing the conditional mean, as shown here:

$$\hat{X}_{n+1} = g(X_1, X_2, \ldots, X_n) = \mathrm{E}(X_{n+1} \mid X_1, X_2, \ldots, X_n)$$

Such that the mean squared error is minimized:

$$\min_g \mathrm{E}\left(X_{n+1} - g(X_1, X_2, \ldots, X_n)\right)^2$$

In general, g is a nonlinear function, but you will want to find a (best) linear predictor. That is, g is a linear combination of past observations such that the following is true:

$$\min_{\mathbf{a}} \mathrm{E}\left(X_{n+1} - \sum_{i=1}^{n} a_i X_{n+1-i}\right)^2$$

To solve for ***a***, you use the equivalent formulation that the prediction errors and the observations are uncorrelated.

$$\mathrm{E}\left(X_{n+1} - \hat{X}_{n+1}\right) X_j = 0, j = 1, 2, \ldots, n$$

Replace $\hat{X}_{n+1}$ with the linear predictor, as shown here:

$$\mathrm{E}\left(X_{n+1} - \sum_{i=1}^{n} a_i X_{n+1-i}\right) X_j = 0, j = 1, 2, \ldots, n$$

Expand it, as shown here:

$$\mathrm{E}(X_{n+1} X_j) = \mathrm{E}\left(X_j \sum_{i=1}^{n} a_i X_{n+1-i}\right), j = 1, 2, \ldots, n$$

$$\mathrm{E}(X_{n+1} X_j) = \sum_{i=1}^{n} a_i \mathrm{E}(X_j X_{n+1-i}), j = 1, 2, \ldots, n$$

$$\begin{cases} \mathrm{E}(X_{n+1} X_1) = \sum_{i=1}^{n} a_i \mathrm{E}(X_1 X_{n+1-i}) \\ \mathrm{E}(X_{n+1} X_2) = \sum_{i=1}^{n} a_i \mathrm{E}(X_2 X_{n+1-i}) \\ \quad\vdots \end{cases}$$

In terms of ACF, you have this:

$$\begin{cases} \gamma(n) = \sum_{i=1}^{n} a_i \gamma(n-i) \\ \gamma(n-i) = \sum_{i=1}^{n} a_i \gamma(n-i-1) \\ \vdots \end{cases}$$

In matrix notation, you have this:

$$\gamma = \Gamma_n \boldsymbol{a}$$

Where $[\Gamma \boldsymbol{n}]_{ij} = \gamma(i-j)$.

Solving this matrix equation will give the best linear predictor of the next-step forecast.

$$\hat{X}_{n+1} = \sum_{i=1}^{n} a_i X_{n+1-i}, \text{ where } \boldsymbol{a} = \Gamma_n^{-1} \gamma$$

In practice, you solve $\boldsymbol{a}$ using an iterative algorithm instead of solving a numerically difficult matrix equation, especially when n is big. The iterations will compute all the conditional expectations $\hat{X}_j$ for $j = 1, 2, \ldots, n, n + 1$. This Yule-Walker equation can be extended for more than one step ahead forecast $\hat{X}_{n+h}$.

In NM Dev, the `ARMAForecastOneStep` class implements the iterative innovation algorithm to compute the one-step forecast. (The `ARMAForecastMultiStep` class computes the h-step forecast.) It takes a series of observations and a model specification and outputs the conditional expectations over time. For example, the following code generates a random time series from an ARMA(1, 1) model and computes the conditional expectations at each time step:

```
println("making forecasts for an ARMA model")

// define an ARMA(1, 1)
val arma11 = ARMAModel(
        doubleArrayOf(0.2), // the AR coefficients
        doubleArrayOf(1.1) // the MA coefficients
)

// create a random number generator from the ARMA model
val sim = ARIMASim(arma11)
sim.seed(1234567890L)

// generate a random time series
val T = 50 // length of the time series
var x: DoubleArray = DoubleArray(T)
for (i in 0 until T) {
    // call the RNG to generate random numbers according to the specification
    x[i] = sim.nextDouble()
}

// compute the one-step conditional expectations for the model
val forecaset = ARMAForecastOneStep(x, arma11)
var x_hat: DoubleArray = DoubleArray(T)
var residuals: DoubleArray = DoubleArray(T)
```

```
for (i in 0 until T) {
    // the one-step conditional expectations
    x_hat[i] = forecaset.xHat(i)
    // the errors
    residuals[i] = x[i] - x_hat[i]
}

println(Arrays.toString(x))
```

The (abridged) output is as follows:

```
[0.1968790947035005, 0.16584033866577874, 0.7910121229310072, 0.10657769691646068,
-1.0371447908191465, 0.04412684959211502, 0.7241722424723148, -1.7538519814924725,
-4.772738896937248, -2.7244783039780023, -1.1110789790665505, -2.106322783331434,
-1.1271763863477884, 0.9965503611140754,
println(Arrays.toString(x_hat))
```

The (abridged) output is as follows:

```
[0.0, 0.11783028083009503, 0.06297686421253082, 0.6826462678185927, -0.42568727132717654,
-0.7032843656741394, 0.632629314138487, 0.22277838517806908, -2.058229893163323,
-3.3247441761833425, -0.016461199464652077, -1.1919709121238073, -1.2353528600412458,
-0.1287408986154927, 1.2083288982851947,
```

Figure 15-18 plots the output. The observations are the red line, and the one-step forecasts are the blue line.

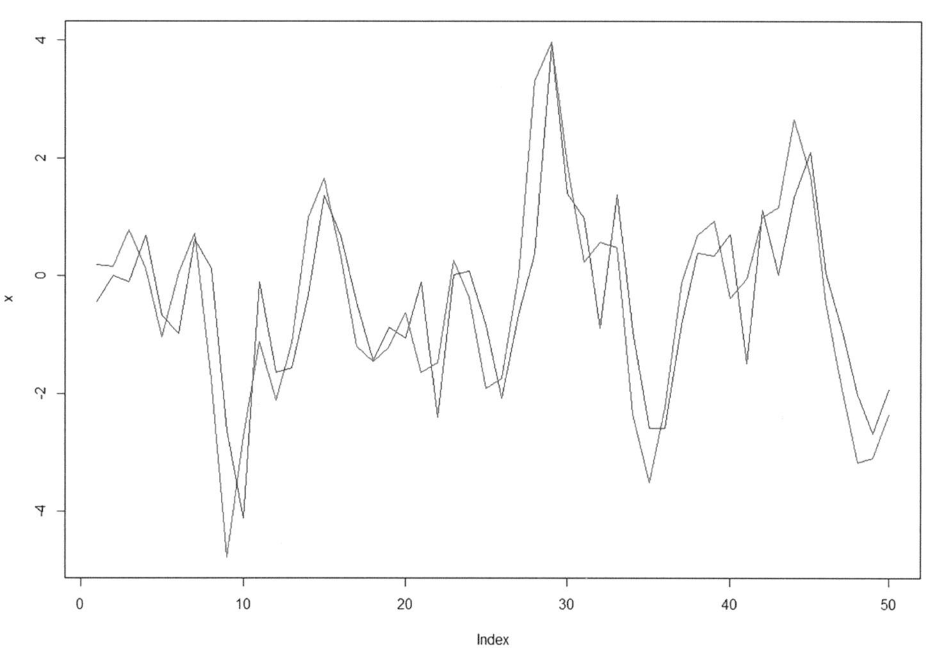

***Figure 15-18.** Observed values (red) versus conditional expectations (blue)*

```
println(Arrays.toString(residuals))
```

The (abridged) output is as follows:

```
[0.1968790947035005, 0.04801005783568371, 0.7280352587184764, -0.576068570902132,
-0.6114575194919699, 0.7474112152662544, 0.09154292833382782, -1.9766303666705416,
-2.7145090037739252, 0.6002658722053402, -1.0946177796018985, -0.9143518712076266,
0.1081764736934574, 1.1252912597295681,
```

Figure 15-19 plots the residuals or errors or differences between observations and the conditional expectations.

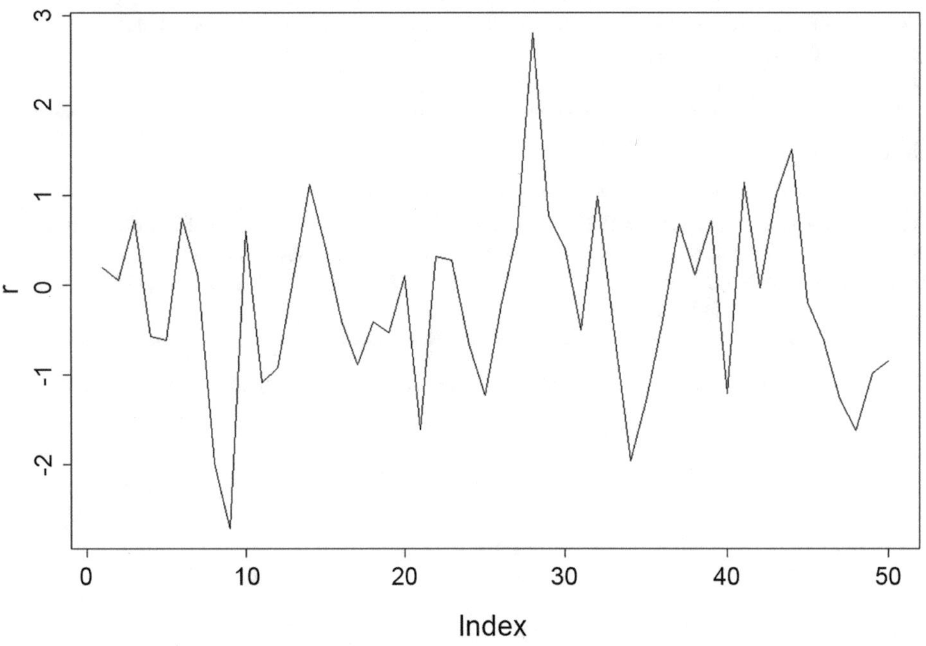

Figure 15-19. *The residuals or errors*

Estimation

In general, given a data set, you use ACF and PACF plots to determine a model to fit the data. If the PACF plot drops sharply after p significant lags and the ACF plot gradually decreases, it is a good indication of an AR(p) process. If the ACF plot drops sharply after q significant lags and the PACF plot gradually decreases, it is a good indication of an MA(q) process. If, on the other hand, both the ACF and PACF plots gradually decrease, then the ARMA process should be considered for modeling. Although there are no cutoff lags for ACF and PACF, where they diminish can be indicative of the correct orders. For example, if both ACF and PACF are small after lag 1, you can try ARMA(1, 1). You should also try a few other competing models, such as ARMA(0, 1), ARMA(1, 0), ARMA(2, 1), ARMA(1, 2), and ARMA(2, 2). You fit the data to each of these models and select the best model in the pool by choosing the one with the smallest AIC and AICc (or BIC). You then check the goodness of fit to validate the selection.

AIC is defined as follows:

$$AIC = -2\ln(L) + 2k$$

Where ln(L) is the log-likelihood function of the model and k is the number of parameters:
AICc is defined as follows:

$$AICc = -2\ln(L) + 2k + \frac{2k(k+1)}{n-k-1}$$

Where ln(L) is the log-likelihood function of the model, k is the number of parameters, and n is the sample size.

To fit each of the possible models, the NM Dev class called `ConditionalSumOfSquares` uses the conditional sum of squares method. It is a maximum likelihood method that all the information in the data is used rather than, say, just the first and second moments as in the method of moments. The likelihood function that NM Dev uses, in terms of the ARMA model parameters $\{\boldsymbol{\phi}, \boldsymbol{\theta}, \sigma^2\}$, is as follows:

$$L(\phi, \theta, \sigma^2) = n\log(\sigma^2) + \frac{1}{\sigma^2}\sum_{t=1}^{n}(X_t - \hat{X}_t)^2$$

It finds a complete specification of the ARMA(p, q) model in terms of ϕ, the AR coefficients; θ, the MA coefficient; and σ^2, the variance of the error term; so that the sum of squared differences between observations X_t and predictions/expectations $\hat{X}_t$ is minimized. Moreover, the class computes the AIC and AICc for model selection. The class signature is as follows:

```
public class ConditionalSumOfSquares implements ARMAFit {
    /**
     * Fit an ARIMA model for the observations using CSS. Note that the
     * algorithm fits only an ARMA model. {@code d} is taken as an input. If the
     * differenced input time series is not zero-mean, it is first demeaned
     * before running the algorithm as in Brockwell and Davis. When reporting
     * the model, we compute the intercept to match the mean.
     *
     * @param x             the time series of observations
     * @param p             the number of AR terms
     * @param d             the order of integration
     * @param q             the number of MA terms
     * @param maxIterations the maximum number of iterations
     */
    public ConditionalSumOfSquares(
            double[] x,
            final int p,
            final int d,
            final int q,
            int maxIterations
    );
    /**
     * Fit an ARIMA model for the observations using CSS. Note that the
     * algorithm fits only an ARMA model. {@code d} is taken as an input. If the
     * differenced input time series is not zero-mean, it is first demeaned
     * before running the algorithm as in Brockwell and Davis. When reporting
     * the model, we compute the intercept to match the mean.
```

```
     *
     * @param x the time series of observations
     * @param p the number of AR terms
     * @param d the order of integration
     * @param q the number of MA terms
     */
    public ConditionalSumOfSquares(
            double[] x,
            final int p,
            final int d,
            final int q
    );
    /**
     * Get the number of parameters for the estimation/fitting. They are the AR
     * terms, MA terms, and variance (sigma^2).
     *
     * @return the number of parameters
     */
    public int nParams();
    /**
     * Get the fitted ARIMA model.
     *
     * @return the fitted ARIMA model
     */
    @Override
    public ARIMAModel getModel();
    /**
     * Get the fitted ARMA model.
     *
     * @return the fitted ARMA model
     */
    public ARMAModel getARMAModel();
    @Override
    public double var();
    /**
     * Get the asymptotic covariance matrix of the estimated parameters,
     * <i>&phi;</i> and <i>&theta;</i>. The estimators are asymptotically
     * normal.
     *
     * @return the asymptotic covariance matrix
     * @see "P. J. Brockwell and R. A. Davis, "Eq. 10.8.27, Thm. 10.8.2, Chapter
     * 10.8, Model Building and Forecasting with ARIMA Processes," Time Series:
     * Theory and Methods, Springer, 2006."
     */
    @Override
    public Matrix covariance();
    /**
     * Get the asymptotic standard errors of the estimated parameters,
     * <i>&phi;</i> and <i>&theta;</i>. The estimators are asymptotically
     * normal.
     *
```

```
     * @return the asymptotic errors
     * @see "P. J. Brockwell and R. A. Davis, "Eq. 10.8.27, Thm. 10.8.2, Chapter
     * 10.8, Model Building and Forecasting with ARIMA Processes," Time Series:
     * Theory and Methods, Springer, 2006."
     */
    @Override
    public ImmutableVector stderr();
    /**
     * Compute the AIC, a model selection criterion.
     *
     * @return the AIC
     * @see
     * <a href="http://en.wikipedia.org/wiki/Akaike_information_criterion">Wikipedia:
     * Akaike
     * information criterion</a>
     */
    @Override
    public double AIC();
    /**
     * Compute the AICc, a model selection criterion.
     *
     * @return the AICc
     * @see "P. J. Brockwell and R. A. Davis, "Eq. 9.2.1, Chapter 9.2, Model
     * Building and Forecasting with ARIMA Processes," Time Series: Theory and
     * Methods, Springer, 2006."
     */
    @Override
    public double AICC();
}
```

To determine whether the chosen ARMA(p, q) model, after fitting the model parameters, is a good fit to the data, you verify that the residuals, $r_t = X_t - \bar{X}_t$, should be a white noise process without serial correlation. You can run the Ljung-Box test on the residuals to check for any nonzero autocorrelation. The degree of freedom for the χ_m^2 test is $m = l - (p + q)$, which is the number of lags to check minus the number of model parameters. If the p-value of the test is smaller than the required significance, say, 5 percent, then there is autocorrelation in the residuals that is not explained by the fitted model. You need to choose a different model. Otherwise, you can conclude that the residuals are independent white noise and hence a good model selection.

The following code demonstrates how to fit a model to the data and test for its goodness of fit. You first create a random time series, $\{X_t\}$, from a (known) model. Then you fit an ARMA(1, 1) model to the data. (At this point, we are just guessing that $p = q = 1$. If it fails the goodness-of-fit test, you would have to choose another pair of orders.) Using the fitted model, you compute the fitted values $\{\bar{X}_t\}$ and the residuals $r_t = X_t - \bar{X}_t$. Finally, test whether the residuals are white noise using the `LjungBox` class up to the first four lags. The null hypotheses is that the ACF for all the four lags are zero. The degree of freedom is therefore $(4 - (1 + 1)) = 2$. (The degree of freedom is reduced by 2 due to the number of model parameters in the ARMA(1, 1) model.)

```
// define an ARMA(1, 1)
val arma11 = ARMAModel(
        doubleArrayOf(0.2), // the AR coefficients
        doubleArrayOf(1.1) // the MA coefficients
)
```

```
// create a random number generator from the ARMA model
val sim = ARIMASim(arma11)
sim.seed(1234567890L)

// generate a random time series
val T = 50 // length of the time series
var x: DoubleArray = DoubleArray(T)
for (i in 0 until T) {
    // call the RNG to generate random numbers according to the specification
    x[i] = sim.nextDouble()
}

// fit an ARMA(1,1) model
val css = ConditionalSumOfSquares(x, 1, 0, 1)
val arma11_css = css.getARMAModel()
println(String.format("The fitted ARMA(1,1) model is %s%n", arma11_css))
println(String.format("The fitted ARMA(1,1) model, demeanded, is %s%n", arma11_css.
getDemeanedModel()))
println(String.format("AIC = %f", css.AIC()))
```

The output is as follows:

```
The fitted ARMA(1,1) model is x_t = -0.25855664657157695 + (0.4087316816737802*x_{t-1}) +
(1.0193696854247496*e_{t-1}) + e_t; var(e_t) = 0.886664, d = 0
The fitted ARMA(1,1) model, demeanded, is x_t = 0.0 + (0.4087316816737802*x_{t-1}) +
(1.0193696854247496*e_{t-1}) + e_t; var(e_t) = 1.000000, d = 0
AIC = 93.971130
```

The following code runs the goodness-of-fit test.

```
// run the goodness-of-fit test
val test = LjungBox(
        residuals,
        4, // check up to the 4-th lag
        2 // number of parameters
)
println(String.format("The test statistic = %f", test.statistics()))
println(String.format("The p-value = %f", test.pValue()))
```

The output is as follows:

```
The test statistic = 2.686421
The p-value = 0.261006
```

The true process is as follows:

$$\begin{Bmatrix} \mu = 0 \\ \phi_1 = 0.2 \\ \theta_1 = 1.1 \\ \sigma^2 = 1 \end{Bmatrix}$$

The fitted process is as follows:

$$\begin{Bmatrix} \mu = -0.2586 \\ \phi_1 = 0.4087 \\ \theta_1 = 1.0194 \\ \sigma^2 = 0.8867 \end{Bmatrix}$$

The test statistic is 2.686421. The p-value is 0.261006, which is bigger than the 5 percent significance level. Thus, you fail to reject the null that none of the autocorrelation coefficients up to lag 4 is zero. You must conclude that the residuals are random white noise. The fitted model is a good fit. Note that although the fitted model does not agree exactly with the true model that generates the data, especially on ϕ_1, it fits the data well. The results are affected by the numerical optimization used, its implementation, and its sample size. If you increase the sample size T to 1000 in the simulation, then the fitted model will match the true model.

Figure 15-20 plots the time series of observed values (red) and the fitted values (blue) from the fitted model. Figure 15-21 plots the residuals, which appear to be much like white noise. Therefore, the model is a good fit to the data.

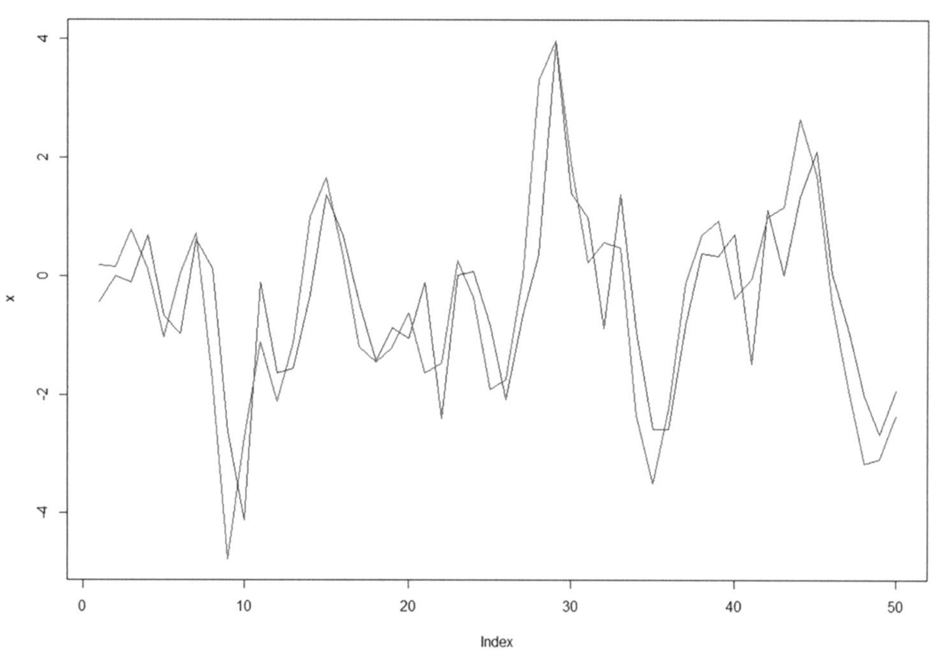

Figure 15-20. *Observed values (red) versus fitted values (blue)*

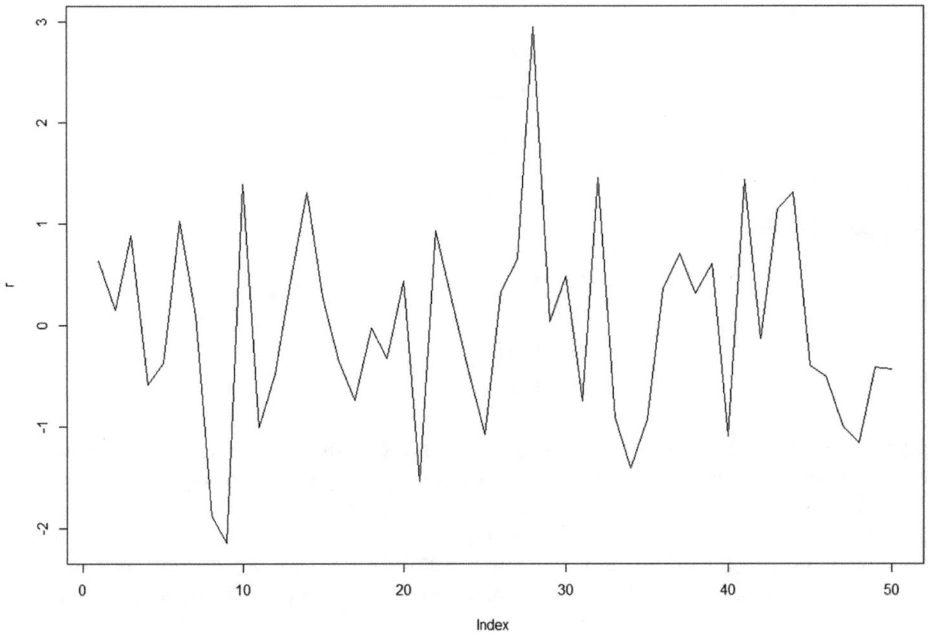

***Figure 15-21.** Residuals from fitting the ARMA(1, 1) model*

15.2.4. ARIMA Model

The processes covered so far—AR, MA, and ARMA—are stationary processes. They are mean-reverting processes that have a tendency to go back to the mean when there is deviation. Their mean is constant over time, and so is their variance. A lot of real-life data, such as in financial data, is not like that. For example, the S&P 500 prices in Figure 15-22, Y_t, clearly exhibit a (stochastic) trend, and the (price) level increases over time. There is no mean or level that the prices seem to be going back to.

***Figure 15-22.** S&P 500 prices from 2015 to 2019*

Unit Root

Consider a simple AR(1) process (zero mean or demeaned):

$$Y_t = \phi_1 Y_{t-1} + \varepsilon_t$$

The differenced series is as follows:

$$\Delta Y_t = Y_t - Y_{t-1} = (\phi_1 - 1) Y_{t-1} + \varepsilon_t = \lambda Y_{t-1} + \varepsilon_t$$

If $\lambda = 0$, then the current level Y_{t-1} has no influence on the future value Y_t. Then $Y_t = \sum_{i=1}^{t} \varepsilon_i$ is simply a sum of the white noise and hence a random walk. On the other hand, if $\lambda < 0$, then the more positive the current value Y_{t-1} is, the more negative the next increment ΔY_t is. In addition, the more negative the current value Y_{t-1} is, the more positive the next increment ΔY_t is. Hence, you have mean reversion. Note that when $\lambda < 0$, you have $\phi_1 < 1$, which is (part of) the stationarity condition for AR(1). On the other hand, when $\lambda = 0$, you have $\phi_1 = 1$. The process is said to have a unit root and is nonstationary.

There are three types of unit root process for when $\phi_1 = 1$: a unit root without drift or time trend, a unit root with drift, and a unit root with drift and deterministic time trend.

Given a white noise process $\{\varepsilon_t\}$ that is i.i.d. and is with zero mean and constant variance σ^2, a unit root process without drift or time trend is as follows:

$$Y_t = Y_{t-1} + \varepsilon_t$$

Or equivalently:

$$Y_t = Y_0 + \sum_{i=1}^{t} \varepsilon_i$$

Then, you have this:

$$\begin{cases} \mathrm{E}(Y \mid Y_0) = Y_0 \\ \mathrm{var}(Y_t \mid Y_0) = \sigma^2 t \end{cases}$$

That is, when $\phi_1 = 1$, the variance of the process is a linear function of time t and hence nonstationary.

A unit root process with drift α is as follows:

$$Y_t = \alpha + Y_{t-1} + \varepsilon_t$$

Or equivalently:

$$Y_t = Y_0 + \alpha t + \sum_{i=1}^{t} \varepsilon_i$$

Then, you have this:

$$\begin{cases} \mathrm{E}(Y_t \mid Y_0) = Y_0 + \alpha t \\ \mathrm{var}(Y_t \mid Y_0) = \sigma^2 t \end{cases}$$

That is, when $\phi_1 = 1$, both the mean and the variance of the process are linear functions of time t and hence nonstationary.

A unit root process with drift and a deterministic time trend is as follows:

$$Y_t = \alpha + \beta t + Y_{t-1} + \varepsilon_t$$

Or equivalently:

$$Y_t = Y_0 + \alpha t + \beta \sum_{i=1}^{t} i + \sum_{i=1}^{t} \varepsilon_i$$

Then, it looks like this:

$$\begin{cases} \mathrm{E}(Y_t \mid Y_0) = Y_0 + \alpha t + \beta \sum_{i=1}^{t} i \\ \mathrm{var}(Y_t \mid Y_0) = \sigma^2 t \end{cases}$$

That is, when $\phi_1 = 1$, both the mean and the variance of the process are linear functions of time *t,* hence are nonstationary. The drift and deterministic trend can be removed, either by differencing or by fitting a polynomial to the data to obtain a time series of residuals. The original time series is said to be trend stationary.

The Dickey-Fuller (DF) hypothesis test checks for a numerical unit root by testing whether $\phi_1 = 1$. The augmented Dickey-Fuller (ADF) test generalizes this idea to a more general autoregressive model, as shown here:

$$\Delta Y_t = \alpha + \beta t + \lambda Y_{t-1} + \delta_1 \Delta Y_{t-1} + \ldots + \delta_{p-1} \Delta Y_{t-p+1} + \varepsilon_t$$

Where α is a constant drift, β is the coefficient of a time trend, and p is the lag order of the autoregressive process. The ADF test tests the null hypothesis that $\lambda = 0$ or that there is a unit root. The alternative hypothesis is that $\lambda < 0$.

$$\begin{cases} H_0 : \lambda = 0 \\ H_1 : \lambda < 0 \end{cases}$$

To compute the test statistics, you first regress Y_t on Y_{t-1} to get the estimated $\hat{\lambda}$ (or $\hat{\phi}_1$) and its sample standard deviation $\hat{\sigma}_{\hat{\lambda}}$. The test statistics is as follows:

$$DF_\lambda = \frac{\hat{\lambda}}{\hat{\sigma}_{\hat{\lambda}}}$$

The test statistics is compared to the relevant critical value from the Dickey-Fuller distribution. As this test is one-sided, you are concerned only with negative values of the test statistic. If the calculated test statistic is less (more negative) than the critical value, then the null hypothesis of $\lambda = 0$ is rejected, and you conclude that there is no unit root and hence stationarity.

The NM Dev class called `AugmentedDickeyFuller` implements the ADF test. There are three different Dickey-Fuller distributions for the three cases mentioned earlier: without drift or time trend ($\alpha = \beta = 0$), with drift ($\alpha \neq 0, \beta = 0$), and with drift and a deterministic time trend ($\alpha \neq 0, \beta \neq 0$). The critical values are different for these cases. The `TrendType.NO_CONSTANT`, `TrendType.CONSTANT`, and `TrendType.CONSTANT_TIME` flags represent these three cases, respectively. The following code demonstrates running the ADF test:

```
val sample: DoubleArray = doubleArrayOf(0.2, 0.3, -0.1, 0.4, -0.5, 0.6, 0.1, 0.2, 0.2, 0.3,
-0.1, 0.4, -0.5, 0.6, 0.1, 0.2)
val adf = AugmentedDickeyFuller(
                sample,
```

```
            TrendType.CONSTANT, // constant drift term
            4, // the lag order
            null
    )

println("H0: " + adf.getNullHypothesis())
println("H1: " + adf.getAlternativeHypothesis())
println(String.format("\nThe p-value for the test = %f", adf.pValue()))
println(String.format("The statistics for the test = %f", adf.statistics()))
```

The output is as follows:

```
H0: there is a unit root in the process, hence non-stationarity
H1: there is no unit root in the process, hence stationarity

the statistics = -2.641969
the p-value = 0.100000
```

The p-value is 0.1, which is too big. You fail to reject the null hypothesis at the 5 percent significance level. You must conclude that this data has a unit root and is not stationary.

You can run the same example in R, which is the de facto standard tool used by statisticians:

```
there is a unit root in the process, hence non-stationarity
there is no unit root in the process, hence stationarity
the p-value for the test = 0.100000
the statistics for the test = -2.641969
```

The R output is as follows:

```
        Augmented Dickey-Fuller Test
data:  c(x, x)
Dickey-Fuller = -2.642, Lag order = 4, p-value = 0.3278
alternative hypothesis: stationary
```

Although the statistics from the code snippets match, the p-values are very different (0.1 from NM Dev versus 0.3278 from R). I believe that the R result is wrong because R does not actually implement the Dickey-Fuller distributions. R has only tables of some critical values. To compute the p-value for a statistic, R uses interpolation from a few critical values in the table. Here is R's computation:

$$\frac{0.9-0.1}{3.24-1.14}=\frac{x-0.1}{3.24-2.642}$$

$$x=\frac{0.8}{3.24-1.14}\left(3.24-2.642\right)+0.1=0.3278$$

The -3.24 and -1.14 values are from Table 4.2c in Banerjee, Dolado, Galbraith, & Hendry (1993).

In contrast, NM Dev implements the three Dickey-Fuller distributions. The p-value is computed from the distribution each time, rather than looking up and interpolating it from a few critical values in a table.

Continuing with the S&P 500 example in Figure 15-22, the following code tests whether there is a unit root in the daily prices:

```
val adf = AugmentedDickeyFuller(spx.toArray())
println(String.format("The p-value for the test = %f", adf.pValue()))
println(String.format("The statistics for the test = %f", adf.statistics()))
```

The output is as follows:

```
the p-value for the test = 0.200000
the statistics for the test = -2.767399
```

The result shows that the p-value is 0.200, so you fail to reject the null at the 5 percent significance level. You must conclude that S&P 500's data has a unit root and is not stationary.

ARIMA(p, d, q)

S&P 500 prices are not stationary according to the ADF test. However, as shown in Section 15.1, the price differences, ΔY_t, are stationary like white noise.

$$\Delta Y_t = Y_t - Y_{t-1}$$

You can write Y_t as the first-order cumulative sum of the differenced series:

$$Y_t = \sum_{k=1}^{t} \Delta Y_k$$

Y_t is said to have the first order of integration or to be integrated of order 1. In mathematics, the word *integration* means summation. In calculus, integration is the sum of infinitesimally small elements; here it is the summation of time series.

More generally, a time series is integrated of order d, denoted as $I(d)$, if it takes d number of differences to obtain a covariance-stationary series. That is, the following is stationary:

$$\Delta^d Y_k = (1-B)^d Y_t$$

Y_t is the d-th order cumulative sum of the differenced series, as shown here:

$$Y_t = \sum_{k=1}^{t} \ldots \sum_{k=1}^{t} {}^{,,d} Y_k$$

In practice, d is hardly beyond 2.

In general, an ARIMA(p, d, q) process Y_t is such that if you do the differencing d times, the new time series $\Delta^d Y_k$ is a stationary ARMA process. The letter I stands for "integration." For instance, ARIMA(0, 1, 0) is a pure random walk that sums up the error terms (although the error terms may have different variances, as you see in Section 15.2.5). The NM Dev class called `ARIMAModel` constructs such a time series. The class signature is as follows:

```
public class ARIMAModel extends ARIMAXModel {
    /**
     * Construct a univariate ARIMA model.
     *
     * @param mu    the intercept (constant) term
     * @param AR    the AR coefficients (excluding the initial 1); {@code null}
     *              if no AR coefficients
     * @param d     the order of integration
     * @param MA    the MA coefficients (excluding the initial 1); {@code null}
     *              if no MA coefficients
     * @param sigma the white noise variance
     */
    public ARIMAModel(double mu, double[] AR, int d, double[] MA, double sigma);
    /**
     * Construct a univariate ARIMA model with unit variance.
     *
     * @param mu the intercept (constant) term
     * @param AR the AR coefficients (excluding the initial 1); {@code null} if
     *           no AR coefficients
     * @param d  the order of integration
     * @param MA the MA coefficients (excluding the initial 1); {@code null} if
     *           no MA coefficients
     */
    public ARIMAModel(double mu, double[] AR, int d, double[] MA);
    /**
     * Construct a univariate ARIMA model with zero-intercept (mu).
     *
     * @param AR    the AR coefficients (excluding the initial 1); {@code null}
     *              if no AR coefficients
     * @param d     the order of integration
     * @param MA    the MA coefficients (excluding the initial 1); {@code null}
     *              if no MA coefficients
     * @param sigma the white noise variance
     */
    public ARIMAModel(double[] AR, int d, double[] MA, double sigma);
    /**
     * Construct a univariate ARIMA model with unit variance and zero-intercept
     * (mu).
     *
     * @param AR the AR coefficients (excluding the initial 1); {@code null} if
     *           no AR coefficients
     * @param d  the order of integration
     * @param MA the MA coefficients (excluding the initial 1); {@code null} if
     *           no MA coefficients
     */
    public ARIMAModel(double[] AR, int d, double[] MA);
    /**
     * Copy constructor.
     *
     * @param that a univariate ARIMA model
     */
```

```
    public ARIMAModel(ARIMAModel that);
    /**
     * Get the ARMA part of this ARIMA model, essentially ignoring the
     * differencing.
     *
     * @return the ARMA part
     */
    public ARMAModel getARMA();
}
```

The NM Dev class called `ARIMASim` constructs a random number generator from an ARIMA specification. It generates a sequence of random numbers that has the distribution based on the model, be it AR, MA, ARMA, or ARIMA. The class signature is as follows:

```
public class ARIMASim implements RandomNumberGenerator {
    /**
     * Construct an ARIMA model.
     *
     * @param arima   an ARIMA model
     * @param lags    the lags of AR length; {@code lags[0]} is \(x_{t-1}\)
     * @param innovations the innovations of MA length; {@code innovations[0]}
     *                    is \(e_{t-1}\)
     * @param rng         a random number generator to generate innovations
     */
    public ARIMASim(
            ARIMAModel arima,
            double[] lags,
            double[] innovations,
            RandomNumberGenerator rng
    );
    /**
     * Construct an ARIMA model.
     * The lags and innovations are initialized to 0.
     *
     * @param arima an ARIMA model
     * @param rng   a random number generator to generate innovations
     */
    public ARIMASim(
            ARIMAModel arima,
            RandomNumberGenerator rng
    );
    /**
     * Construct an ARIMA model, using random standard Gaussian innovations.
     *
     * @param arima an ARIMA model
     */
    public ARIMASim(ARIMAModel arima);
    @Override
    public void seed(long... seeds);
    @Override
    public double nextDouble();
```

ARIMAX(p, d, q)

The ARIMAModel class extends the ARIMAXModel class, which represents an ARIMAX model. An ARIMAX process is such that if you do the differencing d times, the new time series $\Delta^d Y_k$ is a stationary ARMA process with exogenous or independent variables. The letter X stands for "exogenous." Mathematically, you have this:

$$\Delta^d Y_k = (1-B)^d Y_t = X_t = \phi_1 X_{t-1} + \ldots + \phi_p X_{t-p} + \theta_1 \varepsilon_{t-1} + \ldots + \theta_q \varepsilon_{t-q} + \varepsilon_t + \psi \boldsymbol{D_t}$$

$$\phi(B) X_t = \theta(B) \varepsilon_t + \psi \boldsymbol{D_t}$$

One way to deal with such a model is to reinterpret it as a linear regression of X_t on $\boldsymbol{D_t}$, plus stationary mean-reverting ARMA errors u_t, as shown here:

$$X_t = \psi \boldsymbol{D_t} + u_t$$

$$u_t = \phi_1 X_{t-1} + \ldots + \phi_p X_{t-p} + \theta_1 \varepsilon_{t-1} + \ldots + \theta_q \varepsilon_{t-q} + \varepsilon_t$$

Where $\boldsymbol{D_t}$ is an $m \times 1$ vector that contains all m exogenous variables at time t (excluding the intercept term) and its coefficients are represented by an m-dimensional vector $\boldsymbol{\psi}$.

One use of an ARIMAX model is to model the product revenue growth as a linear function of yearly inflation rate, yearly GDP, and yearly population growth rate. The exogenous factors in this example are yearly inflation rate, yearly GDP, and yearly population growth rate. The residuals from the linear regression can then be modeled as an ARMA process. The NM Dev class called ARIMAXModel represents an ARIMAX model. You can construct such an ARIMAX model by specifying ϕ_i, θ_j, and $\boldsymbol{\psi}$. The class signature is as follows:

```
public class ARIMAXModel {
    /**
     * Construct a univariate ARIMAX model.
     *
     * @param mu    the intercept (constant) term
     * @param AR    the AR coefficients (excluding the initial 1); {@code null}
     *              if no AR coefficient
     * @param d     the order of integration
     * @param MA    the MA coefficients (excluding the initial 1); {@code null}
     *              if no MA coefficient
     * @param psi   the coefficients of the deterministic terms (excluding the
     *              intercept term)
     * @param sigma the white noise variance
     */
    public ARIMAXModel(
            double mu,
            double[] AR,
            int d,
            double[] MA,
            double[] psi,
            double sigma
    );
    /**
     * Construct a univariate ARIMAX model with unit variance.
     *
```

```
     * @param mu  the intercept (constant) term
     * @param AR  the AR coefficients (excluding the initial 1); {@code null} if
     *            no AR coefficient
     * @param d   the order of integration
     * @param MA  the MA coefficients (excluding the initial 1); {@code null} if
     *            no MA coefficient
     * @param psi the coefficients of the deterministic terms (excluding the
     *            intercept term)
     */
    public ARIMAXModel(
            double mu,
            double[] AR,
            int d,
            double[] MA,
            double[] psi
    );
    /**
     * Construct a univariate ARIMAX model with zero-intercept (mu).
     *
     * @param AR    the AR coefficients (excluding the initial 1); {@code null}
     *              if no AR coefficient
     * @param d     the order of integration
     * @param MA    the MA coefficients (excluding the initial 1); {@code null}
     *              if no MA coefficient
     * @param psi   the coefficients of the deterministic terms (excluding the
     *              intercept term)
     * @param sigma the white noise variance
     */
    public ARIMAXModel(
            double[] AR,
            int d,
            double[] MA,
            double[] psi,
            double sigma
    );
    /**
     * Construct a univariate ARIMAX model with unit variance and zero-intercept
     * (mu).
     *
     * @param AR  the AR coefficients (excluding the initial 1); {@code null} if
     *            no AR coefficient
     * @param d   the order of integration
     * @param MA  the MA coefficients (excluding the initial 1); {@code null} if
     *            no MA coefficient
     * @param psi the coefficients of the deterministic terms (excluding the
     *            intercept term)
     */
    public ARIMAXModel(
            double[] AR,
            int d,
```

```
        double[] MA,
        double[] psi
);
/**
 * Copy constructor.
 *
 * @param that a univariate ARIMAX model
 */
public ARIMAXModel(ARIMAXModel that);
/**
 * Get the intercept (constant) term.
 *
 * @return the intercept (constant) term
 */
public double mu();
/**
 * Get the <i>i</i>-th AR coefficient; AR(0) = 1.
 *
 * @param i an index
 * @return the <i>i</i>-th AR coefficient
 */
public double AR(int i);
/**
 * Get all the AR coefficients.
 *
 * @return all the AR coefficients
 */
public double[] phi();
/**
 * Get the polynomial <i>(1 - &phi;)</i>.
 * The coefficients (except the initial 1) have the opposite signs to
 * {@link #AR(int)} and
 * {@link #phi()}.
 *
 * @return the polynomial <i>(1 - &phi;)</i>
 */
public Polynomial phiPolynomial();
/**
 * Get the <i>i</i>-th MA coefficient; MA(0) = 1.
 *
 * @param i an index
 * @return the <i>i</i>-th MA coefficient
 */
public double MA(int i);
/**
 * Get all the MA coefficients.
 *
 * @return all the MA coefficients
 */
```

```
public double[] theta();
/**
 * Get the polynomial <i>(1 + &theta;)</i>.
 *
 * @return the polynomial <i>(1 + &theta;)</i>
 */
public Polynomial thetaPolynomial();
/**
 * Get the coefficients of the deterministic terms.
 *
 * @return the coefficients of the deterministic terms; could be
 *         {@code null}
 */
public double[] psi();
/**
 * Get the order of integration.
 *
 * @return the order of integration
 */
public int d();
/**
 * Get the number of AR terms.
 *
 * @return the number of AR terms
 */
public int p();
/**
 * Get the number of MA terms.
 *
 * @return the number of MA terms
 */
public int q();
/**
 * Get the maximum of AR length or MA length.
 *
 * @return max(# AR terms, # MA terms)
 */
public int maxPQ();
/**
 * Get the white noise variance.
 *
 * @return the white noise variance
 */
public double sigma();
/**
 * Get the ARMAX part of this ARIMAX model, essentially ignoring the
 * differencing.
 *
 * @return the ARMAX part
 */
```

```
    public ARMAXModel getARMAX();
    @Override
    public String toString();
```

Estimation

Given a data set, the NM Dev class called AutoARIMAFit automatically constructs a model that best fits the data. It generates a pool of candidates with different model parameters $\{p, d, q\}$ and then selects the best one based on AIC or AICc. Each candidate is fit to the data using the maximum likelihood method, as in Section 15.2.3.4. The class signature is as follows:

```
public class AutoARIMAFit {
    /**
     * Automatically selects and estimates the ARIMA model using custom
     * parameters.
     *
     * @param x            the time series
     * @param maxP         maximum number of AR order considered
     * @param maxD         maximum number of integration order considered
     * @param maxQ         maximum number of MA order considered
     * @param minP         minimum number of AR order considered
     * @param minQ         minimum number of MA order considered
     * @param maxIteration maximum number of iterations for optimization
     */
    public AutoARIMAFit(
            double[] x,
            int maxP,
            int maxD,
            int maxQ,
            int minP,
            int minQ,
            int maxIteration
    );
    /**
     * Automatically selects and estimates the ARIMA model using default
     * parameters.
     *
     * @param x the time series
     */
    public AutoARIMAFit(double[] x);
    /**
     * Selects the optimal ARIMA model by AIC.
     *
     * @return the optimal ARIMA model
     */
    public ARIMAModel optimalModelByAIC();
    /**
     * Selects the optimal ARIMA model by AICC.
     *
```

```
     * @return the optimal ARIMA model
     */
    public ARIMAModel optimalModelByAICC();
}
```

Continuing with the example using the S&P 500, the following code snippet builds an ARIMA model from the S&P 500 daily prices and log returns. Since you already know that the data has a unit root from Section 15.2.4.1, you should expect the order of integration to be 1 in the resultant model, but you do not yet know the AR and MA orders of lag. On the other hand, you should expect the order of integration to be 0 for the log returns as the data is stationary. The code will automatically find the best AR and MA orders of lag.

```
// auto fit an ARIMA model to S&P 500 prices
val fit_sp500_1 = AutoARIMAFit(spx.toArray(), 5, 1, 5, 0, 0, 1000)
val arima1 = fit_sp500_1.optimalModelByAIC()
val arima2 = fit_sp500_1.optimalModelByAICC()
println("The optimal model for S&P500 prices by AIC is:")
println(arima1)
```

The output is as follows:

```
The optimal model for S&P500 prices by AIC is:

x_t = 1.7922553356473905 + (-0.8770604472900667*x_{t-1}+-0.05836375140117205*x_{t-2}) +
(0.857937953677179*e_{t-1}) + e_t; var(e_t) = 416.996308, d = 1
```

```
println("The optimal model for S&P500 prices by AICc is:")
println(arima2)
```

The output is as follows:

```
The optimal model for S&P500 prices by AICc is:

x_t = 1.7922553356473905 + (-0.8770604472900667*x_{t-1}+-0.05836375140117205*x_{t-2}) +
(0.857937953677179*e_{t-1}) + e_t; var(e_t) = 416.996308, d = 1
```

```
// auto fit an ARIMA model to S&P 500 log returns
val fit_sp500_2 = AutoARIMAFit(log_returns, 5, 1, 5, 0, 0, 1000)
val arima3 = fit_sp500_2.optimalModelByAIC()
val arima4 = fit_sp500_2.optimalModelByAICC()
println("The optimal model for S&P500 log returns by AIC is:")
println(arima3)
```

The output is as follows:

```
The optimal model for S&P500 log returns by AIC is:

x_t = 1.906712718546103E-5 + (0.5853547135786259*x_{t-1}+0.36118328122948645*x_{t-2}) +
(-0.6148623312793726*e_{t-1}+-0.41230588621083164*e_{t-2}+0.0547444231494261*e_{t-3}) +
e_t; var(e_t) = 0.000073, d = 0
```

```
println("The optimal model for S&P500 log returns by AICc is:")
println(arima4)
```

The output is as follows:

```
The optimal model for S&P500 log returns by AICc is:

x_t = 1.906712718546103E-5 + (0.5853547135786259*x_{t-1}+0.36118328122948645*x_{t-2}) +
(-0.6148623312793726*e_{t-1}+-0.41230588621083164*e_{t-2}+0.0547444231494261*e_{t-3}) +
e_t; var(e_t) = 0.000073, d = 0
```

Both AIC and AICc select the same models for prices and log returns. The model chosen for S&P 500 prices is as follows:

$$\Delta Y_t = 1.7923 - 0.8771X_{t-1} - 0.0584X_{t-2} + 0.8579\varepsilon_{t-1} + \varepsilon_t$$

This is an ARIMA(2, 1, 1) model.

The model chosen for S&P 500 log returns is as follows:

$$X_t = 0.00002 + 0.5854X_{t-1} + 0.3612X_{t-2} - 0.6149\varepsilon_{t-1} - 0.4123\varepsilon_{t-2} + 0.0547\varepsilon_{t-3} + \varepsilon_t$$

This is an ARMA(2, 3) model. Note that the variance of the error term seems suspiciously small, 0.000073.

Forecast

The NM Dev class called `ARIMAForecast` makes forecasts for an ARIMA time series using the innovative algorithm, as in Section 15.2.3.3. Continuing with the S&P 500 example, the following code snippet predicts the next ten prices:

```
// make price forecasts based on the fitted model
val forecast_prices = ARIMAForecast(spx, arima1)
println("The next 10 price forecasts for sp500 using the ARIMA(2,1,1) model is:")
for (i in 0 until 10) {
    println(forecast_prices.next())
}
```

The output is as follows:

```
The next 10 price forecasts for sp500 using the ARIMA(2,1,1) model is:
[1258]: 3222.504320 (0.000006)
[1259]: 3224.324729 (0.000011)
[1260]: 3224.449506 (0.000016)
[1261]: 3226.026079 (0.000022)
[1262]: 3226.428302 (0.000027)
[1263]: 3227.775769 (0.000032)
[1264]: 3228.362739 (0.000038)
[1265]: 3229.561543 (0.000043)
[1266]: 3230.268117 (0.000048)
[1267]: 3231.370697 (0.000054)
```

Figure 15-23 plots the results. The top blue line shows the actual prices, and the bottom orange one shows the forecasts from the ARIMA(2, 1, 1) model.

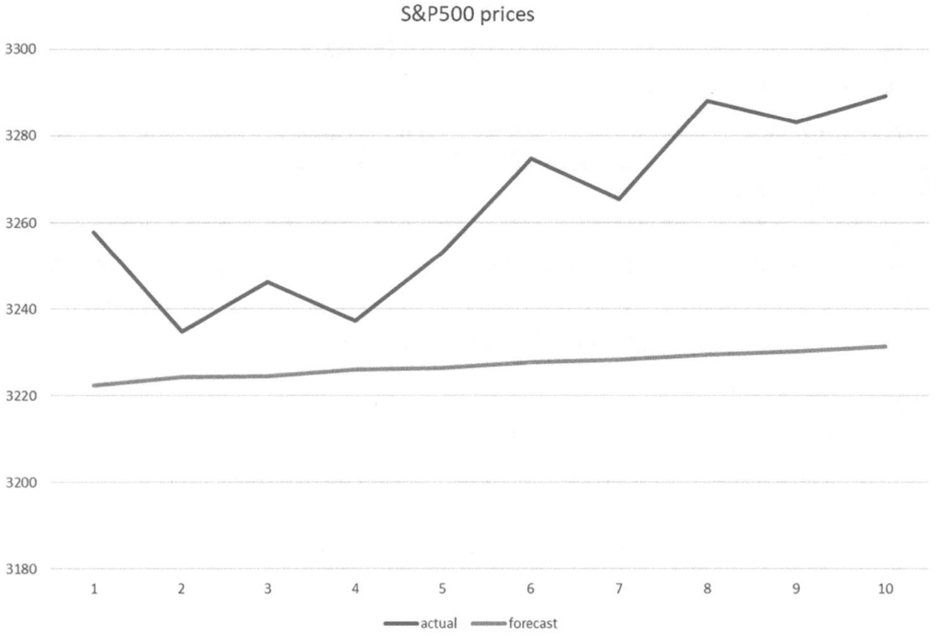

Figure 15-23. *S&P 500 next ten days, actual prices versus forecasts*

The following code snippet predicts the next ten log returns:

```
// forecast log returns based on the fitted model
val forecast_returns = ARIMAForecast(SimpleTimeSeries(log_returns), arima4)
println("The next 10 log return forecasts for sp500 using the ARMA(2, 3) model is:")
for (i in 0 until 10) {
    println(forecast_returns.next())
}
```

The output is as follows:

```
The next 10 price forecasts for sp500 using the ARMA(2,3) model is:
[1257]: -0.000121 (1.000000)
[1258]: 0.000000 (1.000871)
[1259]: -0.000305 (1.005549)
[1260]: -0.000160 (1.005565)
[1261]: -0.000185 (1.006064)
[1262]: -0.000147 (1.006198)
[1263]: -0.000134 (1.006419)
[1264]: -0.000112 (1.006586)
[1265]: -0.000095 (1.006752)
[1266]: -0.000077 (1.006901)
```

Figure 15-24 plots the results. The more volatile blue line shows the actual log returns, and the more stable orange one shows the forecasts from the ARMA(2, 3) model.

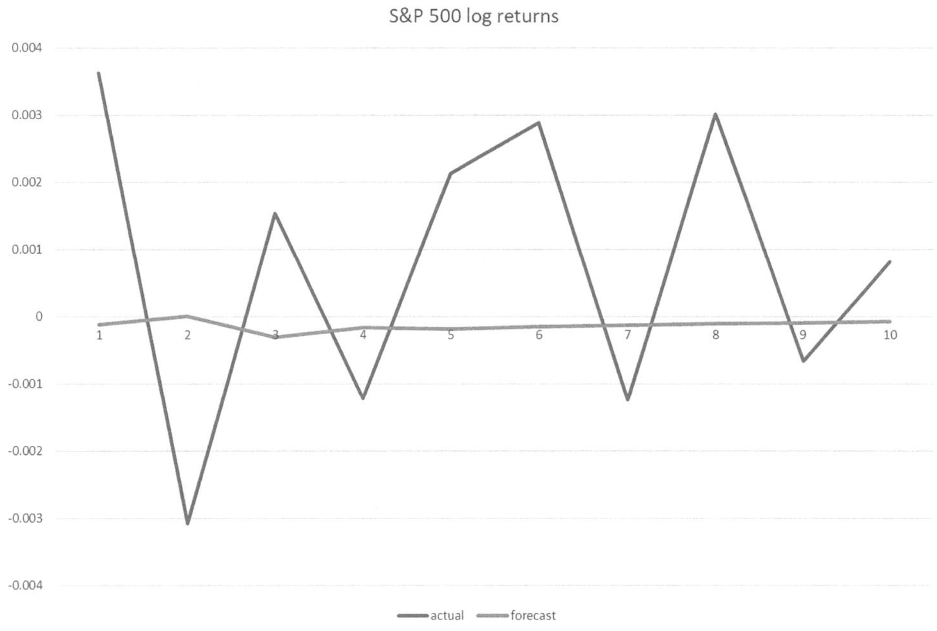

***Figure 15-24.** S&P 500 next ten days, actual log returns versus forecasts*

In Figure 15-23 and Figure 15-24, it is clear that the forecasts or the models severely underestimate the volatility of the data. This is the topic of the next section.

15.2.5. GARCH Model

So far, we have covered the generalized autoregressive conditional heteroskedasticity (GARCH) model, which analyzes the conditional mean of time series. We now introduce the tools to study the volatility or variance of time series. Volatility is important in estimating the forecast error and confidence interval. In finance, volatility is often used as a measure of risk. Figure 15-25 plots the S&P 500 returns. We have already shown that the returns are white noise in Section 15.1.6, but their volatility changes over time. Moreover, periods of large volatility are often followed by periods of large volatility; and periods of small volatility are followed by periods of small volatility. This is called volatility clustering.

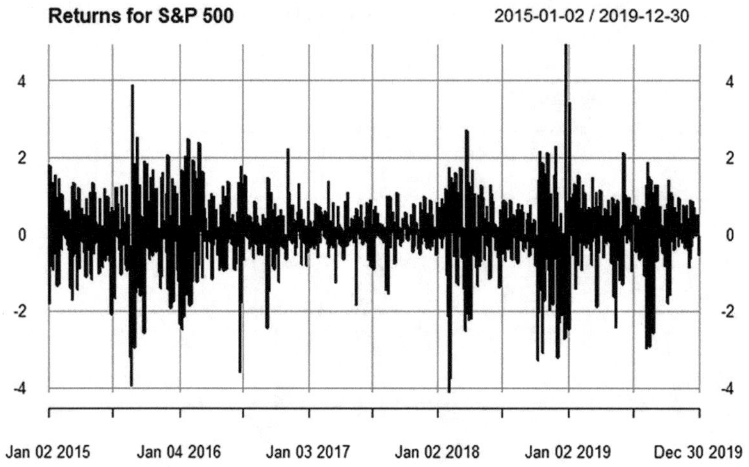

Figure 15-25. *S&P 500 returns*

In Section 15.2.4.4, you saw how to calibrate an ARMA model for the returns. That is, the returned r_t follows an ARMA(p, q) process:

$$r_t = \phi_0 + \sum_{i=1}^{p} \phi_i r_{t-i} + \sum_{j=1}^{q} \theta_j \varepsilon_{t-j} + \varepsilon_t$$

The conditional mean of returns μ_t is as follows:

$$\mu_t = \mathrm{E}\left(r_t \mid r_1, \ldots r_{t-1}\right)$$

$$= \phi_0 + \sum_{i=1}^{p} \phi_i r_{t-i} + \sum_{j=1}^{q} \theta_j \varepsilon_{t-j}$$

$$r_t = \mu_t + \varepsilon_t$$

The conditional variance σ_t^2 is as follows:

$$\sigma_t^2 = \mathrm{var}\left(r_t \mid r_1, \ldots r_{t-1}\right) = \mathrm{E}\left(\left(r_t - \mu_t\right)^2 \mid r_1, \ldots r_{t-1}\right)$$

$$= \mathrm{E}\left(\varepsilon_t^2 \mid r_1, \ldots r_{t-1}\right)$$

ARCH(q)

The error term is as follows:

$$\varepsilon_t = r_t - \mu_t = r_t - \mathrm{E}\left(r_t \mid r_1, \ldots r_{t-1}\right)$$

These ε_t values are split into a stochastic piece z_t and a time-dependent standard deviation σ_t characterizing the typical size of the terms, so that you have this:

$$\varepsilon_t = \sigma_t z_t$$

Where z_t is i.i.d. white noise with zero mean and unit variance.

If you plot the ε_t^2, you'll find that the PACF decays to zero much faster than the ACF. This suggests that an AR process is suitable to model σ_t^2. The autoregressive conditional heteroscedasticity (ARCH) model is a statistical model for time series that describes the variance of the current error term or innovation as a function of the actual sizes of the previous error terms.

$$\sigma_t^2 = \alpha_0 + \alpha_1 \varepsilon_{t-1}^2 + \ldots + \alpha_p \varepsilon_{t-q}^2 = \alpha_0 + \sum_{i=1}^{q} \alpha_i \varepsilon_{t-i}^2$$

Where $\alpha_0 > 0$, $\alpha_i \geq 0$, $i = 1, 2, \ldots, q$, and $\text{var}(\varepsilon_t) < \infty$.

An ARCH(q) model can be estimated using ordinary least squares regression. A hypothesis test for the lag length q of the ARCH effect is as follows. First, estimate the best-fitting autoregressive model AR(q) on the data:

$$y_t = a_0 + a_1 y_{t-1} + \ldots + a_q y_{t-q} + \varepsilon_t$$

Then obtain the squares of the error $\hat{\varepsilon}_t^2$ and regress them on a constant and q-lagged values:

$$\hat{\varepsilon}_t^2 = \hat{\alpha}_0^2 + \sum_{i=1}^{q} \hat{\alpha}_i \hat{\varepsilon}_{t-i}^2$$

Where q is the length of the ARCH lags.

Finally, the null hypothesis is that, in the absence of the ARCH effect, you have $\hat{\alpha}_i = 0$ for all $i = 1, \ldots, q$:

$$H_0 : \hat{\alpha}_1 = \ldots = \hat{\alpha}_q = 0$$

The alternative hypothesis is that, in the presence of the ARCH effect, at least one of the estimated $\hat{\alpha}_i$ coefficients must be significant (nonzero). In a sample of T residuals under the null hypothesis of no ARCH errors, the test statistic is as follows:

$$s = (T - q) R^2$$

where R^2 is R-squared of the regression of $\hat{\varepsilon}_t^2$.

The test statistic follows χ^2 distribution with q degrees of freedom. If s is bigger than the Chi-squared table value, you reject the null hypothesis and conclude that there is an ARCH effect in the ARMA model. If s is smaller than the Chi-squared table value, you do not reject the null hypothesis.

The conditional variance of $\{r_t\}$ can then be written as a sum of past errors or innovations.

$$\text{var}(r_t \mid r_1, \ldots r_{t-1}) = \sigma_t^2 = \alpha_0 + \alpha_1 \varepsilon_{t-1}^2 + \ldots + \alpha_p \varepsilon_{t-q}^2 = \alpha_0 + \sum_{i=1}^{q} \alpha_i \varepsilon_{t-i}^2$$

For ARCH(1), you have this:

$$\varepsilon_t = \sigma_t z_t$$

$$\sigma_t^2 = \alpha_0 + \alpha_1 \varepsilon_{t-1}^2$$

Where $\alpha_0 > 0$, $0 < \alpha_1 < 1$.
The unconditional mean is as follows:

$$E(\varepsilon_t) = E(E(\varepsilon_t | r_1,...r_{t-1}))$$

$$= E(E(\sigma_t z_t | r_1,...r_{t-1}))$$

$$= E(\sigma_t E(z_t | r_1,...r_{t-1}))$$

$$= \sigma_t E(E(z_t | r_1,...r_{t-1})) = 0$$

Because z_t is i.i.d. noise with mean 0.
The unconditional variance is as follows:

$$\text{var}(\varepsilon_t) = E(\varepsilon_t^2)$$

$$= E(E(\varepsilon_t^2 | r_1,...r_{t-1}))$$

$$= E(E(\sigma_t^2 z_t^2 | r_1,...r_{t-1}))$$

$$= E(\sigma_t^2 E(z_t^2 | r_1,...r_{t-1}))$$

$$= E(\sigma_t^2) = E(\alpha_0 + \alpha_1 \varepsilon_{t-1}^2)$$

$$= \alpha_0 + \alpha_1 E(\varepsilon_{t-1}^2)$$

Setting $\text{var}(\varepsilon_t) = \text{var}(\varepsilon_{t-1}) = E(\varepsilon_{t-1}^2)$, you get the following:

$$\text{var}(\varepsilon_t) = \frac{\alpha_0}{1-\alpha_1}$$

The autocovariance function is as follows:

$$\gamma(k) = \text{cov}(\varepsilon_t, \varepsilon_{t-k}) = E(\varepsilon_t \varepsilon_{t-k})$$

$$= E(\sigma_t z_t \sigma_{t-k} z_{t-k})$$

$$= E(z_t) E(\sigma_t \sigma_{t-k} z_{t-k}) = 0$$

Because, again, z_t is i.i.d. noise with mean 0.
Suppose the data is an AR(1) model such that you have this:

$$X_t = \phi_0 + \phi_1 X_{t-1} + \varepsilon_t$$

And ε_t follows ARCH(1).

The unconditional mean of the process is as follows:

$$E(X_t) = \phi_0 + \phi_1 E(X_{t-1}) + E(\varepsilon_t)$$

Since $E(X_t) = E(X_{t-1})$ and $E(\varepsilon_t) = 0$, you have this:

$$E(X_t) = \frac{\phi_0}{1-\phi_1}$$

The unconditional variance of the process is as follows:

$$\text{var}(X_t) = \frac{\text{var}(\varepsilon_t)}{1-\phi_1^2} = \frac{1}{1-\phi_1^2}\frac{\alpha_0}{1-\alpha_1}$$

GARCH(p, q)

If the ARCH model requires a large q or a high order, a generalized autoregressive conditional heteroskedasticity (GARCH) model may be more parsimonious and thus much easier to identify and estimate. A GARCH model is an extension of the ARCH model that incorporates a moving-average component of past variances together with the autoregressive component. Specifically, a GARCH(p, q) model includes p lags of variance terms (e.g., the observations if modeling the white noise residual errors of another process), together with q lags of residual errors from a process.

$$\varepsilon_t = \sigma_t z_t$$

$$\sigma_t^2 = \alpha_0 + \alpha_1 \varepsilon_{t-1}^2 + \alpha_2 \varepsilon_{t-2}^2 + \ldots + \alpha_q \varepsilon_{t-q}^2 + \beta_1 \sigma_{t-1}^2 + \beta_2 \sigma_{t-2}^2 + \ldots + \beta_p \sigma_{t-p}^2 = \alpha_0 + \sum_{i=1}^{q} \alpha_i \varepsilon_{t-i}^2 + \sum_{ij1}^{p} \beta_j \sigma_{t-j}^2$$

Where z_t is i.i.d. white noise with zero mean and unit variance. $\alpha_0 > 0$, $\alpha_{t-i} \geq 0$ for $i = 1, \ldots, q$ and $\beta_{t-j} \geq 0$ for $j = 1, \ldots, p$.

The lag length p in a GARCH(p, q) process can be established in three steps. First, estimate the best-fitting autoregressive model AR(q) on the data.

$$y_t = a_0 + a_1 y_{t-1} + \ldots + a_q y_{t-q} + \varepsilon_t$$

Then compute and plot the autocorrelations of ε^2 as follows:

$$\rho(i) = \frac{\sum_{t=i+1}^{T} \left(\hat{\varepsilon}_t^2 - \hat{\sigma}_t^2\right)\left(\hat{\varepsilon}_{t-1}^2 - \hat{\sigma}_{t-1}^2\right)}{\sum_{t=1}^{T} \left(\hat{\varepsilon}_t^2 - \hat{\sigma}_t^2\right)^2}$$

Finally, the asymptotic, that is for large samples, standard deviation of $\rho(i)$ is $1/\sqrt{T}$. Individual values that are larger than this indicate GARCH errors.

The best identification tool is probably plotting the time series. It is usually easy to spot periods of increased variation here and there in the data. It will be useful to look at the ACF and PACF of both y_t and y_t^2 . For instance, if y_t appears to be white noise and y_t^2 appears to be AR(1), then an ARCH(1) model for the variance may be appropriate. If the PACF of y_t^2 cuts off after lag q, then ARCH(q) may be work. If both ACF and PACF decay slowly, then you can try GARCH.

Given a GARCH(1, 1) process as follows:

$$\varepsilon_t = \sigma_t z_t$$

$$\sigma_t^2 = \alpha_0 + \alpha_1 \varepsilon_{t-1}^2 + \beta_1 \sigma_{t-1}^2$$

The conditional mean is as follows:

$$E(\varepsilon_t | r_1,\ldots,r_{t-1}) = E(\sigma_t z_t | r_1,\ldots,r_{t-1}) = \sigma_t E(z_t | r_1,\ldots,r_{t-1}) = 0$$

The unconditional mean is as follows:

$$E(\varepsilon_t) = E(E(\varepsilon_t | r_1,\ldots,r_{t-1})) = 0$$

The unconditional variance is as follows:

$$\mathrm{var}(\varepsilon_t) = E(\varepsilon_t^2)$$

$$= E(E(\varepsilon_t^2 | r_1,\ldots,r_{t-1})) = E(E(\sigma_t^2 z_t^2 | r_1,\ldots,r_{t-1}))$$

$$= E(\sigma_t^2 E(z_t^2 | r_1,\ldots,r_{t-1})) = E(\sigma_t^2 E(z_t^2))$$

$$= E(\sigma_t^2) = E(\alpha_0 + \alpha_1 \varepsilon_{t-1}^2 + \beta_1 \sigma_{t-1}^2)$$

$$= \alpha_0 + \alpha_1 E(\varepsilon_{t-1}^2) + \beta_1 E(\sigma_{t-1}^2)$$

$$= \alpha_0 + (\alpha_1 + \beta_1) E(\varepsilon_{t-1}^2)$$

$$\mathrm{var}(\varepsilon_t) = \frac{\alpha_0}{1 - \alpha_1 - \beta_1}$$

In NM Dev, you can construct a GARCH model and thus also an ARCH model using the `GARCHModel` class. The class signature is as follows:

```
public class GARCHModel {
    /**
     * Construct a GARCH model.
     *
     * @param a0 the constant term
     * @param a  the ARCH coefficients
     * @param b  the GARCH coefficients
     */
    public GARCHModel(double a0, double[] a, double[] b);
    /**
     * Copy constructor.
     *
     * @param that a GARCH model
     */
```

```
public GARCHModel(GARCHModel that);
/**
 * Get the constant term.
 *
 * @return the constant term
 */
public double a0();
/**
 * Get the ARCH coefficients.
 *
 * @return the ARCH coefficients; could be {@code null}
 */
public double[] alpha();
/**
 * Get the GARCH coefficients.
 *
 * @return the GARCH coefficients; could be {@code null}
 */
public double[] beta();
/**
 * Get the number of GARCH terms.
 *
 * @return the number of GARCH terms
 */
public int p();
/**
 * Get the number of ARCH terms.
 *
 * @return the number of ARCH terms
 */
public int q();
/**
 * Get the maximum of the ARCH length or GARCH length.
 *
 * @return max(# ARCH terms, # GARCH terms)
 */
public int maxPQ();
/**
 * Compute the unconditional variance of the GARCH model.
 *
 * @return the unconditional variance
 */
public double var();
/**
 * Compute the conditional variance based on the past information.
 *
 * @param e2         the last <i>q</i> squared observations
 * @param sigma2_lag the last <i>p</i> conditional variances
 * @return the conditional variance, <i>h(t | F<sub>t</sub>)</i>
 */
```

```
    public double sigma2(double[] e2, double[] sigma2_lag);
    @Override
    public String toString();
}
```

For example, the following code snippet constructs this ARCH(1) process:

$$\sigma_t^2 = 0.2 + 0.212\varepsilon_{t-1}^2$$

```
// σ_t^2 = 0.2 + 0.212 * ε_(t-1)^2
val arch1 = GARCHModel(
                0.2, // constant
                doubleArrayOf(0.212), // ARCH terms
                doubleArrayOf() // no GARCH terms
        )
println(arch1)
println(String.format("conditional variance = %f", arch1.`var`()))
```

The output is as follows:

```
0.2+ 0.212000 * e_{t-1}
conditional variance = 0.253807
```

The following code snippet constructs this GARCH(1, 1) process:

$$\varepsilon_t = \sigma_t z_t$$

$$\sigma_t^2 = 0.2 + 0.212\varepsilon_{t-1}^2 + 0.106\sigma_{t-1}^2$$

```
// σ_t^2= 0.2+0.212ε_(t-1)^2+0.106σ_(t-1)^2
val garch11 = GARCHModel(
                0.2, // constant
                doubleArrayOf(0.212), // ARCH terms
                doubleArrayOf(0.106) // GARCH terms
        )
println(garch11)
println(String.format("conditional variance = %f", garch11.`var`()))
```

The output is as follows:

```
0.2+ 0.212000 * e_{t-1}+ 0.106000 * h_{t-1}
conditional variance = 0.293255
```

The NM Dev class called GARCHSim constructs a random number generator from a GARCH model. It generates a sequence of random numbers with the distribution based on the model, be it ARCH or GARCH. The class signature is as follows:

```
public class GARCHSim implements RandomNumberGenerator {
    /**
     * Simulate an GARCH model.
     *
     * @param model a GARCH model
     * @param z     the innovations; size = q
     * @param rng   a random number generator
     */
    public GARCHSim(
            GARCHModel model,
            double[] z,
            RandomNumberGenerator rng
    );
    /**
     * Simulate an GARCH model.
     * The innovations are initialized to 0.
     *
     * @param model a GARCH model
     * @param rng   a random number generator
     */
    public GARCHSim(
            GARCHModel model,
            RandomNumberGenerator rng
    );
    /**
     * Simulate an GARCH model.
     * The innovations are initialized to 0.
     *
     * @param model a GARCH model
     */
    public GARCHSim(GARCHModel model);
    @Override
    public void seed(long... seeds);
    @Override
    public double nextDouble();
    /**
     * Get the next random (e2_t, h_t).
     *
     * @return the next random (e2_t, h_t)
     */
    public Pair nextPair();
}
```

Note that the nextPair() function generates the next random pair of $\left(\varepsilon_t^2, \sigma_t^2\right)$.

The following code generates a sequence of $\left\{\varepsilon_t^2\right\}$ for the previous GARCH(1, 1) process:

```
// simulate the GARCH process
val sim = GARCHSim(garch11)
sim.seed(1234567890L)
val series: DoubleArray = RNGUtils.nextN(sim, 200)
println(Arrays.toString(series))
```

The (abridged) output is as follows:

```
[0.09464235164181764, -0.04287154757437102, 0.4059365561386082, -0.505733772227959,
0.018704443199705746, 0.10203313531778042, 0.2290917436991943, -1.1774233639361313,
-1.2612835802035602, 0.1202380988464397, -0.3805367043220213, -0.545565537829306,
0.2552633108201118, 0.34673063120199493, 0.3443670090107649, -0.3782080513709261,
-0.21524174277686497, -0.3657868
```

Figure 15-26 shows the output and Figure 15-27 plots the output.

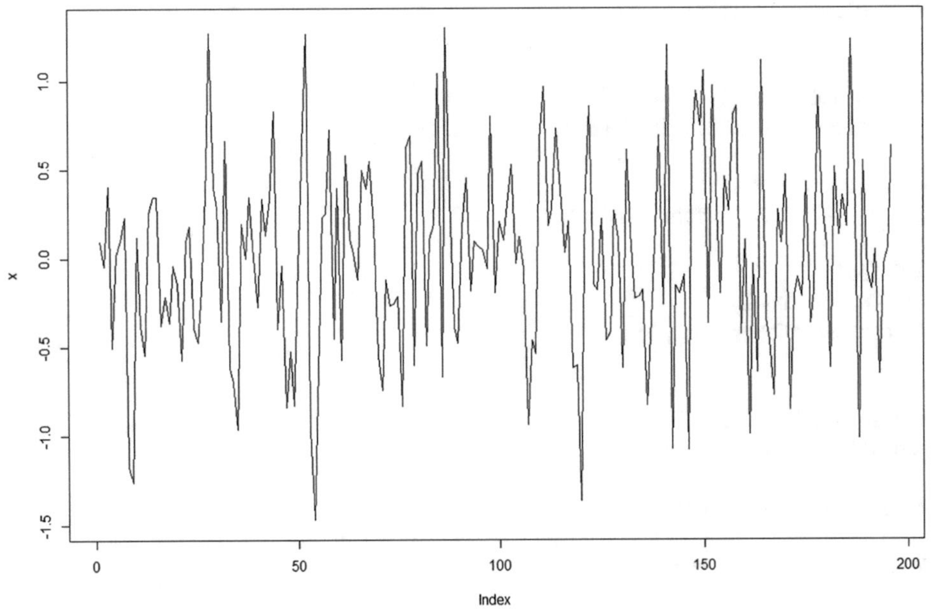

***Figure 15-26.** A simulation of the GARCH process* $\varepsilon_t = \sigma_t z_t$, $\sigma_t^2 = \mathbf{0.2} + \mathbf{0.212}\varepsilon_{t-1}^2 + \mathbf{0.106}\sigma_{t-1}^2$

Estimation

The ARMA (or ARIMA) model gives the (conditional) mean of the time series, and the GARCH (or ARCH) model gives the (conditional) variance. There are two ways to estimate the parameters for the models. One way is to estimate them separately, first ARMA and then GARCH. The other way is to estimate them at the same time.

Here are the steps to estimate the ARMA and GARCH models separately:

1. Fit the given time series $\{X_t\}$ with an ARMA model.
2. Compute the fitted values $\{\hat{X}_t\}$.
3. Get the residuals $Z_t = X_t - \hat{X}_t$.
4. Fit the residuals $\{Z_t\}$ with a GARCH model.

We illustrate these steps by continuing with the S&P 500 example in Section 15.2.5.

Step 1

In that section, you already fit an ARMA model to the log returns of the index data. The model for S&P 500 log returns is an ARMA(2, 3) model.

$$X_t = 0.00002 + 0.5854X_{t-1} + 0.3612X_{t-2} - 0.6149\varepsilon_{t-1} - 0.4123\varepsilon_{t-2} + 0.0547\varepsilon_{t-3} + \varepsilon_t$$

Step 2

In Section 15.2.3.3, you learned how to use the ARMAForecastOneStep class to compute fitted values. The following code snippet computes the fitted values for the log returns per the ARMA model:

```
// compute the conditional means of the model at each time
val log_returns_hat = ARMAForecastOneStep(log_returns, arima4.getARMA())
```

Step 3

The residuals are simply the differences between the observations and the fitted values.

```
// compute the residuals = observations - fitted values
var residuals: DoubleArray = DoubleArray(log_returns.size)
for (t in 0 until log_returns.size) {
    residuals[t] = log_returns[t] - log_returns_hat.xHat(t)
}
println("residuals:")
println(Arrays.toString(residuals))
```

The (abridged) output is as follows:

```
residuals:
[-0.018803861662403516, -0.009667995537079697, 0.009867948291772356, 0.017230524405766275,
-0.008052457343284872, -0.00802263763874365, -0.00388207620190564, -0.006538145657867553,
-0.010089298244179472, 0.012219831049269827, 6.923295906500515E-4, 0.0049467495116336125,
0.014384919218676588, -0.005355196442542493, 0.0027100743427746175, -0.014354852007562454,
-0.01389617168273286, 0.007807679503488708, -0.013934967193129357, 0.01256537802026989,
0.01290446728032751, -0.003443932600304114, ......]
```

Figure 15-27 plots the residuals.

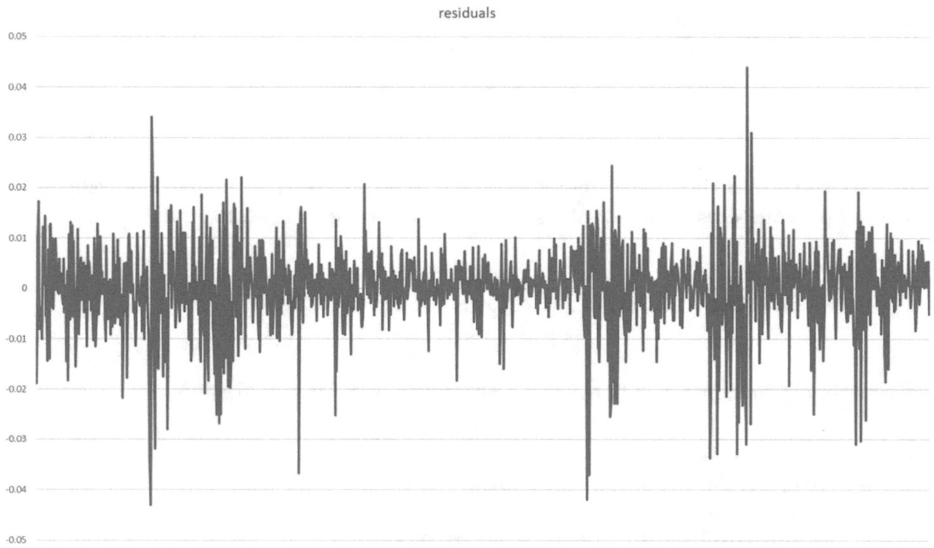

Figure 15-27. *The residuals*

Step 4

Finally, use the NM Dev class called GARCHFit to fit the residuals to a GARCH(1, 1) model:

```
// fit the residuals to a GARCH(1,1) model
val garch_fit = GARCHFit(residuals, 1, 1)
val garch = garch_fit.getModel()
println(String.format("The residual GARCH(1,1) model is: %s", garch))
```

The output is as follows:

```
the residual GARCH(1,1) model is: 8.526563917448361E-6 + 0.240668 * e_{t-1}^2 + 0.603932
* h_{t-1}^2
```

The GARCH model that fits to the residual data is as follows:

$$\varepsilon_t = \sigma_t z_t$$

$$\sigma_t^2 = 0.000008 + 0.240668\varepsilon_{t-1}^2 + 0.603932\sigma_{t-1}^2$$

The complete ARMA-GARCH model for S&P 500 log returns using the two-step approach is therefore as follows:

$$\begin{cases} X_t = 0.00002 + 0.5854X_{t-1} + 0.3612X_{t-2} - 0.6149\varepsilon_{t-1} - 0.4123\varepsilon_{t-2} + 0.0547\varepsilon_{t-3} + \varepsilon_t \\ \varepsilon_t = \sigma_t z_t \\ \sigma_t^2 = 0.000008 + 0.240668\varepsilon_{t-1}^2 + 0.603932\sigma_{t-1}^2 \end{cases}$$

Alternatively, the NM Dev class called ARMAGARCHFit can fit the data to both an ARMA model and a GARCH model jointly in one go. Note that this algorithm will give a (slightly) different result than the two-step approach. ARMAGARCHFit uses the quasi-maximum likelihood estimation (QMLE). It assumes normal distribution for innovations (in the implementation) and uses robust standard errors for inference. Here is the code snippet:

```
// fit both the ARMA and GARCH models in one go
val arma_garch_fit = ARMAGARCHFit(
                log_returns, // the input series
                2, // the order for AR in ARMA model
                3, // the order for MA in ARMA model
                1, // the order for GARCH in GARCH model
                1 // the order for ARCH in GARCH model
        )
println("The ARMA model is:")
println(arma_garch_fit.getARMAGARCHModel().getARMAModel())
println("\nThe GARCH model is:")
println(arma_garch_fit.getARMAGARCHModel().getGARCHModel())
```

The output is as follows:

```
the ARMA model is:
x_t = 1.906712718546103E-5 + (0.5185474463591396*x_{t-1}+0.4510540652006832*x_{t-2}) +
(-0.6106836970210202*e_{t-1}+-0.39996126652483494*e_{t-2}+0.03177641621643222*e_{t-3}) +
e_t; var(e_t) = 1.000000, d = 0
the GARCH model is:
3.355640148051882E-6+ 0.203885 * e_{t-1}+ 0.749625 * h_{t-1}
```

$$\begin{cases} X_t = 0.00001907 + 0.5185X_{t-1} + 0.4511X_{t-2} - 0.6107\varepsilon_{t-1} - 0.4\varepsilon_{t-2} + 0.0318\varepsilon_{t-3} + \varepsilon_t \\ \varepsilon_t = \sigma_t z_t \\ \sigma_t^2 = 0.000003356 + 0.203885\varepsilon_{t-1}^2 + 0.749625\sigma_{t-1}^2 \end{cases}$$

Forecast

An ARMA-GARCH model specifies the dynamics of a stochastic process, predicting the conditional mean and conditional variance. That is:

$$X_t \sim N\left(\hat{X}_t, \sigma_t^2\right)$$

Forecasting $\hat{X}_t$ with ARMA was discussed in Section 15.2.3.3. This section shows how forecasting σ_t^2 for a GARCH(1, 1) model works.

$$\varepsilon_t = \sigma_t z_t$$

$$\sigma_t^2 = \alpha_0 + \alpha_1\varepsilon_{t-1}^2 + \beta_1\sigma_{t-1}^2$$

The one-step forecast is as follows:

$$\sigma_{t+1}^2 = \alpha_0 + \alpha_1 \varepsilon_t^2 + \beta_1 \sigma_t^2$$

The constant α_0 corresponds to the long-run average. The second term $\alpha_1 \varepsilon_t^2$ is the new information that was not available when the previous forecast was made. The third term $\beta_1 \sigma_t^2$ is the forecast that was made in the previous period. The weights on these three terms determine how fast the variance changes with new information and how fast it reverts to its long-run mean.

The two-step forecast is as follows:

$$\sigma_{t+2}^2 = \alpha_0 + \alpha_1 \varepsilon_{t+1}^2 + \beta_1 \sigma_{t+1}^2$$

$$= \alpha_0 + \alpha_1 \sigma_{t+1}^2 z_{t+1}^2 + \beta_1 \sigma_{t+1}^2$$

$$= \alpha_0 + \left(\alpha_1 z_{t+1}^2 + \beta_1\right) \sigma_{t+1}^2$$

$$= \alpha_0 + \left(\alpha_1 + \beta_1\right) \sigma_{t+1}^2$$

In general, for $h \geq 2$, you have the h-step forecast as follows:

$$\sigma_{t+h}^2 = \alpha_0 + \left(\alpha_1 + \beta_1\right) \sigma_{t+h-1}^2$$

15.3. Multivariate Time Series

Many real-life time series are better considered in conjunction with each other because they are intertwined and closely related. For example, a data set of air quality may consist of time series of temperature, pressure, wind speed, and wind direction over time. Each time series alone does not tell you much about air quality, but these component series together give you a more complete picture of reality. Considering the joint properties of multiple time series may also tell you something new that would not otherwise be possible if you considered each independently.

Figure 15-28 plots the prices of the S&P 500 and APPL (Apple stock) from January 1, 1981 to December 12, 2019. Note that AAPL started to become a major player in the market and followed the S&P 500 only since 2008. This was the year when iPhone 3 came out. APPL has had three big sell-offs. It dropped by 46.8 percent from September 2012 to May 2013, during which the S&P 500 rose by 11.7 percent. When APPL fell by 25.8 percent from February 2015 to May 2016, the S&P 500 was flat. During the 36 percent dip by AAPL from its all-time high trading in October 2018 to the close of January 2019, the S&P 500 did not move. When we say APPL is overpriced (or underpriced), it is more meaningful when we compare it to a benchmark such as the S&P 500. We want to study a couple of the time series (AAPL, S&P 500) jointly and study their interdependence and co-movement. Many of the concepts and techniques developed for a univariate time series—such as autoregression, moving-average, stationarity, autocovariance, estimation, and forecast—extend naturally to multivariate time series.

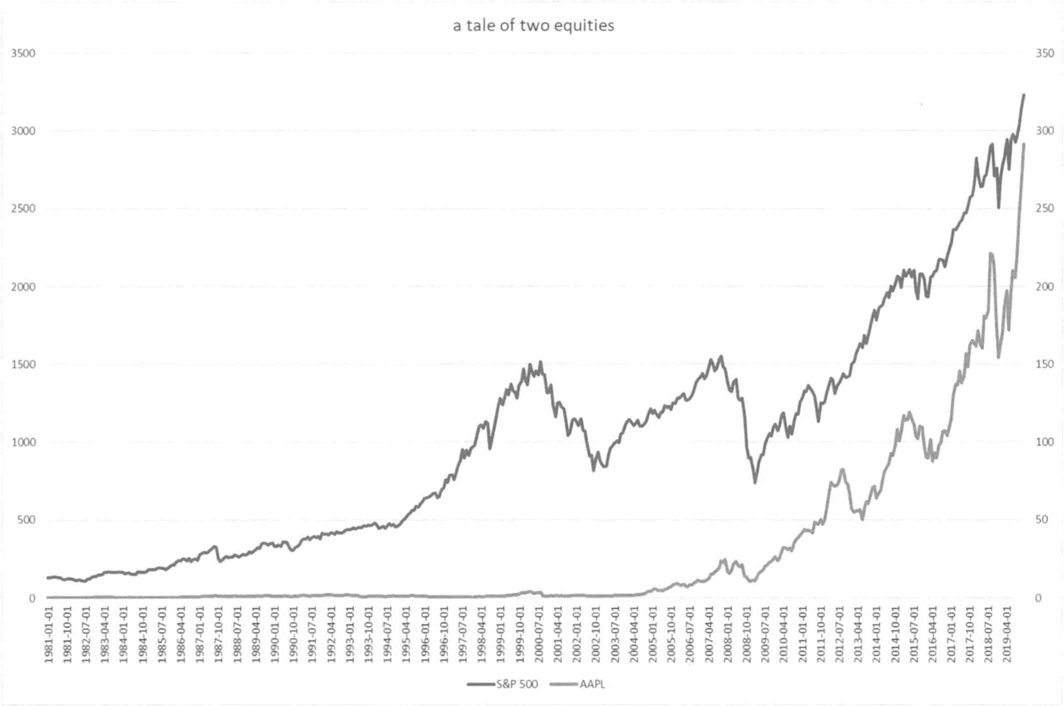

Figure 15-28. *Monthly prices of the S&P 500 and AAPL from 1981 to 2019*

A multivariate time series $\{\boldsymbol{X}_t\}$ consists of m time series $\{X_{ti}, t = 0, \pm1, \pm2, \ldots\}$, $i = 1, \ldots, m$ such that each row in $\boldsymbol{X}_t$ is a univariate time series.

$$\mathbf{X_t} = \left(X_{t1}, \ldots, X_{tm}\right)'$$

A jointly stationary process $\{\boldsymbol{X}_t\}$ implies that every univariate component process $\{X_{ti}\}$ is stationary.

In NM Dev, the data structures to represent multivariate time series, charted in Figure 15-28, mirror those for univariate time series. The top-level interface is `MultivariateTimeSeries`. Depending on the type of the timestamp or index, you have `MultivariateGenericTimeTimeSeries` for any index type as long as it is comparable, `MultivariateRealization` for real-valued time such as for continuous-time stochastic process, and `MultivariateIntTimeTimeSeries` and `MultivariateSimpleTimeSeries` for integer indexed time series.

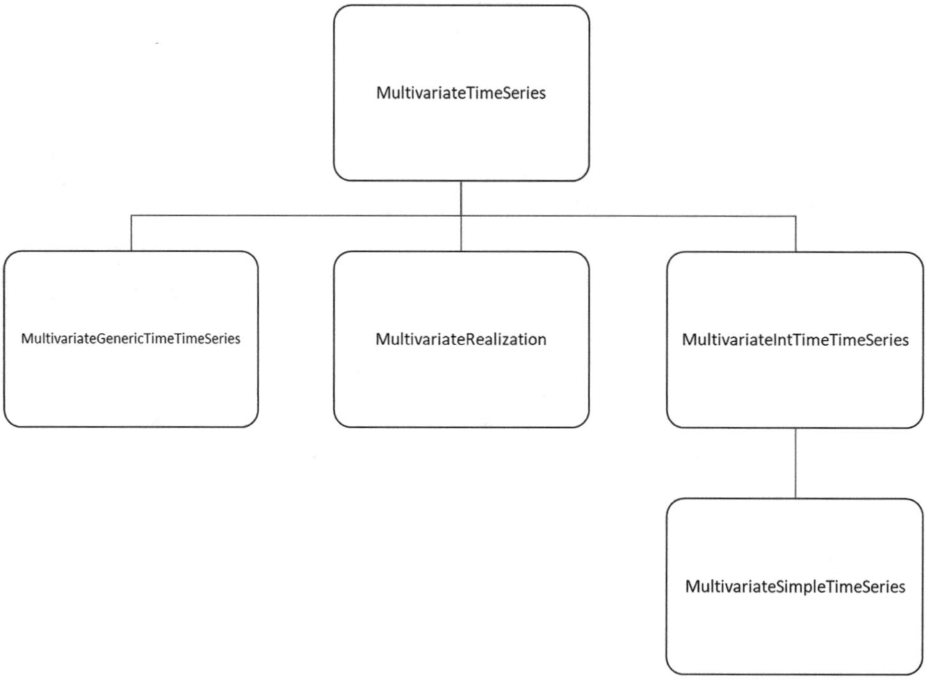

***Figure 15-29.** The hierarchy of classes to represent multivariate time series*

In this section, we mainly use the `MultivariateSimpleTimeSeries` class because we are studying equi-time data. The class signature and the operations that it supports are as follows:

```
public class MultivariateSimpleTimeSeries implements MultivariateIntTimeTimeSeries {
    /**
     * Construct an instance of {@code MultivariateSimpleTimeSeries}.
     *
     * @param values a matrix representation of the time series
     */
    public MultivariateSimpleTimeSeries(Matrix values);
    /**
     * Construct an instance of {@code MultivariateSimpleTimeSeries}.
     *
     * @param values a double array representation of the time series
     */
    public MultivariateSimpleTimeSeries(double[]... values);
    /**
     * Construct an instance of {@code MultivariateSimpleTimeSeries}.
     *
     * @param values a vector representation of the time series
     */
    public MultivariateSimpleTimeSeries(Vector... values);
    /**
     * Construct an instance of {@code MultivariateSimpleTimeSeries} from a
     * univariate time series.
```

```
     *
     * @param ts a univariate time series
     */
    public MultivariateSimpleTimeSeries(IntTimeTimeSeries ts);
    @Override
    public Matrix toMatrix();
    @Override
    public int size();
    @Override
    public int dimension();
    @Override
    public Iterator<Entry> iterator();
    @Override
    public Vector get(int t);
    /**
     * Construct an instance of {@code MultivariateSimpleTimeSeries} by dropping
     * the leading {@code nItems} entries.
     *
     * @param nItems the number of leading entries to be dropped
     * @return a {@code MultivariateSimpleTimeSeries}
     */
    public MultivariateSimpleTimeSeries drop(int nItems);
    /**
     * Construct an instance of {@code MultivariateSimpleTimeSeries} by taking
     * the first difference {@code d} times.
     *
     * @param d the number of differences
     * @return {@code diff(x, lag = 1, differences = d)} as in DoubleUtils
     */
    public MultivariateSimpleTimeSeries diff(int d);
    /**
     * Construct an instance of {@code MultivariateSimpleTimeSeries} by lagging
     * the time series. This operation makes sense only for equidistant data
     * points.
     *
     * @param nLags  the number of lags
     * @param length the length of the lagged time series
     * @return a lagged time series
     */
    public MultivariateSimpleTimeSeries lag(int nLags, int length);
    /**
     * Construct an instance of {@code MultivariateSimpleTimeSeries} by lagging
     * the time series. This operation makes sense only for equidistant data
     * points.
     *
     * @param nLags the number of lags
     * @return a lagged time series
     */
    public MultivariateSimpleTimeSeries lag(int nLags);
    @Override
    public String toString();
}
```

For example, the following code snippet constructs and operates on an integer-indexed, bivariate time series. Each time or row in the time series consists of a pair of real numbers. Note that the NM Dev code has a different convention than the mathematics notation, where each row is a component univariate time series.

```
println("multivariate time series")

// construct a bivariate time series
val X_T0 = MultivariateSimpleTimeSeries(
                DenseMatrix(
                    arrayOf(
                        doubleArrayOf(-1.875, 1.693),
                        doubleArrayOf(-2.518, -0.03),
                        doubleArrayOf(-3.002, -1.057),
                        doubleArrayOf(-2.454, -1.038),
                        doubleArrayOf(-1.119, -1.086),
                        doubleArrayOf(-0.72, -0.455),
                        doubleArrayOf(-2.738, 0.962),
                        doubleArrayOf(-2.565, 1.992),
                        doubleArrayOf(-4.603, 2.434),
                        doubleArrayOf(-2.689, 2.118)
                )))
println("X_T0: " + X_T0)
```

The output is as follows:

```
X_T0: [[-1.875000, 1.693000] , [-2.518000, -0.030000] , [-3.002000, -1.057000] ,
[-2.454000, -1.038000] , [-1.119000, -1.086000] , [-0.720000, -0.455000] , [-2.738000,
0.962000] , [-2.565000, 1.992000] , [-4.603000, 2.434000] , [-2.689000, 2.118000] ]
```

```
// first difference of the bivariate time series
val X_T1 = X_T0.diff(1)
println("diff(1): " + X_T1)
```

The output is as follows:

```
diff(1): [[-0.643000, -1.723000] , [-0.484000, -1.027000] , [0.548000, 0.019000] ,
[1.335000, -0.048000] , [0.399000, 0.631000] , [-2.018000, 1.417000] , [0.173000,
1.030000] , [-2.038000, 0.442000] , [1.914000, -0.316000] ]
```

```
// first order lagged time series
val X_T2 = X_T0.lag(1)
println("lag(1): " + X_T2)
```

The output is as follows:

```
lag(1): [[-1.875000, 1.693000] , [-2.518000, -0.030000] , [-3.002000, -1.057000] ,
[-2.454000, -1.038000] , [-1.119000, -1.086000] , [-0.720000, -0.455000] , [-2.738000,
0.962000] , [-2.565000, 1.992000] , [-4.603000, 2.434000] ]
```

```
// drop the first two items
val X_T3 = X_T0.drop(1)
println("drop(1): " + X_T3)
```

The output is as follows:

```
drop(1): [[-2.518000, -0.030000] , [-3.002000, -1.057000] , [-2.454000, -1.038000] ,
[-1.119000, -1.086000] , [-0.720000, -0.455000] , [-2.738000, 0.962000] , [-2.565000,
1.992000] , [-4.603000, 2.434000] , [-2.689000, 2.118000] ]
```

The following code reads the monthly price data for the S&P 500 and AAPL and computes their log returns:

```
// read the monthly S&P 500 data from a csv file
val spx_arr = DoubleUtils.readCSV2d("./resources/sp500_monthly.csv", true, true)
// convert the csv file into a matrix for manipulation
val spx_M: Matrix = DenseMatrix(spx_arr)
// extract the column of adjusted close prices
val spx_v: Vector = spx_M.getColumn(5) // adjusted closes

// read the monthly AAPL data from a csv file
val appl_arr = DoubleUtils.readCSV2d("./resources/AAPL_monthly.csv", true, true)
// convert the csv file into a matrix for manipulation
val aapl_M: Matrix = DenseMatrix(appl_arr)
// extract the column of adjusted close prices
val aapl_v: Vector = aapl_M.getColumn(5) // adjusted closes

// combine SPX and AAPL to form a bivariate time series
val mts = MultivariateSimpleTimeSeries(cbind(spx_v, aapl_v))
println("(spx, aapl) prices: \n" + mts)

// compute the bivariate time series of log returns
val p1: Matrix = mts.drop(1).toMatrix()
val p: Matrix = mts.toMatrix()
var log_returns_M: Matrix = p1.ZERO() // allocate space for the matrix
for (i in 1 until p1.nRows()) { // matrix and vector index starts from 1
    var r: Double = log10(p1.get(i, 1)) - log10(p.get(i, 1))
    log_returns_M.set(i, 1, r)
    r = log10(p1.get(i, 2)) - log10(p.get(i, 2))
    log_returns_M.set(i, 2, r)
}
// convert a matrix to a multivariate time series
val log_returns = MultivariateSimpleTimeSeries(log_returns_M)
println("(spx, aapl) log_returns: \n" + log_returns)
```

The (abridged) output is as follows:

```
(spx, aapl) prices:
[[129.550003, 0.397911] , [131.270004, 0.373261] , [136.000000, 0.345091] , [132.809998,
0.399671] , [132.589996, 0.466576] , [131.210007, 0.366219] , [130.919998, 0.352133] ,
[122.790001, 0.283467] , [116.180000, 0.214801] , [121.889999, 0.281707] , [126.349998,
0.262339] , [122.550003, 0.311638] , [120.400002, 0.286989] , [113.110001, 0.257057] ,
[111.959999, 0.237690] , [116.440002, 0.207759] , [111.879997, 0.197195] , [109.610001,
0.179588] , [107.089996, 0.190152] , [119.510002, 0.253536] , [120.419998,
```

Figure 15-30 and Figure 15-31 plot the output results. Figure 15-32 is the scatter plot of the log of monthly returns of both equities on the same chart. It clearly shows the co-movement of the time series.

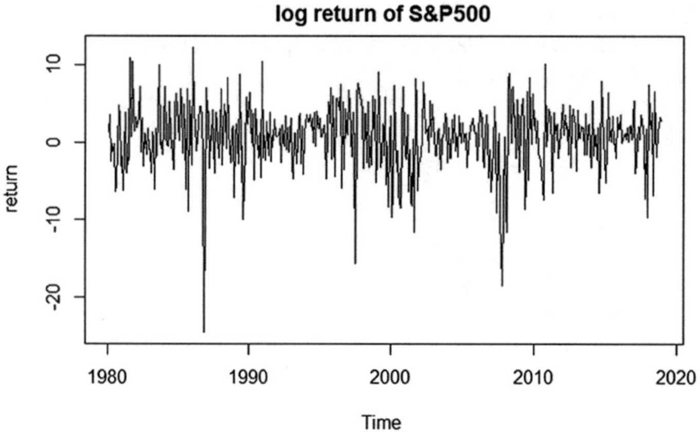

Figure 15-30. *Log monthly returns of the S&P 500 from 1980 to 2019*

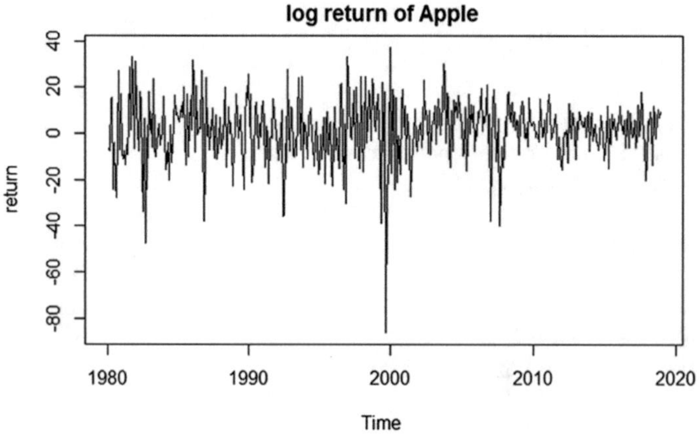

Figure 15-31. *Log monthly returns of AAPL from 1980 to 2019*

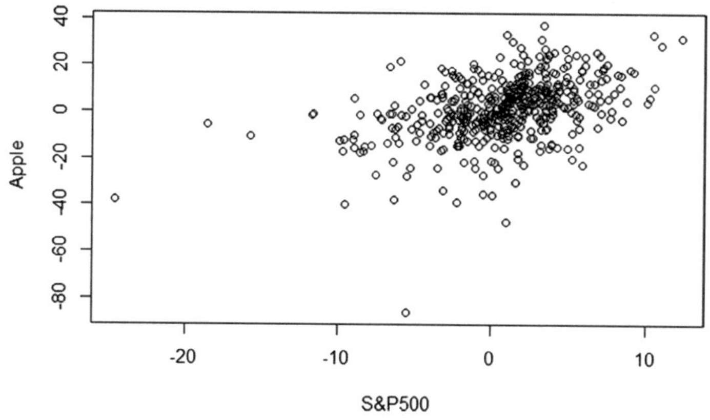

***Figure 15-32.** Scatter plot of log monthly returns of S&P 500 and AAPL*

Let $\boldsymbol{X}_t = \begin{pmatrix} X_{1t} \\ \vdots \\ X_{mt} \end{pmatrix}$, then the mean of $\boldsymbol{X}_t$ is

$$\mu = \mathrm{E}(\boldsymbol{X}_t) = \begin{pmatrix} \mu_1 \\ \vdots \\ \mu_n \end{pmatrix}$$

The cross-covariance function between X_{it} and X_{jt} is a function of the lag distance $k = |\, i - j|$. It is the covariance between lead lag and between pairs of components.

$$\Gamma(k) = \mathrm{cov}(X_t, X_{t+k}) = \mathrm{E}\left((X_t - \mu)(X_{t+k} - \mu)'\right)$$

$$= \mathrm{E}\left(\begin{pmatrix} X_{1t} - \mu_1 \\ \vdots \\ X_{mt} - \mu_m \end{pmatrix}\begin{pmatrix} X_{1t+k} - \mu_1 \\ \vdots \\ X_{mt+k} - \mu_m \end{pmatrix}'\right)$$

$$= \begin{bmatrix} \mathrm{cov}\left(X_{1t}, X_{1(t+k)}\right) & \mathrm{cov}\left(X_{1t}, X_{2(t+k)}\right) & \dots & \mathrm{cov}\left(X_{1t}, X_{m(t+k)}\right) \\ \mathrm{cov}\left(X_{2t}, X_{1(t+k)}\right) & \mathrm{cov}\left(X_{2t}, X_{2(t+k)}\right) & & \mathrm{cov}\left(X_{2t}, X_{m(t+k)}\right) \\ \vdots & & \ddots & \vdots \\ \mathrm{cov}\left(X_{mt}, X_{1(t+k)}\right) & \mathrm{cov}\left(X_{mt}, X_{2(t+k)}\right) & \dots & \mathrm{cov}\left(X_{mt}, X_{m(t+k)}\right) \end{bmatrix}$$

$$= \begin{bmatrix} \gamma_{11}(k) & \gamma_{12}(k) & \dots & \gamma_{1m}(k) \\ \gamma_{21}(k) & \gamma_{22}(k) & & \gamma_{2m}(k) \\ \vdots & & \ddots & \vdots \\ \gamma_{m1}(k) & \gamma_{m2}(k) & \dots & \gamma_{mm}(k) \end{bmatrix}$$

where $i = 1, 2, \ldots, m, j = 1, 2, \ldots, m$ and the following:

$$\gamma_{ij}(k) = E\left[(X_{it} - \mu_i)\left(X_{j(t+k)} - \mu_j\right)\right] = E\left[\left(X_{i(t-k)} - \mu_i\right)\left(X_{jt} - \mu_j\right)\right] = \gamma_{ij}(-k)$$

$\mathbf{\Gamma}(k)$ is called the cross-covariance matrix function for the vector process $\{\mathbf{X}_t\}$. $\gamma_{ij}(k)$ is called the cross-lag covariance. Autocovariance for the i-th component is $\gamma_{ii}(k)$. The matrix $\mathbf{\Gamma}(0)$ is a contemporaneous variance-covariance matrix of process. Covariance between the i-th and j-th components is $\gamma_{ij}(0)$. Variance for the i-th component is $\gamma_{ii}(0)$.

The cross-correlation matrix function for a vector process is given as follows:

$$\rho(k)=\boldsymbol{D}^{-\frac{1}{2}}\Gamma(k)\boldsymbol{D}^{-\frac{1}{2}}=\left[\rho_{ij}(k)\right]$$

for $i = 1, 2, ..., m$ and $j = 1, 2, ..., m$.

$\boldsymbol{D}$ is the diagonal matrix in which the i-th diagonal element is the variance of the i-th component process. That is:

$$\boldsymbol{D}=diag\left[\gamma_{11}(0),\gamma_{22}(0),\ldots,\gamma_{nn}(0)\right]$$

$\rho_{ij}(k)$ is the cross-correlation function between X_{it} and X_{jt}:

$$\rho_{ij}(k)=\frac{\gamma_{ij}(k)}{\left[\gamma_{ii}(0)\gamma_{jj}(0)\right]^{\frac{1}{2}}}$$

$\rho_{ii}(k)$ is the autocorrelation function for the i-th component series X_{it}.

15.3.1. VAR Model

The vector autoregressive model (VAR) is a natural extension of the univariate autoregressive model to multivariate time series. It may provide better forecasts than using a univariate autoregressive model because VAR incorporates structures or dependent relationships among the component time series.

VAR(1)

Consider this VAR(1) model:

$$\begin{pmatrix} X_{1t} \\ \vdots \\ X_{mt} \end{pmatrix} = \begin{pmatrix} \mu_1 \\ \vdots \\ \mu_m \end{pmatrix} + \phi_1 \begin{pmatrix} X_{1(t-1)} \\ \vdots \\ X_{m(t-1)} \end{pmatrix} + \begin{pmatrix} \varepsilon_{1t} \\ \vdots \\ \varepsilon_{mt} \end{pmatrix}$$

In matrix form, it looks like this:

$$\boldsymbol{X}_t = \boldsymbol{\mu} + \boldsymbol{\phi}_1 \boldsymbol{X}_{t-1} + \boldsymbol{\varepsilon}_t$$

Where $\boldsymbol{X}_t$ is an $(m \times 1)$ vector, $\boldsymbol{\mu}$ is an $(m \times 1)$ vector, and $\boldsymbol{\phi}_1$ is an $(m \times m)$ AR coefficient matrix. $\boldsymbol{\varepsilon}_t$ is an $(m \times 1)$ white noise vector with zero mean and covariance matrix structure, as shown here:

$$\operatorname{cov}\left(\varepsilon_t,\varepsilon_{t+k}'\right)=\mathrm{E}\left(\varepsilon_t\varepsilon_{t+k}'\right)=\begin{cases}\Sigma, k=0\\ 0, k\neq 0\end{cases}$$

Where $\mathbf{\Sigma}$ is an $(m \times m)$ symmetric positive definite matrix.

In terms of the backshift operator B, you have this:

$$(\boldsymbol{I}_m - \phi_1 B)\boldsymbol{X}_t = \mu + \varepsilon_t$$

Where $\boldsymbol{I}_m$ is the $(m \times m)$ identity matrix.

VAR(1) is stationary if the roots, z, of the characteristic equation lie outside the complex unit circle, that is, $|z| > 1$.

$\det(\boldsymbol{I}_m - \boldsymbol{\phi}_1 z) = 0$ for $|z| \leq 1$

The ACVF of VAR(1) is as follows:

$$\Gamma(k) = \mathrm{E}\left(\boldsymbol{X}_{t-k}\boldsymbol{X}_t^{'}\right) = \mathrm{E}\left(\boldsymbol{X}_{t-k}\left(\phi_1\boldsymbol{X}_{t-1} + \varepsilon_t\right)^{'}\right)$$

$$= \mathrm{E}\left(\boldsymbol{X}_{t-k}\boldsymbol{X}_{t-1}^{\boldsymbol{c}}\phi_1^{'} + \boldsymbol{X}_{t-k}\varepsilon_t^{'}\right)$$

$$= \Gamma(k-1)\phi_1^{'}$$

For $k \geq 1$.

The variance $\boldsymbol{\Gamma}(0)$ is computed as follows:

$$\mathrm{var}(\mathbf{X}_t) = \phi_1 \,\mathrm{var}(\mathbf{X}_{t-1})\phi_1^{'} + \mathrm{var}(\varepsilon_t)$$

The matrix equation is therefore:

$$\Gamma(0) = \phi_1\Gamma(0)\phi_1^{'} + \mathrm{var}(\Sigma)$$

Solving $\boldsymbol{\Gamma}(0)$ is usually expressed as an infinite sum of the moving-average coefficients.

VAR(p)

More generally, a VAR(p) model is represented as a regression of the lagged values.

$$\begin{pmatrix} X_{1t} \\ \vdots \\ X_{mt} \end{pmatrix} = \begin{pmatrix} \mu_1 \\ \vdots \\ \mu_m \end{pmatrix} + \phi_1 \begin{pmatrix} X_{1(t-1)} \\ \vdots \\ X_{m(t-1)} \end{pmatrix} + \cdots + \phi_p \begin{pmatrix} X_{1(t-p)} \\ \vdots \\ X_{m(t-p)} \end{pmatrix} + \begin{pmatrix} \varepsilon_{1t} \\ \vdots \\ \varepsilon_{mt} \end{pmatrix}$$

where $\boldsymbol{\phi}_i$ is an $(m \times m)$ AR coefficient matrix.

$\boldsymbol{\varepsilon}_t$ is an $(m \times 1)$ white noise vector with zero mean and covariance matrix structure, as shown here:

$$\mathrm{cov}\left(\varepsilon_t, \varepsilon_{\mathbf{t+k}}^{'}\right) = \mathrm{E}\left(\varepsilon_t\varepsilon_{\mathbf{t+k}}^{'}\right) = \begin{cases} \Sigma, k = 0 \\ 0, k \neq 0 \end{cases}$$

where $\boldsymbol{\Sigma}$ is an $(m \times m)$ symmetric positive definite matrix.

In terms of the backshift operator B, you have the following:

$$\boldsymbol{X}_t = \mu + \left(\sum_{i=1}^{p}\phi_i B^i\right)\boldsymbol{X}_t + \varepsilon_t$$

Or the following:

$$\left(\boldsymbol{I}_m - \sum_{i=1}^{p} \phi_i B^i \right) \boldsymbol{X}_t = \mu + \varepsilon_t$$

The stationarity condition is that the characteristic polynomial should have the roots, z, outside the complex unit circle, that is, $|z| > 1$.

$$\det\left(\mathbf{I_m} - \sum_{i=1}^{p} \phi_i z^i \right) = 0 \text{ for } |z| \le 1$$

As an example, a bivariate VAR(p) model can be written as follows:

$$\begin{pmatrix} X_t \\ Y_t \end{pmatrix} = \begin{pmatrix} \mu_1 \\ \mu_2 \end{pmatrix} + \begin{pmatrix} \phi_{11}^1 & \phi_{12}^1 \\ \phi_{21}^1 & \phi_{22}^1 \end{pmatrix} \begin{pmatrix} X_{t-1} \\ Y_{t-1} \end{pmatrix} + \ldots + \begin{pmatrix} \phi_{11}^p & \phi_{12}^p \\ \phi_{21}^p & \phi_{22}^p \end{pmatrix} \begin{pmatrix} X_{t-p} \\ Y_{t-p} \end{pmatrix} + \begin{pmatrix} \varepsilon_{xt} \\ \varepsilon_{yt} \end{pmatrix}$$

In NM Dev, you can construct a VAR model using the `VARModel` class. The class signature is as follows:

```
public class VARModel extends VARMAModel {
    /**
     * Construct a VAR model.
     *
     * @param mu    the intercept (constant) vector
     * @param phi   the AR coefficients (excluding the initial 1)
     * @param sigma the white noise covariance matrix
     */
    public VARModel(Vector mu, Matrix[] phi, Matrix sigma);
    /**
     * Construct a VAR model with unit variance.
     *
     * @param mu  the intercept (constant) vector
     * @param phi the AR coefficients (excluding the initial 1)
     */
    public VARModel(Vector mu, Matrix[] phi);
    /**
     * Construct a VAR model with zero-intercept (mu).
     *
     * @param phi   the AR coefficients (excluding the initial 1)
     * @param sigma the white noise covariance matrix
     */
    public VARModel(Matrix[] phi, Matrix sigma);
    /**
     * Construct a VAR model with unit variance and zero-intercept (mu).
     *
     * @param phi the AR coefficients (excluding the initial 1)
     */
    public VARModel(Matrix[] phi);
    /**
     * Construct a multivariate model from a univariate AR model.
     *
     * @param model a univariate AR model
     */
```

```
    public VARModel(dev.nm.stat.timeseries.linear.univariate.stationaryprocess.arma.
    ARModel model);
    /**
     * Copy constructor.
     *
     * @param that a VAR model
     */
    public VARModel(VARModel that);
}
```

The following code snippet constructs this VAR(1) model:

$$\begin{cases} X_{1t} = 0.7X_{1t-1} + 0.12X_{2t-1} + \varepsilon_t \\ X_{2t} = 0.31X_{1t-1} + 0.6X_{2t-1} + \varepsilon_t \end{cases}$$

Or equivalently:

$$\begin{pmatrix} X_{1t} \\ X_{2t} \end{pmatrix} = \begin{pmatrix} 0.7 & 0.12 \\ 0.31 & 0.6 \end{pmatrix} \begin{pmatrix} X_{1(t-1)} \\ X_{2(t-1)} \end{pmatrix} + \begin{pmatrix} \varepsilon_{1t} \\ \varepsilon_{2t} \end{pmatrix}$$

```
// construct a VAR(1) model
val PHI: Array<Matrix?> = arrayOfNulls<Matrix>(1)
PHI[0] = DenseMatrix(
        arrayOf(
            doubleArrayOf(0.7, 0.12),
            doubleArrayOf(0.31, 0.6)
        ))
val var1 = VARModel(PHI)
println("unconditional mean = " + var1.unconditionalMean())
```

The output is as follows:

```
unconditional mean = [0.000000, 0.000000]
```

VARX(p)

The VARX model is an extension of the VAR model that allows incorporating exogenous variables such as those determined by linear regression. A VARX(p) model is defined as follows:

$$\boldsymbol{X}_t = \mu + \sum_{i=1}^{p} \phi_i \boldsymbol{X}_{t-i} + \psi \boldsymbol{D}_t + \varepsilon_t$$

where $\boldsymbol{D}_t$ is an $(m \times 1)$ vector that contains all exogenous variables at time t (excluding the intercept term) and its coefficients are represented by an m-dimensional vector $\boldsymbol{\psi}$.

In NM Dev, you can construct a VARX model using the `VARXModel` class by specifying ϕ_i and ψ. The class signature is as follows:

```
public class VARXModel extends VARMAXModel {
    /**
     * Construct a VARX model.
     *
     * @param mu    the intercept (constant) vector
     * @param phi   the AR coefficients (excluding the initial 1)
     * @param psi   the coefficients of the deterministic terms (excluding the
     *              intercept)
     * @param sigma the white noise covariance matrix
     */
    public VARXModel(
            Vector mu,
            Matrix[] phi,
            Matrix psi,
            Matrix sigma
    );
    /**
     * Construct a VARX model with unit variance.
     *
     * @param mu  the intercept (constant) vector
     * @param phi the AR coefficients (excluding the initial 1)
     * @param psi the coefficients of the deterministic terms (excluding the
     *            intercept)
     */
    public VARXModel(
            Vector mu,
            Matrix[] phi,
            Matrix psi
    );
    /**
     * Construct a VARX model with zero-mean.
     *
     * @param phi   the AR coefficients (excluding the initial 1)
     * @param psi   the coefficients of the deterministic terms (excluding the
     *              intercept)
     * @param sigma the white noise covariance matrix
     */
    public VARXModel(
            Matrix[] phi,
            Matrix psi,
            Matrix sigma
    );
    /**
     * Construct a VARX model with unit variance and zero-mean.
     *
     * @param phi the AR coefficients (excluding the initial 1)
     * @param psi the coefficients of the deterministic terms (excluding the
     *            intercept)
```

```
     */
    public VARXModel(
            Matrix[] phi,
            Matrix psi
    );
    /**
     * Construct a VARX(p) from a transitory VECM(p).
     *
     * @param vecm a transitory VECM(p)
     */
    public VARXModel(VECMTransitory vecm);
    /**
     * Construct a VARX(p) from a long-run VECM(p).
     *
     * @param vecm a long-run VECM(p)
     */
    public VARXModel(VECMLongrun vecm);
    /**
     * Copy constructor.
     *
     * @param that a VARX model
     */
    public VARXModel(VARXModel that);
}
```

Estimation

There are multiple ways to estimate the model parameters for a VAR(p) model, $\boldsymbol{\mu}$, $\boldsymbol{\phi}_i$, $\boldsymbol{\Sigma}$. Some involve maximum likelihood; some involve some form of linear regression. The simplest way is to perform an OLS regression of a component series, for example, X_{1t}, on the lagged observations, for example, $\{X_{1(t-1)}, X_{2(t-1)}\}$, one at a time for a total of m regressions. The NM Dev class called `VARFit` implements such an estimation algorithm. The following example fits to a data set randomly generated by a known VAR(2) model. You can then compare the estimated model to the true model.

```
// construct a VAR(2) model
val MU: Vector = DenseVector(1.0, 2.0)
val PHI = arrayOf(
    DenseMatrix(
        arrayOf(
            doubleArrayOf(0.2, 0.3),
            doubleArrayOf(0.0, 0.4))),
    DenseMatrix(
        arrayOf(
            doubleArrayOf(0.1, 0.2),
            doubleArrayOf(0.3, 0.1)))
)
val model0 = VARModel(MU, PHI)
```

```
// construct a RNG from the model
val sim = VARIMASim(model0)
sim.seed(1234567891L)

// generate a random multivariate time series
val N = 5000
var ts = arrayOfNulls<DoubleArray>(N)
for (i in 0 until N) {
    ts[i] = sim.nextVector()
}
val mts = MultivariateSimpleTimeSeries(DenseMatrix(ts))

// fit the data to a VAR(2) model
val model1 = VARFit(mts, 2)
println("\nμ = ")
println(model1.mu())
println("\nϕ_1 =")
println(model1.AR(1))
println("\nϕ_2 =")
println(model1.AR(2))
println("\nsigma =")
println(model1.sigma())
```

The output is as follows:

```
μ =
[1.074960, 1.980312]
ϕ _1 =
2x2
        [,1] [,2]
[1,] 0.214364, 0.275072,
[2,] -0.005042, 0.408162,
ϕ _2 =
2x2
         [,1] [,2]
[1,] 0.106844, 0.197318,
[2,] 0.293868, 0.106817,
sigma =
2x2
         [,1] [,2]
[1,] 1.000000, 0.000000,
[2,] 0.000000, 1.000000,
```

The data-generating process has these model parameters:

$$\begin{cases} \mu = \begin{bmatrix} 1 \\ 2 \end{bmatrix} \\ \phi_1 = \begin{bmatrix} 0.2 & 0.3 \\ 0 & 0.4 \end{bmatrix} \\ \phi_2 = \begin{bmatrix} 0.1 & 0.2 \\ 0.3 & 0.1 \end{bmatrix} \\ \Sigma = \begin{bmatrix} 1 & 0 \\ 0 & 1 \end{bmatrix} \end{cases}$$

The estimated model is as follows:

$$\begin{cases} \mu = \begin{bmatrix} 1.074960 \\ 1.980312 \end{bmatrix} \\ \phi_1 = \begin{bmatrix} 0.214364 & 0.275072 \\ -0.005042 & 0.408162 \end{bmatrix} \\ \phi_2 = \begin{bmatrix} 0.106844 & 0.197318 \\ 0.293868 & 0.106817 \end{bmatrix} \\ \Sigma = \begin{bmatrix} 1 & 0 \\ 0 & 1 \end{bmatrix} \end{cases}$$

Thus, the fitted model is reasonably close to the true model.

Continuing with the S&P 500 and AAPL example, let's fit an VAR(1) model to the data:

```
// fit the log returns to an VAR(1) model
val fit = VARFit(log_returns, 1)
println("the estimated phi_1 for var(1) is")
println(fit.AR(1))
```

The output is as follows:

```
the estimated phi_1 for var(1) is
2x2
     [,1] [,2]
[1,] 0.013789, 0.020325,
[2,] 0.027695, 0.060242,
```

The fitted model for the log returns of the S&P 500 X_t and of AAPL Y_t is as follows:

$$\begin{cases} X_t = 0.0149X_{t-1} + 0.0202Y_{t-1} + \varepsilon_{Xt} \\ Y_t = 0.0307X_{t-1} + 0.0599Y_{t-1} + \varepsilon_{Yt} \end{cases}$$

Forecast

NM Dev makes forecasts for a VAR model (or more generally a VARMA model) using the multivariate version of the innovation algorithm, as shown in Section 15.2.3.3. The algorithm needs only the autocovariance structure of the time series for prediction. See Brockwell & Davis (2006) for more details. The NM Dev `MultivariateForecastOneStep` class implements such an algorithm.

For illustration purposes, the following code makes forecasts for a univariate MA(1) process that you treat as a multivariate time series:

$$X_t = \varepsilon_t + \theta\varepsilon_{t-1}$$

The autocovariance function is as follows:

$$\begin{cases} \gamma(0) = \sigma^2\left(1+\theta^2\right) \\ \gamma(1) = \theta\sigma^2 \\ \gamma(k) = 0, k > 1 \end{cases}$$

```
// MA(1) model parameters
val theta: Double = -0.9
val sigma: Double = 1.0

// a multivariate time series (although the dimension is just 1)
val Xt = MultivariateSimpleTimeSeries(
            DenseMatrix(
                arrayOf(
                    doubleArrayOf(-2.58),
                    doubleArrayOf(1.62),
                    doubleArrayOf(-0.96),
                    doubleArrayOf(2.62),
                    doubleArrayOf(-1.36)
                ))
            )

// the autocovariance function
val K = object : MultivariateAutoCovarianceFunction() {

    override fun evaluate(x1: Double, x2: Double): Matrix {
        val i: Int = x1.toInt()
        val j: Int = x2.toInt()

        var k: Double = 0.0

        if (i == j) {
            k = sigma * sigma
            k *= 1 + theta * theta
        }

        if (Math.abs(j - i) == 1) {
            k = theta
            k *= sigma * sigma
```

```
        }

        // γ = 0 otherwise
        val result: DenseMatrix = DenseMatrix(arrayOf(doubleArrayOf(k)))
        return result
    }
}

// run the innovation algorithm
val forecast = MultivariateForecastOneStep(Xt, K)

// making forecasts
for (i in 0..5) {
    println(Arrays.toString(forecast.xHat(i).toArray()))
}
```

The output is as follows:

```
[0.0]
[1.2828729281767954]
[-0.22269169944446712]
[0.5459302808535396]
[-1.632259252377928]
[-0.22241089478200632]
```

Continuing with the S&P 500 and AAPL example, you can use the innovation algorithm to make forecasts of the future log returns for both equities. The NM Dev class called `MultivariateAutoCovarianceFunction` automatically constructs the autocovariance function from a (demeaned) model.

```
val log_returns2 = fit.getDemeanedModel() // demeaned version

// predict the future values using the innovation algorithm
val K = VARMAAutoCovariance(log_returns2, log_returns.size())
val forecast = MultivariateForecastOneStep(log_returns, K)
for (i in 0..5) {
    println(Arrays.toString(forecast.xHat(i).toArray()))
}
```

The output is as follows:

```
[-0.0011136954759254775, -0.0034724968295386954]
[-0.0010870486562220205, -0.0036785428307488867]
[0.002652352403164996, 0.008171489429722277]
[0.0031357055857177477, 0.009321715600157739]
[-0.005096491742666534, -0.014981786357934351]
```

15.3.2. VMA Model

A vector moving-average (VMA) model is a linear combination of a sequence of m-dimensional white noise random vectors.

VMA(1)

Consider a VMA(1) model:

$$\begin{pmatrix} X_{1t} \\ \vdots \\ X_{mt} \end{pmatrix} = \begin{pmatrix} \mu_1 \\ \vdots \\ \mu_m \end{pmatrix} + \theta_1 \begin{pmatrix} \varepsilon_{1(t-1)} \\ \vdots \\ \varepsilon_{m(t-1)} \end{pmatrix} + \begin{pmatrix} \varepsilon_{1t} \\ \vdots \\ \varepsilon_{mt} \end{pmatrix}$$

In matrix notation, you have this:

$$\boldsymbol{X_t} = \mu + \phi_1 \varepsilon_{t-1} + \varepsilon_t$$

Where $\boldsymbol{X_t}$ is an $(m \times 1)$ vector, $\boldsymbol{\mu}$ is an $(m \times 1)$ vector, and $\boldsymbol{\theta_1}$ is an $(n \times n)$ matrix.
ε_t is an $(m \times 1)$ white noise vector with zero mean and covariance matrix structure, as shown here:

$$\text{cov}\left(\varepsilon_t, \varepsilon_{t+k}^{'}\right) = \text{E}\left(\varepsilon_t \varepsilon_{t+k}^{'}\right) = \begin{cases} \Sigma, k = 0 \\ 0, k \neq 0 \end{cases}$$

Where $\boldsymbol{\Sigma}$ is an $(m \times m)$ symmetric positive definite matrix.

VMA(q)

In general, a VMA(q) model of order q is a regression of the observations on the previous white noise, as shown here:

$$\begin{pmatrix} X_{1t} \\ \vdots \\ X_{mt} \end{pmatrix} = \begin{pmatrix} \mu_1 \\ \vdots \\ \mu_m \end{pmatrix} + \theta_1 \begin{pmatrix} \varepsilon_{1(t-1)} \\ \vdots \\ \varepsilon_{m(t-1)} \end{pmatrix} + \ldots + \theta_q \begin{pmatrix} \varepsilon_{1(t-q)} \\ \vdots \\ \varepsilon_{m(t-q)} \end{pmatrix} + \begin{pmatrix} \varepsilon_{1t} \\ \vdots \\ \varepsilon_{mt} \end{pmatrix}$$

Where $\boldsymbol{\theta_i}$ is the $(m \times m)$ MA coefficient matrix.

$\boldsymbol{\varepsilon_t}$ is m-dimensional white noise random vectors with zero mean and covariance matrix structure, as shown here:

$$\text{cov}\left(\varepsilon_t, \varepsilon_{t+k}^{'}\right) = \text{E}\left(\varepsilon_t \varepsilon_{t+k}^{'}\right) = \begin{cases} \Sigma, k = 0 \\ 0, k \neq 0 \end{cases}$$

Where $\boldsymbol{\Sigma}$ is an $(m \times m)$ symmetric positive definite matrix.
In terms of the backshift operator B, you have this:

$$\boldsymbol{X_t} = \mu + \left(\mathbf{I} + \sum_{i=1}^{q} \theta_i B^i\right) \varepsilon_t$$

As in the scalar case, any VMA(q) process is stationary for a finite q. For a VMA(∞) process, it is stationary if the sequence of matrices $\{\theta_i\}_{i=0}^{\infty}$ is absolutely summable. That is, for any $i = 1, 2, \ldots, m$ and $j = 1, 2, \ldots, m$, you have this:

$$\sum_{s=0}^{\infty} \theta_{ij,s} < \infty$$

Where $\theta_{ij,s}$ is the row i and column j element of matrix $\theta_{ij,s}$.

In NM Dev, you can construct a VMA model using the `VMAModel` class. The class signature is as follows:

```
public class VMAModel extends VARMAModel {
    /**
     * Construct a multivariate MA model.
     *
     * @param mu    the intercept (constant) vector
     * @param theta the MA coefficients (excluding the initial 1); {@code null}
     *              if no MA coefficient
     * @param sigma the white noise covariance matrix
     */
    public VMAModel(
            Vector mu,
            Matrix[] theta,
            Matrix sigma
    );
    /**
     * Construct a multivariate MA model with unit variance.
     *
     * @param mu    the intercept (constant) vector
     * @param theta the MA coefficients (excluding the initial 1); {@code null}
     *              if no MA coefficient
     */
    public VMAModel(
            Vector mu,
            Matrix[] theta
    );
    /**
     * Construct a multivariate MA model with zero-mean.
     *
     * @param theta the MA coefficients (excluding the initial 1); {@code null}
     *              if no MA coefficient
     * @param sigma the white noise covariance matrix
     */
    public VMAModel(
            Matrix[] theta,
            Matrix sigma
    );
    /**
     * Construct a multivariate MA model with unit variance and zero-mean.
     *
     * @param theta the MA coefficients (excluding the initial 1); {@code null}
     *              if no MA coefficient
     */
```

```
    public VMAModel(Matrix[] theta);
    /**
     * Construct a multivariate MA model from a univariate MA model.
     *
     * @param model a univariate MA model
     */
    public VMAModel(dev.nm.stat.timeseries.linear.univariate.stationaryprocess.arma.
    MAModel model);
    /**
     * Copy constructor.
     *
     * @param that a multivariate MA model
     */
    public VMAModel(VMAModel that);
}
```

The following code shows how to construct this VMA(1) model:

$$\begin{cases} X_{1t} = 0.5\varepsilon_{1t-1} + 0.16\varepsilon_{2t-1} + \varepsilon_{1t} \\ X_{2t} = -0.7\varepsilon_{1t-1} + 0.28\varepsilon_{2t-1} + \varepsilon_{2t} \end{cases}$$

```
// construct a VAR(1) model
val THETA: Array<Matrix?> = arrayOfNulls<Matrix>(1)
THETA[0] = DenseMatrix(
        arrayOf(
            doubleArrayOf(0.5, 0.16),
            doubleArrayOf(-0.7, 0.28)
        ))
val vma1 = VMAModel(THETA)
println("unconditional mean = " + vma1.unconditionalMean())
```

The output is as follows:

```
unconditional mean = [0.000000, 0.000000]
```

15.3.3. VARMA Model

A multivariate VARMA model is a combination of VAR and VMA models. That is:

$$\begin{pmatrix} X_{1t} \\ \vdots \\ .X_{mt} \end{pmatrix} = \begin{pmatrix} \mu_1 \\ \vdots \\ \mu_m \end{pmatrix} + \phi_1 \begin{pmatrix} X_{1(t-1)} \\ \vdots \\ X_{m(t-1)} \end{pmatrix} + \ldots + \phi_p \begin{pmatrix} X_{1(t-p)} \\ \vdots \\ X_{m(t-p)} \end{pmatrix} + \theta_1 \begin{pmatrix} \varepsilon_{1(t-1)} \\ \vdots \\ \varepsilon_{m(t-1)} \end{pmatrix} + \ldots + \theta_q \begin{pmatrix} \varepsilon_{1(t-q)} \\ \vdots \\ \varepsilon_{m(t-q)} \end{pmatrix} + \begin{pmatrix} \varepsilon_{1t} \\ \vdots \\ \varepsilon_{mt} \end{pmatrix}$$

Where $\boldsymbol{\phi}_i$ is an $(m \times m)$ AR coefficient matrix and $\boldsymbol{\theta}_j$ is an $(m \times m)$ MA coefficient matrix. In matrix notation, you have this:

$$\boldsymbol{X}_t = \mu + \sum_{i=1}^{p} \phi_i \boldsymbol{X}_{t-i} + \sum_{i=1}^{q} \theta_i \varepsilon_{t-i} + \varepsilon_t$$

$\boldsymbol{X}_t$, $\boldsymbol{\mu}$, and $\boldsymbol{\varepsilon}_t$ are m-dimensional vectors.

$\boldsymbol{\varepsilon}_t$ is an $(m \times 1)$ white noise vector with zero mean and covariance matrix structure, as shown here:

$$\text{cov}\left(\varepsilon_t, \varepsilon_{t+k}^{'}\right) = \text{E}\left(\varepsilon_t \varepsilon_{t+k}^{'}\right) = \begin{cases} \Sigma, k = 0 \\ 0, k \neq 0 \end{cases}$$

Where $\boldsymbol{\Sigma}$ is an $(m \times m)$ symmetric positive definite matrix.

In NM Dev, you can construct a VARMA model using the `VARMAModel` class. The class signature is as follows:

```
public class VARMAModel extends VARIMAModel {
    /**
     * Construct a multivariate ARMA model.
     *
     * @param mu    the intercept (constant) vector
     * @param phi   the AR coefficients (excluding the initial 1); {@code null}
     *              if no AR coefficient
     * @param theta the MA coefficients (excluding the initial 1); {@code null}
     *              if no MA coefficient
     * @param sigma the white noise covariance matrix
     */
    public VARMAModel(
            Vector mu,
            Matrix[] phi,
            Matrix[] theta,
            Matrix sigma
    );
    /**
     * Construct a multivariate ARMA model with unit variance.
     *
     * @param mu    the intercept (constant) vector
     * @param phi   the AR coefficients (excluding the initial 1); {@code null}
     *              if no AR coefficient
     * @param theta the MA coefficients (excluding the initial 1); {@code null}
     *              if no MA coefficient
     */
    public VARMAModel(
            Vector mu,
            Matrix[] phi,
            Matrix[] theta
    );
    /**
     * Construct a multivariate ARMA model with zero-intercept (mu).
     *
     * @param phi   the AR coefficients (excluding the initial 1); {@code null}
     *              if no AR coefficient
     * @param theta the MA coefficients (excluding the initial 1); {@code null}
     *              if no MA coefficient
```

```
     * @param sigma the white noise covariance matrix
     */
    public VARMAModel(
            Matrix[] phi,
            Matrix[] theta,
            Matrix sigma
    );
    /**
     * Construct a multivariate ARMA model with unit variance and zero-intercept
     * (mu).
     *
     * @param phi   the AR coefficients (excluding the initial 1); {@code null}
     *              if no AR coefficient
     * @param theta the MA coefficients (excluding the initial 1); {@code null}
     *              if no MA coefficient
     */
    public VARMAModel(
            Matrix[] phi,
            Matrix[] theta
    );
    /**
     * Construct a multivariate model from a univariate ARMA model.
     *
     * @param model a univariate ARMA model
     */
    public VARMAModel(dev.nm.stat.timeseries.linear.univariate.stationaryprocess.arma.
    ARMAModel model);
    /**
     * Copy constructor.
     *
     * @param that a multivariate ARMA model
     */
    public VARMAModel(VARMAModel that);
    /**
     * Compute the multivariate ARMA conditional mean, given all the lags.
     *
     * @param arLags the AR lags
     * @param maLags the MA lags
     * @return the conditional mean
     */
    public Vector conditionalMean(
            Matrix arLags,
            Matrix maLags
    );
    /**
     * Compute the multivariate ARMA unconditional mean.
     *
     * @return the unconditional mean
     */
    public Vector unconditionalMean();
    /**
```

```
     * Get the demeaned version of the time-series model.
     * \[
     * Y_t = (X_t - \mu) = \sum_{i=1}^p \phi_i (X_{t-i} - \mu) + \sum_
     {i=1}^q
     * \theta_j
     * \epsilon_{t-j} + \epsilon_t
* \]

     * &mu; is the unconditional mean.
     *
     * @return the demeaned time series
     */
    public VARMAModel getDemeanedModel();
```

For example, the following code constructs this VARMA(1, 1) for X_t and Y_t:

$$\begin{cases} X_t = 0.7X_{t-1} + 0.5\varepsilon_{t-1} + 0.6\varepsilon_{t-2} + \varepsilon_X \\ Y_t = 0.6\ Y_{t-1} - 0.7\varepsilon_{t-1} + 0.8\varepsilon_{t-2} + \varepsilon_Y \end{cases}$$

```
// construct a VARIMA(1,1) model
val PHI1: Array<Matrix?> = arrayOfNulls<Matrix>(1)
PHI1[0] = DenseMatrix(
        arrayOf(
            doubleArrayOf(0.7, 0.0),
            doubleArrayOf(0.0, 0.6)
        ))
val THETA1: Array<Matrix?> = arrayOfNulls<Matrix>(1)
THETA1[0] = DenseMatrix(
        arrayOf(
            doubleArrayOf(0.5, 0.6),
            doubleArrayOf(-0.7, 0.8)
        ))

val varma11: VARMAModel = VARMAModel(
        PHI1,
        THETA1
)
println("unconditional mean = " + varma11.unconditionalMean())
```

The output is as follows:

```
unconditional mean = [0.000000, 0.000000]
```

For a demeaned VARMA(p, q) process, as shown here:

$$\boldsymbol{X}_t = \sum_{i=1}^{p} \phi_i \boldsymbol{X}_{t-i} + \sum_{i=1}^{q} \theta_i \varepsilon_{t-i} + \varepsilon_t$$

$$\left(\boldsymbol{I}-\sum_{i=1}^{p}\phi_i\boldsymbol{B}^i\right)\boldsymbol{X}_t=\left(\boldsymbol{I}+\sum_{i=1}^{q}\theta_i\boldsymbol{B}^i\right)\varepsilon_t$$

Or it looks like this:

$$\phi(B)\boldsymbol{X}_t=\Theta(B)\varepsilon_t$$

Where:

$$\phi(B)=\left(\boldsymbol{I}-\sum_{i=1}^{p}\phi_iB^i\right)$$

And:

$$\Theta(B)=\left(\boldsymbol{I}+\sum_{i=1}^{q}\theta_iB^i\right)\varepsilon_t$$

$\boldsymbol{I}$ is the identity matrix. $\boldsymbol{\phi}(B)$ and $\boldsymbol{\Theta}(B)$ are matrix-valued polynomials, such that you have this:

$$\phi(z)=\boldsymbol{I}-\phi_1z-\ldots-\phi_pz^p$$

And this:

$$\Theta(z)=\boldsymbol{I}+\theta_1z+\ldots+\theta_qz^q$$

It can be shown that $\boldsymbol{X}_t$ is causal, meaning that $\boldsymbol{X}_t$ can be written as an infinite sum of MA terms, if and only if the roots, z, of the $\boldsymbol{\phi}(z)$ lie outside the complex unit circle, that is, $|z| > 1$.

That is, if and only if this:

$$\det \boldsymbol{\phi}(z) \neq 0, \text{ for } |z| \leq 1$$

Then you have this:

$$\boldsymbol{X}_t=\sum_{i=0}^{\infty}\Psi_i\varepsilon_{t-i}$$

where:

$$\Psi(z)=\sum_{i=0}^{\infty}\Psi_iz^i=\phi^{-1}(z)\Theta(z)$$

On the other hand, it can be shown that $\boldsymbol{X}_t$ is invertible, meaning that $\boldsymbol{X}_t$ can be written as an infinite sum of AR terms, if and only if the roots, z, of the $\boldsymbol{\Theta}(z)$ lie outside the complex unit circle, that is, $|z| > 1$.

That is, if and only if this:

$$\det \boldsymbol{\Theta}(z) \neq 0, \text{ for } |z| \leq 1$$

Then you have the following:

$$\varepsilon_t=\sum_{i=0}^{\infty}\Pi_i\boldsymbol{X}_{t-i}$$

Where:

$$\Pi(z) = \sum_{i=0}^{\infty} \Pi_i z^i = \Theta^{-1}(z)\phi(z)$$

You should usually assume that $\boldsymbol{X}_t$ is stationary, causal, and invertible.

To find the autocovariance function of the process, $\Gamma(k)$, consider post-multiplying the ARMA equation by $\boldsymbol{X}_{t-k}^{'}$ on both sides and taking expectations. The ARMA equation is as follows:

$$\left(\sum_{i=0}^{p} \phi_i \mathbf{X}_{t-i}\right) = \left(\sum_{i=0}^{q} \theta_i \varepsilon_{t-i}\right)$$

$$\phi_0 = \theta_0 = \boldsymbol{I}$$

This gives the following:

$$\sum_{i=0}^{p} \phi_i \mathrm{E}|(\boldsymbol{X}_{t-i} \boldsymbol{X}'_{t-k}) = \sum_{i=0}^{q} \theta_i \mathrm{E}(\varepsilon_{t-i} \boldsymbol{X}'_{t-k})$$

To compute $\mathrm{E}\left(\varepsilon_{t-i} \boldsymbol{X}_{t-k}^{'}\right)$, you can use the infinite-order moving-average representation of the ARMA process (causality).

$$\boldsymbol{X}_{t-k} = \sum_{j=0}^{\infty} \Psi_j \varepsilon_{t-k-j}$$

Putting the two equations together, you get this:

$$\sum_{i=0}^{p} \phi_i \mathrm{E}(\boldsymbol{X}_{t-i} \boldsymbol{X}'_{t-k}) = \sum_{i=0}^{q} \sum_{j=0}^{\infty} \theta_i \mathrm{E}\left(\varepsilon_{t-i} \varepsilon_{t-k-j}^{'}\right) \Psi_j^{'}$$

Note the following:

$$\mathrm{E}\left(\boldsymbol{X}_{t-i} \boldsymbol{X}_{t-k}^{'}\right) = \Gamma(k-i)$$

$$\mathrm{E}\left(\varepsilon_{t-i} \varepsilon_{t-k-j}^{'}\right) = \begin{cases} \Sigma, j = i-k \\ \mathbf{0}, j \neq i-k \end{cases}$$

You can simplify the equation to the following:

$$\sum_{i=0}^{p} \phi_i \Gamma(k-i) = \sum_{i=k}^{q} \theta_i \Sigma \Psi_{i-k}^{'}$$

The autocovariance function for a causal ARMA process can be determined recursively by solving this system of Yule-Walker equations:

$$\Gamma(k) = \begin{cases} -\sum_{i=1}^{p} \phi_i \Gamma(k-i) + \sum_{i=k}^{q} \theta_i \Sigma \Psi_{i-k}^{'}, k \leq q \\ -\sum_{i=1}^{p} \phi_i \Gamma(k-i), k > q \end{cases}$$

In the case of a pure autoregressive process of order p, $\boldsymbol{\theta}_i = \mathbf{0}$ for $i > 1$, there are the following:

$$\begin{cases} \Gamma(0) = -\sum_{i=1}^{p} \phi_i \Gamma(i) + \Sigma \\ \Gamma(k) = -\sum_{i=1}^{p} \phi_i \Gamma(k-i) \end{cases}$$

In the case of a pure moving-average process of order q, $\boldsymbol{\phi}_i = \mathbf{0}$ for $i > 0$, there are the following:

$$\Gamma(k) = \sum_{i=k}^{q} \theta_i \Sigma \theta_{i-k}'$$

For $k = 0, \ldots, q$.

In NM Dev, the `VARMAAutoCovariance` class computes the autocovariance function for a causal VARMA process. The `VARMAAutoCorrelation` class computes the autocorrelation function. Section 15.3.1.5 shows how to compute the autocovariance function for S&P 500 log returns. The following is another example to compute the autocovariance function for a VARMA model:

```
// the AR coefficients
val AR = arrayOf(
    DenseMatrix(
        arrayOf(
            doubleArrayOf(0.5, 0.5),
            doubleArrayOf(0.0, 0.5)))
)

// the MA coefficients
var MA = arrayOf(
    AR[0].t()
)

// SIGMA
val SIGMA: Matrix = DenseMatrix(
                arrayOf(
                    doubleArrayOf(1.0, 0.2),
                    doubleArrayOf(0.2, 1.0)
                ))

// define a VARIMA(1,1) model
val varma11 = VARMAModel(AR, MA, SIGMA)

// compute the autocovariance function for a VARIMA process up to a certain number of lags
val GAMMA = VARMAAutoCovariance(
                varma11,
                10 // number of lags
        )
```

```
// print out the autocovariance function
for (i in 0..5) {
    println(String.format("GAMMA(%d) = %n", i))
    println(GAMMA.evaluate(1.0))
    println()
}
```

The output is as follows:

```
GAMMA(0) =
2x2
         [,1] [,2]
[1,] 5.598667, 3.897333,
[2,] 3.524000, 3.241333,
GAMMA(1) =
2x2
         [,1] [,2]
[1,] 5.598667, 3.897333,
[2,] 3.524000, 3.241333,
GAMMA(2) =
2x2
         [,1] [,2]
[1,] 5.598667, 3.897333,
[2,] 3.524000, 3.241333,
GAMMA(3) =
2x2
         [,1] [,2]
[1,] 5.598667, 3.897333,
[2,] 3.524000, 3.241333,
GAMMA(4) =
2x2
         [,1] [,2]
[1,] 5.598667, 3.897333,
[2,] 3.524000, 3.241333,
GAMMA(5) =
2x2
         [,1] [,2]
[1,] 5.598667, 3.897333,
[2,] 3.524000, 3.241333,
```

15.3.4. VARIMA Model

As with the scalar time series case, when there is a unit root or the data is not stationary, you can take the first difference and model the differences instead. An VARIMA(p, d, q) process is a multivariate time series ***Yt*** such that you have this:

$$\begin{cases} \boldsymbol{X}_t = (\boldsymbol{I} - B)^{\mathrm{d}} \boldsymbol{Y}_t \\ \phi(B)\boldsymbol{X}_t = \Theta(B)\varepsilon_t \end{cases}$$

In NM Dev, the VARIMAModel class represents such a model. The class signature is as follows:

```
public class VARIMAModel extends VARIMAXModel {
    /**
     * Construct a multivariate ARIMA model.
     *
     * @param MU    the intercept (constant) vector
     * @param PHI   the AR coefficients (excluding the initial 1); {@code null}
     *              if no AR coefficient
     * @param d     the order of integration
     * @param THETA the MA coefficients (excluding the initial 1); {@code null}
     *              if no MA coefficient
     * @param SIGMA the white noise covariance matrix
     */
    public VARIMAModel(
            Vector MU,
            Matrix[] PHI,
            int d,
            Matrix[] THETA,
            Matrix SIGMA
    );
    /**
     * Construct a multivariate ARIMA model with unit variance.
     *
     * @param MU    the intercept (constant) vector
     * @param PHI   the AR coefficients (excluding the initial 1); {@code null}
     *              if no AR coefficient
     * @param d     the order of integration
     * @param THETA the MA coefficients (excluding the initial 1); {@code null}
     *              if no MA coefficient
     */
    public VARIMAModel(
            Vector MU,
            Matrix[] PHI,
            int d,
            Matrix[] THETA
    );
    /**
     * Construct a multivariate ARIMA model with zero-intercept (mu).
     *
     * @param PHI   the AR coefficients (excluding the initial 1); {@code null}
     *              if no AR coefficient
     * @param d     the order of integration
     * @param THETA the MA coefficients (excluding the initial 1); {@code null}
     *              if no MA coefficient
     * @param SIGMA the white noise covariance matrix
     */
    public VARIMAModel(
            Matrix[] PHI,
            int d,
            Matrix[] THETA,
```

```
            Matrix SIGMA
    );
    /**
     * Construct a multivariate ARIMA model with unit variance and
     * zero-intercept (mu).
     *
     * @param PHI   the AR coefficients (excluding the initial 1); {@code null}
     *              if no AR coefficient
     * @param d     the order of integration
     * @param THETA the MA coefficients (excluding the initial 1); {@code null}
     *              if no MA coefficient
     */
    public VARIMAModel(
            Matrix[] PHI,
            int d,
            Matrix[] THETA
    );
    /**
     * Construct a multivariate model from a univariate ARIMA model.
     *
     * @param model a univariate ARIMA model
     */
    public VARIMAModel(dev.nm.stat.timeseries.linear.univariate.arima.ARIMAModel model);
    /**
     * Copy constructor.
     *
     * @param that a multivariate ARIMA model
     */
    public VARIMAModel(VARIMAModel that);
    /**
     * Get the ARMA part of this ARIMA model, essentially ignoring the
     * differencing.
     *
     * @return the ARMA part
     */
    public VARMAModel getVARMA();
}
```

For example, this is an VARIMA process:

$$\begin{cases} \Delta \boldsymbol{Y}_t = \boldsymbol{Y}_t - \boldsymbol{Y}_{t-1} = \boldsymbol{c} + \boldsymbol{X}_t \\ X_{1t} = 0.3X_{1t-1} - 0.2X_{2t-1} + 0.2\varepsilon_{1t-1} + \varepsilon_{1t} \\ X_{2t} = 0.05X_{1t-1} + 0.04X_{2t-1} + 0.5\varepsilon_{2t-1} + \varepsilon_{2t} \end{cases}$$

You can also add exogenous variables or factors to the equation. A VARIMAX(p, d, q) model is such that you have this:

$$\begin{cases} \boldsymbol{X}_t = (\boldsymbol{I} - B)^{d} \boldsymbol{Y}_t \\ \phi(B)\boldsymbol{X}_t = \Theta(B)\varepsilon_t + \psi_t \boldsymbol{D}_t \end{cases}$$

Where $\boldsymbol{D}_t$ is a vector that contains all exogenous variables at time t (excluding the intercept term) and its coefficients are represented as vector $\boldsymbol{\psi}_t$.

In NM Dev, the VARIMAXModel class represents such a model. The class signature is as follows:

```
public class VARIMAXModel {
    /**
     * Construct a multivariate ARIMAX model.
     *
     * @param MU    the intercept (constant) vector
     * @param PHI   the AR coefficients (excluding the initial 1); {@code null}
     *              if no AR coefficient
     * @param d     the order of integration
     * @param THETA the MA coefficients (excluding the initial 1); {@code null}
     *              if no MA coefficient
     * @param PSI   the coefficients of the deterministic terms (excluding the
     *              intercept term)
     * @param SIGMA the white noise covariance matrix
     */
    public VARIMAXModel(
            Vector MU,
            Matrix[] PHI,
            int d,
            Matrix[] THETA,
            Matrix PSI,
            Matrix SIGMA
    );
    /**
     * Construct a multivariate ARIMAX model with unit variance.
     *
     * @param MU    the intercept (constant) vector
     * @param PHI   the AR coefficients (excluding the initial 1); {@code null}
     *              if no AR coefficient
     * @param d     the order of integration
     * @param THETA the MA coefficients (excluding the initial 1); {@code null}
     *              if no MA coefficient
     * @param PSI   the coefficients of the deterministic terms (excluding the
     *              intercept term)
     */
    public VARIMAXModel(
            Vector MU,
            Matrix[] PHI,
            int d,
            Matrix[] THETA,
            Matrix PSI
    );
    /**
```

```
 * Construct a multivariate ARIMAX model with zero-intercept (mu).
 *
 * @param PHI   the AR coefficients (excluding the initial 1); {@code null}
 *              if no AR coefficient
 * @param d     the order of integration
 * @param THETA the MA coefficients (excluding the initial 1); {@code null}
 *              if no MA coefficient
 * @param PSI   the coefficients of the deterministic terms (excluding the
 *              intercept term)
 * @param SIGMA the white noise covariance matrix
 */
public VARIMAXModel(
        Matrix[] PHI,
        int d,
        Matrix[] THETA,
        Matrix PSI,
        Matrix SIGMA
);
/**
 * Construct a multivariate ARIMAX model with unit variance and
 * zero-intercept (mu).
 *
 * @param PHI   the AR coefficients (excluding the initial 1); {@code null}
 *              if no AR coefficient
 * @param d     the order of integration
 * @param THETA the MA coefficients (excluding the initial 1); {@code null}
 *              if no MA coefficient
 * @param PSI   the coefficients of the deterministic terms (excluding the
 *              intercept term)
 */
public VARIMAXModel(
        Matrix[] PHI,
        int d,
        Matrix[] THETA,
        Matrix PSI
);
/**
 * Copy constructor.
 *
 * @param that a multivariate ARIMAX model
 */
public VARIMAXModel(VARIMAXModel that);
/**
 * Construct a multivariate ARIMAX model from a univariate ARIMAX model.
 *
 * @param model a univariate ARIMAX model
 */
public VARIMAXModel(
        dev.nm.stat.timeseries.linear.univariate.arima.ARIMAXModel model
```

```
);
/**
 * Get the intercept (constant) vector.
 *
 * @return the intercept (constant) vector
 */
public ImmutableVector mu();
/**
 * Get the <i>i</i>-th AR coefficient; AR(0) = 1.
 *
 * @param i an index
 * @return the <i>i</i>-th AR coefficient
 */
public ImmutableMatrix AR(int i);
/**
 * Get all the AR coefficients.
 *
 * @return all the AR coefficients
 */
public ImmutableMatrix[] phi();
/**
 * Get the <i>i</i>-th MA coefficient; MA(0) = 1.
 *
 * @param i an index
 * @return the <i>i</i>-th MA coefficient
 */
public ImmutableMatrix MA(int i);
/**
 * Get all the MA coefficients.
 *
 * @return all the MA coefficients
 */
public ImmutableMatrix[] theta();
/**
 * Get the coefficients of the deterministic terms.
 *
 * @return the coefficients of the deterministic terms; could be
 *         {@code null}
 */
public ImmutableMatrix psi();
/**
 * Get the order of integration.
 *
 * @return the order of integration
 */
public int d();
/**
 * Get the dimension of multivariate time series.
 *
 * @return the dimension of multivariate time series
 */
```

```
    public int dimension();
    /**
     * Get the number of AR terms.
     *
     * @return the number of AR terms
     */
    public int p();
    /**
     * Get the number of MA terms.
     *
     * @return the number of MA terms
     */
    public int q();
    /**
     * Get the maximum of AR length or MA length.
     *
     * @return max(# AR terms, # MA terms)
     */
    public int maxPQ();
    /**
     * Get the white noise covariance matrix.
     *
     * @return the white noise covariance matrix
     */
    public ImmutableMatrix sigma();
    /**
     * Get the ARMAX part of this ARIMAX model, essentially ignoring the
     * differencing.
     *
     * @return the ARMAX part
     */
    public VARMAXModel getVARMAX();
}
```

The NM Dev class called `VARIMASim` takes a VARIMA model (or any variant of it) and constructs a random number generator that produces a sequence of random vectors that follow the probability distribution of the model. Here's an example:

```
// number of random numbers to generate
val T = 100000

// the mean
val MU: Vector = DenseVector(1.0, 1.0)
// the AR coefficients
val PHI = arrayOf(
    DenseMatrix(
    arrayOf(
        doubleArrayOf(0.5, 0.5),
        doubleArrayOf(0.0, 0.5)
)))
// the MA coefficients
```

```
val THETA = arrayOf(PHI[0])
// the white noise covariance structure
val SIGMA: Matrix = DenseMatrix(
                arrayOf(
                    doubleArrayOf(1.0, 0.2),
                    doubleArrayOf(0.2, 1.0)
                ))

// construct a VARMA model
val VARMA = VARMAModel(MU, PHI, THETA, SIGMA)

// construct a random number generator from a VARMA model
val SIM = VARIMASim(VARMA)
SIM.seed(1234567890L)

// produce the random vectors
val data = arrayOfNulls<DoubleArray>(T)
for (i in 0 until T) {
    data[i] = SIM.nextVector()
}

// statistics about the simulation
// println(String.format("each vector size = %d%n", data[0].size()))
// println(String.format("sample size = %d%n", data.length))

// compute the theoretical mean of the data
// val theoretical_mean: DoubleArray = Inverse(DenseMatrix(arrayOf(doubleArrayOf(2.0,
2.0))).ONE().minus(VARMA.AR(1))).multiply(DenseVector(MU)).toArray()
// println("theoretical mean =")
// println(Arrays.toString(theoretical_mean))

// cast the random data in matrix form for easy manipulation
val dataM: Matrix = MatrixFactory.rbind(DenseMatrix(data))
// compute the sample mean of the data
val sample_mean1: Double = Mean(dataM.getColumn(1).toArray()).value()
val sample_mean2: Double = Mean(dataM.getColumn(2).toArray()).value()
println(String.format("Sample mean of the first variable = %f%n", sample_mean1))
println(String.format("Sample mean of the second variable = %f%n", sample_mean2))

// compute the theoretical covariance of the data
val cov_theoretical: Matrix = DenseMatrix(
        arrayOf(
            doubleArrayOf(811.0 / 135.0, 101.0 / 45.0),
            doubleArrayOf(101.0 / 45.0, 7.0 / 3.0)
        ))
println("Theoretical covariance =")
println(cov_theoretical)

// compute the sample covariance of the data
val sample_cov = SampleCovariance(dataM)
```

```
println("\nSample covariance =")
println(sample_cov)
```

The output is as follows:

```
each vector size = 2
sample size = 100000
theoretical mean =
[4.0, 2.0]
sample mean of the first variable = 3.994879
sample mean of the second variable = 2.005700
theoretical covariance =
2x2
        [,1] [,2]
[1,] 6.007407, 2.244444,
[2,] 2.244444, 2.333333,
sample covariance =
2x2
        [,1] [,2]
[1,] 5.315639, 1.790519,
[2,] 1.790519, 2.340646,
```

Note that the sample statistics for the simulated data match the theoretical statistics reasonably well.

15.4. Cointegration

In time-series analysis and prediction, you usually work with stationary data so that the mean and variance do not vary. It would be rather difficult to make any prediction if the data's statistical properties changed all the time. However, much real-life data such as financial data is not stationary. Although you can do first differencing to make it stationary, you would lose any long-term information in the data. More importantly, differencing does not allow you to discover any (long-term) relationship among the data.

Consider this hypothetical series:

$$\begin{cases} Y_{1t} = \sum_{i=1}^{t} \varepsilon_{1i} \\ Y_{2t} = Y_{1t} + \varepsilon_{2t} \end{cases}$$

Clearly, both Y_{1t} and are Y_{2t} random walk. If you study each of them separately, you would first use differencing to make each of them stationary. But then all you get are two white noise processes. You can tell nothing about them. You certainly would miss out that they are in fact tightly coupled and even share a common (stochastic) trend, namely, Y_{1t}.

$$\begin{cases} \Delta Y_{1t} = \varepsilon_{1t} \\ \Delta Y_{2t} = \varepsilon_{1t} + \left(\varepsilon_{2t} - \varepsilon_{2(t-1)}\right) \end{cases}$$

In finance, most components of the price time series are very much like random walk if you look at each of them individually. However, economic theory tells us that assets in the same sector often share the same common market trend. For example, when in a big bull market, all big-name tech stocks like GOOD, M$FT,

AAPL, and AMZN tend to go up together; when in a bear market, they all sell off at the same time. The CAPM theory popularizes the concept of the "beta" of a stock. The beta, β, of a stock measures how sensitive a stock is to the market movement. It is the sensitivity of the stock's (excess) return R_i to the (excess) market return R_M. In other words, all stocks in the market share a (stochastic) common market trend:

$$\mathrm{E}(R_i) - R_f = \beta_i \left[\mathrm{E}(R_M) - R_f \right]$$

Figure 15-33 plots the price of the S&P 500 and AAPL from 2008 to 2019. Each of them looks like a random walk (and probably is). However, we cannot help but wonder if there is a relationship between them. The distance between them looks more or less stable. Although it is notoriously difficult to predict where the stock market will go in the future, it seems rather easy to predict the distance between the S&P 500 and AAPL. In fact, if you do S&P 500 prices minus (scaled) AAPL prices, their differences are indeed stationary. This reveals that these equities share a common stochastic trend. Figure 15-34 plots the differences.

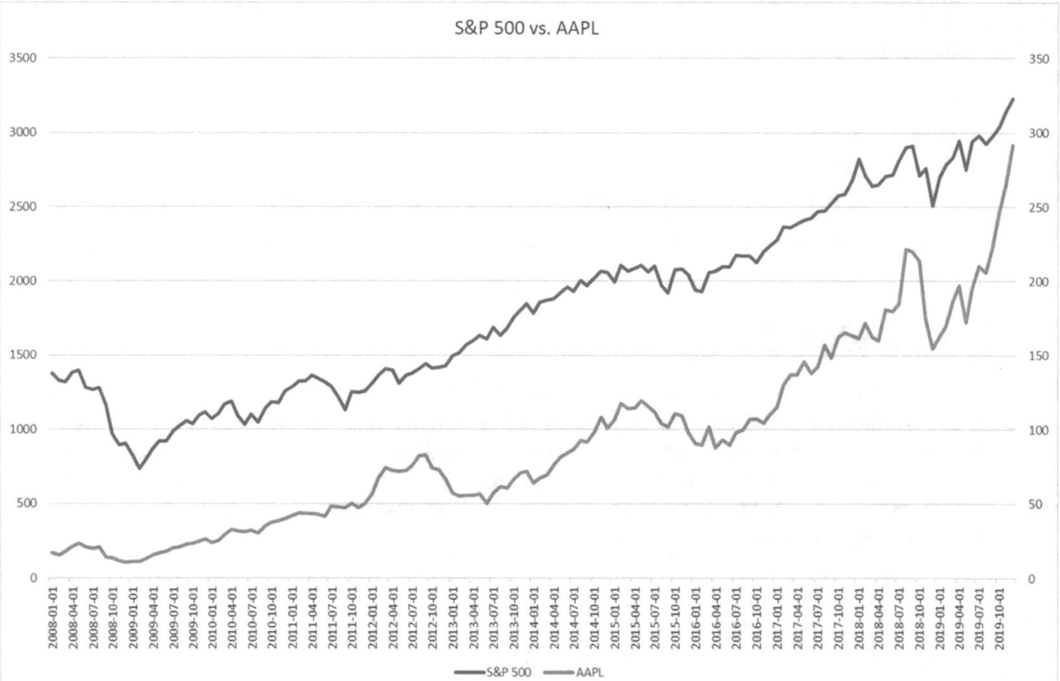

***Figure 15-33.** Monthly prices of the S&P 500 and AAPL from 2008 to 2019*

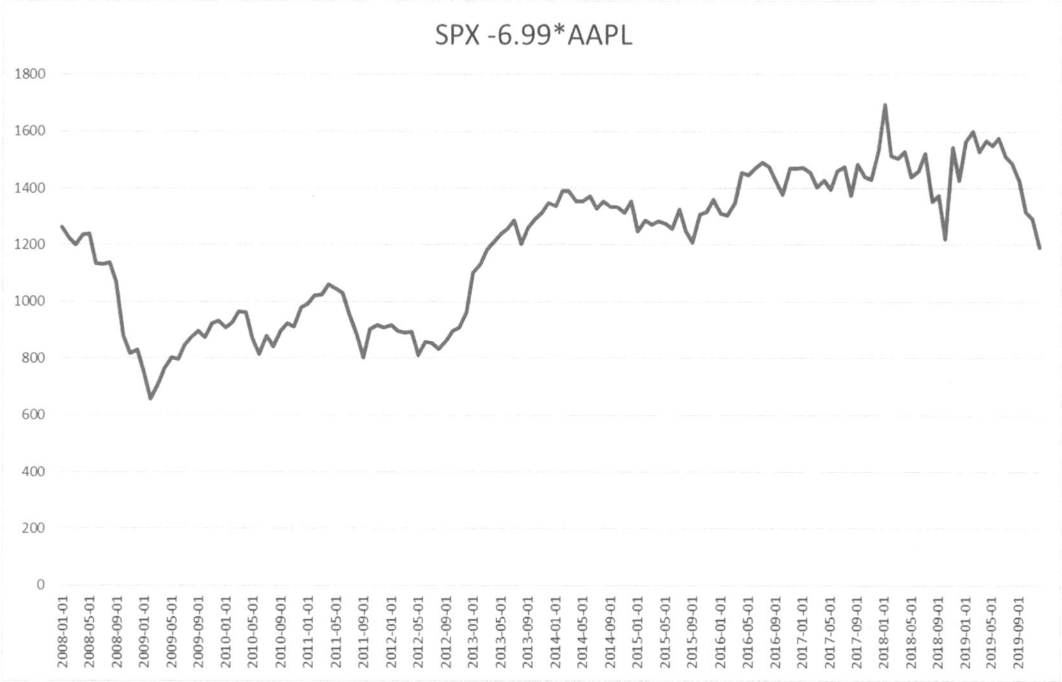

Figure 15-34. *Differences between the S&P 500 and scaled AAPL*

15.4.1. VEC Model

Consider this simple VAR example:

$$\begin{cases} x_t = a_{11}x_{t-1} + a_{12}y_{t-1} + \varepsilon_{xt} \\ y_t = a_{21}x_{t-1} + a_{22}y_{t-1} + \varepsilon_{yt} \end{cases}$$

Take the first difference, as shown here:

$$\begin{cases} x_t - x_{t-1} = (a_{11} - 1)x_{t-1} + a_{12}y_{t-1} + \varepsilon_{xt} \\ y_t - y_{t-1} = a_{21}x_{t-1} + (a_{22} - 1)y_{t-1} + \varepsilon_{yt} \end{cases}$$

Or equivalently, as shown here:

$$\begin{bmatrix} \Delta x_t \\ \Delta y_t \end{bmatrix} = \begin{bmatrix} a_{11} - 1 & a_{12} \\ a_{21} & a_{22} - 1 \end{bmatrix} \begin{bmatrix} x_{t-1} \\ y_{t-1} \end{bmatrix} + \begin{bmatrix} \varepsilon_{xt} \\ \varepsilon_{yt} \end{bmatrix}$$

Suppose you have this:

$$a_{11} = \frac{(1 - a_{22}) - a_{12}a_{21}}{1 - a_{22}}$$

Then you have this:

$$\begin{bmatrix}\Delta x_t \\ \Delta y_t\end{bmatrix}=\begin{bmatrix}\dfrac{-a_{12}a_{21}}{1-a_{22}} & a_{12} \\ a_{21} & a_{22}-1\end{bmatrix}\begin{bmatrix}x_{t-1} \\ y_{t-1}\end{bmatrix}+\begin{bmatrix}\varepsilon_{xt} \\ \varepsilon_{yt}\end{bmatrix}$$

Rearranging terms, you get this:

$$\begin{cases}\Delta x_t=\alpha_x\left(x_{t-1}-\beta y_{t-1}\right)+\epsilon_{xt} \\ \Delta y_t=\alpha_y\left(x_{t-1}-\beta y_{t-1}\right)+\epsilon_{yt}\end{cases}$$

Where:

$$\begin{cases}\alpha_x=\dfrac{-a_{12}a_{21}}{1-a_{22}} \\ \alpha_y=a_{21} \\ \beta=\dfrac{1-a_{22}}{a_{21}}\end{cases}$$

You know that Δx_t, Δy_t, ϵ_{xt}, and ϵ_{yt} are all stationary, so the common factor $(x_{t-1} - \beta y_{t-1})$ must also be stationary. In fact, it is the long-run equilibrium behind both x_t and y_t. β is called the cointegrating coefficient. x_t and y_t are said to be cointegrated and that the cointegrated relationship $x_t - \beta y_t$ is stationary. Suppose the long-run equilibrium spanned by β is 0 (or expected to be 0); then both Δx_t and Δy_t respond only to shocks. α_x and α_y are called the speed of adjustment. Suppose $\alpha_x < 0$ and $\alpha_y > 0$; then $\{x_t\}$ decreases in response to positive deviation from the equilibrium, and $\{y_t\}$ increases in response to positive deviation. In other words, whenever one of the component series deviates from the long-term equilibrium, the α acts like statistical gravity to pull it back to the equilibrium. Figure 15-35 illustrates the concept of cointegration.

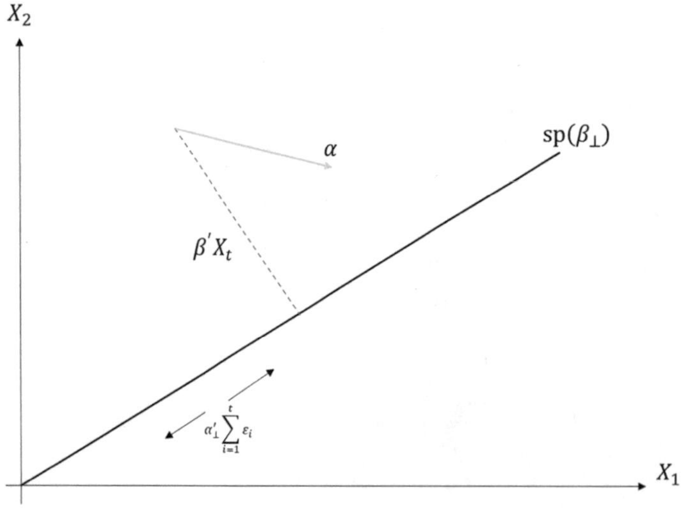

***Figure 15-35.** Cointegration of X_1 and X_2 about a long-term equilibrium spanned by $\beta_\perp$*

In general, you can write a VAR model $\boldsymbol{Y}_t$ in the (transitory) vector error correction model (VECM) as you did for the previous simple example. A VECM has this form:

$$\Delta \boldsymbol{Y}_t = \mu + \Pi \boldsymbol{Y}_{t-1} + \sum_{i=1}^{p-1} \Gamma_i \boldsymbol{Y}_{t-i} + \Psi \boldsymbol{D}_t + \epsilon_t$$

Where $\boldsymbol{\mu}$, $\boldsymbol{Y}_t$ and ϵ_t are m-dimensional vectors. The impact matrix $\boldsymbol{\Pi}$ and the coefficients $\boldsymbol{\Gamma}_i$ of the lagged time series are $(m \times m)$ matrices. $\boldsymbol{D}_t$ is a vector that contains all exogenous variables at time t (excluding the intercept term). Its coefficients are represented by the matrix $\boldsymbol{\Psi}$ from, say, linear regression.

If $\boldsymbol{Y}_t$ is cointegrated, then β exists, and an VECM exists. Moreover, the impact matrix can be decomposed into the following:

$$\Pi = \alpha \beta'$$

In this simple example, you have the following:

$$\begin{bmatrix} \Delta x_t \\ \Delta y_t \end{bmatrix} = \begin{bmatrix} \alpha_x \\ \alpha_y \end{bmatrix} [1 - \beta] \begin{bmatrix} x_t \\ y_t \end{bmatrix} + \begin{bmatrix} \varepsilon_{xt} \\ \varepsilon_{yt} \end{bmatrix}$$

In NM Dev, the `VECMTransitory` class represents the transitory VECM. The class signature is as follows:

```
public class VECMTransitory extends VECM {
    /**
     * Construct a transitory VECM(p) model.
     *
     * @param MU    the intercept (constant) vector
     * @param PI    the impact matrix
     * @param GAMMA the AR coefficients of the lagged differences; {@code null}
     *              if <i>p = 1</i>
     * @param PSI   the coefficients of the deterministic terms (excluding the
     *              intercept term)
     * @param SIGMA the white noise covariance matrix
     */
    public VECMTransitory(
            Vector MU,
            Matrix PI,
            Matrix[] GAMMA,
            Matrix PSI,
            Matrix SIGMA
    );
    /**
     * Construct a transitory VECM(p) model with zero-intercept (mu).
     *
     * @param PI    the impact matrix
     * @param GAMMA the AR coefficients of the lagged differences; {@code null}
     *              if <i>p = 1</i>
     * @param PSI   the coefficients of the deterministic terms (excluding the
     *              intercept term)
     * @param SIGMA the white noise covariance matrix
     */
```

```
    public VECMTransitory(
            Matrix PI,
            Matrix[] GAMMA,
            Matrix PSI,
            Matrix SIGMA
    );
    /**
     * Construct a transitory VECM(p) from a VARX(p).
     *
     * @param varx a VARX model
     */
    public VECMTransitory(VARXModel varx);
    /**
     * Copy constructor.
     *
     * @param that a transitory VECM model
     */
    public VECMTransitory(VECMTransitory that);
}
```

It provides a conversion method between a transitory VECM(p) and a VARX(p) model. Here's an example:

```
// define a VAR(2) model
val varxModel = VARXModel(
        arrayOf(
            DenseMatrix(
                    arrayOf(
                        doubleArrayOf(-0.210, 0.167),
                        doubleArrayOf(0.512, 0.220)
                    )),
            DenseMatrix(
                    arrayOf(
                        doubleArrayOf(0.743, 0.746),
                        doubleArrayOf(-0.405, 0.572)
                    ))
        ),
        null)

// construct a VECM from a VAR
val vecm = VECMTransitory(varxModel)

println("dimension = " + vecm.dimension())
println("PI, the impact matrix = ")
println(vecm.pi())
println("GAMMA = ")
println(vecm.gamma(1))
```

The output is as follows:

```
dimension = 2
PI, the impact matrix =
2x2
        [,1] [,2]
[1,] -0.467000, 0.913000,
[2,] 0.107000, -0.208000,
GAMMA =
2x2
        [,1] [,2]
[1,] -0.743000, -0.746000,
[2,] 0.405000, -0.572000,
```

Consider a VAR(p) model such that the component series $y_{1t}, y_{2t}, \ldots, y_{kt}$ are first-order nonstationary. D_t is an exogenous vector, representing a deterministic trend term, intercept term, and so on.

$$y_t = A_1 y_{t-1} + A_2 y_{t-2} + \ldots + A_p y_{t-p} + \Psi D_t + \mu_t$$

The first-order $I(1)$ process becomes a zero-order $I(0)$ stationary process after taking the first difference:

$$\Delta y_t = \Pi y_{t-1} + \sum_{i=1}^{p-1} \Gamma_i \Delta y_{t-i} + \Psi D_t + \mu_t$$

By matching coefficients, you get the following:

$$\Pi = \sum_{i=1}^{p} A_i - I$$

$$\Gamma_i = -\sum_{j=i+1}^{p} A_j$$

Δy_t and Δy_{t-j}, $j = 1, 2, \ldots, p$, are of $I(0)$. If Πy_{t-1} is also $I(0)$, then there is a cointegration relationship between $y_{1t}, y_{2t}, \ldots, y_{kt}$. You can reduce an $I(1)$ process to an $I(0)$ process by cointegration.

In general, if the time series under consideration has the same integration order y_{it}~$I(d)$ and there exists a certain linear combination (cointegration vector $\boldsymbol{\beta}$) that reduces the combined time series to a lower integration order $\boldsymbol{\beta}' \boldsymbol{Y}_t$~$I(d - b)$, then it is said that there is a significant cointegration relationship between these time series. In other words, the components of an m-dimensional vector $\boldsymbol{Y}_t = (y_{1t}, y_{2t}, \ldots, y_{mt})'$ is called (d, b)-order cointegration, denoted as $\boldsymbol{Y}_t$~CI(d, b).

15.4.2. Johansen Cointegration Test

Let's continue with the simple VAR example.

$$\begin{bmatrix} \Delta x_t \\ \Delta y_t \end{bmatrix} = \begin{bmatrix} \dfrac{-a_{12}a_{21}}{1-a_{22}} & a_{12} \\ a_{21} & a_{22}-1 \end{bmatrix} \begin{bmatrix} x_{t-1} \\ y_{t-1} \end{bmatrix} + \begin{bmatrix} \varepsilon_{xt} \\ \varepsilon_{yt} \end{bmatrix}$$

The impact matrix is as follows:

$$\Pi = \begin{bmatrix} \frac{-a_{12}a_{21}}{1-a_{22}} & a_{12} \\ a_{21} & a_{22}-1 \end{bmatrix}$$

Note that the rows are not linearly independent. Specifically, you have the following:

$$\begin{bmatrix} \frac{-a_{12}a_{21}}{1-a_{22}} & a_{12} \end{bmatrix} \times \frac{-(1-a_{22})}{a_{12}} = \begin{bmatrix} a_{21} & a_{22}-1 \end{bmatrix}$$

In general, the rank of the impact matrix **Π** determines whether and how many cointegrating relationships are among the component series. If **Π** is of full rank, then the VAR system (in levels) is already stationary. If the rank is zero, then there exists no cointegrating relations among the component time series. The interesting case is when the rank is not full rank $r < m$. Determining the rank of **Π**, k, means determining the number of nonzero eigenvalues of **Π**. In numerical computing, you do not just check if a number is 0. **Π** is usually obtained from numerical VAR estimation from data. Eigenvalues of **Π** are computed using a numerical procedure. Chances are that it is almost never 0 after a long series of numerical computations. You therefore need an effective procedure to determine numerical 0 for eigenvalues.

Trace Test

Let the characteristic roots or eigenvalues of matrix **Π** be $\lambda_1 > \lambda_2 > \ldots > \lambda_m$. The number of nonzero eigenvalues r is the number of cointegration vectors. The remaining $m - r$ noncointegration eigenvalues, $\lambda_{r+1}, \ldots \lambda_m$, should be 0. The trace hypothesis test, for each r, tests the following:

$$H_{r0} : \lambda_{r+1} = 0$$

$$H_{r1} : \lambda_{r+1} > 0, r = 0,1,\ldots,k-1$$

The corresponding test statistic is as follows:

$$\eta_r = -T \sum_{i=r+1}^{m} \ln(1-\lambda_i)$$

η_r is called the characteristic root trace statistics.

You can test r in a loop. If η_0 is not significant, you accept H_{00} ($r = 0$), meaning that there is 0 cointegration vector (that is, there is no cointegration relationship). You then stop. If η_0 is significant, rejecting H_{00} means that there is at least one cointegration vector. You next test the significance of η_1. If η_1 is not significant, you accept H_{10}, meaning that there is only one cointegration vector. You then stop. Otherwise, you repeat the process until H_{r0} is accepted, meaning that there are r cointegration vectors. These r cointegration vectors correspond to the largest r eigenvalues.

Maximum Eigenvalue Test

For the Johansen cointegration test, there is another similar hypothesis test to determine r.

$$H_{r0} : \lambda_{r+1} = 0$$

$$H_{r1} : \lambda_{r+1} > 0, r = 0, 1, \ldots, m - 1$$

The test statistic is as follows:

$$\xi_r = -T \ln\left(1 - \lambda_{r+1}\right)$$

You can again test for different r in an iterative manner until you determine the maximum r.
Suppose the rank of $\mathbf{\Pi}$ is r. Then you can decompose $\mathbf{\Pi}$ into the following:

$$\Pi = \alpha \beta'$$

Such that $\mathbf{\Pi}$ is $(m \times m)$ matrix, $\boldsymbol{\alpha}$ $(m \times r)$ and $\boldsymbol{\beta}'$ $(r \times m)$.

$\boldsymbol{\beta}$ can estimated by maximizing the very complicated and long log-likelihood function in Johansen (1995). In NM Dev, the `JohansenTest` class implements Johansen's algorithm and tests to find $\boldsymbol{\beta}$. It computes both the trace and eigen statistics. It supports a number of trend assumptions.

1. `NO_CONSTANT`: This is trend type I: no constant, no linear trend.
2. `RESTRICTED_CONSTANT`: This is trend type II: no restricted constant, no linear trend.
3. `CONSTANT`: This is trend type III: constant, no linear trend.
4. `CONSTANT_RESTRICTED_TIME`: This is trend type IV: constant, restricted linear trend.
5. `CONSTANT_TIME`: This is trend type V: constant, linear trend.

The following code computes the cointegrating relationship between the S&P 500 and AAPL:

```
// read the monthly S&P 500 data from a csv file
val spx_arr = DoubleUtils.readCSV2d("./resources/sp500_monthly.csv", true, true)

// convert the csv file into a matrix for manipulation
val spx_M1: Matrix = DenseMatrix(spx_arr)
// remove the data before 2008
val spx_M2: Matrix = MatrixFactory.subMatrix(spx_M1, 325, spx_M1.nRows(), 1, spx_M1.nCols())
// extract the column of adjusted close prices
val spx_v: Vector = spx_M2.getColumn(5) // adjusted closes

// read the monthly AAPL data from a csv file
val appl_arr = DoubleUtils.readCSV2d("./resources/AAPL_monthly.csv", true, true)
// convert the csv file into a matrix for manipulation
val aapl_M1: Matrix = DenseMatrix(appl_arr)
// remove the data before 2008
val aapl_M2: Matrix = MatrixFactory.subMatrix(aapl_M1, 325, aapl_M1.nRows(), 1, aapl_
M1.nCols())
// extract the column of adjusted close prices
val aapl_v: Vector = aapl_M2.getColumn(5) // adjusted closes

// combine SPX and AAPL to form a bivariate time series
val mts = MultivariateSimpleTimeSeries(cbind(spx_v, aapl_v))
//      println("(spx, aapl) prices: \n" + mts)
```

```
// run cointegration on all combinations of available test and trend types
for (test: Test in Test.values()) {
    for (trend: dev.nm.stat.cointegration.JohansenAsymptoticDistribution.TrendType in dev.
    nm.stat.cointegration.JohansenAsymptoticDistribution.TrendType.values()) {
        val coint = CointegrationMLE(mts, true)
        val johansen = JohansenTest(test, trend, coint.getEigenvalues().size())
        println("alpha:")
        println(coint.alpha())
        println("beta:")
        println(coint.beta())
        println("Johansen test: "
                + test.toString()
                + "\t" + trend.toString()
                + "\t eigenvalues: " + coint.getEigenvalues()
                + "\t statistics: " + johansen.getStats(coint)
        )
        println("")
    }
}

// run ADF test to check if the cointegrated series is indeed stationary
val betas: DoubleArray = doubleArrayOf(-12.673296, -6.995392)
for (beta: Double in betas) {
    println(String.format("testing for beta = %f%n", beta))
    val ci: Vector = spx_v.add(aapl_v.scaled(beta))
    val adf = AugmentedDickeyFuller(
                    ci.toArray(),
                    TrendType.CONSTANT, // constant drift term
                    4, // the lag order
                    null
            )

    println("H0: " + adf.getNullHypothesis())
    println("H1: " + adf.getAlternativeHypothesis())
    println(String.format("the p-value for the test = %f%n", adf.pValue()))
    println(String.format("the statistics for the test = %f%n", adf.statistics()))
    println("")
}
```

The output is as follows:

```
alpha:
2x2
        [,1] [,2]
[1,] 0.014356, -0.025999,
[2,] 0.005514, -0.000736,
beta:
2x2
        [,1] [,2]
[1,] 1.000000, 1.000000,
[2,] -6.995392, -12.673296,
```

```
Johansen test: EIGEN   NO_CONSTANT    eigenvalues: [0.027251, 0.006941]    statistics:
[3.923298, 0.989090]
alpha:
2x2
         [,1] [,2]
[1,] 0.014356, -0.025999,
[2,] 0.005514, -0.000736,
beta:
2x2
         [,1] [,2]
[1,] 1.000000, 1.000000,
[2,] -6.995392, -12.673296,
Johansen test: EIGEN   RESTRICTED_CONSTANT    eigenvalues: [0.027251, 0.006941]
statistics: [3.923298, 0.989090]
alpha:
2x2
         [,1] [,2]
[1,] 0.014356, -0.025999,
[2,] 0.005514, -0.000736,
beta:
2x2
         [,1] [,2]
[1,] 1.000000, 1.000000,
[2,] -6.995392, -12.673296,
Johansen test: EIGEN   CONSTANT    eigenvalues: [0.027251, 0.006941]    statistics:
[3.923298, 0.989090]
alpha:
2x2
         [,1] [,2]
[1,] 0.014356, -0.025999,
[2,] 0.005514, -0.000736,
beta:
2x2
         [,1] [,2]
[1,] 1.000000, 1.000000,
[2,] -6.995392, -12.673296,
Johansen test: EIGEN   CONSTANT_RESTRICTED_TIME    eigenvalues: [0.027251, 0.006941]
statistics: [3.923298, 0.989090]
alpha:
2x2
         [,1] [,2]
[1,] 0.014356, -0.025999,
[2,] 0.005514, -0.000736,
beta:
2x2
         [,1] [,2]
[1,] 1.000000, 1.000000,
[2,] -6.995392, -12.673296,
Johansen test: EIGEN   CONSTANT_TIME    eigenvalues: [0.027251, 0.006941]    statistics:
[3.923298, 0.989090]
alpha:
```

```
2x2
         [,1] [,2]
[1,] 0.014356, -0.025999,
[2,] 0.005514, -0.000736,
beta:
2x2
         [,1] [,2]
[1,] 1.000000, 1.000000,
[2,] -6.995392, -12.673296,
Johansen test: TRACE   NO_CONSTANT   eigenvalues: [0.027251, 0.006941]    statistics:
[4.912388, 0.989090]
alpha:
2x2
         [,1] [,2]
[1,] 0.014356, -0.025999,
[2,] 0.005514, -0.000736,
beta:
2x2
         [,1] [,2]
[1,] 1.000000, 1.000000,
[2,] -6.995392, -12.673296,
Johansen test: TRACE   RESTRICTED_CONSTANT   eigenvalues: [0.027251, 0.006941]
statistics: [4.912388, 0.989090]
alpha:
2x2
         [,1] [,2]
[1,] 0.014356, -0.025999,
[2,] 0.005514, -0.000736,
beta:
2x2
         [,1] [,2]
[1,] 1.000000, 1.000000,
[2,] -6.995392, -12.673296,
Johansen test: TRACE   CONSTANT   eigenvalues: [0.027251, 0.006941]    statistics:
[4.912388, 0.989090]
alpha:
2x2
         [,1] [,2]
[1,] 0.014356, -0.025999,
[2,] 0.005514, -0.000736,
beta:
2x2
         [,1] [,2]
[1,] 1.000000, 1.000000,
[2,] -6.995392, -12.673296,
Johansen test: TRACE   CONSTANT_RESTRICTED_TIME   eigenvalues: [0.027251, 0.006941]
statistics: [4.912388, 0.989090]
alpha:
2x2
         [,1] [,2]
[1,] 0.014356, -0.025999,
```

```
[2,] 0.005514, -0.000736,
beta:
2x2
        [,1] [,2]
[1,] 1.000000, 1.000000,
[2,] -6.995392, -12.673296,
Johansen test: TRACE   CONSTANT_TIME    eigenvalues: [0.027251, 0.006941]     statistics:
[4.912388, 0.989090]
testing for beta = -12.673296
H0: there is a unit root in the process, hence non-stationarity
H1: there is no unit root in the process, hence stationarity
the p-value for the test = 0.520000
the statistics for the test = -1.520184
testing for beta = -6.995392
H0: there is a unit root in the process, hence non-stationarity
H1: there is no unit root in the process, hence stationarity
the p-value for the test = 0.000000
the statistics for the test = -3.683306
```

According to the statistics, there is only one cointegration relationship. The cointegrating beta is -6.995392. The cointegration is as follows:

$$SPX - 6.995392 \times \text{AAPL}$$

You can run the ADF test to the cointegrating time series. The p-value is 0, meaning that you can reject the null. That means that the "distance" between the S&P 500 and AAPL is indeed stationary. When AAPL deviates from the statistical equilibrium, it could mean a trading signal. For the strongly mean-reverting pairs of stocks, you can design trading strategies around them. You can find more details in my other book, *Numerical Methods in Quantitative Trading.* See Figure 15-36.

Figure 15-36. *The SPX and AAPL are cointegrated*

Index

A

B

H. Li, PhD, *Numerical Methods Using Kotlin*, https://doi.org/10.1007/978-1-4842-8826-9

C

D

E

F

G

H

I

J

K

L

M

N

O

Q

R

S

T

U

V

W, X

Y

Z

Printed in the United States
by Baker & Taylor Publisher Services